Sports around the World

Sports around the World

HISTORY, CULTURE, AND PRACTICE

Volume 4: Olympic Medalists and Winners and Champions of Major World Sporting Events

JOHN NAURIGHT
CHARLES PARRISH

 ABC-CLIO

Santa Barbara, California • Denver, Colorado • Oxford, England

Library of Congress Cataloging-in-Publication Data

Nauright, John, 1962–
    Sports around the world : history, culture, and practice / John Nauright, Charles Parrish.
        p. cm.
    Includes bibliographical references and index.
    ISBN 978-1-59884-300-2 (hardback) — ISBN 978-1-59884-301-9 (ebook)
1. Sports—Cross-cultural studies. 2. Sports—Social aspects. I. Parrish, Charles. II. Title.
    GV706.8.N385   2012
    306.4′83—dc23   2011047997

ISBN: 978-1-59884-300-2
EISBN: 978-1-59884-301-9

15 14 13 12 11   1 2 3 4 5

This book is also available on the World Wide Web as an eBook.
Visit www.abc-clio.com for details.

ABC-CLIO, LLC
130 Cremona Drive, P.O. Box 1911
Santa Barbara, California 93116-1911

This book is printed on acid-free paper ∞
Manufactured in the United States of America

For Jenni and Maria, and Ashley, Lauren, Lucas, and Aliana

Contents

VOLUME I: GENERAL TOPICS, AFRICA, ASIA, MIDDLE EAST, AND OCEANIA

Alphabetical List of Entries, xix
Acknowledgments, xxxiii
Introduction: The History, Culture, and Practice of Sports Around the World, xxxvii

General Topics, I

Coaching in Sport, 1
Disabled and Sport, 4
Fédération Internationale de Football Association, 6
Globalization and Sport, 8
Imperialism and Sport, 15
International Olympic Committee, 23
International Relations and Sport, 26
Legal Liability in Sport, 28
Media and Sport, 34
Music and Sport, 37
Olympic Movement, 39
Philosophy of Sport, 45
Sexuality and Sports, 47
Sociology of Sport, 50
Sport Labor Migration, 54
Sport Psychology, 55
Sports Medicine, 59
Sports Museums and Heritage Collections, 63
Tourism and Sport, 67
United Nations and Sport, 69

Africa, Sub-Sahara, 73

SPORTS HISTORY, CULTURE, AND PRACTICE IN SUB-SAHARAN AFRICA, 73
Accra Sports Stadium Disaster (Ghana), 80
African Games, 81

African Nations Cup, Association Football, 83
Antiapartheid Sports Movement (South Africa), 84
Apartheid and Sports in South Africa, 90
Association Football, Cameroon, 94
Association Football, Ghana, 95
Association Football, Nigeria, 96
Association Football, South Africa, 97
Association Football, Sub-Saharan Africa in General, 100
Association Football, Zambia, 101
Athletics, Kenya, 102
Athletics, Rest of Africa, 104
Athletics, South Africa, 105
Bantu Sports Club (Johannesburg, South Africa), 107
Baseball, South Africa, 108
Boxing, South Africa, 109
Commonwealth Games, African Nations, 112
Comrades Marathon (South Africa), 114
Cricket, Kenya, 114
Cricket, South Africa, 115
Cricket, Zimbabwe, 121
Dakar Rally, 123
Ellis Park Stadium Disaster (South Africa), 123
Field Hockey, South Africa, 124
Field Sports, South Africa, 125
FIFA World Cup of 2010 (South Africa), 127
Golf, Sub-Saharan Africa, 129
Hansie Cronje Match-Fixing Scandal (South Africa), 131
Imperialism and Sport, British Colonial Africa, 132
Jeux de la Francophonie of 2005 (Niger), 136
Jukskei (South Africa), 136

Milla, Roger (1952–), 137
Missionaries and Sport in Africa, 138
Netball, South Africa, 139
Olympic Boycott of 1976 (African Nations), 141
Orkney Stadium Disaster (South Africa), 141
Player, Gary (1935–), 142
Pollock, Graeme (1944–), 143
Rebel Sports Tours, South Africa, 143
Robben Island Sports Club (South Africa), 144
Rugby Union Football, Rest of Africa, 146
Rugby Union Football, South Africa, 147
Rugby World Cup of 1995 (South Africa), 152
Rumble in the Jungle (1974), 153
South Africa and the Olympic Games, 154
Sport and International Development in
    Africa, 156
Springbok Emblem (South Africa), 158
Stick Fighting, Africa and Caribbean, 158
Sun City (South Africa), 159
Supreme Council for Sport in Africa, 160
Surfing, South Africa, 161
Swimming, Southern Africa, 162
Tennis, Africa, 163
Traditional Sports, Southern Africa, 165
Tutsi High Jumping (Rwanda), 168
Vuvuzela (South Africa), 169
Weah, George (1966–), 170
Zambian National Football Team Disaster
    (1993), 171

Asia, South and East, 173

SPORTS HISTORY, CULTURE, AND PRACTICE
IN ASIA, 173
    Aikido, 184
    Asian Beach Games, 185
    Asian Football Confederation, 185
    Asian Games, 186
    Asian Winter Games, 188
    Association Football, Central Asia, 189
    Association Football, China, 189
    Association Football, Japan, 190
    Association Football, Korea, 191
    Association Football, South Asia, 193
    Association Football, Southeast Asia, 193
    Athletics, Asia, 194
    Auto Racing, Asia, 195

Badminton, Asia, 196
Baseball, Japan, 197
Baseball, Korea, 200
Baseball, Taiwan, 202
Basketball, China, 203
Boxing, Philippines, 205
British Imperialism and Sports in Asia, 206
Commonwealth Games, Asia, 207
Commonwealth Games of 1998 (Kuala
    Lumpur), 208
Commonwealth Games of 2010 (New
    Delhi), 209
Cricket, Bangladesh, 210
Cricket, India, 210
Cricket, Pakistan, 213
Cricket, Sri Lanka, 215
Dragon Boat Racing, 217
Far Eastern Championship Games, 219
Field Hockey, Asia, 219
FIFA World Cup of 2002 (Japan and South
    Korea), 221
Games of the Newly Emerging Forces, 222
Gender and Sport, Asia, 224
Hong Kong Sevens, 226
Iaidō, 226
Judo, 226
Jujitsu, 227
Kabaddi, 228
Karate, 228
Kendo, 229
Khan, Imran (1952–), 231
Kurash, 232
Macau Grand Prix, 233
Media and Sport (Asia), 233
Mountaineering (Himalayas), 235
Muay Thai, 236
Olympic Council of Asia, 236
Olympic Games of 1940 (Tokyo), 237
Olympic Games of 1964 (Tokyo), 238
Olympic Games of 1988 (Seoul, Republic of
    Korea), 240
Olympic Games of 2008 (Beijing), 242
Olympic Winter Games of 1972 (Sapporo,
    Japan), 243
Olympic Winter Games of 1998 (Nagano,
    Japan), 244

Polo, India, 245
Sepak Takraw, 247
Skating, Short-Track Speed (Asia), 248
Southeast Asian Games, 249
Squash, Asia, 250
Sumo, 250
Table Tennis, Asia, 252
Tae Kwon Do, 253
Tai Chi, 255
Tendulkar, Sachin (1973–), 255
Tennis, Asia, 256
Traditional Sports, Asia, 257
Twenty20 Cricket (India), 259
Two Chinas Issue, 260
U.S. Imperialism and Sport in Asia, 261
Volleyball, Asia, 263
Winter Sports, Asia, 265
Wrestling, Mongolian, 265
Wushu, 266
Yao, Ming (1980–), 267

Middle East and North Africa, 269

SPORTS HISTORY, CULTURE, AND PRACTICE IN THE MIDDLE EAST AND NORTH AFRICA, 269

Arab Women and the Olympic Games, 272
Association Football, Egypt, 273
Association Football, North Africa, 274
Association Football, Palestine, 275
Association Football, Saudi Arabia, 276
Athletics, Middle East and North Africa, 277
Attouga (1945–), 280
Basketball, Israel, 280
Basketball, Lebanon, 281
Ben M'barek, Larbi (1914–1992), 282
Bourguibism and Sport (Tunisia), 283
Cairo Football Derby: Al-Ahly–Zamalek, 283
Camel Racing, 284
Camus, Albert (1913–1960), 285
Cycling, North Africa, 286
Dubai Sports City, 287
Egypt, Sports and Nasserism, 287
Ethnicity and Sectarianism in Divided Societies in the Middle East, 288
Gender and Sport, Middle East and North Africa, 290
Gulf Cooperation Council Games, 292
Hamia, Cherif (1931–), 292
Handball, North Africa, 293
Iran and Sport since the Islamic "Revolution," 293
Iraq, Baath Regime and Sport in, 295
Islamic Solidarity Games of 2005 (Saudi Arabia), 296
Islamism and Sport, 297
L'Équipe FLN (Algeria), 299
Maghrebin Games, 299
Media and Sport in the Arab World, 300
Mediterranean Games of 1975 (Algiers), 301
Mekhloufi, Rachid (1936–), 302
Migrations, Diasporas, and Sports in the Middle East and North Africa, 302
Nakache, Alfred (1915–1983), 305
North Africa and the FIFA World Cup (Association Football), 305
Oman, Sport in, 306
Pan-Africanism and Sport, North Africa, 308
Pan-Arab Nationalism and the Pan-Arab Games, 309
Qatar Asian Games of 2006, 310
Qatar Sports Development and the Bid for the 2016 Olympic Games, 310
Tunis 2001 Mediterranean Games, 311
Women Islamic Games (Iran), 312
Yemen, Sport in the Republic of, 314

Australia, New Zealand, and Oceana, 315

SPORTS HISTORY, CULTURE, AND PRACTICE IN OCEANIA, 315

Aborigines in Sport (Australia), 327
All Blacks (Māori—New Zealand), 329
All Blacks (New Zealand National Rugby Team), 330
America's Cup, Australia and New Zealand, 331
Antiapartheid Campaigns (Australia and Aotearoa/New Zealand), 332
The Ashes, 334
Association Football, Australia, 335
Association Football, New Zealand, 338
Athletics, Australia and New Zealand, 339
Australian Football League, 341
Australian Institute of Sport, 343

Australian Olympic Committee, 347
Australian Open (Tennis), 348
Australian Rules Football, 349
Australian Society for Sports History, 355
Australian Sports Commission, 355
Baseball, Australia, 360
Basketball, Australia and New Zealand, 361
Bodyline (1932–1933), 362
Boxing, Australia, 363
Bradman, Sir Donald (1908–2001), 364
British Commonwealth Games of 1974
    (Christchurch, New Zealand), 365
British Empire and Commonwealth Games of
    1962 (Perth, Australia), 365
British Empire Games of 1938 (Sydney), 366
Brownlow Medal (Australia), 366
Coast to Coast Race (New Zealand), 367
Commonwealth Games, Australia, 368
Commonwealth Games of 1982 (Brisbane), 369
Commonwealth Games of 1990 (Auckland), 370
Commonwealth Games of 2006
    (Melbourne), 371
Court, Margaret (1942–), 372
Cricket, Australia, 372
Cricket, New Zealand, 378
Cricket, Trobriand Islands, 381
Cycling, Australia and New Zealand, 382
Elliott, Herb (1938–), 383
Field Hockey, Australia and New Zealand, 384
Field Sports, Australia and New Zealand, 385
Fraser, Dawn (1937–), 388
Freeman, Cathy (1973–), 388
Golf, Oceania, 389
Goolagong-Cawley, Evonne (1951–), 390
Hadlee, Sir Richard (1951–), 391
The Haka (New Zealand), 392
Henley-on-Todd Regatta, 393
Hillary, Sir Edmund (1919–2008), 393
Hopman Cup (Australia), 394
Horse Racing, Australia and New Zealand, 394
Indigenous (Aboriginal Australian) Cricket Tour
    of England (1868), 396
International Rules Football, 398
Jack Johnson–Tommy Burns Fight, Sydney
    (1908), 398
Jackson, Marjorie (1931–), 399

Laver, Rod (1938–), 399
Lawn Bowling, Australia and New Zealand, 400
Lillee, Dennis Keith (1949–), 402
Lindrum, Walter (1898–1960), 402
Lomu, Jonah (1975–), 403
Lovelock, Jack (1910–1949), 404
Makybe Diva (1999–), 404
McKay, Heather (1941–), 405
Meads, Colin Earl (1936–), 406
Melbourne Cricket Ground, 406
Melbourne Cup, 407
Miller, Keith Ross (1919–2004), 408
Nepia, George (1905–1986), 409
Netball, Australia, 409
Netball, New Zealand, 411
Netball, Pacific Islands, 412
New Zealand All Blacks of 1905 ("The
    Originals"), 413
New Zealand All Blacks of 1924 ("The
    Invincibles"), 415
New Zealand Olympic Committee, 415
Nga Taonga Takaro (Traditional Māori Games,
    New Zealand), 416
Norman, Greg (1955–), 422
Norman, Peter (1942–2006), 423
Olympic Games of 1956 (Melbourne), 423
Olympic Games of 2000 (Sydney), 425
Phar Lap (1926–1932), 427
Ranfurly Shield (New Zealand), 428
Rose, Lionel (1948–), 428
Rowing/Sculling, Australia and New
    Zealand, 429
Rugby League Football, Australia, 431
Rugby League Football, New Zealand, 433
Rugby Sevens, 434
Rugby Union Football, Australia, 434
Rugby Union Football, New Zealand, 439
Rugby Union Football, Pacific Islands, 445
Rugby World Cup of 1987 (New Zealand and
    Australia), 447
Rugby World Cup of 2003 (Australia), 447
Sailing, Australia and New Zealand, 448
Sheffield Shield, 449
Short Track Speed Skating, Australia, 450
Singh, Vijay (1963–), 450
Snell, Peter (1938–), 451

Softball, Australia, 451

South Sydney District Rugby League Club Ltd vs. News Limited, 453

Springbok Tour of New Zealand (1981) (South African Rugby Tour), 454

Super 15 Rugby, 456

Super League "War," 456

Surfing, Australia and New Zealand, 457

Surf Lifesaving, Australia, 460

Swimming, Australia, 462

Sydney Organising Committee for the Olympic Games, 464

Sydney Paralympic Organising Committee, 465

Sydney to Hobart Yacht Race (Australia), 466

TAB (Totalisator Agency Board), Australia, 466

Thorpe, Ian (1982–), 468

Traditional Sports, Australian Aboriginal and Torres Strait Islander Peoples, 468

Trumper, Victor Thomas (1877–1915), 472

Underarm Bowling Incident, Cricket (Australia), 472

Warne, Shane (1969–), 473

Wilding, Anthony (1883–1915), 473

Woodchopping, 474

World Series Cricket, 474

VOLUME 2: BRITISH ISLES AND EUROPE

Alphabetical List of Entries, xix

Acknowledgments, xxxiii

Introduction: The History, Culture, and Practice of Sports Around the World, xxxvii

British Isles, I

SPORTS HISTORY, CULTURE, AND PRACTICE IN THE BRITISH ISLES, I

Animal Blood Sports, British Isles, 13

Anti-Apartheid Movement, British Isles, 15

Archery, 17

Army Physical Training Corps (Great Britain), 18

Ascot, 19

Association Football, England and Wales, 19

Association Football, Scotland, 26

Athletics, British Isles, 29

Badminton, British Isles, 31

Badminton House, 32

Bandy, 33

Barmy Army, 34

Basketball, British Isles, 35

Beckham, David (1975–), 36

Best, George (1946–2005), 38

Billiards, 38

Botham, Sir Ian (1955–), 39

Boxing, British Isles, 40

British Imperialism and Sport, 44

British Olympic Association, 50

Camogie (Ireland), 51

Cardiff Arms Park, 52

Central Council for Physical Recreation, 53

Chariots of Fire (1981), 54

Commonwealth Games, England, 55

Commonwealth Games, Northern Ireland, 56

Commonwealth Games, Scotland, 57

Commonwealth Games, Wales, 58

Commonwealth Games of 1958 (Cardiff), 59

Corinthians, 60

Cotswold Games (England), 60

Coursing (British Isles), 61

Cricket, England, 61

Croquet, 68

Curling, Scotland, 69

Darts, 69

Doggett's Coat and Badge (England), 71

Epsom Downs Racecourse (England), 71

Eton Wall Game (England), 73

Fanzines (British Isles), 73

Field Hockey, British Isles, 74

Field Sports, British Isles, 76

FIFA World Cup of 1966 (England), 80

Fives, England, 83

Football, Gaelic, 83

Footballers' Wives, 85

Foxhunting, British Isles, 86

Gaelic Athletic Association, 89

Gender and Sport, British Isles, 93

Gleneagles Agreement, 98

Golf, British Isles, 98

Grace, W. G. (1848–1915), 105

Grand National, 106

Hammond, Wally (1903–1965), 107

Hampden Park, 108

Hampden Park Riot of 1909, 108
Henley Royal Regatta, England, 109
Highland Games, Scotland, 109
Hillsborough Disaster, England, 111
Hobbs, Sir John Berry (1882–1963), 112
Hooliganism, British Isles, 113
Horse Racing, British Isles, 115
Hurling, 121
Ice Hockey, British Isles, 122
Imperial/International Cricket Council, 123
Irish Diaspora and Sport, 125
Isle of Man Motorcycle Races, 126
Knur and Spell, England, 126
Lawn Bowling, British Isles, 127
Literature and Sport, British Isles, 128
London Marathon, 132
Manchester United Munich Air Disaster, 133
Marylebone Cricket Club, 134
Matthews, Sir Stanley (1915–2000), 135
Mountain Climbing, British Isles, 136
Much Wenlock Games, England, 139
Murrayfield Stadium, 139
Muscular Christianity, 140
Netball, British Isles, 143
Newmarket, England, 146
Northern Ireland, Sport and Sectarianism in, 146
The Old Firm: Glasgow Celtic and Glasgow
    Rangers Football Clubs, Scotland, 148
Olympic Games of 1908 (London), 150
Olympic Games of 1948 (London), 151
Olympic Games of 2012 (London), 153
Open Championship (British Open), 155
Pedestrianism, 156
Polo, Britain, 157
Premier League, 159
Punting, England, 160
Quoits, Great Britain, 161
Race and Sport, British Isles, 162
Racewalking, 168
Ranjitsinhji, K. S. (1872–1933), 168
Real Tennis, 169
Rowing/Sculling, British Isles, 169
Royal and Ancient Golf Club, 171
Rugby League, Great Britain, 172
Rugby Union Football, England, 175
Rugby Union Football, Ireland, 179

Rugby Union Football, Scotland, 182
Rugby Union Football, Wales, 183
Rugby World Cup of 1991 (United Kingdom and
    France), 188
Rugby World Cup of 1999 (Wales), 189
Six Nations Rugby Championship, 190
Snooker, 190
Speedway, 192
Squash, British Isles, 193
Stoolball, 193
Swimming, England, 194
Tartan Army, Scotland, 196
Taylor Report, 197
Tennis, British Isles, 198
This Sporting Life, 202
Tug-of-War, 202
Twickenham Stadium, 203
Underwater Hockey, 204
Vardon, Harry (1870–1937), 205
"Vitaï Lampada," 206
Walker Cup, 206
Warner, Sir Pelham (1873–1963), 207
Water Polo, 207
Wembley Stadium, 208
Wightman Cup, 209
Wimbledon, 210
Wisden Cricketers' Almanack, 215
Wolfenden Committee Report (1960), 215
Workers' Sport, British Isles, 216

Europe, 219

SPORTS HISTORY, CULTURE, AND PRACTICE IN EUROPE, 219

Ancient Olympic Games and Greek Sporting
    Festivals, 226
Ancient Roman Sport, 230
Armand Césari Stadium Disaster, 233
Association Football, France, 234
Association Football, Germany, 235
Association Football, Italy, 236
Association Football, The Netherlands, 239
Association Football, Nordic Countries, 240
Association Football, Portugal, 241
Association Football, Spain, 242
Ballesteros, Severiano (1957–2011), 244
Baseball, Europe, 245

Baseball, Finnish, 246

Basketball, Europe, 249

Basketball, Italy, 251

Basketball, Russia, the Former Soviet Union, and
the Baltic Countries, 253

Basketball, Yugoslav Countries, 255

Beckenbauer, Franz (1945–), 257

Becker, Boris (1967–), 257

Blatter, Joseph S. (1936–), 258

Book of the Courtier (Castiglione), 259

Borg, Björn (1956–), 260

Bosman Ruling, 1995, 261

Bullfighting, 263

Bundesliga Match-Fixing Scandal of 2005
(Germany), 264

Camp Nou (Spain), 265

Champions League, 266

Comăneci, Nadia (1961–), 267

Cricket, Netherlands, 268

Cruyff, Johan (1947–), 269

DanceSport, 270

Dassler Family (Adidas and Puma), 273

De Coubertin, Pierre Frédy, Baron
(1863–1937), 274

Deutsche Demokratische Republik (East
Germany) and Sport, 275

Deutscher Olympischer Sportbund, 280

Diem, Carl (1882–1962), 283

Doping, Tour de France, 283

European Committee for Sports History, 286

European Union and Sport, 287

Fédération Internationale de Natation, 289

Federer, Roger (1981–), 290

Fencing, 291

FIFA World Cup of 1958 (Sweden), 293

FIFA World Cup of 1974 (West Germany), 294

FIFA World Cup of 1982 (Spain), 297

FIFA World Cup of 1990 (Italy), 298

FIFA World Cup of 1998 (France), 300

FIFA World Cup of 2006 (Germany), 301

Fistball, 304

Folk Sports and Traditional Games, Europe, 304

Formula One Auto Racing, 312

French Open Tennis Championships, 315

Gender and Sport, Europe, 317

Golf, Europe, 321

Graf, Stefanie Maria "Steffi" (1969–), 322

Greco-Roman Wrestling, 323

Gymnastics, Czech, 325

Gymnastics, Danish, 326

Gymnastics, German (*Turnen*), 327

Gymnastics, Romania, 331

Gymnastics, Soviet/Russian, 333

Gymnastics, Swedish, 334

Handball, Team, 335

Henie, Sonja (1912–1969), 338

Heysel Stadium Disaster (Belgium), 338

Hooliganism, European Football (Soccer), 339

Hungary vs. Soviet Union Olympic Water Polo
Match of 1956, 342

Ice Hockey, Europe, 343

Indurain, Miguel (1964–), 348

International Amateur Athletic Federation, 349

International Society for the History of Physical
Education and Sport, 351

Italian Football Scandal of 2006 (Calciopoli), 351

Jeux de la Francophonie, 352

Jousting, 353

Kaatsen, 355

Karaiskakis Stadium Disaster, 356

Killy, Jean-Claude (1943–), 357

Klammer, Franz (1953–), 358

Kolven, 358

Korbut, Olga (1955–), 359

Korfball, 360

Lacoste, René (1904–1996), 360

La Liga, 361

Langer, Bernhard (1957–), 362

Lapta, 363

La Soule, 363

Lenglen, Suzanne (1899–1938), 364

Maccabiah Games, 364

Martial Arts, Europe, 366

Massey, Arnaud (1877–1950), 367

Merckx, Eddy (1945–), 368

Modern Pentathlon, 369

Motorcycle Racing (Europe), 369

Nadal, Rafael (1986–), 371

Navratilova, Martina (1956–), 372

Nurmi, Paavo (1897–1973), 372

Olympic Games of 1896 (Athens), 374

Olympic Games of 1900 (Paris), 376

Olympic Games of 1912 (Stockholm), 377
Olympic Games of 1920 (Antwerp), 379
Olympic Games of 1924 (Paris), 380
Olympic Games of 1928 (Amsterdam), 381
Olympic Games of 1936 (Berlin), 383
Olympic Games of 1952 (Helsinki), 387
Olympic Games of 1960 (Rome), 389
Olympic Games of 1972 (Munich), 390
Olympic Games of 1980 (Moscow), 392
Olympic Games of 1992 (Barcelona, Spain), 394
Olympic Games of 2004 (Athens), 396
Olympic Winter Games of 1924 (Chamonix), 397
Olympic Winter Games of 1928 (St. Moritz), 398
Olympic Winter Games of 1936 (Garmisch-Partenkirchen), 399
Olympic Winter Games of 1948 (St. Moritz), 400
Olympic Winter Games of 1952 (Oslo), 400
Olympic Winter Games of 1956 (Cortina), 401
Olympic Winter Games of 1964 (Innsbruck), 402
Olympic Winter Games of 1968 (Grenoble), 403
Olympic Winter Games of 1976 (Innsbruck), 404
Olympic Winter Games of 1984 (Sarajevo), 406
Olympic Winter Games of 1992 (Albertville), 407
Olympic Winter Games of 1994 (Lillehammer), 408
Olympic Winter Games of 2006 (Turin/Torino), 410
Pankration, 412
Pelota, 413
Petanque, Bocce, Boules, 414
Platini, Michel (1955–), 415
Prost, Alain (1955–), 415
Puskas, Ferenc (1927–2006), 416
Rallying/World Rally Championship, 416
Rock Climbing, 417
Rugby Union Football, France, 418
Rugby Union Football, Italy, 422
Running of the Bulls, 425
Samaranch, Juan Antonio (1920–2010), 426
San Siro Stadium, 426
Santiago Bernabéu Stadium, 427
Schmeling, Max (1905–2005), 427
Schumacher, Michael (1969–), 428
Schwingen (Switzerland), 428
Serie A (Italy), 429

Skiing, Alpine (Europe), 430
Skiing, Nordic, 435
Sliding Sports (Bobsleigh, Luge, and Skeleton), 438
Sokol Movement (Czech Republic, Slovakia, Czechoslovakia), 442
Sorenstam, Annika (1970–), 443
Spartakiads, 444
Speed Skating, Europe, 445
Table Tennis, Europe, 448
Total Football (Netherlands), 450
Tour de France, 450
Tretiak, Vladislav (1952–), 456
Union of European Football Associations, 457
Volata, 458
Weightlifting (Europe), 458
Witt, Katerina (1965–), 459
Women's Olympics, 460
Worker Sport, Europe, 461
World Anti-Doping Agency, 464
Wrestling, Brittany (Gouren), 465
Wrestling, Iceland (Glima), 466
Yashin, Lev Ivanovic (1929–1990), 466
Zatopek, Emil (1922–2000), 467
Zidane, Zinedine (1972–), 467
Zoff, Dino (1942–), 468

VOLUME 3: LATIN AMERICA AND NORTH AMERICA

Alphabetical List of Entries, xix
Acknowledgments, xxxiii
Introduction: The History, Culture, and Practice of Sports Around the World, xxxvii

Latin America and the Caribbean, 1

SPORTS HISTORY, CULTURE, AND PRACTICE IN LATIN AMERICA AND THE CARIBBEAN, 1
Alianza Lima Air Tragedy (Peru), 12
Altitude Ban, FIFA, 13
Andres Escobar Murder (Colombia), 14
Association Football, Argentina, 14
Association Football, Bolivia, 24
Association Football, Brazil, 25
Association Football, Caribbean, 32
Association Football, Central America, 34

Association Football, Mexico, 36

Association Football, Pacific Coast of South America, 38

Association Football, Paraguay, 47

Association Football, Uruguay, 48

Athletics, Caribbean, 50

Auto Racing, Latin America, 53

Azteca Stadium (Mexico), 55

Baseball, Central and South America, 55

Baseball, Cuba, 57

Baseball, Dominican Republic, 60

Baseball, Dutch West Indies, 64

Baseball, Mexico, 65

Baseball, Puerto Rico, 66

Basketball, Latin America, 68

Bolivarian Games, 70

Bolt, Usain (1986–), 71

Boxing, Latin America, 71

Brazilian Soccer Match–Fixing Scandal of 2005, 78

Bueno, Maria (1939–), 78

Capoeira, Brazil, 79

Central American and Caribbean Games, 81

Central American Games, 82

Chávez, Julio César (1962–), 83

Clemente, Roberto (1934–1972), 84

Commonwealth Games of 1966 (Jamaica), 85

Conejo, Luis Gabelo (1960–), 86

CONMEBOL, 86

Copa América, 87

Copa Libertadores, 88

Cricket, West Indies, 89

Di Stéfano, Alfredo (1926–), 94

Estadio Centenario (Uruguay), 94

Estadio Mateo Flores Disaster of 1996 (Guatemala), 95

Estadio Monumental (Argentina), 96

Estadio Nacional (Chile), 97

Estadio Nacional Disaster of 1964 (Lima, Peru), 97

Fangio, Juan Manuel (1911–1995), 98

Fast Bowling, West Indies (Cricket), 98

Field Hockey, Argentina, 99

FIFA World Cup of 1930 (Uruguay), 99

FIFA World Cup of 1950 (Brazil), 100

FIFA World Cup of 1962 (Chile), 102

FIFA World Cup of 1970 (Mexico), 103

FIFA World Cup of 1978 (Argentina), 103

FIFA World Cup of 1986 (Mexico), 104

FIFA World Cup of 2014 (Brazil), 107

Football War (El Salvador and Honduras), 107

Futsal (Uruguay), 108

Gender and Sport, Latin America and the Caribbean, 109

Golf, Latin America and the Caribbean, 111

Havelange, João (1916–), 112

James, C. L. R. (1901–1989), 113

Linares, Omar "El Niño" (1967–), 114

Luta Livre (Brazil), 115

Maracanã Stadium (Brazil), 115

Maradona, Diego (1960–), 116

Netball, West Indies, 117

Ochoa, Lorena (1981–), 118

Olympic Games of 1968 (Mexico City), 119

Olympic Games of 2016 (Rio de Janeiro), 120

Pan American Games, 121

Pato (Argentina), 124

Pelé (1940–), 125

Polo, Argentina, 126

Porta, Hugo (1951–), 128

Puerta 12 Tragedy (Buenos Aires, Argentina), 129

Rally Argentina, 130

Rugby Union Football, Argentina, 130

Sabatini, Gabriela (1970–), 135

Sanchez, Hugo (1958–), 136

Senna, Ayrton (1960–1994), 136

Sobers, Sir Garfield (1936–), 137

Softball, Latin America, 137

South American Games, 138

Tennis, Latin America, 139

Traditional Sports and Games, Latin America, 141

Vasco da Gama Stadium Disaster of 2000 (Brazil), 144

Vilas, Guillermo (1952–), 144

Volleyball, Brazil, 145

North America, 147

SPORTS HISTORY, CULTURE, AND PRACTICE IN NORTH AMERICA, 147

Aaron, Hank (1934–), 158

ABC's Wide World of Sports, 159
Aboriginal Mascot Issue, North America, 160
Ali, Muhammad (1942–), 161
All American Girls Professional Baseball
    League, 163
America's Cup, United States, 164
Arena Football, 165
Armstrong, Lance (1971–), 166
Ashe, Arthur (1943–1993), 167
Association Football, United States and
    Canada, 168
Athletics, United States (Field Events), 171
Athletics, United States (Track Events), 175
Augusta National Golf Club, 177
Baseball, United States, 177
Baseball Hall of Fame (United States), 185
Basquette, 186
"Battle of the Sexes" (Tennis Match), 187
Beach Volleyball (United States and
    Canada), 188
Black Sox Scandal (1919), 189
Bodybuilding, 190
Boston Marathon, 192
Broomball, 193
Brundage, Avery (1887–1975), 194
Bryant, Kobe (1978–), 195
Bryant, Paul "Bear" (1913–1983), 196
Camp, Walter (1859–1925), 196
Chamberlain, Wilt (1936–1999), 197
Commonwealth Games, Canada, 199
Curling, North America, 200
Cycling, North America, 202
Davis Cup (Tennis), 204
Dempsey, William Harrison "Jack"
    (1895–1983), 205
Didrikson, Mildred Ella (1911–1956), 207
DiMaggio, Joe (1914–1999), 208
Disc Golf, 209
Drag Racing, 210
Dubin Inquiry, 210
Ederle, Gertrude (1906–2003), 211
Extreme Sports, 213
Fenway Park, 214
Field of Dreams (1989), 215
Figure Skating, North America, 216
Football, American, 218

Football, Canadian, 225
Foxhunting, North America, 229
Frontier Sports, Canada, 230
Gehrig, Lou (1903–1941), 231
Gender and Sport, Canada, 232
Gender and Sport, United States, 234
Gibson, Althea (1927–2003), 239
Golf, United States and Canada, 240
Grange, Harold (1903–1991), 246
Green Bay Packers, 247
Gretzky, Wayne (1961–), 247
Hamm, Mia (1972–), 248
Handball, United States, 250
Hanlan, Edward (1855–1908), 251
Harlem Globetrotters, 251
Hockey Night in Canada, 252
Horse Racing, United States, 253
Horseshoes (Horseshoe Pitching), 263
Ice Hockey, Canada, 264
Ice Hockey, United States, 271
Iditarod Dogsled Race, 274
IndyCar Auto Racing, 275
Jai Alai, 278
James, LeBron (1984–), 278
Johnson, Ben, Scandal at the 1988 Olympics, 279
Johnson, Jack (1878–1946), 280
Jones, Robert (Bobby) Tyre (1902–1971), 281
Jordan, Michael (1963–), 282
Kahanamoku, Duke (1890–1968), 284
Kentucky Derby, 285
King, Billie Jean (1943–), 286
Knight, Philip Hamson (1938–), and Nike
    Corporation, 287
Lacrosse, 288
Lombardi, Vince (1918–1970), 290
Louis, Joe (1914–1981), 291
Major League Baseball, 292
Major League Soccer, United States, 294
Man o'War (1917–1947), 295
Mantle, Mickey (1931–1995), 296
Marciano, Rocky (1923–1969), 297
Mays, Willie (1931–), 298
Miniature Golf, 299
"Miracle on Ice" of 1980, 301
Monday Night Football, United States, 302
Namath, Joseph William (1943–), 303

National Association for Stock Car Auto Racing, 304

National Basketball Association, 308

National Collegiate Athletic Association, 310

National Football League, 312

National Football League Championship Game of 1958, 315

National Hockey League, 315

Native American Sports, 317

Negro Baseball Leagues, 320

Nicklaus, Jack (1940–), 322

North American Soccer League, 323

North American Society for Sport History, 324

O'Dea, Pat (1872–1962), 325

Olympic Summer Games of 1904, 325

Olympic Summer Games of 1932, 327

Olympic Summer Games of 1976, 328

Olympic Summer Games of 1984, 328

Olympic Summer Games of 1996, 331

Olympic Winter Games of 1932, 333

Olympic Winter Games of 1980, 334

Olympic Winter Games of 1988, 334

Olympic Winter Games of 2002, 335

Olympic Winter Games of 2010, 337

Outrigger Canoe Racing, 339

Owens, Jesse (1913–1980), 340

Paddleball, 341

Paintball, 342

Palmer, Arnold (1929–), 343

Patrick, Danica (1982–), 344

Phelps, Michael (1985–), 345

Pigeon Racing, 346

Ping-Pong Diplomacy, 346

Pool (Pocket Billiards), North America, 347

President's Council on Fitness, Sports, and Nutrition, 348

Race and Sport, North America, 349

Racquetball, 356

Richard Riot, 357

Ringette, 358

Ripken, Cal, Jr. (1960–), 359

Robinson, Jackie (1919–1972), 360

Rockne, Knute (1888–1931), 361

Rocky, 362

Rodeo, 363

Roller Derby, 364

Rose Bowl, 365

Rowing/Sculling, Canada, 366

Rowing/Sculling, United States, 367

Rugby Union Football, Canada, 369

Rugby Union Football, United States, 370

Ruth, George Herman (1895–1948), 372

Ryder Cup, 374

Sailboarding, 380

Sailing, North America, 380

Sandow, Eugen (1867–1925), 382

Seabiscuit (1933–1947), 383

Secretariat (1970–1989), 384

Sexuality and Sport, North America, 385

Snowboarding, 386

Softball, 387

Spalding, Albert Goodwill (1850–1915), 389

Spalding World Baseball Tour, 390

Speed Skating, North America, 391

Speedball, 393

Spitz, Mark (1950–), 394

Steroid Scandal in Baseball and the Mitchell Report, 395

Sullivan, John L. (1858–1918), 396

Summit on Ice of 1972 (Canada–Soviet Union Ice Hockey Series), 397

Super Bowl, 398

Swimming, Canada, 399

Swimming, United States, 400

Synchronized Swimming, 405

Ten-pin Bowling, 406

Thorpe, Jim (1888–1953), 408

Title IX, 410

Tonya Harding–Nancy Kerrigan Scandal, 411

Trampoline, 412

Triathlon, 412

Truck and Tractor Pulling, 413

Ultimate, 414

Unitas, Johnny (1933–2002), 415

U.S. Open Golf Championship, 415

U.S. Open of 1913 (Golf), 417

U.S. Open Tennis Championship, 418

Volleyball, United States, 421

Waterskiing, 422

Weissmuller, Johnny (1904–1984), 423

Williams, Esther (1921–), 424

Women's National Basketball Association, 424

Women's Sports Foundation, 425
Wooden, John (1910–2010), 425
Woods, Tiger (1975–), 426
World Hockey Association, 427
World Series (United States), 428
X Games, 429

VOLUME 4: OLYMPIC MEDALISTS AND WINNERS AND CHAMPIONS OF MAJOR WORLD SPORTING EVENTS

Alphabetical List of Entries, xix
Acknowledgments, xxxiii

Introduction: The History, Culture, and Practice of Sports Around the World, xxxvii

Olympic Medalists—Summer Olympics, 1

Olympic Medalists—Winter Olympics, 221

Winners and Champions of Major World Sporting Events, 261

Select Bibliography, 365

Editors and Contributors, 379

Index, 391

Alphabetical List of Entries

Aaron, Hank (1934–), 3.158

ABC's Wide World of Sports, 3.159

Aboriginal Mascot Issue, North America, 3.160

Aborigines in Sport (Australia), 1.327

Accra Sports Stadium Disaster (Ghana), 1.80

African Games, 1.81

African Nations Cup, Association Football, 1.83

Aikido, 1.184

Ali, Muhammad (1942–), 3.161

Alianza Lima Air Tragedy (Peru), 3.12

All American Girls Professional Baseball League, 3.163

All Blacks (Māori—New Zealand), 1.329

All Blacks (New Zealand National Rugby Team), 1.330

Altitude Ban, FIFA, 3.13

America's Cup, Australia and New Zealand, 1.331

America's Cup, United States, 3.164

Ancient Olympic Games and Greek Sporting Festivals, 2.226

Ancient Roman Sport, 2.230

Andres Escobar Murder (Colombia), 3.14

Animal Blood Sports, British Isles, 2.13

Antiapartheid Campaigns (Australia and Aotearoa/New Zealand), 1.332

Anti-Apartheid Movement, British Isles, 2.15

Antiapartheid Sports Movement (South Africa), 1.84

Apartheid and Sports in South Africa, 1.90

Arab Women and the Olympic Games, 1.272

Archery, 2.17

Arena Football, 3.165

Armand Césari Stadium Disaster, 2.233

Armstrong, Lance (1971–), 3.166

Army Physical Training Corps (Great Britain), 2.18

Ascot, 2.19

Ashe, Arthur (1943–1993), 3.167

The Ashes, 1.334

Asian Beach Games, 1.185

Asian Football Confederation, 1.185

Asian Games, 1.186

Asian Winter Games, 1.188

Association Football, Argentina, 3.14

Association Football, Australia, 1.335

Association Football, Bolivia, 3.24

Association Football, Brazil, 3.25

Association Football, Cameroon, 1.94

Association Football, Caribbean, 3.32

Association Football, Central America, 3.34

Association Football, Central Asia, 1.189

Association Football, China, 1.189

Association Football, Egypt, 1.273

Association Football, England and Wales, 2.19

Association Football, France, 2.234

Association Football, Germany, 2.235

Association Football, Ghana, 1.95

Association Football, Italy, 2.236

Association Football, Japan, 1.190

Association Football, Korea, 1.191

Association Football, Mexico, 3.36

Association Football, The Netherlands, 2.239

Association Football, New Zealand, 1.338

Association Football, Nigeria, 1.96

Association Football, Nordic Countries, 2.240

Association Football, North Africa, 1.274

Association Football, Pacific Coast of South America, 3.38

Association Football, Palestine, 1.275

Association Football, Paraguay, 3.47

Association Football, Portugal, 2.241

Association Football, Saudi Arabia, 1.276

Association Football, Scotland, 2.26

Association Football, South Africa, 1.97

Association Football, South Asia, 1.193

Association Football, Southeast Asia, 1.193

Association Football, Spain, 2.242

Association Football, Sub-Saharan Africa in General, 1.100

Association Football, United States and Canada, 3.168

Association Football, Uruguay, 3.48

Association Football, Zambia, 1.101

Athletics, Asia, 1.194

Athletics, Australia and New Zealand, 1.339

Athletics, British Isles, 2.29

Athletics, Caribbean, 3.50

Athletics, Kenya, 1.102

Athletics, Middle East and North Africa, 1.277

Athletics, Rest of Africa, 1.104

Athletics, South Africa, 1.105

Athletics, United States (Field Events), 3.171

Athletics, United States (Track Events), 3.175

Attouga (1945–), 1.280

Augusta National Golf Club, 3.177

Australian Football League, 1.341

Australian Institute of Sport, 1.343

Australian Olympic Committee, 1.347

Australian Open (Tennis), 1.348

Australian Rules Football, 1.349

Australian Society for Sports History, 1.355

Australian Sports Commission, 1.355

Auto Racing, Asia, 1.195

Auto Racing, Latin America, 3.53

Azteca Stadium (Mexico), 3.55

Badminton, Asia, 1.196

Badminton, British Isles, 2.31

Badminton House, 2.32

Ballesteros, Severiano (1957–), 2.244

Bandy, 2.33

Bantu Sports Club (Johannesburg, South Africa), 1.107

Barmy Army, 2.34

Baseball, Australia, 1.360

Baseball, Central and South America, 3.55

Baseball, Cuba, 3.57

Baseball, Dominican Republic, 3.60

Baseball, Dutch West Indies, 3.64

Baseball, Europe, 2.245

Baseball, Finnish, 2.246

Baseball, Japan, 1.197

Baseball, Korea, 1.200

Baseball, Mexico, 3.65

Baseball, Puerto Rico, 3.66

Baseball, South Africa, 1.108

Baseball, Taiwan, 1.202

Baseball, United States, 3.177

Baseball Hall of Fame (United States), 3.185

Basketball, Australia and New Zealand, 1.361

Basketball, British Isles, 2.35

Basketball, China, 1.203

Basketball, Europe, 2.249

Basketball, Israel, 1.280

Basketball, Italy, 2.251

Basketball, Latin America, 3.68

Basketball, Lebanon, 1.281

Basketball, Russia, the Former Soviet Union, and the Baltic Countries, 2.253

Basketball, Yugoslav Countries, 2.255

Basquette, 3.186

"Battle of the Sexes" (Tennis Match), 3.187

Beach Volleyball (United States and Canada), 3.188

Beckenbauer, Franz (1945–), 2.257

Becker, Boris (1967–), 2.257

Beckham, David (1975–), 2.36

Ben M'barek, Larbi (1914–1992), 1.282

Best, George (1946–2005), 2.38

Billiards, 2.38

Black Sox Scandal (1919), 3.189

Blatter, Joseph S. (1936–), 2.258

Bodybuilding, 3.190

Bodyline (1932–1933), 1.362

Bolivarian Games, 3.70

Bolt, Usain (1986–), 3.71

Book of the Courtier (Castiglione), 2.259

Borg, Björn (1956–), 2.260

Bosman Ruling, 1995, 2.261

Boston Marathon, 3.192

Botham, Sir Ian (1955–), 2.39

Bourguibism and Sport (Tunisia), 1.283

Boxing, Australia, 1.363

Boxing, British Isles, 2.40

Boxing, Latin America, 3.71

Boxing, Philippines, 1.205

Boxing, South Africa, 1.109

Bradman, Sir Donald (1908–2001), 1.364

Brazilian Soccer Match–Fixing Scandal of 2005, 3.78

British Commonwealth Games of 1974 (Christchurch, New Zealand), 1.365

British Empire and Commonwealth Games of 1962 (Perth, Australia), 1.365

British Empire Games of 1938 (Sydney), 1.366

British Imperialism and Sport, 2.44

British Imperialism and Sports in Asia, 1.206

British Olympic Association, 2.50

Broomball, 3.193

Brownlow Medal (Australia), 1.366

Brundage, Avery (1887–1975), 3.194

Bryant, Kobe (1978–), 3.195

Bryant, Paul "Bear" (1913–1983), 3.196

Bueno, Maria (1939–), 3.78

Bullfighting, 2.263

Bundesliga Match-Fixing Scandal of 2005 (Germany), 2.264

Cairo Football Derby: Al-Ahly–Zamalek, 1.283

Camel Racing, 1.284

Camogie (Ireland), 2.51

Camp, Walter (1859–1925), 3.196

Camp Nou (Spain), 2.265

Camus, Albert (1913–1960), 1.285

Capoeira, Brazil, 3.79

Cardiff Arms Park, 2.52

Central American and Caribbean Games, 3.81

Central American Games, 3.82

Central Council for Physical Recreation, 2.53

Chamberlain, Wilt (1936–1999), 3.197

Champions League, 2.266

Chariots of Fire (1981), 2.54

Chávez, Julio César (1962–), 3.83

Clemente, Roberto (1934–1972), 3.84

Coaching in Sport, 1.1

Coast to Coast Race (New Zealand), 1.367

Comăneci, Nadia (1961–), 2.267

Commonwealth Games, African Nations, 1.112

Commonwealth Games, Asia, 1.207

Commonwealth Games, Australia, 1.368

Commonwealth Games, Canada, 3.199

Commonwealth Games, England, 2.55

Commonwealth Games, Northern Ireland, 2.56

Commonwealth Games, Scotland, 2.57

Commonwealth Games, Wales, 2.58

Commonwealth Games of 1958 (Cardiff), 2.59

Commonwealth Games of 1966 (Jamaica), 3.85

Commonwealth Games of 1982 (Brisbane), 1.369

Commonwealth Games of 1990 (Auckland), 1.370

Commonwealth Games of 1998 (Kuala Lumpur), 1.208

Commonwealth Games of 2006 (Melbourne), 1.371

Commonwealth Games of 2010 (New Delhi), 1.209

Comrades Marathon (South Africa), 1.114

Conejo, Luis Gabelo (1960–), 3.86

CONMEBOL, 3.86

Copa América, 3.87

Copa Libertadores, 3.88

Corinthians, 2.60

Cotswold Games (England), 2.60

Coursing (British Isles), 2.61

Court, Margaret (1942–), 1.372

Cricket, Australia, 1.372

Cricket, Bangladesh, 1.210

Cricket, England, 2.61

Cricket, India, 1.210

Cricket, Kenya, 1.114

Cricket, Netherlands, 2.268

Cricket, New Zealand, 1.378

Cricket, Pakistan, 1.213

Cricket, South Africa, 1.115

Cricket, Sri Lanka, 1.215

Cricket, Trobriand Islands, 1.381

Cricket, West Indies, 3.89

Cricket, Zimbabwe, 1.121

Croquet, 2.68

Cruyff, Johan (1947–), 2.269

Curling, North America, 3.200

Curling, Scotland, 2.69

Cycling, Australia and New Zealand, 1.382

Cycling, North Africa, 1.286

Cycling, North America, 3.202

Dakar Rally, 1.123

DanceSport, 2.270

Darts, 2.69

Dassler Family (Adidas and Puma), 2.273

Davis Cup (Tennis), 3.204

De Coubertin, Pierre Frédy, Baron (1863–1937), 2.274

Dempsey, William Harrison "Jack" (1895–1983), 3.205

Deutsche Demokratische Republik (East Germany) and Sport, 2.275

Deutscher Olympischer Sportbund, 2.280

Didrikson, Mildred Ella (1911–1956), 3.207

Diem, Carl (1882–1962), 2.283

DiMaggio, Joe (1914–1999), 3.208

Disabled and Sport, 1.4

Disc Golf, 3.209

Di Stéfano, Alfredo (1926–), 3.94

Doggett's Coat and Badge (England), 2.71

Doping, Tour de France, 2.283

Dragon Boat Racing, 1.217

Drag Racing, 3.210

Dubai Sports City, 1.287

Dubin Inquiry, 3.210

Ederle, Gertrude (1906–2003), 3.211

Egypt, Sports and Nasserism, 1.287

Elliott, Herb (1938–), 1.383

Ellis Park Stadium Disaster (South Africa), 1.123

Epsom Downs Racecourse (England), 2.71

Estadio Centenario (Uruguay), 3.94

Estadio Mateo Flores Disaster of 1996 (Guatemala), 3.95

Estadio Monumental (Argentina), 3.96

Estadio Nacional (Chile), 3.97

Estadio Nacional Disaster of 1964 (Lima, Peru), 3.97

Ethnicity and Sectarianism in Divided Societies in the Middle East, 1.288

Eton Wall Game (England), 2.73

European Committee for Sports History, 2.286

European Union and Sport, 2.287

Extreme Sports, 3.213

Fangio, Juan Manuel (1911–1995), 3.98

Fanzines (British Isles), 2.73

Far Eastern Championship Games, 1.219

Fast Bowling, West Indies (Cricket), 3.98

Fédération Internationale de Football Association, 1.6

Fédération Internationale de Natation, 2.289

Federer, Roger (1981–), 2.290

Fencing, 2.291

Fenway Park, 3.214

Field Hockey, Argentina, 3.99

Field Hockey, Asia, 1.219

Field Hockey, Australia and New Zealand, 1.384

Field Hockey, British Isles, 2.74

Field Hockey, South Africa, 1.124

Field of Dreams (1989), 3.215

Field Sports, Australia and New Zealand, 1.385

Field Sports, British Isles, 2.76

Field Sports, South Africa, 1.125

FIFA World Cup of 1930 (Uruguay), 3.99

FIFA World Cup of 1950 (Brazil), 3.100

FIFA World Cup of 1958 (Sweden), 2.293

FIFA World Cup of 1962 (Chile), 3.102

FIFA World Cup of 1966 (England), 2.80

FIFA World Cup of 1970 (Mexico), 3.103

FIFA World Cup of 1974 (West Germany), 2.294

FIFA World Cup of 1978 (Argentina), 3.103

FIFA World Cup of 1982 (Spain), 2.297

FIFA World Cup of 1986 (Mexico), 3.104

FIFA World Cup of 1990 (Italy), 2.298

FIFA World Cup of 1998 (France), 2.300

FIFA World Cup of 2002 (Japan and South Korea), 1.221

FIFA World Cup of 2006 (Germany), 2.301

FIFA World Cup of 2010 (South Africa), 1.127

FIFA World Cup of 2014 (Brazil), 3.107

Figure Skating, North America, 3.216

Fistball, 2.304

Fives, England, 2.83

Folk Sports and Traditional Games, Europe, 2.304

Football, American, 3.218

Football, Canadian, 3.225

Football, Gaelic, 2.83

Footballers' Wives, 2.85

Football War (El Salvador and Honduras), 3.107

Formula One Auto Racing, 2.312

Foxhunting, British Isles, 2.86

Foxhunting, North America, 3.229

Fraser, Dawn (1937–), 1.388

Freeman, Cathy (1973–), 1.388

French Open Tennis Championships, 2.315

Frontier Sports, Canada, 3.230

Futsal (Uruguay), 3.108

Gaelic Athletic Association, 2.89

Games of the Newly Emerging Forces, 1.222

Gehrig, Lou (1903–1941), 3.231

Gender and Sport, Asia, 1.224

Gender and Sport, British Isles, 2.93

Gender and Sport, Canada, 3.232

Gender and Sport, Europe, 2.317

Gender and Sport, Latin America and the Caribbean, 3.109

Gender and Sport, Middle East and North Africa, 1.290

Gender and Sport, United States, 3.234

Gibson, Althea (1927–2003), 3.239

Gleneagles Agreement, 2.98

Globalization and Sport, 1.8

Golf, British Isles, 2.98

Golf, Europe, 2.321

Golf, Latin America and the Caribbean, 3.111

Golf, Oceania, 1.389

Golf, Sub-Saharan Africa, 1.129

Golf, United States and Canada, 3.240

Goolagong-Cawley, Evonne (1951–), 1.390

Grace, W. G. (1848–1915), 2.105

Graf, Stefanie Maria "Steffi" (1969–), 2.322

Grand National, 2.106

Grange, Harold (1903–1991), 3.246

Greco-Roman Wrestling, 2.323

Green Bay Packers, 3.247

Gretzky, Wayne (1961–), 3.247

Gulf Cooperation Council Games, 1.292

Gymnastics, Czech, 2.325

Gymnastics, Danish, 2.326

Gymnastics, German (*Turnen*), 2.327

Gymnastics, Romania, 2.331

Gymnastics, Soviet/Russian, 2.333

Gymnastics, Swedish, 2.334

Hadlee, Sir Richard (1951–), 1.391

The Haka (New Zealand), 1.392

Hamia, Cherif (1931–), 1.292

Hamm, Mia (1972–), 3.248

Hammond, Wally (1903–1965), 2.107

Hampden Park, 2.108

Hampden Park Riot of 1909, 2.108

Handball, North Africa, 1.293

Handball, Team, 2.335

Handball, United States, 3.250

Hanlan, Edward (1855–1908), 3.251

Hansie Cronje Match-Fixing Scandal (South Africa), 1.131

Harlem Globetrotters, 3.251

Havelange, João (1916–), 3.112

Henie, Sonja (1912–1969), 2.338

Henley-on-Todd Regatta, 1.393

Henley Royal Regatta, England, 2.109

Heysel Stadium Disaster (Belgium), 2.338

Highland Games, Scotland, 2.109

Hillary, Sir Edmund (1919–2008), 1.393

Hillsborough Disaster, England, 2.111

Hobbs, Sir John Berry (1882–1963), 2.112

Hockey Night in Canada, 3.252

Hong Kong Sevens, 1.226

Hooliganism, British Isles, 2.113

Hooliganism, European Football (Soccer), 2.339

Hopman Cup (Australia), 1.394

Horse Racing, Australia and New Zealand, 1.394

Horse Racing, British Isles, 2.115

Horse Racing, United States, 3.253

Horseshoes (Horseshoe Pitching), 3.263

Hungary vs. Soviet Union Olympic Water Polo Match of 1956, 2.342

Hurling, 2.121

Iaidō, 1.226

Ice Hockey, British Isles, 2.122

Ice Hockey, Canada, 3.264

Ice Hockey, Europe, 2.343

Ice Hockey, United States, 3.271

Iditarod Dogsled Race, 3.274

Imperial/International Cricket Council, 2.123

Imperialism and Sport, 1.15

Imperialism and Sport, British Colonial
    Africa, 1.132

Indigenous (Aboriginal Australian) Cricket Tour of
    England (1868), 1.396

Indurain, Miguel (1964–), 2.348

IndyCar Auto Racing, 3.275

International Amateur Athletic Federation, 2.349

International Olympic Committee, 1.23

International Relations and Sport, 1.26

International Rules Football, 1.398

International Society for the History of Physical
    Education and Sport, 2.351

Iran and Sport since the Islamic "Revolution", 1.293

Iraq, Baath Regime and Sport in, 1.295

Irish Diaspora and Sport, 2.125

Islamic Solidarity Games of 2005 (Saudi
    Arabia), 1.296

Islamism and Sport, 1.297

Isle of Man Motorcycle Races, 2.126

Italian Football Scandal of 2006 (Calciopoli), 2.351

Jack Johnson–Tommy Burns Fight, Sydney
    (1908), 1.398

Jackson, Marjorie (1931–), 1.399

Jai Alai, 3.278

James, C. L. R. (1901–1989), 3.113

James, LeBron (1984–), 3.278

Jeux de la Francophonie, 2.352

Jeux de la Francophonie of 2005 (Niger), 1.136

Johnson, Ben, Scandal at the 1988 Olympics, 3.279

Johnson, Jack (1878–1946), 3.280

Jones, Robert Tyre (1902–1971), 3.281

Jordan, Michael (1963–), 3.282

Jousting, 2.353

Judo, 1.226

Jujitsu, 1.227

Jukskei (South Africa), 1.136

Kaatsen, 2.355

Kabaddi, 1.228

Kahanamoku, Duke (1890–1968), 3.284

Karaiskakis Stadium Disaster, 2.356

Karate, 1.228

Kendo, 1.229

Kentucky Derby, 3.285

Khan, Imran (1952–), 1.231

Killy, Jean-Claude (1943–), 2.357

King, Billie Jean (1943–), 3.286

Klammer, Franz (1953–), 2.358

Knight, Philip Hamson (1938–), and Nike
    Corporation, 3.287

Knur and Spell, England, 2.126

Kolven, 2.358

Korbut, Olga (1955–), 2.359

Korfball, 2.360

Kurash, 1.232

Lacoste, René (1904–1996), 2.360

Lacrosse, 3.288

La Liga, 2.361

Langer, Bernhard (1957–), 2.362

Lapta, 2.363

La Soule, 2.363

Laver, Rod (1938–), 1.399

Lawn Bowling, Australia and New Zealand, 1.400

Lawn Bowling, British Isles, 2.127

Legal Liability in Sport, 1.28

Lenglen, Suzanne (1899–1938), 2.364

L'Équipe FLN (Algeria), 1.299

Lillee, Dennis Keith (1949–), 1.402

Linares, Omar "El Niño" (1967–), 3.114

Lindrum, Walter (1898–1960), 1.402

Literature and Sport, British Isles, 2.128

Lombardi, Vince (1918–1970), 3.290

Lomu, Jonah (1975–), 1.403

London Marathon, 2.132

Louis, Joe (1914–1981), 3.291

Lovelock, Jack (1910–1949), 1.404

Luta Livre (Brazil), 3.115

Macau Grand Prix, 1.233

Maccabiah Games, 2.364

Maghrebin Games, 1.299

Major League Baseball, 3.292

Major League Soccer, United States, 3.294

Makybe Diva (1999–), 1.404

Manchester United Munich Air Disaster, 2.133

Man o' War (1917–1947), 3.295

Mantle, Mickey (1931–1995), 3.296

Maracanã Stadium (Brazil), 3.115

Maradona, Diego (1960–), 3.116

Marciano, Rocky (1923–1969), 3.297

Martial Arts, Europe, 2.366

Marylebone Cricket Club, 2.134

Massey, Arnaud (1877–1950), 2.367

Matthews, Sir Stanley (1915–2000), 2.135

Mays, Willie (1931–), 3.298

McKay, Heather (1941–), 1.405

Meads, Colin Earl (1936–), 1.406

Media and Sport, 1.34

Media and Sport (Asia), 1.233

Media and Sport in the Arab World, 1.300

Mediterranean Games of 1975 (Algiers), 1.301

Mekhloufi, Rachid (1936–), 1.302

Melbourne Cricket Ground, 1.406

Melbourne Cup, 1.407

Merckx, Eddy (1945–), 2.368

Migrations, Diasporas, and Sports in the Middle East and North Africa, 1.302

Milla, Roger (1952–), 1.137

Miller, Keith Ross (1919–2004), 1.408

Miniature Golf, 3.299

"Miracle on Ice" of 1980, 3.301

Missionaries and Sport in Africa, 1.138

Modern Pentathlon, 2.369

Monday Night Football, United States, 3.302

Motorcycle Racing (Europe), 2.369

Mountain Climbing, British Isles, 2.136

Mountaineering (Himalayas), 1.235

Muay Thai, 1.236

Much Wenlock Games, England, 2.139

Murrayfield Stadium, 2.139

Muscular Christianity, 2.140

Music and Sport, 1.37

Nadal, Rafael (1986–), 2.371

Nakache, Alfred (1915–1983), 1.305

Namath, Joseph William (1943–), 3.303

National Association for Stock Car Auto Racing, 3.304

National Basketball Association, 3.308

National Collegiate Athletic Association, 3.310

National Football League, 3.312

National Football League Championship Game of 1958, 3.315

National Hockey League, 3.315

Native American Sports, 3.317

Navratilova, Martina (1956–), 2.372

Negro Baseball Leagues, 3.320

Nepia, George (1905–1986), 1.409

Netball, Australia, 1.409

Netball, British Isles, 2.143

Netball, New Zealand, 1.411

Netball, Pacific Islands, 1.412

Netball, South Africa, 1.139

Netball, West Indies, 3.117

Newmarket, England, 2.146

New Zealand All Blacks of 1905 ("The Originals"), 1.413

New Zealand All Blacks of 1924 ("The Invincibles"), 1.415

New Zealand Olympic Committee, 1.415

Nga Taonga Takaro (Traditional Māori Games, New Zealand), 1.416

Nicklaus, Jack (1940–), 3.322

Norman, Greg (1955–), 1.422

Norman, Peter (1942–2006), 1.423

North Africa and the FIFA World Cup (Association Football), 1.305

North American Soccer League, 3.323

North American Society for Sport History, 3.324

Northern Ireland, Sport and Sectarianism in, 2.146

Nurmi, Paavo (1897–1973), 2.372

Ochoa, Lorena (1981–), 3.118

O'Dea, Pat (1872–1962), 3.325

The Old Firm: Glasgow Celtic and Glasgow Rangers Football Clubs, Scotland, 2.148

Olympic Boycott of 1976 (African Nations), 1.141

Olympic Council of Asia, 1.236

Olympic Games of 1896 (Athens), 2.374

Olympic Games of 1900 (Paris), 2.376

Olympic Games of 1908 (London), 2.150

Olympic Games of 1912 (Stockholm), 2.377

Olympic Games of 1920 (Antwerp), 2.379

Olympic Games of 1924 (Paris), 2.380

Olympic Games of 1928 (Amsterdam), 2.381

Olympic Games of 1936 (Berlin), 2.383

Olympic Games of 1940 (Tokyo), 1.237

Olympic Games of 1948 (London), 2.151

Olympic Games of 1952 (Helsinki), 2.387

Olympic Games of 1956 (Melbourne), 1.423

Olympic Games of 1960 (Rome), 2.389

Olympic Games of 1964 (Tokyo), 1.238

Olympic Games of 1968 (Mexico City), 3.119

Olympic Games of 1972 (Munich), 2.390

Olympic Games of 1980 (Moscow), 2.392

Olympic Games of 1988 (Seoul, Republic of Korea), 1.240

Olympic Games of 1992 (Barcelona), 2.394

Olympic Games of 2000 (Sydney), 1.425

Olympic Games of 2004 (Athens), 2.396

Olympic Games of 2008 (Beijing), 1.242

Olympic Games of 2012 (London), 2.153

Olympic Games of 2016 (Rio de Janeiro), 3.120

Olympic Movement, 1.39

Olympic Summer Games of 1904, 3.325

Olympic Summer Games of 1932, 3.327

Olympic Summer Games of 1976, 3.328

Olympic Summer Games of 1984, 3.328

Olympic Summer Games of 1996, 3.331

Olympic Winter Games of 1924 (Chamonix), 2.397

Olympic Winter Games of 1928 (St. Moritz), 2.398

Olympic Winter Games of 1932, 3.333

Olympic Winter Games of 1936 (Garmisch-Partenkirchen), 2.399

Olympic Winter Games of 1948 (St. Moritz), 2.400

Olympic Winter Games of 1952 (Oslo), 2.400

Olympic Winter Games of 1956 (Cortina), 2.401

Olympic Winter Games of 1964 (Innsbruck), 2.402

Olympic Winter Games of 1968 (Grenoble), 2.403

Olympic Winter Games of 1972 (Sapporo, Japan), 1.243

Olympic Winter Games of 1976 (Innsbruck), 2.404

Olympic Winter Games of 1980, 3.334

Olympic Winter Games of 1984 (Sarajevo), 2.406

Olympic Winter Games of 1988, 3.334

Olympic Winter Games of 1992 (Albertville), 2.407

Olympic Winter Games of 1994 (Lillehammer), 2.408

Olympic Winter Games of 1998 (Nagano, Japan), 1.244

Olympic Winter Games of 2002, 3.335

Olympic Winter Games of 2006 (Turin/Torino), 2.410

Olympic Winter Games of 2010, 3.337

Oman, Sport in, 1.306

Open Championship (British Open), 2.155

Orkney Stadium Disaster (South Africa), 1.141

Outrigger Canoe Racing, 3.339

Owens, Jesse (1913–1980), 3.340

Paddleball, 3.341

Paintball, 3.342

Palmer, Arnold (1929–), 3.343

Pan-Africanism and Sport, North Africa, 1.308

Pan American Games, 3.121

Pan-Arab Nationalism and the Pan-Arab Games, 1.309

Pankration, 2.412

Pato (Argentina), 3.124

Patrick, Danica (1982–), 3.344

Pedestrianism, 2.156

Pelé (1940–), 3.125

Pelota, 2.413

Petanque, Bocce, Boules, 2.414

Phar Lap (1926–1932), 1.427

Phelps, Michael (1985–), 3.345

Philosophy of Sport, 1.45

Pigeon Racing, 3.346

Ping-Pong Diplomacy, 3.346

Platini, Michel (1955–), 2.415

Player, Gary (1935–), 1.142

Pollock, Graeme (1944–), 1.143

Polo, Argentina, 3.126

Polo, Britain, 2.157

Polo, India, 1.245

Pool (Pocket Billiards), North America, 3.347

Porta, Hugo (1951–), 3.128

Premier League, 2.159

President's Council on Fitness, Sports, and Nutrition, 3.348

Prost, Alain (1955–), 2.415

Puerta 12 Tragedy (Buenos Aires, Argentina), 3.129

Punting, England, 2.160

Puskas, Ferenc (1927–2006), 2.416

Qatar Asian Games of 2006, 1.310

Qatar Sports Development and the Bid for the 2016 Olympic Games, 1.310

Quoits, Great Britain, 2.161

Race and Sport, British Isles, 2.162

Race and Sport, North America, 3.349

Racewalking, 2.168

Racquetball, 3.356

Rally Argentina, 3.130

Rallying/World Rally Championship, 2.416

Ranfurly Shield (New Zealand), 1.428

Ranjitsinhji, K. S. (1872–1933), 2.168

Real Tennis, 2.169

Rebel Sports Tours, South Africa, 1.143

Richard Riot, 3.357

Ringette, 3.358

Ripken, Cal, Jr. (1960–), 3.359

Robben Island Sports Club (South Africa), 1.144

Robinson, Jackie (1919–1972), 3.360

Rock Climbing, 2.417

Rockne, Knute (1888–1931), 3.361

Rocky, 3.362

Rodeo, 3.363

Roller Derby, 3.364

Rose, Lionel (1948–), 1.428

Rose Bowl, 3.365

Rowing/Sculling, Australia and New Zealand, 1.429

Rowing/Sculling, British Isles, 2.169

Rowing/Sculling, Canada, 3.366

Rowing/Sculling, United States, 3.367

Royal and Ancient Golf Club, 2.171

Rugby League, Great Britain, 2.172

Rugby League Football, Australia, 1.431

Rugby League Football, New Zealand, 1.433

Rugby Sevens, 1.434

Rugby Union Football, Argentina, 3.130

Rugby Union Football, Australia, 1.434

Rugby Union Football, Canada, 3.369

Rugby Union Football, England, 2.175

Rugby Union Football, France, 2.418

Rugby Union Football, Ireland, 2.179

Rugby Union Football, Italy, 2.422

Rugby Union Football, New Zealand, 1.439

Rugby Union Football, Pacific Islands, 1.445

Rugby Union Football, Rest of Africa, 1.146

Rugby Union Football, Scotland, 2.182

Rugby Union Football, South Africa, 1.147

Rugby Union Football, United States, 3.370

Rugby Union Football, Wales, 2.183

Rugby World Cup of 1987 (New Zealand and Australia), 1.447

Rugby World Cup of 1991 (United Kingdom and France), 2.188

Rugby World Cup of 1995 (South Africa), 1.152

Rugby World Cup of 1999 (Wales), 2.189

Rugby World Cup of 2003 (Australia), 1.447

Rumble in the Jungle (1974), 1.153

Running of the Bulls, 2.425

Ruth, George Herman (1895–1948), 3.372

Ryder Cup, 3.374

Sabatini, Gabriela (1970–), 3.135

Sailboarding, 3.380

Sailing, Australia and New Zealand, 1.448

Sailing, North America, 3.380

Samaranch, Juan Antonio (1920–2010), 2.426

Sánchez, Hugo (1958–), 3.136

Sandow, Eugen (1867–1925), 3.382

San Siro Stadium, 2.426

Santiago Bernabéu Stadium, 2.427

Schmeling, Max (1905–2005), 2.427

Schumacher, Michael (1969–), 2.428

Schwingen (Switzerland), 2.428

Seabiscuit (1933–1947), 3.383

Secretariat (1970–1989), 3.384

Senna, Ayrton (1960–1994), 3.136

Sepak Takraw, 1.247

Serie A (Italy), 2.429

Sexuality and Sport, North America, 3.385

Sexuality and Sports, 1.47

Sheffield Shield, 1.449

Short Track Speed Skating, Australia, 1.450

Singh, Vijay (1963–), 1.450

Six Nations Rugby Championship, 2.190

Skating, Short-Track Speed (Asia), 1.248

Skiing, Alpine (Europe), 2.430

Skiing, Nordic, 2.435

Sliding Sports (Bobsleigh, Luge, and Skeleton), 2.438

Snell, Peter (1938–), 1.451

Snooker, 2.190

Snowboarding, 3.386

Sobers, Sir Garfield (1936–), 3.137

Sociology of Sport, 1.50

Softball, 3.387

Softball, Australia, 1.451

Softball, Latin America, 3.137

Sokol Movement (Czech Republic, Slovakia, Czechoslovakia), 2.442

Sorenstam, Annika (1970–), 2.443

South Africa and the Olympic Games, 1.154

South American Games, 3.138

Southeast Asian Games, 1.249

South Sydney District Rugby League Club Ltd vs. News Limited, 1.453

Spalding, Albert Goodwill (1850–1915), 3.389

Spalding World Baseball Tour, 3.390

Spartakiads, 2.444

Speed Skating, Europe, 2.445

Speed Skating, North America, 3.391

Speedball, 3.393

Speedway, 2.192

Spitz, Mark (1950–), 3.394

Sport and International Development in Africa, 1.156

Sport Labor Migration, 1.54

Sport Psychology, 1.55

Sports Medicine, 1.59

Sports Museums and Heritage Collections, 1.63

Springbok Emblem (South Africa), 1.158

Springbok Tour of New Zealand (1981) (South African Rugby Tour), 1.454

Squash, Asia, 1.250

Squash, British Isles, 2.193

Steroid Scandal in Baseball and the Mitchell Report, 3.395

Stick Fighting, Africa and Caribbean, 1.158

Stoolball, 2.193

Sullivan, John L. (1858–1918), 3.396

Summit on Ice of 1972 (Canada–Soviet Union Ice Hockey Series), 3.397

Sumo, 1.250

Sun City (South Africa), 1.159

Super Bowl, 3.398

Super 15 Rugby, 1.456

Super League "War", 1.456

Supreme Council for Sport in Africa, 1.160

Surfing, Australia and New Zealand, 1.457

Surfing, South Africa, 1.161

Surf Lifesaving, Australia, 1.460

Swimming, Australia, 1.462

Swimming, Canada, 3.399

Swimming, England, 2.194

Swimming, Southern Africa, 1.162

Swimming, United States, 3.400

Sydney Organising Committee for the Olympic Games, 1.464

Sydney Paralympic Organising Committee, 1.465

Sydney to Hobart Yacht Race (Australia), 1.466

Synchronized Swimming, 3.405

TAB (Totalisator Agency Board), Australia, 1.466

Table Tennis, Asia, 1.252

Table Tennis, Europe, 2.448

Tae Kwon Do, 1.253

Tai Chi, 1.255

Tartan Army, Scotland, 2.196

Taylor Report, 2.197

Tendulkar, Sachin (1973–), 1.255

Tennis, Africa, 1.163

Tennis, Asia, 1.256

Tennis, British Isles, 2.198

Tennis, Latin America, 3.139

Ten-pin Bowling, 3.406

This Sporting Life, 2.202

Thorpe, Ian (1982–), 1.468

Thorpe, Jim (1888–1953), 3.408

Title IX, 3.410

Tonya Harding–Nancy Kerrigan Scandal, 3.411

Total Football (Netherlands), 2.450

Tour de France, 2.450

Tourism and Sport, 1.67

Traditional Sports, Asia, 1.257

Traditional Sports, Australian Aboriginal and Torres Strait Islander Peoples, 1.468

Traditional Sports, Southern Africa, 1.165

Traditional Sports and Games, Latin America, 3.141

Trampoline, 3.412

Tretiak, Vladislav (1952–), 2.456

Triathlon, 3.412

Truck and Tractor Pulling, 3.413

Trumper, Victor Thomas (1877–1915), 1.472

Tug-of-War, 2.202

Tunis 2001 Mediterranean Games, 1.311

Tutsi High Jumping (Rwanda), 1.168

Twenty20 Cricket (India), 1.259

Twickenham Stadium, 2.203

Two Chinas Issue, 1.260

Ultimate, 3.414

Underarm Bowling Incident, Cricket (Australia), 1.472

Underwater Hockey, 2.204

Union of European Football Associations, 2.457

Unitas, Johnny (1933–2002), 3.415

United Nations and Sport, 1.69

U.S. Imperialism and Sport in Asia, 1.261

U.S. Open Golf Championship, 3.415

U.S. Open of 1913 (Golf), 3.417

U.S. Open Tennis Championship, 3.417

Vardon, Harry (1870–1937), 2.205

Vasco da Gama Stadium Disaster of 2000 (Brazil), 3.144

Vilas, Guillermo (1952–), 3.144

"Vitaï Lampada", 2.206

Volata, 2.458

Volleyball, Asia, 1.263

Volleyball, Brazil, 3.145

Volleyball, United States, 3.421

Vuvuzela (South Africa), 1.169

Walker Cup, 2.206

Warne, Shane (1969–), 1.473

Warner, Sir Pelham (1873–1963), 2.207

Water Polo, 2.207

Waterskiing, 3.422

Weah, George (1966–), 1.170

Weightlifting (Europe), 2.458

Weissmuller, Johnny (1904–1984), 3.423

Wembley Stadium, 2.208

Wightman Cup, 2.209

Wilding, Anthony (1883–1915), 1.473

Williams, Esther (1921–), 3.424

Wimbledon, 2.210

Winter Sports, Asia, 1.265

Wisden Cricketers' Almanack, 2.215

Witt, Katerina (1965–), 2.459

Wolfenden Committee Report (1960), 2.215

Women Islamic Games (Iran), 1.312

Women's National Basketball Association, 3.424

Women's Olympics, 2.460

Women's Sports Foundation, 3.425

Woodchopping, 1.474

Wooden, John (1910–2010), 3.425

Woods, Tiger (1975–), 3.426

Worker Sport, Europe, 2.461

Workers' Sport, British Isles, 2.217

World Anti-Doping Agency, 2.464

World Hockey Association, 3.427

World Series (United States), 3.428

World Series Cricket, 1.474

Wrestling, Brittany (*Gouren*), 2.465

Wrestling, Iceland (*Glima*), 2.466

Wrestling, Mongolian, 1.265

Wushu, 1.266

X Games, 3.429

Yao, Ming (1980–), 1.267

Yashin, Lev Ivanovic (1929–1990), 2.466

Yemen, Sport in the Republic of, 1.314

Zambian National Football Team Disaster (1993), 1.171

Zatopek, Emil (1922–2000), 2.467

Zidane, Zinedine (1972–), 2.467

Zoff, Dino (1942–), 2.468

Acknowledgments

Sports Around the World: History, Culture, and Practice is not merely a new encyclopedia of sports. It explores sports and sporting cultures around the world in some unique ways. You will find entries on the same sport in different countries as well as entries on sports and areas of the world often overlooked. It goes without saying that a project of this magnitude has required thousands of human hours to produce. Four years and some 300 contributors later, we are here with a finished product. When ABC-CLIO approached one of us to revamp the encyclopedic discussion of sport with a different approach, it remained to be seen if we could all actually pull this off. *Sports Around the World: History, Culture, and Practice* really does move away from the traditional encyclopedic approach and provides greater depth of analysis of sports wherever they are played around the world. After all, how can Brazilian, Italian, and Ghanaian soccer be given full treatment in a single entry on association football (soccer)? Kenyan running is quite different from Jamaican running, and cricket history and culture in India are certainly different from Australia.

Many people, a number of them colleagues or advanced students, stepped in to fill gaps that appeared late in the day. These entries are no less important than those written by the many recognized experts in sports history and sports studies. Several generations of scholars interested in sport have led the charge, some with decades of experience under their belt and some who are only a few steps ahead of many of you reading these volumes.

We would particularly like to thank our regional editors: Daryl Adair (Oceania), Dean Allen (sub-Saharan Africa, coeditor), Mahfoud Amara (Middle East and North Africa), Timothy J. L. Chandler and Daryl Leeworthy (British Isles), Lise Joern and Verner Møller (Europe), and Charles Little (Asia outside the Middle East). John Nauright coedited the sub-Saharan Africa section, and Charles Parrish edited Latin America and the Caribbean with invaluable advice from Joe "Jose" Arbena. A couple of editors stepped in to fill gaps at the last minute, and they certainly made the overall process of coordination easier. Many authors may be well known to some readers, and we would like to thank those who, in some cases despite bouts of severe and even life-threatening illness, have contributed to the project without the need to do so. Particular thanks go to (in no particular order) Henning Eichberg, John Bale, Verner Møller, Maarten van Bottenburg, Louise Mansfield, Paul Darby, Colin Tatz, Bill Murray, Mike Huggins, Phil Dine, Mark Dyreson, Rob Ruck, S. W. Pope, Mike Lomax, Thierry Terret, Arnd Krüger, Gertrud Pfister, Jørn Hansen, Jerry Gems, Alan Cobley, David R. Black, Mike Silk, Chris Bolsmann, Malcolm MacLean, Greg Ryan, Carol

Osborne, Toni Bruce, Scarlett Cornelissen, Kamilla Swart, David Hassan, Joe Bradley, Dick McGehee, Mark Nagel, Julie Stevens, Ian Ritchie, Brett Hutchins, and Marek Waic, among many others, all of whom have established themselves as premier scholars in the fields of sports and leisure studies. Others are sure to become well known as sports studies scholars in the future and were eager to assist when asked. We would like in particular to thank up-and-coming (or already arrived) international stars such as Michelle Sikes, Emily Houghton, Philani Nongogo, Risto Rasku, Sine Agergaard, Thomas Fletcher, Chris Gaffney, James McBean, Anand Rampersand, and Sarah and Aaron Zipp, among others. No less important have been the contributions by our colleagues in the School of Recreation, Health, and Tourism at George Mason University: Jatin Ambegnakor, Robert Baker, Dominique Banville, Chris Elzey, Craig Esherick, Jim Kozlowski, R. Pierre Rodgers, and last but certainly not least, our guru David Wiggins. John Nauright's research students at George Mason and at the University of the West Indies, Cave Hill in Barbados, and Aarhus University in Denmark also made important contributions, namely Jason Carlson, Nicole Hitpas, Jørgen B. Kjær, Molly McManamon, Kelsey Moore, Anna Outratova (also of Charles University in Prague), Liz Ryan, Rwany Sibaja, Jill Singleton, Dae Song, and Daniel Zimmet at George Mason; Philip Forde, Rommel Green, and Sasha Sutherland at Cave Hill; and Line Jensen at Aarhus. Jill Singleton in particular did much to get this project off the ground through invaluable administrative assistance as well as contributing many greatly needed entries. A couple of former students of John's at Georgia Southern University and the University of Abertay Dundee also penned excellent entries, particularly John Stockstill and Andrea Giampiccoli, both of whom always answer the call for assistance when needed.

We would also like to extend thanks to our editors and other support staff at ABC-CLIO, particularly John Wagner, who came to the project midway through the process. John stepped right in without missing a beat to help us keep the project moving forward. Our copyediting team was also sensational.

Last but most importantly, we have to thank our long-suffering families for putting up with this monumental project that has been hanging over our heads for the past several years. John Nauright particularly wants to start by thanking Charlie Parrish for coming on board and making the completion of the project possible. (Whoever thought this project could be run by one editor is crazy; even crazier is that John began by wrongly thinking he could do just that.) Without Charlie as an equal partner, this project would have taken double the time if not longer. It goes without saying that one should never put his or her fate in the hands of 200-plus academics when there is a deadline ahead; however, we believed that this project could make an innovative contribution to the reference work literature on sports. We fired up the coffeepot many nights around 11:00 p.m. after the normal family members in our households had quite sensibly gone to sleep. We exchanged many late-night emails with colleagues. Of course, Daryl Adair in Sydney, Australia, for example, was actually operating a civilized work schedule when we exchanged messages at an unseemly hour here in Virginia. John wanted to say to Papa that he actually did find something good that happens after midnight, so I hope they have Kindles up in heaven.

We lost Papa (aka Dr. Michael Edward Hodges) during the course of this project after he finally lost his courageous and inspiring battle with cancer. He is greatly missed. His support and the support of my extended family have meant more to me than they know.

John would like to thank his daughters Ashley and Lauren for putting up with a distracted dad, for indulging my long hours in front of computer screens that don't love you back, and, to Ashley, for compiling some of the lists in Volume 4. Lauren's volleyball games were a welcome diversion from this project. Shiloh the Wonder Dog also provided me with many needed moments of escape. I am immensely proud of them and love them for all the joy they bring me every day. Most importantly, I want to thank Jenni for not leaving us sad and alone even though there are many times that we are certain the thought crossed her mind! She has given me so much, and I could not have completed this project without her amazing support, encouragement, patience, and love.

Charlie would also like to extend thanks to his children Lucas and Aliana for the much-needed moments of laughter and joy they provided throughout the duration of this project. Additional gratitude is extended to family members both near and abroad for taking interest in this endeavor and constantly inquiring on its progress. In particular, I want to express thanks to Maria for coping with the inconveniences related to my involvement with this project. Her support, encouragement, and understanding were invaluable and provided the additional motivation to extend my efforts well beyond the midnight hour. Finally, I want to acknowledge the enduring support of my grandfather L. M. "Leon" Lassiter. He passed away during this project, yet his wit and wisdom live on through the many lives he touched.

Introduction: The History, Culture, and Practice of Sports Around the World

What is sport or what are sports? Why should we study it/them, let alone produce a four-volume encyclopedia on sports around the world? For the purposes of this project, we have defined sport as rule-bound physical activities that are played at informal and formal levels from a young age into old age. Some sports will be familiar to you and readily identifiable in everyone's mind as a sport. Examples of these include association football or soccer, baseball, basketball, tennis, and hockey. Other sports are sometimes open for debate: Is motor racing a sport? What about golf? Many games contain an element of physical activity. You use your hands and arms to move a chess piece, for example, and anyone who has witnessed a game of dominos in Barbados knows that the tiles should be slammed down on the table with authority, although the players sit or stand around the playing area. We have therefore chosen to limit our coverage in these volumes to those activities that are widely agreed to be sports. We do not expect that the argument of what is and what is not a sport will be settled here, nor should it be.

Another argument, and one that many teachers and academics have offered for decades, is that sport is not important or is a sideline to the really meaningful things in life. No one can deny in the 21st century that sports are relevant to billions of people around the world. More people watch the FIFA World Cup Final in soccer than any other event, with estimates as high as 700 million or 800 million watching on television. More people watch debates about who should be president of the Barcelona Football Club than who should lead the country of Spain. Having said this, in real terms, sports are, on the one hand, important parts of the everyday existence of millions of people around the world, yet on the other hand, they are less important than other forms of business in terms of financial turnover or profits made (or in most cases not made!). In this collection of essays and entries on sports, we present an overview of what sports are around the world, how they are practiced, and where they take place, and we discuss the most significant figures in sports, past and present.

Whether you are interested in famous sports people, learning more about a specific sport, or learning more about sports in different regions of the world, *Sports Around the World: History, Culture, and Practice* is for you. While there are many more sources of information on sports available in print and online than in the past, precious few sources bring together experts from around the world who view sports critically but fairly and present information that holds up to academic scrutiny while at the same time communicating information to nonspecialist readers. These volumes are not meant to be stuffed away on some professor's shelf to look impressive to those who happen to stop by. Rather, *Sports Around the World* is meant to be a reference work for high school and university students, readers with general interest in sporting topics, journalists, people working in the sports industry, and sports fans, particularly those looking for information on a particular sport.

It is not possible to encompass the full history of world sport in one reference, but we touch on major themes and key events and processes that have shaped the modern sporting world. Modern sport and sporting competitions have long fueled passions and keen debate both during the times in which events took place and afterward as historic events. Historians of sport seek to examine the phenomenon of sports, placing sports, sports organizations, and sporting events in their appropriate social, cultural, political, and economic contexts.

Sports Around the World offers more than 850 entries arranged by region and written by more than 250 scholars and experts in various sports, sporting events, and related topics. Each regional section begins with a general essay discussing sports history, culture, and practice in the region, and each entry concludes with a listing of current print and electronic information resources on the entry topic. Entries are listed alphabetically within regional sections. Volume 1 includes essays on important general topics; Africa, Sub-Sahara; Asia, East and South; Australia, New Zealand, and Oceania; and the Middle East and North Africa. Volume 2 covers the British Isles and Europe, and Volume 3 covers Latin America and the Caribbean and North America. Volume 4 includes lists of Olympic medal winners for every Olympics since 1896 as well as the winners of many other major world sporting events, such as the World Series and the FIFA World Cup. Volume 4 also includes a detailed subject index providing quick and easy access to the wealth of information within the entries.

Sports has its roots in ritual activities of premodern societies and in most cases was linked to what David Sansone has called the ritual sacrifice of human energy. In comparing rituals and physical contests among the ancient Greeks and Native Americans, Sansone found commonalities linked to the release of human energy that surrounded sporting competitions in both regions of the world.

Much of what has been written about the history of sport, at least in the West, has followed the classical pattern of Western history as being a story of Western civilization emerging in the ancient Near East, Greece, and Rome; passing through Europe in the Middle Ages; and developing more fully in the early modern and modern eras. Our view of sports history today is largely one seen through the lens of 19th-century scholars who sought ancient origins for civilization and viewed sport as an activity promoted by the ancient Greeks, corrupted by the Romans, and mostly marginalized after the fall of the Roman Empire to develop as popular recreations particularly linked to folk festivals. Among elites in Europe, physical competitions remained popular but were particularly centered on horsemanship, swordsmanship, and marksmanship. In other parts of the world, physical activities, games, and contests that resemble modern sport in some ways also took place. As author David Sansome has pointed out, much of these premodern physical practices, whether in ancient Greece, Mexico, or China, were related to the ritual sacrifice of human energy. Although many of the sports that have become global in scope originated in Western Europe and North America, other influences have also been important. It has been the work of sports historians to understand the nature of sports throughout human history and the role of sociologists of sport to examine the meaning of sports in contemporary societies and cultures. In addition to these professional researchers, many journalists and enthusiasts have also contributed to the literature on sports. Many of the best works on sport are listed in the suggestions for further reading found at the ends of entries.

The Practice of Sports History and Sports Studies

Sporting traditions are made and perpetuated in several ways. They are formed through lived and shared experiences but are also mediated through newspapers, popular periodicals, television, radio, the Internet and other forms of new media, and books and articles written for the popular and academic markets. As the social, cultural, political, and economic roles of sport increased during the 20th century, sport became something that many thought worth writing and reading about.

Sports history began as a hobby for many or was written by sports journalists, but it is not on the sidelines anymore, with many historians turning their attention to sport as a viable area for study. Historians of sport are no longer forced to advance elaborate justifications for their chosen field of study or couch their research within the history of popular culture or leisure or as a novel way of engaging key issues within the historical profession (as was the case 20 or 30 years ago). Sport history was a fledgling area that had been embraced by only a relative handful of scholars prior to the early 1970s. However, over time it became linked to the new social history and flourished during the late 20th century and has finally achieved mainstream academic legitimacy and acclaim. Practitioners are no longer forced to encounter the smirks and repressed laughs from so-called (and professed) mainstream historians. Meanwhile, many journalists, particularly with experience of a particular team or city, have contributed to the information that we have about sport in the past.

The key dynamic in the development of this subdiscipline has been engagement with wider trends within social and cultural history along with a latent interest in critical social theory. A young generation of historians who came into the profession during the 1970s and early 1980s challenged many of the prevailing assumptions held by historians about how best to study the past. Armed with new assumptions, questions, topics, and methods, the new historians fundamentally shifted their collective attention from political events and big ideas toward the processes and experiences of everyday life. In particular, the new social history drew upon two prominent European intellectual trends: the notion of total history championed by scholars connected to the French journal *Annales* (an attempt to incorporate all of the human and social sciences so to as to re-create the totality of the past), and history from the bottom up, as advanced by various British Marxist-influenced historians, such as E. P. Thompson, who employed an analysis of society that emphasized the role of human agency and class struggle in the making of history. In addition to these two fundamentally European schools of historical scholarship, the new historians incorporated the work of social theorists and thereby expanded their understanding of concepts such as society, culture, community, and power.

Sport historians also borrowed from anthropology and sociology and examined the complex relationships between sport and social structures. The most prominent example of this emergent trend within sport history was Allen Guttmann, whose wide interdisciplinary training and command of European languages enabled him to define a new social scientifically based interpretive paradigm informed by Weberian sociology and modernization theory. Simultaneously, sport historians were investigating the socially constructed ideas of race, class, gender, ethnicity, and national identities surrounding modern sport. One can easily look back on the flood of sports historical research produced during the 1980s as a first golden age of sports history.

The bulk of assessments of the state of the field published during the past 20 or so years has rarely subjected sports history's existence to a critique but instead has provided a gentler assessment of its steady ascendancy. Such periodic progress reports have been common within the English-language historiography of North America and the United Kingdom and have been supported by the North American Society for Sport History and the British Society for Sport History in their official journals, *Journal of Sport History* and the *Sport Historian* (renamed *Sport in History* in 2003), respectively. The other key sport history journals are *International Journal of the History of Sport* (formerly the *British Journal of Sports History,* which began in 1984), *Sporting Traditions* (launched in 1984 by the Australian Society for Sport History), and *Sport History Review* (formerly the *Canadian Journal of History of Sport,* established in 1973). A number of important contributions in the international history of sport were also published in the *Journal of Olympic History, Olympika, Stadion, Internationale Zeitschrift für Geschichte des Sports,* and *Revue Internationale d'Histoire du Sport.*

While the field has been driven internally by the publication of research in scholarly journals, monographs and occasional trade books have externally elevated the stature of sport history. A dramatic expansion of the literature occurred during the 1980s and 1990s, aided by the establishment of several book series and the sustained interest of university presses and commercial publishers in the United States and the United Kingdom. In the United Kingdom, Frank Cass Press (now subsumed by Routledge) and Routledge led the way. In the United States, the University of Illinois Press was a publisher of sports history, while SUNY Press and the University of Minnesota Press produced important series in sports studies. Lately the University of Arkansas Press has begun to publish key works in sports history. The University of Nebraska Press has recently published many journalistic and popular texts on the history of sport, especially baseball. While the number of presses that focus on sport is limited, anyone interested in learning about sport in history as well as in contemporary society has plenty from which to choose.

In addition to the historical study of sport and studies in the sociology and cultural studies of sport, other key subdisciplinary fields have emerged, particularly the philosophy of sport (including ethics), sport law, and, most significantly, sport management. Some of this work informs the discussion in many of the entries in this collection. In American universities, sports studies has largely been taken over by sport management as a degree program of study, and it appears that European universities are heading slowly in the same direction. The assumption has been that sport management provides practical training for those who are interested in pursuing careers in sport that are not focused on scientific training. The argument goes that sport is becoming more and more of a business, and therefore trained professionals should be educated to take on the roles of running sports teams, leagues, and major events.

Although the bulk of the periodical literature has appeared in sport-related journals, some notable contributions have been published in leading mainstream historical journals as well, and books on sport are more commonly reviewed in mainstream history and sociology journals than they were in the past. Intelligent writing on sport has also appeared in many nonsporting journals as well as much popular literature. A good example comes from the American weekly magazine *Sports Illustrated,* where writers such as Rick Reilly and S. L. Price present well-thought-out critiques of sports. They have also produced books on sport that are well worth reading. Price's 2009 book *Far Afield: A Sportswriting Odyssey,* recounting the year he spent living in France with his family, provides great insight into the differences between American and European sporting cultures. Frank Foer, editor of the American critical magazine *New Republic,* tackles the subject of globalization through an exploration of soccer cultures around the world in his provocatively titled *How Soccer Explains the World: An Unlikely Theory of Globalization.*

Given the assumed conservative nature surrounding sport, it might be surprising to learn that leftist writers have weighed in on sports subjects for many years. Che Guevara edited a rugby journal when he was a student in Argentina, Fidel Castro has played and written about sport, former Jamaican prime minister Michael Manly has written a detailed history of West Indian cricket, and West Indian Marxist-influenced scholar C. L. R. James has produced one of the best sports books of all time with his *Beyond a Boundary,* written in 1963. While developing this project, we also learned that Leon Trotsky was a sportsman in Russia. Nelson Mandela has stated that sport has the power "to change the world." On the other side of the political spectrum, noted conservative columnist and television analyst George F. Will has written at length about sport, most significantly about baseball. Conservative American presidents Ronald Reagan, George H. W. Bush, and George W. Bush had lifelong engagement with sport. Gerald Ford was an All-American college football player, and Dwight D. Eisenhower and William Howard Taft popularized golf, and Richard Nixon was obsessed with sport and used sporting metaphors widely. Democratic presidents have also embraced sport. John F. Kennedy, despite his many injuries, was known for sailing and his family football games, while Barack Obama plays basketball as often as possible. In the United Kingdom, Prime Minister John Major was notorious for his love of sport and indeed tried to salvage his political career by using hoped-for sporting success by English athletes or teams in his plans to call a general election. Around the world political leaders have embraced sport, while at the same time sporting leaders, particularly those heading major organizations such as the International Olympic Committee (IOC) and the Fédération Internationale de Football Association (International Federation of Football Associations, FIFA), the governing body for world soccer, have become decidedly political.

In every corner of the world, sport is definitely much more than a business. Millions of people pour their hearts and souls into sport each and every week of the year, following their team, their player, or their country in ways that make sport different from other businesses. You can go into the store and decide to buy a new shirt. If you get home and it doesn't fit or you change your mind, you simply return it. It is not a life-and-death matter. In sport, it has never been that simple. While modern sport in its current organizational and commercialized form has been around for 100 years or more, it remains more powerful as a cultural and political force than its economic impact might indicate. Millions and millions of people in all corners of the globe wear their heart on their sleeve in support of their team. And sport can actually be a life-and-death matter. El Salvador and Honduras famously fought a war sparked by a soccer match controversy, and the Colombian defender Andreas Escobar was killed after scoring an own goal (i.e., a goal against his own team) in the 1994 World Cup. Stadium disasters have occurred in many countries: Bradford, Hillsborough, and Heysel are names easily recited by any follower of soccer in England.

Sports leagues are unique entities in capitalist economies, because unlike other areas of business, sports leagues need to cooperate to succeed. Yet, there is not one accepted model of business practice in the organization of professional sports internationally. This makes sport different and not easily tied down by principles taught only in schools of business. In fact, some argue that it is a mistake to even think of sports teams as businesses. Yes, they should be run professionally, but they should be viewed more in the form of a public trust than a limited liability company. The North American practice is to have single leagues that exist as private entities shared by the owners of professional teams. In much of the rest of the world, professional sports operates on a promotion-relegation system whereby teams can move up or down between leagues depending on their performance. If a team finishes last in the National Football League (NFL), there is no threat of it dropping to a lower league. In fact, the team is rewarded with the first draft pick for the following season. In 2009, the powerful English soccer club Newcastle United performed poorly and was relegated to the league below the Premier League. This relegation will cost the club millions of pounds in lost television revenue, further jeopardizing its ability to compete with the top clubs and ensuring that a swift rebound is needed to restore the club's position. In Australia, teams have traditionally been publically owned. This has resulted in fan-led campaigns to save beleaguered teams threatened with mergers or relocations. Attempts to create North American models of sport ownership largely failed in Australia because it was anathema to Aussie sporting practices. In the Nordic countries and other parts of Europe, the multisport club format is common; it caters to mass participation and elite sport within a single entity. These examples point to the need to understand the social and cultural role of sport in any given society, which is as important as understanding the sport marketplace in and of itself.

Sport is one of the most significant shapers of collective identity in the contemporary world and is a powerful force in human societies. Often sporting events and people's reactions to them are the clearest public manifestations of culture and collective identities in a given society. Frequently sport is inscribed with the power to liberate and elevate the human spirit—to create moments of escape from the mundane. Sport is also highly nostalgic; it allows us to relive great moments and to hope for them to appear again in the next match or season. We hope that some of the magic of sport as well as an understanding of the problems and complexities of sports appear here in these volumes.

John Nauright

Note: This essay is adapted from two introductory essays written by John Nauright and S. W. Pope in 2009 for their coedited collections *The New Sport Management*

Reader (Morgantown: Fitness Information Technology, 2009) and *The Routledge Companion to Sports History* (London: Routledge, 2010).

Further Reading

Allison, L., ed. 2005. *The Global Politics of Sport: The Role of Global Institutions in Sport.* London: Routledge.

Arnaud, P., and G. Garrier, eds. 1992. *Jeux et sports dans l'histoire,* 2 vols. Paris: CTHS.

Arnaud, P., and T. Terret 1996. *Histoire du sport feminine.* Paris: L'Harmattan.

Bairner, A. 2001. *Sport, Nationalism and Globalization: European and North American Perspectives.* Albany: SUNY Press.

Baker, W. 1988. *Sports in the Western World.* Urbana: University of Illinois Press.

Baker, W. 2007. *Playing with God: Religion and Modern Sport.* Cambridge, MA: Harvard University Press.

Bale, J., and M. Cronin, eds. 2003. *Sport and Postcolonialism.* Oxford: Berg.

Booth, D. 2001. *The Field: Truth and Fiction in Sports History.* London: Routledge.

Burstyn, V. 1999. *The Rites of Men: Manhood, Politics, and the Culture of Sport.* Toronto: University of Toronto Press.

Cahn, S. 1994. *Coming On Strong: Gender and Sexuality in Twentieth Century Women's Sport.* Cambridge, MA: Harvard University Press.

Carter, J. 1988. *Sports and Pastimes of the Middle Ages.* Lanham, MD: University Press of America.

Coakley, J., and E. Dunning, eds. 2000. *Handbook of Sports Studies.* London: Sage.

Cox, R., G. Jarvie, and W. Vamplew, eds. 2000. *Encyclopedia of British Sport.* Oxford: ABC-CLIO.

Decker, W., and J-P. Thullier. 2004. *Le sport dans l'Antiquité: Égypt, Grèce et Rome.* Paris: Picard.

Diem, C. 1960. *Weltgeschichte des Sports.* Stuttgart: Cotta.

Eichberg, H., J. Bale, and C. Philo. 1998. *Body Cultures: Essays on Sport, Space and Identity.* London: Routledge.

Elias, N., and E. Dunning. 1986. *Quest for Excitement: Sport and Leisure in the Civilizing Process.* Oxford: Blackwell.

Foer, F. 2005. *How Soccer Explains the World: An Unlikely Theory of Globalization.* New York: HarperCollins.

Giulianotti, R. 2004. *Sport and Modern Social Theorists.* Harlow, UK: Palgrave.

Giulianotti, R., and R. Robertson. 2007. *Globalization and Sport.* Oxford: Blackwell.

Gruneau, R. 1999. *Class, Sports and Social Development.* 2nd ed. Champaign, IL: Human Kinetics.

Guttmann, A. 1978. *From Ritual to Record: The Nature of Modern Sports.* New York: Columbia University Press.

Guttmann, A. 1991. *Women's Sports: A History.* New York: Columbia University Press.

Guttmann, A. 1992. *The Olympics: A History of the Modern Games.* Urbana: University of Illinois Press.

Guttmann, A. 1994. *Games and Empires: Modern Sports and Cultural Imperialism.* New York: Columbia University Press.

Guttmann 2004. *Sports: The First Five Millennia.* Amherst: University of Massachusetts Press.

Hall, M. A. 1996. *Feminism and Sporting Bodies: Essays on Theory and Practice.* Champaign, IL: Human Kinetics.

Hargreaves, J. 1994. *Sporting Females: Critical Issues in the History and Sociology of Women's Sports.* London: Routledge.

Hill, J. 2007. *Sport and the Literary Imagination: Essays in History, Literature and Sport.* New York: Peter Lang.

Hoberman, J. 1992. *Mortal Engines: The Science of Human Performance and the Dehumanization of Sport.* New York: Free Press.

Hoberman, J. 2005. *Testosterone Dreams: Rejuvenation, Aphrodisia, Doping.* Berkeley: University of California Press.

Holt, R. 1989. *Sport and the British: A Modern History.* Oxford: Clarendon.

Huizinga, J. 1950. *Homo Ludens: A Study of the Play Element in Culture.* Boston: Beacon.

James, C. L. R. 1963. *Beyond a Boundary.* London: Stanley Paul.

Kyle, D. 2007. *Sport and Spectacle in the Ancient World.* London: Blackwell.

LaFeber, W. 2002. *Michael Jordan and the New Global Capitalism.* New and expanded ed. New York: Norton.

Maguire, J. 1999. *Globalization and Sports.* Cambridge, UK: Polity.

Mandell, R. 1984. *Sport: A Cultural History.* New York: Columbia University Press.

Mangan, J. A. 1981. *Athleticism in the Victorian and Edwardian Public School.* Cambridge: Cambridge University Press.

Mangan, J. A. 1987. *The Games Ethic and Imperialism: Aspects of the Diffusion of an Ideal.* Harmondsworth, UK: Viking.

Messner, M. 1992. *Power at Play: Sports and the Problem of Masculinity.* Boston: Beacon.

Miller, T., G. Lawrence, J. McKay, and D. Rowe 2001. *Globalization and Sport: Playing the World.* London: Sage.

Møller, V., and J. Nauright, eds. 2003. *The Essence of Sport.* Odense: University Press of Southern Denmark.

Nauright, J., and T. J. L. Chandler, eds. 1996. *Making Men: Rugby and Masculine Identity.* London: Frank Cass.

Nauright, J., and S. W. Pope, eds. 2009. *The New Sport Management Reader.* Morgantown, WV: Fitness Information Technology.

Phillips, M., ed. 2006. *Deconstructing Sports History: A Postmodern Analysis.* Albany: SUNY Press.

Pope, S. W., and J. Nauright, eds. 2010. *The Routledge Companion to Sports History.* London: Routledge.

Sansone, D. 1988. *Greek Athletics and the Genesis of Sport.* Berkeley: University of California Press.

Simson, V., and A. Jennings 1992. *The Lords of the Rings: Power, Money and Drugs in the Modern Olympics.* New York: Simon and Schuster.

Van Bottenburg, M. 2001. *Global Games.* Urbana: University of Illinois Press.

Vertinsky, P. 1994. *The Eternally Wounded Woman: Women, Doctors and Exercise in the Late Nineteenth Century.* Urbana: University of Illinois Press.

Wagg, S., and D. Andrews, eds. 2007. *East Plays West: Sport and the Cold War.* London: Routledge.

Young, D. 1984. *The Olympic Myth of Greek Amateur Athletics.* Chicago: Ares.

Olympic Medalists—Summer Olympics

Archery

Men's Au Chapelet, 33-Meter

Year	Gold	Silver	Bronze
1900	Huber Van Innis (Belgium)	Victor Thibaud (France)	Charles Frédéric Petit (France)

Men's Au Chapelet, 50-Meter

Year	Gold	Silver	Bronze
1900	Eugène Mougin (France)	Henri Helle (France)	Emile Mercier (France)

Men's Au Cordon Doré, 33-Meter

Year	Gold	Silver	Bronze
1900	Hubert Van Innis (Belgium)	Victor Thibaud (France)	Charles Frédéric Petit (France)

Men's Au Cordon Doré, 50-Meter

Year	Gold	Silver	Bronze
1900	Henri Herouin (France)	Hubert Van Innis (Belgium)	Emile Fisseux (France)

Men's Continental Style, 50-Meter

Year	Gold	Silver	Bronze
1908	Eugène G. Grisot (France)	Gustave Cabaret (France)	Louis Vernet (France)

Men's Double American Round

Year	Gold	Silver	Bronze
1904	George Philipp Bryant (United States)	Robert Williams (United States)	William Henry Thompson (United States)

Men's York Round

Year	Gold	Silver	Bronze
1908	Henry Barber Richardson (United States)	Reginald B. Brooks-King (Great Britain)	William Dod (Great Britain)

Men's Double York Round

Year	Gold	Silver	Bronze
1904	George Philipp Bryant (United States)	Robert Williams (United States)	William Henry Thompson (United States)

Women's Double Columbia Round

Year	Gold	Silver	Bronze
1904	Matilda Scott Howell (United States)	Emma C. Cooke (United States)	Jessie Pollock (United States)

Women's National Round

Year	Gold	Silver	Bronze
1908	Sybil Fenton Quenni Newall (Great Britain)	Charlotte Dod (Great Britain)	Beatrice Geraldine Hill-Lowe (Great Britain)

Women's Double National Round

Year	Gold	Silver	Bronze
1904	Matilda Scott Howell (United States)	Emma C. Cooke (United States)	Jessie Pollock (United States)

Men's Individual Fixed Bird Target, Large Birds

Year	Gold	Silver	Bronze
1920	Edmond Cloetens (Belgium)	Louis Van de Perck (Belgium)	Firmin Flamand (Belgium)

Men's Team Fixed Bird Target, Large Birds

Year	Gold	Silver	Bronze
1920	Edmond Cloetens, Louis van de Perck, Firmin Flamand, Edmond van Moer, Joseph Hermans, Auguste Van de Verre (Belgium)	Not awarded	Not awarded

Men's Individual Fixed Bird Target, Small Birds

Year	Gold	Silver	Bronze
1920	Edmond Van Moer (Belgium)	Louis Van de Perck (Belgium)	Joseph Hermans (Belgium)

Men's Team Fixed Bird Target, Small Birds

Year	Gold	Silver	Bronze
1920	Edmond Cloetens, Louis van de Perck, Firmin Flamand, Edmond van Moer, Joseph Hermans, Auguste Van de Verre (Belgium)	Not awarded	Not awarded

Men's Individual Moving Bird Target, 28-Meter

Year	Gold	Silver	Bronze
1920	Hubert Van Innis (Belgium)	Léonce Gaston Quentin (France)	Not awarded

Men's Individual Moving Bird Target, 33-Meter

Year	Gold	Silver	Bronze
1920	Hubert Van Innis (Belgium)	Julien Louis Brule (France)	Not awarded

Men's Individual Moving Bird Target, 50-Meter

Year	Gold	Silver	Bronze
1920	Hubert Van Innis (Belgium)	Julien Louis Brule (France)	Not awarded

Men's Team Moving Bird Target, 28-Meter

Year	Gold	Silver	Bronze
1920	Janus Theeuwes, Driekske van Bussel, Joep Packbiers, Janus van Merrienboer, Jo van Gastel, Theo Willems, Piet de Brouwer, Tiest van Gestel (Netherlands)	Hubert Van Innis, Alphonse Allaert, Edmond de Knibber, Louis Delcon, Jérome De Maeyer, Pierre van Thielt, Louis Fierens, Louis van Beeck (Belgium)	Julien Brulé, Léonce Quentin, Pascal Fauvel, Eugène Grisot, Eugène Richez, Artur Mabellon, Léon Epin, Paul Leroy (France)

Men's Team Moving Bird Target, 33-Meter

Year	Gold	Silver	Bronze
1920	Hubert Van Innis, Pierre van Thielt, Jérome De Maeyer, Alphonse Allaert, Edmond de Knibber, Louis Delcon, Louis van Beeck, Louis Fierens (Belgium)	Julien Brulé, Léonce Quentin, Pascal Fauvel, Eugène Grisot, Eugène Richez, Artur Mabellon, Léon Epin, Paul Leroy (France)	Not awarded

Men's Team Moving Bird Target, 50-Meter

Year	Gold	Silver	Bronze
1920	Hubert Van Innis, Pierre van Thielt, Jérome De Maeyer, Alphonse Allaert, Edmond de Knibber, Louis Delcon, Louis van Beeck, Louis Fierens (Belgium)	Julien Brulé, Léonce Quentin, Pascal Fauvel, Eugène Grisot, Eugène Richez, Artur Mabellon, Léon Epin, Paul Leroy (France)	Not awarded

Men's Individual, FITA Olympic Round 70-Meter

Year	Gold	Silver	Bronze
1992	Sebastien Flute (France)	Chung Jae-Hun (South Korea)	Simon Terry (Great Britain)
1996	Justin Huish (United States)	Magnus Petersson (Sweden)	Oh Kyo-Moon (South Korea)
2000	Simon Fairweather (Australia)	Viktor Wunderle (United States)	Wietse Van Alten (Netherlands)
2004	Marco Galiazzo (Italy)	Horishi Yamamoto (Japan)	Tim Cuddihy (Australia)
2008	Viktor Ruban (Ukraine)	Park Kyung-Mo (South Korea)	Baie Badenov (Russian Federation)

Women's Individual, FITA Olympic Round 70-Meter

Year	Gold	Silver	Bronze
1992	Cho Youn-Jeong (South Korea)	Kim Soo-Nyung (South Korea)	Natalia Valeeva (Unified Team)
1996	Kim Kyung-Wook (South Korea)	Ying He (China)	Olena Sadovnycha (Ukraine)
2000	Yun Mi-Jin (South Korea)	Kim Nam-Soon (South Korea)	Kim Soo-Nyung (South Korea)
2004	Sung-Hyun Park (South Korea)	Lee Sung-Jin (South Korea)	Alison Williamson (Great Britain)
2008	Zhang Juan Juan (China)	Park Sung-Hyun (South Korea)	Yun Ok-Hee (South Korea)

Men's Team, FITA Olympic Round 70-Meter

Year	Gold	Silver	Bronze
1992	Juan Holgado, Alfonso Menéndez, Antonio Vázquez (Spain)	Ismo Falck, Jari Lipponen, Tomi Poikolainen (Finland)	Steven Hallard, Richard Priestman, Simon Terry (Great Britain)
1996	Justin Huish, Butch Johnson, Rod White (United States)	Jang Yong-Ho, Kim Bo-Ram, Oh Kyo-Moon (South Korea)	Matteo Bisiani, Michele Frangilli, Andrea Parenti (Italy)
2000	Oh Kyo-Moon, Jang Yong-Ho, Kim Chung-Tae (South Korea)	Matteo Bisiani, Michele Frangilli, Ilario Di Buò (Italy)	Butch Johnson, Rod White, Vic Wunderle (United States)
2004	Im Dong-Hyun, Jang Yong-Ho, Park Kyung-Mo (South Korea)	Chen Szu-Yuan, Liu Ming-Huang, Wang Cheng-Pang (Taiwan)	Dmytro Hrachov, Viktor Ruban, Oleksandr Serdyuk (Ukraine)
2008	Im Dong-Hyun, Lee Chang-Hwan, Park Kyung-Mo (South Korea)	Ilario Di Buò, Marco Galiazzo, Mauro Nespoli (Italy)	Jiang Lin, Li Wenquan, Xue Haifeng (China)

Women's Team, FITA Olympic Round 70-Meter

Year	Gold	Silver	Bronze
1992	Cho Youn-Jeong, Kim Soo-Nyung, Lee Eun-Kyung (South Korea)	Ma Xiangjun, Wang Hong, Wang Xiaozhu (China)	Lyudmila Arzhannikova, Khatuna Kvrivichvili, Natalia Valeeva (Unified Team)
1996	Kim Jo-Sun, Kim Kyung-Wook, Yoon Hye-Young (South Korea)	Barbara Mensing, Cornelia Pfohl, Sandra Wagner-Sachse (Germany)	Iwona Dzięcioł, Katarzyna Klata, Joanna Nowicka (Poland)
2000	Kim Jo-Sun, Kim Kyung-Wook, Yoon Hye-Young (South Korea)	Olena Sadovnycha, Nataliya Burdeyna, Kateryna Serdyuk (Ukraine)	Barbara Mensing, Cornelia Pfohl, Sandra Wagner-Sachse (Germany)
2004	Lee Sung-Jin, Park Sung-Hyun, Yun Mi-Jin (South Korea)	He Ying, Lin Sang, Zhang Juan Juan (China)	Chen Li Ju, Wu Hui-Ju, Yuan Shu-Chi (Taiwan)
2008	Joo Hyun-Jung, Park Sung-Hyun, Yun Ok-Hee (South Korea)	Chen Ling, Guo Dan, Zhang Juan Juan (China)	Virginie Arnold, Sophie Dodemont, Bérengère Schuh (France)

Men's Individual FITA Round

Year	Gold	Silver	Bronze
1972	John Chester Williams (United States)	Gunnar Jervill (Sweden)	Kyösti Kalevi Laasonen (Finland)
1976	Darrell Owen Pace (United States)	Hiroshi Michinaga (Japan)	Giancarlo Ferrari (Italy)
1980	Tomi Poikolainen (Finland)	Boris Isachenko (Soviet Union)	Giancarlo Ferrari (Italy)
1984	Darrell Owen Pace (United States)	Richard Lee McKinney (United States)	Hiroshi Yamamoto (Japan)
1988	Jay Barrs (United States)	Park Sung-Soo (South Korea)	Vladimir Esheev (Soviet Union)

Women's Individual FITA Round

Year	Gold	Silver	Bronze
1972	Doreen Viola Hansen Wilber (United States)	Irena Szydlowska (Poland)	Emma Gapchenko (Soviet Union)
1976	Luann Marie Ryon (United States)	Valentina Kovpan (Soviet Union)	Zebiniso Rustamove (Soviet Union)
1980	Keto Losaberidze (Soviet Union)	Natalia Butuzova (Soviet Union)	Paivi Meriluotoaaltonen (Finland)
1984	Seo Hyang-Soon (South Korea)	Ling-Juan Li (China)	Kim Jin-Ho (South Korea)
1988	Kim Soo-Nyung (South Korea)	Wang Hee-Kyung (South Korea)	Yun Young-Sook (South Korea)

Men's Team FITA Round

Year	Gold	Silver	Bronze
1988	Chun In-Soo, Lee Han-Sup, Park Sung-Soo (South Korea)	Jay Barrs, Richard McKinney, Darrell Pace (United States)	Steven Hallard, Richard Priestman, Leroy Watson (Great Britain)

Women's Team FITA Round

Year	Gold	Silver	Bronze
1988	Kim Soo-Nyung, Wang Hee-Kyung, Yun Young-Sook (South Korea)	Lilies Handayani, Nurfitriyana Saiman, Kusuma Wardhani (Indonesia)	Deborah Ochs, Denise Parker, Melanie Skillman (United States)

Men's Sur la perche à la herse

Year	Gold	Silver	Bronze
1900	Emmanuel Foulon (Belgium)	Auguste Serrurier Jr. (France) Emile Druart (Belgium)	Not awarded

Men's Sur la perche à la pyramide

Year	Gold	Silver	Bronze
1900	Émile Grumiaux (France)	Auguste Serrurier (France)	Louis Glineux (Belgium)

Men's Team Elimination Round

Year	Gold	Silver	Bronze
1988	Chun In-Soo, Lee Han-Sup, Park Sung-Soo (South Korea)	Jay Barrs, Richard McKinney, Darrell Pace (United States)	Steven Hallard, Richard Priestman, Leroy Watson (Great Britain)

Women's Team Elimination Round

Year	Gold	Silver	Bronze
1988	Kim Soo-Nyung, Wang Hee-Kyung, Yun Young-Sook (South Korea)	Lilies Handayani, Nurfitriyana Saiman, Kusuma Wardhani (Indonesia)	Deborah Ochs, Denise Parker, Melanie Skillman (United States)

Men's Double FITA Elimination Round

Year	Gold	Silver	Bronze
1988	Jay Barrs (United States)	Park Sung-Soo (South Korea)	Vladimir Echeev (Soviet Union)

Women's Double FITA Elimination Round

Year	Gold	Silver	Bronze
1988	Kim Soo-Nyung (South Korea)	Wang Hee-Kyung (South Korea)	Yun Young-Sook (South Korea)

Artistic Gymnastics

Men's Team Event

Year	Gold	Silver	Bronze
1904	John Grieb, Anton Heida, Max Hess, Philip Kassel, Julius Lenhart, Ernst Reckeweg (United States)	Emil Beyer, John Bissinger, Arthur Rosenkampff, Julian Schmitz, Otto Steffen, Max Wolf (United States)	John Duha, Charles Krause, George Mayer, Robert Maysack, Philip Schuster, Edward Siegler (United States)
1908	Gösta Åsbrink, Carl Bertilsson, Hjalmar Cedercrona, Andreas Cervin, Rudolf Degermark, Carl Folcker, Sven Forssman, Erik Granfelt, Carl Hårleman, Nils Hellsten, Gunnar Höjer, Arvid Holmberg, Carl Holmberg, Oswald Holmberg, Hugo Jahnke, John Jarlén, Gustaf Johnsson, Rolf Johnsson, Nils von Kantzow, Sven Landberg, Olle Lanner, Axel Ljung, Osvald Moberg, Carl Martin Norberg, Erik Norberg, Tor Norberg, Axel Norling, Daniel Norling, Gösta Olson, Leonard Peterson, Sven Rosén, Gustaf Rosenquist, Axel Sjöblom, Birger Sörvik, Haakon Sörvik, Karl Johan Svensson, Karl Gustaf Vinqvist, Nils Widforss (Sweden)	Arthur Amundsen, Carl Albert Andersen, Otto Authén, Hermann Bohne, Trygve Bøyesen, Oskar Bye, Conrad Carlsrud, Sverre Grøner, Harald Halvorsen, Harald Hansen, Petter Hol, Eugen Ingebretsen, Ole Iversen, Per Mathias Jespersen, Sigge Johannessen, Nicolai Kiær, Carl Klæth, Thor Larsen, Rolf Lefdahl, Hans Lem, Anders Moen, Frithjof Olsen, Carl Alfred Pedersen, Paul Pedersen, Sigvard Sivertsen, John Skrataas, Harald Smedvik, Andreas Strand, Olaf Syvertsen, Thomas Thorstensen (Norway)	Eino Forsström, Otto Granström, Johan Kemp, Iivari Kyykoski, Heikki Lehmusto, John Lindroth, Yrjö Linko, Edvard Linna, Matti Markkanen, Kaarlo Mikkolainen, Veli Nieminen, Kaarlo Kustaa Paasia, Arvi Pohjanpää, Aarne Pohjonen, Eino Railio, Heikki Riipinen, Arno Saarinen, Einar Werner Sahlstein, Aarne Salovaara, Karl Sandelin, Elis Sipilä, Viktor Smeds, Kaarlo Soinio, Kurt Enoch Stenberg, Väinö Tiiri, Karl Magnus Wegelius (Finland)

Year	Gold	Silver	Bronze
1912	Pietro Bianchi, Guido Boni, Alberto Braglia, Giuseppe Domenichelli, Carlo Fregosi, Alfredo Gollini, Francesco Loi, Luigi Maiocco, Giovanni Mangiante, Lorenzo Mangiante, Serafino Mazzarochi, Guido Romano, Paolo Salvi, Luciano Savorini, Adolfo Tunesi, Giorgio Zampori, Umberto Zanolini, Angelo Zorzi (Italy)	József Bittenbinder, Imre Erdődy, Samu Fóti, Imre Gellért, Győző Haberfeld, Ottó Hellmich, István Herczeg, József Keresztessy, Lajos Kmetykó, János Krizmanich, Elemér Pászti, Árpád Pédery, Jenő Rittich, Ferenc Szüts, Ödön Téry, Géza Tuli (Hungary)	Albert Betts, William Cowhig, Sidney Cross, Harold Dickason, Herbert Drury, Bernard Franklin, Leonard Hanson, Samuel Hodgetts, Charles Luck, William MacKune, Ronald McLean, Alfred Messenger, Henry Oberholzer, Edward Pepper, Edward Potts, Reginald Potts, George Ross, Charles Simmons, Arthur Southern, William Titt, Charles Vigurs, Samuel Walker, John Whitaker (Great Britain)
1916: Olympics not held			
1920	Arnaldo Andreoli, Ettore Bellotto, Pietro Bianchi, Fernando Bonatti, Luigi Cambiaso, Luigi Contessi, Carlo Costigliolo, Luigi Costigliolo, Giuseppe Domenichelli, Roberto Ferrari, Carlo Fregosi, Romualdo Ghiglione, Ambrogio Levati, Francesco Loi, Vittorio Lucchetti, Luigi Maiocco, Ferdinando Mandrini, Lorenzo Mangiante, Antonio Marovelli, Michele Mastromarino, Giuseppe Paris, Manlio Pastorini, Ezio Roselli, Paolo Salvi, Giovanni Tubino, Giorgio Zampori, Angelo Zorzi (Italy)	Eugenius Auwerkerken, Théophile Bauer, François Claessens, Augustus Cootmans, Frans Gibens, Albert Haepers, Domien Jacob, Félicien Kempeneers, Jules Labéeu, Hubert Lafortune, Auguste Landrieu, Charles Lannie, Constant Loriot, Nicolaas Moerloos, Ferdinand Minnaert, Louis Stoop, Jean Van Guysse, Alphonse Van Mele, François Verboven, Jean Verboven, Julien Verdonck, Joseph Verstraeten, Georges Vivex, Julianus Wagemans (Belgium)	Georges Berger, Émile Bouchès, René Boulanger, Alfred Buyenne, Eugène Cordonnier, Léon Delsarte, Lucien Démanet, Paul Durin, Georges Duvant, Fernand Fauconnier, Arthur Hermann, Albert Hersoy, André Higelin, Auguste Hoël, Louis Kempe, Georges Lagouge, Paulin Lemaire, Ernest Lespinasse, Émile Martel, Jules Pirard, Eugène Pollet, Georges Thurnherr, Marco Torrès, François Walker, Julien Wartelle, Paul Wartelle (France)
1924	Luigi Cambiaso, Mario Lertora, Vittorio Lucchetti, Luigi Maiocco, Ferdinando Mandrini, Francesco Martino, Giuseppe Paris, Giorgio Zampori (Italy)	Eugène Cordonnier, Léon Delsarte, François Gangloff, Jean Gounot, Arthur Hermann, André Higelin, Joseph Huber, Albert Séguin (France)	Hans Grieder, August Güttinger, Jean Gutweninger, Georges Miez, Otto Pfister, Antoine Rebetez, Carl Widmer, Josef Wilhelm (Switzerland)
1928	Hans Grieder, August Güttinger, Hermann Hänggi, Eugen Mack, Georges Miez, Otto Pfister, Eduard Steinemann, Melchior Wezel (Switzerland)	Josef Effenberger, Jan Gajdoš, Jan Koutný, Emanuel Löffler, Bedřich Šupčík, Ladislav Tikal, Ladislav Vácha, Václav Veselý (Czechoslovakia)	Eduard Antonijević, Dragutin Cioti, Stane Derganc, Boris Gregorka, Anton Malej, Ivan Porenta, Josip Primožič, Leon Štukelj (Yugoslavia)
1932	Oreste Capuzzo, Savino Guglielmetti, Mario Lertora, Romeo Neri, Franco Tognini (Italy)	Frank Haubold, Frank Cumiskey, Al Jochim, Fred Meyer, Michael Schuler (United States)	Mauri Nyberg-Noroma, Ilmari Pakarinen, Heikki Savolainen, Einari Teräsvirta, Martti Uosikkinen (Finland)
1936	Franz Beckert, Konrad Frey, Alfred Schwarzmann, Willi Stadel, Inno Stangl, Walter Steffens, Matthias Volz, Ernst Winter (Germany)	Karl Frei, Christian Kipfer, Walter Lehmann, Robert Lucy, Michael Reusch, Josef Stalder, Emil Studer, Melchior Thalmann (Switzerland)	Mauri Nyberg-Noroma, Veikko Pakarinen, Aleksanteri Saarvala, Heikki Savolainen, Esa Seeste, Einari Teräsvirta, Eino Tukiainen, Martti Uosikkinen (Finland)
1940–1944: Olympics not held			
1948	Paavo Aaltonen, Veikko Huhtanen, Kalevi Laitinen, Olavi Rove, Aleksanteri Saarvala, Sulo Salmi, Heikki Savolainen, Einari Teräsvirta (Finland)	Karl Frei, Christian Kipfer, Walter Lehmann, Robert Lucy, Michael Reusch, Josef Stalder, Emil Studer, Melchior Thalmann (Switzerland)	László Baranyai, Jozsef Fekete, Gyözö Mogyorosi, János Mogyorósi-Klencs, Ferenc Pataki, Lajos Sántha, Lajos Tóth, Ferenc Várkõi (Hungary)

Year	Gold	Silver	Bronze
1952	Vladimir Belyakov, Iosif Berdiev, Viktor Chukarin, Evgeny Korolkov, Dmytro Leonkin, Valentin Muratov, Mikhail Perelman, Grant Shaginyan (Soviet Union)	Hans Eugster, Ernst Fivian, Ernst Gebedinger, Jack Günthard, Hans Schwarzentruber, Josef Stalder, Melchior Thalmann, Jean Tschabold (Switzerland)	Paavo Aaltanen, Kalevi Laitinen, Onni Lappalainen, Kaino Lempinen, Berndt Lindfors, Olavi Rove, Heikki Savolainen, Kalevi Viskari (Finland)
1956	Albert Azarian, Viktor Chukarin, Valentin Muratov, Boris Shakhlin, Pavel Stolbov, Yuri Titov (Soviet Union)	Nobuyuki Aihara, Akira Kono, Masumi Kubota, Takashi Ono, Masao Takemoto, Shinji Tsukawaki (Japan)	Raime Heinonen, Olavi Laimuvirta, Onni Lappalainen, Berndt Lindfors, Martti Mansikka, Kalevi Suciemi (Finland)
1960	Nobuyuki Aihara, Yukio Endo, Takashi Mitsukuri, Takashi Ono, Masao Takemoto, Shuji Tsurumi (Japan)	Albert Azaryan, Valery Kerdemilidi, Nikolai Miligulo, Vladimir Portnoi, Boris Shakhlin, Yuri Titov (Soviet Union)	Giovanni Carminucci, Pasquale Carminucci, Gianfranco Marzolla, Franco Menichelli, Orlando Polmonari, Angelo Vicardi (Italy)
1964	Yukio Endo, Takuji Hayata, Takashi Mitsukuri, Takashi Ono, Shuji Tsurumi, Haruhiro Yamashita (Japan)	Sergei Diomidov, Viktor Leontev, Viktor Lisitsky, Boris Shakhlin, Yuri Titov, Yuri Tsapenko (Soviet Union)	Siegfried Fülle, Philipp Fürst, Erwin Koppe, Klaus Köste, Günter Lyhs, Peter Weber (East Germany)
1968	Yukio Endo, Sawao Kato, Takeshi Kato, Eizo Kenmotsu, Akinori Nakayama, Mitsuo Tsukahara (Japan)	Sergei Diomidov, Valery Iljinykh, Valery Karasev, Viktor Klimenko, Victor Lisitsky, Mikhail Voronin (Soviet Union)	Gunter Beier, Matthias Brehme, Gerhard Dietrich, Siegfried Fulle, Klaus Köste, Peter Weber (East Germany)
1972	Shigeru Kasamatsu, Sawao Kato, Eizo Kenmotsu, Akinori Nakayama, Teruichi Okamura, Mitsuo Tsukahara (Japan)	Nikolai Andrianov, Viktor Klimenko, Alexander Maleev, Edvard Mikaelian, Vladimir Schukin, Mikhail Voronin (Soviet Union)	Matthias Brehme, Wolfgang Klotz, Klaus Köste, Jürgen Paeke, Reinhard Rychly, Wolfgang Thune (East Germany)
1976	Shun Fujimoto, Hisato Igarashi, Hiroshi Kajiyama, Sawao Kato, Eizo Kenmotsu, Mitsuo Tsukahara (Japan)	Nikolai Andrianov, Alexander Dityatin, Gennadi Kryssin, Vladimir Marchenko, Vladimir Markelov, Vladimir Tikhonov (Soviet Union)	Roland Brückner, Rainer Hanschke, Bernd Jager, Wolfgang Klotz, Lutz Mack, Michael Nikolay (East Germany)
1980	Nikolai Andrianov, Eduard Azaryan, Alexander Dityatin, Bogdan Makuts, Vladimir Markelov, Alexander Tkachev (Soviet Union)	Ralf-Peter Hemmann, Lutz Hoffmann, Lutz Mack, Michael Nikolay, Andreas Bronst, Roland Brückner (East Germany)	Ferenc Donath, Gyorgy Guczoghy, Zoltan Kelemen, Peter Kovacs, Zoltán Magyar, Istvan Vamos (Hungary)
1984	Bart Conner, Timothy Daggett, Mitchell Gaylord, James Hartung, Scott Johnson, Peter Vidmar (United States)	Li Ning, Li Xiaoping, Li Yuejiu, Lou Yun, Tong Fei, Xu Zhiqiang (China)	Koji Gushiken, Noritoshi Hirata, Nobuyuki Kajitani, Shinji Morisue, Koji Sotomura, Kyoji Yamawaki (Japan)
1988	Vladimir Artemov, Dmitri Bilozertchev, Vladimir Gogoladze, Sergei Kharkov, Valeri Liukin, Vladimir Nouvikov (Soviet Union)	Holger Behrendt, Ralf Buechner, Ulf Hoffmann, Sylvio Kroll, Sven Tippelt, Andreas Wecker (East Germany)	Yukio Iketani, Hiroyuki Konishi, Koichi Mizushima, Daisuke Nishikawa, Toshiharu Sato, Takahiro Yameda (Japan)
1992	Valery Belenky, Igor Korobchinski, Grigory Misutin, Vitaly Scherbo, Rustam Sharipov, Alexei Voropaev (Unified Team)	Guo Linyao, Li Chunyang, Li Dashuang, Li Ge, Li Jing, Li Xiaoshuang (China)	Yutaka Aihara, Takashi Chinen, Yoshiaki Hatakeda, Yukio Iketani, Masayuki Matsunaga, Daisuke Nishikawa (Japan)
1996	Sergei Kharkov, Nikolai Kryukov, Alexei Nemov, Yevgeni Podgorny, Dmitri Trush, Dmitri Vasilenko, Alexei Voropaev (Russia)	Fan Bin, Fan Hongbin, Huang Huadong, Huang Liping, Li Xiaoshuang, Shen Jian, Zhang Jinjing (China)	Igor Korobchinski, Oleg Kosiak, Grigory Misutin, Vladimir Shamenko, Rustam Sharipov, Oleksandr Svetlichny, Yuri Yermakov (Ukraine)

Year	Gold	Silver	Bronze
2000	Huang Xu, Li Xiaopeng, Xiao Junfeng, Xing Aowei, Yang Wei, Zheng Lihui (China)	Oleksandr Beresh, Valeri Goncharov, Ruslan Mezentsev, Valeri Pereshkura, Oleksandr Svetlichny, Roman Zozulia (Ukraine)	Maxim Aleshin, Alexei Bondarenko, Dmitri Drevin, Nikolai Kryukov, Alexei Nemov, Yevgeni Podgorny (Russia)
2004	Takehiro Kashima, Hisashi Mizutori, Daisuke Nakano, Hiroyuki Tomita, Naoya Tsukahara, Isao Yoneda (Japan)	Jason Gatson, Morgan Hamm, Paul Hamm, Brett McClure, Blaine Wilson, Guard Young (United States)	Marian Drăgulescu, Ilie Daniel Popescu, Dan Nicolae Potra, Răzvan Dorin Şelariu, Ioan Silviu Suciu, Marius Urzică (Romania)
2008	Chen Yibing, Huang Xu, Li Xiaopeng, Xiao Qin, Yang Wei, Zou Kai (China)	Takehiro Kashima, Takuya Nakase, Makoto Okiguchi, Koki Sakamoto, Hiroyuki Tomita, Kōhei Uchimura (Japan)	Alexander Artemev, Raj Bhavsar, Joe Hagerty, Jonathan Horton, Justin Spring, Kai Wen Tan (United States)

Women's Team Event

Year	Gold	Silver	Bronze
1928	Estella Agsteribbe, Jacomina van den Berg, Alida van den Bos, Petronella Burgerhof, Elka de Levie, Helena Nordheim, Ans Polak, Petronella van Randwijk, Hendrika van Rumt, Jud Simons, Jacoba Stelma, Anna van der Vegt (Netherlands)	Bianca Ambrosetti, Lavinia Gianoni, Luigina Giavotti, Virginia Giorgi, Germana Malabarba, Clara Marangoni, Luigina Perversi, Diana Pizzavini, Luisa Tanzini, Carolina Tronconi, Ines Vercesi, Rita Vittadini (Italy)	Annie Broadbent, Lucy Desmond, Margaret Hartley, Amy Jagger, Isobel Judd, Jessie Kite, Marjorie Moreman, Edith Pickles, Ethel Seymour, Ada Smith, Hilda Smith, Doris Woods (Great Britain)
1932: Event not held			
1936	Anita Bärwirth, Erna Bürger, Isolde Frölian, Friedl Iby, Trudi Meyer, Paula Pöhlsen, Julie Schmitt, Käthe Sohnemann (Germany)	Jaroslava Bajerová, Vlasta Děkanová, Božena Dobešová, Vlasta Foltová, Anna Hřebřinová, Matylda Pálfyová, Zdeňka Veřmiřovská, Marie Větrovská (Czechoslovakia)	Margit Csillik, Margit Kalocsai, Ilona Madary, Gabriella Mészáros, Margit Nagy, Olga Tőrös, Judit Tóth, Eszter Voit (Hungary)
1940–1944: Olympics not held			
1948	Zdenka Honsová, Marie Kovářová, Miloslava Misáková, Milena Müllerová, Vera Ruzickova, Olga Silhanová, Bozena Srncová, Zdeňka Veřmiřovská (Czechoslovakia)	Edit Parényi-Weckinger, Mária Zalai-Kövi, Irén Kárpáti-Karcsics, Erzsébet Gulyás-Köteles, Erzsébet Balázs, Olga Tass, Anna Fehér, Margit Nagy-Sandor (Hungary)	Ladislava Bakanic, Marian Barone, Consetta Lenz, Dorothy Dalton, Meta Elste, Helen Schifano, Clara Schroth, Anita Simonis (United States)
1952	Nina Bocharova, Pelageya Danilova, Maria Gorokhovskaya, Ekaterina Kalinchuk, Galina Minaicheva, Galina Shamrai, Galina Urbanovich (Soviet Union)	Andrea Bodo, Irén Daruházi-Karcsics, Erzsebet Gulyas, Ágnes Keleti, Margit Korondi, Edit Parényi-Weckinger, Olga Tass, Mária Zalai-Kövi (Hungary)	Hana Bobkova, Alena Chadimova, Jana Rabasova, Alena Reichova, Matylda Sinova, Bozena Srncova, Vera Vancurova, Eva Vechtova (Czechoslovakia)
1956	Polina Astakhova, Ludmila Egorova, Lidia Kalinina, Larissa Latynina, Tamara Manina, Sofia Muratova (Soviet Union)	Andrea Bodo, Karolyne Gulyas, Ágnes Keleti, Alice Kertesz, Margit Korondi, Olga Tass (Hungary)	Georgeta Hurmuzachi, Sonia Iovan, Elena Leuşteanu, Elena Mărgărit, Elena Săcălici, Emilia Vătăşoiu (Romania)
1960	Polina Astakhova, Lidia Ivanova, Larissa Latynina, Tamara Lyukhina, Sofia Muratova, Margarita Nikolaeva (Soviet Union)	Eva Bosáková, Věra Čáslavská, Matylda Matoušková, Hana Růžičková, Ludmila Švédová, Adolfina Tačová (Czechoslovakia)	Atanasia Ionescu, Sonia Iovan, Elena Leuşteanu, Emilia Vătăşoiu-Liţă, Elena Niculescu, Uta Poreceanu (Romania)

Year	Gold	Silver	Bronze
1964	Larissa Latynina, Polina Astakhova, Tamara Manina, Elena Volchetskaya, Tamara Zamotailova, Ludmila Gromova (Soviet Union)	Věra Čáslavská, Jaroslava Sedláčková, Adolfína Tkačíková, Mária Krajčírová, Hana Lišková, Jana Kubičková (Czechoslovakia)	Keiko Ikeda, Toshiko Aihara, Kiyoko Ono, Taniko Nakamura, Hiroko Tsuji, Ginko Chiba (Japan)
1968	Ludmilla Tourischeva, Zinaida Voronina, Larissa Petrik, Lyubov Burda, Olga Karaseva, Natalia Kuchinskaya (Soviet Union)	Věra Čáslavská, Bohumila Řimnáčová, Miroslava Skleničková, Mária Krajčírová, Hana Lišková, Jana Kubičková (Czechoslovakia)	Karin Janz, Erika Zuchold, Maritta Bauerschmidt, Ute Starke, Marianne Noack, Magdalena Schmidt (East Germany)
1972	Ludmilla Tourischeva, Olga Korbut, Tamara Lazakovich, Lyubov Burda, Elvira Saadi, Antonina Koshel (Soviet Union)	Karin Janz, Erika Zuchold, Angelika Hellmann, Irene Abel, Christine Schmitt, Richarda Schmeisser (East Germany)	Ilona Bekesi, Monika Csaszar, Krisztina Medveczky, Aniko Kery, Marta Kelemen, Zsuzsa Nagy (Hungary)
1976	Maria Filatova, Svetlana Grozdova, Nellie Kim, Olga Korbut, Elvira Saadi, Ludmilla Tourischeva (Soviet Union)	Nadia Comăneci, Mariana Constantin, Georgeta Gabor, Anca Grigoraş, Gabriela Truşcă, Teodora Ungureanu (Romania)	Carola Dombeck, Gitta Escher, Kerstin Gerschau, Angelika Hellmann, Marion Kische, Steffi Kraker (East Germany)
1980	Yelena Davydova, Maria Filatova, Nellie Kim, Elena Naimushina, Natalia Shaposhnikova, Stella Zakharova (Soviet Union)	Nadia Comăneci, Rodica Dunca, Emilia Eberle, Melita Ruhn, Dumitriţa Turner, Cristina Elena Grigoraş (Romania)	Maxi Gnauck, Silvia Hindorff, Steffi Kraker, Katharina Rensch, Karola Sube, Birgit Suss (East Germany)
1984	Ecaterina Szabo, Laura Cutina, Simona Păucă, Cristina Elena Grigoraş, Mihaela Stănuleţ, Lavinia Agache (Romania)	Mary Lou Retton, Julianne McNamara, Kathy Johnson, Michelle Dusserre, Tracee Talavera, Pamela Bileck (United States)	Ma Yanhong, Wu Jiani, Chen Yongyan, Zhou Ping, Zhou Qiurui, Huang Qun (China)
1988	Svetlana Baitova, Elena Shevchenko, Olga Strazheva, Natalia Laschenova, Svetlana Boginskaya, Yelena Shushunova (Soviet Union)	Camelia Voinea, Celestina Popa, Eugenia Golea, Gabriela Potorac, Aurelia Dobre, Daniela Silivaş (Romania)	Martina Jentsch, Gabriele Faehnrich, Ulrike Klotz, Betti Schieferdecker, Dörte Thümmler, Dagmar Kersten (East Germany)
1992	Svetlana Boginskaya, Tatiana Gutsu, Oksana Chusovitina, Tatiana Lysenko, Elena Grudneva, Rozalia Galiyeva (Unified Team)	Lavinia Miloşovici, Gina Gogean, Cristina Bontaş, Mirela Paşca, Maria Neculiţă, Vanda Hădărean (Romania)	Shannon Miller, Kim Zmeskal, Dominique Dawes, Wendy Bruce, Betty Okino, Kerri Strug (United States)
1996	Amanda Borden, Amy Chow, Dominique Dawes, Shannon Miller, Dominique Moceanu, Jaycie Phelps, Kerri Strug (United States)	Elena Dolgopolova, Rozalia Galiyeva, Elena Grosheva, Svetlana Khorkina, Dina Kochetkova, Yevgeniya Kuznetsova, Oksana Lyapina (Russia)	Simona Amânar, Gina Gogean, Ionela Loaieş, Alexandra Marinescu, Lavinia Miloşovici, Mirela Ţugurlan (Romania)
2000	Andreea Răducan, Maria Olaru, Simona Amânar, Loredana Boboc, Andreea Isărescu, Claudia Presacan (Romania)	Yelena Produnova, Svetlana Khorkina, Yekaterina Lobaznyuk, Elena Zamolodchikova, Anastasiya Kolesnikova, Anna Chepeleva (Russia)	Amy Chow, Jamie Dantzscher, Dominique Dawes, Kristen Maloney, Elise Ray, Tasha Schwikert (United States)
2004	Oana Ban, Alexandra Eremia, Cătălina Ponor, Monica Roşu, Nicoleta Daniela Şofronie, Silvia Stroescu (Romania)	Mohini Bhardwaj, Annia Hatch, Terin Humphrey, Courtney Kupets, Courtney McCool, Carly Patterson (United States)	Ludmila Ezhova, Svetlana Khorkina, Maria Krioutchkova, Anna Pavlova, Elena Zamolodchikova, Natalia Ziganchina (Russia)
2008	Yang Yilin, Cheng Fei, Jiang Yuyuan, Deng Linlin, He Kexin, Li Shanshan (China)	Shawn Johnson, Nastia Liukin, Chellsie Memmel, Samantha Peszek, Alicia Sacramone, Bridget Sloan (United States)	Andreea Acatrinei, Gabriela Drăgoi, Andreea Grigore, Sandra Izbaşa, Steliana Nistor, Anamaria Tămârjan (Romania)

Men's Individual All-Around

Year	Gold	Silver	Bronze
1900	Gustave Sandras (France)	Noël Bas (France)	Lucien Démanet (France)
1904	Julius Lenhart (United States)	Wilhelm Weber (Germany)	Adolf Spinnler (Switzerland)
1908	Alberto Braglia (Italy)	Walter Tysall (Great Britain)	Louis Ségura (France)
1912	Alberto Braglia (Italy)	Louis Ségura (France)	Adolfo Tunesi (Italy)
1916: Olympics not held			
1920	Giorgio Zampori (Italy)	Marco Torrés (France)	Jean Gounot (France)
1924	Leon Štukelj (Yugoslavia)	Robert Pražák (Czechoslovakia)	Bedřich Šupčík (Czechoslovakia)
1928	Georges Miez (Switzerland)	Hermann Hänggi (Switzerland)	Leon Štukelj (Yugoslavia)
1932	Romeo Neri (Italy)	István Pelle (Hungary)	Heikki Savolainen (Finland)
1936	Alfred Schwarzmann (Germany)	Eugen Mack (Switzerland)	Konrad Frey (Germany)
1940–1944: Olympics not held			
1948	Veikko Huhtanen (Finland)	Walter Lehmann (Switzerland)	Paavo Aaltonen (Finland)
1952	Viktor Chukarin (Soviet Union)	Grant Shaginyan (Soviet Union)	Josef Stalder (Switzerland)
1956	Viktor Chukarin (Soviet Union)	Takashi Ono (Japan)	Yuri Titov (Soviet Union)
1960	Boris Shakhlin (Soviet Union)	Takashi Ono (Japan)	Yuri Titov (Soviet Union)
1964	Yukio Endo (Japan)	Viktor Lisitsky (Soviet Union) Boris Shakhlin (Soviet Union) Shuji Tsurumi (Japan)	Not awarded
1968	Sawao Kato (Japan)	Mikhail Voronin (Soviet Union)	Akinori Nakayama (Japan)
1972	Sawao Kato (Japan)	Eizo Kenmotsu (Japan)	Akinori Nakayama (Japan)
1976	Nikolai Andrianov (Soviet Union)	Sawao Kato (Japan)	Mitsuo Tsukahara (Japan)
1980	Alexander Dityatin (Soviet Union)	Nikolai Andrianov (Soviet Union)	Stoyan Deltchev (Hungary)
1984	Koji Gushiken (Japan)	Peter Vidmar (United States)	Li Ning (China)
1988	Vladimir Artemov (Soviet Union)	Valeri Liukin (Soviet Union)	Dmitry Bilozerchev (Soviet Union)
1992	Vitaly Scherbo (Unified Team)	Grigory Misutin (Unified Team)	Valery Belenky (Unified Team)
1996	Li Xiaonshuang (China)	Alexei Nemov (Russia)	Vitaly Scherbo (Belarus)
2000	Alexei Nemov (Russia)	Yang Wei (China)	Oleksandr Beresh (Ukraine)
2004	Paul Hamm (United States)	Kim Dae-Eun (South Korea)	Yang Tae-Young (South Korea)
2008	Yang Wei (China)	Kōhei Uchimura (Japan)	Benoît Caranobe (France)

Women's Individual All-Around

Year	Gold	Silver	Bronze
1952	Maria Gorokhovskaya (Soviet Union)	Nina Bocharova (Soviet Union)	Margit Korondi (Hungary)
1956	Larissa Latynina (Soviet Union)	Ágnes Keleti (Hungary)	Sofia Muratova (Soviet Union)
1960	Larissa Latynina (Soviet Union)	Sofia Muratova (Soviet Union)	Polina Astakhova (Soviet Union)
1964	Věra Čáslavská (Czechoslovakia)	Larissa Latynina (Soviet Union)	Polina Astakhova (Soviet Union)
1968	Věra Čáslavská (Czechoslovakia)	Zinaida Voronina (Soviet Union)	Natalia Kuchinskaya (Soviet Union)
1972	Ludmila Tourischeva (Soviet Union)	Karin Janz (East Germany)	Tamara Lazakovich (Soviet Union)
1976	Nadia Comăneci (Romania)	Nellie Kim (Soviet Union)	Ludmila Tourischeva (Soviet Union)
1980	Elena Davydova (Soviet Union)	Maxi Gnauck (East Germany) Nadia Comăneci (Romania)	Not awarded
1984	Mary Lou Retton (United States)	Ecaterina Szabo (Romania)	Simona Păucă (Romania)
1988	Elena Shushunova (Soviet Union)	Daniela Silivaş (Romania)	Svetlana Boginskaya (Soviet Union)
1992	Tatia Gutsu (Unified Team)	Shannon Miller (United States)	Lavinia Miloşovici (Romania)
1996	Lilia Podkopayeva (Ukraine)	Gina Gogean (Romania)	Simona Amânar (Romania) Lavinia Miloşovici (Romania)
2000	Simona Amânar (Romania)	Maria Olaru (Romania)	Liu Xuan (China)

Year	Gold	Silver	Bronze
2004	Carly Patterson (United States)	Svetlana Khorkina (Russia)	Zhang Nan (China)
2008	Nastia Liukin (United States)	Shawn Johnson (United States)	Yang Yilin (China)

Women's Balance Beam

Year	Gold	Silver	Bronze
1952	Nina Bocharova (Soviet Union)	Maria Gorokhovskaya (Soviet Union)	Margit Korondi (Hungary)
1956	Ágnes Keleti (Hungary)	Eva Bosáková (Czechoslovakia) Tamara Manina (Soviet Union)	Not awarded
1960	Eva Bosáková (Czechoslovakia)	Larissa Latynina (Soviet Union)	Sofia Muratova (Soviet Union)
1964	Věra Čáslavská (Czechoslovakia)	Tamara Manina (Soviet Union)	Larissa Latynina (Soviet Union)
1968	Natalia Kuchinskaya (Soviet Union)	Věra Čáslavská (Czechoslovakia)	Larissa Petrik (Soviet Union)
1972	Olga Korbut (Soviet Union)	Tamara Lazakovich (Soviet Union)	Karin Janz (East Germany)
1976	Nadia Comăneci (Romania)	Olga Korbut (Soviet Union)	Teodora Ungureanu (Romania)
1980	Nadia Comăneci (Romania)	Elena Davydova (Soviet Union)	Natalia Shaposhnikova (Soviet Union)
1984	Simona Păucă (Romania) Ecaterina Szabo (Romania)	Not awarded	Kathy Johnson (United States)
1992	Tatiana Lysenko (Unified Team)	Lu Li (China) Shannon Miller (United States)	Not awarded
1996	Shannon Miller (United States)	Lilia Podkopayeva (Ukraine)	Gina Gogean (Romania)
2000	Liu Xuan (China)	Ekaterina Lobazniouk (Russia)	Elena Produnova (Russia)
2004	Cătălina Ponor (Romania)	Carly Patterson (United States)	Alexandra Eremia (Romania)
2008	Shawn Johnson (United States)	Nastia Liukin (United States)	Cheng Fei (China)

Women's Vault

Year	Gold	Silver	Bronze
1952	Ekaterina Kalinchuk (Soviet Union)	Maria Gorokhovskaya (Soviet Union)	Galina Minaicheva (Soviet Union)
1956	Larissa Latynina (Soviet Union)	Tamara Manina (Soviet Union)	Olga Tass (Hungary) Ann-Sofi Colling (Sweden)
1960	Margarita Nikolaeva (Soviet Union)	Sofia Muratova (Soviet Union)	Larissa Latynina (Soviet Union)
1964	Věra Čáslavská (Czechoslovakia)	Larissa Latynina (Soviet Union) Birgit Radochla (Germany)	Not awarded
1968	Věra Čáslavská (Czechoslovakia)	Erika Zuchold (East Germany)	Zinaida Voronina (Soviet Union)
1972	Karin Janz (East Germany)	Erika Zuchold (East Germany)	Ludmila Tourischeva (Soviet Union)
1976	Nellie Kim (Soviet Union)	Ludmila Tourischeva (Soviet Union)	Nadia Comăneci (Romania)
1980	Natalia Shaposhnikova (Soviet Union)	Steffi Kraker (East Germany)	Melita Rühn (Romania)
1984	Ecaterina Szabo (Romania)	Mary Lou Retton (United States)	Lavinia Agache (Romania)
1988	Svetlana Boginskaya (Soviet Union)	Gabriela Potorac (Romania)	Daniela Silivaș (Romania)
1992	Lavinia Miloşovici (Romania) Henrietta Ónodi (Hungary)	Not awarded	Tatiana Lysenko (Unified Team)
1996	Simona Amânar (Romania)	Mo Huilan (China)	Gina Gogean (Romania)
2000	Elena Zamolodchikova (Russia)	Andrea Răducan (Romania)	Ekaterina Lobazniouk (Russia)
2004	Monica Roşu (Romania)	Annia Hatch (United States)	Anna Pavlova (Russia)
2008	Hong Un-Jong (North Korea)	Oksana Chusovitina (Germany)	Cheng Fei (People Republic of China)

Women's Uneven Bars

Year	Gold	Silver	Bronze
1952	Margit Korondi (Hungary)	Maria Gorokhovskaya (Soviet Union)	Ágnes Keleti (Hungary)
1956	Ágnes Keleti (Hungary)	Larissa Latynina (Soviet Union)	Sofia Muratova (Soviet Union)
1960	Polina Astakhova (Soviet Union)	Larissa Latynina (Soviet Union)	Tamara Lyukhina (Soviet Union)
1964	Polina Astakhova (Soviet Union)	Katalin Makray (Hungary)	Larissa Latynina (Soviet Union)
1968	Věra Čáslavská (Czechoslovakia)	Karin Janz (East Germany)	Zinaida Voronna (Soviet Union)
1972	Karin Janz (East Germany)	Olga Korbut (Soviet Union)	Erika Zuchold (East Germany)
1976	Nadia Comăneci (Romania)	Teodora Ungureanu (Romania)	Marta Egervari (Hungary)
1980	Maxi Gnauck (East Germany)	Emilia Eberle (Romania)	Steffi Kraker (East Germany) Melita Ruhn (Romania) Maria Filatova (Soviet Union)
1984	Ma Yanhong (China) Julianne McNamara (United States)	Not awarded	Mary Lou Retton (United States)
1988	Daniela Silivaş (Romania)	Dagmar Kersten (East Germany)	Elena Shushunova (Soviet Union)
1992	Lu Li (China)	Tatiana Gutsu (Unified Team)	Shannon Miller (United States)
1996	Svetlana Khorkina (Russia)	Bi Wenjing (China) Amy Chow (United States)	Not awarded
2000	Svetlana Khorkina (Russia)	Ling Jie (China)	Yang Yun (China)
2004	Émilie Le Pennec (France)	Terin Humphrey (United States)	Courtney Kupets (United States)
2008	He Kexin (China)	Nastia Liukin (United States)	Yang Yilin (China)

Women's Floor Exercise

Year	Gold	Silver	Bronze
1952	Ágnes Keleti (Hungary)	Maria Gorokhovskaya (Soviet Union)	Margit Korondi (Hungary)
1956	Ágnes Keleti (Hungary) Larissa Latynina (Soviet Union)	Not awarded	Elena Leuşteanu (Romania)
1960	Larissa Latynina (Soviet Union)	Polina Astakhova (Soviet Union)	Tamara Lyukhina (Soviet Union)
1964	Larissa Latynina (Soviet Union)	Polina Astakhova (Soviet Union)	Aniko Janosi-Ducza (Hungary)
1968	Larissa Petrik (Soviet Union) Věra Čáslavská (Czechoslovakia)	Not awarded	Natalia Kuchinskaya (Soviet Union)
1972	Olga Korbut (Soviet Union)	Ludmila Tourischeva (Soviet Union)	Tamara Lazakovich (Soviet Union)
1976	Nellie Kim (Soviet Union)	Ludmila Tourischeva (Soviet Union)	Nadia Comăneci (Romania)
1980	Nellie Kim (Soviet Union) Nadia Comăneci (Romania)	Not awarded	Natalia Shaposhnikova (Soviet Union) Maxi Gnauck (East Germany)
1984	Ecaterina Szabo (Romania)	Julianne McNamara (United States)	Mary Lou Retton (United States)
1988	Daniela Silivaş (Romania)	Svetlana Boginskaya (Soviet Union)	Diana Doudeva (Bulgaria)
1992	Lavinia Miloşovici (Romania)	Henrietta Ónodi (Hungary)	Cristina Bontaş (Romania) Shannon Miller (United States) Tatiana Gutsu (Unified Team)
1996	Lilia Podkopayeva (Ukraine)	Simona Amânar (Romania)	Dominique Dawes (United States)
2000	Elena Zamolodchikova (Russia)	Svetlana Khorkina (Russia)	Simona Amânar (Romania)
2004	Cătălina Ponor (Romania)	Nicoleta Daniela Şofronie (Romania)	Patricia Moreno (Spain)
2008	Sandra Izbaşa (Romania)	Shawn Johnson (United States)	Nastia Liukin (United States)

Men's Club Swinging

Year	Gold	Silver	Bronze
1904	Edward Hennig (United States)	Emil Voigt (United States)	Ralph Wilson (United States)

Men's Combined Three Events

Year	Gold	Silver	Bronze
1904	Adolf Spinnler (Switzerland)	Julius Lenhart (United States)	Wilhelm Weber (Germany)

Men's Combined Four Events

Year	Gold	Silver	Bronze
1904	Anton Heida (United States)	George Eyser (United States)	William Merz (United States)

Men's Floor Exercise

Year	Gold	Silver	Bronze
1932	István Pelle (Hungary)	Georges Miez (Switzerland)	Mario Lertora (Italy)
1936	Georges Miez (Switzerland)	Josef Walter (Switzerland)	Konrad Frey (Germany) Eugen Mack (Switzerland)
1940–1944: Olympics not held			
1948	Ferenc Pataki (Hungary)	János Mogyorósi-Klencs (Hungary)	Zdenek Ruzicka (Czechoslovakia)
1952	William Thoresson (Sweden)	Jerzy Jokiel (Poland) Tadao Uesako (Japan)	Not awarded
1956	Valentin Muratov (Soviet Union)	Nobuyuki Aihara (Japan) William Thoresson (Sweden) Viktor Chukarin (Soviet Union)	Not awarded
1960	Nobuyuki Aihara (Japan)	Yuri Titov (Soviet Union)	Franco Menichelli (Italy)
1964	Franco Menichelli (Italy)	Yukio Endo (Japan) Viktor Lisitsky (Soviet Union)	Not awarded
1968	Sawao Kato (Japan)	Akinori Nakayama (Japan)	Takeshi Kato (Japan)
1972	Nikolai Andrianov (Soviet Union)	Akinori Nakayama (Japan)	Shigeru Kasamatsu (Japan)
1976	Nikolai Andrianov (Soviet Union)	Vladimir Marchenko (Soviet Union)	Peter Kormann (United States)
1980	Roland Brückner (East Germany)	Nikolay Andrianov (Soviet Union)	Alexander Dityatin (Soviet Union)
1984	Li Ning (China)	Lou Yun (China)	Koji Sotomura (Japan) Philippe Vatuone (France)
1988	Sergei Kharkov (Soviet Union)	Vladimir Marchenko (Soviet Union)	Lou Yun (China) Yukio Iketani (Japan)
1992	Li Xiaoshuang (China)	Yukio Iketani (Japan) Grigory Misutin (Unified Team)	Not awarded
1996	Ioannis Melissanidis (Greece)	Li Xiaoshuang (China)	Alexei Nemov (Russia)
2000	Igors Vihrovs (Latvia)	Alexei Nemov (Russia)	Jordan Jovtchev (Bulgaria)
2004	Kyle Shewfelt (Canada)	Marian Drăgulescu (Romania)	Jordan Jovtchev (Bulgaria)
2008	Zou Kai (China)	Gervasio Deferr (Spain)	Anron Golotsutskov (Russia)

Men's Pommel Horse

Year	Gold	Silver	Bronze
1896	Louis Zutter (Switzerland)	Hermann Weingärtner (Germany)	Not awarded
1900: Event not held			
1904	Anton Heida (United States)	George Eyser (United States)	William Merz (United States)
1908–1920: Event not held			
1924	Josef Wilhelm (Switzerland)	Jean Gutweninger (Switzerland)	Antoine Rebetez (Switzerland)
1928	Hermann Hänggi (Switzerland)	Georges Miez (Switzerland)	Heikki Savolainen (Finland)
1932	István Pelle (Hungary)	Omero Bonoli (Italy)	Frank Haubold (United States)

Year	Gold	Silver	Bronze
1936	Konrad Frey (Germany)	Eugen Mack (Switzerland)	Albert Bachmann (Switzerland)
1940–1944: Olympics not held			
1948	Paavo Aaltonen (Finland) Veikko Huhtanen (Finland) Heikki Savolainen (Finland)	Not awarded	Not awarded
1952	Viktor Chukarin (Soviet Union)	Grant Shaginyan (Soviet Union) Evgeny Korolkov (Soviet Union)	Not awarded
1956	Boris Shakhlin (Soviet Union)	Takeshi Ono (Japan)	Viktor Chukarin (Soviet Union)
1960	Eugen Ekman (Finland) Boris Shakhlin (Soviet Union)	Not awarded	Shuji Tsurumi (Japan)
1964	Miroslav Cerar (Yugoslavia)	Shuji Tsurumi (Japan)	Yuri Tsapenko (Soviet Union)
1968	Miroslav Cerar (Yugoslavia)	Olli Laiho (Finland)	Mikhail Voronin (Soviet Union)
1972	Viktor Klimenko (Soviet Union)	Sawao Kato (Japan)	Eizo Kenmotsu (Japan)
1976	Zoltán Magyar (Hungary)	Eizo Kenmotsu (Japan)	Nikolai Andrianov (Soviet Union) Michael Nikolay (East Germany)
1980	Zoltán Magyar (Hungary)	Alexander Dityatin (Soviet Union)	Michael Nikolay (East Germany)
1984	Li Ning (China) Peter Vidmar (United States)	Not awarded	Timothy Daggett (United States)
1988	Lyubomir Gueraskov (Bulgaria) Zsolt Borkai (Hungary) Dmitri Bilozertchev (Soviet Union)	Not awarded	Not awarded
1992	Vitaly Scherbo (Unified Team) Pae Gil-Su (North Korea)	Not awarded	Andreas Wecker (Germany)
1996	Li Donghua (Switzerland)	Marius Urzică (Romania)	Alexei Nemov (Russia)
2000	Marius Urzică (Romania)	Eric Poujade (France)	Alexei Nemov (Russia)
2004	Teng Haibin (China)	Marius Urzică (Romania)	Takehiro Kashima (Japan)
2008	Xiao Qin (China)	Filip Ude (Croatia)	Louis Smith (Great Britain)

Men's Rings

Year	Gold	Silver	Bronze
1896	Ioannis Mitropoulos (Greece)	Hermann Weingärtner (Germany)	Not awarded
1900: Event not held			
1904	Herman Glass (United States)	William Merz (United States)	Emil Voigt (United States)
1908–1920: Event not held			
1924	Francesco Martino (Italy)	Roert Pražák (Czechoslovakia)	Ladislav Vácha (Czechoslovakia)
1928	Leon Štukelj (Yugoslavia)	Ladislav Vácha (Czechoslovakia)	Emanuel Löffler (Czechoslovakia)
1932	George Gulack (United States)	Bill Denton (United States)	Giovanni Lattuada (Italy)
1936	Alois Hudec (Czechoslovakia)	Leon Štukelj (Yugoslavia)	Matthias Volz (Germany)
1940–1944: Olympics not held			
1948	Karl Frei (Switzerland)	Michael Reusch (Switzerland)	Zdenek Ruzicka (Czechoslovakia)
1952	Grant Shaginyan (Soviet Union)	Viktor Chukarin (Soviet Union)	Dmitri Leonkin (Soviet Union) Hans Eugster (Switzerland)
1956	Albert Azarian (Soviet Union)	Valentin Muratov (Soviet Union)	Masao Takemoto (Japan) Masumi Kubota (Japan)
1960	Albert Azarian (Soviet Union)	Boris Shakhlin (Soviet Union)	Takeshi Ono (Japan) Velik Kapsazov (Bulgaria)
1964	Takuji Hayata (Japan)	Franco Menichelli (Italy)	Boris Shakhlin (Soviet Union)
1968	Akinori Nakayama (Japan)	Mikhail Voronin (Soviet Union)	Sawao Kato (Japan)
1972	Akinori Nakayama (Japan)	Mikhail Voronin (Soviet Union)	Mitsuo Tsukahara (Japan)
1976	Nikolai Andrianov (Soviet Union)	Alexander Dityatin (Soviet Union)	Danut Grecu (Romania)
1980	Alexander Dityatin (Soviet Union)	Alexander Tkachev (Soviet Union)	Jiri Tabak (Czechoslovakia)
1984	Koji Gushiken (Japan) Li Ning (China)	Not awarded	Mitchell Gaylord (United States)

Year	Gold	Silver	Bronze
1988	Holger Behrendt (East Germany) Dimitri Bilozertchev (Soviet Union)	Not awarded	Sven Tippelt (East Germany)
1992	Vitaly Scherbo (Unified Team)	Li Jing (China)	Andreas Wecker (Germany) Li Xiaoshuang (China)
1996	Jury Chechi (Italy)	Szilveszter Csollány (Hungary) Dan Burincă (Romania)	Not awarded
2000	Szilveszter Csollány (Hungary)	Dimosthenis Tampakos (Greece)	Jordan Jovtchev (Bulgaria)
2004	Dimosthenis Tampakos (Greece)	Jordan Jovtchev (Bulgaria)	Juri Chechi (Italy)
2008	Chen Yibing (China)	Yang Wei (China)	Oleksandr Vorobiov (Ukraine)

Men's Vault

Year	Gold	Silver	Bronze
1896	Carl Schuhmann (Germany)	Louis Zutter (Switzerland)	Hermann Weingärtner (Germany)
1900: Event not held			
1904	George Eyser (United States) Anton Heida (United States)	Not awarded	William Merz (United States)
1908–1920: Event not held			
1924	Frank Kriz (United States)	Jan Koutný (Czechoslovakia)	Bohumil Mořkovský (Czechoslovakia)
1928	Eugen Mack (Switzerland)	Emanuel Löffler (Czechoslovakia)	Stane Derganc (Yugoslavia)
1932	Savino Guglielmetti (Italy)	Al Jochim (United States)	Ed Carmichael (United States)
1936	Alfred Schwarzmann (Germany)	Eugen Mack (Switzerland)	Matthias Volz (Germany)
1940–1944: Olympics not held			
1948	Paavo Aaltonen (Finland)	Olavi Rove (Finland)	Ferenc Pataki (Hungary) János Mogyorósi-Klencs (Hungary) Leo Sotornik (Czechoslovakia)
1952	Viktor Chukarin (Soviet Union)	Masao Takemoto (Japan)	Takashi Ono (Japan) Tada Uesako (Japan)
1956	Helmut Bantz (Germany) Valentin Muratov (Soviet Union)	Not awarded	Yuri Titov (Soviet Union)
1960	Boris Shakhlin (Soviet Union) Takashi Ono (Japan)	Not awarded	Vladimir Portnoi (Soviet Union)
1964	Haruhiro Yamashita (Japan)	Viktor Lisitsky (Soviet Union)	Hannu Rantakari (Finland)
1968	Mikhail Voronin (Soviet Union)	Yukio Endo (Japan)	Sergei Diomidov (Soviet Union)
1972	Klaus Köste (East Germany)	Viktor Klimenko (Soviet Union)	Nikolai Andrianov (Soviet Union)
1976	Nikolai Andrianov (Soviet Union)	Mitsuo Tsukahara (Japan)	Hiroshi Kajiyama (Japan)
1980	Nikolai Andrianov (Soviet Union)	Alexander Dityatin (Soviet Union)	Roland Brückner (East Germany)
1984	Lou Yun (China)	Mitchell Gaylord (United States) Koji Gushiken (Japan) Shinji Morisue (Japan)	Not awarded
1988	Lou Yun (China)	Sylvio Kroll (East Germany)	Park Jong-Hoon (South Korea)
1992	Vitaly Scherbo (Unified Team)	Grigory Misutin (Unified Team)	Yoo Ok-Ryul (South Korea)
1996	Alexei Nemov (Russia)	Yeo Hong-Chul (South Korea)	Vitaly Scherbo (Belarus)
2000	Gervasio Deferr (Spain)	Alexei Bondarenko (Russia)	Leszek Blanik (Poland)
2004	Gervasio Deferr (Spain)	Jevgēņijs Saproņenko (Latvia)	Marian Drăgulescu (Romania)
2008	Leszek Blanik (Poland)	Thomas Bouhail (France)	Anton Golotsutskov (Russia)

Men's Parallel Bars

Year	Gold	Silver	Bronze
1896	Alfred Flatow (Germany)	Louis Zutter (Switzerland)	Not awarded
1900: Event not held			

Year	Gold	Silver	Bronze
1904	George Eyser (United States)	Anton Heida (United States)	John Duha (United States)
1908–1920: Event not held			
1924	August Güttinger (Switzerland)	Robert Pražák (Czechoslovakia)	Giorgio Zampori (Italy)
1928	Ladislav Vácha (Czechoslovakia)	Josip Primožič (Yugoslavia)	Hermann Hänggi (Switzerland)
1932	Romeo Neri (Italy)	István Pelle (Hungary)	Heikki Savolainen (Finland)
1936	Konrad Frey (Germany)	Michael Reusch (Switzerland)	Alfred Schwarzmann (Germany)
1940–1944: Olympics not held			
1948	Michael Reusch (Switzerland)	Veikko Huhtanen (Finland)	Josef Stalder (Switzerland) Christian Kipfer (Switzerland)
1952	Hans Eugster (Switzerland)	Viktor Chukarin (Soviet Union)	Josef Stalder (Switzerland)
1956	Viktor Chukarin (Soviet Union)	Masumi Kubota (Japan)	Takeshi Ono (Japan) Masa Takemoto (Japan)
1960	Boris Shakhlin (Soviet Union)	Giovanni Carminucci (Italy)	Takeshi Ono (Japan)
1964	Yukio Endo (Japan)	Shuji Tsurumi (Japan)	Franco Menichelli (Italy)
1968	Akinori Nakayama (Japan)	Mikhail Voronin (Soviet Union)	Vladimir Klimenko (Soviet Union)
1972	Sawao Kato (Japan)	Shigeru Kasamatsu (Japan)	Eizo Menmotsu (Japan)
1976	Sawao Kato (Japan)	Nikolai Andrianov (Soviet Union)	Mitsuo Tsukahara (Japan)
1980	Alexander Tkachev (Soviet Union)	Alexander Dityatin (Soviet Union)	Roland Brückner (East Germany)
1984	Bart Conner (United States)	Nobuyuki Kajitani (Japan)	Mitchell Gaylord (United States)
1988	Vladimir Artemov (Soviet Union)	Valeri Liukin (Soviet Union)	Sven Tippelt (East Germany)
1992	Vitaly Scherbo (Unified Team)	Li Jing (China)	Igor Korobscinski (Unified Team) Guo Linyao (China) Masayuki Matsunaga (Japan)
1996	Rustam Sharipov (Ukraine)	Jair Lynch (United States)	Vitaly Scherbo (Belarus)
2000	Li Xiaopeng (China)	Lee Joo-Hyung (South Korea)	Alexei Nemov (Russia)
2004	Valeri Goncharov (Ukraine)	Hiroyuki Tomita (Japan)	Li Xiaopeng (China)
2008	Li Xiaopeng (China)	Yoo Won-Chul (South Korea)	Anton Fokin (Uzbekistan)

Men's Horizontal Bar

Year	Gold	Silver	Bronze
1896	Hermann Weingärtner (Germany)	Alfred Flatow (Germany)	Not awarded
1900: Event not held			
1904	Anton Heida (United States) Edward Hennig (United States)	Not awarded	George Eyser (United States)
1908–1920: Event not held			
1924	Leon Štukelj (Yugoslavia)	Jean Gutweninger (Switzerland)	André Higelin (France)
1928	Georges Miez (Switzerland)	Romeo Neri (Italy)	Eugen Mack (Switzerland)
1932	Dallas Bixler (United States)	Heikki Savolainen (Finland)	Einari Teräsvirta (Finland)
1936	Aleksanteri Saarvala (Finland)	Konrad Frey (Germany)	Alfred Schwarzmann (Germany)
1940–1944: Olympics not held			
1948	Josef Stalder (Switzerland)	Walter Lehmann (Switzerland)	Veikko Huhtanen (Finland)
1952	Jack Günthard (Switzerland)	Josef Stalder (Switzerland) Alfred Schwarzmann (Germany)	Not awarded
1956	Takeshi Ono (Japan)	Yuri Titov (Soviet Union)	Masao Takemoto (Japan)
1960	Takeshi Ono (Japan)	Masao Takemoto (Japan)	Boris Shakhlin (Soviet Union)
1964	Boris Shakhlin (Soviet Union)	Yuri Titov (Soviet Union)	Miroslav Cerar (Yugoslavia)
1968	Mikhail Voronin (Soviet Union) Akinori Nakayama (Japan)	Not awarded	Eizo Kenmotsu (Japan)
1972	Mitsuo Tsukahara (Japan)	Sawao Kato (Japan)	Shigeru Kasamatsu (Japan)
1976	Mitsuo Tsukahara (Japan)	Eizo Kenmotsu (Japan)	Eberhard Gienger (West Germany) Henri Boerio (France)
1980	Stoyan Deltchev (Bulgaria)	Alexander Dityatin (Soviet Union)	Nikolai Andrianov (Soviet Union)

Year	Gold	Silver	Bronze
1984	Shinji Morisue (Japan)	Tong Fei (China)	Koji Gushiken (Japan)
1988	Vladimir Artemov (Soviet Union) Valeri Liukin (Soviet Union)	Not awarded	Holger Behrendt (East Germany)
1992	Trent Dimas (United States)	Grigory Misutin (Unified Team) Andreas Wecker (Germany)	Not awarded
1996	Andreas Wecker (Germany)	Krasimir Dounec (Bulgaria)	Vitaly Scherbo (Belarus) Fan Bin (China) Alexei Nemov (Russia)
2000	Alexei Nemov (Russia)	Benjamin Varonian (France)	Lee Joo-Hyung (South Korea)
2004	Igor Cassina (Italy)	Paul Hamm (United States)	Isao Yoneda (Japan)
2008	Zou Kai (China)	Jonathan Horton (United States)	Fabian Hambüchen (Germany)

Men's Rope Climbing

Year	Gold	Silver	Bronze
1896	Nikolaos Andriakopoulos (Greece)	Thomas Xenakis (Greece)	Fritz Hoffmann (Germany)
1900: Event not held			
1904	George Eyser (United States)	Charles Krause (United States)	Emil Voigt (United States)
1908–1920: Event not held			
1924	Bedřich Šupčík (Czechoslovakia)	Albert Séguin (France)	Ladislav Vácha (Czechoslovakia) August Güttinger (Switzerland)
1928: Event not held			
1932	Raymond Bass (United States)	William Galbraith (United States)	Thomas Connolly (United States)

Men's Indian Clubs

Year	Gold	Silver	Bronze
1932	George Roth (United States)	Philip Erenberg (United States)	William Kuhlemeier (United States)

Men's Sidehorse Vault

Year	Gold	Silver	Bronze
1924	Albert Séguin (France)	Jean Gounot (France) François Gangloff (France)	Not awarded

Men's Tumbling

Year	Gold	Silver	Bronze
1932	Raymond Bass (United States)	Edwin Gross (United States)	William Herrmann (United States)

Men's Team Horizontal Bar

Year	Gold	Silver	Bronze
1896	Konrad Böcker, Alfred Flatow, Gustav Flatow, Georg Hillmar, Fritz Hoffmann, Fritz Manteuffel, Karl Neukirch, Richard Röstel, Gustav Schuft, Carl Schuhmann, Hermann Weingärtner (Germany)	Not awarded	Not awarded

Men's Team Free System

Year	Gold	Silver	Bronze
1912	Isak Abrahamsen, Hans Beyer, Hartmann Bjørnsen, Alfred Engelsen, Bjarne Johnsen, Sigurd Jørgensen, Knud Leonard Knudsen, Alf Lie, Rolf Lie, Tor Lund, Petter Martinsen, Per Mathiesen, Jacob Opdahl, Nils Opdahl, Bjarne Pettersen, Frithjof Sælen, Øistein Schirmer, Georg Selenius, Sigvard Sivertsen, Robert Sjursen, Einar Strøm, Gabriel Thorstensen, Thomas Thorstensen, Nils Voss (Norway)	Kaarlo Ekholm, Eino Forsström, Eero Hyvärinen, Mikko Hyvärinen, Tauno Ilmoniemi, Ilmari Keinänen, Jalmari Kivenheimo, Karl Lund, Aarne Pelkonen, Ilmari Pernaja, Arvid Rydman, Eino Saastamoinen, Aarne Salovaara, Heikki Sammallahti, Hannes Sirola, Klaus Suomela, Lauri Tanner, Väinö Tiiri, Kaarlo Vähämäki, Kaarlo Vasama (Finland)	Axel Andersen, Hjalmart Andersen, Halvor Birch, Wilhelm Grimmelmann, Arvor Hansen, Christian Hansen, Marius Hansen, Charles Jensen, Hjalmar Peter Johansen, Poul Jørgensen, Carl Krebs, Vigo Madsen, Lukas Nielsen, Rikard Nordstrøm, Steen Olsen, Oluf Olsson, Carl Pedersen, Oluf Pedersen, Niels Petersen, Christian Svendsen (Denmark)
1916: Olympics not held			
1920	Georg Albertsen, Rudolf Andersen, Viggo Dibbern, Aage Frandsen, Hugo Helsten, Harry Holm, Herold Jansson, Robert Johnsen, Christian Juhl, Vilhelm Lange, Svend Madsen, Peder Marcussen, Peder Møller, Niels Turin Nielsen, Steen Olsen, Christian Pedersen, Hans Rønne, Harry Sørensen, Christian Thomas, Knud Vermehren (Denmark)	Alf Aanning, Karl Aas, Jørgen Andersen, Gustav Bayer, Jørgen Bjørnstad, Asbjørn Bodahl, Eilert Bøhm, Trygve Bøyesen, Ingolf Davidsen, Håkon Endreson, Jacob Erstad, Harald Færstad, Hermann Helgesen, Petter Hol, Otto Johannessen, John Anker Johansen, Torbjørn Kristoffersen, Henrik Nielsen, Jacob Opdahl, Arthur Rydstrøm, Frithjof Sælen, Bjørn Skjærpe, Wilhelm Steffensen, Olav Sundal, Reidar Tønsberg, Lauritz Wigand-Larsen (Norway)	Not awarded

Men's Team Swedish System

Year	Gold	Silver	Bronze
1912	Per Bertilsson, Carl-Ehrenfried Carlberg, Nils Granfelt, Curt Hartzell, Oswald Holmberg, Anders Hylander, Axel Janse, Boo Kullberg, Sven Landberg, Per Nilsson, Benkt Norelius, Axel Norling, Daniel Norling, Sven Rosén, Nils Silfverskiöld, Carl Silfverstrand, John Sörenson, Yngve Stiernspetz, Carl-Erik Svensson, Karl Johan Svensson, Knut Torell, Edward Wennerholm, Claes Wersäll, David Wiman (Sweden)	Peter Andersen, Valdemar Bøggild, Søren Peter Christensen, Ingvald Eriksen, George Falcke, Torkild Garp, Hans Trier Hansen, Johannes Hansen, Rasmus Hansen, Jens Kristian Jensen, Søren Alfred Jensen, Karl Kirk, Jens Kirkegaard, Olaf Kjems, Carl Larsen, Jens Peter Laursen, Marius Lefèrve, Povl Mark, Einar Olsen, Hans Pedersen, Hans Eiler Pedersen, Olaf Pedersen, Peder Larsen Pedersen, Aksel Sørensen, Martin Thau, Søren Thorborg, Kristen Vadgaard, Johannes Vinther (Denmark)	Arthur Amundsen, Jørgen Andersen, Trygve Bøyesen, Georg Brustad, Conrad Christensen, Oscar Engelstad, Marius Eriksen, Axel Henry Hansen, Petter Hol, Eugen Ingebretsen, Olaf Ingebretsen, Olof Jacobsen, Erling Jensen, Thor Jensen, Frithjof Olsen, Oscar Olstad, Edvin Paulsen, Carl Alfred Pedersen, Paul Pedersen, Rolf Robach, Sigurd Smebye, Torleif Torkildsen (Norway)
1916: Olympics not held			

Year	Gold	Silver	Bronze
1920	Fausto Acke, Albert Andersson, Arvid Andersson-Holtman, Helge Bäckander, Bengt Bengtsson, Fabian Biörck, Erik Charpentier, Sture Ericsson-Ewréus, Konrad Granström, Helge Gustafsson, Åke Häger, Ture Hedman, Sven Johnson, Sven-Olof Jonsson, Karl Lindahl, Edmund Lindmark, Bengt Mohrberg, Frans Persson, Klas Särner, Curt Sjöberg, Gunnar Söderlindh, John Sörenson, Erik Svensén, Gösta Törner (Sweden)	Johannes Birk, Frede Hansen, Frederik Hansen, Kristian Hansen, Hans Jakobsen, Aage Jørgensen, Alfred Frøkjær Jørgensen, Alfred Ollerup Jørgensen, Arne Jørgensen, Knud Kirkeløkke, Jens Lambæk, Kristian Larsen, Kristian Madsen, Niels Erik Nielsen, Niels Kristian Nielsen, Dynes Pedersen, Hans Pedersen, Johannes Pedersen, Peter Dorf Pedersen, Rasmus Rasmussen, Hans Christian Sørensen, Hans Laurids Sørensen, Søren Sørensen, Georg Vest, Aage Walther (Denmark)	Paul Arets, Léon Bronckaert, Léopold Clabots, Jean-Baptiste Claessens, Léon Darrien, Lucien Dehoux, Ernest Deleu, Émile Duboisson, Ernest Dureuil, Joseph Fiems, Marcel Hansen, Louis Henin, Omer Hoffman, Félix Logiest, Charles Maerschalck, René Paenhuijsen, Arnold Pierrot, René Pinchart, Gaspard Pirotte, Augustien Pluys, Léopold Son, Édouard Taeymans, Pierre Thiriar, Henri Verhavert (Belgium)

Men's Triathlon

Year	Gold	Silver	Bronze
1904	Adolf Spinnler (Switzerland)	Julius Lenhart (United States)	Wilhelm Weber (Germany)

Women's Team Portable Apparatus

Year	Gold	Silver	Bronze
1952	Karin Lindberg, Ann-Sofi Pettersson, Evy Berggren, Gun Roring, Gota Pettersson, Irgrid Sandahi (Sweden)	Maria Horokhovska, Nina Bocharova, Galina Minaicheva, Galina Urbanovich, Pelageva Danilova, Galina Shamrai (Soviet Union)	Margit Korondi, Ágnes Keleti, Edit Perenyi-Weckinger, Olga Tass, Erzsebet Gulyas, Maria Zalai-Kovi (Hungary)
1956	Anrea Bodo, Karolyne Gulyas, Ágnes Keleti, Alice Kertesz, Margit Korondi, Olga Tass (Hungary)	Karin Lindberg, Ann-Sofi Pettersson, Eva Rönström, Evy Berggren, Doris Hedberg, Maud Karlén (Sweden)	Polina Astakhova, Ludmila Egorova, Lidia Kalinina, Larissa Latynina, Tamara Manina, Sofia Muratova (Soviet Union) Helena Rakoczy, Natalia Kot, Danuta Nowak-Stachow, Dorota Horzonek-Jokiel, Barbara Wilk-Ślizowska, Lidia Szczerbińska (Poland)

Athletics

Men's 100-Meter

Year	Gold	Silver	Bronze
1896	Thomas Burke (United States)	Fritz Hofmann (Germany)	Alajos Szokolyi (Hungary) Francis Lane (United States)
1900	Francis Jarvis (United States)	Walter B. John Tewksbury (United States)	Stanley Rowley (Australia)
1904	Archie Hahm (United States)	John Nathaniel Cartmell (United States)	William Hogenson (United States)
1908	Reginald Walker (South Africa)	James Rector (United States)	Robert Kerr (Canada)
1912	Ralph Craig (United States)	I. Alvah Meyer (United States)	Donald Lippincott (United States)
1916: Olympics not held			
1920	Charles Paddock (United States)	Morris Kirksey (United States)	Harry Edward (Great Britain)

Year	Gold	Silver	Bronze
1924	Harold Abrahams (Great Britain)	Jackson Scholz (United States)	Arthur Porritt (New Zealand)
1928	Percy Williams (Canada)	John Edward London (Great Britain)	Georg Lammers (Germany)
1932	Eddie Tolan (United States)	Ralph Metcalfe (United States)	Arthur Jonath (Germany)
1936	Jesse Owens (United States)	Ralph Metcalfe (United States)	Martinus Osendarp (Netherlands)
1940–1944: Olympics not held			
1948	Harrison Dillard (United States)	Harold Norwood Ewell (Great Britain)	Lloyd Labeach (Panama)
1952	Lindy Remigino (United States)	Herbert McKenley (Jamaica)	Emmanuel McDonald Bailey (Great Britain)
1956	Robert Joseph Morrow (United States)	Walter Thane Baker (United States)	Hector Hogan (Australia)
1960	Armin Hary (Germany)	David Sime (United States)	Peter Radford (Great Britain)
1964	Robert Hays (United States)	Enrique Figuerola Camue (Cuba)	Henry Winston "Harry" Jerome (Canada)
1968	James Ray Hines (United States)	Lennox Miller (Jamaica)	Charles Edward Greene (United States)
1972	Valery Borzov (Soviet Union)	Robert Taylor (United States)	Lennox Miller (Jamaica)
1976	Hasely Crawford (Trinidad and Tobago)	Donald Quarrie (Jamaica)	Valery Borzov (Soviet Union)
1980	Allan Wells (Great Britain)	Silvio Leonard Sarria (Cuba)	Peter Petrov (Bulgaria)
1984	Carl Lewis (United States)	Samuel Louis Graddy (United States)	Ben Johnson (Canada)
1988	Carl Lewis (United States)	Linford Christie (Great Britain)	Calvin Smith (United States)
1992	Linford Christie (Great Britain)	Frank Fredericks (Namibia)	Dennis Mitchell (United States)
1996	Donovan Bailey (Canada)	Frank Fredericks (Namibia)	Ato Bolden (Trinidad and Tobago)
2000	Maurice Greene (United States)	Ato Boldon (Trinidad and Tobago)	Obadele Thompson (Barbados)
2004	Justin Gatlin (United States)	Francis Obikwelu (Portugal)	Maurice Greene (United States)
2008	Usain Bolt (Jamaica)	Richard Thompson (Trinidad and Tobago)	Walter Dix (United States)

Men's 200-Meter

Year	Gold	Silver	Bronze
1900	John Tewksbury (United States)	Norman Pritchard (India)	Stanley Rowley (Australia)
1904	Archie Hahn (United States)	Nathaniel Cartmell (United States)	William Hogenson (United States)
1908	Bobby Kerr (Canada)	Robert Cloughen (United States)	Nathaniel Cartmell (United States)
1912	Ralph Craig (United States)	Don Lippincott (United States)	William Applegarth (Great Britain)
1916: Olympics not held			
1920	Allen Woodring (United States)	Charles Paddock (United States)	Harry Edward (Great Britain)
1924	Jackson Scholz (United States)	Charles Paddock (United States)	Eric Liddell (Great Britain)
1928	Percy Williams (Canada)	Walter Rangeley (Great Britain)	Helmut Körnig (Germany)
1932	Eddie Tolan (United States)	George Simpson (United States)	Ralph Metcalfe (United States)
1936	Jesse Owens (United States)	Matthew Robinson (United States)	Tinus Osendarp (Netherlands)
1940–1944: Olympics not held			
1948	Mel Patton (United States)	Barney Ewell (United States)	Lloyd LaBeach (Panama)
1952	Andy Stanfield (United States)	Thane Baker (United States)	James Gathers (United States)
1956	Bobby Joe Morrow (United States)	Andy Stanfield (United States)	Thane Baker (United States)
1960	Livio Berruti (Italy)	Lester Carney (United States)	Abdoulaye Seye (France)
1964	Henry Carr (United States)	Paul Drayton (United States)	Edwin Roberts (Trinidad and Tobago)
1968	Tommie Smith (United States)	Peter Norman (Australia)	John Carlos (United States)
1972	Valeri Borzov (Soviet Union)	Larry Black (United States)	Pietro Mennea (Italy)
1976	Don Quarrie (Jamaica)	Millard Hampton (United States)	Dwayne Evans (United States)

Year	Gold	Silver	Bronze
1980	Pietro Mennea (Italy)	Allan Wells (Great Britain)	Don Quarrie (Jamaica)
1984	Carl Lewis (United States)	Kirk Baptiste (United States)	Thomas Jefferson (United States)
1988	Joe DeLoach (United States)	Carl Lewis (United States)	Robson da Silva (Brazil)
1992	Michael Marsh (United States)	Frankie Fredericks (Namibia)	Michael Bates (United States)
1996	Michael Johnson (United States)	Frankie Fredericks (Namibia)	Ato Boldon (Trinidad and Tobago)
2000	Konstantinos Kenteris (Greece)	Darren Campbell (Great Britain)	Ato Boldon (Trinidad and Tobago)
2004	Shawn Crawford (United States)	Bernard Williams (United States)	Justin Gatlin (United States)
2008	Usain Bolt (Jamaica)	Shawn Crawford (United States)	Walter Dix (United States)

Men's 400-Meter

Year	Gold	Silver	Bronze
1896	Tom Burke (United States)	Herbert Jamison (United States)	Charles Gmelin (Great Britain)
1900	Max Long (United States)	William Holland (United States)	Ernst Schultz (Denmark)
1904	Harry Hillman (United States)	Frank Waller (United States)	Herman Groman (United States)
1908	Wyndham Halswelle (Great Britain)	Not awarded	Not awarded
1912	Charles Reidpath (United States)	Hanns Braun (Germany)	Edward Lindberg (United States)
1916: Olympics not held			
1920	Bevil Rudd (South Africa)	Guy Butler (Great Britain)	Nils Engdahl (Sweden)
1924	Eric Liddell (Great Britain)	Horatio Fitch (United States)	Guy Butler (Great Britain)
1928	Ray Barbuti (United States)	James Ball (Canada)	Joachim Büchner (Germany)
1932	Bill Carr (United States)	Ben Eastman (United States)	Alexander Wilson (Canada)
1936	Archie Williams (United States)	Godfrey Brown (Great Britain)	James LuValle (United States)
1940–1944: Olympics not held			
1948	Arthur Wint (Jamaica)	Herb McKenley (Jamaica)	Mal Whitfield (United States)
1952	George Rhoden (Jamaica)	Herb McKenley (Jamaica)	Ollie Matson (United States)
1956	Charlie Jenkins (United States)	Karl-Freidrich Haas (Germany)	Voitto Hellstén (Finland) Ardalion Ignatyev (Soviet Union)
1960	Otis Davis (United States)	Carl Kaufmann (Germany)	Malcolm Spence (South Africa)
1964	Michael Larrabee (United States)	Wendell Mottley (Trinidad and Tobago)	Andrzej Badeński (Poland)
1968	Lee Evans (United States)	Larry James (United States)	Ron Freeman (United States)
1972	Vincent Matthews (United States)	Wayne Collett (United States)	Julius Sang (Kenya)
1976	Alberto Juantorena (Cuba)	Frederick Newhouse (United States)	Herman Frazier (United States)
1980	Viktor Markin (Soviet Union)	Rick Mitchell (Australia)	Frank Schaffer (East Germany)
1984	Alonzo Babers (United States)	Gabriel Tiacoh (Ivory Coast)	Antonia McKay (United States)
1988	Steve Lewis (United States)	Butch Reynolds (United States)	Danny Everett (United States)
1992	Quincy Watts (United States)	Steve Lewis (United States)	Samson Kitur (Kenya)
1996	Michael Johnson (United States)	Roger Black (Great Britain)	Davis Kamoga (Uganda)
2000	Michael Johnson (United States)	Alvin Harrison (United States)	Greg Haughton (Jamaica)
2004	Jeremy Wariner (United States)	Otis Harris (United States)	Derrick Brew (United States)
2008	LaShawn Merritt (United States)	Jeremy Wariner (United States)	David Neville (United States)

Men's 800-Meter

Year	Gold	Silver	Bronze
1896	Edwin Flack (Great Britain)	Nándor Dáni (Hungary)	Dimitrious Golemis (Greece)
1900	Alfred Tysoe (Great Britain)	John Cregan (United States)	David Hall (United States)
1904	Jim Lightbody (United States)	Howard Valentine (United States)	Emil Breitkreutz (United States)
1908	Mel Sheppard (United States)	Emilio Lunghi (Italy)	Hanns Braun (Germany)
1912	Ted Meredith (United States)	Mel Sheppard (United States)	Ira Davenport (United States)

Year	Gold	Silver	Bronze
1916: Olympics not held			
1920	Albert Hill (Great Britain)	Earl Eby (United States)	Bevil Rudd (South Africa)
1924	Douglas Lowe (Great Britain)	Paul Martin (Switzerland)	Schuyler Enck (United States)
1928	Douglas Lowe (Great Britain)	Erik Byléhn (Sweden)	Hermann Engelhard (Germany)
1932	Thomas Hampson (Great Britain)	Alexander Wilson (Canada)	Phil Edwards (Canada)
1936	John Woodruff (United States)	Mario Lanzi (Italy)	Phil Edwards (Canada)
1940–1944: Olympics not held			
1948	Mal Whitfield (United States)	Arthur Wint (Jamaica)	Marcel Hansenne (France)
1952	Mal Whitfield (United States)	Arthur Wint (Jamaica)	Heinz Ulzheimer (Germany)
1956	Tom Courtney (United States)	Derek Johnson (Great Britain)	Audun Boysen (Norway)
1960	Peter Snell (New Zealand)	Roger Moens (Belgium)	George Kerr (British West Indies)
1964	Peter Snell (New Zealand)	Bill Crothers (Canada)	Wilson Kiprugut (Kenya)
1968	Ralph Doubell (Australia)	Wilson Kiprugut (Kenya)	Tom Farrell (United States)
1972	Dave Wottle (United States)	Yevgeni Arzhanov (Soviet Union)	Mike Boit (United States)
1976	Alberto Juantorena (Cuba)	Ivo van Damme (Belgium)	Rick Wohlhuter (United States)
1980	Steve Ovett (Great Britain)	Sebastian Coe (Great Britain)	Kikolay Kirov (Soviet Union)
1984	Joaquim Cruz (Brazil)	Sebastian Coe (Great Britain)	Earl Jones (United States)
1988	Paul Ereng (Kenya)	Joaquim Cruz (Brazil)	Saïd Aouita (Morocco)
1992	William Tanui (Kenya)	Nixon Kiprotich (Kenya)	Johnny Gray (United States)
1996	Vebjørn Rodal (Norway)	Hezekiél Sepeng (South Africa)	Fred Onyancha (Kenya)
2000	Nils Schumann (Germany)	Wilson Kipketer (Denmark)	Djabir Saïd-Guerni (Algeria)
2004	Yuriy Borzakovskiy (Russia)	Mbulaeni Mulaudzi (South Africa)	Wilson Kipketer (Denmark)
2008	Wilfred Bungei (Kenya)	Ismail Ahmed Ismail (Sudan)	Alfred Kirwa Yego (Kenya)

Men's 1,500-Meter

Year	Gold	Silver	Bronze
1896	Edwin Flack (Great Britain)	Arthur Blake (United States)	Albin Lermusiaux (France)
1900	Charles Bennett (Great Britain)	Henri Dloge (France)	John Bray (United States)
1904	Jim Lightbody (United States)	William Verner (United States)	Lacey Hearn (United States)
1908	Mel Sheppard (United States)	Harold A. Wilson (Great Britain)	Norman Hallows (Great Britain)
1912	Arnold Jackson (Great Britain)	Abel Kiviat (United States)	Norman Taber (United States)
1916: Olympics not held			
1920	Albert Hill (Great Britain)	Philip Noel-Baker (Great Britain)	Lawrence Shields (United States)
1924	Paavo Nurmi (Finland)	Willy Schärer (Switzerland)	Henry Stallard (Great Britain)
1928	Harri Larva (Finland)	Jules Ladoumegue (France)	Eino Purje (Finland)
1932	Luigi Beccali (Italy)	Jerry Cornes (Great Britain)	Phil Edwards (Canada)
1936	Jack Lovelock (New Zealand)	Glenn Cunningham (United States)	Luigi Beccali (Italy)
1940–1944: Olympics not held			
1948	Henry Eriksson (Sweden)	Lennart Strand (Sweden)	Wim Slijkhuis (Netherlands)
1952	Josy Barthel (Luxembourg)	Bob McMillen (United States)	Werner Lueg (Germany)
1956	Ron Delany (Ireland)	Klaus Richtzenhain (Germany)	John Landy (Australia)
1960	Herb Elliott (Australia)	Michel Jazy (France)	István Rózsavölgyi (Hungary)
1964	Peter Snell (New Zealand)	Josef Odložil (Czechoslovakia)	John Davies (New Zealand)
1968	Kipchoge Keino (Kenya)	Jim Ryun (United States)	Bodo Tümmler (West Germany)
1972	Pekka Vasala (Finland)	Kipchoge Keino (Kenya)	Rod Dixon (New Zealand)
1976	John Walker (New Zealand)	Ivo van Damme (Belgium)	Paul-Heins Wellmann (West Germany)
1980	Sebastian Coe (Great Britain)	Jürgen Straub (East Germany)	Steve Ovett (Great Britain)
1984	Sebastian Coe (Great Britain)	Steve Cram (Great Britain)	José Manuel Abascal (Spain)
1988	Peter Rono (Kenya)	Peter Elliott (Great Britain)	Jens-Peter Herold (East Germany)
1992	Fermin Cacho Ruiz (Spain)	Rachid El Basir (Morocco)	Mohammed Suleiman (Qatar)

Year	Gold	Silver	Bronze
1996	Noureddine Morceli (Algeria)	Fermín Cacho (Spain)	Stephen Kipkorir (Kenya)
2000	Noah Ngeny (Kenya)	Hicham El Guerrouj (Morocco)	Nernard Lagat (Kenya)
2004	Hicham El Guerrouj (Morocco)	Bernard Lagat (Kenya)	Rui Silva (Portugal)
2008	Asbel Kipruto Kiprop (Kenya)	Nicholas Willis (New Zealand)	Mehdi Baala (France)

Men's 5,000-Meter

Year	Gold	Silver	Bronze
1912	Hannes Kolehmainen (Finland)	Jean Bouin (France)	George Hutson (Great Britain)
1916: Olympics not held			
1920	Joseph Guillemot (France)	Paavo Nurmi (Finland)	Eric Backman (Sweden)
1924	Paavo Nurmi (Finland)	Ville Ritola (Finland)	Edvin Wide (Sweden)
1928	Ville Ritola (Finland)	Paavo Nurmi (Finland)	Edvin Wide (Sweden)
1932	Lauri Leftinen (Finland)	Ralph Hill (United States)	Hauri Virtanen (Finland)
1936	Gunnar Höckert (Finland)	Lauri Lehtinen (Finland)	Henry Jonsson (Sweden)
1940–1944: Olympics not held			
1948	Gaston Reiff (Belgium)	Emil Zátopek (Czechoslovakia)	Wim Slijkhuis (Netherlands)
1952	Emil Zátopek (Czechoslovakia)	Alain Mimoun (France)	Herbert Schade (Germany)
1956	Vladimir Kuts (Soviet Union)	Gordon Pirie (Great Britain)	Derek Ibbotson (Great Britain)
1960	Murray Halberg (New Zealand)	Hans Grodotzki (Germany)	Kazimierz Zimny (Hungary)
1964	Bob Schul (United States)	Harald Norpoth (Germany)	Bill Dellinger (United States)
1968	Mohammed Gammoudi (Tunisia)	Kipchoge Keino (Kenya)	Naftali Temu (Kenya)
1972	Lasse Virén (Finland)	Mohammed Gammoudi (Tunisia)	Ian Stewart (Great Britain)
1976	Lasse Virén (Finland)	Dick Quax (New Zealand)	Klaus-Peter Hildenbrand (West Germany)
1980	Miruts Yifter (Ethiopia)	Suleiman Nyambui (Tanzania)	Kaarlo Maaninka (Finland)
1984	Saïd Aouita (Morocco)	Markus Ryffel (Switzerland)	António Leitão (Portugal)
1988	John Ngugi (Kenya)	Dieter Baumann (West Germany)	Hansjörg Kunze (East Germany)
1992	Dieter Baumann (West Germany)	Paul Bitok (Kenya)	Fita Bayisa (Ethiopia)
1996	Vénuste Niyongabo (Burundi)	Paul Bitok (Kenya)	Salah Hissou (Morocco)
2000	Million Wolde (Ethiopia)	Ali Saïdi-Sief (Algeria)	Brahim Lahlafi (Morocco)
2004	Hicham El Guerrouj (Morocco)	Kenenisa Bekele (Ethiopia)	Eliud Kipchoge (Kenya)
2008	Kenenisa Bekele (Ethiopia)	Eliud Kipchoge (Kenya)	Edwin Cheruiyot Soi (Kenya)

Men's 10,000-Meter

Year	Gold	Silver	Bronze
1912	Hannes Kolehmainen (Finland)	Lewis Tewanima (United States)	Albin Stenroos (Finland)
1916: Olympics not held			
1920	Paavo Nurmi (Finland)	Joseph Guillemot (France)	James Wilson (Great Britain)
1924	Ville Ritola (Finland)	Edvin Wide (Sweden)	Eero Berg (Finland)
1928	Paavo Nurmi (Finland)	Ville Ritola (Finland)	Edvin Wide (Sweden)
1932	Janusz Kusociński (Poland)	Volmari Iso-Hollo (Finland)	Lauri Virtanen (Finland)
1936	Ilmari Salminen (Finland)	Arvo Askola (Finland)	Volmari Iso-Hollo (Finland)
1940–1944: Olympics not held			
1948	Emil Zátopek (Czechoslovakia)	Alain Mimoun (France)	Bertil Albertsson (Sweden)
1952	Emil Zátopek (Czechoslovakia)	Alain Mimoun (France)	Aleksandr Anufriyev (Soviet Union)
1956	Vladamir Kuts (Soviet Union)	József Kovács (Hungary)	Allan Lawrence (Australia)
1960	Pyotr Bolotnikov (Soviet Union)	Hans Grodotzki (West Germany)	David Power (Australia)
1964	Billy Mills (United States)	Mohammed Gammoudi (Tunisia)	Ron Clarke (Australia)
1968	Naftali Temu (Kenya)	Mamo Wolde (Ethiopia)	Mohammed Gammoudi (Tunisia)
1972	Lasse Virén (Finland)	Emiel Puttemans (Belgium)	Miruts Yifter (Ethiopia)

Year	Gold	Silver	Bronze
1976	Lasse Virén (Finland)	Carlos Lopes (Portugal)	Brendan Foster (Great Britain)
1980	Miruts Yifter (Ethiopia)	Kaarlo Maaninka (Finland)	Mohamed Kedir (Ethiopia)
1984	Alberto Cova (Italy)	Mike McLeod (Great Britain)	Mike Musyoki (Kenya)
1988	Brahim Boutayeb (Morocco)	Salvatore Antibo (Italy)	Kipkemboy Kimeli (Kenya)
1992	Khalid Skah (Morocco)	Richard Chelimo (Kenya)	Addis Abebe (Ethiopia)
1996	Halie Gebrselassie (Ethiopia)	Paul Tergat (Kenya)	Salah Hissou (Morocco)
2000	Haile Gebrselassie (Ethiopia)	Paul Tergat (Kenya)	Assefa Mezgebu (Ethiopia)
2004	Kenenisa Bekele (Ethiopia)	Sileshi Sihine (Ethiopia)	Zersenay Tadese (Eritrea)
2008	Kenenisa Bekele (Ethiopia)	Sileshi Sihine (Ethiopia)	Micah Kogo (Kenya)

Men's 110-Meter Hurdles

Year	Gold	Silver	Bronze
1896	Thomas Curtis (United States)	Grantley Goulding (Great Britain)	Not awarded
1900	Alvin Kraenzlein (United States)	John McLean (United States)	Frederick Moloney (United States)
1904	Frederick Schule (United States)	Thaddeus Shideler (United States)	Lesley Ashburner (United States)
1908	Forrest Smithson (United States)	John Garrels (United States)	Arthur Shaw (United States)
1912	Frederick Kelly (United States)	James Wendell (United States)	Martin Hawkins (United States)
1916: Olympics not held			
1920	Earl Thomson (Canada)	Harold Barron (United States)	Frederic Murray (United States)
1924	Daniel Kinsey (United States)	Sydnet Atkinson (South Africa)	Sten Pettersson (Sweden)
1928	Sydnet Atkinson (South Africa)	Steve Anderson (United States)	John Collier (United States)
1932	George Saling (United States)	Percy Beard (United States)	Donald Finlay (Great Britain)
1936	Forrest Towns (United States)	Donald Finlay (Great Britain)	Frederick Pollard (United States)
1940–1944: Olympics not held			
1948	William Porter (United States)	Clyde Scott (United States)	Craig Dixon (United States)
1952	Harrison Dillard (United States)	Jack Davis (United States)	Arthur Barnard (United States)
1956	Lee Calhoun (United States)	Jack Davis (United States)	Joel Shankle (United States)
1960	Lee Calhoun (United States)	William May (United States)	Hayes Jones (United States)
1964	Hayes Jones (United States)	Blaine Lindgren (United States)	Anotoly Mikhailov (Soviet Union)
1968	Willie Davenport (United States)	Ervin Hall (United States)	Eddy Ottoz (Italy)
1972	Rodney Milburn (United States)	Guy Drut (France)	Thomas Hill (United States)
1976	Guy Drut (France)	Alejandro Casañas (Cuba)	Willie Davenport (United States)
1980	Thomas Munkelt (East Germany)	Alejandro Casañas (Cuba)	Aleksandr Puchkov (Soviet Union)
1984	Roger Kingdom (United States)	Greg Foster (United States)	Arto Bryggare (Finland)
1988	Roger Kingdom (United States)	Colin Jackson (Great Britain)	Tonie Campbess (United States)
1992	Mark McKoy (Canada)	Tony Dees (United States)	Jack Pierce (United States)
1996	Allen Johnson (United States)	Mark Crear (United States)	Florian Schwarthoff (Germany)
2000	Anier Garcia (Cuba)	Terrence Trammell (United States)	Mark Crear (United States)
2004	Liu Xiang (China)	Terrence Trammell (United States)	Anier Garcia (Cuba)
2008	Dayron Robles (Cuba)	David Payne (United States)	David Oliver (United States)

Men's 400-Meter Hurdles

Year	Gold	Silver	Bronze
1900	John Tewksbury (United States)	Henri Tauzin (France)	George Orton (Canada)
1904	Harry Hillman (United States)	Frank Waller (United States)	George Poage (United States)
1908	Charles Bacon (United States)	Harry Hillman (United States)	Leonard Tremeer (Great Britain)
1912: Event not held			
1916: Olympics not held			
1920	Frank Loomis (United States)	John Norton (United States)	August Desch (United States)
1924	Morgan Taylor (United States)	Erik Vilen (Finland)	Ivan Riley (United States)

Year	Gold	Silver	Bronze
1928	David Burghley (Great Britain)	Frank Cuhel (United States)	Morgan Taylor (United States)
1932	Bob Tisdall (Ireland)	Glenn Hardin (United States)	Morgan Taylor (United States)
1936	Glenn Hardin (United States)	John Loaring (Canada)	Miguel White (Philippines)
1940–1944: Olympics not held			
1948	Roy Cochran (United States)	Duncan White (Ceylon)	Rune Larsson (Sweden)
1952	Charles Moore (United States)	Yuri Lituyev (Soviet Union)	John Holland (New Zealand)
1956	Glenn Davis (United States)	Eddie Southern (United States)	Joshua Culbreath (United States)
1960	Glenn Davis (United States)	Crifton Crushman (United States)	Richard Howard (United States)
1964	Rex Cawley (United States)	John Cooper (United States)	Salvatore Morale (Italy)
1968	David Hemery (Great Britain)	Gerhard Hennige (West Germany)	John Sherwood (Great Britain)
1972	John Akii-Bua (Uganda)	Ralph Mann (United States)	David Hemery (Great Britain)
1976	Edwin Moses (United States)	Michael Shine (United States)	Yevgeny Gavrilenko (Soviet Union)
1980	Volker Beck (East Germany)	Vasili Arkhipenko (Soviet Union)	Gary Oakes (Great Britain)
1984	Edwin Moses (United States)	Danny Harris (United States)	Harald Schmid (West Germany)
1988	Andre Phillips (United States)	Amadou Dia Ba (Senegal)	Edwin Moses (United States)
1992	Kevin Young (United States)	Winthrop Graham (Jamaica)	Kriss Akabusi (Great Britain)
1996	Derrick Adkins (United States)	Samuel Matete (Zambia)	Calvin Davis (United States)
2000	Angelo Taylor (United States)	Hadi Al Somayli (Saudi Arabia)	Llewellyn Herbert (South Africa)
2004	Félix Sánchez (Dominican Republic)	Danny McFarlane (Jamaica)	Naman Keïta (France)
2008	Angelo Taylor (United States)	Karron Clement (United States)	Bershawn Jackson (United States)

Men's 3,000-Meter Steeplechase

Year	Gold	Silver	Bronze
1920	Percy Hodge (Great Britain)	Patrick Flynn (United States)	Ernesto Ambrosini (Italy)
1924	Ville Ritola (Finland)	Elias Katz (Finland)	Paul Bontemps (France)
1928	Toivo Loukola (Finland)	Paavo Nurmi (Finland)	Ove Andersen (Finland)
1932	Volmari Iso-Hollo (Finland)	Thomas Evenson (Great Britain)	Joe McCluskey (United States)
1936	Volmari Iso-Hollo (Finland)	Kaarlo Tuominen (Finland)	Alfred Dompert (Germany)
1940–1944: Olympics not held			
1948	Tore Sjöstrand (Sweden)	Erik Elmsäter (Sweden)	Göte Hagström (Sweden)
1952	Horace Ashenfelter (United States)	Vladimir Kazantsev (Soviet Union)	John Disley (Great Britain)
1956	Chris Brasher (Great Britain)	Sándor Rozsnyói (Hungary)	Ernst Larsen (Norway)
1960	Zdzisław Krzyszkowiak (Poland)	Nikolai Sokolov (Soviet Union)	Semen Rzhischin (Soviet Union)
1964	Gaston Roelants (Belgium)	Justins Dog (Great Britain)	Ivan Belyayev (Soviet Union)
1968	Amos Biwott (Kenya)	Benjamin Kogo (Kenya)	George Young (United States)
1972	Kipchoge Keino (Kenya)	Ben Jipcho (Kenya)	Tapio Kantanen (Finland)
1976	Anders Gärderud (Sweden)	Bronisław Malinowski (Poland)	Frank Baumgartl (East Germany)
1980	Bronisław Malinowski (Poland)	Filbert Bayi (Tanzania)	Eshetu Tura (Ethiopia)
1984	Julius Korir (Kenya)	Joseph Mahmoud (France)	Brian Diemer (United States)
1988	Julius Kariuki (Kenya)	Peter Koech (Kenya)	Mark Rowland (Great Britain)
1992	Matthew Birir (Kenya)	Patrick Sang (Kenya)	William Mutwol (Kenya)
1996	Joseph Keter (Kenya)	Moses Kiptanui (Kenya)	Alessandro Lambruschini (Italy)
2000	Reuben Kosgei (Kenya)	Wilson Boit Kipketer (Kenya)	Ali Ezzine (Morocco)
2004	Ezekiel Kemboi (Kenya)	Brimin Kipruto (Kenya)	Paul Kipsiele Koech (Kenya)
2008	Brimin Kiprop Kipruto (Kenya)	Mahiedine Mekhissi-Benabbad (France)	Richard Kipkemboi Mateelong (Kenya)

Men's 4 × 100-Meter Relay

Year	Gold	Silver	Bronze
1912	David Jacobs, Henry Macintosh, Victor d'Arcy, William Applegarth (Great Britain)	Ivan Möller, Charles Luther, Ture Person, Knut Lindberg (Sweden)	Not awarded
1916: Olympics not held			
1920	Charlie Paddock, Jackson Scholz, Loren Murchison, Morris Kirksey (United States)	René Lorain, René Tirard, René Mourlon, Émile Ali-Khan (France)	Agne Holmström, William Petersson, Sven Malm, Nils Sandström (Sweden)
1924	Lorean Murchison, Louis Clarke, Frank Hussey, Alfred LeConey (United States)	Harold Abrahams, Walter Rangeley, William Nichol, Lancelot Royle (Great Britain)	Jan de Vries, Jacob Boot, Harry Broos, Marinus van den Berge (Netherlands)
1928	Frank Wykoff, James Quinn, Charles Borah, Henry Russell (United States)	Georg Lammers, Richard Corts, Hubert Houben, Helmut Körnig (Germany)	Cyril Gil, Teddy Smouha, Walter Rangeley, Jack London (Great Britain)
1932	Robert Kiesel, Emmett Toppino, Hector Dyer, Frank Wykoff (United States)	Helmut Körnig, Friedrich Hendrix, Erich Borchmeyer, Arthur Jonath (Germany)	Giuseppe Castelli, Ruggero Maregatti, Gabriele Salviati, Edgardo Toetti (Italy)
1936	Jesse Owens, Ralph Metcalfe, Foy Draper, Frank Wykoff (United States)	Orazio Mariani, Gianni Caldana, Elio Ragni, Tullio Gonnelli (Italy)	Wilhelm Leichum, Erich Borchmeyer, Erwin Gillmeister, Gerd Hornberger (Germany)
1940–1944: Olympics not held			
1948	Barney Ewell, Lorenzo Wright, Harrison Dillard, Mel Patton (United States)	John Archer, John Gregory, Alastair McCorquodale, Kenneth Jones (Great Britain)	Michele Tito, Enrico Perucconi, Antonio Siddi, Carlo Monti (Italy)
1952	Dean Smith, Harrison Dillard, Lindy Remigino, Andy Stanfield (United States)	Boris Tokaryev, Levan Kalyayev, Levan Sanadze, Vladimir Sukharyev (Soviet Union)	László Zarándi, Géza Varasdi, György Csányi, Béla Goldoványi (Hungary)
1956	Ira Murchison, Leamon King, Thane Baker, Bobby Joe Morrow (United States)	Leonid Bartenev, Boris Tokaryev, Yuri Konovalov, Vladimir Sukharyev (Soviet Union)	Lothar Knörzer, Leonhard Pohl, Heinz Fütterer, Manfred Germar (United Team of Germany)
1960	Bernd Cullmann, Armin Hary, Walter Mahlendorf, Martin Lauer (United Team of Germany)	Gusman Kosanov, Leonid Bartenev, Yuri Konovalov, Edvin Ozoliņš (Soviet Union)	Peter Radford, David Jones, David Segal, Neville Whitehead (Great Britain)
1964	Paul Drayton, Gerry Ashworth, Richard Stebbins, Bob Hayes (United States)	Andrzej Zieliński, Wiesław Maniak, Marian Foik, Marian Dudziak (Poland)	Paul Genevay, Bernard Laidebeur, Claude Piquemal, Jocelyn Delecour (France)
1968	Charles Greene, Mel Pender, Ronnie Ray Smith, Jim Hines (United States)	Hermes Ramírez, Juan Morales, Pablo Montes, Enrique Figuerola (Cuba)	Gérard Fenouil, Jocelyn Delecour, Claude Piquemal, Roger Bambuck (France)
1972	Larry Black, Robert Taylor, Gerald Tinker, Eddie Hart (United States)	Aleksandr Kornelyuk, Vladimir Lovetsky, Juris Silovs, Valeri Borzov (Soviet Union)	Jobst Hirscht, Karlheinz Klotz, Gerhard Wucherer, Klaus Ehl (West Germany)
1976	Harvey Glance, Johnny Jones, Millard Hampton, Steve Riddick (United States)	Manfred Kokot, Jörg Pfeifer, Klaus-Dieter Kurrat, Alexander Thieme (East Germany)	Aleksandr Aksinin, Nikolay Kolesnikov, Juris Silovs, Valeri Borzov (Soviet Union)
1980	Vladimir Muravyov, Nikolay Sidorov, Aleksandr Aksinin, Andrey Prokofyev (Soviet Union)	Krzysztof Zwoliński, Zenon Licznerski, Leszek Dunecki, Marian Woronin (Poland)	Antoine Richard, Pascal Barré, Patrick Barré, Hermann Panzo (France)
1984	Sam Graddy, Ron Brown, Calvin Smith, Carl Lewis (United States)	Albert Lawrence, Greg Meghoo, Don Quarrie, Ray Stewart (Jamaica)	Ben Johnson, Tony Sharpe, Desai Williams, Sterling Hinds (Canada)
1988	Viktor Bryzhin, Vladimir Krylov, Vladimir Muravyov, Vitaliy Savin (Soviet Union)	Elliot Bunney, John Regis, Mike McFarlane, Linford Christie (Great Britain)	Bruno Marie-Rose, Daniel Sangouma, Gilles Quenehervé, Max Morinière (France)

Year	Gold	Silver	Bronze
1992	Michael Marsh, Leroy Burrell, Dennis Mitchell, Carl Lewis, James Jett (United States)	Oluyemi Kayode, Chidi Imoh, Olapade Adeniken, Davidson Ezinwa, Osmond Ezinwa (Nigeria)	Andrés Simón, Joel Lamela, Joel Isasi, Jorge Aguilera (Cuba)
1996	Robert Esmie, Glenroy Gilbert, Bruny Surin, Donovan Bailey, Carlton Chambers (Canada)	Jon Drummond, Tim Harden, Michael Marsh, Dennis Mitchell, Tim Montgomery (United States)	Arnaldo da Silva, Robson da Silva, Edson Ribeiro, André da Silva (Brazil)
2000	Jon Drummond, Bernard Williams, Brian Lewis, Maurice Greene, Tim Montgomery, Kenneth Brokenburr (United States)	Vicente de Lima, Edson Ribeiro, André da Silva, Claudinei da Silva, Cláudio Souza (Brazil)	José Ángel César, Luis Alberto Pérez-Rionda, Ivan García, Freddy Mayola (Cuba)
2004	Jason Gardener, Darren Campbell, Marlon Devonish, Mark Lewis-Francis (Great Britain)	Shawn Crawford, Justin Gatlin, Coby Miller, Maurice Greene, Darvis Patton (United States)	Olusoji Fasuba, Uchenna Emedolu, Aaron Egbele, Deji Aliu (Nigeria)
2008	Usain Bolt, Asafa Powell, Nesta Carter, Michael Frater, Dwight Thomas (Jamaica)	Emmanuel Callender, Richard Thompson, Aaron Armstrong, Marc Burns, Keston Bledman (Trinidad and Tobago)	Naoki Tsukahara, Shingo Suetsugu, Shinji Takahira, Nobuharu Asahara (Japan)

Men's 4 × 400-Meter Relay

Year	Gold	Silver	Bronze
1912	Mel Sheppard, Edward Lindberg, Ted Meredith, Charles Reidpath (United States)	Charles Lelong, Robert Schurrer, Pierre Failliot, Charles Poulenard (France)	George Nicol, Ernest Henley, James Soutter, Cyril Seedhouse (Great Britain)
1916: Olympics not held			
1920	Cecil Griffiths, Robert Lindsay, John Ainsworth-Davies, Guy Butler (Great Britain)	Harry Davel, Clarence Oldfield, Jack Oosterlaak, Bevil Rudd (South Africa)	Georges André, Gaston Féry, Maurice Delvart, Jean Delvaux (France)
1924	Commodore Cochran, Alan Helffrich, Oliver MacDonald, William Stevenson (United States)	Artur Svensson, Erik Byléhn, Gustaf Weijnarth, Nils Engdahl (Sweden)	Edward Toms, George Renwick, Richard Ripley, Guy Butler (Great Britain)
1928	George Baird, Emerson Spencer, Frederick Alderman, Ray Barbuti (United States)	Otto Neumann, Harry Storz, Richard Krebs, Hermann Engelhard (Germany)	Alex Wilson, Phil Edwards, Stanley Glover, James Ball (Canada)
1932	Ivan Fuqua, Edgar Ablowich, Karl Warner, Bill Carr (United States)	Crew Stoneley, Thomas Hampson, David Burghley, Godfrey Rampling (Great Britain)	Ray Lewis, James Ball, Phil Edwards, Alex Wilson (Canada)
1936	Freddie Wolff, Godfrey Rampling, Bill Roberts, Godfrey Brown (Great Britain)	Harold Cagle, Robert Young, Edward O'Brien, Alfred Fitch (United States)	Helmut Hamann, Friedrich von Stülpnagel, Harry Voigt, Rudolf Harbig (Germany)
1940–1944: Olympics not held			
1948	Arthur Harnden, Clifford Bourland, Roy Cochran, Mal Whitfield (United States)	Jean Kerebel, François Schewetta, Robert Chef d'Hotel, Jacques Lunis (France)	Kurt Lundquist, Lars Wolfbrandt, Folke Alnevik, Rune Larsson (Sweden)
1952	Arthur Wint, Leslie Laing, Herb McKenley, George Rhoden (Jamaica)	Ollie Matson, Gerald Cole, Charles Moore, Mal Whitfield (United States)	Hans Geister, Günther Steines, Heinz Ulzheimer, Karl-Friedrich Haas (Germany)
1956	Charles Jenkins, Lou Jones, Jesse Mashburn, Tom Courtney (United States)	Graham Gipson, Leon Gregory, David Lean, Kevan Gosper (Australia)	Peter Higgins, Michael Wheeler, John Salisbury, Derek Johnson (Great Britain)
1960	Jack Yerman, Earl Young, Glenn Davis, Otis Davis (United States)	Joachim Reske, Manfred Kinder, Johannes Kaiser, Carl Kaufmann (Germany)	Malcolm Spence, James Wedderburn, Keith Gardner, George Kerr (British West Indies)

Year	Gold	Silver	Bronze
1964	Ollan Cassell, Michael Larrabee, Ulis Williams, Henry Carr (United States)	Timothy Graham, Adrian Metcalfe, John Cooper, Robbie Brightwell (Great Britain)	Edwin Skinner, Kenneth Bernard, Edwin Roberts, Wendell Mottley (Trinidad and Tobago)
1968	Vincent Matthews, Ron Freeman, Larry James, Lee Evans (United States)	Daniel Rudisha, Munyoro Nyamau, Naftali Bon, Charles Asati (Kenya)	Helmar Müller, Manfred Kinder, Gerhard Hennige, Martin Jellinghaus (West Germany)
1972	Charles Asati, Munyoro Nyamau, Robert Ouko, Julius Sang (Kenya)	Martin Reynolds, Alan Pascoe, David Hemery, David Jenkins (Great Britain)	Gilles Bertould, Daniel Velasques, Francis Kerbiriou, Jacques Carette (France)
1976	Herman Frazier, Benny Brown, Fred Newhouse, Maxie Parks (United States)	Ryszard Podlas, Jan Werner, Zbigniew Jaremski, Jerzy Pietrzyk (Poland)	Franz-Peter Hofmeister, Lothar Krieg, Harald Schmid, Bernd Herrmann (West Germany)
1980	Remigijus Valiulis, Mikhail Linge, Nikolay Chernetsky, Viktor Markin (Soviet Union)	Klaus Thiele, Andreas Knebel, Frank Schaffer, Volker Beck (East Germany)	Stefano Malinverni, Mauro Zuliani, Roberto Tozzi, Pietro Mennea (Italy)
1984	Sunder Nix, Ray Armstead, Alonzo Babers, Antonio McKay (United States)	Kriss Akabusi, Garry Cook, Todd Bennett, Philip Brown (Great Britain)	Sunday Uti, Moses Ugbusien, Rotimi Peters, Innocent Egbunike (Nigeria)
1988	Danny Everett, Steve Lewis, Kevin Robinzine, Butch Reynolds (United States)	Howard Davis, Devon Morris, Winthrop Graham, Bertland Cameron (Jamaica)	Norbert Dobeleit, Edgar Itt, Jörg Vaihinger, Ralf Lübke (West Germany)
1992	Andrew Valmon, Quincy Watts, Michael Johnson, Steve Lewis, Darnell Hall, Charles Jenkins (United States)	Lázaro Martínez, Héctor Herrera, Norberto Téllez, Roberto Hernández (Cuba)	Roger Black, David Grindley, Kriss Akabusi, John Regis, Du'aine Ladejo, Mark Richardson (Great Britain)
1996	LaMont Smith, Alvin Harrison, Derek Mills, Anthuan Maybank, Jason Rouser (United States)	Iwan Thomas, Jamie Baulch, Mark Richardson, Roger Black, Du'aine Ladejo, Mark Hylton (Great Britain)	Michael McDonald, Roxbert Martin, Greg Haughton, Davian Clarke, Dennis Blake, Garth Robinson (Jamaica)
2000	Alvin Harrison, Antonio Pettigrew, Calvin Harrison, Michael Johnson (United States)*	Clement Chukwu, Jude Monye, Sunday Bada, Enefiok Udo-Obong, Nduka Awazie, Fidelis Gadzama (Nigeria)	Michael Blackwood, Greg Haughton, Christopher Williams, Danny McFarlane, Sanjay Ayre, Michael McDonald (Jamaica)
2004	Otis Harris, Derrick Brew, Jeremy Wariner, Darold Williamson, Kelly Willie, Andrew Rock (United States)	John Steffensen, Mark Ormrod, Patrick Dwyer, Clinton Hill (Australia)	James Godday, Musa Audu, Saul Weigopwa, Enefiok Udo Obong (Nigeria)
2008	LaShawn Merritt, Angelo Taylor, David Neville, Jeremy Wariner, Kerron Clement, Reggie Witherspoon (United States)	Andretti Bain, Michael Mathieu, Andrae Williams, Chris Brown, Avard Moncur, Ramon Miller (Bahamas)	Maksim Dyldin, Vladislav Frolov, Anton Kokorin, Denis Alekseyev (Russia)

* The U.S. team was disqualified in 2004 due to Jerome Young's use of performance-enhancing drugs.

Men's Marathon

Year	Gold	Silver	Bronze
1896	Spiridon Louis (Greece)	Kharilaos Vasilakos (Greece)	Gyula Kellner (Hungary)
1900	Michel Théato (France)	Émile Champion (France)	Ernst Fast (Sweden)
1904	Thomas J. Hicks (United States)	Albert Coray (United States)	Arthur Newton (United States)
1908	Johnny Hayes (United States)	Charles Heffron (South Afirca)	Joseph Forshaw (United States)
1912	Kenneth McArthur (South Africa)	Christian Gitsham (South Africa)	Gaston Strobino (United States)
1916: Olympics not held			
1920	Hannes Kolehmainen (Finland)	Jüri Lossmann (Estonia)	Valerio Arri (Italy)
1924	Albin Stenroos (Finland)	Romeo Bertini (Italy)	Clarence DeMar (United States)
1928	Boughera El Ouafi (France)	Manuel Plaza (Chile)	Martti Marttelin (Finland)
1932	Juan Carlos Zabala (Argentina)	Samuel Ferris (Great Britain)	Armas Toivonen (Finland)
1936	Son Kitei (Japan)	Ernest Harper (Great Britain)	Nan Shoryu (Japan)

Year	Gold	Silver	Bronze
1940–1944: Olympics not held			
1948	Delfo Cabrera (Argentina)	Thomas Richards (Great Britain)	Etienne Gailly (Belgium)
1952	Emil Zátopek (Czechoslovakia)	Reinaldo Gorno (Argentina)	Gustaf Jansson (Sweden)
1956	Alain Mimoun (France)	Franjo Mihalić (Yugoslavia)	Veikko Karvonen (Finland)
1960	Abebe Bikila (Ethiopia)	Rhadi Ben Abdesselam (Morocco)	Barry Magee (New Zealand)
1964	Abebe Bikila (Ethiopia)	Basil Heatley (Great Britain)	Kokichi Tsuburaya (Japan)
1968	Mamo Wolde (Ethiopia)	Kenji Kimihara (Japan)	Mike Ryan (New Zealand)
1972	Frank Shorter (United States)	Karel Lismont (Belgium)	Mamo Wolde (Ethiopia)
1976	Waldemar Cierpinski (East Germany)	Frank Shorter (United States)	Karel Lismont (Belgium)
1980	Waldemar Cierpinski (East Germany)	Gerard Nijboer (Netherlands)	Setymkul Dzhumanazarov (Soviet Union)
1984	Carlos Lopes (Portugal)	John Treacy (Ireland)	Charlie Spedding (Great Britain)
1988	Gelindo Bordin (Italy)	Douglas Wakiihuri (Kenya)	Hussein Ahmed Salah (Djibouti)
1992	Hwang Young-Cho (South Korea)	Koichi Morishita (Japan)	Stephan Freigang (Germany)
1996	Josia Thugwane (South Africa)	Lee Bong-Ju (South Korea)	Erick Wainaina (Kenya)
2000	Gezahgne Abera (Ethiopia)	Erick Wainaina (Kenya)	Tesfaye Tola (Ethiopia)
2004	Stefano Baldini (Italy)	Mebrahtom Keflezighi (United States)	Vanderlei de Lima (Brazil)
2008	Samuel Wanjiru (Kenya)	Jaouad Gharib (Morocco)	Tsegay Kebede (Ethiopia)

Men's 20-Kilometer Walk

Year	Gold	Silver	Bronze
1956	Leonid Spirin (Soviet Union)	Antanas Mikenas (Soviet Union)	Bruno Junk (Soviet Union)
1960	Vladimir Golubnichy (Soviet Union)	Noel Freeman (Australia)	Stanley Vickers (Great Britain)
1964	Kenneth Matthews (Great Britain)	Dieter Lindner (Germany)	Volodymyr Holubnychy (Soviet Union)
1968	Volodymyr Holubnychy (Soviet Union)	José Pedraza (Mexico)	Nikolay Smaga (Soviet Union)
1972	Peter Frenkel (East Germany)	Volodymyr Holubnychy (Soviet Union)	Hans Reimann (East Germany)
1976	Daniel Bautista (Mexico)	Hans-Georg Reimann (East Germany)	Peter Frenkel (East Germany)
1980	Maurizio Damilano (Italy)	Piotr Pochinchuk (Soviet Union)	Roland Wieser (East Germany)
1984	Ernesto Canto (Mexico)	Raúl González (Mexico)	Maurizio Damilano (Italy)
1988	Jozef Pribilinec (Czechoslovakia)	Ronald Weigel (East Germany)	Maurizio Damilano (Italy)
1992	Daniel Plaza (Spain)	Guillaume LeBlanc (Canada)	Giovanni De Benedictis (Italy)
1996	Jefferson Pérez (Ecuador)	Ilya Markov (Russia)	Bernardo Segura (Mexico)
2000	Robert Korzeniowski (Poland)	Noé Hernández (Mexico)	Vladimir Andreyev (Russia)
2004	Ivano Brugnetti (Italy)	Francisco Javier Fernández (Spain)	Nathan Deaks (Australia)
2008	Valeriy Borchin (Russia)	Jefferson Pérez (Ecuador)	Jared Tallent (Australia)

Men's 50-Kilometer Walk

Year	Gold	Silver	Bronze
1932	Thomas Green (Great Britain)	Jānis Daliņš (Latvia)	Ugo Frigerio (Italy)
1936	Harold Whitlock (Great Britain)	Arthur Schwab (Switzerland)	Adalberts Bubenko (Latvia)
1940–1944: Olympics not held			
1948	John Ljunggren (Sweden)	Gaston Godel (Switzerland)	Tebbs Lloyd-Johnson (Great Britain)
1952	Giuseppe Dordoni (Italy)	Josef Dolezal (Czechoslovakia)	Antal Róka (Hungary)

Year	Gold	Silver	Bronze
1956	Norman Read (New Zealand)	Yevgeni Mashinskov (Soviet Union)	John Ljunggren (Sweden)
1960	Don Thompson (Great Britain)	John Ljunggren (Sweden)	Abdon Pamich (Italy)
1964	Abdon Pamich (Italy)	Paul Nihill (Great Britain)	Ingvar Pettersson (Sweden)
1968	Christoph Höhne (Germany)	Antal Kill (Hungary)	Larry Young (United States)
1972	Bernd Kannenberg (West Germany)	Veniamin Soldatenko (Soviet Union)	Larry Young (United States)
1976: Event not held			
1980	Hartwig Gauder (East Germany)	Jorge Llopart (Spain)	Evgeni Ivchenko (Soviet Union)
1984	Raúl González (Mexico)	Bo Gustafsson (Sweden)	Sandro Bellucci (Italy)
1988	Vyacheslav Ivanenko (Soviet Union)	Ronald Weigel (East Germany)	Hartwig Gauder (East Germany)
1992	Andrey Perlov (Unified Team)	Carlos Mercenario (Mexico)	Ronald Weigel (Germany)
1996	Robert Korzeniowski (Poland)	Mikhail Shchennikov (Russia)	Valentí Massana (Spain)
2000	Robert Korzeniowski (Poland)	Aigars Fadejevs (Latvia)	Joel Sánchez Guerrero (Mexico)
2004	Robert Korzeniowski (Poland)	Denis Nizhegorodov (Russia)	Aleksey Voyevodin (Russia)
2008	Alex Schwazer (Italy)	Jared Tallent (Australia)	Denis Nizhegorodov (Netherlands)

Men's Long Jump

Year	Gold	Silver	Bronze
1896	Ellery Clark (United States)	Robert Garrett (United States)	James Connolly (United States)
1900	Alvin Kraenzlein (United States)	Myer Prinstein (United States)	Patrick Leahy (Great Britain)
1904	Meyer Prinstein (United States)	Daniel Frank (United States)	Robert Strangland (United States)
1908	Frank Irons (United States)	Daniel Kelly (United States)	Calvin Bricker (Canada)
1912	Albert Gutterson (United States)	Calvin Bricker (Canada)	Georg Åberg (Sweden)
1916: Olympics not held			
1920	William Petersson (Sweden)	Carl Johnson (United States)	Erik Abrahamsson (Sweden)
1924	William DeHart Hubbard (United States)	Edward Gourdin (United States)	Sverre Hansen (Norway)
1928	Edward Hamm (United States)	Silvio Cator (Haiti)	Alfred Bates (United States)
1932	Ed Gordon (United States)	Lambert Redd (United States)	Chuhei Nambu (Japan)
1936	Jesse Owens (United States)	Luz Long (Germany)	Naoto Tajima (Japan)
1940–1944: Olympics not held			
1948	Willie Stelle (United States)	Theo Bruce (Australia)	Herbert Douglas (United States)
1952	Jerome Biffle (United States)	Meredith Gourdine (United States)	Ödön Földessy (Hungary)
1956	Greg Bell (United States)	John Bennett (United States)	Jorma Valkama (Finland)
1960	Ralph Boston (United States)	Irvin Roberson (United States)	Igor Ter-Ovanesyan (Soviet Union)
1964	Lynn Davies (Great Britain)	Ralph Boston (United States)	Igor Ter-Ovanesyan (Soviet Union)
1968	Bob Beamon (United States)	Klaus Beer (East Germany)	Ralph Boston (United States)
1972	Randy Williams (United States)	Hans Baumgartner (West Germany)	Arnie Robinson (United States)
1976	Arnie Robinson (United States)	Randy Williams (United States)	Frank Wartenberg (East Germany)
1980	Lutz Dombrowski (East Germany)	Frank Paschek (East Germany)	Valeriy Podluzhniy (Soviet Union)
1984	Carl Lewis (United States)	Gary Honey (Australia)	Giovanni Evangelisti (Italy)
1988	Carl Lewis (United States)	Mike Powell (United States)	Larry Myricks (United States)
1992	Carl Lewis (United States)	Mike Powell (United States)	Joe Greene (United States)
1996	Carl Lewis (United States)	James Beckford (Jamaica)	Joe Greene (United States)
2000	Iván Pedroso (Cuba)	Jai Taurima (Australia)	Roman Shchurenko (Ukraine)
2004	Dwight Phillips (United States)	John Moffitt (United States)	Joan Lino Martínez (Spain)
2008	Irving Saladino (Panama)	Khotso Mokoena (South Africa)	Ibrahim Camejo (Cuba)

Men's Triple Jump

Year	Gold	Silver	Bronze
1896	James Connolly (United States)	Alexandre Tufféri (France)	Ioannis Persakis (Greece)
1900	Meyer Prinstein (United States)	James Connolly (United States)	Lewis Sheldon (United States)
1904	Meyer Prinstein (United States)	Frederick Englehardt (United States)	Robert Stangland (United States)
1908	Timothy Ahearne (Great Britain)	John Garfield MacDonald (Canada)	Edvard Larsen (Norway)
1912	Gustaf Lindblom (Sweden)	Georg Åberg (Sweden)	Erik Almlöf (Sweden)
1916: Olympics not held			
1920	Vilho Tuulos (Finland)	Folke Jansson (Sweden)	Erik Almlöf (Sweden)
1924	Nick Winter (Australia)	Luis Brunetto (Argentina)	Vilho Tuulos (Finland)
1928	Mikio Oda (Japan)	Levi Casey (United States)	Vilho Tuulos (Finland)
1932	Chuhei Nambu (Japan)	Erik Svensson (Sweden)	Kenkichi Oshima (Japan)
1936	Naoto Tajima (Japan)	Masao Harada (Japan)	Jack Metcalfe (Australia)
1940–1944: Olympics not held			
1948	Arne Åhman (Sweden)	George Avery (Australia)	Ruhi Sarialp (Turkey)
1952	Adhemar da Silva (Brazil)	Leonid Shcherbakov (Soviet Union)	Arnoldo Devonish (Venezuela)
1956	Adhemar da Silva (Brazil)	Vilhjálmur Einarsson (Iceland)	Vitold Kreer (Soviet Union)
1960	Józef Szmidt (Poland)	Cladimir Goryaev (Soviet Union)	Vitold Kreer (Soviet Union)
1964	Józef Szmidt (Poland)	Oleg Fedoseev (Soviet Union)	Victor Kravchenko (Soviet Union)
1968	Viktor Saneyev (Soviet Union)	Nelson Prudêncio (Brazil)	Giuseppe Gentile (Italy)
1972	Viktor Saneyev (Soviet Union)	Jörg Drehmel (East Germany)	Nelson Prudêncio (Brazil)
1976	Viktor Saneyev (Soviet Union)	James Butts (United States)	João Carlos de Oliveira (Brazil)
1980	Jaak Uudmäe (Soviet Union)	Viktor Saneev (Soviet Union)	João Carlos de Oliveira (Brazil)
1984	Al Joyner (United States)	Mike Conley (United States)	Keith Connor (Great Britain)
1988	Hristo Markov (Bulgaria)	Igor Lapshin (Soviet Union)	Aleksandr Kovalenko (Soviet Union)
1992	Mike Conley (United States)	Charles Simpkins (United States)	Frank Rutherford (Bahamas)
1996	Kenny Harrison (United States)	Jonathan Edwards (Great Britain)	Yoelbi Quesada (Cuba)
2000	Jonathan Edwards (Great Britain)	Yoel García (Cuba)	Denis Kapustin (Russia)
2004	Christian Olsson (Sweden)	Marian Oprea (Romania)	Danil Burkenya (Russia)
2008	Nelson Évora (Portugal)	Phillips Idowu (Great Britain)	Leevan Sands (Bahamas)

Men's High Jump

Year	Gold	Silver	Bronze
1896	Ellery Claek (United States)	James Connolly (United States) Robert Garrett (United States)	Not awarded
1900	Irving Baxter (United States)	Patrick Leahy (Great Britain)	Lajos Gönczy (Hungary)
1904	Samuel Jones (United States)	Garrett Serviss (United States)	Paul Weinstein (Germany)
1908	Harry Porter (United States)	Georges André (France) Cornelius Leahy (Great Britain) István Somodi (Hungary)	Not awarded
1912	Alma Richards (United States)	Hans Liesche (Germany)	George Horine (United States)
1916: Olympics not held			
1920	Richmond Landon (United States)	Harold Muller (United States)	Bo Ekulund (Sweden)
1924	Harold Osborn (United States)	Leroy Brown (United States)	Pierre Lewden (France)
1928	Robert Wade King (United States)	Benjamin Hedges (United States)	Claude Ménard (France)
1932	Duncan McNaughton (Canada)	Robert van Osdel (United States)	Simeon Toribio (Philippines)
1936	Cornelius Johnson (United States)	David Albritton (United States)	Delos Thurber (United States)
1940–1944: Olympics not held			
1948	John Winter (Australia)	Bjorn Paulson (Norway)	George Stanich (United States)

Year	Gold	Silver	Bronze
1952	Walter Davis (United States)	Kenneth Wiesner (United States)	José da Conceição (Brazil)
1956	Charles Dumas (United States)	Charles Porter (United States)	Igor Kashkarov (Soviet Union)
1960	Robert Shavlakadze (Soviet Union)	Valeriy Brumel (Soviet Union)	John Thomas (United States)
1964	Valeriy Brumel (Soviet Union)	John Thomas (United States)	John Rambo (United States)
1968	Dick Fosberry (United States)	Ed Caruthers (United States)	Valentin Gavrilov (Soviet Union)
1972	Jüri Tarmak (Soviet Union)	Stefan Junge (East Germany)	Dwight Stones (United States)
1976	Jacek Wszoła (Poland)	Greg Joy (Canada)	Dwight Stones (United States)
1980	Gerd Wessig (East Germany)	Jacek Wszoła (Poland)	Jörg Freimuth (East Germany)
1984	Dietmar Mögenburg (West Germany)	Patrik Sjöberg (Sweden)	Jianhua Zhu (China)
1988	Gennadiy Avdeyenko (Soviet Union)	Hollis Conway (United States)	Rudolf Povarnitsyn (Soviet Union) Patrik Sjöberg (Sweden)
1992	Javier Sotomayor (Cuba)	Patrik Sjöberg (Sweden)	Hollis Conway (United States) Tim Forsyth (Australia) Artur Partyka (Poland)
1996	Charles Austin (United States)	Artur Partyka (Poland)	Steve Smith (Great Britain)
2000	Sergey Klyugin (Russia)	Javier Sotomayor (Cuba)	Abderrahmane Hammad (Algeria)
2004	Stefan Holm (Sweden)	Matt Hemingway (United States)	Jaroslav Bába (Czech Republic)
2008	Andrey Silnov (Russia)	Germaine Mason (Great Britain)	Yaraslav Rybakov (Russia)

Men's Pole Vault

Year	Gold	Silver	Bronze
1896	Welles Hoyt (United States)	Albert Tyler (United States)	Evangelos Damaskos (Greece) Ioannis Theodoeopoulos (Greece)
1900	Irving Baxter (United States)	Meredith Colket (United States)	Carl-Albert Andersen (Norway)
1904	Charles Dvorak (United States)	LeRoy Samse (United States)	Louis Wilkins (United States)
1908	Edward Cook (United States) Alfred Gilbert (United States)	Not awarded	Edward Archibald (Canada) Charles Jacobs (United States) Bruno Söderström (Sweden)
1912	Harry Babcock (United States)	Frank Nelson (United States) Marc Wright (United States)	William Halpenny (Canada) Frank Murphy (United States) Bertil Uggla (Sweden)
1916: Olympics not held			
1920	Frank Foss (United States)	Henry Petersen (Denmark)	Edwin Myers (United States)
1924	Lee Barnes (United States)	Glen Graham (United States)	James Brooker (United States)
1928	Sabin Carr (United States)	William Droegemuller (United States)	Charles McGinnis (United States)
1932	William Miller (United States)	Shuhei Nishida (Japan)	George Jefferson (United States)
1936	Earle Meadows (United States)	Shuhei Nishida (Japan)	Sueo Ōe (Japan)
1940–1944: Olympics not held			
1948	Guinn Smith (United States)	Erkki Kataja (Finland)	Robert Richards (United States)
1952	Bob Richards (United States)	Donald Laz (United States)	Ragnar Lundberg (Sweden)
1956	Bob Richards (United States)	Bob Gutowski (United States)	Georgios Roubanis (Greece)
1960	Don Bragg (United States)	Ron Morris (United States)	Eeles Landström (Finland)
1964	Fred Hansen (United States)	Wolfgang Reinhardt (Germany)	Klaum Lehnertz (Germany)
1968	Bob Seagren (United States)	Claus Schiprowski (Germany)	Wolfgang Nordwig (East Germany)
1972	Wolfgang Nordwig (East Germany)	Robert Seagren (United States)	Jan Johnson (United States)
1976	Tadeusz Ślusarski (Poland)	Anrri Kalliomäki (Finland)	David Roberts (United States)
1980	Władysław Kozakiewicz (Poland)	Konstantin Volkov (Soviet Union) Tadeusz Ślusarski (Poland)	Not awarded

Year	Gold	Silver	Bronze
1984	Pierre Quinon (France)	Mike Tully (United States)	Earl Bell (United States) Thierry Vigneron (France)
1988	Sergey Bubka (Soviet Union)	Rodion Gataullin (Soviet Union)	Grigoriy Yegorov (Soviet Union)
1992	Maksim Tarasov (Unified Team)	Igor Trandenkov (Unified Team)	Javier García (Spain)
1996	Jean Galfione (France)	Igor Trandenkov (Russia)	Andrei Tivontchik (Germany)
2000	Nick Hysong (United States)	Lawrence Johnson (United States)	Maksim Tarasov (Russia)
2004	Timothy Mack (United States)	Toby Stevenson (United States)	Giuseppe Gibilisco (Italy)
2008	Steven Hooker (Australia)	Evgeny Lukyanenko (Russia)	Denys Yurchenko (Ukraine)

Men's Shot Put

Year	Gold	Silver	Bronze
1896	Robert Garrett (United States)	Miltiades Gouskos (Greece)	Georgios Papasideris (Greece)
1900	Richard Sheldon (United States)	Josiah McCracken (United States)	Robert Garrett (United States)
1904	Ralph Rose (United States)	Wesley Coe (United States)	Lawrence Feuerbach (United States)
1908	Ralph Rose (United States)	Denis Horgan (Great Britain)	John Garrels (United States)
1912	Patrick McDonald (United States)	Ralph Rose (United States)	Lawrence Whitney (United States)
1916: Olympics not held			
1920	Ville Pörhölä (Finland)	Elmer Niklander (Finland)	Harry Liversedge (United States)
1924	Clarence Houser (United States)	Glenn Hartranft (United States)	Ralph Hills (United States)
1928	John Kuck (United States)	Herman Brix (United States)	Emil Hirschfeld (Germany)
1932	Leo Sexton (United States)	Harlow Rothert (United States)	František Douda (Czechoslovakia)
1936	Hans Woellke (Germany)	Sulo Bärlund (Finland)	Gerhard Stöck (Germany)
1940–1944: Olympics not held			
1948	Wilbur Thompson (United States)	Jim Delaney (United States)	Jim Fuchs (United States)
1952	William Parry O'Brian (United States)	Darrow Hooper (United States)	Jim Fuchs (United States)
1956	William Parry O'Brian (United States)	Bill Nieder (United States)	Jiří Skobla (Czechoslovakia)
1960	Bill Nieder (United States)	William Parry O'Brian (United States)	Dallas Long (United States)
1964	Dallas Long (United States)	Randy Matson (United States)	Vilmos Varju (Hungary)
1968	Randy Matson (United States)	George Woods (United States)	Eduard Gushchin (Soviet Union)
1972	Władysław Komar (Poland)	George Woods (United States)	Hartmut Briesenick (East Germany)
1976	Udo Beyer (East Germany)	Yevgeny Mironov (Soviet Union)	Aleksandr Baryshnikov (Soviet Union)
1980	Vladimir Kiselyov (Soviet Union)	Aleksandr Baryshnikov (Soviet Union)	Udo Beyer (East Germany)
1984	Alessandro Andrei (Italy)	Michael Carter (United States)	Dave Laut (United States)
1988	Ulf Timmermann (East Germany)	Randy Barnes (United States)	Werner Günthör (Switzerland)
1992	Mike Stulce (United States)	Jim Doehring (United States)	Vyacheslav Lykho (Unified Team)
1996	Randy Barnes (United States)	John Godina (United States)	Oleksandr Bagach (Ukraine)
2000	Arsi Harju (Finland)	Adam Nelson (United States)	John Godina (United States)
2004	Yuriy Bilonoh (Ukraine)	Adam Nelson (United States)	Joachim Olsen (Denmark)
2008	Tomasz Majewski (Poland)	Christian Cantwell (United States)	Andrei Mikhnevich (Belarus)

Men's Discus

Year	Gold	Silver	Bronze
1896	Robert Garrett (United States)	Panagiotis Paraskevopoulos (Greece)	Soritios Versis (Greece)
1900	Rudolf Bauer (Hungary)	František Janda-Suk (Bohemia)	Richard Sheldon (United States)

Year	Gold	Silver	Bronze
1904	Martin Sheridan (United States)	Ralph Rose (United States)	Nicolaos Georgandas (Greece)
1908	Martin Sheridan (United States)	Merritt Giffin (United States)	Marquis Horr (United States)
1912	Armas Taipale (Finland)	Richard Byrd (United States)	James Duncan (United States)
1916: Olympics not held			
1920	Elmer Niklander (Finland)	Armas Taipale (Finland)	Gus Pope (United States)
1924	Clarence Houser (United States)	Vilho Niittymaa (Finland)	Thomas Lieb (United States)
1928	Clarence Houser (United States)	Antero Kivi (Finland)	James Corson (United States)
1932	John Anderson (United States)	Henri LaBorde (United States)	Paul Winter (France)
1936	Ken Carpenter (United States)	Gordon Dunn (United States)	Giorgio Oberweger (Italy)
1940–1944: Olympics not held			
1948	Adolfo Consolini (Italy)	Giuseppe Tosi (Italy)	Fortune Gordien (United States)
1952	Sim Iness (United States)	Adolfo Consolini (Italy)	James Dillion (United States)
1956	Al Oerter (United States)	Fortune Gordien (United States)	Desmond Koch (United States)
1960	Al Oerter (United States)	Rink Babka (United States)	Dich Cochran (United States)
1964	Al Oerter (United States)	Ludvik Danek (Czechoslovakia)	Dave Weill (United States)
1968	Al Oerter (United States)	Lothar Milde (East Germany)	Ludvík Daněk (Czechoslovakia)
1972	Ludvík Daněk (Czechoslovakia)	Jay Silvester (United States)	Ricky Bruch (Sweden)
1976	Mac Wilkins (United States)	Wolfgang Schmidt (East Germany)	John Powell (United States)
1980	Viktor Rashchupkin (Soviet Union)	Imrich Bugár (Czechoslovakia)	Luis Delís (Cuba)
1984	Rolf Danneberg (West Germany)	Mac Wilkins (United States)	John Powell (United States)
1988	Jürgen Schult (East Germany)	Romas Ubartas (Soviet Union)	Rolf Danneberg (West Germany)
1992	Romas Ubartas (Lithuania)	Jürgen Schult (Germany)	Roberto Moya (Cuba)
1996	Lars Riedel (Germany)	Vladimir Dubrovshchik (Belarus)	Vasiliy Kaptyukh (Belarus)
2000	Virgilijus Alekna (Lithuania)	Lars Reidel (Germany)	Frantz Kruger (South Africa)
2004	Virgilijus Alekna (Lithuania)	Zoltán Kővágó (Hungary)	Aleksander Tammert (Estonia)
2008	Gerd Kanter (Estonia)	Piotr Małachowski (Poland)	Virgilijus Alekna (Lithuania)

Men's Hammer Throw

Year	Gold	Silver	Bronze
1900	John Flanagan (United States)	Truxtun Hare (United States)	Josiah McCracken (United States)
1904	John Jesus Flanagan (United States)	John DeWitt (United States)	Ralph Rose (United States)
1908	John Jesus Flanagan (United States)	Matt McGrath (United States)	Con Walsh (Canada)
1912	Matt McGrath (United States)	Guncan Gillis (Canada)	Clarence Childs (United States)
1916: Olympics not held			
1920	Patrick Ryan (United States)	Carl Johan Lind (Sweden)	Basil Bennett (United States)
1924	Fred Tootell (United States)	Matt McGrath (United States)	Malcolm Nokes (Great Britain)
1928	Pat O'Callaghan (Ireland)	Ossian Skiöld (Sweden)	Edmund Black (United States)
1932	Pat O'Callaghan (Ireland)	Ville Pörhölä (Finland)	Peter Zaremba (United States)
1936	Karl Hein (Germany)	Erwin Blask (Germany)	Fred Warngård (Sweden)
1940–1944: Olympics not held			
1948	Imre Nemeth (Hungary)	Ivan Gubijan (Yugoslavia)	Bob Bennett (United States)
1952	József Csermák (Hungary)	Karl Storch (Germany)	Imre Németh (Hungary)
1956	Harold Connolly (United States)	Mikhail Krivonosov (Soviet Union)	Anatoli Samotsvetov (Soviet Union)
1960	Vasili Rudenkov (Soviet Union)	Gyula Zsivótzky (Hungary)	Tadeusz Rut (Poland)
1964	Romuald Klim (Soviet Union)	Gyula Zsivótzky (Hungary)	Uwe Beyer (Germany)
1968	Gyula Zsivótzky (Hungary)	Romuald Klim (Soviet Union)	Lázár Lovász (Hungary)
1972	Anatoli Bondarchuk (Soviet Union)	Kochen Sachse (East Germany)	Vasili Khmelevski (Soviet Union)

Year	Gold	Silver	Bronze
1976	Yurir Sedykh (Soviet Union)	Aleksei Spiridonov (Soviet Union)	Anatoly Bondarchuk (Soviet Union)
1980	Yuriy Sedykh (Soviet Union)	Sergey Litvinov (Soviet Union)	Jüri Tamm (Soviet Union)
1984	Juha Tiainen (Finland)	Karl-Hand Riehm (Germany)	Klaus Ploghaus (Germany)
1988	Sergey Litvinov (Soviet Union)	Yuriy Sedykh (Soviet Union)	Jüri Tamm (Soviet Union)
1992	Andrey Abduvaliyev (Unified Team)	Igor Astapkovich (Unified Team)	Igor Nikulin (Unified Team)
1996	Balázs Kiss (Hungary)	Lance Deal (United States)	Oleksandr Krykun (Ukraine)
2000	Szymon Ziółkowski (Poland)	Nicola Vizzoni (Italy)	Igor Astapkovich (Belarus)
2004	Koji Murofushi (Japan)	Ivan Tsikhan (Belarus)	Eşref Apak (Turkey)
2008	Primož Kozmus (Slovenia)	Vadim Devyatovskiy (Belarus)	Ivan Tsikhan (Belarus)

Men's Javelin

Year	Gold	Silver	Bronze
1908	Eric Lemming (Sweden)	Arne Halse (Norway)	Otto Nilsson (Sweden)
1912	Eric Lemming (Sweden)	Juho Saaristo (Finland)	Mór Kóczán (Hungary)
1916: Olympics not held			
1920	Jonni Myyrä (Finland)	Urho Peltonen (Finland)	Pekka Johansson (Finland)
1924	Jonni Myyrä (Finland)	Gunnar Lindström (Sweden)	Eugene Oberst (United States)
1928	Erik Lundqvist (Sweden)	Béla Szepes (Hungary)	Olav Sunde (Norway)
1932	Matti Järvinen (Finland)	Matti Sippala (Finland)	Eino Penttilä (Finland)
1936	Gerhard Stöck (Germany)	Yrjo Nikkanen (Finland)	Kalervo Toivonen (Finland)
1940–1944: Olympics not held			
1948	Tapio Rautavaara (Finland)	Steve Seymour (United States)	József Várszegi (Hungary)
1952	Cyrus Young (United States)	Bill Miller (United States)	Toivo Hyytiäinen (Finland)
1956	Egil Danielsen (Norway)	Janusz Sidło (Poland)	Viktor Tsybulenko (Soviet Union)
1960	Viktor Tsybulenko (Soviet Union)	Walter Krüger (Germany)	Gergely Kulcsár (Hungary)
1964	Pauli Nevala (Finland)	Gergely Kulcsár (Hungary)	Jānis Lūsis (Soviet Union)
1968	Jānis Lūsis (Soviet Union)	Jorma Kinnunen (Finland)	Gergely Kulcsár (Hungary)
1972	Klaus Wolfermann (Germany)	Jānis Lūsis (Soviet Union)	Bill Schmidt (United States)
1976	Miklós Németh (Hungary)	Hannu Siitonrn (Finland)	Gheorghe Mgelea (Romania)
1980	Dainis Kūla (Soviet Union)	Aleksandr Makarov (Soviet Union)	Jüri Tamm (Soviet Union)
1984	Arto Härkönen (Finland)	Dave Ottley (Great Britain)	Kenth Eldebrink (Sweden)
1988	Tapio Korjus (Finland)	Jan Železný (Czechoslovakia)	Seppo Räty (Finland)
1992	Jan Železný (Czechoslovakia)	Seppo Räty (Finland)	Steve Backley (Great Britain)
1996	Jan Železný (Czech Republic)	Steve Backley (Great Britain)	Seppo Räty (Finland)
2000	Jan Železný (Czech Republic)	Steve Backley (Great Britain)	Sergey Makarov (Russia)
2004	Andreas Thorkildsen (Norway)	Cadims Vasilevskis (Latvia)	Sergey Makarov (Russia)
2008	Andreas Thorkildsen (Norway)	Ainārs Kovals (Latvia)	Tero Pitkämäki (Finland)

Men's Decathalon

Year	Gold	Silver	Bronze
1904	Tom Kiely (Great Britain)	Adam Gunn (United States)	Thomas Hare (United States)
1908: Event not held			
1912	Hugo Wieslander (Sweden) Jim Thorpe (United States)	Charles Lomberg (Sweden)	Gösta Holmér (Sweden)
1916: Olympics not held			
1920	Helge Løvland (Norway)	Brutus Hamilton (United States)	Bertil Ohlson (Sweden)
1924	Harold Osborn (United States)	Emerson Norton (United States)	Aleksander Klumberg (Estonia)
1928	Paavo Yrjölä (Finland)	Akilles Järvinen (Finland)	John Doherty (United States)
1932	James Bausch (United States)	Akilles Järvinen (Finland)	Wolrad Everle (Germany)

Year	Gold	Silver	Bronze
1936	Glenn Morris (United States)	Robert Claek (United States)	Jack Parker (United States)
1940–1944: Olympics not held			
1948	Bob Mathias (United States)	Ignance Heinrich (France)	Floyd Simmons (United States)
1952	Bob Mathias (United States)	Milt Campbell (United States)	Floyd Simmons (United States)
1956	Milt Campbell (United States)	Rafer Johnson (United States)	Vasili Kuznetsov (Soviet Union)
1960	Rafer Johnson (United States)	Yang Chuan-Kwang (China)	Vasili Kuznetsov (Soviet Union)
1964	Willi Holdorf (Germany)	Rein Aun (Soviet Union)	Hans-Joachim Walde (Germany)
1968	Bill Toomey	Hans-Joachim Walde (Germany)	Kurt Bendlin (Germany)
1972	Nikolai Avilov (Soviet Union)	Leonid Litvinenko (Soviet Union)	Ryszard Katus (Poland)
1976	Bruce Jenner (United States)	Guido Kratschmer (Germany)	Nikolai Avilov (Soviet Union)
1980	Daley Thompson (Great Britain)	Yuriy Kutsenko (Soviet Union)	Sergey Zhelanov (Soviet Union)
1984	Daley Thompson (Great Britain)	Jürgen Hingsen (Germany)	Siegfried Wentz (West Germany)
1988	Christian Schenk (East Germany)	Torsten Voss (East Germany)	Dave Steen (Canada)
1992	Robert Změlík (Czechoslovakia)	Antonio Peñalver (Spain)	Dave Johnson (United States)
1996	Dan O'Brien (United States)	Frank Busemann (Germany)	Tomáš Dvořák (Czech Republic)
2000	Erki Nool (Estonia)	Roman Šebrle (Czech Republic)	Chris Huffins (United States)
2004	Roman Šebrle (Czech Republic)	Bryan Clay (United States)	Dmitriy Karpov (Kazakhstan)
2008	Bryan Clay (United States)	Andrei Krauchanka (Belarus)	Leonel Suárez (Cuba)

Men's 60-Meter

Year	Gold	Silver	Bronze
1900	Alvin Kraenzlein (United States)	John Tewksbury (United States)	Stanley Rowley (Australia)
1904	Archie Hahn (United States)	William Hogenson (United States)	Fay Moulton (United States)

Men's 200-Meter Hurdles

Year	Gold	Silver	Bronze
1900	Alvin Kraenzlein (United States)	Norman Pritchard (India)	Walter Tewksbury (United States)
1904	Harry Hillman (United States)	Frank Castleman (United States)	George Poage (United States)

Men's 2,500-Meter Steeplechase

Year	Gold	Silver	Bronze
1900	George Orton (Canada)	Sidney Robinson (Great Britain)	Jacques Chastanié (France)

Men's 2,590-Meter Steeplechase

Year	Gold	Silver	Bronze
1904	Jim Lightbody (United States)	John Daly (Great Britain)	Arthur Newton (United States)

Men's 3,200-Meter Steeplechase

Year	Gold	Silver	Bronze
1908	Arthur Russell (Great Britain)	Archie Robertson (Great Britain)	John Eisele (United States)

Men's 4,000-Meter Steeplechase

Year	Gold	Silver	Bronze
1904	John Rimmer (Great Britain)	Charles Bennett (Great Britain)	Sidney Robinson (Great Britain)

Men's Medley Relay

Year	Gold	Silver	Bronze
1908	William Hamilton, Nathaniel Cartmell, John Taylor, Mel Sheppard (United States)	Arthur Hoffmann, Hans Eicke, Otto Trieloff, Hanns Braun (Germany)	Pál Simon, Frigyes Wiesner, József Nagy, Ödön Bodor (Hungary)

Men's 3,000-Meter Team Race

Year	Gold	Silver	Bronze
1912	Tell Berna, George Bonhag, Abel Kiviat, Louis Scott, Norman Taber (United States)	Bror Fock, Nils Frykberg, Thorild Olsson, Ernst Wide, John Zander (Sweden)	William Cottrill, George Hutson, William Moore, Edward Owen, Cyril Porter (Great Britain)
1916: Olympics not held			
1920	Horace Brown, Ivan Dresser, Arlie Schardt (United States)	Charles Blewitt, Albert Hill, William Seagrove (Great Britain)	Eric Backman, Sven Lundgren, Edvin Wide (Sweden)
1924	Elias Katz, Paavo Nurmi, Ville Ritola (Finland)	Harry Johnston, Bernhard McDonald, George Webber (Great Britain)	William Cox, Edward Kirby, Willard Tibbetts (United States)

Men's 5,000-Meter Team Race

Year	Gold	Silver	Bronze
1900	Charles Bennett, John Rimmer, Sidney Robinson, Alfred Tysoe (Great Britain), Stanley Rowley (Australia)	Henri Deloge, Gaston Ragueneau, Jacques Chastanié, André Castanet, Michel Champoudry (France)	Not awarded

Men's 3-Mile Team Race

Year	Gold	Silver	Bronze
1908	Joseph Deakin, Archie Robertson, William Coales (Great Britain)	John Eisele, George Bonhag, Herbert Trube (United States)	Louis de Fleurac, Joseph Dreher, Paul Lizandier (France)

Men's 4-Mile Team Race

Year	Gold	Silver	Bronze
1904	Arthur Newton, George Underwood, Paul Pilgrim, Howard Valentine, David Munson (United States)	Jim Lightbody, William Verner, Lacey Hearn, Sidney Hatch (United States), Albert Coray (France)	Not awarded

Men's 5-Mile Race

Year	Gold	Silver	Bronze
1908	Emil Voigt (Great Britain)	Edward Owen (Great Britain)	John Svanberg (Sweden)

Men's 3,000-Meter Walk

Year	Gold	Silver	Bronze
1920	Ugo Frigerio (Italy)	George Parker (Australia)	Richard Remer (United States)

Men's 3,500-Meter Walk

Year	Gold	Silver	Bronze
1908	George Larner (Great Britain)	Ernest Webb (Great Britain)	Harry Kerr (Australasia)

Men's 10,000-Meter Walk

Year	Gold	Silver	Bronze
1912	George Goulding (Canada)	Ernest Webb (Great Britain)	Fernando Altimani (Italy)
1920	Ugo Frigerio (Italy)	Joseph Pearman (United States)	Charles Gunn (Great Britain)
1924	Ugo Frigerio (Italy)	Gordon Goodwin (Great Britain)	Cecil McMaster (South Africa)
1948	John Mikaelsson (Sweden)	Ingemar Johansson (Sweden)	Fritz Schwab (Switzerland)
1952	John Mikaelsson (Sweden)	Fritz Schwab (Switzerland)	Bruno Junk (Soviet Union)

Men's 10-Mile Walk

Year	Gold	Silver	Bronze
1908	George Larner (Great Britain)	Ernest Webb (Great Britain)	Edward Spencer (Great Britain)

Men's Triathlon

Year	Gold	Silver	Bronze
1904	Max Emmerich (United States)	John Grieb (United States)	William Merz (United States)

Men's Pentathlon

Year	Gold	Silver	Bronze
1912	Ferdinand Bie (Norway) Jim Thorpe (United States)	James Donahue (United States)	Frank Lukeman (Canada)
1920	Eero Lehtonen (Finland)	Everett Bradley (United States)	Hugo Lahtinen (Finland)
1924	Eero Lehtonen (Finland)	Elemér Somfay (Hungary)	Robert LeGendre (United States)

Men's Standing Long Jump

Year	Gold	Silver	Bronze
1900	Ray Ewry (United States)	Irving Baxter (United States)	Émile Torcheboeuf (France)
1904	Ray Ewry (United States)	Charles King (United States)	John Biller (United States)
1908	Ray Ewry (United States)	Konstantinos Tsiklitiras (Greece)	Martin Sheridan (United States)
1912	Konstantinos Tsiklitiras (Greece)	Platt Adams (United States)	Benjamis Adams (United States)

Men's Standing Triple Jump

Year	Gold	Silver	Bronze
1900	Ray Ewry (United States)	Irving Baxter (United States)	Robert Garrett (United States)
1904	Ray Ewry (United States)	Charles King (United States)	Joseph Stadler (United States)

Men's Standing High Jump

Year	Gold	Silver	Bronze
1900	Ray Ewry (United States)	Irving Baxter (United States)	Lewis Sheldon (United States)
1904	Ray Ewry (United States)	Joseph Stadler (United States)	Lawson Roberton (United States)
1908	Ray Ewry (United States)	John Biller (United States)	Konstantinos Tsiklitiras (Greece)
1912	Platt Adams (United States)	Benjamin Adams (United States)	Konstantinos Tsiklitiras (Greece)

Men's 56-Pound Weight Throw

Year	Gold	Silver	Bronze
1904	Étienne Desmarteau (Canada)	John Jesus Flanagan (United States)	James Mitchell (United States)
1920	Patrick McDonald (United States)	Patrick Ryan (United States)	Carl Johan Lind (Sweden)

Men's Shot Put, Two-handed

Year	Gold	Silver	Bronze
1912	Ralph Rose (United States)	Patrick McDonald (United States)	Elmer Niklander (Finland)

Men's Discus, Ancient Style

Year	Gold	Silver	Bronze
1908	Martin Sheridan (United States)	Marquis Horr (United States)	Verner Järvinen (Finland)

Men's Discus, Two-handed

Year	Gold	Silver	Bronze
1912	Armas Taipale (Finland)	Elmer Niklander (Finland)	Emil Magnisson (Sweden)

Men's Javelin, Freestyle

Year	Gold	Silver	Bronze
1908	Eric Lemming (Sweden)	Michalis Dorizas (Greece)	Arne Halse (Norway)

Men's Javelin, Two-handed

Year	Gold	Silver	Bronze
1912	Julius Saaristo (Finland)	Väinö Siikaniemi (Finland)	Urho Peltonen (Finland)

Men's Individual Cross-Country

Year	Gold	Silver	Bronze
1912	Hannes Kolehmainen (Finland)	Hjalmar Andersson (Sweden)	John Eke (Sweden)
1916: Olympics not held			
1920	Paavo Nurmi (Finland)	Eric Bachman (Sweden)	Heikki Liimatainen (Finland)
1924	Paavo Nurmi (Finland)	Ville Ritola (Finland)	Earl Johnson (United States)

Men's Team Cross-Country

Year	Gold	Silver	Bronze
1912	Hjalmar Andersson, John Eke, Josef Ternström (Sweden)	Hannes Kolehmainen, Jalmari Eskola, Albin Stenroos (Finland)	Frederick Hibbins, Ernest Glover, Thomas Humphreys (Great Britain)
1916: Olympics not held			
1920	Paavo Nurmi, Heikki Liimatainen, Teodor Koskenniemi (Finland)	James Wilson, Frank Hegarty, Alfred Nichols (Great Britain)	Eric Backman, Gustaf Mattsson, Hilding Ekman (Sweden)
1924	Paavo Nurmi, Ville Ritola, Heikki Liimatainen (Finland)	Earl Johnson, Arthur Studenroth, August Fager (United States)	Henri Lauvaux, Gaston Heuet, Maurice Norland (France)

Men's 1,500-Meter Wheelchair

Year	Gold	Silver	Bronze
2004	Rawat Tana (Thailand)	Robert Figl (Germany)	Saul Mendoza (Mexico)

Women's 100-Meter Dash

Year	Gold	Silver	Bronze
1928	Betty Robinson (United States)	Bobbie Rosenfeld (Canada)	Ethel Smith (Canada)
1932	Stanisława Walasiewicz (Poland)	Hilda Strike (Canada)	Wilhelmina von Bremen (United States)
1936	Helen Stephens (United States)	Stanisława Walasiewicz (Poland)	Käthe Krauß (Germany)
1940–1944: Olympics not held			

Year	Gold	Silver	Bronze
1948	Fanny Blankers-Koen (Netherlands)	Dorothy Manley (Great Britain)	Shirley Strickland (Australia)
1952	Marjorie Jackson (Australia)	Daphne Hasenjager (South Africa)	Shirley Strickland de la Hunty (Australia)
1956	Betty Cuthbert (United States)	Christa Stubnich (Germany)	Marlene Matthews (Australia)
1960	Wilma Rudolph (United States)	Dorothy Hyman (Great Britain)	Giuseppina Leone (Italy)
1964	Wyomia Tyus (United States)	Edith McGuire (United States)	Ewa Kłobukowska (Poland)
1968	Wyomia Tyus (United States)	Barbara Ferrell (United States)	Irena Szewińska (Poland)
1972	Renate Stecher (East Germany)	Raelene Boyle (Australia)	Silvia Chibás (Cuba)
1976	Annegret Richter (Germany)	Renate Stecher (East Germany)	Inge Helton (Germany)
1980	Lyudmila Kondratyeva (Soviet Union)	Marlies Göhr (East Germany)	Ingrid Auerswald (East Germany)
1984	Evelyn Ashford (United States)	Alice Brown (United States)	Merlene Ottey (Jamaica)
1988	Florence Griffith-Joyner (United States)	Evelyn Ashford-Washington (United States)	Heike Daute-Drechsler (East Germany)
1992	Gail Devers (United States)	Juliet Cuthbert (Jamaica)	Irina Privalove (Unified Team)
1996	Gail Devers (United States)	Marlene Ottey (Jamaica)	Gwen Torrence (United States)
2000	Marion Jones* (United States)	Ekaterini Thanou (Greece) Tanya Lawrence (Jamaica)	Merlene Ottey (Jamaica)
2004	Yulia Nesterenko (Belarus)	Lauryn Williams (United States)	Veronica Campbell (Jamaica)
2008	Shelly-Ann Fraser (Jamaica)	Sherone Simpson (Jamaica) Jerron Stewart (Jamaica)	Not awarded

* Medal stripped in 2003 due to use of performance-enhancing drugs.

Women's 200-Meter

Year	Gold	Silver	Bronze
1948	Fanny Blankers-Koen (Netherlands)	Audrey Williamson (Great Britain)	Audrey Patterson (United States)
1952	Marjorie Jackson (Australia)	Puck Brouwer (Netherlands)	Nadezhda Khnykina-Dvalishvili (Soviet Union)
1956	Betty Cuthbert (United States)	Christa Stubnich (Germany)	Marlene Matthews (Australia)
1960	Wilma Rudolph (United States)	Jutta Heine (Germany)	Dorothy Hyman (Great Britain)
1964	Edith McGuire (United States)	Irena Kirzenstein (Poland)	Marilyn Black (Australia)
1968	Irena Szewińska (Poland)	Raelene Boyle (Australia)	Jenny Lamy (Australia)
1972	Renate Stecher (East Germany)	Raelene Boyle (Australia)	Irena Szewińska (Poland)
1976	Bärbel Eckert (East Germany)	Annegret Richter (Germany)	Renate Stecher (East Germany)
1984	Valerie Brisco-Hooks (United States)	Florence Griffith (United States)	Merlene Ottey (Jamaica)
1988	Florence Griffith-Joyner (United States)	Grace Jackson (Jamaica)	Heike Daute-Drechsler (East Germany)
1992	Gwen Torrenc (United States)	Julia Cuthbert (Jamaica)	Merlene Ottey (Jamaica)
1996	Marie-José Pérec (France)	Merlene Ottey (Jamaica)	Mary Onyali (Nigeria)
2000	Pauline Davis-Thompson (Bahamas)	Susanthika Jayasinghe (Sri Lanka)	Beverly McDonald (Jamaica)
2004	Veronica Campbell (Jamaica)	Allyson Felix (United States)	Debbie Ferguson (Bahamas)
2008	Veronica Campbell-Brown (Jamaica)	Allyson Felix (United States)	Kerron Stewart (Jamaica)

Women's 400-Meter

Year	Gold	Silver	Bronze
1964	Betty Cuthbert (Australia)	Ann Packer (Great Britain)	Judy Amoore (Australia)
1968	Colette Besson (France)	Lillian Board (Great Britain)	Natalya Pechonkina (Soviet Union)

Year	Gold	Silver	Bronze
1972	Monika Zehrt (East Germany)	Rita Wilden (Germany)	Kathy Hammond (United States)
1976	Irena Szewińska (Poland)	Christina Brehmer (East Germany)	Ellen Streidt (East Germany)
1980	Marita Koch (East Germany)	Jarmila Kratochvílová (Czechoslovakia)	Christina Lathan (East Germany)
1984	Valerie Brisco-Hooks (United States)	Chandra Cheeseborough (United States)	Kathy Smallwood-Cook (Great Britain)
1988	Olga Vladykina-Bryzgina (Soviet Union)	Petra Muller (East Germany)	Olga Nazarova (Soviet Union)
1992	Marie-José Pérec (France)	Olge Bryzgina (Unified Team)	Ximena Restrepo (Colombia)
1996	Marie-José Pérec (France)	Cathy Freeman (Australia)	Falilat Ogunkoya (Nigeria)
2000	Cathy Freeman (Australia)	Lorraice Graham (Jamaica)	Jathatine Merry (Great Britain)
2004	Tonique Williams-Darling (Bahamas)	Ana Guevata (Mexico)	Natalya Antyukh (Russia)
2008	Christine Ohuruogu (Great Britain)	Shericka Williams (Jamaica)	Sanya Richards (United States)

Women's 800-Meter

Year	Gold	Silver	Bronze
1928	Line Radke (Germany)	Kinue Hitomi (Japan)	Inga Gentzel (Sweden)
1932–1936: Event not held			
1940–1944: Olympics not held			
1948–1956: Event not held			
1960	Lyudmila Lysenko (Soviet Union)	Brenda Jones (Australia)	Ursula Donath (Germany)
1964	Ann Packer (Great Britain)	Maryvonne Dupureur (France)	Marise Chamberlain (New Zealand)
1968	Madeline Manning (United States)	Ilona Silai (Romania)	Maria Gommers (Netherlands)
1972	Hildegard Falck (Germany)	Nijolė Sabaitė (Soviet Union)	Gunhild Hoffmeister (East Germany)
1976	Tatyana Kazankina (Soviet Union)	Nikolina Shtereva (Bulgaria)	Elfi Zinn (East Germany)
1980	Nadezhda Olizarenko (Soviet Union)	Olga Mineeva (Soviet Union)	Tatyana Providokhina (Soviet Union)
1984	Doina Melinte (Romania)	Kim Gallagher (United States)	Fita Lovin (Romania)
1988	Sigrun Ludvigs-Wodars (East Germany)	Christine Wachtel (East Germany)	Kim Gallagher (United States)
1992	Ellen van Langen (Netherlands)	Lilita Nurutdinova (Unified Team)	Ana Fidelia Quirot (Cuba)
1996	Svetlana Masterkova (Russia)	Ana Fidelia Quirot (Cuba)	Maria de Lurdes Mutola (Mozambique)
2000	Maria de Lurdes Mutola (Mozambique)	Stephanie Graf (Austria)	Kelly Holmes (Great Britain)
2004	Kelly Holmes (Great Britain)	Hasna Benhassi (Morocco)	Jolanda Čeplak (Slovenia)
2008	Pamela Jelimo (Kenya)	Janeth Jepkosgei Busienei (Kenya)	Hasna Benhassi (Morocco)

Women's 1,500-Meter

Year	Gold	Silver	Bronze
1972	Ludmila Bragina (Soviet Union)	Gunhild Hoffmeister (East Germany)	Paola Pigni (Italy)
1976	Tatyana Kazankina (Soviet Union)	Gunhild Hoffmeister (East Germany)	Ulrike Klapezynski (East Germany)
1980	Tatyana Kazankina (Soviet Union)	Christiane Wartenberg (East Germany)	Nadezhda Olizarenko (Soviet Union)
1984	Gabriella Dorio (Italy)	Doina Melinte (Romania)	Maricica Puică (Romania)
1988	Paula Ilie-Ivan (Romania)	Laimutė Baikauskaitė (Soviet Union)	Tetyana Samolenko (Soviet Union)

Year	Gold	Silver	Bronze
1992	Hassiba Boulmerka (Algeria)	Lyudmila Togachova (Unified Team)	Qu Yunxia (China)
1996	Svetlana Masterkova (Russia)	Gabriela Szabo (Romania)	Theresia Kiesl (Austria)
2000	Nouria Mérah-Benida (Algeria)	Violeta Beclea (Romania)	Gabriela Szabo (Romania)
2004	Kelly Holmes (Great Britain)	Tatyana Tomashova (Russia)	Maria Cioncan (Romania)
2008	Nancy Jebet Lagat (Kenya)	Iryna Lishchynska (Ukraine)	Nataliya Tobias (Ukraine)

Women's 5,000-Meter

Year	Gold	Silver	Bronze
1996	Wang Junxia (China)	Pauline Konga (Kenya)	Roberta Brunet (Italy)
2000	Gabriela Szabo (Romania)	Sonia O'Sullivan (Ireland)	Gete Wami (Ethiopia)
2004	Meseret Defar (Ethiopia)	Isabella Ochichi (Kenya)	Tirunesh Dibaba (Ethiopia)
2008	Tiruneh Dibaba (Ethiopia)	Elvan Abeylegesse (Turkey)	Meseret Defar (Ethiopia)

Women's 10,000-Meter

Year	Gold	Silver	Bronze
1988	Olga Bondarenko (Soviet Union)	Liz McColgan (Great Britain)	Yelena Zhupiyeva-Vyazova (Soviet Union)
1992	Derartu Tulu (Ethiopia)	Elana Meter (South Africa)	Lynn Jennings (United States)
1996	Fernanda Ribeiro (Portugal)	Wang Junxia (China)	Gete Wami (Ethiopia)
2000	Derartu Tulu (Ethiopia)	Gete Wami (Ethiopia)	Fernanda Ribeiro (Portugal)
2004	Xing Huina (China)	Ejagayehu Dibaba (Ethiopia)	Derartu Tulu (Ethiopia)
2008	Tirunesh Dibaba (Ethiopia)	Elvan Abeylegesse (Turkey)	Shalane Flanagan (United States)

Women's Marathon

Year	Gold	Silver	Bronze
1984	Joan Benoit (United States)	Grete Waitz (Norway)	Rosa Mota (Portugal)
1988	Rosa Mota (United States)	Lisa Martin (Australia)	Katrin Dörre (East Germany)
1992	Valentina Yegorova (Unified Team)	Yuko Arimori (Japan)	Lorraine Moller (New Zealand)
1996	Fatuma Roba (Ethiopia)	Valentina Yegorova (Russia)	Yuko Arimori (Japan)
2000	Naoko Takahashi (Japan)	Lidia Simon (Romania)	Joyce Chepchumba (Kenya)
2004	Mitzuki Noguchi (Japan)	Catherine Ndereba (Kenya)	Deena Kastor (United States)
2008	Constantina Di ă-Tomescu (Romania)	Catherine Ndereba (Kenya)	Zhou Chunxiu (China)

Women's 100-Meter Hurdles

Year	Gold	Silver	Bronze
1972	Annelie Ehehardt (East Germany)	Valeria Bufanu (Romania)	Karin Balzer (East Germany)
1976	Johanna Schaller (East Germany)	Tatiana Anisimova (Soviet Union)	Natalya Lebedeva (Soviet Union)
1980	Vera Komisova (Soviet Union)	Johanna Klier (East Germany)	Lucyna Langer (Poland)
1984	Benita Fitzgerald (United States)	Shirley Strong (Great Britain)	Michèle Chardonnet (France) Kim Turner (United States)
1988	Yordanka Donkova (Bulgaria)	Gloria Kovarik-Siebert (East Germany)	Claudia Reidick-Zazckiewicz (Germany)
1992	Voula Patoulidou (Greece)	LaVonna Martin (United States)	Yordanka Donkova (Bulgaria)
1996	Ludmila Engquist (Sweden)	Brigita Bukovec (Slovenia)	Patricia Girard (France)
2000	Olga Shishigina (Kazakhstan)	Glory Alozie (Nigeria)	Melissa Morrison (United States)
2004	Joanne Hayes (United States)	Olena Krasovska (Ukraine)	Melissa Morrison (United States)
2008	Dawn Harper (United States)	Sally McLellan (Australia)	Priscilla Lopes-Schliep (Canada)

Women's 400-Meter Hurdles

Year	Gold	Silver	Bronze
1984	Nawal El Moutawakel (Morocco)	Judi Brown (United States)	Cristeana Cojocaru (Romania)
1988	Debbie Flintoff-King (Australia)	Tatyana Ledovskaya (Soviet Union)	Ellen Neumann-Fiedler (East Germany)
1992	Sally Gunnell (Great Britain)	Sandra Farmer-Patrick (United States)	Janeene Vickers (United States)
1996	Deon Hemmings (Jamaica)	Kim Batten (United States)	Tonja Buford-Bailey (United States)
2000	Irina Privalova (Russia)	Deon Hemmings (Jamaica)	Nezha Bidouane (Morocco)
2004	Fani Halkia (Greece)	Ionela Târlea-Manolache (Romania)	Tetuana Tereshchuk-Antipova (Ukraine)
2008	Maleine Walker (Jamaica)	Sheena Tosta (United States)	Tasha Danvers (Great Britain)

Women's 3,000-Meter Steeplechase

Year	Gold	Silver	Bronze
2008	Gulnara Samitova-Galkina (Russia)	Eunice Jepkorir (Kenya)	Yekaterina Volkova (Russia)

Women's 4 × 100-Meter Relay

Year	Gold	Silver	Bronze
1928	Fanny Rosenfeld, Ethel Smith, Jane Bell, Myrtle Cook (Canada)	Mary Washburn, Jessie Cross, Loretta McNeil, Betty Robinson (United States)	Rosa Kellner, Helene Schmidt, Anni Holdmann, Helene Junker (Germany)
1932	Mary Carew, Evelyn Furtsc, Annette Rogers, Wilhelmina von Bremen (United States)	Mildred Fizzell, Lilian Palmer, Mary Frizzel, Hilda Strike (Canada)	Eileen Hiscock, Gwendoline Porter, Violet Webb, Nellie Halstead (Great Britain)
1936	Harriet Bland, Annette Rogers, Betty Robinson, Helen Stephens (United States)	Eileen Hiscock, Violet Olney, Audrey Brown, Barbara Burke (Great Britain)	Dorothy Brookshaw, Mildred Dolson, Hilda Cameron, Aileen Meagher (Canada)
1940–1944: Olympics not held			
1948	Xenia Stad-de Jong, Netty Witziers-Timmer, Gerda van der Kade-Koudijs, Fanny Blankers-Koen (Netherlands)	Shirley Strickland, June Maston, Elizabeth McKinnon, Joyce King (Australia)	Viola Myers, Nancy MacKay, Diane Foster, Patricia Jones (Canada)
1952	Mae Faggs, Barbara Jones, Janet Moreau, Catherine Hardy (United States)	Ursula Knab, Maria Sander, Helga Klein, Marga Petersen (Germany)	Sylvia Cheeseman, June Foulds, Jean Desforges, Heather Armitage (Great Britain)
1956	Shirley Strickland de la Hunty, Norma Croker, Fleur Mellor, Betty Cuthbert (Australia)	Anne Pashley, Jean Scrivens, June Foulds, Heather Armitage (Great Britain)	Mae Faggs, Margaret Matthews, Wilma Rudolph, Isabelle Daniels (United States)
1960	Martha Hudson, Lucinda Williams, Barbara Jones, Wilma Rudolph (United States)	Martha Langbein, Annie Biechl, Brunhilde Hendrix, Jutta Heine (Germany)	Teresa Wieczorek, Barbara Janiszewska, Celina Jesionowska, Halina Richter (Poland)
1964	Teresa Ciepły, Irena Kirszenstein, Halina Górecka, Ewa Kłobukowska (Poland)	Willye White, Wyomia Tyus, Marilyn White, Edith McGuire (United States)	Janet Simpson, Mary Rand, Daphne Arden, Dorothy Hyman (Great Britain)
1968	Barbara Ferrell, Margaret Bailes, Mildrette Netter, Wyomia Tyus (United States)	Marlene Elejarde, Fulgencia Romay, Violetta Quesada, Miguelina Cobián (Cuba)	Lyudmila Zharkova, Galina Bukharina, Vera Popkova, Lyudmila Samotyosova (Soviet Union)
1972	Christiane Krause, Ingrid Mickler-Becker, Annegret Richter, Heide Rosendahl (Germany)	Evelyn Kaufer, Christina Heinich, Bärbel Struppert, Renate Stecher (East Germany)	Marlene Elejarde, Carmen Valdés, Fulgencia Romay, Silvia Chibás (Cuba)

Year	Gold	Silver	Bronze
1976	Marlies Oelsner, Renate Stecher, Carla Bodendorf, Bärbel Eckert (East Germany)	Elvira Possekel, Inge Helten, Annegret Richter, Annegret Kroniger (Germany)	Tatyana Prorochenko, Lyudmila Maslakova, Nadezhda Besfamilnaya, Vera Anisimova (Soviet Union)
1980	Romy Müller, Bärbel Wöckel, Ingrid Auerswald, Marlies Göhr (East Germany)	Vera Komisova, Lyudmila Maslakova, Vera Anisimova, Natalya Bochina (Soviet Union)	Heather Hunte, Kathy Smallwood-Cook, Beverley Goddard, Sonia Lannaman (Great Britain)
1984	Alice Brown, Jeanette Bolden, Chandra Cheeseborough, Evelyn Ashford (United States)	Angela Bailey, Marita Payne, Angella Taylor-Issajenko, France Gareau (Canada)	Simone Jacobs, Kathy Smallwood-Cook, Beverley Callander, Heather Oakes (Great Britain)
1988	Alice Brown, Sheila Echols, Florence Griffith Joyner, Evelyn Ashford (United States)	Silke Möller, Kerstin Behrendt, Ingrid Auerswald, Marlies Göhr (East Germany)	Lyudmila Kondratyeva, Galina Malchugina, Marina Zhirova, Natalya Pomoschnikova (Soviet Union)
1992	Evelyn Ashford, Esther Jones, Carlette Guidry, Gwen Torrence, Michelle Finn (United States)	Olga Bogoslovskaya, Galina Malchugina, Marina Trandenkova, Irina Privalova (Unified Team)	Beatrice Utondu, Faith Idehen, Christy Opara-Thompson, Mary Onyali (Nigeria)
1996	Gail Devers, Inger Miller, Chryste Gaines, Gwen Torrence, Carlette Guidry (United States)	Eldece Clarke, Chandra Sturrup, Savatheda Fynes, Pauline Davis-Thompson, Debbie Ferguson (Bahamas)	Michelle Freeman, Juliet Cuthbert, Nikole Mitchell, Merlene Ottey, Gillian Russell, Andrea Lloyd (Jamaica)
2000	Sevatheda Fynes, Chandra Sturrup, Pauline Davis-Thompson, Debbie Ferguson, Eldece Clarke-Lewis (Bahamas)	Tanya Lawrence, Veronica Campbell, Beverly McDonald, Merlene Ottey, Merlene Frazer (Jamaica)	Chryste Gaines, Torri Edwards, Nanceen Perry, Marion Jones (United States)
2004	Tayna Lawrence, Sherone Simpson, Aleen Bailey, Veronica Campbell, Beverly McDonald (Jamaica)	Olga Fyodorova, Yuliya Tabakova, Irina Khabarova, Larisa Kruglova (Russia)	Véronique Mang, Muriel Hurtis, Sylviane Félix, Christine Arron (France)
2008	Yuliya Chermoshanskaya, Yuliya Gushchina, Aleksandra Fedoriva, Yevgeniya Polyakova (Russia)	Kim Gevaert, Élodie Ouédraogo, Hanna Mariën, Olivia Borlée (Belgium)	Halimat Ismaila, Oludamola Osayomi, Agnes Osazuwa, Gloria Kemasuode, Franca Idoko (Nigeria)

Women's 4 × 400-Meter Relay

Year	Gold	Silver	Bronze
1972	Dagmar Käsling, Rita Kühne, Helga Seidler, Monika Zehrt (East Germany)	Mable Fergerson, Madeline Manning, Cheryl Toussaint, Kathy Hammond (United States)	Anette Rückes, Inge Bödding, Hildegard Falck, Rita Wilden (Germany)
1976	Doris Maletzki, Brigitte Rohde, Ellen Streidt, Christina Brehmer (East Germany)	Debra Sapenter, Sheila Ingram, Pamela Jiles, Rosalyn Bryant (United States)	Inta Kļimoviča, Lyudmila Aksenova, Natalya Sokolova, Nadezhda Ilyina (Soviet Union)
1980	Tatyana Prorochenko, Tatyana Goistchik, Nina Zyuskova, Irina Nazarova (Soviet Union)	Gabriele Löwe, Barbara Krug, Christina Lathan, Marita Koch (East Germany)	Linsey MacDonald, Michelle Probert, Joslyn Hoyte-Smith, Donna Hartley (Great Britain)
1984	Lillie Leatherwood, Sherri Howard, Valerie Brisco-Hooks, Chandra Cheeseborough (United States)	Charmaine Crooks, Jillian Richardson, Molly Killingbeck, Marita Payne (Canada)	Heike Schulte-Mattler, Ute Thimm, Heidi-Elke Gaugel, Gaby Bußmann (Germany)
1988	Tatyana Ledovskaya, Olga Nazarova, Mariya Pinigina, Olga Bryzgina (Soviet Union)	Denean Howard, Diane Dixon, Valerie Brisco-Hooks, Florence Griffith Joyner (United States)	Dagmar Neubauer-Rübsam, Kirsten Emmelmann, Sabine Busch, Petra Müller (East Germany)

Year	Gold	Silver	Bronze
1992	Yelena Ruzina, Lyudmila Dzhigalova, Olga Nazarova, Olga Bryzgina, Marina Shmonina, Liliya Nurutdinova (Unified Team)	Natasha Kaiser, Gwen Torrence, Jearl Miles, Rochelle Stevens, Denean Hill, Dannette Young (United States)	Phylis Smith, Sandra Douglas, Jennifer Stoute, Sally Gunnell (Great Britain)
1996	Rochelle Stevens, Maicel Malone, Kim Graham, Jearl Miles, Linetta Wilson (United States)	Bisi Afolabi, Fatima Yusuf, Charity Opara, Falilat Ogunkoya (Nigeria)	Uta Rohländer, Linda Kisabaka, Anja Rücker, Grit Breuer (Germany)
2000	Jearl Miles Clark, Monique Hennagan, Marion Jones, LaTasha Colander, Andrea Anderson (United States)	Sandie Richards, Catherine Scott, Deon Hemmings, Lorraine Graham, Charmaine Howell, Michelle Burgher (Jamaica)	Yuliya Sotnikova, Svetlana Goncharenko, Olga Kotlyarova, Irina Privalova, Natalya Nazarova, Olesya Zykina (Russia)
2004	DeeDee Trotter, Monique Henderson, Sanya Richards, Monique Hennagan, Crystal Cox, Moushaumi Robinson (United States)	Olesya Krasnomovets, Natalya Nazarova, Olesya Zykina, Natalya Antyukh, Tatyana Firova, Natalya Ivanova (Russia)	Novlene Williams, Michelle Burgher, Nadia Davy, Sandie Richards, Ronetta Smith (Jamaica)
2008	Mary Wineberg, Allyson Felix, Monique Henderson, Sanya Richards (United States)	Yuliya Gushchina, Lyudmila Litvinova, Tatyana Firova, Anastasiya Kapachinskaya (Russia)	Shericka Williams, Shereefa Lloyd, Rosemarie Whyte, Novlene Williams (Jamaica)

Women's 20-Kilometer Walk

Year	Gold	Silver	Bronze
2000	Liping Wang (China)	Kjersti Plätzer (Norway)	María Vasco (Spain)
2004	Athanasia Tsoumeleka (Greece)	Olimpiada Ivanova (Russia)	Jane Saville (Australia)
2008	Olga Kaniskina (Russia)	Kjersti Plätzer (Norway)	Elisa Riguado (Italy)

Women's High Jump

Year	Gold	Silver	Bronze
1928	Ethel Catherwood (Canada)	Lien Gisolf (Netherlands)	Mildred Wiley (United States)
1932	Jean Shiley (United States)	Babe Didrikson (United States)	Eva Dawes (Canada)
1936	Ibolya Csák (Hungary)	Dorothy Odam (Great Britain)	Elfriede Kaun (Germany)
1940–1944: Olympics not held			
1948	Alice Cochman (United States)	Dorothy Tyler-Odam (Great Britain)	Micheline Ostermeyer (France)
1952	Esther Brand (South Africa)	Sheila Lerwill (Great Britain)	Aleksandra Chudina (Soviet Union)
1956	Mildred McDaniel (United States)	Thelma Hopkins (Great Britain)	Maria Pisareva (Soviet Union)
1960	Iolanda Balaş (Romania)	Dorothy Shirley (Great Britain)	Jarosława Jóźwiakowska (Poland)
1964	Iolanda Balaş (Romania)	Michele Brown (Australia)	Taisia Chenchik (Soviet Union)
1968	Miloslava Rezková (Czechoslovakia)	Antonina Okorokova (Soviet Union)	Valentina Kozyr (Soviet Union)
1972	Heidi Rosendahl (Germany)	Diana Yorgova (Hungary)	Eva Šuranová (Czechoslovakia)
1976	Angela Voigt (East Germany)	Kathy McMillan (United States)	Lidiya Alfeyeva (Soviet Union)
1980	Sara Simeoni (Italy)	Urszula Kielan (Poland)	Jutta Kirst (East Germany)
1984	Ulrike Meyfarth (East Germany)	Sara Simeoni (Italy)	Joni Huntley (United States)
1988	Louise Ritter (United States)	Stefka Kostadinova (Bulgaria)	Tamara Bykova (Soviet Union)
1992	Heike Henkel (Germany)	Galina Astafei (Romania)	Ioamnet Quintero (Cuba)
1996	Stefka Kostadinova (Bulgaria)	Niki Bakogianni (Greece)	Inha Babakova (Ukraine)
2000	Yelena Yelesina (Russia)	Hestrie Cloete (South Africa)	Kajsa Bergqvist (Sweden)
2004	Yelena Slesarenko (Russia)	Hestrie Cloete (South Africa)	Viktoriya Styopina (Ukraine)
2008	Tia Hellebaut (Belgium)	Blanka Vlašić (Croatia)	Anna Chicherove (Russia)

Women's Pole Vault

Year	Gold	Silver	Bronze
2000	Stacy Dragila (United States)	Tatiana Grigorieva (Australia)	Vala Flosadóttir (Iceland)
2004	Yelena Isinbayeva (Russia)	Scetlana Feofanova (Russia)	Anna Rogowska (Poland)
2008	Yelena Isinbayeva (Russia)	Jennifer Stuczynski (United States)	Svetlana Feofanova (Russia)

Women's Triple Jump

Year	Gold	Silver	Bronze
1996	Inessa Kravets (Ukraine)	Inna Lasovkaya (Russia)	Šárka Kašpárková (Czech Republic)
2000	Tereza Marinova (Bulgaria)	Tatyana Lebedeva (Russia)	Olena Hovorova (Ukraine)
2004	Françoise Mbango Etone (Cameroon)	Hrysopiyi Devetzi (Greece)	Tatyana Lebedeva (Russia)
2008	Françoise Mbango Etone (Cameroon)	Tatyana Lebedeva (Russia)	Hrysopiyi Devetzi (Greece)

Women's Long Jump

Year	Gold	Silver	Bronze
1948	Olga Gyarmati (Hungary)	Noemí Simonetto de Portela (Argentina)	Ann-Britt Leyman (Sweden)
1952	Yvette Williams (New Zealand)	Aleksandra Chudina (Soviet Union)	Shirley Cawley (Great Britain)
1956	Elżbieta Krzesińska (Poland)	Willye White (United States)	Nadezhda Khnykina-Dvalishvili (Soviet Union)
1960	Vera Kolashnikova (Soviet Union)	Elżbieta Krzesińska (Poland)	Hildrun Claus (Germany)
1964	Mary Rand (Great Britain)	Irena Kirszenstein (Poland)	Tatyana Schelkonova (Soviet Union)
1968	Viorica Viscopoleanu (Romania)	Sheila Sherwood (Great Britain)	Tatyana Talysheva (Soviet Union)
1972	Heidi Rosendahl (Germany)	Diana Yorgova (Bulgaria)	Eva Šuranová (Czechoslovakia)
1976	Angela Voigt (East Germany)	Kathy McMillan (United States)	Lidiya Alfeyeva (Soviet Union)
1980	Tatyana Kolpakova (Soviet Union)	Brigitte Wujak (East Germany)	Tatyana Skachko (Soviet Union)
1984	Anişoara Cuşmir-Stanciu (Romania)	Vali Ionescu (Romania)	Sue Hearnshaw (Great Britain)
1988	Jackie Joyner-Kersee (United States)	Heike Daute-Drechsler (East Germany)	Galina Chistyakova (Soviet Union)
1992	Heike Drechsler (Germany)	Inessa Kravets (Unified Team)	Jackie Joyner-Kersee (United States)
1996	Chioma Ajunwa (Nigeria)	Fiona May (Italy)	Jackie Joyner-Kersee (United States)
2000	Heike Drechsler (Germany)	Fiona May (Italy)	Tatyana Kotova (Russia)
2004	Tatyana Lebedeva (Russia)	Irina Simagina (Russia)	Tatyana Kotova (Russia)
2008	Maurren Maggi (Brazil)	Tatyana Lebedeva (Russia)	Blessing Okagbare (Nigeria)

Women's Shot Put

Year	Gold	Silver	Bronze
1948	Micheline Ostermeyer (France)	Amelia Piccinini (Italy)	Ine Schäffer (Austria)
1952	Galina Zybina (Soviet Union)	Marianne Werner (Germany)	Klavdia Tochonova (Soviet Union)
1956	Tamara Tyshkevich (Soviet Union)	Galina Zybina (Soviet Union)	Marianne Werner (United Team of Germany)
1960	Tamara Press (Soviet Union)	Johanna Lüttge (United Team of Germany)	Earlene Brown (United States)
1964	Tamara Press (Soviet Union)	Renate Culmberger (United Team of Germany)	Galina Zybina (Soviet Union)

Year	Gold	Silver	Bronze
1968	Margitta Gummel (East Germany)	Marita Lange (East Germany)	Nadezhda Chizhova (Soviet Union)
1972	Nadezhda Chizhova (Soviet Union)	Matgitta Gummel (East Germany)	Ivanka Hristova (Bulgaria)
1976	Ivanka Hristova (Bulgaria)	Nadezhda Chizhova (Soviet Union)	Helena Fibingerová (Czechoslovakia)
1980	Ilona Schoknecht-Slupianek (East Germany)	Svetlana Krachevskaia (Soviet Union)	Margitta Droese-Pufe (East Germany)
1984	Claudia Losch (West Germany)	Mihaela Loghin (Romania)	Gael Martin (Australia)
1988	Natalya Lisovskaya (Soviet Union)	Kathrin Neimk (East Germany)	Li Meisu (China)
1992	Svetlana Krivelyova (Unified Team)	Huang Zhihong (China)	Kathrin Neimke (Germany)
1996	Astrid Kumbernuss (Germany)	Sui Xinmei (China)	Irina Khudoroshkina (Russia)
2000	Yanina Karolchik (Belarus)	Larisa Peleshenko (Russia)	Astrid Kumbernuss (Germany)
2004	Yumileidi Cumbá (Cuba)	Nadine Kleinert (Germany)	Svetlana Krivelyova (Russia)
2008	Valerie Vili (New Zealand)	Natallia Mikhnevich (Belarus)	Nadzeya Astapchuk (Belarus)

Women's Discus

Year	Gold	Silver	Bronze
1928	Halina Konopacka (Poland)	Lillian Copeland (United States)	Ruth Svedberg (Sweden)
1932	Lillian Copeland (United States)	Ruth Osborn (United States)	Jadwiga Wajs (Poland)
1936	Gisela Mauermayer (Germany)	Jadwiga Wajs (Poland)	Paula Mollenhauer (Germany)
1940–1944: Olympics not held			
1948	Micheline Ostermeyer (France)	Edera Cordiale (Italy)	Jacqueline Mazeas (France)
1952	Nina Romashkova (Soviet Union)	Elizaveta Bagryantseva (Soviet Union)	Nina Dumbadze (Soviet Union)
1956	Olga Fikotová (Czechoslovakia)	Irina Beglyakova (Soviet Union)	Nina Romashkova (Soviet Union)
1960	Nina Romashkova (Soviet Union)	Tamara Press (Soviet Union)	Lia Manoliu (Romania)
1964	Tamara Press (Soviet Union)	Ingrid Lotz (United Team of Germany)	Lia Manoliu (Romania)
1968	Lia Manoliu (Romania)	Liesel Westermann (West Germany)	Jolán Kleiber (Hungary)
1972	Faina Melnik (Soviet Union)	Argentina Menis (Romania)	Vasilka Stoeva (Bulgaria)
1976	Evelin Schlaak (East Germany)	Maria Vergova (Bulgaria)	Gabriele Hinzmann (East Germany)
1980	Evelin Jahl (East Germany)	Maria Vergova-Petkova (Bulgaria)	Tatyana Lesovaya (Soviet Union)
1984	Ria Stalman (Netherlands)	Leslie Deniz (United States)	Florenţa Crăciunescu (Romania)
1988	Martina Opitz-Hellmann (East Germany)	Diana Sachse-Gansky (East Germany)	Tsvetanka Khristova (Bulgaria)
1992	Maritza Martén (Cuba)	Tsvetanka Khristova (Bulgaria)	Daniela Costian (Australia)
1996	Ilke Wyludda (Germany)	Natalya Sadova (Russia)	Ellina Zvereva (Belarus)
2000	Ellina Zvereva (Belarus)	Anastasía Kelesídou (Greece)	Iryna Yatchenko (Belarus)
2004	Natalya Sadova (Russia)	Anastasía Kelesídou (Greece)	Iryna Yatchenko (Belarus)
2008	Stephanie Brown Trafton (United States)	Yarelis Barrios (Cuba)	Olena Antonova (Ukraine)

Women's Javelin

Year	Gold	Silver	Bronze
1932	Babe Didrikson (United States)	Ellen Braumüller (Germany)	Tilly Fleischer (Germany)
1936	Tilly Fleischer (Germany)	Luise Krüger (Germany)	Maria Kwaśniewska (Poland)
1940–1944: Olympics not held			
1948	Herma Bauma (Austria)	Kaisa Parviainen (Finland)	Lily Carlstedt (Denmark)
1952	Dana Zátopková (Czechoslovakia)	Aleksandra Chudina (Soviet Union)	Elena Gorchakova (Soviet Union)

Year	Gold	Silver	Bronze
1956	Inese Yaunzeme (Soviet Union)	Marlene Ahrens (Chile)	Nadezhda Konyaeva (Soviet Union)
1960	Elvīra Ozolina (Soviet Union)	Dana Zátopková (Czechoslovakia)	Birutė Kalėdienė (Soviet Union)
1964	Mihaela Peneş (Romania)	Márta Rudas (Hungary)	Elena Gorchakova (Soviet Union)
1968	Angéla Németh (Hungary)	Mihaela Peneş (Romania)	Eva Janko (Austria)
1972	Ruth Fuchs (East Germany)	Jacqueline Todten (East Germany)	Kate Schmidt (United States)
1976	Ruth Fuchs (East Germany)	Marion Becker (Germany)	Kate Schmidt (United States)
1980	Maria Colon (Cuba)	Saida Gunba (Soviet Union)	Ute Hommola (East Germany)
1984	Tessa Sanderson (Great Britain)	Tiina Lillak (Finland)	Fatima Whitbread (Great Britain)
1988	Petra Felke (East Germany)	Fatima Whitbread (Great Britain)	Beate Kock (East Germany)
1992	Silke Renk (Germany)	Natalya Shikolenko (Unified Team)	Karen Forkel (Germany)
1996	Heli Rantanen (Finland)	Louise McPaul (Australia)	Trine Hattestad (Norway)
2000	Trine Hattestad (Norway)	Mirela Manjani-Tzelili (Greece)	Osleidys Menéndez (Cuba)
2004	Osleidys Menéndez (Cuba)	Steffi Nerius (Germany)	Mirela Manjani (Greece)
2008	Barbora Špotáková (Czechoslovakia)	Mariya Abakumova (Russia)	Christina Obergföll (Germany)

Women's Hammer Throw

Year	Gold	Silver	Bronze
2000	Kamila Skolimowska (Poland)	Olga Kuzenkova (Russia)	Kirsten Münchow (Germany)
2004	Olga Kuzenkova (Russia)	Yipsi Moreno (Cuba)	Yunaika Crawford (Cuba)
2008	Aksana Miankova (Belarus)	Yipsi Moreno (Cuba)	Zhang Wenxiu (China)

Women's Heptathlon

Year	Gold	Silver	Bronze
1984	Glynis Nunn (Australia)	Jackie Joyner (United States)	Sabine Everts (West Germany)
1988	Jackie Joyner-Kersee (United States)	Sabine Everts (West Germany)	Anke Behmer (East Germany)
1992	Jackie Joyner-Kersee (United States)	Irina Belova (Unified Team)	Sabine Braun (Germany)
1996	Ghada Shouaa (Syria)	Natalya Sazanovich (Belarus)	Denise Lewis (Great Britain)
2000	Denise Lewis (Great Britain)	Yelena Prokhorova (Russia)	Natallia Sazanovich (Belarus)
2004	Carolina Klüft (Sweden)	Austra Skujytė (Lithuania)	Kelly Sotheryon (Great Britain)
2008	Nataliya Dobrynska (Ukraine)	Hyleas Fountain (United States)	Tatyana Chernova (Russia)

Women's 80-Meter Hurdles

Year	Gold	Silver	Bronze
1932	Babe Didrikson (United States)	Evelyne Hall (United States)	Marjorie Clark (South Africa)
1936	Trebisonda Valla (Italy)	Anni Steuer (Germany)	Betty Taylor (Canada)
1940–1944: Olympics not held			
1948	Fanny Blankers-Koen (Netherlands)	Maureen Gardner (Great Britain)	Shirley Strickland (Australia)
1952	Shirley Strickland de la Hunty (Australia)	Mariya Golubnichaya (Soviet Union)	Maria Sander (Germany)
1956	Shirley Strickland de la Hunty (Australia)	Gisela Köhler (United Team of Germany)	Norma Thrower (Australia)
1960	Irina Press (Soviet Union)	Carole Quinton (Great Britain)	Gisela Köhler-Birkemeyer (United Team of Germany)
1964	Karin Balzer (United Team of Germany)	Teresa Ciepły (Poland)	Pam Kilborn (Australia)
1968	Maureen Caird (Australia)	Pam Kilborn (Australia)	Chi Cheng (China)

Women's Pentathlon

Year	Gold	Silver	Bronze
1964	Irina Press (Soviet Union)	Mary Rand (Great Britain)	Galina Bystrova (Soviet Union)
1968	Ingrid Becker (West Germany)	Liese Prokop (Austria)	Annamária Tóth (Hungary)
1972	Mary Peters (Great Britain)	Heide Rosendahl (Germany)	Burglinde Pollak (East Germany)
1976	Siegrun Siegl (East Germany)	Christine Laser (East Germany)	Burglinde Pollak (East Germany)
1980	Nadezhda Tkachenko (Soviet Union)	Olga Rukavishnikova (Soviet Union)	Olga Kuragina (Soviet Union)

Women's 3,000-Meter

Year	Gold	Silver	Bronze
1984	Maricica Puică (Romania)	Wendy Sly (Great Britain)	Lynn Williams (Canada)
1988	Tetyana Samolenko (Soviet Union)	Paula Ivan (Romania)	Yvonne Murray (Great Britain)
1992	Yelena Romanova (Unified Team)	Tetyana Dorovskikh (Unified Team)	Angela Chalmers (Canada)

Women's 10,000-Meter Walk

Year	Gold	Silver	Bronze
1992	Chen Yueling (China)	Yelena Nikolayeva (Unified Team)	Li Chunxiu (China)
1996	Yelena Nikolayeva (Unified Team)	Elisabetta Perrone (Italy)	Wang Yan (China)

Women's 800-Meter Wheelchair

Year	Gold	Silver	Bronze
2004	Chantel Petitclerc (Canada)	Eliza Stanovich (Australia)	Louise Sauvage (Australia)

Men's 10-Mile Walk

Year	Gold	Silver	Bronze
1908	George Edward Larner (Great Britain)	Ernest Webb (Great Britain)	Edward Adams Spencer (Great Britain)

Men's 6.4-Kilogram Stone Throw

Year	Gold	Silver	Bronze
1906	Nikolaos Georgantas (Greece)	Martin Sheridan (United States)	Mikhail Dorizas (Greece)

Badminton

Men's Singles

Year	Gold	Silver	Bronze
1992	Alan Budikusuma (Indonesia)	Ardy Wiranata (Indonesia)	Thomas Stuer-Lauridsen (Denmark) Hermawan Susanto (Indonesia)
1996	Poul-Erik Høyer Larsen (Denmark)	Dong Jiong (China)	Rashid Sidek (Malaysia)
2000	Ji Xinpeng (China)	Hendrawan (Indonesia)	Xia Xuanze (China)
2004	Taufik Hidayat (Indonesia)	Shon Seung-Mo (South Korea)	Sony Dwi Kuncoro (Indonesia)
2008	Lin Dan (China)	Lee Chong Wei (Malaysia)	Chen Jin (China)

Women's Singles

Year	Gold	Silver	Bronze
1992	Susi Susanti (Indonesia)	Bang Soo-Hyun (South Korea)	Huang Hua (China) Tang Jiuhong (China)
1996	Bang Soo-Hyun (South Korea)	Mia Audina (Indonesia)	Susi Susanti (Indonesia)
2000	Gong Zhichao (China)	Camilla Martin (Denmark)	Ye Zhaoying (China)
2004	Zhang Ning (China)	Mia Audina (Netherlands)	Zhou Mi (China)
2008	Zhang Ning (China)	Xie Xingfang (China)	Maria Kristin Yulianti (Indonesia)

Men's Doubles

Year	Gold	Silver	Bronze
1992	Kim Moon-Soo, Park Joo-Bong (South Korea)	Eddy Hartano, Rudy Gunawan (Indonesia)	Li Yongbo, Tian Bingyi (China) Razif Sidek, Jalani Sidek (Malaysia)
1996	Ricky Subagja, Rexy Mainaka (Indonesia)	Cheah Soon Kit, Yap Kim Hock (Malaysia)	Denny Kantano, Antonius Ariantho (Indonesia) Qun Yiyuan, Liu Jianjun (China)
2000	Tony Gunawan, Candra Wijaya (China)	Lee Dong-Soo, Yoo Yong-Sung (South Korea)	Ha Tae-Kwon, Kim Dong-Moon (South Korea)
2004	Kim Dong-Moon, Ha Yae-Kwon (South Korea)	Lee Dong-Soo, Yoo Yong-Sung (South Korea)	Eng Hian, Flandy Limpele (Indonesia)
2008	Markis Kido, Hendra Setiawan (Indonesia)	Cai Yun, Fu Haifeng (China)	Lee Jae-Jin, Hwang Ji-Man (South Korea)

Women's Doubles

Year	Gold	Silver	Bronze
1992	Hwang Hye-Young, Chung So-Young (South Korea)	Guan Weizhen, Nong Qunhua (China)	Gil Young-ah, Lin Yan Fen (China)
1996	Ge Fei, Gu Jun (China)	Gil Young-Ah, Jang Hye-Ock (South Korea)	Qun Yiyuan, Tang Yongshu (China)
2000	Ge Fei, Gu Jun (China)	Huang Nanyan, Yang Wei (China)	Gao Ling, Qin Yiyuan (China)
2004	Zhang Jiewen, Yang Wei (China)	Huang Sui, Gao Ling (China)	Ra Kyung-Min, Lee Kyung-Won (South Korea)
2008	Du Jing, Yu Yang (China)	Lee Kyung-Won, Lee Hyo-Jung (South Korea)	Zhang Yawen, Wei Yili (China)

Mixed Doubles

Year	Gold	Silver	Bronze
1996	Kim Dong-Moon, Gil Young-Ah (South Korea)	Park Joo-Bong, Ra Kyung-Min (South Korea)	Liu Jianjun, Sun Man (China)
2000	Zhang Jun, Gao Ling (China)	Tri Kusharyanto, Minarti Timur (Indonesia)	Simon Archer, Joanne Goode (Great Britain)
2004	Zhang Jun, Gao Ling (China)	Nathan Robertson, Gail Emms (Great Britain)	Jens Eriksen, Mette Schjoldager (Denmark)
2008	Lee Yong-Dae, Lee Hyo-Jung (South Korea)	Nova Widianto, Lilyana Natsir (Indonesia)	He Hanbin, Yu Yang (China)

Baseball

Men's Baseball

Year	Gold	Silver	Bronze
1992	Omar Ajete, Rolando Arrojo, José Raúl Delgado Diez, Giorge Diaz Loren, Osvaldo Fernández, José Estrada González, Lourdes Gourriel, Orlando Hernández, Alberto Hernández, Orestes Kindelán, Omar Linares, Germán Mesa, Víctor Mesa, Antonio Pacheco, Juan Padilla, Luis Ulacia, Ermidelio Urrutia, Jorge Luis Valdés, Lázaro Vargas (Cuba)	Chang Cheng-Hsien, Chang Wen-Chung, Chang Yaw-Teing, Chen Chi-Hsin, Chen Wei-Chen, Chiang Tai-Chuan, Huang Chung-Yi, Huang Wen-Po, Jong Yeu-Jeng, Ku Kuo-Chian, Kuo Lee Chien-Fu, Liao Ming-Hsiung, Lin Chao-Huang, Lin Kun-Han, Lo Chen-Jung, Lo Kuo-Chong, Pai Kun-Hong, Tsai Ming-Hung, Wang Kuang-Shih, Wu Shih-Hsih (Taiwan)	Tomohito Ito, Shinichiro Kawabata, Masahito Kohiyama, Hirotami Kojima, Hiroki Kokubo, Takashi Miwa, Hiroshi Nakamoto, Masafumi Nishi, Kazutaka Nishiyama, Koichi Oshima, Hiroyuki Sakaguchi, Shinichi Sato, Yasuhiro Sato, Masanori Sugiura, Kento Sugiyama, Yasunori Takami, Akihiro Togo, Koji Tokunaga, Shigeki Wakabayashi, Katsumi Watanabe (Japan)
1996	Omar Ajete, Miguel Caldés Luis, José Contreras, Jorge Fumero, José Estrada González, Alberto Hernández, Rey Isaac, Orestes Kindelán, Pedro Luis Lazo, Omar Linares, Omar Luis, Juan Manrique, Eliecer Montes de Oca, Antonio Pacheco, Juan Padilla, Eduardo Paret, Ormari Romero, Antonio Scull, Luis Ulacia, Lázaro Vargas (Cuba)	Kosuke Fukudome, Tadahito Iguchi, Makoto Imaoka, Takeo Kawamura, Jutaro Kimura, Takashi Kurosu, Takao Kuwamoto, Nobuhiko Matsunaka, Koichi Misawa, Masahiko Mori, Masao Morinaka, Daishin Nakamura, Masahiro Nojima, Hideaki Okubo, Hitoshi Ono, Yasuyuki Saigo, Tomoaki Sato, Masanori Sugiura, Takayuki Takabayashi, Yoshitomo Tani (Japan)	Chad Allen, Kris Benson, R. A. Dickey, Troy Glaus, Chad Green, Seth Greisinger, Kip Harkrider, A. J. Hinch, Jacque Jones, Billy Koch, Mark Kotsay, Matt Lecroy, Travis Lee, Braden Looper, Brian Loyd, Warren Morris, Augie Ojeda, Jim Parque, Jeff Weaver, Jason Williams (United States)
2000	Brent Abernathy, Kurt Ainsworth, Pat Borders, Sean Burroughs, John Cotton, Travis Dawkins, Adam Everett, Ryan Franklin, Chris George, Shane Heams, Marcus Jensen, Mike Kinkade, Rick Krivda, Doug Mientkiewicz, Mike Neill, Roy Oswalt, Jon Rauch, Anthony Sanders, Bobby Seay, Ben Sheets, Brad Wilkerson, Todd Williams, Ernie Young, Tim Young (United States)	Omar Ajete, Yovany Aragon, Miguel Caldés, Danel Castro, José Contreras, Yobal Dueñas, Yasser Gómez, José Ibar, Orestes Kindelán, Pedro Luis Lazo, Omar Linares, Oscar Macías, Juan Manrique, Javier Méndez, Rolando Meriño, Germán Mesa, Antonio Pacheco, Ariel Pestano, Gabriel Pierre, Maels Rodríguez, Antonio Scull, Luis Ulacia, Lázaro Valle, Norge Luis Vera (Cuba)	Chang Song-Ho, Chong Tae-Hyon, Chung Min-Tae, Chung Soo-Keun, Hong Sung-Heon, Jang Sung-Ho, Jin Pil-jung, Kim Dong-Joo, Kim Han-Soo, Kim Ki-Tae, Kim Soo-Kyung, Kim Tae-Gyun, Koo Dae-Sung, Lee Byung-Kyu, Lee Seung-Ho, Lee Seung-Yeop, Lim Chang-Yong, Lim Sun-Dong, Park Jae-Hong, Park Jin-Man, Park Jong-Ho, Park Kyung-Oan, Park Seok-Jin, Son Min-Han, Song Jin-Woo (South Korea)
2004	Danny Betancourt, Luis Borroto, Frederich Cepeda, Yorelvis Charles, Michel Enríquez, Norberto González, Yulieski Gourriel, Pedro Luis Lazo, Roger Machado, Jonder Martínez, Frank Montieth, Vicyohandri Odelín, Adiel Palma, Eduardo Paret, Ariel Pestano, Alexei Ramírez, Eriel Sánchez, Antonio Scull, Carlos Tabares, Yoandri Urgelles, Osmani Urrutia, Manuel Vega, Norge Luis Vera (Cuba)	Craig Anderson, Thomas Brice, Adrian Burnside, Gavin Fingleson, Paul Gonzalez, Nick Kimpton, Brendan Kingman, Craig Lewis, Graeme Lloyd, Dave Nilsson, Trent Oeltjen, Wayne Ough, Chris Oxspring, Brett Roneberg, Ryan Rowland Smith, John Stephens, Phil Stockman, Brett Tamburrino, Richard Thompson, Andrew Utting, Rodney Van Buizen, Ben Wigmore, Glenn Williams, Jeff Williams (Australia)	Ryoji Aikawa, Yuya Ando, Atsushi Fujimoto, Kosuke Fukudome, Hirotoshi Ishii, Hisashi Iwakuma, Hitoki Iwase, Kenji Johjima, Makoto Kaneko, Takuya Kimura, Masahide Kobayashi, Hiroki Kuroda, Daisuke Matsuzaka, Daisuke Miura, Shinya Miyamoto, Arihito Muramatsu, Norihiro Nakamura, Michihiro Ogasawara, Naoyuki Shimizu, Yoshinobu Takahashi, Yoshitomo Tani, Koji Uehara, Kazuhiro Wada, Tsuyoshi Wada (Japan)

Year	Gold	Silver	Bronze
2008	Bong Jung-Keun, Chong Tae-Hyon, Han Ki-Joo, Jang Won-Sam, Jeong Keun-Woo, Jin Kab-Yong, Kang Min-Ho, Kim Dong-Joo, Kim Hyun-Soo, Kim Kwang-Hyun, Kim Min-Ho, Kim Min-Jae, Ko Young-Min, Kwon Hyuk, Lee Dae-Ho, Lee Jin-Young, Lee Jong-Wook, Lee Seung-Yeop, Lee Taek-Keun, Lee Yong-Kyu, Oh Seung-Hwan, Ryu Hyun-Jin, Song Seung-Jun, Yoon Suk-MinSouth (South Korea)	Alexei Bell, Frederich Cepeda, Alfredo Despaigne, Giorvis Duvergel, Michel Enríquez, Norberto González, Yulieski Gourriel, Miguel Lahera, Pedro Luis Lazo, Jonder Martínez, Alexander Mayeta, Rolando Meriño, Vicyohandri Odelín, Adiel Palma, Eduardo Paret, Yadier Pedroso, Ariel Pestano, Luis Rodríguez, Elier Sánchez, Eriel Sánchez, Yoandry Urgellés, Norge Luis Vera (Cuba)	Brett Anderson, Jake Arrieta, Brian Barden, Matt Brown, Trevor Cahill, Jeremy Cummings, Jason Donald, Brian Duensing, Dexter Fowler, John Gall, Mike Hessman, Kevin Jepsen, Brandon Knight, Michael Koplove, Matt LaPorta, Lou Marson, Blaine Neal, Jayson Nix, Nate Schierholtz, Jeff Stevens, Stephen Strasburg, Taylor Teagarden, Terry Tiffee, Casey Weathers (United States)

Basketball

Men's Basketball

Year	Gold	Silver	Bronze
1936	Sam Balter, Ralph Bishop, Joe Fortenberry, Tex Gibbons, Francis Johnson, Carl Knowles, Frank Lubin, Art Mollner, Donald Piper, Jack Ragland, Willard Schmidt, Carl Shy, Duane Swanson, Bill Wheatley (United States)	Gordon Aitchison, Ian Allison, Art Chapman, Chuck Chapman, Edward Dawson, Irving Meretsky, Doug Peden, James Stewart, Malcolm Wiseman (Canada)	Carlos Borja, Víctor Borja, Rodolfo Choperena, Luis de la Vega, Raúl Fernández, Andrés Gómez, Silvio Hernández, Francisco Martínez, Jesús Olmos, José Pamplona, Greer Skousen (Mexico)
1940–1944: Olympics not held			
1948	Cliff Barker, Don Barksdale, Ralph Beard, Lew Beck, Vince Boryla, Gordon Carpenter, Alex Groza, Wah Wah Jones, Bob Kurland, Ray Lumpp, Robert Pitts, Jesse Renick, Jackie Robinson, Kenny Rollins (United States)	André Barrais, Michel Bonnevie, André Buffière, René Chocat, René Dérency, Maurice Desaymonnet, André Even, Maurice Girardot, Fernand Guillou, Raymond Offner, Jacques Perrier, Yvan Quénin, Lucien Rebuffic, Pierre Thiolon (France)	Algodão Bráz, Ruy de Freitas, Marcus Vinícius Dias, Affonso Évora, Alexandre Gemignani, Alfredo da Motta, Alberto Marson, Nilton Pacheco, Massinet Sorcinelli (Brazil)
1952	Ron Bontemps, Marc Freiberger, Wayne Glasgow, Charlie Hoag, Bill Hougland, John Keller, Dean Kelley, Bob Kenney, Bob Kurland, Bill Lienhard, Clyde Lovellette, Frank McCabe, Dan Pippin, Howie Williams (United States)	Stepas Butautas, Nodar Dzhordzhi-kiya, Anatoly Konev, Otar Korkiya, Heino Kruus, Ilmar Kullam, Justinas Lagunavičius, Joann Lõssov, Aleksandr Moiseyev, Yuri Ozerov, Kazys Petkevičius, Stasys Stonkus, Maigonis Valdmanis, Viktor Vlasov (Soviet Union)	Martín Acosta y Lara, Enrique Baliño, Victorio Cieslinskas, Héctor Costa, Nelson Demarco, Héctor García Otero, Tabaré Larre Borges, Adesio Lombardo, Roberto Lovera, Sergio Matto, Wilfredo Peláez, Carlos Roselló (Uruguay)
1956	K. C. Jones, Burdette Haldorson, Carl Cain, Gilbert Ford, Richard Boushka, James Walsh, Charles Darling, William Evans, Bill Hougland, Robert Jeangerard, Bill Russell, Ronald Tomsic (United States)	Arkadi Bochkaryov, Maigonis Valdmanis, Viktor Zubkov, Jānis Krūmiņš, Algirdas Lauritėnas, Valdis Muižnieks, Yuri Ozerov, Kazys Petkevičius, Michail Semyonov, Stasys Stonkus, Michail Studenezki, Vladimir Torban (Soviet Union)	Carlos Blixen, Ramiro Cortes, Héctor Costa, Nelson Chelle, Nelson Demarco, Héctor García, Carlos Gonzáles, Sergio Matto, Oscar Moglia, Raúl Mera, Ariel Olascoaga, Milton Scarón (Uruguay)

Year	Gold	Silver	Bronze
1960	Jay Arnette, Walt Bellamy, Bob Boozer, Terry Dischinger, Burdette Haldorson, Darrall Imhoff, Allen Kelley, Lester Lane, Jerry Lucas, Oscar Robertson, Adrian Smith, Jerry West (United States)	Yury Komeyev, Jānis Krūmiņš, Guram Minaschvili, Valdis Muižnieks, Cesars Ozers, Aleksandr Petrov, Mikhail Semyonov, Vladimir Ugrekelidze, Maigonis Valdmanis, Albert Valtin, Gennadi Volnov, Viktor Zubkov (Soviet Union)	Edson Bispo dos Santos, Moyses Blas, Waldemar Blatkauskas, Algodão Carmo de Souza, Carlos Domingos Massoni, Waldyr Geraldo Boccardo, Wlamir Marques, Amaury Antônio Pasos, Fernando Pereira de Freitas, Antonio Salvador Sucar, Jatyr Eduardo Schall (Brazil)
1964	Jim Barnes, Bill Bradley, Larry Brown, Joe Caldwell, Mel Counts, Dick Davies, Walt Hazzard, Lucious Jackson, John McCaffrey, Jeff Mullins, Jerome Shipp, George Wilson (United States)	Armenak Alachachian, Nikolai Bagley, Vyacheslav Chrynin, Juris Kalnins, Yury Korneyev, Jānis Krūmiņš, Jaak Lipso, Levan Mosechvili, Valdis Muižnieks, Aleksandr Petrov, Aleksandr Travin, Gennadi Volnov (Soviet Union)	Edson Bispo dos Santos, Friedrich Wilhelm Braun, Carmo de Souza, Carlos Domingos Massoni, Wlamir Marques, Victor Mirshawka, Amaury Antônio Pasos, Ubiratan Pereira Maciel, Antonio Salvador Sucar, Jatyr Eduardo Schall, José Edvar Simoes, Sergio de Toledo Machado (Brazil)
1968	Michael Barrett, John Clawson, Donald Dee, Calvin Fowler, Spencer Haywood, Bill Hosket, Jim King, Glynn Saulters, Charles Scott, Michael Silliman, Kenneth Spain, Joseph White (United States)	Dragutin Čermak, Krešimir Ćosić, Vladimir Cvetković, Ivo Daneu, Radivoj Korać, Trajko Rajković, Zoran Maroević, Dragoslav Ražnatović, Petar Skansi, Damir Solman, Nikola Plećaš, Aljoša Zorga (Yugoslavia)	Anatoli Polivoda, Anatoli Krikun, Vadim Kapranov, Vladimir Andreev, Sergei Kovalenko, Modestas Paulauskas, Jaak Lipso, Gennadi Volnov, Priit Tomson, Zurab Sakandelidze, Yury Selichov, Sergei Belov (Soviet Union)
1972	Anatoli Polivoda, Modestas Paulauskas, Zurab Sakandelidze, Alzhan Zharmukhamedov, Aleksandr Boloshev, Ivan Edeshko, Sergei Belov, Mikheil Korkiya, Ivan Dvorny, Gennadi Volnov, Alexander Belov, Sergei Kovalenko (Soviet Union)	Kenneth Davis, Doug Collins, Tom Henderson, Mike Bantom, Robert Jones, Dwight Jones, James Forbes, Jim Brewer, Tom Burleson, Tom McMillen, Kevin Joyce, Ed Ratleff (United States)	Juan Domecq, Ruperto Herrera, Juan Roca, Pedro Chappé, José Miguel Alvarez Pozo, Rafael Canizares, Conrado Perez, Miguel Calderon, Tomas Herrera, Oscar Varona, Alejandro Urgelles, Franklin Standard (Cuba)
1976	Phil Ford, Steve Sheppard, Adrian Dantley, Walter Davis, Quinn Buckner, Ernie Grunfeld, Kenneth Carr, Scott May, Tate Armstrong, Tom LaGarde, Phil Hubbard, Mitch Kupchak (United States)	Blagoje Georgievski, Dragan Kićanović, Vinko Jelovac, Rajko Žižić, Željko Jerkov, Andro Knego, Zoran Slavnić, Krešimir Ćosić, Damir Šolman, Žarko Varajić, Dražen Dalipagić, Mirza Delibašić (Yugoslavia)	Vladimir Arsamaskov, Aleksandr Salnikov, Valeri Miloserdov, Alzhan Zharmukhamedov, Andrei Makeyev, Ivan Edeshko, Sergei Belov, Vladimir Tkachenko, Anatoli Myshkin, Mikheil Korkiya, Alexander Belov, Vladimir Zhigily (Soviet Union)
1980	Andro Knego, Dragan Kićanović, Rajko Žižić, Mihovil Nakić, Željko Jerkov, Branko Skroče, Zoran Slavnić, Krešimir Ćosić, Ratko Radovanović, Duje Krstulović, Dražen Dalipagić, Mirza Delibašić (Yugoslavia)	Romeo Sacchetti, Roberto Brunamonti, Michael Silvester, Enrico Gilardi, Fabrizio Della Fiori, Marco Solfrini, Marco Bonamico, Dino Meneghin, Renato Villalta, Renzo Vecchiato, Pierluigi Marzorati, Pietro Generali (Italy)	Stanislav Eremin, Valeri Miloserdov, Sergei Tarakanov, Aleksandr Salnikov, Andrei Lopatov, Nikolai Derugin, Sergei Belov, Vladimir Tkachenko, Anatoli Myshkin, Sergėjus Jovaiša, Alexander Belostenny, Vladimir Zhigily (Soviet Union)

Year	Gold	Silver	Bronze
1984	Steve Alford, Leon Wood, Patrick Ewing, Vern Fleming, Alvin Robertson, Michael Jordan, Joe Kleine, Jon Koncak, Wayman Tisdale, Chris Mullin, Sam Perkins, Jeffrey Turner (United States)	José Manuel Beirán, José Luis Llorente, Fernando Arcega, Josep Maria Margall, Andrés Jiménez, Fernando Romay, Fernando Martín Espina, Juan Antonio Corbalán, Ignacio Solozábal, Juan Domingo de la Cruz, Juan Manuel López Iturriaga, Juan Antonio San Epifanio (Spain)	Dražen Petrović, Aleksandar Petrović, Nebojša Zorkić, Rajko Žižić, Ivan Sunara, Emir Mutapčić, Sabit Hadžić, Andro Knego, Ratko Radovanović, Mihovil Nakić-Vojnović, Dražen Dalipagić, Branko Vukićević (Yugoslavia)
1988	Aleksandr Volkov, Tiit Sokk, Sergei Tarakanov, Šarūnas Marčiulionis, Igors Miglinieks, Valerij Tichonenko, Rimas Kurtinaitis, Arvydas Sabonis, Viktor Pankrashkin, Valdemaras Chomičius, Alexander Belostenny, Valery Goborov (Soviet Union)	Dražen Petrović, Zdravko Radulović, Zoran Čutura, Toni Kukoč, Žarko Paspalj, Željko Obradović, Jure Zdovc, Stojko Vranković, Vlade Divac, Franjo Arapović, Dino Rađa, Danko Cvjetičanin (Yugoslavia)	Mitch Richmond, Charles E. Smith, Charles D. Smith, Bimbo Coles, Jeff Grayer, Willie Anderson, Stacey Augmon, Dan Majerle, Danny Manning, J. R. Reid, David Robinson, Hersey Hawkins (United States)
1992	Charles Barkley, Larry Bird, Clyde Drexler, Patrick Ewing, Magic Johnson, Michael Jordan, Christian Laettner, Karl Malone, Chris Mullin, Scottie Pippen, David Robinson, John Stockton (United States)	Vladan Alanović, Franjo Arapović, Danko Cvjetičanin, Alan Gregov, Arijan Komazec, Toni Kukoč, Aramis Naglić, Velimir Perasović, Dražen Petrović, Dino Rađa, Žan Tabak, Stojko Vranković (Croatia)	Romanas Brazdauskis, Valdemaras Chomičius, Darius Dimavičius, Gintaras Einikis, Sergėjus Jovaiša, Artūras Karnišovas, Gintaras Krapikas, Rimas Kurtinaitis, Šarūnas Marčiulionis, Alvydas Pazdrazdis, Arvydas Sabonis, Arūnas Visockas (Lithuania)
1996	Charles Barkley, Grant Hill, Anfernee Hardaway, David Robinson, Scottie Pippen, Mitch Richmond, Reggie Miller, Karl Malone, John Stockton, Shaquille O'Neal, Gary Payton, Hakeem Olajuwon (United States)	Miroslav Berić, Dejan Bodiroga, Predrag Danilović, Vlade Divac, Aleksandar Đorđević, Nikola Lončar, Saša Obradović, Žarko Paspalj, Željko Rebrača, Zoran Savić, Dejan Tomašević, Milenko Topić (Yugoslavia)	Gintaras Einikis, Andrius Jurkūnas, Artūras Karnišovas, Rimas Kurtinaitis, Darius Lukminas, Šarūnas Marčiulionis, Tomas Pačėsas, Arvydas Sabonis, Saulius Štombergas, Rytis Vaišvila, Eurelijus Žukauskas, Mindaugas Žukauskas (Lithuania)
2000	Shareef Abdur-Rahim, Ray Allen, Vin Baker, Vince Carter, Kevin Garnett, Tim Hardaway, Allan Houston, Jason Kidd, Antonio McDyess, Alonzo Mourning, Gary Payton, Steve Smith (United States)	Jim Bilba, Yann Bonato, Makan Dioumassi, Laurent Foirest, Thierry Gadou, Cyril Julian, Crawford Palmer, Antoine Rigaudeau, Stéphane Risacher, Laurent Sciarra, Moustapha Sonko, Frédéric Weis (France)	Dainius Adomaitis, Gintaras Einikis, Andrius Giedraitis, Šarūnas Jasikevičius, Kęstutis Marčiulionis, Darius Maskoliūnas, Tomas Masiulis, Ramūnas Šiškauskas, Darius Songaila, Saulius Štombergas, Mindaugas Timinskas, Eurelijus Žukauskas (Lithuania)
2004	Carlos Delfino, Gabriel Fernández, Emanuel Ginóbili, Leonardo Gutiérrez, Wálter Herrmann, Alejandro Montecchia, Andrés Nocioni, Fabricio Oberto, Pepe Sánchez, Luis Scola, Hugo Sconochini, Rubén Wolkowyski (Argentina)	Gianluca Basile, Massimo Bulleri, Roberto Chiacig, Giacomo Galanda, Luca Garri, Denis Marconato, Michele Mian, Gianmarco Pozzecco, Nikola Radulović, Alex Righetti, Rodolfo Rombaldoni, Matteo Soragna (Italy)	Carmelo Anthony, Carlos Boozer, Tim Duncan, Allen Iverson, LeBron James, Richard Jefferson, Stephon Marbury, Shawn Marion, Lamar Odom, Emeka Okafor, Amar'e Stoudemire, Dwyane Wade (United States)

Year	Gold	Silver	Bronze
2008	Carlos Boozer, Jason Kidd, LeBron James, Deron Williams, Michael Redd, Dwyane Wade, Kobe Bryant, Dwight Howard, Chris Bosh, Chris Paul, Tayshaun Prince, Carmelo Anthony (United States)	Pau Gasol, Rudy Fernández, Ricky Rubio, Juan Carlos Navarro, José Calderón, Felipe Reyes, Carlos Jiménez, Raül López, Berni Rodríguez, Marc Gasol, Álex Mumbrú, Jorge Garbajosa (Spain)	Carlos Delfino, Manu Ginóbili, Román González, Leonardo Gutiérrez, Juan Pedro Gutiérrez, Federico Kammerichs, Andrés Nocioni, Fabricio Oberto, Antonio Porta, Pablo Prigioni, Paolo Quinteros, Luis Scola (Argentina)

Women's Basketball

Year	Gold	Silver	Bronze
1976	Olga Barysheva, Tamara Daunienė, Natalya Klimova, Tatyana Ovechkina, Angelė Rupšienė, Nadezhda Shuvayeva, Nadezhda Zakharova, Uljana Semjonova, Raisa Kurvyakova, Nelli Feryabnikova, Olga Sukharnova, Tatiana Zakharova-Nadirova (Soviet Union)	Cindy Brogdon, Susan Rojcewicz, Ann Meyers, Lusia Harris, Nancy Dunkle, Charlotte Lewis, Nancy Lieberman, Gail Marquis, Patricia Roberts, Mary Anne O'Connor, Patricia Head, Julienne Simpson (United States)	Krasimira Bogdanova, Diana Dilova, Krasimira Gyurova, Penka Metodieva, Snezhana Mikhaylova, Girgina Skerlatova, Mariya Stoyanova, Margarita Shtarkelova, Petkana Makaveeva, Nadka Golcheva, Penka Stoyanova, Todorka Yordanova (Bulgaria)
1980	Olga Barysheva, Tatyana Ivinskaya, Nelli Feryabnikova, Vida Beselienė, Tatyana Ovechkina, Angelė Rupšienė, Lyubov Sharmay, Uljana Semjonova, Tatiana Zakharova-Nadirova, Olga Sukharnova, Nadezhda Shuvayeva, Lyudmila Rogozhina (Soviet Union)	Krasimira Bogdanova, Vanya Dermendzhieva, Silviya Germanova, Petkana Makaveeva, Nadka Golcheva, Penka Stoyanova, Evladiya Slavcheva, Kostadinka Radkova, Snezhana Mikhaylova, Angelina Mikhaylova, Penka Metodieva, Diana Dilova (Bulgaria)	Vera Djurašković, Mersada Bečirspahić, Jelica Komnenović, Mira Bjedov, Vukica Mitić, Sanja Ožegović, Sofija Pekić, Marija Tonković, Zorica Djurković, Vesna Despotović, Biljana Majstorović, Jasmina Perazić (Yugoslavia)
1984	Teresa Edwards, Lea Henry, Lynette Woodard, Anne Donovan, Cathy Boswell, Cheryl Miller, Janice Lawrence, Cindy Noble, Kim Mulkey, Denise Curry, Pamela McGee, Carol Menken-Schaudt (United States)	Aei-Young Choi, Eun-Sook Kim, Hyung-Sook Lee, Kyung-Hee Choi, Mi-Ja Lee, Kyung-Ja Moon, Hwa-Soon Kim, Myung-Hee Jeong, Young-Hee Kim, Jung-A Sung, Chan-Sook Park (South Korea)	Chen Yuefang, Li Xiaoqin, Ba Yan, Song Xiaobo, Qui Chen, Wang Jun, Xiu Lijuan, Zheng Haixia, Cong Xuedi, Zhang Hui, Liu Qing, Zhang Yueqin (China)
1988	Teresa Edwards, Kamie Ethridge, Cynthia Brown, Anne Donovan, Teresa Weatherspoon, Bridgette Gordon, Vicky Bullett, Andrea Lloyd, Katrina McClain, Jennifer Gillom, Cynthia Cooper, Suzanne McConnell (United States)	Stojna Vangelovska, Mara Lakić, Zana Lelas, Eleonora Wild, Kornelija Kvesić, Danira Nakić, Slađana Golić, Polona Dornik, Razija Mujanović, Vesna Bajkuša, Andjelija Arbutina, Bojana Milošević (Yugoslavia)	Olga Buryakina, Yelena Khudashova, Vitalija Tuomaitė, Olga Yakovleva, Galina Savitskaya, Aleksandra Leonova, Olga Yevkova, Irina Sumnikova, Irina Minkh, Irina Gerlits, Olesya Barel, Natalya Zasulskaya (Soviet Union)
1992	Elen Bunatyants, Irina Sumnikova, Marina Tkachenko, Irina Minkh, Irina Gerlits, Svetlana Zaboluyeva, Natalya Zasulskaya, Yelena Zhirko, Yelena Tornikidu, Yelena Shvaybovich, Yelena Khudashova, Yelena Baranova (Unified Team)	Cong Xuedi, He Jun, Li Dongmei, Li Xin, Liu Jun, Liu Qing, Peng Ping, Wang Fang, Zhan Shuping, Zheng Dongmei, Zheng Haixia (China)	Vicky Bullett, Daedra Charles, Cynthia Cooper, Clarissa Davis, Medina Dixon, Teresa Edwards, Tammy Jackson, Carolyn Jones, Katrina McClain, Suzanne McConnell, Vickie Orr, Teresa Weatherspoon (United States)

Year	Gold	Silver	Bronze
1996	Jennifer Azzi, Ruthie Bolton, Teresa Edwards, Venus Lacy, Lisa Leslie, Rebecca Lobo, Katrina McClain, Nikki McCray, Carla McGhee, Dawn Staley, Katy Steding, Sheryl Swoopes (United States)	Roseli Gustavo, Marta Sobral, Silvia Andrea Santos Luz, Alessandra Oliveira, Cintia Santos, Claudia Maria Pastor, Hortência Adriana Santos, Maria Angelica, Janeth Arcain, Maria Paula Gonçalves da Silva, Leila Sobral (Brazil)	Robyn Maher, Rachael Sporn, Michele Timms, Michelle Brogan, Trisha Fallon, Allison Cook, Carla Boyd, Sandy Brondello, Shelley Sandie, Fiona Robinson, Michelle Chandler (Australia)
2000	Teresa Edwards, Yolanda Griffith, Chamique Holdsclaw, Ruthie Bolton, Lisa Leslie, Nikki McCray, DeLisha Milton-Jones, Katie Smith, Dawn Staley, Sheryl Swoopes, Natalie Williams, Kara Wolters (United States)	Carla Boyd, Sandy Brondello, Trisha Fallon, Michelle Griffiths, Kristi Harrower, Jo Hill, Lauren Jackson, Annie La Fleur, Shelley Sandie, Rachael Sporn, Michele Timms, Jennifer Whittle (Australia)	Janeth Arcain, Ilisaine David, Lilian Concalves, Helen Luz Silvinha, Cláudia das Neves, Alessandra Oliveira, Adriana Moisés Pinto, Adriana Santos, Cintia Santos, Kelly Santos, Marta Sobral (Brazil)
2004	Sue Bird, Swin Cash, Tamika Catchings, Yolanda Griffith, Shannon Johnson, Lisa Leslie, Ruth Riley, Katie Smith, Dawn Staley, Sheryl Swoopes, Diana Taurasi, Tina Thompson (United States)	Suzy Batkovic, Sandy Brondello, Trisha Fallon, Kristi Harrower, Lauren Jackson, Natalie Porter, Alicia Poto, Belinda Snell, Rachael Sporn, Laura Summerton, Penny Taylor, Allison Tranquilli (Australia)	Anna Arkhipova, Olga Arteshina, Yelena Baranova, Diana Goustilina, Maria Kalmykova, Elena Karpova, Ilona Korstin, Irina Osipova, Oxana Rakhmatulina, Tatiana Shchegoleva, Maria Stepanova, Natalia Vodopyanova (Russia)
2008	Seimone Augustus, Sue Bird, Tamika Catchings, Sylvia Fowles, Kara Lawson, Lisa Leslie, DeLisha Milton-Jones, Candace Parker, Cappie Pondexter, Katie Smith, Diana Taurasi, Tina Thompson (United States)	Erin Phillips, Tully Bevilaqua, Jennifer Screen, Penny Taylor, Suzy Batkovic, Hollie Grima, Kristi Harrower, Laura Summerton, Belinda Snell, Emma Randall, Rohanee Cox, Lauren Jackson (Australia)	Marina Kuzina, Oxana Rakhmatulina, Natalia Vodopyanova, Becky Hammon, Marina Karpunina, Tatiana Shchegoleva, Ilona Korstin, Maria Stepanova, Yekaterina Lisina, Irina Sokolovskaya, Svetlana Abrosimova, Irina Osipova (Russia)

Basque Pelota

Men's Cesta Punta

Year	Gold	Silver	Bronze
1900	José de Amézola y Aspizúa, Francisco Villota Baquiola (Spain)	Maurice Durquetty, Etchegaray* (France)	Not awarded
1904–1912: Event not held			
1916: Olympics not held			
1920: Event not held			
1924	Sagrana*, José Andrés Garate, Santamaría* (Spain)	Camino*, Harizpe*, Magescas* (France)	Not awarded
1928–1936: Event not held			
1940–1944: Olympics not held			
1948–1964: Event not held			
1968	Mirapeix*, Mirapeix*, Beascoechea*, Arrien* (Spain)	Etcheverry*, Camy*, Borra*, Fourneau* (France)	Hamui*, Hamui*, Andrade*, Lanzagorta* (Mexico)
1972–1988: Event not held			

Year	Gold	Silver	Bronze
1992	Alejandro Celaya Goyogana, Andoni Oianguren Arizmendi, Josu Mugartegui Lejardi, Juan Antonio Compañón Duque (Spain)	Michel Ahadoberry, Philippe Etcheberry, Pierre Bordes, Pierre Etchalus (France)	Francisco J. Valdes Basaguren, Juan Pablo Valdés Basaguren, Xavier Ugartechea Escofet (Mexico)

* Full name not known.

Men's Frontenis

Year	Gold	Silver	Bronze
1968	Loaiza*, Hernandez*, Sanciprian* (Mexico)	Sehter*, Utge* (Argentina)	Garraus*, Lersundi*, Irigaray* (Spain)
1972–1988: Event not held			
1992	Edgar Salazar Sepúlveda, Jaime Salazar Sepúlveda, Luis Alberto Mercadillo Muñiz, Roberto Iniestra Estudillo (Mexico)	Ferran Velasco Moreno, José Luis Roig Azpitarte, Pedro Fite Villacampa, Ricardo Font de Mora Perez (Spain)	Alejandro García de la Vega, Gerardo Gabriel Romano Checa, Guillermo Filippo Manzanelli, Luis A. Cimadamore Guarneri (Argentina)

* Full name not known.

Women's Frontenis

Year	Gold	Silver	Bronze
1992	Miriam Aracely Muñoz Cadena, Rosa Maria Flores Buendia (Mexico)	Cristina Ortiz Bonanad, Estefanía Navarrete Ibáñez, Maria Teresa Palacios Moya, Rosa Maria Martinez Jimeno (Spain)	Haymed Valdes Blanco, Martha E. Dominguez Gonzalez (Cuba)

Men's Pala Corta

Year	Gold	Silver	Bronze
1992	Daniel García Jiménez, Pedro Hernandez Ripoll, Rafael Araujo Guardamino, Ricardo Garrido Llanos (Spain)	Arturo Medina Alanis, Fernando lniestra Estudillo, José Antonio Musi Chaya, Roberto Iniestra Estudillo (Mexico)	Ismael Felix Gonzalez Vazquez, Manuel Anduiza Garcia, Ricardo A. González Rocha (Cuba)

Men's Paleta, Leather Pelote

Year	Gold	Silver	Bronze
1968	Bareilts*, Bareilts*, Berrotaran*, Goicoechea* (France)	Ancizu*, Caballero*, Reyzabal*, Casado* (Spain)	Sanchez*, Beltran*, Del Valle* (Mexico)
1972–1988: Event not held			
1992	Fernando Elortondo Echeverría, Fernando Luis Abadia Barreiro, Juan Jose Miro Bonaudo, Ricardo A. Bizzozero Elias (Argentina)	Fernando Mendiluce Maisonave, Javier Juan Ubanell Ibarrola, Luis Altadill Garro, Pedro Jose Egaña García (Spain)	Carlito Arenas, Christophe Cazemayor, Jean-Luc Cambos, Jean-Marc Petrissans (France)

* Full name not known.

Men's Paleta, Rubber Pelote

Year	Gold	Silver	Bronze
1968	Becerra*, Rendon*, Gastelu-mendi*, Baltazar* (Mexico)	Sehter*, Utge*, Goyeche*, Caresella* (Argentina)	Iroldi*, D'Alba*, Bell* (Uruguay)
1972–1988: Event not held			

Year	Gold	Silver	Bronze
1992	Eduardo F. Ross Rossetti, Gerardo Gabriel Romano Checa, Juan Jose Miro Bonaudo, Reinaldo Ramon Ross Rossetti (Argentina)	Gabriel Amadoz, Marc Lassalle, Patrick Lissar (France)	Juan Pagoaga Chivite, Miguel Irizar Muñoz, Miguel Maria Sagarazazu, Mikel Eguinoa Landa (Spain)

* Full name not known.

Men's Fronton, Paleta

Year	Gold	Silver	Bronze
1992	Óscar Insausti Guelbenzu, Miguel Ángel Uros Murillo, Luis Tejada Hervás, Juan Pablo García Jiménez (Spain)	Luis Alberto Mercadillo Muñiz, José Antonio Musi Chaya, Pedro Aguirre Lesaca, Fernando Iniestra Estudillo (Mexico)	Gustavo A. Canut Garramiola, Guillermo Filippo Manzanelli, Fernando Elortondo Echeverría, Carlos Gustavo Huete Torres (Argentina)

Men's Fronton, Bare-handed

Year	Gold	Silver	Bronze
1968	Esquisabel*, Basabe*, Sacristan*, Iruzubieta* (Spain)	Arrillaga*, Minondo*, Lissar*, Etchegoin* (France)	Hernández*, Tovar*, Rivero*, Izquierdo* (Mexico)
1972–1988: Event not held			
1992	Rubén Beloki Iribarren, Jon Baceta Ciarsolo (Spain)	Bernard Muguida, Philippe Hirigoyen (France)	Eusebio López Carrillo, José A. Quesada Lugones (Cuba)

* Full name not known.

Men's Fronton, Doubles Bare-handed

Year	Gold	Silver	Bronze
1992	Alfredo Valerdi Aguirre, Iñaki Lujambio Ansa, Jose Angel Balanza Tobias, Juan Manuel Fernandez Garcia (Spain)	Daniel Mutuberria, Martin Bergara, Pascal Juzan, Roger Espil (France)	Francisco Javier Vera Quirós, Luis A. Izquierdo Ramirez, Pedro Olivos Jiménez, Pedro Santamaría Saldaña (Mexico)

Men's Trinquet, Doubles Bare-handed

Year	Gold	Silver	Bronze
1992	Alfredo Zea García, Horacio Saldaña Jiménez, Pedro Santamaría Saldaña, Raul Saldaña Jimenez (Mexico)	Jesús Ruiz Bastida, Joaquin Larrañaga Larrañaga, Miguel Choperena, Oskar Goñi Matxiñena (Spain)	Etienne Sallaberry, Jean Pierre Falxa, Pascal Cotabarren, Rene Muscarditz (France)

Beach Volleyball

Men's Beach Volleyball

Year	Gold	Silver	Bronze
1996	Karch Kiraly, Kent Steffes (United States)	Michael Dodd, Mike Whitmarsh (United States)	John Child, Mark Heese (Canada)
2000	Dain Blanton, Eric Fonoimoana (United States)	Zé Marco de Melo, Ricardo Santos (Brazil)	Axel Hager, Jörg Ahmann (Germany)
2004	Ricardo Santos, Emanuel Rego (Brazil)	Javier Bosma, Pablo Herrera (Spain)	Stefan Kobel, Patrick Heuscher (Switzerland)
2008	Phil Dalhausser, Todd Rogers (United States)	Márcio Araújo, Fábio Luiz Magalhães (Brazil)	Ricardo Santos, Emanuel Rego (Brazil)

Women's Beach Volleyball

Year	Gold	Silver	Bronze
1996	Jackie Silva, Sandra Pires (Brazil)	Mônica Rodrigues, Adriana Samuel (Brazil)	Natalie Cook, Kerri Pottharst (Australia)
2000	Natalie Cook, Kerri Pottharst (Australia)	Adriana Behar, Shelda Bede (Brazil)	Adriana Samuel, Sandra Pires (Brazil)
2004	Kerri Walsh, Misty May (United States)	Shelda Bede, Adriana Behar (Brazil)	Holly McPeak, Elaine Youngs (United States)
2008	Kerri Walsh, Misty May-Treanor (United States)	Wang Jie, Tian Jia (China)	Xue Chen, Zhang Xi (China)

Boxing

Light Flyweight

Year	Gold	Silver	Bronze
1968	Francisco Rodríguez (Venezuela)	Jee Yong-Ju (South Korea)	Hubert Skrzypczak (Poland) Harlan Marbley (United States)
1972	György Gedo (Hungary)	Kim U-Gil (North Korea)	Ralph Evans (Great Britain) Enrique Rodriguez (Spain)
1976	Jorge Hernández (Cuba)	Li Byong-Uk (North Korea)	Orlando Maldonado (Puerto Rico) Payao Poontarat (Thailand)
1980	Shamil Sabirov (Soviet Union)	Hipolito Ramos (Cuba)	Li Byong-Uk (North Korea) Ismail Mustafov (Bulgaria)
1984	Paul Gonzales (United States)	Salvatore Todisco (Italy)	Marcelino Bolivar (Venezuela) Keith Mwila (Zambia)
1988	Ivailo Marinov (Bulgaria)	Michael Carbajal (United States)	Leopoldo Serantes (Philippines) Róbert Isaszegi (Hungary)
1992	Rogelio Marcelo (Cuba)	Daniel Petrov (Bulgaria)	Jan Quast (Germany) Roel Velasco (Philippines)
1996	Daniel Petrov (Bulgaria)	Mansueto Velasco (Philippines)	Oleg Kiryukhin (Ukraine) Rafael Lozano (Spain)
2000	Brahim Asloum (France)	Rafael Lozano (Spain)	Maikro Romero (Cuba) Kim Un-Chol (North Korea)
2004	Yan Bhartelemy (Cuba)	Atagün Yalçınkaya (Turkey)	Zou Shuming (China) Sergey Kazakov (Russia)
2008	Zou Shiming (China)	Pürevdorjiin Serdamba (Mongolia)	Paddy Barnes (Ireland) Yampier Hernández (Cuba)

Flyweight

Year	Gold	Silver	Bronze
1904	George Finnegan (United States)	Miles Burke (United States)	Not awarded
1908–1912: Event not held			
1916: Olympics not held			
1920	Frankie Genaro (United States)	Anders Petersen (Denmark)	William Cuthbertson (Great Britain)
1924	Fidel La Barba (United States)	James McKenzie (Great Britain)	Raymond Fee (United States)
1928	Antal Kocsis (Hungary)	Armand Apell (France)	Carlo Cavagnoli (Italy)
1932	István Énekes (Hungary)	Francisco Cabañas (Mexico)	Louis Salica (United States)
1936	Willy Kaiser (Germany)	Gavino Matta (Italy)	Louis Laurie (United States)
1940–1944: Olympics not held			
1948	Pascual Pérez (Argentina)	Spartaco Bandinelli (Italy)	Han Soo-Ann (South Korea)

Year	Gold	Silver	Bronze
1952	Nate Brooks (United States)	Edgar Basel (Germany)	Anatoli Bulakov (Soviet Union) Willie Toweel (South Africa)
1956	Terence Spinks (Great Britain)	Mircea Dobrescu (Romania)	John Caldwell (Ireland) René Libeer (France)
1960	Gyula Török (Hungary)	Sergei Sivko (Soviet Union)	Abdel Moneim El-Guindi (Egypt) Kiyoshi Tanabe (Japan)
1964	Fernando Atzori (Italy)	Artur Olech (Poland)	Robert John Carmody (United States) Stanislav Sorokin (Soviet Union)
1968	Ricardo Delgado (Mexico)	Artur Olech (Poland)	Servílio de Oliveira (Brazil) Leo Rwabdogo (Uganda)
1972	Georgi Kostadinov (Bulgaria)	Leo Rwabwogo (Uganda)	Leszek Blazynski (Poland) Douglas Rodríguez (Cuba)
1976	Leo Randolph (United States)	Ramón Duvalón (Cuba)	Leszek Błażyński (Poland) David Torosyan (Soviet Union)
1980	Petar Lesov (Bulgaria)	Viktor Miroshnichenko (Soviet Union)	Hugh Russell (Ireland) János Váradi (Hungary)
1984	Steve McCrory (United States)	Redzep Redzepovski (Yugoslavia)	Eyüp Can (Turkey) Ibrahim Bilali (Kenya)
1988	Kim Kwang-Sun (South Korea)	Andreas Tews (East Germany)	Mario González (Mexico) Timofey Skryabin (Soviet Union)
1992	Choi Chol-Su (North Korea)	Raúl González (Cuba)	István Kovács (Hungary) Timothy Austin (United States)
1996	Maikro Romero (Cuba)	Bulat Jumadilov (Kazakhstan)	Zoltan Lunka (Germany) Albert Pakeyev (Russia)
2000	Wijan Ponlid (Thailand)	Bulat Jumadilov (Kazakhstan)	Jérôme Thomas (France) Vladimir Sidorenko (Ukraine)
2004	Yuriorkis Gamboa (Cuba)	Jérôme Thomas (France)	Fuad Aslanov (Azerbaijan) Rustamhodza Rahimov (Germany)
2008	Somjit Jongjohor (Thailand)	Andry Laffita (Cuba)	Georgy Balakshin (Russia) Vincenzo Picardi (Italy)

Bantamweight

Year	Gold	Silver	Bronze
1904	Oliver Kirk (United States)	George Finnegan (United States)	Not awarded
1908	A. Henry Thomas (Great Britain)	John Condon (Great Britain)	William Webb (Great Britain)
1912: Event not held			
1916: Olympics not held			
1920	Clarence Walker (South Africa)	Clifford Graham (Canada)	George McKenzie (Italy)
1924	William H. Smith (South Africa)	Salvatore Tripoli (Great Britain)	Jean Ces (France)
1928	Vittorio Tamagnini (Italy)	John Daley (United States)	Harry Isaacs (South Africa)
1932	Horace Gwynne (Canada)	Hans Ziglarski (Germany)	José Villanueva (Philippines)
1936	Ulderico Sergo (Italy)	Jack Wilson (United States)	Fidel Ortiz (Mexico)
1940–1944: Olympics not held			
1948	Tibor Csík (Hungary)	Gianbattista Zuddas (Italy)	Juan Evangelista Venegas (Puerto Rico)
1952	Pentti Hämäläinen (Finland)	John McNally (Ireland)	Kang Joon-Ho (South Korea) Gennady Garbuzov (Soviet Union)
1956	Wolfgang Behrendt (Germany)	Song Soon-Chun (South Korea)	Caludio Barrientos (Chile) Frederick Gilroy (Ireland)
1960	Oleg Grigoryev (Soviet Union)	Primo Zamparini (Italy)	Brunon Bendig (Poland) Oliver Taylor (Australia)
1964	Takao Sakurai (Japan)	Chung Shin-Cho (South Korea)	Juan Fabila Mendoza (Mexico) Washington Rodríguez (Uruguay)

Year	Gold	Silver	Bronze
1968	Valerian Sokolov (Soviet Union)	Eridadi Mukwanga (Uganda)	Eiji Morioka (Japan) Chang Kyou-Chul (South Korea)
1972	Orlando Martinez (Cuba)	Alfonso Zamora (Mexico)	George Turpin (Great Britain) Ricardo Carreras (United States)
1976	Gu Yong-Ju (North Korea)	Charles Mooney (United States)	Patrick Cowdell (Great Britain) Viktor Rybakov (Soviet Union)
1980	Juan Hernández (Cuba)	Bernardo Piñango (Venezuela)	Michael Anthony (Guyana) Dumitru Cipere (Romania)
1984	Maurizio Stecca (Italy)	Héctor López (Mexico)	Dale Walters (Canada) Pedro Nolasco (Dominican Republic)
1988	Kennedy McKinney (United States)	Aleksandar Hristov (Bulgaria)	Jorge Julio Rocha (Colombia) Phajol Moolsan (Thailand)
1992	Joel Casamayor (Cuba)	Wayne McCullough (Ireland)	Lee Gwang-Sik (North Korea) Mohammed Achik (Morocco)
1996	István Kovács (Hungary)	Arnaldo Mesa (Cuba)	Vichai Khadpo (Thailand) Raimkul Malakhbekov (Russia)
2000	Guillermo Rigondeaux (Cuba)	Raimkul Malakhbekov (Russia)	Sergiy Danylchenko (Ukraine) Clarence Vinson (United States)
2004	Guillermo Rigondeaux (Cuba)	Worapoj Petchkoom (Thailand)	Aghase Mammadov (Azerbaijan) Bahodirjon Sooltonov (Uzbekistan)
2008	Enkhbatyn Badar-Uugan (Mongolia)	Yankiel León (Cuba)	Bruno Julie (Mauritius) Veaceslav Gojan (Moldova)

Featherweight

Year	Gold	Silver	Bronze
1904	Oliver Kirk (United States)	Frank Haller (United States)	Frederick Gilmore (United States)
1908	Richard Gunn (Great Britain)	Charles Morris (United States)	High Roddin (Great Britain)
1912: Event not held			
1916: Olympics not held			
1920	Paul Fritsch (France)	Jean Gachet (France)	Edoardo Garzena (Italy)
1924	Jackie Fields (United States)	Joseph Salas (United States)	Pedro Quartucci (Argentina)
1928	Bep van Klaveren (Netherlands)	Victor Peralta (Argentina)	Harold Devine (United States)
1932	Carmelo Robledo (Argentina)	Josef Schleinkofer (Germany)	Allan Carlsson (Sweden)
1936	Oscar Casanovas (Argentina)	Charles Catterall (South Africa)	Josef Miner (Germany)
1940–1944: Olympics not held			
1948	Ernesto Formenti (Italy)	Dennis Sheperd (South Africa)	Aleksy Antkiewicz (Poland)
1952	Ján Zachara (Czechoslovakia)	Sergio Caprari (Italy)	Joseph Ventaja (France) Leonard Leisching (South Africa)
1956	Vladimir Safronov (Soviet Union)	Thomas Nicholls (Great Britain)	Henryk Niedźwiedzki (Poland) Pentti Hämäläinen (Finland)
1960	Francesco Musso (Italy)	Jerzy Adamski (Poland)	William Meyers (South Africa) Jorma Limmonen (Finland)
1964	Stanislav Stepashkin (Soviet Union)	Anthony Villanueva (Philippines)	Heinz Schulz (Germany) Charles Broan (United States)
1968	Antonio Roldán (Mexico)	Alberto Robinson (United States)	Philip Waruinge (Kenya) Ivan Mihailov (Belarus)
1972	Boris Kuznetsov (Soviet Union)	Philip Waruinge (Kenya)	Clementa Rojas (Columbia) Andras Botos (Hungary)
1976	Ángel Herrera (Cuba)	Richard Nowakowski (East Germany)	Leszek Kosedowski (Poland) Juan Paredes (Mexico)
1980	Rudi Fink (East Germany)	Adolfo Horta (Cuba)	Viktor Rybakov (Soviet Union) Krzysztof Kosedowski (Poland)

Year	Gold	Silver	Bronze
1984	Meldrick Taylor (United States)	Peter Konyegwachie (Nigeria)	Omar Catari (Venezuela) Türgüt Aykaç (Turkey)
1988	Giovanni Parisi (Italy)	Daniel Dumitrescu (Romania)	Lee Jae-Hyul (South Korea) Abdelhak Achik (Morocco)
1992	Andreas Tews (Germany)	Faustino Reyes (Spain)	Hocine Soltani (Algeria) Ramazi Palyani (Turkey)
1996	Kamsing Somluck (Thailand)	Serafim Todorov (Bulgaria)	Pablo Chacón (Argentina) Floyd Mayweather Jr. (United States)
2000	Bekzat Sattarkhanov (Kazakhstan)	Ricardo Juarez (United States)	Tahar Tamsamani (Morocco) Kamil Djamaloudinov (Russia)
2004	Alexei Tichtchenko (Russia)	Kim Song-Guk (North Korea)	Vitali Tajbert (Germany) Jo Seok-Hwan (South Korea)
2008	Vasyl Lomachenko (Ukraine)	Khedafi Djelkhir (France)	Yakup Kılıç (Turkey) Shahin Imranov (Azerbaijan)

Lightweight

Year	Gold	Silver	Bronze
1904	Harry Spangler (United States)	Russell van Horn (United States)	Peter Sturholdt (United States)
1908	Frederick Grace (Great Britain)	Frederick Spiller (Great Britain)	Harry Johnson (Great Britain)
1912: Event not held			
1916: Olympics not held			
1920	Samuel Mosberg (United States)	Gotfred Johansen (Denmark)	Clarence Newton (Canada)
1924	Hans Jacob Nielsen (Denmark)	Alfredo Copello (Argentina)	Frederick Boylstein (United States)
1928	Carlo Orlandi (Italy)	Stephen Halaiko (United States)	Gunmar Berggren (Sweden)
1932	Lawrence Stevens (South Africa)	Thure Ahlqvist (Sweden)	Nathan Bor (United States)
1936	Imre Harangi (Hungary)	Nikolai Stepulov (Estonia)	Erik Ågren (Sweden)
1940–1944: Olympics not held			
1948	Gerald Dreyer (South Africa)	Joseph Vissers (Belgium)	Svend Wad (Denmark)
1952	Aureliano Bolognesi (Italy)	Aleksy Antkiewicz (Poland)	Gheorghe Fiat (Romania) Erkki Pakkanen (Finland)
1956	Richard McTaggart (Great Britain)	Harry Kurschat (Germany)	Anatoly Lagetko (Soviet Union) Anthony Byrne (Ireland)
1960	Kazimierz Paździor (Poland)	Sandro Lopopolo (Italy)	Abel Laudonio (Argentina) Richard McTaggart (Great Britain)
1964	Jozef Grudzien (Poland)	Velikton Barannikov (Soviet Union)	Jim McCourt (Ireland) Ronald Allen Harris (United States)
1968	Ronald W. Harris (United States)	Józef Grudzień (Poland)	Zvonimir Vujin (Yugoslavia) Calistrat Cutov (Romania)
1972	Jan Szczepanski (Poland)	László Orbán (Hungary)	Samuel Mbugua (Kenya) Alfonso Pérez (Colombia)
1976	Howard Davis (United States)	Simion Cutov (Romania)	Ace Rusevski (Yugoslavia) Vassily Solomin (Soviet Union)
1980	Ángel Herrera (Cuba)	Viktor Demyanenko (Soviet Union)	Kazimierz Adach (Poland) Richard Nowakowski (East Germany)
1984	Pernell Whitaker (United States)	Luis Ortiz (Puerto Rico)	Chun Chil-Sung (South Korea) Martin Ndongo-Ebanga (Cameroon)
1988	Andreas Zülow (East Germany)	George Cramne (Sweden)	Nergüin Enkhbat (Mongolia) Romallis Ellis (United States)
1992	Oscar De La Hoya (United States)	Marco Rudolph (Germany)	Namjilyn Bayarsaikhan (Mongolia) Hong Sung-Sik (South Korea)

Year	Gold	Silver	Bronze
1996	Hocine Soltani (Algeria)	Tontcho Tontchev (Bulgaria)	Terrance Cauthen (United States) Leonard Doroftei (Romania)
2000	Mario Kindelán (Cuba)	Andriy Kotelnyk (Ukraine)	Cristián Bejarano (Mexico) Alexandr Maletin (Russia)
2004	Mario Kindelán (Cuba)	Amir Khan (Great Britain)	Serik Yeleuov (Kazakhstan) Murat Khrachev (Russia)
2008	Aleksei Tishchenko (Russia)	Daouda Sow (France)	Hrachik Javakhyan (Armenia) Yordenis Ugás (Cuba)

Light Welterweight

Year	Gold	Silver	Bronze
1952	Charles Adkins (United States)	Viktor Mednov (Soviet Union)	Bruno Visintin (Italy) Erkki Mallenius (Finland)
1956	Vladimir Yengibaryan (Soviet Union)	Franco Nenci (Italy)	Constantin Dumitrescu (Romania) Henry Loubscher (South Africa)
1960	Bohumil Němeček (Czechoslovakia)	Clement Quartey (Ghana)	Quincy Daniels (United States) Marian Kasprzyk (Poland)
1964	Jerzy Kulej (Poland)	Yevgeni Frolov (Soviet Union)	Habib Galhia (Tunisia) Eddia Blay (Ghana)
1968	Jerzy Kulej (Poland)	Enriques Requeiferos (Cuba)	Arto Nilsson (Finland) James Wallington (United States)
1972	Ray Seales (United States)	Angel Angelov (Belarus)	Issaka Dabore (Nigeria) Zvonimir Vujin (Yugoslavia)
1976	Ray Leonard (United States)	Andrés Aldama (Cuba)	Vladimir Kolev (Bulgaria) Kazimierz Szczerba (Poland)
1980	Patrizio Oliva (Italy)	Serik Konakbaev (Soviet Union)	Anthony Willis (Great Britain) Jose Aguilar (Cuba)
1984	Jerry Page (United States)	Dhawee Umponmaha (Thailand)	Mircea Fulger (Romania) Mirko Puzović (Yugoslavia)
1988	Vyacheslav Yanovski (Soviet Union)	Grahame Cheney (Australia)	Lars Myrberg (Sweden) Reiner Gies (Germany)
1992	Héctor Vinent (Cuba)	Mark Leduc (Canada)	Jyei Kjäll (Finland) Leonard Doroftei (Romania)
1996	Héctor Vinent (Cuba)	Oktay Urkal (Germany)	Fathi Missaoui (Tunisia) Bolat Niyazymbetov (Kazakhstan)
2000	Mahammatkodir Abdoollayev (Uzbekistan)	Ricardo Williams (United States)	Mohamed Allalou (Algeria) Diógenes Luña (Cuba)
2004	Manus Boonjumnong (Thailand)	Yudel Johnson (Cuba)	Boris Georgiev (Bulgaria) Ionuţ Gheorghe (Romania)
2008	Manuel Félix Díaz (Dominican Republic)	Manus Boonjumnong (Thailand)	Roniel Iglesias (Cuba) Alexis Vastine (France)

Welterweight

Year	Gold	Silver	Bronze
1904	Albert Young (United States)	Harry Spanjer (United States)	Joseph Lydon (United States)
1908–1912: Event not held			
1916: Olympics not held			
1920	Bert Schneider (Canada)	Alexander Ireland (Great Britain)	Frederick Colberg (United States)
1924	Jean Delarge (Belgium)	Héctor Méndez (Argentina)	Douglas Lewis (Canada)
1928	Ted Morgan (New Zealand)	Raúl Landini (Argentina)	Raymond Smillie (Canada)
1932	Edward Flynn (United States)	Erich Campe (Germany)	Bruno Ahlberg (Finland)
1936	Sten Suvio (Finland)	Michael Murach (Germany)	Gerhard Pedersen (Denmark)
1940–1944: Olympics not held			
1948	Július Torma (Czechoslovakia)	Horace Herring (United States)	Alessandro D'Ottavio (Italy)

Year	Gold	Silver	Bronze
1952	Zygmunt Chychla (Poland)	Sergei Scherbakov (Soviet Union)	Günther Heidemann (Germany) Victor Jörgensen (Denmark)
1956	Nicolae Linca (Romania)	Fred Tiedt (Ireland)	Kevin Hogarth (Australia) Nicholas Gargano (Great Britain)
1960	Giovanni Benvenuti (Italy)	Yuri Radonyak (Soviet Union)	Leszek Drogosz (Poland) Jimmy Lloyd (Great Britain)
1964	Marian Kasprzyk (Poland)	Ričardas Tamulis (Soviet Union)	Pertti Purhonen (Finland) Silvano Bertini (Italy)
1968	Manfred Wolke (East Germany)	Joseph Bessala (Cameroon)	Mario Guilloti (Argentina) Vladimir Musalimov (Soviet Union)
1972	Emilio Correa (Cuba)	János Kajdi (Hungary)	Jesse Valdez (United States) Richard Murunga (Kenya)
1976	Jochen Bachfeld (East Germany)	Pedro Gamarro (Venezuela)	Reinhard Skricek (Germany) Victor Zilberman (Romania)
1980	Andrés Aldama (Cuba)	John Mugabi (Uganda)	Karl-Heinz Krüger (East Germany) Kazimierz Szczerba (Poland)
1984	Mark Breland (United States)	An Young-Su (South Korea)	Joni Nyman (Finland) Luciano Bruno (Italy)
1988	Robert Wangila (Kenya)	Laurent Boudouani (France)	Jan Dydak (Poland) Kenneth Gould (United States)
1992	Michael Carruth (Ireland)	Juan Hernández Sierra (Cuba)	Anibal Acevedo (Puerto Rico) Arkhom Chenglai (Thailand)
1996	Oleg Saitov (Russia)	Juan Hernández Sierra (Cuba)	Daniel Santos (Puerto Rico) Marian Simion (Romania)
2000	Oleg Saitov (Russia)	Sergey Dotsenko (Ukraine)	Vitalie Gruşac (Moldova) Dorel Simion (Romania)
2004	Bakhtiyar Artayev (Kazakhstan)	Lorenzo Aragón (Cuba)	Kim Jung-Joo (South Korea) Oleg Saitov (Russia)
2008	Bakhyt Sarsekbayev (Kazakhstan)	Carlos Banteaux Suárez (Cuba)	Hanati Silamu (China) Kim Jung-Joo (South Korea)

Light Middleweight

Year	Gold	Silver	Bronze
1952	László Papp (Hungary)	Theunis van Schalkwyk (South Africa)	Boris Tishin (Soviet Union) Eladio Herrera (Argentina)
1956	László Papp (Hungary)	José Torres (United States)	John McCormack (Great Britain) Zbigniew Pietrzykowski (Poland)
1960	Wilbert McClure (United States)	Carmelo Bossi (Italy)	William Fisher (Great Britain) Boris Lagutin (Soviet Union)
1964	Boris Lagutin (Soviet Union)	Joseph Gonzales (France)	Nojim Maiyegun (Nigeria) Józef Grzesiak (Poland)
1968	Boris Lagutin (Soviet Union)	Rolando Garbey (Cuba)	John Lee Baldwin (United States) Günther Meier (Germany)
1972	Dieter Kottysch (Germany)	Wiesław Rudkowski (Poland)	Peter Tiepold (East Germany) Alan Minter (Great Britain)
1976	Jerzy Rybicki (Poland)	Tadija Kačar (Yugoslavia)	Rolando Garbey (Cuba) Viktor Savchenko (Soviet Union)
1980	Armando Martínez (Cuba)	Aleksandr Koshkyn (Soviet Union)	Jan Franek (Czechoslovakia) Detlef Kästner (East Germany)
1984	Frank Tate (United States)	Shawn O'Sullivan (Canada)	Christophe Tiozzo (France) Manfred Zielonka (West Germany)
1988	Park Si-Hun (South Korea)	Roy Jones Jr. (United States)	Raymond Downey (Canada) Richard Woodhall (Great Britain)

Year	Gold	Silver	Bronze
1992	Juan Carlos Lemus (Cuba)	Orhan Delibaş (Netherlands)	György Mizsei (Hungary) Robin Reid (Great Britain)
1996	David Reid (United States)	Alfredo Duvergel (Cuba)	Yermakhan Ibraimov (Kazakhstan) Karim Tulaganov (Kazakhstan)
2000	Yermakhan Ibraimov (Kazakhstan)	Marian Simion (Romania)	Pornchai Thongburan (Thailand) Jermain Taylor (United States)

Middleweight

Year	Gold	Silver	Bronze
1904	Charles Mayer (United States)	Benjamin Spradley (United States)	Not awarded
1908	Johnny Douglas (Great Britain)	Reginald Baker (Australasia)	William Philo (Great Britain)
1912: Event not held			
1916: Olympics not held			
1920	Harry Mallin (Great Britain)	Georges Prud'Homme (Canada)	Moe Herscovitch (Canada)
1924	Harry Mallin (Great Britain)	John Elliott (Great Britain)	Joseph Jules Beecken (Belgium)
1928	Piero Toscani (Italy)	Jan Heřmánek (Czechoslovakia)	Léonard Steyaert (Belgium)
1932	Carmen Barth (United States)	Amado Azar (Argentina)	Ernest Peirce (South Africa)
1936	Jean Despeaux (France)	Henry Tiller (Norway)	Raúl Villareal (Argentina)
1940–1944: Olympics not held			
1948	László Papp (Hungary)	John Wright (Great Britain)	Ivano Fontana (Italy)
1952	Floyd Patterson (United States)	Vasile Ti (Romania)	Boris Nikolov (Bulgaria) Stig Sjölin (Sweden)
1956	Gennadi Schatkov (Soviet Union)	Ramón Tapia (Chile)	Gilbert Chapron (France) Victor Zalzar (Argentina)
1960	Eddie Crook Jr. (United States)	Tadeusz Walasek (Poland)	Yevgeny Feofanov (Soviet Union) Ion Monea (Romania)
1964	Valeri Popenchenko (Soviet Union)	Emil Schulz (Germany)	Franco Valle (Italy) Tadeusz Walasek (Poland)
1968	Chris Finnegan (Great Britain)	Aleksei Kiselyov (Soviet Union)	Agustin Zaragoza (Mexico) Al Jones (United States)
1972	Vyacheslav Lemechev (Soviet Union)	Reima Virtanen (Finland)	Prince Amartey (Ghana) Marvin Johnson (United States)
1976	Michael Spinks (United States)	Rufat Riskiyev (Soviet Union)	Luis Felipe Martínez (Cuba) Alec Năstac (Romania)
1980	José Gómez (Cuba)	Viktor Savchenko (Soviet Union)	Valentin Silaghi (Romania) Jerzy Rybicki (Poland)
1984	Shin Joon-Sup (South Korea)	Virgil Hill (United States)	Aristides González (Puerto Rico) Mohamed Zaoui (Algeria)
1988	Henry Maske (East Germany)	Egerton Marcus (Canada)	Chris Sande (Kenya) Hussain Shah Syed (Pakistan)
1992	Ariel Hernández (Cuba)	Chris Byrd (United States)	Chris Johnson (Canada) Lee Seung-Bae (South Korea)
1996	Ariel Hernández (Cuba)	Malik Beyleroğlu (Turkey)	Rhoshii Wells (United States) Mohamed Bahari (Algeria)
2000	Jorge Gutiérrez (Cuba)	Gaydarbek Gaydarbekov (Russia)	Vugar Alakparov (Azerbaijan) Zsolt Erdei (Hungary)
2004	Gaydarbek Gaydarbekov (Russia)	Gennadiy Golovkin (Kazakhstan)	Suriya Prasathinphimai (Thailand) Andre Dirrell (United States)
2008	James DeGale (Great Britain)	Emilio Correa (Cuba)	Darren Sutherland (Ireland) Vijender Singh (India)

Light Heavyweight

Year	Gold	Silver	Bronze
1920	Eddie Eagan (United States)	Sverre Sørsdal (Norway)	Harold Franks (Great Britain)
1924	Harry Mitchell (Great Britain)	Thyge Petersen (Denmark)	Sverre Sørsdal (Norway)
1928	Victor Avendaño (Argentina)	Ernst Pistulla (Germany)	Karel Miljon (Netherlands)
1932	David Carstens (South Africa)	Gino Rossi (Italy)	Peter Jørgensen (Denmark)
1936	Roger Michelot (France)	Richard Vogt (Germany)	Francisco Risiglione (Argentina)
1940–1944: Olympics not held			
1948	George Hunter (South Africa)	Donald Scott (Great Britain)	Muaro Cía (Argentina)
1952	Norvel Lee (United States)	Antonio Pacenza (Argentina)	Anatoly Perov (Soviet Union) Harry Siljander (Finland)
1956	James Boyd (United States)	Gheorghe Negrea (Romania)	Carlos Lucas (Chile) Romualdas Murauskas (Soviet Union)
1960	Cassius Clay (Muhammad Ali) (United States)	Zbigniew Pietrzykowski (Poland)	Anthony Madigan (Australia) Giulio Saraudi (Italy)
1964	Cosimo Pinto (Italy)	Aleksei Kiselyov (Soviet Union)	Alexander Nikolov (Bulgaria) Zbigniew Pietrzykowski (Poland)
1968	Daniel Poznyak (Soviet Union)	Ion Monea (Romania)	Georgi Stankov (Bulgaria) Stanislaw Dragan (Poland)
1972	Mate Parlov (Yugoslavia)	Gilberto Carrillo (Cuba)	Isaac Ikhouria (Nigeria) Janusz Gortat (Poland)
1976	Leon Spinks (United States)	Sixto Soria (Cuba)	Kostică Dafinoiu (Romania) Janusz Gortat (Poland)
1980	Slobodan Kacar (Yugoslavia)	Pawel Skrzecz (Poland)	Herbert Bauch (East Germany) Ricardo Rojas (Cuba)
1984	Anton Josipović (Yugoslavia)	Kavin Barry (New Zealand)	Evander Holyfield (United States) Mustapha Moussa (Algeria)
1988	Andrew Maynard (United States)	Nurmagomed Shanavazov (Soviet Union)	Damir Škaro (Yugoslavia) Henryk Petrich (Poland)
1992	Torsten May (Germany)	Rostislav Zaulichniy (Unified Team)	Wojciech Bartnik (Poland) Zoltán Béres (Hungary)
1996	Vasilii Jirov (Kazakhstan)	Lee Seung-Bae (South Korea)	Antonio Tarver (United States) Thomas Ulrich (Germany)
2000	Alexandre Lebziak (Russia)	Rudolf Kraj (Czech Republic)	Andiy Fedchuk (Ukraine) Sergey Mihaylov (Uzbekistan)
2004	Andre Ward (United States)	Magomed Aripgadjiev (Belarus)	Ahmed Ismail (Egypt) Utkirbek Haydarov (Uzbekistan)
2008	Zhang Xiaping (China)	Kenneth Rgan (Ireland)	Tony Jeffries (Great Britain) Yerkebuian Shynaliyev (Kazakhstan)

Heavyweight

Year	Gold	Silver	Bronze
1904	Samuel Berger (United States)	Charles Mayer (United States)	William Michaels (United States)
1908	Albert Oldman (Great Britain)	Sydney Evans (Great Britain)	Frederick Parks (Great Britain)
1912: Event not held			
1916: Olympics not held			
1920	Ronald Rawson (Great Britain)	Søren Petersen (Denmark)	Albert Eluère (France)
1924	Otto von Porat (Norway)	Søren Petersen (Denmark)	Alfredo Porzio (Argentina)
1928	Arturo Rodríguez (Argentina)	Nils Ramm (Sweden)	Michael Michaelsen (Denmark)
1932	Santiago Lovell (Argentina)	Luigi Rovati (Italy)	Frederick Feary (United States)
1936	Herbert Runge (Germany)	Guillermo Lovell (Argentina)	Erling Nilsen (Norway)
1940–1944: Olympics not held			

Year	Gold	Silver	Bronze
1948	Rafael Iglesias (Argentina)	Gunnar Nilsson (Sweden)	John Arthur (South Africa)
1952	Ed Sanders (United States)	Ingemar Johansson (Sweden)	Ilkka Koshki (Finland) Andries Nieman (South Africa)
1956	Pete Rademacher (United States)	Lev Mukhin (Soviet Union)	Daniel Bekker (South Africa) Giacomo Bozzano (Italy)
1960	Francesco de Piccoli (Italy)	Daniel Bekker (South Africa)	Josef Němec (Czechoslovakia) Giulio Saraudi (Italy)
1964	Joe Frazier (United States)	Hans Huber (Germany)	Giuseppe Ros (Italy) Vadim Yemelyanov (Soviet Union)
1968	George Foreman (United States)	Ionas Chepulis (Soviet Union)	Giorgio Bambini (Italy) Joaquín Rocha (Mexico)
1972	Teófilo Stevenson (Cuba)	Ion Alexe (Romania)	Hasse Thomsén (Sweden) Peter Hussing (Germany)
1976	Teófilo Stevenson (Cuba)	Mircea Şimon (Romania)	Clarence Hill (Bermuda) John Tate (United States)
1980	Teófilo Stevenson (Cuba)	Piotr Zaev (Soviet Union)	István Lévai (Hungary) Jürgen Fanghänel (East Germany)
1984	Henry Tillman (United States)	Willie DeWit (Canada)	Angelo Musone (Italy) Arnold Vanderlyde (Netherlands)
1988	Ray Mercer (United States)	Baik Hyun-Man (South Korea)	Andrzej Golota (Poland) Arnold Vanderlyde (Holland)
1992	Félix Savón (Cuba)	David Izonritei (Nigeria)	Arnold Vanderlyde (Netherlands) David Tua (New Zealand)
1996	Félix Savón (Cuba)	David Defiagbon (Canada)	Nate Jones (United States) Luan Krasniqi (Germany)
2000	Félix Savón (Cuba)	Sultan Ibragimov (Russia)	Vladimer Tchanturia (Georgia) Sebastian Köber (Germany)
2004	Odlanier Solis (Cuba)	Viktar Zuyev (Belarus)	Mohamed Elsayed (Egypt) Naser Al Shami (Syria)
2008	Rakhim Chakhkiev (Russia)	Clementa Russo (Italy)	Osmay Acosta (Cuba) Deontay Wilder (United States)

Super Heavyweight

Year	Gold	Silver	Bronze
1984	Tyrell Biggs (United States)	Francesco Damiani (Italy)	Robert Wells (Great Britain) Aziz Salihu (Yugoslavia)
1988	Lennox Lewis (Canada)	Riddick Bowe (United States)	Aleksandr Miroshnichenko (Soviet Union) Janusz Zarenkiewicz (Poland)
1992	Roberto Balado (Cuba)	Richardo Igbineghu (Nigeria)	Brian Nielsen (Denmark) Svilen Rusinov (Bulgaria)
1996	Wladimir Klitschko (Ukraine)	Paea Wolfgram (Tonga)	Duncan Dokiwari (Nigeria) Alexei Lezin (Russia)
2000	Audley Harrison (Great Britain)	Mukhtarkhan Dildabekov (Kazakhstan)	Paolo Vidoz (Italy) Rustam Saidov (Uzbekistan)
2004	Alexander Povetkin (Russia)	Mohamed Aly (Egypt)	Michel López Núñez (Cuba) Roberto Cammarelle (Italy)
2008	Roberto Cammarelle (Italy)	Zhang Zhilei (China)	Vyacheslav Glazkov (Ukraine) David Price (Great Britain)

Canoe/Kayak, Flatwater

Men's Canoe, Single 500-Meter

Year	Gold	Silver	Bronze
1976	Aleksandr Togov (Soviet Union)	John Wood (Canada)	Matija Ljubek (Yugoslavia)
1980	Sergei Postrekhin (Soviet Union)	Lyubomir Lyubenov (Bulgaria)	Olaf Heukrodt (East Germany)
1984	Larry Cain (Canada)	Henning Lynge Jakobsen (Denmark)	Costic Olaru (Romania)
1988	Olaf Heukrodt (East Germany)	Michał Śliwiński (Soviet Union)	Martin Marinov (Bulgaria)
1992	Nikolay Bukhalov (Bulgaria)	Michał Śliwiński (Soviet Union)	Olaf Heukrodt (East Germany)
1996	Martin Doktor (Czechoslovakia)	Slavomír Kňazovický (Slovakia)	Imre Pulai (Hungary)
2000	György Kolonics (Hungary)	Maxim Opalev (Russia)	Andreas Dittmer (Germany)
2004	Andreas Dittmer (Germany)	David Cal (Spain)	Maxim Opalev (Russia)
2008	Maxim Opalev (Russia)	David Cal (Spain)	Iurii Cheban (Ukraine)

Men's Canoe, Single 1,000-Meter

Year	Gold	Silver	Bronze
1936	Frank Amyot (Canada)	Bohuslav Karlik (Czechoslovakia)	Erich Koschik (Germany)
1940–1944: Olympics not held			
1948	Josef Holeček (Czechoslovakia)	Douglas Bennett (Canada)	Robert Boutigny (France)
1952	Josef Holeček (Czechoslovakia)	János Parti (Hungary)	Olavi Ojanperä (Finland)
1956	Leon Rotman (Romania)	István Hernek (Hungary)	Gennady Bukharin (Soviet Union)
1960	János Parti (Hungary)	Aleksandr Silayev (Soviet Union)	Leon Rotman (Romania)
1964	Jürgen Eschert (United Team of Germany)	Andrei Igorov (Romania)	Yevgeny Penyayev (Soviet Union)
1968	Tibor Tatai (Hungary)	Detlef Lewe (Germany)	Vitaly Galkov (Soviet Union)
1972	Reinhard Eiben (East Germany)	Reinhold Kauder (Germany)	James McEwan (United States)
1976	Matija Ljubek (Yugoslavia)	Vasyl Yurchenko (Soviet Union)	Tamás Wichmann (Hungary)
1980	Lyubomir Lyubenov (Bulgaria)	Sergei Postrekhin (Soviet Union)	Eckhard Leue (East Germany)
1984	Ulrich Eicke (Germany)	Larry Cain (Canada)	Henning Lynge Jakobsen (Denmark)
1988	Ivans Klementyev (Soviet Union)	Jörg Schmidt (East Germany)	Nikolay Bukhalov (Bulgaria)
1992	Nikolay Bukhalov (Bulgaria)	Ivans Klementjevs (Latvia)	György Zala (Hungary)
1996	Martin Doktor (Czechoslovakia)	Ivans Klementjevs (Latvia)	György Zala (Hungary)
2000	Andreas Dittmer (Germany)	Ledis Balceiro (Cuba)	Stephan Giles (Canada)
2004	David Cal (Spain)	Andreas Dittmer (Germany)	Attila Vajda (Hungary)
2008	Attila Vajda (Hungary)	David Cal (Spain)	Thomas Hall (Canada)

Men's Canoe, Single 10,000-Meter

Year	Gold	Silver	Bronze
1948	František Čapek (Czechoslovakia)	Frank Havens (United States)	Norman Lane (Canada)
1952	Frank Havens (United States)	Gábor Novák (Hungary)	Alfréd Jindra (Czechoslovakia)
1956	Leon Rotman (Romania)	János Parti (Hungary)	Gennady Bukharin (Soviet Union)

Men's Canoe, Double 500-Meter

Year	Gold	Silver	Bronze
1976	Serhei Petrenko, Aleksandr Vinogradov (Soviet Union)	Andrzej Gronowicz, Jerzy Opara (Poland)	Tamás Buday, Oszkár Frey (Hungary)
1980	László Foltán, István Vaskuti (Hungary)	Ivan Potzaichin, Petre Capusta (Romania)	Borislav Ananiev, Nikolai Ilkov (Bulgaria)

Year	Gold	Silver	Bronze
1984	Matija Ljubek, Mirko Nišović (Yugoslavia)	Ivan Patzaichin, Toma Simionov (Romania)	Enrique Míguez, Narcisco Suárez (Spain)
1988	Viktor Reneysky, Nicolae Juravschi (Soviet Union)	Marek Dopierała, Marek Łbik (Poland)	Philippe Renaud, Joël Bettin (France)
1996	György Kolonics, Csaba Horváth (Hungary)	Viktor Reneysky, Nicolae Juravschi (Moldova)	Grigore Obreja, Gheorghe Andriev (Romania)
2000	Ferenc Novák, Imre Pulai (Hungary)	Daniel Jędraszko, Paweł Baraszkiewicz (Poland)	Mitică Pricop, Florin Popescu (Romania)
2004	Meng Guanliang, Yang Wenjun (China)	Ibrahim Rojas, Ledis Balceiro (Cuba)	Alexander Kostoglod, Aleksandr Kovalyov (Russia)
2008	Meng Guanliang, Yang Wenjun (China)	Sergey Ulegin, Alexander Kostoglod (Russia)	Christian Gille, Thomasz Wylenzek (Germany)

Men's Canoe, Double 1,000-Meter

Year	Gold	Silver	Bronze
1936	Vladimír Syrovátka, Jan Brzák-Felix (Czechoslovakia)	Rupert Weinstabl, Karl Proisl (Austria)	Frank Saker, Harvey Charters (Canada)
1940–1944: Olympics not held			
1948	Jan Brzák-Felix, Bohumil Kudrna (Czechoslovakia)	Steven Lysak, Stephen Macknowski (United States)	Georges Dransart, Georges Gandil (France)
1952	Bent Peder Rasch, Finn Haunstoft (Denmark)	Jan Brzák-Felix, Bohumil Kudrna (Czechoslovakia)	Egon Drews, Wilfried Soltau (Germany)
1956	Alexe Dumitru, Simion Ismailciuc (Romania)	Pavel Kharin, Gratsian Botev (Soviet Union)	Károly Wieland, Ferenc Mohácsi (Hungary)
1960	Leonid Geishtor, Sergei Makarenko (Soviet Union)	Aldo Dezi, Francesco La Macchia (Italy)	Imre Farkas, András Törő (Hungary)
1964	Andrei Khimich, Stepan Oshchepkov (Soviet Union)	Jean Boudehen, Michel Chapuis (France)	Peer Nielsen, John Sørensen (Denmark)
1968	Ivan Patzaichin, Serghei Covaliov (Romania)	Tamás Wichmann, Gyula Petrikovics (Hungary)	Naum Prokupets, Mikhail Zamotin (Soviet Union)
1972	Vladas Česiūnas, Yuri Lobanov (Soviet Union)	Ivan Patzaichin, Serghei Covaliov (Romania)	Fedia Damianov, Ivan Burtchin (Bulgaria)
1976	Serhei Petrenko, Aleksandr Vinogradov (Soviet Union)	Gheorghe Danielov, Gheorghe Simionov (Romania)	Tamás Buday, Oszkár Frey (Hungary)
1980	Ivan Patzaichin, Toma Simionov (Romania)	Olaf Heukrodt, Uwe Madeja (East Germany)	Vasyl Yurchenko, Yuri Lobanov (Soviet Union)
1984	Ivan Patzaichin, Toma Simionov (Romania)	Matija Ljubek, Mirko Nišović (Yugoslavia)	Didier Hoyer, Eric Renaud (France)
1988	Viktor Reneysky, Nicolae Juravschi (Soviet Union)	Olaf Heukrodt, Ingo Spelly (East Germany)	Marek Dopierała, Marek Łbik (Poland)
1992	Ulrich Papke, Ingo Spelly (Germany)	Christian Frederiksen, Arne Nielsson (Denmark)	Didier Hoyer, Olivier Boivin (France)
1996	Gunar Kirchbach, Andreas Dittmer (Germany)	Marcel Glavan, Antonel Borsan (Romania)	György Kolonics, Csaba Horváth (Hungary)
2000	Mitică Pricop, Florin Popescu (Romania)	Ibrahim Rojas, Leobaldo Pereira (Cuba)	Stefan Uteß, Lars Kober (Germany)
2004	Christian Gille, Tomasz Wylenzek (Germany)	Aleksandr Kostoglod, Aleksandr Kovalyov (Russia)	György Kozmann, György Kolonics (Hungary)
2008	Andrei Bahdanovich, Aliaksandr Bahdanovich (Belarus)	Christian Gille, Tomasz Wylenzek (Germany)	György Kozmann, Tamás Kiss (Hungary)

Men's Canoe, Double 10,000-Meter

Year	Gold	Silver	Bronze
1936	Václav Mottl, Zdeněk Škrland (Czechoslovakia)	Frank Saker, Harvey Charters (Canada)	Rupert Weinstabl, Karl Proisl (Austria)
1940–1944: Olympics not held			
1948	Steven Lysak, Stephen Macknowski (United States)	Václav Havel, Jiří Pecka (Czechoslovakia)	Georges Dransart, Georges Gandil (France)
1952	Georges Turlier, Jean Laudet (France)	Kenneth Lane, Donald Hawgood (Canada)	Egon Drews, Wilfried Soltau (Germany)
1956	Pavel Kharin, Gratsian Botev (Soviet Union)	Georges Dransart, Marcel Renaud (France)	Imre Farkas, József Hunics (Hungary)

Men's Folding Kayak, Single 10,000-Meter

Year	Gold	Silver	Bronze
1936	Gregory Hradetzky (Austria)	Henri Eberhardt (France)	Xaver Hörmann (Germany)

Men's Folding Kayak, Double 10,000-Meter

Year	Gold	Silver	Bronze
1936	Sven Johansson, Erik Bladström (Sweden)	Willi Horn, Erich Hanisch (Germany)	Piet Wijdekop, Cees Wijdekop (Netherlands)

Men's Kayak, Single 500-Meter

Year	Gold	Silver	Bronze
1976	Vasile Dîba (Romania)	Zoltán Sztanity (Hungary)	Rüdiger Helm (East Germany)
1980	Vladimir Parfenovich (Soviet Union)	John Sumegi (Australia)	Vasile Dîba (Romania)
1984	Ian Ferguson (New Zealand)	Lars-Erik Moberg (Sweden)	Bernard Brégeon (France)
1988	Zsolt Gyulay (Hungary)	Andreas Stähle (East Germany)	Paul MacDonald (New Zealand)
1992	Mikko Kolehmainen (Finland)	Zsolt Gyulai (Hungary)	Knut Holmann (Norway)
1996	Antonio Rossi (Italy)	Knut Holmann (Norway)	Piotr Markiewicz (Poland)
2000	Knut Holmann (Norway)	Petar Merkov (Bulgaria)	Michael Kolganov (Israel)
2004	Adam van Koeverden (Canada)	Nathan Baggaley (Australia)	Ian Wynne (Great Britain)
2008	Ken Wallace (Australia)	Adam van Koeverden (Canada)	Tim Brabants (Great Britain)

Men's Kayak, Single 1,000-Meter

Year	Gold	Silver	Bronze
1936	Gregory Hradetzky (Austria)	Helmut Cämmerer (Germany)	Jaap Kraaier (Netherlands)
1940–1944: Olympics not held			
1948	Gert Fredriksson (Sweden)	Johan Andersen (Denmark)	Henri Eberhardt (France)
1952	Gert Fredriksson (Sweden)	Thorvald Strömberg (Finland)	Louis Gantois (France)
1956	Gert Fredriksson (Sweden)	Igor Pissarov (Soviet Union)	Lajos Kiss (Hungary)
1960	Erik Hansen (Denmark)	Imre Szöllösi (Hungary)	Gert Fredriksson (Sweden)
1964	Rolf Peterson (Sweden)	Mihály Hesz (Hungary)	Aurel Vernescu (Romania)
1968	Mihály Hesz (Hungary)	Aleksandr Shaparenko (Soviet Union)	Erik Hansen (Denmark)
1972	Aleksandr Shaparenko (Soviet Union)	Rolf Peterson (Sweden)	Géza Csapó (Hungary)
1976	Rüdiger Helm (East Germany)	Géza Csapó (Hungary)	Vasile Dîba (Romania)
1980	Rüdiger Helm (East Germany)	Alain Lebas (France)	Ion Bîrlădeanu (Romania)
1984	Alan Thompson (New Zealand)	Milan Janić (Yugoslavia)	Greg Barton (United States)
1988	Greg Barton (United States)	Grant Davies (Australia)	André Wohllebe (East Germany)

Year	Gold	Silver	Bronze
1992	Clint Robinson (Australia)	Knut Holmann (Norway)	Greg Barton (United States)
1996	Knut Holmann (Norway)	Beniamino Bonomi (Italy)	Clint Robinson (Australia)
2000	Knut Holmann (Norway)	Petar Merkov (Bulgaria)	Tim Brabants (Great Britain)
2004	Eirik Verås Larsen (Norway)	Ben Fouhy (New Zealand)	Adam van Koeverden (Canada)
2008	Tim Brabants (Great Britain)	Eirik Verås Larsen (Norway)	Ken Wallace (Australia)

Men's Kayak, Single 10,000-Meter

Year	Gold	Silver	Bronze
1936	Gregory Hradetzky (Austria)	Henri Eberhardt (France)	Xaver Hörmann (Germany)
1940–1944: Olympics not held			
1948	Gert Fredriksson (Sweden)	Kurt Wires (Finland)	Eivind Skabo (Norway)
1952	Thorvald Strömberg (Finland)	Gert Fredriksson (Sweden)	Michael Scheuer (Germany)
1956	Gert Fredriksson (Sweden)	Ferenc Hatlaczky (Hungary)	Michael Scheuer (Germany)

Men's Kayak, Double 500-Meter

Year	Gold	Silver	Bronze
1976	Joachim Mattern, Bernd Olbricht (East Germany)	Serhei Nahorny, Vladimir Romanovsky (Soviet Union)	Larion Serghei, Policarp Malîhin (Romania)
1980	Vladimir Parfenovich, Sergei Chukhray (Soviet Union)	Herminio Menéndez, Guillermo del Riego (Spain)	Rüdiger Helm, Bernd Olbricht (East Germany)
1984	Ian Ferguson, Paul MacDonald (New Zealand)	Per-Inge Bengtsson, Lars-Erik Moberg (Sweden)	Hugh Fisher, Alwyn Morris (Canada)
1988	Ian Ferguson, Paul MacDonald (New Zealand)	Igor Nagaev, Viktor Denisov (Soviet Union)	Attila Ábrahám, Ferenc Csipes (Hungary)
1992	Kay Bluhm, Torsten Gutsche (Germany)	Maciej Freimut, Wojciech Kurpiewski (Poland)	Bruno Dreossi, Antonio Rossi (Italy)
1996	Kay Bluhm, Torsten Gutsche (Germany)	Beniamino Bonomi, Daniele Scarpa (Italy)	Andrew Trim, Daniel Collins (Australia)
2000	Zoltán Kammerer, Botond Storcz (Hungary)	Andrew Trim, Daniel Collins (Australia)	Ronald Rauhe, Tim Wieskötter (Germany)
2004	Ronald Rauhe, Tim Wieskötter (Germany)	Clint Robinson, Nathan Baggaley (Australia)	Raman Piatrushenka, Vadzim Makhneu (Belarus)
2008	Saúl Craviotto, Carlos Pérez (Spain)	Ronald Rauhe, Tim Wieskötter (Germany)	Raman Piatrushenka, Vadzim Makhneu (Belarus)

Men's Kayak, Double 1,000-Meter

Year	Gold	Silver	Bronze
1936	Adolf Kainz, Alfons Dorfner (Austria)	Ewald Tilker, Fritz Bondroit (Germany)	Nicolaas Tates, Wim van der Kroft (Netherlands)
1940–1944: Olympics not held			
1948	Hans Berglund, Lennart Klingström (Sweden)	Ejvind Hansen, Jakob Jensen (Denmark)	Thor Axelsson, Nils Björklöf (Finland)
1952	Kurt Wires, Yrjö Hietanen (Finland)	Lars Glasser, Ingemar Hedberg (Sweden)	Maximilian Raub, Herbert Wiedermann (Austria)
1956	Michael Scheuer, Meinrad Miltenberger (Germany)	Mikhail Kaaleste, Anatoli Demitkov (Soviet Union)	Maximilian Raub, Herbert Wiedermann (Austria)
1960	Gert Fredriksson, Sven-Olov Sjödelius (Sweden)	András Szente, György Mészáros (Hungary)	Stefan Kapłaniak, Władysław Zieliński (Poland)
1964	Sven-Olov Sjödelius, Gunnar Utterberg (Sweden)	Antonius Geurts, Paulus Hoekstra (Netherlands)	Heinz Büker, Holger Zander (Germany)
1968	Aleksandr Shaparenko, Volodymyr Morozov (Soviet Union)	Csaba Giczy, István Timár (Hungary)	Gerhard Seibold, Günther Pfaff (Austria)

Year	Gold	Silver	Bronze
1972	Nikolai Gorbachev, Viktor Kratasyuk (Soviet Union)	József Deme, János Rátkai (Hungary)	Władysław Szuszkiewicz, Rafał Piszcz (Poland)
1976	Serhei Nahorny, Vladimir Romanovsky (Soviet Union)	Joachim Mattern, Bernd Olbricht (East Germany)	Zoltán Bakó, István Szabó (Hungary)
1980	Vladimir Parfenovich, Sergei Chukhray (Soviet Union)	István Szabó, István Joós (Hungary)	Luis Gregorio Ramos, Herminio Menéndez (Spain)
1984	Hugh Fisher, Alwyn Morris (Canada)	Bernard Brégeon, Patrick Lefoulon (France)	Barry Kelly, Grant Kenny (Australia)
1988	Greg Barton, Norman Bellingham (United States)	Ian Ferguson, Paul MacDonald (New Zealand)	Peter Foster, Kelvin Graham (Australia)
1992	Kay Bluhm, Torsten Gutsche (Germany)	Kalle Sundqvist, Gunnar Olsson (Sweden)	Grzegorz Kotowicz, Dariusz Białkowski (Poland)
1996	Daniele Scarpa, Antonio Rossi (Italy)	Kay Bluhm, Torsten Gutsche (Germany)	Andrian Dushev, Milko Kazanov (Bulgaria)
2000	Antonio Rossi, Beniamino Bonomi (Italy)	Markus Oscarsson, Henrik Nilsson (Sweden)	Krisztián Bártfai, Krisztián Veréb (Hungary)
2004	Markus Oscarsson, Henrik Nilsson (Sweden)	Antonio Rossi, Beniamino Bonomi (Italy)	Eirik Verås Larsen, Nils Olav Fjeldheim (Norway)
2008	Andreas Ihle, Martin Hollstein (Germany)	Kim Wraae Knudsen, René Holten Poulsen (Denmark)	Andrea Facchin, Antonio M. Scaduto (Italy)

Men's Kayak, Double 10,000-Meter

Year	Gold	Silver	Bronze
1936	Paul Wevers, Ludwig Landen (Germany)	Viktor Kalisch, Karl Steinhuber (Austria)	Tage Fahlborg, Helge Larsson (Sweden)
1940–1944: Olympics not held			
1948	Gunnar Akerlund, Hans Wetterström (Sweden)	Ivar Mathisen, Knut Ostby (Norway)	Thor Axelsson, Nils Björklöf (Finland)
1952	Kurt Wires, Yrjö Hietanen (Finland)	Gunnar Akerlund, Hans Wetterström (Sweden)	Ferenc Varga, József Gurovits (Hungary)
1956	János Urányi, László Fábián (Hungary)	Fritz Briel, Theodor Kleine (Germany)	Dennis Green, Walter Brown (Australia)

Men's Kayak, Single 4 × 500-Meter

Year	Gold	Silver	Bronze
1960	Dieter Krause, Günther Perleberg, Paul Lange, Friedhelm Wentzke (Germany)	Imre Szöllősi, Imre Kemecsey, András Szente, György Mészáros (Hungary)	Erik Hansen, Helmuth Sorensen, Arne Hoyer, Erling Jessen (Denmark)

Men's Kayak, Fours 1,000-Meter

Year	Gold	Silver	Bronze
1964	Nikolai Chuzhikov, Anatoli Grishin, Vyacheslav Ionov, Volodymyr Morozov (Soviet Union)	Günther Perleberg, Bernhard Schulze, Friedhelm Wentzke, Holger Zander (Germany)	Simion Cuciuc, Atanase Sciotnic, Mihai Turcas, Aurel Vernescu (Romania)
1968	Steinar Amundsen, Tore Berger, Egil Soby, Jan Johansen (Norway)	Anton Calenic, Haralambie Ivanov, Dimitrie Ivanov, Mihai Turcas (Romania)	Csaba Giczy, Imre Szöllősi, István Timár, István Csizmadia (Hungary)
1972	Yuri Filatov, Yuri Stetsenko, Volodymyr Morozov, Valeri Didenko (Soviet Union)	Aurel Vernescu, Mihai Zafiu, Roman Vartolomeu, Atanase Sciotnic (Romania)	Egil Soby, Steinar Amundsen, Tore Berger, Jan Johansen (Norway)
1976	Sergei Chukhray, Aleksandr Degtyarev, Yuri Filatov, Vladimir Morozov (Soviet Union)	José María Esteban, José Ramón López, Herminio Menéndez, Luis Gregorio Ramos (Spain)	Frank-Peter Bischof, Bernd Duvigneau, Rüdiger Helm, Jürgen Lehnert (East Germany)

Year	Gold	Silver	Bronze
1980	Rüdiger Helm, Bernd Olbricht, Harald Marg, Bernd Duvigneau (East Germany)	Mihai Zafiu, Vasile Dîba, Ion Geantă, Nicusor Esanu (Romania)	Borislav Borisov, Bozhidar Milenkov, Lazar Khristov, Ivan Manev (Bulgaria)
1984	Grant Bramwell, Ian Ferguson, Paul MacDonald, Alan Thompson (New Zealand)	Per-Inge Bengtsson, Tommy Karls, Lars-Erik Moberg, Thomas Ohlsson (Sweden)	Francois Barouh, Philippe Boccara, Pascal Boucherit, Didier Vavasseur (France)
1988	Zsolt Gyulay, Ferenc Csipes, Sándor Hódosi, Attila Ábrahám (Hungary)	Aleksandr Motuzenko, Sergey Kirsanov, Igor Nagayev, Viktor Denisov (Soviet Union)	Kay Bluhm, André Wohllebe, Andreas Stähle, Hans-Jörg Bliesener (East Germany)
1992	Mario Von Appen, Oliver Kegel, Thomas Reineck, André Wohllebe (Germany)	Ferenc Csipes, Zsolt Gyulay, Attila Ábrahám, László Fidel (Hungary)	Ramon Andersson, Kelvin Graham, Ian Rowling, Steven Wood (Australia)
1996	Thomas Reineck, Olaf Winter, Detlef Hofmann, Mark Zabel (Germany)	András Rajna, Gábor Horváth, Ferenc Csipes, Attila Adrovicz (Hungary)	Oleg Gorobiy, Sergey Verlin, Georgiy Tsybulnikov, Anatoli Tishchenko (Russia)
2000	Zoltán Kammerer, Botond Storcz, Ákos Vereckei, Gábor Horváth (Hungary)	Jan Schäfer, Mark Zabel, Björn Bach, Stefan Ulm (Germany)	Grzegorz Kotowicz, Adam Seroczyński, Dariusz Białkowski, Marek Witkowski (Poland)
2004	Zoltán Kammerer, Botond Storcz, Ákos Vereckei, Gábor Horváth (Hungary)	Andreas Ihle, Mark Zabel, Björn Bach, Stefan Ulm (Germany)	Richard Riszdorfer, Michal Riszdorfer, Erik Vlček, Juraj Bača (Slovakia)
2008	Raman Piatrushenka, Aliaksei Abalmasau, Artur Litvinchuk, Vadzim Makhneu (Belarus)	Richard Riszdorfer, Michal Riszdorfer, Erik Vlček, Juraj Tarr (Slovakia)	Lutz Altepost, Norman Bröckl, Torsten Eckbrett, Björn Goldschmidt (Germany)

Women's Kayak, Single 500-Meter

Year	Gold	Silver	Bronze
1948	Karen Hoff (Denmark)	Alida van der Anker-Doedens (Netherlands)	Fritzi Schwingl (Austria)
1952	Sylvi Saimo (Finland)	Gertrude Liebhart (Austria)	Nina Savina (Soviet Union)
1956	Yelizaveta Dementyeva (Soviet Union)	Therese Zenz (United Team of Germany)	Tove Søby (Denmark)
1960	Antonina Seredina (Soviet Union)	Therese Zenz (United Team of Germany)	Daniela Walkowiak (Poland)
1964	Lyusmila Khvedosyuk (Soviet Union)	Hilde Lauer (Romania)	Marcia Jones (United States)
1968	Lyudmila Pinayeva (Soviet Union)	Renate Breuer (West Germany)	Viorica Dumitru (Romania)
1972	Yulia Ryabchinskaya (Soviet Union)	Mieke Jaapies (Netherlands)	Anna Pfeffer (Hungary)
1976	Carola Zirzow (East Germany)	Tatiana Korshunova (Soviet Union)	Klára Rajnai (Hungary)
1980	Birgit Fischer (East Germany)	Vanja Gesheva (Bulgaria)	Antonina Melnikova (Soviet Union)
1984	Agneta Andersson (Sweden)	Barbara Schüttpelz (West Germany)	Annemiek Derckx (Netherlands)
1988	Vanja Gesheva (Bulgaria)	Birgit Schmidt (East Germany)	Izabela Dylewska (Poland)
1992	Birgit Schmidt (Germany)	Rita Kőbán (Hungary)	Izabela Dylewska (Poland)
1996	Rita Kőbán (Hungary)	Caroline Brunet (Canada)	Josefa Idem (Italy)
2000	Josefa Idem (Italy)	Caroline Brunet (Canada)	Katrin Borchert (Australia)
2004	Natasa Janics (Hungary)	Josefa Idem (Italy)	Caroline Brunet (Canada)
2008	Inna Osypenko-Radomska (Ukraine)	Josefa Idem (Italy)	Katrin Wagner-Augustin (Germany)

Women's Kayak, Double 500-Meter

Year	Gold	Silver	Bronze
1960	Mariya Shubina, Antonina Seredina (Soviet Union)	Therese Zenz, Ingrid Hartmann (United Team of Germany)	Klára Fried-Bánfalvi, Vilma Egresi (Hungary)
1964	Roswitha Esser, Annemarie Zimmermann (United Team of Germany)	Francine Fox, Glorianne Perrier (United States)	Hilde Lauer, Cornelia Sideri (Romania)
1968	Roswitha Esser, Annemarie Zimmermann (West Germany)	Anna Pfeffer, Katalin Rozsnyói (Hungary)	Lyudmila Pinayeva, Antonina Seredina (Soviet Union)
1972	Lyudmila Pinayeva, Yekaterina Kuryshko (Soviet Union)	Ilse Kaschube, Petra Grabowski (East Germany)	Maria Nichiforov, Viorica Dumitru (Romania)
1976	Nina Gopova, Galina Kreft (Soviet Union)	Anna Pfeffer, Klára Rajnai (Hungary)	Bärbel Köster, Carola Zirzow (East Germany)
1980	Carsta Genäuß, Martina Bischof (East Germany)	Galina Kreft, Nina Gopova (Soviet Union)	Éva Rakusz, Mária Zakariás (Hungary)
1984	Agneta Andersson, Anna Olsson (Sweden)	Alexandra Barre, Sue Holloway (Canada)	Josefa Idem, Barbara Schüttpelz (West Germany)
1988	Birgit Schmidt, Anke Nothnagel (East Germany)	Vanja Gesheva, Diana Paliiska (Bulgaria)	Annemiek Derckx, Annemarie Cox (Netherlands)
1992	Ramona Portwich, Anke von Seck (Germany)	Agneta Andersson, Susanne Gunnarsson (Sweden)	Rita Kőbán, Éva Dónusz (Hungary)
1996	Susanne Gunnarsson, Agneta Andersson (Sweden)	Birgit Fischer, Ramona Portwich (Germany)	Anna Wood, Katrin Borchert (Australia)
2000	Birgit Fischer, Katrin Wagner (Germany)	Katalin Kovács, Szilvia Szabó (Hungary)	Aneta Pastuszka, Beata Sokołowska (Poland)
2004	Katalin Kovács, Natasa Janics (Hungary)	Birgit Fischer, Carolin Leonhardt (Germany)	Aneta Pastuszka, Beata Sokołowska (Poland)
2008	Katalin Kovács, Natasa Janics (Hungary)	Beata Mikołajczyk, Aneta Konieczna (Poland)	Marie Delattre, Anne-Laure Viard (France)

Women's Kayak, Fours 500-Meter

Year	Gold	Silver	Bronze
1984	Agafia Constantin, Nastasia Ionescu, Tecla Marinescu, Maria Ştefan (Romania)	Agneta Andersson, Anna Olsson, Eva Karlsson, Susanne Wiberg (Sweden)	Alexandra Barre, Lucie Guay, Sue Holloway, Barbara Olmstead (Canada)
1988	Birgit Schmidt, Anke Nothnagel, Ramona Portwich, Heike Singer (East Germany)	Erika Géczi, Erika Mészáros, Éva Rakusz, Rita Kőbán (Hungary)	Vanja Gesheva, Diana Paliiska, Ogniana Petkova, Borislava Ivanova (Bulgaria)
1992	Rita Kőbán, Éva Dónusz, Erika Mészáros, Kinga Czigány (Hungary)	Katrin Borchert, Ramona Portwich, Birgit Schmidt, Anke Von Seck (Germany)	Anna Olsson, Agneta Andersson, Maria Haglund, Susanne Rosenqvist (Sweden)
1996	Anett Schuck, Birgit Fischer, Manuela Mucke, Ramona Portwich (Germany)	Gabi Müller, Ingrid Haralamow, Sabine Eichenberger, Daniela Baumer (Switzerland)	Susanne Rosenqvist, Anna Olsson, Ingela Ericsson, Agneta Andersson (Sweden)
2000	Birgit Fischer, Manuela Mucke, Anett Schuck, Katrin Wagner (Germany)	Rita Kőbán, Katalin Kovács, Szilvia Szabó, Erzsébet Viski (Hungary)	Raluca Ioniţă, Mariana Limbău, Elena Radu, Sanda Toma (Romania)
2004	Birgit Fischer, Maike Nollen, Katrin Wagner, Carolin Leonhardt (Germany)	Katalin Kovács, Szilvia Szabó, Erzsébet Viski, Kinga Bóta (Hungary)	Inna Osypenko, Tetyana Semykina, Hanna Balabanova, Olena Cherevatova (Ukraine)
2008	Fanny Fischer, Nicole Reinhardt, Katrin Wagner-Augustin, Conny Waßmuth (Germany)	Katalin Kovács, Gabriella Szabó, Danuta Kozák, Natasa Janics (Hungary)	Lisa Oldenhof, Hannah Davis, Chantal Meek, Lyndsie Fogarty (Australia)

Canoe/Kayak Slalom

Men's Canoe, Double

Year	Gold	Silver	Bronze
1972	Walter Hofmann, Rolf-Dieter Amend (East Germany)	Hans-Otto Schumacher, Wilhelm Baues (West Germany)	Jean-Louis Olry, Jean-Claude Olry (France)
1976–1988: Event not held			
1992	Joe Jacobi, Scott Strausbaugh (United States)	Jiří Rohan, Miroslav Šimek (Czechoslovakia)	Franck Adisson, Wilfrid Forgues (France)
1996	Franck Adisson, Wilfrid Forgues (France)	Jiří Rohan, Miroslav Šimek (Czech Republic)	Andre Ehrenberg, Michael Senft (Germany)
2000	Pavol Hochschorner, Peter Hochschorner (Slovakia)	Krzysztof Kołomański, Michał Staniszewski (Poland)	Marek Jiras, Tomáš Máder (Czech Republic)
2004	Pavol Hochschorner, Peter Hochschorner (Slovakia)	Marcus Becker, Stefan Henze (Germany)	Jaroslav Volf, Ondřej Štěpánek (Czech Republic)
2008	Pavol Hochschorner, Peter Hochschorner (Slovakia)	Ondřej Štěpánek, Jaroslav Volf (Czech Republic)	Mikhail Kuznetsov, Dmitry Larionov (Russia)

Men's Canoe, Single

Year	Gold	Silver	Bronze
1972	Reinhard Eiben (East Germany)	Reinhold Kauder (West Germany)	James McEwan (United States)
1976–1988: Event not held			
1992	Lukáš Pollert (Czechoslovakia)	Gareth Marriott (Great Britain)	Jacky Avril (France)
1996	Michal Martikán (Slovakia)	Lukáš Pollert (Czech Republic)	Patrice Estanguet (France)
2000	Tony Estanguet (France)	Michal Martikán (Slovakia)	Juraj Minčík (Slovakia)
2004	Tony Estanguet (France)	Michal Martikán (Slovakia)	Stefan Pfannmöller (Germany)
2008	Michal Martikán (Slovakia)	David Florence (Great Britain)	Robin Bell (Australia)

Men's Kayak, Single

Year	Gold	Silver	Bronze
1972	Siebert Horn (East Germany)	Norbert Sattler (Austria)	Harald Gimpel (East Germany)
1976–1988: Event not held			
1992	Pierpaolo Ferrazzi (Italy)	Sylvain Curinier (France)	Jochem Lettmann (Germany)
1996	Oliver Fix (Germany)	Andraž Vehovar (Slovenia)	Thomas Becker (Germany)
2000	Thomas Schmidt (Germany)	Paul Ratcliffe (Great Britain)	Pierpaolo Ferrazzi (Italy)
2004	Benoît Peschier (France)	Campbell Walsh (Great Britain)	Fabien Lefèvre (France)
2008	Alexander Grimm (Germany)	Fabien Lefèvre (France)	Benjamin Boukpeti (Togo)

Women's Kayak, Single

Year	Gold	Silver	Bronze
1972	Angelika Bahmann (East Germany)	Gisela Grothaus (West Germany)	Magdalena Wunderlich (West Germany)
1976–1988: Event not held			
1992	Elisabeth Micheler-Jones (Germany)	Danielle Woodward (Australia)	Dana Chladek (United States)
1996	Štěpánka Hilgertová (Czech Republic)	Dana Chladek (United States)	Myriam Fox-Jerusalmi (France)
2000	Štěpánka Hilgertová (Czech Republic)	Brigitte Guibal (France)	Anne-Lise Bardet (France)
2004	Elena Kaliská (Slovakia)	Rebecca Giddens (United States)	Helen Reeves (Great Britain)
2008	Elena Kaliská (Slovakia)	Jacqueline Lawrence (Australia)	Violetta Oblinger-Peters (Austria)

Cricket

Men's Cricket

Year	Gold	Silver	Bronze
1900	C. B. K. Beachcroft, Arthur Birkett, Alfred Bowerman, George Buckley, Francis Burchell, Frederick Christian, Harry Corner, Frederick Cuming, William Donne, Alfred Powlesland, John Symes, Montagu Toller (Great Britain)	W. Andersen*, W. T. Attrill, J. Braid*, W. Browning*, R. Horne*, T. H. Jordan, Arthur McEvoy, D. Robinson*, F. Rogues*, A. J. Schneidau, Henry Terry, Philip Tomalin (France)	Not awarded

* Full name not known.

Croquet

Men's Croquet Singles, One Ball

Year	Gold	Silver	Bronze
1900	Aumoitte* (France)	Johin* (France)	Waydelich* (France)

* Full name not known.

Men's Croquet Singles, Two Balls

Year	Gold	Silver	Bronze
1900	Waydelich* (France)	Vignerot* (France)	Sautereau* (France)

* Full name not known.

Men's Croquet Doubles

Year	Gold	Silver	Bronze
1900	Aumoitte*, Johin* (France)	Not awarded	Not awarded

* Full name not known.

Cycling, BMX

Men's BMX

Year	Gold	Silver	Bronze
2008	Māris Štrombergs (Latvia)	Mike Day (United States)	Donny Robinson (United States)

Women's BMX

Year	Gold	Silver	Bronze
2008	Anne-Caroline Chausson (France)	Laëtitia Le Corguillé (France)	Jill Kintner (United States)

Cycling, Road

Men's Individual Road Race

Year	Gold	Silver	Bronze
1896	Aristidis Konstantinidis (Greece)	August von Gödrich (Germany)	Edward Battel (Great Britain)
1900–1912: Event not held			
1916: Olympics not held			
1920–1924: Event not held			
1928	Henry Hansen (Denmark)	Frank Southall (Great Britain)	Gösta Carlsson (Sweden)
1932	Attilio Pavesi (Italy)	Guglielmo Segato (Italy)	Bernhard Britz (Sweden)
1936	Robert Charpentier (France)	Guy Lapébie (France)	Ernst Nievergelt (Switzerland)
1940–1944: Olympics not held			
1948	José Beyaert (France)	Gerrit Voorting (Netherlands)	Lode Wouters (Belgium)
1952	André Noyelle (Belgium)	Robert Grondelaers (Belgium)	Edi Ziegler (Germany)
1956	Ercole Baldini (Italy)	Arnaud Geyre (France)	Alan Jackson (Great Britain)
1960	Viktor Kapitonov (Soviet Union)	Livio Trapè (Italy)	Willy van den Berghen (Belgium)
1964	Mario Zanin (Italy)	Kjeld Rodian (Denmark)	Walter Godefroot (Belgium)
1968	Pierfranco Vianelli (Italy)	Leif Mortensen (Denmark)	Gösta Pettersson (Sweden)
1972	Hennie Kuiper (Netherlands)	Clyde Sefton (Australia)	Not awarded
1976	Bernt Johansson (Sweden)	Giuseppe Martinelli (Italy)	Mieczysław Nowicki (Poland)
1980	Lothar Thoms (East Germany)	Aleksandr Panfilov (Soviet Union)	David Weller (Jamaica)
1984	Alexi Grewal (United States)	Steve Bauer (Canada)	Dag Otto Lauritzen (Norway)
1988	Olaf Ludwig (Germany)	Bernd Gröne (West Germany)	Christian Henn (West Germany)
1992	Fabio Casartelli (Italy)	Erik Dekker (Netherlands)	Dainis Ozols (Latvia)
1996	Pascal Richard (Switzerland)	Rolf Sørensen (Denmark)	Max Sciandri (Great Britain)
2000	Jan Ullrich (Germany)	Alexandre Vinokouroz (Kazakhstan)	Andreas Klöden (Germany)
2004	Paolo Bettini (Italy)	Sérgio Paulinho (Portugal)	Axel Merckx (Belgium)
2008	Samuel Sánchez (Spain)	Fabian Cancellara (Switzerland)	Alexandr Kolobnev (Russia)

Men's Team Road Race

Year	Gold	Silver	Bronze
1912	Erik Friborg, Algot Lönn, Ragnar Malm, Axel Persson (Sweden)	Frederick Grubb, William Hammond, Leon Meredith, Charles Moss (Great Britain)	Albert Krushel, Alvin Loftes, Walter Martin, Carl Schutte (United States)
1916: Olympics not held			
1920	Fernand Canteloube, Georges Detreille, Marcel Gobillot, Achille Souchard (France)	Sigfrid Lundberg, Ragnar Malm, Axel Persson, Harry Stenqvist (Sweden)	Albert De Bunné, Jean Janssens, André Vercruysse, Albert Wyckmans (Belgium)
1924	Armand Blanchonnet, René Hamel, André Leducq, Georges Wambst (France)	Rik Hoevenaers, Alphonse Parfondry, Jean Van Den Bosch, Fernand Saivé (Belgium)	Gunnar Sköld, Erik Bohlin, Ragnar Malm, Erik Bjurberg (Sweden)
1928	Henry Hansen, Orla Jørgensen, Leo Nielsen (Denmark)	Jack Lauterwasser, John Middleton, Frank Southall (Great Britain)	Gösta Carlsson, Erik Jansson, Georg Johnsson (Sweden)
1932	Giuseppe Olmo, Attilio Pavesi, Guglielmo Segato (Italy)	Henry Hansen, Leo Nielsen, Frode Sørensen (Denmark)	Arne Berg, Bernhard Britz, Sven Höglund (Sweden)
1936	Robert Charpentier, Robert Dorgebray, Guy Lapébie (France)	Edgar Buchwalder, Ernst Nievergelt, Kurt Ott (Switzerland)	Auguste Garrebeek, Armand Putzeys, François Vandermotte (Belgium)
1940–1944: Olympics not held			
1948	Léon Delathouwer, Eugène van Roosbroeck, Lode Wouters (Belgium)	Robert John Maitland, Ian Scott, Gordon Thomas (Great Britain)	José Beyaert, Jacques Dupont, Alain Moineau (France)

Year	Gold	Silver	Bronze
1952	Robert Grondelaers, André Noyelle, Lucien Victor (Belgium)	Dino Bruni, Gianni Ghidini, Vincenzo Zucconelli (Italy)	Jacques Anquetil, Claude Rouer, Alfred Tonello (France)
1956	Arnaud Geyre, Maurice Moucheraud, Michel Vermeulin (France)	Arthur Brittain, William Holmes, Alan Jackson (Great Britain)	Reinhold Pommer, Gustav-Adolf Schur, Horst Tüller (Germany)

Men's Time Trial, Individual

Year	Gold	Silver	Bronze
1912	Rudolph Lewis (South Africa)	Frederick Grubb (Great Britain)	Carl Schutte (United States)
1916: Olympics not held			
1920	Harry Stenqvist (Sweden)	Henry Kaltenbrun (South Africa)	Fernand Cateloube (France)
1924	Armand Blanchonnet (France)	Henri Hoevenaers (Belgium)	René Hamel (France)
1928–1936: Event not held			
1940–1944: Olympics not held			
1948–1992: Event not held			
1996	Miguel Indurain (Spain)	Abraham Olano (Spain)	Chris Boardman (Great Britain)
2000	Jason Queally (Great Britain)	Stefan Nimke (Germany)	Shane Kelly (Australia)
2004	Chris Hoy (Great Britain)	Arnaud Tournant (France)	Stefan Nimke (Germany)
2008	Fabian Cancellara (Switzerland)	Gustav Erik Larsson (Sweden)	Levi Leipheimer (United States)

Men's Time Trial, Team

Year	Gold	Silver	Bronze
1960	Livio Trapè, Antonio Bailetti, Ottavio Cogliati, Giacomo Fornoni (Italy)	Gustav-Adolf Schur, Egon Adler, Erich Hagen, Günter Lörke (Germany)	Aleksei Petrov, Viktor Kapitonov, Yevgeny Klevtsov, Yury Melikhov (Soviet Union)
1964	Bart Zoet, Evert Dolman, Gerben Karstens, Jan Pieterse (Netherlands)	Ferruccio Manza, Severino Andreoli, Luciano Dalla Bona, Pietro Guerra (Italy)	Sture Pettersson, Sven Hamrin, Erik Pettersson, Gösta Pettersson (Sweden)
1968	Joop Zoetemelk, Fedor den Hertog, Jan Krekels, René Pijnen (Netherlands)	Sture Pettersson, Tomas Pettersson, Erik Pettersson, Gösta Pettersson (Sweden)	Pierfranco Vianelli, Giovanni Bramucci, Vittorio Marcelli, Mauro Simonetti (Italy)
1972	Valery Yardy, Gennady Komnatov, Valery Likhachov, Boris Shukov (Soviet Union)	Ryszard Szurkowski, Edward Barcik, Lucjan Lis, Stanisław Szozda (Poland)	Not awarded
1976	Aavo Pikkuus, Valery Chaplygin, Anatoly Chukanov, Vladimir Kaminsky (Soviet Union)	Ryszard Szurkowski, Tadeusz Mytnik, Mieczysław Nowicki, Stanisław Szozda (Poland)	Jørn Lund, Verner Blaudzun, Gert Frank, Jørgen Hansen (Denmark)
1980	Yury Kashirin, Oleg Logvin, Sergei Shelpakov, Anatoly Yarkin (Soviet Union)	Falk Boden, Bernd Drogan, Olaf Ludwig, Hans-Joachim Hartnick (East Germany)	Michal Klasa, Vlastibor Konečný, Alipi Kostadinov, Jiří Škoda (Czechoslovakia)
1984	Marcello Bartalini, Marco Giovannetti, Eros Poli, Claudio Vandelli (Italy)	Alfred Achermann, Richard Trinkler, Laurent Vial, Benno Wiss (Switzerland)	Ron Kiefel, Clarence Knickman, Davis Phinney, Andrew Weaver (United States)
1988	Jan Schur, Uwe Ampler, Mario Kummer, Maik Landsmann (East Germany)	Andrzej Sypytkowski, Joachim Halupczok, Zenon Jaskuła, Marek Lesniewski (Poland)	Michel Lafis, Anders Jarl, Björn Johansson, Jan Karlsson (Sweden)
1992	Michael Rich, Bernd Dittert, Christian Meyer, Uwe Peschel (Germany)	Andrea Peron, Flavio Anastasia, Luca Colombo, Gianfranco Contri (Italy)	Jean-Louis Harel, Hervé Boussard, Didier Faivre-Pierret, Philippe Gaumont (France)

Women's Individual Road Race

Year	Gold	Silver	Bronze
1984	Connie Carpenter (United States)	Rebecca Twigg (United States)	Sandra Schumacher (West Germany)

Year	Gold	Silver	Bronze
1988	Monique Knol (Netherlands)	Jutta Niehaus (West Germany)	Laima Zilporite (Soviet Union)
1992	Kathryn Watt (Australia)	Jeannie Longo-Ciprelli (France)	Monique Knol (Netherlands)
1996	Jeannie Longo-Ciprelli (France)	Imelda Chiappa (Italy)	Clara Hughes (Canada)
2000	Leontien Zijlaard (Netherlands)	Hanka Kupfernagel (Germany)	Diana Žiliūtė (Lithuania)
2004	Sara Carrigan (Australia)	Judith Arndt (Germany)	Olga Slyusareva (Russia)
2008	Nicole Cooke (Great Britain)	Emma Johansson (Sweden)	Tatiana Guderzo (Italy)

Women's Individual Time Trial

Year	Gold	Silver	Bronze
1996	Zulfiya Zabirova (Russia)	Jeannie Longo-Ciprelli (France)	Clara Hughes (Canada)
2000	Leontien Zijlaard (Netherlands)	Mari Holden (United States)	Jeannie Longo-Ciprelli (France)
2004	Leontien Zijlaard (Netherlands)	Deirdre Demet-Barry (United States)	Karin Thürig (Switzerland)
2008	Kristin Armstrong (United States)	Emma Pooley (Great Britain)	Karin Thürig (Switzerland)

Cycling, Track

Men's ¼-Mile

Year	Gold	Silver	Bronze
1904	Marcus Hurley (United States)	Burton Downing (United States)	Teddy Billington (United States)

Men's ⅓-Mile

Year	Gold	Silver	Bronze
1904	Marcus Hurley (United States)	Burton Downing (United States)	Teddy Billington (United States)

Men's ½-Mile

Year	Gold	Silver	Bronze
1904	Marcus Hurley (United States)	Teddy Billington (United States)	Burton Downing (United States)

Men's 1-Mile

Year	Gold	Silver	Bronze
1904	Marcus Hurley (United States)	Burton Downing (United States)	Teddy Billington (United States)

Men's 2-Mile

Year	Gold	Silver	Bronze
1904	Burton Downing (United States)	Oscar Goerke (United States)	Marcus Hurley (United States)

Men's 5-Mile

Year	Gold	Silver	Bronze
1904	Charles Schlee (United States)	George E. Wiley (United States)	Arthur F. Andrews (United States)

Men's 25-Mile

Year	Gold	Silver	Bronze
1904	Burton Downing (United States)	Arthur F. Andrews (United States)	George E. Wiley (United States)

Men's 660-Yard

Year	Gold	Silver	Bronze
1908	Victor Johnson (Great Britain)	Émile Demangel (France)	Karl Neumer (Germany)

Men's 5-Kilometer

Year	Gold	Silver	Bronze
1908	Benjamin Jones (Great Britain)	Maurice Schilles (France)	André Auffray (France)

Men's 10-Kilometer

Year	Gold	Silver	Bronze
1896	Paul Masson (France)	Léon Flameng (France)	Adolf Schmal (Austria)

Men's 20-Kilometer

Year	Gold	Silver	Bronze
1908	Clarence Kingsbury (Great Britain)	Benjamin Jones (Great Britain)	Joseph Werbrouck (Belgium)

Men's 25-Kilometer

Year	Gold	Silver	Bronze
1900	Louis Bastien (France)	Louis Hildebrand (France)	Auguste Daumain (France)

Men's 50-Kilometer

Year	Gold	Silver	Bronze
1920	Henry George (Belgium)	Cyril Alden (Great Britain)	Piet Ikelaar (Netherlands)
1924	Ko Willems (Netherlands)	Cyril Alden (Great Britain)	Harry Wyld (Great Britain)

Men's 100-Kilometer

Year	Gold	Silver	Bronze
1896	Léon Flameng (France)	Georgios Kolettis (Greece)	Not awarded
1900–1904: Event not held			
1908	Charles Bartlett (Great Britain)	Charles Denny (Great Britain)	Octave Lapize (France)

Men's 12-Hour Race

Year	Gold	Silver	Bronze
1896	Adolf Schmal (Austria)	Frank Keeping (Great Britain)	Not awarded

Men's Madison

Year	Gold	Silver	Bronze
2000	Brett Airken, Scott McGrory (Australia)	Etienne De Wilde, Matthew Gilmore (Belgium)	Silvio Martinello, Marco Villa (Italy)
2004	Graeme Brown, Stuart O'Grady (Australia)	Franco Marvulli, Bruno Risi (Switzerland)	Rob Hayles, Bradlet Wiggins (Great Britain)
2008	Juan Curuchet, Walter Pérez (Argentina)	Joan Llaneras, Antonio Tauler (Spain)	Mikhail Ignatyev, Alexei Markov (Russia)

Men's Point Race

Year	Gold	Silver	Bronze
1984	Roger Ilegems (Belgium)	Uwe Messerschmidt (Germany)	José Youshimatz (Mexico)
1988	Dan Frost (Denmark)	Leo Peelen (Netherlands)	Marat Ganeyev (Soviet Union)
1992	Giovanni Lombardi (Italy)	Léon van Bon (Netherlands)	Cédric Mathy (Belgium)

Year	Gold	Silver	Bronze
1996	Silvio Martinello (Italy)	Brian Walton (Canada)	Stuart O'Grady (Australia)
2000	Juan Llaneras (Spain)	Milton Wynants (Uruguay)	Aleksei Markov (Russia)
2004	Mikhail Ignatyev (Russia)	Joan Llaneras (Spain)	Guido Fulst (Germany)
2008	Joan Llaneras (Spain)	Roger Kluge (Germany)	Chris Newton (Great Britain)

Men's Individual Pursuit

Year	Gold	Silver	Bronze
1964	Jiri Daller (Czechoslovakia)	Giorgio Ursi (Italy)	Preben Isaksson (Denmark)
1968	Daniel Rebillard (France)	Mogens Jensen (Denmark)	Xaver Kurmann (Switzerland)
1972	Knut Knudsen (Norway)	Xaver Kurmann (Switzerland)	Hans Lutz (West Germany)
1976	Gregor Braun (West Germany)	Herman Ponsteen (Netherlands)	Thomas Huschke (East Germany)
1980	Robert Dill-Bundi (Switzerland)	Alain Bondue (France)	Hans-Henrik Ørsted (Denmark)
1984	Mark Gorski (United States)	Nelson Vails (United States)	Tsutomo Sakamoto (Japan)
1988	Gintautas Union (Soviet Union)	Dean Woods (Australia)	Bernd Dittert (East Germany)
1992	Chris Boardman (Great Britain)	Jens Lehmann (Germany)	Gary Anderson (New Zealand)
1996	Andrea Collinelli (Italy)	Philippe Ermenault (France)	Bradley McGee (Australia)
2000	Robert Bartko (Germany)	Jens Lehmann (Germany)	Bradley McGee (Australia)
2004	Bradley Wiggins (Great Britain)	Brad McGee (Australia)	Sergi Escobar (Spain)
2008	Bradley Wiggins (Great Britain)	Hayden Roulston (New Zealand)	Steven Burke (Great Britain)

Men's Tandem

Year	Gold	Silver	Bronze
1908	André Auffray, Maurice Schilles (France)	Frederick Hamlin, Horace Johnson (Great Britain)	Colin Brooks, Walter Isaacs (Great Britain)
1912: Event not held			
1916: Olympics not held			
1920	Thomas Lance, Harry Ryan (Great Britain)	William Smith, James Walker (South Africa)	Frans de Vreng, Piet Ikelaar (Netherlands)
1924	Lucien Choury, Jean Cugnot (France)	Edmund Hansen, Willy Hansen (Denmark)	Gerard Bosch van Drakestein, Maurice Peeters (Netherlands)
1928	Bernhard Leene, Daan van Dijk (Netherlands)	Ernest Chambers, John Sibbit (Great Britain)	Hans Bernhardt, Karl Köther (Germany)
1932	Louis Chaillot, Maurice Perrin (France)	Ernest Chambers, Stanley Chambers (Great Britain)	Harald Christensen, Willy Gervin (Denmark)
1936	Ernst Ihbe, Carl Lorenz (Germany)	Bernhard Leene, Hendrik Ooms (Netherlands)	Pierre Georget, Georges Maton (France)
1940–1944: Event not held			
1948	Renato Perona, Ferdinando Teruzzi (Italy)	Alan Bannister, Reg Harris (Great Britain)	Gaston Fron, René Faye (France)
1952	Lionel Cox, Russell Mockridge (Australia)	Raymond Robinson, Thomas Shardelow (South Africa)	Antonio Maspes, Cesare Pinarello (Italy)
1956	Joey Browne, Anthony Marchant (Australia)	Ladislav Fouček, Václav Machek (Czechoslovakia)	Giuseppe Ogna, Cesare Pinarello (Italy)
1960	Giuseppe Beghetto, Sergio Bianchetto (Italy)	Jürgen Simon, Lothar Stäber (Germany)	Vladimir Leonov, Boris Vasilyev (Soviet Union)
1964	Sergio Bianchetto, Angelo Damiano (Italy)	Imants Bodnieks, Viktor Logunov (Soviet Union)	Willi Fuggerer, Klaus Kobusch (Germany)
1968	Daniel Morelon, Pierre Trentin (France)	Leijn Loevesijn, Jan Janssen (Netherlands)	Daniel Goens, Robert van Lancker (Belgium)
1972	Vladimir Semenets, Igor Tselovalnykov (Soviet Union)	Jürgen Geschke, Werner Otto (East Germany)	Andrzej Bek, Benedykt Kocot (Poland)

Men's 1-Kilometer Time Trial

Year	Gold	Silver	Bronze
1896	Paul Masson (France)	Stamatios Nikolopoulos (Greece)	Léon Flameng (France)
1900–1912: Event not held			
1916: Olympics not held			
1920–1924: Event not held			
1928	Willy Hansen (Denmark)	Gerard Bosch van Drakestein (Netherlands)	Dunc Gray (Australia)
1932	Dunc Gray (Australia)	Jacobus van Egmond (Netherlands)	Charles Rampelberg (France)
1936	Arie van Vliet (Netherlands)	Pierre Georget (France)	Rudolf Karsch (Germany)
1940–1944: Olympics not held			
1948	Jacques Dupont (France)	Pierre Nihant (Belgium)	Tommy Godwin (Great Britain)
1952	Russell Mockridge (Australia)	Marino Morettini (Italy)	Raymond Tobinson (South Aftica)
1956	Leandro Faggin (Italy)	Ladislav Fouček (Czechoslovakia)	Alfred Swift (South Africa)
1960	Sante Gaiadone (Italy)	Dieter Gieseler (Germany)	Rostislav Vargashkin (Soviet Union)
1964	Jiří Daler (Czechoslovakia)	Giorgio Ursi (Italy)	Preben Isaksson (Denmark)
1968	Pierre Trentin (France)	Niels Fredborg (Denmark)	Janusz Kierzkowski (Poland)
1972	Niels Fredborg (Denmark)	Daniel Clark (Australia)	Jürgen Schütze (East Germany)
1976	Klaus-Jürgen Grünke (East Germany)	Michel Vaarten (Belgium)	Niels Fredborg (Denmark)
1980	Lothar Thoms (East Germany)	Aleksandr Panfilov (Soviet Union)	David Weller (Jamaica)
1984	Fredy Schmidtke (West Germany)	Curt Harnett (Canada)	Fabrice Colas (France)
1988	Aleksandr Kirichenko (Soviet Union)	Martin Vinnicombe (Australia)	Robert Lechner (West Germany)
1992	José Manuel Moreno (Spain)	Shane Kelly (Australia)	Erin Hartwell (United States)
1996	Florian Rousseau (France)	Erin Hartwell (United States)	Takanobu Jumonji (Japan)
2000	Jason Queally (Great Britain)	Stefan Nimke (Germany)	Shane Kelly (Australia)
2004	Chris Hoy (Great Britain)	Arnaud Tournant (France)	Stefan Nimke (Germany)

Men's Keirin

Year	Gold	Silver	Bronze
2000	Florian Rousseau (France)	Gary Neiwand (Australia)	Jens Fiedler (Germany)
2004	Ryan Bayley (Australia)	José Antonio Escuredo (Spain)	Shane Kelly (Australia)
2008	Chris Hoy (Great Britain)	Ross Edgar (Great Britain)	Kiyofumi Nagai (Japan)

Men's Team Pursuit

Year	Gold	Silver	Bronze
1908	Benjamin Jones, Clarence Kingsbury, Leonard Meredith, Ernest Payne (Great Britain)	Max Götze, Rudolf Katzer, Hermann Martens, Karl Neumer (Germany)	William Anderson, Walter Andrews, Frederick McCarthy, William Morton (Canada)
1912: Event not held			
1916: Olympics not held			
1920	Arnaldo Carli, Ruggero Ferrario, Franco Giorgetti, Primo Magnani (Italy)	Cyril Alden, Horace Johnson, William Stewart, Albert White (Great Britain)	Harry Goosen, Henry Kaltenbrun, William Smith, James Walker (South Africa)
1924	Angelo de Martino, Alfredo Dinale, Aurelio Menegazzi, Francesco Zucchetti (Italy)	Józef Lange, Jan Lazarski, Tomasz Stankiewicz, Franciszek Szymczyk (Poland)	Jean van den Bosch, Léonard Daghelinckx, Henri Hoevenaers, Ferdinand Saive (Belgium)
1928	Marco Cattaneo, Cesare Facciani, Mario Lusiani, Luigi Tasselli (Italy)	Janus Braspennincx, Piet van der Horst, Johannes Maas, Jan Pijnenburg (Netherlands)	George Southall, Harry Wyld, Leonard Wyld, Percy Wyld (Great Britain)

Year	Gold	Silver	Bronze
1932	Nino Borsari, Marco Cimatti, Alberto Ghilardi, Paolo Pedretti (Italy)	Paul Chocque, Amédée Fournier, René Legrèves, Henri Mouillefarine (France)	William Harvell, Charles Holland, Ernest Johnson, Frank Southall (Great Britain)
1936	Robert Charpentier, Jean Goujon, Guy Lapébie, Roger-Jean Le Nizerhy (France)	Bianco Bianchi, Mario Gentili, Armando Latini, Severino Rigoni (Italy)	Harry Hill, Ernest Johnson, Charles King, Ernest Mills (Great Britain)
1940–1944: Olympics not held			
1948	Pierre Adam, Serge Blusson, Charles Coste, Fernand Decanali (France)	Arnaldo Benfenati, Guido Bernardi, Anselmo Citterio, Rino Pucci (Italy)	Robert Geldard, Tommy Godwin, David Ricketts, Wilfred Waters (Great Britain)
1952	Loris Campana, Mino de Rossi, Guido Messina, Marino Morettini (Italy)	George Estman, Robert Fowler, Thomas Shardelow, Alfred Swift (South Africa)	Donald Burgess, George Newberry, Alan Newton, Ronald Stretton (Great Britain)
1956	Antonio Domenicali, Leandro Faggin, Franco Gandini, Valentino Gasparella (Italy)	René Bianchi, Jean Graczyk, Jean-Claude Lecante, Michel Vermeulin (France)	Donald Burgess, Michael Gambrill, John Geddes, Thomas Simpson (Great Britain)
1960	Luigi Arienti, Franco Testa, Mario Vallotto, Marino Vigna (Italy)	Bernd Barleben, Peter Gröning, Manfred Klieme, Siegfried Köhler (Germany)	Arnold Belgardt, Leonid Kolumbet, Stanislav Moskvin, Viktor Romanov (Soviet Union)
1964	Lothar Claesges, Karlheinz Henrichs, Karl Link, Ernst Streng (Germany)	Vincenzo Mantovani, Carlo Rancati, Luigi Roncaglia, Franco Testa (Italy)	Henk Cornelisse, Gerard Koel, Jaap Oudkerk, Cor Schuuring (Netherlands)
1968	Gunnar Asmussen, Mogens Jensen, Per Jørgensen, Reno Olsen (Denmark)	Udo Hempel, Karlheinz Henrichs, Jürgen Kissner, Karl Link (West Germany)	Lorenzo Bosisio, Cipriano Chemello, Giorgio Morbiato, Luigi Roncaglia (Italy)
1972	Günther Schumacher, Jürgen Colombo, Günter Haritz, Udo Hempel (West Germany)	Uwe Unterwalder, Thomas Huschke, Heinz Richter, Herbert Richter (East Germany)	William Moore, Michael Bennett, Ian Hallam, Ronald Keeble (Great Britain)
1976	Peter Vonhof, Gregor Braun, Hans Lutz, Günther Schumacher (West Germany)	Viktor Sokolov, Vladimir Osokin, Aleksandr Perov, Vitaly Petrakov (Soviet Union)	Ian Hallam, Ian Banbury, Michael Bennett, Robin Croker (Great Britain)
1980	Viktor Manakov, Valery Movchan, Vladimir Osokin, Vitaly Petrakov (Soviet Union)	Gerald Mortag, Uwe Unterwalder, Matthias Wiegand, Volker Winkler (East Germany)	Teodor Černý, Martin Penc, Jiří Pokorný, Igor Sláma (Czechoslovakia)
1984	Michael Grenda, Kevin Nichols, Michael Turtur, Dean Woods (Australia)	David Grylls, Steve Hegg, Patrick McDonough, Leonard Nitz (United States)	Reinhard Alber, Rolf Gölz, Roland Günther, Michael Marx (West Germany)
1988	Viatcheslav Ekimov, Artūras Kasputis, Dmitry Nelyubin, Gintautas Umaras (Soviet Union)	Carsten Wolf, Steffen Blochwitz, Roland Hennig, Dirk Meier (East Germany)	Scott McGrory, Dean Woods, Brett Dutton, Wayne McCarny, Stephen McGlede (Australia)
1992	Stefan Steinweg, Andreas Walzer, Guido Fulst, Michael Glöckner, Jens Lehmann (Germany)	Stuart O'Grady, Brett Aitken, Stephen McGlede, Shaun O'Brien (Australia)	Jan Petersen, Michael Sandstød, Ken Frost, Jimmi Madsen, Klaus Nielsen (Denmark)
1996	Chistophe Capelle, Philippe Ermenault, Jean-Michel Monin, Francis Moreau (France)	Eduard Gritsun, Nikolay Kuznetsov, Alexei Markov, Anton Shantyr (Russia)	Brett Aitken, Stuart O'Grady, Timothy O'Shannessey, Dean Woods (Australia)
2000	Guido Fulst, Robert Bartko, Daniel Becke, Jens Lehmann (Germany)	Sergiy Chernyavsky, Sergiy Matveyev, Alexander Symonenko, Oleksandr Fedenko (Ukraine)	Paul Manning, Chris Newton, Bryan Steel, Bradley Wiggins (Great Britain)
2004	Graeme Brown, Brett Lancaster, Brad McGee, Luke Roberts (Australia)	Steve Cummings, Rob Hayles, Paul Manning, Bradley Wiggins (Great Britain)	Carlos Castaño, Sergi Escobar, Asier Maeztu, Carlos Torrent (Spain)
2008	Ed Clancy, Paul Manning, Geraint Thomas, Bradley Wiggins (Great Britain)	Casper Jørgensen, Jens-Erik Madsen, Michael Mørkøv, Alex Nicki Rasmussen, Michael Færk Christensen (Denmark)	Sam Bewley, Hayden Roulston, Marc Ryan, Jesse Sergent, Westley Gough (New Zealand)

Men's Individual Sprint

Year	Gold	Silver	Bronze
1896	Paul Masson (France)	Stamatios Nikolopoulos (Greece)	Léon Flameng (France)
1900	Georges Taillandier (France)	Fernand Sanz (France)	John Henry Lake (United States)
1904: Event not held			
1908	Not awarded*	Not awarded*	Not awarded*
1912: Event not held			
1916: Olympics not held			
1920	Maurice Peeters (Netherlands)	Horace Johnson (Great Britain)	Harry Ryan (Great Britain)
1924	Lucien Michard (France)	Jacob Meijer (Holland)	Jean Cugnot (France)
1928	Roger Beaufrand (France)	Antoine Mazairac (Netherlands)	Willy Hansen (Denmark)
1932	Jacobus van Egmond (Netherlands)	Louis Chaillot (France)	Bruno Pellizzari (Italy)
1936	Toni Merkens (Germany)	Arie van Vliet (Netherlands)	Louis Chaillot (France)
1940–1944: Olympics not held			
1948	Mario Ghella (Italy)	Reg Harris (Great Britain)	Axel Schandorff (Denmark)
1952	Enzo Sacchi (Italy)	Lionel Cox (Australia)	Werner Potzernheim (Germany)
1956	Michel Rousseau (France)	Guglielmo Pesenti (Italy)	Dick Ploog (Australia)
1960	Sante Gaiardoni (Italy)	Leo Sterckx (Belgium)	Valentino Gasparella (Italy)
1964	Giovanni Pettenella (Italy)	Sergio Bianchetto (Italy)	Daniel Morelon (France)
1968	Daniel Morelon (France)	Giurdano Turrini (Italy)	Pierre Trentin (France)
1972	Daniel Morelon (France)	John Nicholson (Australia)	Omar Pkhakadze (Soviet Union)
1976	Anton Tkáč (Czechoslovakia)	Daniel Morelon (France)	Jürgen Geschke (East Germany)
1980	Lutz Heßlich (East Germany)	Yave Cahard (France)	Sergei Kopylov (Soviet Union)
1984	Mark Gorski (United States)	Nelson Vails (United States)	Tsutomo Sakamoto (Japan)
1988	Lutz Heßlich (East Germany)	Nikolay Kovsh (Soviet Union)	Gary Neiwand (Australia)
1992	Jens Fiedler (Germany)	Gary Neiwand (Australia)	Curtis Harnett (Canada)
1996	Jens Fiedler (Germany)	Marty Nothstein (United States)	Curtis Harnett (Canada)
2000	Marty Nothstein (United States)	Florian Rousseau (France)	Jens Fiedler (Germany)
2004	Ryan Bayley (Australia)	Theo Bos (Netherlands)	René Wolff (Germany)
2008	Chris Hoy (Great Britain)	Jason Kenny (Great Britain)	Mickaël Bourgain (France)

* No medals awarded, as the race was declared void due to time.

Men's Team Sprint

Year	Gold	Silver	Bronze
2000	Florian Rousseau, Arnaud Tournant, Laurent Gané (France)	Chris Hoy, Craig MacLean, Jason Queally (Great Britain)	Gary Neiwand, Sean Eadie, Darryn Hill (Australia)
2004	Jens Fiedler, Stefan Nimke, René Wolff (Germany)	Toshiaki Fushimi, Masaki Inoue, Tomohiro Nagatsuka (Japan)	Mickaël Bourgain, Laurent Gané, Arnaud Tournant (France)
2008	Chris Hoy, Jason Kenny, Jamie Staff (Great Britain)	Grégory Baugé, Kévin Sireau, Arnaud Tournant (France)	René Enders, Maximilian Levy, Stefan Nimke (Germany)

Women's Individual Sprint

Year	Gold	Silver	Bronze
1988	Erika Salumäe (Soviet Union)	Christa Luding (East Germany)	Connie Young (United States)
1992	Erika Salumäe (Estonia)	Annett Neumann (Germany)	Ingrid Haringa (Netherlands)
1996	Félicia Ballanger (France)	Michelle Ferris (Australia)	Ingrid Haringa (Netherlands)
2000	Félicia Ballanger (France)	Oksana Grishina (Russia)	Iryna Yanovych (Ukraine)
2004	Lori-Ann Muenzer (Canada)	Tamilla Abassova (Russia)	Anna Meares (Australia)
2008	Victoria Pendleton (Great Britain)	Anna Meares (Australia)	Guo Shuang (China)

Women's 3,000-Meter Individual Pursuit

Year	Gold	Silver	Bronze
1992	Petra Roßner (Germany)	Kathryn Watt (Australia)	Rebecca Twigg (United States)
1996	Antonella Bellutti (Italy)	Marion Clignet (France)	Judith Arndt (Germany)
2000	Leontien Zijlaard (Netherlands)	Marion Clignet (France)	Yvonne McGregor (Great Britain)
2004	Sarah Ulmer (New Zealand)	Katie Mactier (Australia)	Leontien van Moorsel (Netherlands)
2008	Rebecca Romero (Great Britain)	Wendy Houvenaghel (Great Britain)	Lesya Kalitovska (Ukraine)

Women's Points Race

Year	Gold	Silver	Bronze
1996	Nathalie Lancien (France)	Ingrid Haringa (Netherlands)	Lucy Tyler-Sharman (Australia)
2000	Antonella Bellutti (Italy)	Leontien Zijlaard (Netherlands)	Olga Slioussareva (Russia)
2004	Olga Slyusareva (Russia)	Belem Guerrero Méndez (Mexico)	María Luisa Calle (Colombia)
2008	Marianne Vos (Netherlands)	Yoanka González (Cuba)	Leire Olaberría (Spain)

Women's 500-Meter Time Trial

Year	Gold	Silver	Bronze
2000	Félicia Ballanger (France)	Michelle Ferris (Australia)	Cuihua Jiang (China)
2004	Anna Meares (Australia)	Jiang Yonghua (China)	Natallia Tsylinskaya (Belarus)

Men's 1,980-Yard Team Pursuit

Year	Gold	Silver	Bronze
1908	Benjamin Jones, Clarence Kingsbury, Leon Meredith, Ernest Payne (Great Britain)	Max Götze, Rudolf Katzer, Hermann Martens, Karl Neumer (Germany)	William Anderson, Walter Andrews, Frederick McCarthy, William Morton (Canada)

Men's 1-Kilometer Pursuit

Year	Gold	Silver	Bronze
1928	Roger Beaufrand (France)	Antonius Hendrikus Mazairac (Netherlands)	Willy Falck Hansen (Denmark)

Men's Olympic Sprint

Year	Gold	Silver	Bronze
2000	Arnaud Tournant, Florian Rousseau, Laurent Gane (France)	Chris Hoy, Craig MacLean, Jason Queally (Great Britain)	Darryn Hill, Garry Malcolm Neiwand, Sean Eadie (Australia)

Men's One Lap (660-Yard) Sprint

Year	Gold	Silver	Bronze
1908	Victor Louis Johnson (Great Britain)	Emile Demangel (France)	Karl Neumer (Germany)

Mountain Bike

Men's Cross-Country

Year	Gold	Silver	Bronze
1996	Bart Brentjens (Netherlands)	Thomas Frischknecht (Switzerland)	Miguel Martinez (France)
2000	Miguel Martinez (France)	Filip Meirhaeghe (Belgium)	Christoph Sauser (Switzerland)
2004	Julien Absalon (France)	José Antonio Hermida (Spain)	Bart Brentjens (Netherlands)
2008	Julien Absalon (France)	Jean-Christophe Péraud (France)	Nino Schurter (Switzerland)

Women's Cross-Country

Year	Gold	Silver	Bronze
1996	Paola Pezzo (Italy)	Alison Sydor (Canada)	Susan DeMattei (United States)
2000	Paola Pezzo (Italy)	Barbara Blatter (Switzerland)	Margarita Fullana (Spain)
2004	Gunn-Rita Dahle (Norway)	Marie-Hélène Prémont (Canada)	Sabine Spitz (Germany)
2008	Sabine Spitz (Germany)	Maja Włoszczowska (Poland)	Irina Kalentieva (Russia)

Diving

Men's 10-Meter Platform

Year	Gold	Silver	Bronze
1904	George Sheldon (United States)	Georg Hoffmann (Germany)	Alfred Brunschweiger (Germany) Frank Kehoe (United States)
1908	Hjalmar Johansson (Sweden)	Karl Malmström (Sweden)	Arvid Spångberg (Sweden)
1912	Erik Aldlerz (Sweden)	Albert Zürner (Germany)	Gustaf Blomgren (Sweden)
1916: Olympics not held			
1920	Clarence Pinkston (United States)	Erik Adlerz (Sweden)	Harry Prieste (United States)
1924	Albert White (United States)	David Fall (United States)	Clarence Pinkston (United States)
1928	Pete Desjardins (United States)	Farid Simaika (Egypt)	Michael Galitzen (United States)
1932	Harold Smith (United States)	Michael Galitzen (United States)	Frank Kurtz (United States)
1936	Marshall Wayne (United States)	Elbert Root (United States)	Hermann Stork (Germany)
1940–1944: Olympics not held			
1948	Sammy Lee (United States)	Bruce Harlan (United States)	Joaquín Capilla (Mexico)
1952	Sammy Lee (United States)	Joaquín Capilla (Mexico)	Günther Haase (Germany)
1956	Joaquín Capilla (Mexico)	Gary Robian (United States)	Richard Connor (United States)
1960	Bob Webster (United States)	Gary Tobian (United States)	Brian Phelps (Great Britain)
1964	Bob Webster (United States)	Klaus Dibiasi (Italy)	Thomas Gompf (United States)
1968	Klaus Dibiasi (Italy)	Alvaro Gaxiola (Mexico)	Edwin Young (United States)
1972	Klaus Dibiasi (Italy)	Richard Rydze (United States)	Giorgio Cagnotto (Italy)
1976	Klaus Dibiasi (Italy)	Greg Louganis (United States)	Vladimir Aleynik (Soviet Union)
1980	Frank Hoffmann (East Germany)	Vladimir Aleynik (Soviet Union)	David Ambartsumyan (Soviet Union)
1984	Greg Louganis (United States)	Bruce Kimball (United States)	Li Kongzheng (China)
1988	Greg Louganis (United States)	Xiong Ni (China)	Jesús Mena (Mexico)
1992	Sun Shuwei (China)	Scott Donie (United States)	Xiong Ni (China)
1996	Dmitri Sautin (Russia)	Jan Hempel (Germany)	Xiong Ni (China)
2000	Tian Liang (China)	Hu Jia (China)	Dmitri Sautin (Russia)
2004	Hu Jia (China)	Mathew Helm (Australia)	Tian Liang (China)
2008	Matthew Mitcham (Australia)	Zhou Lüxin (China)	Gleb Galperin (Russia)

Men's 3-Meter Springboard

Year	Gold	Silver	Bronze
1908	Albert Zürner (Germany)	Kurt Behrens (Germany)	George Gaidzik (United States) Gottlob Walz (Germany)
1912	Paul Günther (Germany)	Hans Luber (Germany)	Kurt Behrens (Germany)
1916: Olympics not held			
1920	Louis Kuehn (United States)	Clarence Pinkston (United States)	Louis Balbach (United States)
1924	Albert White (United States)	Pete Desjardins (United States)	Clarence Pinkston (United States)
1928	Pete Desjardins (United States)	Michael Galitzen (United States)	Farid Simaika (Egypt)
1932	Michael Galitzen (United States)	Harold Smith (United States)	Richard Degener (United States)
1936	Richard Degener (United States)	Marshall Wayne (United States)	Alan Greene (United States)
1940–1944: Olympics not held			
1948	Bruce Harlan (United States)	Miller Anderson (United States)	Sammy Lee (United States)
1952	David Browning (United States)	Miller Anderson (United States)	Bob Clotworthy (United States)
1956	Bob Clotworthy (United States)	Donald Harper (United States)	Joaquín Capilla (Mexico)
1960	Gary Tobian (United States)	Samuel Hall (United States)	Juan Botella (Mexico)
1964	Kenneth Sitzberger (United States)	Francis Gorman (United States)	Lawrence Andreasen (United States)
1968	Bernard Wrightson (United States)	Klaus Dibiasi (Italy)	James Henry (United States)
1972	Vladimir Vasin (Soviet Union)	Giorgio Cagnotto (Italy)	Craig Lincoln (United States)
1976	Phil Boggs (United States)	Giorgio Cagnotto (Italy)	Aleksandr Kosenkov (Soviet Union)
1980	Aleksandr Portnov (Soviet Union)	Carlos Girón (Mexico)	Giorgio Cagnotto (Italy)
1984	Greg Louganis (United States)	Tan Liangde (China)	Ronald Merriott (United States)
1988	Greg Louganis (United States)	Tan Liangde (China)	Li Deliang (China)
1992	Mark Lenzi (United States)	Tan Liangde (China)	Dmitri Sautin (Unified Team)
1996	Xiong Ni (China)	Yu Zhuocheng (China)	Mark Lenzi (United States)
2000	Xiong Ni (China)	Fernando Platas (Mexico)	Dmitri Sautin (Russia)
2004	Peng Bo (China)	Alexandre Despatie (Canada)	Dmitri Sautin (Russia)
2008	He Chong (China)	Alexandre Despatie (Canada)	Qin Kai (China)

Men's Synchronized 10-Meter Platform

Year	Gold	Silver	Bronze
2000	Dmitri Sautin, Igor Lukashin (Russia)	Hu Jua & Tian Liang (China)	Jan Hempel & Heiko Meyer (Germany)
2004	Tian Liang, Yang Jinghui (China)	Peter Waterfield, Leon Taylor (Great Britain)	Lathew Helm, Robert Newbery (Australia)
2008	Lin Yue, Huo Liang (China)	Patrick Hausding, Sascha Klein (Germany)	Gleb Galperin, Dmitriy Dobroskok (Russia)

Men's Synchronized 3-Meter Springboard

Year	Gold	Silver	Bronze
2000	Xiong Ni, Xiao Hailiang (China)	Dmitri Sautin, Alexandre Dobroskok (Russia)	Robert Newbery, Dean Pullar (Australia)
2004	Thomas Bimis, Nikolaos Siranidis (Greece)	Tobias Schellenberg, Andreas Wels (Germany)	Steven Barnett, Robert Newbery (Australia)
2008	Wang Feng, Qin Kai (China)	Dmitri Sautin, Yuriy Kunakov (Russia)	Illya Kvasha, Oleksiy Prygorov (Ukraine)

Men's Plunge for Distance

Year	Gold	Silver	Bronze
1904	William Dickey (United States)	Edgar Adams (United States)	Leo Joseph Goodwin (United States)

Men's Plain High Diving

Year	Gold	Silver	Bronze
1912	Erik Adlerz (Sweden)	Hjalmar Johansson (Sweden)	John Jansson (Sweden)
1916: Olympics not held			
1920	Arvid Wallman (Sweden)	Nils Skoglund (Sweden)	John Jansson (Sweden)
1924	Dick Eve (Australia)	John Jansson (Sweden)	Harold Clarke (Great Britain)

Women's 10-Meter Platform

Year	Gold	Silver	Bronze
1912	Greta Johansson (Sweden)	Lisa Regnell (Sweden)	Isabelle White (Great Britain)
1916: Olympics not held			
1920	Stefanie Clausen (Denmark)	Beatrice Armstrong (Great Britain)	Eva Olliwier (Sweden)
1924	Caroline Smith (United States)	Elizabeth Becker (United States)	Hjördis Töpel (Sweden)
1928	Elizabeth Becker-Pinkson (United States)	Georgia Coleman (United States)	Laura Sjöqvist (Sweden)
1932	Dorothy Poynton (United States)	Georgia Coleman (United States)	Marion Roper (United States)
1936	Dorothy Poynton-Hill (United States)	Velma Dunn (United States)	Käthe Köhler (Germany)
1940–1944: Olympics not held			
1948	Vicki Graves (United States)	Patsy Elsener (United States)	Blirte Christoffersen (Denmark)
1952	Pat McCormick (United States)	Paula Myers (United States)	Juno Stover-Irwin (United States)
1956	Pat McCormick (United States)	Juno Stover-Irwin (United States)	Paula Pope (United States)
1960	Ingrid Krämer (Germany)	Paula Pope (United States)	Ninel Krutova (Soviet Union)
1964	Lesley Bush (United States)	Ingrid Krämer (Germany)	Galina Alekseeva (Soviet Union)
1968	Milena Duchková (Czechoslovakia)	Natalya Lobanova (Soviet Union)	Ann Peterson (United States)
1972	Ulrika Knape (Sweden)	Milena Duchková (Czechoslovakia)	Marina Janicke (East Germany)
1976	Elena Vaytsekhovskaya (Soviet Union)	Ulrika Knape (Sweden)	Deborah Wilson (United States)
1980	Martina Jäschke (East Germany)	Servard Emirzian (Soviet Union)	Liana Tsotadze (Soviet Union)
1984	Zhou Jihong (China)	Michele Mitchell (United States)	Wendy Wyland (United States)
1988	Xu Yanmei (China)	Michelle Mitchell (United States)	Wendy Williams (United States)
1992	Fu Mingxia (China)	Yelena Miroshina (Unified Team)	Mary Ellen Clark (United States)
1996	Fu Mingxia (China)	Annika Walter (Germany)	Mary Ellen Clark (United States)
2000	Laura Wilkinson (United States)	Li Na (China)	Anne Montminy (Canada)
2004	Chantelle Newbery (Australia)	Lao Lishi (China)	Loudy Tourky (Australia)
2008	Chen Ruolin (China)	Émilie Heymans (Canada)	Wang Xin (China)

Women's 3-Meter Springboard

Year	Gold	Silver	Bronze
1920	Aileen Riggin (United States)	Helen Wainwright (United States)	Thelma Payne (United States)
1924	Elizabeth Becker (United States)	Aileen Riggin (United States)	Caroline Fletcher (United States)
1928	Helen Meany (United States)	Dorothy Poynton (United States)	Georgia Coleman (United States)
1932	Georgia Coleman (United States)	Katherine Rawls (United States)	Jane Fauntz (United States)
1936	Marjorie Gestring (United States)	Katherine Rawls (United States)	Dorothy Poynton-Hill (United States)

Year	Gold	Silver	Bronze
1940–1944: Olympics not held			
1948	Vivki Graves (United States)	Zoe Ann Olsen (United States)	Patsy Elsener (United States)
1952	Pat McCormick (United States)	Madeleine Moreau (France)	Zoe-Ann Olsen-Jensen (United States)
1956	Pat McCormick (United States)	Jeanne Stunyo (United States)	Irene MacDonald (Canada)
1960	Ingrid Krämer (Germany)	Paula Pope (United States)	Elizabeth Ferris (Great Britain)
1964	Ingrid Krämer (Germany)	Jeanne Collier (United States)	Mary Willard (United States)
1968	Susanne Gossick (United States)	Tamara Pogosheva (Soviet Union)	Keala O'Sullivan (United States)
1972	Micki King (United States)	Ulrika Knape (Sweden)	Marina Janiche (East Germany)
1976	Jennifer Chandler (United States)	Christa Köhler (East Germany)	Cynthia Potter (United States)
1980	Irina Kalinina (Soviet Union)	Martina Pröeber (East Germany)	Karin Guthke (East Germany)
1984	Sylvie Bernier (Canada)	Kelly McCormick (United States)	Christina Seufert (United States)
1988	Gao Min (China)	Li Qing (China)	Kelly McCormick (United States)
1992	Gao Min (China)	Irina Lashko (Unified Team)	Brita Baldus (Germany)
1996	Fu Mingxia (China)	Irina Lashko (Russia)	Annie Pelletier (Canada)
2000	Fu Mingxia (China)	Guo Jingjing (China)	Dörte Lindner (Germany)
2004	Guo Jingjing (China)	Wu Minxia (China)	Yulia Pakhalina (Russia)
2008	Guo Jingjing (China)	Yuliya Pakhalina (Russia)	Wu Minxia (China)

Women's Synchronized 10-Meter Platform

Year	Gold	Silver	Bronze
2000	Li Na, Sang Xue (China)	Émilie Heymans, Anne Montminy (Canada)	Rebecca Gilmore, Loudy Tourky (Australia)
2004	Lao Lishi, Li Ting (China)	Natalie Goncharova, Yulia Koltunova (Russia)	Blythe Hartley, Émilie Heymans (Canada)
2008	Wang Xin, Chen Ruolin (China)	Briony Cole, Melissa Wu (Australia)	Paola Espinosa, Tatiana Ortiz (Mexico)

Women's Synchronized 3-Meter Springboard

Year	Gold	Silver	Bronze
2000	Vera Ilina, Ioulia Pakhalina (Russia)	Fu Mingxia, Guo Jingjing (China)	Ganna Sorokina, Olena Zhupina (Ukraine)
2004	Wu Minxia, Guo Jingjing (China)	Vera Ilina, Yulia Pakhalina (Russia)	Irina Lashko, Chantelle Newbery (Australia)
2008	Guo Jingjing, Wu Minxia (China)	Yuliya Pakhalina, Anastasia Pozdnyakova (Russia)	Ditte Kotzian, Heike Fischer (Germany)

Equestrian

Men's Jumping

Year	Gold	Silver	Bronze
1900	Aimé Haegeman (Belgium)	Georges van der Poële (Belgium)	Louis de Champsavin (France)

Men's High Jump

Year	Gold	Silver	Bronze
1900	Dominique Gardères (France) Giovanni Giorgio Trissino (Italy)	Not awarded	Georges van der Poële (Belgium)

Men's Long Jump

Year	Gold	Silver	Bronze
1900	Constant van Langhendonck (Belgium)	Giovanni Giorgio Trissino (Italy)	Pierre de Bellegarde (France)

Mixed Individual Dressage

Year	Gold	Silver	Bronze
1912	Carl Bonde (Sweden)	Gustaf Adolf Boltenstern (Sweden)	Hans von Blixen-Finecke (Sweden)
1916: Olympics not held			
1920	Janne Lundblad (Sweden)	Bertil Sandström (Sweden)	Hans von Rosen (Sweden)
1924	Ernst Linder (Sweden)	Bertil Sandström (Sweden)	Xavier Lesage (France)
1928	Carl Freiherr von Langen (Germany)	Charles Marion (France)	Ragnar Olson (Sweden)
1932	Xavier Lesage (France)	Charles Marion (France)	Hiram Tuttle (United States)
1936	Heinz Pollay (Germany)	Friedrich Gerhard (Germany)	Alois Podhajsky (Austria)
1940–1944: Olympics not held			
1948	Hans Moser (Switzerland)	André Jousseaume (France)	Gustaf Adolf Boltenstern Jr. (Sweden)
1952	Henri Saint Cyr (Sweden)	Lis Hartel (Denmark)	André Jousseaume (Germany)
1956	Henri Saint Cyr (Sweden)	Lis Hartel (Denmark)	Liselott Linsenhoff (United Team of Germany)
1960	Sergei Filatov (Soviet Union)	Gustav Fischer (Switzerland)	Josef Neckermann (United Team of Germany)
1964	Heni Chammartin (Switzerland)	Harry Boldt (United Team of Germany)	Sergei Filatov (Soviet Union)
1968	Ivan Kizimov (Soviet Union)	Josef Neckermann (West Germany)	Reiner Klimke (West Germany)
1972	Liselott Linsenhogg (West Germany)	Yelena Petushkova (Soviet Union)	Josef Neckermann (West Germany)
1976	Christine Stückelberger (Switzerland)	Harry Boldt (West Germany)	Reiner Klimke (West Germany)
1980	Elisabeth Theurer (Austria)	Yuri Kovshov (Soviet Union)	Viktor Ugryumov (Soviet Union)
1984	Reiner Klimke (West Germany)	Anne Jensen-Tornblad (Denmark)	Otto Hoger (Switzerland)
1988	Nicole Uphoff (West Germany)	Margit Otto-Crepin (France)	Christine Stückelberger (Switzerland)
1992	Nicole Uphoff (Germany)	Isabell Werth (Germany)	Klaus Balkenhol (Germany)
1996	Isabell Werth (Germany)	Anky van Grunsven (Netherlands)	Sven Rothenberger (Netherlands)
2000	Anky van Grunsven (Netherlands)	Isabell Werth (Germany)	Ulla Salzgeber (Germany)
2004	Anky van Grunsven (Netherlands)	Ulla Salzgeber (Germany)	Beatriz Ferrer-Salat (Spain)
2008	Anky van Grunsven (Netherlands)	Isabell Werth (Germany)	Heike Kemmer (Germany)

Mixed Team Dressage

Year	Gold	Silver	Bronze
1928	Carl Freiherr von Langen, Hermann Linkenbach, Eugen Freiherr von Lotzbeck (Germany)	Ragnar Olson, Janne Lundblad, Carl Bonde (Sweden)	Jan van Reede, Pierre Versteegh, Gerard le Heux (Netherlands)
1932	Xavier Lesage, Charles Marion, André Jousseaume (France)	Bertil Sandström, Thomas Byström, Gustaf Adolf Boltenstern Jr. (Sweden)	Hiram Tuttle, Isaac Kitts, Alvin Moore (United States)
1936	Heinz Pollay, Friedrich Gerhard, Hermann von Oppeln-Bronikowski (Germany)	André Jousseaume, Gérard de Ballorre, Daniel Gillois (France)	Gregor Adlercreutz, Sven Colliander, Folke Sandström (Sweden)

Year	Gold	Silver	Bronze
1940–1944: Olympics not held			
1948	André Jousseaume, Jean Saint-Fort Paillard, Maurice Buret (France)	Robert Borg, Earl Foster Thomson, Frank Henry (United States)	Fernando Paes, Francisco Valadas, Luís Mena e Silva (Portugal)
1952	Henri Saint Cyr, Gustaf Adolf Boltenstern Jr., Gehnäll Persson (Sweden)	Gottfried Trachsel, Henri Chammartin, Gustav Fischer (Switzerland)	Heinz Pollay, Ida von Nagel, Fritz Thiedemann (Germany)
1956	Henri Saint Cyr, Gehnäll Persson, Gustaf Adolf Boltenstern Jr. (Sweden)	Liselott Linsenhoff, Hannelore Weygand, Anneliese Küppers (Germany)	Gottfried Trachsel, Henri Chammartin, Gustav Fischer (Switzerland)
1960: Event not held			
1964	Harry Boldt, Reiner Klimke, Josef Neckermann (Germany)	Henri Chammartin, Gustav Fischer, Marianne Gossweiler (Switzerland)	Sergei Filatov, Ivan Kizimov, Ivan Kalita (Soviet Union)
1968	Josef Neckermann, Reiner Klimke, Liselott Linsenhoff (West Germany)	Yelena Petushkova, Ivan Kizimov, Ivan Kalita (Soviet Union)	Henri Chammartin, Marianne Gossweiler, Gustav Fischer (Switzerland)
1972	Yelena Petushkova, Ivan Kizimov, Ivan Kalita (Soviet Union)	Karin Schlüter-Schmidt, Liselott Linsenhoff, Josef Neckermann (West Germany)	Ulla Håkansson, Ninna Swaab, Maud von Rosen (Sweden)
1976	Harry Boldt, Reiner Klimke, Gabriela Grillo (West Germany)	Christine Stückelberger, Ulrich Lehmann, Doris Ramseier (Switzerland)	Hilda Gurney, Dorothy Morkis, Edith Master (United States)
1980	Yuri Kovshov, Viktor Ugryumov, Vera Misevich (Soviet Union)	Petar Mandajiev, Svetoslav Ivanov, Gheorghi Gadjev (Bulgaria)	Anghelache Donescu, Dumitru Veliku, Petre Rosca (Romania)
1984	Reiner Klimke, Uwe Sauer, Hubert Krug (West Germany)	Otto Hofer, Christine Stückelberger, Amy De Bary (Switzerland)	Ulla Hakansson, Louise Nathorst, Ingamay Bylund (Sweden)
1988	Reiner Klimke, Ann-Kathrin Linsenhoff, Monica Theodorescu, Nicole Uphoff (West Germany)	Otto Josef Hofer, Christine Stückelberger, Daniel Ramseier, Samuel Schetzmann (Switzerland)	Cynthia Neale-Ishoy, Eva Pracht, Gina Smith, Ashley Nicoll (Canada)
1992	Klaus Balkenhol, Nicole Uphoff, Monica Theodorescu, Isabell Werth (Germany)	Tineke Bartels, Anky van Grunsven, Ellen Bontje, Annemarie Sanders (Netherlands)	Robert Dover, Carol Lavell, Charlotte Bredahl, Michael Poulin (United States)
1996	Klaus Balkenhol, Martin Schaudt, Monica Theodorescu, Isabell Werth (Germany)	Tineke Bartels, Anky van Grunsven, Sven Rothenberger, Gonnelien Rothenberger (Netherlands)	Robert Dover, Michelle Gibson, Steffen Peters, Guenter Seidel (United States)
2000	Isabell Werth, Nadine Capellmann, Ulla Salzgeber, Alexandra Simons de Ridder (Germany)	Ellen Bontje, Anky van Grunsven, Arjen Teeuwissen, Coby van Baalen (Netherlands)	Susan Blinks, Robert Dover, Guenter Seidel, Christine Traurig (United States)
2004	Heike Kemmer, Hubertus Schmidt, Martin Schaudt, Ulla Salzgeber (Germany)	Beatriz Ferrer-Salat, Juan Antonio Jimenez, Ignacio Rambla, Rafael Soto (Spain)	Lisa Wilcox, Günter Seidel, Deborah McDonald, Robert Dovery (United States)
2008	Heike Kemmer, Nadine Capellmann, Isabell Werth (Germany)	Hans Peter Minderhoud, Imke Schellekens-Bartels, Anky van Grunsven (Netherlands)	Anne van Olst, Princess Nathalie of Sayn-Wittgenstein-Berleburg, Andreas Helgstrand (Denmark)

Mixed Individual Eventing

Year	Gold	Silver	Bronze
1912	Axel Nordlander (Sweden)	Friedrich von Rochow (Germany)	Jean Cariou (France)
1916: Olympics not held			
1920	Helmer Mörner (Sweden)	Åge Lundström (Sweden)	Ettore Caffaratti (Italy)
1924	Adolph van der Voort van Zijp (Netherlands)	Frode Kirkenbjerg (Denmark)	Sloan Doak (United States)

Year	Gold	Silver	Bronze
1928	Charles Pahud de Mortanges (Netherlands)	Gerard de Kruijff (Netherlands)	Bruno Neumann (Germany)
1932	Charles Pahud de Mortanges (Netherlands)	Earl Foster Thomson (United States)	Clarence von Rosen Jr. (Sweden)
1936	Ludwig Stubbendorf (Germany)	Earl Foster Thomson (United States)	Hans Linding (Denmark)
1940–1944: Olympics not held			
1948	Bernard Chevallier (France)	Frank Henry (United States)	Robert Selfelt (Sweden)
1952	Hans von Blixen-Finecke Jr. (Sweden)	Guy Lefrant (France)	Wilhelm Büsing (Germany)
1956	Petrus Kastenman (Sweden)	August Lütke-Westhues (United Team of Germany)	Francis Weldon (Great Britain)
1960	Lawrence Morgan (Australia)	Neale Labis (Australia)	Anton Bühler (Switzerland)
1964	Mauro Checcoli (Italy)	Carlos Moratorio (Argentina)	Fritz Ligges (United Team of Germany)
1968	Jean-Jacques Guyon (France)	Derek Allhusen (Great Britain)	Michael Page (United States)
1972	Richard Meade (Great Britain)	Alessandro Argenton (Italy)	Jan Jönsson (Sweden)
1976	Edmund Coffin (United States)	Michael Plumb (United States)	Karl Schultz (West Germany)
1980	Federico Euro Roman (Italy)	Aleksandr Blinov (Soviet Union)	Yuri Salnikov (Soviet Union)
1984	Mark Todd (New Zealand)	Karen Stives (United States)	Virginia Leng (Great Britain)
1988	Mark Todd (New Zealand)	Ian Stark (Great Britain)	Virginia Leng (Great Britain)
1992	Matthew Ryan (Australia)	Herbert Bloecker (Germany)	Blyth Tait (New Zealand)
1996	Blyth Tait (New Zealand)	Sally Clark (New Zealand)	Kerry Millikin (United States)
2000	David O'Connor (United States)	Andrew Hoy (Australia)	Mark Todd (New Zealand)
2004	Leslie Law (Great Britain)	Kimberly Severson (United States)	Pippa Finnell (Great Britain)
2008	Hinrich Romeike (Germany)	Gina Miles (United States)	Kristina Cook (Great Britain)

Mixed Team Eventing

Year	Gold	Silver	Bronze
1912	Axel Nordlander, Nils Adlercreutz, Ernst Casparsson, Henric Horn af Åminne (Sweden)	Friedrich von Rochow, Richard von Schaesberg, Eduard von Lütcken, Carl von Moers (Germany)	Ben Lear, John Montgomery, Guy Henry, Ephraim Graham (United States)
1916: Olympics not held			
1920	Helmer Mörner, Åge Lundström, Georg von Braun, Gustaf Dyrsch (Sweden)	Ettore Caffaratti, Garibaldi Spighi, Giulio Cacciandra, Carlo Asinari (Italy)	Roger Moeremans d'Emaüs, Oswald Lints, Jules Bonvalet, Jacques Misonne (Belgium)
1924	Adolph van der Voort van Zijp, Charles Pahud de Mortanges, Gerard de Kruijff, Antonius Colenbrander (Netherlands)	Claës König, Torsten Sylvan, Gustaf Hagelin, Carl Gustaf Lewenhaupt (Sweden)	Alberto Lombardi, Alessandro Alvisi, Emanuele Beraudo di Pralormo, Tommaso Lequio di Assaba (Italy)
1928	Charles Pahud de Mortanges, Gerard de Kruijff, Adolph van der Voort van Zijp (Netherlands)	Bjart Ording, Arthur Qvist, Eugen Johansen (Norway)	Michał Antoniewicz, Józef Trenkwald, Karol Rómmel (Poland)
1932	Earl Foster Thomson, Harry Chamberlin, Edwin Argo (United States)	Charles Pahud de Mortanges, Karel Schummelketel, Aernout van Lennep (Netherlands)	Not awarded
1936	Ludwig Stubbendorf, Rudolf Lippert, Konrad Freiherr von Wangenheim (Germany)	Henryk Roycewicz, Zdzisław Kawecki, Seweryn Kulesza (Poland)	Alec Scott, Edward Howard-Vyse, Richard Fanshawe (Great Britain)
1940–1944: Olympics not held			
1948	Frank Henry, Charles Anderson, Earl Foster Thomson (United States)	Robert Selfelt, Olof Stahre, Sigurd Svensson (Sweden)	Humberto Mariles, Raúl Campero, Joaquín Solano (Mexico)

Year	Gold	Silver	Bronze
1952	Hans von Blixen-Finecke Jr., Olof Stahre, Folke Frölén (Sweden)	Wilhelm Büsing, Klaus Wagner, Otto Rothe (Germany)	Charles Hough Jr., Walter Staley Jr., John Wofford (United States)
1956	Francis Weldon, Arthur Rook, Bertie Hill (Great Britain)	August Lütke-Westhues, Otto Rothe, Klaus Wagner (Germany)	John Rumble, Jim Elder, Brian Herbinson (Canada)
1960	Lawrence Morgan, Neale Lavis, Bill Roycroft (Australia)	Anton Bühler, Hans Schwarzenbach, Rudolf Günthardt (Switzerland)	Jack le Goff, Guy Lefrant, Jehan le Roy (France)
1964	Mauro Checcoli, Paolo Angioni, Giuseppe Ravano (Italy)	Michael Page, Kevin Freeman, John Plumb (United States)	Fritz Ligges, Horst Karsten, Gerhard Schulz (Germany)
1968	Derek Allhusen, Richard Meade, Reuben Jones (Great Britain)	Michael Page, James C. Wofford, John Plumb (United States)	Wayne Roycroft, Brien Cobcroft, Bill Roycroft (Australia)
1972	Richard Meade, Mary Gordon-Watson, Bridget Parker, Mark Phillips (Great Britain)	Kevin Freeman, Bruce Davidson, John Plumb, James C. Wofford (United States)	Harry Klugmann, Ludwig Gössing, Karl Schultz, Horst Karsten (West Germany)
1976	Edmund Coffin, Michael Plumb, Bruce Davidson, Mary Anne Tauskey (United States)	Karl Schultz, Herbert Blöcker, Helmut Rethemeier, Otto Ammermann (West Germany)	Wayne Roycroft, Mervyn Bennet, Bill Roycroft, Denis Pigott (Australia)
1980	Aleksandr Blinov, Yuri Salnikov, Valery Volkov, Sergei Rogozhin (Soviet Union)	Federico Euro Roman, Anna Casagrande, Mauro Roman, Marina Sciocchetti (Italy)	Yocupicio Manuel Mendivil, Rios David Barcena, Soto Jose Luis Perez, Lopez Fabian Vazquez (Mexico)
1984	Michael Plumb, Karen Stives, Torrance Fleischmann, Bruce Davidson (United States)	Virginia Leng, Ian Stark, Diana Clapham, Lucinda Green (Great Britain)	Bettina Overesch, Burkhard Tesdorpf, Claus Erhorn, Dietmar Hogrefe (West Germany)
1988	Claus Erhorn, Matthias Andreas Baumann, Thies Kaspareit, Ralf Ehrenbrink (West Germany)	Captain Mark Phillips, Karen Straker, Virginia Leng, Ian Stark (Great Britain)	Mark Todd, Margaret Knighton, Andrew Bennie, Tinks Pottinger (New Zealand)
1992	David Green, Gillian Rolton, Andrew Hoy, Matthew Ryan (Australia)	Blyth Tait, Andrew Nicholson, Mark Todd, Victoria Latta (New Zealand)	Herbert Bloecker, Ralf Ehrenbrink, Matthias Baumann, Cord Mysegages (Germany)
1996	Wendy Schaeffer, Gillian Rolton, Andrew Hoy, Phillip Dutton (Australia)	Karen O'Connor, David O'Connor, Bruce Davidson, Jill Henneberg (United States)	Blyth Tait, Andrew Nicholson, Vaughn Jefferis, Victoria Latta (New Zealand)
2000	Phillip Dutton, Andrew Hoy, Stuart Tinney, Matt Ryan (Australia)	Ian Stark, Jeanette Brakewell, Pippa Funnell, Leslie Law (Great Britain)	Nina Fout, Karen O'Connor, David O'Connor, Linden Wiesman (United States)
2004	Arnaud Boiteau, Cédric Lyard, Didier Courrèges, Jean Teulère, Nicolas Touzaint (France)	Jeanette Brakewell, Mary King, Leslie Law, Pippa Funnell, William Fox-Pitt (Great Britain)	Kimberly Severson, Darren Chiacchia, John Williams, Amy Tryon, Julie Richards (United States)
2008	Peter Thomsen, Frank Ostholt, Andreas Dibowski, Ingrid Klimke, Hinrich Romeike (Germany)	Shane Rose, Sonja Johnson, Lucinda Fredericks, Clayton Fredericks, Megan Jones (Australia)	Sharon Hunt, Daisy Dick, William Fox-Pitt, Kristina Cook, Mary King (Great Britain)

Mixed Individual Jumping

Year	Gold	Silver	Bronze
1912	Jean Cariou (France)	Rabod von Kröcher (Germany)	Emmanuel de Blommaert (Belgium)
1916: Olympics not held			
1920	Tommaso Lequio di Assaba (Italy)	Alessandro Valerio (Italy)	Carl Gustaf Lewenhaupt (Sweden)
1924	Alphonse Gemuseus (Switzerland)	Tommaso Lequio di Assaba (Italy)	Adam Królikiewicz (Poland)
1928	František Ventura (Czechoslovakia)	Pierre Bertran de Balanda (France)	Charles-Gustave Kuhn (Switzerland)
1932	Takeichi Nishi (Japan)	Harry Chamberlin (United States)	Clarence von Rosen Jr. (Sweden)
1936	Kurt Hasse (Germany)	Henri Rang (Romania)	József von Platthy (Hungary)

Year	Gold	Silver	Bronze
1940–1944: Olympics not held			
1948	Humberto Mariles (Mexico)	Rubén Uriza (Mexico)	Jean-François d'Orgeix (France)
1952	Pierre Jonquères d'Oriola (France)	Óscar Cristi (Chile)	Fritz Thiedemann (Germany)
1956	Hans Günter Winkler (United Team of Germany)	Raimondo D'Inzeo (Italy)	Piero D'Inzeo (Italy)
1960	Raimondo D'Inzeo (Italy)	Piero D'Inzeo (Italy)	David Broome (Great Britain)
1964	Pierre Jonquères d'Oriola (France)	Hermann Schridde (United Team of Germany)	Peter Robeson (Great Britain)
1968	William Steinkraus (United States)	Marion Coakes (Great Britain)	David Broome (Great Britain)
1972	Graziano Mancinelli (Italy)	Ann Moore (Great Britain)	Neal Shapiro (United States)
1976	Alwin Schockemöhle (West Germany)	Michel Vaillancourt (Canada)	François Mathy (Belgium)
1980	Jan Kowalczyk (Poland)	Nikolai Korolkov (Soviet Union)	Joaquin Pérez (Mexico)
1984	Joseph Fargis (United States)	Conrad Homfeld (United States)	Heidi Robbiani (Switzerland)
1988	Pierre Durand Jr. (France)	Greg Best (United States)	Karsten Huck (West Germany)
1992	Ludger Beerbaum (Germany)	Piet Raymakers (Netherlands)	Norman Dello Joio (United States)
1996	Ulrich Kirchhoff (Germany)	Wilhelm Melliger (Switzerland)	Alexandra Ledermann (France)
2000	Jeroen Dubbeldam (Netherlands)	Albert Voorn (Netherlands)	Khaled Al Eid (Saudi Arabia)
2004	Rodrigo Pessoa (Brazil)	Chris Kappler (United States)	Marco Kutscher (Germany)
2008	Eric Lamaze (Canada)	Rolf-Göran Bengtsson (Sweden)	Beezie Madden (United States)

Mixed Team Show Jumping

Year	Gold	Silver	Bronze
1912	Gustaf Lewenhaupt, Gustaf Kilman, Hans von Rosen, Fredrik Rosencrantz (Sweden)	Michel Dufourt, Jean Cariou, Bernard Meyer, Albert Seigner (France)	Sigismund Freyer, Wilhelm von Hohenau, Ernst Deloch, Prince Friedrich Karl of Prussia (Germany)
1916: Olympics not held			
1920	Claës König, Hans von Rosen, Daniel Norling, Frank Martin (Sweden)	Henri Laame, André Coumans, Herman de Gaiffier d'Hestroy, Herman d'Oultromont (Belgium)	Ettore Caffaratti, Alessandro Alvisi, Giulio Cacciandra, Carlo Asinari (Italy)
1924	Åke Thelning, Axel Ståhle, Åge Lundström (Sweden)	Alphonse Gemuseus, Werner Stuber, Hans Bühler (Switzerland)	António Borges, Hélder de Souza, José Mouzinho (Portugal)
1928	José Navarro Morenes, José Álvarez de Bohórquez, Julio García Fernández (Spain)	Kazimierz Gzowski, Kazimierz Szosland, Michał Antoniewicz (Poland)	Karl Hansén, Carl Björnstjerna, Ernst Hallberg (Sweden)
1932	Not awarded*	Not awarded*	Not awarded*
1936	Kurt Hasse, Marten von Barnekow, Heinz Brandt (Germany)	Johan Greter, Jan de Bruine, Henri van Schaik (Netherlands)	José Beltrão, Domingos de Sousa, Luís Mena e Silva (Portugal)
1940–1944: Olympics not held			
1948	Humberto Mariles, Rubén Uriza, Alberto Valdés (Mexico)	Jaime García, José Navarro Morenes, Marcellino Gavilán (Spain)	Harry Llewellyn, Henry Nicoll, Arthur Carr (Great Britain)
1952	Wilfred White, Douglas Stewart, Harry Llewellyn (Great Britain)	Óscar Cristi, César Mendoza, Ricardo Echeverría (Chile)	William Steinkraus, Arthur McCashin, John William Russell (United States)
1956	Hans Günter Winkler, Fritz Thiedemann, Alfons Lütke-Westhues (United Team of Germany)	Raimondo D'Inzeo, Piero D'Inzeo, Salvatore Oppes (Italy)	Wilfred White, Pat Smythe, Peter Robeson (Great Britain)

Year	Gold	Silver	Bronze
1960	Hans Günter Winkler, Fritz Thiedemann, Alwin Schockemöhle (United Team of Germany)	Frank Chapot, William Steinkraus, George H. Morris (United States)	Raimondo D'Inzeo, Piero D'Inzeo, Antonio Oppes (Italy)
1964	Hermann Schridde, Kurt Jarasinski, Hans Günter Winkler (United Team of Germany)	Pierre Jonquères d'Oriola, Janou Lefèbvre, Guy Lefrant (France)	Piero D'Inzeo, Raimondo D'Inzeo, Graziano Mancinelli (Italy)
1968	James Day, Thomas Gayford, Jim Elder (Canada)	Jean Rozier, Janou Lefèbvre, Pierre Jonquères d'Oriola (France)	Hermann Schridde, Alwin Schockemöhle, Hans Günter Winkler (West Germany)
1972	Fritz Ligges, Gerhard Wiltfang, Hartwig Steenken, Hans Günter Winkler (West Germany)	William Steinkraus, Neal Shapiro, Kathryn Kusner, Frank Chapot (United States)	Vittorio Orlandi, Raimondo D'Inzeo, Graziano Mancinelli, Piero D'Inzeo (Italy)
1976	Hubert Parot, Jean-Marcel Rozier, Marc Roguet, Michel Roche (France)	Alwin Schockemöhle, Hans Günter Winkler, Sönke Sönksen, Paul Schockemöhle (West Germany)	Eric Wauters, François Mathy, Edgar-Henri Cuepper, Stanny Van Paesschen (Belgium)
1980	Vyacheslav Chukanov, Viktor Poganovsky, Viktor Asmaev, Nikolai Korolkov (Soviet Union)	Marian Kozicki, Jan Kowalczyk, Wiesław Hartman, Janusz Bobik (Poland)	Joaquin Perez Heras, Jesus Gomez Portugal, Valencia Gerardo Tazzer, Alberto Valdes Lacarra (Mexico)
1984	Joseph Fargis, Conrad Homfeld, Leslie Howard, Melanie Smith (United States)	Michael Whitaker, John Whitaker, Steven Smith, Timothy Grubb (Great Britain)	Paul Schockemöhle, Peter Luther, Franke Sloothaak, Fritz Ligges (West Germany)
1988	Ludger Beerbaum, Wolfgang Brinkmann, Dirk Hafemeister, Franke Sloothaak (West Germany)	Greg Best, Lisa Ann Jacquin, Anne Kursinski, Joseph Fargis (United States)	Hubert Bourdy, Frédéric Cottier, Michel Robert, Pierre Durand Jr. (France)
1992	Piet Raymakers, Bert Romp, Jan Tops, Jos Lansink (Netherlands)	Boris Boor, Joerg Muenzner, Hugo Simon, Thomas Fruehmann (Austria)	Hervé Godignon, Hubert Bourdy, Michel Robert, Eric Navet (France)
1996	Franke Sloothaak, Lars Nieberg, Ulrich Kirchhoff, Ludger Beerbaum (Germany)	Peter Leone, Leslie Burr-Howard, Anne Kursinski, Michael R. Matz (United States)	Luiz Azevedo, Alvaro Miranda Neto, Andre Johannpeter, Rodrigo Pessoa (Brazil)
2000	Ludger Beerbaum, Lars Nieberg, Marcus Ehning, Otto Becker (Germany)	Markus Fuchs, Beat Maendli, Lesley McNaught, Willi Melliger (Switzerland)	Rodrigo Pessoa, Luiz Felipe De Azevedo, Álvaro Miranda Neto, Andre Johannpeter (Brazil)
2004	Peter Wylde, McLain Ward, Beezie Madden, Chris Kappler (United States)	Rolf-Göran Bengtsson, Malin Baryard, Peter Eriksson, Peder Fredericson (Sweden)	Otto Becker, Marco Kutscher, Christian Ahlmann (Germany)
2008	McLain Ward, Laura Kraut, Will Simpson, Beezie Madden (United States)	Jill Henselwood, Eric Lamaze, Ian Millar, Mac Cone (Canada)	Christina Liebherr, Pius Schwizer, Niklaus Schurtenberger, Steve Guerdat (Switzerland)

* No medals awarded, as no team completed the course.

Mixed Individual Vaulting

Year	Gold	Silver	Bronze
1920	Daniel Bouckaert (Belgium)	Field* (France)	Louis Finet (Belgium)

* Full name not known.

Mixed Team Vaulting

Year	Gold	Silver	Bronze
1920	Daniel Bouckaert, Louis Finet, Van Ranst (Belgium)	Field*, Salins*, Cauchy* (France)	Carl Green, Anders Mårtensson, Oskar Nilsson (Sweden)

* Full name not known.

Mixed Individual Figure Riding

Year	Gold	Silver	Bronze
1920	T. Bouckaert* (Belgium)	Field* (France)	T. Finet* (Belgium)

* Full name not known.

Mixed Team Figure Riding

Year	Gold	Silver	Bronze
1920	T. Bouckaert*, T. Fiinet*, Van Cauwenberg*, Van Ranst*, Van Schauwbroeck* (Belgium)	Cauchy*, Field*, Salins* (France)	Anders Märtensson, Carl Green, Oskar Nilsson (Sweden)

* Full name not known.

Fencing

Men's Individual Foil

Year	Gold	Silver	Bronze
1896	Eugène-Henri Gravelotte (France)	Henri Callot (France)	Perikles Pierrakos-Mavromichalis (Greece)
1900	Émile Coste (France)	Henri Masson (France)	Marcel Jacques Boulenger (France)
1904	Ramón Fonst (Cuba)	Albertson Van Zo Post (Cuba)	Charles Tatham (Cuba)
1908: Event not held			
1912	Nedo Nadi (Italy)	Pietro Speciale (Italy)	Richard Verderber (Austria)
1916: Olympics not held			
1920	Nedo Nadi (Italy)	Philippe Cattiau (France)	Roger Ducret (France)
1924	Roger Ducret (France)	Philippe Cattiau (France)	Maurice E. Van Damme (Belgium)
1928	Lucien Gaudin (France)	Erwin Casmir (Germany)	Giulio Gaudini (Italy)
1932	Gustavo Marzi (Italy)	Joseph L. Lewis (United States)	Giulio Gaudini (Italy)
1936	Giulio Gaudini (Italy)	Edward Gardère (France)	Giorgio Bocchino (Italy)
1940–1944: Olympics not held			
1948	Jehan Buhan (France)	Christian d'Oriola (France)	Lajos Maszlay (Hungary)
1952	Christian d'Oriola (France)	Edoardo Mangiarotti (Italy)	Manlio Di Rosa (Italy)
1956	Christian d'Oriola (France)	Giancarlo Bergamini (Italy)	Antonio Spallino (Italy)
1960	Viktor Zhdanovich (Soviet Union)	Yuri Sisikin (Soviet Union)	Albert Axelrod (Soviet Union)
1964	Egon Franke (Poland)	Jean Claude Magnan (France)	Daniel Revenu (France)
1968	Ion Drîmbă (Romania)	Jenö Kamuti (Hungary)	Daniel Revenu (France)
1972	Witold Woyda (Poland)	Jenő Kamuti (Hungary)	Christian Noël (France)
1976	Fabio dal Zotto (Italy)	Aleksander Romankov (Soviet Union)	Bernard Talvard (France)
1980	Vladimir Smirnov (Soviet Union)	Pascal Jolyot (France)	Aleksander Romankov (Soviet Union)
1984	Mauro Numa (Italy)	Matthias Behr (West Germany)	Stefano Cerioni (Italy)
1988	Stefano Cerioni (Italy)	Udo Wagner (East Germany)	Aleksander Romankov (Soviet Union)
1992	Philippe Omnes (France)	Sergei Golubitsky (Unified Team)	Elvis Gregory (Cuba)
1996	Alessandro Puccini (Italy)	Lionel Plumenail (France)	Franck Boidin (France)
2000	Kim Young-Ho (South Korea)	Ralf Bissdorf (Germany)	Dmitriy Shevchenko (Russia)
2004	Brice Guyart (France)	Salvatore Sanzo (Italy)	Andrea Cassarâ (Italy)
2008	Benjamin Kleibrink (Germany)	Yuki Ota (Japan)	Salvatore Sanzo (Italy)

Men's Masters Foil

Year	Gold	Silver	Bronze
1896	Leonidas Pyrgos (Greece)	Jean Maurice Perronet (France)	Not awarded
1900	Lucein Mérignac (France)	Alphonse Kirchhoffer (France)	Jean-Baptiste Mimiague (France)

Men's Team Foil

Year	Gold	Silver	Bronze
1904	Ramón Fonst, Albertson Van Zo Post, Manuel Díaz (Cuba)	Charles Tatham, Charles Townsend, Arthur Fox (United States)	Not awarded
1908–1912: Event not held			
1916: Olympics not held			
1920	Aldo Nadi, Nedo Nadi, Olivier Abelardo, Pietro Speciale, Rodolfo Terlizzi, Oreste Puliti, Tommaso Constantino, Baldo Baldi (Italy)	Andrè Labattut, Georges Trombert, Marcel Perrot, Lucien Gaudin, Philippe Cattiau, Roger Ducret, Gaston Amson, Lionel Bony De Castellane (France)	Francis Honeycutt, Arthur Lyon, Robert Sears, Henry Breckin-ridge, Harold Rayner (United States)
1924	Lucien Gaudin, Philippe Cattiau, Jacques Coutrot, Roger Ducret, Henri Jobier, Andre Labattut, Guy de Lauget, Josef Peroteaux (France)	Désire Beurain, Charles Crahay, Orphile Ferdnand De Montigny, Maurice E. Van Damme, Marcel L. Berre, Albert de Roocker (Belgium)	Laszló Berti, Sándor Pósta, Zoltán Ozoray Schenker, Ödön Tersztyánszky, István Lich-teneckert (Hungary)
1928	Ugo Pignotti, Giulio Gaudini, Giorgio Pessina, Gioachino Guaragna, Oreste Puliti, Giorgio Chiavacci (Italy)	Philippe Cattiau, Roger Ducret, André Labattut, Lucien Gaudin, Raymond Flacher, André Gaboriaud (France)	Roberto Larraz, Raul Anganuzzi, Luis Lucchetti, Hector Lucchetti, Carmelo Camet (Argentina)
1932	Edward Gardère, René Bondoux, René Bougnol, René Lemoine, Philippe Cattiau, Jean Piot (France)	Giulio Gaudini, Gustavo Marzi, Ugo Pignotti, Gioachino Guaragna, Rodolfo Terlizzi, Giorgio Pessina (Italy)	George Charles Calnan, Richard Clarke Steere, Joseph L. Levis, Dernell Every, Hugh Vincent Alessandroni, Frank Righeimer (United States)
1936	Giorgio Bocchino, Manlio Di Rosa, Gioachino Guaragna, Ciro Verratti, Giulio Gaudini, Gustavo Marzi (Italy)	Edward Gardère, André Gardere, Jacques Coutrot, René Bougnol, René Bondoux, René Lemoine (France)	Siegfried Lerdon, August Heim, Erwin Casmir, Julius Eisenecker, Stefan Rosenbauer, Otto Adam (Germany)
1940–1944: Olympics not held			
1948	Adrien Rommel, Christian d'Oriola, Andre Bonin, Jacques Lataste, Jehan Buhan, René Bougnol (France)	Saverio Ragno, Renzo Nostini, Manlio Di Rosa, Giorgio Pellini, Edoardo Mangiarotti, Giuliano Nostini (Italy)	André Van De Werve De Vorsselaer, Paul Louis Jean Valcke, Raymond Bru, Georges Camille De Bourgignon, Henri Paternoster, Edouard Yves (Belgium)
1952	Christian d'Oriola, Jacques Lataste, Jehan Buhan, Claude Netter, Jacques Noël, Adrien Rommel (France)	Giancarlo Bergamini, Antonio Spallino, Manlio Di Rosa, Giorgio Pellini, Edoardo Mangiarotti, Renzo Nostini (Italy)	Endre Palócz, Tibor Berczelly, Endre Tilli, Aladár Gerevich, József Sákovics, Lajos Maszlay (Hungary)
1956	Vittorio Lucarelli, Luigi Arturo Carpaneda, Manlio Di Rosa, Giancarlo Bergamini, Antonio Spallino, Edoardo Mangiarotti (Italy)	Bernard Baudoux, Rene Coicaud, Claude Netter, Roger Closset, Christian d'Oriola, Jacques Lataste (France)	Lajos Somodi, József Gyuricza, Endre Tilli, József Marosi, Mihály Fülöp, József Sákovics (Hungary)
1960	Viktor Zhdanovich, Mark Midler, Yury Rudov, Yuri Sisikin, German Sveshnikov (Soviet Union)	Alberto Pellegrino, Luigi Carpaneda, Mario Culetto, Aldo Aureggi, Edoardo Mangiarotti (Italy)	Jürgen Theuerkauff, Tim Gerresheim, Eberhard Mehl, Jürgen Brecht (Germany)

Year	Gold	Silver	Bronze
1964	Viktor Zhdanovich, Yuri Sharov, Yuri Sisikin, German Sveshnikov, Mark Midler (Soviet Union)	Witold Woyda, Zbigniew Skrudlik, Ryszard Parulski, Egon Franke, Janusz Rozycki (Poland)	Jacky Courtillat, Jean-Claude Magnan, Christian Noël, Daniel Revenu, Pierre Rodocanachi (France)
1968	Daniel Revenu, Gilles Berolatti, Christian Noël, Jean-Claude Magnan, Jacques Dimont (France)	German Sveshnikov, Yuri Shadov, Vasili Stankovich, Viktor Putyatin, Yuri Sisikin (Soviet Union)	Witold Woyda, Zbigniew Skrudlik, Ryszard Parulski, Egon Franke, Adam Lisewski (Poland)
1972	Marek Dabrowski, Jerzy Kaczmarek, Lech Koziejowski, Witold Woyda, Arkadiusz Godel (Poland)	Vladimir Denisov, Anatoli Kotetsev, Leonid Romanov, Vasili Stankovich, Viktor Putyatin (Soviet Union)	Jean-Claude Magnan, Christian Noël, Daniel Revenu, Bernard Talvard, Gilles Berolatti (France)
1976	Matthias Behr, Thomas Bach, Harald Hein, Klaus Reichert, Erik Sens-Gorius (Germany)	Fabio dal Zotto, Carlo Montano, Stefano Simoncelli, Giovanni Battista Coletti, Attilio Calatroni (Italy)	Christian Noël, Bernard Talvard, Didier Flament, Frederic Pietruszka, Daniel Revenu (France)
1980	Didier Flament, Pascal Joylot, Bruno Boscherie, Philippe Bonin, Frederic Pietruszka (France)	Alexandr Romankov, Vladimir Smirnov, Sarbizhan Ruziev, Ashot Karagian, Vladimir Lapitsky (Soviet Union)	Adam Robak, Bogusław Zych, Lech Koziejowski, Marian Sypniewski (Poland)
1984	Mauro Numa, Andrea Borella, Stefano Cerioni, Angelo Scuri, Andrea Cipressa (Italy)	Matthias Behr, Matthias Gey, Harald Hein, Frank Beck, Klaus Reichert (West Germany)	Philippe Omnes, Patrick Groc, Frederic Pietruszka, Pascal Jolyot, Marc Cerboni (France)
1988	Vladimir Aptiaouri, Anvar Ibraguimov, Boris Koretsky, Ilgar Mamedov, Alexandr Romankov (Soviet Union)	Matthias Behr, Thomas Enders, Matthias Gey, Ulrich Schreck, Thorsten Wiedner (West Germany)	István Busa, Zsolt Érsek, Róbert Gátai, Pál Szekeres, István Szelei (Hungary)
1992	Udo Wagner, Ulrich Schreck, Thorsten Weidner, Alexander Koch, Ingo Weissenborn (Germany)	Elvis Gregory, Guillermo Betancourt Scull, Oscar García Perez, Tulio Diaz Babier, Hermenegildo Garcia Marturell (Cuba)	Marian Sypniewski, Piotr Kiełpikowski, Adam Krzesiński, Cezary Siess, Ryszard Sobczak (Poland)
1996	Dmitriy Shevchenko, Ilgar Mamedov, Vladislav Pavlovich (Russia)	Piotr Kielpikowski, Adam Krzesinski, Ryszard Sobczak (Poland)	Elvis Gregory, Rolando Leon, Oscar García Perez (Cuba)
2000	Jean-Noel Ferrari, Brice Guyart, Patrice Lhotellier, Lionel Plumenail (France)	Dong Zhaozhi, Wang Haibin, Ye Chong, Zhang Jie (China)	Daniele Crosta, Gabriele Magni, Salvatore Sanzo, Matteo Zennaro (Italy)
2004	Andrea Cassara, Salvatore Sanzo, Simone Vanni (Italy)	Dong Zhaozhi, Wang Haibin, Wu Hanxiong, Ye Chong (China)	Renal Ganeev, Youri Moltchan, Rouslan Nassiboulline, Viatcheslav Pozdniakov (Russia)

Men's Individual Épée

Year	Gold	Silver	Bronze
1900	Ramón Fonst (Cuba)	Louis Perrée (France)	Léon Sée (France)
1904	Ramón Fonst (Cuba)	Charles Tatham (Cuba)	Albertson Van Zo Post (Cuba)
1908	Gaston Alibert (France)	Alexandre Lippmann (France)	Eugène Olivier (France)
1912	Paul Anspach (Belgium)	Ivan Joseph Martin Osiier (Denmark)	Philippe le Hardy de Beaulieu (Belgium)
1916: Event not held			
1920	Armand Massard (France)	Alexandre Lippmann (France)	Gustave Buchard (France)
1924	Charles Delporte (Belgium)	Roger Ducret (France)	Nils Hellsten (Sweden)
1928	Lucien Gaudin (France)	Georges Buchard (France)	George Calnan (United States)
1932	Giancarlo Cornaggia Medici (Italy)	Georges Buchard (France)	Carlo Agostoni (Italy)
1936	Franco Riccardi (Italy)	Saverio Ragno (Italy)	Giancarlo Cornaggia Medici (Italy)
1940–1944: Olympics not held			

Year	Gold	Silver	Bronze
1948	Luigi Cantone (Italy)	Oswald Zappelli (Switzerland)	Edoardo Mangiarotti (Italy)
1952	Edoardo Mangiarotti (Italy)	Dario Mangiarotti (Italy)	Oswald Zappelli (Switzerland)
1956	Carlo Pavesi (Italy)	Giuseppe Delfino (Italy)	Edoardo Mangiarotti (Italy)
1960	Giuseppe Delfino (Italy)	Allan Jay (Great Britain)	Bruno Khabarov (Soviet Union)
1964	Grigory Kriss (Soviet Union)	Henry Hoskyns (Great Britain)	Guram Kostava (Soviet Union)
1968	Gyözö Kulcsar (Hungary)	Grigory Kriss (Soviet Union)	Gianluigi Saccaro (Italy)
1972	Csaba Fenyvesi (Hungary)	Jacques Ladegaillerie (France)	Győző Kulcsár (Hungary)
1976	Alexander Pusch (West Germany)	Hans-Jürgen Hehn (West Germany)	Gyözö Kulcsar (Hungary)
1980	Johan Harmenberg (Sweden)	Ernő Kolczonay (Hungary)	Philippe Riboud (France)
1984	Philippe Boisse (France)	Björne Väggö (Sweden)	Philippe Riboud (France)
1988	Arnd Schmitt (West Germany)	Philippe Riboud (France)	Andrei Chouvalov (Soviet Union)
1992	Éric Srecki (France)	Pavel Kolobkov (Unified Team)	Jean-Michel Henry (France)
1996	Aleksandr Beketov (Russia)	Ivan Trevejo (Cuba)	Géza Imre (Hungary)
2000	Pavel Kolobkov (Russia)	Hughes Obry (France)	Lee Sang-Ki (South Korea)
2004	Marcel Fischer (Switzerland)	Wang Lei (China)	Pavel Kolobkov (Russia)
2008	Matteo Tagliariol (Italy)	Fabrice Jeannet (France)	José Luis Abajo (Spain)

Men's Masters Épée

Year	Gold	Silver	Bronze
1900	Albert Robery Ayat (France)	Émile Bougnol (France)	Henri Laurent (France)

Men's Team Épée

Year	Gold	Silver	Bronze
1908	Gaston Alibert, Henri-Georges Berger, Charles Collignon, Eugène Olivier (France)	Charles Leaf Daniell, Cecil Haig, Martin Holt, Robert Montgomerie (Great Britain)	Paul Anspach, Desire Beaurain, Ferdinand Feyerick, François Rom (Belgium)
1912	Paul Anspach, Henri Anspach, Robert Hennet, Orphile de Montigny, Jacques Ochs, François Rom, Gaston Salmon, Victor Willems (Belgium)	Edgar Seligman, Edgar Amphlett, Robert Montgomerie, John Blake, Percival Dawson, Arthur Everitt, Sydney Mertineau, Martin Holt (Great Britain)	Adrianus de Jong, Willem van Blijenburgh, Jetze Doorman, Leonardus Salomonson, George van Rossem (Netherlands)
1916: Event not held			
1920	Aldo Nadi, Nedo Nadi, Abelardo Olivier, Giovanni Canova, Dino Urbani, Tullio Bozza, Andrea Marrazzi, Antonio Allochio, Tommaso Constantino, Paolo Thaon di Revel (Italy)	Paul Anspach, Léon Tom, Ernest Gevers, Félix Goblet D'aviella, Victor Boin, Joseph De Craecker, Maurice De Wee, Philippe Le Hardy De Beaulieu, Orphile Fernand De Montigny (Belgium)	Armand Massard, Alexandre Lippmann, Gustave Buchard, Georges Casanova, Georges Trombert, Gaston Amson, Émile Moreau (France)
1924	Lucien Gaudin, Georges Buchard, Roger Ducret, André Labatut, Lionel Liottel, Alexandre Lippmann, Georges Tainturier (France)	Paul Anspach, Joseph De Craecker, Charles Delporte, Orphile Fernand De Montigny, Ernest Gevers, Léon Tom (Belgium)	Giulio Basletta, Marcello Bertinetti, Giovanni Canova, Vincenzo Cuccia, V. Montegazza, Oreste Moricca (Italy)
1928	Giulio Basletta, Marcello Bertinetti, Giancarlo Cornaggia-Medici, Carlo Agostoni, Renzo Minoli, Franco Riccardi (Italy)	Géo Buchard, Gaston Amson, Émile Cornic, Bernard Schmetz, René Barbier (France)	Paulo Leal, Mário de Noronha, Jorge de Paiva, Frederico Paredes, João Sassetti, Henrique da Silveira (Portugal)
1932	Fernand Jourdant, Bernard Schmetz, Georges Tainturier, Georges Buchard, Jean Piot, Philippe Cattiau (France)	Saverio Ragno, Giancarlo Cornaggia Medici, Franco Riccardi, Carlo Agostoni, Renzo Minoli (Italy)	George Charles Calnan, Gustave Marinius Heiss, Frank Stahl Jr. Righeimer, Tracy Jaeckel, Curtis Charles Shears, Miguel Angel De Capriles (United States)

Year	Gold	Silver	Bronze
1936	Alfredo Pezzana, Edoardo Mangiarotti, Saverio Ragno, Giancarlo C. Cornaggia-Medici, Giancarlo Brusati, Franco Riccardi (Italy)	Hans Drakenberg, Hans Granfelt, Gustaf Dyrssen, Gustav Almgren, Birger Cederin, Sven Thofelt (Sweden)	Henri Dulieux, Philippe Cattiau, Georges Buchard, Paul Wormser, Michel Pécheux, Bernard Schmetz (France)
1940–1944: Olympics not held			
1948	Maurice Huet, Michel Pécheux, Marcel Desprets, Edouard Artigas, Henri Guerin, Henri Lepage (France)	Luigi Cantone, Marc Antonio Mandruzzato, Carlo Agostoni, Edoardo Mangiarotti, Fiorenzo Marini, Dario Mangiarotti (Italy)	Frank Cervell, Carl Forssell, Bengt Ljungquist, Sven Thofelt, Per Hjalmar Carleson, Arne Tollbom (Sweden)
1952	Roberto Battaglia, Carlo Pavesi, Franco Bertinetti, Giuseppe Delfino, Dario Mangiarotti, Edoardo Mangiarotti (Italy)	Berndt-Otto Rehbinder, Bengt Ljungquist, Per Hjalmar Carleson, Carl Forssell, Sven Fahlman, Lennart Magnusson (Sweden)	Otto Rüfenacht, Paul Meister, Oswald Zappelli, Willy Fitting, Mario Valota, Paul Barth (Switzerland)
1956	Giuseppe Delfino, Franco Bertinetti, Alberto Pellegrino, Giorgio Anglesio, Carlo Pavesi, Edoardo Mangiarotti (Italy)	Bela Rerrich, Ambrus Nagy, Barnabas Berzsenyi, Jozsef Marosi, Jozsef Sakovics, Lajos Balthazár (Hungary)	Yves Dreyfus, Rene Queyroux, Daniel Dagallier, Claude Nigon, Armand Mouyal (France)
1960	Giuseppe Delfino, Alberto Pellegrino, Carlo Pavesi, Edoardo Mangiarotti, Fiorenzo Marini, Gianluigi Saccaro (Italy)	Allan Jay, Michael Howard, John Pelling, Henry Hoskyns, Raymond Harrison, Michael Alexander (Great Britain)	Valentin Chernikov, Guram Kostava, Arnold Chernushevich, Bruno Khabarov, Aleksandr Pavlovsky (Soviet Union)
1964	Árpád Bárány, Tamás Gábor, István Kausz, Győző Kulcsár, Zoltán Nemere (Hungary)	Giovan Battista Breda, Giuseppe Delfino, Gianfranco Paolucci, Alberto Pellegrino, Gianluigi Saccaro (Italy)	Claude Bourquard, Claude Brodin, Jacques Brodin, Yves Dreyfus, Jack Guittet (France)
1968	Csaba Fenyvesi, Zoltan Nemere, Pál Schmitt, Gyözö Kulcsar, Pal Nagy (Hungary)	Grigory Kriss, Iosif Vitebsky, Aleksei Nikanchikov, Yuri Smolyakov, Viktor Modzalevsky (Soviet Union)	Bogdan Andrzejewski, Michał Butkiewicz, Bogdan Gonsior, Henryk Nielaba, Kazimierz Barburski (Poland)
1972	Sándor Erdös, Csaba Fenyvesi, Gyözö Kulcsar, Pál Schmitt, Istvan Osztrics (Hungary)	Guy Evequoz, Daniel Giger, Christian Kauter, Peter Lötscher, François Suchanecki (Switzerland)	Viktor Modzalevsky, Sergei Paramonov, Igor Valetov, Georgi Zažitski, Grigori Kriss (Soviet Union)
1976	Carl von Essen, Hans Jacobson, Rolf Edling, Leif Högström, Göran Flodström (Sweden)	Alexander Pusch, Hans-Jürgen Hehn, Reinhold Behr, Volker Fischer, Hanns Jana (West Germany)	François Suchanecki, Michel Poffet, Daniel Giger, Christian Kauter, Jean-Blaise Evequoz (Switzerland)
1980	Philippe Riboud, Patrick Picot, Hubert Gardas, Philippe Boisse, Michel Salesse (France)	Piotr Jabłkowski, Andrzej Lis, Leszek Swornowski, Ludomir Chronowski, Mariusz Strzałka (Poland)	Ashot Karagian, Boris Lukomsky, Aleksander Abushackmetov, Aleksander Mozhaev, Vladimir Smirnov (Soviet Union)
1984	Elmar Borrmann, Volker Fischer, Gerhard Heer, Rafael Nickel, Alexander Pusch (West Germany)	Philippe Boisse, Jean-Michel Henry, Olivier Lenglet, Philippe Riboud, Michel Salesse (France)	Stefano Bellone, Sandro Cuomo, Cosimo Ferro, Roberto Manzi, Angelo Mazzoni (Italy)
1988	Frederic Delpla, Jean-Michel Henry, Olivier Lenglet, Philippe Riboud, Éric Srecki (France)	Elmar Borrman, Volker Fischer, Thomas Gerull, Alexander Pusch, Arnd Schmitt (West Germany)	Andrei Chuvalov, Pavel Kolobkov, Vladimir Reznichenko, Mikhail Tishko, Igor Tikhomirov (Soviet Union)
1992	Elmar Borrman, Robert Felisiak, Arnd Schmitt, Uwe Proske, Vladimir Reznichenko (Germany)	Iván Kovács, Krisztián Kulcsár, Ferenc Hegedűs, Ernő Kolczonay, Gábor Totola (Hungary)	Pavel Kolobkov, Andrei Chuvalov, Sergei Kravchuk, Sergei Kostarev, Valery Zakharevich (Unified Team)
1996	Sandro Cuomo, Angelo Mazzoni, Maurizio Randazzo (Italy)	Aleksandr Beketov, Pavel Kolobkov, Valery Zakharevich (Russia)	Jean-Michel Henry, Robert Leroux, Éric Srecki (France)

Year	Gold	Silver	Bronze
2000	Angelo Mazzoni, Paolo Milanoli, Maurizio Randazzo, Alfredo Rota (Italy)	Jean-François di Martino, Robert Leroux, Hughes Obry, Éric Srecki (France)	Nelson Loyola, Candido Alberto Maya, Carlos Pedroso, Ivan Trevejo (Cuba)
2004	Fabrice Jeannet, Jérôme Jeannet, Hugues Obry, Érik Boisse (France)	Gábor Boczkó, Krisztián Kulcsár, Iván Kovács, Géza Imre (Hungary)	Sven Schmid, Jörg Fiedler, Daniel Strigel (Germany)
2008	Jérôme Jeannet, Fabrice Jeannet, Ulrich Robeiri (France)	Robert Andrzejuk, Tomasz Motyka, Adam Wiercioch, Radosław Zawrotniak (Poland)	Stefano Carozzo, Diego Confalonieri, Alfredo Rota, Matteo Tagliariol (Italy)

Men's Individual Sabre

Year	Gold	Silver	Bronze
1896	Ioannis Georgiadis (Greece)	Telemachos Karakalos (Greece)	Holger Nielsen (Denmark)
1900	Georges de la Falaise (France)	Léon Thiébaut (France)	Siegfried Flesch (Austria)
1904	Manuel Díaz (Cuba)	William Grebe (United States)	Albertson Van Zo Post (Cuba)
1908	Jenő Fuchs (Hungary)	Béla Zulawszky (Hungary)	Vilém Goppold von Lobsdorf (Bohemia)
1912	Jenő Fuchs (Hungary)	Béla Békessy (Hungary)	Ervin Mészáros (Hungary)
1916: Event not held			
1920	Nedo Nadi (Italy)	Aldo Nadi (Italy)	Adrianus De Jong (Netherlands)
1924	Sándor Pósta (Hungary)	Roger Ducret (France)	János Garay (Hungary)
1928	Odön Tersztyánszky (Hungary)	Attila Petschauer (Hungary)	Bino Bini (Italy)
1932	György Piller (Hungary)	Giulio Gaudini (Italy)	Endre Kabos (Hungary)
1936	Endre Kabos (Hungary)	Gustavo Marzi (Italy)	Aladár Gerevich (Hungary)
1940–1944: Olympics not held			
1948	Aladár Gerevich (Hungary)	Vinvenzo Pinton (Italy)	Pál Kovács (Hungary)
1952	Pál Kovács (Hungary)	Aladár Gerevich (Hungary)	Tibor Berczelly (Hungary)
1956	Rudolf Kárpáti (Hungary)	Jerzy Pawłowski (Poland)	Lev Kuznetsov (Soviet Union)
1960	Rudolf Kárpáti (Hungary)	Zoltán Horváth (Hungary)	Wladimiro Calarese (Italy)
1964	Tibor Pézsa (Hungary)	Claude Arabo (France)	Umar Mavlikhanov (Soviet Union)
1968	Jerzy Pawłowski (Poland)	Mark Rakita (Soviet Union)	Tibor Pézsa (Hungary)
1972	Viktor Sidyak (Soviet Union)	Péter Maróth (Hungary)	Vladimir Nazlymov (Soviet Union)
1976	Viktor Krovopuskov (Soviet Union)	Vladimir Nazlymov (Soviet Union)	Viktor Sidyak (Soviet Union)
1980	Viktor Krovopuskov (Soviet Union)	Mikhail Burtsev (Soviet Union)	Imre Gedővári (Hungary)
1984	Jean-François Lamour (France)	Marco Marin (Italy)	Peter Westbrook (United States)
1988	Jean-François Lamour (France)	Janusz Olech (Poland)	Giovanni Scalzo (Italy)
1992	Bence Szabó (Hungary)	Marco Marin (Italy)	Jean-François Lamour (France)
1996	Stanislav Pozdniakov (Russia)	Sergey Sharikov (Russia)	Damien Touya (France)
2000	Mihai Claudiu Covaliu (Romania)	Mathieu Gourdain (France)	Wiradech Kothny (Germany)
2004	Aldo Montano (Italy)	Zsolt Nemcsik (Hungary)	Vladislav Tretiak (Ukraine)
2008	Zhong Man (China)	Nicolas Lopez (France)	Mihai Covaliu (Romania)

Men's Masters Sabre

Year	Gold	Silver	Bronze
1900	Antonio Conte (Italy)	Italo Santelli (Italy)	Milan Neralić (Austria)

Men's Team Sabre

Year	Gold	Silver	Bronze
1908	Jenő Fuchs, Oszkár Gerde, Péter Tóth, Lajos Werkner, Dezső Földes (Hungary)	Marcello Bertinetti, Riccardo Nowak, Abelardo Olivier, Alessandro Pirzio-Biroli, Sante Ceccherini (Italy)	Vlastimil Lada-Sázavský, Vilém Goppold von Lobsdorf, Bedřich Schejbal, Jaroslav Šourek-Tuček, Otakar Lada (Bohemia)
1912	Jenő Fuchs, László Berti, Ervin Mészáros, Dezső Földes, Oszkár Gerde, Zoltán Ozoray Schenker, Péter Tóth, Lajos Werkner (Hungary)	Richard Verderber, Otto Herschmann, Rudolf Cvetko, Friedrich Golling, Andreas Suttner, Albert Bogen, Reinhold Trampler (Austria)	Willem van Blijenburgh, George van Rossem, Adrianus de Jong, Jetze Doorman, Dirk Scalongne, Hendrik de Jongh (Netherlands)
1916: Event not held			
1920	Aldo Nadi, Nedo Nadi, Francesco Gargano, Oreste Puliti, Giorgio Santelli, Dino Urbani, Federico Secondo Cesarano, Baldo Baldi (Italy)	Jean Margraff, Marc Marie Jean Perrodon, Henri Marie Raoul De Saint Germain, Georges Trombert (France)	Jan Van Der Wiel, Adrianus De Jong, Jetze Doorman, Willem Van Blijenburgh, Louis Delaunoy, Salomon Zeldenrust (Netherlands)
1924	Renato Anselmi, Guido Balzarini, Marcello Bertinetti, Bino Bini, Vincenzo Cuccia, Oreste Moricca, Oreste Puliti, Giulio Sarrocchi (Italy)	László Berti, János Garay, Sándor Pósta, József Rády, Zoltán Ozoray Schenker, László Széchy, Ödön Tersztyánszky, Jenő Uhlyárik (Hungary)	Adrianus De Jong, Jetze Doorman, Hendrik Scherpenhuyzen, Jan Van Der Wiel, Maarten Hendrik Van Dulm, Henri Jacob Wynoldy-Daniels (Netherlands)
1928	Ödön Tersztyánszky, János Garay, Attila Petschauer, József Rády, Sándor Gombos, Gyula Glykais (Hungary)	Bino Bini, Oreste Puliti, Giulio Sarrocchi, Renato Anselmi, Emilio Salafia, Gustavo Marzi (Italy)	Adam Papée, Tadeusz Friedrich, Kazimierz Laskowski, Władysław Segda, Aleksander Małecki, Jerzy Zabielski (Poland)
1932	Endre Kabos, Attila Petschauer, Ernő Nagy, Gyula Glykais, György Piller, Aladár Gerevich (Hungary)	Gustavo Marzi, Giulio Gaudini, Renato Anselmi, Emilio Salafia, Arturo De Vecchi, Ugo Pignotti (Italy)	Tadeusz Friedrich, Marian Suski, Władysław Dobrowolski, Władysław Segda, Leszek Lubicz, Adam Papée (Poland)
1936	Pál Kovács, Tibor Berczelly, Imre Rajczy, Aladár Gerevich, Endre Kabos, László Rajcsányi (Hungary)	Vincenzo Pinton, Aldo Masciotta, Athos Tanzini, Aldo Montano, Gustavo Marzi, Giulio Gaudini (Italy)	Hans Jörger, Julius Eisenecker, August Heim, Erwin Casmir, Richard Wahl, Hans Esser (Germany)
1940–1944: Olympics not held			
1948	László Rajcsányi, Bertalan Papp, Aladár Gerevich, Tibor Berczelly, Rudolf Kárpáti, Pál Kovács (Hungary)	Carlo Turcato, Gastone Darè, Vincenzo Pinton, Mauro Racca, Renzo Nostini, Aldo Montano (Italy)	Miguel Angel De Capriles, Norman Cohn-Armitage, George Vitez Worth, Dean Victor Cetrulo, James Hummitzsch Flynn, Tibor Andrew Nyilas (United States)
1952	Bertalan Papp, László Rajcsányi, Rudolf Kárpáti, Tibor Berczelly, Aladár Gerevich, Pál Kovács (Hungary)	Giorgio Pellini, Vincenzo Pinton, Renzo Nostini, Mauro Racca, Gastone Darè, Roberto Ferrari (Italy)	Maurice Piot, Jacques Lefèvre, Bernard Morel, Jean Laroyenne, Jean François Tournon, Jean Levavasseur (France)
1956	Attila Keresztes, Aladár Gerevich, Rudolf Kárpáti, Jenő Hámori, Pál Kovács, Dániel Magay (Hungary)	Zygmunt Pawlas, Jerzy Pawłowski, Wojciech Zabłocki, Andrzej Ryszard Piątkowski, Marian Kuszewski, Ryszard Zub (Poland)	Yakov Rylsky, David Tyshler, Lev Kuznetsov, Yevgeny Cherepovsky, Leonid Bogdanov (Soviet Union)
1960	Tamás Mendelényi, Rudolf Kárpáti, Pál Kovács, Zoltán Horváth, Gábor Delneky, Aladár Gerevich (Hungary)	Andrzej Piatkowski, Emil Ochyra, Wojciech Zabłocki, Jerzy Pawłowski, Ryszard Zub, Marian Kuszewski (Poland)	Wladimiro Calarese, Giampaolo Calanchini, Pierluigi Chicca, Roberto Ferrari, Mario Ravagnan (Italy)
1964	Boris Melnikov, Nugzar Asatiani, Mark Rakita, Yakov Rylsky, Umar Mavlikhanov (Soviet Union)	Giampaolo Calanchini, Wladimiro Calarese, Pierluigi Chicca, Mario Ravagnan, Cesare Salvadori (Italy)	Emil Ochyra, Jerzy Pawłowski, Ryszard Zub, Andrzej Piatkowski, Wojciech Zabłocki (Poland)

Year	Gold	Silver	Bronze
1968	Vladimir Nazlymov, Viktor Sidyak, Eduard Vinokurov, Mark Rakita, Umar Mavlikhanov (Soviet Union)	Wladimiro Calarese, Pierluigi Chicca, Michele Maffei, Cesare Salvadori, Rolando Rigoli (Italy)	Tamás Kovács, János Kalmár, Péter Bakonyi, Miklós Meszéna, Tibor Pézsa (Hungary)
1972	Michele Maffei, Mario Aldo Montano, Mario Tullio Montano, Rolando Rigoli, Cesare Salvadori (Italy)	Viktor Bashenov, Vladimir Nazlymov, Viktor Sidyak, Eduard Vinokurov, Mark Rakita (Soviet Union)	Pál Gerevich, Tamás Kovács, Péter Marót, Tibor Pézsa, Péter Bakonyi (Hungary)
1976	Viktor Krovopuskov, Eduard Vinokurov, Viktor Sidyak, Vladimir Nazlymov, Mikhail Burtsev (Soviet Union)	Mario Aldo Montano, Michele Maffei, Angelo Arcidiacono, Tommaso Montano, Mario Tullio Montano (Italy)	Daniel Irimiciuc, Ioan Pop, Marin Mustata, Corneliu Marin, Alexandru Nilca (Romania)
1980	Mikhail Burtsev, Viktor Krovopuskov, Viktor Sidjak, Vladimir Nazlymov, Nikolai Alekhin (Soviet Union)	Michele Maffei, Mario Aldo Montano, Marco Romano, Ferdinando Meglio, Giovanni Scalzo (Italy)	Imre Gedővári, Rudolf Nébald, Pál Gerevich, Ferenc Hammang, György Nébald (Hungary)
1984	Marco Marin, Gianfranco Dalla Barba, Giovanni Scalzo, Ferdinando Meglio, Angelo Arcidiacono (Italy)	Jean-François Lamour, Pierre Guichot, Hervé Granger-Veyron, Philippe Delrieu, Franck Ducheix (France)	Marin Mustata, Ioan Pop, Alexandru Chiculita, Corneliu Marin, Vilmos Szabo (Romania)
1988	Imre Bujdosó, László Csongrádi, Imre Gedővári, György Nébald, Bence Szabó (Hungary)	Andrei Alshan, Mikhail Burtsev, Sergei Koryakin, Sergei Mindirgassov, Heorhiy Pohosov (Soviet Union)	Massimo Cavaliere, Gianfranco Dalla Barba, Marco Marin, Ferdinando Meglio, Giovanni Scalzo (Italy)
1992	Grigory Kiriyenko, Aleksander Chirchov, Heorhiy Pohosov, Vadim Gutzeit, Stanislav Pozdniakov (Unified Team)	Bence Szabó, Csaba Köves, György Nébald, Péter Abay, Imre Bujdosó (Hungary)	Jean-François Lamour, Jean-Philippe Daurelle, Franck Ducheix, Hervé Grainger-Veyron, Pierre Guichot (France)
1996	Stanislav Pozdniakov, Grigory Kiriyenko, Sergey Sharikov (Russia)	Csaba Köves, József Navarrete, Bence Szabó (Hungary)	Rafaello Caserta, Luigi Tarantino, Toni Terenzi (Italy)
2000	Serguei Charikov, Alexei Frossine, Stanislav Pozdniakov (Russia)	Mathieu Gourdain, Julien Pillet, Cedric Seguin, Damien Touya (France)	Dennis Bauer, Wiradech Kothny, Eero Lehmann, Alexander Weber (Germany)
2004	Julien Pillet, Damien Touya, Gael Touya (France)	Aldo Montano, Gianpiero Pastore, Luigi Tarantino (Italy)	Sergey Sharikov, Alexei Diatchenko, Stanislav Pozdniakov, Alexey Yakimenko (Russia)
2008	Nicolas Lopez, Julien Pillet, Boris Sanson (France)	Tim Morehouse, Jason Rogers, Keeth Smart, James Williams (United States)	Aldo Montano, Diego Occhiuzzi, Giampiero Pastore, Luigi Tarantino (Italy)

Men's Amateurs-Masters Épée

Year	Gold	Silver	Bronze
1900	Albert Robert Ayat (France)	Ramón Fonst (Cuba)	Léon Sée (France)

Men's Single Stick

Year	Gold	Silver	Bronze
1904	Albertson Van Zo Post (Cuba)	William O'Connor (United States)	William Grebe (United States)

Women's Individual Foil

Year	Gold	Silver	Bronze
1924	Ellen Osiier (Denmark)	Gladis Davis (Great Britain)	Grete Heckscher (Denmark)
1928	Helene Mayer (Germany)	Muriel Freeman (Great Britain)	Olga Oelkers (Germany)
1932	Ellen Preis (Austria)	Judy Guinness (Great Britain)	Erna Bogen (Hungary)
1936	Ilona Elek (Hungary)	Helene Mayer (Germany)	Ellen Preis (Austria)

Year	Gold	Silver	Bronze
1940–1944: Olympics not held			
1948	Ilona Elek (Hungary)	Karen Lachmann (Denmark)	Ellen Mueller (Austria)
1952	Irene Camber (Italy)	Ilona Elek (Hungary)	Karen Lachmann (Denmark)
1956	Gillian Sheen (Great Britain)	Olga Orban (Romania)	Renée Garilhe (France)
1960	Adelheid Schmid (United Team of Germany)	Valentina Rastvorova (Soviet Union)	Maria Vicol (Romania)
1964	Ildikó Újlaky-Rejtő (Hungary)	Helga Mees (United Team of Germany)	Antonella Ragno (Italy)
1968	Elena Novikova-Belova (Soviet Union)	Pilar Roldán (Mexico)	Ildikó Újlaky-Rejtő (Hungary)
1972	Antonella Ragno-Lonzi (Italy)	Ildikó Bóbis (Hungary)	Galina Gorokhova (Soviet Union)
1976	Ildikó Schwarczenberger (Hungary)	Maria Consolata Collino (Italy)	Elena Novikova-Belova (Soviet Union)
1980	Pascale Trinquet (France)	Magda Maros (Hungary)	Barbara Wysoczańska (Poland)
1984	Luan Jujie (China)	Cornelia Hanisch (West Germany)	Dorina Vaccaroni (Italy)
1988	Anja Fichtel-Mauritz (West Germany)	Sabine Bau (West Germany)	Zita Funkenhauser (West Germany)
1992	Giovanna Trillini (Italy)	Wang Huifeng (China)	Tatiana Sadovskaya (Unified Team)
1996	Laura Badea (Romania)	Calentina Vezzali (Italy)	Giovanna Trillini (Italy)
2000	Valentina Vezzali (Italy)	Rita Koenig (Germany)	Giovanna Trillini (Italy)
2004	Valentina Vezzali (Italy)	Giovanna Trillini (Italy)	Sylwia Gruchała (Poland)
2008	Valentina Vezzali (Italy)	Nam Hyun-Hee (South Korea)	Margherita Granbassi (Italy)

Women's Team Foil

Year	Gold	Silver	Bronze
1960	Valentina Prudskova, Alexandra Zabelina, Lyudmila Shishova, Tatyana Petrenko, Galina Gorokhova, Valentina Rastvorova (Soviet Union)	Györgyi Marvalics, Ildikó Újlaky-Rejtő, Magdolna Nyári, Katalin Juhász, Lídia Dömölky (Hungary)	Bruna Colombetti, Velleda Cesari, Claudia Pasini, Irene Camber, Antonella Ragno-Lonzi (Italy)
1964	Paula Marosi, Katalin Juhász, Judit Ágoston, Lídia Dömölky, Ildikó Újlaky-Rejtő (Hungary)	Lyudmila Shishova, Valentina Prudskova, Valentina Rastvorova, Tatyana Samusenko, Galina Gorokhova (Soviet Union)	Heidi Schmid, Helga Mees, Rosemarie Scherberger, Gudrun Theuerkauff (United Team of Germany)
1968	Aleksandra Zabelina, Tatyana Samusenko, Elena Novikova-Belova, Galina Gorokhova, Svetlana Tširkova (Soviet Union)	Lídia Dömölky, Ildikó Bóbis, Ildikó Újlaky-Rejtő, Mária Gulácsy, Paula Marosi (Hungary)	Ecaterina Iencic-Stahl, Ileana Gyulai-Drimba-Jenei, Maria Vicol, Olga Orban-Szabo, Ana Dersidan-Ene-Pascu (Romania)
1972	Elena Novikova-Belova, Galina Gorokhova, Tatyana Samusenko, Aleksandra Zabelina, Svetlana Tširkova (Soviet Union)	Ildikó Bóbis, Ildikó Újlaky-Rejtő, Ildikó Schwarczenberger, Mária Szolnoki, Ildikó Rónay (Hungary)	Ileana Gyulai-Drimba-Jenei, Ana Dersidan-Ene-Pascu, Ecaterina Iencic-Stahl, Olga Orban-Szabo (Romania)
1976	Elena Novikova-Belova, Olga Knyazeva, Valentina Sidorova, Nailia Gilizova, Valentina Nikonova (Soviet Union)	Brigitte Latrille-Gaudin, Brigitte Gapais-Dumont, Christine Muzio, Veronique Trinquet, Claudette Herbster-Josland (France)	Ildikó Schwarczenberger, Edit Kovács, Magda Maros, Ildikó Újlaky-Rejtő, Ildikó Bóbis (Hungary)
1980	Brigitte Latrille-Gaudin, Pascale Trinquet, Isabelle Begard, Veronique Brouquier, Christine Muzio (France)	Valentina Sidorova, Nailia Giliazova, Elena Novikova-Belova, Irina Ushakova, Larisa Tsagaraeva (Soviet Union)	Ildikó Schwarczenberger, Magda Maros, Gertrúd Stefanek, Zsuzsanna Szőcs, Edit Kovács (Hungary)

Year	Gold	Silver	Bronze
1984	Ute Kircheis-Wessel, Christiane Weber, Cornelia Hanisch, Sabine Bischoff, Zita Funkenhauser (Germany)	Aurora Dan, Monica Weber-Koszto, Rozalia Oros, Marcela Modovan-Zsak, Elisabeta Guzganu-Tufan (Romania)	Laurence Modaine, Pascale Trinquet-Hachin, Brigitte Latrille-Gaudin, Veronique Brouquier, Anne Meygret (France)
1988	Sabine Bau, Anja Fichtel-Mauritz, Zita Funkenhauser, Anette Klug, Christiane Weber (Germany)	Francesca Bortolozzi Borella, Annapia Gandolfi, Lucia Traversa, Dorina Vaccaroni, Margherita Zalaffi (Italy)	Zsuzsa Jánosi, Edit Kovács, Gertrúd Stefanek, Zsuzsanna Szőcs, Katalin Tuschák (Hungary)
1992	Diana Bianchedi, Francesca Bortolozzi Borella, Giovanna Trillini, Dorina Vaccaroni, Margherita Zalaffi (Italy)	Sabine Bau, Zita Funkenhauser, Annette Dobmeier, Anja Fichtel-Mauritz, Monika Weber-Koszto (Germany)	Reka Szabo-Lazar, Claudia Grigorescu, Elisabeta Tufan, Laura Badea, Roxana Dumitrescu (Romania)
1996	Francesca Bortolozzi-Borella, Giovanna Trillini, Valentina Vezzali (Italy)	Laura Badea, Reka Szabo, Roxana Scarlat (Romania)	Anja Fichtel Mauritz, Sabine Bau, Monika Weber-Koszto (Germany)
2000	Diana Bianchedi, Annamaria Giacometti, Giovanna Trillini, Valentina Vezzali (Italy)	Sylwia Gruchała, Magdalena Mroczkiewicz, Anna Rybicka, Barbara Wolnicka (Poland)	Sabine Bau, Rita Koenig, Gesine Schiel, Monika Weber (Germany)
2004: Event not held			
2008	Svetlana Boiko, Aida Shanayeva, Viktoria Nikishina, Yevgeniya Lamonova (Russia)	Emily Cross, Hanna Thompson, Erinn Smart (United States)	Valentina Vezzali, Giovanna Trillini, Margherita Granbassi, Ilaria Salvatori (Italy)

Women's Individual Épée

Year	Gold	Silver	Bronze
1996	Laura Flessel (France)	Valerie Barlois (France)	Gyöngyi Szalay (Hungary)
2000	Tímea Nagy (Hungary)	Gianna Hablützel-Bürki (Switzerland)	Laura Flessel-Colovic (France)
2004	Tímea Nagy (Hungary)	Laura Flessel-Colovic (France)	Maureen Nisima (France)
2008	Britta Heidemann (Germany)	Ana Maria Brânză (Romania)	Ildikó Mincza-Nébald (Hungary)

Women's Team Épée

Year	Gold	Silver	Bronze
1996	Laura Flessel, Sophie Moresee-Pichot, Valerie Barlois (France)	Laura Chiesa, Elisa Uga, Margherita Zalaffi (Italy)	Maria Mazina, Yuliya Garayeva, Karina Aznavourian (Russia)
2000	Karina Aznavourian, Oxana Ermakova, Tatiana Logounova, Maria Mazina (Russia)	Gianna Hablützel-Bürki, Sophie Lamon, Diana Romagnoli, Tabea Steffen (Switzerland)	Li Na, Liang Qin, Liu Yingqing, Yang Shaoqi (China)
2004	Karina Aznavourian, Oxana Ermakova, Tatiana Logounova, Anna Sivkova (Russia)	Claudia Bokel, Imke Duplitzer, Britta Heidemann (Germany)	Sarah Daninthe, Laura Flessel-Colovic, Hajnalka Kiraly Picot, Maureen Nisima (France)

Women's Individual Sabre

Year	Gold	Silver	Bronze
2004	Mariel Zagunis (United States)	Tan Xue (China)	Sada Jacobson (United States)
2008	Mariel Zagunis (United States)	Sada Jacobson (United States)	Becca Ward (United States)

Women's Team Sabre

Year	Gold	Silver	Bronze
2008	Olha Zhovnir, Olga Kharlan, Halyna Pundyk, Olena Khomrova (Ukraine)	Bao Yingying, Huang Haiyang, Ni Hong, Tan Xue (China)	Sada Jacobson, Becca Ward, Mariel Zagunis (United States)

Football (Soccer)

Men's Football (Soccer)

Year	Gold	Silver	Bronze
1900	John H. Jones, Claude Buckenham, William Gosling, Alfred Chalk, T. E. Burridge, William Quash, Arthur Turner, F. G. Spackman, J. Nicholas, James Zealley, A. Haslam (Great Britain)	Pierre Allemane, Louis Bach, Alfred Bloch, Fernand Canelle, Duparc, Eugène Fraysse, Virgile Gaillard, Georges Garnier, R. Grandjean, Lucien Huteau, Marcel Lamberg, Maurice Macaine, Gaston Peltier (France)	Albert Delbecque, Hendrik van Heuckelum, Raul Kelecom, Marcel Leboutte, Lucien Londot, Ernest Moreau de Melen, Edmond Neefs, Georges Pelgrims, Alphonse Renier, Emile Spannoghe, Eric Thornton (Belgium)
1904	George Ducker, John Fraser, John Gourlay, Alexander Hall, Albert Johnston, Robert Lane, Ernest Linton, Gordon McDonald, Frederick Steep, Tom Taylor, William Twaits, Otto Christman, Albert Henderson (Canada)	Charles Bartliff, Warren Brittingham, Oscar Brockmeyer, Alexander Cudmore, Charles January, John January, Thomas January, Raymond Lawler, Joseph Lydon, Louis Menges, Peter Ratican (United States)	George Cooke, Thomas Cooke, Cormic Cosgrove, Dierkes, Martin Dooling, Frank Frost, Claude Jameson, Henry Jameson, Johnson, O'Connell, Harry Tate (United States)
1908	Horace Bailey, Arthur Berry, Frederick Chapman, Walter Corbett, Harold Hardman, Robert Hawkes, Kenneth Hunt, Herbert Smith, Harold Stapley, Clyde Purnell, Vivian Woodward, George Barlow, Albert Bell, Ronald Brebner, W. Crabtree, Walter Daffern, Thomas Porter, Albert Scothern (Great Britain)	Peter Marius Andersen, Harald Bohr, Charles Buchwald, Ludvig Drescher, Johannes Gandil, Harald Hansen, August Lindgren, Kristian Middelboe, Nils Middelboe, Sophus Nielsen, Oskar Nørland, Bjørn Rasmussen, Vilhelm Wolfhagen, Magnus Beck, Ødbert E. Bjarnholt, Knud Hansen, Einar Middelboe (Denmark)	Reinier Beeuwkes, Frans de Bruyn Kops, Karel Heijting, Jan Kok, Bok de Korver, Emil Mundt, Louis Otten, Jops Reeman, Edu Snethlage, Ed Sol, Jan Thomée, Caius Welcker, Jan van den Berg, Lo la Chapelle, Vic Gonsalves, John Heijting, Tonie van Renterghem (Netherlands)
1912	Arthur Berry, Ronald Brebner, Thomas Burn, Joseph Dines, Edward Hanney, Gordon Hoare, Arthur Knight, Henry Littlewort, Ivan Sharpe, Harold Walden, Vivian Woodward, Douglas McWhirter, Harold Stamper, Gordon Wright (Great Britain)	Paul Berth, Charles Buchwald, Hjalmar Christoffersen, Harald Hansen, Sophus Hansen, Ivar Lykke, Nils Middelboe, Sophus Nielsen, Anthon Olsen, Axel Petersen, Vilhelm Wolfhagen, Emil Jørgensen, Oskar Nørland, Poul Nielsen, Axel Thufason, Svend Aage Castella, Ludvig Drescher, Axel Dyrberg, Viggo Malmquist, Christian Morville (Denmark)	Nico Bouvy, Huug de Groot, Bok de Korver, Nico de Wolf, Constant Feith, Just Göbel, Dirk Lotsy, Caesar ten Cate, Jan van Breda Kolff, Jan Vos, David Wijnveldt, Piet Bouman, Joop Boutmy, Ge Fortgens, Jan van der Sluis (Netherlands)
1916: Olympics not held			
1920	Félix Balyu, Désiré Bastin, Mathieu Bragard, Robert Coppée, Jean De Bie, André Fierens, Emile Hanse, Georges Hebdin, Louis van Hege, Henri Larnoe, Joseph Musch, Fernand Nisot, Armand Swartenbroeks, Oscar Verbeeck (Belgium)	Patricio Arabolaza, Mariano Arrate, Juan Artola, José María Belauste, Sabino Bilbao, Agustín Eizaguirre, Ramón Equiazábal, Ramón Gil, Domingo Gómez-Acedo, Silverio Izaguirre, Rafael Moreno, Luis Otero, Francisco Pagazaurtundúa, José Samitier, Agustín Sancho, Félix Sesúmaga, Pedro Vallana, Joaquín Vázquez, Ricardo Zamora (Spain)	Arie Bieshaar, Leo Bosschart, Evert Bulder, Jaap Bulder, Harry Dénis, Jan van Dort, Ber Groosjohan, Felix von Heijden, Frits Kuipers, Dick MacNeill, Jan de Natris, Oscar van Rappard, Henk Steeman, Ben Verweij (Netherlands)

Year	Gold	Silver	Bronze
1924	José Andrade, Pedro Arispe, Pedro Céa, Alfredo Ghierra, Andrés Mazali, José Nasazzi, José Naya, Pedro Petrone, Ángel Romano, Héctor Scarone, Humberto Tomasina, Antonio Urdinarán, Santos Urdinarán, José Vidal, Alfredo Zibechi, Pedro Casella, Luis Chiappara, Pedro Etchegoyen, Zoilo Saldombide, Pascual Somma, Fermín Uriarte, Pedro Zingone (Uruguay)	Max Abegglen, Félix Bédouret, Walter Dietrich, Karl Ehrenbolger, Paul Fässler, Edmond Kramer, Adolphe Mengotti, August Oberhauser, Robert Pache, Aron Pollitz, Hans Pulver, Rudolf Ramseyer, Adolphe Reymond, Paul Schmiedlin, Paul Sturzenegger, Charles Bouvier, Gustav Gottenkieny, Jean Haag, Marcel Katz, Louis Richard, Teo Schär, Walter Weiler (Switzerland)	Axel Alfredsson, Charles Brommesson, Gustaf Carlsson, Albin Dahl, Sven Friberg, Fritjof Hillén, Konrad Hirsch, Gunnar Holmberg, Per Kaufeldt, Tore Keller, Rudolf Kock, Sigfrid Lindberg, Sven Lindqvist, Evert Lundquist, Sten Mellgren, Sven Rydell, Harry Sundberg, Thorsten Svensson, Karl Gustafsson, Vigor Lindberg, Gunnar Olsson, Robert Zander (Sweden)
1928	José Andrade, Pedro Arispe, Juan Arremón, René Borjas, Antonio Campolo, Adhemar Canavesi, Héctor Castro, Pedro Céa, Lorenzo Fernández, Roberto Figueroa, Alvaro Gestido, Andrés Mazali, José Nasazzi, Pedro Petrone, Juan Piriz, Héctor Scarone, Santos Urdinarán, Peregrino Anselmo, Venancio Bartibas, Fausto Batignani, Ángel Melogno, Domingo Tejera (Uruguay)	Ludovico Bidoglio, Ángel Bossio, Saúl Calandra, Adolfo Carricaberry, Roberto Cherro, Octavio Díaz, Juan Evaristo, Manuel Ferreira, Enrique Gainzarain, Ángel Médici, Luis Monti, Rodolfo Orlandini, Raimundo Orsi, Fernando Paternoster, Feliciano Perducca, Domingo Tarasconi, Alfredo Helman, Segundo Luna, Pedro Ochoa, Natalio Perinetti, Luis Weihmuller, Adolfo Zumelz (Argentina)	Adolfo Baloncieri, Elvio Banchero, Delfo Bellini, Fulvio Bernardini, Umberto Caligaris, Giampiero Combi, Giovanni De Prâ, Pietro Genovesi, Antonio Janni, Virgilio Levratto, Mario Magnozzi, Silvio Pietroboni, Alfredo Pitto, Enrico Rivolta, Virginio Rosetta, Gino Rossetti, Angelo Schiavio, Valentino Degani, Attilio Ferraris, Felice Gasperi, Pietro Pastore, Andrea Vivian (Italy)
1932: Event not held			
1936	Giuseppe Baldo, Sergio Bertoni, Carlo Biagi, Giulio Cappelli, Alfredo Foni, Annibale Frossi, Francesco Gabriotti, Ugo Locatelli, Libero Marchini, Alfonso Negro, Achille Piccini, Pietro Rava, Luigi Scarabello, Bruno Venturini (Italy)	Franz Fuchsberger, Max Hofmeister, Eduard Kainberger, Karl Kainberger, Martin Kargl, Josef Kitzmüller, Anton Krenn, Ernst Künz, Adolf Laudon, Franz Mandl, Klement Steinmetz, Karl Wahlmüller, Walter Werginz (Austria)	Arne Brustad, Nils Eriksen, Odd Frantzen, Sverre Hansen, Rolf Holmberg, Øivind Holmsen, Fredrik Horn, Magnar Isaksen, Henry Johansen, Jørgen Juve, Reidar Kvammen, Alf Martinsen, Magdalon Monsen, Frithjof Ulleberg (Norway)
1940–1944: Olympics not held			
1948	Torsten Lindberg, Karl Svensson, Knut Nordahl, Erik Nilsson, Birger Rosengren, Bertil Nordahl, Sune Andersson, Gunnar Gren, Gunnar Nordahl, Henry Carlsson, Nils Liedholm, Barje Leander (Sweden)	Franjo Šoštarić, Miroslav Brozović, Branko Stanković, Zlatko Čajkovski, Miodrag Jovanović, Aleksandar Atanacković, Prvoslav Mihajlović, Rajko Mitić, Franjo Wölfl, Stjepan Bobek, Željko Čajkovski, Kosta Tomašević, Ljubomir Lovrić, Zvonko Cimermančić, Bernard Vukas (Yugoslavia)	John Hansen, Karl Aage Hansen, Ivan Jensen, Viggo Jensen, Knud Lundberg, Eigil Nielsen, Knud Børge Overgaard, Axel Pilmark, Johannes Pløger, Carl Aage Præst, Holger Seebach, Jørgen Leschly Sørensen, Dion Ørnvold, Knud Bastrup-Birk, Hans Colberg, Edvin Hansen, Jørgen W. Hansen, Erik Kuld Jensen, Ove Jensen, Per Knudsen, Poul Petersen, Erling Sørensen (Denmark)
1952	Gyula Grosics, Jenő Dálnoki, Mihály Lantos, Imre Kovács, Gyula Lóránt, József Bozsik, László Budai, Sándor Kocsis, Nándor Hidegkuti, Ferenc Puskás, Zoltán Czibor, Jenő Buzánszky, József Zakariás, Lajos Csordás, Péter Palotás (Hungary)	Vladimir Beara, Branko Stanković, Tomislav Crnković, Zlatko Čajkovski, Ivan Horvat, Vujadin Boškov, Tihomir Ognjanov, Rajko Mitić, Bernard Vukas, Stjepan Bobek, Branko Zebec (Yugoslavia)	Karl Svensson, Lennart Samuelsson, Erik Nilsson, Holger Hansson, Bengt Gustavsson, Gösta Lindh, Sylve Bengtsson, Gösta Löfgren, Ingvar Rydell, Yngve Brodd, Gösta Sandberg, Olof Ahlund (Sweden)

Year	Gold	Silver	Bronze
1956	Lev Yashin, Nikolai Tishchenko, Mikhail Ogonkov, Aleksei Paramonov, Anatoli Bashashkin, Igor Netto, Boris Tatushin, Anatoli Isayev, Eduard Streltsov, Valentin Ivanov, Vladimir Ryzhkin, Boris Kuznetsov, Yozhef Betsa, Sergei Salnikov, Boris Razinsky, Anatoli Maslyonkin, Anatoli Ilyin, Nikita Simonyan (Soviet Union)	Petar Radenković, Mladen Koščak, Nikola Radović, Ivan Šantek, Ljubiša Spajić, Dobroslav Krstić, Dragoslav Šekularac, Zlatko Papec, Sava Antić, Todor Veselinović, Muhamed Mujić, Blagoje Vidinić, Ibrahim Biogradlić, Luka Lipošinović (Yugoslavia)	Stefan Bozhkov, Georgi Naydenov, Kiril Rakarov, Manol Manolov, Nikola Kovachev, Panayot Panayotov, Ivan Kolev, Krum Yanev, Gavril Stoyanov, Todor Diev, Yosif Yosifov, Georgi Dimitrov, Milcho Goranov, Dimitar Milanov (Bulgaria)
1960	Andrija Anković, Vladimir Durković, Milan Galić, Fahrudin Jusufi, Tomislav Knez, Borivoje Kostić, Aleksandar Kozlina, Dušan Maravić, Željko Matuš, Željko Perušić, Novak Roganović, Velimir Sombolac, Milutin Šoškić, Silvester Takač, Blagoje Vidinić, Ante Žanetić (Yugoslavia)	Paul Andersen, John Danielsen, Henning Enoksen, Henry From, Bent Hansen, Poul Jensen, Hans Christian Nielsen, Harald Nielsen, Flemming Nielsen, Poul Pedersen, Jørn Sørensen, Tommy Troelsen, Erik Gaardhøje, Jørgen Hansen, Henning Helbrandt, Bent Krog, Erling Linde Larsen, Poul Mejer, Finn Sterobo (Denmark)	Flórian Albert, Jenő Dálnoki, Zoltán Dudás, János Dunai, Lajos Faragó, János Göröcs, Ferenc Kovács, Dezső Novák, Pál Orosz, László Pál, Tibor Pál, Gyula Rákosi, Imre Sátori, Ernő Solymosi, Gábor Török, Pál Várhidi, Oszkár Vilezsál (Hungary)
1964	Ferenc Bene, Tibor Csernai, János Farkas, József Gelei, Kálmán Ihász, Sándor Katona, Imre Komora, Ferenc Nógrádi, Dezső Novák, Árpád Orbán, Károly Palotai, Antal Szentmihályi, Gusztáv Szepesi, Zoltán Varga (Hungary)	Jan Brumovský, Ludovít Cvetler, Ján Geleta, František Knebort, Karel Knesl, Karel Lichtnégl, Vojtech Masný, Štefan Matlák, Ivan Mráz, Karel Nepomucký, Zdeněk Pičman, František Schmucker, Anton Švajlen, Anton Urban, František Valošek, Josef Vojta, Vladimír Weiss (Czechoslovakia)	Gerd Backhaus, Wolfgang Barthels, Bernd Bauchspieß, Gerhard Körner, Otto Fräßdorf, Henning Frenzel, Dieter Engelhardt, Herbert Pankau, Manfred Geisler, Jürgen Heinsch, Klaus Lisiewicz, Jürgen Nöldner, Peter Rock, Klaus-Dieter Seehaus, Hermann Stöcker, Werner Unger, Klaus Urbanczyk, Eberhard Vogel, Manfred Walter, Horst Weigang (United Team of Germany)
1968	István Básti, Antal Dunai, Lajos Dunai, Ernő Noskó, Dezső Novák, Károly Fatér, László Fazekas, István Juhász, László Keglovich, Lajos Kocsis, Iván Menczel, László Nagy, Miklós Páncsics, István Sárközi, Lajos Szűcs, Zoltan Szarka, Miklós Szalai, Gábor Sárközi (Hungary)	Stoyan Yordanov, Atanas Gerov, Georgi Hristakiev, Milko Gaydarski, Kiril Ivkov, Ivaylo Georgiev, Tsvetan Dimitrov, Evgeni Yanchovski, Petar Zhekov, Atanas Hhristov, Asparuh Donev, Kiril Hristov, Georgi Ivanov, Todor Nikolov, Yancho Dimitrov, Ivan Zafirov, Mihail Gyonin, Georgi Vasilev (Bulgaria)	Kenzo Yokoyama, Hiroshi Katayama, Masakatsu Miyamoto, Yoshitada Yamaguchi, Mitsuo Kamata, Ryozo Suzuki, Kiyoshi Tomizawa, Takaji Mori, Aritatsu Ogi, Eizo Yuguchi, Shigeo Yaegashi, Teruki Miyamoto, Masashi Watanabe, Yasuyuki Kuwahara, Kunishige Kamamoto, Ikuo Matsumoto, Ryuichi Sugiyama, Masahiro Hamazaki (Japan)

Year	Gold	Silver	Bronze
1972	Hubert Kostka, Zbigniew Gut, Jerzy Gorgoń, Zygmunt Anczok, Lesław Ćmikiewicz, Zygmunt Maszczyk, Jerzy Kraska, Kazimierz Deyna, Zygfryd Szołtysik, Włodzimierz Lubański, Robert Gadocha, Ryszard Szymczak, Antoni Szymanowski, Joachim Marx, Grzegorz Lato, Marian Ostafiński, Kazimierz Kmiecik (Poland)	István Géczi, Péter Vépi, Miklós Páncsics, Péter Juhász, Lajos Szűcs, Mihály Kozma, Antal Dunai, Lajos Kű, Béla Váradi, Ede Dunai, László Bálint, Lajos Kocsis, Kálmán Tóth, László Branikovics, József Kovács, Csaba Vidács, Adám Rothermel (Hungary)	Oleg Blokhin, Murtaz Khurtsilava, Yuri Istomin, Vladimir Kaplichny, Viktor Kolotov, Evgeny Lovchev, Sergei Olshansky, Evhen Rudakov, Vyacheslav Semyonov, Gennady Yevriuzhikin, Oganes Zanazanyan, Andrei Yakubik, Arkady Andreasyan, Revaz Dzodzuashvili, Yozhef Sabo, Yuri Yeliseyev, Vladimir Onischenko, Anatoliy Kuksov, Vladimir Pilguy (Soviet Union)
			Jürgen Croy, Manfred Zapf, Konrad Weise, Bernd Bransch, Jürgen Pommerenke, Jürgen Sparwasser, Hans-Jürgen Kreische, Joachim Streich, Wolfgang Seguin, Peter Ducke, Frank Ganzera, Lothar Kurbjuweit, Eberhard Vogel, Harald Irmscher, Ralf Schulenberg, Reinhard Häfner, Siegmar Watzlich (East Germany)
1976	Hans-Ulrich Grapenthin, Wilfried Gröbner, Jürgen Croy, Gerd Weber, Hans-Jürgen Dörner, Konrad Weise, Lothar Kurbjuweit, Reinhard Lauck, Gerd Heidler, Reinhard Häfner, Hans-Jürgen Riediger, Bernd Bransch, Martin Hoffmann, Gerd Kische, Wolfram Löwe, Hartmut Schade, Dieter Riedel (East Germany)	Jan Tomaszewski, Piotr Mowlik, Antoni Szymanowski, Jerzy Gorgoń, Wojciech Rudy, Władysław Żmuda, Zygmunt Maszczyk, Grzegorz Lato, Henryk Wawrowski, Henryk Kasperczak, Roman Ogaza, Kazimierz Kmiecik, Kazimierz Deyna, Andrzej Szarmach, Henryk Wieczorek, Lesław Ćmikiewicz, Jan Benigier (Poland)	Vladimir Astapovsky, Anatoly Konjkov, Viktor Matvienko, Mykhailo Fomenko, Stefan Reshko, Vladimir Troshkin, David Kipiani, Vladimir Onischenko, Viktor Kolotov, Vladimir Veremeev, Oleg Blokhin, Leonid Buryak, Vladimir Fyodorov, Aleksandr Minayev, Viktor Zvyagintsev, Leonid Nazarenko, Aleksandr Prokhorov (Soviet Union)
1980	Stanislav Seman, Luděk Macela, Josef Mazura, Libor Radimec, Zdeněk Rygel, Petr Němec, Ladislav Vízek, Jan Berger, Jindřich Svoboda, Luboš Pokluda, Werner Lička, Rostislav Václavíček, Jaroslav Netolička, Oldřich Rott, František Štambacher, František Kunzo (Czechoslovakia)	Bodo Rudwaleit, Arthur Ullrich, Lothar Hause, Frank Uhlig, Frank Baum, Rudiger Schnuphase, Frank Terletzki, Wolfgang Steinbach, Jurgen Bahringer, Werner Peter, Dieter Kühn, Norbert Trieloff, Matthias Müller, Matthias Liebers, Bernd Jakubowski, Wolf-Rudiger Netz (East Germany)	Rinat Dasayev, Tengiz Sulakvelidze, Aleksandr Chivadze, Vagiz Khidiyatullin, Oleg Romantsev, Sergey Shavlo, Sergey Andreyev, Volodymyr Bezsonov, Yuri Gavrilov, Fyodor Cherenkov, Valery Gazzaev, Vladimir Pilguy, Sergej Baltacha, Sergei Nikulin, Khoren Oganesian, Aleksandr Prokopenko (Soviet Union)
1984	William Ayache, Michel Bensoussan, Michel Bibard, Dominique Bijotat, François Brisson, Patrick Cubaynes, Patrice Garande, Philippe Jeannol, Guy Lacombe, Jean-Claude Lemoult, Jean Philippe Rohr, Albert Rust, Didier Senac, Jean-Christophe Thouvenel, Jose Toure, Daniel Xuereb, Jean Louis Zanon (France)	Jorge Luis da Silva Brum, David Cortez Silva, Milton Cruz, Luís Henrique Dias, Andre Luiz Ferreira, Mauro Galvão, Antonio José Gil, João Leiehart Neto, Gilmar Popoca, Sylvio Paiva, Gilmar Rinaldi, Ademir Roque Kaefer, Paulo Santos, Ronaldo Silva, Carlos Caetano Bledorn Verri, Francisco Vidal, Luiz Carlos Winck (Brazil)	Mirsad Baljić, Mehmed Baždarević, Vlado Čapljić, Borislav Cvetković, Stjepan Deverić, Milko Djurovski, Marko Elsner, Nenad Gračan, Tomislav Ivković, Srečko Katanec, Branko Miljuš, Mitar Mrkela, Jovica Nikolić, Ivan Pudar, Ljubomir Radanović, Admir Smajić, Dragan Stojković (Yugoslavia)

Year	Gold	Silver	Bronze
1988	Dmitri Kharine, Gela Ketashvili, Igor Sklyarov, Oleksiy Cherednyk, Arvydas Janonis, Vadym Tyshchenko, Yevgeni Kuznetsov, Igor Ponomaryov, Aleksandr Borodyuk, Igor Dobrovolski, Vladimir Liuty, Evgeni Jarovenko, Sergei Fokin, Vladimir Tatarchuk, Alexei Mikhailichenko, Aleksei Prudnikov, Viktor Losev, Sergei Gorlukovich, Yuri Savichev, Arminas Narbekovas (Soviet Union)	Cláudio Taffarel, José Carlos Araújo, Jorge de Amorim Campos Oliveira, Luís Carlos Winck, André Cruz, Joao Santos Batista, Ricardo Gomes, Ademir Roque Kaefer, Iomar do Nascimento, Valdo Filho, Edmar Bernardes dos Santos, Jorge Luís Andrade da Silva, Hamilton De Souza, Milton de Souza Filho, Geovani Silva, Sergio Donizete Luiz, José Roberto Gama de Oliveira, Aloísio Pires Alves, Romário de Souza Faria (Brazil)	Oliver Reck, Michael Schulz, Armin Görtz, Wolfgang Funkel, Thomas Hörster, Olaf Janßen, Rudolf Bommer, Holger Fach, Jürgen Klinsmann, Wolfram Wuttke, Frank Mill, Uwe Kamps, Roland Grahammer, Thomas Häßler, Christian Schreier, Fritz Walter, Ralf Sievers, Gerhard Kleppinger, Karlheinz Riedle, Gunnar Sauer (Germany)
1992	José Emilio Amavisca, Rafael Berges, Santiago Cañizares, Abelardo Albert Ferrer, Josep Guardiola, Miguel Hernández Sánchez, Antonio Jimenez Sistachs, Mikel Lasa, Juan Manuel López, Javier Manjarín, Luis Enrique, Kiko Narváez, Alfonso Pérez Muñoz, Antonio Pinilla, Francisco Soler Atencia, Gabriel Vidal, Roberto Solozábal, David Villabona, Francisco Veza (Spain)	Dariusz Adamczuk, Marek Bajor, Jerzy Brzęczek, Marek Koźmiński, Dariusz Gęsior, Marcin Jałocha, Tomasz Łapiński, Tomasz Wałdoch, Aleksander Kłak, Andrzej Kobylański, Ryszard Staniek, Wojciech Kowalczyk, Andrzej Juskowiak, Grzegorz Mielcarski, Piotr Świerczewski, Mirosław Walógóra, Dariusz Kosela, Arkadiusz Onyszko, Dariusz Szubert, Tomasz Wieszczycki (Poland)	Joachin Yaw Acheampong, Simon Addo, Sammi Adjei, Maxwell Konadu, Mamood Amadu, Isaac Asare, Frank Amankwah, Nii Lamptey, Bernard Aryee, Kwame Ayew, Mohammed Gargo, Mohammed Kalilu, Ibrahim Dossey, Samuel Osei Kuffour, Samuel Kumah, Anthony Mensah, Alex Nyarko, Yaw Preko, Shamo Quaye, Oli Rahman (Ghana)
1996	Daniel Amokachi, Emmanuel Amunike, Tijani Babangida, Celestine Babayaro, Emmanuel Babayaro, Teslim Fatusi, Victor Ikpeba, Dosu Joseph, Nwankwo Kanu, Garba Lawal, Abiodon Obafemi, Kingsley Obiekwu, Uche Okechukwu, Jay-Jay Okocha, Sunday Oliseh, Mobi Oparaku, Wilson Oruma, Taribo West (Nigeria)	Matias Almeyda, Roberto Ayala, Christian Bassedas, Carlos Bossio, Pablo Cavallero, José Chamot, Hernán Crespo, Marcelo Delgado, Marcelo Gallardo, Claudio López, Gustavo Adrián López, Hugo Morales, Ariel Ortega, Pablo Paz, Hector Pineda, Roberto Sensini, Diego Simeone, Javier Zanetti (Argentina)	Nélson de Jesus Silva, José Marcelo Ferreira, Aldair Nascimento dos Santos, Ronaldo Luís Nazário de Lima, Flávio Conceição, Roberto Carlos, José Roberto Gama de Oliveira, Alexandre da Silva Mariano, Osvaldo Giroldo Júnior, Rivaldo Vítor Borba Ferreira, Sávio Bortolini Pimentel, Danrlei de Deus Hinterholz, Narciso dos Santos, André Luiz, José Elias Moedim Júnior, Marcelinho Paulista, Luiz Carlos Bombonato Goulart, Ronaldo Guiaro (Brazil)
2000	Samuel Eto'o, Serge Mimpo, Clément Beaud, Aaron Nguimbat, Joël Epalle, Modeste M'bami, Patrice Abanda, Nicolas Alnoudji, Daniel Bekono, Serge Branco, Lauren, Carlos Kameni, Patrick Mboma, Albert Meyong, Daniel Ngom Kome, Geremi, Patrick Suffo, Pierre Wome (Cameroon)	David Albelda, Iván Amaya, Miguel Ángel Angulo, Daniel Aranzubia, Joan Capdevila, Jordi Ferrón, Gabriel García, Xavier Hernández, Jesus María Lacruz, Albert Luque, Carlos Marchena, Felip Ortiz, Carles Puyol, José María Romero, Ismael Ruiz, Raúl Tamudo, Antonio Velamazán, Unai Vergara (Spain)	Pedro Reyes, Nelson Tapia, Iván Zamorano, Javier di Gregorio, Cristian Álvarez, Francisco Arrué, Pablo Contreras, Sebastián González, David Henríquez, Manuel Ibarra, Claudio Maldonado, Reinaldo Navia, Rodrigo Núñez, Rafael Olarra, Patricio Ormazábal, David Pizarro, Rodrigo Tello, Mauricio Rojas (Chile)

Year	Gold	Silver	Bronze
2004	German Lux, Wilfredo Caballero, Roberto Ayala, Fabricio Coloccini, Gabriel Heinze, Clemente Rodríguez, Leandro Fernández, Javier Mascherano, Kily González, Andres D'Alessandro, Luis González, Nicolás Medina, Cesar Delgado, Carlos Tévez, Mauro Rosales, Javier Saviola, Mariano González, Luciano Figueroa (Argentina)	Rodrigo Romero, Emilio Martínez, Julio Manzur, Carlos Gamarra, José Devaca, Celso Esquivel, Pablo Giménez, Edgar Barreto, Fredy Barreiro, Diego Figueredo, Aureliano Torres, Pedro Benitez, Julio César Enciso, Julio González, Ernesto Cristaldo, Osvaldo Díaz, José Cardozo, Diego Barreto (Paraguay)	Ivan Pelizzoli, Marco Amelia, Emiliano Moretti, Matteo Ferrari, Andrea Barzagli, Cesare Bovo, Giorgio Chiellini, Daniele Bonera, Giampiero Pinzi, Angelo Palombo, Andrea Pirlo, Daniele De Rossi, Marco Donadel, Alberto Gilardino, Simone Del Nero, Giuseppe Sculli, Andrea Gasbarroni, Giandomenico Mesto (Italy)
2008	Óscar Ustari, Ezequiel Garay, Luciano Fabián Monzón, Pablo Zabaleta, Fernando Gago, Federico Fazio, José Ernesto Sosa, Éver Banega, Ezequiel Lavezzi, Juan Román Riquelme, Ángel Di María, Nicolás Pareja, Lautaro Acosta, Javier Mascherano, Lionel Messi, Sergio Agüero, Diego Buonanotte, Sergio Romero, Nicolas Navarro (Argentina)	Ambruse Vanzekin, Chibuzor Okonkwo, Onyekachi Apam, Dele Adeleye, Monday James, Chinedu Obasi, Sani Kaita, Victor Nsofor Obinna, Promise Isaac, Solomon Okoronkwo, Oluwafemi Ajilore, Olubayo Adefemi, Peter Odemwingie, Efe Ambrose, Victor Anichebe, Emmanuel Ekpo, Ikechukwu Ezenwa, Oladapo Olufemi (Nigeria)	Diego Alves, Renan Brito Soares, Márcio Rafael Ferreira de Souza, Alex Silva, Thiago Silva, Marcelo Vieira da Silva Júnior, Ilson Pereira Dias Júnior, Breno Borges, Anderson Hernanes de Carvalho Andrade Lima, Anderson Luís de Abreu Oliveira, Lucas Pezzini Leiva, Ronaldo de Assis Moreira, Ramires Santos do Nascimento, Diego Ribas da Cunha, Thiago Neves, Alexandre Pato, Rafael Sóbis, João Alves de Assis Silva (Brazil)

Women's Football (Soccer)

Year	Gold	Silver	Bronze
1996	Mary Harvey, Cindy Parlow, Carla Overbeck, Tiffany Roberts, Brandi Chastain, Staci Wilson, Shannon MacMillan, Mia Hamm, Michelle Akers-Stahl, Julie Foudy, Carin Gabarra, Kristine Lilly, Joy Fawcett, Tisha Venturini, Tiffeny Milbrett, Briana Scurry (United States)	Zhong Honglian, Wang Liping, Fan Yunjie, Yu Hongqi, Xie Huilin, Zhao Lihong, Wei Haiying, Shui Qingxia, Sun Wen, Liu Ailing, Sun Qingmei, Wen Lirong, Liu Ying, Chen Yufeng, Shi Guihong, Gao Hong (China)	Bente Nordby, Agnete Carlsen, Gro Espeseth, Nina Nymark Andersen, Merete Myklebust, Hege Riise, Anne Nymark Andersen, Heidi Støre, Marianne Pettersen, Linda Medalen, Brit Sandaune, Kjersti Thun, Tina Svensson, Tone Haugen, Trine Tangeraas, Ann-Kristin Aarønes, Tone Gunn Frustøl, Reidun Seth, Ingrid Sternhoff (Norway)
2000	Gro Espeseth, Bente Nordby, Marianne Pettersen, Hege Riise, Kristin Bekkevold, Ragnhild Gulbrandsen, Solveig Gulbrandsen, Margunn Haugenes, Ingeborg Hovland, Christine Bøe Jensen, Silje Jørgensen, Monica Knudsen, Gøril Kringen, Unni Lehn, Dagny Mellgren, Anita Rapp, Brit Sandaune, Bente Kvitland (Norway)	Brandi Chastain, Joy Fawcett, Julie Foudy, Mia Hamm, Kristine Lilly, Tiffeny Milbrett, Carla Overbeck, Cindy Parlow, Briana Scurry, Lorrie Fair, Shannon MacMillan, Siri Mullinix, Christie Pearce, Nikki Serlenga, Danielle Slaton, Kate Sobrero, Sara Whalen (United States)	Ariane Hingst, Melanie Hoffmann, Steffi Jones, Renate Lingor, Maren Meinert, Sandra Minnert, Claudia Mueller, Birgit Prinz, Silke Rottenberg, Kerstin Stegemann, Bettina Wiegmann, Tina Wunderlich, Nicole Brandebusemeyer, Nadine Angerer, Doris Fitschen, Jeannette Goette, Stefanie Gottschlich, Inka Grings (Germany)

Year	Gold	Silver	Bronze
2004	Briana Scurry, Heather Mitts, Christie Rampone, Cat Reddick, Lindsay Tarpley, Brandi Chastain, Shannon Boxx, Angela Hucles, Mia Hamm, Aly Wagner, Julie Foudy, Cindy Parlow, Kristine Lilly, Joy Fawcett, Kate Markgraf, Abby Wambach, Heather O'Reilly, Kristin Luckenbill (United States)	Andréia Suntaque, Marlisa Wahlbrink, Mônica Angélica de Paula, Tânia Maria Pereira Ribeiro, Juliana Ribeiro Cabral, Daniela Alves Lima, Rosana dos Santos Augusto, Renata Costa, Aline Pellegrino, Miraildes Maciel Mota, Elaine Estrela Moura, Andréia dos Santos, Delma Gonçalves, Marta Vieira da Silva, Cristiane Rozeira de Souza Silva, Roseli de Belo, Dayane de Fátima Rocha, Grazielle Pinheiro Nascimento (Brazil)	Silke Rottenberg, Kerstin Stegeman, Kerstin Garefrekes, Steffi Jones, Sarah Günther, Viola Odebrecht, Pia Wunderlich, Petra Wimbersky, Birgit Prinz, Renate Lingor, Martina Müller, Navina Omilade, Sandra Minnert, Isabell Bachor, Sonja Fuss, Conny Pohlers, Ariane Hingst, Nadine Angerer (Germany)
2008	Hope Solo, Heather Mitts, Christie Rampone, Rachel Buehler, Lindsay Tarpley, Natasha Kai, Shannon Boxx, Amy Rodriguez, Heather O'Reilly, Aly Wagner, Carli Lloyd, Lauren Cheney, Tobin Heath, Stephanie Cox, Kate Markgraf, Angela Hucles, Lori Chalupny, Nicole Barnhart (United States)	Andréia Suntaque, Simone Gomes Jatobá, Andréia Rosa, Tânia Maria Pereira Ribeiro, Renata Costa, Andréia dos Santos, Daniela Alves Lima, Miraildes Maciel Mota, Ester Aparecida dos Santos, Marta Vieira da Silva, Cristiane Rozeira de Souza Silva, Bárbara Micheline do Monte Barbosa, Francielle Manoel Alberto, Delma Gonçalves, Fabiana da Silva Simões, Érika Cristiano dos Santos, Maurine Dornelles Gonçalves, Rosana dos Santos Augusto (Brazil)	Nadine Angerer, Kerstin Stegemann, Saskia Bartusiak, Babett Peter, Annike Krahn, Linda Bresonik, Melanie Behringer, Sandra Smisek, Birgit Prinz, Renate Lingor, Anja Mittag, Ursula Holl, Célia Okoyino da Mbabi, Simone Laudehr, Fatmire Bajramaj, Conny Pohlers, Ariane Hingst, Kerstin Garefrekes (Germany)

Golf

Men's Individual

Year	Gold	Silver	Bronze
1900	Charles Sands (United States)	Walter Rutherford (Great Britain)	David Robertson (Great Britain)
1904	George Lyon (Canada)	Chandler Egan (United States)	Burt McKinnie (United States) Francis Newton (United States)

Women's Individual

Year	Gold	Silver	Bronze
1900	Margaret Ives Abbott (United States)	Pauline Whittier (United States)	Daria Pratt (United States)

Men's Team

Year	Gold	Silver	Bronze
1904	Robert Hunter, Chandler Egan, Kenneth Edwards, Clement Smoot, Walter Egan, Daniel Sawyer, Edward Cummins, Mason Phelps, Nathaniel Moore, Warren Wood (United States)	Albert Lambert, Stuart Stickney, Burt McKinnie, William Stickney, Ralph McKittrick, Frederick Semple, Francis Newton, Henry Potter, John Cady, John Maxwell (United States)	Douglass Cadwallader, Allen Lard, Jesse Carleton, Simeon Price, Harold Weber, John Rahm, Arthur Hussey, Orus Jones, Harold Fraser, George Oliver (United States)

Handball

Men's Handball

Year	Gold	Silver	Bronze
1936	Willy Bandholz, Wilhelm Baumann, Helmut Berthold, Helmut Braselmann, Wilhelm Brinkmann, Georg Dascher, Kurt Dossin, Fritz Fromm, Hermann Hansen, Erich Herrmann, Heinrich Keimig, Hans Keiter, Alfred Klingler, Arthur Knautz, Heinz Körvers, Karl Kreutzberg, Wilhelm Müller, Günther Ortmann, Edgar Reinhardt, Fritz Spengler, Rudolf Stahl, Hans Theilig (Germany)	Franz Bartl, Franz Berghammer, Franz Bistricky, Franz Brunner, Johann Houschka, Emil Juracka, Ferdinand Kiefler, Josef Krejci, Otto Licha, Friedrich Maurer, Anton Perwein, Siegfried Powolny, Siegfried Purner, Walter Reisp, Alfred Schmalzer, Alois Schnabel, Ludwig Schuberth, Johann Tauscher, Jaroslav Volak, Leopold Wohlrab, Friedrich Wurmböck, Johann Zehetner (Austria)	Max Blösch, Rolf Fäs, Burkhard Gantenbein, Willy Gysi, Erland Herkenrath, Ernst Hufschmid, Willy Hufschmid, Werner Meyer, Georg Mischon, Willy Schäfer, Werner Scheurmann, Edy Schmid, Erich Schmitt, Eugen Seiterle, Max Streib, Robert Studer, Rudolf Wirz (Switzerland)
1940–1944: Olympics not held			
1948–1968: Event not held			
1972	Abaz Arslanagić, Petar Fajfrić, Hrvoje Horvat, Milorad Karalić, Đorđe Lavrnić, Milan Lazarević, Zdravko Miljak, Slobodan Mišković, Branislav Pokrajac, Nebojša Popović, Miroslav Pribanić, Albin Vidović, Zoran Živković, Zdenko Zorko (Yugoslavia)	Ladislav Beneš, František Brůna, Vladimír Haber, Vladimír Jarý, Jiří Kavan, Arnošt Klimčík, Jaroslav Konečný, František Králík, Jindřich Krepindl, Vincent Lafko, Andrej Lukošík, Pavel Mikeš, Peter Pospíšil, Ivan Satrapa, Zdeněk Škára, Jaroslav Škarvan (Czechoslovakia)	Ştefan Birtalan, Adrian Cosma, Marin Dan, Alexandru Dincă, Cristian Gaţu, Gheorghe Gruia, Roland Gunesch, Gabriel Kicsid, Ghiţă Licu, Cornel Penu, Valentin Samungi, Simion Schöbel, Werner Stöckl, Constantin Tudosie, Radu Voina (Romania)
1976	Aleksandr Anpilogov, Yevgeni Chernyshov, Anatoli Fedyukin, Valeri Gassy, Vasily Ilyin, Mykhaylo Ishchenko, Yuri Kidyaev, Yury Klimov, Vladimir Kravtsov, Serhiy Kushniryuk, Yuriy Lahutyn, Vladimir Maksimov, Oleksandr Rezanov, Mykola Tomyn (Soviet Union)	Ştefan Birtalan, Adrian Cosma, Cezar Drăgăniă, Alexandru Fölker, Cristian Gaţu, Mircea Grabovschi, Roland Gunesch, Gabriel Kicsid, Ghiţă Licu, Nicolae Munteanu, Cornel Penu, Werner Stöckl, Constantin Tudosie, Radu Voina (Romania)	Zdzisław Antczak, Janusz Brzozowski, Piotr Cieśla, Jan Gmyrek, Alfred Kałuziński, Jerzy Klempel, Zygfryd Kuchta, Jerzy Melcer, Ryszard Przybysz, Henryk Rozmiarek, Andrzej Sokołowski, Andrzej Szymczak, Mieczysław Wojczak, Włodzimierz Zieliński (Poland)
1980	Hans-Georg Beyer, Lothar Doering, Günter Dreibrodt, Ernst Gerlach, Klaus Gruner, Rainer Höft, Hans-Georg Jaunich, Hartmut Krüger, Peter Rost, Dietmar Schmidt, Wieland Schmidt, Siegfried Voigt, Frank-Michael Wahl, Ingolf Wiegert (East Germany)	Aleksandr Anpilogov, Vladimir Belov, Yevgeni Chernyshov, Anatoli Fedyukin, Mykhaylo Ishchenko, Aleksandr Karshakevich, Yuri Kidyaev, Vladimir Kravtsov, Serhiy Kushniryuk, Viktor Makhorin, Voldemaras Novickis, Vladimir Repev, Mykola Tomyn, Aleksey Zhuk (Soviet Union)	Ştefan Birtalan, Iosif Boroş, Adrian Cosma, Cezar Drăgăniă, Marian Dumitru, Cornel Durău, Alexandru Fölker, Claudiu Ionescu, Nicolae Munteanu, Vasile Stîngă, Lucian Vasilache, Neculai Vasilcă, Radu Voina, Maricel Voinea (Romania)
1984	Zlatan Arnautović, Mirko Bašić, Jovica Elezović, Mile Isaković, Pavle Jurina, Milan Kalina, Slobodan Kuzmanovski, Dragan Mladenović, Zdravko Rađenović, Momir Rnić, Branko Štrbac, Veselin Vujović, Veselin Vuković, Zdravko Zovko (Yugoslavia)	Jochen Fraatz, Thomas Happe, Arnulf Meffle, Rüdiger Neitzel, Michael Paul, Dirk Rauin, Siegfried Roch, Michael Roth, Ulrich Roth, Martin Schwalb, Uwe Schwenker, Thomas Springel, Andreas Thiel, Klaus Wöller, Erhard Wunderlich (West Germany)	Mircea Bedivan, Dumitru Berbece, Iosif Boroş, Alexandru Buligan, Gheorghe Covaciu, Gheorghe Dogărescu, Marian Dumitru, Cornel Durău, Alexandru Fölker, Nicolae Munteanu, Vasile Oprea, Adrian Simion, Vasile Stîngă, Neculai Vasilcă, Maricel Voinea (Romania)

Year	Gold	Silver	Bronze
1988	Vyacheslav Atavin, Igor Chumak, Valery Gopin, Aleksandr Karshakevich, Andrey Lavrov, Yuri Nesterov, Voldemaras Novickis, Aleksandr Rymanov, Konstantin Sharovarov, Yuri Shevtsov, Georgi Sviridenko, Aleksandr Tuchkin, Andrey Tyumentsev, Mikhail Vasilev (Soviet Union)	Choi Suk-Jae, Kang Jae-Won, Kim Jae-Hwan, Koh Suk-Chang, Lee Sang-Hyo, Lim Jin-Suk, Noh Hyun-Suk, Oh Young-Ki, Park Do-Hun, Park Young-Dae, Shim Jae-Hong, Shin Young-Suk, Yoon Tae-Il (South Korea)	Mirko Bašić, Jožef Holpert, Boris Jarak, Slobodan Kuzmanovski, Muhamed Memić, Alvaro Načinović, Goran Perkovac, Zlatko Portner, Iztok Puc, Rolando Pušnik, Momir Rnić, Zlatko Saračević, Irfan Smajlagić, Ermin Velić, Veselin Vujović (Yugoslavia)
1992	Andrey Barbashinsky, Serhiy Bebeshko, Igor Chumak, Talant Duyshebaev, Yuriy Gavrilov, Valery Gopin, Oleg Grebnev, Oleg Kiselyov, Vasily Kudinov, Andrey Lavrov, Igor Vasilev, Mikhail Yakimovich (Unified Team)	Magnus Andersson, Robert Andersson, Anders Bäckegren, Per Carlén, Magnus Cato, Erik Hajas, Robert Hedin, Patrik Liljestrand, Ola Lindgren, Mats Olsson, Staffan Olsson, Axel Sjöblad, Tommy Souraniemi, Tomas Svensson, Pierre Thorsson, Magnus Wislander (Sweden)	Philippe Debureau, Philippe Gardent, Denis Lathoud, Pascal Mahé, Philippe Médard, Gaël Monthurel, Laurent Munier, Frédéric Perez, Alain Portes, Thierry Perreux, Éric Quintin, Jackson Richardson, Stéphane Stoecklin, Jean-Luc Thiébaut, Denis Tristant, Frédéric Volle (France)
1996	Patrik Čavar, Valner Franković, Slavko Goluža, Bruno Gudelj, Vladimir Jelčić, Božidar Jović, Nenad Kljaić, Venio Losert, Valter Matošević, Zoran Mikulić, Alvaro Načinović, Goran Perkovac, Iztok Puc, Zlatko Saračević, Irfan Smajlagić, Vladimir Šuster (Croatia)	Magnus Andersson, Robert Andersson, Per Carlén, Martin Frändesjö, Erik Hajas, Robert Hedin, Andreas Larsson, Ola Lindgren, Stefan Lövgren, Mats Olsson, Staffan Olsson, Johan Petersson, Tomas Svensson, Tomas Sivertsson, Pierre Thorsson, Magnus Wislander (Sweden)	David Barrufet, Talant Duyshebaev, Mateo Garralda, Rafael Guijosa, Demetrio Lozano, Enric Masip, Jordi Nuñez, Jesús Olalla, Juan Pérez, Xavier O'Callaghan, Antonio Carlos Ortega, Antonio Ugalde, Iñaki Urdangarín, Alberto Urdiales, Andrei Xepkin (Spain)
2000	Dmitry Filippov, Vyacheslav Gorpishin, Oleg Khodkov, Eduard Koksharov, Denis Krivoshlykov, Vasily Kudinov, Stanislav Kulinchenko, Dmitry Kuzelev, Andrey Lavrov, Igor Lavrov, Sergey Pogorelov, Pavel Sukosyan, Dmitri Torgovanov, Aleksandr Tuchkin, Lev Voronin (Russia)	Magnus Andersson, Martin Boquist, Martin Frändesjö, Mathias Franzén, Peter Gentzel, Andreas Larsson, Ola Lindgren, Stefan Lövgren, Staffan Olsson, Johan Petersson, Tomas Svensson, Tomas Sivertsson, Pierre Thorsson, Ljubomir Vranjes, Magnus Wislander (Sweden)	David Barrufet, Talant Duyshebaev, Mateo Garralda, Rafael Guijosa, Demetrio Lozano, Enric Masip, Jordi Nuñez, Jesús Olalla, Juan Pérez, Xavier O'Callaghan, Antonio Carlos Ortega, Antonio Ugalde, Iñaki Urdangarín, Alberto Urdiales, Andrei Xepkin (Spain)
2004	Ivano Balić, Davor Dominiković, Mirza Džomba, Slavko Goluža, Nikša Kaleb, Blaženko Lacković, Venio Losert, Valter Matošević, Petar Metličić, Vlado Šola, Denis Špoljarić, Goran Šprem, Igor Vori, Vedran Zrnić (Croatia)	Markus Baur, Frank von Behren, Mark Dragunski, Henning Fritz, Pascal Hens, Jan Olaf Immel, Torsten Jansen, Florian Kehrmann, Stefan Kretzschmar, Klaus-Dieter Petersen, Christian Ramota, Christian Schwarzer, Daniel Stephan, Christian Zeitz, Volker Zerbe (Germany)	Mikhail Chipurin, Aleksandr Gorbatikov, Vyacheslav Gorpishin, Vitali Ivanov, Eduard Koksharov, Alexey Kostygov, Denis Krivoshlykov, Vasily Kudinov, Oleg Kuleshov, Andrey Lavrov, Sergey Pogorelov, Alexey Rastvortsev, Dmitri Torgovanov, Aleksandr Tuchkin (Russia)

Year	Gold	Silver	Bronze
2008	Luc Abalo, Joël Abati, Cédric Burdet, Didier Dinart, Jérôme Fernandez, Bertrand Gille, Guillaume Gille, Olivier Girault, Michaël Guigou, Nikola Karabatić, Daouda Karaboué, Christophe Kempe, Daniel Narcisse, Thierry Omeyer, Cédric Paty (France)	Sturla Ásgeirsson, Arnór Atlason, Logi Geirsson, Snorri Guðjónsson, Hreiðar Guðmundsson, Róbert Gunnarsson, Björgvin Páll Gústavsson, Ásgeir Örn Hallgrímsson, Ingimundur Ingimundarson, Sverre Andreas Jakobsson, Alexander Petersson, Guðjón Valur Sigurðsson, Sigfús Sigurðsson, Ólafur Stefánsson (Iceland)	David Barrufet, Jon Belaustegui, David Davis, Alberto Entrerríos, Raúl Entrerríos, Rubén Garabaya, Juanín García, José Javier Hombrados, Demetrio Lozano, Cristian Malmagro, Carlos Prieto, Albert Rocas, Iker Romero, Víctor Tomás (Spain)

Women's Handball

Year	Gold	Silver	Bronze
1976	Lyubov Odynokova, Lyudmyla Bobrus, Aldona Česaitytė, Tetyana Hlushchenko, Larysa Karlova, Mariya Litoshenko, Nina Lobova, Tetyana Kocherhina, Lyudmyla Panchuk, Rafiga Shabanova, Nataliya Tymoshkina, Lyudmila Shubina, Zinaida Turchyna, Halyna Zakharova (Soviet Union)	Gabriele Badorek, Hannelore Burosch, Roswitha Krause, Waltraud Kretzschmar, Evelyn Matz, Liane Michaelis, Eva Paskuy, Kristina Richter, Christina Rost, Silvia Siefert, Marion Tietz, Petra Uhlig, Christina Voß, Hannelore Zober (East Germany)	Éva Angyal, Mária Berzsenyi, Ágota Bujdosó, Klára Csíkné, Zsuzsanna Kéziné, Katalin Lakiné, Rozália Lelkesné, Márta Megyeriné, Ilona Nagy, Marianna Nagy, Erzsébet Németh, Amália Sterbinszky, Borbála Tóth Harsányi, Mária Vadászné (Hungary)
1980	Larysa Karlova, Tetyana Kocherhina, Valentyna Lutayeva, Aldona Nenénienė, Lyubov Odynokova, Iryna Palchykova, Lyudmila Poradnyk, Yuliya Safina, Larisa Savkina, Sigita Strečen, Nataliya Tymoshkina, Zinaida Turchyna, Olha Zubaryeva (Soviet Union)	Svetlana Anastasovska, Mirjana Đurica, Radmila Drljača, Katica Ileš, Slavica Jeremić, Svetlana Kitić, Jasna Merdan, Vesna Milosević, Mirjana Ognjenović, Vesna Radović, Radmila Savić, Ana Titlić, Biserka Višnjić, Zorica Vojinović (Yugoslavia)	Birgit Heinecke, Roswitha Krause, Waltraud Kretzschmar, Katrin Krüger, Kornelia Kunisch, Evelyn Matz, Kristina Richter, Christina Rost, Sabine Röther, Renate Rudolph, Marion Tietz, Petra Uhlig, Claudia Wunderlich, Hannelore Zober (East Germany)
1984	Svetlana Anastasovska, Alenka Cuderman, Svetlana Dašić-Kitić, Slavica Đukić, Dragica Đurić, Mirjana Đurica, Emilija Erčić, Ljubinka Janković, Jasna Kolar-Merdan, Ljiljana Mugoša, Svetlana Mugoša, Mirjana Ognjenović, Zorica Pavićević, Jasna Ptujec, Biserka Višnjić (Yugoslavia)	Han Hwa-Soo, Jeong Hyoi-Soon, Jeung Soon-Bok, Kim Choon-Rye, Kim Kyung-Soon, Kim Mi-Sook, Kim Ok-Hwa, Lee Soon-Ei, Lee Young-Ja, Shon Mi-Na, Sung Kyung-Hwa, Yoon Byung-Soon, Yoon Soo-Kyung (South Korea)	Chen Zhen, Gao Xiumin, He Jianping, Li Lan, Liu Liping, Liu Yumei, Sun Xiulan, Wang Linwei, Wang Mingxing, Wu Xingjiang, Zhang Weihong, Zhang Peijun, Zhu Juefeng (China)
1988	Ki Mi-Sook, Kim Choon-Rye, Kim Hyun-Mee, Kim Kyung-Soon, Kim Myung-Soon, Lee Ki-Soon, Lim Mi-Kyung, Shon Mi-Na, Song Ji-Hyun, Suk Min-Hee, Sung Kyung-Hwa, Lee Mi-Young (South Korea)	Kjerstin Andersen, Berit Digre, Marthe Eliasson, Susann Goksør, Trine Haltvik, Hanne Hegh, Hanne Hogness, Vibeke Johnsen, Kristin Midthun, Karin Pettersen, Karin Singstad, Annette Skotvoll, Ingrid Steen, Heidi Sundal, Cathrine Svendsen (Norway)	Natalya Anisimova, Maryna Bazhanova, Tatyana Dzhandzhgava, Elina Guseva, Tetyana Horb, Larysa Karlova, Natalya Lapitskaya, Svitlana Mankova, Nataliya Matryuk, Natalya Morskova, Olena Nemashkalo, Nataliya Rusnachenko, Olha Semenova, Yevheniya Tovstohan, Zinaida Turchyna (Soviet Union)

Year	Gold	Silver	Bronze
1992	Cha Jae-Kyung, Han Hyun-Sook, Han Sun-Hee, Hong Jeong-Ho, Jang Ri-Ra, Kim Hwa-Sook, Lee Ho-Youn, Lee Mi-Young, Lim O-Kyeong, Min Hye-Sook, Moon Hyang-Ja, Nam Eun-Young, Oh Sung-Ok, Park Jeong-Lim, Park Kap-Sook (South Korea)	Hege Kirsti Frøseth, Tonje Sagstuen, Hanne Hogness, Heidi Sundal, Susann Goksør, Cathrine Svendsen, Mona Dahle, Siri Eftedal, Henriette Henriksen, Ingrid Steen, Karin Pettersen, Annette Skotvoll, Kristine Duvholt, Heidi Tjugum (Norway)	Natalya Anisimova, Maryna Bazhanova, Svetlana Bogdanova, Galina Borzenkova, Natalya Deryugina, Tatyana Dzhandzhgava, Lyudmila Gudz, Elina Guseva, Tetyana Horb, Larisa Kiselyova, Natalya Morskova, Galina Onoprienko, Svetlana Pryakhina (Unified Team)
1996	Anja Andersen, Camilla Andersen, Kristine Andersen, Heidi Astrup, Tina Bøttzau, Marianne Florman, Conny Hamann, Anja Hansen, Anette Hoffman, Tonje Kjærgaard, Janne Kolling, Susanne Lauritsen, Gitte Madsen, Lene Rantala, Gitte Sunesen, Anne Dorthe Tanderup (Denmark)	Cho Eun-Hee, Han Sun-Hee, Hong Jeong-Ho, Huh Soon-Young, Kim Cheong-Sim, Kim Eun-Mi, Kim Jeong-Mi, Kim Mi-Sim, Kim Rang, Kwag Hye-Jeong, Lee Sang-Eun, Lim O-Kyeong, Moon Hyang-Ja, Oh Sung-Ok, Oh Yong-Ran, Park Jeong-Lim (South Korea)	Éva Erdős, Andrea Farkas, Beáta Hoffmann, Anikó Kántor, Erzsébet Kocsis, Beatrix Kökény, Eszter Mátéfi, Auguszta Mátyás, Anikó Meksz, Anikó Nagy, Helga Németh, Ildikó Pádár, Beáta Siti, Anna Szántó, Katalin Szilágyi, Beatrix Tóth (Hungary)
2000	Lene Rantala, Camilla Andersen, Tina Bøttzau, Janne Kolling, Tonje Kjærgaard, Karen Brødsgaard, Katrine Fruelund, Maja Grønbæk, Christina Hansen, Anette Hoffman, Lotte Kiærskou, Karin Mortensen, Anja Nielsen, Rikke Petersen, Mette Vestergaard (Denmark)	Beatrix Balogh, Rita Deli, Ágnes Farkas, Andrea Farkas, Anikó Kántor, Beatrix Kökény, Anita Kulcsár, Dóra Lőwy, Anikó Nagy, Ildikó Pádár, Katalin Pálinger, Krisztina Pigniczki, Bojana Radulovics, Judith Simics, Beáta Siti (Hungary)	Kristine Duvholt, Trine Haltvik, Heidi Tjugum, Susann Goksør Bjerkrheim, Ann Cathrin Eriksen, Kjersti Grini, Elisabeth Hilmo, Mia Hundvin, Tonje Larsen, Cecilie Leganger, Jeanette Nilsen, Marianne Rokne, Brigitte Sættem, Monica Sandve, Else-Marthe Sørlie (Norway)
2004	Louise Nørgaard, Rikke Skov, Henriette Mikkelsen, Mette Vestergaard, Rikke Jørgensen, Camilla Thomsen, Karin Mortensen, Lotte Kiærskou, Trine Jensen, Katrine Fruelund, Rikke Schmidt, Kristine Andersen, Karen Brødsgaard, Line Daugaard, Josephine Touray (Denmark)	Oh Yong-Ran, Woo Sun-Hee, Huh Soon-Young, Lee Gong-Joo, Jang So-Hee, Kim Hyun-Ok, Kim Cha-Youn, Oh Seong-Ok, Huh Young-Sook, Moon Kyeong-Ha, Lim O-Kyeong, Lee Sang-Eun, Myoung Bok-Hee, Choi Im-jeong, Moon Pil-Hee (South Korea)	Nataliya Borysenko, Ganna Burmystrova, Tetyana Shynkarenko, Maryna Vergelyuk, Olena Yatsenko, Ganna Siukalo, Olena Radchenko, Olena Tsygitsa, Galyna Markushevska, Lyudmyla Shevchenko, Iryna Honcharova, Nataliya Lyapina, Anastasiya Borodina, Larysa Zaspa, Oxana Rayhel (Ukraine)
2008	Ragnhild Aamodt, Karoline Dyhre Breivang, Marit Malm Frafjord, Gro Hammerseng, Katrine Lunde Haraldsen, Kari Aalvik Grimsbø, Kari Mette Johansen, Tonje Larsen, Kristine Lunde, Else-Marthe Sørlie Lybekk, Tonje Nøstvold, Katja Nyberg, Linn-Kristin Riegelhuth, Gøril Snorroeggen (Norway)	Yekaterina Andryushina, Irina Bliznova, Yelena Dmitriyeva, Anna Kareyeva, Yekaterina Marennikova, Yelena Polenova, Irina Poltoratskaya, Lyudmila Postnova, Oxana Romenskaya, Natalia Shipilova, Maria Sidorova, Inna Suslina, Emiliya Turey, Yana Uskova (Russia)	Bae Min-Hee, Choi Im-Jeong, Hong Jeong-Ho, Huh Soon-Young, Kim Cha-Youn, Kim Nam-Sun, Kim O-Na, Lee Min-Hee, Moon Pil-Hee, Oh Seong-Ok, Oh Yong-Ran, Park Chung-Hee, Song Hai-Rim (South Korea)

Field Hockey

Men's Field Hockey

Year	Gold	Silver	Bronze
1908	Louis Baillon, Harry Freeman, Eric Green, Gerald Logan, Alan Noble, Edgar Page, Reggie Pridmore, Percy Rees, John Yate Robinson, Stanley Shoveller, Harvey Wood (Great Britain)	Allman-Smith, Henry Brown, Walter Campbell, William Graham, Richard Gregg, Edward Holmes, Robert Kennedy, Henry Murphy, Walter Peterson, Charles Power, Frank Robinson (Great Britain)	Alexander Burt, John Burt, Alastair Denniston, Charles Foulkes, Hew Fraser, James Harper-Orr, Ivan Laing, Hugh Neilson, William Orchardson, Norman Stevenson, Hugh Walker (Great Britain)
			Connah, Llewellyn Evans, Arthur Law, Richard Lyne, Wilfred Pallott, Frederick Phillips, Edward Richards, Charles Shephard, Bertrand Turnbull, Philip Turnbull, James Williams (Great Britain)
1912: Event not held			
1916: Olympics not held			
1920	Charles Atkin, John Bennett, Colin Campbell, Harold Cassels, Harold Cooke, Eric Crockford, Reginald Crummack, Harry Haslam, Arthur Leighton, Charles Marcon, John McBryan, George McGrath, Stanley Shoveller, William Smith, Cyril Wilkinson (Great Britain)	Hans Bjerrum, Ejvind Blach, Niels Blach, Steen Due, Thorvald Eigenbrod, Frands Faber, Hans Jørgen Hansen, Hans Herlak, Henning Holst, Erik Husted, Paul Metz, Andreas Rasmussen (Denmark)	André Becquet, Pierre Chibert, Raoul Daufresne de la Chevalerie, Fernand de Montigny, Charles Delelienne, Louis Diercxsens, Robert Gevers, Adolphe Goemaere, Charles Gniette, Raymond Keppens, René Strauwen, Pierre Valcke, Maurice van den Bemden, Jean van Nerom (Belgium)
1924: Event not held			
1928	Richard Allen, Dhyan Chand, Maurice Gateley, William Goodsir-Cullen, Leslie Hammond, Feroze Khan, George Marthins, Rex Norris, Broome Pinniger, Michael Rocque, Frederic Seaman, Ali Shaukat, Jaipal Singh, Sayed Yusuf, Kher Singh Gill (India)	Jan Ankerman, Jan Brand, Rein de Waal, Emile Duson, Gerrit Jannink, Adriaan Katte, August Kop, Ab Tresling, Paul van de Rovaart, Robert van der Veen, Haas Visser 't Hooft, C. J. J. Hardebeck, T. F. Hubrecht, G. Leembruggen, H. J. L. Mangelaar Meertens, Otto Muller von Czernicki, W. J. van Citters, C. J. van der Hagen, Tonny van Lierop, J. J. van Tienhoven van den Bogaard, J. M. van Voorst van Beest, N. Wenholt (Netherlands)	Bruno Boche, Georg Brunner, Heinz Förstendorf, Erwin Franzkowiak, Werner Freyberg, Theodor Haag, Hans Haußmann, Kurt Haverbeck, Aribert Heymann, Herbert Hobein, Fritz Horn, Karl-Heinz Irmer, Herbert Kemmer, Herbert Müller, Werner Proft, Gerd Strantzen, Rolf Wollner, Heinz Wöltje, Erich Zander, Fritz Lincke, Heinz Schäfer, Kurt Weiß (Germany)
1932	Richard Allen, Muhammad Aslam, Lal Bokhari, Frank Brewin, Richard Carr, Dhyan Chand, Leslie Hammond, Arthur Hind, Sayed Jaffar, Masud Minhas, Broome Pinniger, Gurmit Singh Kullar, Roop Singh, William Sullivan, Carlyle Tapsell (India)	Shunkichi Hamada, Junzo Inohara, Sadayoshi Kobayashi, Haruhiko Kon, Kenichi Konishi, Hiroshi Nagata, Eiichi Nakamura, Yoshio Sakai, Katsumi Shibata, Akio Sohda, Toshio Usami (Japan)	William Boddington, Harold Brewster, Roy Coffin, Amos Deacon, Horace Disston, Samuel Ewing, James Gentle, Henry Greer, Lawrence Knapp, David McMullin, Leonard O'Brien, Charles Sheaffer, Frederick Wolters (United States)

Year	Gold	Silver	Bronze
1936	Richard Allen, Dhyan Chand, Ali Dara, Lionel Emmett, Peter Fernandes, Joseph Galibardy, Earnest Goodsir-Cullen, Mohammed Hussain, Sayed Jaffar, Ahmed Khan, Ahsan Khan, Mirza Masood, Cyril Michie, Baboo Nimal, Joseph Phillips, Shabban Shahab-ud-Din, Garewal Singh, Roop Singh, Carlyle Tapsell (India)	Hermann auf der Heide, Ludwig Beisiegel, Erich Cuntz, Karl Dröse, Alfred Gerdes, Werner Hamel, Harald Huffmann, Erwin Keller, Herbert Kemmer, Werner Kubitzki, Paul Mehlitz, Karl Menke, Fritz Messner, Detlef Okrent, Heinrich Peter, Heinz Raack, Carl Ruck, Hans Scherbart, Heinz Schmalix, Tito Warnholtz, Kurt Weiß, Erich Zander (Germany)	Henk de Looper, Jan de Looper, Aat de Roos, Rein de Waal, Piet Gunning, Inge Heybroek, Hans Schnitger, René Sparenberg, Ernst van den Berg, Ru van der Haar, Tonny van Lierop, Max Westerkamp (Netherlands)
1940–1944: Olympics not held			
1948	Leslie Claudius, Keshav Dutt, Walter D'Souza, Lawrie Fernandes, Ranganathan Francis, Gerry Glacken, Akhtar Hussain, Patrick Jansen, Amir Kumar, Kishan Lal, Leo Pinto, Jaswant Singh Rajput, Latif-ur-Rehman, Reginald Rodrigues, Balbir Singh Sr., Randhir Singh Gentle, Grahanandan Singh, K. D. Singh, Trilochan Singh, Maxie Vaz (India)	Robert Adlard, Norman Borrett, David Brodie, Ronald Davis, William Griffiths, Frederick Lindsay, William Lindsay, John Peake, Frank Reynolds, George Sime, Michael Walford, William White (Great Britain)	André Boerstra, Henk Bouwman, Piet Bromberg, Harry Derckx, Han Drijver, Dick Esser, Roepie Kruize, Jenne Langhout, Dick Loggere, Ton Richter, Eddy Tiel, Wim van Heel (Netherlands)
1952	Leslie Claudius, Meldric Daluz, Keshav Dutt, Chinadorai Deshmutu, Ranganathan Francis, Raghbir Lal, Govind Perumal, Muniswamy Rajgopal, Balbir Singh Dosanjh, Randhir Singh Gentle, Udham Singh, Dharam Singh, Grahanandan Singh, K. D. Singh (India)	Jules Ancion, André Boerstra, Harry Derckx, Han Drijver, Dick Esser, Roepie Kruize, Dick Loggere, Lau Mulder, Eddy Tiel, Wim van Heel, Leonard Wery (Netherlands)	Denys Carnill, John Cockett, John Conroy, Graham Dadds, Derek Day, Dennis Eagan, Robin Fletcher, Roger Midgley, Richard Norris, Neil Nugent, Anthony Nunn, Anthony John Robinson, John Paskin Taylor (Great Britain)
1956	Leslie Claudius, Ranganathan Francis, Haripal Kaushik, Amir Kumar, Raghbir Lal, Shankar Lakshman, Govind Perumal, Amit Singh Bakshi, Raghbir Singh Bhola, Balbir Singh Dosanjh, Hardyal Singh Garchey, Randhir Singh Gentle, Balkishan Singh Grewal, Gurdev Singh Kullar, Udham Singh Kullar, Bakshish Singh, Charles Stephen (India)	Akhtar Hussain, Munir Dar, Ghulam Rasool, Habibur Rehman, Anwar Ahmed Khan, Habib Ali Kiddie, Latifur Rehman, Manzoor Hussain Atif, Qazi Musarrat Hussain, Motiullah, Naseer Bunda, Noor Alam, Zakir Hussain (Pakistan)	Gunter Brennecke, Hugo Budinger, Werner Delmes, Hugo Dollheiser, Eberhard Ferstl, Alfred Lücker, Helmut Nonn, Wolfgang Nonn, Heinz Radzikowski, Werner Rosenbaum, Gunther Ullerich (United Team of Germany)
1960	Hamid Abdul, Rashid Abdul, Waheed Abdul, Ahmad Bashir, Rasul Ghulam, Anwar Khan, Aslam Khursheed, Habib Kiddi, Hussain Manzoor, Ahmed Mushtaq, Ullah Mutti, Ahmad Nasir, Alam Noor (Pakistan)	Joseph Antic, Leslie Claudius, Jaman Lal Sharma, Mohinder Lal, Shankar Lakshman, John Peter, Govind Sawant, Raghbir Singh Bhola, Udham Singh Kullar, Charanjit Singh, Jaswant Singh, Joginder Singh, Prithipal Singh (India)	Pedro Amat, Francisco Caballer, Juan Calzado, José Colomer, Carlos Iglesias, Jose Dinares, Eduardo Dualde, Joaquin Dualde, Rafael Egusquiza, Ignacio Macaya, Pedro Murua, Pedro Roig, Luis Usoz, Narciso Ventallo (Spain)

Year	Gold	Silver	Bronze
1964	Haripal Kaushik, Mohinder Lal, Shankar Lakshman, Bandu Patil, John Peter, Ali Sayed, Udham Singh Kullar, Charanjit Singh, Darshan Singh, Dharam Singh, Gurbux Singh, Harbinder Singh, Jagjit Singh, Joginder Singh, Prithipal Singh (India)	Hamid Abdul, Mohammad Asad Malik, Munir Dar, Mahmud Khalid, Anwar Khan, Nawaz Khizar, Azam Khurshid, Muhammad Manna, Hussain Manzoor, Rashid Muhammad, Ullah Mutti, Tariq Niazi, Saeed Anwar, Aziz Tariq, Hayat Zafar, Uddin Zaka (Pakistan)	Mervyn Crossman, Paul Dearing, Raymond Evans, Brian Glencross, Robin Hodder, John McBryde, Donald McWatters, Patrick Nilan, Eric Pearce, Julian Pearce, Desmond Piper, Donald Smart, Anthony Waters, Graham Wood (Australia)
1968	Abdul Rasheed, Jahangir Butt, Tanvir Dar, Gulraiz Akhtar, Khalid Mahmood, Mohammad Asad Malik, Mohammad Ashfaq, Tariq Niazi, Riaz Ahmad, Riazuddin, Saeed Anwar, Tariq Aziz, Zakir Hussain (Pakistan)	Paul Dearing, Raymond Evans, Brian Glencross, Robert Haigh, Donald Martin, James Mason, Patrick Nilan, Eric Pearce, Gordon Pearce, Julian Pearce, Desmond Piper, Fred Quine, Ronald Riley, Donald Smart (Australia)	Rajendra Christy, Krishnanurthy Perumal, John Peter, Inamur Rehaman, Munir Sait, Ajitpal Singh, Balbir Singh (I), Balbir Singh (II), Balbir Singh (III), Gurbux Singh, Harbinder Singh, Harmik Singh, Inder Singh, Prithipal Singh, Tarsem Singh (India)
1972	Wolfgang Baumgart, Horst Drose, Dieter Freise, Werner Kaess-mann, Carsten Keller, Detlef Kittstein, Ulrich Klaes, Peter Kraus, Michael Krause, Michael Peter, Wolfgang Rott, Fritz Schmidt, Rainer Seifert, Wolfgang Strodter, Eckart Suhl, Eduard Thelen, Peter Trump, Ulrich Vos (West Germany)	Rashid Abdul, Rasool Akhtar, Ul Akhtar, Jahangir Butt, Ur Fazal, Ud Islah, Mohammad Asad Malik, Shahnaz Muhammad, Uz-Zaman Munawar, Ahmad Riaz, Saeed Anwar, Saleem Sherwani, Iftikar Syed, Mudassar Syed, Muhammad Zahid (Pakistan)	B. P. Govinda, Cornelius Charles, Manuel Frederick, Michael Kindo, Ashok Kumar, M. P. Ganesh, Krishnanurthy Perumal, Ajitpal Singh, Harbinder Singh, Harcharan Singh, Harmik Singh, Kulwant Singh, Mukhbain Singh, Virinder Singh (India)
1976	Paul Ackerley, Jeff Archibald, Arthur Borren, Alan Chesney, John Christensen, Greg Dayman, Tony Ineson, Barry Maister, Selwyn Maister, Trevor Manning, Alan McIntyre, Neil McLeod, Arthur Parkin, Mohan Patel, Ramesh Patel, Les Wilson (New Zealand)	David Bell, Greg Browning, Ric Charlesworth, Ian Cooke, Barry Dancer, Douglas Golder, Robert Haigh, Wayne Hammond, Jim Irvine, Malcolm Poole, Robert Proctor, Graeme Reid, Ronald Riley, Trevor Smith, Terry Walsh (Australia)	Rashid Abdul, Rasool Akhtar, Mahmood Arshad, Arshad Chaudhry, Khan Haneef, Ud Islah, Sami Khan, Hassan Manzoor, Hussain Manzoor, Uz-Zaman Munawar, Zia Qamar, Nazim Salim, Shahnaz Sheikh, Saleem Sherwani, Iftikar Syed, Mudassar Syed (Pakistan)
1980	Vasudevan Baskaran, Bir Bhadur Chettri, Sylvanus Dung Dung, Merwyn Fernandes, Zafar Iqbal, Maharaj Krishan Kaushik, Charanjit Kumar, Sommayya Maneypande, Allan Schofield, Mohamed Shahid, Davinder Singh, Gurmail Singh, Amarjit Singh Rana, Rajinder Singh, Ravinder Pal Singh, Surinder Singh Sodhi (India)	Juan Amat, Juan Arbós, Jaime Arbós, Javier Cabot, Ricardo Cabot, Miguel Chaves, Juan Coghen, Miguel de Paz, Francisco Fábregas, José Garcia, Rafael Garralda, Santiago Malgosa, Paulino Monsalve, Juan Pellón, Carlos Roca, Jaime Zumalacárregui (Spain)	Sos Airapetian, Minneula Azizov, Valeri Belyakov, Viktor Deputatov, Aleksandr Goncha-rov, Aleksandr Gusev, Sergei Klevtsov, Viacheslav Lampeev, Aleksandr Miasnikov, Mikhail Nichepurenko, Leonid Pavlovski, Sergei Pleshakov, Vladimir Pleshakov, Aleksandr Sychyov, Oleg Zagorodnev, Farit Zigangirov (Soviet Union)
1984	Rashid Abdul, Tauqeer Dar, Ahmed Ishtiaq, Ullah Kaleem, Hameed Khalid, Hanir Khan, Shahid Ali Khan, Hussain Manzoor, Ayaz Mehmood, Ghulam Moin Ud Din, Ahmed Mushtaq, Akhtar Naeem, Ali Nasir, Zia Qasim, Hassan Sardar, Saleem Sherwani (Pakistan)	Christian Bassemir, Stefan Blöcher, Dirk Brinkmann, Heiner Dopp, Carsten Fischer, Tobias Frank, Volker Fried, Thomas Gunst, Horst-Ulrich Hänel, Karl-Joachim Hurter, Andreas Keller, Reinhard Krull, Michael Peter, Thomas Reck, Ekkhard Schmidt-Opper, Markku Slawyk (West Germany)	Paul Barber, Stephen Batchelor, Kulbir Bhaura, Robert Cattrall, Richard Dodds, James Duthie, Norman Hughes, Sean Kerly, Richard Leman, Stephen Martin, William McConnell, Veryan Pappin, Jon Potter, Mark Precious, Ian Taylor, David Westcott (Great Britain)

Year	Gold	Silver	Bronze
1988	Paul Barber, Stephen Batchelor, Kulbir Bhaura, Robert Clift, Richard Dodds, David Faulkner, Russell Garcia, Martyn Grimley, Sean Kerly, Jimmy Kirkwood, Richard Leman, Stephen Martin, Veryan Pappin, Jon Potter, Imran Sherwani, Ian Taylor (Great Britain)	Stefan Blöcher, Dirk Brinkmann, Thomas Brinkmann, Heiner Dopp, Hans-Henning Fastrich, Carsten Fischer, Tobias Frank, Volker Fried, Horst-Ulrich Hänel, Michael Hilgers, Andreas Keller, Michael Metz, Andreas Mollandin, Thomas Reck, Christian Schliemann, Ekkhard Schmidt-Opper (West Germany)	Marc Benninga, Floris Jan Bovelander, Jacques Brinkman, Maurits Crucq, Marc Delissen, Cees Jan Diepeveen, Patrick Faber, Ronald Jansen, Rene Klaassen, Hendrik Kooijman, Hidde Kruize, Frank Leistra, Erik Parlevliet, Gert Schlatmann, Tim Steens, Taco van den Honert (Netherlands)
1992	Andreas Becker, Christian Blunck, Carsten Fischer, Volker Fried, Michael Hilgers, Andreas Keller, Michael Knauth, Oliver Kurtz, Christian Mayerhöfer, Sven Meinhardt, Michael Metz, Klaus Michler, Christopher Reitz, Stefan Saliger, Jan-Peter Tewes, Stefan Tewes (Germany)	John Bestall, Warren Birmingham, Lee Bodimeade, Ashley Carey, Gregory Corbitt, Stephen Davies, Damon Diletti, Lachlan Dreher, Lachlan Elmer, Dean Evans, Paul Lewis, Graham Reid, Jay Stacy, David Wansbrough, Ken Wark, Michael York (Australia)	Saeed Anjum, Hasan Farhat, Khalid Bashir, Muhammad Khawaja, Mansoor Ahmed, Asif Muhammad, Ikhlaq Muhammad, Mohammad Khalid Sr, Qamar Muhammad, Hussain Musaddaq, Rana Mujahid, Shahbaz Ahmed, Muhammad Shahbaz, Shahid Ali Khan, Tahir Zaman, Wasim Feroz (Pakistan)
1996	Floris Jan Bovelander, Jacques Brinkman, Maurits Crucq, Teun de Nooijer, Marc Delissen, Jeroen Delmee, Ronald Jansen, Erik Jazet, Leo Gebbink, Bram Lomans, Taco van den Honert, Tycho van Meer, Wouter van Pelt, Remco van Wijk, Stephan Veen, Guus Vogels (Netherlands)	Jaime Amat, Pablo Amat, Javier Arnau, Jordi Arnau, Oscar Barrena, Ignacio Cobos, Juan Dinarés, Juan Escarré, Xavier Escudé, Juantxo García-Mauriño, Antonio González, Ramón Jufresa, Joaquín Malgosa, Victor Pujol, Ramón Sala, Pablo Usoz (Spain)	Stuart Carruthers, Baeden Choppy, Stephen Davies, Damon Diletti, Lachlan Dreher, Lachlan Elmer, Brendan Garard, Paul Gaudoin, Mark Hager, Paul Lewis, Grant Smith, Matthew Smith, Daniel Sproule, Jay Stacy, Ken Wark, Michael York (Australia)
2000	Jacques Brinkman, Jaap-Derk Buma, Teun de Nooijer, Jeroen Delmee, Marten Eikelboom, Piet-Hein Geeris, Ronald Jansen, Erik Jazet, Bram Lomans, Sander van der Weide, Wouter van Pelt, Diederik van Weel, Remco van Wijk, Stephan Veen, Guus Vogels, Peter Windt (Netherlands)	Han Hyung-Bae, Hwang Jong-Hyun, Jeon Hong-Kwon, Jeon Jong-Ha, Ji Seung-Hwan, Kang Keon-Wook, Kim Chel-Hwan, Kim Jung-Chul, Kim Kyung-Seok, Kim Yong-Bae, Kim Yoon, Lim Jong-Chun, Lim Jung-Woo, Seo Jong-Ho, Song Seung-Tae, Yeo Woon-Kon (South Korea)	Michael Brennan, Adam Commens, Stephen Davies, Damon Diletti, Lachlan Dreher, Jason Duff, Troy Elder, James Elmer, Paul Gaudoin, Stephen Holt, Brent Livermore, Daniel Sproule, Jay Stacy, Craig Victory, Matthew Wells, Michael York (Australia)
2004	Michael Brennan, Travis Brooks, Dean Butler, Liam de Young, Jamie Dwyer, Nathan Eglington, Troy Elder, Bevan George, Robert Hammond, Mark Hickman, Mark Knowles, Brent Livermore, Michael McCann, Stephen Mowlam, Grant Schubert, Matthew Wells (Australia)	Matthijs Brouwer, Ronald Brouwer, Teun de Nooijer, Jeroen Delmee, Geert-Jan Derikx, Rob Derikx, Marten Eikelboom, Floris Evers, Erik Jazet, Karel Klaver, Jesse Mahieu, Rob Reckers, Taeke Taekema, Sander van der Weide, Klaas Veering, Guus Vogels (Netherlands)	Clemens Arnold, Christoph Bechmann, Sebastian Biederlack, Philipp Crone, Eike Duckwitz, Christoph Eimer, Björn Emmerling, Florian Kunz, Björn Michel, Sascha Reinelt, Justus Scharowsky, Christian Schulte, Tibor Weißenborn, Timo Weß, Matthias Witthaus, Christopher Zeller (Germany)
2008	Philip Witte, Maximilian Mueller, Sebastian Biederlack, Carlos Nevado, Moritz Fuerste, Jan-Marco Montag, Tobias Hauke, Tibor Weißenborn, Benjamin Weß, Niklas Meinert, Timo Weß, Oliver Korn, Christopher Zeller, Max Weinhold, Matthias Witthaus, Florian Keller, Philipp Zeller (Germany)	Francisco Cortes, Santiago Freixa, Francisco Fábregas, Victor Sojo, Alex Fabregas, Pablo Amat, Eduardo Tubau, Roc Oliva, Juan Fernandez, Ramon Alegre, Xavier Ribas, Albert Sala, Rodrigo Garza, Sergi Enrique, Eduard Arbos, David Alegre (Spain)	Jamie Dwyer, Liam de Young, Rob Hammond, Mark Knowles, Eddie Ockenden, David Guest, Luke Doerner, Grant Schubert, Bevan George, Andre Smith, Stephen Lambert, Eli Matheson, Matthew Wells, Travis Brooks, Kiel Brown, Fergus Kavanagh, Des Abbott (Australia)

Women's Field Hockey

Year	Gold	Silver	Bronze
1980	Elizabeth Chase, Sandra Chick, Gillian Cowley, Patricia Davies, Sarah English, Maureen George, Ann Grant, Susan Huggett, Patricia McKillop, Brenda Phillips, Christine Prinsloo, Sonia Robertson, Anthea Stewart, Helen Volk, Linda Watson (Zimbabwe)	Milada Blazková, Jirina Cermáková, Jirina Hájková, Berta Hrubá, Ida Hubácková, Jirina Kadlecová, Jarmila Králícková, Jirina Krízová, Alena Kyselicová, Jana Lahodová, Kveta Petrícková, Viera Podhányiová, Iveta Sránková, Marie Sykorová, Marta Urbanová, Lenka Vymazalová (Czechoslovakia)	Liailia Akhmerova, Natalia Buzunova, Natalia Bykova, Tatiana Embakhtova, Nadezhda Filippova, Liudmila Frolova, Lidia Glubokova, Nelli Gorbatkova, Elena Guryeva, Galina Inzhuvatova, Alina Kham, Natella Krasnikova, Nadezhda Ovechkina, Tatiana Shvyganova, Galina Viuzhanina, Valentina Zazdravnykh (Soviet Union)
1984	Carina Benninga, Fieke Boekhorst, Marjolein Eijsvogel, Det de Beus, Irene Hendriks, Elsemiek Hillen, Sandra Le Poole, Anneloes Nieuwenhuizen, Martine Ohr, Alette Pos, Lisette Sevens, Marieke van Doorn, Aletta van Manen, Sophie von Weiler, Laurien Willemse, Margriet Zegers (Netherlands)	Gabriele Appel, Dagmar Breiken, Beate Deininger, Elke Drull, Birgit Hagen, Birgit Hahnm, Martina Koch, Sigrid Landgraf, Corinna Lingnau, Christina Moser, Patricia Ott, Hella Roth, Gabriele Schley, Susanne Schmid, Ursula Thielemann, Andrea Weiermann-Lietz (West Germany)	Beth Anders, Beth Beglin, Regina Buggy, Gwen Cheeseman, Sheryl Johnson, Christine Larson-Mason, Kathleen McGahey, Anita Miller, Leslie Milne, Charlene Morett, Diane Moyer, Marcella Place, Karen Shelton, Brenda Stauffer, Julie Staver, Judy Strong (United States)
1988	Tracey Belbin, Deborah Bowman, Lee Capes, Michelle Capes, Sally Carbon, Elsbeth Clement, Loretta Dorman, Maree Fish, Rechelle Hawkes, Lorraine Hillas, Kathleen Partridge, Sharon Patmore, Jackie Pereira, Alexandra Pisani, Kim Small, Liane Tooth (Australia)	Chang Eun-Jung, Cho Ki-Hyang, Choi Choon-Ok, Chung Eun-Kyung, Chung Sang-Hyun, Han Gum Shil, Han Ok-Kyung, Hwang Keum-Sook, Jin Won-Sim, Kim Mi-Sun, Kim Soon-Duk, Kim Young-Sook, Lim Kye-Sook, Park Soon-Ja, Seo Hyo-Sun, Seo Kwang-Mi (South Korea)	Willemien Aardenburg, Carina Benninga, Marjolein Eijsvogel, Yvonne Buter, Det de Beus, Annemieke Fokke, Noor Holsboer, Helen van der Ben, Lisanne Lejeune, Anneloes Nieuwenhuizen, Martine Ohr, Marieke van Doorn, Aletta van Manen, Sophie von Weiler, Laurien Willemse, Ingrid Wolff (Netherlands)
1992	María Carmen Barea, Sonia Barrio, Mercedes Coghen, Celia Corres, Natalia Dorado, Nagore Gabellanes, Marívi González, Anna Maiques, Silvia Manrique, Elisabeth Maragall, María Isabel Martínez, Teresa Motos, Nuria Olivé, Virginia Ramírez, María Ángeles Rodríguez, Maider Tellería (Spain)	Britta Becker, Tanja Dickenscheid, Nadine Ernsting-Krienke, Christine Ferneck, Eva Hagenbäumer, Franziska Hentschel, Caren Jungjohann, Katrin Kauschke, Irina Kuhnt, Heike Lätzsch, Susanne Müller, Tina Peters, Simone Thomaschinski, Bianca Weiß, Anke Wild, Susie Wollschläger (Germany)	Jill Atkins, Lisa Bayliss, Karen Brown, Vickey Dixon, Susan Fraser, Wendy Fraser, Kathryn Johnson, Sandy Lister, Jackie McWilliams, Tammy Miller, Helen Morgan, Mary Nevill, Mandy Nicholls, Alison Ramsay, Jane Sixsmith, Joanne Thompson (Great Britain)
1996	Michelle Andrews, Alyson Annan, Louise Dobson, Renita Farrell, Juliet Haslam, Rechelle Hawkes, Clover Maitland, Karen Marsden, Jenny Morris, Jackie Pereira, Nova Peris-Kneebone, Katrina Powell, Lisa Powell, Danni Roche, Kate Starre, Liane Tooth (Australia)	Chang Eun-Jung, Cho Eun-Jung, Choi Eun-Kyung, Choi Mi-Soon, Jeon Young-Sun, Jin Deok-San, Kim Myung-Ok, Kown Soo-Hyun, Kwon Chang Sook, Lee Eun-Kyung, Lee Eun-Young, Lee Ji-Young, Lim Jeong-Sook, Oh Seung-Shin, Woo Hyun-Jung, You Jae-Sook (South Korea)	Stella de Heij, Wietske de Ruiter, Mijntje Donners, Willemijn Duyster, Noor Holsboer, Nicole Koolen, Ellen Kuipers, Jeannette Lewin, Suzanne Plesman, Florentine Steenberghe, Margje Teeuwen, Carole Thate, Jacqueline Toxopeus, Fleur van de Kieft, Dillianne van den Boogaard, Suzan van der Wielen (Netherlands)

Year	Gold	Silver	Bronze
2000	Michelle Andrews, Alyson Annan, Louise Dobson, Renita Farrell, Juliet Haslam, Rechelle Hawkes, Clover Maitland, Karen Marsden, Jenny Morris, Jackie Pereira, Nova Peris-Kneebone, Katrina Powell, Lisa Powell, Danni Roche, Kate Starre, Liane Tooth (Australia)	Magdalena Aicega, Mariela Antoniska, Inés Arrondo, Luciana Aymar, María Paz Ferrari, Anabel Gambero, Agustina García, María de la Paz Hernández, Laura Maiztegui, Mercedes Margalot, Karina Masotta, Vanina Oneto, Jorgelina Rimoldi, Cecilia Rognoni, Ayelén Stepnik, Paola Vukojicic (Argentina)	Minke Booij, Ageeth Boomgaardt, Julie Deiters, Mijntje Donners, Fatima Moreira de Melo, Clarinda Sinnige, Hanneke Smabers, Minke Smabers, Margje Teeuwen, Carole Thate, Daphne Touw, Fleur van de Kieft, Dillianne van den Boogaard, Macha van der Vaart, Suzan van der Wielen, Myrna Veenstra (Netherlands)
2004	Tina Bachmann, Caroline Casaretto, Nadine Ernsting-Krienke, Franziska Gude, Mandy Haase, Natascha Keller, Denise Klecker, Anke Kühn, Heike Lätzsch, Badri Latif, Sonja Lehmann, Silke Müller, Fanny Rinne, Marion Rodewald, Louisa Walter, Julia Zwehl (Germany)	Minke Booij, Chantal de Bruijn, Lisanne de Roever, Mijntje Donners, Sylvia Karres, Fatima Moreira de Melo, Eefke Mulder, Maartje Scheepstra, Janneke Schopman, Clarinda Sinnige, Minke Smabers, Jiske Snoeks, Macha van der Vaart, Miek van Geenhuizen, Lieve van Kessel (Netherlands)	Magdalena Aicega, Mariela Antoniska, Inés Arrondo, Luciana Aymar, Claudia Burkart, Marina di Giacomo, Agustina García, Mariana González, Alejandra Gulla, María de la Paz Hernández, Mercedes Margalot, Vanina Oneto, Cecilia Rognoni, Mariné Russo, Ayelén Stepnik, Paola Vukojicic (Argentina)
2008	Maartje Goderie, Maartje Paumen, Naomi van As, Minke Smabers, Marilyn Agliotti, Minke Booij, Wieke Dijkstra, Sophie Polkamp, Ellen Hoog, Lidewij Welten, Lisanne de Roever, Miek van Geenhuizen, Eva de Goede, Janneke Schopman, Eefke Mulder, Fatima Moreira de Melo (Netherlands)	Ren Ye, Zhang Yimeng, Gao Lihua, Chen Qiuqi, Zhao Yudiao, Li Hongxia, Cheng Hui, Tang Chunling, Zhou Wanfeng, Ma Yibo, Fu Baorong, Pan Fengzhen, Huang Junxia, Song Qungling, Li Shuang, Chen Zhaoxia (China)	Paola Vukojicic, Belén Succi, Magdalena Aicega, Mercedes Margalot, Mariana Rossi, Noel Barrionuevo, Giselle Kañevsky, Claudia Burkart, Luciana Aymar, Mariné Russo, Mariana González Oliva, Soledad García, Alejandra Gulla, María de la Paz Hernández, Carla Rebecchi, Rosario Luchetti (Argentina)

Jeu de Paume

Men's Individual

Year	Gold	Silver	Bronze
1908	Jay Gould (United States)	Eustace Miles (Great Britain)	Neville Bulwer-Lytton (Great Britain)

Judo

Men's Extra Lightweight

Year	Gold	Silver	Bronze
1980	Thierry Rey (France)	José Rodríguez (Cuba)	Aramby Emizh (Soviet Union) Tibor Kincses (Hungary)
1984	Shinji Hosokawa (Japan)	Kim Kae-Yup (South Korea)	Neil Eckersley (Great Britain) Edward Liddie (United States)
1988	Kim Kae-Yup (South Korea)	Kevin Asano (United States)	Shinji Hosokawa (Japan) Amiran Totikashvili (Soviet Union)
1992	Nazim Guseynov (Unified Team)	Yoon Hyun (South Korea)	Tadanori Koshino (Japan) Richard Trautmann (Germany)

Year	Gold	Silver	Bronze
1996	Tadahiro Nomura (Japan)	Girolamo Giovinazzo (Italy)	Richard Trautmann (Germany) Dorjpalamyn Narmandakh (Mongolia)
2000	Tadahiro Nomura (Japan)	Jung Bu-Kyung (South Korea)	Manolo Poulot (Cuba) Aidyn Smagulov (Kyrgyzstan)
2004	Tadahiro Nomura (Japan)	Nestor Khergiani (Georgia)	Khashbaataryn Tsagaanbaatar (Mongolia) Choi Min-Ho (South Korea)
2008	Choi Min-Ho (South Korea)	Ludwig Paischer (Austria)	Rishod Sobirov (Uzbekistan) Ruben Houkes (Netherlands)

Men's Half Lightweight

Year	Gold	Silver	Bronze
1980	Nikolai Solodukhin (Soviet Union)	Tsendiin Damdin (Mongolia)	Ilian Nedkov (Bulgaria) Janusz Pawłowski (Poland)
1984	Yoshiyuki Matsuoka (Japan)	Hwang Jung-Oh (South Korea)	Marc Alexandre (France) Josef Reiter (Austria)
1988	Lee Kyung-Keun (South Korea)	Janusz Pawłowski (Poland)	Bruno Carabetta (France) Yosuke Yamamoto (Japan)
1992	Rogério Sampaio (Brazil)	József Csák (Hungary)	Israel Hernández (Cuba) Udo Quellmalz (Germany)
1996	Udo Quellmalz (Germany)	Yukimasa Nakamura (Japan)	Israel Hernández (Cuba) Henrique Guimarães (Brazil)
2000	Hüseyin Özkan (Turkey)	Larbi Benboudaoud (France)	Girolamo Giovinazzo (Italy) Giorgi Vazagashvili (Georgia)
2004	Masato Uchishiba (Japan)	Jozef Krnáč (Slovakia)	Georgi Georgiev (Bulgaria) Yordanis Arencibia (Cuba)
2008	Masato Uchishiba (Japan)	Bengamin Darbelet (France)	Yordanis Arencibia (Cuba) Pak Chol Min (North Korea)

Men's Lightweight

Year	Gold	Silver	Bronze
1964	Takehide Nakatani (Japan)	Eric Hänni (Switzerland)	Oleg Stepanov (Soviet Union) Ārons Bogoļubovs (Soviet Union)
1968: Event not held			
1972	Takao Kawaguchi (Japan)	Not awarded	Kim Yong-Ik (North Korea) Jean-Jacques Mounier (France)
1976	Héctor Rodríguez (Cuba)	Chang Eun-Kyung (South Korea)	Felice Marani (Italy) József Tuncsik (Hungary)
1980	Ezio Gamba (Italy)	Neil Adams (Great Britain)	Ravdangiin Davaadalai (Mongolia) Karl-Heinz Lehmann (East Germany)
1984	Ahn Byeong-Keun (South Korea)	Ezio Gamba (Italy)	Kerrith Brown (Great Britain) Luis Onmura (Brazil)
1988	Marc Alexandre (France)	Sven Loll (East Germany)	Mike Swain (United States) Georgy Tenadze (Soviet Union)
1992	Toshihiko Koga (Japan)	Bertalan Hajtós (Hungary)	Chung Hoon (South Korea) Oren Smadja (Israel)
1996	Kenzo Nakamura (Japan)	Kwak Dae-Sung (South Korea)	Christophe Gagliano (France) Jimmy Pedro (United States)
2000	Giuseppe Maddaloni (Italy)	Tiago Camilo (Brazil)	Anatoly Laryukov (Belarus) Vsevolods Zeļonijs (Latvia)
2004	Lee Won-Hee (South Korea)	Vitaliy Makarov (Russia)	Leandro Guilheiro (Brazil) Jimmy Pedro (United States)
2008	Elnur Mammadli (Azerbaijan)	Wang Ki-Chun (South Korea)	Rasul Boqiev (Tajikistan) Leandro Guilheiro (Brazil)

Men's Half Middleweight

Year	Gold	Silver	Bronze
1972	Toyokazu Nomura (Japan)	Anton Zajkowski (Poland)	Dietmar Hötger (East Germany) Anatoliy Novikov (Soviet Union)
1976	Vladimir Nevzorov (Soviet Union)	Koji Kuramoto (Japan)	Marian Tałaj (Poland) Patrick Vial (France)
1980	Shota Khabareli (Soviet Union)	Juan Ferrer (Cuba)	Harald Heinke (East Germany) Bernard Tchoullouyan (France)
1984	Frank Wieneke (Germany)	Neil Adams (Great Britain)	Mircea Frăţică (Romania) Michel Nowak (France)
1988	Waldemar Legień (Poland)	Frank Wieneke (Germany)	Torsten Bréchôt (East Germany) Bashir Varaev (Soviet Union)
1992	Hidehiko Yoshida (Japan)	Jason Morris (United States)	Bertrand Damaisin (France) Kim Byung-Joo (South Korea)
1996	Djamel Bouras (France)	Toshihiko Koga (Japan)	Soso Liparteliani (Georgia) Cho In-Chul (South Korea)
2000	Makoto Takimoto (Japan)	Cho In-Chul (South Korea)	Nuno Delgado (Portugal) Aleksei Budõlin (Estonia)
2004	Ilias Iliadis (Greece)	Roman Gontyuk (Ukraine)	Dmitri Nossov (Russia) Flávio Canto (Brazil)
2008	Ole Bischof (Germany)	Kim Jae-Bum (South Korea)	Tiago Camilo (Brazil) Roman Gontiuk (Ukraine)

Men's Middleweight

Year	Gold	Silver	Bronze
1964	Isao Okano (Japan)	Wolfgang Hofmann (Germany)	James Bregman (United States) Kim Eui-Tae (South Korea)
1968: Event not held			
1972	Shinobu Sekine (Japan)	Oh Seung-Lip (South Korea)	Jean-Paul Coche (France) Brian Jacks (Great Britain)
1976	Isamu Sonoda (Japan)	Valeriy Dvoynikov (Soviet Union)	Slavko Obadov (Yugoslavia) Park Young-Chul (South Korea)
1980	Jürg Röthlisberger (Switzerland)	Isaac Azcuy (Cuba)	Detlef Ultsch (East Germany) Aleksandrs Jackevičs (Soviet Union)
1984	Peter Seisenbacher (Austria)	Robert Berland (United States)	Walter Carmona (Brazil) Seiki Nose (Japan)
1988	Peter Seisenbacher (Austria)	Vladimir Shestakov (Soviet Union)	Akinobu Osako (Japan) Ben Spijkers (Netherlands)
1992	Waldemar Legień (Poland)	Pascal Tayot (France)	Nicolas Gill (Canada) Hirotaka Okada (Japan)
1996	Jean Ki-Young (South Korea)	Armen Bagdasarov (Uzbekistan)	Marko Spittka (Germany) Mark Huizinga (Netherlands)
2000	Mark Huizinga (Netherlands)	Carlos Honorato (Brazil)	Frédéric Demontfaucon (France) Ruslan Mashurenko (Ukraine)
2004	Zurab Zviadauri (Georgia)	Hiroshi Izumi (Japan)	Mark Huizinga (Netherlands) Khasanbi Taov (Russia)
2008	Irakli Tsirekidze (Georgia)	Amar Benikhlef (Algeria)	Hesham Mesbah (Egypt) Sergei Aschwanden (Switzerland)

Men's Half Heavyweight

Year	Gold	Silver	Bronze
1972	Shota Chochishvili (Soviet Union)	David Starbrook (Great Britain)	Paul Barth (Germany) Chiaki Ishii (Brazil)

Year	Gold	Silver	Bronze
1976	Kazuhiro Ninomiya (Japan)	Ramaz Khharshiladze (Soviet Union)	Jürg Röthlisberger (Switzerland) David Starbrook (Great Britain)
1980	Robert Van de Walle (Belgium)	Tengiz Khubuluri (Soviet Union)	Dietmar Lorenz (East Germany) Henk Numan (Netherlands)
1984	Ha Hyoung-Zoo (South Korea)	Douglas Vieira (Brazil)	Bjarni Friðriksson (Iceland) Günther Neureuther (Germany)
1988	Aurélio Miguel (Brazil)	Marc Meiling (Germany)	Dennis Stewart (Great Britain) Robert Van de Walle (Belgium)
1992	Antal Kovács (Hungary)	Raymond Stevens (Great Britain)	Theo Mijer (Netherlands) Dmitri Sergeyev (Unified Team)
1996	Paweł Nastula (Poland)	Kim Min-Soo (South Korea)	Stéphane Traineau (France) Aurélio Miguel (Brazil)
2000	Kosei Inoue (Japan)	Nicolas Gill (Canada)	Yuri Stepkine (Russia) Stéphane Traineau (France)
2004	Ihar Makarau (Belarus)	Jang Sung-Ho (South Korea)	Ariel Zeevi (Israel) Michael Jurack (Germany)
2008	Naidangiin Tüvshinbayar (Mongolia)	Askhat Zhitkeyev (Kazakhstan)	Movlud Miraliyev (Azerbaijan) Henk Grol (Netherlands)

Men's Heavyweight

Year	Gold	Silver	Bronze
1964	Isao Inokuma (Japan)	Doug Rogers (Canada)	Parnaoz Chikviladze (Soviet Union) Anzor Kiknadze (Soviet Union)
1968: Event not held			
1972	Willem Ruska (Netherlands)	Klaus Glahn (Germany)	Motoki Nichimura (Japan) Givi Onashvili (Soviet Union)
1976	Sergei Novikov (Soviet Union)	Günther Neureuther (Germany)	Allen Coage (United States) Sumio Endo (Japan)
1980	Angelo Parisi (France)	Dimitar Zaprianov (Bulgaria)	Radomir Kovačević (Yugoslavia) Vladimír Kocman (Czechoslovakia)
1984	Hitoshi Saito (Japan)	Angelo Parisi (France)	Mark Berger (Canada) Cho Yong-Chul (South Korea)
1988	Hitoshi Saito (Japan)	Henry Stöhr (East Germany)	Cho Yong-Chul (South Korea) Grigory Verichev (Soviet Union)
1992	David Khakhaleishvili (Unified Team)	Naoya Ogawa (Japan)	Imre Csosz (Hungary) David Douillet (France)
1996	David Douillet (France)	Ernesto Pérez (Spain)	Frank Möller (Germany) Harry Van Barneveld (Belgium)
2000	David Douillet (France)	Shinichi Shinohara (Japan)	Indrek Pertelson (Estonia) Tamerlan Tmenov (Russia)
2004	Keiji Suzuki (Japan)	Tamerlan Tmenov (Russia)	Indrek Pertelson (Estonia) Dennis van der Geest (Netherlands)
2008	Satoshi Ishii (Japan)	Abdullo Tangriev (Uzbekistan)	Teddy Riner (France) Oscar Braison (Cuba)

Men's Open Category

Year	Gold	Silver	Bronze
1964	Anton Geesink (Netherlands)	Akio Kaminaga (Japan)	Theodore Boronovskis (Australia) Klaus Glahn (Germany)
1968: Event not held			
1972	Willem Ruska (Netherlands)	Vitali Kuznetsov (Soviet Union)	Jean-Claude Brondani (France) Angelo Parisi (Great Britain)

Year	Gold	Silver	Bronze
1976	Haruki Uemura (Japan)	Keith Remfry (Great Britain)	Cho Jae-Gi (South Korea) Shota Chochishivili (Soviet Union)
1980	Dietmar Lorenz (East Germany)	Angelo Parisi (France)	Arthur Mapp (Great Britain) András Ozsvár (Hungary)
1984	Yasuhiro Yamashita (Japan)	Mohamed Ali Rashwan (Egypt)	Mihai Cioc (Romania) Arthur Schnabel (Germany)

Women's Extra Lightweight

Year	Gold	Silver	Bronze
1992	Cécile Nowak (France)	Ryoko Tamura (Japan)	Amarilis Savón (Cuba) Hülya Şenyurt (Turkey)
1996	Kye Sun-Hi (North Korea)	Ryoko Tamura (Japan)	Yolanda Soler (Spain) Amarilis Savon (Cuba)
2000	Ryoko Tamura (Japan)	Lioubov Brouletova (Russia)	Anna-Maria Gradante (Germany) Ann Simons (Belgium)
2008	Alina Alexandra Dumitru (Romania)	Yanet Bermoy (Cuba)	Paulo Pareto (Argentina) Ryoko Tani (Japan)

Women's Half Lightweight

Year	Gold	Silver	Bronze
1992	Almudena Muñoz (Spain)	Noriko Mizoguchi (Japan)	Li Zhongyun (China) Sharon Rendle (Great Britain)
1996	Marie-Claire Restoux (France)	Hyun Sook-Hee (South Korea)	Noriko Sugawara (Japan) Legna Verdecia (Cuba)
2000	Legna Verdecia (Cuba)	Noriko Mizoguchi (Japan)	Kye Sun-Hi (North Korea) Liu Yuxiang (China)
2004	Xian Dongmei (China)	Yuki Yokosawa (Japan)	Ilse Heylen (Belgium) Amarilis Savón (Cuba)
2008	Xian Dongmei (China)	An Kum-Ae (North Korea)	Soraya Haddad (Algeria) Misato Nakamura (Japan)

Women's Lightweight

Year	Gold	Silver	Bronze
1992	Miriam Blasco (Spain)	Nicola Fairbrother (Great Britain)	Driulis González (Cuba) Chiyori Tateno (Japan)
1996	Driulis González (Cuba)	Jung Sun-Yong (South Korea)	Isabel Fernández (Spain) Marisbel Lomba (Belgium)
2000	Isabel Fernández (Spain)	Driulis González (Cuba)	Kie Kusakabe (Japan) Maria Pekli (Australia)
2004	Yvonne Bönisch (Germany)	Kye Sun-Hui (North Korea)	Deborah Gravenstijn (Netherlands) Yurisleidy Lupetey (Cuba)
2008	Giulia Quintavalle (Italy)	Deborah Gravenstijn (Netherlands)	Xu Yan (China) Ketleyn Quadros (Brazil)

Women's Half Middleweight

Year	Gold	Silver	Bronze
1992	Cathérine Fleury (France)	Yael Arad (Israel)	Elena Petrova (Unified Team) Zhang Di (China)
1996	Yuko Emoto (Japan)	Gella Vandecaveye (Belgium)	Jenny Gal (Netherlands) Jung Sung-Sook (South Korea)
2000	Séverine Vandenhende (France)	Li Shufang (China)	Gella Vandecaveye (Belgium) Jung Sung-Sook (South Korea)

Year	Gold	Silver	Bronze
2004	Ayumi Tanimoto (Japan)	Claudia Heill (Austria)	Driulis González (Cuba) Urška Žolnir (Slovenia)
2008	Ayumi Tanimoto (Japan)	Lucie Décosse (France)	Elisabeth Willeboordse (Netherlands) Won Ok-Im (North Korea)

Women's Middleweight

Year	Gold	Silver	Bronze
1992	Odalis Revé (Cuba)	Emanuela Pierantozzi (Italy)	Kate Howey (Great Britain) Heidi Rakels (Belgium)
1996	Cho Min-Sun (South Korea)	Aneta Szczepańska (Poland)	Wang Xianbo (China) Claudia Zwiers (Netherlands)
2000	Sibelis Veranes (Cuba)	Kate Howey (Great Britain)	Cho Min-Sun (South Korea) Ylena Scapin (Italy)
2004	Masae Ueno (Japan)	Edith Bosch (Netherlands)	Qin Dongya (China) Annett Böhm (Germany)
2008	Masae Ueno (Japan)	Anaysi Hernández (Cuba)	Ronda Rousey (United States) Edith Bosch (Netherlands)

Women's Half Heavyweight

Year	Gold	Silver	Bronze
1992	Kim Mi-Jung (South Korea)	Yoko Tanabe (Japan)	Irene de Kok (Netherlands) Laetitia Meignan (France)
1996	Ulla Werbrouck (Belgium)	Yoko Tanabe (Japan)	Ylenia Scapin (Italy) Diadenis Luna (Cuba)
2000	Tang Lin (China)	Céline Lebrun (France)	Simona Richter (Romania) Emanuela Pierantozzi (Italy)
2004	Noriko Anno (Japan)	Liu Xia (China)	Yurisel Laborde (Cuba) Lucia Morico (Italy)
2008	Yang Xiuli (China)	Yalennis Castillo (Cuba)	Jeong Gyeong-Mi (South Korea) Stéphanie Possamaï (France)

Women's Heavyweight

Year	Gold	Silver	Bronze
1992	Zhuang Xiaoyan (China)	Estela Rodríguez (Cuba)	Natalia Lupino (France) Yoko Sakaue (Japan)
1996	Sun Fuming (China)	Estela Rodríguez (Cuba)	Johanna Hagn (Germany) Christine Cicot (France)
2000	Yuan Hua (China)	Daima Beltrán (Cuba)	Kim Seon-Young (South Korea) Mayumi Yamashita (Japan)
2004	Maki Tsukada (Japan)	Daima Beltrán (Cuba)	Tea Donguzashvili (Russia) Sun Fuming (China)
2008	Tong Wen (China)	Maki Tsukada (Japan)	Idalis Ortiz (Cuba) Lucija Polavder (Slovenia)

Lacrosse

Men's Lacrosse

Year	Gold	Silver	Bronze
1904	Eli Blanchard, William Brennaugh, George Bretz, William Burns, George Cattanach, George Cloutier, Sandy Cowan, Jack Flett, Benjamin Jamieson, Stuart Laidlaw, Hilliard Lyle, Lawrence Pentland (Canada)	Bjorn Neidks, Patrick Crogan, J. W. Dowling, Gibson*, Robert Hunter, Murphy*, Partridge*, George Passmore, William T. Passmore, Ross*, Sullivan*, A. H. Venn, Woods* (United States)	Black Hawk, Black Eagle, Almighty Voice, Flat Iron, Spotted Tail, Half Moon, Lightfoot, Snake Eater, Red Jacket, Night Hawk, Man Afraid Soap, Rain in Face (Canada)
1908	Patrick Brennan, John Broderick, George Campbell, Angus Dillon, Frank Dixon, Richard Louis Duckett, J. Fyon*, Tommy Gorman, Ernest Hamilton, Henry Hoobin, Albert Hara*, Clarence McKerrow, David McLeod*, George Rennie, Alexander Turnbull (Canada)	Gustav Alexander, J. Alexander*, L. Blockey*, George Buckland, E. O. Dutton, V. G. Gilbey*, S. N. Hayes, F. S. Johnsin*, Wilfrid Johnson, Edward Jones, R. G. W. Martin, G. Mason, G. J. Mason*, J. Parker-Smith, H. W. Ramsay, Charles Scott, H. Shorrocks*, Norman Whitley (Great Britain)	Not awarded

* Full name not known.

Modern Pentathlon

Men's Individual

Year	Gold	Silver	Bronze
1912	Gösta Lilliehöök (Sweden)	Gösta Åsbrink (Sweden)	Georg de Laval (Sweden)
1916: Olympics not held			
1920	Gustaf Dyrssen (Sweden)	Erik de Laval (Sweden)	Gösta Runö (Sweden)
1924	Bo Lindman (Sweden)	Gustaf Dyrssen (Sweden)	Bertil Uggla (Sweden)
1928	Sven Thofelt (Sweden)	Bo Lindman (Sweden)	Helmut Kahl (Germany)
1932	Johan Gabriel Oxenstierna (Sweden)	Bo Lindman (Sweden)	Richard Mayo (United States)
1936	Gotthard Handrick (Germany)	Charles Leonard (United States)	Silvano Abba (Italy)
1940–1944: Olympics not held			
1948	William Grut (Sweden)	George Moore (United States)	Gösta Gärdin (Sweden)
1952	Lars Hall (Sweden)	Gábor Benedek (Hungary)	István Szondy (Hungary)
1956	Lars Hall (Sweden)	Olavi Mannonen (Finland)	Väinö Korhonen (Finland)
1960	Ferenc Németh (Hungary)	Imre Nagy (Hungary)	Robert Beck (United States)
1964	Ferenc Németh (Hungary)	Igor Novikov (Soviet Union)	Albert Mokeev (Soviet Union)
1968	Björn Ferm (Sweden)	András Balczó (Hungary)	Pavel Lednev (Soviet Union)
1972	András Balczó (Hungary)	Boris Onischenko (Soviet Union)	Pavel Lednev (Soviet Union)
1976	Janusz Pyciak-Peciak (Poland)	Pavel Lednev (Soviet Union)	Jan Bartu (Czechoslovakia)
1980	Anatoly Starostin (Soviet Union)	Tamás Szombathelyi (Hungary)	Pavel Lednev (Soviet Union)
1984	Daniele Masala (Italy)	Svante Rasmuson (Sweden)	Carlo Massullo (Italy)
1988	Martinek János (Hungary)	Carlo Massullo (Italy)	Vakhtang Iagorashvili (Soviet Union)
1992	Arkadiusz Skrzypaszek (Poland)	Attila Mizsér (Hungary)	Eduard Zenovka (Unified Team)
1996	Alexandre Paryguin (Kazakhstan)	Eduard Zenovka (Russia)	János Martinek (Hungary)
2000	Dmitri Svatkovsky (Russia)	Gábor Balogh (Hungary)	Pavel Dovgal (Belarus)

Year	Gold	Silver	Bronze
2004	Andrew Moiseev (Russia)	Andrejus Zadneprovskis (Lithuania)	Libor Capalini (Czech Republic)
2008	Andrew Moiseev (Russia)	Edvinas Krungolcas (Lithuania)	Andrejus Zadneprovskis (Lithuania)

Men's Team

Year	Gold	Silver	Bronze
1952	Gábor Benedek, Aladár Kovácsi, István Szondy (Hungary)	Lars Hall, Torsten Lindqvist, Claes Egnell (Sweden)	Olavi Mannonen, Lauri Vilkko, Olavi Rokka (Finland)
1956	Igor Novikov, Aleksandr Tarasov, Ivan Deryugin (Soviet Union)	George Lambert, William Andre, Jack Daniels (United States)	Olavi Mannonen, Vaino Korhonen, Berndt Katter (Finland)
1960	Ferenc Németh, Imre Nagy, András Balczó (Hungary)	Igor Novikov, Nikolay Tatarinov, Hanno Selg (Soviet Union)	Robert Beck, George Lambert, Jack Daniels (United States)
1964	Igor Novikov, Albert Mokeyev, Viktor Mineyev (Soviet Union)	James Moore, David Kirkwood, Paul Pesthy (United States)	Ferenc Török, Imre Nagy, Ottó Török (Hungary)
1968	András Balczó, István Móna, Ferenc Török (Hungary)	Boris Onishchenko, Pavel Lednyov, Stasys Šaparnis (Soviet Union)	Raoul Gueguen, Lucien Guiguet, Jean-Pierre Giudicelli (France)
1972	Boris Onishchenko, Pavel Lednyov, Vladimir Shmelyov (Soviet Union)	András Balczó, Zsigmond Villányi, Pál Bakó (Hungary)	Risto Hurme, Veikko Salminen, Martti Ketelä (Finland)
1976	Jim Fox, Danny Nightingale, Adrian Parker (Great Britain)	Ján Bártu, Bohumil Starnovský, Jiří Adam (Czechoslovakia)	Tamás Kancsal, Tibor Maracskó, Szvetiszláv Sasics (Hungary)
1980	Anatoli Starostin, Pavel Lednyov, Yevgeny Lipeyev (Soviet Union)	Tamás Szombathelyi, Tibor Maracskó, László Horváth (Hungary)	Svante Rasmuson, Lennart Pettersson, George Horváth (Sweden)
1984	Daniele Masala, Pier Paolo Cristofori, Carlo Massullo (Italy)	Michael Storm, Robert Gregory Losey, Dean Glenesk (United States)	Paul Four, Didier Boube, Joël Bouzou (France)
1988	János Martinek, Attila Mizsér, László Fábián (Hungary)	Carlo Massullo, Daniele Masala, Gianluca Tiberti (Italy)	Richard Phelps, Dominic Mahony, Graham Brookhouse (Great Britain)
1992	Arkadiusz Skrzypaszek, Dariusz Goździak, Maciej Czyżowicz (Poland)	Anatoli Starostin, Dmitri Svatkovskiy, Eduard Zenovka (Unified Team)	Gianluca Tiberti, Carlo Massullo, Roberto Bomprezzi (Italy)

Women's Individual

Year	Gold	Silver	Bronze
2000	Stephanie Cook (Great Britain)	Emily De Riel (United States)	Kate Allenby (Great Britain)
2004	Zsuzsanna Vörös (Hungary)	Jeļena Rubļevska (Latvia)	Georgina Harland (Great Britain)
2008	Lena Schöneborn (Germany)	Heather Fell (Great Britain)	Victoria Tereshuk (Ukraine)

Polo

Men's Polo

Year	Gold	Silver	Bronze
1900	Denis St. George Daly, Alfred Rawlinson, John Beresford (Great Britain), Foxhall Parker Keene, Frank MacKey (United States)	Walter Buckmaster, Jean de Madre, Frederick Freake (Great Britain), Walter McCreery (United States)	Edouard Alphonse de Rothschild, Robert Fournier-Sarlovèze, Maurice Raoul-Duval (France), Frederick Agnew Gill (Great Britain), Eustaquio de Escandón, Manuel de Escandón, Pablo de Escandón (Mexico), Guillermo Hayden Wright (United States)

Year	Gold	Silver	Bronze
1904: Event not held			
1908	Charles Darley Miller, George Arthur Miller, Patteson Womersley Nickalls, Herbert Haydon Wilson (Great Britain)	Walter Buckmaster, Frederick Freake, Walter Jones, John Wodehouse (Great Britain) John Hardress Lloyd, John Paul McCann, Percy O'Reilly, Auston Rotherham (Great Britain)	Not awarded
1912: Event not held			
1916: Olympics not held			
1920	Teignmouth Melville, Frederick Barrett, John Wodehouse, Vivian Noverre Lockett (Great Britain)	Leopoldo de La Maza, Justo de San Miguel, Álvaro de Figueroa, José de Figueroa (Spain)	Arthur Harris, Terry Allen, John Montgomery, Nelson Margetts (United States)
1924	Arturo Kenny, Juan Miles, Guillermo Naylor, Juan Nelson, Enrique Padilla (Argentina)	Elmer Boeseke, Tommy Hitchcock Jr., Frederick Roe, Rodman Wanamaker (United States)	Frederick Barrett, Dennis Bingham, Fred Guest, Kinnear Wise (Great Britain)
1928–1932: Event not held			
1936	Luis Duggan, Roberto Cavanagh, Andrés Gazzotti, Manuel Andrada, Diego Cavanagh (Argentina)	Bryan Fowler, William Hinde, David Dawnay, Humphrey Patrick Guinness (Great Britain)	Juan Gracia, Julio Mueller, Antonio Nava, Alberto Ramos (Mexico)

Rackets

Men's Individual

Year	Gold	Silver	Bronze
1908	Evan Noel (Great Britain)	Henry Leaf (Great Britain)	John Jacob Astor (Great Britain) Henry Brougham (Great Britain)

Men's Doubles

Year	Gold	Silver	Bronze
1908	Vane Pennell, John Jacob Astor (Great Britain)	Edmund Bury, Cecil Browning (Great Britain)	Evan Noel, Henry Leaf (Great Britain)

Rhythmic Gymnastics

Women's Individual All-Around

Year	Gold	Silver	Bronze
1984	Lori Fung (Canada)	Doina Stainculescu (Romania)	Regina Weber (Germany)
1988	Marina Lobatch (Soviet Union)	Adriana Dunavska (Bulgaria)	Alexandra Timoshenko (Soviet Union)
1992	Alexandra Timoshenko (Soviet Union)	Carolina Pascual (Spain)	Oxana Skaldina (Unified Team)
1996	Ekaterina Serebrianskaya (Ukraine)	Yanina Batyrchina (Russia)	Elena Vitrichenko (Ukraine)
2000	Yulia Barsukova (Russia)	Yulia Raskina (Belarus)	Alina Kabaeva (Russia)
2004	Alina Kabaeva (Russia)	Irina Tchachina (Russia)	Anna Bessonova (Ukraine)
2008	Evgeniya Kanaeva (Russia)	Inna Zhukova (Belarus)	Anna Bessonova (Ukraine)

Women's Team All-Around

Year	Gold	Silver	Bronze
1996	Marta Baldó, Nuria Cabanillas, Estela Giménez, Lorena Guréndez, Tania Lamarca, Estíbaliz Martínez (Spain)	Valentina Kevlian, Maria Koleva, Maja Tabakova, Ivelina Taleva, Viara Vatachka (Bulgaria)	Yevgeniya Bochkaryova, Irina Dzyuba, Yuliya Ivanova, Yelena Krivoshey, Olga Shtyrenko, Angelina Yushkova (Russia)
2000	Irina Belova, Yelena Shalamova, Natalia Lavrova, Mariya Netesova, Vera Shimanskaya, Irina Zilber (Russia)	Tatyana Ananko, Tatyana Belan, Anna Glazkova, Irina Ilyenkova, Maria Lazuk, Olga Puzhevich (Belarus)	Eirini Aindili, Evangelia Christodoulou, Maria Georgatou, Zacharoula Karyami, Charikleia Pantazi, Anna Pollatou (Greece)
2004	Olesya Belugina, Olga Glatskikh, Tatiana Kurbakova, Natalia Lavrova, Yelena Posevina, Elena Murzina (Russia)	Elisa Blanchi, Fabrizia D'Ottavio, Marinella Falca, Daniela Masseroni, Elisa Santoni, Laura Vernizzi (Italy)	Zhaneta Ilieva, Eleonora Kezhova, Zornitsa Marinova, Kristina Ranguelova, Galina Tancheva, Vladislava Tancheva (Bulgaria)
2008	Margarita Aliychuk, Anna Gavrilenko, Tatiana Gorbunova, Yelena Posevina, Daria Shkurikhina, Natalia Zuyeva (Russia)	Cai Tongtong, Chou Tao, Lü Yuanyang, Sui Jianshuang, Sun Dan, Zhang Shuo (China)	Olesya Babushkina, Anastasia Ivankova, Ksenia Sankovich, Zinaida Lunina, Glafira Martinovich, Alina Tumilovich (Belarus)

Roque

Men's Individual

Year	Gold	Silver	Bronze
1904	Charles Jacobus (United States)	Smith Streeter (United States)	Charles Brown (United States)

Rowing

Men's Single Sculls

Year	Gold	Silver	Bronze
1900	Hermann Barrelet (France)	André Gaudin (France)	George Saint Ashe (Great Britain)
1904	Frank Greer (United States)	James Juvenal (United States)	Constance Titus (United States)
1908	Harry Blackstaffe (Great Britain)	Alexander McCulloch (Great Britain)	Bernhard von Gaza (Germany) Károly Levitzky (Hungary)
1912	William Kinnear (Great Britain)	Polydore Veirman (Belgium)	Everard Butler (Canada) Mart Kuusik (Russia)
1916: Olympics not held			
1920	Jack Kelly (United States)	Jack Beresford (Great Britain)	Clarence Hadfield D'Arcy (New Zealand)
1924	Jack Beresford (Great Britain)	William Gilmore (United States)	Josef Schneider (Switzerland)
1928	Henry Pearce (Australia)	Kenneth Myers (United States)	Theodore Collet (Great Britain)
1932	Henry Pearce (Australia)	William Miller (United States)	Guillermo Douglas (Uruguay)
1936	Gustav Schäfer (Germany)	Josef Hasenöhrl (Austria)	Daneil Barrow (United States)
1940–1944: Olympics not held			
1948	Mervyn Wood (Australia)	Eduardo Risso (Uruguay)	Romolo Catasta (Italy)
1952	Yuri Tyukalov (Soviet Union)	Mervyn Wood (Australia)	Teodor Kocerka (Poland)
1956	Vyacheslav Ivanov (Soviet Union)	Stuart MacKenzie (Australia)	John B. Kelly Jr. (United States)
1960	Vyacheslav Ivanov (Soviet Union)	Achim Hill (Germany)	Teodor Kocerka (Poland)
1964	Vyacheslav Ivanov (Soviet Union)	Achim Hill (Germany)	Gottfried Kottmann (Switzerland)

Year	Gold	Silver	Bronze
1968	Henri Wienese (Netherlands)	Jochen Meißner (Germany)	Alberto Demiddi (Argentina)
1972	Yuri Malishev (Soviet Union)	Alberto Demiddi (Argentina)	Wolfgang Güldenpfennig (East Germany)
1976	Pertti Karppinen (Finland)	Peter-Michael Kolbe (West Germany)	Joachim Dreifke (East Germany)
1980	Pertti Karppinen (Finland)	Vasil Yakusha (Soviet Union)	Peter Kersten (East Germany)
1984	Pertti Karppinen (Finland)	Peter-Michael Kolbe (West Germany)	Robert Mills (Canada)
1988	Thomas Lange (East Germany)	Peter Michael Kolbe (West Germany)	Eric Verdonk (New Zealand)
1992	Thomas Lange (East Germany)	Václav Chalupa (Czechoslovakia)	Kajetan Broniewski (Poland)
1996	Xeno Müller (Switzerland)	Derek Porter (Canada)	Thomas Lange (Germany)
2000	Rob Waddell (New Zealand)	Xeno Müller (Switzerland)	Marcel Hacker (Germany)
2004	Olaf Tufte (Norway)	Jüri Jaanson (Estonia)	Ivo Yanakiev (Bulgaria)
2008	Olaf Tufte (Norway)	Ondřej Synek (Czech Republic)	Mahé Drysdale (New Zealand)

Men's Double Sculls

Year	Gold	Silver	Bronze
1904	John Mulcahy, William Varley (United States)	Jamie McLoughlin, John Hoben (United States)	Joseph Ravannack, John Wells (United States)
1908–1912: Event not held			
1916: Olympics not held			
1920	Jack Kelly, Paul Costello (United States)	Erminio Dones, Peitro Annoni (Italy)	Alfred Plé, Gaston Giran (France)
1924	Paul Costello, Jack Kelly (United States)	Marc Detton, Jean-Pierre Stock (France)	Rudolph Bosshard, Heinrich Thoma (Switzerland)
1928	Paul Costello, Charles McIlvaine (United States)	Joseph Wright Jr., Jack Guest (Canada)	Leo Losert, Viktor Flessl (Austria)
1932	Kenneth Myers, William Gilmore (United States)	Herbert Buhtz, Gerhard Boetzelen (Germany)	Charles Pratt, Noël de Mille (Canada)
1936	Jack Beresford, Dick Southwood (Great Britain)	Willi Kaidel, Joachim Pirsch (Germany)	Roger Verey, Jerzy Ustupski (Poland)
1940–1944: Olympics not held			
1948	Dickie Burnell, Bert Bushnell (Great Britain)	Ebbe Parsner, Aage Larsen (Denmark)	William Jones, Juan Rodríguez (Uruguay)
1952	Tranquilo Cappozzo, Eduardo Guerrero (Argentina)	Georgiy Zhylin, Ihor Yemchuk (Soviet Union)	Miguel Seijas, Juan Rodríguez (Uruguay)
1956	Aleksandr Berkutov, Yuri Tyukalov (Soviet Union)	Pat Costello, Jim Gardiner (United States)	Murray Riley, Mervyn Wood (Australia)
1960	Václav Kozák, Pavol Schmidt (Czechoslovakia)	Aleksandr Berkutov, Yuri Tyukalov (Soviet Union)	Ernst Hürlimann, Rolf Larcher (Switzerland)
1964	Boris Dubrovsky, Oleg Tyurin (Soviet Union)	Seymour Cromwell, Jim Storm (United States)	Vladimír Andrs, Pavel Hofmann (Czechoslovakia)
1968	Anatoly Sass, Aleksandr Timoshinin (Soviet Union)	Henricus Droog, Leendert van Dis (Netherlands)	John Nunn, Bill Maher (United States)
1972	Aleksandr Timoshinin, Gennadi Korshikov (Soviet Union)	Frank Hansen, Svein Thøgersen (Norway)	Joachim Böhmer, Hans-Ulrich Schmied (East Germany)
1976	Frank Hansen, Alf Hansen (Norway)	Chris Baillieu, Michael Hart (Great Britain)	Hans-Ulrich Schmied, Jürgen Bertow (East Germany)
1980	Joachim Dreifke, Klaus Kröppelien (East Germany)	Zoran Pančić, Milorad Stanulov (Yugoslavia)	Zdeněk Pecka, Václav Vochoska (Czechoslovakia)
1984	Brad Alan Lewis, Paul Enquist (United States)	Pierre-Marie Deloof, Dirk Crois (Belgium)	Zoran Pancic, Milorad Stanulov (Yugoslavia)
1988	Nico Rienks, Ronald Flourijn (Netherlands)	Beat Schwerzmann, Ueli Bodenmann (Switzerland)	Aleksandr Marchenko, Vasily Yakusha (Soviet Union)

Year	Gold	Silver	Bronze
1992	Peter Antonie, Stephen Hawkins (Australia)	Arnold Jonke, Christoph Zerbst (Austria)	Nico Rienks, Henk-Jan Zwolle (Netherlands)
1996	Agostino Abbagnale, Davide Tizzano (Italy)	Steffen Skår Størseth, Kjetil Undset (Norway)	Frederic Kowal, Samuel Barathay (France)
2000	Luka Špik, Iztok Čop (Slovenia)	Olaf Tufte, Fredrik Bekken (Norway)	Giovanni Calabrese, Nicola Sartori (Italy)
2004	Sébastien Vieilledent, Adrien Hardy (France)	Luka Špik, Iztok Čop (Slovenia)	Rossano Galtarossa, Alessio Sartoti (Italy)
2008	David Crawshay, Scott Brennan (Australia)	Tõnu Endrekson, Jüri Jaanson (Estonia)	Matthew Wells, Stephen Rowbotham (Great Britain)

Men's Quadruple Sculls

Year	Gold	Silver	Bronze
1976	Wolfgang Güldenpfennig, Rüdiger Reiche, Karl Heinz Bussert, Michael Wolfgramm (East Germany)	Yevgeny Duleev, Yuri Yakimov, Aivar Lazdenieks, Vitautas Butkus (Soviet Union)	Jaroslav Helebrand, Zdeněk Pecka, Václav Vochoska, Vladek Lacina (Czechoslovakia)
1980	Frank Dundr, Carsten Bunk, Uwe Heppner, Martin Winter (East Germany)	Yuri Shapochka, Yevgeny Barbakov, Valery Kleshnev, Nikolai Dovgan (Soviet Union)	Mincho Nikolov, Lyubomir Petrov, Ivo Rusev, Bogdan Dobrev (Bulgaria)
1984	Albert Hedderich, Raimund Hörmann, Dieter Wiedenmann, Michael Dürsch (West Germany)	Paul Reedy, Gary Gullock, Timothy McLaren, Anthony Lovrich (Australia)	Doug Hamilton, Mike Hughes, Phil Monckton, Bruce Ford (Canada)
1988	Agostino Abbagnale, Davide Tizzano, Gianluca Farina, Piero Poli (Italy)	Alf Hansen, Rolf Thorsen, Lars Bjønness, Vetle Vinje (Norway)	Jens Köppen, Steffen Zühlke, Steffen Bogs, Heiko Habermann (East Germany)
1992	Andreas Hajek, Michael Steinbach, Stephan Volkert, André Willms (Germany)	Kjetil Undset, Per Sætersdal, Lars Bjønness, Rolf Thorsen (Norway)	Alessandro Corona, Gianluca Farina, Rossano Galtarossa, Filippo Soffici (Italy)
1996	Andreas Hajek, Stephan Volkert, André Steiner, André Willms (Germany)	Tim Young, Eric Mueller, Brian Jamieson, Jason Gailes (United States)	Janusz Hooker, Boden Joseph Hanson, Duncan Free, Ronald Snook (Australia)
2000	Agostino Abbagnale, Alessio Sartori, Rossano Galtarossa, Simone Raineri (Italy)	Jochem Verberne, Dirk Lippits, Diederik Simon, Michiel Bartman (Netherlands)	Marco Geisler, Andreas Hajek, Stephan Volkert, André Willms (Germany)
2004	Nikolai Spinev, Igor Kravtsov, Aleksei Svirin, Sergei Fedorovtsev (Russia)	David Kopřiva, Tomáš Karas, Jakub Hanák, David Jirka (Czech Republic)	Sergij Grin, Sergij Bilushchenko, Oleg Lykov, Leonid Shaposhnikov (Ukraine)
2008	Konrad Wasielewski, Marek Kolbowicz, Michał Jeliński, Adam Korol (Poland)	Luca Agamennoni, Simone Venier, Rossano Galtarossa, Simone Raineri (Italy)	Jonathan Coeffic, Pierre-Jean Peltier, Julien Bahain, Cédric Berrest (France)

Men's Coxless Pair

Year	Gold	Silver	Bronze
1904	Robert Farnan, Joseph Ryan (United States)	John Mulcahy, William Varley (United States)	John Joachim, Joseph Buerger (United States)
1908	John Fenning, Gordon Thomson (Great Britain)	George Fairbairn, Philip Verdon (Great Britain)	Frederick Toms, Norway Jackes (Canada)
			Martin Stahnke, Willy Düskow (Germany)
1912: Event not held			
1916: Olympics not held			
1920: Event not held			
1924	Teun Beijnen, Willy Rösingh (Netherlands)	Maurice Bouton, Georges Piot (France)	Not awarded

Year	Gold	Silver	Bronze
1928	Bruno Müller, Kurt Moeschter (Germany)	Terence O'Brien, Robert Nisbet (Great Britain)	Paul McDowell, John Schmitt (United States)
1932	Lewis Clive, Hugh Edwards (Great Britain)	Cyril Stiles, Fred Thompson (New Zealand)	Henryk Budziński, Jan Krenz-Mikołajczak (Poland)
1936	Willi Eichhorn, Hugo Strauß (Germany)	Harry Larsen, Peter Olsen (Denmark)	Horacio Podestá, Julio Curatella (Argentina)
1940–1944: Olympics not held			
1948	Jack Wilson, Ran Laurie (Great Britain)	Hans Kalt, Josef Kalt (Switzerland)	Felice Fanetti, Bruno Boni (Italy)
1952	Charlie Logg, Tom Price (United States)	Michel Knuysen, Bob Baetens (Belgium)	Kurt Schmid, Hans Kalt (Switzerland)
1956	James Fifer, Duvall Hecht (United States)	Igor Buldakov, Viktor Ivanov (Soviet Union)	Alfred Sageder, Josef Kloimstein (Austria)
1960	Valentin Boreyko, Oleg Golovanov (Soviet Union)	Alfred Sageder, Josef Kloimstein (Austria)	Veli Lehtelä, Toimi Pitkänen (Finland)
1964	George Hungerford, Roger Jackson (Canada)	Steven Blaisse, Ernst Veenemans (Netherlands)	Michael Schwan, Wolfgang Hottenrott (Germany)
1968	Jörg Lucke, Heinz-Jürgen Bothe (East Germany)	Larry Hough, Tony Johnson (United States)	Peter Christiansen, Ib Larsen (Denmark)
1972	Siegfried Brietzke, Wolfgang Mager (East Germany)	Heinrich Fischer, Alfred Bachmann (Switzerland)	Roel Luynenburg, Ruud Stokvis (Netherlands)
1976	Jörg Landvoigt, Bernd Landvoigt (East Germany)	Calvin Coffey, Mike Staines (United States)	Peter van Roye, Thomas Strauß (West Germany)
1980	Jörg Landvoigt, Bernd Landvoigt (East Germany)	Yuri Pimenov, Nikolay Pimenov (Soviet Union)	Charles Wiggin, Malcolm Carmichael (Great Britain)
1984	Petru Iosub, Valer Toma (Romania)	Fernando Climent, Luis María Lasúrtegui (Spain)	Hans Magnus Grepperud, Sverre Løken (Norway)
1988	Andy Holmes, Steve Redgrave (Great Britain)	Dănuţ Dobre, Dragoş Neagu (Romania)	Sadik Mujkič, Bojan Preseren (Yugoslavia)
1992	Matthew Pinsent, Steve Redgrave (Great Britain)	Colin Ettingshausen, Peter Holtzenbein (Germany)	Iztok Čop, Denis Žvegelj (Slovenia)
1996	Steven Redgrave, Matthew Pinsent (Great Britain)	David Weightman, Robert Geoffrey Scott (Australia)	Michael Andrieux, Jean Christoph Rolland (France)
2000	Michel Andrieux, Jean-Christophe Rolland (France)	Ted Murphy, Sebastian Bea (United States)	Matthew Long, James Tomkins (Australia)
2004	Drew Ginn, James Tomkins (Australia)	Siniša Skelin, Nikša Skelin (Croatia)	Donovan Cech, Ramon di Clemente (South Africa)
2008	Drew Ginn, Duncan Free (Australia)	David Calder, Scott Frandsen (Canada)	Nathan Twaddle, George Bridgewater (New Zealand)

Men's Coxed Pairs

Year	Gold	Silver	Bronze
1900	François Brandt, Roelof Klein, Hermanus Brockmann (Netherlands), Unknown Cox (France)	Lucien Martinet, René Waleff, Unknown Cox (France)	Carlos Deltour, Antoine Védrenne, Raoul Paoli (France)
1904–1912: Event not held			
1916: Olympics not held			
1920	Ercole Olgeni, Giovanni Scatturin, Guido De Filip (Italy)	Gabriel Poix, Maurice Bouton, Ernest Barberolle (France)	Édouard Candeveau, Alfred Felber, Paul Piaget (Switzerland)
1924	Édouard Candeveau, Alfred Felber, Émile Lachapelle (Switzerland)	Ercole Olgeni, Giovanni Scatturin, Gino Sopracordevole (Italy)	Leon Butler, Harold Wilson, Edward Jennings (United States)
1928	Hans Schöchlin, Karl Schöchlin, Hans Bourquin (Switzerland)	Armand Marcelle, Edouard Marcelle, Henri Préaux (France)	Léon Flament, François de Coninck, Georges Anthony (Belgium)

Year	Gold	Silver	Bronze
1932	Joseph Schauers, Charles Kieffer, Edward Jennings (United States)	Jerzy Braun, Janusz Ślązak, Jerzy Skolimowski (Poland)	Anselme Brusa, André Giriat, Pierre Brunet (France)
1936	Gerhard Gustmann, Herbert Adamski, Dieter Arend (Germany)	Almiro Bergamo, Guido Santin, Luciano Negrini (Italy)	Marceau Fourcade, Georges Tapie, Noël Vandernotte (France)
1940–1944: Olympics not held			
1948	Finn Pedersen, Tage Henriksen, Carl Andersen (Denmark)	Giovanni Steffè, Aldo Tarlao, Alberto Radi (Italy)	Antal Szendey, Béla Zsitnik, Róbert Zimonyi (Hungary)
1952	Raymond Salles, Gaston Mercier, Bernard Malivoire (France)	Heinz Manchen, Helmut Heinhold, Helmut Noll (Germany)	Svend Pedersen, Paul Svendsen, Jorgen Frantzen (Denmark)
1956	Arthur Ayrault, Conn Findlay, Armin Seiffert (United States)	Karl-Heinrich von Groddeck, Horst Arndt, Rainer Borkowsky (United Team of Germany)	Ihor Yemchuk, Georgiy Zhylin, Vladimir Petrov (Soviet Union)
1960	Bernhard Knubel, Karl Renneberg, Klaus Zerta (United Team of Germany)	Antanas Bagdonavičius, Zigmas Jukna, Igor Rudakov (Soviet Union)	Richard Draeger, Conn Findlay, Henry Mitchell (United States)
1964	Edward Ferry, Conn Findlay, Kent Mitchell (United States)	Jacques Morel, Georges Morel, Jean Claude Darouy (France)	Jan Just Bos, Herman Rouwé, Frederik Hartsuiker (Netherlands)
1968	Primo Baran, Renzo Sambo, Bruno Cipolla (Italy)	Herman Suselbeek, Hadriaan van Nes, Roderick Rijnders (Netherlands)	Jørn Krab, Harry Jørgensen, Preben Krab (Denmark)
1972	Wolfgang Gunkel, Jörg Lücke, Klaus-Dieter Neubert (East Germany)	Oldřich Svojanovský, Pavel Svojanovský, Vladimír Petříček (Czechoslovakia)	Ştefan Tudor, Petre Ceapura, Ladislau Lovrenschi (Romania)
1976	Harald Jährling, Friedrich Ulrich, Georg Spohr (East Germany)	Dmitri Bekhterev, Yuri Shurkalov, Yuri Lorentsson (Soviet Union)	Oldřich Svojanovský, Pavel Svojanovský, Ludvík Vébr (Czechoslovakia)
1980	Harald Jährling, Friedrich-Wilhelm Ulrich, Georg Spohr (East Germany)	Viktor Pereverzev, Gennady Kryuchkin, Aleksandr Lukyanov (Soviet Union)	Dusko Mrduljas, Zlatko Celent, Josip Reic (Yugoslavia)
1984	Carmine Abbagnale, Giuseppe Abbagnale, Giuseppe di Capua (Italy)	Dimitrie Popescu, Vasile Tomoiagă, Dumitru Răducanu (Romania)	Kevin Still, Robert Espeseth, Doug Herland (United States)
1988	Giuseppe di Capua, Carmine Abbagnale, Giuseppe Abbagnale (Italy)	Mario Streit, Detlef Kirchhoff, René Rensch (East Germany)	Patrick Sweeney, Andy Holmes, Steve Redgrave (Great Britain)
1992	Garry Herbert, Greg Searle, Jonny Searle (Great Britain)	Giuseppe di Capua, Carmine Abbagnale, Giuseppe Abbagnale (Italy)	Dimitrie Popescu, Dumitru Răducanu, Nicolaie Taga (Romania)

Men's Coxless Fours

Year	Gold	Silver	Bronze
1904	Arthur Stockhoff, August Erker, George Dietz, Albert Nasse (United States)	Frederck Suerig, Martin Formanack, Charles Aman, Michael Begley (United States)	Gustav Voerg, John Freitag, Louis Helm, Frank Dummerth (United States)
1908	Collier Cudmore, James Angus Gillan, Duncan Mackinnon, John Somers-Smith (Great Britain)	Philip Filleul, Harold Barker, John Fenning, Gordon Thomson (Great Britain)	Gordon Balfour, Becher Gale, Charles Riddy, Geoffrey Taylor (Canada), Hermannus Höfte, Albertus Wielsma, Johan Burk, Bernardus Croon (Netherlands)
1912: Event not held			
1916: Olympics not held			
1920: Event not held			
1924	Charles Eley, James MacNabb, Robert Morrison, Terence Sanders (Great Britain)	Archibald Black, George MacKay, Colin Finlayson, William Wood (Canada)	Emile Albrecht, Alfred Probst, Eugen Sigg, Hans Walter (Switzerland)

Year	Gold	Silver	Bronze
1928	John Lander, Michael Warriner, Richard Beesly, Edward Vaughan Bevan (Great Britain)	Charles Karle, William Miller, George Healis, Ernest Bayer (United States)	Cesare Rossi, Pietro Freschi, Umberto Bonadè, Paolo Gennari (Italy)
1932	John Badcock, Hugh Edwards, Jack Beresford, Rowland George (Great Britain)	Karl Aletter, Ernst Gaber, Walter Flinsch, Hans Maier (Germany)	Antonio Ghiardello, Francesco Cossu, Giliante D'Este, Antonio Garzoni Provenzani (Italy)
1936	Rudolf Eckstein, Anton Rom, Martin Karl, Wilhelm Menne (Germany)	Thomas Bristow, Alan Barrett, Peter Jackson, John Sturrock (Great Britain)	Hermann Betschart, Hans Homberger, Alex Homberger, Karl Schmid (Switzerland)
1940–1944: Olympics not held			
1948	Giuseppe Moioli, Elio Morille, Giovanni Invernizzi, Francesco Faggi (Italy)	Helge Halkjær, Aksel Bonde Hansen, Helge Muxoll Schrøder, Ib Larsen (Denmark)	Frederick Kingsbury, Stuart Griffing, Gregory Gates, Robert Perew (United States)
1952	Duje Bonačić, Velimir Valenta, Mate Trojanović, Petar Šegvić (Yugoslavia)	Pierre Blondiaux, Jean-Jacques Guissart, Marc Bouissou, Roger Gautier (France)	Veikko Lommi, Kauko Wahlsten, Oiva Lommi, Lauri Nevalainen (Finland)
1956	Archibald McKinnon, Lorne Loomer, Walter D'Hondt, Donald Arnold (Canada)	John Welchli, John McKinlay, Arthur McKinlay, James McIntosh (United States)	René Guissart, Yves Delacour, Gaston Mercier, Guy Guillabert (France)
1960	Arthur Ayrault, Ted Nash, John Sayre, Rusty Wailes (United States)	Tullio Baraglia, Renato Bosatta, Giancarlo Crosta, Giuseppe Galante (Italy)	Igor Akhremchik, Yuri Bachurov, Valentin Morkovkin, Anatoly Tarabrin (Soviet Union)
1964	John Hansen, Bjørn Hasløv, Erik Petersen, Kurt Helmudt (Denmark)	John Russell, Hugh Wardell-Yerburgh, William Barry, John James (Great Britain)	Geoffrey Picard, Richard Lyon, Theodore Mittet, Ted Nash (United States)
1968	Frank Forberger, Frank Rühle, Dieter Grahn, Dieter Schubert (East Germany)	Zoltán Melis, József Csermely, György Sarlós, Antal Melis (Hungary)	Renato Bosatta, Pier Conti-Manzini, Tullio Baraglia, Abramo Albini (Italy)
1972	Frank Forberger, Frank Rühle, Dieter Grahn, Dieter Schubert (East Germany)	Dick Tonks, Dudley Storey, Ross Collinge, Noel Mills (New Zealand)	Joachim Ehrig, Peter Funnekötter, Franz Held, Wolfgang Plottke (West Germany)
1976	Siegfried Brietzke, Andreas Decker, Stefan Semmler, Wolfgang Mager (East Germany)	Ole Nafstad, Arne Bergodd, Finn Tveter, Rolf Andreassen (Norway)	Raul Arnemann, Nikolai Kuznetsov, Valeri Dolinin, Anushavan Gasan-Dzhalalov (Soviet Union)
1980	Jürgen Thiele, Andreas Decker, Stefan Semmler, Siegfried Brietzke (East Germany)	Aleksei Kamkin, Valeri Dolinin, Aleksandr Kulagin, Vitaly Yeliseyev (Soviet Union)	John Beattie, Ian McNuff, David Townsend, Martin Cross (Great Britain)
1984	Les O'Connell, Shane O'Brien, Conrad Robertson, Keith Trask (New Zealand)	David Clark, Johnathan Smith, Phillip Stekl, Alan Forney (United States)	Michael Jessen, Lars Nielsen, Per Rasmussen, Erik Christiansen (Denmark)
1988	Roland Schröder, Ralf Brudel, Olaf Förster, Thomas Greiner (East Germany)	Raoul Rodriguez, Thomas Bohrer, Richard Kennelly, David Krmpotich (United States)	Guido Grabow, Volker Grabow, Norbert Keßlau, Joerg Puttlitz (West Germany)
1992	Andrew Cooper, Nicholas Green, Mike McKay, James Tomkins (Australia)	Jeffrey McLaughlin, William Burden, Thomas Bohrer, Patrick Manning (United States)	Milan Janša, Sadik Mujkič, Sašo Mirjanič, Janez Klemenčič (Slovenia)
1996	Nicholas Green, Drew Ginn, James Tomkins, Mike McKay (Australia)	Bertrand Vecten, Olivier Moncelet, Daniel Fauche, Giles Bosquet (France)	Greg Searle, Jonny Searle, Rupert Obholzer, Tim Foster (Great Britain)
2000	James Cracknell, Steve Redgrave, Tim Foster, Matthew Pinsent (Great Britain)	Walter Molea, Riccardo Dei Rossi, Lorenzo Carboncini, Carlo Mornati (Italy)	James Stewart, Ben Dodwell, Geoffrey Stewart, Bo Hanson (Australia)
2004	Steve Williams, James Cracknell, Ed Coode, Matthew Pinsent (Great Britain)	Cameron Baerg, Thomas Herschmiller, Jake Wetzel, Barney Williams (Canada)	Lorenzo Porzio, Dario Dentale, Luca Agamennoni, Raffaello Leonardo (Italy)
2008	Tom James, Steve Williams, Pete Reed, Andrew Triggs-Hodge (Great Britain)	Matt Ryan, James Marburg, Cameron McKenzie-McHarg, Francis Hegerty (Australia)	Julien Desprès, Benjamin Rondeau, Germain Chardin, Dorian Mortelette (France)

Men's Coxed Fours

Year	Gold	Silver	Bronze
1900	Henri Bouckaert, Jean Cau, Émile Delchambre, Henri Hazebroucq, Charlot* (France)	Georges Lumpp, Charles Perrin, Daniel Soubeyran, Émile Wegelin, Unknown Cox (France)	Wilhelm Carstens, Julius Körner, Adolf Möller, Hugo Rüster, Gustav Moths (Germany)
	Gustav Goßler, Oskar Goßler, Walter Katzenstein, Waldemar Tietgens, Carl Goßler (Germany)	Coenraad Hiebendaal, Geert Lotsij, Paul Lotsij, Johannes Terwogt, Hermanus Brockmann (Netherlands)	Ernst Felle, Otto Fickeisen, Carl Lehle, Hermann Wilker, Franz Kröwerath (Germany)
1904–1908: Event not held			
1912	Albert Arnheiter, Hermann Wilker, Rudolf Fickeisen, Otto Fickeisen, Karl Leister (Germany)	Julius Beresford, Karl Vernon, Charles Rought, Bruce Logan, Geoffrey Carr (Great Britain)	Erik Bisgaard, Rasmus Frandsen, Mikael Simonsen, Poul Thymann, Ejgil Clemmensen (Denmark)
1916: Olympics not held			
1920	Willy Brüderlin, Max Rudolf, Paul Rudolf, Hans Walter, Paul Staub (Switzerland)	Kenneth Myers, Carl Klose, Franz Federschmidt, Erich Federschmidt, Sherman Clark (United States)	Birger Var, Theodor Klem, Henry Larsen, Per Gulbrandsen, Thoralf Hagen (Norway)
1924	Emile Albrecht, Alfred Probst, Eugen Sigg, Hans Walter, Émile Lachapelle (Switzerland)	Eugène Constant, Louis Gressier, Georges Lecointe, Raymond Talleux, Ernest Barberolle (France)	Robert Gerhardt, Sidney Jelinek, Edward Mitchell, Henry Welsford, John Kennedy (United States)
1928	Valerio Perentin, Giliante D'Este, Nicolò Vittori, Giovanni Delise, Renato Petronio (Italy)	Ernst Haas, Joseph Meyer, Otto Bucher, Karl Schwegler, Fritz Bösch (Switzerland)	Franciszek Bronikowski, Edmund Jankowski, Leon Birkholc, Bernard Ormanowski, Bolesław Drewek (Poland)
1932	Hans Eller, Horst Hoeck, Walter Meyer, Joachim Spremberg, Carlheinz Neumann (Germany)	Bruno Vattovaz, Giovanni Plazzer, Riccardo Divora, Bruno Parovel, Giovanni Scher (Italy)	Jerzy Braun, Janusz Ślązak, Stanisław Urban, Edward Kobyliński, Jerzy Skolimowski (Poland)
1936	Hans Maier, Walter Volle, Ernst Gaber, Paul Söllner, Fritz Bauer (Germany)	Hermann Betschart, Hans Homberger, Alex Homberger, Karl Schmid, Rolf Spring (Switzerland)	Fernand Vandernotte, Marcel Vandernotte, Jean Cosmat, Marcel Chauvigné, Noël Vandernotte (France)
1940–1944: Olympics not held			
1948	Warren Westlund, Robert Martin, Robert Will, Gordon Giovanelli, Allan Morgan (United States)	Rudolf Reichling, Erich Schriever, Emil Knecht, Pierre Stebler, André Moccand (Switzerland)	Erik Larsen, Børge Nielsen, Henry Larsen, Harry Knudsen, Jørgen Olsen (Denmark)
1952	Karel Mejta, Jiří Havlis, Jan Jindra, Stanislav Lusk, Miroslav Koranda (Czechoslovakia)	Rico Bianchi, Karl Weidmann, Heinrich Scheller, Émile Ess, Walter Leiser (Switzerland)	Carl Lovested, Alvin Ulbrickson, Richard Wahlstrom, Matthew Leanderson, Albert Rossi (United States)
1956	Albert Winkler, Romano Sgheiz, Angelo Vanzin, Franco Trincavelli, Ivo Stefanoni (Italy)	Olle Larsson, Gösta Eriksson, Ivar Aronsson, Evert Gunnarsson, Bertil Göransson (Sweden)	Kauko Hänninen, Reino Poutanen, Veli Lehtelä, Toimi Pitkänen, Matti Niemi (Finland)
1960	Gerd Cintl, Horst Effertz, Klaus Riekemann, Jürgen Litz, Michael Obst (Germany)	Robert Dumontois, Claude Martin, Jacques Morel, Guy Nosbaum, Jean Klein (France)	Fulvio Balatti, Romano Sgheiz, Franco Trincavelli, Giovanni Zucchi, Ivo Stefanoni (Italy)
1964	Peter Neusel, Bernhard Britting, Joachim Werner, Egbert Hirschfelder, Juergen Oelke (Germany)	Renato Bosatta, Emilio Trivini, Giuseppe Galante, Franco De Pedrina, Giovanni Spinola (Italy)	Lex Mullink, Jan Van De Graaff, F. R. Van De Graaff, Robert Van De Graaff, Marius Klumperbeek (Netherlands)
1968	Dick Joyce, Ross Collinge, Dudley Storey, Warren Cole, Simon Dickie (New Zealand)	Peter Kremtz, Manfred Gelpke, Roland Göhler, Klaus Jacob, Dieter Semetzky (East Germany)	Denis Oswald, Peter Bolliger, Hugo Waser, Jakob Grob, Gottlieb Fröhlich (Switzerland)

Year	Gold	Silver	Bronze
1972	Peter Berger, Hans-Johann Färber, Gerhard Auer, Alois Bierl, Uwe Benter (West Germany)	Dietrich Zander, Reinhard Gust, Eckhard Martens, Rolf Jobst, Klaus-Dieter Ludwig (East Germany)	Otakar Mareček, Karel Neffe, Vladimír Jánoš, František Provazník, Vladimír Petříček (Czechoslovakia)
1976	Vladimir Eshinov, Nikolai Ivanov, Mikhail Kuznetsov, Aleksandr Klepikov, Aleksandr Lukyanov (Soviet Union)	Andreas Schulz, Rüdiger Kunze, Walter Diessner, Ullrich Diessner, Johannes Thomas (East Germany)	Johann Faerber, Ralph Kubail, Siegfried Fricke, Peter Niehusen, Hartmut Wenzel (West Germany)
1980	Dieter Wendisch, Ullrich Diessner, Walter Diessner, Gottfried Döhn, Andreas Gregor (East Germany)	Artūrs Garonskis, Dimants Krišjānis, Dzintars Krišjānis, Žoržs Tikmers, Juris Bērziņš (Soviet Union)	Grzegorz Stellak, Adam Tomasiak, Grzegorz Nowak, Ryszard Stadniuk, Ryszard Kubiak (Poland)
1984	Richard Budgett, Martin Cross, Adrian Ellison, Andy Holmes, Steve Redgrave (Great Britain)	Edward Ives, Thomas Kiefer, Michael Bach, Gregory Springer, John Stillings (United States)	Brett Hollister, Kevin Lawton, Barrie Mabbott, Don Symon, Ross Tong (New Zealand)
1988	Bernd Niesecke, Hendrik Reiher, Karsten Schmelling, Bernd Eichwurzel, Frank Klawonn (East Germany)	Dimitrie Popescu, Ioan Snep, Vasile Tomoiagă, Ladislau Lovrenschi, Valentin Robu (Romania)	Chris White, Ian Wright, Andrew Bird, Greg Johnston, George Keys (New Zealand)
1992	Iulica Ruican, Viorel Talapan, Dimitrie Popescu, Dumitru Răducanu, Nicolaie Taga (Romania)	Ralf Brudel, Uwe Kellner, Thoralf Peters, Karsten Finger, Hendrik Reiher (Germany)	Wojciech Jankowski, Maciej Lasicki, Jacek Streich, Tomasz Tomiak, Michał Cieślak (Poland)

* Full name not known.

Men's Coxed Fours, Inriggers

Year	Gold	Silver	Bronze
1912	Ejler Allert, Jørgen Hansen, Carl Møller, Carl Pedersen, Poul Hartmann (Denmark)	Ture Rosvall, William Bruhn-Möller, Conrad Brunkman, Herman Dahlbäck, Wilhelm Wilkens (Sweden)	Claus Høyer, Reidar Holter, Magnus Herseth, Frithjof Olstad, Olav Bjørnstad (Norway)

Men's Eights

Year	Gold	Silver	Bronze
1900	William Carr, Harry DeBaecke, John Exley, John Geiger, Edwin Hedley, James Juvenal, Roscoe Lockwood, Edward Marsh, Louis Abell (United States)	Jules De Bisschop, Prospère Bruggeman, Oscar De Somville, Oscar De Cock, Maurice Hemelsoet, Marcel Van Crombrugge, Frank Odberg, Maurice Verdonck, Alfred van Landeghem (Belgium)	François Brandt, Johannes van Dijk, Roelof Klein, Ruurd Leegstra, Walter Middelberg, Hendrik Offerhaus, Walter Thijssen, Henricus Tromp, Hermanus Brockmann (Netherlands)
1904	Frederick Cresser, Michael Gleason, Frank Schell, James Flanagan, Charles Armstrong, Harry Lott, Joseph Dempsey, John Exley, Louis Abell (United States)	Arthur Bailey, William Rice, George Reiffenstein, Phil Boyd, George Strange, William Wadsworth, Donald MacKenzie, Joseph Wright, Thomas Loudon (Canada)	Not awarded

Year	Gold	Silver	Bronze
1908	Albert Gladstone, Frederick Kelly, Banner Johnstone, Guy Nickalls, Charles Burnell, Ronald Sanderson, Raymond Etherington-Smith, Henry Bucknall, Gilchrist Maclagan (Great Britain)	Oscar Taelman, Marcel Morimont, Rémy Orban, Georges Mijs, François Vergucht, Polydore Veirman, Oscar De Somville, Rodolphe Poma, Alfred van Landeghem (Belgium)	Irvine Robertson, Joseph Wright, Julius Thomson, Walter Lewis, Gordon Balfour, Becher Gale, Charles Riddy, Geoffrey Taylor, Douglas Kertland (Canada) Frank Jerwood, Eric Powell, Oswald Carver, Edward Williams, Henry Goldsmith, Harold Kitching, John Burn, Douglas Stuart, Richard Boyle (Great Britain)
1912	Edgar Burgess, Sidney Swann, Leslie Wormwald, Ewart Horsfall, James Angus Gillan, Arthur Garton, Alister Kirby, Philip Fleming, Henry Wells (Great Britain)	William Fison, William Parker, Thomas Gillespie, Beaufort Burdekin, Frederick Pitman, Arthur Wiggins, Charles Littlejohn, Robert Bourne, John Walker (Great Britain)	Otto Liebing, Max Bröske, Max Vetter, Willi Bartholomae, Fritz Bartholomae, Werner Dehn, Rudolf Reichelt, Hans Matthiae, Kurt Runge (Germany)
1916: Olympics not held			
1920	Virgil Jacomini, Edwin Graves, William Jordan, Edward Moore, Alden Sanborn, Donald Johnston, Vincent Gallagher, Clyde King, Sherman Clark (United States)	Ewart Horsfall, Guy Oliver Nickalls, Richard Lucas, Walter James, John Campbell, Sebastian Earl, Ralph Shove, Sidney Swann, Robin Johnstone (Great Britain)	Theodor Nag, Conrad Olsen, Adolf Nilsen, Håkon Ellingsen, Thore Michelsen, Arne Mortensen, Karl Nag, Tollef Tollefsen, Thoralf Hagen (Norway)
1924	Leonard Carpenter, Howard Kingsbury, Alfred Lindley, John Miller, James Rockefeller, Frederick Sheffield, Benjamin Spock, Alfred Wilson, Laurence Stoddard (United States)	Arthur Bell, Robert Hunter, William Langford, Harold Little, John Smith, Warren Snyder, Norman Taylor, William Wallace, Ivor Campbell (Canada)	Antonio Cattalinich, Francesco Cattalinich, Simeone Cattalinich, Giuseppe Grivelli, Latino Galasso, Pietro Ivanov, Bruno Sorich, Carlo Toniatti, Vittorio Gliubich (Italy)
1928	Marvin Stalder, John Brinck, Francis Frederick, William Thompson, William Dally, James Workman, Hubert A. Caldwell, Peter Donlon, Donald Blessing (United States)	Jamie Hamilton, Guy Oliver Nickalls, John Badcock, Donald Gollan, Harold Lane, Gordon Killick, Jack Beresford, Harold West, Arthur Sulley (Great Britain)	Frederick Hedges, Frank Fiddes, John Hand, Herbert Richardson, Jack Murdoch, Athol Meech, Edgar Norris, William Ross, John Donnelly (Canada)
1932	Edwin Salisbury, James Blair, Duncan Gregg, David Dunlap, Burton Jastram, Charles Chandler, Harold Tower, Winslow Hall, Norris Graham (United States)	Vittorio Cioni, Mario Balleri, Renato Bracci, Dino Barsotti, Roberto Vestrini, Guglielmo Del Bimbo, Enrico Garzelli, Renato Barbieri, Cesare Milani (Italy)	Earl Eastwood, Joseph Harris, Stanley Stanyar, Harry Fry, Cedric Liddell, William Thoburn, Donald Boal, Albert Taylor, George MacDonald (Canada)
1936	Herbert Morris, Charles Day, Gordon Adam, John White, James McMillin, George Hunt, Joseph Rantz, Donald Hume, Robert Moch (United States)	Guglielmo Del Bimbo, Dino Barsotti, Oreste Grossi, Enzo Bartolini, Mario Checcacci, Dante Secchi, Ottorino Quaglierini, Enrico Garzelli, Cesare Milani (Italy)	Alfred Rieck, Helmut Radach, Hans Kuschke, Heinz Kaufmann, Gerd Völs, Werner Loeckle, Hans-Joachim Hannemann, Herbert Schmidt, Wilhelm Mahlow (Germany)
1940–1944: Olympics not held			
1948	Ian Turner, David Turner, James Hardy, George Ahlgren, Lloyd Butler, David Brown, Justus Smith, John Stack, Ralph Purchase (United States)	Christopher Barton, Michael Lapage, Guy Richardson, Ernest Bircher, Paul Massey, Charles Lloyd, David Meyrick, Alfred Mellows, Jack Dearlove (Great Britain)	Kristoffer Lepsøe, Thorstein Kråkenes, Hans Hansen, Halfdan Gran Olsen, Harald Kråkenes, Leif Næss, Thor Pedersen, Carl Monssen, Sigurd Monssen (Norway)

Year	Gold	Silver	Bronze
1952	Frank Shakespeare, William Fields, James Dunbar, Richard Murphy, Robert Detweiler, Henry Procter, Wayne Frye, Edward Stevens, Charles Manring (United States)	Yevgeny Brago, Vladimir Rodimushkin, Aleksei Komarov, Igor Borisov, Slava Amiragov, Leonid Gissen, Yevgeny Samsonov, Vladimir Kryukov, Igor Polyakov (Soviet Union)	Robert Tinning, Ernest Chapman, Nimrod Greenwood, David Anderson, Geoffrey Williamson, Mervyn Finlay, Edward Pain, Phillip Cayzer, Tom Chessell (Australia)
1956	Thomas Charlton, David Wight, John Cooke, Donald Beer, Caldwell Esselstyn, Charles Grimes, Rusty Wailes, Robert Morey, William Becklean (United States)	Philip Kueber, Richard McClure, Robert Wilson, David Helliwell, Donald Pretty, William McKerlich, Douglas McDonald, Lawrence West, Carlton Ogawa (Canada)	Michael Aikman, David Boykett, Angus Benfield, James Howden, Garth Manton, Walter Howell, Adrian Monger, Bryan Doyle, Harold Hewitt (Australia)
1960	Manfred Rulffs, Walter Schröder, Frank Schepke, Kraft Schepke, Karl-Heinrich von Groddeck, Karl-Heinz Hopp, Klaus Bittner, Hans Lenk, Willi Padge (United Team of Germany)	Donald Arnold, Walter D'Hondt, Nelson Kuhn, John Lecky, Lorne Loomer, Archibald MacKinnon, William McKerlich, Glen Mervyn, Sohen Biln (Canada)	Bohumil Janoušek, Jan Jindra, Jiří Lundák, Stanislav Lusk, Václav Pavkovič, Luděk Pojezný, Jan Švéda, Josef Věntus, Miroslav Koníček (Czechoslovakia)
1964	Joseph Amlong, Thomas Amlong, Harold Budd, Emory Clark, Stanley Cwiklinski, Hugh Foley, William Knecht, William Stowe, Róbert Zimonyi (United States)	Klaus Aeffke, Klaus Bittner, Karl-Heinrich von Groddeck, Hans-Jurgen Wallbrecht, Klaus Behrens, Jurgen Schroeder, Jürgen Plagemann, Horst Meyer, Thomas Ahrens (United Team of Germany)	Petr Čermák, Jiří Lundák, Jan Mrvík, Július Toček, Josef Věntus, Luděk Pojezný, Bohumil Janoušek, Richard Nový, Miroslav Koníček (Czechoslovakia)
1968	Horst Meyer, Wolfgang Hottenrott, Dirk Schreyer, Egbert Hirschfelder, Rüdiger Henning, Jörg Siebert, Lutz Ulbricht, Nikolaus Ott, Günther Thiersch (West Germany)	Alfred Duval, David Douglas, Michael Morgan, John Ranch, Joseph Frazio, Gary Pearce, Peter Dickson, Robert Shirlaw, Alan Grover (Australia)	Zigmas Jukna, Aleksandr Martyshkin, Antanas Bagdonavičius, Vytautas Briedis, Vladimir Sterlik, Valentyn Kravchuk, Juozas Jagelavičius, Viktor Suslin, Yuri Lorentsson (Soviet Union)
1972	Tony Hurt, Wybo Veldman, Dick Joyce, John Hunter, Lindsay Wilson, Athol Earl, Trevor Coker, Gary Robertson, Simon Dickie (New Zealand)	Lawrence Terry, Franklin Hobbs, Peter Raymond, Timothy Mickelson, Eugene Clapp, William Hobbs, Cleve Livingston, Michael Livingston, Paul Hoffman (United States)	Hans-Joachim Borzym, Jörg Landvoigt, Harold Dimke, Manfred Schneider, Hartmut Schreiber, Manfred Schmorde, Bernd Landvoigt, Heinri Mederow, Dietmar Schwarz (East Germany)
1976	Bernd Baumgart, Gottfried Döhn, Werner Klatt, Hans Joachim Luck, Dieter Wendisch, Roland Kostulski, Ulrich Karnatz, Karl Heins Prudohl, Karl Heinz Danielovski (East Germany)	Richard Lester, John Yallop, Timothy Crooks, Hugh Matheson, David Maxwell, James Clark, Fred Smallbone, Leonard Robertson, Patrick Sweeney (Great Britain)	Ivan Sutherland, Trevor Coker, Peter Dignan, Lindsay Wilson, Athol Earl, Dave Rodger, Alex McLean, Tony Hurt, Simon Dickie (New Zealand)
1980	Bernd Krauss, Hans-Peter Koppe, Ulrich Kons, Jörg Friedrich, Jens Doberschütz, Ulrich Karnatz, Uwe Dühring, Bernd Höing, Klaus-Dieter Ludwig (East Germany)	Duncan McDougall, Allan Whitwell, Henry Clay, Chris Mahoney, Andrew Justice, John Pritchard, Malcolm McGowan, Richard Stanhope, Colin Moynihan (Great Britain)	Viktor Kokdshin, Andrey Tishchenko, Aleksandr Tkachenko, Jonas Pintskus, Jonas Normantas, Andrei Lugin, Aleksandr Mantsevich, Igor Maistrenko, Grigory Dmitrienko (Soviet Union)
1984	Blair Horn, Dean Crawford, Michael Evans, Paul Steele, Grant Main, Mark Evans, Kevin Neufeld, Pat Turner, Brian McMahon (Canada)	Chip Lubsen, Andrew Sudduth, John Terwilliger, Christopher Penny, Tom Darling, Fred Borchelt, Charles Clapp III, Bruce Ibbetson, Bob Jaugstetter (United States)	Craig Muller, Clyde Hefer, Samuel Patten, Tim Willoughby, Ian Edmunds, James Battersby, Ion Popa, Stephen Evans, Gavin Thredgold (Australia)

Year	Gold	Silver	Bronze
1988	Bahne Rabe, Eckhardt Schultz, Ansgar Wessling, Wolfgang Maennig, Matthias Mellinghaus, Thomas Möllenkamp, Thomas Domian, Armin Eichholz, Manfred Klein (West Germany)	Viktor Omelyanovich, Vasily Tikhonov, Andrey Vasilyev, Pavel Gurkovsky, Nikolay Kumarov, Aleksandr Lukvanov, Veniamin But, Viktor Diduk, Aleksandr Dumchev (Soviet Union)	Mike Teti, Jonathan Smith, Ted Patton, John Rusher, Peter Nordell, Jeffrey McLaughlin, Doug Burden, John Pescatore, Seth Bauer (United States)
1992	Darren Barber, Andrew Crosby, Michael Forgeron, Robert Marland, Terence Paul, Derek Porter, Michael Rascher, Bruce Robertson, John Wallace (Canada)	Iulica Ruican, Viorel Talapan, Vasile Nastase, Claudiu Marin, Dănuţ Dobre, Valentin Robu, Vasile Mastacan, Ioan Vizitiu, Marin Gheorghe (Romania)	Roland Baar, Armin Eichholz, Detlef Kirchhoff, Manfred Klein, Bahne Rabe, Frank Richter, Hans Sennewald, Thorsten Streppelhoff, Ansgar Wessling (Germany)
1996	Koos Maasdijk, Ronald Florijn, Jeroen Duyster, Michiel Bartman, Henk-Jan Zwolle, Niels van der Zwan, Niels van Steenis, Diederik Simon, Nico Rienks (Netherlands)	Mark Kleinschmidt, Detlef Kirchhoff, Wolfram Huhn, Roland Baar, Marc Weber, Ulrich Viefers, Peter Thiede, Thorsten Streppelhoff, Frank Jörg Richter (Germany)	Pavel Melnikov, Andrei Glukhov, Anton Chermashentsev, Aleksandr Lukyanov, Nikolai Aksyonov, Dmitri Rozinkevich, Sergei Matveyev, Roman Monchenko, Vladimir Volodenkov, Vladimir Sokolov (Russia)
2000	Andrew Lindsay, Ben Hunt-Davis, Simon Dennis, Louis Attrill, Luka Grubor, Kieran West, Fred Scarlett, Steve Trapmore, Rowley Douglas (Great Britain)	Christian Ryan, Alastair Gordon, Nick Porzig, Robert Jahrling, Mike McKay, Stuart Welch, Daniel Burke, Jaime Fernandez, Brett Hayman (Australia)	Igor Francetić, Tihomir Franković, Tomislav Smoljanović, Nikša Skelin, Siniša Skelin, Krešimir Čuljak, Igor Boraska, Branimir Vujević, Silvijo Petriško (Croatia)
2004	Jason Read, Wyatt Allen, Chris Ahrens, Joseph Hansen, Matt Deakin, Dan Beery, Beau Hoopman, Bryan Volpenhein, Peter Cipollone (United States)	Matthijs Vellenga, Gijs Vermeulen, Jan-Willem Gabriëls, Daniël Mensch, Geert Jan Derksen, Gerritjan Eggenkamp, Diederik Simon, Michiel Bartman, Chun Wei Cheung (Netherlands)	Stefan Szczurowski, Stuart Reside, Stuart Welch, James Stewart, Geoffrey Stewart, Boden Hanson, Mike McKay, Stephen Stewart, Michael Toon (Austria)
2008	Kevin Light, Ben Rutledge, Andrew Byrnes, Jake Wetzel, Malcolm Howard, Dominic Seiterle, Adam Kreek, Kyle Hamilton, Brian Price (Canada)	Alex Partridge, Tom Stallard, Tom Lucy, Richard Egington, Josh West, Alastair Heathcote, Matthew Langridge, Colin Smith, Acer Nethercott (Great Britain)	Beau Hoopman, Matt Schnobrich, Micah Boyd, Wyatt Allen, Daniel Walsh, Steven Coppola, Josh Inman, Bryan Volpenhein, Marcus McElhenney (United States)

Men's Lightweight Double Sculls

Year	Gold	Silver	Bronze
1996	Michael Gier, Markus Gier (Switzerland)	Maarten van der Linden, Pepijn Aardewijn (Netherlands)	Bruce Hick, Anthony Edwards (Australia)
2000	Tomasz Kucharski, Robert Sycz (Poland)	Elia Luini, Leonardo Pettinari (Norway)	Pascal Touron, Thibaud Chapelle (France)
2004	Tomasz Kucharski, Robert Sycz (Poland)	Fréderic Dufour, Pascal Touron (France)	Vasileios Polymeros, Nikolaos Skiathitis (Greece)
2008	Zac Purchase, Mark Hunter (Great Britain)	Dimitrios Mougios, Vasileios Polymeros (Greece)	Mads Reinholdt Rasmussen, Rasmus Nicholai Quist Hansen (Denmark)

Men's Lightweight Coxless Fours

Year	Gold	Silver	Bronze
1996	Victor Feddersen, Niels Henriksen, Thomas Poulsen, Eskild Ebbesen (Denmark)	Brian Peaker, Jeffrey Lay, Dave Boyes, Gavin Hassett (Canada)	Marc Schneider, Jeff Pfaendtner, David Collins, William Carlucci (United States)
2000	Laurent Porchier, Jean-Christophe Bette, Yves Hocdé, Xavier Dorfmann (France)	Simon Burgess, Anthony Edwards, Darren Balmforth, Robert Richards (Australia)	Søren Madsen, Thomas Ebert, Eskild Ebbesen, Victor Feddersen (Denmark)
2004	Thor Kristensen, Thomas Ebert, Stephan Mølvig, Eskild Ebbesen (Denmark)	Glen Loftus, Anthony Edwards, Ben Cureton, Simon Burgess (Australia)	Lorenzo Bertini, Catello Amarante, Salvatore Amitrano, Bruno Mascarenhas (Italy)
2008	Thomas Ebert, Morten Jørgensen, Eskild Ebbesen, Mads Andersen (Denmark)	Łukasz Pawłowski, Bartłomiej Pawełczak, Miłosz Bernatajtys, Paweł Rańda (Poland)	Iain Brambell, Jon Beare, Mike Lewis, Liam Parsons (Canada)

Women's Single Sculls

Year	Gold	Silver	Bronze
1976	Christine Scheiblich (East Germany)	Joan Lind (United States)	Yelena Antonova (Soviet Union)
1980	Sanda Toma (Romania)	Antonina Makhina (Soviet Union)	Martina Schröter (East Germany)
1984	Valeria Răcilă (Romania)	Charlotte Geer (United States)	Ann Haesebrouck (Belgium)
1988	Jutta Behrendt (East Germany)	Anne Marden (United States)	Magdalena Gueorguieva (Bulgaria)
1992	Elisabeta Lipă (Romania)	Annelies Braedael (Belgium)	Silken Laumann (Canada)
1996	Ekaterina Karsten (Belarus)	Silken Laumann (Canada)	Trine Hansen (Denmark)
2000	Ekaterina Karsten (Belarus)	Rumyana Neykova (Bulgaria)	Katrin Rutschow-Stomporowski (Germany)
2004	Katrin Rutschow-Stomporowski (Germany)	Ekaterina Karsten (Belarus)	Rumyana Neykova (Bulgaria)
2008	Rumyana Neykova (Bulgaria)	Michelle Guerette (United States)	Ekaterina Karsten (Belarus)

Women's Double Sculls

Year	Gold	Silver	Bronze
1976	Svetlana Otsetova, Zdravka Yordanova (Bulgaria)	Sabine Jahn, Petra Boesler (East Germany)	Leonora Kaminskaitė, Genovaitė Ramoškienė (Soviet Union)
1980	Yelena Khloptseva, Larisa Popova (Soviet Union)	Cornelia Linse, Heidi Westphal (East Germany)	Olga Homeghi, Valeria Rosca Racila (Romania)
1984	Mariora Popescu, Elisabeta Oleniuc (Romania)	Greet Hellemans, Nicolette Hellemans (Netherlands)	Daniele Laumann, Silken Laumann (Canada)
1988	Birgit Peter, Martina Schröter (East Germany)	Elisabeta Lipă, Veronica Cogeanu (Romania)	Stefka Madina, Violeta Ninova (Bulgaria)
1992	Kerstin Köppen, Kathrin Boron (Germany)	Veronica Cochelea, Elisabeta Lipă (Romania)	Xiaoli Gu, Huali Lu (China)
1996	Kathleen Heddle, Marnie McBean (Canada)	Xiuyun Zhang, Cao Mianying (China)	Irene Eijs, Eeke van Nes (Netherlands)
2000	Jana Thieme, Kathrin Boron (Germany)	Pieta van Dishoeck, Eeke van Nes (Netherlands)	Birutė Šakickienė, Kristina Poplavskaja (Lithuania)
2004	Georgina Evers-Swindell, Caroline Evers-Swindell (New Zealand)	Peggy Waleska, Britta Oppelt (Germany)	Sarah Winckless, Elise Laverick (Great Britain)
2008	Georgina Evers-Swindell, Caroline Evers-Swindell (New Zealand)	Annekatrin Thiele, Christiane Huth (Germany)	Elise Laverick, Anna Bebington (Great Britain)

Women's Quadruple Sculls

Year	Gold	Silver	Bronze
1976	Anke Borchman, Jutta Lau, Viola Poley, Roswietha Zobelt, Liane Weigelt (East Germany)	Anna Kondrachina, Mira Bryunina, Larisa Alexandrova, Galina Ermolaeva, Nadezhda Chernyshova (Soviet Union)	Ioana Tudoran, Maria Micşa, Felicia Afrăsiloaie, Elisabeta Lazăr, Elena Giurcă (Romania)
1980	Sybille Reinhardt, Jutta Ploch, Jutta Lau, Roswietha Zobelt, Liane Buhr (East Germany)	Antonina Pustovit, Yelena Matievskaya, Olga Vasilchenko, Nadezhda Lyubimova, Nina Cheremisina (Soviet Union)	Mariana Serbezova, Roumeliana Bontcheva, Doloress Nakova, Anka Bakova, Anka Gheorghieva (Bulgaria)
1984	Titie Taran, Anisoara Sorohan, Ioana Badea, Sofia Corban, Ecaterina Oancia (Romania)	Anne Marden, Lisa Rohde, Joan Lind, Virginia Gilder, Kelly Rickon (United States)	Hanne Eriksen, Birgitte Hanel, Charlotte Koefoed, Bodil Rasmussen, Jette Sørensen (Denmark)
1988	Kerstin Foerster, Kristina Mundt, Beate Schramm, Jana Sorgers (East Germany)	Irina Kalimbet, Svetlana Maziy, Inna Frolova, Antonina Makhina (Soviet Union)	Anişoara Bălan, Anişoara Minea, Veronica Cogeanu, Elisabeta Lipă (Romania)
1992	Sybille Schmidt, Birgit Peter, Kerstin Müller, Kristina Mundt (Germany)	Anişoara Dobre, Doina Ignat, Constanţa Burcică, Veronica Cochelea (Romania)	Antonina Zelikovich, Tetiana Ustiuzhanina, Ekaterina Karsten, Yelena Khloptseva (Unified Team)
1996	Katrin Rutschow-Stomporowski, Jana Sorgers, Kerstin Köppen, Kathrin Boron (Germany)	Svetlana Maziy, Dina Myftakhutdinova, Inna Frolova, Olena Ronzhyna (Ukraine)	Laryssa Biesenthal, Diane O'Grady, Kathleen Heddle, Marnie McBean (Canada)
2000	Manja Kowalski, Meike Evers, Manuela Lutze, Kerstin Kowalski (Germany)	Guin Batten, Gillian Lindsay, Katherine Grainger, Miriam Batten (Great Britain)	Oksana Dorodnova, Irina Fedotova, Yuliya Levina, Larisa Merk (Russia)
2004	Kathrin Boron, Meike Evers, Manuela Lutze, Kerstin El Qalqili (Germany)	Alison Mowbray, Debbie Flood, Frances Houghton, Rebecca Romero (Great Britain)	Dana Faletic, Rebecca Sattin, Amber Bradley, Kerry Hore (Australia)
2008	Tang Bin, Xi Aihua, Jin Ziwei, Zhang Yangyang (China)	Annie Vernon, Debbie Flood, Frances Houghton, Katherine Grainger (Great Britain)	Britta Oppelt, Manuela Lutze, Kathrin Boron, Stephanie Schiller (Germany)

Women's Coxless Pairs

Year	Gold	Silver	Bronze
1976	Siyka Kelbecheva, Stoyanka Gruycheva (Bulgaria)	Angelika Noack, Sabine Dähne (East Germany)	Edith Eckbauer, Thea Einöder (West Germany)
1980	Ute Steindorf, Cornelia Klier (East Germany)	Malgorzata Dluzewska, Czeslawa Koscianska (Poland)	Siika Barboulova, Stoyanka Kubatova (Bulgaria)
1984	Rodica Arba, Elena Horvat (Romania)	Tricia Smith, Elizabeth Craig (Canada)	Ellen Becker, Iris Völkner (West Germany)
1988	Olga Homeghi, Rodica Arba (Romania)	Radka Stoyanova, Lalka Berberova (Bulgaria)	Nicola Paybe, Lynley Hannen (New Zealand)
1992	Kathleen Heddle, Marnie McBean (Canada)	Ingeburg Schwerzmann, Stefani Werremeier (Germany)	Stephanie Pierson, Anna Seaton (United States)
1996	Megan Leanne Still, Kate Elizabeth Slatter (Australia)	Misst Schwen, Karen Kraft (United States)	Christine Gosse, Helene Cortin (France)
2000	Georgeta Damian, Doina Ignat (Romania)	Rachael Taylor, Kate Slatter (Australia)	Melissa Ryan, Karen Kraft (United States)
2004	Georgeta Damian, Viorica Susanu (Romania)	Katherine Grainger, Cath Bishop (Great Britain)	Yuliya Bichyk, Natallia Helakh (Belarus)
2008	Georgeta Andrunache, Viorica Susanu (Romania)	Wu You, Gao Yulan (China)	Yuliya Bichyk, Natallia Helakh (Belarus)

Women's Coxed Fours

Year	Gold	Silver	Bronze
1976	Karin Metze, Bianka Schwede, Gabriele Lohs, Andrea Kurth, Sabine Heß (East Germany)	Kapka Georgieva, Ginka Gyurova, Mariyka Modeva, Lilyana Vaseva, Reni Yordanova (Bulgaria)	Lyudmila Krokhina, Lidiya Krylova, Galina Mishenina, Anna Pasokha, Nadezhda Sevostyanova (Soviet Union)
1980	Silvia Fröhlich, Ramona Kapheim, Angelika Noack, Romy Saalfeld, Kirsten Wenzel (East Germany)	Nadezhda Filipova, Ginka Gurova, Mariika Modeva, Rita Todorova, Iskra Velinova (Bulgaria)	Nina Cheremisina, Maria Fadeeva, Svetlana Semenova, Galina Sovetnikova, Marina Studneva (Soviet Union)
1984	Chira Apostol, Olga Homeghi-Bularda, Viorica Ioja, Florica Lavric, Maria Fricioiu (Romania)	Barbara Armbrust, Marilyn Brain, Angela Schneider, Lesley Thompson, Jane Tregunno (Canada)	Karen Brancourt, Susan Chapman, Margot Foster, Robin Grey-Gardner, Susan Lee (Australia)
1988	Gerlinde Doberschütz, Carola Hornig, Sylvia Rose, Birte Siech, Martina Walther (East Germany)	Hu Ya-Dong, Li Rong-Hua, Yang Xiao, Zhang Xiang-Hua, Zhou Shouying (China)	Herta Anitas, Doina Snep-Balan, Veronica Necula, Ecaterina Oancia, Marioara Trasca (Romania)

Women's Coxless Fours

Year	Gold	Silver	Bronze
1992	Jennifer Barnes, Jessica Monroe, Brenda Taylor, Kay Worthington (Canada)	Shelagh Donohoe, Cynthia Eckert, Carol Feeney, Amy Fuller (United States)	Antje Frank, Annette Hohn, Gabriele Mehl, Birte Siech (Germany)

Women's Eights

Year	Gold	Silver	Bronze
1976	Brigitte Ahrenholz, Henrietta Ebert, Viola Goretzki, Monika Kallies, Christiane Knetsch, Helma Lehmann, Irina Müller, Ilona Richter, Marina Wilke (East Germany)	Olga Guzenko, Olga Kolkova, Klavdiya Kozenkova, Olga Pugovskaya, Nadezhda Roshchina, Nadezhda Rozgon, Lyubov Talalaeva, Nelli Tarakanova, Elena Zubko (Soviet Union)	Carol Brown, Anita Defrantz, Carolyn Graves, Marion Greig, Margaret McCarthy, Gail Ricketson, Lynn Silliman, Anne Warner, Jacqueline Zoch (United States)
1980	Martina Boesler, Christiane Knetsch, Gabriele Lohs, Karin Metze, Kersten Neisser, Ilona Richter, Marita Sandig, Birgit Schütz, Marina Wilke (East Germany)	Nina Frolova, Mariya Payun, Olga Pivovarova, Nina Preobrazhen-skaya, Nadezhda Prishchepa, Tatyana Stetsenko, Yelena Tereshina, Nina Umanets, Valentina Zhulina (Soviet Union)	Angelica Aposteanu, Elena Bondar, Florica Bucur, Maria Constanti-nescu, Yelena Dobritoiu, Rodica Frintu, Ana Iliuta, Rodica Puscatu-Arba, Marlena Zagoni (Romania)
1984	Betsy Beard, Carol Bower, Jeanne Flanagan, Carie Graves, Kathy Keeler, Harriet Metcalf, Kristine Norelius, Shyril O'Steen, Kristen Thorsness (United States)	Mihaela Armasescu, Doina Balan, Adriana Bazon, Camelia Diaconescu, Viorica Ioja, Aneta Mihaly, Aurora Plesca, Lucia Sauca, Marioara Trasca (Romania)	Lynda Cornet, Marieke van Drogenbroek, Harriet van Ettekoven, Greet Hellemans, Nicolette Hellemans, Martha Laurijsen, Catharina Neelissen, Anne Quist, Wiljon Vaandrager (Netherlands)
1988	Ramona Balthasar, Kathrin Haacker, Anja Kluge, Daniela Neunast, Beatrix Schröer, Uta Stange, Annegret Strauch, Ute Wild, Judith Zeidler (East Germany)	Herta Anitas, Mihaela Armasescu, Doina Balan, Adriana Bazon, Olga Homeghi, Veronica Necula, Ecaterina Oancia, Rodica Puscatu, Marioara Trasca (Romania)	Han Yaqin, He Yanwen, Hu Ya-Dong, Li Rong-Hua, Yang Xiao, Zhang Xiang-Hua, Zhang Yali, Zhou Shouying, Zhou Xiuhua (China)

Year	Gold	Silver	Bronze
1992	Jennifer Barnes, Shannon Crawford, Megan Delehanty, Kathleen Heddle, Marnie McBean, Jessica Monroe, Brenda Taylor, Lesley Thompson, Kay Worthington (Canada)	Adriana Bazon, Iulia Bulie, Elena Georgescu, Viorica Lepădatu, Veronica Necula, Ioana Olteanu, Maria Padurariu, Doina Robu, Doina Snep (Romania)	Sylvia Dördelmann, Kathrin Haacker, Christiane Harzendorf, Daniela Neunast, Cerstin Petersmann, Dana Pyritz, Ute Schell, Annegret Strauch, Judith Zeidler (Germany)
1996	Veronica Cochela, Liliana Gafencu, Elena Georgescu, Doina Ignat, Elisabeta Lipă, Ioana Olteanu, Marioara Popescu, Doina Spircu, Anca Tanase (Romania)	Alison Korn, Theresa Luke, Maria Maunder, Heather McDermid, Jessica Monroe, Emma Robinson, Lesley Thompson, Tosha Tsang, Anna van der Kamp (Canada)	Tamara Davydenko, Natalya Lavrinenko, Yelena Mikulich, Aleksandra Pankina, Yaroslava Pavlovich, Valentina Skrabatun, Natalia Stasyuk, Natalya Volchek, Marina Znak (Belarus)
2000	Veronica Cochela, Georgeta Damian, Maria Magdalena Dumitrache, Liliana Gafencu, Elena Georgescu, Doina Ignat, Elisabeta Lipă, Ioana Olteanu, Viorica Susanu (Romania)	Tessa Appeldoorn, Carin ter Beek, Pieta van Dishoeck, Elien Meijer, Eeke van Nes, Nelleke Penninx, Martijntje Quik, Anneke Venema, Marieke Westerhof (Netherlands)	Buffy Alexander, Laryssa Biesenthal, Heather Davis, Alison Korn, Theresa Luke, Heather McDermid, Emma Robinson, Lesley Thompson, Dorota Urbaniak (Canada)
2004	Aurica Barascu, Georgeta Damian, Rodica Florea, Liliana Gafencu, Elena Georgescu, Doina Ignat, Elisabeta Lipă, Ioana Papuc, Viorica Susanu (Romania)	Alison Cox, Caryn Davies, Megan Dirkmaat, Kate Johnson, Laurel Korholz, Samantha Magee, Anna Mickelson, Lianne Nelson, Mary Whipple (United States)	Annemiek de Haan, Hurnet Dekkers, Nienke Hommes, Annemarieke van Rumpt, Sarah Siegelaar, Marlies Smulders, Helen Tanger, Froukje Wegman, Ester Workel (Netherlands)
2008	Erin Cafaro, Lindsay Shoop, Anna Goodale, Elle Logan, Anna Cummins, Susan Francia, Caroline Lind, Caryn Davies, Mary Whipple (United States)	Femke Dekker, Marlies Smulders, Nienke Kingma, Roline Repelaer van Driel, Annemarieke van Rumpt, Helen Tanger, Sarah Siegelaar, Annemiek de Haan, Ester Workel (Netherlands)	Constanţa Burcică, Viorica Susanu, Rodica Şerban, Enikő Barabás, Simona Muşat, Ioana Papuc, Georgeta Andrunache, Doina Ignat, Elena Georgescu (Romania)

Women's Lightweight Double Sculls

Year	Gold	Silver	Bronze
1996	Camelia Macoviciuc, Constanţa Burcică (Romania)	Teresa Z. Bell, Lindsay Burns (United States)	Virginia Lee, Rebecca Joyce (Australia)
2000	Constanţa Burcică, Angela Alupei (Romania)	Valerie Viehoff, Claudia Blasberg (Germany)	Christine Collins, Sarah Garner (United States)
2004	Constanţa Burcică, Angela Alupei (Romania)	Daniela Reimer, Claudia Blasberg (Germany)	Kirsten van der Kolk, Marit van Eupen (Netherlands)
2008	Kirsten van der Kolk, Marit van Eupen (Netherlands)	Sanna Stén, Minna Nieminen (Finland)	Melanie Kok, Tracy Cameron (Canada)

Rugby

Men's Rugby

Year	Gold	Silver	Bronze
1900	Alexandre Pharamond, Frantz Reichel, Jean Collas, Constantin Henriquez de Zubiera, Auguste Giroux, André Rischmann, Léon Binoche, Charles Gondouin, Albert Roosevelt, Hubert Lefèbvre, Emile Sarrade, Wladimir Aïtoff, Joseph Olivier, Jean-Guy Gauthier, A. Albert, Victor Larchandet, Jean Hervé (France)	Hermann Kreuzer, Arnold Landvoigt, Heinrich Reitz, Jacob Herrmann, Erich Ludwig, Hugo Betting, August Schmierer, Fritz Muller, Adolf Stockhausen, Hans Latscha, Willy Hofmeister, Georg Wenderoth, Eduard Poppe, Richard Ludwig, Albert Amrhein (Germany)	Not awarded
		F. C. Bayliss, J. Henry Birtles, James Cantion, Arthur Darby, Clement Deykin, L. Hood, M. L. Logan, H. A. Loveitt, Herbert Nicol, V. Smith, M. W. Talbot, Joseph Wallis, Claude Whittindale, Raymond Whittindale, Francis Wilson (Great Britain)	
1904: Event not held			
1908	Phil Carmichael, Charles Russell, Daniel Carroll, Jack Hickey, Frank Smith, Chris McKivat, Arthur McCabe, Thomas Griffen, John Barnett, Patrick McCue, Sydney Middleton, Tom Richards, Malcolm McArthur, Charles McMurtrie, Robert Craig (Australia)	Edward Jackett, Barney Solomon, Bert Solomon, L. F. Dean, J. T. Jose, Thomas Wedge, James Davey, Richard Jackett, E. J. Jones, Arthur Wilson, Nicholas Tregurtha, A. Lawrey, C. R. Marshall, A. Willcocks, John Trevaskis (Great Britain)	Not awarded
1912: Event not held			
1916: Olympics not held			
1920	Daniel Carroll, Charles Doe, George Fish, James Fitzpatrick, Joseph Hunter, Morris Kirksey, Charles Mehan, John Muldoon, John O'Neil, John Patrick, Cornelius Righter, Colby Slater, Rudolph Scholz, Robert L. Templeton, Charles Lee Tilden Jr., James Winston, Heaton Wrenn (United States)	Alfred Eluère, Jean Bruneval, André Chilo, Grenet, François Borde, René Crabos, Edouard Bader, Raoul Thiercelin, Adolphe Bousquet, Curtet, Jacques Forestier, Raymond Berrurier, Eugène Soulie, Maurice Labeyrie, Robert Levasseur, Constant Lamaigniere, Pierre Petiteau, Robert Thierry (France)	Not awarded
1924	Philip Clark, Norman Cleaveland, Hugh Cunningham, Dudley DeGroot, Robert Devereux, George Dixon, Charles Doe, Linn Farrish, Edward Graff, Joseph Hunter, Richard Hyland, Caesar Mannelli, Charles Mehan, John Muldoon, John O'Neil, John Patrick, William Rogers, Rudolph Scholz, Colby Slater, Norman Slater, Charles Lee Tilden Jr., Edward Turkington, Alan Valentine, Alan Williams (United States)	René Araou, Jean Bayard, Louis Beguet, André Béhotéguy, Alexandre Bioussa, Etienne Bonnes, François Borde, Adolphe Bousquet, Aimé Cassayet-Armagnac, Clément Dupont, Albert Dupouy, Jean Etcheberry, Henri Galau, Gilbert Gérintès, Raoul Got, Adolphe Jaureguy, René Lasserre, Marcel-Frédéric Lubin-Lebrère, Etienne Piquiral, Jean Vaysse (France)	Dumitru Armasel, Gheorghe Bentia, Theodor Florian, Ion Girlisteanu, Nicolae Marasco, Theodor Marian, Sorin Michailesco, Paul Nedelcovici, Iosif Nemesch, Eugen Sfetescu, Mircea Sfetescu, Soare Sterian, Anastasie Tanasescu, Mihail Vardala, Paul Vidrashcu, Dumitru Volvoreanu (Romania)

Year	Gold	Silver	Bronze
1928–1932: Event not held			
1936*	Maurice Savy, Pierre Geschwind, Jean Coderc, Joseph Desclaux, Maurice Celhay, Georges Libaros, Pierre Thiers, Francis Daguerre, Andre Rochon, Marcel Laurent, Andre Goyard, Etienne Ithurra, Lucien Cognet, Francois Raynal, Louis Dupont (France)	Germany**	Riccardo Centinari, Aurelio Cazzini, Giulio Rizzoli, Francesco Vinci III, Renzo Maffioli, Giuseppe Piana, Mario Campagna, Tommaso Fattori, Sandro Bonfante, Guglielmo Zoffoli, Angelo Albonico, Vincenzo Bertolotto, Giuseppe Visentin, Ivan Aloisio, Arturo re Garbagnati (Italy)

* The 1936 rugby union tournament was held in Berlin prior to that year's Summer Olympics and was informally associated with them but was not an official demonstration sport or sanctioned Olympic event.

** The roster for the 1936 German rugby union team was unavailable to our researchers at the time of this printing.

Sailing

Mixed .5–1-Ton

Year	Gold	Silver	Bronze
1900	John H. Gretton, Linton Hope, Lorne Campbell (Great Britain)	Jacques Baudrier, Jean Lebret, Marcotte*, Valton*, William Martin (France)	E. Michelet*, F. Michelet*, France

* Full name not known.

Mixed .5-Ton

Year	Gold	Silver	Bronze
1900	Pierre Gervais (France)	Texier*, Texier*, Jean Charcot, Robert Linzeler (France)	Henri Monnot (France)

* Full name not known.

Mixed 10–20-Ton

Year	Gold	Silver	Bronze
1900	Emile Billard, P. Perquer* (France)	Jean Le Duc Decazes (France)	Edward Hore (Great Britain)

* Full name not known.

Mixed 10-Meter

Year	Gold	Silver	Bronze
1912	Filip Ericsson, Carl Hellström, Paul Isberg, Humbert Lundén, Herman Nyberg, Harry Rosenswärd, Erik Wallerius, Harald Wallin (Sweden)	Waldemar Björkstén, Jacob Björnström, Bror Brenner, Allan Franck, Emil Lindh, Adolf Pekkalainen, Harry Wahl (Finland)	Ester Beloselsky, Ernest Brasche, Karl Lindblom, Nikolaï Puschnitsky, Aleksandr Rodionov, Iossif Schomaker, Philip Strauch (Russia)
1916: Olympics not held			
1920	Charles Arentz, Willy Gilbert, Robert Giertsen, Arne Sejersted, Halfdan Schjött, Trygve Schjøtt, Otto Falkenberg (Norway)* Erik Herseth, Sigurd Holter, Ingar Nielsen, Ole Sørensen, Petter Jamvold, Gunnar Jamvold, Claus Juell (Norway)**	Not awarded	Not awarded

* According to 1919 rules.

** According to 1907 rules.

Mixed 12-Foot Dinghy

Year	Gold	Silver	Bronze
1920	Johan Hin, Cornelis Hin, Frans Hin (Netherlands)	Arnoud van der Biesen, Petrus Beukers (Netherlands)	Not awarded

Mixed Individual 12-Foot Dinghy

Year	Gold	Silver	Bronze
1928	Sven Thorell (Sweden)	Henrik Robert (Norway)	B. Broman* (Finland)

* Full name not known.

Mixed 12-Meter

Year	Gold	Silver	Bronze
1908	Thomas Glen-Coats, John Downes, John Buchanan, James Bunten, Arthur Downes, David Dunlop, John Mackenzie, Albert Martin, Gerald Tait, John Aspin (Great Britain)	Charles MacIver, James Kenion, James Baxter, William Davidson, John Jellico, Thomas Littledale, Charles MacLeod-Robertson, John Spence, John Adam, Cecil MacIver (Great Britain)	Not awarded
1912	Johan Anker, Nils Bertelsen, Eilert Falch-Lund, Halfdan Hansen, Arnfinn Heje, Magnus Konow, Alfred Larsen, Petter Larsen, Christian Staib, Carl Thaulow (Norway)	Per Bergman, Dick Bergström, Kurt Bergström, Hugo Clason, Folke Johnson, Sigurd Kander, Nils Lamby, Erik Lindqvist, Nils Persson, Richard Sällström (Sweden)	Max Alfthan, Erik Hartvall, Jarl Hulldén, Sigurd Juslén, Ernst Krogius, Eino Sandelin, Johan Silén (Finland)
1916: Olympics not held			
1920	Johan Friele, Olav Örvig, Arthur Allers, Christen Wiese, Martin Borthen, Egill Reimers, Kaspar Hassel, Thor Ørvig, Erik Ørvig (Norway)* Henrik Østervold, Jan Østervold, Ole Østervold, Hans Naess, Halvor Mögster, Halvor Birkeland, Rasmus Birkeland, Kristian Østervold, Lauritz Christiansen (Norway)*	Not awarded	Not awarded

* According to 1919 rules.
** According to 1907 rules.

Mixed 18-Foot Dinghy

Year	Gold	Silver	Bronze
1920	Francis Richards, Thomas Hedberg (Great Britain)	Not awarded	Not awarded

Mixed 2–3-Ton

Year	Gold	Silver	Bronze
1900	William Exshaw (Great Britain), Frédéric Blanchy, Jacques Le Lavasseur (France)	Susse*, Doucet*, Godinet*, Mialaret* (France)	Auguste Donny (France)

* Full name not known.

Mixed 30-Square Meter

Year	Gold	Silver	Bronze
1920	Tore Holm, Yngve Holm, Axel Rydin, Georg Tengwall (Sweden)	Not awarded	Not awarded

Mixed 3–10-Ton

Year	Gold	Silver	Bronze
1900	Howard Taylor, Edward Hore, H. N. Jefferson (Great Britain)	Maurice Gufflet, A. Dubos*, J. Dubos*, Robert Gufflet, Charly Guiraist (France)	M. MacHenry* (United States)

* Full name not known.

Mixed 40-Square Meter

Year	Gold	Silver	Bronze
1920	Gösta Lundqvist, Rolf Steffenburg, Gösta Bengtsson, Axel Calvert (Sweden)	Gustaf Svensson, Ragnar Svensson, Percy Almstedt, Erik Mellbin (Sweden)	Not awarded

Men's 470 Two-Person Dinghy

Year	Gold	Silver	Bronze
1988	Thierry Peponnet, Luc Pillot (France)	Tõnu Tõniste, Toomas Tõniste (Soviet Union)	John Shadden, Charles McKee (United States)
1992	Jordi Calafat, Francisco Sanchez (Spain)	Morgan Reeser, Kevin Burnham (United States)	Tõnu Tõniste, Toomas Tõniste (Estonia)
1996	Yevhen Braslavets, Ihor Matviyenko (Ukraine)	John Merricks, Ian Walker (Great Britain)	Victor Rocha, Nuno Barreto (Portugal)
2000	Tom King, Mark Turnbull (Australia)	Paul Foerster, Robert Merrick (United States)	Juan de la Fuente, Javier Conte (Argentina)
2004	Paul Foerster, Kevin Burnham (United States)	Nick Rogers, Joe Glanfield (Great Britain)	Kazuto Seki, Kenjiro Todoroki (Japan)
2008	Nathan Wilmot, Malcolm Page (Australia)	Nick Rogers, Joe Glanfield (Great Britain)	Nicolas Charbonnier, Olivier Bausset (France)

Women's 470 Two-Person Dinghy

Year	Gold	Silver	Bronze
1988	Allison Jolly, Lynne Jewell (United States)	Marit Söderström, Birgitta Bengtsson (Sweden)	Larisa Moskalenko, Irina Shunikhovskaya (Soviet Union)
1992	Theresa Zabell, Patricia Guerra (Spain)	Leslie Egnot, Jan Shearer (New Zealand)	J. J. Isler, Pamela Healy (United States)
1996	Begona Via Dufresne, Theresa Zabell (Spain)	Yumiko Shige, Yurie Alicia Kinoshita (Japan)	Olena Pakholchik, Ruslana Taran (Ukraine)
2000	Jenny Armstrong, Belinda Stowell (Australia)	J. J. Isler, Sarah Glaser (United States)	Ruslana Taran, Olena Pakholchyk (Ukraine)
2004	Sofia Bekatorou, Aimilia Tsoulfa (Greece)	Natalia Vía Dufresne, Sandra Azón (Spain)	Therese Torgersson, Vendela Zachrisson (Sweden)
2008	Elise Rechichi, Tessa Parkinson (Australia)	Marcelien de Koning, Lobke Berkhout (Netherlands)	Fernanda Oliveira, Isabel Swan (Brazil)

Mixed 49er Skiff

Year	Gold	Silver	Bronze
2000	Jyrki Jarvi, Thomas Johanson (Finland)	Ian Barker, Simon Hiscocks (Great Britain)	Charles McKee, Jonathan Dunn McKee (United States)
2004	Iker Martinez de Lizarduy, Xabier Fernández (Spain)	Georgii Leonchuk, Rodion Luka (Ukraine)	Chris Draper, Simon Hiscocks (Great Britain)
2008	Jonas Warrer, Martin Kirketerp Ibsen (Denmark)	Iker Martinez de Lizarduy, Xabier Fernández (Spain)	Hannes Peckolt, Jan Peter Peckolt (Germany)

Mixed 5.5-Meter

Year	Gold	Silver	Bronze
1952	Britton Chance, Sumner White, Edgar White, Michael Schoettle (United States)	Peder Lunde, Vibeke Lunde, Børre Falkum-Hansen (Norway)	Folke Wassén, Carl-Erik Ohlson, Magnus Wassén (Sweden)
1956	Lars Thörn, Hjalmar Karlsson, Sture Stork (Sweden)	Robert Perry, Neil Kennedy-Cochran-Patrick, John Dillon, David Bowker (Great Britain)	Jock Sturrock, Devereaux Mytton, Douglas Buxton (Australia)
1960	George O'Day, James Hunt, David Smith (United States)	William Berntsen, Sören Hancke, Steen Christensen (Denmark)	Henri Copponex, Manfred Metzger, Pierre Girard (Switzerland)
1964	William Northam, Peter O'Donnell, James Sargeant (Australia)	Lars Thörn, Sture Stork, Arne Karlsson (Sweden)	John J. McNamara, Francis Scully, Joseph Batchelder (United States)
1968	Ulf Sundelin, Jörgen Sundelin, Peter Sundelin (Sweden)	Louis Noverraz, Bernhard Dunand, Marcel Stern (Switzerland)	Robin Aisher, Adrian Jardine, Paul Anderson (Great Britain)

Mixed 6.5-Meter

Year	Gold	Silver	Bronze
1920	Johan Carp, Petrus Wernink, Bernard Carp (Netherlands)	Albert Weil, Félix Picon, Robert Monier (France)	Not awarded

Mixed 6-Meter

Year	Gold	Silver	Bronze
1908	Thomas McMeekin, Gilbert Laws, Charles Crichton (Great Britain)	Léon Huybrechts, Louis Huy-brechts, Henri Weewauters (Belgium)	Henri Arthus, Louis Potheau, Pierre Rabot (France)
1912	Amédée Thubé, Gaston Thubé, Jacques Thubé (France)	Steen Herschend, Hans Meulen-gracht-Madsen, Sven Thomsen (Denmark)	Otto Aust, Eric Sandberg, Harald Sandberg (Sweden)
1916: Olympics not held			
1920	Andreas Brecke, Paal Kaasen, Ingolf Rød (Norway)* Emile Cornellie, Florimond Cornellie, Frédéric Bruynseels (Belgium)**	Léon Huybrechts, Charles van den Bussche, John Klotz (Belgium)* Einar Torgensen, Andreas Knudsen, Leif Erichsen (Norway)**	Henrik Agersborg, Trygve Pedersen, Einar Berntsen (Norway)**
1924	Eugen Lunde, Christopher Dahl, Anders Lundgren (Norway)	Knud Degn, Christian Nielsen, Vilhelm Vett (Denmark)	Johan Carp, Anthonij Guépin, Jan Vreede (Netherlands)
1928	Crown Prince Olav (later King Olav V), Johan Anker, Erik Anker, Håkon Bryhn (Norway)	Vilhelm Vett, Nils Otto Møller, Aage Høy-Petersen, Peter Schlütter, Sven Linck (Denmark)	Nikolai Vekšin, William von Wirén, Eberhard Vogdt, Georg Faehlmann, Andreas Faehlmann (Estonia)
1932	Tore Holm, Martin Hindorff, Olle Åkerlund, Åke Bergqvist (Sweden)	Robert Carlson, Temple Ashbrook, Frederic Conant, Charles Smith, Donald Douglas, Emmett Davis (United States)	Philip Rogers, Gerald Wilson, Gardner Boultbee, Kenneth Glass (Canada)

Year	Gold	Silver	Bronze
1936	Christopher Boardman, Miles Bellville, Russell Harmer, Charles Leaf, Leonard Martin (Great Britain)	Magnus Konow, Karsten Konow, Fredrik Meyer, Vaadjuv Nyqvist, Alf Tveten (Norway)	Sven Salén, Lennart Ekdahl, Martin Hindorff, Torsten Lord, Dagmar Salén (Sweden)
1940–1944: Olympics not held			
1948	Herman Whiton, Alfred Loomis, James Weekes, James Smith, Michael Mooney (United States)	Enrique Sieburger Sr., Enrique Sieburger Jr., Emilio Homps, Rufino Rodriguez de la Torre, Rodolfo Rivademar, Julio Sieburger (Argentina)	Tore Holm, Torsten Lord, Martin Hindorff, Carl Robert Ameln, Gösta Salén (Sweden)
1952	Herman Whiton, Eric Ridder, Julian Roosevelt, John Morgan, Everard Endt, Emelyn Whiton (United States)	Finn Ferner, Johan Ferner, Erik Heiberg, Carl Mortensen, Tor Arneberg (Norway)	Ernst Westerlund, Paul Sjöberg, Ragnar Jansson, Jonas Konto, Rolf Turkka (Finland)

* According to 1919 rules.

** According to 1907 rules.

Mixed 7-Meter

Year	Gold	Silver	Bronze
1908	Charles Rivett-Carnac, Frances Rivett-Carnac, Norman Bingley, Richard Dixon (Great Britain)	Not awarded	Not awarded
1912: Event not held			
1916: Olympics not held			
1920	William Maddison, Dorothy Wright, Robert Coleman, Cyril Wright (Great Britain)	Johann Faye, Christian Dick, Sten Abel, Neils Neilsen (Norway)	Not awarded

Mixed 8-Meter

Year	Gold	Silver	Bronze
1908	Blair Cochrane, Arthur Wood, Henry Sutton, John Rhodes, Charles Campbell (Great Britain)	Carl Hellström, Edmund Thormählen, Erik Wallerius, Eric Sandberg, Harald Wallin (Sweden)	Philip Hunloke, Alfred Hughes, Frederick Hughes, George Ratsey, William Ward (Great Britain)
1912	Thomas Aas, Andreas Brecke, Torleiv Corneliussen, Thoralf Glad, Christian Jebe (Norway)	Emil Henriques, Bengt Heyman, Alvar Thiel, Herbert Westermark, Nils Westermark (Sweden)	Arthur Ahnger, Erik Lindh, Bertil Tallberg, Gunnar Tallberg, Georg Westling (Finland)
1916: Olympics not held			
1920	Magnus Konow, Reidar Marthiniussen, Ragnar Vik, Thorleif Christoffersen (Norway)* Carl Ringvold, Thorleif Holbye, Tellef Wagle, Kristoffer Olsen, Alf Jacobsen (Norway)**	Jens Salvesen, Lauritz Schmidt, Finn Schiander, Nils Thomas, Ralph Tschudi (Norway)*	Albert Grisar, Willy de l'Arbre, Léopold Standaert, Henri Weewauters, Georges Hellebuyck (Belgium)*
1924	Rick Bockelie, Harald Hagen, Ingar Nielsen, Carl Ringvold, Carl Ringvold Jr. (Norway)	Edwin Jacob, Thomas Riggs, Walter Riggs, Ernest Roney, Harold Fowler (Great Britain)	Louis Breguet, Pierre Gauthier, Robert Girardet, André Guerrier, Georges Mollard (France)
1928	Donatien Bouché, Carl de la Sablière, André Derrien, Virginie Hériot, André Lesauvage, Jean Lesieur (France)	Gerard de Vries Lentsch, Maarten de Wit, Lambertus Doedes, Hendrik Kersken, Johannes van Hoolwerff, Cornelis van Staveren (Netherlands)	Clarence Hammar, Tore Holm, Carl Sandblom, John Sandblom, Philip Sandblom, Wilhelm Törsleff (Sweden)

Year	Gold	Silver	Bronze
1932	John Biby, William Cooper, Carl Dorsey, Owen Churchill, Robert Sutton, Pierpont Davis, Alan Morgan, Alphonse Burnand, Thomas Webster, John Huettner, Richard Moore, Kenneth Carey (United States)	Ernest Cribb, Harry Jones, Peter Gordon, Hubert Wallace, Ronald Maitland, George Gyles (Canada)	Not awarded
1936	Giovanni Reggio, Bruno Bianchi, Luigi De Manincor, Domenico Mordini, Luigi Poggi, Enrico Poggi (Italy)	Olaf Ditlev-Simonsen, Hans Struksnæs, Lauritz Schmidt, Nordahl Wallem, Jacob Thams, John Ditlev-Simonsen (Norway)	Hans Howaldt, Alfried Krupp von Bohlen und Halbach, Felix Scheder-Bieschin, Eduard Mohr, Otto Wachs, Fritz Bischoff (Germany)

* According to 1919 rules.

** According to 1907 rules.

Men's Board (Division II)

Year	Gold	Silver	Bronze
1988	Anthony Kendall (New Zealand)	Jan Boersma (Netherlands Antilles)	Michael Gebhardt (United States)

Men's Board (Lechner)

Year	Gold	Silver	Bronze
1992	Franck David (France)	Lars Kleppich (Australia)	Mike Gebhardt (United States)

Women's Board (Mistral)

Year	Gold	Silver	Bronze
1984	Karen Morch (Canada)	Anne Gardnew-Nelson (United States)	Andrea Livingston (United States)
1988–1992: Event not held			
1996	Lai Shan Lee (Hong Kong, China)	Barbara Kendall (New Zealand)	Alessandra Sensini (Italy)
2000	Alessandra Sensini (Italy)	Amelie Lux (Germany)	Barbara Kendall (New Zealand)
2004	Faustine Merret (France)	Jian Yin (China)	Alessandra Sensini (Italy)

Men's Board (Windglider)

Year	Gold	Silver	Bronze
1984	Stephan Van Den Berg (Netherlands)	Randal Scott Steele (United States)	Anthony Bruce Kendall (New Zealand)

Mixed Dragon

Year	Gold	Silver	Bronze
1948	Thor Thorvaldsen, Sigve Lie, Haakon Barfod (Norway)	Folke Bohlin, Hugo Johnson, Gösta Brodin (Sweden)	William Berntsen, Ole Berntsen, Klaus Baess (Denmark)
1952	Sigve Lie, Haakon Barfod, Thor Thorvaldsen (Norway)	Per Gedda, Sidney Boldt-Christmas, Erland Almqvist (Sweden)	Theodor Thomsen, Erich Natusch, Georg Nowka (Germany)
1956	Folke Bohlin, Bengt Palmquist, Leif Wikström (Sweden)	Ole Berntsen, Cyril Andresen, Christian von Bülow (Denmark)	Graham Mann, Ronald Backus, Jonathan Janson (Great Britain)
1960	Crown Prince Constantine (later King Constantine II), Odysseus Eskidioglou, Georgios Zaimis (Greece)	Jorge Salas, Héctor Calegaris, Jorge Del Rio (Argentina)	Antonio Cosentino, Antonio Ciciliano, Giulio De Stefano (Italy)
1964	Ole Berntsen, Christian von Bülow, Ole Poulsen (Denmark)	Peter Ahrendt, Ulrich Mense, Wilfred Lorenz (United Team of Germany)	Lowell North, Charles Rogers, Richard Deaver (United States)

Year	Gold	Silver	Bronze
1968	George Friedrichs, Barton Jahncke, Gerald Schreck (United States)	Aage Birch, Poul Richard Høj Jensen, Niels Markussen (Denmark)	Paul Borowski, Karl-Heinz Thun, Konrad Weichert (East Germany)
1972	John Cuneo, Thomas Anderson, John Shaw (Australia)	Paul Borowski, Konrad Weichert, Karl-Heinz Thun (East Germany)	Donald Cohan, Charles Horter, John Marshall (United States)

Mixed Finn Heavyweight Dinghy

Year	Gold	Silver	Bronze
2008	Ben Ainslie (Great Britain)	Guillaume Florent (France)	Zach Railey (United States)

Mixed Firefly Class

Year	Gold	Silver	Bronze
1948	Paul Elvstrom (Denmark)	Ralph Evans (United States)	Jacobus De Jong (Netherlands)

Mixed Fleet (Soling)

Year	Gold	Silver	Bronze
1972	Harry Melges, William Bentsen, William Allen (United States)	Stig Wennerströ, Bo Knape, Stefan Krook (Sweden)	David Miller, John Ekels, Paul Cote (Canada)
1976	Poul Richard Høj Jensen, Valdemar Bandolowski, Erik Hansen (Denmark)	John Kolius, Walter Glasgow, Richard Hoepfner (United States)	Dieter Below, Michael Zachries, Olaf Engelhardt (East Germany)
1980	Valdemar Bandolowski, Erik Hansen, Poul Richard Høj Jensen (Denmark)	Alexandr Budnikov, Boris Budnikov, Nikolay Poliakov (Soviet Union)	Tasos Boudouris, Tasos Gavrilis, Aristidis Rapanakis (Greece)
1984	Robbie Haines, Ed Trevalyan, Rod Davis (United States)	Torben Grael, Daniel Adler, Ronaldo Senfft (Brazil)	Hans Fogh, John Kerr, Stephen Calder (Canada)
1988	Jochen Schümann, Thomas Flach, Bernd Jäkel (East Germany)	John Kostecki, William Baylis, Robert Billingham (United States)	Jesper Bank, Jan Mathiasen, Steen Secher (Denmark)
1992	Jesper Bank, Steen Secher, Jesper Seier (Denmark)	Kevin Mahaney, James Brady, Douglas Kern (United States)	Lawrie Smith, Robert Cruikshank, Ossie Stewart (Great Britain)
1996	Thomas Flach, Bernd Jäkel, Jochen Schümann (Germany)	Georgi Shayduko, Igor Skalin, Dmitri Shabanov (Russia)	Jim Barton, Jeff Madrigali, Kent Massey (United States)
2000	Jesper Bank, Henrik Blakskjær, Thomas Jacobsen (Denmark)	Jochen Schümann, Gunnar Bahr, Ingo Borkowski (Germany)	Paul Davis, Herman Johannessen, Espen Stokkeland (Norway)

Mixed Fleet (Yngling)

Year	Gold	Silver	Bronze
2004	Sarah Ayton, Shirley Robertson, Sarah Webb (Great Britain)	Ganna Kalinina, Svitlana Matevusheva, Ruslana Taran (Ukraine)	Dorte Jensen, Helle Jespersen, Christina Otzen (Denmark)
2008	Sarah Ayton, Sarah Webb, Pippa Wilson (Great Britain)	Mandy Mulder, Annemieke Bes, Merel Witteveen (Netherlands)	Sofia Bekatorou, Sofia Papadopoulou, Virginia Kravarioti (Greece)

Mixed Flying Dutchman

Year	Gold	Silver	Bronze
1960	Peder Lunde Jr., Bjørn Bergvall (Norway)	Hans Fogh, Ole Erik Petersen (Denmark)	Rolf Mulka, Ingo Von Bredow (Germany)
1964	Earle Wells, Helmer Pedersen (New Zealand)	Keith Musto, Tony Morgan (Great Britain)	Harry Melges, William Bentsen (United States)
1968	Rodney Pattisson, Iain MacDonald-Smith (Great Britain)	Ullrich Libor, Peter Naumann (West Germany)	Reinaldo Conrad, Burkhard Cordes (Brazil)

Year	Gold	Silver	Bronze
1972	Rodney Pattisson, Christopher Davies (Great Britain)	Yves Pajot, Marc Pajot (France)	Ullrich Libor, Peter Naumann (West Germany)
1976	Jörg Diesch, Eckart Diesch (West Germany)	Rodney Pattisson, Julian Brooke-Houghton (Great Britain)	Reinaldo Conrad, Peter Ficker (Brazil)
1980	Alejandro Abascal Garcia, Miguel Noguer Castellvi (Spain)	David Wilkins, James Wilkinson (Ireland)	Szabólcs Detre, Zsolt Detre (Hungary)
1984	Jonathan McKee, Carl Buchan (United States)	Terry McLaughlin, Evert Bastet (Canada)	Jonathan Richards, Peter Allam (Great Britain)
1988	Jørgen Bojsen-Møller, Christian Grønborg (Denmark)	Ole Pollen, Erik Björkum (Norway)	Frank McLaughlin, John Millen (Canada)
1992	Luis Doreste, Domingo Manrique (Spain)	Stephen Bourdow, Paul Foerster (United States)	Jens Bojsen-Møller, Jørgen Bojsen-Møller (Denmark)

Men's Laser One-Person Dinghy

Year	Gold	Silver	Bronze
1996	Robert Scheidt (Brazil)	Ben Ainslie (Great Britain)	Peer Moberg (Norway)
2000	Ben Ainslie (Great Britain)	Robert Scheidt (Brazil)	Michael Blackburn (Australia)
2004	Robert Scheidt (Brazil)	Andreas Geritzer (Austria)	Vasilij Žbogar (Slovenia)
2008	Paul Goodison (Great Britain)	Vasilij Žbogar (Slovenia)	Diego Romero (Italy)

Women's Laser Radial One-Person Dinghy

Year	Gold	Silver	Bronze
2008	Anna Tunnicliffe (United States)	Gintarė Volungevičiūtė (Lithuania)	Xu Lijia (China)

Mixed Olympic Class Monotype

Year	Gold	Silver	Bronze
1924	Léon Huybrechts (Belgium)	Henrik Robert (Norway)	Hans Erik Dittmar (Finland)
1932	Jacques Lebrun (France)	Adriaan Maas (Netherlands)	Santiago Cansino (Spain)
1936	Daniel Kagchelland (Netherlands)	Werner Krogmann (Germany)	Peter Scott (Great Britain)

Mixed Open Class

Year	Gold	Silver	Bronze
1900	Lorne Campbell Currie, John H. Gretton, Linton Hope, Algernon Maudslay (Great Britain)	Paul Wiesner, George Naue, Heinrich Peters, Ottokar Weise (Germany)	E. Michelet*, F. Michelet* (France)

* Full name not known.

Men's RS:X Windsurfer

Year	Gold	Silver	Bronze
2008	Tom Ashley (New Zealand)	Julien Bontemps (France)	Shahar Zubari (Israel)

Women's RS:X Windsurfer

Year	Gold	Silver	Bronze
2008	Jian Yin (China)	Alessandra Sensini (Italy)	Bryony Shaw (Great Britain)

Mixed Sharpie 12-Meter

Year	Gold	Silver	Bronze
1956	Peter Mander, Jack Cropp (New Zealand)	Rolland Tasker, John Scott (Australia)	Jasper Blackall, Terence Smith (Great Britain)

Women's Single-handed Dinghy

Year	Gold	Silver	Bronze
1992	Linda Andersen (Norway)	Natalia Via Dufresne (Spain)	Julia Trotman (United States)
1996	Kristine Roug (Denmark)	Margriet Matthijsse (Netherlands)	Courtenay Becker-Dey (United States)
2000	Shirley Robertson (Great Britain)	Margriet Matthijsse (Netherlands)	Serena Amato (Argentina)
2004	Siren Sunby (Norway)	Lenka Smidova (Czech Republic)	Signe Livbjerg (Denmark)

Men's Single-handed Dinghy (Finn)

Year	Gold	Silver	Bronze
1952	Paul Bert Elvstrøm (Denmark)	Charles Currey (Great Britain)	Richard Sarby (Sweden)
1956	Paul Bert Elvstrøm (Denmark)	André Nelis (Belgium)	John Marvin (United States)
1960	Paul Bert Elvstrøm (Denmark)	Aleksandr Tsutselov (Soviet Union)	André Nelis (Belgium)
1964	Wilhelm Kuhweide (Germany)	Peter Barrett (United States)	Henning Wind (Denmark)
1968	Valentin Mankin (Soviet Union)	Hubert Raudaschl (Austria)	Fabio Albarelli (Italy)
1972	Serge Maury (France)	Ilias Hatzipavlis (Greece)	Viktor Potapov (Soviet Union)
1976	Jochen Schümann (East Germany)	Andrei Balashov (Soviet Union)	John Bertrand (Australia)
1980	Esko Rechardt (Finland)	Wolfgang Mayrhofer (Austria)	Andrei Balashov (Soviet Union)
1984	Russell Coutts (New Zealand)	John Bertrand (United States)	Terry Neilson (Canada)
1988	Jose Doreste (Spain)	Peter Holmberg (U.S. Virgin Islands)	John Cutler (New Zealand)
1992	José van der Ploeg (Spain)	Brian Ledbetter (United States)	Craig Monk (New Zealand)
1996	Mateusz Kusznierewicz (Poland)	Sébastien Godefroid (Belgium)	Roy Heiner (Netherlands)
2000	Iain Percy (Great Britain)	Luca Devoti (Italy)	Fredrik Lööf (Sweden)
2004	Ben Ainslie (Great Britain)	Rafael Trujillo (Spain)	Mateusz Kusznierewicz (Poland)
2008	Ben Ainslie (Great Britain)	Zach Railey (United States)	Guillaume Florent (France)

Men's Star

Year	Gold	Silver	Bronze
1932	Gilbert Gray, Andrew Libano (United States)	George Colin Ratsey, Peter Jaffe (Great Britain)	Gunnar Asther, Daniel Sundén-Cullberg (Sweden)
1936	Peter Bischoff, Hans-Joachim Weise (Germany)	Arvid Laurin, Uno Wallentin (Sweden)	Bob Maas, Willem de Vries Lentsch (Netherlands)
1940–1944: Olympics not held			
1948	Hilary Smart, Paul Smart (United States)	Carlos de Cardenas Culmell, Carlos de Cardenas Pla (Cuba)	Adriaan Maas, Edward Stutterheim (Netherlands)
1952	Agostino Straulino, Nicolò Rode (Italy)	John Price, John Reid (United States)	Joaquim Mascarenhas de Fiúza, Francisco de Andrade (Portugal)
1956	Herbert Williams, Lawrence Low (United States)	Agostino Straulino, Nicolò Rode (Italy)	Durward Knowles, Sloane Farrington (Bahamas)
1960	Timir Pinegin, Fyodor Shutkov (Soviet Union)	Mario Gentil, Jose Gentil (Portugal)	William Parks, Robert Halperin (United States)
1964	Durward Knowles, Cecil Cooke (Bahamas)	Richard Stearns, Lynn Williams (United States)	Pelle Pettersson, Holger Sundström (Sweden)
1968	Lowell North, Peter Barrett (United States)	Peder Lunde Jr., Per Olav Wiken (Norway)	Franco Cavallo, Camilo Gargano (Italy)
1972	David Forbes, Scott Anderson (Australia)	Pelle Petterson, Stellan Westerdahl (Sweden)	Wilhelm Kuhweide, Karsten Meyer (Germany)
1976: Event not held			
1980	Valentin Mankin, Aleksandr Muzychenko (Soviet Union)	Karl Ferstl, Hubert Raudaschl (Austria)	Giorgio Gorla, Alfio Peraboni (Italy)

Year	Gold	Silver	Bronze
1984	William E. Buchan, Steven Erickson (United States)	Joachim Griese, Michael Marcour (West Germany)	Giorgio Gorla, Alfio Peraboni (Italy)
1988	Michael McIntyre, Bryn Vaile (Great Britain)	Mark Reynolds, Harold Haenel (United States)	Torben Grael, Nelson Falcão (Brazil)
1992	Mark Reynolds, Harold Haenel (United States)	Roderick Davis, Donald Cowie (New Zealand)	Ross MacDonald, Eric Jespersen (Canada)
1996	Torben Grael, Marcelo Ferreira (Brazil)	Hans Wallen, Bobby Lohse (Sweden)	Colin Beashel, David Giles (Australia)
2000	Mark Reynolds, Harold Haenel (United States)	Ian Walker, Mark Covell (Great Britain)	Torben Grael, Marcelo Ferreira (Brazil)
2004	Marcelo Ferreira, Torben Grael (Brazil)	Ross MacDonald, Mike Wolfs (Canada)	Pascal Rambeau, Xavier Rohart (France)
2008	Iain Percy, Andrew Simpson (Great Britain)	Robert Scheidt, Bruno Prada (Brazil)	Fredrik Lööf, Anders Ekström (Sweden)

Mixed Swallow (Golondrina)

Year	Gold	Silver	Bronze
1948	Stewart Morris, David Bond (Great Britain)	Duarte de Almeida Bello, Fernando Pinto Coelho Bello (Portugal)	Lockwood Pirie, Owen Torrey (United States)

Mixed Tempest

Year	Gold	Silver	Bronze
1972	Valentin Mankin, Vitali Dyrdyra (Soviet Union)	Alan Warren, David Hunt (Great Britain)	Glenn Foster, Peter Dean (United States)
1976	John Albrechtson, Ingvar Hansson (Sweden)	Valentin Mankin, Vladislav Akimenko (Soviet Union)	Dennis Conner, Conn Findlay (United States)

Mixed Tornado Multihall

Year	Gold	Silver	Bronze
1976	Reginald White, John Osborn (Great Britain)	David McFaull, Michael Rothwell (United States)	Jörg Spengler, Jörg Schmall (West Germany)
1980	Lars Sigurd Bjorkström, Alexandre Welter (Brazil)	Peter Due, Per Kjærgaard (Denmark)	Goran Marstrom, Jorgen Ragnarsson (Sweden)
1984	Rex Sellers, Chris Timms (New Zealand)	Randy Smyth, Jay Glaser (United States)	Christopher Cairns, John Anderson (Australia)
1988	Jean Le Deroff, Nicolas Hénard (France)	Chris Timms, Rex Sellers (New Zealand)	Lars Grael, Clinio Freitas (Brazil)
1992	Yves Loday, Nicolas Hénard (France)	Randy Smyth, Keith Notary (United States)	Mitch Booth, John Forbes (Australia)
1996	Jose Ballester, Fernando Leon (Spain)	Mitch Booth, Andrew Landenberger (Australia)	Lars Grael, Kiko Pellicano (Brazil)
2000	Roman Hagara, Hans Peter Steinacher (Austria)	John Forbes, Darren Bundock (Australia)	Roland Gäbler, René Schwall (Germany)
2004	Roman Hagara, Hans-Peter Steinacher (Austria)	John Lovell, Charlie Ogeltree (United States)	Santiago Lange, Carlos Espínola (Argentina)
2008	Antón Paz, Fernando Echavarri (Spain)	Darren Bundock, Glenn Ashby (Australia)	Santiago Lange, Carlos Espínola (Argentina)

Shooting

Men's 1,000-Yard Free Rifle, Prone

Year	Gold	Silver	Bronze
1908	Joshua Millner (Great Britain)	Kellogg Casey (United States)	Maurice Blood (Great Britain)

Men's Individual 100-Meter Running Deer, Single Shot

Year	Gold	Silver	Bronze
1908	Oscar Swahn (Sweden)	Ted Ranken (Great Britain)	Alexander Rogers (Great Britain)
1912	Alfred Swahn (Sweden)	Åke Lundeberg (Sweden)	Nestori Toivonen (Finland)
1916: Olympics not held			
1920	Otto Olsen (Norway)	Alfred Swahn (Sweden)	Harald Natvig (Norway)
1924	John Boles (United States)	Cyril Mackworth-Praed (Great Britain)	Otto Olsen (Norway)

Men's Team 100-Meter Running Deer, Single Shot

Year	Gold	Silver	Bronze
1908	Arvid Knöppel, Ernst Rosell, Alfred Swahn, Oscar Swahn (Sweden)	Walter Ellicott, William Russell Lane-Joynt, Charles Nix, Ted Ranken (Great Britain)	Not awarded
1912	Alfred Swahn, Oscar Swahn, Åke Lundeberg, Per-Olof Arvidsson (Sweden)	William McDonnell, Walter Winans, William Leuschner, William Libbey (United States)	Axel Londen, Nestori Toivonen, Iivar Väänänen, Ernst Rosenqvist (Finland)
1916: Olympics not held			
1920	Einar Liberg, Ole Lilloe-Olsen, Harald Natvig, Hans Nordvik, Otto Olsen (Norway)	Yrjö Kolho, Kalle Lappalainen, Toivo Tikkanen, Nestori Toivonen, Karl Magnus Wegelius (Finland)	Thomas Brown, Willis A. Lee, Lawrence Nuesslein, Carl Osburn, Lloyd Spooner (United States)
1924	Einar Liberg, Ole Lilloe-Olsen, Harald Natvig, Otto Olsen (Norway)	Otto Hultberg, Mauritz Johansson, Fredric Landelius, Alfred Swahn (Sweden)	John Boles, Raymond Coulter, Dennis Fenton, Walter Stokes (United States)

Men's Individual 100-Meter Running Deer, Double Shot

Year	Gold	Silver	Bronze
1908	Walter Winans (United States)	Ted Ranken (Great Britain)	Oscar Swahn (Sweden)
1912	Åke Lundeberg (Sweden)	Edward Benedicks (Sweden)	Oscar Swahn (Sweden)
1916: Olympics not held			
1920	Ole Lilloe-Olsen (Norway)	Fredric Landelius (Sweden)	Einar Liberg (Norway)
1924	Ole Lilloe-Olsen (Norway)	Cyril Mackworth-Praed (Great Britain)	Alfred Swahn (Sweden)

Men's Team 100-Meter Running Deer, Double Shot

Year	Gold	Silver	Bronze
1920	Harald Natvig, Ole Lilloe-Olsen, Einar Liberg, Hans Nordvik, Thorstein Johansen (Norway)	Alfred Swahn, Oscar Swahn, Fredric Landelius, Bengt Lagercrantz, Edward Benedicks (Sweden)	Toivo Tikkanen, Karl Magnus Wegelius, Nestori Toivonen, Vilho Vauhkonen, Yrjö Kolho (Finland)
1924	Cyril Mackworth-Praed, Philip Neame, Herbert Perry, Allen Whitty (Great Britain)	Einar Liberg, Ole Lilloe-Olsen, Harald Natvig, Otto Olsen (Norway)	Axel Ekblom, Mauritz Johansson, Fredric Landelius, Alfred Swahn (Sweden)

Men's Individual 100-Meter Running Deer, Combined

Year	Gold	Silver	Bronze
1952	John Larsen (Norway)	Olof Skoldberg (Sweden)	Tauno Vilhelmi Maki (Finland)
1956	Vitali Romanenko (Soviet Union)	Olof Skoldberg (Sweden)	Vladimir Sevryugin (Soviet Union)

Men's 10-Meter Air Pistol

Year	Gold	Silver	Bronze
1988	Tanyu Kiryakov (Bulgaria)	Erich Buljung (United States)	Xu Haifeng (China)
1992	Wang Yifu (China)	Nonka Matova (Bulgaria)	Małgorzata Książkiewicz (Poland)
1996	Robert Di Donna (Italy)	Wang Yifu (China)	Tanyu Kiryakov (Bulgaria)
2000	Franck Dumoulin (France)	Wang Yifu (China)	Igor Basinski (Belarus)
2004	Wang Yifu (China)	Mikhail Nestruyev (Russia)	Vladimir Isakov (Russia)
2008	Pang Wei (China)	Jin Jong-Oh (South Korea)	Jason Turner (United States)

Women's 10-Meter Air Pistol

Year	Gold	Silver	Bronze
1988	Jasna Šekarić (Yugoslavia)	Nino Salukvadze (Soviet Union)	Marina Dobrantcheva (Soviet Union)
1992	Marina Logvinenko (Unified Team)	Jasna Šekarić (Independent Participant)	Maria Grozdeva (Bulgaria)
1996	Olga Klochneva (Russia)	Marina Logvinenko (Russia)	Maria Grozdeva (Bulgaria)
2000	Tao Luna (China)	Jasna Šekarić (Yugoslavia)	Annemarie Forder (Australia)
2004	Olena Kostevych (Ukraine)	Jasna Šekarić (Serbia and Montenegro)	Maria Grozdeva (Bulgaria)
2008	Guo Wenjun (China)	Natalia Paderina (Russia)	Nino Salukvadze (Georgia)

Men's 10-Meter Air Rifle

Year	Gold	Silver	Bronze
1984	Philippe Heberlé (France)	Andreas Kronthaler (Austria)	Barry Dagger (Great Britain)
1988	Goran Maksimović (Yugoslavia)	Nicolas Berthelot (France)	Johann Riederer (West Germany)
1992	Yuri Fedkin (Unified Team)	Franck Badiou (France)	Johann Riederer (Germany)
1996	Artem Khadjibekov (Russia)	Wolfram Waibel (Austria)	Jean-Pierre Amat (France)
2000	Cai Yalin (China)	Artem Khadjibekov (Russia)	Yevgeni Aleinikov (Russia)
2004	Zhu Qinan (China)	Li Jie (China)	Jozef Gönci (Slovakia)
2008	Abhinav Bindra (India)	Zhu Qunan (China)	Henri Häkkinen (Finland)

Women's 10-Meter Air Rifle

Year	Gold	Silver	Bronze
1984	Pat Spurgin (United States)	Edith Gufler (Italy)	Wu Xiaoxuan (China)
1988	Irina Chilova (Soviet Union)	Silvia Sperber (Germany)	Anna Maloukhina (Soviet Union)
1992	Yeo Kab-Soon (South Korea)	Vesela Letcheva (Bulgaria)	Aranka Binder (Independent Olympic Participant)
1996	Renata Mauer (Poland)	Petra Horneber (West Germany)	Aleksandra Ivošev (Yugoslavia)
2000	Nancy Johnson (United States)	Kang Cho-Hyun (South Korea)	Gao Jing (China)
2004	Du Li (China)	Lioubov Galkina (Russia)	Kateřina Kůrková (Czech Republic)
2008	Kateřina Emmons (Czech Republic)	Lioubov Galkina (Russia)	Snježana Pejčić (Croatia)

Men's 10-Meter Running Target

Year	Gold	Silver	Bronze
1992	Michael Jakosits (Germany)	Anatoli Asrabayev (Unified Team)	Luboš Račanský (Czechoslovakia)
1996	Yang Ling (China)	Xiao Jun (China)	Miroslav Januš (Czech Republic)
2000	Yang Ling (China)	Oleg Moldovan (Moldova)	Niu Zhiyuan (China)
2004	Manfred Kurzer (Germany)	Aleksandr Blinov (Russia)	Dimitri Lykin (Russia)

Men's 25-Meter Military Pistol

Year	Gold	Silver	Bronze
1896	John Paine (United States)	Sumner Paine (United States)	Nikolaos Morakis (Greece)

Men's 25-Meter Rapid-Fire Pistol

Year	Gold	Silver	Bronze
1896	Ioannis Phrangoudis (Greece)	Georgios Orphanidis (Greece)	Holger Nielsen (Denmark)
1900	Maurice Larrouy (France)	Léon Moreaux (France)	Eugéne Balme (France)
1904–1912: Event not held			
1916: Olympics not held			
1920: Event not held			
1924	Henry Bailey (United States)	Vilhelm Carlberg (Sweden)	Lennart Hannelius (Finland)
1928: Event not held			
1932	Renzo Morigi (Italy)	Heinz Hax (Germany)	Domenico Matteucci (Italy)
1936	Cornelius van Oyen (Germany)	Heinz Hax (Germany)	Torsten Ullman (Sweden)
1940–1944: Olympics not held			
1948	Károly Takács (Hungary)	Carlos Valiente Diaz Saez (Argentina)	Sven Lundquist (Sweden)
1952	Károly Takács (Hungary)	Szilard Kun (Hungary)	Gheorghe Lichiardopol (Romania)
1956	Stefan Petrescu (Romania)	Yevgeni Cherkasov (Soviet Union)	Gheorghe Lichiardopol (Romania)
1960	William McMillan (United States)	Pentti Linnosvuo (Finland)	Alexander Zabelin (Soviet Union)
1964	Pentti Linnosvuo (Finland)	Ion Tripsa (Romania)	Lubomír Nácovský (Czechoslovakia)
1968	Józef Zapędzki (Poland)	Marcel Rosca (Romania)	Renart Suleimanov (Soviet Union)
1972	Józef Zapędzki (Poland)	Ladislav Falta (Czechoslovakia)	Viktor Torshin (Soviet Union)
1976	Norbert Klaar (East Germany)	Jürgen Wiefel (East Germany)	Roberto Ferraris (Italy)
1980	Corneliu Ion (Romania)	Jürgen Wiefel (East Germany)	Gerhard Petritsch (Austria)
1984	Takeo Kamachi (Japan)	Corneliu Ion (Romania)	Rauno Bies (Finland)
1988	Afanasijs Kuzmins (Soviet Union)	Ralf Schumann (East Germany)	Zoltán Kovács (Hungary)
1992	Ralf Schumann (Germany)	Afanasijs Kuzmins (Latvia)	Vladimir Vokhmtanin (Unified Team)
1996	Ralf Schumann (Germany)	Emil Milev (Bulgaria)	Vladimir Vokhmtanin (Kazakhstan)
2000	Sergei Alifirenko (Russia)	Michel Ansermet (Switzerland)	Iulian Raicea (Romania)
2004	Ralf Schumann (Germany)	Sergei Poliakov (Russia)	Sergei Alifirenko (Russia)
2008	Oleksandr Petriv (Ukraine)	Ralf Schumann (Germany)	Christian Reitz (Germany)

Men's Individual 25-Meter Small Bore Rifle

Year	Gold	Silver	Bronze
1912	Vilhelm Carlberg (Sweden)	Johan Hübner von Holst (Sweden)	Gideon Ericsson (Sweden)

Men's Team 25-Meter Small-Bore Rifle

Year	Gold	Silver	Bronze
1912	Eric Carlberg, G. Vilhelm Carlberg, Gustav Boivie, Johan Hübner von Holst (Sweden)	Joseph Pepe, William Edwin Pimm, William Kensett Styles, William Milne (Great Britain)	Frederick S. Hird, William F. Leushner, Warren A. Sprout, William Neil McDonnell (United States)

Men's Small-Bore Rifle

Year	Gold	Silver	Bronze
1908	John Fleming (Great Britain)	Michael Matthews (Great Britain)	William Marsden (Great Britain)

Men's Team 300-Meter + 600-Meter Rifle

Year	Gold	Silver	Bronze
1920	Joseph Jackson, Willis A. Lee, Carl Osburn, Oliver Schriver, Lloyd Spooner (United States)	Albert Helgerud, Otto Olsen, Jacob Onsrud, Østen Østensen, Olaf Sletten (Norway)	Eugen Addor, Joseph Jehle, Fritz Kuchen, Werner Schneeberger, Weibel* (Switzerland)

* Full name not known.

Mixed 300-Meter Rifle, 3 Positions

Year	Gold	Silver	Bronze
1900	Emil Kellenberger (Switzerland)	Anders Peter Nielsen (Denmark)	Paul van Asbroeck (Belgium) Ole Østmo (Norway)
1904–1908: Event not held			
1912	Paul Colos (France)	Lars Jørgen Madsen (Denmark)	Niels Larsen (Denmark)
1916: Olympics not held			
1920	Morris Fisher (United States)	Niels Larsen (Denmark)	Østen Østensen (Norway)
1924–1936: Event not held			
1940–1944: Olympics not held			
1948	Emil Grunig (Switzerland)	Pauli Aapeli Janhonen (Finland)	Willy Røgeberg (Norway)
1952	Anatoli Bogdanov (Soviet Union)	Robert Bürchler (Switzerland)	Lev Weinstein (Soviet Union)
1956	Vasili Borisov (Soviet Union)	Allan Erdman (Soviet Union)	Vilho Ylönen (Finland)
1960	Hubert Hammerer (Austria)	Hans Rudolph Spillmann (Switzerland)	Vassily Borssov (Soviet Union)
1964	Gary Anderson (United States)	Shota Kveliashvili (Soviet Union)	Martin Gunnarsson (United States)
1968	Gary Anderson (United States)	Valentin Kornev (Soviet Union)	Kurt Müller (Switzerland)

Men's 50-Meter Rifle, 3 Positions

Year	Gold	Silver	Bronze
1952	Erling Asbjørn Kongshaug (Norway)	Vilho Ylönen (Finland)	Boris Andreyev (Soviet Union)
1956	Anatoli Bogdanov (Soviet Union)	Otakar Hořínek (Czechoslovakia)	John Sundberg (Sweden)
1960	Viktor Shamburkin (Soviet Union)	Marat Nijasov (Soviet Union)	Klaus Zähringer (United Team of Germany)
1964	Lones Wigger (United States)	Velitchko Christov (Bulgaria)	László Hammerl (Hungary)
1968	Bernd Klingner (West Germany)	John Writer (United States)	Vitali Parkhimovich (Soviet Union)
1972–1980: Event not held			
1984	Malcolm Cooper (Great Britain)	Daniel Nipov (Switzerland)	Alister Allan (Great Britain)
1988	Malcolm Cooper (Great Britain)	Alister Allan (Great Britain)	Kirill Ivanov (Soviet Union)
1992	Gracha Petikian (Unified Team)	Robert Foth (United States)	Ryohei Koba (Japan)
1996	Jean-Pierre Amat (France)	Sergey Belyayev (Kazakhstan)	Wolfram Waibel (Austria)
2000	Rajmond Debevec (Slovakia)	Juha Hirvi (Finland)	Harald Stenvaag (Norway)

Year	Gold	Silver	Bronze
2004	Zia Zhanbo (China)	Michael Anti (United States)	Christian Planer (Austria)
2008	Qiu Jian (China)	Jury Sukhorukov (Ukraine)	Rajmond Debevec (Slovakia)

Mixed 50-Meter Rifle, 3 Positions

Year	Gold	Silver	Bronze
1972	John Writer (United States)	Lanny Bassham (United States)	Werner Lippoldt (East Germany)
1976	Lanny Bassham (United States)	Margaret Murdock (United States)	Werner Seibold (West Germany)
1980	Viktor Vlassov (Soviet Union)	Bernd Hartstein (East Germany)	Sven Johansson (Sweden)

Men's 50-Meter Rifle, Prone

Year	Gold	Silver	Bronze
1908	Arthur Carnell (Great Britain)	Harold Humby (Great Britain)	George Barnes (Great Britain)
1912	Frederick Hird (United States)	William Milne (Great Britain)	Harold Burt (Great Britain)
1916: Olympics not held			
1920: Event not held			
1924	Pierre Coquelin de Lisle (France)	Marcus Dinwiddie (United States)	Josias Hartmann (Switzerland)
1928: Event not held			
1932	Bertil Rönnmark (Sweden)	Gustavo Huet (Mexico)	Zoltán Soós Hradetzky (Hungary)
1936	Willy Røgeberg (Norway)	Ralf Berszenyi (Hungary)	Władysław Karaś (Poland)
1940–1944: Olympics not held			
1948	Arthur Cook (United States)	Walter Thomsen (United States)	Jonas Jonsson (Sweden)
1952	Iosif Sîrbu (Romania)	Boris Andreyev (Soviet Union)	Arthur Jackson (United States)
1956	Gerald Ouellette (Canada)	Vasily Borisov (Soviet Union)	Stuart Boa (Canada)
1960	Peter Kohnke (United Team of Germany)	James Enoch Hill (United States)	Forcella Pelliccioni (Venezuela)
1964	Lázló Hammerl (Hungary)	Lones Wigger (United States)	Tommy Pool (United States)
1968	Jan Kůrka (Czechoslovakia)	Lázló Hammerl (Hungary)	Ian Ballinger (New Zealand)
1972–1980: Event not held			
1984	Edward Etzel (United States)	Michel Bury (France)	Michael Sullivan (Great Britain)
1988	Miroslav Varga (Czechoslovakia)	Cha Young-Chul (South Korea)	Attila Záhonyi (Hungary)
1992	Lee Eun-Chul (South Korea)	Harald Stenvaag (Norway)	Stevan Pletikosić (Independent)
1996	Christian Klees (Germany)	Sergey Belyayev (Kazakhstan)	Jozef Gönci (Slovakia)
2000	Jonas Edman (Sweden)	Torben Grimmel (Denmark)	Sergei Martynov (Belarus)
2004	Matthew Emmons (United States)	Christian Lusch (Germany)	Sergei Martynov (Belarus)
2008	Artur Ayvazian (Ukraine)	Matthew Emmons (United States)	Warren Potent (Australia)

Mixed 50-Meter Rifle, Prone

Year	Gold	Silver	Bronze
1972	Li Ho-Jun (North Korea)	Victor Auer (United States)	Nicolae Rotaru (Romania)
1976	Karlheinz Smieszek (West Germany)	Ulrich Lind (West Germany)	Gennadi Lushchikov (Soviet Union)
1980	Károly Varga (Hungary)	Hellfried Heilfort (East Germany)	Petar Zaprianov (Bulgaria)

Women's 50-Meter Rifle, 3 Positions

Year	Gold	Silver	Bronze
1984	Wu Xiaoxuan (China)	Ulrike Holmer (West Germany)	Wanda Jewell (United States)
1988	Silvia Sperber (West Germany)	Vessela Letcheva (Bulgaria)	Valentina Cherkasova (Soviet Union)
1992	Launi Meili (United States)	Nonka Matova (Bulgaria)	Małgorzata Książkiewicz (Poland)
1996	Aleksandra Ivošev (Yugoslavia)	Irina Gerasimenok (Russia)	Renata Mauer (Poland)

Year	Gold	Silver	Bronze
2000	Renata Mauer (Poland)	Tatiana Goldobina (Russia)	Maria Feklistova (Russia)
2004	Lioubov Galkina (Russia)	Valentina Turisini (Italy)	Wang Chengyi (China)
2008	Du Li (China)	Kateřina Emmons (Czech Republic)	Eglis Yaima Cruz (Cuba)

Women's 25-Meter Pistol

Year	Gold	Silver	Bronze
1984	Linda Thom (Canada)	Ruby Fox (United States)	Patricia Dench (Australia)
1988	Nino Salukvadze (Soviet Union)	Tomoko Hasegawa (Japan)	Jasna Šekarić (Yugoslavia)
1992	Marina Logvinenko (Unified Team)	Li Duihong (China)	Dorjsürengiin Mönkhbayar (Mongolia)
1996	Li Duihong (China)	Diana Yorgova (Yugoslavia)	Marina Logvinenko (Russia)
2000	Maria Grozdeva (Bulgaria)	Tao Luna (China)	Lalita Yauhleuskaya (Belarus)
2004	Maria Grozdeva (Bulgaria)	Lenka Hyková (Czech Republic)	Irada Ashumova (Azerbaijan)
2008	Chen Ying (China)	Otrydyn Gündegmaa (Mongolia)	Munkhbayar Dorjsuren (Germany)

Men's Individual 25-Meter Military Pistol

Year	Gold	Silver	Bronze
1896	John Paine (United States)	Sumner Paine (United States)	Nikolaos Morakis (Greece)

Men's Team 50-Meter Military Pistol

Year	Gold	Silver	Bronze
1900	Friedrich Lüthi, Paul Probst, Louis Richardet, Karl Röderer, Konrad Stäheli (Switzerland)	Louis Duffoy, Maurice Lecoq, Léon Moreaux, Achille Paroche, Trinité (France)	Solko van den Bergh, Antonius Bouwens, Dirk Boest Gips, Henrik Sillem, Anthony Sweijs (Netherlands)
1904–1908: Event not held			
1912	Alfred Lane, Henry Sears, Peter Dolfen, John Dietz (United States)	Georg de Laval, Eric Carlberg, Vilhelm Carlberg, Erik Boström (Sweden)	Horatio Poulter, Hugh Durant, Albert Kempster, Charles Stewart (Great Britain)

Men's Individual 200-Meter Rifle

Year	Gold	Silver	Bronze
1896	Pantelis Karasevdas (Greece)	Pavlos Pavlidis (Greece)	Nicolaos Trikupis (Greece)

Men's Individual 300-Meter Free Rifle

Year	Gold	Silver	Bronze
1896	Georgios Orphanidis (Greece)	Ioannis Phrangoudis (Greece)	Viggo Jensen (Denmark)

Men's Team 300-Meter Military Rifle

Year	Gold	Silver	Bronze
1900	Franz Böckli, Alfred Grütter, Emil Kellenberger, Louis Richardet, Konrad Stäheli (Switzerland)	Olaf Frydenlund, Hellmer Hermandsen, Ole Østmo, Ole Sæther, Tom Seeberg (Norway)	Auguste Cavadini, Maurice Lecoq, Léon Moreaux, Achille Paroche, René Thomas (France)
1904: Event not held			
1908	William Leuschner, William Martin, Charles Winder, Kellogg Casey, Ivan Eastman, Charles Benedict (United States)	Harcourt Ommundsen, Fleetwood Varley, Arthur Fulton, Philip Richardson, William Padgett, John Martin (Great Britain)	William Smith, Charles Crowe, Bruce Williams, Dugald McInnis, William Eastcott, S. Harry Kerr (Canada)

Year	Gold	Silver	Bronze
1912	Cornelius Burdette, Allan Briggs, Harry Adams, John Jackson, Carl Osburn, Warren Sprout (United States)	Harcourt Ommundsen, Henry Burr, Edward Skilton, James Reid, Edward Parnell, Arthur Fulton (Great Britain)	Mauritz Eriksson, Werner Jernström, Tönnes Björkman, Carl Björkman, Bernhard Larsson, Hugo Johansson (Sweden)
1916: Olympics not held			
1920	Lars Jørgen Madsen, Niels Larsen, Anders Peterson, Erik Sætter-Lassen, Anders Peter Nielsen (Denmark)	Carl Osburn, Lawrence Nuesslein, Lloyd Spooner, Willis Lee, Thomas Brown (United States)	Olle Ericsson, Hugo Johansson, Leon Lagerlöf, Walfrid Hellman, Mauritz Eriksson (Sweden)

Men's Individual 600-Meter Military Rifle

Year	Gold	Silver	Bronze
1920	Hugo Johansson (Sweden)	Mauritz Eriksson (Sweden)	Lloyd Spooner (United States)

Men's Team 600-Meter Military Rifle

Year	Gold	Silver	Bronze
1920	Dennis Fenton, Gunnery Schriver, Willis A. Lee, Lloyd Spooner, Joseph Jackson (United States)	David Smith, Robert Bodley, Ferdinand Buchanan, George Harvey, Fred Morgan (South Africa)	Mauritz Eriksson, Hugo Johansson, Gustaf Adolf Jonsson, Erik Blomqvist, Erik Ohlsson (Sweden)

Mixed 50-Meter Running Target

Year	Gold	Silver	Bronze
1972	Yakov Zheleznyak (Soviet Union)	Helmut Bellingrodt (Colombia)	John Kynoch (Great Britain)
1976	Aleksandr Gazov (Soviet Union)	Aleksandr Kedyarov (Soviet Union)	Jerzy Greszkiewicz (Poland)
1980	Igor Sokolov (Soviet Union)	Thomas Pfeffer (East Germany)	Aleksandr Gazov (Soviet Union)

Men's 50-Meter Running Target

Year	Gold	Silver	Bronze
1984	Li Yuwei (China)	Helmut Bellingrodt (Colombia)	Huang Shiping (China)
1988	Tor Heiestad (Norway)	Huang Shiping (China)	Gennadi Avramenko (Soviet Union)

Men's 25-Yard Rifle, Disappearing Target

Year	Gold	Silver	Bronze
1908	William Styles (Great Britain)	Harold Hawkins (Great Britain)	Edward Amoore (Great Britain)

Men's 25-Yard Rifle, Moving Target

Year	Gold	Silver	Bronze
1908	John Fleming (Great Britain)	Maurice Matthews (Great Britain)	William Marsden (Great Britain)

Men's 50-Yard + 100-Yard Rifle, Stationary Target

Year	Gold	Silver	Bronze
1908	Arthur Carnell (Great Britain)	Harold Humby (Great Britain)	George Barnes (Great Britain)

Men's 25-Meter Small-Bore Rifle, Disappearing Target

Year	Gold	Silver	Bronze
1912	Vilhelm Carlberg (Sweden)	Johan Hübner von Holst (Sweden)	Gideon Ericsson (Sweden)

Men's 300-Meter Rifle, 3 Positions

Year	Gold	Silver	Bronze
1908	Albert Helgerud (Norway)	Harry Simon (United States)	Ole Sæther (Norway)
1912	Paul Colas (France)	Lars Jorgen Madsen (Denmark)	Niels Larsen (Denver)
1916: Olympics not held			
1920	Morris Fisher (United States)	Niels Larsen (Denmark)	Østen Østensen (Norway)
1924	Morris Fisher (United States)	Carl Osburn (United States)	Niels Larsen (Denver)
1928–1936: Event not held			
1940–1944: Olympics not held			
1948	Emil Grünig (Switzerland)	Pauli Aapeli Janhonen (Finland)	Willy Røgeberg (Norway)
1952	Anatoli Bogdanov (Soviet Union)	Robert Bürchler (Switzerland)	Lev Vainshtein (Soviet Union)
1956	Vasily Borisov (Soviet Union)	Allan Erdman (Soviet Union)	Vilho Ylönen (Finland)
1960	Hubert Hammerer (Austria)	Hansrudi Spillmann (Switzerland)	Vasily Borisov (Soviet Union)
1964	Gary Anderson (United States)	Shota Kveliashvili (Soviet Union)	Martine Gunnarsson (United States)
1968	Gary Anderson (United States)	Valentin Kornev (Soviet Union)	Kurt Müller (Switzerland)

Mixed 300-Meter Rifle, 3 Positions

Year	Gold	Silver	Bronze
1972	Lones Wigger (United States)	Boris Melnik (Soviet Union)	Lajos Papp (Hungary)

Men's 600-Meter Rifle, Prone

Year	Gold	Silver	Bronze
1912	Paul Colas (France)	Carl Osburn (United States)	John Jackson (United States)

Men's 1,000-Yard Free Rifle, Prone

Year	Gold	Silver	Bronze
1908	Joshua Millner (Great Britain)	Kellogg Casey (United States)	Maurice Blood (Great Britain)

Men's Team 30-Meter Pistol

Year	Gold	Silver	Bronze
1912	Eric Carlberg, Vilhelm Carlberg, Johan Hübner von Holst, Paul Palén (Sweden)	Amos Kash, Nikolai Melnitsky, Pavel Voyloshnikov, Grigori Panteleimonov (Russia)	Hugh Durant, Albert Kempster, Charles Stewart, Horatio Poulter (Great Britain)
1916: Olympics not held			
1920	Louis Harant, Alfred Lane, Carl Frederick, James H. Snook, Michael Kelly (United States)	Alexandros Theofilakis, Ioannis Theofilakis, Georgios Moraitinis, Alexandros Vrasivanopoulos, Iason Sappas (Greece)	Fritz Zulauf, Joseph Jehle, Gustave Amoudruz, Hans Egli, Domenico Giamgonini (Switzerland)

Men's Team 50-Meter Pistol

Year	Gold	Silver	Bronze
1908	James Gorman, Irving Calkins, John Dietz, Charles Axtell (United States)	Paul Van Asbroeck, Reginald Storms, Charles Paumier du Verger, Rene Englebert (Belgium)	Jesse Wallingford, Geoffrey Coles, Henry Lynch-Staunton, Walter Ellicott (Great Britain)
1912: Event not held			
1916: Olympics not held			
1920	Carl Frederick, Alfred Lane, Raymond Bracken, James H. Snook, Michael Kelly (United States)	Anders Andersson, Casimir Reuterskiöld, Gunnar Gabrielsson, Sigvard Hultcrantz, Anders Johnson (Sweden)	Afrânio da Costa, Sebastião Wolf, Dario Barbosa, Fernando Soledade, Guilherme Paraense (Brazil)

Men's Team 25-Meter Rifle

Year	Gold	Silver	Bronze
1912	Johan Hübner von Holst, Eric Carlberg, Vilhelm Carlberg, Gustaf Boivie (Sweden)	William Pimm, Joseph Pepé, William Milne, William Styles (Great Britain)	Frederick Hird, Warren Sprout, William McDonnell, William Leuschner (United States)

Men's Team 50-Meter Rifle

Year	Gold	Silver	Bronze
1908	Edward Amoore, Harold Humby, Maurice Matthews, William Pimm (Great Britain)	Eric Carlberg, Vilhelm Carlberg, Franz-Albert Schartau, Johan Hübner von Holst (Sweden)	Henri Bonnefoy, Paul Colas, Léon Lécuyer, André Regaud (France)
1912	William Pimm, Edward Lessimore, Joseph Pepé, Robert Murray (Great Britain)	Arthur Nordenswan, Eric Carlberg, Ruben Örtegren, Vilhelm Carlberg (Sweden)	Warren Sprout, William Leuschner, Frederick Hird, Carl Osburn (United States)
1916: Olympics not held			
1920	Lawrence Nuesslein, Arthur Rothrock, Willis Lee, Dennis Fenton, Gunnery Schriver (United States)	Sigvard Hultcrantz, Erik Ohlsson, Leon Lagerlöf, Ragnar Stare, Olle Ericsson (Sweden)	Østen Østensen, Olaf Sletten, Anton Olsen, Sigvart Johansen, Albert Helgerud (Norway)

Men's Team 300-Meter Rifle

Year	Gold	Silver	Bronze
1908	Julius Braathe, Albert Helgerud, Einar Liberg, Olaf Sæther, Ole Sæther, Gudbrand Skatteboe (Norway)	Per-Olof Arvidsson, Janne Gustafsson, Axel Jansson, Gustaf Adolf Jonsson, Claës Rundberg, Gustav-Adolf Sjöberg (Sweden)	Eugène Balme, Raoul de Boigne, Albert Courquin, Léon Johnson, Maurice Lecoq, André Parmentier (France)
1912	Mauritz Eriksson, Hugo Johansson, Erik Blomqvist, Carl Björkman, Bernhard Larsson, Gustaf Jonsson (Sweden)	Gudbrand Skatteboe, Ole Sæther, Østen Østensen, Albert Helgerud, Olaf Sæther, Einar Liberg (Norway)	Ole Olsen, Lars Jørgen Madsen, Niels Larsen, Niels Andersen, Laurits Larsen, Jens Hajslund (Denmark)
1916: Olympics not held			
1920	Joseph Jackson, Willis Lee, Gunnery Schriver, Carl Osburn, Lloyd Spooner (United States)	Otto Olsen, Albert Helgerud, Olaf Sletten, Østen Østensen, Jacob Onsrud (Norway)	Fritz Kuchen, Albert Tröndle, Arnold Rösli, Walter Lienhard, Caspar Widmer (Switzerland)
1924	Raymond Coulter, Joseph Crockett, Morris Fisher, Sidney Hinds, Walter Stokes (United States)	Paul Colas, Albert Courquin, Pierre Hardy, Georges Roes, Emile Rumeau (France)	Ludovic Augustin, Destin Destine, Saint Eloi Metullus, Astrel Rolland, Ludovic Valborge (Haiti)

Men's Team Trap

Year	Gold	Silver	Bronze
1908	Alexander Maunder, James Pike, Charles Palmer, John Postans, Frank Moore, Peter Easte (Great Britain)	Walter Ewing, George Beattie, Arthur Westover, Mylie Fletcher, George Vivian, Donald McMackon (Canada)	George Whitaker, Gerald Skinner, John Butt, William Morris, Harold Creasy, Richard Hutton (Great Britain)
1912	Charles Billings, Ralph Spotts, John H. Hendrickson, James Graham, Edward Gleason, Frank Hall (United States)	John Butt, William Grosvenor, Harold Humby, Alexander Maunder, Charles Palmer, George Whitaker (Great Britain)	Erich Graf von Bernstorff, Franz von Zeldlitz und Leipe, Horst Goeldel, Albert Preuss, Erland Koch, Alfred Goeldel (Germany)
1916: Olympics not held			
1920	Mark Arie, Horace Bonser, Jay Clark, Forest McNeir, Frank Troeh, Frank Wright (United States)	Albert Bosquet, Joseph Cogels, Émile Dupont, Edouard Fesinger, Henri Quersin, Louis Van Tilt (Belgium)	Per Kinde, Fredric Landelius, Erik Lundquist, Karl Richter, Erik Sökjer-Petersén, Alfred Swahn (Sweden)

Year	Gold	Silver	Bronze
1924	Frederick Etchen, Frank Hughes, John Noel, Clarence Platt, Samuel Sharman, William Silkworth (United States)	William Barnes, George Beattie, John Black, Robert Montgomery, Samuel Newton, Samuel Vance (Canada)	Werner Ekman, Konrad Huber, Robert Huber, Georg Nordblad, Toivo Tikkanen, Karl Magnus Wegelius (Finland)

Men's Individual Trap

Year	Gold	Silver	Bronze
1900	Roger de Barbarin (France)	Rene Guyot (France)	Justinien de Clary (France)
1904: Event not held			
1908	Walter Ewing (Canada)	George Beattie (Canada)	Alexander Maunder Anastasios Metaxas (Greece)
1912	James Graham (United States)	Alfred Goeldel (Germany)	Harry Blau (Russia)
1916: Olympics not held			
1920	Mark Arie (United States)	Frank Troeh (United States)	Frank Wright (United States)
1924	Gyula Halasy (Hungary)	Konrad Huber (Finland)	Frank Hughes (United States)
1928–1936: Event not held			
1940–1944: Olympics not held			
1948: Event not held			
1952	George Generaux (Canada)	Knut Holmqvist (Sweden)	Hans Liljedahl (Sweden)
1956	Galliano Rossini (Italy)	Adam Smelczyński (Poland)	Alessandro Ciceri (Italy)
1960	Ion Dumitrescu (Romania)	Galliano Rossini (Italy)	Sergei Kalinin (Soviet Union)
1964	Ennio Mattarelli (Italy)	Pavel Senichev (Soviet Union)	William Morris (United States)
1968	John Braithwaite (Great Britain)	Thomas Garrigus (United States)	Kurt Czekalla (East Germany)
1972–1992: Event not held			
1996	Michael Diamond (Australia)	Josh Lakatos (United States)	Lance Bede (United States)
2000	Michael Diamond (Australia)	Ian Peel (Great Britain)	Giovanni Pellielo (Italy)
2004	Aleksei Alipov (Russia)	Giovanni Pellielo (Italy)	Adam Vella (Australia)
2008	David Kostelecký (Czech Republic)	Giovanni Pellielo (Italy)	Aleksei Alipov (Russia)

Mixed Individual Trap

Year	Gold	Silver	Bronze
1972	Angelo Scalzone (Italy)	Michel Carrega (France)	Silvano Basagni (Italy)
1976	Donald Haldeman (United States)	Armando Da Silva Marques (Portugal)	Ubaldesco Baldi (Italy)
1980	Luciano Giovannetti (Italy)	Rustam Yambulatov (Soviet Union)	Jörg Damme (East Germany)
1984	Luciano Giovannetti (Italy)	Francisco Boza (Peru)	Daniel Carlisle (United States)
1988	Dmitry Monakov (Soviet Union)	Miloslav Bednařík (Czechoslovakia)	Frans Peeters (Belgium)
1992	Petr Hrdlička (Czechoslovakia)	Kazumi Watanabe (Japan)	Marco Venturini (Italy)

Men's Individual Double Trap

Year	Gold	Silver	Bronze
1996	Russell Mark (Australia)	Albano Pera (Italy)	Zhang Bing (China)
2000	Richard Faulds (Great Britain)	Russell Mark (Australia)	Fehaid Al Deehani (Kuwait)
2004	Ahmed Al Maktoum (United Arab Emirates)	Rajyavardhan Singh Rathore (India)	Wang Zheng (China)
2008	Walton Eller (United States)	Francesco D'Aniello (Italy)	Hu Binyuan (China)

Men's Skeet

Year	Gold	Silver	Bronze
1968	Evgeni Petrov (Soviet Union)	Romano Garagnani (Italy)	Konrad Wirnhier (West Germany)
1972–1992: Event not held			
1996	Ennio Falco (Italy)	Mirosław Rzepkowski (Poland)	Andrea Benelli (Italy)
2000	Mykola Milchev (Ukraine)	Petr Málek (Czech Republic)	James Graves (United States)
2004	Andrea Benelli (Italy)	Marko Kemppainen (Finland)	Juan Miguel Rodríguez (Cuba)
2008	Vincent Hancock (United States)	Tore Brovold (Norway)	Anthony Terras (France)

Mixed Skeet

Year	Gold	Silver	Bronze
1972	Konrad Wirnhier (West Germany)	Evgeni Petrov (Soviet Union)	Michael Buchheim (East Germany)
1976	Josef Panáček (Czechoslovakia)	Eric Swinkels (Netherlands)	Wiesław Gawlikowski (Poland)
1980	Hans Kjeld Rasmussen (Denmark)	Lars-Göran Carlsson (Sweden)	Roberto Castrillo (Cuba)
1984	Matthew Dryke (United States)	Ole Riber Rasmussen (Denmark)	Luca Scribani Rossi (Italy)
1988	Axel Wegner (East Germany)	Alfonso de Iruarrizaga (Chile)	Jorge Guardiola (Spain)
1992	Zhang Shan (China)	Juan Giha (Peru)	Bruno Rossetti (Italy)

Women's Trap

Year	Gold	Silver	Bronze
2000	Dana Gudzinevičiūtė (Lithuania)	Delphine Racinet (France)	Gao E (China)
2004	Suzanne Balogh (Australia)	María Quintanal (Spain)	Lee Bo-Na (South Korea)
2008	Satu Mäkelä-Nummela (Finland)	Zuzana Štefečeková (Slovakia)	Corey Cogdell (United States)

Women's Skeet

Year	Gold	Silver	Bronze
2000	Zemfira Meftakhetdinova (Azerbaijan)	Svetlana Demina (Russia)	Diána Igaly (Hungary)
2004	Diána Igaly (Hungary)	Wei Ning (China)	Zemfira Meftakhetdinova (Azerbaijan)
2008	Chiara Cainero (Italy)	Kim Rhode (United States)	Christine Brinker (Germany)

Women's Individual Double Trap

Year	Gold	Silver	Bronze
1996	Kim Rhode (United States)	Susanne Kiermayer (Germany)	Deserie Huddleston (Australia)
2000	Pia Hansen (Sweden)	Deborah Gelisio (Italy)	Kim Rhode (United States)
2004	Kim Rhode (United States)	Lee Bo-Na (South Korea)	Gao E (China)

Men's 50-Meter Pistol

Year	Gold	Silver	Bronze
1896	Summer Paine (United States)	Holger Nielsen (Denmark)	Joannis Phrangoudis (Greece)
1900	Karl Röderer (Switzerland)	Achille Paroche (France)	Konrad Stäheli (Switzerland)
1904: Event not held			
1908	Paul Van Asbroeck (Belgium)	Réginald Storms (Belgium)	James Gorman (United States)
1912	Alfred Lane (United States)	Peter Dolfen (United States)	Charles Stewart (Great Britain)
1916: Olympics not held			
1920	Karl Frederick (United States)	Afrânio da Costa (Brazil)	Alfred Lane (United States)
1924–1932: Event not held			
1936	Torsten Ullman (Sweden)	Erich Krempel (Germany)	Charles des Jammonières (France)
1940–1944: Olympics not held			

Year	Gold	Silver	Bronze
1948	Edwin Vasquez Cam (Peru)	Rudolf Schnyder (Switzerland)	Torsten Ullman (Sweden)
1952	Huelet Benner (United States)	Angel Leon de Gozalo (Spain)	Ambrus Balogh (Hungary)
1956	Pentti Linnosvuo (Finland)	Makhmud Umarov (Soviet Union)	Offutt Pinion (United States)
1960	Alexei Gushchin (Soviet Union)	Makhmud Umarov (Soviet Union)	Yoshihisa Yoshikawa (Japan)
1964	Väinö Markkanen (Finland)	Franklin Green (United States)	Yoshihisa Yoshikawa (Japan)
1968	Grigori Kosych (Soviet Union)	Heinz Mertel (West Germany)	Harald Vollmar (East Germany)
1972–1980: Event not held			
1984	Xu Haifeng (China)	Ragnar Skanåker (Sweden)	Wang Yifu
1988	Sorin Babii (Romania)	Ragnar Skanåker (Sweden)	Igor Basinski (Soviet Union)
1992	Kanstantsin Lukashyk (Unified Team)	Wang Yifu (China)	Ragnar Skanåker (Sweden)
1996	Boris Kokorev (Russia)	Igor Basinski (Belarus)	Roberto Di Donna (Italy)
2000	Tanyu Kiryakov (Bulgaria)	Igor Basinski (Belarus)	Martin Tenk (Czech Republic)
2004	Mikhail Nestruyev (Russia)	Jin Jong-Oh (South Korea)	Kim Jong-Su (North Korea)
2008	Jin Jong-Oh (South Korea)	Tan Zongliang (China)	Vladimir Isakov (Russia)

Mixed 50-Meter Pistol

Year	Gold	Silver	Bronze
1972	Ragnar Skanåker (Sweden)	Daniel Iuga (Romania)	Rudolf Dollinger (Austria)
1976	Uwe Pottech (East Germany)	Harald Vollmar (East Germany)	Rudolf Dollinger (Austria)
1980	Aleksandr Melentiev (Soviet Union)	Harald Vollmar (East Germany)	Lubtcho Diakov (Bulgaria)

Men's Rifle, Moving Target

Year	Gold	Silver	Bronze
1908	John Fleming (Great Britain)	Maurice Matthews (Great Britain)	William Marsden (Great Britain)

Men's 300-Meter Military Rifle, Kneeling

Year	Gold	Silver	Bronze
1900	Konrad Stäheli (Switzerland)	Emil Kellenberger (Switzerland) Anders Peter Nielsen (Denmark)	Not awarded

Men's 300-Meter Military Rifle, Prone

Year	Gold	Silver	Bronze
1900	Achille Paroche (France)	Anders Peter Nielsen (Denmark)	Ole Østmo (Norway)
1904–1912: Event not held			
1916: Olympics not held			
1920	Otto Olsen (Norway)	Léon Johnson (France)	Fritz Kuchen (Switzerland)

Men's 300-Meter Military Rifle, Standing

Year	Gold	Silver	Bronze
1900	Lars Jørgen Madsen (Denmark)	Ole Østmo (Norway)	Charles Paumier (Belgium)

Softball

Women's Softball

Year	Gold	Silver	Bronze
1996	Laura Berg, Gillian Boxx, Sheila Cornell, Lisa Fernandez, Michele Granger, Lori Harrigan, Dionna Harris, Kim Maher, Leah O'Brien, Dot Richardson, Julie Smith, Michele Smith, Shelly Stokes, Danielle Tyler, Christa Lee Williams (United States)	An Zhongxin, Chen Hong, He Liping, Lei Li, Liu Xuqing, Liu Yaju, Ma Ying, Ou Jingbai, Tao Hua, Wang Lihong, Wang Ying, Wei Qiang, Xu Jian, Yan Fang, Zhang Chunfang (China)	Joanne Brown, Kim Cooper, Carolyn Crudgington, Kerry Dienelt, Peta Edebone, Tanya Harding, Jennifer Holliday, Jocelyn Lester, Sally McDermid, Francine McRae, Haylea Petrie, Nicole Richardson, Melanie Roche, Natalie Ward, Brooke Wilkins (Australia)
2000	Christie Ambrosi, Laura Berg, Jennifer Brundage, Crystl Bustos, Sheila Cornell, Lisa Fernandez, Lori Harrigan, Danielle Henderson, Jennifer McFalls, Stacey Nuveman, Leah O'Brien, Dot Richardson, Michele Smith, Michelle Venturella, Christa Lee Williams (United States)	Misako Ando, Yumiko Fujii, Taeko Ishikawa, Kazue Ito, Yoshimi Kobayashi, Shiori Koseki, Mariko Masubuchi, Naomi Matsumoto, Emi Naito, Haruka Saito, Juri Takayama, Hiroko Tamoto, Reika Utsugi, Miyo Yamada, Noriko Yamaji (Japan)	Sandra Allen, Joanne Brown, Kerry Dienelt, Peta Edbone, Sue Fairhurst, Selina Follas, Fiona Hanes, Kelly Hardie, Tanya Harding, Sally McDermid, Simmone Morrow, Melanie Roche, Natalie Titcume, Natalie Ward, Brooke Wilkins (Australia)
2004	Leah Amico, Laura Berg, Crystl Bustos, Lisa Fernandez, Jennie Finch, Tairia Flowers, Amanda Freed, Lori Hannigan, Lovieanne Jung, Kelly Kretschman, Jessica Mendoza, Stacey Nuveman, Cat Osterman, Janny Topping, Natasha Watley (United States)	Sandra Allen, Marissa Carpadios, Fiona Crawford, Amanda Doman, Peta Edebone, Tanya Harding, Natalie Hodgskin, Simmone Morrow, Tracey Mosley, Stacey Porter, Melanie Roche, Natalie Titcume, Natalie Ward, Brooke Wilkins, Kerry Wyborn (Australia)	Emi Inui, Kazue Ito, Yumi Iwabuchi, Masumi Mishina, Emi Naito, Haruka Saito, Hiroko Sakai, Naoko Sakamoto, Rie Sato, Yuki Sato, Juri Takayama, Yukiko Ueno, Reika Utsugi, Eri Yamada, Noriko Yamaji (Japan)
2008	Naho Emoto, Motoko Fujimoto, Megu Hirose, Emi Inui, Sachiko Ito, Ayumi Karino, Satoko Mabuchi, Yukiyo Mine, Masumi Mishina, Rei Nishiyama, Hiroko Sakai, Rie Sato, Mika Someya, Yukiko Ueno, Eri Yamada (Japan)	Monica Abbott, Laura Berg, Crystl Bustos, Andrea Duran, Jennie Finch, Tairia Flowers, Victoria Galindo, Lovieanne Jung, Kelly Kretschman, Lauren Lappin, Caitlin Lowe, Jessica Mendoza, Stacey Nuveman, Cat Osterman, Natasha Wiley (United States)	Jodie Bowering, Kylie Cronk, Kelly Hardie, Tanya Harding, Sandy Lewis, Simmone Morrow, Tracey Mosley, Stacey Porter, Melanie Roche, Justine Smethurst, Danielle Stewart, Natalie Titcume, Natalie Ward, Belinda Wright, Kerry Wyborn (Australia)

Swimming

Men's 1,000-Meter Freestyle

Year	Gold	Silver	Bronze
1900	John Arthur Jarvis (Great Britain)	Otto Wahle (Austria)	Zoltan Halmay (Hungary)

Women's 100-Meter Backstroke

Year	Gold	Silver	Bronze
1924	Sybil Bauer (United States)	Phyllis Harding (Great Britain)	Aileen Riggin (United States)
1928	Maria Braun (Netherlands)	Ellen King (Great Britain)	Margaret Cooper (Great Britain)
1932	Eleanor Holm (United States)	Philomenia Mealing (Australia)	Elizabeth Davies (Great Britain)

Year	Gold	Silver	Bronze
1936	Dina Senff (Netherlands)	Hendrika Mastenbroek (Netherlands)	Alice Bridges (United States)
1940–1944: Olympics not held			
1948	Karen Harup (Denmark)	Suzanne Zimmerman (United States)	Judith Davies (Australia)
1952	Joan Harrison (South Africa)	Geertje Wielema (Netherlands)	Jean Stewart (New Zealand)
1956	Judith Grinham (Great Britain)	Carin Cone (United States)	Margaret Edwards (Great Britain)
1960	Lynn Burke (United States)	Natalie Steward (Great Britain)	Satoko Tanaka (Japan)
1964	Kathleen Ferguson (United States)	Christine Caron (France)	Virginia Duenkel (United States)
1968	Kaye Marie Hall (United States)	Elaine Tanner (Canada)	Jane Ellen Swagerty (United States)
1972	Melissa Louise Belote (United States)	Andrea Gyarmati (Hungary)	Susanne Jean Atwood (United States)
1976	Ulrike Richter (East Germany)	Birgit Treiber (East Germany)	Nancy Ellen Garapick (Canada)
1980	Rica Reinisch (East Germany)	Ina Kleber (East Germany)	Petra Riedel (East Germany)
1984	Theresa Andrews (United States)	Elizabeth Mitchell (United States)	Jolanda De Rover (Netherlands)
1988	Kristin Otto (East Germany)	Krisztina Egerszegi (Hungary)	Cornelia Sirch (East Germany)
1992	Krisztina Egerszegi (Hungary)	Tunde Szabo (Hungary)	Lea Loveless (United States)
1996	Beth Botsford (United States)	Whitney Hedgepeth (United States)	Marianne Kriel (South Africa)
2000	Diana Mocanu (Romania)	Mai Nakamura (Japan)	Nina Alexandorvna Zhivanevskaya (Spain)
2004	Natalie Coughlin (United States)	Kirsty Coventry (Zimbabwe)	Laure Manaudou (France)
2008	Natalie Coughlin (United States)	Kirsty Coventry (Zimbabwe)	Margaret Hoelzer (United States)

Men's 100-Meter Backstroke

Year	Gold	Silver	Bronze
1904	Walter Brack (Germany)	Georg Hoffman (Germany)	Georg Zacharias (Germany)
1908	Arno Bieberstein (Germany)	Hans Dam (Denmark)	Herbert Nickall (Great Britain)
1912	Harry Hebner (United States)	Otto Fahr (Germany)	Paul Kellner (Germany)
1916: Olympics not held			
1920	Warren Kealoha (United States)	Raymond Kegeris (United States)	Gerard Blitz (Belgium)
1924	Warren Kealoha (United States)	Paul Wyatt (United States)	Istvan Bartha (Hungary)
1928	George Harold Kojac (United States)	Walter Laufer (United States)	Paul Wyatt (United States)
1932	Masaji Kiyokawa (Japan)	Toshio Iriye (Japan)	Kentaro Kawatsu (Japan)
1936	Adolph Kiefer (United States)	Albert Van de Weghe (United States)	Masaji Kiyokawa (Japan)
1940–1944: Olympics not held			
1948	Allen Stack (United States)	Robert Cowell (United States)	Georges Vallerey Jr. (France)
1952	Yoshinobu Oyakawa (United States)	Gilbert Bozon (France)	Jack Taylor (United States)
1956	David Theile (Australia)	John Monckton (Australia)	Frank McKinney (United States)
1960	David Theile (Australia)	Frank McKinney (United States)	Robert Bennett (United States)
1964: Event not held			
1968	Roland Matthes (East Germany)	Charles Hickcox (United States)	Ronald Mills (United States)
1972	Roland Matthes (East Germany)	Michael Stamm (United States)	John Murphy (United States)
1976	John Phillips Naber (United States)	Peter Rocca (United States)	Roland Matthes (East Germany)
1980	Bengt Baron (Sweden)	Viktor Kuznetsov (Soviet Union)	Vladimir Dolgov (Soviet Union)
1984	Richard Carey (United States)	David Wilson (United States)	Michael West (Canada)
1988	Daichi Suzuki (Japan)	David Berkoff (United States)	Igor Polyanski (Soviet Union)
1992	Mark Tewksbury (Canada)	Jeff Rouse (United States)	David Berkoff (United States)
1996	Jeff Rouse (United States)	Rodolfo Falcon Cabrera (Cuba)	Neisser Bent (Cuba)

Year	Gold	Silver	Bronze
2000	Lenny Krayzelburg (United States)	Matthew Welsh (Australia)	Stev Theloke (Germany)
2004	Aaron Peirsol (United States)	Markus Rogan (Austria)	Tomomi Morita (Japan)
2008	Aaron Peirsol (United States)	Matt Grevers (United States)	Arkady Vyatchanin (Russia) Hayden Stoeckel (Australia)

Men's 100-Meter Breaststroke

Year	Gold	Silver	Bronze
1968	Donald McKenzie (United States)	Vladimir Kosinsky (Soviet Union)	Nikolai Pankin (Soviet Union)
1972	Nobutaka Taguchi (Japan)	Thomas Bruce (United States)	John Hencken (United States)
1976	John Hencken (United States)	David Wilkie (Great Britain)	Arvidas Yozaitis (Soviet Union)
1980	Dunkan Goodhew (Great Britain)	Arsen Miskarov (Soviet Union)	Peter Evans (Australia)
1984	Steven Lundquist (United States)	Victor Davis (Canada)	Peter Evans (Australia)
1988	Adrian Moorhouse (Great Britain)	Karoly Guttler (Hungary)	Dmitri Volkov (Soviet Union)
1992	Nelson Diebel (United States)	Norbert Rozsa (Hungary)	Philip Rogers (Australia)
1996	Frederick Deburghgraeve (Belgium)	Jeremy Linn (United States)	Mark Warnecke (Germany)
2000	Domenico Fioravanti (Italy)	Ed Moses (United States)	Roman Sludnov (Russia)
2004	Kosuke Kitajima (Japan)	Brendan Hansen (United States)	Hugues Duboscq (France)
2008	Kosuke Kitajima (Japan)	Alexander Oen (Norway)	Hugues Duboscq (France)

Women's 100-Meter Breaststroke

Year	Gold	Silver	Bronze
1968	Djurdjica Bjedov (Yugoslavia)	Galina Prozumenschikova-Stepanova (Soviet Union)	Sharon Wichman (United States)
1972	Catherine Carr (United States)	Galina Prozumenschikova-Stepanova (Soviet Union)	Djurdjica Bjedov (Yugoslavia)
1976	Hannelore Anke (East Germany)	Lyubov Rusanova (Soviet Union)	Marina Koshevaya (Soviet Union)
1980	Ute Geweniger (East Germany)	Elvira Vasilkova (Soviet Union)	Susanne Nielsson (Denmark)
1984	Petra Van Staveren (Netherlands)	Anne Ottenbrite (Canada)	Catherine Poirot (France)
1988	Tania Bogomilova-Dangalakova (Bulgaria)	Antoaneta Frankeva (Bulgaria)	Silke Horner (East Germany)
1992	Elena Rudkovskaya (Unified Team)	Anita Nall (United States)	Samantha Riley (Australia)
1996	Penelope Heyns (South Africa)	Amanda Beard (United States)	Samantha Riley (Australia)
2000	Megan Quann (United States)	Leisel Jones (Australia)	Penelope Heyns (South Africa)
2004	Xuejuan Luo (China)	Brooke Hanson (Australia)	Leisel Jones (Australia)
2008	Leisel Jones (Australia)	Rebecca Soni (United States)	Mima Jukic (Austria)

Women's 100-Meter Butterfly

Year	Gold	Silver	Bronze
1956	Shelley Mann (United States)	Nancy Ramey (United States)	Mary Sears (United States)
1960	Carolyn Schuler (United States)	Marianne Heemskerk (Netherlands)	Janice Andrew (Australia)
1964	Sharon Stouder (United States)	Aagje Kok (Netherlands)	Kathleen Ellis (United States)
1968	Lynette McClements (Australia)	Eleanor Daniel (United States)	Susanne Shields (United States)
1972	Mayumi Aoki (Japan)	Roswitha Beier (East Germany)	Andrea Gyarmati (Hungary)
1976	Kornelia Ender (East Germany)	Andrea Pollack (East Germany)	Wendy Boglioli (United States)
1980	Caren Metschuck (East Germany)	Andrea Pollack (East Germany)	Christiane Knacke (East Germany)
1984	Mary Meagher (United States)	Jenna Leigh Johnson (United States)	Karin Seick (West Germany)
1988	Kristin Otto (East Germany)	Birte Weigang (East Germany)	Hong Qian (China)

Year	Gold	Silver	Bronze
1992	Hong Qian (China)	Christine Ahmann-Leighton (United States)	Catherine Plewinski (France)
1996	Amy Van Dyken (United States)	Limin Liu (China)	Angel Martino (United States)
2000	Inge De Bruijn (Netherlands)	Martina Moravcova (Slovakia)	Dara Torres (United States)
2004	Petria Thomas (Australia)	Otylia Jedrzejczak (Poland)	Inge De Bruijn (Netherlands)
2008	Lisbeth Trickett (Australia)	Christine Magnuson (United States)	Jessicah Schipper (Australia)

Men's 100-Meter Butterfly

Year	Gold	Silver	Bronze
1968	Douglas Russell (United States)	Mark Spitz (United States)	Ross Wales (United States)
1972	Mark Spitz (United States)	Bruce Robertson (Canada)	Jerry Heidenreich (United States)
1976	Matthew Vogel (United States)	Joseph Bottom (United States)	Gary Hall (United States)
1980	Par Arvidsson (Sweden)	Roger Pyttel (East Germany)	David Lopez-Zubero Purcell (Spain)
1984	Michael Gross (West Germany)	Pablo Morales (United States)	Glenn Buchanan (Australia)
1988	Anthony Nesty (Suriname)	Matthew Biondi (United States)	Andrew Jameson (Great Britain)
1992	Pablo Morales (United States)	Rafal Szukala (Poland)	Anthony Nesty (Suriname)
1996	Denis Pankratov (Russia)	Scott Miller (Australia)	Vladislav Kulikov (Russia)
2000	Lars Frolander (Sweden)	Michael Klim (Australia)	Geoff Huegill (Australia)
2004	Michael Phelps (United States)	Ian Crocker (United States)	Andriy Serdinov (Ukraine)
2008	Michael Phelps (United States)	Milorad Cavic (Serbia)	Andrew Lauterstein (Australia)

Men's 100-Meter Freestyle

Year	Gold	Silver	Bronze
1896	Alfred Hajos (Hungary)	Otto Herschmann (Austria)	
1900: Event not held			
1904	Zoltan Halmay (Hungary)	Charles Daniels (United States)	J. Scott Leary (United States)
1908	Charles Daniels (United States)	Zoltan Halmay (Hungary)	Harald Julin (Sweden)
1912	Duke Kahanamoku (United States)	Cecil Healy (Australasia)	Kenneth Huszagh (United States)
1916: Olympics not held			
1920	Duke Kahanamoku (United States)	Pua Kela Kealoha (United States)	William Harris (United States)
1924	Johnny Weissmuller (United States)	Duke Kahanamoku (United States)	Samuel Kahanamoku (United States)
1928	Johnny Weissmuller (United States)	Istvan Barany (Hungary)	Katsuo Takaishi (Japan)
1932	Yasuji Mioyazaki (Japan)	Tatsugo Kawaishi (Japan)	Albert Schwartz (United States)
1936	Ferenc Csik (Hungary)	Masanori Yusa (Japan)	Shigeo Arai (Japan)
1940–1944: Olympics not held			
1948	Walter Ris (United States)	Alan Ford (United States)	Geza Kadas (Hungary)
1952	Clark Scholes (United States)	Hiroshi Suzuki (Japan)	Goran Larsson (Sweden)
1956	Jon Henricks (Australia)	John Devitt (Australia)	Gary Chapman (Australia)
1960	John Devitt (Australia)	Lance Larson (United States)	Manoel Dos Santos (Brazil)
1964	Donald Schollander (United States)	Robert McGregor (Great Britain)	Hans-Joachim Klein (United Team of Germany)
1968	Michael Wenden (Australia)	Kenneth Walsh (United States)	Mark Spitz (United States)
1972	Mark Spitz (United States)	Jerry Heidenreich (United States)	Vladimir Bure (Soviet Union)
1976	James Montgomery (United States)	Jack Babashoff (United States)	Peter Nocke (West Germany)
1980	Jorg Woithe (East Germany)	Per Holmertz (Sweden)	Per Johansson (Sweden)
1984	Ambrose Iv Gaines (United States)	Marcus Stockwell (Australia)	Per Johansson (Sweden)
1988	Matthew Biondi (United States)	Christopher Jacobs (United States)	Stephan Caron (France)

Year	Gold	Silver	Bronze
1992	Alexander Popov (Unified Team)	Gustavo Borges (Brazil)	Stephan Caron (France)
1996	Alexander Popov (Unified Team)	Gary Hall (United States)	Gustavo Borges (Brazil)
2000	Pieter Van Den Hoogenband (Netherlands)	Alexander Popov (Russia)	Gary Hall (United States)
2004	Pieter Van Den Hoogenband (Netherlands)	Roland Schoeman (South Africa)	Ian Thorpe (Australia)
2008	Alain Bernard (France)	Eamon Sullivan (Australia)	Cesar Cielo Filho (Brazil) Jason Lezak (United States)

Women's 100-Meter Freestyle

Year	Gold	Silver	Bronze
1912	Fanny Durack (Australasia)	Wilhelmina Wylie (Australasia)	Jennie Fletcher (Great Britian)
1916: Olympics not held			
1920	Ethelda Bleibtry (United States)	Irene Guest (United States)	Frances Schroth (United States)
1924	Ethel Lackie (United States)	Mariechen Wehselau (United States)	Gertrude Ederle (United States)
1928	Albina Osipowich (United States)	Eleanor Saville (United States)	Margaret Cooper (Great Britain)
1932	Helene Madison (United States)	Willemyntje Den Ouden (Netherlands)	Eleanor Saville (United States)
1936	Hendrika Mastenbroek (Netherlands)	Jeanette Campbell (Argentina)	Gisela Arendt-Jacobs (Germany)
1940–1944: Olympics not held			
1948	Greta Andersen (Denmark)	Ann Curtis (United States)	Marie-Louise Linssen-Vaessen (Netherlands)
1952	Katalin Szoke (Hungary)	Johanna Termeulen (Netherlands)	Judith Temes (Hungary)
1956	Dawn Fraser (Australia)	Lorraine Crapp (Australia)	Faith Leech (Australia)
1960	Dawn Fraser (Australia)	Susan Von Saltza (United States)	Natalie Steward (Great Britain)
1964	Dawn Fraser (Australia)	Sharon Stouder (United States)	Kathleen Ellis (United States)
1968	Jane Henne (United States)	Susan Pedersen (United States)	Linda Gustavson (United States)
1972	Alexandra Neilson (United States)	Shirley Babashoff (United States)	Shane Gould (Australia)
1976	Kornelia Ender (East Germany)	Petra Priemer (East Germany)	Enith Brigitha (Netherlands)
1980	Barbara Krause (East Germany)	Caren Metschuck (East Germany)	Ines Diers (East Germany)
1984	Carolyn Steinseifer (United States) Nancy Hogshead (United States)		Annemarie Verstappen (Netherlands)
1988	Kristin Otto (East Germany)	Yong Zhuang (China)	Catherine Plewinski (France)
1992	Yong Zhuang (China)	Jenny Thompson (United States)	Franziska Van Almsick (Germany)
1996	Jingyi Le (China)	Sandra Voelker (Germany)	Angel Martino (United States)
2000	Inge De Bruijn (Netherlands)	Dara Torres (United States) Jenny Thompson (United States)	Therese Alshammar (Sweden)
2004	Jodie Henry (Australia)	Inge de Bruijn (Netherlands)	Natalie Coughlin (United States)
2008	Britta Steffen (Germany)	Lisbeth Trickett (Australia)	Natalie Coughlin (United States)

Men's 100-Meter Freestyle for Sailors

Year	Gold	Silver	Bronze
1896	Ioannis Malokinis (Greece)	Spiridon Chasapis (Greece)	Dimitrios Drivas (Greece)

Men's 1,200-Meter Freestyle

Year	Gold	Silver	Bronze
1896	Alfred Hajos (Hungary)	Joannis Andreou (Greece)	Efstathios Chorophas (Greece)

Men's 1,500-Meter Freestyle

Year	Gold	Silver	Bronze
1900	John Jarvis (Great Britain)	Otto Wahle (Austria)	Zoltan Halmay (Hungary)
1904	Emil Rausch (Germany)	Geza Kiss (Hungary)	Francis Gailey (United States)
1908	Henry Taylor (Great Britain)	Thomas Battersby (Great Britain)	Frank Beaurepaire (Australasia)
1912	George Hodgson (Canada)	John Hatfield (Great Britain)	Harold Hardwick (Australasia)
1916: Olympics not held			
1920	Norman Ross (United States)	George Vernot (Canada)	Frank Beaurepaire (Australia)
1924	Andrew Charlton (Australia)	Arne Borg (Sweden)	Frank Beaurepaire (Australia)
1928	Arne Borg (Sweden)	Andrew Charlton (Australia)	Clarence Crabbe (United States)
1932	Kusuo Kitamura (Japan)	Shozo Makino (Japan)	James Cristy (United States)
1936	Noboru Terada (Japan)	Jack Medica (United States)	Shunpei Uto (Japan)
1940–1944: Olympics not held			
1948	James Mclane (United States)	John Marshall (Australia)	Gyorgy Mitro (Hungary)
1952	Ford Konno (United States)	Shiro Hashizume (Japan)	Tetsuo Okamoto (Brazil)
1956	Murray Rose (Australia)	Tsuyoshi Yamanaka (Japan)	George Breen (United States)
1960	John Konrads (Australia)	Murray Rose (Australia)	George Breen (United States)
1964	Robert Windle (Australia)	John Nelson (United States)	Allan Wood (Australia)
1968	Michael Burton (United States)	John Kinsella (United States)	Gregory Brough (Australia)
1972	Michael Burton (United States)	Graham Windeatt (Australia)	Douglas Northway (United States)
1976	Brian Goodell (United States)	Robert Hackett (United States)	Stephen Holland (Australia)
1980	Vladimir Salnikov (Soviet Union)	Aleksandr Chaev (Soviet Union)	Maxwell Metzker (Australia)
1984	Michael O'Brien (United States)	George Dicarlo (United States)	Stefan Pfeiffer (West Germany)
1988	Vladimir Salnikov (Soviet Union)	Stefan Pfeiffer (West Germany)	Uwe Dassler (East Germany)
1992	Kieren Perkins (Australia)	Glen Housman (Australia)	Jorg Hoffman (Germany)
1996	Kieren Perkins (Australia)	Daniel Kowalski (Australia)	Graeme Smith (Great Britain)
2000	Grant Hackett (Australia)	Kieren Perkins (Australia)	Chris Thompson (United States)
2004	Grant Hackett (Australia)	Larsen Jensen (United States)	David Davies (Great Britain)
2008	Oussama Mellouli (Tunisia)	Grant Hackett (Australia)	Ryan Cochrane (Canada)

Women's 200-Meter Backstroke

Year	Gold	Silver	Bronze
1968	Lillian Watson (United States)	Elaine Tanner (Canada)	Kaye Hall (United States)
1972	Melissa Belote (United States)	Susanne Atwood (United States)	Donna Gurr (Canada)
1976	Ulrike Richter (East Germany)	Birgit Treiber (East Germany)	Nancy Garapick (Canada)
1980	Rica Reinisch (East Germany)	Comelia Polit (East Germany)	Birgit Treiber (East Germany)
1984	Jolanda De Rover (Netherlands)	Amy White (United States)	Aneta Patrascoiu (Romania)
1988	Krisztina Egerszegi (Hungary)	Kathrin Zimmermann (East Germany)	Comelia Sirch (East Germany)
1992	Krisztina Egerszegi (Hungary)	Dagmar Hase (Germany)	Nicole Stevenson (Australia)
1996	Krisztina Egerszegi (Hungary)	Whitney Hedgepeth (United States)	Cathleen Rund (Germany)
2000	Diana Mocanu (Romania)	Rozana Maracineanu (France)	Miki Nakao (Japan)
2004	Kirsty Coventry (Zimbabwe)	Stanislava Komarova (Russia)	Antje Bucshschulte (Germany) Reiko Nakamura (Japan)
2008	Kirsty Coventry (Zimbabwe)	Margaret Hoelzer (United States)	Reiko Nakamura (Japan)

Men's 200-Meter Backstroke

Year	Gold	Silver	Bronze
1900	Ernst Hoppenberg (Germany)	Karl Ruberl (Austria)	Johannes Drost (Netherlands)
1904–1912: Event not held			
1916: Olympics not held			
1920–1936: Event not held			

Year	Gold	Silver	Bronze
1940–1944: Olympics not held			
1948–1960: Event not held			
1964	Jedward Graef (United States)	Gary Dilley (United States)	Robert Bennett (United States)
1968	Roland Matthes (East Germany)	Mitchell Ivey (United States)	Jack Horsley (United States)
1972	Roland Matthes (East Germany)	Michael Stamm (United States)	Mitchell Ivey (United States)
1976	John Naber (United States)	Peter Rocca (United States)	Daniel Harrigan (United States)
1980	Sandor Wladar (Hungary)	Zoltan Verraszto (Hungary)	Mark Kerry (Australia)
1984	Richard Carey (United States)	Frederic Delcourt (France)	Cameron Henning (Canada)
1988	Igor Polyanski (Soviet Union)	Frank Baltrusch (East Germany)	Paul Kingsman (New Zealand)
1992	Martin Lopez-Zubero (Spain)	Vladimir Selkov (Unified Team)	Stefano Battistelli (Italy)
1996	Brad Bridgewater (United States)	Tripp Schwenk (United States)	Emanuele Merisi (Italy)
2000	Lenny Krayzelburg (United States)	Aaron Peirsol (United States)	Matthew Welsh (Australia)
2004	Aaron Peirsol (United States)	Markus Rogan (Austria)	Razvan Florea (Romania)
2008	Ryan Lochte (United States)	Aaron Peirsol (United States)	Arkady Vyatchanin (Russia)

Men's 200-Meter Breaststroke

Year	Gold	Silver	Bronze
1908	Frederick Holman (Great Britain)	William Robinson (Great Britain)	Pontus Hansson (Sweden)
1912	Walter Bathe (Germany)	Willy Lutzow (Germany)	Kurt Malisch (Germany)
1916: Olympics not held			
1920	Hakan Malmrot (Sweden)	Tor Henning (Sweden)	Arvo Aaltonen (Finland)
1924	Robert Skelton (United States)	Joseph De Combe (Belgium)	William Kirshbaum (United States)
1928	Yoshiyuki Tsuruta (Japan)	Erich Rademacher (Germany)	Teofilo Yldefonso (Philippines)
1932	Yoshiyuki Tsuruta (Japan)	Reizo Koike (Japan)	Teofilo Yldefonso (Philippines)
1936	Tetsuo Hamuro (Japan)	Erwin Sietas (Germany)	Reizo Koike (Japan)
1940–1944: Olympics not held			
1948	Joseph Verdeur (United States)	Keith Carter (United States)	Robert Sohl (United States)
1952	John Davies (Australia)	Bowen Stassforth (United States)	Herbert Klein (Germany)
1956	Masaru Furukawa (Japan)	Masahiro Yoshimura (Japan)	Kharis Yunichev (Soviet Union)
1960	William Mulliken (United States)	Yoshihiko Osaki (Japan)	Wieger Mensonides (Netherlands)
1964	Lawrence O'Brien (Australia)	Georgi Prokopenko (Soviet Union)	Chester Jastremski (United States)
1968	Felipe Munoz (Mexico)	Vladimir Kosinsky (Soviet Union)	Brian Job (United States)
1972	John Hencken (United States)	David Wilkie (Great Britain)	Nobutaka Taguchi (Japan)
1976	David Wilkie (Great Britain)	John Hencken (United States)	Richard Colella (United States)
1980	Robertas Zhulpa (Soviet Union)	Alban Vermes (Hungary)	Arsen Miskarov (Soviet Union)
1984	Victor Davis (Canada)	Glenn Beringen (Australia)	Etienne Dagon (Switzerland)
1988	Jozsef Szabo (Hungary)	Nick Gillingham (Great Britain)	Sergio Lopez Miro (Spain)
1992	Mike Barrowman (United States)	Norbert Rozsa (Hungary)	Nick Gillingham (Great Britain)
1996	Norbert Rozsa (Hungary)	Karoly Guttler (Hungary)	Andrey Korneyev (Russia)
2000	Domenico Fioravanti (Italy)	Terence Parkin (South Africa)	Davide Rummolo (Italy)
2004	Kosuke Kitajima (Japan)	Daniel Gyurta (Hungary)	Brendan Hansen (United States)
2008	Kosuke Kitajima (Japan)	Brenton Rickard (Australia)	Hugues Duboscq (France)

Women's 200-Meter Breaststroke

Year	Gold	Silver	Bronze
1924	Lucille Morton (Great Britain)	Agnes Geraghty (United States)	Gladys Carson (Great Britain)
1928	Hilde Schrader (Germany)	Mietje Baron (Netherlands)	Charlotte Muhe (Germany)
1932	Clare Dennis (Australia)	Hideko Maehata (Japan)	Else Jacobsen (Denmark)
1936	Hideko Maehata (Japan)	Martha Genenger (Germany)	Inge Sorensen (Denmark)
1940–1944: Olympics not held			
1948	Petronella Van Vliet (Netherlands)	Beatrice Lyons (Australia)	Eva Novak-Gerard (Hungary)

Year	Gold	Silver	Bronze
1952	Eva Szekely (Hungary)	Eva Novak-Gerard (Hungary)	Helen Gordon-McKay (Great Britain)
1956	Ursala Happe-Krey (United Team Germany)	Eva Szekely (Hungary)	Eva-Maria Ten Elsen (United Team Germany)
1960	Anita Lonsbrough (Great Britain)	Wiltrud Urselmann (United Team Germany)	Barbara Gobel (United Team Germany)
1964	Galina Prozumenschikova-Stepanova (Soviet Union)	Claudia Kolb (United States)	Svetlana Babanina (Soviet Union)
1968	Sharon Wichman (United States)	Djurdjica Bjedov (Yugoslavia)	Galina Prozumenschikova-Stepanova (Soviet Union)
1972	Beverley Whitfield (Australia)	Dana Schoenfield (United States)	Galina Prozumenschikova-Stepanova (Soviet Union)
1976	Marina Koshevaya (Soviet Union)	Marina Yurchenya (Soviet Union)	Lyubov Rusanova (Soviet Union)
1980	Lina Kachushite (Soviet Union)	Svetlana Varganova (Soviet Union)	Yulia Bogdanova (Soviet Union)
1984	Anne Ottenbrite (Canada)	Susan Rapp (United States)	Ingrid Lempereur (Belgium)
1988	Silke Horner (East Germany)	Xiao-Min Huang (China)	Antoaneta Frenkeva (Bulgaria)
1992	Kyoko Iwasaki (Japan)	Li Lin (China)	Anita Nall (United States)
1996	Penelope Heyns (South Africa)	Amanda Beard (United States)	Agnes Kovacs (Hungary)
2000	Agnes Kovacs (Hungary)	Kristy Kowal (United States)	Amanda Beard (United States)
2004	Amanda Beard (United States)	Leisel Jones (Australia)	Anne Poleska (Germany)
2008	Rebecca Soni (United States)	Leisel Jones (Australia)	Sara Nordenstam (Norway)

Men's 200-Meter Butterfly

Year	Gold	Silver	Bronze
1956	William Yorzyk (United States)	Takashi Ishimoto (Japan)	Gyorgy Tumpek (Hungary)
1960	Michael Troy (United States)	Neville Hayes (Australia)	John Gillanders (United States)
1964	Kevin Berry (Australia)	Carl Robie (United States)	Frederick Schmidt (United States)
1968	Carl Robie (United States)	Martyn Woodroffe (Great Britain)	John Ferris (United States)
1972	Mark Spitz (United States)	Gary Hall (United States)	Robin Backhaus (United States)
1976	Michael Bruner (United States)	Steven Gregg (United States)	William Forrester (United States)
1980	Sergei Fesenko (Soviet Union)	Philip Hubble (Great Britain)	Roger Pyttel (East Germany)
1984	Jonathan Sieben (Australia)	Michael Gross (West Germany)	Rafael Vidal Castro (Venezuela)
1988	Michael Gross (West Germany)	Benny Leo Nielsen (Denmark)	Anthony Mosse (New Zealand)
1992	Melvin Stewart (United States)	Danyon Loader (New Zealand)	Franck Esposito (France)
1996	Denis Pankratov (Russia)	Tom Malchow (United States)	Scott Goodman (Australia)
2000	Tom Malchow (United States)	Denys Sylantyev (Ukraine)	Justin Norris (Australia)
2004	Michael Phelps (United States)	Takashi Yamamoto (Japan)	Stephen Parry (Great Britain)
2008	Michael Phelps (United States)	Laszlo Cseh (Hungary)	Takeshi Matsuda (Japan)

Women's 200-Meter Butterfly

Year	Gold	Silver	Bronze
1968	Aagje Kok (Netherlands)	Helga Lindner (East Germany)	Eleanor Daniel (United States)
1972	Karen Moe-Thornton (United States)	Lynn Colella (United States)	Eleanor Daniel (United States)
1976	Andrea Pollack (East Germany)	Ulrike Tauber (East Germany)	Rosemarie Kother-Gabriel (East Germany)
1980	Ines Geissler (East Germany)	Sybille Schonrock (East Germany)	Michelle Ford (Australia)
1984	Mary Meagher (United States)	Karen Phillips (Australia)	Ina Beyermann (West Germany)
1988	Kathleen Nord (East Germany)	Birte Weigang (East Germany)	Mary Meagher (United States)
1992	Summer Sanders (United States)	Xiaohong Wang (China)	Susan O'Neill (Australia)
1996	Susan O'Neill (Australia)	Petria Thomas (Australia)	Michelle Smith (Ireland)
2000	Misty Hyman (United States)	Susan O'Neill (Australia)	Petria Thomas (Australia)

Year	Gold	Silver	Bronze
2004	Otylia Jedrzejczak (Poland)	Petria Thomas (Australia)	Yuko Nakanishi (Japan)
2008	Zige Liu (China)	Liuyang Jiao (China)	Jessicah Schipper (Australia)

Men's 200-Meter Freestyle

Year	Gold	Silver	Bronze
1900	Frederick Lane (Australia)	Zoltan Halmay (Hungary)	Karl Ruberl (Austria)
1904	Charles Daniels (United States)	Francis Gailey (United States)	Emil Rausch (Germany)
1908–1912: Event not held			
1916: Olympics not held			
1920–1936: Event not held			
1940–1944: Olympics not held			
1948–1964: Event not held			
1968	Michael Wenden (Australia)	Donald Schollander (United States)	John Nelson (United States)
1972	Mark Spitz (United States)	Robert Genter (United States)	Werner Lampe (West Germany)
1976	Bruce Furniss (United States)	John Naber (United States)	James Montgomery (United States)
1980	Sergei Koplyakov (Soviet Union)	Andrei Krylov (Soviet Union)	Graeme Brewer (Australia)
1984	Michael Gross (West Germany)	Michael Heath (United States)	Thomas Fahrner (West Germany)
1988	Duncan Armstrong (Australia)	Anders Holmertz (Sweden)	Matthew Biondi (United States)
1992	Evgueni Sadovyi (Unified Team)	Anders Holmertz (Sweden)	Antti Kasvio (Finland)
1996	Danyon Loader (New Zealand)	Gustavo Borges (Brazil)	Daniel Kowalski (Australia)
2000	Pieter Van Den Hoogenband (Netherlands)	Ian Thorpe (Australia)	Massimiliano Rosolino (Italy)
2004	Ian Thorpe (Australia)	Pieter Van Den Hoogenband (Netherlands)	Michael Phelps (United States)
2008	Michael Phelps (United States)	Park Tae-Hwan (South Korea)	Peter Vanderkaay (United States)

Women's 200-Meter Freestyle

Year	Gold	Silver	Bronze
1968	Deborah Meyer (United States)	Jane Henne (United States)	Jane Barkman (United States)
1972	Shane Gould (Australia)	Shirley Babashoff (United States)	Keena Rothhammer (United States)
1976	Kornelia Ender (East Germany)	Shirley Babashoff (United States)	Enith Brigitha (Netherlands)
1980	Barbara Krause (East Germany)	Ines Diers (East Germany)	Carmela Schmidt (East Germany)
1984	Mary Wayte (United States)	Cynthia Woodhead (United States)	Annemarie Verstappen (Netherlands)
1988	Heike Friedrich (East Germany)	Silvia Poll Ahrens (Costa Rica)	Manuela Stellmach (East Germany)
1992	Nicole Haislett (United States)	Franziska Van Almsick (Germany)	Kerstin Kielgass (Germany)
1996	Claudia Ahrens (Costa Rica)	Franziska Van Almsick (Germany)	Dagmar Hase (Germany)
2000	Susan O'Neill (Australia)	Martina Moravcova (Slovakia)	Claudia Ahrens (Costa Rica)
2004	Camelia Potec (Romania)	Federica Pellegrini (Italy)	Solenne Figues (France)
2008	Federica Pellegrini (Italy)	Sare Isakovic (Slovenia)	Jiaying Pang (China)

Women's 200-Meter Individual Medley

Year	Gold	Silver	Bronze
1968	Claudia Kolb (United States)	Susan Pedersen (United States)	Jane Henne (United States)
1972	Shane Gould (Australia)	Kornelia Ender (East Germany)	Lynn Vidali (United States)
1976–1980: Event not held			
1984	Tracy Caulkins (United States)	Nancy Hogshead (United States)	Michelle Pearson (Australia)
1988	Daniela Hunger (Germany)	Elena Dendeberova (Soviet Union)	Noemi Lung (Romania)
1992	Li Lin (China)	Summer Sanders (United States)	Daniela Hunger (Germany)
1996	Michelle Smith (Ireland)	Marianne Limpert (Canada)	Li Lin (China)

Year	Gold	Silver	Bronze
2000	Yana Klochkova (Ukraine)	Beatrice Caslaru (Romania)	Christina Teuscher (United States)
2004	Yana Klochkova (Ukraine)	Amanda Beard (United States)	Kirsty Coventry (Zimbabwe)
2008	Stephanie Rice (Australia)	Kirsty Coventry (Zimbabwe)	Natalie Coughlin (United States)

Men's 200-Meter Individual Medley

Year	Gold	Silver	Bronze
1968	Charles Hickcox (United States)	Gregory Buckingham (United States)	John Ferris (United States)
1972	Gunnar Larsson (Sweden)	Alexander McKee (United States)	Steven Furniss (United States)
1976–1980: Event not held			
1984	Alexander Baumann (Canada)	Pablo Morales (United States)	Neil Cochran (Great Britain)
1988	Tamas Darnyi (Hungary)	Patrick Kuhl (East Germany)	Vadim Yaroshchuk (Soviet Union)
1992	Tamas Darnyi (Hungary)	Gregory Burgess (United States)	Attila Czene (Hungary)
1996	Attila Czene (Hungary)	Jani Sievinen (Finland)	Curtis Myden (Canada)
2000	Massimiliano Rosolino (Italy)	Tom Dolan (United States)	Tom Wilkens (United States)
2004	Michael Phelps (United States)	Ryan Lochte (United States)	George Bovell (Trinidad and Tobago)
2008	Michael Phelps (United States)	Laszlo Cseh (Hungary)	Ryan Lochte (United States)

Men's 200-Meter Obstacle Event

Year	Gold	Silver	Bronze
1900	Frederick Lane (Australia)	Otto Wahle (Austria)	Peter Kemp (Great Britain)

Men's 200-Meter Team Swimming

Year	Gold	Silver	Bronze
1900	Ernest Hoppenberg, Herbert Von Petersdorff, Julius Frey, Max Hainle, Max Schone (Germany)	Bertrand, Cadet, Maurice Hochepied, Verbecke, Victor Hochepied (France)	Desire Merchez, Houben, Jean Leuillieux, Louis Martin, Tartara (France)

Men's 4,000-Meter Freestyle

Year	Gold	Silver	Bronze
1900	John Jarvis (Great Britain)	Zoltan Halmay (Hungary)	Louis Martin (France)

Men's 400-Meter Breaststroke

Year	Gold	Silver	Bronze
1904	Georg Zacharias (Germany)	Walter Brack (Germany)	Henry Handy (United States)
1908: Event not held			
1912	Walter Bathe (Germany)	Tor Henning (Sweden)	Percy Courtman (Great Britain)
1916: Olympics not held			
1920	Hakan Malmrot (Sweden)	Tor Henning (Sweden)	Arvo Aaltonen (Finland)

Men's 400-Meter Freestyle

Year	Gold	Silver	Bronze
1896	Paul Neumann (Austria)	Antonios Pepanos (Greece)	Efstathios Chorophas (Greece)
1900: Event not held			
1904	Charles Daniels (United States)	Francis Gailey (United States)	Otto Wahle (Austria)
1908	Henry Taylor (Great Britain)	Frank Beaurepaire (Australasia)	Otto Scheff (Austria)
1912	George Hodgson (Canada)	John Hatfield (Great Britain)	Harold Hardwick (Australasia)
1916: Olympics not held			
1920	Norman Ross (United States)	Ludy Langer (United States)	George Vernot (Canada)

Year	Gold	Silver	Bronze
1924	JohnnyWeissmuller (United States)	Arne Borg (Sweden)	Andrew Charlton (Australia)
1928	Victoriano Zorrilla (Argentina)	Andrew Charlton (Australia)	Arne Borg (Sweden)
1932	Clarence Crabbe (United States)	Jean Taris (France)	Tsutomu Oyokota (Japan)
1936	Jack Medica (United States)	Shunpei Uto (Japan)	Shozo Makino (Japan)
1940–1944: Olympics not held			
1948	William Smith (United States)	James Mclane (United States)	John Marshall (Australia)
1952	Jean Boiteux (France)	Ford Konno (United States)	Per-Olof Ostrand (Sweden)
1956	Murray Rose (Australia)	Tsuyoshi Yamanaka (Japan)	George Breen (United States)
1960	Murray Rose (Australia)	Tsuyoshi Yamanaka (Japan)	John Konrads (Australia)
1964	Donald Schollander (United States)	Frank Wiegand (Unified Team)	Allan Wood (Australia)
1968	Michael Burton (United States)	Ralph Hutton (Canada)	Alain Mosconi (France)
1972	Bradford Cooper (Australia)	Robert Genter (United States)	Thomas McBreen (United States)
1976	Brian Goodell (United States)	Timothy Shaw (United States)	Vladimir Raskatov (Soviet Union)
1980	Vladimir Salnikov (Soviet Union)	Andrei Krylov (Soviet Union)	Ivar Stukolkin (Soviet Union)
1984	George Dicarlo (United States)	John Mykkanen (United States)	Justin Lemberg (Australia)
1988	Uwe Dassler (East Germany)	Duncan Armstrong (Australia)	Artur Wojdat (Poland)
1992	Evgueni Sadovyi (Unified Team)	Kieren Perkins (Australia)	Anders Holmertz (Sweden)
1996	Danyon Loader (New Zealand)	Paul Palmer (Great Britain)	Daniel Kowalski (Australia)
2000	Ian Thorpe (Australia)	Massimiliano Rosolino (Italy)	Klete Keller (United States)
2004	Ian Thorpe (Australia)	Grant Hackett (Australia)	Klete Keller (United States)
2008	Park Tae-Hwan (South Korea)	Lin Zhang (China)	Larsen Jensen (United States)

Women's 400-Meter Freestyle

Year	Gold	Silver	Bronze
1920	Ethelda Bleibtrey (United States)	Margaret Woodbridge (United States)	Frances Schroth (United States)
1924	Martha Norelius (United States)	Helen Wainwright (United States)	Gertrude Ederle (United States)
1928	Martha Norelius (United States)	Maria Braun (Netherlands)	Josephine McKim (United States)
1932	Helene Madison (United States)	Lenore Kight-Wingard (United States)	Jenny Maakal (South Africa)
1936	Hendrika Mastenbroek (Netherlands)	Ragnild Hveger (Denmark)	Lenore Kight-Wingard (United States)
1940–1944: Olympics not held			
1948	Ann Curtis (United States)	Karen Harup (Denmark)	Catherine Gibson (Great Britain)
1952	Valeria Gyenge (Hungary)	Eva Novak-Gerard (Hungary)	Evelyn Kawamoto (United States)
1956	Lorraine Crapp (Australia)	Dawn Fraser (Australia)	Sylvia Ruuska (United States)
1960	Susan Von Saltza (United States)	Jane Cederqvist (Sweden)	Catharina Lagerberg (Netherlands)
1964	Virginia Duenkel (United States)	Marilyn Ramenofsky (United States)	Therese Stickles (United States)
1968	Deborah Meyer (United States)	Linda Gustavson (United States)	Karen Moras (Australia)
1972	Shane Gould (Australia)	Novella Calligaris (Italy)	Gudrun Wegner (East Germany)
1976	Petra Thumer (East Germany)	Shirley Babashoff (United States)	Shannon Smith (Canada)
1980	Ines Diers (East Germany)	Petra Schneider (East Germany)	Carmela Schmidt (East Germany)
1984	Tiffany Lisa Cohen (United States)	Sarah Hardcastle (Great Britain)	June Croft (Great Britain)
1988	Janet Evans (United States)	Heike Friedrich (East Germany)	Anke Mohring (East Germany)
1992	Dagmar Hase (Germany)	Janet Evans (United States)	Hayley Lewis (Australia)
1996	Michelle Smith (Ireland)	Dagmar Hase (Germany)	Kirsten Vlieghuis (Netherlands)
2000	Brooke Bennett (United States)	Diana Munz (United States)	Claudia Ahrens (Costa Rica)
2004	Laure Manaudou (France)	Otylia Jedrzejczak (Poland)	Kaitlin Sandeno (United States)
2008	Rebecca Adlington (Great Britain)	Katie Hoff (United States)	Joanne Jackson (Great Britain)

Women's 400-Meter Individual Medley

Year	Gold	Silver	Bronze
1964	Donna De Varona (United States)	Sharon Finneran (United States)	Martha Randall (United States)
1968	Claudia Kolb (United States)	Lynn Vidali (United States)	Sabine Steinbach (East Germany)
1972	Gail Neall (Australia)	Leslie Cliff (Canada)	Novella Calligaris (Italy)
1976	Ulrike Tauber (East Germany)	Cheryl Gibson (Canada)	Rebecca Smith (Canada)
1980	Petra Schneider (East Germany)	Sharron Davies (Great Britain)	Agnieszka Czopek (Poland)
1984	Tracy Caulkins (United States)	Suzanne Landells (Australia)	Petra Zindler (West Germany)
1988	Janet Evans (United States)	Noemi Lung (Romania)	Daniela Hunger (East Germany)
1992	Krisztina Egerszegi (Hungary)	Li Lin (China)	Summer Sanders (United States)
1996	Michelle Smith (Ireland)	Allison Wagner (United States)	Krisztina Egerszegi (Hungary)
2000	Yana Klochkova (Ukraine)	Yasuko Tajima (Japan)	Beatrice Caslaru (Romania)
2004	Yana Klochkova (Ukraine)	Kaitlin Sandeno (United States)	Georgina Bardach (Argentina)
2008	Stephanie Rice (Australia)	Kirsty Coventry (Zimbabwe)	Katie Hoff (United States)

Men's 400-Meter Individual Medley

Year	Gold	Silver	Bronze
1964	Richard Roth (United States)	Roy Saari (United States)	Gerhard Hetz (United Team of Germany)
1968	Charles Hickcox (United States)	Gary Hall (United States)	Michael Holthaus (West Germany)
1972	Gunnar Larsson (Sweden)	Alexander McKee (United States)	Andras Hargitay (Hungary)
1976	Rodney Strachan (United States)	Alexander McKee (United States)	Andrei Smirnov (Soviet Union)
1980	Aleksandr Sidorenko (Soviet Union)	Sergei Fesenko (Soviet Union)	Zoltan Verraszto (Hungary)
1984	Alexander Baumann (Canada)	Ricardo Prado (Brazil)	Robert Woodhouse (Australia)
1988	Tamas Darnyi (Hungary)	David Wharton (United States)	Stefano Battistelli (Italy)
1992	Tamas Darnyi (Hungary)	Eric Namesnik (United States)	Luca Sacchi (Italy)
1996	Tom Dolan (United States)	Eric Namesnik (United States)	Curtis Myden (Canada)
2000	Tom Dolan (United States)	Erik Vendt (United States)	Curtis Myden (Canada)
2004	Michael Phelps (United States)	Erik Vendt (United States)	Laszlo Cseh (Hungary)
2008	Michael Phelps (United States)	Laszlo Cseh (Hungary)	Ryan Lochte (United States)

Women's 4 × 100-Meter Freestyle Relay

Year	Gold	Silver	Bronze
1912	Belle Moore, Jennie Fletcher, Annie Speirs, Irene Steer (Great Britain)	Wally Dressel, Louise Otto, Hermine Stindt, Grete Rosenberg (Germany)	Margarete Adler, Klara Milch, Josephine Sticker, Berta Zahourek (Austria)
1916: Olympics not held			
1920	Margaret Woodbridge, Frances Schroth, Irene Guest, Ethelda Bleibtrey (United States)	Hilda James, Constance Jeans, Charlotte Radcliffe, Grace McKenzie (Great Britain)	Aina Berg, Emily Machnow, Carin Nilsson, Jane Gylling (Sweden)
1924	Euphrasia Donnelly, Gertrude Ederle, Ethel Lackie, Mariechen Wehselau (United States)	Florence Barker, Constance Jeans, Grace McKenzie, Iris Tanner (Great Britain)	Aina Berg, Gurli Ewerlund, Wivan Pettersson, Hjordis Topel (Sweden)
1928	Eleanor Garatti, Adelaide Lambert, Martha Norelius, Albina Osipowich (United States)	Joyce Cooper, Ellen King, Cissie Stewart, Iris Tanner (Great Britain)	Marie Bedford, Freddie van der Goes, Rhoda Rennie, Kathleen Russell (South Africa)
1932	Helen Johns, Helene Madison, Josephine McKim, Eleanor Saville (United States)	Corrie Laddé, Willy den Ouden, Puck Oversloot, Maria Vierdag (Netherlands)	Joyce Cooper, Valerie Davies, Edna Hughes, Helen Varcoe (Great Britain)
1936	Rie Mastenbroek, Willy den Ouden, Jopie Selbach, Tini Wagner (Netherlands)	Gisela Arendt, Ruth Halbsguth, Leni Lohmar, Ingeborg Schmitz (Germany)	Mavis Freeman, Bernice Lapp, Olive McKean, Katherine Rawls (United States)

Year	Gold	Silver	Bronze
1940–1944: Olympics not held			
1948	Marie Corridon, Thelma Kalama, Brenda Helser, Ann Curtis (United States)	Eva Riis, Karen Harup, Greta Andersen, Fritze Carstensen (Denmark)	Irma Heijting-Schuhmacher, Margot Marsman, Marie-Louise Linssen-Vaessen, Hannie Termeulen (Netherlands)
1952	Ilona Novák, Judit Temes, Eva Novak, Katalin Szoke (Hungary)	Marie-Louise Linssen-Vaessen, Koosje van Voorn, Hannie Termeulen, Irm Heijting-Schuhmacher (Netherlands)	Jacqueline Lavine, Marilee Stepan, Joan Alderson-Rosazza, Evelyn Kawamoto (United States)
1956	Dawn Fraser, Faith Leech, Sandra Morgan, Lorraine Crapp (Australia)	Sylvia Ruuska, Shelley Mann, Nancy Simons, Joan Alderson-Rosazza (United States)	Natalie Myburgh, Susan Roberts, Moira Abernethy, Jeanette Myburgh (South Africa)
1960	Joan Spillane, Shirley Stobs, Carolyn Wood, Chris von Saltza (United States)	Dawn Fraser, Ilsa Konrads, Lorraine Crapp, Alva Colguhuon (Australia)	Christel Steffin, Heidi Pechstein, Gisela Weiss, Ursula Brunner (Germany)
1964	Sharon Stouder, Donna de Varona, Lillian Watson, Kathleen Ellis (United States)	Robyn Thorn, Janice Murphy, Lynette Bell, Dawn Fraser (Australia)	Pauline van der Wildt, Toos Beumer, Winnie ven Weerden-burg, Erica Terpstra (Netherlands)
1968	Jane Barkman, Linda Gustavson, Susan Pedersen, Jan Henne (United States)	Gabriele Wetzko, Roswitha Krause, Uta Schmuck, Gabriele Perthes (East Germany)	Angela Coughlan, Marilyn Corson, Elaine Tanner, Marion Lay (Canada)
1972	Shirley Babashoff, Jane Barkman, Jennifer Kemp, Sandra Neilson (United States)	Andrea Eife, Kornelia Ender, Elke Sehmisch, Gabriele Wetzko (East Germany)	Gudrun Beckmann, Heidemarie Reineck, Angela Steinbach, Jutta Weber (West Germany)
1976	Kim Peyton, Wendy Boglioli, Jill Sterkel, Shirley Babashoff (United States)	Kornelia Ender, Petra Priemer, Andrea Pollack, Claudia Hempel (East Germany)	Gail Amundrud, Barbara Clark, Becky Smith, Anne Jardin (Canada)
1980	Barbara Krause, Caren Metschuck, Ines Diers, Sarina Hulsenbeck (East Germany)	Carina Ljungdahl, Tina Gustafsson, Agneta Martensson, Agneta Eriksson (Sweden)	Conny van Bentum, Wilma van Velsen, Reggie de Jong, Annelies Maas (Netherlands)
1984	Jenna Johnson, Carrie Steinseifer, Dara Torres, Nancy Hogshead (United States)	Annemarie Verstappen, Elles Voskes, Desi Reijers, Conny van Bentum (Netherlands)	Iris Zscherpe, Susanne Schuster, Christiane Pielke, Karin Seick (West Germany)
1988	Kristin Otto, Katrin Meibner, Daniela Hunger, Manuela Stellmach (East Germany)	Marianne Muis, Mildred Muis, Conny van Bentum, Karin Brienesse (Netherlands)	Mary Wayte, Mitzi Kremer, Laura Walker, Dara Torres (United States)
1992	Nicole Haislett, Angel Martino, Jenny Thompson, Dara Torres (United States)	Le Jingyi, Lu Bin, Zhuang Yong, Yang Wenyi (China)	Franziska van Almsick, Daniela Hunger, Simone Osygus, Manuela Stellmach (Germany)
1996	Angel Martino, Amy Van Dyken, Catherine Fox, Jenny Thompson (United States)	Le Jingyi, Na Chao, Yun Nian, Shan Ying (China)	Sandra Völker, Simone Osygus, Antje Buschschulte, Franziska van Almsick (Germany)
2000	Amy Van Dyken, Courtney Shealy, Jenny Thompson, Dara Torres (United States)	Manon van Rooijen, Wilma van Hofwegen, Inge de Bruijn, Thamar Henneken (Netherlands)	Johanna Sjöberg, Therese Alshammar, Louise Johncke, Anna-Karin Kammerling (Sweden)
2004	Alice Mills, Libby Lenton, Petria Thomas, Jodie Henry (Australia)	Kara Lynn Joyce, Natalie Coughlin, Amanda Weir, Jenny Thompson (United States)	Chantal Groot, Inge Dekker, Marleen Veldhuis, Inge de Bruijn (Netherlands)
2008	Inge Dekker, Ranomi Kromowi-djojo, Femke Heemskerk, Marleen Veldhuis (Netherlands)	Natalie Coughlin, Lacey Nymeyer, Kara Lynn Joyce, Dara Torres (United States)	Cate Campbell, Alice Mills, Melanie Schlanger, Lisbeth Trickett (Australia)

Men's 4 × 100-Meter Freestyle Relay

Year	Gold	Silver	Bronze
1964	Stephen Clark, Mike Austin, Gary Ilman, Don Schollander (United States)	Horst Löffler, Frank Wiegand, Uwe Jacobsen, Hans-Joachim Klein (Germany)	David Dickson, Peter Doak, John Ryan, Bob Windle (Australia)
1968	Zachary Zorn, Stephen Rerych, Kenneth Walsh, Mark Spitz (United States)	Georgi Kulikov, Viktor Mazanov, Semyon Belitz-Geyman, Leonid Ilyichov (Soviet Union)	Greg Rogers, Robert Cusack, Bob Windle, Michael Wenden (Australia)
1972	David Edgar, John Murphy, Jerry Heidenreich, Mark Spitz (United States)	Vladimir Bure, Viktor Mazanov, Viktor Aboimov, Igor Grivennikov (Soviet Union)	Roland Matthes, Wilfried Hartung, Peter Bruch, Lutz Unger (East Germany)
1976–1980: Event not held			
1984	Chris Cavanaugh, Michael Heath, Matt Biondi, Rowdy Gaines (United States)	Greg Fasala, Neil Brooks, Michael Delany, Mark Stockwell (Australia)	Thomas Lejdström, Bengt Baron, Mikael Om, Per Johansson (Sweden)
1988	Chris Jacobs, Troy Dalbey, Tom Jager, Matt Biondi, Doug Gjertsen (United States)	Gennadiy Prigoda, Yuri Bashkatov, Nikolai Yevseyev, Vladimir Tkachenko, Raimundas Mazuolis (Soviet Union)	Dirk Richter, Thomas Flemming, Lars Hinneburg, Steffen Zesner (East Germany)
1992	Joe Hudepohl, Matt Biondi, Tom Jager, Jon Olsen (United States)	Pavlo Khnykin, Gennadily Prigoda, Yuri Bashkatov, Alexander Popov (Unified Team)	Dirk Richter, Christian Troger, Steffen Zesner, Mark Pinger (Germany)
1996	Jon Olsen, Josh Davis, Bradley Schumacher, Gary Hall Jr. (United States)	Roman Yegorov, Alexander Popov, Vladimir Predkin, Vladimir Pyshnenko (Russia)	Christian Tröger, Bengt Zikarsky, Bjorn Zikarsky, Mark Pinger (Germany)
2000	Michael Klim, Chris Fydler, Ashley Callus, Ian Thorpe (Australia)	Anthony Ervin, Neil Walker, Jason Lezak, Gary Hall Jr. (United States)	Fernando Scherer, Gustavo Borges, Carlos Jayme, Edvaldo Valerio (Brazil)
2004	Roland Schoeman, Lyndon Ferns, Darian Townsend, Ryk Neethling (South Africa)	Johan Kenkhuis, Mitja Zastrow, Klaas-Erik Zwering, Pieter van den Hoogenband (Netherlands)	Ian Crocker, Michael Phelps, Neil Walker, Jason Lezak (United States)
2008	Michael Phelps, Garrett Weber-Gale, Cullen Jones, Jason Lezak (United States)	Amaury Leveaux, Fabien Gilot, Frederick Bousquet, Alain Bernard (France)	Eamon Sullivan, Andrew Lauterstein, Ashley Callus, Matt Targett (Australia)

Men's 4 × 100-Meter Medley Relay

Year	Gold	Silver	Bronze
1960	Frank McKinney, Paul Hait, Lance Larson, Jeff Farrell (United States)	David Theile, Terry Gathercole, Neville Hayes, Goeff Shipton (Australia)	Kazuo Tomita, Koichi Hirakida, Yoshihiko Osaki, Keigo Shimuzu (Japan)
1964	Harold Mann, William Craig, Fred Schmidt, Stephen Clark (United States)	Ernst Kuppers, Egon Henninger, Horst-Gunther Gregor, Hans-Joachim Klein (Germany)	Peter Reynolds, Ian O'Brien, Kevin Berry, David Dickson (Australia)
1968	Charles Hickcox, Don McKenzie, Douglas Russell, Kenneth Walsh (United States)	Roland Matthes, Egon Henninger, Horst-Gunter Gregor, Frank Wiegand (East Germany)	Yuri Gromak, Vladimir Nemshilov, Vladimir Kosinsky, Leonid Ilyichov (Soviet Union)
1972	Mike Stamm, Tom Bruce, Mark Spitz, Jerry Heidenreich (United States)	Roland Matthes, Klaus Katzur, Hartmut Flockner, Lutz Unger (East Germany)	Erik Fish, William Mahony, Bruce Robertson, Robert Kasting (Canada)
1976	John Naber, John Hencken, Matt Vogel, Jim Montgomery (United States)	Stephen Pickell, Graham Smith, Clay Evans, Gary MacDonald (Canada)	Klaus Steinbach, Walter Kusch, Michael Kraus, Peter Nocke (West Germany)
1980	Mark Kerry, Peter Evans, Mark Tonelli, Neil Brooks (Australia)	Viktor Kuznetsov, Arsen Miskarov, Yevgeni Seredin, Sergey Kopliakov (Soviet Union)	Gary Abraham, Duncan Goodhew, David Lowe, Martin Smith (Great Britain)
1984	Rick Carey, Steve Lundquist, Pablo Morales, Rowdy Gaines (United States)	Mike West, Victor Davis, Tom Ponting, Sandy Gross (Canada)	Mark Kerry, Peter Evans, Glenn Buchanan, Mark Stockwell (Australia)

Year	Gold	Silver	Bronze
1988	David Berkoff, Richard Schroeder, Matt Biondi, Chris Jacobs (United States)	Mark Tewksbury, Victor Davis, Tom Ponting, Sandy Goss (Canada)	Igor Polyansky, Dmitri Volkov, Vadim Yaroshchuk, Gennadiy Prigoda (Soviet Union)
1992	Jeff Rouse, Nelson Diebel, Pablo Morales, Jon Olsen, David Berkoff, Hans Dersch, Melvin Stewart, Matt Biondi (United States)	Vladimir Selkov, Vasili Ivanov, Pavlo Khnykin, Alexander Popov, Vladimir Pyshnenko, Vladislav Kulikov, Dmitri Volkov (Unified Team)	Mark Tewksbury, Jonathan Cleveland, Marcel Gery, Stephen Clarke, Tom Ponting (Canada)
1996	Jeff Rouse, Jeremy Linn, Mark Henderson, Gary Hall Jr., Josh Davis, Kurt Grote, John Hargis, Tripp Schwenk (United States)	Vladimir Selkov, Stanislav Lopukhov, Denis Pankratov, Alexander Popov, Roman Ivanovsky, Vladislav Kulikov, Roman Yegorov (Russia)	Steven Dewick, Phil Rogers, Scott Miller, Michael Klim, Toby Haenen (Australia)
2000	Lenny Krayzelburg, Ed Moses, Ian Crocker, Gary Hall Jr., Neil Walker, Tommy Hannan, Jason Lezak (United States)	Matt Welsh, Regan Harrison, Geoff Huegill, Michael Klim, Josh Watson, Ryan Mitchell, Adam Pine, Ian Thorpe (Australia)	Stev Theloke, Jens Kruppa, Thomas Rupprath, Torsten Spanneberg (Germany)
2004	Aaron Peirsol, Brendan Hansen, Ian Crocker, Jason Lezak, Lenny Krayzelburg, Mark Gangloff, Michael Phelps, Neil Walker (United States)	Steffen Driesen, Jens Kruppa, Thomas Rupprath, Lars Conrad, Helge Meeuw (Germany)	Tomomi Morita, Kosuke Kitajima, Takashi Yamamoto, Yoshihiro Okumura (Japan)
2008	Aaron Peirsol, Brendan Hansen, Michael Phelps, Jason Lezak, Matt Grevers, Mark Gangloff, Ian Corcker, Garrett Weber-Gale (United States)	Hayden Stoeckel, Brenton Rickard, Andrew Lauterstein, Eamon Sullivan, Ashley Delaney, Christian Sprenger, Adam Pine, Matt Targett (Australia)	Junichi Miyashita, Kosuke Kitajima, Takuro Fujii, Hisayoshi Sato (Japan)

Women's 4 × 100-Meter Medley Relay

Year	Gold	Silver	Bronze
1960	Lynn Burke, Patty Kempner, Carolyn Schuler, Chris von Saltza (United States)	Marilyn Wilson, Rosemary Lassig, Jan Andrew, Dawn Fraser (Australia)	Ingrid Schmidt, Ursula Kuper, Barbel Fuhrmann, Ursel Brunner (Germany)
1964	Cathy Ferguson, Cynthia Goyette, Sharon Stouder, Kathleen Ellis (United States)	Corrie Winkel, Klenie Bimolt, Ada Kok, Erica Terpstra (Netherlands)	Tatyana Savelyeva, Svetlana Babanina, Tatyana Devyatova, Natalya Ustinova (Soviet Union)
1968	Kaye Hall, Catie Ball, Ellie Daniel, Susan Pedersen (United States)	Lynne Watson, Judy Playfair, Lyn McClements, Janet Steinbeck (Australia)	Angelika Kraus, Uta Frommater, Heike Hustede, Heidemarie Reineck (West Germany)
1972	Melissa Belote, Catherine Carr, Deena Deardurff, Sandra Neilson (United States)	Christine Herbst, Renate Vogel, Roswitha Beier, Kornelia Ender (East Germany)	Gudrun Beckmann, Vreni Eberle, Silke Pielen, Heidemarie Reineck (West Germany)
1976	Ulrike Richter, Hannelore Anke, Andrea Pollack, Kornelia Ender, Birgit Treiber, Carola Nitschke, Rosemarie Gabriel (East Germany)	Linda Jezek, Lauri Siering, Camille Wright, Shirley Babashoff, Lelei Fonoimoana, Wendy Boglioli (United States)	Wendy Hogg, Robin Corsiglis, Susan Sloan, Anne Jardin, Deborah Clarke (Canada)
1980	Rica Reinisch, Ute Geweniger, Andrea Pollack, Caren Metschuck (East Germany)	Helen Jameson, Margaret Kelly, Ann Osgerby, June Croft (Great Britain)	Elena Kruglova, Elvira Vasilkova, Alla Grishchenkova, Natalya Strunnikova (Soviet Union)
1984	Theresa Andrews, Tracy Caulkins, Mary Meagher, Nancy Hogshead (United States)	Svenja Schlicht, Ute Hasse, Ina Beyermann, Karin Seick (West Germany)	Reema Abdo, Anne Ottenbrite, Michelle MacPherson, Pamela Rai (Canada)
1988	Kristin Otto, Silke Horner, Birte Weigang, Katrin Meibner (East Germany)	Beth Barr, Tracey McFarlane, Janel Jorgensen, Mary Wayte (United States)	Lori Melien, Allison Higson, Jane Kerr, Andrea Nugent (Canada)

Year	Gold	Silver	Bronze
1992	Crissy Ahmann-Leighton, Lea Loveless, Anita Nall, Jenny Thompson, Janie Wagstaff, Megan Kleine, Summer Sanders, Nicole Haislett (United States)	Franziska van Almsick, Jana Dorries, Dagmar Hase, Daniela Hungar, Daniela Brendel, Bettina Ustrowski, Simone Osygus (Germany)	Nina Zhivanevskaya, Olga Kirichenko, Nataliya Meshch-eryakova, Yelena Rudkovskaya, Yelena Chubina (Unified Team)
1996	Beth Botsford, Amanda Bear, Angel Martino, Amy Van Dyken, Catherine Fox, Whitney Hedgepeth, Kristine Quance, Jenny Thompson (United States)	Nicole Stevenson, Samantha Riley, Susie O'Neill, Sarah Ryan, Helen Denman, Angela Kennedy (Australia)	Chen Yan, Han Xue, Cai Huijue, Shan Ying (China)
2000	Dara Torres, Barbara Bedford, Megan Quann, Jenny Thompson, Courtney Shealy, Ashley Tappin, Amy Van Dyken, Staciana Stitts (United States)	Petria Thomas, Leisel Jones, Susie O'Neill, Dyana Calub, Giaan Rooney, Tamee White, Sarah Ryan (Australia)	Masami Tanaka, Sumika Minamoto, Mai Nakamura, Junko Onishi (Japan)
2004	Giaan Rooney, Leisel Jones, Petria Thomas, Jodie Henry, Brooke Hanson, Alice Mills, Jessicah Schipper (Australia)	Natalie Coughlin, Amanda Beard, Jenny Thompson, Kara Lynn Joyce, Haley Cope, Tara Kirk, Rachel Komisarz, Amanda Weir (United States)	Antje Buschschulte, Sarah Poewe, Franziska van Almsick, Daniela Gotz (Germany)
2008	Emily Seebohm, Leisel Jones, Jessicah Schipper, Lisbeth Trickett, Tarnee White, Felicity Galvez, Shayne Reese (Australia)	Natalie Coughlin, Rebecca Soni, Christine Magnuson, Dara Torres, Margaret Hoelzer, Megan Jendrick, Elaine Breeden, Kara Lynn Joyce (United States)	Zhao Jing, Sun Ye, Zhou Yafei, Pang Jiaying, Xu Tianlongzi (China)

Women's 4 × 200-Meter Freestyle Relay

Year	Gold	Silver	Bronze
1996	Trina Jackson, Christina Teuscher, Sheila Taormina, Jenny Thompson, Lisa Jacob, Annette Salmeen, Ashley Whitney (United States)	Franziska van Almsick, Kerstin Kielgass, Anke Scholz, Dagmar Hase, Meike Freitag, Simone Osygus (Germany)	Julia Greville, Nicole Stevenson, Emma Johnson, Susie O'Neill, Lise Mackie (Australia)
2000	Diana Munz, Jenny Thompson, Samantha Arsenault, Lindsay Benko, Julia Stowers, Kim Black (United States)	Giann Rooney, Petria Thomas, Kirsten Thomson, Susie O'Neill, Jacinta van Lint, Elke Graham (Australia)	Franziska van Almsick, Antje Buschschulte, Sara Harstick, Kerstin Kielgass, Meike Freitag, Britta Steffen (Germany)
2004	Natalie Coughlin, Carly Piper, Dana Vollmer, Kaitlin Sandeno, Lindsay Benko, Rhi Jeffrey, Rachel Komisarz (United States)	Zhu Yingwen, Xu Yanwei, Yang Yu, Pang Jiaying, Li Ji (China)	Franziska van Almsick, Petra Dallmann, Antje Buschschulte, Hannah Stockbauer, Janina Gotz, Sara Harstick (Germany)
2008	Stephanie Rice, Bronte Barratt, Kylie Palmer, Linda Mackenzie, Felicity Galvez, Angie Bainbridge, Melanie Schlanger, Lara Davenport (Australia)	Yang Yu, Qianwei Zhu, Miao Tan, Jiaying Pang, Jingzhi Tang (China)	Allison Schmitt, Natalie Coughlin, Caroline Burckle, Katie Hoff, Christine Marshall, Kim Vandenberg, Julia Smit (United States)

Men's 4 × 200-Meter Freestyle Relay

Year	Gold	Silver	Bronze
1908	John Derbyshire, William Foster, Paul Radmilovic, Henry Taylor (Great Britain)	Zoltan Halmay, Bela Las Torres, Jozsef Munk, Imre Zachar (Hungary)	Charles Daniels, Leo Goodwin, Harry Hebner, Leslie Rich (Great Britain)
1912	Leslie Boardman, Malcolm Champion, Harold Hardwick, Cecil Healy (Australasia)	Harry Hebner, Kenneth Huszagh, Duke Kahanamoku, Perry McGillivray (United States)	Thomas Battersby, William Foster, Jack Hatfield, Henry Taylor (Great Britain)

1916: Olympics not held

Year	Gold	Silver	Bronze
1920	Duke Kahanamoku, Pua Kealoha, Perry McGillivray, Norman Ross (United States)	Frank Beaurepaire, Henry Hay, William Herald, Ivan Stedman (Australia)	Harold Annison, Edward Peter, Leslie Savage, Henry Taylor (Great Britain)
1924	Ralph Breyer, Harrison Glancy, Richard Howell, Wallace O'Connor, Johnny Weissmuller (United States)	Frank Beaurepaire, Boy Charlton, Moss Christie, Ernest Henry, Ivan Stedman (Australia)	Ake Borg, Arne Borg, Thor Henning, Gosta Persson, Orvar Trolle, Georg Werner (Sweden)
1928	Austin Clapp, George Kojac, Walter Laufer, Johnny Weissmuller (United States)	Nobuo Arai, Tokuhei Sada, Katsuo Takaishi, Hiroshi Yoneyama (Japan)	Garnet Ault, Munroe Bourne, Walter Spence, James Thompson (Canada)
1932	Yasuji Miyazaki, Hisakichi Toyoda, Takashi Yokoyama, Masanori Yusa (Japan)	Frank Booth, George Fissler, Maiola Kalili, Manuella Kalili (United States)	Istvan Barany, Laszlo Szabados, Andras Szekely, Andras Wanie (Hungary)
1936	Shigeo Arai, Shigeo Sugiura, Masahura Taguchi, Masanori Yusa (Japan)	Ralph Flanagan, John Macionis, Jack Medica, Paul Wolf (United States)	Oszkar Abay-Nemes, Ferenc Csik, Odon Grof, Arpad Lengyel (Hungary)
1940–1944: Olympics not held			
1948	Walter Ris, James McLane, Wallace Wolf, William Smith (United States)	Elemer Szatmari, Gyorgy Mitro, Imre Nyeki, Geza Kadas (Hungary)	Joseph Bernardo, Rene Cornu, Henri Padou, Alexandre Jany (France)
1952	Wayne Moore, Bill Woolsey, Ford Konno, James McLane (United States)	Hiroshi Suzuki, Yoshihiro Hamaguchi, Toru Goto, Teijiro Tanikawa (Japan)	Joseph Bernardo, Aldo Eminente, Alexandre Jany, Jean Boiteux (France)
1956	Kevin O'Halloran, John Devitt, Murray Rose, Jon Henricks (Australia)	Dick Hanley, George Breen, Bill Woolsey, Ford Konno (United States)	Vitali Sorokin, Vladimir Struzha-nov, Gennadi Nikolaev, Boris Nikitin (Soviet Union)
1960	George Harrison, Richard Blick, Michael Troy, Jeff Farrell (United States)	Makoto Fukui, Hiroshi Ishii, Tsuyoshi Yamanaka, Tatsuo Fujimoto (Japan)	David Dickson, John Devitt, Murray Rose, John Konrads (Australia)
1964	Stephen Clark, Roy Saari, Gary Ilman, Don Schollander (United States)	Horst-Gunther Gregor, Gerhard Hetz, Frank Wiegand, Hans-Joachim Klein (Germany)	Makoto Fukui, Kunihiro Iwasaki, Toshio Shoji, Yukiaki Okabe (Japan)
1968	John Nelson, Stephen Rerych, Mark Spitz, Don Schollander (United States)	Greg Rogers, Graham White, Bob Windle, Michael Wenden (Australia)	Vladimir Bure, Semyon Belitz-Geyman, Georgi Kulikov, Leonid Ilyichov (Soviet Union)
1972	John Kinsella, Fred Tyler, Steve Genter, Mark Spitz (United States)	Klaus Steinbach, Werner Lampe, Hans Vosseler, Hans Fassnacht (West Germany)	Inor Grivennikov, Viktor Mazanov, Georgi Kulikov, Vladimir Bure (Soviet Union)
1976	Mike Bruner, Bruce Furniss, John Naber, Jim Montgomery (United States)	Vladimir Raskatov, Andrei Bogdanov, Sergey Kopliakov, Andrei Krylov (Soviet Union)	Alan McClatchey, David Dunne, Gordon Downie, Brian Brinkley (Great Britain)
1980	Sergey Koplyakov, Vladimir Salnikov, Ivar Stukolkin, Andrey Krylov (Soviet Union)	Frank Pfutze, Jorg Woithe, Detlev Grabs, Rainer Strohbach (East Germany)	Jorge Fernandes, Marcus Mattioli, Ciro Delgado, Djan Madruga (Brazil)
1984	Michael Heath, David Larson, Jeff Float, Bruce Hayes (United States)	Thomas Fahmer, Dirk Korthals, Alexander Schowtka, Michael Gross (West Germany)	Neil Cochran, Paul Easter, Paul Howe, Andrew Astbury (Great Britain)
1988	Troy Dalbey, Matt Cetlinski, Doug Gjertsen, Matt Biondi (United States)	Uwe Dabler, Sven Lodziewski, Thomas Flemming, Steffen Zesner (East Germany)	Erik Hochstein, Thomas Fahmer, Rainer Henkel, Michael Gross (West Germany)
1992	Dmitry Lepikov, Vladimir Pyshnenko, Veniamin Tayanov-ich, Yevgeny Sadovyi, Aleksey Kudryavtsev, Yury Mukhin (Unified Team)	Christer Wallin, Anders Holmertz, Tommy Werner, Lars Frolander (Sweden)	Joe Hudepohl, Melvin Stewart, Joe Olsen, Doug Gjertsen, Scott Jaffe, Daniel Jorgensen (United States)

Year	Gold	Silver	Bronze
1996	Josh Davis, Joe Hudepohl, Bradley Schumacher, Ryan Berube, Jon Olsen (United States)	Christer Wallin, Anders Holmertz, Lars Frolander, Anders Lyrbring (Sweden)	Aimo Heilmann, Christian Keller, Christian Troger, Steffen Zesner, Konstantin Dubrovin, Oliver Lampe (Germany)
2000	Todd Pearson, Ian Thorpe, Bill Kirby, Michael Klim, Grant Hackett, Daniel Kowalski (Australia)	Jamie Rauch, Josh Davis, Scott Goldblatt, Klete Keller, Nate Dusing, Chad Carvin (United States)	Martijn Zuijdweg, Johan Kenkhuis, Pieter van den Hoogenband, Marcel Wouda, Mark van der Zijden (Netherlands)
2004	Michael Phelps, Ryan Lochte, Peter Vanderkaay, Klete Keller, Scott Goldblatt, Dan Ketchum (United States)	Grant Hackett, Michael Klim, Nicholas Sprenger, Ian Thorpe, Antony Matkovich, Todd Pearson, Craig Stevens (Australia)	Emiliano Brembilla, Massimiliano Rosolino, Simone Carcato, Filippo Magnini, Federico Cappellazzo, Matteo Pelliciari (Italy)
2008	Michael Phelps, Ryan Lochte, Ricky Berens, Peter Vanderkaay, David Walters, Erik Vendt, Klete Keller (United States)	Nikita Lobintsev, Evgeny Lagunov, Danila Izotov, Alexander Sukhorukov, Mikhail Polischuk (Russia)	Patrick Murphy, Grant Hackett, Grant Brits, Nick Ffrost, Kirk Palmer, Leith Brodie (Australia)

Men's 4 × 50-Yard Freestyle Relay

Year	Gold	Silver	Bronze
1904	Joseph Ruddy, Leo Goodwin, Louis Handley, Charles Daniels (United States)	David Hammond, William Tuttle, Hugo Goetz, Raymond Thorne (United States)	Amedee Reyburn, Gwynne Evans, Marquard Schwarz, William Orthwein (United States)

Women's 50-Meter Freestyle

Year	Gold	Silver	Bronze
1988	Kristin Otto (East Germany)	Yang Wenyi (China)	Katrin Meibner (East Germany) Jill Sterkel (United States)
1992	Wenyi Yang (China)	Yong Zhuang (China)	Angel Martino (United States)
1996	Amy Van Dyken (United States)	Le Jingyi (China)	Sandra Volker (Germany)
2000	Inge de Bruijn (Netherlands)	Therese Alshammar (Sweden)	Dara Torres (United States)
2004	Inge de Bruijn (Netherlands)	Malia Metella (France)	Libby Lenton (Australia)
2008	Britta Steffen (Germany)	Dara Torres (United States)	Cate Campbell (Australia)

Men's 50-Meter Freestyle

Year	Gold	Silver	Bronze
1988	Matt Biondi (United States)	Tom Jager (United States)	Gennady Prigoda (Soviet Union)
1992	Alexander Popov (Russia)	Matt Biondi (United States)	Tom Jager (United States)
1996	Alexander Popov (Russia)	Gary Hall Jr. (United States)	Fernando Scherer (Brazil)
2000	Anthony Ervin (United States) Gary Hall Jr. (United States)		Peter van den Hoogenband (Netherlands)
2004	Gary Hall Jr. (United States)	Duje Draganja (Croatia)	Roland Mark Schoeman (South Africa)
2008	Cesar Cielo Filho (Brazil)	Amaury Leveaux (France)	Alain Bernard (France)

Women's 800-Meter Freestyle

Year	Gold	Silver	Bronze
1968	Debbie Meyer (United States)	Pam Kruse (United States)	Maria Teresa Ramirez (Mexico)
1972	Keena Rothhammer (United States)	Shane Gould (Australia)	Novella Calligaris (Italy)
1976	Petra Thumer (East Germany)	Shirley Babashoff (United States)	Wendy Weinberg (United States)
1980	Michelle Ford (Australia)	Ines Diers (East Germany)	Heike Dahne (East Germany)
1984	Tiffany Cohen (United States)	Michelle Richardson (United States)	Sarah Hardcastle (Great Britain)

Year	Gold	Silver	Bronze
1988	Janet Evans (United States)	Astrid Strauss (East Germany)	Julie McDonald (Australia)
1992	Janet Evans (United States)	Hayley Lewis (Australia)	Jana Henke (Germany)
1996	Brooke Bennett (United States)	Dagmar Hase (Germany)	Kirsten Vlieghuis (Netherlands)
2000	Brooke Bennett (United States)	Yana Klochkova (Ukraine)	Kaitlin Sandeno (United States)
2004	Ai Shibata (Japan)	Laure Manaudou (France)	Diana Munz (United States)
2008	Rebecca Adlington (Great Britain)	Alessia Filippi (Italy)	Lotte Friis (Denmark)

Men's 880-Yard Freestyle

Year	Gold	Silver	Bronze
1904	Emil Rausch (Germany)	Francis Gailey (United States)	Geza Kiss (Hungary)

Men's Marathon 10-Kilometer

Year	Gold	Silver	Bronze
2008	Maarten van der Weijden (Netherlands)	David Davies (Great Britain)	Thomas Lurz (Germany)

Women's Marathon 10-Kilometer

Year	Gold	Silver	Bronze
2008	Larisa Ilchenko (Russia)	Keri-Anne Payne (Great Britain)	Cassandra Patten (Great Britain)

Men's Underwater Swimming

Year	Gold	Silver	Bronze
1900	Charles de Vendeville (France)	Andre Six (France)	Peder Lykkeberg (Denmark)

Synchronized Swimming

Women's Duet

Year	Gold	Silver	Bronze
1984	Candy Costie, Tracie Ruiz (United States)	Sharon Hambrook, Kelly Kryczka (Canada)	Saeko Kimura, Miwako Motoyoshi (Japan)
1988	Michelle Cameron, Carolyn Waldo (Canada)	Karen Josephson, Sarah Josephson (United States)	Mikako Kotani, Miyako Tanaka (Japan)
1992	Karen Josephson, Sarah Josephson (United States)	Penny Vilagos, Vicky Vilagos (Canada)	Fumiko Okuno, Aki Takayama (Japan)
1996: Event not held			
2000	Olga Brusnikina, Maria Kisseleva (Russia)	Miya Tachibana, Miho Takeda (Japan)	Virginie Dedieu, Myriam Lignot (France)
2004	Anastasia Davydova, Anastasia Ermakova (Russia)	Miya Tachibana, Miho Takeda (Japan)	Alison Bartosik, Anna Kozlova (United States)
2008	Anastasia Davydova, Anastasia Ermakova (Russia)	Andrea Fuentes, Gemma Mengual (Spain)	Saho Harada, Emiko Suzuki (Japan)

Women's Solo

Year	Gold	Silver	Bronze
1984	Tracie Ruiz (United States)	Carolyn Waldo (Canada)	Miwako Motoyoshi (Japan)
1988	Carolyn Waldo (Canada)	Tracie Ruiz (United States)	Mikako Kotani (Japan)
1992	Kristen Babb-Sprague (United States) Sylvie Frechette (Canada)	Not awarded	Fumiko Okuno (Japan)

Women's Team

Year	Gold	Silver	Bronze
1996	Suzannah Bianco, Tammy Cleland, Becky Dyroen-Lancer, Heather Pease, Jill Savery, Nathalie Schneyder, Heather Simmons-Carrasco, Jill Sudduth, Emily Lesueur, Margot Thien (United States)	Karen Clark, Sylvie Frechette, Janice Bremner, Karen Fonteyne, Christine Larsen, Erin Woodley, Cari Read, Lisa Alexander, Valerie Hould-Marchand, Kasia Kulesza (Canada)	Miya Tachibana, Akiko Kawase, Rei Jimbo, Miho Takeda, Raika Fujii, Miho Kawabe, Junko Tanaka, Riho Nakajima, Mayuko Fujiki, Kaori Takahashi (Japan)
2000	Yelena Azarova, Olga Brusnikina, Maria Kisseleva, Olga Novokshchenova, Irina Pershina, Yelena Soya, Yuliya Vasilyeva, Olga Vasyukova, Yelena Antonova (Russia)	Ayano Egami, Raika Fujii, Yoko Isoda, Rei Jimbo, Miya Tachibana, Miho Takeda, Yoko Yoneda, Yuko Yoneda, Juri Tatsumi (Japan)	Lyne Beaumont, Claire Carver-Dias, Erin Chan, Catherine Garceau, Fanny Letourneau, Kirstin Normand, Jacinthe Taillon, Reidun Tatham, Jessica Chase (Canada)
2004	Yelena Azarova, Olga Brusnikina, Anastasia Davydova, Anastasia Ermakova, Elvira Khasyanova, Maria Kisseleva, Olga Novokshchenova, Anna Shorina, Mariya Gromova (Russia)	Michiyo Fujimaru, Saho Harada, Kanako Kitao, Emiko Suzuki, Miya Tachibana, Miho Takeda, Juri Tatsumi, Yoko Yoneda (Japan)	Alison Bartosik, Tamara Crow, Erin Dobratz, Rebecca Jasontek, Anna Kozlova, Sara Lowe, Lauren McFall, Stephanie Nesbitt, Kendra Zanotto (United States)
2008	Anatasia Davydova, Anastasia Ermakova, Maria Gromova, Natalia Ishchenko, Elvira Khasyanova, Olga Kuzhela, Yelena Ovchinnikova, Anna Shorina, Svetlana Romashina (Russia)	Alba Maria Cabello, Raquel Corral, Andrea Fuentes, Gemma Mengual, Thais Henriquez, Laura Lopez, Gisela Moron, Irina Rodriguez, Paola Tirados (Spain)	Gu Beibei, Huang Xuechen, Jiang Tingting, Jiang Wenwen, Liu Ou, Luo Qian, Sun Qiuting, Wang Na, Zhang Xiaohuan (China)

Table Tennis

Men's Doubles

Year	Gold	Silver	Bronze
1988	Chen Longcan, Wei Qingguang (China)	Ilija Lupulesku, Zoran Primorac (Yugoslavia)	Ahn Jae-Hyung, Yoo Nam-Kyu (South Korea)
1992	Lu Lin, Wang Tao (China)	Steffen Fetzner, Jorg Robkopf (Germany)	Kang Hee-Chan, Lee Chul-Seung (South Korea) Kim Taek-Soo, Yoo Nam-Kyu (South Korea)
1996	Liu Guoliang, Kong Linghui (China)	Lu Lin, Wang Tao (China)	Lee Chul-Seung, Yoo Nam-Kyu (South Korea)
2000	Wang Liqin, Yan Sen (China)	Liu Guoliang, Kong Linghui (China)	Jean-Philippe Gatien, Patrick Chila (France)
2004	Chen Qi, Ma Lin (China)	Ko Lai Chak, Li Ching (Hong Kong)	Michael Maze, Finn Tugwell (Denmark)

Women's Doubles

Year	Gold	Silver	Bronze
1988	Hyun Jung-Hwa, Yang Young-Ja (South Korea)	Chen Jing, Jiao Zhimin (China)	Jasna Fazlic, Gordana Perkucin (Yugoslavia)
1992	Deng Yaping, Qiao Hong (China)	Chen Zihe, Gao Jun (China)	Li Bun-Hui, Yu Sun-Bok (North Korea) Hyun Jung-Hwa, Hong Cha-Ok (South Korea)

Year	Gold	Silver	Bronze
1996	Deng Yaping, Qiao Hong (China)	Liu-Wei, Qiao Yunping (China)	Park Hae-Jung, Ryu Ji-Hae (South Korea)
2000	Li Ju, Wang Nan (China)	Sun Jin, Yang Ying (China)	Kim Moo-Kyo, Ryu Ji-Hae (South Korea)
2004	Wang Nan, Zhang Yining (China)	Lee Eun-Sil, Seok Eun-Mi (South Korea)	Guo Yue, Niu Jianfeng (China)

Men's Singles

Year	Gold	Silver	Bronze
1988	Yoo Nam-Kyu (South Korea)	Kim Ki-Taik (South Korea)	Erik Lindh (Sweden)
1992	Jan-Ove Waldner (Sweden)	Jean-Philippe Gatien (France)	Kim Taek-Soo (South Korea) Ma Wenge (China)
1996	Liu Guoliang (China)	Wang Tao (China)	Jorg Robkopf (Germany)
2000	Kong Linghui (China)	Jan-Ove Waldner (Sweden)	Liu Gouliang (China)
2004	Ryu Seung-Min (South Korea)	Wang Hao (China)	Wang Liqin (China)
2008	Ma Lin (China)	Wang Hao (China)	Wang Liqin (China)

Women's Singles

Year	Gold	Silver	Bronze
1988	Chen Jing (China)	Li Huifen (China)	Jiao Zhimin (China)
1992	Deng Yaping (China)	Qiao Hong (China)	Li Bun-Hui (North Korea) Hyun Jung-Hwa (South Korea)
1996	Deng Yaping (China)	Chen Jing (Taiwan)	Qiao Hong (China)
2000	Wang Nan (China)	Li Ju (China)	Chen Jing (Taiwan)
2004	Zhang Yining (China)	Kim Hyang-Mi (North Korea)	Kim Kyung-Ah (South Korea)
2008	Zhang Yining (China)	Wang Nan (China)	Guo Yue (China)

Men's Team

Year	Gold	Silver	Bronze
2008	Wang Hao, Ma Lin, Wang Liqin (China)	Dimitrij Ovcharov, Timo Boll, Christian Suss (Germany)	Oh Sang-Eun, Ryu Seung-Min, Yoon Jae-Young (South Korea)

Women's Team

Year	Gold	Silver	Bronze
2008	Guo Yue, Wang Nan, Zhang Yining (China)	Feng Tianwei, Li Jiawei, Wang Yuegu (Singapore)	Dang Ye-Seo, Kim Kyung-Ah, Park Mi-Young (South Korea)

Taekwondo

Men's Flyweight

Year	Gold	Silver	Bronze
2000	Michail Mouroutsos (Greece)	Gabriel Esparza (Spain)	Huang Chih-hsiung (Taiwan)
2004	Chu Mu-Yen (Taiwan)	Oscar Salazar (Mexico)	Tamer Bayoumi (Egypt)
2008	Guillermo Perez (Mexico)	Yulis Gabriel Mercedes (Dominican Republic)	Rohullah Nikpai (Afghanistan) Chu Mu-Yen (Taiwan)

Men's Lightweight

Year	Gold	Silver	Bronze
2000	Steven Lopez (United States)	Sin Joon-Sik (South Korea)	Hadi Saei (Iran)
2004	Hadi Saei (Iran)	Huang Chih-Hsiung (Taiwan)	Song Myeong-Seob (South Korea)
2008	Son Tae-Jin (South Korea)	Mark Lopez (United States)	Servet Tazegul (Turkey) Sung Yu-Chi (Taiwan)

Men's Middleweight

Year	Gold	Silver	Bronze
2000	Angel Matos (Cuba)	Faissal Ebnoutalib (Germany)	Victor Estrada (Mexico)
2004	Steven Lopez (United States)	Bahri Tannkulu (Turkey)	Yousef Karami (Iran)
2008	Hadi Saei (Iran)	Mauro Sarmiento (Italy)	Zhu Guo (China) Steven Lopez (United States)

Men's Heavyweight

Year	Gold	Silver	Bronze
2000	Kim Kyong-Hun (South Korea)	Daniel Trenton (Australia)	Pascal Gentil (France)
2004	Moon Dae-Sung (South Korea)	Alexandros Nikolaidis (Greece)	Pascal Gentil (France)
2008	Cha Dong-Min (South Korea)	Alexandros Nikolaidis (Greece)	Chika Chukwumerije (Nigeria) Arman Chilmanov (Kazakhstan)

Women's Flyweight

Year	Gold	Silver	Bronze
2000	Lauren Burns (Australia)	Urbia Melendez (Cuba)	Chi Shu-Ju (Chinese Taipei)
2004	Chen Shih-Hsin (Chinese Taipei)	Yanelis Labrada (Cuba)	Yaowapa Boorapolchai (Thailand)
2008	Wu Jingyu (China)	Buttree Puedpong (Thailand)	Daynellis Montejo (Cuba) Dalia Contreras (Venezuela)

Women's Lightweight

Year	Gold	Silver	Bronze
2000	Jung Jae-Eun (South Korea)	Tran Hieu Ngan (Vietnam)	Hamide Bikcin Tosun (Turkey)
2004	Jang Ji-Won (South Korea)	Nia Abdallah (United States)	Iridia Salazar (Mexico)
2008	Lim Su-Jeong (South Korea)	Azize Tannkulu (Turkey)	Diana Lopez (United States) Martina Zubcic (Croatia)

Women's Middleweight

Year	Gold	Silver	Bronze
2000	Lee Sun-Hee (South Korea)	Trude Gundersen (Norway)	Yoriko Okamoto (Japan)
2004	Luo Wei (China)	Elisavet Mystakidou (Greece)	Hwang Kyung-Sun (South Korea)
2008	Hwang Kyung-Seon (South Korea)	Karine Sergerie (Canada)	Gwladys Epangue (France) Sandra Saric (Croatia)

Women's Heavyweight

Year	Gold	Silver	Bronze
2000	Chen Zhong (China)	Natalia Ivanova (Russia)	Dominique Bosshart (Canada)
2004	Chen Zhong (China)	Myriam Baverel (France)	Adriana Carmona (Venezuela)
2008	Maria Espinoza (Mexico)	Nina Solheim (Norway)	Sarah Stevenson (Great Britain) Natalia Falavigna (Brazil)

Tennis

Men's Doubles

Year	Gold	Silver	Bronze
1896	John Pius Boland (Great Britain), Friedrich Traun (Germany)	Demetrios Petrokokkinos, Dionysios Kasdaglis (Greece)	Edwin Flack (Australia), George S. Robertson (Great Britain)
1900	Lawrence Doherty, Reginald Doherty (Great Britain)	Max Decugis (France), Basil Spalding de Garmendia (United States)	Harold Mahoney, Arthur Norris (Great Britain) Andre Prevost, Georges de la Chapelle (France)
1904	Beals Wright, Edgar Leonard (United States)	Robert LeRoy, Alphonzo Bell (United States)	Clarence Gamble, Arthur Wear (United States) Joseph Wear, Allen West (United States)
1908	George Hillyard, Reginald Doherty (Great Britain)	Josiah Ritchie, James Parke (Great Britain)	Clement Cazalet, Charles Dixon (Great Britain)
1912	Harold Kitson, Charles Winslow (South Africa)	Felix Pipes, Arthur Zborzil (Austria)	Albert Canet, Edouard Meny de Marangue (France)
1916: Olympics not held			
1920	Oswald Turnbull, Max Woosnam (Great Britain)	Ichiya Kumagae, Seiichiro Kashio (Japan)	Pierre Albarran, Max Decugis (France)
1924	Francis Hunter, Vincent Richards (United States)	Jacques Brugnon, Henri Cochet (France)	Jean Borotra, Rene Lacoste (France)
1928–1936: Event not held			
1940–1944: Olympics not held			
1948–1964: Event not held			
1968	Rafael Osuna, Vicente Zarazua (Mexico)	Juan Gisbert, Manuel Santana (Spain)	Pierre Darmon (France), Joaquin Loyo-Mayo (Mexico)
1972–1984: Event not held			
1988	Ken Flach, Robert Seguso (United States)	Emilio Sanchez, Sergio Casal (Spain)	Miloslav Mecir, Milan Srejber (Czechoslovakia) Stefan Edberg, Anders Jarryd (Sweden)
1992	Boris Becker, Michael Stich (Germany)	Wayne Ferreira, Piet Norval (South Africa)	Goran Ivanisevic, Goran Prpic (Croatia) Javier Frana, Christian Miniussi (Argentina)
1996	Todd Woodbridge, Mark Woodforde (Australia)	Neil Broad, Tim Henmen (Great Britain)	Marc-Kevin Goellner, David Prinosil (Germany)
2000	Sebastien Lareau, Daniel Nestor (Canada)	Todd Woodbridge, Mark Woodforde (Australia)	Alex Corretja, Albert Costa (Spain)
2004	Fernando Gonzalez, Nicolas Massu (Chile)	Nicolas Kiefer, Rainer Schuttler (Germany)	Mario Ancic, Ivan Ljubicic (Croatia)
2008	Roger Federer, Stanislas Wawrinka (Switzerland)	Simon Aspelin, Thomas Johansson (Sweden)	Bob Bryan, Mike Bryan (United States)

Women's Doubles

Year	Gold	Silver	Bronze
1920	Kathleen McKane, Winifred McNair (Great Britain)	Geraldine Beamish, Dorothy Holman (Great Britain)	Elisabeth d'Ayen, Suzanne Lenglen (France)
1924	Hazel Wightman, Helen Wills Moody (United States)	Phyllis Covell, Kathleen McKane (Great Britain)	Evelyn Colyer, Dorothy Shepherd-Barron (Great Britain)
1928–1964: Event not held			
1968	Edda Buding, Helga Niessen (West Germany)	Rosa Maria Darmon (France), Julie Heldman (United States)	Jane Bartkowicz, Valerie Ziegenfuss (United States)

Year	Gold	Silver	Bronze
1972–1984: Event not held			
1988	Pam Shriver, Zina Garrison (United States)	Jana Novotna, Helena Sukova (Czechoslovakia)	Elizabeth Smylie, Wendy Turnbull (Australia) Steffi Graf, Claudia Kohde-Kilsch (West Germany)
1992	Gigi Fernandez, Mary Joe Fernandez (United States)	Conchita Martinez, Arantxa Sanchez Vicario (Spain)	Leila Meskhi, Natasha Zvereva (Unified Team) Nicole Bradtke, Rachel McQuillan (Australia)
1996	Gigi Fernandez, Mary Joe Fernandez (United States)	Jana Novotna, Helena Sukova (Czech Republic)	Conchita Martinez, Arantxa Sanchez Vicario (Spain)
2000	Venus Williams, Serena Williams (United States)	Kristie Boogert, Miriam Oremans (Netherlands)	Els Callens, Dominique van Roost (Belgium)
2004	Li Ting, Sun Tiantian (China)	Conchita Martinez, Virginia Ruano Pascual (Spain)	Paola Suarez, Patricia Tarabini (Argentina)
2008	Serena Williams, Venus Williams (United States)	Anabel Medina Garrigues, Virginia Ruano Pascual (Spain)	Yan Zi, Zheng Jie (China)

Men's Singles

Year	Gold	Silver	Bronze
1896	John Pius Boland (Great Britain)	Dionysios Kasdaglis (Greece)	Konstantinos Paspatis (Greece) Momcsillo Tapavicza (Hungary)
1900	Lawrence Doherty (Great Britain)	Harold Mahoney (Great Britain)	Reginald Doherty (Great Britain) Arthur Norris (Great Britain)
1904	Beals Wright (United States)	Robert LeRoy (United States)	Alphonzo Bell (United States) Edgar Leonard (United States)
1908	Josiah Ritchie (Great Britain)	Otto Froitzheim (Germany)	Wilberforce Eaves (Great Britain)
1912	Charles Winslow (South Africa)	Harold Kitson (South Africa)	Oscar Kreuzer (Germany)
1916: Olympics not held			
1920	Louis Raymond (South Africa)	Ichiya Kumagae (Japan)	Charles Winslow (South Africa)
1924	Vincent Richards (United States)	Henri Cochet (France)	Umberto De Morpurgo (Italy)
1928–1964: Event not held			
1968	Manuel Santana (Spain)	Manuel Orantes (Spain)	Herbert Fitzgibbon (United States)
1972–1980: Event not held			
1984	Stefan Edberg (Sweden)	Francisco Maciel (Mexico)	Jimmy Arias (United States) Paolo Canè (Italy)
1988	Miloslav Mecir (Czechoslovakia)	Tim Mayotte (United States)	Stefan Edberg (Sweden) Brad Gilbert (United States)
1992	Marc Rosset (Switzerland)	Jordi Arrese (Spain)	Goran Ivanisevic (Croatia) Andrei Cherkasov (Unified Team)
1996	Andre Agassi (United States)	Sergi Bruguera (Spain)	Leander Paes (India)
2000	Yevgeny Kafelnikov (Russia)	Tommy Haas (Germany)	Arnaud Di Pasquale (France)
2004	Nicolas Massu (China)	Mardy Rish (United States)	Fernando Gonzalez (Chile)
2008	Rafael Nadal (Spain)	Fernando Gonzalez (Chile)	Novak Djokovic (Serbia)

Women's Singles

Year	Gold	Silver	Bronze
1900	Charlotte Cooper (Great Britain)	Helene Prevost (France)	Marion Jones (United States) Hedwiga Rosenbaumova (Bohemia)
1904: Event not held			
1908	Dorothea Chambers (Great Britain)	Penelope Boothby (Great Britain)	Joan Winch (Great Britain)
1912	Marguerite Broquedis (France)	Dorothea Koring (Germany)	Molla Bjurstedt (Norway)
1916: Olympics not held			

Year	Gold	Silver	Bronze
1920	Suzanne Lenglen (France)	Dorothy Holman (Great Britain)	Kathleen McKane (Great Britain)
1924	Helen Wills Moody (United States)	Julie Vlasto (France)	Kathleen McKane (Great Britain)
1928–1964: Event not held			
1968	Helga Niessen (West Germany)	Jane Bartkowicz (United States)	Julie Heldman (United States)
1972–1980: Event not held			
1984	Steffi Graf (West Germany)	Sabrina Goleš (Yugoslavia)	Raffaella Reggi (Italy) Catherine Tanvier (France)
1988	Steffi Graf (West Germany)	Gabriela Sabatini (Argentina)	Zina Garrison (United States) Manuela Maleeva (Bulgaria)
1992	Jennifer Capriati (United States)	Steffi Graf (Germany)	Mary Joe Fernandez (United States) Arantxa Sanchez Vicario (Spain)
1996	Lindsay Davenport (United States)	Arantxa Sanchez Vicario (Spain)	Jana Novotna (Czech Republic)
2000	Venus Williams (United States)	Elena Dementieva (Russia)	Monica Seles (United States)
2004	Justine Henin (Belgium)	Amelie Mauresmo (France)	Alicia Molik (Australia)
2008	Elena Dementieva (Russia)	Dinara Safina (Russia)	Vera Zvonareva (Russia)

Mixed Doubles

Year	Gold	Silver	Bronze
1900	Charlotte Cooper, Reginald Doherty (Great Britain)	Helene Prevost (France), Harold Mahoney (Great Britain)	Marion Jones (United States), Lawrence Doherty (Great Britain) Hedwiga Rosenbaumova (Bohemia), Archibald Warden (Great Britain)
1904–1908: Event not held			
1912	Dorothea Koring, Charles Dixon (Great Britain)	Helen Aitchison, Herbert Barrett (Great Britain)	Sigrid Fick, Gunner Setterwall (Sweden)
1916: Olympics not held			
1920	Suzanne Lenglen, Max Decugis (France)	Kathleen McKane, Maxwell Woosnam (Great Britain)	Milada Skrbkova, Ladislav Zelma (Czechoslovakia)
1924	Hazel Wightman, Richard Williams (United States)	Marion Jessup, Vincent Richards (United States)	Kornelia Bouman, Hendrik Timmer (Netherlands)

Men's Singles Indoor

Year	Gold	Silver	Bronze
1908	Arthur Gore (Great Britain)	George Caridia (Great Britain)	Josiah Ritchie (Great Britain)
1912	Andre Gobert (France)	Charles Dixon (Great Britain)	Anthony Wilding (Australasia)

Men's Doubles Indoor

Year	Gold	Silver	Bronze
1908	Arthur Gore, Herbert Barrett (Great Britain)	George Caridia, George Simond (Great Britain)	Wollmar Bostrom, Gunnar Setterwall (Sweden)
1912	Maurice Germot, Andre Gobert (France)	Carl Kempe, Gunnar Setterwall (Sweden)	Alfred Beamish, Charles Dixon (Great Britain)

Women's Singles Indoor

Year	Gold	Silver	Bronze
1908	Gwendoline Eastlake-Smith (Great Britain)	Angela Greene (Great Britain)	Martha Alderstrahle (Sweden)
1912	Edith Hannam (Great Britain)	Sofie Castenschiold (Denmark)	Mabel Parton (Great Britain)

Mixed Doubles Indoor

Year	Gold	Silver	Bronze
1912	Edith Hannam, Charles Dixon (Great Britain)	Helen Aitchison, Herbert Barrett (Great Britain)	Sigrid Fick, Gunnar Setterwall (Sweden)

Trampoline

Women's Individual

Year	Gold	Silver	Bronze
2000	Irina Karavaeva (Russia)	Oxana Tsyhulyeva (Ukraine)	Karen Cockburn (Canada)
2004	Anna Dogonadze (Germany)	Karen Cockburn (Canada)	Huang Shanshan (China)
2008	He Wenna (China)	Karen Cockburn (Canada)	Ekaterina Khilko (Uzbekistan)

Men's Individual

Year	Gold	Silver	Bronze
2000	Alexander Moskalenko (Russia)	Ji Wallace (Australia)	Mathieu Turgeon (Canada)
2004	Yuri Nikitin (Ukraine)	Alexander Moskalenko (Russia)	Henrik Stehlik (Germany)
2008	Lu Chunlong (China)	Jason Burnett (Canada)	Dong Dong (China)

Triathlon

Men's Individual

Year	Gold	Silver	Bronze
2000	Simon Whitfield	Stephan Vuckovic (Germany)	Jan Rehula (Czech Republic)
2004	Hamish Carter (New Zealand)	Bevan Docherty (New Zealand)	Sven Riederer (Switzerland)
2008	Jan Frodeno (Germany)	Simon Whitfield (Canada)	Bevan Docherty (New Zealand)

Women's Individual

Year	Gold	Silver	Bronze
2000	Brigitte McMahon (Switzerland)	Michellie Jones (Australia)	Magali Messmer (Switzerland)
2004	Kate Allen (Austria)	Loretta Harrop (Australia)	Susan Williams (United States)
2008	Emma Snowsill (Australia)	Vanessa Fernandes (Portugal)	Emma Moffatt (Australia)

Tug-of-War

Men's Tug-of-War

Year	Gold	Silver	Bronze
1900	Edgar Aabye (Denmark), August Nilsson (Sweden), Eugen Schmidt (Denmark), Gustaf Soderstrom (Sweden), Karl Staaf (Sweden), Charles Winckler (Denmark)	Raymond Basset, Jean Collas, Charles Gondouin, Joseph Roffo, Emile Sarrade, Constantin Henriquez de Zubiera (France)	Not awarded

Year	Gold	Silver	Bronze
1904	Patrick Flanagan, Sidney Johnson, Oscar Olson, Conrad Magnusson, Henry Seiling (United States)	Max Braun, August Rodenberg, Charles Rose, William Seiling, Orrin Upshaw (United States)	Oscar Friede, Charles Haberkorn, Harry Jacobs, Frank Kugler, Charles Thias (United States)
1908	Edward Barrett, John Duke, Frederick Goodfellow, Frederick Humphreys, William Hirons, Albert Ireton, Frederick Merriman, Edwin Mills, John James Shepherd (Great Britain)	James Clarke, Thomas Butler, Charles Foden, William Greggan, Alexander Kidd, Daniel McDonald Lowey, Patrick Philbin, George Smith, Thomas Swindlehurst (Great Britain)	Walter Chaffe, Joseph Dowler, Ernest Ebbage, Thomas Homewood, Alexander Munro, William Slade, Walter Tammas, T. J. Williams, James Woodget (Great Britain)
1912	Arvid Andersson, Adolf Bergman, Johan Edman, Erik Algot Fredriksson, Carl Jonsson, Erik Larsson, August Gustafsson, Herbert Lindstrom (Sweden)	Alexander Munro, John Sewell, John James Shepherd, Joseph Dowler, Edwin Mills, Frederick Humphreys, Mathias Hynes, Walter Chaffe (Great Britain)	Not awarded
1916: Olympics not held			
1920	George Canning, Frederick Humphreys, Frederick Holmes, Edwin Mills, John Sewell, John James Shepherd, Harry Stiff, Ernest Thorn (Great Britain)	Wilhelmus Bekkers, Johannes Hengeveld, Sijtse Jansma, Henk Janssen, Antonius van Noon, Marinus van Rekum, Willem van Rekum (Netherlands)	Edouard Bourguignon, Alphonse Ducatillon, Remy Maertens, Christin Piek, Henri Pintens, Charles Van den Broeck, Francois Van Hoorenbeek, Gustave Wuyts (Belgium)

Volleyball

Men's Volleyball

Year	Gold	Silver	Bronze
1964	Ivans Bugajenkovs, Nikolay Burobin, Yuri Chesnokov, Vazha K'ach'arava, Valeri Kalachikhin, Vitali Kovalenko, Staņislavs Lugailo, Georgi Mondzolevski, Yuriy Poyarkov, Eduard Sibiryakov, Yuriy Venherovsky, Dmitri Voskoboynikov (Soviet Union)	Milan Čuda, Bohumil Golián, Zdeněk Humhal, Petr Kop, Josef Labuda, Josef Musil, Karel Paulus, Boris Perušič, Pavel Schenk, Václav Šmídl, Josef Šorm, Ladislav Toman (Czechoslovakia)	Yutaka Demachi, Tsutomu Koyama, Sadatoshi Sugahara, Naohiro Ikeda, Yasutaka Sato, Toshiaki Kosedo, Tokihiko Higuchi, Masayuki Minami, Takeshi Tokutomi, Teruhisa Moriyama, Yūzo Nakamura, Katsutoshi Nekoda (Japan)
1968	Olegs Antropovs, Ivans Bugajenkovs, Volodymyr Byelyayev, Volodymyr Ivanov, Valeri Kravchenko, Yevhen Lapinsky, Vasilijus Matuševas, Viktor Mikhalchuk, Georgi Mondzolevski, Yuriy Poyarkov, Eduard Sibiryakov, Borys Tereshchuk (Soviet Union)	Naohiro Ikeda, Kenji Kimura, Isao Koizumi, Masayuki Minami, Yasuaki Mitsumori, Jungo Morita, Katsutoshi Nekoda, Seiji Oko, Tetsuo Satō, Kenji Shimaoka, Mamoru Shiragami, Tadayoshi Yokota (Japan)	Bohumil Golián, Zdeněk Groessl, Petr Kop, Drahomír Koudelka, Josef Musil, Vladimír Petlák, Antonín Procházka, Pavel Schenk, Josef Smolka, František Sokol, Jiří Svoboda, Lubomír Zajíček (Czechoslovakia)
1972	Yoshihide Fukao, Kenji Kimura, Masayuki Minami, Jungo Morita, Yūzo Nakamura, Katsutoshi Nekoda, Tetsuo Nishimoto, Yasuhiro Noguchi, Seiji Oko, Tetsuo Satō, Kenji Shimaoka, Tadayoshi Yokota (Japan)	Horst Hagen, Wolfgang Löwe, Wolfgang Maibohm, Jürgen Maune, Horst Peter, Eckehard Pietzsch, Siegfried Schneider, Arnold Schulz, Rudi Schumann, Rainer Tscharke, Wolfgang Webner, Wolfgang Weise (East Germany)	Viktor Borshch, Yefim Chulak, Vyacheslav Domani, Vladimir Kondra, Valeri Kravchenko, Yevhen Lapinsky, Vladimir Patkin, Yuriy Poyarkov, Vladimir Putyatov, Aleksandr Saprykin, Yuri Starunsky, Leonid Zayko (Soviet Union)

Year	Gold	Silver	Bronze
1976	Bronisław Bebel, Ryszard Bosek, Wiesław Gawłowski, Marek Karbarz, Lech Łasko, Zbigniew Lubiejewski, Mirosław Rybaczewski, Włodzimierz Sadalski, Edward Skorek, Włodzimierz Stefański, Tomasz Wójtowicz, Zbigniew Zarzycki (Poland)	Vladimir Chernyshov, Yefim Chulak, Vladimir Dorokhov, Aleksandr Ermilov, Vladimir Kondra, Oleh Molyboha, Anatoliy Polishchuk, Aleksandr Savin, Pāvels Seļivanovs, Yuri Starunsky, Vladimir Ulanov, Vyacheslav Zaytsev (Soviet Union)	Alfredo Figueredo, Víctor García, Diego Lapera, Leonel Marshall Steward Sr., Ernesto Martínez, Lorenzo Martínez, Jorge Pérez, Antonio Rodríguez, Carlos Salas, Victoriano Sarmientos, Jesús Savigne, Raúl Vilches (Cuba)
1980	Vladimir Chernyshov, Vladimir Dorokhov, Aleksandr Ermilov, Vladimir Kondra, Valeriy Kryvov, Fedir Lashchonov, Viljar Loor, Oleh Molyboha, Yuriy Panchenko, Aleksandr Savin, Pāvels Seļivanovs, Vyacheslav Zaytsev (Soviet Union)	Yordan Angelov, Dimitar Dimitrov, Stefan Dimitrov, Stoyan Gunchev, Hristo Iliev, Petko Petkov, Kaspar Simeonov, Hristo Stoyanov, Mitko Todorov, Tsano Tsanov, Emil Valtchev, Dimitar Zlatanov (Bulgaria)	Marius Căta-Chiţiga, Valter Chifu, Laurenţiu Dumănoiu, Günther Enescu, Dan Gîrleanu, Sorin Macavei, Viorel Manole, Florin Mina, Corneliu Oros, Nicolae Pop, Constantin Sterea, Nicu Stoian (Romania)
1984	Douglas Dvorak, Dave Saunders, Steven Salmons, Paul Sunderland, Rich Duwelius, Steve Timmons, Craig Buck, Marc Waldie, Chris Marlowe, Aldis Berzins, Patrick Powers, Karch Kiraly (United States)	Amauri Ribeiro, Antônio Carlos Gueiros Ribeiro, Bernard Rajzman, Bernardo Rezende, Domingos Lampariello Neto, Fernando Roscio de Ávila, Marcus Vinícius Simões Freire, José Montanaro Jr., Renan Dal Zotto, Rui Campos do Nascimento, William Carvalho da Silva, Mário Xandó de Oliveira Neto (Brazil)	Franco Bertoli, Francesco Dall'Olio, Giancarlo Dametto, Guido De Luigi, Giovanni Errichiello, Giovanni Lanfranco, Andrea Lucchetta, Pier Paolo Lucchetta, Marco Negri, Piero Rebaudengo, Paolo Vecchi, Fabio Vullo (Italy)
1988	Troy Tanner, David Saunders, Jonathon Root, Robert Ctvrtlik, Robert Partie, Steve Timmons, Craig Buck, Scott Fortune, Ricci Luyties, Jeffrey Stork, Eric Sato, Charles Kiraly (United States)	Yuri Panchenko, Andrei Kuznetsov, Viacheslav Zaitsev, Igor Runov, Vladimir Shkurikhin, Yevgeni Krasilnikova, Raimundas Vilde, Valeri Losev, Yuri Sapega, Oleksandr Sorokalet, Yaroslav Antonov, Yuri Cherednik (Soviet Union)	Claudio Zulianello, Daniel Castellani, Esteban Martinez, Alejandro Diz, Daniel Colla, Carlos Weber, Hugo Conte, Waldo Kantor, Raul Quiroga, Jon Uriate, Esteban de Palma, Juan Cuminetti (Argentina)
1992	Amauri Ribeiro, Antonio Carlos Gouveia, Douglas Chiarotti, Giovane Gávio, Janelson Carvalho, Jorge Edson Brito, Mauricio Lima, Marcelo Negrao, Paulo Andre Silva, Andre Feilpe Ferreira, Talmo Oliveira, Alexandre Samuel (Brazil)	Edwin Benne, Peter Blange, Ron Boudrie, Henk-Jan Held, Martin van der Horst, Marko Klok, Olof van der Meulen, Jan Posthuma, Avital Selinger, Martin Teffer, Ronald Zoodsma, Ron Zwerver (Netherlands)	Nick Becker, Carlos Briceno, Bob Ctvrtlik, Scott Fortune, Dan Greenbaum, Brent Hilliard, Bryan Ivie, Douglas Partie, Bob Samuelson, Eric Sato, Jeff Stork, Steve Timmons (United States)
1996	Peter Blangé, Guido Görtzen, Rob Grabert, Henk-Jan Held, Misha Latuhihin, Jan Posthuma, Brecht Rodenburg, Richard Schuil, Bas van de Goor, Mike van de Goor, Olof van der Meulen, Ron Zwerver (Netherlands)	Lorenzo Bernardi, Vigor Bovolenta, Marco Bracci, Luca Cantagalli, Andrea Gardini, Andrea Giani, Pasquale Gravina, Marco Meoni, Samuele Papi, Andrea Sartoretti, Paolo Tofoli, Andrea Zorzi (Italy)	Vladimir Batez, Dejan Brđović, Đorđe Đurić, Andrija Gerić, Nikola Grbić, Vladimir Grbić, Rajko Jokanović, Slobodan Kovač, Đula Mešter, Žarko Petrović, Željko Tanasković, Goran Vujević (Yugoslavia)
2000	Vladimir Batez, Slobodan Kovač, Slobodan Boškan, Đula Mešter, Vasa Mijić, Nikola Grbić, Vladimir Grbić. Andrija Gerić, Goran Vujević, Ivan Miljković, Veljko Petković, Igor Vušurović (Yugoslavia)	Vadim Khamuttskikh, Ruslan Olikhver, Valeri Goryushev, Igor Shulepov, Aleksey Kazakov, Evgeni Mitkov, Sergey Tetyukhin, Roman Yakovlev, Konstantin Ushakov, Aleksandr Gerasimov, Ilya Savelev, Aleksey Kuleshov (Russia)	Andrea Gardini, Marco Meoni, Pasquale Gravina, Luigi Mastrangelo, Paolo Tofoli, Samuele Papi, Andrea Sartoretti, Marco Bracci, Simone Rosalba, Mirko Corsano, Andrea Giani, Alessandro Fei (Italy)

Year	Gold	Silver	Bronze
2004	Anderson Rodrigues, Andre Nascimento, Andre Heller, Dante Amaral, Giberto Godoy Filho, Giovane Gávio, Gustavo Endres, Mauricio Lima, Nalbert Bitencourt, Ricardo Garcia, Rodrigo Santana, Sergio Santos (Brazil)	Matej Cernic, Alberto Cisolla, Paolo Cozzi, Alessandro Fei, Andrea Giani, Luigi Mastrangelo, Samuele Papi, Damiano Pippi, Andrea Sartoretti, Venceslav Simeonov, Paolo Tofoli, Valerio Vermiglio (Italy)	Pavel Abramov, Sergei Baranov, Stanislav Dineykin, Andrey Egorchev, Aleksey Kazakov, Vadim Khamuttskikh, Taras Khtey, Aleksandr Kosarev, Aleksey Kuleshov, Sergey Tetyukhin, Konstantin Ushakov, Aleksey Verbov (Russia)
2008	Lloy Ball, Sean Rooney, David Lee, Richard Lambourne, William Priddy, Ryan Millar, Riley Salmon, Thomas Hoff, Clayton Stanley, Kevin Hansen, Gabriel Gardner, Scott Touzinsky (United States)	Bruno Rezende, Marcelo Elgarten, Andre Heller, Samuel Fuchs, Gilberto Godoy Filho, Murilo Endres, Andre Nascimento, Sergio Santos, Anderson Rodrigues, Gustavo Endres, Rodrigo Santana, Dante Amaral (Brazil)	Alexander Korneev, Semen Poltavskiy, Alexander Kosarev, Sergey Grankin, Sergey Tetyukhin, Vadim Khamuttskikh, Yury Berezhko, Alexey Ostapenko, Alexander Volkov, Alexey Verbov, Maxim Mikhaylov, Alexey Kuleshov (Russia)

Women's Volleyball

Year	Gold	Silver	Bronze
1964	Yuko Fujimoto, Yuriko Handa, Sata Isobe, Masae Kasai, Masako Kondo, Katsumi Matsumura, Yoshiko Matsumura, Emiko Miyamoto, Setsuko Sasaki, Ayano Shibuki, Yoko Shinozaki, Kinuko Tanida (Japan)	Antonina Ryzhova, Astra Biltauer, Ninel Lukanina, Lyudmila Buldakova, Nelli Abramova, Tamara Tikhonina, Valentina Kamenek-Vinogradova, Inna Ryskal, Marita Katusheva, Tatyana Roshchina, Valentina Mishak, Lyudmila Gureyeva (Soviet Union)	Hanna Busz, Krystyna Czajkowska, Maria Golimowska, Barbara Hermel, Krystyna Jakubowska, Danuta Kordaczuk, Krystyna Krupa, Józefa Ledwig, Jadwiga Marko, Jadwiga Rutkowska, Maria Śliwka, Zofia Szczęśniewska (Poland)
1968	Lyudmila Buldakova, Lyudmila Mikhailovskaya, Tatyana Veinberga, Vera Lantratova, Vera Galuskha-Duyunova, Tatyana Sarycheva, Tatyana Ponyaneva-Tretyakova, Nina Smoleeva, Inna Ryskal, Galina Leontyeva, Roza Salikhova, Valentina Kamenek-Vinogradova (Soviet Union)	Sachiko Fukunaka, Makiko Furukawa, Keiko Hama, Setsuko Inoue, Toyoko Iwahara, Yōko Kasahara, Yukiyo Kojima, Sumie Oinuma, Aiko Onozawa, Kunie Shishikura, Suzue Takayama, Setsuko Yoshida (Japan)	Halina Aszkiełowicz, Lidia Chmielnicka, Krystyna Czajkowska, Krystyna Jakubowska, Krystyna Krupa, Jadwiga Książek, Józefa Ledwig, Barbara Niemczyk, Krystyna Ostromęcka, Elżbieta Porzec, Zofia Szczęśniewska, Wanda Wiecha (Poland)
1972	Lyudmila Borozna, Lyudmila Buldakova, Vera Galushka-Duyunova, Tatyana Gonobobleva, Natalya Kudreva, Galina Leontyeva, Tatyana Ponyaeva-Tretyakova, Inna Ryskal, Roza Salikhova, Tatyana Sarycheva, Nina Smoleeva, Lyubov Turina (Soviet Union)	Makiko Furukawa, Keiko Hama, Takako Iida, Toyoko Iwahara, Katsumi Matsumura, Sumie Oinuma, Mariko Okamoto, Seiko Shimakage, Michiko Shiokawa, Takako Shirai, Noriko Yamashita, Yaeko Yamazaki (Japan)	Hwang He-Suk, Jang Ok-Rim, Jong Ok-Jin, Kang Ok-Sun, Kim Zung-Bok, Kim Myong-Suk, Kim Su-Dae, Kim Yeun-Ja, Paek Myong-Suk, Ri Chun-Ok, Ryom Chun-Ja (North Korea)
1976	Yuko Arakida, Takako Iida, Katsuko Kanesaka, Kiyomi Kato, Echiko Maeda, Noriko Matsuda, Mariko Okamoto, Takako Shirai, Shoko Takayanagi, Hiromi Yano, Juri Yokoyama, Mariko Yoshida (Japan)	Larisa Bergen, Liudmila Chernyshova, Olga Kozakova, Natalya Kushnir, Nina Muradyan, Liliya Osadchaya, Anna Rostova, Lyubov Rudovskaya, Inna Ryskal, Lyudmila Shchetinina, Nina Smoleeva, Zoya Yusova (Soviet Union)	Baik Myung-Sun, Byon Kyung-Ja, Chang Hee-Sook, Jo Hea-Jung, Jung Soon-Ok, Lee Soon-Bok, Lee Soon-Ok, Ma Kum-Ja, Park Mi-Kum, Yoon Young-Nae, Yu Jung-Hyae, Yu Kyung-Hwa (South Korea)

Year	Gold	Silver	Bronze
1980	Elena Akhaminova, Elena Andreiuk, Svetlana Badulina, Liudmila Chernyshova, Liubov Kozyreva, Lidia Loginova, Irina Makogonova, Svetlana Nikishina, Larisa Pavlova, Nadezhda Radzevich, Natalia Razumova, Olga Solovova (Soviet Union)	Katharina Bullin, Barbara Czekalla, Brigitte Fetzer, Andrea Heim, Ute Kostrzewa, Heike Lehmann, Christine Mummhardt, Karin Püschel, Karla Roffeis, Martina Schmidt, Annette Schultz, Anke Westendorf (East Germany)	Verka Borisova, Tsvetana Bozhurina, Rositsa Dimitrova, Tanya Dimitrova, Maya Georgieva, Margarita Gerasimova, Tanya Gogova, Valentina Ilieva, Rumyana Kaisheva, Anka Khristolova, Silviya Petrunova, Galina Stancheva (Bulgaria)
1984	Hou Yuzhu, Jiang Ying, Lang Ping, Li Yanjun, Liang Yan, Su Huijuan, Yang Xiaojun, Yang Xilan, Zhang Rongfang, Zheng Meizhu, Zhou Xiaolan, Zhu Ling (China)	Jeanne Beauprey, Carolyn Becker, Linda Chisholm, Rita Crockett, Laurie Flachmeier, Debbie Green, Flo Hyman, Rose Magers, Kimberly Ruddins, Julie Vollertsen, Paula Weishoff, Susan Woodstra (United States)	Yumi Egami, Norie Hiro, Miyoko Hirose, Kyoko Ishida, Yoko Kagabu, Yuko Mitsuya, Keiko Miyajima, Kimie Morita, Kumi Nakada, Emiko Odaka, Sachiko Otani, Kayoko Sugiyama (Japan)
1988	Valentina Ogienko, Elena Volkova, Marina Kumysh, Irina Smirnova, Tatyana Sidorenko, Irina Parkhomchuk, Tatyana Krainova, Olga Shkurnova, Marina Nikulina, Elena Ovchinnikova, Olga Krivosheeva, Svetlana Korytova (Soviet Union)	Luisa Cervera, Alejandra de la Guerra, Denisse Fajardo, Miriam Gallardo, Rosa García, Sonia Heredia, Katherine Horny, Natalia Málaga, Gabriela Pérez del Solar, Cecilia Tait, Gina Torrealva, Cenaida Uribe (Peru)	Guo-Jun Li, Hong Zhao, Yu-Zhu Hou, Ya-Jun Wang, Xi-Lan Yang, Huijuan Su, Ying Jiang, Yong-Mei Cui, Xiao-Jun Yang, Mei-Zhu Zheng, Dan Wu, Yue-Ming Li (China)
1992	Regla Bell, Mercedes Calderón, Magaly Carvajal, Marlenis Costa, Idalmis Gato, Lilia Izquierdo, Norka Latamblet, Mireya Luis, Tania Ortiz, Raisa O'Farril, Regla Torres (Cuba)	Valentina Ogienko, Natalya Morozova, Marina Nikoulina, Elena Tyurina, Irina Smirnova, Tatyana Sidorenko, Tatiana Menchova, Yevgeniya Artamonova, Galina Lebedeva, Svetlana Vassilevskaia, Elena Tcheboukina, Svetlana Koritova (Unified Team)	Liane Sato, Paula Weishoff, Yoko Zetterlund, Elaina Oden, Kimberley Oden, Teee Sanders, Caren Kemner, Ruth Lawanson, Tammy Liley, Janet Cobbs, Tara Cross-Battle, Lori Endicott (United States)
1996	Taismary Agüero, Regla Bell, Magaly Carvajal, Marlenis Costa, Ana Fernández, Mirka Francia, Idalmis Gato, Lilia Izquierdo, Mireya Luis, Raisa O'Ferrill, Yumilka Ruiz, Regla Torres (Cuba)	Cui Yong-Mei, He Qi, Lai Yawen, Li Yan, Liu Xiaoning, Pan Wenli, Sun Yue, Wang Lina, Wang Yi, Wang Ziling, Wu Yongmei, Zhu Yunying (China)	Ana Ida Alvares, Leila Barros, Filo Bodziak, Hilma Caldeira, Ana Connelly, Marcia Cunha, Virna Dias, Ana Moser, Ana Sanglard, Hélia Souza, Sandra Suruagy, Fernanda Venturini (Brazil)
2000	Taismary Agüero, Zoila Barros, Regla Bell, Marlenis Costa, Ana Fernández, Mirka Francia, Idalmis Gato, Lilia Izquierdo, Mireya Luis, Yumilka Ruiz, Martha Sanchez, Regla Torres (Cuba)	Yevgeniya Artamonova, Anastasiya Belikova, Lioubov Kilic, Yekaterina Gamova, Yelena Godina, Tatyana Gracheva, Natalya Morozova, Olga Potachova, Inessa Korkmaz, Elizaveta Tishchenko, Elena Tyurina, Yelena Vasilevskaya (Russia)	Leila Barros, Erika Coimbra, Janina Conceição, Virna Dias, Kely Fraga, Ricarda Lima, Katia Lopes, Elisangela Oliveira, Walewska Oliveira, Karin Rodrigues, Raquel Silva, Helia Souza (Brazil)
2004	Chen Jing, Feng Kun, Li Shan, Liu Yanan, Song Nina, Wang Lina, Yang Hao, Zhang Na, Zhang Ping, Zhang Yuehong, Zhao Ruirui, Zhou Suhong (China)	Yevgeniya Artamonova, Lioubov Kılıç, Olga Chukanova, Yekaterina Gamova, Aleksandra Korukovets, Olga Nikolaeva, Yelena Plotnikova, Natalya Safronova, Marina Sheshenina, Irina Tebenikhina, Elizaveta Tishchenko, Elena Tyurina (Russia)	Zoila Barros, Rosir Calderon, Nancy Carrillo, Ana Fernández, Maybelis Martinez, Liana Mesa, Anniara Muñoz, Yaima Ortíz, Daimí Ramírez, Yumilka Ruiz, Marta Sánchez, Dulce Tellez (Cuba)

Year	Gold	Silver	Bronze
2008	Walewska Oliveira, Carolina Albuquerque, Marianne Steinbrecher, Paula Pequeno, Thaisa Menezes, Hélia Souza, Valeska Menezes, Fabiana Claudino, Welissa Gonzaga, Jaqueline Carvalho, Sheilla Castro, Fabiana de Oliveira (Brazil)	Ogonna Nnamani, Danielle Scott-Arruda, Tayyiba Haneef-Park, Lindsey Berg, Stacy Sykora, Nicole Davis, Heather Bown, Jennifer Joines, Kim Glass, Robyn Ah Mow-Santos, Kim Willoughby, Logan Tom (United States)	Wang Yimei, Feng Kun, Yang Hao, Liu Yanan, Wei Qiuyue, Xu Yunli, Zhou Suhong, Zhao Ruirui, Xue Ming, Li Juan, Zhang Na, Ma Yunwen (China)

Water Motorsports

Men's Open Class A

Year	Gold	Silver	Bronze
1908	Emile Thubron (France)	Not awarded	Not awarded

Men's Class B

Year	Gold	Silver	Bronze
1908	Isaac Thomas Thornycroft, Bernard Redwood, John Field-Richards (Great Britain)	Not awarded	Not awarded

Men's Class C

Year	Gold	Silver	Bronze
1908	Isaac Thomas Thornycroft, Bernard Redwood, John Field-Richards (Great Britain)	Not awarded	Not awarded

Water Polo

Men's Water Polo

Year	Gold	Silver	Bronze
1900	Thomas Coe, John Derbyshire, Peter Kemp, William Lister, Arthur Robertson, Eric Robinson, George Wilkinson (Great Britain)	Henri Cohen, Jean De Backer, Victor De Behr, Fernand Feyaerts, Oscar Grégoire, Albert Michant, Victor Sonnemans (Belgium)	Thomas Burgess, Coulon*, Alphonse Decuyper, Jules Clévenot, Fardelle*, Favier*, Louis Laufray, Leriche*, Louis Martin, Désiré Mérchez, Henri Peslier, Pesloy*, Charles Treffel, Paul Vasseur (France)
1904	David Bratton, George Van Cleaf, Leo Goodwin, Louis Handley, David Hesser, Joseph Ruddy, James Steen (United States)	Rex Beach, Jerome Steever, Edwin Swatek, Charles Healy, Frank Kehoe, David Hammond, William Tuttle (United States)	John Meyers, Manfred Toeppen, Gwynne Evans, Amedee Reyburn, Fred Schreiner, Augustus Goessling, William Orthwein (United States)
1908	George Cornet, Charles Forsyth, George Nevinson, Paul Radmilovic, Charles Smith, Thomas Thould, George Wilkinson (Great Britain)	Victor Boin, Herman Donners, Fernand Feyaerts, Oscar Grégoire, Herman Meyboom, Albert Michant, Joseph Pletinckx (Belgium)	Robert Andersson, Erik Bergvall, Pontus Hanson, Harald Julin, Torsten Kumfeldt, Axel Runström, Gunnar Wennerström (Sweden)

Year	Gold	Silver	Bronze
1912	Isaac Bentham, Charles Bugbee, George Cornet, Arthur Edwin Hill, Paul Radmilovic, Charles Smith, George Wilkinson (Great Britain)	Robert Andersson, Vilhelm Andersson, Erik Bergqvist, Max Gumpel, Pontus Hanson, Harald Julin, Torsten Kumfeldt (Sweden)	Victor Boin, Félicien Courbet, Herman Donners, Albert Durant, Oscar Grégoire, Herman Meyboom, Joseph Pletinckx (Belgium)
1916: Olympics not held			
1920	Charles Bugbee, William Henry Dean, Christopher Jones, William Peacock, Noel Purcell, Paul Radmilovic, Charles Smith (Great Britain)	René Bauwens, Gérard Blitz, Maurice Blitz, Pierre Dewin, Albert Durant, Paul Gailly, Pierre Nijs, Joseph Pletinckx (Belgium)	Erik Andersson, Robert Andersson, Vilhelm Andersson, Nils Backlund, Erik Bergqvist, Max Gumpel, Pontus Hanson, Harald Julin, Theodor Nauman, Torsten Kumfeldt (Sweden)
1924	R. Bertrand*, A. Fasani*, Albert Delborgies, Albert Mayaud, Georges Rigal, Henri Padou, J. Perol*, Jean Lasquin, Noël Delberghe, Paul Dujardin, Robert Desmettre (France)	Gérard Blitz, Maurice Blitz, Joseph Cludts, Joseph De Combe, Pierre Dewin, Albert Durant, Georges Fleurix, Paul Gailly, Joseph Pletinckx, Jules Thiry, Jean-Pierre Vermetten (Belgium)	Arthur Austin, Elmer Collett, Henry Jamison Handy, Oliver Horn, Frederick Lauer, George Mitchell, John Norton, Wallace O'Connor, George Schroth, Herbert Vollmer, Johnny Weissmuller (United States)
1928	Max Amann, Karl Bähre, Emil Benecke, Johann Blank, Otto Cordes, Fritz Gunst, Erich Rademacher, Joachim Rademacher (Germany)	István Barta, Olivér Halassy, Márton Homonnai, Sándor Ivády, Alajos Keserű, Ferenc Keserű, József Vértesy (Hungary)	Émile Bulteel, Henri Cuvelier, Paul Dujardin, Jules Keignaert, Henri Padou, Ernest Roger, Albert Thévenon, Achille Tribouillet, Albert Vandeplancke (France)
1932	István Barta, György Bródy, Olivér Halassy, Márton Homonnai, Sándor Ivády, Alajos Keserű, Ferenc Keserű, János Németh, Miklós Sárkány, József Vértesy (Hungary)	Emil Benecke, Otto Cordes, Hans Eckstein, Fritz Gunst, Erich Rademacher, Joachim Rademacher, Hans Schulze, Heiko Schwartz (Germany)	Austin Clapp, Philip Daubenspeck, Charles Finn, Charles McCallister, Wallace O'Connor, Cal Strong, Herbert Wildman (United States)
1936	Mihály Bozsi, Jenő Brandi, György Bródy, Olivér Halassy, Kálmán Hazai, Márton Homonnai, György Kutasi, György Kutasi, János Németh, Miklós Sárkány, Sándor Tarics (Hungary)	Bernhard Baier, Fritz Gunst, Josef Hauser, Alfred Kienzle, Paul Klingenburg, Heinrich Krug, Hans Schneider, Hans Schulze, Gustav Schürger, Helmuth Schwenn, Fritz Stolze (Germany)	Gérard Blitz, Albert Castelyns, Pierre Coppieters, Joseph De Combe, Henri De Pauw, Henri Disy, Fernand Isselé, Edmond Michiels, Henri Stoelen (Belgium)
1940–1944: Olympics not held			
1948	Ermenegildo Arena, Emilio Bulgarelli, Pasquale Buonocore, Aldo Ghira, Mario Majoni, Geminio Ognio, Gianfranco Pandolfini, Tullo Pandolfini, Cesare Rubini (Italy)	Jenő Brandi, Oszkár Csuvik, Dezső Fábián, Dezső Gyarmati, Endre Győrfi, Miklós Holop, László Jeney, Dezső Lemhényi, Károly Szittya, István Szivós (Hungary)	Cor Braasem, Hennie Keetelaar, Nijs Korevaar, Joop Rohner, Frits Ruimschotel, Piet Salomons, Frits Smol, Hans Stam, Ruud van Feggelen (Netherlands)
1952	Róbert Antal, Antal Bolvári, Dezső Fábián, Dezső Gyarmati, István Hasznos, László Jeney, György Kárpáti, Dezső Lemhényi, Kálmán Markovits, Miklós Martin, Károly Szittya, István Szivós, György Vizvári (Hungary)	Veljko Bakašun, Marko Brainović, Vladimir Ivković, Zdravko Ježić, Zdravko-Ćiro Kovačić, Ivo Kurtini, Lovro Radonjić, Ivo Štakula, Boško Vuksanović (Yugoslavia)	Ermenegildo Arena, Lucio Ceccarini, Renato De Sanzuane, Raffaello Gambino, Salvatore Gionta, Maurizio Mannelli, Geminio Ognio, Carlo Peretti, Enzo Polito, Cesare Rubini, Renato Traiola (Italy)
1956	Antal Bolvári, Ottó Boros, Dezső Gyarmati, István Hevesi, László Jeney, Tivadar Kanizsa, György Kárpáti, Kálmán Markovits, Mihály Mayer, István Szivós, Ervin Zádor (Hungary)	Ivo Cipci, Tomislav Franjković, Vladimir Ivković, Zdravko Ježić, Hrvoje Kačić, Zdravko-Ćiro Kovačić, Lovro Radonjić, Marijan Žužej (Yugoslavia)	Viktor Ageev, Pyotr Breus, Boris Goykhman, Nodar Gvakhariya, Vyacheslav Kurennoy, Boris Markarov, P'et're Mshveni- yeradze, Valentin Prokopov, Mikhail Ryzhak, Yury Shlyapin (Soviet Union)

Year	Gold	Silver	Bronze
1960	Amedeo Ambron, Danio Bardi, Giuseppe D'Altrui, Salvatore Gionta, Giancarlo Guerrini, Franco Lavoratori, Gianni Lonzi, Luigi Mannelli, Rosario Parmegiani, Eraldo Pizzo, Dante Rossi, Brunello Spinelli (Italy)	Viktor Ageev, Givi Chikvanaia, Leri Gogoladze, Boris Goykhman, Yury Grigorovsky, Anatoly Kartashov, Vyacheslav Kurennoy, P'et're Mshveni-yeradze, Vladimir Novikov, Yevgeny Saltsyn, Vladimir Semyonov (Soviet Union)	András Bodnár, Ottó Boros, Zoltán Dömötör, László Felkai, Dezső Gyarmati, István Hevesi, László Jeney, Tivadar Kanizsa, György Kárpáti, András Katona, János Konrád, Kálmán Markovits, Mihály Mayer, Péter Rusorán (Hungary)
1964	Miklós Ambrus, András Bodnár, Ottó Boros, Zoltán Dömötör, László Felkai, Dezső Gyarmati, Tivadar Kanizsa, György Kárpáti, János Konrád, Mihály Mayer, Dénes Pócsik, Péter Rusorán (Hungary)	Ozren Bonačić, Zoran Janković, Milan Muškatirović, Antun Nardeli, Franjo Nonković, Vinko Rosić, Mirko Sandić, Zlatko Šimenc, Božidar Stanišić, Karlo Stipanić, Ivo Trumbić (Yugoslavia)	Viktor Ageev, Zenon Bortkevich, Eduard Egorov, Igor Grabovsky, Boris Grishin, Nikolai Kalashnikov, Nikolay Kuznetsov, Vladimir Kuznetsov, Leonid Osipov, Boris Popov, Vladimir Semyonov (Soviet Union)
1968	Ozren Bonačić, Dejan Dabović, Zdravko Hebel, Zoran Janković, Ronald Lopatini, Uroš Marović, Đorđe Perišić, Miroslav Poljak, Mirko Sandić, Karlo Stipanić, Ivo Trumbić (Yugoslavia)	Aleksei Barkalov, Oleg Bovin, Givi Chikvanaya, Aleksandr Dolgushin, Yuri Grigorovsky, Boris Grishin, Vadim Gulyaev, Leonid Osipov, Vladimir Semyonov, Aleksandr Shidlovsky, Vyacheslav Skok (Soviet Union)	András Bodnár, Zoltán Dömötör, László Felkai, Ferenc Konrád, János Konrád, Mihály Mayer, Endre Molnár, Dénes Pócsik, László Sárosi, János Steinmetz, István Szívós Jr. (Hungary)
1972	Anatoli Akimov, Aleksei Barkalov, Aleksandr Dolgushin, Aleksandr Dreval, Vadim Gulyaev, Aleksandr Kabanov, Nikolai Melnikov, Leonid Osipov, Aleksandr Shidlovsky, Vladimir Shmudsky, Viacheslav Sobchenko (Soviet Union)	András Bodnár, Tibor Cservenyák, Tamás Faragó, István Görgényi, Zoltán Kásás, Ferenc Konrád, István Magas, Endre Molnár, Dénes Pócsik, László Sárosi, István Szívós Jr. (Hungary)	Peter Asch, Steven Barnett, Bruce Bradley, Stanley Cole, James Ferguson, Eric Lindroth, John Parker, Gary Sheerer, James Slatton, Russell Webb, Barry Weitzenberg (United States)
1976	Gábor Csapó, Tibor Cservenyák, Tamás Faragó, György Gerendás, György Horkai, György Kenéz, Ferenc Konrád, Endre Molnár, László Sárosi, Attila Sudár, István Szívós Jr. (Hungary)	Alberto Alberani, Silvio Barac-chini, Luigi Castagnola, Vincenzo D'Angelo, Gianni de Magistris, Riccardo de Magistris, Marcello del Duca, Alessandro Ghibellini, Sante Marsili, Umberto Panerai, Roldano Simeoni (Italy)	Alex Boegschoten, Ton Buunk, Piet de Zwarte, Andy Hoepel-man, Evert Kroon, Nico Landeweerd, Hans Smits, Gijze Stroboer, Rik Toonen, Hans van Zeeland, Jan Evert Veer (Netherlands)
1980	Vladimir Akimov, Aleksei Barkalov, Evgeni Grishin, Mikhail Ivanov, Aleksandr Kabanov, Sergei Kotenko, Georgi Mschvenieradze, Mait Riisman, Erkin Shagaev, Evgeni Sharonov, Viacheslav Sobchenko (Soviet Union)	Milivoj Bebić, Zoran Gopčević, Milorad Krivokapić, Boško Lozica, Predrag Manojlović, Zoran Mustur, Damir Polić, Zoran Roje, Ratko Rudić, Slobodan Trifunović, Luka Vezilić (Yugoslavia)	Gábor Csapó, Tamás Faragó, György Gerandás, Károly Hauszler, György Horkai, István Kiss, László Kuncz, Endre Molnár, Attila Sudár, István Szívós Jr., István Udvardi (Hungary)
1984	Dragan Andrić, Milivoj Bebić, Perica Bukić, Veselin Đuho, Milorad Krivokapić, Deni Lušić, Igor Milanović, Tomislav Paškvalin, Zoran Petrović, Andrija Popović, Zoran Roje, Goran Sukno, Božo Vuletić (Yugoslavia)	Douglas Burke, Peter Campbell, Jody Campbell, Christopher Dorst, Gary Figueroa, Andrew McDonald, Kevin Robertson, Terry Schroeder, Timothy Shaw, John Siman, Jon Svendsen, Joseph Vargas, Craig Wilson (United States)	Santiago Chalmowsky, Armando Fernández, Roland Freund, Rainer Hoppe, Thomas Huber, Thomas Loebb, Werner Obschernikat, Rainer Ossel-mann, Frank Otto, Peter Röhle, Jurgen Schroder, Hagen Stamm, Dirk Theismann (West Germany)

Year	Gold	Silver	Bronze
1988	Dragan Andrić, Tomislav Bezmalinović, Perica Bukić, Veselin Đuho, Igor Gočanin, Deni Lušić, Igor Milanović, Tomislav Paškvalin, Renko Posinković, Goran Radenović, Dubravko Šimenc, Aleksandar Šoštar, Mirko Vičević (Yugoslavia)	James Bergeson, Gregory Boyer, Peter Campbell, Jeff Campbell, Jody Campbell, Christopher Duplanty, Michael Evans, Douglas Kimbell, Edward Klass, Alan Mouchawar, Kevin Robertson, Terry Schroeder, Craig Wilson (United States)	Dmitri Apanassenko, Viktor Berendyuga, Mikhail Giorgadze, Evgeni Grishin, Mikhail Ivanov, Aleksandr Kolotov, Sergei Kotenko, Sergei Markoch, Nurlan Mendygaliev, Georgi Mschvenieradze, Sergey Naumov, Evgeni Sharonov, Nikolai Smirnov (Soviet Union)
1992	Francesco Attolico, Gianni Averaimo, Alessandro Bovo, Paolo Caldarella, Alessandro Campagna, Marco D'Altrui, Massimiliano Ferretti, Mario Fiorillo, Ferdinando Gandolfi, Amedeo Pomilio, Francesco Porzio, Giuseppe Porzio, Carlo Silipo (Italy)	Daniel Ballart, Manuel Estiarte, Pedro Francisco García, Salvador Gómez, Marco Antonio González, Rubén Michavila, Miguel Ángel Oca, Sergi Pedrerol, Josep Picó, Jesús Miguel Rollán, Ricardo Sánchez, Jordi Sans, Manuel Silvestre (Spain)	Dmitri Apanassenko, Andrei Belofastov, Evgueni Charonov, Dmitry Gorshkov, Vladimir Karaboutov, Aleksandr Kolotov, Andriy Kovalenko, Nikolay Kozlov, Serguei Markotch, Sergey Naumov, Alexandre Ogorodnikov, Alexandre Tchiguir (Unified Team)
1996	Josep María Abarca, Angel Luis Andreo, Daniel Ballart, Manuel Estiarte, Pedro Francisco García, Salvador Gómez, Ivan Moro, Miguel Ángel Oca, Jorge Payá, Sergi Pedrerol, Jesús Miguel Rollán, Jordi Sans, Carles Sans (Spain)	Maro Balić, Perica Bukić, Damir Glavan, Igor Hinić, Vjekoslav Kobešćak, Joško Kreković, Ognjen Kržić, Dubravko Šimenc, Siniša Školneković, Ratko Štritof, Tino Vegar, Renato Vrbičić, Zdeslav Vrdoljak (Croatia)	Alberto Angelini, Francesco Attolico, Fabio Bencivenga, Alessandro Bovo, Alessandro Calcaterra, Roberto Calcaterra, Marco Gerini, Alberto Ghibellini, Luca Giustolisi, Amedeo Pomilio, Francesco Postiglione, Carlo Silipo, Leonardo Sottani (Italy)
2000	Tibor Benedek, Péter Biros, Rajmund Fodor, Tamás Kásás, Gergely Kiss, Zoltán Kósz, Tamás Märcz, Tamás Molnár, Barnabás Steinmetz, Zoltán Szécsi, Bulcsú Székely, Zsolt Varga, Attila Vári (Hungary)	Roman Balashov, Dmitri Dugin, Sergei Garbuzov, Dmitry Gorshkov, Yuri Yatsev, Nikolay Kozlov, Nikolai Maksimov, Andrei Rekechinski, Dmitri Stratan, Revaz Tchomakhidze, Aleksandr Yeryshov, Marat Zakirov, Irek Zinnourov (Russia)	Aleksandar Ćirić, Danilo Ikodinović, Viktor Jelenić, Nikola Kuljača, Aleksandar Šapić, Dejan Savić, Aleksandar Šoštar, Petar Trbojević, Veljko Uskoković, Jugoslav Vasović, Vladimir Vujasinović, Nenad Vukanić, Predrag Zimonjić (Yugoslavia)
2004	Tibor Benedek, Péter Biros, Rajmund Fodor, István Gergely, Tamás Kásás, Gergely Kiss, Norbert Madaras, Tamás Molnár, Ádám Steinmetz, Zoltán Szécsi, Tamás Varga, Attila Vári (Hungary)	Aleksandar Ćirić, Vladimir Gojković, Danilo Ikodinović, Viktor Jelenić, Predrag Jokić, Nikola Kuljača, Slobodan Nikić, Aleksandar Šapić, Dejan Savić, Denis Šefik, Petar Trbojević, Vanja Udovičić, Vladimir Vujasinović (Serbia and Montenegro)	Roman Balashov, Revaz Tchomak-hidze, Aleksandr Fyodorov, Serguei Garbouzov, Dmitry Gorshkov, Nikolay Kozlov, Nikolai Maximov, Andrei Reketchinski, Dmitri Stratan, Alexander Yerishev, Vitaly Yurchik, Marat Zakirov, Irek Zinnourov (Russia)
2008	Tibor Benedek, Péter Biros, István Gergely, Norbert Hosnyánszky, Tamás Kásás, Zoltán Szécsi, Gábor Kis, Gergely Kiss, Norbert Madaras, Tamás Molnár, Dániel Varga, Dénes Varga, Tamás Varga (Hungary)	Tony Azevedo, Ryan Bailey, Layne Beaubien, Brandon Brooks, Peter Hudnut, Tim Hutten, J. W. Krumpholz, Rick Merlo, Merrill Moses, Jeff Powers, Jesse Smith, Peter Varellas, Adam Wright (United States)	Aleksandar Ćirić, Filip Filipović, Živko Gocić, Branko Peković, Duško Pijetlović, Andrija Prlainović, Nikola Rađen, Aleksandar Šapić, Dejan Savić, Denis Šefik, Slobodan Soro, Vanja Udovičić, Vladimir Vujasinović (Serbia)

* Full name not recorded

Women's Water Polo

Year	Gold	Silver	Bronze
2000	Naomi Castle, Joanne Fox, Bridgette Gusterson, Simone Hankin, Yvette Higgins, Kate Hooper, Bronwyn Mayer, Gail Miller, Melissa Mills, Debbie Watson, Liz Weekes, Danielle Woodhouse, Taryn Woods (Australia)	Robin Beauregard, Ellen Estes, Ericka Lorenz, Heather Moody, Bernice Orwig, Maureen O'Toole, Nicolle Payne, Heather Petri, Kathy Sheehy, Coralie Simmons, Julie Swail, Brenda Villa, Courtney Johnson (United States)	Marina Akobiya, Ekaterina Anikeeva, Sofia Konukh, Maria Koroleva, Natalia Kutuzova, Svetlana Kuzina, Yuliya Petrova, Tatiana Petrova, Galina Rytova, Elena Smurova, Elena Tokun, Irina Tolkunova, Ekaterina Vassilieva (Russia)
2004	Carmela Allucci, Alexandra Araujo, Silvia Bosurgi, Francesca Conti, Tania di Mario, Elena Gigli, Melania Grego, Giusy Malato, Martina Miceli, Maddalena Musumeci, Cinzia Ragusa, Noémi Tóth, Manuela Zanchi (Italy)	Dimitra Asilian, Georgia Ellinaki, Eftychia Karagianni, Angeliki Karapataki, Stavroula Kozom-poli, Georgia Lara, Kyriaki Liosi, Aniopi Melidoni, Antonia Moraiti, Evangelia Moraitidou, Anthoula Mylonaki, Aikaterini Oikonomopoulou, Antigoni Roumpesi (Greece)	Robin Beauregard, Margaret Dingeldein, Ellen Estes, Jacqueline Frank, Natalie Golda, Ericka Lorenz, Heather Moody, Thalia Munro, Nicolle Payne, Heather Petri, Kelly Rulon, Amber Stachowski, Brenda Villa (United States)
2008	Mieke Cabout, Daniëlle de Bruijn, van den Berg, Rianne Guiche-laar, Biurakn Hakhverdian, Noeki Klein, Simone Koot, Ilse van der Meijden, Yasemin Smit, Iefke van Belkum, Gillian van den Berg, Marieke van den Ham (Netherlands)	Elizabeth Armstrong, Patty Cardenas, Kami Craig, Natalie Golda, Alison Gregorka, Brittany Hayes, Jaime Hipp, Heather Petri, Jessica Steffens, Moriah van Norman, Brenda Villa, Lauren Wenger, Elsie Windes (United States)	Gemma Beadsworth, Nikita Cuffe, Suzie Fraser, Taniele Gofers, Kate Gynther, Amy Hetzel, Bronwen Knox, Emma Knox, Alicia McCormack, Melissa Rippon, Rebecca Rippon, Jenna Santoromito, Mia Santoromito (Australia)

Water Skiing

Men's Slalom

Year	Gold	Silver	Bronze
1972	Roby Zucchi (Italy)	Wayne Grimditch (United States)	Jean-Michel Jamin (France)

Men's Figure Skiing

Year	Gold	Silver	Bronze
1972	Ricky McCormick (United States)	Wayne Grimditch (United States)	Karl-Heinz Benzinger (West Germany)

Men's Jump

Year	Gold	Silver	Bronze
1972	Ricky McCormick (United States)	Max Hofer (Italy)	Hagen Klie (West Germany)

Women's Slalom

Year	Gold	Silver	Bronze
1972	Liz Allen-Shetter (United States)	Willy Staehle (Netherlands)	Pat Messner (Canada)

Women's Figure Skiing

Year	Gold	Silver	Bronze
1972	Willy Staehle (Netherlands)	Kaye Thurlow (Australia)	Sylvie Maurial (France)

Women's Jump

Year	Gold	Silver	Bronze
1972	Sylvie Maurial (France)	Kaye Thurlow (Australia)	Liz Allen-Shetter (United States)

Weightlifting

Men's One-hand Lift

Year	Gold	Silver	Bronze
1896	Launceston Elliot (Great Britain)	Viggo Jensen (Denmark)	Alexandros Nikolopoulos (Greece)

Men's Two-hand Lift

Year	Gold	Silver	Bronze
1896	Viggo Jensen (Denmark)	Launceston Elliot (Great Britain)	Sotirios Versis (Greece)
1900: Event not held			
1904	Perikles Kakousis (Greece)	Oscar Osthoff (United States)	Frank Kugler (United States)

Men's All-Around Dumbbell

Year	Gold	Silver	Bronze
1904	Oscar Osthoff (United States)	Frederick Winters (United States)	Frank Kugler (United States)

Men's Flyweight

Year	Gold	Silver	Bronze
1972	Zygmunt Smalcerz (Poland)	Lajos Szűcs (Hungary)	Sándor Holczreiter (Hungary)
1976	Aleksandr Voronin (Soviet Union)	György Kőszegi (Hungary)	Mohammad Nassiri (Iran)
1980	Kanybek Osmanliev (Soviet Union)	Choi Ho-Bong (North Korea)	Han Gyong-Si (North Korea)
1984	Zeng Guoqiang (China)	Zhou Peishun (China)	Kazushito Manabe (Japan)
1988	Sevdalin Marinov (Bulgaria)	Chun Byung-Kwan (South Korea)	He Zhuoqiang (China)
1992	Ivan Ivanov (Bulgaria)	Lin Qisheng (China)	Traian Cihărean (Romania)
1996	Halil Mutlu (Turkey)	Zhang Xiangsen (China)	Sevdalin Minchev (Bulgaria)

Men's Bantamweight

Year	Gold	Silver	Bronze
1948	Joseph DePietro (United States)	Julian Creus (Great Britain)	Richard Tom (United States)
1952	Ivan Udodov (Soviet Union)	Mahmoud Namjoo (Iran)	Ali Mirzaei (Iran)
1956	Charles Vinci (United States)	Vladimir Stogov (Soviet Union)	Mahmoud Namjoo (Iran)
1960	Charles Vinci (United States)	Yoshinobu Miyake (Japan)	Esmaeil Elmkhah (Iran)
1964	Aleksei Vakhonin (Soviet Union)	Imre Földi (Hungary)	Shiro Ishinoseki (Japan)
1968	Mohammad Nassiri (Iran)	Imre Földi (Hungary)	Henryk Trębicki (Poland)
1972	Imre Földi (Hungary)	Mohammad Nassiri (Iran)	Gennadi Chetin (Soviet Union)
1976	Norair Nurikyan (Bulgaria)	Grzegorz Cziura (Poland)	Kenkichi Ando (Japan)
1980	Daniel Núñez (Cuba)	Yurik Sarkisian (Soviet Union)	Tadeusz Dembonczyk (Poland)
1984	Wu Shude (China)	Lai Runming (China)	Masahiro Kotaka (Japan)
1988	Oksen Mirzoyan (Soviet Union)	He Yingqiang (Soviet Union)	Liu Shoubin (China)
1992	Chun Byung-Kwan (South Korea)	Liu Shoubin (China)	Luo Jianming (China)
1996	Tang Lingsheng (China)	Leonidas Sampanis (Greece)	Nikolay Pechalov (Bulgaria)
2000	Halil Mutlu (Turkey)	Wu Wenxiong (China)	Zhang Xiangxiang (China)
2004	Halil Mutlu (Turkey)	Wu Meijin (China)	Sedat Artuç (Turkey)
2008	Long Qingquan (China)	Hoang Anh Tuan (Vietnam)	Eko Yuli Irawan (Indonesia)

Men's Featherweight

Year	Gold	Silver	Bronze
1920	Frans De Haes (Belgium)	Alfred Schmidt (Estonia)	Eugène Ryther (Switzerland)
1924	Pierino Gabetti (Italy)	Andreas Stadler (Austria)	Arthur Reinmann (Switzerland)
1928	Franz Andrysek (Austria)	Pierino Gabetti (Italy)	Hans Wölpert (Germany)

Year	Gold	Silver	Bronze
1932	Raymond Suvigny (France)	Hans Wölpert (Germany)	Anthony Terlazzo (United States)
1936	Anthony Terlazzo (United States)	Saleh Soliman (Egypt)	Ibrahim Shams (Egypt)
1940–1944: Olympics not held			
1948	Mahmoud Fayad (Egypt)	Rodney Wilkes (Trinidad and Tobago)	Jafar Salmassi (Iran)
1952	Rafael Chimishkyan (Soviet Union)	Nikolai Saksonov (Soviet Union)	Rodney Wilkes (Trinidad and Tobago)
1956	Isaac Berger (United States)	Yevgeni Minaev (Soviet Union)	Marian Zieliński (Poland)
1960	Yevgeni Minaev (Soviet Union)	Isaac Berger (United States)	Sebastiano Mannironi (Italy)
1964	Yoshinobu Miyake (Japan)	Isaac Berger (United States)	Mieczysław Nowak (Poland)
1968	Yoshinobu Miyake (Japan)	Dito Shanidze (Soviet Union)	Yoshiyuku Miyake (Japan)
1972	Norair Nurikyan (Bulgaria)	Dito Shanidze (Soviet Union)	Janos Benedek (Hungary)
1976	Nikolay Kolesnikov (Soviet Union)	Georghi Todorov (Bulgaria)	Kazumasa Hirai (Japan)
1980	Viktor Mazin (Soviet Union)	Stefan Dimitrov (Bulgaria)	Marek Seweryn (Poland)
1984	Chen Weiqiang (Soviet Union)	Gelu Radu (Romania)	Tsai Wen-Yee (Taiwan)
1988	Naim Süleymanoğlu (Turkey)	Stefan Topurov (Bulgaria)	Ye Huanming (China)
1992	Naim Süleymanoğlu (Turkey)	Nikolay Pechalov (Bulgaria)	He Yingqiang (China)
1996	Naim Süleymanoğlu (Turkey)	Valerios Leonidas (Greece)	Xiao Jiangang (China)
2000	Nikolay Pechalov (Croatia)	Leonidas Sampanis (Greece)	Gennady Oleshchuk (Belarus)
2004	Shi Zhiyong (China)	Le Maosheng (China)	Israel José Rubio (Venezuela)
2008	Zhang Xiangxiang (China)	Diego Fernando Salazar (Colombia)	Triyatno (Indonesia)

Men's Lightweight

Year	Gold	Silver	Bronze
1920	Alfred Neuland (Estonia)	Louis Williquet (Belgium)	Georges Rooms (Belgium)
1924	Edmond Decottignies (France)	Anton Zwerina (Austria)	Bohumil Durdis (Czechoslovakia)
1928	Hans Haas (Austria) Kurt Helbig (Germany)	Not awarded	Fernand Arnout (France)
1932	René Duverger (France)	Hans Haas (Austria)	Gastone Pierini (Italy)
1936	Robert Fein (Austria) Anwar Mesbah (Egypt)	Not awarded	Karl Jansen (Germany)
1940–1944: Olympics not held			
1948	Ibrahim Shams (Egypt)	Attia Hamouda (Egypt)	James Halliday (Great Britain)
1952	Tommy Kono (United States)	Yevgeni Lopatin (Soviet Union)	Verdi Barberis (Australia)
1956	Ihor Rybak (Soviet Union)	Ravil Khabutdinov (Soviet Union)	Kim Chang-Hee (South Korea)
1960	Viktor Bushev (Soviet Union)	Tan Howe Liang (Singapore)	Abdul Wahid Aziz (Iraq)
1964	Waldemar Baszanowski (Poland)	Vladimir Kaplunov (Soviet Union)	Marian Zieliński (Poland)
1968	Waldemar Baszanowski (Poland)	Parviz Jalayer (Iran)	Marian Zieliński (Poland)
1972	Mukharby Kirzhinov (Soviet Union)	Mladen Kutchev (Bulgaria)	Zbigniew Kaczmarek (Poland)
1976	Petro Korol (Soviet Union)	Daniel Senet (France)	Kazimierz Czarnecki (Poland)
1980	Yanko Rusev (Bulgaria)	Joachim Kunz (East Germany)	Mincho Pachov (Bulgaria)
1984	Yao Jingyuan (China)	Andrei Socaci (Romania)	Jouni Grönman (Finland)
1988	Joachim Kunz (East Germany)	Israil Militosyan (Soviet Union)	Li Jinhe (China)
1992	Israil Militosyan (Unified Team)	Yoto Yotov (Bulgaria)	Andreas Behm (Germany)
1996	Zhan Xugang (China)	Kim Myong-Nam (South Korea)	Attila Feri (Hungary)
2000	Galabin Boevski (Bulgaria)	Georgi Markov (Bulgaria)	Segey Lavrenov (Belarus)
2004	Zhang Guozheng (China)	Lee Bae-Young (South Korea)	Nikolay Pechalov (Croatia)
2008	Liao Hui (China)	Vencelas Dabaya-Tientcheu (France)	Tigran Gevorg Martirosyan (Armenia)

Men's Middleweight

Year	Gold	Silver	Bronze
1920	Henri Gance (France)	Pietro Bianchi (Italy)	Albert Pettersson (Sweden)
1924	Carlo Galimberti (Italy)	Alfred Neuland (Estonia)	Jaan Kikkas (Estonia)
1928	Roger François (France)	Carlo Galimberti (Italy)	Guus Scheffer (Netherlands)
1932	Rudolf Ismayr (Germany)	Carlo Galimberti (Italy)	Karl Hipfinger (Austria)
1936	Khadr El Touni (Egypt)	Rudolf Ismayr (Germany)	Adolf Wagner (Germany)
1940–1944: Olympics not held			
1948	Frank Spellman (United States)	Peter George (United States)	Kim Sung-Jip (South Korea)
1952	Peter George (United States)	Gérard Gratton (Canada)	Kim Sung-Jip (South Korea)
1956	Fyodor Bogdanovsky (Soviet Union)	Peter George (United States)	Ermanno Pignatti (Italy)
1960	Aleksandr Kurynov (Soviet Union)	Tommy Kono (United States)	Gyözö Veres (Hungary)
1964	Hans Zdražila (Czechoslovakia)	Viktor Kurentsov (Soviet Union)	Masashi Ouchi (Japan)
1968	Viktor Kurentsov (Soviet Union)	Masashi Ouchi (Japan)	Karoly Bakos (Hungary)
1972	Yordan Bikov (Bulgaria)	Mohamed Traboulsi (Lebanon)	Anselmo Silvino (Italy)
1976	Yordan Mitkov (Bulgaria)	Vartan Militosyan (Soviet Union)	Peter Wenzel (East Germany)
1980	Asen Zlatev (Bulgaria)	Oleksander Pervy (Soviet Union)	Nedelcho Kolev (Bulgaria)
1984	Karl-Heinz Radschinsky (West Germany)	Jacques Demers (Canada)	Dragomir Cioroslan (Romania)
1988	Borislav Gidikov (Bulgaria)	Ingo Steinhofel (East Germany)	Aleksandr Varbanov (Bulgaria)
1992	Fedor Kassapu (Unified Team)	Pablo Lara Rodriguez (Cuba)	Kim Myong-Ham (North Korea)
1996	Pablo Lara Rodriguez (Cuba)	Yoto Yotov (Bulgaria)	Jon Chol-Nam (North Korea)
2000	Zhan Xugang (China)	Viktor Mitrou (Greece)	Arsen Melikyan (Armenia)
2004	Taner Sagir (Turkey)	Sergey Filimonov (Kazakhstan)	Oleg Perepetchenov (Russia)
2008	Sa Jae-Hyouk (South Korea)	Li Hongli (China)	Gevorg Davtyan (Armenia)

Men's Light Heavyweight

Year	Gold	Silver	Bronze
1920	Ernest Cadine (France)	Fritz Hünenberger (Switzerland)	Erik Pettersson (Sweden)
1924	Charles Rigoulot (France)	Fritz Hünenberger (Switzerland)	Leopold Friedrich (Austria)
1928	El Sayed Nosseir (Egypt)	Louis Hostin (France)	Jan Verheijen (Netherlands)
1932	Louis Hostin (France)	Svend Olsen (Denmark)	Henry Duey (United States)
1936	Louis Hostin (France)	Eugen Deutsch (Germany)	Ibrahim Wasif (Egypt)
1940–1944: Olympics not held			
1948	Stanley Stanczyk (United States)	Harold Sakata (United States)	Gösta Magnusson (Sweden)
1952	Trofim Lomakin (Soviet Union)	Stanley Stanczyk (United States)	Arkady Vorobyov (Soviet Union)
1956	Tommy Kono (United States)	Vasili Stepanov (Soviet Union)	James George (United States)
1960	Ireneusz Palinski (Poland)	James George (United States)	Jan Bochenek (Poland)
1964	Rudolf Plyukfelder (Soviet Union)	Géza Tóth (Hungary)	Gyõzõ Veres (Hungary)
1968	Boris Selitsky (Soviet Union)	Vladimir Belyayev (Soviet Union)	Norbert Ozimek (Poland)
1972	Leif Jenssen (Norway)	Norbert Ozimek (Poland)	György Horvath (Hungary)
1976	Valery Shary (Soviet Union)	Trendafil Stoitchev (Bulgaria)	Peter Baczako (Hungary)
1980	Yurik Vardanian (Soviet Union)	Blagoi Blagoev (Bulgaria)	Dušan Poliačik (Czechoslovakia)
1984	Petre Becheru (Romania)	Robert Kabbas (Australia)	Ryoji Isaoka (Japan)
1988	Israil Arsamakov (Soviet Union)	Istvan Messzi (Hungary)	Lee Kyung-Kun (South Korea)
1992	Pyrros Dimas (Greece)	Krzysztof Siemion (Poland)	Ibragim Samadov (Unified Team)*
1996	Pyrros Dimas (Greece)	Marc Huster (Germany)	Andrzej Cofalik (Poland)
2000	Pyrros Dimas (Greece)	Marc Huster (Germany)	Giorgi Asanidze (Georgia)
2004	Giorgi Asanidze (Georgia)	Andrei Rybakou (Belarus)	Pyrros Dimas (Greece)
2008	Lu Yong (China)	Andrei Rybakou (Belarus)	Tigran Vardan Martirosyan (Armenia)

* Medal revoked due to conduct on podium.

Men's Middle Heavyweight

Year	Gold	Silver	Bronze
1952	Norbert Schemansky (United States)	Grigory Novak (Soviet Union)	Lennox Kilgour (Trinidad and Tobago)
1956	Arkady Vorobyov (Soviet Union)	David Sheppard (United States)	Jean Debuf (France)
1960	Arkady Vorobyov (Soviet Union)	Trofim Lomakin (Soviet Union)	Louis Martin (Great Britain)
1964	Vladimir Golovanov (Soviet Union)	Louis Martin (Great Britain)	Ireneusz Paliński (Poland)
1968	Kaarlo Kangasmiemi (Finland)	Jaan Talts (Soviet Union)	Marek Gołąb (Poland)
1972	Andon Nikolov (Bulgaria)	Atanas Shopov (Bulgaria)	Hans Bettembourg (Sweden)
1976	David Rigert (Soviet Union)	Lee James (United States)	Atanas Shopov (Bulgaria)
1980	Peter Baczako (Hungary)	Rumen Aleksandrov (Bulgaria)	Frank Mantek (East Germany)
1984	Nicu Vlad (Romania)	Dumitru Petre (Romania)	David Merver (Great Britain)
1988	Anatoly Khrapaty (Soviet Union)	Nail Mukhamedyarov (Soviet Union)	Slawomir Zawada (Poland)
1992	Kakhi Kakhiashvili (Unified Team)	Sergey Syrtsoc (Unified Team)	Sergiusz Wolczaniecki
1996	Aelksei Petrov (Russia)	Leonidas Kokas (Greece)	Oliver Caruso (Germany)
2000	Akakios Kakiasvilis (Greece)	Szymon Kolecki (Poland)	Aleksei Petrov (Russia)
2004	Milen Dobrev (Bulgaria)	Khadjimourad Akkayev (Russia)	Eduard Tyukin (Russia)
2008	Ilya Ilin (Kazakhstan)	Szymon Kolecki (Poland)	Khadjimourad Akkayev (Russia)

Men's Heavyweight

Year	Gold	Silver	Bronze
1920	Filippo Bottino (Italy)	Joseph Alzin (Luxembourg)	Louis Bernot (France)
1924	Giuseppe Tonani (Italy)	Franz Aigner (Austria)	Harald Tammer (Estonia)
1928	Josef Strassberger (Germany)	Arnold Luhaäär (Estonia)	Jaroslav Skobla (Czechoslovakia)
1932	Jaroslav Skobla (Czechoslovakia)	Václav Pšenička (Czechoslovakia)	Josef Strassberger (Germany)
1936	Josef Manger (Germany)	Václav Pšenička (Czechoslovakia)	Arnold Luhaäär (Estonia)
1940–1944: Olympics not held			
1948	John Davis (United States)	Norbert Schemansky (United States)	Abraham Charite (Netherlands)
1952	John Davis (United States)	James Bradford (United States)	Humberto Selvetti (Argentina)
1956	Paul Anderson (United States)	Humberto Selvetti (Argentina)	Alberto Pigiani (Italy)
1960	Yury Vlasov (Soviet Union)	James Bradford (United States)	Norbert Schemansky (United States)
1964	Leonid Zhabotinsky (Soviet Union)	Yury Vlasov (Soviet Union)	Norbert Schemansky (United States)
1968	Leonid Zhabotinsky (Soviet Union)	Serge Reding (Belgium)	Joseph Dube (United States)
1972	Jaan Talts (Soviet Union)	Aleksandr Krachev	Stefan Grützner (East Germany)
1976	Yuri Zaitsev (Soviet Union)	Krastiu Semerdzhiev (Bulgaria)	Tadeusz Rutkowski (Poland)
1980	Leonid Taranenko (Soviet Union)	Valentin Hristov (Bulgaria)	György Szalai (Hungary)
1984	Norberto Oberburger (Italy)	Stefan Tasnadi (Romania)	Guy Carlton (United States)
1988	Yury Zakharevitch (Soviet Union)	József Jacsó (Hungary)	Ronny Weller (East Germany)
1992	Ronny Weller (Germany)	Artour Akoev (Unified Team)	Stefan Botev (Bulgaria)
1996	Timur Taymazov (Ukraine)	Sergey Syrtsov (Russia)	Nicu Vlad (Romania)
2000	Hossein Tavakkoli (Iran)	Alan Tsagaev (Bulgaria)	Said Asaad (Qatar)
2004	Dmitry Berestov (Russia)	Ihor Razoronov (Ukraine)	Gleb Pisarevskiy (Russia)
2008	Andrei Aramnau (Belarus)	Dmitry Klokov (Ukraine)	Dmitry Lapikov (Russia)

Men's First Heavyweight

Year	Gold	Silver	Bronze
1980	Ota Zaremba (Czechoslovakia)	Igor Nitikin (Soviet Union)	Alberto Blanco (Cuba)
1984	Rolf Milser (West Germany)	Vasile Groapa (Romania)	Pekka Niemi (Finland)
1988	Pavel Kuznetsov (Soviet Union)	Nicu Vlad (Romania)	Peter Immesberger (West Germany)
1992	Vikkor Tregubov (Unified Team)	Timur Taymazov (Unified Team)	Waldemar Malak (Poland)
1996	Kakhi Kakhiashvili (Greece)	Anatoly Khrapaty (Kazakhstan)	Denys Gotfrid (Ukraine)

Men's Super Heavyweight

Year	Gold	Silver	Bronze
1972	Vasiliy Alekseyev (Soviet Union)	Rudolf Mang (West Germany)	Gerd Bonk (East Germany)
1976	Vasiliy Alekseyev (Soviet Union)	Gerd Bonk (East Germany)	Helmut Losch (East Germany)
1980	Sultan Rakhmanov (Soviet Union)	Jürgen Heuser (East Germany)	Tadeusz Rutkowski (Poland)
1984	Dean Lukin (Australia)	Mario Martinez (United States)	Manfred Nerlinger (West Germany)
1988	Aleksandr Kurlovich (Soviet Union)	Manfred Nerlinger (West Germany)	Martin Zawieja (West Germany)
1992	Aleksandr Kurlovich (Unified Team)	Leonid Taranenko (Unified Team)	Manfred Nerlinger (Germany)
1996	Andrei Chemerkin (Russia)	Ronny Weller (Germany)	Stefan Botev (Australia)
2000	Hossein Rezazadeh (Iran)	Ronny Weller (Germany)	Andrei Chemerkin (Russia)
2004	Hossein Rezazadeh (Iran)	Viktors Ščerbatihs (Latvia)	Velichko Cholakov (Bulgaria)
2008	Matthias Steiner (Germany)	Evgeny Chigishev (Russia)	Viktors Ščerbatihs (Latvia)

Women's Flyweight

Year	Gold	Silver	Bronze
2000	Tara Nott (United States)	Raema Lisa Rumbewas (Indonesia)	Sri Indriyani (Indonesia)
2004	Nurcan Taylan (Turkey)	Li Zhuo (China)	Aree Wiratthaworn (Thailand)
2008	Chen Xiexia (China)	Sibel Özkan (Turkey)	Chen Wei Ling (Taiwan)

Women's Featherweight

Year	Gold	Silver	Bronze
2000	Yang Xia (China)	Li Fengying (Taiwan)	Winami Binti Slamet (Indonesia)
2004	Udomporn Polsak (Thailand)	Raema Lisa Rumbewas (Indonesia)	Mabel Mosquera (Colombia)
2008	Prapawadee Jaroenrattanatarakoon (Thailand)	Yoon Jin-Hee (South Korea)	Nastassia Novikova (Belarus)

Women's Lightweight

Year	Gold	Silver	Bronze
2000	Soraya Jiménez (Mexico)	Ri Song-Hui (North Korea)	Khassaraporn Suta (Thailand)
2004	Chen Yangqing (China)	Ri Song-Hui (North Korea)	Wandee Kameaim (Thailand)
2008	Chen Yangqing (China)	Marina Shainova (Russia)	O Jong-Ae (North Korea)

Women's Middleweight

Year	Gold	Silver	Bronze
2000	Chen Xiaomin (China)	Valentina Popova (Russia)	Ioanna Khatziioannou (Greece)
2004	Nataliya Shakun (Ukraine)	Hanna Batsiushka (Belarus)	Tatsiana Stukalava (Belarus)
2008	Pak Hyon-Suk (North Korea)	Irina Nekrassova (Kazakhstan)	Lu Ying-chi (Taiwan)

Women's Light Heavyweight

Year	Gold	Silver	Bronze
2000	Lin Weining (China)	Erzsébet Márkus (Hungary)	Karnam Malleswari (India)
2004	Liu Chunhong (China)	Eszter Krutzler (Hungary)	Zarema Kasaeva (Russia)
2008	Liu Chunhong (China)	Oxana Slivenko (Russia)	Natalya Davydova (Ukraine)

Women's Heavyweight

Year	Gold	Silver	Bronze
2000	María Isabel Urrutia (Colombia)	Ruth Ogbeifo (Nigeria)	Kuo Yi-hang (Taiwan)
2004	Pawina Thongsuk (Thailand)	Nataliya Zabolotnaya (Russia)	Valentina Popova (Russia)
2008	Cao Lei (China)	Alla Vazhenina (Kazakhstan)	Nadezhda Yevstyukhina (Russia)

Women's Super Heavyweight

Year	Gold	Silver	Bronze
2000	Ding Meiyuan (China)	Agata Wróbel (Poland)	Cheryl Haworth (United States)
2004	Tang Gonghong (China)	Jang Mi-Ran (South Korea)	Agata Wróbel (Poland)
2008	Jang Mi-Ran (South Korea)	Olha Korobka (Ukraine)	Mariya Grabovetskaya (Kazakhstan)

Freestyle Wrestling

Men's Bantamweight

Year	Gold	Silver	Bronze
1904	Isidor Niflot (United States)	August Weaver (United States)	Louis Strebler (United States)
1908	George Mehnert (United States)	William Press (Great Britain)	Aubert Cote (Canada)
1912: Event not held			
1916: Olympics not held			
1920: Event not held			
1924	Kustaa Pihlajamäki (Finland)	Kaarlo Mäkinen (Finland)	Bryan Hines (United States)
1928	Kaarlo Mäkinen (Finland)	Edmond Spapen (Belgium)	James Trifunov (Canada)
1932	Robert Pearce (United States)	Ödön Zombori (Hungary)	Aatos Jaskari (Finland)
1936	Ödön Zombori (Hungary)	Ross Flood (United States)	Johannes Herbert (Germany)
1940–1944: Olympics not held			
1948	Nasuh Akar (Turkey)	Gerald Leeman (United States)	Charles Kouyos (France)
1952	Shohachi Ishii (Japan)	Rashid Mamedbekov (Soviet Union)	Khasaba Dadasaheb Jadhav (India)
1956	Mustafa Dağıstanlı (Turkey)	Mehdi Yaghoubi (Iran)	Mikhail Shahkov (Soviet Union)
1960	Terrence McCann (United States)	Nezhdet Zalev (Bulgaria)	Tadeusz Trojanowski (Poland)
1964	Yojiro Uetake (Japan)	Hüseyin Akbaş (Turkey)	Aydin Ibragimov (Soviet Union)
1968	Yojiro Uetake (Japan)	Donald Behm (United States)	Aboutaleb Talebi (Iran)
1972	Hideaki Yanagida (Japan)	Richard Sanders (United States)	László Klinga (Hungary)
1976	Vladimir Yumin (Soviet Union)	Hans-Dieter Brüchert (East Germany)	Masao Arai (Japan)
1980	Sergei Beloglazov (Soviet Union)	Li Ho-Pyong (North Korea)	Dugarsürengiin Oyuunbold (Mongolia)
1984	Hideaki Tomiyama (Japan)	Barry Davis (United States)	Kim Eui-Kon (South Korea)
1988	Sergei Beloglazov (Soviet Union)	Askari Mohammadian (Iran)	Noh Kyung-Sun (South Korea)
1992	Alejandro Puerto (Cuba)	Sergei Smal (Unified Team)	Kim Yon-Sik (North Korea)
1996	Kendall Cross (United States)	Guivi Sissaouri (Canada)	Ri Yong-Sam (North Korea)

Year	Gold	Silver	Bronze
2000	Alireza Dabir (Iran)	Yevgen Buslovych (Ukraine)	Terry Brands (United States)
2004	Mavlet Batirov (Russia)	Stephen Abas (United States)	Chikara Tanabe (Japan)
2008	Henry Cejudo (United States)	Tomohiro Matsunaga (Japan)	Besik Kudukhov (Russia) Radoslav Velikov (Bulgaria)

Men's Featherweight

Year	Gold	Silver	Bronze
1904	Benjamin Bradshaw (United States)	Theodore McLear (United States)	Charles Clapper (United States)
1908	George Dole (United States)	James Slim (Great Britain)	William McKie (Great Britain)
1912: Event not held			
1916: Olympics not held			
1920	Charles E. Ackerly (United States)	Samuel Gerson (United States)	Philip Bernard (Great Britain)
1924	Robin Reed (United States)	Chester Newton (United States)	Katsutoshi Naito (Japan)
1928	Allie Morrison (United States)	Kustaa Pihlajamäki (Finland)	Hans Minder (Switzerland)
1932	Hermanni Pihlajamäki (Finland)	Edgar Nemir (United States)	Einar Karlsson (Sweden)
1936	Kustaa Pihlajamäki (Finland)	Francis Millard (United States)	Gösta Frändfors (Sweden)
1940–1944: Olympics not held			
1948	Gazanfer Bilge (Turkey)	Ivar Sjölin (Sweden)	Adolf Muller (Switzerland)
1952	Bayram Şit (Turkey)	Nasser Givehchi (Iran)	Josiah Henson (United States)
1956	Shozo Sasahara (Japan)	Joseph Mewis (Belgium)	Erkki Penttilä (Finland)
1960	Mustafa Dağıstanlı (Turkey)	Stancho Kolev (Bulgaria)	Vladimir Rubashvili (Soviet Union)
1964	Osamu Watanabe (Japan)	Stancho Kolev (Bulgaria)	Nodar Khokhashvili (Soviet Union)
1968	Masaaki Kaneko (Japan)	Enyu Todorov (Bulgaria)	Shamseddin Seyed-Abbasi (Iran)
1972	Zagalav Abdulbekov (Soviet Union)	Vehbi Akdağ (Turkey)	Ivan Krastev (Bulgaria)
1976	Yang Jung-Mo (South Korea)	Zevegiin Oidov (Mongolia)	Gene Davis (United States)
1980	Magomedgasan Abushev (Soviet Union)	Miho Dukov (Bulgaria)	Georgios Hatziioannidis (Greece)
1984	Randall Lewis (United States)	Kosei Akaishi (Japan)	Lee Jung-Keun (South Korea)
1988	John Smith (United States)	Stepan Sarkisyan (Soviet Union)	Simeon Shterev (Bulgaria)
1992	John Smith (United States)	Askari Mohammadian (Iran)	Lázaro Reinoso (Cuba)
1996	Tom Brands (United States)	Jan Jae-Sung (South Korea)	Elbrus Tedeyev (Ukraine)
2000	Mourad Oumakhanov (Russia)	Serafim Barzakov (Bulgaria)	Jang Jae-Sung (South Korea)
2004	Yandro Quintana (Cuba)	Masoud Mostafa-Jokar (Iran)	Kenji Inoue (Japan)
2008	Mavlet Batirov (Russia)	Vasyl Fedoryshyn (Ukraine)	Morad Mohammadi (Iran) Kenichi Yumoto (Japan)

Men's Lightweight

Year	Gold	Silver	Bronze
1904	Otto Roehm (United States)	Rudolph Tesing (United States)	Albert Zirkel (United States)
1908	George de Relwyskow (Great Britain)	William Wood (Great Britain)	Albert Gingell (Great Britain)
1912: Event not held			
1916: Olympics not held			
1920	Kalle Anttila (Finland)	Gottfrid Svensson (Sweden)	Peter Wright (Great Britain)
1924	Russell Vis (United States)	Volmar Wikström (Finland)	Arvo Haavisto (Finland)
1928	Osvald Käpp (Estonia)	Charles Pacôme (France)	Eino Augusti Leino (Finland)
1932	Charles Pacôme (France)	Károly Kárpáti (Hungary)	Gustaf Klarén (Sweden)
1936	Károly Kárpáti (Hungary)	Wolfgang Ehrl (Germany)	Hermanni Pihlajamäki (Finland)

Year	Gold	Silver	Bronze
1940–1944: Olympics not held			
1948	Celal Atik (Turkey)	Gösta Frändfors (Sweden)	Hermann Baumann (Switzerland)
1952	Olle Anderberg (Sweden)	Jay Thomas Evans (United States)	Jahanbakht Towfigh (Iran)
1956	Imam-Ali Habibi (Iran)	Shigeru Kasahara (Japan)	Alimbeg Bestayev (Soviet Union)
1960	Shelby Wilson (United States)	Vladimir Rubashvili (Soviet Union)	Enyu Valchev (Bulgaria)
1964	Enyu Valchev (Bulgaria)	Klaus Rost (United Team of Germany)	Iwao Horiuchi (Japan)
1968	Abdollah Movahed (Iran)	Enyu Valchev (Bulgaria)	Danzandarjaagiin Sereeter (Mongolia)
1972	Dan Gable (United States)	Kikuo Wada (Japan)	Ruslan Ashuraliyev (Soviet Union)
1976	Pavel Pinigin (Soviet Union)	Lloyd Keaser (United States)	Yasaburo Sugawara (Japan)
1980	Saipulla Absaidov (Soviet Union)	Ivan Yankov (Bulgaria)	Šaban Sejdi (Yugoslavia)
1984	You In-Tak (South Korea)	Andrew Rein (United States)	Jukka Rauhala (Finland)
1988	Arsen Fadzayev (Soviet Union)	Park Jang-Soon (South Korea)	Nate Carr (United States)
1992	Arsen Fadzayev (Unified Team)	Valentin Getzov (Bulgaria)	Kosei Akaishi (Japan)
1996	Vadim Bogiyev (Russia)	Townsend Saunders (United States)	Zaza Zazirov (Ukraine)
2000	Daniel Igali (Canada)	Arsen Gitinov (Russia)	Lincoln McIlravy (United States)
2004	Elbrus Tedeyev (Ukraine)	Jamill Kelly (United States)	Makhach Murtazaliev (Russia)
2008	Ramazan Şahin (Turkey)	Andriy Stadnik (Ukraine)	Sushil Kumar (India) / Otar Tushishvili (Georgia)

Men's Welterweight

Year	Gold	Silver	Bronze
1904	Charles Ericksen (United States)	William Bechmann (United States)	Jerry Winholtz (United States)
1908–1912: Event not held			
1916: Olympics not held			
1920: Event not held			
1924	Hermann Gehri (Switzerland)	Eino Leino (Finland)	Otto Müller (Switzerland)
1928	Arvo Haavisto (Finland)	Lloyd Appleton (United States)	Maurice Letchford (Canada)
1932	Jack van Bebber (United States)	Daniel MacDonald (Canada)	Eino Leino (Finland)
1936	Frank Lewis (United States)	Thure Andersson (Sweden)	Joseph Schleimer (Canada)
1940–1944: Olympics not held			
1948	Yaşar Doğu (Turkey)	Richard Garrard (Australia)	Leland Merrill (United States)
1952	William Smith (United States)	Per Berlin (Sweden)	Abdollah Mojtabavi (Iran)
1956	Mitsuo Ikeda (Japan)	İbrahim Zengin (Turkey)	Vakhtang Balavadze (Soviet Union)
1960	Douglas Blubaugh (United States)	İsmail Ogan (Turkey)	Muhammed Bashir (Pakistan)
1964	İsmail Ogan (Turkey)	Guliko Sagaradze (Soviet Union)	Mohammad Ali Sanatkaran (Iran)
1968	Mahmut Atalay (Turkey)	Daniel Robin (France)	Tömöriin Artag (Mongolia)
1972	Wayne Wells (United States)	Jan Karlsson (Sweden)	Adolf Seger (West Germany)
1976	Jiichiro Date (Japan)	Mansour Barzegar (Iran)	Stanley Dziedzic (United States)
1980	Valentin Raychev (Bulgaria)	Jamtsyn Davaajav (Mongolia)	Dan Karabin (Czechoslovakia)
1984	David Schultz (United States)	Martin Knosp (West Germany)	Šaban Sejdi (Yugoslavia)
1988	Kenny Monday (United States)	Adlan Varayev (Soviet Union)	Rahmat Sukra (Bulgaria)
1992	Park Jang-Soon (South Korea)	Kenny Monday (United States)	Amir Reza Khadem (Iran)
1996	Buvaisar Saitiev (Russia)	Park Jang-Soon (South Korea)	Takuya Ota (Japan)
2000	Brandon Slay (United States)	Moon Eui-Jae (South Korea)	Adem Bereket (Turkey)
2004	Buvaisar Saitiev (Russia)	Gennadiy Laliyev (Kazakhstan)	Iván Fundora (Cuba)
2008	Buvaisar Saitiev (Russia)	Soslan Tigiev (Uzbekistan)	Murad Gaidarov (Bulgaria) / Kiril Terziev (Bulgaria)

Men's Middleweight

Year	Gold	Silver	Bronze
1908	Stanley Bacon (Great Britain)	George de Relwyskow (Great Britain)	Frederick Beck (Great Britain)
1912: Event not held			
1916: Olympics not held			
1920	Eino Leino (Finland)	Väinö Penttala (Finland)	Charles Johnson (United States)
1924	Fritz Hagmann (Switzerland)	Pierre Ollivier (Belgium)	Vilho Pekkala (Finland)
1928	Ernst Kyburz (Switzerland)	Donald Stockton (Canada)	Samuel Rabin (Great Britain)
1932	Ivar Johansson (Sweden)	Kyösti Luukko (Finland)	József Tunyogi (Hungary)
1936	Emile Poilvé (France)	Richard Voliva (United States)	Ahmet Kireçci (Turkey)
1940–1944: Olympics not held			
1948	Glen Brand (United States)	Adil Candemir (Turkey)	Erik Lindén (Sweden)
1952	David Tsimakuridze (Soviet Union)	Gholamreza Takhti (Iran)	György Gurics (Hungary)
1956	Nikola Stanchev (Bulgaria)	Daniel Hodge (United States)	Georgi Skhirtladze (Soviet Union)
1960	Hasan Güngör (Turkey)	Georgi Skhirtladze (Soviet Union)	Hans Antonsson (Sweden)
1964	Prodan Gardzhev (Bulgaria)	Hasan Güngör (Turkey)	Daniel Brand (United States)
1968	Boris Gurevich (Soviet Union)	Jigjidiin Mönkhbat (Mongolia)	Prodan Gardzhev (Bulgaria)
1972	Levan Tediashvili (Soviet Union)	John Peterson (United States)	Vasile Iorga (Romania)
1976	John Peterson (United States)	Viktor Novozhilov (Soviet Union)	Adolf Seger (West Germany)
1980	Ismail Abilov (Bulgaria)	Magomedkhan Aratsilov (Soviet Union)	István Kovács (Hungary)
1984	Mark Schultz (United States)	Hideyuki Nagashima (Japan)	Christopher Rinke (Canada)
1988	Han Myung-Woo (South Korea)	Necmi Gençalp (Turkey)	Jozef Lohyňa (Czechoslovakia)
1992	Kevin Jackson (United States)	Elmadi Jabrailov (Unified Team)	Rasoul Khadem (Iran)
1996	Khadzhimurad Magomedov (Russia)	Yang Hyun-Moo (South Korea)	Amir Reza Khadem (Iran)
2000	Adam Saitiev (Russia)	Yoel Romero (Cuba)	Mogamed Ibragimov (Macedonia)
2004	Cael Sanderson (United States)	Moon Eui-Jae (South Korea)	Sazhid Sazhidov (Russia)
2008	Revaz Mindorashvili (Georgia)	Yusup Abdulsalomov (Tajikistan)	Taras Danko (Ukraine) Georgy Ketoyev (Russia)

Men's Heavyweight

Year	Gold	Silver	Bronze
1904	Bernhoff Hansen (United States)	Frank Kugler (United States)	Fred Warmbold (United States)
1908	Con O'Kelly (Great Britain)	Jacob Gundersen (Norway)	Edward Barrett (Great Britain)
1912: Event not held			
1916: Olympics not held			
1920	Robert Ruth (Switzerland)	Nat Pendleton (United States)	Fred Mayer (United States) Ernst Nilsson (Sweden)
1924	Harry Steel (United States)	Henri Wernli (Switzerland)	Andrew McDonald (Great Britain)
1928	Johan Richthoff (Sweden)	Aukusti Sihvola (Finland)	Edmond Dame (Austria)
1932	Johan Richthoff (Sweden)	John Riley (United States)	Nikolaus Hirschl (Austria)
1936	Kristjan Palusalu (Estonia)	Josef Klapuch (Czechoslovakia)	Hjalmar Nyström (Finland)
1940–1944: Olympics not held			
1948	Gyula Bóbis (Hungary)	Bertil Antonsson (Sweden)	Joseph Armstrong (Australia)
1952	Arsen Mekokishvili (Soviet Union)	Bertil Antonsson (Sweden)	Kenneth Richmond (Great Britain)
1956	Hamit Kaplan (Turkey)	Hussein Mehmedov (Bulgaria)	Taisto Kangasniemi (Finland)
1960	Wilfried Dietrich (United Team of Germany)	Hamit Kaplan (Turkey)	Savkuds Dzarasov (Soviet Union)
1964	Aleksandr Ivanitsky (Soviet Union)	Lyutvi Akhmedov (Bulgaria)	Hamit Kaplan (Turkey)
1968	Alexander Medved (Soviet Union)	Osman Duraliev (Bulgaria)	Wilfried Dietrich (West Germany)

Year	Gold	Silver	Bronze
1972	Ivan Yarygin (Soviet Union)	Khorloogiin Bayanmönkh (Mongolia)	József Csatári (Hungary)
1976	Ivan Yarygin (Soviet Union)	Russell Hellickson (United States)	Dimo Kostov (Bulgaria)
1980	Ilya Mate (Soviet Union)	Slavcho Chervenkov (Bulgaria)	Július Strnisko (Czechoslovakia)
1984	Lou Banach (United States)	Joseph Atiyeh (Syria)	Vasile Puşcaşu (Romania)
1988	Vasile Puşcaşu (Romania)	Leri Khabelov (Soviet Union)	William Scherr (United States)
1992	Leri Khabelov (Unified Team)	Heiko Balz (Germany)	Ali Kayalı (Turkey)
1996	Kurt Angle (United States)	Abbas Jadidi (Iran)	Arawat Sabejew (Germany)
2000	Sagid Murtazaliev (Russia)	Islam Bairamukov (Kazakhstan)	Eldar Kurtanidze (Georgia)
2004	Khadjimourat Gatsalov (Russia)	Magomed Ibragimov (Uzbekistan)	Alireza Heidari (Iran)
2008	Shirvani Muradov (Russia)	Taimuraz Tigiyev (Kazakhstan)	Georgi Gogshelidze (Georgia) Khetag Gazyumov (Azerbaijan)

Men's Super Heavyweight

Year	Gold	Silver	Bronze
1972	Alexander Medved (Soviet Union)	Osman Duraliev (Bulgaria)	Chris Taylor (United States)
1976	Soslan Andiyev (Soviet Union)	József Balla (Hungary)	Ladislau Şimon (Romania)
1980	Soslan Andiyev (Soviet Union)	József Balla (Hungary)	Adam Sandurski (Poland)
1984	Bruce Baumgartner (United States)	Robert Molle (Canada)	Ayhan Taşkın (Turkey)
1988	David Gobezhishvili (Soviet Union)	Bruce Baumgartner (United States)	Andreas Schröder (East Germany)
1992	Bruce Baumgartner (United States)	Jeffrey Thue (Canada)	David Gobezhishvili (Unified Team)
1996	Mahmut Demir (Turkey)	Aleksei Medvedev (Belarus)	Bruce Baumgartner (United States)
2000	David Musul'bes (Russia)	Artur Taymazov (Uzbekistan)	Alexis Rodríguez (Cuba)
2004	Artur Taymazov (Uzbekistan)	Alireza Rezaei (Iran)	Aydin Polatçi (Turkey)
2008	Artur Taymazov (Uzbekistan)	Bakhtiyar Akhmedov (Russia)	David Musul'bes (Slovakia) Marid Mutalimov (Kazakhstan)

Women's Flyweight

Year	Gold	Silver	Bronze
2004	Irina Merleni (Ukraine)	Chiharu Icho (Japan)	Patricia Miranda (United States)
2008	Carol Huynh (Canada)	Chiharu Icho (Japan)	Mariya Stadnik (Azerbaijan) Irina Merleni (Ukraine)

Women's Lightweight

Year	Gold	Silver	Bronze
2004	Saori Yoshida (Japan)	Tonya Verbeek (Canada)	Anna Gornis (France)
2008	Saori Yoshida (Japan)	Xu Li (China)	Tonya Verbeek (Canada) Jackeline Renteria (Colombia)

Women's Middleweight

Year	Gold	Silver	Bronze
2004	Kaori Icho (Japan)	Sara McMann (United States)	Lise Legrand (France)
2008	Kaori Icho (Japan)	Alena Kartashova (Russia)	Randi Miller (United States) Yelena Shalygina (Kazakhstan)

Women's Heavyweight

Year	Gold	Silver	Bronze
2004	Wang Xu (China)	Guzel Manyurova (Russia)	Kyoko Hamaguchi (Japan)
2008	Wang Xu (China)	Stanka Zlateva (Bulgaria)	Kyoko Hamaguchi (Japan) Agnieszka Wieszczek (Poland)

Men's Light Flyweight

Year	Gold	Silver	Bronze
1904	Robert Curry (United States)	John Hein (United States)	Gustav Thiefenthaler (United States)
1908–1912: Event not held			
1916: Olympics not held			
1920–1936: Event not held			
1940–1944: Olympics not held			
1948–1968: Event not held			
1972	Roman Dmitriyev (Soviet Union)	Ognyan Nikolov (Bulgaria)	Ebrahim Javadi (Iran)
1976	Khasan Isaev (Bulgaria)	Roman Dmitriyev (Soviet Union)	Akria Kudo (Japan)
1980	Claudio Pollio (Italy)	Jang Se-Hong (North Korea)	Sergei Kornilayev (Soviet Union)
1984	Bobby Weaver (United States)	Takashi Irie (Japan)	Son Gab-Do (South Korea)
1988	Takashi Kobayashi (Japan)	Ivan Tzonov (Bulgaria)	Sergei Karamchakov (Soviet Union)
1992	Kim Il (North Korea)	Kim Jong-Shin (South Korea)	Vougar Oroudjov (Unified Team)
1996	Kim Il (North Korea)	Armen Mkertchian (Armenia)	Alexis Vila (Cuba)

Men's Flyweight

Year	Gold	Silver	Bronze
1904	George Mehnert (United States)	Gustave Bauer (United States)	William Nelson (United States)
1908–1912: Event not held			
1916: Olympics not held			
1920–1936: Event not held			
1940–1944: Olympics not held			
1948	Lennart Viitala (Finland)	Halit Balamir (Turkey)	Thure Johansson (Sweden)
1952	Hasan Gemici (Turkey)	Yushu Kitano (Japan)	Mahmoud Mollaghasemi (Iran)
1956	Mirian Tsalkalamanidze (Soviet Union)	Mohammad Ali Khojastehpour (Iran)	Hüseyin Akbaş (Turkey)
1960	Ahmet Bilek (Turkey)	Masayuki Matsubara (Japan)	Ebrahim Seifpour (Iran)
1964	Yoshikatsu Yoshida (Japan)	Chang Chang-Sun (South Korea)	Ali Akbar Heidari (Iran)
1968	Shigeo Nakata (Japan)	Richard Sanders (United States)	Chimedbazaryn Damdinsharav (Mongolia)
1972	Kiyomi Kato (Japan)	Arsen Alakhverdiyev (Soviet Union)	Kim Gwong-Hyong (North Korea)
1976	Yuji Takada (Japan)	Alexander Ivanov (Soviet Union)	Jeon Hae-Sup (South Korea)
1980	Anatoli Beloglazov (Soviet Union)	Władysław Stecyk (Poland)	Nermedin Selimov (Bulgaria)
1984	Šaban Trstena (Yugoslavia)	Kim Jong-Kyu (South Korea)	Yuji Takada (Japan)
1988	Mitsuru Sato (Japan)	Šaban Trstena (Yugoslavia)	Vladimir Toguzov (Soviet Union)
1992	Li Hak-Son (North Korea)	Zeke Jones (United States)	Valentin Jordanov (Bulgaria)
1996	Valentin Jordanov (Bulgaria)	Namig Abdullayev (Azerbaijan)	Maulen Mamyrov (Kazakhstan)
2000	Namig Abdullayev (Azerbaijan)	Sammie Henson (United States)	Amiran Kardanov (Greece)

Men's Light Heavyweight

Year	Gold	Silver	Bronze
1920	Anders Larsson (Sweden)	Charles Courant (Switzerland)	Walter Maurer (United States)
1924	John Spellman (United States)	Rudolf Svensson (Sweden)	Charles Courant (Switzerland)
1928	Thure Sjöstedt (Sweden)	Arnold Bögli (Switzerland)	Henri Lefèbre (France)
1932	Peter Mehringer (United States)	Thure Sjöstedt (Sweden)	Eddie Scarf (Australia)
1936	Knut Fridell (Sweden)	August Neo (Estonia)	Erich Siebert (Germany)
1940–1944: Olympics not held			
1948	Henry Wittenberg (United States)	Fritz Stöckli (Switzerland)	Bengt Fahlqvist (Sweden)

Year	Gold	Silver	Bronze
1952	Viking Palm (Sweden)	Henry Wittenberg (United States)	Adil Atan (Turkey)
1956	Gholamreza Takhti (Iran)	Boris Kulayev (Soviet Union)	Peter Blair (United States)
1960	İsmet Atlı (Turkey)	Gholamreza Takhti (Iran)	Anatoly Albul (Soviet Union)
1964	Alexander Medved (Soviet Union)	Ahmet Ayık (Turkey)	Said Musatafov (Bulgaria)
1968	Ahmet Ayık (Turkey)	Shota Lomidze (Soviet Union)	József Csatári (Hungary)
1972	Ben Peterson (United States)	Gennadi Strakhov (Soviet Union)	Károly Bajkó (Hungary)
1976	Levan Tediashvili (Soviet Union)	Ben Peterson (United States)	Stelică Morcov (Romania)
1980	Sanasar Oganisyan (Soviet Union)	Uwe Neupert (East Germany)	Aleksander Cichoń (Poland)
1984	Ed Banach (United States)	Akira Ota (Japan)	Noel Loban (Great Britain)
1988	Makharbek Khadartsev (Soviet Union)	Akira Ota (Japan)	Kim Tae-Woo (South Korea)
1992	Makharbek Khadartsev (Unified Team)	Kenan Simsek (Turkey)	Christopher Campbell (United States)
1996	Rasoul Khadem (Iran)	Makharbek Khadartsev (Russia)	Eldar Kurtanidze (Georgia)

Greco-Roman Wrestling

Men's Bantamweight

Year	Gold	Silver	Bronze
1924	Eduard Pütsep (Estonia)	Anselm Ahlfors (Finland)	Väinö Ikonen (Finland)
1928	Kurt Leucht (Germany)	Jindřich Maudr (Czechoslovakia)	Giovanni Gozzi (Italy)
1932	Jakob Brendel (Germany)	Marcello Nizzola (Italy)	Louis François (France)
1936	Márton Lőrincz (Hungary)	Egon Svensson (Sweden)	Jakob Brendel (Germany)
1940–1944: Olympics not held			
1948	Kurt Pettersén (Sweden)	Ali Mahmoud Hassan (Egypt)	Halil Kaya (Turkey)
1952	Imre Hódos (Hungary)	Zakaria Chibab (Lebanon)	Artem Teryan (Soviet Union)
1956	Konstantin Vyrupayev (Soviet Union)	Edvin Vesterby (Sweden)	Francisc Horvat (Romania)
1960	Oleg Karavayev (Soviet Union)	Ion Cernea (Romania)	Dinko Petrov (Bulgaria)
1964	Masamitsu Ichiguchi (Japan)	Vladlen Trostyansky (Soviet Union)	Ion Cernea (Romania)
1968	János Varga (Hungary)	Ion Baciu (Romania)	Ivan Kochergin (Soviet Union)
1972	Rustam Kazakov (Soviet Union)	Hans-Jürgen Veil (West Germany)	Risto Björlin (Finland)
1976	Pertti Ukkola (Finland)	Ivan Frgić (Yugoslavia)	Farhat Mustafin (Soviet Union)
1980	Shamil Serikov (Soviet Union)	Józef Lipień (Poland)	Benni Ljungbeck (Sweden)
1984	Pasquale Passarelli (West Germany)	Masaki Eto (Japan)	Haralambos Holidis (Greece)
1988	András Sike (Hungary)	Stoyan Balov (Bulgaria)	Haralambos Holidis (Greece)
1992	An Han-Bong (South Korea)	Rifat Yildiz (Germany)	Sheng Zetian (China)
1996	Yuriy Melnichenko (Kazakhstan)	Dennis Hall (United States)	Sheng Zetian (China)
2000	Armen Nazarian (Bulgaria)	Kim In-Sub (South Korea)	Sheng Zetian (China)
2004	István Majoros (Hungary)	Geidar Mamedaliyev (Russia)	Artiom Kiouregkian (Greece)
2008	Nazyr Mankiev (Russia)	Rovshan Bayramov (Azerbaijan)	Park Eun-Chul (South Korea) Roman Amoyan (Armenia)

Men's Featherweight

Year	Gold	Silver	Bronze
1912	Kaarlo Koskelo (Finland)	Georg Gerstäcker (Germany)	Otto Lasanen (Finland)
1916: Olympics not held			
1920	Oskari Friman (Finland)	Heikki Kähkönen (Finland)	Fritiof Svensson (Sweden)

Year	Gold	Silver	Bronze
1924	Kalle Anttila (Finland)	Aleksanteri Toivola (Finland)	Eric Malmberg (Sweden)
1928	Voldemar Väli (Estonia)	Eric Malmberg (Sweden)	Gerolamo Quaglia (Italy)
1932	Giovanni Gozzi (Italy)	Wolfgang Ehrl (Germany)	Lauri Koskela (Finland)
1936	Yaşar Erkan (Turkey)	Aarne Reini (Finland)	Einar Karlsson (Sweden)
1940–1944: Olympics not held			
1948	Mehmet Oktav (Turkey)	Olle Anderberg (Sweden)	Ferenc Tóth (Hungary)
1952	Yakov Punkin (Soviet Union)	Imre Polyák (Hungary)	Abdel Al-Rashid (Egypt)
1956	Rauno Mäkinen (Finland)	Imre Polyák (Hungary)	Roman Dzeneladze (Soviet Union)
1960	Müzahir Sille (Turkey)	Imre Polyák (Hungary)	Konstantin Vyrupayev (Soviet Union)
1964	Imre Polyák (Hungary)	Roman Rurua (Soviet Union)	Branislav Martinović (Yugoslavia)
1968	Roman Rurua (Soviet Union)	Hideo Fujimoto (Japan)	Simion Popescu (Romania)
1972	Georgi Markov (Bulgaria)	Heinz-Helmut Wehling (East Germany)	Kazimierz Lipień (Poland)
1976	Kazimierz Lipień (Poland)	Nelson Davydyan (Soviet Union)	László Réczi (Hungary)
1980	Stelios Mygiakis (Greece)	István Tóth (Hungary)	Boris Kramorenko (Soviet Union)
1984	Kim Weon-Kee (South Korea)	Kent-Olle Johansson (Sweden)	Hugo Dietsche (Switzerland)
1988	Kamandar Madzhidov (Soviet Union)	Zhivko Vangelov (Bulgaria)	An Dae-Hyun (South Korea)
1992	Mehmet Akif Pirim (Turkey)	Sergei Martynov (Unified Team)	Juan Marén (Cuba)
1996	Włodzimierz Jan Zawadzki (Poland)	Juan Marén (Cuba)	Mehmet Akif Pirim (Turkey)
2000	Varteres Samourgachev (Russia)	Juan Marén (Cuba)	Akaki Chachua (Georgia)
2004	Jung Ji-Hyun (South Korea)	Roberto Monzón (Cuba)	Armen Nazarian (Bulgaria)
2008	Islambek Albiev (Russia)	Vitaliy Rahimov (Azerbaijan)	Nurbakyt Tengizbayev (Kazakhstan) Ruslan Tumenbaev (Kyrgyzstan)

Men's Lightweight

Year	Gold	Silver	Bronze
1908	Enrico Porro (Italy)	Nikolay Orlov (Russia)	Arvid Lindén (Finland)
1912	Emil Väre (Finland)	Gustaf Malmström (Sweden)	Edvin Mattiasson (Sweden)
1916: Olympics not held			
1920	Emil Väre (Finland)	Taavi Tamminen (Finland)	Frithjof Andersen (Norway)
1924	Oskari Friman (Finland)	Lajos Keresztes (Hungary)	Källe Westerlund (Finland)
1928	Lajos Keresztes (Hungary)	Eduard Sperling (Germany)	Edvard Westerlund (Finland)
1932	Eric Malmberg (Sweden)	Abraham Kurland (Denmark)	Eduard Sperling (Germany)
1936	Lauri Koskela (Finland)	Josef Herda (Czechoslovakia)	Voldemar Väli (Estonia)
1940–1944: Olympics not held			
1948	Gustav Freij (Sweden)	Aage Eriksen (Norway)	Károly Ferencz (Hungary)
1952	Shazam Safin (Soviet Union)	Gustav Freij (Sweden)	Mikuláš Atanasov (Czechoslovakia)
1956	Kyösti Lehtonen (Finland)	Rıza Doğan (Turkey)	Gyula Tóth (Hungary)
1960	Avtandil Koridze (Soviet Union)	Branislav Martinović (Yugoslavia)	Gustav Freij (Sweden)
1964	Kazim Ayvaz (Turkey)	Valeriu Bularca (Romania)	David Gvantseladze (Soviet Union)
1968	Muneji Munemura (Japan)	Stevan Horvat (Yugoslavia)	Petros Galaktopoulos (Greece)
1972	Shamil Khisamutdinov (Soviet Union)	Stoyan Apostolov (Bulgaria)	Gian-Matteo Ranzi (Italy)
1976	Suren Nalbandyan (Soviet Union)	Ştefan Rusu (Romania)	Heinz-Helmut Wehling (East Germany)
1980	Ştefan Rusu (Romania)	Andrzej Supron (Poland)	Lars-Erik Skiöld (Sweden)
1984	Vlado Lisjak (Yugoslavia)	Tapio Sipilä (Finland)	James Martinez (United States)
1988	Levon Julfalakyan (Soviet Union)	Kim Sung-Moon (South Korea)	Tapio Sipilä ((Finland)

Year	Gold	Silver	Bronze
1992	Attila Repka (Hungary)	Islam Dugushiev (Unified Team)	Rodney Smith (United States)
1996	Ryszard Wolny (Poland)	Ghani Yalouz (France)	Aleksandr Tretyakov (Russia)
2000	Filiberto Azcuy (Cuba)	Katsuhiko Nagata (Japan)	Aleksei Glushkov (Russia)
2004	Farid Mansurov (Azerbaijan)	Şeref Eroğlu (Turkey)	Mkhitar Manukyan (Kazakhstan)
2008	Steeve Guenot (France)	Kanatbek Begaliev (Kyrgyzstan)	Armen Vardanyan (Ukraine)
			Mikhail Siamionau (Belarus)

Men's Welterweight

Year	Gold	Silver	Bronze
1932	Ivar Johansson (Sweden)	Väinö Kajander (Finland)	Ercole Gallegati (Italy)
1936	Rudolf Svedberg (Sweden)	Fritz Schäfer (Germany)	Eino Virtanen (Finland)
1940–1944: Olympics not held			
1948	Gösta Andersson (Sweden)	Miklós Szilvási (Hungary)	Henrik Hansen (Denmark)
1952	Miklós Szilvási (Hungary)	Gösta Andersson (Sweden)	Khalil Taha (Lebanon)
1956	Mithat Bayrak (Turkey)	Vladimir Maneyev (Soviet Union)	Per Berlin (Sweden)
1960	Mithat Bayrak (Turkey)	Günter Maritschnigg (United Team of Germany)	René Schiermeyer (France)
1964	Anatoly Kolesov (Soviet Union)	Kiril Petkov (Bulgaria)	Bertil Nystrom (Sweden)
1968	Rudolf Vesper (East Germany)	Daniel Robin (France)	Károly Bajkó (Hungary)
1972	Vítězslav Mácha (Czechoslovakia)	Petros Galaktopoulos (Greece)	Jan Karlsson (Sweden)
1976	Anatoly Bykov (Soviet Union)	Vítězslav Mácha (Czechoslovakia)	Karl-Heinz Helbing (West Germany)
1980	Ferenc Kocsis (Hungary)	Anatoly Bykov (Soviet Union)	Mikko Huhtala (Finland)
1984	Jouko Salomäki (Finland)	Roger Tallroth (Sweden)	Ştefan Rusu (Romania)
1988	Kim Young-Nam (South Korea)	Daulet Turlykhanov (Soviet Union)	Józef Tracz (Poland)
1992	Mnatsakan Iskandaryan (Unified Team)	Józef Tracz (Poland)	Torbjörn Kornbakk (Sweden)
1996	Filiberto Azcuy (Cuba)	Marko Asell (Finland)	Józef Tracz (Poland)
2000	Murat Kardanov (Russia)	Matt Lindland (United States)	Marko Yli-Hannuksela (Finland)
2004	Aleksandr Dokturishvili (Uzbekistan)	Marko Yli-Hannuksela (Finland)	Varteres Samourgachev (Russia)
2008	Manuchar Kvirkelia (Georgia)	Chang Yongxiang (China)	Yavor Yanakiev (Bulgaria)
			Christophe Guenot (France)

Men's Middleweight

Year	Gold	Silver	Bronze
1908	Frithiof Mårtensson (Sweden)	Mauritz Andersson (Sweden)	Anders Andersen (Denmark)
1912	Claes Johansson (Sweden)	Martin Klein (Russia)	Alfred Asikainen (Finland)
1916: Olympics not held			
1920	Carl Westergren (Sweden)	Arthur Lindfors (Finland)	Masa Perttilä (Finland)
1924	Edvard Westerlund (Finland)	Arthur Lindfors (Finland)	Roman Steinberg (Estonia)
1928	Väinö Kokkinen (Finland)	László Papp (Hungary)	Albert Kusnets (Estonia)
1932	Väinö Kokkinen (Finland)	Jean Földeák (Germany)	Axel Cadier (Sweden)
1936	Ivar Johansson (Sweden)	Ludwig Schweickert (Germany)	József Palotás (Hungary)
1940–1944: Olympics not held			
1948	Axel Grönberg (Sweden)	Muhlis Tayfur (Turkey)	Ercole Gallegati (Italy)
1952	Axel Grönberg (Sweden)	Kalervo Rauhala (Finland)	Nikolay Belov (Soviet Union)
1956	Givi Kartoziya (Soviet Union)	Dimitar Dobrev (Bulgaria)	Rune Jansson (Sweden)
1960	Dimitar Dobrev (Bulgaria)	Lothar Metz (United Team of Germany)	Ion Taranu (Romania)
1964	Branislav Simić (Yugoslavia)	Jiří Kormaník (Czechoslovakia)	Lothar Metz (United Team of Germany)

Year	Gold	Silver	Bronze
1968	Lothar Metz (East Germany)	Valentin Oleynik (Soviet Union)	Branislav Simić (Yugoslavia)
1972	Csaba Hegedűs (Hungary)	Anatoly Nazarenko (Soviet Union)	Milan Nenadić (Yugoslavia)
1976	Momir Petković (Yugoslavia)	Vladimir Cheboksarov (Soviet Union)	Ivan Kolev (Bulgaria)
1980	Gennadi Korban (Soviet Union)	Jan Dołgowicz (Poland)	Pavel Pavlov (Bulgaria)
1984	Ion Draica (Romania)	Dimitrios Thanopoulos (Greece)	Sören Claeson (Sweden)
1988	Mikhail Mamiashvili (Soviet Union)	Tibor Komáromi (Hungary)	Kim Sang-Kyu (South Korea)
1992	Péter Farkas (Hungary)	Piotr Stępień (Poland)	Daulet Turlykhanov (Unified Team)
1996	Hamza Yerlikaya (Turkey)	Thomas Zander (Germany)	Valeriy Tsilent (Belarus)
2000	Hamza Yerlikaya (Turkey)	Sándor Bárdosi (Hungary)	Mukhran Vakhtangadze (Georgia)
2004	Alexei Mishin (Russia)	Ara Abrahamian (Sweden)	Viachaslau Makaranka (Belarus)
2008	Andrea Minguzzi (Italy)	Zoltán Fodor (Hungary)	Nazmi Avluca (Turkey)

Men's Heavyweight

Year	Gold	Silver	Bronze
1912	Yrjö Saarela (Finland)	Johan Olin (Finland)	Søren Marinus Jensen (Denmark)
1916: Olympics not held			
1920	Adolf Lindfors (Finland)	Poul Hansen (Denmark)	Martti Nieminen (Finland)
1924	Henri Deglane (France)	Edil Rosenqvist (Finland)	Rajmund Badó (Hungary)
1928	Rudolf Svensson (Sweden)	Hjalmar Nyström (Finland)	Georg Gehring (Germany)
1932	Carl Westergren (Sweden)	Josef Urban (Czechoslovakia)	Nikolaus Hirschl (Austria)
1936	Kristjan Palusalu (Estonia)	John Nyman (Sweden)	Kurt Hornfischer (Germany)
1940–1944: Olympics not held			
1948	Ahmet Kireçci (Turkey)	Tor Nilsson (Sweden)	Guido Fantoni (Italy)
1952	Johannes Kotkas (Soviet Union)	Josef Růžička (Czechoslovakia)	Tauno Kovanen (Finland)
1956	Anatoly Parfyonov (Soviet Union)	Wilfried Dietrich (United Team of Germany)	Adelmo Bulgarelli (Italy)
1960	Ivan Bogdan (Soviet Union)	Wilfried Dietrich (United Team of Germany)	Bohumil Kubát (Czechoslovakia)
1964	István Kozma (Hungary)	Anatoly Roshchin (Soviet Union)	Wilfried Dietrich (United Team of Germany)
1968	István Kozma (Hungary)	Anatoly Roshchin (Soviet Union)	Petr Kment (Czechoslovakia)
1972	Nicolae Martinescu (Romania)	Nikolai Yakovenko (Soviet Union)	Ferenc Kiss (Hungary)
1976	Nikolai Balboshin (Soviet Union)	Kamen Goranov (Bulgaria)	Andrzej Skrzydlewski (Poland)
1980	Georgi Raikov (Bulgaria)	Roman Bierła (Poland)	Vasile Andrei (Romania)
1984	Vasile Andrei (Romania)	Greg Gibson (United States)	Jožef Tertei (Yugoslavia)
1988	Andrzej Wroński (Poland)	Gerhard Himmel (West Germany)	Dennis Kosolowski (United States)
1992	Héctor Milián (Cuba)	Dennis Kosolowski (United States)	Sergei Demyashkevich (Unified Team)
1996	Andrzej Wroński (Poland)	Sergey Lishtvan (Belarus)	Mikael Ljungberg (Sweden)
2000	Mikael Ljungberg (Sweden)	Davyd Saldadze (Ukraine)	Garrett Lowney (United States)
2004	Karam Gaber (Egypt)	Ramaz Nozadze (Georgia)	Mehmet Özal (Turkey)
2008	Aslanbek Khushtov (Russia)	Mirko Englich (Germany)	Adam Wheeler (United States)
			Asset Mambetov (Kazakhstan)

Men's Super Heavyweight

Year	Gold	Silver	Bronze
1908	Richárd Weisz (Hungary)	Aleksandr Petrov (Russia)	Søren Marinus Jensen (Denmark)
1912: Event not held			
1916: Olympics not held			

Year	Gold	Silver	Bronze
1920–1936: Event not held			
1940–1944: Olympics not held			
1948–1968: Event not held			
1972	Anatoly Roshchin (Soviet Union)	Alexander Tomov (Bulgaria)	Victor Dolipschi (Romania)
1976	Alexander Kolchinsy (Soviet Union)	Alexander Tomov (Bulgaria)	Roman Codreanu (Romania)
1980	Alexander Kolchinsy (Soviet Union)	Alexander Tomov (Bulgaria)	Hassan Bechara (Lebanon)
1984	Jeff Blatnick (United States)	Refik Memišević (Yugoslavia)	Victor Dolipschi (Romania)
1988	Alexander Karelin (Soviet Union)	Rangel Gerovski (Bulgaria)	Tomas Johansson (Sweden)
1992	Alexander Karelin (Unified Team)	Tomas Johansson (Sweden)	Ioan Grigoraş (Romania)
1996	Alexander Karelin (Russia)	Matt Ghaffari (United States)	Sergei Mureiko (Moldova)
2000	Rulon Gardner (United States)	Alexander Karelin (Russia)	Dmitry Debelka (Belarus)
2004	Khasan Baroyev (Russia)	Georgiy Tsurtsumia (Kazakhstan)	Rulon Gardner (United States)
2008	Mijaín López (Cuba)	Khasan Baroyev (Russia)	Mindaugas Mizgaitis (Lithuania) Yuri Patrikeyev (Armenia)

Men's Light Flyweight

Year	Gold	Silver	Bronze
1972	Gheorghe Berceanu (Romania)	Rahim Ali-Abadi (Iran)	Stefan Angelov (Bulgaria)
1976	Alexei Shumakov (Soviet Union)	Gheorghe Berceanu (Romania)	Stefan Angelov (Bulgaria)
1980	Zhaksylyk Ushkempirov (Soviet Union)	Constantin Alexandru (Romania)	Ferenc Seres (Hungary)
1984	Vincenzo Maenza (Italy)	Markus Scherer (West Germany)	Ikuzo Saito (Japan)
1988	Vincenzo Maenza (Italy)	Andrzej Głąb (Poland)	Bratan Tzenov (Bulgaria)
1992	Oleg Kucherenko (Unified Team)	Vincenzo Maenza (Italy)	Wilber Sánchez (Cuba)
1996	Sim Kwon-Ho (South Korea)	Aleksandr Pavlov (Belarus)	Zafar Guliyev (Russia)

Men's Flyweight

Year	Gold	Silver	Bronze
1948	Pietro Lombardi (Italy)	Kenan Olcay (Turkey)	Reino Kangasmäki (Finland)
1952	Boris Gurevich (Soviet Union)	Ignazio Fabra (Italy)	Leo Honkala (Finland)
1956	Nikolai Solovyov (Soviet Union)	Ignazio Fabra (Italy)	Dursun Ali Eğribaş (Turkey)
1960	Dumitru Pîrvulescu (Romania)	Osman Sayed (Egypt)	Mohammad Paziraei (Iran)
1964	Tsutomu Hanahara (Japan)	Angel Kerezov (Bulgaria)	Dimitru Pîrvulescu (Romania)
1968	Petar Kirov (Bulgaria)	Vladimir Bakulin (Soviet Union)	Miroslav Zeman (Czechoslovakia)
1972	Petar Kirov (Bulgaria)	Koichiro Hirayama (Japan)	Giuseppe Bognanni (Italy)
1976	Vitali Konstantinov (Soviet Union)	Nicu Gingă (Romania)	Koichiro Hirayama (Japan)
1980	Vakhtang Blagidze (Soviet Union)	Lajos Rácz (Hungary)	Mladen Mladenov (Bulgaria)
1984	Atsuji Miyahara (Japan)	Daniel Aceves (Mexico)	Bang Dae-Du (South Korea)
1988	Jon Rønningen (Norway)	Atsuji Miyahara (Japan)	Lee Jae-Suk (South Korea)
1992	Jon Rønningen (Norway)	Alfred Ter-Mkrtychyan (Unified Team)	Min Kyung-Gab (South Korea)
1996	Armen Nazarian (Armenia)	Brandon Paulson (United States)	Andriy Kalashnikov (Ukraine)
2000	Sim Kwon-Ho (South Korea)	Lázaro Rivas (Cuba)	Kang Yong-Gyun (North Korea)

Men's Light Heavyweight

Year	Gold	Silver	Bronze
1908	Verner Weckman (Finland)	Yrjö Saarela (Finland)	Carl Jensen (Denmark)
1912	Not awarded	Anders Ahlgren (Sweden) Ivar Böhling (Finland)	Béla Varga (Hungary)

Year	Gold	Silver	Bronze
1916: Olympics not held			
1920	Claes Johansson (Sweden)	Edil Rosenqvist (Finland)	Johannes Eriksen (Denmark)
1924	Carl Westergren (Sweden)	Rudolf Svensson (Sweden)	Onni Pellinen (Finland)
1928	Ibrahim Moustafa (Egypt)	Adolf Rieger (Germany)	Onni Pellinen (Finland)
1932	Rudolf Svensson (Sweden)	Onni Pellinen (Finland)	Mario Gruppioni (Italy)
1936	Axel Cadier (Sweden)	Edwins Bietags (Latvia)	August Neo (Estonia)
1940–1944: Olympics not held			
1948	Karl-Erik Nilsson (Sweden)	Kelpo Gröndahl (Finland)	Ibrahim Orabi (Egypt)
1952	Kelpo Gröndahl (Finland)	Shalva Chikhladze (Soviet Union)	Karl-Erik Nilsson (Sweden)
1956	Valentin Nikolayev (Soviet Union)	Petko Sirakov (Bulgaria)	Karl-Erik Nilsson (Sweden)
1960	Tevfik Kış (Turkey)	Krali Bimbalov (Bulgaria)	Givi Kartoziya (Soviet Union)
1964	Boyan Radev (Bulgaria)	Per Svensson (Sweden)	Heinz Kiehl (United Team of Germany)
1968	Boyan Radev (Bulgaria)	Nikolai Yakovenko (Soviet Union)	Nicolae Martinescu (Romania)
1972	Valeri Rezantsev (Soviet Union)	Josip Čorak (Yugoslavia)	Czesław Kwieciński (Poland)
1976	Valeri Rezantsev (Soviet Union)	Stoyan Ivanov (Bulgaria)	Czesław Kwieciński (Poland)
1980	Norbert Növényi (Hungary)	Igor Kanygin (Soviet Union)	Petre Dicu (Romania)
1984	Steve Fraser (United States)	Ilie Matei (Romania)	Frank Andersson (Sweden)
1988	Atanas Komchev (Bulgaria)	Harri Koskela (Finland)	Vladimir Popov (Soviet Union)
1992	Maik Bullmann (Germany)	Hakkı Başar (Turkey)	Georgi Koguashvili (Unified Team)
1996	Vyacheslav Oleynyk (Ukraine)	Jacek Fafiński (Poland)	Maik Bullmann (Germany)

Men's Open

Year	Gold	Silver	Bronze
1896	Carl Schuhmann (Germany)	Georgios Tsitas (Greece)	Stephanos Christopoulos (Greece)

Olympic Medalists—Winter Olympics

Alpine Skiing

Men's Alpine Combined

Year	Gold	Silver	Bronze
1936	Franz Pfnür (Germany)	Gustav Lantschner (Germany)	Emile Allais (France)
1940–1944: Olympics not held			
1948	Henri Oreiller (France)	Karl Molitor (Switzerland)	James Couttet (France)
1952–1984: Event not held			
1988	Hubert Strolz (Austria)	Bernhard Gstrein (Austria)	Paul Accola (Switzerland)
1992	Josef Polig (Italy)	Gianfranco Martin	Steve Locher (Switzerland)
1994	Lasse Kjus (Norway)	Kjetil Andre Aamodt (Norway)	Harald Christian Strand Nilsen
1998	Mario Reiter (Austria)	Lasse Kjus (Norway)	Christian Mayer (Austria)
2002	Kjetil Andre Aamodt (Norway)	Bode Miller (United States)	Benjamin Raich (Austria)
2006	Kjetil Andre Aamodt (Norway)	Hermann Meier (Austria)	Andreas Schiferrer (Austria)
2010	Ted Ligety (United States)	Ivica Kotelić (Croatia)	Rainer Shönfelder (Austria)

Women's Alpine Combined

Year	Gold	Silver	Bronze
1936	Christl Cranz (Germany)	Käthe Grasegger (Germany)	Laila Schou Nilsen (Norway)
1940–1944: Olympics not held			
1948	Trude Beiser (Austria)	Gretchen Fraser (United States)	Erika Mahringer (Austria)
1952–1984: Event not held			
1988	Anita Wachter (Austria)	Brigitte Oertli (Switzerland)	Maria Walliser (Switzerland)
1992	Petra Kronberger (Austria)	Anita Wachter (Austria)	Florence Masnada (France)
1994	Pernilla Wiberg (Sweden)	Vreni Schneider (Switzerland)	Alenka Dovžan (Slovenia)
1998	Katja Seizinger (Germany)	Martina Ertl (Germany)	Hilde Gerg (Germany)
2002	Janic Kostelić (Croatia)	Renate Götschl (Austria)	Martina Ertl (Germany)
2006	Janic Kostelić (Croatia)	Marlies Schild (Austria)	Anja Pärson (Sweden)
2010	Maria Riesch (Germany)	Julia Mancuso (United States)	Anja Pärson (Sweden)

Women's Downhill

Year	Gold	Silver	Bronze
1948	Hedy Schlunegger (Switzerland)	Trude Beiser (Austria)	Resi Hammerer (Austria)
1952	Trude Jochum-Beiser (Austria)	Annemarie Buchner (Germany)	Giuliana Minuzzo (Italy)
1956	Madeleine Berthod (Switzerland)	Frieda Dänzer (Switzerland)	Lucille Wheeler (Canada)
1960	Heidi Biebl (United Team of Germany)	Penelope Pitou (United States)	Traudl Hecher (Austria)
1964	Christl Haas (Austria)	Edith Zimmermann (Austria)	Traudl Hecher (Austria)
1968	Olga Pall (Austria)	Isabelle Mir (France)	Christl Haas (Austria)

Year	Gold	Silver	Bronze
1972	Marie-Theres Nadig (Switzerland)	Annemarie Pröll (Austria)	Susan Corrock (United States)
1976	Rosi Mittermeier (West Germany)	Brigitte Totschnig (Austria)	Cindy Nelson (United States)
1980	Annemarie Moser-Pröll (Austria)	Hanni Wenzel (Liechtenstein)	Marie-Theres Nadig (Switzerland)
1984	Michela Figini (Switzerland)	Maria Walliser (Switzerland)	Olga Charvátová (Czechoslovakia)
1988	Marina Kiehl (West Germany)	Brigitte Oertli (Switzerland)	Karen Percy (Canada)
1992	Kerrin Lee-Gartner (Canada)	Hilary Lindh (United States)	Veronika Wallinger (Austria)
1994	Katja Seizinger (Germany)	Picabo Street (United States)	Isolde Kostner (Italy)
1998	Katja Seizinger (Germany)	Pernilla Wiberg (Sweden)	Florence Masnada (France)
2002	Carole Montillet (France)	Isolde Kostner (Italy)	Renate Götschl (Austria)
2006	Michaela Dorfmeister (Austria)	Martina Schild (Switzerland)	Anja Pärson (Sweden)
2010	Lindsey Vonn	Julia Mancuso (United States)	Elisabeth Görgl (Austria)

Women's Slalom

Year	Gold	Silver	Bronze
1948	Gretchen Fraser (United States)	Antoinette Meyer (Switzerland)	Erika Mahringer (Austria)
1952	Andrea Mead-Lawrence (United States)	Ossi Reichert (Germany)	Annemarie Buchner (Germany)
1956	Renée Colliard (Switzerland)	Regina Schöpf (Austria)	Yevgeniya Sidorova (Soviet Union)
1960	Anne Heggtveit (Canada)	Betsy Snite (United States)	Barbara Henneberger (United Team of Germany)
1964	Christine Goitschel (France)	Marielle Goitschel (France)	Jean Saubert (United States)
1968	Marielle Goitschel (France)	Nancy Greene (Canada)	Annie Famose (France)
1972	Barbara Cochran (United States)	Danièle Debernard (France)	Florence Steurer (France)
1976	Rosi Mittermeier (West Germany)	Claudia Giordani (Italy)	Hanni Wenzel (Liechtenstein)
1980	Hanni Wenzel (Liechtenstein)	Christa Kinshofer (West Germany)	Erika Haas (Switzerland)
1984	Paoletta Magoni (Italy)	Perrine Pelen (France)	Ursula Konzett (Liechtenstein)
1988	Vreni Schneider (Switzerland)	Mateja Svet (Yugoslavia)	Christa Kinshofer (West Germany)
1992	Petra Kronberger (Austria)	Annelise Coberger (New Zealand)	Blanca Fernández Ochoa (Spain)
1994	Vreni Schneider (Switzerland)	Elfi Eder (Austria)	Katja Koren (Slovenia)
1998	Hilde Gerg (Germany)	Deborah Compagnoni (Italy)	Zali Steggall (Australia)
2002	Janica Kostelić (Croatia)	Laure Péquegnot (France)	Anja Pärson (Sweden)
2006	Anja Pärson (Sweden)	Nicole Hosp (Austria)	Marlies Schild (Austria)
2010	Maria Riesch (Germany)	Marlies Schild (Austria)	Šárka Záhrobská (Czech Republic)

Women's Giant Slalom

Year	Gold	Silver	Bronze
1952	Andrea Mead-Lawrence (United States)	Dagmar Rom (Austria)	Annemarie Buchner (Germany)
1956	Ossi Reichert (United Team of Germany)	Putzi Frandl (Austria)	Thea Hochleitner (Austria)
1960	Yvonne Rüegg (Switzerland)	Penelope Pitou (United States)	Giuliana Minuzzo (Italy)
1964	Marielle Goitschel (France)	Christine Goitschel (France) Jean Saubert (United States)	Not awarded
1968	Nancy Greene (Canada)	Annie Famose (France)	Fernande Bochatay (Switzerland)
1972	Marie-Theres Nadig (Switzerland)	Annemarie Pröll (Austria)	Wiltrud Drexel (Austria)
1976	Kathy Kreiner (Canada)	Rosi Mittermeier (West Germany)	Danièle Debernard (France)
1980	Hanni Wenzel (Liechtenstein)	Irene Epple (West Germany)	Perrine Pelen (France)
1984	Debbie Armstrong (United States)	Christin Cooper (United States)	Perrine Pelen (France)
1988	Vreni Schneider (Switzerland)	Christa Kinshofer (West Germany)	Maria Walliser (Switzerland)
1992	Pernilla Wiberg (Sweden)	Diann Roffe (United States) Anita Wachter (Austria)	Not awarded
1994	Deborah Compagnoni (Italy)	Martina Ertl (Germany)	Vreni Schneider (Switzerland)

Year	Gold	Silver	Bronze
1998	Deborah Compagnoni (Italy)	Alexandra Meissnitzer (Austria)	Katja Seizinger (Germany)
2002	Janica Kostelić (Croatia)	Anja Pärson (Sweden)	Sonja Nef (Switzerland)
2006	Julia Mancuso (United States)	Tanja Poutiainen (Finland)	Anna Ottosson (Sweden)
2010	Viktoria Rebensburg (Germany)	Tina Maze (Slovenia)	Elisabeth Goergl (Austria)

Women's Super G

Year	Gold	Silver	Bronze
1988	Sigrid Wolf (Austria)	Michela Figini (Switzerland)	Karen Percy (Canada)
1992	Deborah Compagnoni (Italy)	Carole Merle (France)	Katja Seizinger (Germany)
1994	Diann Roffe (United States)	Svetlana Gladysheva (Russia)	Isolde Kostner (Italy)
1998	Picabo Street (United States)	Michaela Dorfmeister (Austria)	Alexandra Meissnitzer (Austria)
2002	Daniela Ceccarelli (Italy)	Janica Kostelić (Croatia)	Karen Putzer (Italy)
2006	Michaela Dorfmesiter (Austria)	Janica Kostelić (Croatia)	Alexandra Meissnitzer (Austria)
2010	Andrea Fischbacher (Austria)	Tina Maze (Slovenia)	Lindsey Vonn (United States)

Men's Downhill

Year	Gold	Silver	Bronze
1948	Henri Oreiller (France)	Franz Gabl (Austria)	Karl Molitor (Switzerland) Rolf Olinger (Switzerland)
1952	Zeno Colò (Italy)	Othmar Schneider (Austria)	Christian Pravda (Austria)
1956	Toni Sailer (Austria)	Raymond Fellay (Switzerland)	Anderl Molterer (Austria)
1960	Jean Vuarnet (France)	Hans-Peter Lanig (United Team of Germany)	Guy Périllat (France)
1964	Egon Zimmermann (Austria)	Léo Lacroix (France)	Wolfgang Bartels (United Team of Germany)
1972	Bernhard Russi (Switzerland)	Roland Collombin (Switzerland)	Heinrich Messner (Italy)
1976	Franz Klammer (Austria)	Bernhard Russi (Switzerland)	Herbert Plank (Italy)
1980	Leonhard Stock (Austria)	Peter Wirnsberger (Austria)	Steve Podborski (Canada)
1984	Bill Johnson (United States)	Peter Müller (Switzerland)	Anton Steiner (Austria)
1988	Pirmin Zurbriggen (Switzerland)	Peter Müller (Switzerland)	Franck Piccard (France)
1992	Patrick Ortlieb (Austria)	Franck Piccard (France)	Günther Mader (Austria)
1994	Tommy Moe (United States)	Kjetil André Aamodt (Norway)	Ed Podivinsky (Canada)
1998	Jean-Luc Crétier (France)	Lasse Kjus (Norway)	Hannes Trinkl (Austria)
2002	Fritz Strobl (Austria)	Lasse Kjus (Norway)	Stephan Eberharter (Austria)
2006	Antoine Dénériaz (France)	Michael Walchhofer (Austria)	Bruno Kernen (Switzerland)
2010	Didier Défago (Switzerland)	Aksel Lund Svindal (Norway)	Bode Miller (United States)

Men's Giant Slalom

Year	Gold	Silver	Bronze
1952	Stein Eriksen (Norway)	Christian Pravda (Austria)	Toni Spiess (Austria)
1956	Toni Sailer (Austria)	Anderl Molterer (Austria)	Walter Schuster (Austria)
1960	Roger Staub (Switzerland)	Josef Stiegler (Austria)	Enrst Hinterseet (Austria)
1964	François Bonlieu (France)	Karl Schranz (Austria)	Josef Stiegler (Austria)
1968	Jean-Claude Killy (France)	Willy Favre (Switzerland)	Heini Messner (Austria)
1972	Gustav Thöni (Italy)	Edmund Bruggman (Switzerland)	Werner Mattle (Switzerland)
1976	Heini Hemmi (Switzerland)	Ernst Good (Switzerland)	Ingemar Stenmark (Sweden)
1980	Ingemar Stenmark (Sweden)	Andreas Wenzel (Liechtenstein)	Hans Enn (Austria)
1984	Max Julen (Switzerland)	Jure Franko (Yugoslavia)	Andreas Wenzel (Liechtenstein)
1988	Alberto Tomba (Italy)	Hubert Strolz (Austria)	Pirmin Zurbriggen (Switzerland)
1992	Alberto Tomba (Italy)	Marc Girardelli (Luxembourg)	Kjetl André Aamodt (Norway)
1994	Markus Wasmeier (Germany)	Urs Kälin (Switzerland)	Christian Mayer (Austria)

Year	Gold	Silver	Bronze
1998	Hermann Maier (Austria)	Stephan Eberharter (Austria)	Michael von Grünigen (Switzerland)
2002	Stephan Eberharter (Austria)	Bode Miller (United States)	Lasse Kjus (Norway)
2006	Benjamin Raich (Austria)	Joël Chenal (France)	Hermann Maier (Austria)
2010	Carlo Junka (Switzerland)	Kjetil Jansrud (Norway)	Aksel Lund Svindal (Norway)

Men's Super G

Year	Gold	Silver	Bronze
1988	Franck Piccard (France)	Helmut Mayer (Austria)	Lars-Börje Eriksson (Sweden)
1992	Kjetil André Aamodt (Norway)	Marc Girardelli (Luxembourg)	Jan Einar Thorsen (Norway)
1994	Markus Wasmeier (Germany)	Tommy Moe (United States)	Kjetil André Aamodt (Norway)
1998	Hermann Maier (Austria)	Didier Cuche (Switzerland) Hans Knauß (Austria)	Not awarded
2002	Kjetil André Aamodt (Norway)	Stephan Eberharter (Austria)	Andreas Schifferer (Austria)
2006	Kjetil André Aamodt (Norway)	Hermann Maier (Austria)	Ambrosi Hoffmann (Switzerland)
2010	Aksel Lund Svindal (Norway)	Bode Miller (United States)	Andrew Weibrecht (United States)

Men's Slalom

Year	Gold	Silver	Bronze
1948	Edy Reinalter (Switzerland)	James Couttet (France)	Henri Oreiller (France)
1952	Othmar Schneider (Austria)	Stein Eriksen (Norway)	Guttorm Berge (Norway)
1956	Toni Sailer (Austria)	Chiharu Igaya (Japan)	Stig Sollander (Sweden)
1960	Ernst Hinterseer (Austria)	Matthias Leitner (Austria)	Charles Bozon (France)
1964	Josef Stiegler (Austria)	Billy Kidd (United States)	James Heuga (United States)
1968	Jean-Claude Killy (France)	Herbert Huber (Austria)	Alfred Matt (Austria)
1972	Francisco Fernández Ochoa (Spain)	Gustav Thöni (Italy)	Roland Thöni (Italy)
1976	Piero Gros (Italy)	Gustav Thöni (Italy)	Willi Frommelt (Liechtenstein)
1980	Ingemar Stenmark (Sweden)	Phil Mahre (United States)	Jacques Lüthy (Switzerland)
1984	Phil Mahre (United States)	Steve Mahre (United States)	Didier Bouvet (France)
1988	Alberto Tomba (Italy)	Frank Wörndl (West Germany)	Paul Frommelt (Liechtenstein)
1992	Finn Christian Jagge (Norway)	Alberto Tomba (Italy)	Michael Tritscher (Austria)
1994	Thomas Stangassinger (Austria)	Alberto Tomba (Italy)	Jure Košir (Slovenia)
1998	Hans Petter Buraas (Norway)	Ole Kristian Furuseth (Norway)	Thomas Sykora (Austria)
2002	Jean-Pierre Vidal (France)	Sébastien Amiez (France)	Benjamin Raich (Austria)
2006	Benjamin Raich (Austria)	Reinfried Herbst (Austria)	Rainer Schönfelder (Austria)
2010	Giuliano Razzoli (Italy)	Ivica Kostelić (Croatia)	André Myhrer (Sweden)

Bobsleigh

Men's Four-Man

Year	Gold	Silver	Bronze
1924	Eduard Scherrer, Alfred Neveu, Alfred Schläppi, Heinrich Schläppi (Switzerland)	Ralph Broome, Thomas Arnold, Alexander Richardson, Rodney Soher (Great Britain)	Charles Mulder, René Mortiuax, Paul Van den Broek, Victor Verscheuren, Henri Willems (Belgium)
1928: Event not held			
1932	William Fiske, Eddie Eagan, Clifford Grey, Jay O'Brien (United States)	Henry Homburger, Percy Bryant, Francis Stevens, Edmund Horton (United States)	Hans Mehlhorn, Max Ludwig, Hanns Kilian, Sebastian Huber (Germany)

Year	Gold	Silver	Bronze
1936	Pierre Musy, Arnold Gartmann, Charles Bouvier, Joseph Beerli (Switzerland)	Reto Capadrutt, Hans Aichele, Fritz Feierabend, Hans Bütikofer (Switzerland)	Frederick McEvoy, James Cardno, Guy Dugdale, Charles Green (Great Britain)
1940–1944: Olympics not held			
1948	Francis Tyler, Patrick Martin, Edward Rimkus, William D'Amico (United States)	Max Houben, Freddy Mansveld, Louis-Georges Niels, Jacques Mouvet (Belgium)	James Bickford, Thomas Hicks, Donald Dupree, William Dupree (United States)
1952	Andreas Ostler, Friedrich Kuhn, Lorenz Nieberl, Franz Kemser (Germany)	Stanley Benham, Patrick Martin, Howard Crossett, James Atkinson (United States)	Fritz Feierabend, Albert Madörin, André Filippini, Stephan Waser (Switzerland)
1956	Franz Kapus, Gottfried Diener, Robert Alt, Heinrich Angst (Switzerland)	Eugenio Monti, Ulrico Girardi, Renzo Alverà (Italy)	Arthur Tyler, William Dodge, Charles Butler, James Lamy (United States)
1960: Event not held			
1964	Vic Emery, Peter Kirby, Douglas Anakin, John Emery (Canada)	Erwin Thaler, Adolf Koxeder, Josef Nairz, Reinhold Durnthaler (Austria)	Eugenio Monti, Sergio Siorpaes, Benito Rigoni, Gildo Siorpaes (Italy)
1968	Eugenio Monti, Luciano de Paolis, Roverto Zandonella, Mario Armano (Italy)	Erwin Thaler, Reinhold Durnthaler, Herbert Gruber, Josef Eder (Austria)	Jean Wicki, Hans Candrian, Willi Hofmann, Walter Graf (Switzerland)
1972	Jean Wicki, Edy Hubacher, Hans Leutnegger, Werner Carmichael (Switzerland)	Nevio de Zordo, Gianni Bonichon, Adriano Frassinelli, Corrado dal Fabbro (Italy)	Wolfgang Zimmerer, Peter Utzschneider, Stefan Gaisreiter, Walter Steinbauer (West Germany)
1976	Meinhard Nehmer, Jochen Babcock, Bernhard Germeshausen, Bernhard Lehmann (East Germany)	Erich Schärer, Ulrich Bächli, Rudolf Marti, Joseph Benz (Switzerland)	Wolfgang Zimmerer, Peter Utzschneider, Bodo Bittner, Manfred Schumann (West Germany)
1980	Meinhard Nehmer, Bogdan Musiol, Bernhard Germeshausen, Hans-Jürgen Gerhardt (East Germany)	Erich Schärer, Ulrich Bächli, Rudolf Marti, Joseph Benz (Switzerland)	Horst Schönau, Roland Wetzig, Detlef Richter, Andreas Kirchner (East Germany)
1984	Wolfgang Hoppe, Roland Wetzig, Dietmar Schauerhammer, Andreas Kirchner (East Germany)	Bernhard Lehmann, Bogdan Musiol, Ingo Voge, Eberhard Weise (East Germany)	Silvio Giobellina, Heinz Stettler, Urs Salzmann, Rico Freiermuth (Switzerland)
1988	Ekkehard Fasser, Kurt Maier, Marcel Fässler, Werner Stocker (Switzerland)	Wolfgang Hoppe, Dietmar Schauerhammer, Bogdan Musiol, Ingo Voge (East Germany)	Janis Kipurs, Guntis Osis, Juris Tone, Vladimir Koslov (Soviet Union)
1992	Ingo Appelt, Harald Winkler, Gerhard Haidacher, Thomas Schroll (Austria)	Wolfgang Hoppe, Bogdan Musiol, Axel Kühn, René Hannemann (Germany)	Gustav Weder, Donat Acklin, Lorenz Schindelholz, Curdin Morell (Switzerland)
1994	Harald Czudaj, Karsten Brannasch, Olaf Hampel, Alexander Szelig (Germany)	Gustav Weder, Donat Acklin, Kurt Maier, Domenico Semeraro (Switzerland)	Wolfgang Hoppe, Ulf Hielscher, René Hannemann, Carsten Embach (Germany)
1998	Christoph Langen, Markus Zimmermann, Marco Jakobs, Olaf Hampel (Germany)	Marcel Rohner, Markus Nüssli, Markus Wasser, Beat Seitz (Switzerland)	Bruno Mingeon, Emmanuel Hostache, Éric Le Chanony, Max Robert (France) Sean Olsson, Dean Ward, Courtney Rumbolt, Paul Attwood (Great Britain)
2002	André Lange, Enrico Kühn, Kevin Kuske, Carsten Embach (Germany)	Todd Hays, Randy Jones, Bill Schuffenhauer, Garrett Hines (United States)	Brian Shimer, Mike Kohn, Doug Sharp, Dan Steele (United States)
2006	Kevin Kuske, René Hoppe, Martin Putze, André Lange (Germany)	Alexey Voyevoda, Alexei Seliverstov, Filipp Yegorov, Alexandr Zubkov (Russia)	Martin Annen, Cedric Grand, Thomas Lamparter, Beat Hefti (Switzerland)
2010	Steve Holcomb, Steve Mesler, Curtis Tomasevicz, Justin Olsen (United States)	André Lange, Kevin Kuske, Alexander Rödiger, Martin Putze (Germany)	Lyndon Rush, David Biasset, Lascelles Brown, Chris le Bihan (Canada)

Men's Five-Man

Year	Gold	Silver	Bronze
1928	William Fiske, Nion Rocker, Geoffrey Mason, Clifford Grey, Richard Parke (United States)	Jennison Heaton, David Granger, Lyman Hine, Thomas Doe, Jay O'Brien (United States)	Hanns Kilian, Hans Hess, Sebastian Huber, Valentin Krempl, Hanns Nägle (Germany)

Men's Two-Man

Year	Gold	Silver	Bronze
1932	Hubert Stevens, Curtis Stevens (United States)	Reto Capadrutt, Oscar Geier (Switzerland)	John Heaton, Robert Minton (United States)
1936	Ivan Brown, Alan Washbond (United States)	Fritz Feierabend, Joseph Beerli (Switzerland)	Gilbert Colgate, Richard Lawrence (United States)
1940–1944: Olympics not held			
1948	Felix Endrich, Friedrich Waller (Germany)	Fritz Feierabend, Paul Eberhard (Switzerland)	Frederick Fortune, Schuyler Carron (United States)
1952	Andreas Ostler, Lorenz Nieberl (Germany)	Stanley Benham, Patrick Martin (United States)	Fritz Feierabend, Stephan Waser (Switzerland)
1956	Lamberto Dalla Costa, Giacomo Conti (Italy)	Eugenio Monti, Renzo Alverâ (Italy)	Max Angst, Harry Warburton (Switzerland)
1960: Event not held			
1964	Anthony Nash, Robin Dixon (Great Britain)	Sergio Zardini, Romano Bonagura (Italy)	Eugenio Monti, Sergio Siorpaes (Italy)
1968	Eugenio Monti, Luciano de Paolis (Italy)	Horst Floth, Pepi Bader (West Germany)	Ion Panturu, Nicolae Neagoe (Romania)
1972	Wolfgang Zimmerer, Peter Utzschneider (West Germany)	Horst Floth, Pepi Bader (West Germany)	Jean Wicki, Edy Hubacher (Switzerland)
1976	Meinhard Mehmer, Bernhard Germeschausen (East Germany)	Wolfgang Zimmerer, Manfred Schumann (West Germany)	Erich Schärer, Joseph Benz (Switzerland)
1980	Erich Schärer, Joseph Benz (Switzerland)	Bernhard Germeschausen, Hans-Jürgen Gerhardt (East Germany)	Meinhard Nehmer, Bogdan Musiol (East Germany)
1984	Wolfgang Hoppe, Dietmar Schauerhammer (East Germany)	Bernhard Lehmann, Bogdan Musiol (East Germany)	Zintis Ekmanis, Vladimir Aleksandrov (Soviet Union)
1988	Janis Kipurs, Vladimir Koslov (Soviet Union)	Wolfgang Hoppe, Bogdan Musiol (East Germany)	Bernhard Lehmann, Mario Hoyer (East Germany)
1992	Gustav Weder, Donat Acklin (Switzerland)	Rudolf Lochner, Markus Zimmermann (Germany)	Christoph Langen, Günther Eger (Germany)
1994	Gustav Weder, Donat Acklin (Switzerland)	Reto Götschi, Guido Acklin (Switzerland)	Günther Huber, Stefano Ticci (Italy)
1998	Pierre Lueders, David MacEachern (Canada) Günther Huber, Antonio Tartaglia (Italy)	Not awarded	Christoph Langen, Markus Zimmermann (Germany)
2002	Christoph Langen, Markus Zimmermann (Germany)	Christian Reich, Steve Anderhub (Switzerland)	Martin Annen, Beat Hefti (Switzerland)
2006	Kevin Kuske, André Lange (Germany)	Pierre Lueders, Lascelles Brown (Canada)	Martin Annen, Beat Hefti (Switzerland)
2010	Kevin Kuske, André Lange (Germany)	Richard Adjei, Thomas Florschütz (Germany)	Alexey Voyevoda, Alexandr Zubkov (Russia)

Women's Two-Man

Year	Gold	Silver	Bronze
2002	Jill Bakken, Vonetta Flowers (United States)	Sandra Prokoff, Ulrike Holzner (Germany)	Susi Erdmann, Nicole Herschmann (Germany)
2006	Sandra Kiriasis, Anja Schneider-heinze (Germany)	Shauna Rohbock, Valerie Fleming (United States)	Gerda Weissensteiner, Jennifer Isacco (Italy)
2010	Kaillie Humphries, Heather Moyse (Canada)	Helen Upperton, Shelley-Ann Brown (Canada)	Erin Pac, Elana Meyers (United States)

Cross-Country Skiing

Men's 18-Kilometer

Year	Gold	Silver	Bronze
1924	Thorleif Haug (Norway)	Johan Grøttumsbråten (Norway)	Tapani Niku (Finland)
1928	Johan Grøttumsbråten (Norway)	Ole Hegge (Norway)	Reidar Ødegaard (Norway)
1932	Sven Utterström (Sweden)	Axel Wikström (Sweden)	Veli Saarinen (Finland)
1936	Erik August Larsson (Sweden)	Oddbjørn Hagen (Norway)	Pekka Niemi (Finland)
1940–1944: Olympics not held			
1948	Martin Lundström (Sweden)	Nils Östensson (Sweden)	Gunnar Eriksson (Sweden)
1952	Hallgeir Brenden (Norway)	Tapio Mäkelä (Finland)	Paavo Lonkila (Finland)

Men's 15-Kilometer

Year	Gold	Silver	Bronze
1956	Hallgeir Brenden (Norway)	Sixten Jernberg (Sweden)	Pavel Kolchin (Soviet Union)
1960	Håkon Brusveen (Norway)	Sixten Jernberg (Sweden)	Veikko Hakulinen (Finland)
1964	Eero Mäntyranta (Finland)	Harald Grønningen (Norway)	Sixten Jernberg (Sweden)
1968	Harald Grønningen (Norway)	Eero Mäntyranta (Finland)	Gunnar Larsson (Sweden)
1972	Sven-Åke Lundbäck (Sweden)	Fyodor Simashev (Soviet Union)	Ivar Formo (Norway)
1976	Nikolay Bazhukov (Soviet Union)	Yevgeny Belyayev (Soviet Union)	Arto Koivisto (Finland)
1980	Thomas Wassberg (Sweden)	Juha Mieto (Finland)	Ove Aunli (Norway)
1984	Gunde Svan (Sweden)	Aki Karvonen (Finland)	Harri Kirvesniemi (Finland)
1988	Mikhail Devyatyarov (Soviet Union)	Pål Gunnar Mikkelsplass (Norway)	Vladimir Smirnov (Soviet Union)
1992–1998: Event not held			
2002	Andrus Veerpalu (Estonia)	Frode Estil (Norway)	Jaak Mae (Estonia)
2006	Andrus Veerpalu (Estonia)	Lukáš Bauer (Czech Republic)	Tobias Angerer (Germany)
2010	Dario Cologna (Switzerland)	Pietro Piller Cottrer (Italy)	Lukáš Bauer (Czech Republic)

Men's 50-Kilometer

Year	Gold	Silver	Bronze
1924	Thorleif Haug (Norway)	Thoralf Strømstad (Norway)	Johan Grøttumsbråten (Norway)
1928	Per-Erik Hedlund (Sweden)	Gustaf Jonsson (Sweden)	Volger Andersson (Sweden)
1932	Veli Saarinen (Finland)	Väinö Liikkinen (Finland)	Arne Rustadstuen (Norway)
1936	Elis Wiklund (Sweden)	Axel Wikström (Sweden)	Nils-Joel Englund (Sweden)
1940–1944: Olympics not held			
1948	Nils Karlsson (Sweden)	Harald Eriksson (Sweden)	Benjamin Vanninen (Finland)
1952	Veikko Hakulinen (Finland)	Eero Kolehmainen (Finland)	Magnar Estenstad (Norway)
1956	Sixten Jernberg (Sweden)	Veikko Hakulinen (Finland)	Fyodor Terentyev (Soviet Union)
1960	Kalevi Hämäläinen (Finland)	Veikko Hakulinen (Finland)	Rolf Rämgård (Sweden)
1964	Sixten Jernberg (Sweden)	Assar Rönnlund (Sweden)	Arto Tiainen (Finland)

Year	Gold	Silver	Bronze
1968	Ole Ellefsæter (Norway)	Vyacheslav Vedenin (Soviet Union)	Josef Haas (Switzerland)
1972	Pål Tyldum (Norway)	Magne Myrmo (Norway)	Vyacheslav Vedenin (Soviet Union)
1976	Ivar Formo (Norway)	Gert-Dietmar Klause (East Germany)	Benny Södergren (Sweden)
1980	Nikolay Zimyatov (Soviet Union)	Juha Mieto (Finland)	Alexander Zavyalov (Soviet Union)
1984	Thomas Wassberg (Sweden)	Gunde Svan (Sweden)	Aki Karvonen (Finland)
1988	Gunde Svan (Sweden)	Maurilio De Zolt (Italy)	Andy Grünenfelder (Switzerland)
1992	Bjørn Dæhlie (Norway)	Maurilio De Zolt (Italy)	Giorgio Vanzetta (Italy)
1994	Vladimir Smirnov (Kazakhstan)	Mika Myllylä (Finland)	Sture Sivertsen (Norway)
1998	Bjørn Dæhlie (Norway)	Niklas Jonsson (Sweden)	Christian Hoffmann (Austria)
2002	Mikhail Ivanov (Russia)	Andrus Veerpalu (Estonia)	Odd-Bjørn Hjelmeset (Norway)
2006	Giorgio Di Centa (Italy)	Yevgeny Dementyev (Russia)	Mikhail Botvinov (Austria)
2010	Petter Northug (Norway)	Axel Teichmann (Germany)	Johan Olsson (Sweden)

Men's 4 × 10-Kilometer Relay

Year	Gold	Silver	Bronze
1936	Sulo Nurmela, Klaes Karppinen, Matti Lähde, Kalle Jalkanen (Finland)	Oddbjørn Hagen, Olaf Hoffsbakken, Sverre Brodahl, Bjarne Iversen (Norway)	John Berger, Erik August Larsson, Arthur Häggblad, Martin Matsbo (Sweden)
1940–1994: Olympics not held			
1948	Nils Östensson, Nils Täpp, Gunnar Eriksson, Martin Lundström (Sweden)	Lauri Silvennoinen, Teuvo Laukkanen, Sauli Rytky, August Kiuru (Finland)	Erling Evensen, Olav Økern, Reidar Nyborg, Olav Hagen (Norway)
1952	Heikki Hasu, Paavo Lonkila, Urpo Korhonen, Tapio Mäkelä (Finland)	Magnar Estenstad, Mikal Kirkholt, Martin Stokken, Hallgeir Brenden (Norway)	Nils Täpp, Sigurd Andersson, Enar Josefsson, Martin Lundström (Sweden)
1956	Fyodor Terentyev, Pavel Kolchin, Nikolay Anikin, Vladimir Kuzin (Soviet Union)	August Kiuru, Jorma Kortelainen, Arvo Viitanen, Veikko Hakulinen (Finland)	Lennart Larsson, Gunnar Samuelsson, Per-Erik Larsson, Sixten Jernberg (Sweden)
1960	Toimi Alatalo, Eero Mäntyranta, Väinö Huhtala, Veikko Hakulinen (Finland)	Harald Grønningen, Hallgeir Brenden, Einar Østby, Håkon Brusveen (Norway)	Anatoly Shelyukhin, Gennady Vaganov, Aleksey Kuznetsov, Nikolay Anikin (Soviet Union)
1964	Karl-Åke Asph, Sixten Jernberg, Janne Stefansson, Assar Rönnlund (Sweden)	Väinö Huhtala, Arto Tiainen, Kalevi Laurila, Eero Mäntyranta (Finland)	Ivan Utrobin, Gennady Vaganov, Igor Voronchikhin, Pavel Kolchin (Soviet Union)
1968	Odd Martinsen, Pål Tyldum, Harald Grønningen, Ole Ellefsæter (Norway)	Jan Halvarsson, Bjarne Andersson, Gunnar Larsson, Assar Rönnlund (Sweden)	Kalevi Oikarainen, Hannu Taipale, Kalevi Laurila, Eero Mäntyranta (Finland)
1972	Vladimir Voronkov, Yuri Skobov, Fyodor Simashev, Vyacheslav Vedenin (Soviet Union)	Oddvar Brå, Pål Tyldum, Ivar Formo, Johs Harviken (Norway)	Alfred Kälin, Albert Giger, Alois Kälin, Eduard Hauser (Switzerland)
1976	Matti Pitkänen, Juha Mieto, Pertti Teurajärvi, Arto Koivisto (Finland)	Pål Tyldum, Einar Sagstuen, Ivar Formo, Odd Martinsen (Norway)	Yevgeny Belyayev, Nikolay Bazhukov, Sergey Savelyev, Ivan Garanin (Soviet Union)
1980	Vasily Rochev, Nikolay Bazhukov, Tevgeny Belyayev, Nikolay Zimyatov (Soviet Union)	Lars-Erik Eriksen, Per Knut Aaland, Ove Aunli, Oddvar Brå (Norway)	Harri Kirvesniemi, Pertti Teurajärvi, Matti Pitkänen, Juha Mieto (Finland)
1984	Thomas Wassberg, Benny Kohlberg, Jan Ottosson, Gunde Svan (Sweden)	Alexander Batyuk, Alexander Zavylov, Vladimir Nikitin, Nikolay Zimyatov (Soviet. Union)	Kari Ristanen, Juha Mieto, Harri Kirvesniemi, Aki Karvonen (Finland)

Year	Gold	Silver	Bronze
1988	Jan Ottosson, Thomas Wassberg, Gunde Svan, Torgny Mogren (Sweden)	Vladimir Smirnov, Vladimir Sakhnov, Mikhail Devyatyarov, Alexey Prokurorov (Soviet Union)	Radim Nyč, Václav Korunka, Pavel Benc, Ladislav Švanda (Czechoslovakia)
1992	Terje Langli, Vegard Ulvang, Kristen Skjeldal, Bjørn Dæhlie (Norway)	Giuseppe Pulie, Marco Albarello, Giorgio Vanzetta, Silvio Fauner (Italy)	Mika Kuusisto, Harri Kirvesniemi, Jari Räsänen, Jari Isometsä (Finland)
1994	Maurilio De Zolt, Marco Albarello, Giorgio Vanzetta, Silvio Fauner (Italy)	Sture Sivertsen, Vegard Ulvang, Thomas Alsgaard, Bjørn Dæhlie (Norway)	Mika Myllylä, Harri Kirvesniemi, Jari Räsänen, Jari Isometsä (Finland)
1998	Sture Sivertsen, Erling Jevne, Bjørn Dæhlie, Thomas Alsgaard (Norway)	Marco Albarello, Fulvio Valbusa, Fabio Maj, Silvio Fauner (Italy)	Harri Kirvesniemi, Mika Myllylä, Sami Repo, Jari Isometsä (Finland)
2002	Anders Aukland, Frode Estil, Kristen Skjedal, Thomas Alsgaard (Norway)	Fabio Maj, Giorgio De Centa, Pietro Piller Cottrer, Cristian Zorzi (Italy)	Jens Filbrich, Andreas Schlütter, Tobias Angerer, René Sommerfeldt (Germany)
2006	Fulvio Valbusa, Giorgio Di Centa, Pietro Piller Cottrer, Cristian Zorzi (Italy)	Andreas Schlütter, Jens Filbrich, René Sommerfeldt, Tobias Angerer (Germany)	Mats Larsson, Johan Olsson, Anders Södergren, Mathias Fredriksson (Sweden)
2010	Daniel Rickardsson, Johan Olsson, Anders Södergren, Marcus Hellner (Sweden)	Martin Johnsrud Sundby, Odd-Bjørn Hjelmeset, Lars Berger, Petter Northug (Norway)	Martin Jakš, Lukáš Bauer, Jiří Magál, Martin Koukal (Czech Republic)

Men's 10-Kilometer Classical Interval + 15-Kilometer Freestyle Pursuit

Year	Gold	Silver	Bronze
1992	Bjørn Dæhlie (Norway)	Vegard Ulvang (Norway)	Giorgio Vanzetta (Italy)
1994	Bjørn Dæhlie (Norway)	Vladimir Smirnov (Kazakhstan)	Silvio Fauner (Italy)
1998	Thomas Alsgaard (Norway)	Bjørn Dæhlie (Norway)	Vladimir Smirnov (Kazakhstan)

Men's 10-Kilometer Classical Interval + 10-Kilometer Freestyle Pursuit

Year	Gold	Silver	Bronze
2002	Thomas Alsgaard (Norway) Frode Estil (Norway)	Not awarded	Per Elofsson (Sweden)

Men's 15-Kilometer Classical Interval + 15-Kilometer Freestyle Pursuit

Year	Gold	Silver	Bronze
2006	Yevgeny Dementyev (Russia)	Frode Estil (Norway)	Pietro Piller Cottrer (Italy)
2010	Marcus Hellner (Sweden)	Tobias Angerer (Germany)	Johan Olsson (Sweden)

Men's 1.5-Kilometer Sprint

Year	Gold	Silver	Bronze
2002	Tor Arne Hetland (Norway)	Peter Schlickenrieder (Germany)	Cristian Zorzi (Italy)
2006	Björn Lind (Sweden)	Roddy Darragon (France)	Thobias Fredriksson (Sweden)
2010	Nikita Kriukov (Russia)	Alexander Panzhinskiy (Russia)	Petter Northug (Norway)

Men's Team Sprint

Year	Gold	Silver	Bronze
2006	Thobias Fredriksson, Björn Lind (Sweden)	Jens Arne Svartedal, Tor Arne Hetland (Norway)	Ivan Alypov, Vasili Rotchev (Russia)
2010	Øystein Pettersen, Petter Northug (Norway)	Tim Tscharnke, Axel Teichmann (Germany)	Nikolay Morilov, Alexey Petukhov (Russia)

Women's 10-Kilometer

Year	Gold	Silver	Bronze
1952	Lydia Wideman (Finland)	Mirja Hietamies (Finland)	Siiri Rantanen (Finland)
1956	Lyubov Kozyreva (Soviet Union)	Radya Yeroshina (Soviet Union)	Sonja Edström (Sweden)
1960	Maria Gusakova (Soviet Union)	Lyubov Kozyreva (Soviet Union)	Radya Yeroshina (Soviet Union)
1964	Klavdiya Boyarskikh (Soviet Union)	Yevdokiya Mekshilo (Soviet Union)	Maria Gusakova (Soviet Union)
1968	Toini Gustafsson (Sweden)	Berit Mørdre Lammedal (Norway)	Inger Aufles (Norway)
1972	Galina Kulakova (Soviet Union)	Alevtina Olyunina (Soviet Union)	Marjatta Kajosmaa (Finland)
1976	Raisa Smetanina (Soviet Union)	Helena Takalo (Finland)	Galina Kulakova (Soviet Union)
1980	Barbara Petzold (East Germany)	Hilkka Riihivuori (Finland)	Helena Takalo (Finland)
1984	Marja-Liisa Hämäläinen (Finland)	Raisa Smetanina (Soviet Union)	Britt Pettersen (Norway)
1988	Vida Vencienė (Soviet Union)	Raisa Smetanina (Soviet Union)	Marjo Maitkainen (Finland)
1992–1998: Event not held			
2002	Bente Skari (Norway)	Yuliya Chepalova (Russia)	Stefania Belmondo (Italy)
2006	Kristina Šmigun-Vähi (Estonia)	Marit Bjørgen (Norway)	Hilde G. Pedersen (Norway)
2010	Charlotte Kalla (Sweden)	Kristina Šmigun-Vähi (Estonia)	Marit Bjørgen (Norway)

Women's 3 × 5-Kilometer Relay

Year	Gold	Silver	Bronze
1956	Sirkka Polkunen, Mirja Hietamies, Siiri Rantanen (Finland)	Lyubov Kozyreva, Alevtina Kolchina, Radya Yeroshina (Soviet Union)	Irma Johansson, Anna-Lisa Eriksson, Sonja Edström (Sweden)
1960	Irma Johansson, Britt Strandberg, Sonja Ruthström-Edström (Sweden)	Radya Yeroshina, Maria Gusakova, Lyubov Kozyreva (Soviet Union)	Siiri Rantanen, Eeva Ruoppa, Toini Pöysti (Finland)
1964	Alevtina Kolchina, Yevdokiya Mekshilo, Klavdiya Boyarskikh (Soviet Union)	Barbro Martinsson, Britt Strandberg, Toini Gustafsson (Sweden)	Senja Pusula, Toini Pöysti, Mirja Lehtonen (Finland)
1968	Inger Aufles, Babben Enger Damon, Berit Mørdre Lammedal (Norway)	Britt Strandberg, Toini Gustafsson, Barbro Martinsson (Sweden)	Alevtina Kolchina, Rita Achkina, Galina Kulakova (Soviet Union)
1972	Lyubov Mukhachyova, Alevtina Olyunina, Galina Kulakova (Soviet Union)	Helena Takalo, Hilkka Riihivuori, Marjatta Kajosmaa (Finland)	Inger Aufles, Åslaug Dahl, Berit Mørdre (Norway)

Women's 4 × 5-Kilometer Relay

Year	Gold	Silver	Bronze
1976	Nina Fyodorova, Zinaida Amosova, Raisa Smetanina, Galina Kulakova (Soviet Union)	Liisa Suikhonen, Marjatta Kajosmaa, Hilkka Riihivuori, Helena Takalo (Finland)	Monika Debertshäuser, Sigrun Krause, Barbara Petzold, Veronika Hesse (East Germany)
1980	Marlies Rostock, Carola Anding, Veronika Schmidt, Barbara Petzold (East Germany)	Nina Fyodorova, Nina Rocheva, Galina Kulakova, Raisa Smetanina (Soviet Union)	Britt Pettersen, Anette Bøe, Marit Myrmæl, Berit Aunli (Norway)
1984	Inger Helene Nybråten, Anne Jahren, Britt Pettersen, Berit Aunli (Norway)	Dagmar Švubová, Blanka Paulů, Gabriela Svobodová, Květa Jeriová (Czech Republic)	Pirkko Määttä, Eija Hyytiäinen, Marjo Matikainen, Marja-Liisa Kirvesniemi (Finland)
1988	Svetlana Nageykina, Nina Gavrilyuk, Tamara Tikhonova, Anfisa Reztsova (Soviet Union)	Trude Dybendahl, Marit Wold, Anne Jahren, Marianne Dahlmo (Norway)	Pirkko Määttä, Marja-Liisa Kirvesniemi, Marjo Matikainen, Jaana Savolainen (Finland)
1992	Yelena Välbe, Raisa Smetanina, Larisa Lazutina, Lyubov Yegorova (Unified Team)	Solveig Pedersen, Inger Helene Nybråten, Trude Dybendahl, Elin Nilsen (Norway)	Bice Vanzetta, Manuela Di Centa, Gabriella Paruzzi, Stefania Belmondo (Italy)

Year	Gold	Silver	Bronze
1994	Yelena Välbe, Larisa Lazutina, Nina Gavrilyuk, Lyubov Yegorova (Russia)	Trude Dybendahl, Inger Helene Nybråten, Elin Nilsen, Anita Moen (Norway)	Bice Vanzetta, Manuela Di Centa, Gabriella Paruzzi, Stefania Belmondo (Italy)
1998	Nina Gavrilyuk, Olga Danilova, Yelena Välbe, Larisa Lazutina (Russia)	Bente Martinsen, Marit Mikkelsplass, Elin Nilsen, Anita Moen-Guidon (Norway)	Karin Moroder, Gabriella Paruzzi, Manuela Di Centa, Stefania Belmondo (Italy)
2002	Manuela Henkel, Viola Bauer, Claudia Künzel, Evi Sachenbacher-Stehle (Germany)	Marit Bjørgen, Bente Skari, Hilde G. Pedersen, Anita Moen (Norway)	Andrea Huber, Laurence Rochat, Brigitte Albrecht Loretain, Natascia Leonardi Cortesi (Switzerland)
2006	Natalia Baranova-Masolkina, Larisa Kurkina, Yuliya Chepalova, Yevgeniya Medvedeva (Russia)	Stefanie Böhler, Viola Bauer, Evi Sachenbacher-Stehle, Claudia Künzel (Germany)	Arianna Follis, Gabriella Paruzzi, Antonella Confortola, Sabina Balbusa (Italy)
2010	Vibeke Skofterud, Therese Johaug, Kristin Størmer Steira, Marit Bjørgen (Norway)	Katrin Zeller, Evi Sachenbacher-Stehle, Miriam Gössner, Claudia Nystad (Germany)	Pirjo Muranen, Virpi Kuitunen, Riitta-Liisa Roponen, Aino-Kaisa Saarinen (Finland)

Women's 20-Kilometer

Year	Gold	Silver	Bronze
1984	Marja-Liisa Kirvesniemi (Finland)	Raisa Smetanina (Soviet Union)	Anne Jahren (Norway)
1988	Tamara Tikhonova (Soviet Union)	Anfisa Reztsova (Soviet Union)	Raisa Smetanina (Soviet Union)

Women's 30-Kilometer

Year	Gold	Silver	Bronze
1992	Stefania Belmondo (Italy)	Lyubov Yegorova (Unified Team)	Yelena Välbe (Unified Team)
1994	Manuela Di Centa (Italy)	Marit Wold (Norway)	Marja-Liisa Kirvesniemi (Finland)
1998	Yuliya Chepalova (Russia)	Stefania Belmondo (Italy)	Larisa Lazutina (Russia)
2002	Gabriella Paruzzi (Italy)	Stefania Belmondo (Italy)	Bente Skari (Norway)
2006	Kateřina Neumannová (Czech Republic)	Yuliya Chepalova (Russia)	Justyna Kowalczyk (Poland)
2010	Justyna Kowalczyk (Poland)	Marit Bjørgen (Norway)	Aino-Kaisa Saarinen (Finland)

Women's Combined 5-Kilometer + 10-Kilometer Pursuit

Year	Gold	Silver	Bronze
1992	Lyubov Yegorova (Unified Team)	Stefania Belmondo (Italy)	Yelena Välbe (Unified Team)
1994	Lyubov Yegorova (Russia)	Manuela Di Centa (Italy)	Stefania Belmondo (Italy)
1998	Larisa Lazutina (Russia)	Olga Danilova (Russia)	Kateřina Neumannová (Czech Republic)

Women's Combined 5-Kilometer + 5-Kilometer Pursuit

Year	Gold	Silver	Bronze
2002	Beckie Scott (Canada)	Kateřina Neumannová (Czech Republic)	Viola Bauer (Germany)

Women's Combined 7.5-Kilometer + 7.5-Kilometer Pursuit

Year	Gold	Silver	Bronze
2006	Kristina Šmigun (Estonia)	Kateřina Neumannová (Czech Republic)	Yevgeniya Medvedeva (Russia)
2010	Marit Bjørgen (Norway)	Anna Haag (Sweden)	Justyna Kowalczyk (Poland)

Women's Individual Sprint

Year	Gold	Silver	Bronze
2002	Yuliya Chepalova (Russia)	Evi Sachenbacher (Germany)	Anita Moen (Norway)
2006	Chandra Crawford (Canada)	Claudia Künzel (Germany)	Alyona Sidko (Russia)
2010	Marit Bjørgen (Norway)	Justyna Kowalczyk (Poland)	Petra Majdič (Slovenia)

Women's Team Sprint

Year	Gold	Silver	Bronze
2006	Lina Andersson, Anna Dahlberg (Sweden)	Sara Renner, Beckie Scott (Canada)	Aino-Kaisa Saarinen, Virpi Kuitunen (Finland)
2010	Evi Sachenbacher-Stehle, Claudia Nystad (Germany)	Charlotte Kalla, Anna Haag (Sweden)	Irina Khazova, Natalya Korostelyova (Russia)

Women's 5-Kilometer

Year	Gold	Silver	Bronze
1964	Klavdiya Boyarskikh (Soviet Union)	Mirja Lehtonen (Finland)	Alevtina Kolchina (Soviet Union)
1968	Toini Gustafsson (Sweden)	Galina Kulakova (Soviet Union)	Alevtina Kolchina (Soviet Union)
1972	Galina Kulakova (Sweden)	Marjatta Kajosmaa (Finland)	Helena Šikolová (Czech Republic)
1976	Helena Takalo (Finland)	Raisa Smetanina (Soviet Union)	Nina Fyodorova (Soviet Union)
1980	Raisa Smetanina (Soviet Union)	Hilkka Riihivuori (Finland)	Květa Jeriová (Czech Republic)
1984	Marja-Liisa Hämäläinen (Finland)	Berit Aunli (Norway)	Květa Jeriová (Czech Republic)
1988	Marjo Matikainen (Finland)	Tamara Tikhonova (Soviet Union)	Vida Venciené (Soviet Union)
1992	Marjut Lukkarinen (Finland)	Lyubov Yegorova (Unified Team)	Yelena Välbe (Unified Team)
1994	Lyubov Yegorova (Russia)	Manuela Di Centa (Italy)	Marja-Liisa Kirvesniemi (Finland)
1998	Larisa Lazutina (Russia)	Kateřina Neumannová (Czech Republic)	Bente Martinsen (Norway)

Women's 15-Kilometer

Year	Gold	Silver	Bronze
1992	Lyubov Yegorova (Unified Team)	Marjut Lukkarinen (Finland)	Yelena Välbe (Unified Team)
1994	Manuela Di Centa (Italy)	Lyubov Yegorova (Russia)	Nina Gavrilyuk (Russia)
1998	Olga Danilova (Russia)	Larisa Lazutina (Russia)	Anita Moen-Guidon (Norway)
2002	Stefania Belmondo (Italy)	Kateřina Neumannová (Czech Republic)	Yuliya Chepalova (Russia)

Men's 30-Kilometer Mass Start

Year	Gold	Silver	Bronze
1956	Veikko Hakulinen (Finland)	Sixten Jernberg (Sweden)	Pavel Kolchin (Soviet Union)
1960	Sixten Jernberg (Sweden)	Rolf Rämgård (Sweden)	Nikolay Anikin (Soviet Union)
1964	Eero Mäntyranta (Finland)	Harald Grønningen (Norway)	Igor Voronchikin (Soviet Union)
1968	Franco Nones (Italy)	Odd Martinsen (Norway)	Eero Mäntyranta (Finland)
1972	Vyacheslav Vedenin (Soviet Union)	Pål Tyldum (Norway)	Johs Harviken (Norway)
1976	Sergey Savelyev (Soviet Union)	Bill Koch (United States)	Ivan Garanin (Soviet Union)
1980	Nikolay Zimyatov (Soviet Union)	Vassily Rochev (Soviet Union)	Ivan Lebanov (Bulgaria)
1984	Nikolay Zimyatov (Soviet Union)	Alexander Zavyalov (Soviet Union)	Gunde Svan (Sweden)
1988	Alexey Prokurorov (Soviet Union)	Vladimir Smirnov (Soviet Union)	Vegard Ulvang (Norway)
1992	Vegard Ulvang (Norway)	Bjørn Dæhlie (Norway)	Terje Langli (Norway)
1994	Thomas Alsgaard (Norway)	Bjørn Dæhlie (Norway)	Mika Myllylä (Finland)
1998	Mika Myllylä (Finland)	Erling Jevne (Norway)	Silvio Fauner (Italy)
2002	Christian Hoffmann (Austria)	Mikhail Botvinov (Austria)	Kristen Skjeldal (Norway)

Men's 10-Kilometer Pursuit

Year	Gold	Silver	Bronze
1992	Vegard Ulvang (Norway)	Marco Albarello (Italy)	Christer Majbäck (Sweden)
1994	Björn Daehlie (Norway)	Vladimir Smirnov (Kazakhstan)	Marco Albarello (Italy)
1998	Björn Daehlie (Norway)	Marcus Gandler (Austria)	Mika Myllylae (Finland)
2002	Frode Estil (Norway) Thomas Alsgaard (Norway)	Not awarded	Per Elofsson (Sweden)

Women's 5-Kilometer Pursuit

Year	Gold	Silver	Bronze
2002	Beckie Scott (Canada)	Katerina Neumannova (Czech Republic)	Viola Bauer (Germany)

Curling

Men's Curling

Year	Gold	Silver	Bronze
1924*	William K. Jackson, Robin Welsh, Thomas Murray, Laurence Jackson, D. G. Astley, John McLeod, William Brown, John T. S. Robertson-Aikman, R. Cousin (Great Britain)	Johan Petter Åhlén, Carl-Axel Pettersson, Karl-Erik Wahlberg, Carl Axel Kronlund, Ture Ödlund, Carl Wilhelm Petersén, Erik O. Severin, Victor Wetterström (Sweden)	F. Cournollet**, Georges André, Armand Bénédic, P. Canivet**, R. Planque**, H. Aldeert** (France)
1928–1994: Event not held			
1998	Patrick Hürlimann, Patrik Lörtscher, Daniel Müller, Diego Perren, Dominic Andres (Switzerland)	Mike Harris, Richard Hart, Collin Mitchell, George Karrys, Paul Savage (Canada)	Eigil Ramsfjell, Jan Thoresen, Stig-Arne Gunnestad, Tore Torvbråten, Anthon Grimsmo (Norway)
2002	Pål Trulsen, Lars Vågberg, Flemming Davanger, Bent Ånund Ramsfjell, Torger Nergård (Norway)	Kevin Martin, Don Walchuk, Carter Rycroft, Don Bartlett, Ken Tralnberg (Canada)	Andreas Schwaller, Christof Schwaller, Markus Eggler, Damian Grichting, Marco Ramstein (Switzerland)
2006	Brad Gushue, Mark Nichols, Russ Howard, Jamie Korab, Mike Adam (Canada)	Markku Uusipaavalniemi, Wille Mäkelä, Kalle Kiiskinen, Teemu Salo, Jani Sullanmaa (Finland)	Pete Fenson, Shawn Rojeski, Jospeh Polo, John Shuster, Scott Baird (United States)
2010	Kevin Martin, John Morris, Marc Kennedy, Ben Hebert, Adam Enright (Canada)	Thomas Ulsrud, Torger Nergård, Christoffer Svae, Håvard Vad Petersson, Thomas Løvold (Norway)	Ralph Stöckli, Jan Hauser, Markus Eggler, Simon Strübin, Toni Müller (Switzerland)

* Awarded retroactively in 2006.

** Full name not known.

Women's Curling

Year	Gold	Silver	Bronze
1998	Sanra Schmirler, Jan Betker, Joan McCusker, Marcia Gudereit, Atina Ford (Canada)	Helena Black Lavrsen, Margit Pörtner, Dorthe Holm, Trine Qvist, Jane Bidstrup (Denmark)	Elisabet Gustafson, Katarina Nyberg, Louise Marmont, Elisabeth Persson, Margaretha Lindahl (Sweden)
2002	Rhona Martin, Deborah Knox, Fiona MacDonald, Janice Rankin, Margaret Morton (Great Britain)	Luzia Ebnöther, Mirjam Ott, Tanya Frei, Laurence Bidaud, Nadia Röthlisberger (Switzerland)	Kelley Law, Julie Skinner, Georgina Wheatcroft, Diane Nelson, Cheryl Noble (Canada)

Year	Gold	Silver	Bronze
2006	Anette Norberg, Eva Lund, Cathrine Lindahl, Anna Svärd, Ulrika Bergman (Sweden)	Mirjam Ott, Binia Beeli, Valeria Spälty, Michèle Moser, Manuela Kormann (Switzerland)	Shannon Kleibrink, Amy Nixon, Glenys Bakker, Christine Keshen, Sandra Jenkins (Canada)
2010	Anette Norberg, Eva Lund, Cathrine Lindahl, Anna Le Moine, Kajsa Bergström (Sweden)	Cheryl Bernard, Susan O'Connor, Carolyn Darbyshire, Cori Bartel, Kristie Moore (Canada)	Wang Bingyu, Liu Yin, Yue Qingshuang, Zhou Yan, Liu Jinli (China)

Ice Hockey

Men's Ice Hockey

Year	Gold	Silver	Bronze
1920	Robert Benson, Walter Byron, Fred Fredrickson, Chris Fridfinnson, Magnus Goodman, Haldor Halderson, Konrad Johannesson, Allan Woodman (Canada)	Raymond Bonney, Anthony Conroy, Herbert Drury, Edward Fitzgerald, George Geran, Frank Goheen, Joseph McCormick, Lawrence McCormick, Frank Synott, Leon Tuck, Cyril Weidenborner (United States)	Karel Hartmann, Vilém Loos, Jan Palouš, Jan Peka, Karel Pešek, Josef Šroubek, Otakar Vindyš, Adolf Dušek, Karel Wälzer (Czechoslovakia)
1924	Jack Cameron, Ernie Collett, Bert McCaffrey, Harold McMunn, Duncan Munro, Beattie Ramsay, Cyril Slater, Reginald Smith, Harry Watson (Canada)	Clarence Abel, Herbert Drury, Alphonse Lacroix, John Langley, John Lyons, Justin McCarthy, Willard Rice, Irving Small, Frank Synott (United States)	William Anderson, Lorne Carr-Harris, Colin Carruthers, Eric Carruthers, Guy Clarkson, Ross Cuthbert, George Holmes, Hamilton Jukes, Edward Pitblado, Blaine Sexton (Great Britain)
1928	Charles Delahay, Frank Fisher, Louis Hudson, Norbert Mueller, Herbert Plaxton, Hugh Plaxton, Roger Plaxton, John Porter, Frank Sullivan, Joseph Sullivan, Ross Taylor, David Trottier (Canada)	Carl Abrahamsson, Emil Bergman, Birger Holmqvist, Gustaf Johansson, Henry Johansson, Nils Johansson, Ernst Karlberg, Erik Larsson, Bertil Linde, Sigfrid Öberg, Wilhelm Petersén, Kurt Sucksdorff (Sweden)	Giannin Andreossi, Mezzi Andreossi, Robert Breiter, Louis Dufour, Charles Fasel, Albert Geromini, Fritz Kraatz, Arnold Martignoni, Heini Meng, Anton Morosani, Luzius Rüedi, Richard Torriani (Switzerland)
1932	William Cockburn, Clifford Crowley, Albert Duncanson, George Garbutt, Roy Hinkel, Victor Lindquist, Norman Malloy, Walter Monson, Kenneth Moore, Romeo Rivers, Harold Simpson, Hugh Sutherland, Stanley Wagner, Alston Wise (Canada)	Osborne Anderson, John Bent, John Chase, John Cookman, Douglas Everett, Franklin Farrel, Joseph Fitzgerald, Edwin Frazier, John Garrison, Gerard Hallock, Robert Livingston, Francis Nelson, Winthrop Palmer, Gordon Smith (United States)	Rudi Ball, Alfred Heinrich, Erich Herker, Gustav Jaenecke, Werner Korff, Walter Leinweber, Erich Römer, Martin Schröttle, Marquardt Slevogt, Georg Strobl (Germany)
1936	Alexander Archer, James Borland, Edgar Brenchley, James Chappell, John Coward, Gordon Dailley, John Davey, Carl Erhardt, James Foster, John Kilpatrick, Archibald Stinchcombe, Robert Wyman (Great Britain)	Mazwell Deacon, Hugh Farquharson, Kenneth Farmer, James Haggarty, Walter Kitchen, Raymond Milton, Francis Moore, Herman Murray, Arthur Nash, David Neville, Alexander Sinclair, Ralph St. Germain, William Thomson (Canada)	John Garrison, August Kammer, Philip LaBatte, John Lax, Thomas Moone, Elbridge Ross, Paul Rowe, Francis Shaughnessy, Gordon Smith, Francis Spain, Frank Stubbs (United States)

1940–1944: Olympics not held

Year	Gold	Silver	Bronze
1948	Murray Dowey, Bernard Dunster, Jean Gravelle, Patrick Guzzo, Walter Halder, Thomas Hibberd, Henri-André Laperriere, John Lecompte, George Mara, Albert Roméo Renaud, Reginald Schroeter, Irving Taylor (Canada)	Vladimír Bouzek, Augustin Bubník, Jaroslav Drobný, Přemysl Hajný, Zdeněk Jarkovský, Vladimír Kobranov, Stanislav Konopásek, Bohumil Modrý, Miloslav Pokorný, Václav Roziňák, Miroslav Sláma, Karel Stibor, Vilibald Šťovík, Ladislav Troják, Josef Trousílek, Oldřich Zábrodský, Vladimír Zábrodský (Czechoslovakia)	Hans Bänninger, Alfred Bieler, Heinrich Boller, Ferdinand Cattini, Hans Cattini, Hans Dürst, Walter Paul Dürst, Emil Handschin, Heini Lohrer, Werner Lohrer, Reto Perl, Gebhard Poltera, Ulrich Poltera, Beat Rüedi, Otto Schubiger, Richard Torriani, Hans-Martin Trepp (Switzerland)
1952	George Abel, John Davies, Billy Dawe, Robert Dickson, Donald Gauf, William Gibson, Ralph Hansch, Robert Meyers, David Miller, Eric Paterson, Thomas Pollock, Allan Purvis, Gordon Robertson, Louis Secco, Francis Sullivan, Bob Watt (Canada)	Ruben Bjorkman, Leonard Ceglarski, Joseph Czarnota, Richard Desmond, Andre Gambucci, Clifford Harrison, Gerald Kilmartin, John Mulhern, John Noah, Arnold Oss, Robert Rompre, James Sedin, Alfred Van Allen, Donald Whiston, Ken Yackel (United States)	Göte Almqvist, Åke Andersson, Hans Andersson-Tvilling, Stig Andersson-Tvilling, Lars Björn, Göte Blomqvist, Thord Flodqvist, Erik Johansson, Rune Johansson, Sven Tumba Johansson, Erik Lassas, Holger Nurmela, Hans Öberg, Lars Pettersson, Lars Svensson, Sven Thunman (Sweden)
1956	Yevgeny Babich, Vsevolod Bobrov, Alexei Guryshev, Nikolay Khlystov, Valentin Kuzin, Yuri Krylov, Alfred Kuchevsky, Grigory Mkrtychan, Viktor Nikiforov, Yuri Pantyukhov, Nikolaï Puchkov, Viktor Shuvalov, Genrikh Sidorenkov, Nikolai Sologubov, Ivan Tregubov, Dmitry Ukolov, Aleksandr Uvarov (Soviet Union)	Wendell Anderson, Wellington Burtnett, Eugene Campbell, Gordon Christian, Bill Cleary, Richard Dougherty, Willard Ikola, John Matchefts, John Mayasich, Daniel McKinnon, Richard Meredith, Weldon Olson, John Pettroske, Kenneth Purpur, Don Rigazio, Richard Rodenheiser, Edward Sampson (United States)	Denis Brodeur, Charles Brooker, William Colvin, Alfred Horne, Arthur Hurst, Byrle Klinck, Paul Knox, Ken Laufman, Howard Lee, James Logan, Floyd Martin, Jack McKenzie, Donald Rope, George Scholes, Gerry Theberge, Robert White, Keith Woodall (Canada)
1960	Bill Christian, Roger Christian, Bill Cleary, Bob Cleary, Eugene Grazia, Paul Johnson, Jack Kirrane, John Mayasich, Jack McCartan, Robert McVey, Richard Meredith, Weldon Olson, Edwyn Owen, Rodney Paavola, Lawrence Palmer, Richard Rodenheiser, Tommy Williams (United States)	Bob Attersley, Maurice Benoit, James Connelly, Jack Douglas, Fred Etcher, Robert Forhan, Don Head, Harold Hurley, Ken Laufman, Floyd Martin, Robert McKnight, Cliff Pennington, Donald Rope, Bobby Rousseau, George Samolenko, Harry Sinden, Darryl Sly (Canada)	Veniamin Alexandrov, Aleksandr Almetov, Yuri Baulin, Mikhail Bychkov, Vladimir Grebennikov, Yevgeny Groshev, Nikolai Karpov, Alfred Kuchevsky, Konstantin Loktev, Stanislav Petukhov, Viktor Pryazhnikov, Nikolai Puchkov, Genrikh Sidorenkov, Nikolai Sologubov, Yury Tsitsinov, Viktor Yakushev, Evgeni Yerkin (Soviet Union)
1964	Veniamin Alexandrov, Aleksandr Almetov, Vitaly Davydov, Anatoli Firsov, Eduard Ivanov, Viktor Konovalenko, Victor Kuzkin, Konstantin Loktev, Boris Mayorov, Stanislav Petukhov, Alexander Ragulin, Vyacheslav Starshinov, Leonid Volkov, Victor Yakushev, Boris Zaitzev, Oleg Zaytsev (Soviet Union)	Anders Andersson, Gert Blomé, Lennart Häggroth, Lennart Johansson, Nils Johansson, Sven Tumba Johansson, Lars-Eric Lundvall, Eilert Määttä, Hans Mild, Nils Nilsson, Bert-Ola Nordlander, Carl-Göran Öberg, Uno Öhrlund, Ronald Petters-son, Ulf Sterner, Roland Stoltz, Kjell Svensson (Sweden)	Vlastimil Bubník, Josef Černý, Jiří Dolana, Vladimír Dzurilla, Jozef Golonka, František Gregor, Jiří Holík, Jaroslav Jiřík, Jan Klapáč, Vladimír Nadrchal, Rudolf Potsch, Stanislav Prýl, Ladislav Šmíd, Stanislav Sventek, František Tikal, Miroslav Vlach, Jaroslav Walter (Czechoslovakia)

Year	Gold	Silver	Bronze
1968	Veniamin Alexandrov, Viktor Blinov, Vitaly Davydov, Anatoli Firsov, Anatoly Ionov, Viktor Konovalenko, Victor Kuzkin, Boris Mayorov, Yevgeni Mishakov, Yuri Moiseev, Victor Polupanov, Alexander Ragulin, Igor Romishevsky, Vyacheslav Starshinov, Vladimir Vikulov, Oleg Zaytsev, Yevgeni Zimin, Victor Zinger (Soviet Union)	Josef Černý, Vladimír Dzurilla, Jozef Golonka, Jan Havel, Petr Hejma, Jiří Holík, Josef Horešovský, Jan Hrbatý, Jaroslav Jiřík, Jan Klapáč, Jiří Kochta, Oldřich Macháč, Karel Masopust, Vladimír Nadrchal, Václav Nedomanský, František Pospíšil, František Ševčík, Jan Suchý (Czechoslovakia)	Roger Bourbonnais, Ken Broderick, Ray Cadieux, Paul Conlin, Gary Dineen, Brian Glennie, Ted Hargreaves, Fran Huck, Marshall Johnston, Barry MacKenzie, Bill MacMillan, Steve Monteith, Morris Mott, Terry O'Malley, Danny O'Shea, Gerry Pinder, Herb Pinder, Wayne Stephenson (Canada)
1972	Yury Blinov, Vitaly Davydov, Anatoli Firsov, Valeri Kharlamov, Victor Kuzkin, Victor Kuzkin, Vladimir Lutchenko, Aleksandr Maltsev, Boris Mikhailov, Yevgeni Mishakov, Alexander Pashkov, Vladimir Petrov, Alexander Ragulin, Igor Romishevsky, Vladimir Shadrin, Vladislav Tretiak, Gennadiy Tsygankov, Valeri Vasiliev, Vladimir Vikulov, Alexander Yakushev, Yevgeni Zimin (Soviet Union)	Kevin Ahearn, Larry Bader, Henry Boucha, Charles Brown, Keith Christiansen, Mike Curran, Robbie Ftorek, Mark Howe, Stuart Irving, Jim McElmury, Dick McGlynn, Bruce McIntosh, Tom Mellor, Ronald Naslund, Wally Olds, Tim Regan, Frank Sanders, Craig Sarner, Peter Sears, Timothy Sheehy (United States)	Vladimír Bednár, Josef Černý, Vladimír Dzurilla, Richard Farda, Ivan Hlinka, Jiří Holeček, Jaroslav Holík, Jiří Holík, Oldřich Macháč, Vladimír Martinec, Václav Nedomanský, Eduard Novák, František Pospíšil, Bohuslav Šťastný, Rudolf Tajcnár, Karel Vohralík (Czechoslovakia)
1976	Boris Aleksandrov, Sergei Babinov, Aleksandr Gusev, Sergei Kapustin, Valeri Kharlamov, Vladimir Lutchenko, Yuri Lyapkin, Aleksandr Maltsev, Boris Mikhailov, Vladimir Petrov, Vladimir Shadrin, Victor Shalimov, Aleksandr Sidelnikov, Vladislav Tretiak, Gennadiy Tsygankov, Valeri Vasiliev, Alexander Yakushev, Viktor Zhluktov (Soviet Union)	Josef Augusta, Jiří Bubla, Milan Chalupa, Jiří Crha, Miroslav Dvořák, Bohuslav Ebermann, Ivan Hlinka, Jiří Holeček, Jiří Holík, Milan Kajkl, Oldřich Macháč, Vladimír Martinec, Eduard Novák, Jiří Novák, Milan Nový, Jaroslav Pouzar, František Pospíšil, Bohuslav Šťastný (Czechoslovakia)	Klaus Auhuber, Ignaz Berndaner, Wolfgang Boos, Lorenz Funk, Martin Hinterstocker, Udo Kiessling, Walter Köberle, Ernst Köpf, Anton Kehle, Erich Kühnhackl, Stefan Metz, Franz Reindl, Rainer Philipp, Alois Schloder, Rudolf Thanner, Rudolf Thanner, Josef Völk, Ferenc Vozar, Erich Weishaupt (West Germany)
1980	Bill Baker, Neal Broten, Dave Christian, Steve Christoff, Jim Craig, Mike Eruzione, John Harrington, Steve Janaszak, Mark Johnson, Rob McClanahan, Ken Morrow, Jack O'Callahan, Mike Ramsey, Mark Pavelich, Buzz Schneider, Dave Silk, Bob Suter, Eric Strobel, Mark Wells, Phil Verchota (United States)	Helmuts Balderis, Zinetula Bilyaletdinov, Viacheslav Fetisov, Aleksandr Golikov, Vladimir Golikov, Alexei Kasatonov, Valeri Kharlamov, Vladimir Krutov, Yuri Lebedev, Sergei Makarov, Aleksandr Maltsev, Boris Mikhailov, Vladimir Myshkin, Vasili Pervukhin, Vladimir Petrov, Aleksandr Skvortsov, Sergei Starikov, Vladislav Tretiak, Valeri Vasiliev, Viktor Zhluktov (Soviet Union)	Mats Åhlberg, Sture Andersson, Bo Berglund, Håkan Eriksson, Jan Eriksson, Thomas Eriksson, Leif Holmgren, Tomas Jonsson, Pelle Lindbergh, Bengt Lundholm, William Löfquist, Per Lundqvist, Lars Molin, Mats Näslund, Lennart Norberg, Tommy Samuelsson, Dan Söderström, Mats Waltin, Ulf Weinstock (Sweden)

Year	Gold	Silver	Bronze
1984	Zinetula Bilyaletdinov, Sergei Shepelev, Nikolai Drozdetsky, Viacheslav Fetisov, Aleksandr Geramisov, Alexei Kasatonov, Andrei Khomutov, Vladimir Kovin, Aleksandr Kozhevnikov, Vladimir Krutov, Igor Larionov, Sergei Makarov, Vladimir Myshkin, Vasili Pervukhin, Aleksandr Skvortsov, Sergei Starikov, Igor Stelnov, Vladislav Tretiak, Viktor Tyumenev, Mikhail Vasiliev (Soviet Union)	Jaroslav Benák, Vladimír Caldr, Milan Chalupa, František Černík, Miloslav Hořava, Jiří Hrdina, Arnold Kadlec, Jaroslav Korbela, Jiří Králík, Vladimír Kýhos, Jiří Lála, Igor Liba, Vincent Lukáč, Dušan Pašek, Pavel Richter, Jaromír Šindel, Radoslav Svoboda, Eduard Uvíra (Czechoslovakia)	Thomas Åhlén, Pelle Eklund, Thomas Eklund, Bo Eriksson, Håkan Eriksson, Peter Gradin, Mats Hessel, Peter Hjälm, Göran Lindblom, Tommy Mörth, Leif-Håkan Nordin, Rolf Ridderwall, Jens Öhling, Thomas Rundqvist, Tomas Sandström, Håkan Södergren, Mats Thelin, Michael Thelvén, Mats Waltin, Göte Wälitalo (Sweden)
1988	Ilya Byakin, Vyacheslav Bykov, Aleksandr Chernykh, Viacheslav Fetisov, Alexei Gusarov, Valeri Kamensky, Alexei Kasatonov, Andrei Khomutov, Aleksandr Kozhevnikov, Igor Kravchuk, Vladimir Krutov, Igor Larionov, Andrei Lomakin, Sergei Makarov, Alexander Mogilny, Sergei Mylnikov, Vitali Samoilov, Anatoli Semenov, Sergei Starikov, Igor Stelnov, Sergei Svetlov, Sergei Yashin (Soviet Union)	Timo Blomqvist, Kari Eloranta, Raimo Helminen, Iiro Järvi, Esa Keskinen, Erkki Laine, Kari Laitinen, Erkki Lehtonen, Jyrki Lumme, Reijo Mikkolainen, Jarmo Myllys, Teppo Numminen, Janne Ojanen, Arto Ruotanen, Reijo Ruotsalainen, Simo Saarinen, Kai Suikkanen, Timo Susi, Jukka Tammi, Jari Torkki, Pekka Tuomisto, Jukka Virtanen (Finland)	Mikael Andersson, Peter Åslin, Bo Berglund, Jonas Bergqvist, Anders Bergman, Thom Eklund, Anders Eldebrink, Peter Eriksson, Thomas Eriksson, Michael Hjälm, Lars Ivarsson, Mikael Johansson, Lars Karlsson, Mats Kihlström, Peter Lindmark, Lars Molin, Jens Öhling, Lars-Gunnar Pettersson, Thomas Rundqvist, Tommy Samuelsson, Ulf Sandström, Håkan Södergren (Sweden)
1992	Sergei Bautin, Igor Boldin, Nikolai Borschevsky, Vyacheslav Butsayev, Vyacheslav Bykov, Evgeny Davydov, Alexei Gusarov, Darius Kasparaitis, Nikolai Khabibulin, Yuri Khmylev, Andrei Khomutov, Andrei Kovalenko, Alexei Kovalev, Igor Kravchuk, Vladimir Malakhov, Dmitri Mironov, Sergei Petrenko, Vitali Prokhorov, Mikhail Shtalenkov, Andrei Trefilov, Dmitri Yushkevich, Alexei Zhamnov, Alexei Zhitnik, Sergei Zubov (Unified Team)	Dave Archibald, Todd Brost, Sean Burke, Kevin Dahl, Curt Giles, Dave Hannan, Gord Hynes, Fabian Joseph, Joé Juneau, Trevor Kidd, Patrick Lebeau, Chris Lindberg, Eric Lindros, Kent Manderville, Adrien Plavsic, Dan Ratushny, Sam St. Laurent, Brad Schlegel, Wally Schreiber, Randy Smith, Dave Tippett, Brian Tutt, Jason Woolley (Canada)	Patrik Augusta, Petr Bříza, Jaromír Dragan, Leo Gudas, Miloslav Hořava, Petr Hrbek, Otakar Janecký, Tomáš Jelínek, Drahomír Kadlec, Kamil Kašťák, Robert Lang, Igor Liba, Ladislav Lubina, František Procházka, Petr Rosol, Bedřich Ščerban, Jiří Šlégr, Richard Šmehlík, Róbert Švehla, Oldřich Svoboda, Radek T'oupal, Peter Veselovský, Richard Žemlička (Czechoslovakia)
1994	Håkan Algotsson, Jonas Bergqvist, Charles Berglund, Andreas Dackell, Christian Due-Boje, Niklas Eriksson, Peter Forsberg, Roger Hansson, Roger Johansson, Tomas Jonsson, Jörgen Jönsson, Kenny Jönsson, Patrik Juhlin, Patric Kjellberg, Håkan Loob, Mats Näslund, Stefan Örnskog, Leif Rohlin, Daniel Rydmark, Tommy Salo, Fredrik Stillman, Magnus Svensson (Sweden)	Mark Astley, Adrian Aucoin, David Harlock, Corey Hirsch, Todd Hlushko, Greg Johnson, Fabian Joseph, Paul Kariya, Chris Kontos, Manny Legacé, Ken Lovsin, Derek Mayer, Petr Nedvěd, Dwayne Norris, Greg Parks, Allain Roy, Jean-Yves Roy, Brian Savage, Brad Schlegel, Wally Schreiber, Chris Therien, Todd Warriner, Brad Werenka (Canada)	Mika Alatalo, Erik Hämäläinen, Raimo Helminen, Timo Jutila, Sami Kapanen, Esa Keskinen, Marko Kiprusoff, Saku Koivu, Pasi Kuivalainen, Janne Laukkanen, Tero Lehterä, Jere Lehtinen, Mikko Mäkelä, Jarmo Myllys, Mika Nieminen, Janne Ojanen, Marko Palo, Ville Peltonen, Pasi Sormunen, Mika Strömberg, Jukka Tammi, Petri Varis, Hannu Virta (Finland)

Year	Gold	Silver	Bronze
1998	Josef Beránek, Jan Čaloun, Roman Čechmánek, Jiří Dopita, Roman Hamrlík, Dominik Hašek, Milan Hejduk, Jaromír Jágr, František Kučera, Robert Lang, David Moravec, Pavel Patera, Libor Procházka, Martin Procházka, Robert Reichel, Martin Ručínský, Vladimír Růžička, Jiří Šlégr, Richard Šmehlík, Jaroslav Špaček, Martin Straka, Petr Svoboda (Czech Republic)	Pavel Bure, Valeri Bure, Oleg Shevtsov, Sergei Fedorov, Sergei Gonchar, Alexei Gusarov, Alexei Zhitnik, Valeri Kamensky, Darius Kasparaitis, Andrei Kovalenko, Igor Kravchuk, Sergei Krivokrasov, Boris Mironov, Dmitri Mironov, Aleksey Morozov, Sergei Nemchinov, Mikhail Shtalenkov, German Titov, Andrei Trefilov, Alexei Yashin, Dmitri Yushkevich, Valeri Zelepukin, Alexei Zhamnov (Russia)	Aki-Petteri Berg, Tuomas Grönman, Raimo Helminen, Sami Kapanen, Saku Koivu, Jari Kurri, Janne Laukkanen, Jere Lehtinen, Juha Lind, Jyrki Lumme, Jarmo Myllys, Mika Nieminen, Janne Niinimaa, Teppo Numminen, Ville Peltonen, Kimmo Rintanen, Teemu Selänne, Ari Sulander, Jukka Tammi, Esa Tikkanen, Kimmo Timonen, Antti Törmänen, Juha Ylönen (Finland)
2002	Ed Belfour, Rob Blake, Eric Brewer, Martin Brodeur, Theoren Fleury, Adam Foote, Simon Gagné, Jarome Iginla, Curtis Joseph, Ed Jovanovski, Paul Kariya, Mario Lemieux, Eric Lindros, Al MacInnis, Scott Niedermayer, Joe Nieuwendyk, Owen Nolan, Michael Peca, Chris Pronger, Joe Sakic, Brendan Shanahan, Ryan Smyth, Steve Yzerman (Canada)	Tony Amonte, Tom Barrasso, Chris Chelios, Adam Deadmarsh, Chris Drury, Mike Dunham, Bill Guerin, Phil Housley, Brett Hull, John LeClair, Brian Leetch, Aaron Miller, Mike Modano, Tom Poti, Brian Rafalski, Mike Richter, Jeremy Roenick, Brian Rolston, Gary Suter, Keith Tkachuk, Doug Weight, Mike York, Scott Young (United States)	Maxim Afinogenov, Ilya Bryzgalov, Pavel Bure, Valeri Bure, Pavel Datsyuk, Sergei Fedorov, Sergei Gonchar, Darius Kasparaitis, Nikolai Khabibulin, Ilya Kovalchuk, Alexei Kovalev, Igor Kravchuk, Oleg Kvasha, Igor Larionov, Vladimir Malakhov, Daniil Markov, Boris Mironov, Andrei Nikolishin, Yegor Podomatsky, Sergei Samsonov, Oleg Tverdovsky, Alexei Yashin, Alexei Zhamnov (Russia)
2006	Daniel Alfredsson, P. J. Axelsson, Christian Bäckman, Peter Forsberg, Mika Hannula, Niclas Hävelid, Tomas Holmström, Jörgen Jönsson, Kenny Jönsson, Niklas Kronwall, Nicklas Lidström, Stefan Liv, Henrik Lundqvist, Fredrik Modin, Samuel Påhlsson, Mikael Samuelsson, Daniel Sedin, Henrik Sedin, Mats Sundin, Ronnie Sundin, Mikael Tellqvist, Daniel Tjärnqvist, Henrik Zetterberg, Mattias Öhlund (Sweden)	Niklas Bäckström, Aki-Petteri Berg, Niklas Hagman, Jukka Hentunen, Jussi Jokinen, Olli Jokinen, Niko Kapanen, Mikko Koivu, Saku Koivu, Lasse Kukkonen, Antti Laaksonen, Jere Lehtinen, Toni Lydman, Antti-Jussi Niemi, Ville Nieminen, Antero Niittymäki, Fredrik Norrena, Petteri Nummelin, Teppo Numminen, Ville Peltonen, Jarkko Ruutu, Sami Salo, Teemu Selänne, Kimmo Timonen (Finland)	Jan Bulis, Petr Čajánek, Patrik Eliáš, Martin Erat, Dominik Hašek, Milan Hejduk, Aleš Hemský, Milan Hnilička, Jaromír Jágr, František Kaberle, Tomáš Kaberle, Aleš Kotalík, Filip Kuba, Pavel Kubina, Robert Lang, Marek Malík, Rostislav Olesz, Václav Prospal, Martin Ručínský, Dušan Salfický, Jaroslav Špaček, Martin Straka, Tomáš Vokoun, David Výborný, Marek Židlický (Czech Republic)
2010	Patrice Bergeron, Dan Boyle, Martin Brodeur, Sidney Crosby, Drew Doughty, Marc-André Fleury, Ryan Getzlaf, Dany Heatley, Jarome Iginla, Duncan Keith, Roberto Luongo, Patrick Marleau, Brenden Morrow, Rick Nash, Scott Niedermayer, Corey Perry, Chris Pronger, Mike Richards, Brent Seabrook, Eric Staal, Joe Thornton, Jonathan Toews, Shea Weber (Canada)	David Backes, Dustin Brown, Ryan Callahan, Chris Drury, Tim Gleason, Erik Johnson, Jack Johnson, Patrick Kane, Ryan Kesler, Phil Kessel, Jamie Langenbrunner, Ryan Malone, Ryan Miller, Brooks Orpik, Zach Parise, Joe Pavelski, Jonathan Quick, Brian Rafalski, Bobby Ryan, Paul Stastny, Ryan Suter, Tim Thomas, Ryan Whitney (United States)	Niklas Bäckström, Valtteri Filppula, Niklas Hagman, Jarkko Immonen, Olli Jokinen, Niko Kapanen, Miikka Kiprusoff, Mikko Koivu, Saku Koivu, Lasse Kukkonen, Jere Lehtinen, Sami Lepistö, Toni Lydman, Antti Miettinen, Antero Niittymäki, Janne Niskala, Ville Peltonen, Joni Pitkänen, Jarkko Ruutu, Tuomo Ruutu, Sami Salo, Teemu Selänne, Kimmo Timonen (Finland)

Women's Ice Hockey

Year	Gold	Silver	Bronze
1998	Chris Bailey, Laurie Baker, Alana Blahoski, Lisa Brown-Miller, Karyn Bye, Colleen Coyne, Sara Decosta, Tricia Dunn-Luoma, Cammi Granato, Katie King, Shelley Looney, Sue Merz, Allison Mleczko, Tara Mounsey, Vicki Movsessian, Jenny Potter, Angela Ruggiero, Sarah Tueting, Gretchen Ulion, Sandra Whyte (United States)	Jennifer Botterill, Thérèse Brisson, Cassie Campbell, Judy Diduck, Nancy Drolet, Lori Dupuis, Danielle Goyette, Geraldine Heaney, Jayna Hefford, Becky Kellar, Kathy McCormack, Karen Nystrom, Lesley Reddon, Manon Rhéaume, Laura Schuler, Fiona Smith, France St-Louis, Vicky Sunohara, Hayley Wickenheiser, Stacy Wilson (Canada)	Sari Fisk, Kirsi Hänninen, Satu Huotari, Marianne Ihalainen, Johanna Ikonen, Sari Krooks, Emma Laaksonen, Sanna Lankosaari, Katja Lehto, Marika Lehtimäki, Riikka Nieminen, Marja-Helena Pälvilä, Tuula Puputti, Karoliina Rantamäki, Tiia Reima, Katja Riipi, Päivi Salo, Maria Selin, Liisa-Maria Sneck, Petra Vaarakallio (Finland)
2002	Dana Antal, Kelly Bechard, Jennifer Botterill, Thérèse Brisson, Cassie Campbell, Isabelle Chartrand, Lori Dupuis, Danielle Goyette, Geraldine Heaney, Jayna Hefford, Becky Kellar, Caroline Ouellette, Cherie Piper, Cheryl Pounder, Tammy Lee Shewchuk, Sami Jo Small, Colleen Sostorics, Kim St-Pierre, Vicky Sunohara, Hayley Wickenheiser (Canada)	Chris Bailey, Laurie Baker, Karyn Bye, Julie Chu, Natalie Darwitz, Sara Decosta, Tricia Dunn-Luoma, Cammi Granato, Courtney Kennedy, Andrea Kilbourne, Katie King, Shelley Looney, Sue Merz, Allison Mleczko, Tara Mounsey, Jenny Potter, Angela Ruggiero, Sarah Tueting, Lyndsay Wall, Krissy Wendell (United States)	Annica Åhlén, Lotta Almblad, Anna Andersson, Gunilla Andersson, Emelie Berggren, Kristina Bergstrand, Ann-Louise Edstrand, Joa Elfsberg, Erika Holst, Nanna Jansson, Maria Larsson, Ylva Lindberg, Ulrica Lindström, Kim Martin, Josefin Pettersson, Maria Rooth, Danijela Rundqvist, Evelina Samuelsson, Therese Sjölander, Anna Vikman (Sweden)
2006	Meghan Agosta, Gillian Apps, Jennifer Botterill, Cassie Campbell, Gillian Ferrari, Danielle Goyette, Jayna Hefford, Becky Kellar, Gina Kingsbury, Charline Labonté, Carla MacLeod, Caroline Ouellette, Cherie Piper, Cheryl Pounder, Colleen Sostorics, Kim St-Pierre, Vicky Sunohara, Sarah Vaillancourt, Katie Weatherston, Hayley Wickenheiser (Canada)	Cecilia Andersson, Gunilla Andersson, Jenni Asserholt, Ann-Louise Edstrand, Joa Elfsberg, Emma Eliasson, Erika Holst, Nanna Jansson, Ylva Lindberg, Jenny Lindqvist, Kristina Lundberg, Kim Martin, Frida Nevalainen, Emilie O'Konor, Maria Rooth, Danijela Rundqvist, Therese Sjölander, Katarina Timglas, Anna Vikman, Pernilla Winberg (Sweden)	Caitlin Cahow, Julie Chu, Natalie Darwitz, Pam Dreyer, Tricia Dunn-Luoma, Molly Engstrom, Chanda Gunn, Jamie Hagerman, Kim Insalaco, Kathleen Kauth, Courtney Kennedy, Katie King, Kristin King, Sarah Parsons, Jenny Potter, Helen Resor, Angela Ruggiero, Kelly Stephens, Lyndsay Wall, Krissy Wendell (United States)
2010	Meghan Agosta, Gillian Apps, Tessa Bonhomme, Jennifer Botterill, Jayna Hefford, Haley Irwin, Rebecca Johnston, Becky Kellar, Gina Kingsbury, Charline Labonté, Carla MacLeod, Meaghan Mikkelson, Caroline Ouellette, Cherie Piper, Marie-Philip Poulin, Kim St-Pierre, Colleen Sostorics, Shannon Szabados, Sarah Vaillancourt, Catherine Ward, Hayley Wickenheiser (Canada)	Kacey Bellamy, Caitlin Cahow, Lisa Chesson, Julie Chu, Natalie Darwitz, Meghan Duggan, Molly Engstrom, Hilary Knight, Jocelyne Lamoureux, Monique Lamoureux, Erika Lawler, Gisele Marvin, Brianne McLaughlin, Jenny Schmidgall-Potter, Angela Ruggiero, Molly Schaus, Kelli Stack, Karen Thatcher, Jessie Vetter, Kerry Weiland, Jinelle Zaugg-Siergiej (United States)	Anne Helin, Jenni Hiirikoski, Venla Hovi, Michelle Karvinen, Mira Kuisma, Emma Laaksonen, Rosa Lindstedt, Terhi Mertanen, Heidi Pelttari, Mariia Posa, Annina Rajahuhta, Karoliina Rantamäki, Noora Räty, Mari Saarinen, Saija Sirviö, Nina Tikkinen, Minnamari Tuominen, Saara Tuominen, Linda Välimäki, Anna Vanhatalo, Marjo Voutilainen (Finland)

Figure Skating

Mixed Ice Dancing

Year	Gold	Silver	Bronze
1976	Lyudmila Pakhomova, Alexander Gorshkov (Soviet Union)	Irina Moiseyeva, Andrei Minenkov (Soviet Union)	Colleen O'Connor, James Millns (United States)
1980	Natalia Linichuk, Gennadi Karponossov (Soviet Union)	Krisztina Regőczy, András Sallay (Hungary)	Irina Moiseyeva, Andrei Minenkov (Soviet Union)
1984	Jayne Torvill, Christopher Dean (Great Britain)	Natalia Bestemianova, Andrei Bukin (Soviet Union)	Marina Klimova, Sergei Ponomarenko (Soviet Union)
1988	Natalia Bestemianova, Andrei Bukin (Soviet Union)	Marina Klimova, Sergei Ponomarenko (Soviet Union)	Tracy Wilson, Robert McCall (Canada)
1992	Marina Klimova, Sergei Ponomarenko (Unified Team)	Isabelle Duchesnay, Paul Duchesnay (France)	Maya Usova, Alexander Zhulin (Unified Team)
1994	Oksana Grishuk, Evgency Platov (Russia)	Maya Usova, Alexander Zhulin (Russia)	Jayne Torvill, Christopher Dean (Great Britain)
1998	Oksana Grishuk, Evgency Platov (Russia)	Anjelika Krylova, Oleg Ovsyannikov (Russia)	Marina Anissina, Gwendel Peizerat (France)
2002	Marina Anissina, Gwendel Peizerat (France)	Irina Lobacheva, Ilia Averbukh (Russia)	Barbara Fusar-Poli, Maurizio Margaglio (Italy)
2006	Tatiana Navka, Roman Kostomarov (Russia)	Tanith Belbin, Benjamin Agosto (United States)	Elena Grushina, Ruslan Goncharov (Ukraine)
2010	Tessa Virtue, Scott Moir (Canada)	Meryl Davis, Charlie White (United States)	Oksana Domnina, Maxim Shabalin (Russia)

Men's Singles

Year	Gold	Silver	Bronze
1908	Ulrich Salchow (Sweden)	Richard Johansson (Sweden)	Per Thorén (Sweden)
1912: Event not held			
1916: Olympics not held			
1920	Gillis Grafström (Sweden)	Andreas Krogh (Norway)	Martin Stixrud (Norway)
1924	Gillis Grafström (Sweden)	Willy Böckl (Austria)	Georges Gautschi (Switzerland)
1928	Gillis Grafström (Sweden)	Willy Böckl (Austria)	Robert van Zeebroeck (Belgium)
1932	Karl Schäfer (Austria)	Gillis Grafström (Sweden)	Montgomery Wilson (Canada)
1936	Karl Schäfer (Austria)	Ernst Baier (Germany)	Felix Kaspar (Austria)
1940–1944: Olympics not held			
1948	Dick Button (United States)	Hans Gerschwiler (Switzerland)	Edi Rada (Austria)
1952	Dick Button (United States)	Helmut Seibt (Austria)	James Grogan (United States)
1956	Hayes Alan Jenkins (United States)	Ronnie Robertson (United States)	David Jenkins (United States)
1960	David Jenkins (United States)	Karol Divín (Czechoslovakia)	Donald Jackson (Canada)
1964	Manfred Schnelldorfer (United Team of Germany)	Alain Calmat (France)	Scott Allen (United States)
1968	Wolfgang Schwarz (Austria)	Timothy Wood (United States)	Patrick Péra (France)
1972	Ondrej Nepela (Czechoslovakia)	Sergei Chetvertukhin (Soviet Union)	Patrick Péra (France)
1976	John Curry (Great Britain)	Vladimir Kovalev (Soviet Union)	Toller Cranston (Canada)
1980	Robin Cousins (Great Britain)	Jan Hoffman (East Germany)	Charles Tickner (United States)
1984	Scott Hamilton (United States)	Brian Orser (Canada)	Josef Sabovčík (Czechoslovakia)
1988	Brian Boitano (United States)	Brian Orser (Canada)	Viktor Petrenko (Soviet Union)
1992	Viktor Petrenko (Unified Team)	Paul Wylie (United States)	Petr Barna (Czechoslovakia)
1994	Alexei Urmanov (Russia)	Elvis Stojko (Canada)	Philippe Candeloro (France)
1998	Ilia Kulik (Russia)	Elvis Stojko (Canada)	Philippe Candeloro (France)
2002	Alexei Yagudin (Russia)	Evgeni Plushenko (Russia)	Timothy Goebel (United States)
2006	Evgeni Plushenko (Russia)	Stéphane Lambiel (Switzerland)	Jeffrey Buttle (Canada)
2010	Evan Lysacek (United States)	Evgeni Plushenko (Russia)	Daisuke Takahashi (Japan)

Men's Special Figures

Year	Gold	Silver	Bronze
1908	Nikolai Panin (Russia)	Arthur Cumming (Great Britain)	Geoffrey Hall-Say (Great Britain)

Women's Singles

Year	Gold	Silver	Bronze
1908	Madge Syers (Great Britain)	Elsa Rendschmidt (Germany)	Dorothy Greenhough-Smith (Great Britain)
1912: Event not held			
1916: Olympics not held			
1920	Magda Julin (Sweden)	Svea Norén (Sweden)	Theresa Weld (United States)
1924	Herma Szabo (Austria)	Beatrix Loughran (United States)	Ethel Muckelt (Great Britain)
1928	Sonja Henie (Norway)	Fritzi Burger (Austria)	Beatrix Loughran (United States)
1932	Sonja Henie (Norway)	Fritzi Burger (Austria)	Maribel Vinson (United States)
1936	Sonja Henie (Norway)	Cecilia Colledge (Great Britain)	Vivi-Anne Hultén (Sweden)
1940–1944: Olympics not held			
1948	Barbara Ann Scott (Canada)	Eva Pawlik (Austria)	Jeannette Altwegg (Great Britain)
1952	Jeannette Altwegg (Great Britain)	Tenley Albright (United States)	Jacqueline du Bief (France)
1956	Tenley Albright (United States)	Carol Heiss (United States)	Ingrid Wendl (Austria)
1960	Carol Heiss (United States)	Sjoukje Dijkstra (Netherlands)	Barbara Roles (United States)
1964	Sjoukje Dijkstra (Netherlands)	Regine Heitzer (Austria)	Petra Burka (Canada)
1968	Peggy Fleming (United States)	Gabriele Seyfert (East Germany)	Hana Mašková (Czechoslovakia)
1972	Beatrix Schuba (Austria)	Karen Magnussen (Canada)	Janet Lynn (United States)
1976	Dorothy Hamill (United States)	Dianne de Leeuw (Netherlands)	Christine Errath (East Germany)
1980	Anett Pötzsch (East Germany)	Linda Fratianne (United States)	Dagmar Lurz (West Germany)
1984	Katarina Witt (East Germany)	Rosalynn Sumners (United States)	Kira Ivanova (Soviet Union)
1988	Katarina Witt (East Germany)	Elizabeth Manley (Canada)	Debi Thomas (United States)
1992	Kristi Yamaguchi (United States)	Midori Ito (Japan)	Nancy Kerrigan (United States)
1994	Oksana Baiul (Ukraine)	Nancy Kerrigan (United States)	Chen Lu (China)
1998	Tara Lipinski (United States)	Michelle Kwan (United States)	Chen Lu (China)
2002	Sarah Hughes (United States)	Irina Slutskaya (Russia)	Michelle Kwan (United States)
2006	Shizuka Arakawa (Japan)	Sasha Cohen (United States)	Irina Slutskaya (Russia)
2010	Yuna Kim (South Korea)	Mao Asada (Japan)	Joannie Rochette (Canada)

Mixed Pairs

Year	Gold	Silver	Bronze
1908	Anna Hübler, Heinrich Burger (Germany)	Phyllis Johnson, James H. Johnson (Great Britain)	Madge Syers, Edgar Syers (Great Britain)
1912: Event not held			
1916: Olympics not held			
1920	Ludowika Jakobsson, Walter Jakobsson (Finland)	Alexia Bryn, Yngvar Bryn (Norway)	Phyllis Johnson, Basil Williams (Great Britain)
1924	Helene Engelmann, Alfred Berger (Austria)	Ludowika Jakobsson, Walter Jakobsson (Finland)	Andrée Joly, Pierre Brunet (France)
1928	Andrée Joly, Pierre Brunet (France)	Lilly Scholz, Otto Kaiser (Austria)	Melitta Brunner, Ludwig Wrede (Austria)
1932	Andrée Joly, Pierre Brunet (France)	Beatrix Loughran, Sherwin Badger (United States)	Emília Rotter, László Szollás (Hungary)
1936	Maxi Herber, Ernst Baier (Germany)	Ilse Pausin, Erik Pausin (Austria)	Emília Rotter, László Szollás (Hungary)
1940–1944: Olympics not held			
1952	Ria Falk, Paul Falk (Germany)	Karol Kennedy, Peter Kennedy (United States)	Marianna Nagy, László Nagy (Hungary)

Year	Gold	Silver	Bronze
1956	Sissy Schwarz, Kury Oppelt (Austria)	Frances Dafoe, Norris Bowden (Canada)	Marianna Nagy, László Nagy (Hungary)
1960	Barbara Wagner, Robert Paul (Canada)	Marika Kilius, Hans-Jürgen Bäumler (United Team of Germany)	Nancy Ludington, Ronald Ludington (United States)
1964	Ludmila Belousova, Oleg Protopopov (Soviet Union)	Marika Kilius, Hans-Jürgen Bäumler (United Team of Germany)	Debbi Wilkes, Guy Revell (Canada)
1968	Ludmila Belousova, Oleg Protopopov (Soviet Union)	Tatyana Zhuk, Aleksandr Gorelik (Soviet Union)	Margot Glockshuber, Wolfgang Danne (West Germany)
1972	Irina Rodnina, Alexei Ulanov (Soviet Union)	Lyudmila Smirnova, Andrei Suraikin (Soviet Union)	Manuela Groß, Uwe Kagelmann (East Germany)
1976	Irina Rodnina, Alexander Zaitsev (Soviet Union)	Romy Kermer, Rolf Österreich (East Germany)	Manuela Groß, Uwe Kagelmann (East Germany)
1980	Irina Rodnina, Alexander Zaitsev (Soviet Union)	Marina Cherkasova, Sergei Shakhrai (Soviet Union)	Manuela Mager, Uwe Bewersdorf (East Germany)
1984	Elena Valova, Oleg Vasiliev (Soviet Union)	Kitty Carruthers, Peter Carruthers (United States)	Larisa Selezneva, Oleg Makarov (Soviet Union)
1988	Ekaterina Gordeeva, Sergei Grinkov (Soviet Union)	Elena Valova, Oleg Vasiliev (Soviet Union)	Jill Watson, Peter Oppegard (United States)
1992	Natalia Mishkutenok, Artur Dmitriev (Unified Team)	Elena Bechke, Denis Petrov (Unified Team)	Isabelle Brasseur, Lloyd Eisler (Canada)
1994	Ekaterina Gordeeva, Sergei Grinkov (Russia)	Natalia Mishkutenok, Artur Dmitriev (Russia)	Isabelle Brasseur, Lloyd Eisler (Canada)
1998	Oksana Kazakova, Artur Dmitriev (Russia)	Elena Berezhnaya, Anton Sikharulidze (Russia)	Mandy Wötzel, Ingo Steuer (Germany)
2002	Elena Berezhnaya, Anton Sikharulidze (Russia) Jamie Salé, David Pelletier (Canada)	Not awarded	Shen Xue, Zhao Hongbo (China)
2006	Tatiana Totmianina, Maxim Marinin (Russia)	Zhang Dan, Zhang Hao (China)	Shen Xue, Zhao Hongbo (China)
2010	Shen Xue, Zhao Hongbo (China)	Pan Qing, Tong Jian (China)	Aliona Savchenko, Robin Szolkowy (Germany)

Freestyle Skiing

Men's Moguls

Year	Gold	Silver	Bronze
1992	Edgar Grospiron (France)	Olivier Allamand (France)	Nelson Carmichael (United States)
1994	Jean-Luc Brassard (Canada)	Sergey Shupletsov (Russia)	Edgar Grospiron (France)
1998	Jonny Moseley (United States)	Janne Lahtela (Finland)	Sami Mustonen (Finland)
2002	Janne Lahtela (Finland)	Travis Mayer (United States)	Richard Gay (France)
2006	Dale Begg-Smith (Australia)	Mikko Ronkainen (Finland)	Toby Dawson (United States)
2010	Alexandre Bilodeau (Canada)	Dale Begg-Smith (Australia)	Bryon Wilson (United States)

Men's Aerials

Year	Gold	Silver	Bronze
1994	Andreas Schönbächler (Switzerland)	Philippe LaRoche (Canada)	Lloyd Langlois (Canada)
1998	Eric Bergoust (United States)	Sébastien Foucras (France)	Smitri Dashinski (Belarus)
2002	Aleš Valenta (Czechoslovakia)	Joe Pack (United States)	Aleksei Grishin (Belarus)

Year	Gold	Silver	Bronze
2006	Han Xiaopeng (China)	Joe Pack (United States)	Vladimir Lebedev (Russia)
2010	Aleksei Grishin (Belarus)	Jeret Peterson (United States)	Liu Zhongqing (China)

Men's Ski Cross

Year	Gold	Silver	Bronze
2010	Michael Schmid (Switzerland)	Andreas Matt (Austria)	Audun Grønvold (Norway)

Women's Moguls

Year	Gold	Silver	Bronze
1992	Donna Weinbrecht (United States)	Yelizaveta Kozhevnikova (Unified Team)	Stine Lise Hattestad (Norway)
1994	Stine Lise Hattestad (Norway)	Elizabeth McIntyre (United States)	Yelizaveta Kozhevnikova (Russia)
1998	Tae Satoya (Japan)	Tatjana Mittermayer (Germany)	Kari Traa (Norway)
2002	Kari Traa (Norway)	Shannon Bahrke (United States)	Tae Satoya (Japan)
2006	Jennifer Heil (Canada)	Kari Traa (Norway)	Sandra Laoura (France)
2010	Hannah Kearney (United States)	Jennifer Heil (Canada)	Shannon Bahrke (United States)

Women's Aerials

Year	Gold	Silver	Bronze
1994	Lina Cheryazova (Uzbekistan)	Marie Lindgren (Sweden)	Hilde Synnøve Lid (Norway)
1998	Nikki Stone (United States)	Xu Nannan (China)	Colette Brand (Switzerland)
2002	Alisa Camplin (Australia)	Veronica Brenner (Canada)	Deidra Dionne (Canada)
2006	Evelyne Leu (Switzerland)	Li Nina (China)	Alisa Camplin (Australia)
2010	Lydia Lassila (Australia)	Li Nina (China)	Guo Xinxin (China)

Women's Ski Cross

Year	Gold	Silver	Bronze
2010	Ashleigh McIvor (Canada)	Hedda Berntsen (Norway)	Marion Josserand (France)

Women's Ballet

Year	Gold	Silver	Bronze
1992	Cornelia Kissling (Switzerland)	Cathy Fechoz (France)	Sharon Petzold (United States)

Men's Ballet

Year	Gold	Silver	Bronze
1992	Fabrice Becker (France)	Rune Kristiansen (Norway)	Lane Spina (United States)

Luge

Men's Singles

Year	Gold	Silver	Bronze
1964	Thomas Köhler (Unified Team of Germany)	Klaus Bonsack (Unified Team of Germany)	Hans Plenk (Unified Team of Germany)
1968	Manfred Schmid (Austria)	Thomas Köhler (East Germany)	Klaus Bonsack (East Germany)
1972	Wolfgang Scheidel (East Germany)	Harald Ehrig (East Germany)	Wolfram Fiedler (East Germany)
1976	Dettlef Günther (East Germany)	Josef Fendt (West Germany)	Hans Rinn (East Germany)
1980	Bernhard Glass (East Germany)	Paul Hildgartner (Italy)	Anton Winkler (West Germany)

Year	Gold	Silver	Bronze
1984	Paul Hildgartner (Italy)	Sergey Danilin (Soviet Union)	Valery Dudin (Soviet Union)
1988	Jens Müller (Germany)	Georg Hackl (West Germany)	Yuri Kharchendo (Soviet Union)
1992	Georg Hackl (Germany)	Markus Prock (Austria)	Markus Schmidt (Austria)
1994	Georg Hackl (Germany)	Markus Prock (Austria)	Armin Zöggeler (Italy)
1998	Georg Hackl (Germany)	Armin Zöggeler (Italy)	Jens Müller (Germany)
2002	Armin Zöggeler (Italy)	Georg Hackl (Germany)	Markus Prock (Austria)
2006	Armin Zöggeler (Italy)	Albert Demtschenko (Russia)	Mārtins Rubenis (Latvia)
2010	Felix Loch (Germany)	David Möller (Germany)	Armin Zöggeler (Italy)

Women's Singles

Year	Gold	Silver	Bronze
1964	Ortrun Enderlein (Unified Team of Germany)	Ilse Geisler (Unified Team of Germany)	Helene Thurner (Austria)
1968	Erica Lechner (Italy)	Christina Schmuck (West Germany)	Angelika Dünhaupt (West Germany)
1972	Anna-Maria Müller (East Germany)	Ute Rührold (East Germany)	Margit Schumann (East Germany)
1976	Margit Schumann (East Germany)	Ute Rührold (East Germany)	Elisabeth Demleitner (West Germany)
1980	Vera Zozula (Soviet Union)	Melitta Sollmann (East Germany)	Ingrida Amantova (Soviet Union)
1984	Steffi Martin (East Germany)	Bettina Schmidt (East Germany)	Ute Weiss (East Germany)
1988	Steffi Walter (East Germany)	Ute Oberhoffner (East Germany)	Cerstin Schmidt (East Germany)
1992	Doris Neuner (Austria)	Angelika Neuner (Austria)	Susi Erdmann (Germany)
1994	Gerda Weissensteiner (Italy)	Susi Erdmann (Germany)	Andrea Tagwerker (Austria)
1998	Silke Kraushaar (Germany)	Barbara Niedernhuber (Germany)	Angelika Neuner (Austria)
2002	Sylke Otto (Germany)	Barbara Niedernhuber (Germany)	Silke Kraushaar (Germany)
2006	Sylke Otto (Germany)	Silke Kraushaar (Germany)	Tatjana Hüfner (Germany)
2010	Tatjana Hüfner (Germany)	Nina Reithmayer (Austria)	Natalie Geisenberger (Germany)

Mixed Doubles

Year	Gold	Silver	Bronze
1964	Josef Feistmantl, Manfred Stengl (Austria)	Reinhold Senn, Helmut Thaler (Austria)	Walter Aussendorfer, Sigisfredo Mair (Italy)
1968	Klaus Bonsack, Thomas Köhler (East Germany)	Manfred Schmid, Ewald Walch (Austria)	Wolfgang Winkler, Fritz Nachmann (West Germany)
1972	Horst Hörnlein, Reinhard Bredow (East Germany) / Paul Hildgartner, Walter Plaikner (Italy)	Not awarded	Klaus Bonsack, Wolfram Fiedler (East Germany)
1976	Hans Rinn, Norbert Hahn (East Germany)	Hans Brandner, Balthasar Schwarm (West Germany)	Rudolf Schmid, Franz Schachner (Austria)
1980	Hans Rinn, Norbert Hahn (East Germany)	Peter Gschnitzer, Karl Brunner (Italy)	Georg Fluckinger, Karl Schrott (Austria)
1984	Hans Stangassinger, Franz Wembacher (West Germany)	Yevgeny Belousov, Aleksandr Belyakov (Soviet Union)	Jörg Hoffmann, Jochen Pietzsch (East Germany)
1988	Jörg Hoffmann, Jochen Pietzsch (East Germany)	Stefan Krause, Jan Behrendt (East Germany)	Thomas Schwab, Wolfgang Staudinger (West Germany)
1992	Stefan Krausse, Jan Behrendt (Germany)	Yves Mankel, Thomas Rudolph (Germany)	Hansjörg Raffl, Norbert Huber (Italy)
1994	Kurt Brugger, Wilfried Huber (Italy)	Hansjörg Raffl, Norbert Huber (Italy)	Stefan Krausse, Jan Behrendt (Germany)
1998	Stefan Krausse, Jan Behrendt (Germany)	Chris Thorpe, Gordon Sheer (United States)	Mark Grimmette, Brian Martin (United States)

Year	Gold	Silver	Bronze
2002	Patric Leitner, Alexander Resch (Germany)	Mark Grimmette, Brian Martin (United States)	Chris Thorpe, Clay Ives (United States)
2006	Andreas Linger, Wolfgang Linger (Austria)	André Florschütz, Torsten Wustlich (Germany)	Gerhard Plankensteiner, Oswald Haselrieder (Italy)
2010	Andreas Linger, Wolfgang Linger (Austria)	Andris Šics, Juris Šics (Latvia)	Patric Leitner, Alexander Resch (Germany)

Nordic Combined

Men's 18-Kilometer/15-Kilometer Individual Gundersen

Year	Gold	Silver	Bronze
1924	Thorleif Haug (Norway)	Thoralf Strømstad (Norway)	Johan Grøttumsbråten (Norway)
1928	Johan Grøttumsbråten (Norway)	Hans Vinjarengen (Norway)	Jon Snersrud (Norway)
1932	Johan Grøttumsbråten (Norway)	Ole Stenen (Norway)	Hans Vinjarengen (Norway)
1936	Oddbjørn Hagen (Norway)	Olaf Hoffsbakken (Norway)	Sverre Brodahl (Norway)
1940–1944: Olympics not held			
1948	Heikki Hasu (Finland)	Martti Huhtala (Finland)	Sven Israelsson (Sweden)
1952	Simon Slåttvik (Norway)	Heikki Hasu (Finland)	Sverre Stenersen (Norway)
1956	Sverre Stenersen (Norway)	Bengt Eriksson (Sweden)	Franciszek Gąsienica Groń (Poland)
1960	Georg Thoma (United Team of Germany)	Tormod Knutsen (Norway)	Nikolay Gusakov (Soviet Union)
1964	Tormod Knutsen (Norway)	Nikolay Kiselyov (Soviet Union)	Georg Thoma (United Team of Germany)
1968	Franz Keller (West Germany)	Alois Kälin (Switzerland)	Andreas Kunz (East Germany)
1972	Ulrich Wehling (East Germany)	Rauno Miettinen (Finland)	Karl-Heinz Luck (East Germany)
1976	Ulrich Wehling (East Germany)	Urban Hettich (West Germany)	Konrad Winkler (East Germany)
1980	Ulrich Wehling (East Germany)	Jouko Karjalainen (Finland)	Konrad Winkler (East Germany)
1984	Tom Sandberg (Norway)	Jouko Karjalainen (Finland)	Jukka Ylipulli (Finland)
1988	Hippolyt Kempf (Switzerland)	Klaus Sulzenbacher (Austria)	Allar Levandi (Soviet Union)
1992	Fabrice Guy (France)	Sylvain Guillaume (France)	Klaus Sulzenbacher (Austria)
1994	Fred Børre Lundberg (Norway)	Takanori Kono (Japan)	Bjarte Engen Vik (Norway)
1998	Bjarte Engen Vik (Norway)	Samppa Lajunen (Finland)	Valeri Stolyarov (Russia)
2002	Samppa Lajunen (Finland)	Jaakko Tallus (Finland)	Felix Gottwald (Austria)
2006	Georg Hettich (Germany)	Felix Gottwald (Austria)	Magnus Moan (Norway)

Men's 10-Kilometer Individual Normal Hill

Year	Gold	Silver	Bronze
2010	Jason Lamy-Chappuis (France)	Johnny Spillane (United States)	Alessandro Pittin (Italy)

Men's 3 × 10-Kilometer Team

Year	Gold	Silver	Bronze
1988	Thomas Müller, Hans-Peter Pohl, Hubert Schwarz (West Germany)	Fredy Glanzmann, Hippolyt Kempf, Andreas Schaad (Switzerland)	Hansjörg Aschenwald, Günther Csar, Klaus Sulzenbacher (Austria)
1992	Reiichi Mikata, Takanori Kono, Kenji Ogiwara (Japan)	Knut Tore Apeland, Fred Børre Lundberg, Trond-Einar Elden (Norway)	Klaus Ofner, Stefan Kreiner, Klaus Sulzenbacher (Austria)
1994	Takanori Kono, Masashi Abe, Kenji Ogiwara (Japan)	Knut Tore Apeland, Bjarte Engen Vik, Fred Børre Lundberg (Norway)	Jean-Yves Cuendet, Hippolyt Kempf, Andreas Schaad (Switzerland)

Men's 4 × 5-Kilometer Team

Year	Gold	Silver	Bronze
1998	Halldor Skard, Kenneth Braaten, Bjarte Engen Vik, Fred Börre Lundberg (Norway)	Samppa Lajunen, Jari Mantila, Tapio Nurmela, Hannu Manninen (Finland)	Sylvain Guillaume, Nicolas Bal, Ludovic Roux, Fabrice Guy (France)
2002	Jari Mantila, Hannu Manninen, Jaakko Tallus, Samppa Lajunen (Finland)	Björn Kircheisen, Georg Hettich, Marcel Höhlig, Ronny Ackermann (Germany)	Christoph Bieler, Michael Gruber, Mario Stecher, Felix Gottwald (Austria)
2006	Michael Gruber, Christoph Bieler, Felix Gottwald, Mario Stecher (Austria)	Björn Kircheisen, Georg Hettich, Ronny Ackermann, Jens Gaiser (Germany)	Antti Kuisma, Anssi Koivuranta, Jaakko Tallus, Hannu Manninen (Finland)
2010	Bernhard Gruber, Felix Gottwald, Mario Stecher, David Kreiner (Austria)	Brett Camerota, Todd Lodwick, Johnny Spillane, Bill Demong (United States)	Johannes Rydzek, Tino Edelmann, Eric Frenzel, Björn Kircheisen (Germany)

Men's 7.5-Kilometer Sprint

Year	Gold	Silver	Bronze
2002	Samppa Lajunen (Finland)	Ronny Ackermann (Germany)	Felix Gottwald (Austria)
2006	Felix Gottwald (Austria)	Magnus Moan (Norway)	Georg Hettich (Germany)

Men's 10-Kilometer Individual Large Hill

Year	Gold	Silver	Bronze
2010	Bill Demong (United States)	Johnny Spillane (United States)	Bernhard Gruber (Austria)

Speed Skating

Men's 500-Meter

Year	Gold	Silver	Bronze
1924	Charles Jewtraw (United States)	Oskar Olsen (Norway)	Roald Larsen (Norway) /, Clas Thunberg (Finland)
1928	Bernt Evensen (Norway), Clas Thunberg (Finland)	Not awarded	Jaakko Friman (Finland)
1932	Jack Shea (United States)	Bernt Evensen (Norway)	Alexander Hurd (Canada)
1936	Ivar Ballangrud (Norway)	Georg Krog (Norway)	Leo Freisinger (United States)
1940–1944: Olympics not held			
1948	Finn Helgesen (Norway)	Ken Bartholomew (United States) Thomas Byberg (Norway) Bob Fitzgerald (United States)	Not awarded
1952	Ken Henry (United States)	Don McDermott (United States)	Gordon Audley (Canada) Arne Johansen (Norway)
1956	Yevgeny Grishin (Soviet Union)	Rafayel Grach (Soviet Union)	Alv Gjestvang (Norway)
1960	Yevgeny Grishin (Soviet Union)	Bill Disney (United States)	Rafayel Grach (Soviet Union)
1964	Terry McDermott (United States)	Alv Gjestvang (Norway) Yevgeny Grishin (Soviet Union) Vladimir Orlov (Soviet Union)	Not awarded
1968	Erhard Keller (West Germany)	Terry McDermott (United States) Magne Thomassen (Norway)	Not awarded
1972	Erhard Keller (West Germany)	Hasse Börjes (Sweden)	Valery Muratov (Soviet Union)
1976	Yevgeny Kulikov (Soviet Union)	Valery Muratov (Soviet Union)	Dan Immerfall (United States)
1980	Eric Heiden (United States)	Yevgeny Kulikov (Soviet Union)	Lieuwe de Boer (Netherlands)
1984	Sergey Fokichev (Soviet Union)	Yoshihiro Kitazawa (Japan)	Gaétan Boucher (Canada)
1988	Uwe-Jens Mey (East Germany)	Jan Ykema (Netherlands)	Akira Kuroiwa (Japan)

Year	Gold	Silver	Bronze
1992	Uwe-Jens Mey (Germany)	Toshiyuki Kuroiwa (Japan)	Junichi Inoue (Japan)
1994	Aleksandr Golubev (Russia)	Sergey Klevchenya (Russia)	Manabu Horii (Japan)
1998	Hiroyasu Shimizu (Japan)	Jeremy Wotherspoon (Canada)	Kevin Overland (Canada)
2002	Casey FitzRandolph (United States)	Hiroyasu Shimizu (Japan)	Kip Carpenter (United States)
2006	Joey Cheek (United States)	Dmitry Dorofeyev (Russia)	Lee Kang-Seok (South Korea)
2010	Mo Tae-Bum (South Korea)	Keiichiro Nagashima (Japan)	Joji Kato (Japan)

Men's 1,000-Meter

Year	Gold	Silver	Bronze
1976	Peter Mueller (United States)	Jørn Didriksen (Norway)	Valery Muratov (Soviet Union)
1980	Eric Heiden (United States)	Gaétan Boucher (Canada)	Vladimir Lobanov (Soviet Union)
1984	Gaétan Boucher (Canada)	Sergey Khlebnikov (Soviet Union)	Kai Arne Engelstad (Norway)
1988	Nikolay Gulyayev (Soviet Union)	Uwe-Jens Mey (East Germany)	Igor Zhelezovski (Soviet Union)
1992	Olaf Zinke (Germany)	Kim Yoon-man (South Korea)	Yukinori Miyabe (Japan)
1994	Dan Jansen (United States)	Igor Zhelezovski (Belarus)	Sergey Klevchenya (Russia)
1998	Ids Postma (Netherlands)	Jan Bos (Netherlands)	Hiroyasu Shimizu (Japan)
2002	Gerard van Velde (Netherlands)	Jan Bos (Netherlands)	Joey Cheek (United States)
2006	Shani Davis (United States)	Joey Cheek (United States)	Erben Wennemars (Netherlands)
2010	Shani Davis (United States)	Mo Tae-Bum (Japan)	Chad Hedrick (United States)

Men's 1,500-Meter

Year	Gold	Silver	Bronze
1924	Clas Thunberg (Finland)	Roald Larsen (Norway)	Sigurd Moen (Norway)
1928	Clas Thunberg (Finland)	Bernt Evensen (Norway)	Ivar Ballangrud (Norway)
1932	Jack Shea (United States)	Alex Hurd (Canada)	Willy Logan (Canada)
1936	Charles Mathiesen (Norway)	Ivar Ballangrud (Norway)	Birger Wasenius (Finland)
1940–1944: Olympics not held			
1948	Sverre Farstad (Norway)	Åke Seyffarth (Sweden)	Odd Lundberg (Norway)
1952	Hjalmar Andersen (Norway)	Wim van der Voort (Netherlands)	Roald Aas (Norway)
1956	Yevgeny Grishin (Soviet Union) Yuri Mikhaylov (Soviet Union)	Not awarded	Toivo Salonen (Finland)
1960	Roald Aas (Norway) Yevgeny Grishin (Soviet Union)	Not awarded	Boris Stenin (Soviet Union)
1964	Ants Antson (Soviet Union)	Kees Verkerk (Netherlands)	Villy Haugen (Norway)
1968	Kees Verkerk (Netherlands)	Ivar Eriksen (Norway) Ard Schenk (Netherlands)	Not awarded
1972	Ard Schenk (Netherlands)	Roar Grønvold (Norway)	Göran Claeson (Sweden)
1976	Jan Egil Storholt (Norway)	Yuri Kondakov (Soviet Union)	Hans van Helden (Netherlands)
1980	Eric Heiden (United States)	Kay Arne Stenshjemmet (Norway)	Terje Andersen (Norway)
1984	Gaétan Boucher (Canada)	Sergey Khlebnikov (Soviet Union)	Oleg Bozhev (Soviet Union)
1988	André Hoffmann (East Germany)	Eric Flaim (United States)	Michael Hadschieff (Austria)
1992	Johan Olav Koss (Norway)	Ådne Søndrål (Norway)	Leo Visser (Netherlands)
1994	Johan Olav Koss (Norway)	Rintje Ritsma (Netherlands)	Falko Zandstra (Netherlands)
1998	Ådne Søndrål (Norway)	Ids Postma (Netherlands)	Rintje Ritsma (Netherlands)
2002	Derek Parra (United States)	Jochem Uytdehaage (Netherlands)	Ådne Søndrål (Norway)
2006	Enrico Fabris (Italy)	Shani Davis (United States)	Chad Hedrick (United States)
2010	Mark Tuitert (Netherlands)	Shani Davis (United States)	Håvard Bøkko (Norway)

Men's 5,000-Meter

Year	Gold	Silver	Bronze
1924	Clas Thunberg (Finland)	Julius Skutnabb (Finland)	Roald Larsen (Norway)
1928	Ivar Ballangrud (Norway)	Julius Skutnabb (Finland)	Bernt Evensen (Norway)
1932	Irving Jaffee (United States)	Eddie Murphy (United States)	Willy Logan (Canada)
1936	Ivar Ballangrud (Norway)	Birger Wasenius (Finland)	Antero Ojala (Finland)
1940–1944: Olympics not held			
1948	Reidar Liaklev (Norway)	Odd Lundberg (Norway)	Göthe Hedlund (Sweden)
1952	Hjalmar Andersen (Norway)	Kees Broekman (Netherlands)	Sverre Haugli (Norway)
1956	Boris Shilkov (Soviet Union)	Sigge Ericsson (Sweden)	Oleg Goncharenko (Soviet Union)
1960	Viktor Kosichkin (Soviet Union)	Knut Johannesen (Norway)	Jan Pesman (Netherlands)
1964	Knut Johannesen (Norway)	Per Ivar Moe (Norway)	Fred Anton Maier (Norway)
1968	Fred Anton Maier (Norway)	Kees Verkerk (Netherlands)	Peter Nottet (Netherlands)
1972	Ard Schenk (Netherlands)	Roar Grønvold (Norway)	Sten Stensen (Norway)
1976	Sten Stensen (Norway)	Piet Kleine (Netherlands)	Hans van Helden (Netherlands)
1980	Eric Heiden (United States)	Kay Arne Stenshjemet (Norway)	Tom Erik Oxholm (Norway)
1984	Tomas Gustafson (Sweden)	Igor Malkov (Soviet Union)	René Schøfisch (East Germany)
1988	Tomas Gustafson (Sweden)	Leo Visser (Netherlands)	Gerard Kemkers (Netherlands)
1992	Geir Karlstad (Norway)	Falko Zandstra (Netherlands)	Leo Visser (Netherlands)
1994	Johann Olav Koss (Norway)	Kjell Storelid (Norway)	Rintje Ritsma (Netherlands)
1998	Gianni Romme (Netherlands)	Rintje Ritsma (Netherlands)	Bart Veldkamp (Belgium)
2002	Jochem Uytdehaage (Netherlands)	Derek Parra (United States)	Jens Boden (Germany)
2006	Chad Hedrick (United States)	Sven Kramer (Netherlands)	Enrico Fabris (Italy)
2010	Sven Kramer (Netherlands)	Lee Seung-Hoon (South Korea)	Ivan Skobrev (Russia)

Men's 10,000-Meter

Year	Gold	Silver	Bronze
1924	Julius Skutnabb (Finland)	Clas Thunberg (Finland)	Roald Larsen (Norway)
1928: Event not held			
1932	Irving Jaffee (United States)	Ivar Ballangrud (Norway)	Franck Stack (Canada)
1936	Ivar Ballangrud (Norway)	Birger Wasenius (Finland)	Max Stiepl (Austria)
1940–1944: Olympics not held			
1948	Åke Seyffarth (Sweden)	Lassi Parkkinen (Finland)	Pentti Lammio (Finland)
1952	Hjalmar Andersen (Norway)	Kees Broekman (Netherlands)	Carl-Erik Asplund (Sweden)
1956	Sigge Ericsson (Sweden)	Knut Johannesen (Norway)	Oleg Goncharenko (Soviet Union)
1960	Knut Johannesen (Norway)	Viktor Kosichkin (Soviet Union)	Kjell Bäckman (Sweden)
1964	Johnny Nilsson (Sweden)	Fred Anton Maier (Norway)	Knut Johannesen (Norway)
1968	Johnny Höglin (Sweden)	Fred Anton Maier (Norway)	Örjan Sandler (Sweden)
1972	Ard Schenk (Netherlands)	Kees Verkerk (Netherlands)	Sten Stensen (Norway)
1976	Piet Kleine (Netherlands)	Sten Stensen (Norway)	Hans van Helden (Netherlands)
1980	Eric Heiden (United States)	Piet Kleine (Netherlands)	Tom Erik Oxholm (Norway)
1984	Igor Malkov (Soviet Union)	Tomas Gustafson (Sweden)	René Schöfisch (East Germany)
1988	Tomas Gustafson (Sweden)	Michael Hadschieff (Austria)	Leo Visser (Netherlands)
1992	Bart Veldkamp (Netherlands)	Johann Olav Koss (Norway)	Geir Karlstad (Norway)
1994	Johann Olav Koss (Norway)	Kjell Storelid (Norway)	Bart Veldkamp (Netherlands)
1998	Gianni Romme (Netherlands)	Bob de Jong (Netherlands)	Rintje Ritsma (Netherlands)
2002	Jochem Uytdehaage	Gianni Romme (Netherlands)	Lasse Sætre (Norway)
2006	Bob de Jong (Netherlands)	Chad Hedrick (United States)	Carl Verheijen (Netherlands)
2010	Lee Seung-Hoon (South Korea)	Ivan Skobrev (Russia)	Bob de Jong (Netherlands)

Men's Team Pursuit

Year	Gold	Silver	Bronze
2006	Matteo Anesi, Stefano Donagrandi, Enrico Fabris, Ippolito Sanfratello (Italy)	Arne Dankers, Steven Elm, Denny Morrison, Jason Parker, Justin Warsylewicz (Canada)	Jan Blokhuijsen, Sven Kramer, Simon Kuipers, Mark Tuitert (Netherlands)
2010	Mathieu Giroux, Lucas Makowsy, Denny Morrison (Canada)	Brian Hansen, Chad Hedrick, Jonathan Kuck, Trevor Marsicano (United States)	Jan Blokhuijsen, Sven Kramer, Simon Kuipers, Mark Tuitert (Netherlands)

Women's 500-Meter

Year	Gold	Silver	Bronze
1960	Helga Haase (United Team of Germany)	Nataliya Donchenko (Soviet Union)	Jeanne Ashworth (United States)
1964	Lidiya Skoblikova (Soviet Union)	Irina Egorova (Soviet Union)	Tatyana Sidorova (Soviet Union)
1968	Lyudmila Titova (Soviet Union)	Jenny Fish (United States) Dianne Holum (United States) Mary Meyers (United States)	Not awarded
1972	Anne Henning (United States)	Vera Krasnova (Soviet Union)	Lyudmila Titova (Soviet Union)
1976	Sheila Young (United States)	Cathy Priestner (Canada)	Tatyana Averina (Soviet Union)
1980	Karin Enke (East Germany)	Leah Poulos-Mueller (United States)	Natalya Petrusyova (Soviet Union)
1984	Christa Rothenburger (East Germany)	Karin Enke (East Germany)	Natalya Shive (Soviet Union)
1988	Bonnie Blair (United States)	Christa Rothenburger (East Germany)	Karin Enke (East Germany)
1992	Bonnie Blair (United States)	Ye Qiaobo (China)	Christa Luding (Germany)
1994	Bonnie Blair (United States)	Susan Auch (Canada)	Franziska Schenk (Germany)
1998	Catriona Le May Doan (Canada)	Susan Auch (Canada)	Tomomi Okazaki (Japan)
2002	Catriona Le May Doan (Canada)	Monique Garbrecht-Enfeldt (Germany)	Sabine Völker (Germany)
2006	Svetlana Zhurova (Russia)	Wang Manli (China)	Ren Hui (China)
2010	Lee Sang-Hwa (South Korea)	Jenny Wolf (Germany)	Wang Beixing (China)

Women's 1,000-Meter

Year	Gold	Silver	Bronze
1960	Klara Guseva (Soviet Union)	Helga Haase (United Team of Germany)	Tamara Rylova (Soviet Union)
1964	Lidiya Skoblikova (Soviet Union)	Irina Egorova (Soviet Union)	Kaija Mustonen (Finland)
1968	Carry Geijssen (Netherlands)	Lyudmila Titova (Soviet Union)	Dianne Holum (United States)
1972	Monika Pflug (West Germany)	Atje Keulen-Deelstra (Netherlands)	Anne Henning (United States)
1976	Tatyana Averina (Soviet Union)	Leah Poulos (United States)	Sheila Young (United States)
1980	Natalya Petrusyova (Soviet Union)	Leah Poulos-Mueller (United States)	Sylvia Albrecht (East Germany)
1984	Karin Enke (East Germany)	Andrea Schöne (East Germany)	Natalya Petrusyova (Soviet Union)
1988	Christa Rothenburger (East Germany)	Karin Enke (East Germany)	Bonnie Blair (United States)
1992	Bonnie Blair (United States)	Ye Qiaobo (China)	Monique Garbrecht (Germany)
1994	Bonnie Blair (United States)	Anke Baier (Germany)	Ye Qiaobo (China)
1998	Marianne Timmer (Netherlands)	Christine Witty (United States)	Catriona Le May Doan (Canada)
2002	Christine Witty (United States)	Sabine Völker (Germany)	Jennifer Rodriguez (United States)
2006	Marianne Timmer (Netherlands)	Cindy Klassen (Canada)	Anni Friesinger (Germany)
2010	Christine Nesbitt (Canada)	Annette Gerritsen (Netherlands)	Laurine van Riessen (Netherlands)

Women's 1,500-Meter

Year	Gold	Silver	Bronze
1960	Lidiya Skoblikova (Soviet Union)	Elwira Seroczynska (Poland)	Helena Pilejczyk (Poland)
1964	Lidiya Skoblikova (Soviet Union)	Kaija Mustonen (Finland)	Berta Kolokoltseva (Soviet Union)
1968	Kaija Mustonen (Finland)	Carry Geijssen (Netherlands)	Stien Kaiser (Netherlands)
1976	Galina Stepanskaya (Soviet Union)	Sheila Young (United States)	Tatyana Averina (Soviet Union)
1976	Dianne Holum (United States)	Stien Baas-Kaiser (Netherlands)	Atje Keulen-Deelstra (Netherlands)
1980	Annie Borckink (Netherlands)	Ria Visser (Netherlands)	Sabine Becker (East Germany)
1984	Karin Enke (East Germany)	Andrea Schöne (East Germany)	Natalya Petrusyova (Soviet Union)
1988	Yvonne van Gennip (Netherlands)	Karin Enke (East Germany)	Andrea Ehrig (East Germany)
1992	Jacqueline Börner (Germany)	Gunda Niemann (Germany)	Seiko Hashimoto (Japan)
1994	Ernese Hunyady (Austria)	Svetlana Fedotkina (Russia)	Gunda Niemann (Germany)
1998	Marianne Timmer (Netherlands)	Grunda Niemann-Stirnemann (Germany)	Christine Witty (United States)
2002	Anni Friesinger (Germany)	Sabine Völker (Germany)	Jennifer Rodriguez (United States)
2006	Cindy Klassen (Canada)	Kristina Groves (Canada)	Ireen Wüst (Netherlands)
2010	Ireen Wüst (Netherlands)	Kristina Groves (Canada)	Martina Sáblíková (Czech Republic)

Women's 3,000-Meter

Year	Gold	Silver	Bronze
1960	Lidiya Skoblikova (Soviet Union)	Valentina Stenina (Soviet Union)	Eevi Huttunen (Finland)
1964	Lidiya Skoblikova (Soviet Union)	Han Pil-Hwa (North Korea) Valentina Stenina (Soviet Union)	Not awarded
1968	Ans Schut (Netherlands)	Kaija Mustonen (Finland)	Stien Kaiser (Netherlands)
1972	Stien Baas-Kaiser (Netherlands)	Dianne Holum (United States)	Atje Keulen-Deelstra (Netherlands)
1976	Tatyana Averina (Soviet Union)	Andrea Mitscherlich (East Germany)	Lisbeth Korsmo (Norway)
1980	Bjørg Eva Jensen (Norway)	Sabine Becker (East Germany)	Beth Heiden (United States)
1984	Andrea Schöne (East Germany)	Karin Enke (East Germany)	Gabi Schöbrunn (East Germany)
1988	Yvonne van Gennip (Netherlands)	Andrea Ehrig (East Germany)	Gabi Zange-Schöbrunn (East Germany)
1992	Gunda Niemann (Germany)	Heike Warnicke (Germany)	Ernese Hunyady (Austria)
1994	Svetlana Bazhanova (Russia)	Ernese Hunyady (Austria)	Claudia Pechstein (Germany)
1998	Gunda Niemann-Stirnemann (Germany)	Claudia Pechstein (Germany)	Anni Friesinger (Germany)
2002	Claudia Pechstein (Germany)	Renate Groenewold (Netherlands)	Cindy Klassen (Canada)
2006	Ireen Wüst (Netherlands)	Renate Groenewold (Netherlands)	Cindy Klassen (Canada)
2010	Martina Sáblíková (Czech Republic)	Stephanie Beckert (Germany)	Kristina Groves (Canada)

Women's 5,000-Meter

Year	Gold	Silver	Bronze
1988	Yvonne van Gennip (Netherlands)	Andrea Ehrig (East Germany)	Gabi Zange (East Germany)
1992	Gunda Niemann (Germany)	Heike Warnicke (Germany)	Claudia Pechstein (Germany)
1994	Claudia Pechstein (Germany)	Gunda Niemann (Germany)	Hiromi Yamamoto (Japan)
1998	Claudia Pechstein (Germany)	Gunda Niemann-Stirnemann (Germany)	Lyudmila Prokasheva (Kazakhstan)
2002	Claudia Pechstein (Germany)	Gretha Smit (Netherlands)	Clara Hughes (Canada)
2006	Clara Hughes (Canada)	Claudia Pechstein (Germany)	Cindy Kassen (Canada)
2010	Martina Sáblíková (Czech Republic)	Stephanie Beckert (Germany)	Clara Hughes (Canada)

Women's Team Pursuit

Year	Gold	Silver	Bronze
2006	Daniela Anschütz-Thoms, Anni Friesinger, Lucille Opitz, Claudia Pechstein, Sabine Völker (Germany)	Kristina Groves, Clara Hughes, Cindy Klassen, Christine Nesbitt, Shannon Rempel (Canada)	Yekaterina Abramova, Varvara Barysheva, Galina Likhachova, Yekaterina Lobysheva, Svetlana Vysokova (Russia)
2010	Daniela Anschütz-Thoms, Stephanie Beckert, Anni Friesinger-Postma, Katrin Mattscherodt (Germany)	Masako Hozumi, Nao Kodaira, Maki Tabata (Japan)	Katarzyna Bachleda-Curuś, Katarzyna Woźniak, Luiza Złotkowska (Poland)

Men's All-Round

Year	Gold	Silver	Bronze
1924	Clas Thunberg (Finland)	Roald Larsen (Norway)	Julius Skutnabb (Finland)

Skeleton

Men's Skeleton

Year	Gold	Silver	Bronze
1928	Jennison Heaton (United States)	John Heaton (United States)	David Carnegie (United Kingdom)
1932–1936: Event not held			
1940–1944: Olympics not held			
1948	Nino Bibbia (Italy)	John Heaton (United States)	John Crammond (United Kingdom)
1952–1998: Event not held			
2002	Jimmy Shea (United States)	Martin Rettl (Austria)	Gregor Stähli (Switzerland)
2006	Duff Gibson (Canada)	Jeff Pain (Canada)	Gregor Stähli (Switzerland)
2010	Jon Montgomery (Canada)	Martins Dukurs (Latvia)	Alexander Tretiakov (Russia)

Women's Skeleton

Year	Gold	Silver	Bronze
2002	Tristan Gale (United States)	Lea Ann Parsley (United States)	Alex Coomber (United Kingdom)
2006	Maya Pedersen (Switzerland)	Shelley Rudman (United Kingdom)	Mellisa Hollingsworth-Richards (Canada)
2010	Amy Williams (United Kingdom)	Kerstin Szymkowiak (Germany)	Anja Huber (Germany)

Ski Jumping

Men's Individual Normal Hill

Year	Gold	Silver	Bronze
1964	Veikko Kankkonen (Finland)	Toralf Engan (Norway)	Torgeir Brandtzæg (Norway)
1968	Jiří Raška (Czechoslovakia)	Reinhold Bachler (Austria)	Baldur Preiml (Austria)
1972	Yukio Kasaya (Japan)	Akitsugu Konno (Japan)	Selji Aochi (Japan)
1976	Hans-Georg Aschenbach (East Germany)	Jochen Danneberg (East Germany)	Karl Schnabl (Austria)
1980	Toni Innauer (Austria)	Manfred Deckert (East Germany) Hirokazu Yagi (Japan)	Not awarded
1984	Jens Weißflog (East Germany)	Matti Nykänen (Finland)	Jari Puikkonen (Finland)

Year	Gold	Silver	Bronze
1988	Matti Nykänen (Finland)	Pavel Ploc (Czechoslovakia)	Jiří Malec (Czechoslovakia)
1992	Ernst Vettori (Austria)	Martin Höllwarth (Austria)	Toni Nieminen (Finland)
1994	Espen Bredesen (Norway)	Lasse Ottesen (Norway)	Dieter Thoma (Germany)
1998	Jani Soininen (Finland)	Kazuyoshi Funaki (Japan)	Andreas Widhölzl (Austria)
2002	Simon Ammann (Switzerland)	Sven Hannawald (Germany)	Adam Małysz (Poland)
2006	Lars Bystøl (Norway)	Matti Hautamäki (Finland)	Roar Ljøkelsøy (Norway)
2010	Simon Ammann (Switzerland)	Adam Małysz (Poland)	Gregor Schlierenzauer (Austria)

Men's Individual Large Hill

Year	Gold	Silver	Bronze
1924	Jacob Tullin Thams (Norway)	Narve Bonna (Norway)	Anders Haugen (United States)
1928	Alf Andersen (Norway)	Sigmund Ruud (Norway)	Rudolf Burkert (Czechoslovakia)
1932	Birger Ruud (Norway)	Hans Beck (Norway)	Kaare Wahlberg (Norway)
1936	Birger Ruud (Norway)	Sven Eriksson (Sweden)	Reidar Andersen (Norway)
1940–1944: Olympics not held			
1948	Petter Hugsted (Norway)	Birger Ruud (Norway)	Thorleif Schjelderup (Norway)
1952	Arnfinn Bergmann (Norway)	Torbjørn Falkanger (Norway)	Karl Holmstrøm (Sweden)
1956	Antti Hyvärinen (Finland)	Aulis Kallakorpi (Finland)	Harry Glass (Unified Team of Germany)
1960	Helmut Recknagel (Unified Team of Germany)	Niilo Halonen (Finland)	Otto Leodolter (Austria)
1964	Toralf Engan (Norway)	Veikko Kankkonen (Finland)	Torgeir Brandtzæg (Norway)
1968	Vladimir Belussov (Soviet Union)	Jiří Raška (Czechoslovakia)	Lars Grini (Norway)
1972	Wojciech Fortuna (Poland)	Walter Steiner (Switzerland)	Rainer Schmidt (East Germany)
1976	Karl Schnabl (Austria)	Anton Innauer (Austria)	Henry Glaß (East Germany)
1980	Jouko Törmänen (Finland)	Hubert Neuper (Austria)	Jari Puikkonen (Finland)
1984	Matti Nykänen (Finland)	Jens Weißflog (East Germany)	Pavel Ploc (Czechoslovakia)
1988	Matti Nykänen (Finland)	Erik Johnsen (Norway)	Mataž Debelak (Yugoslavia)
1992	Toni Nieminen (Finland)	Martin Höllwarth (Austria)	Heinz Kuttin (Austria)
1994	Jens Weißflog (Germany)	Espen Bredesen (Norway)	Andreas Goldberger (Austria)
1998	Kazuyoshi Funaki (Japan)	Jani Soininen (Finland)	Masahiko Harada (Japan)
2002	Simon Amman (Switzerland)	Adam Małysz (Poland)	Matti Hautamäki (Finland)
2006	Thomas Morgenstern (Austria)	Andreas Kofler (Austria)	Lars Bystøl (Norway)
2010	Simon Amman (Switzerland)	Adam Małysz (Poland)	Gregor Schlierenzauer (Austria)

Men's Team Large Hill

Year	Gold	Silver	Bronze
1988	Ari-Pekka Nikkola, Matti Nykänen, Tuomo Ylipuli, Jari Puikkonen (Finland)	Primož Ulaga, Matjaž Zupan, Matjaž Debelak, Miran Tepeš (Yugoslavia)	Ole Christian Eidhammer, Jon Inge Kjørum, Ole Gunnar Fidjestøl, Erik Johnsen (Norway)
1992	Ari-Pekka Nikkola, Mika Laitinen, Risto Laakkonen, Toni Nieminen (Finland)	Heinz Kuttin, Ernst Vettori, Martin Höllwarth, Andreas Felder (Austria)	František Jež, Tomáš Goder, Jaroslav Sakala, Jiří Parma (Czechoslovakia)
1994	Hansjörg Jäkle, Christof Duffner, Dieter Thoma, Jens Weißflog (Germany)	Jinya Nishikata, Takanobu Okabe, Noriaki Kasai, Masahiko Harada (Japan)	Heinz Kuttin, Christian Moser, Stefan Horngacher, Andreas Goldberger (Austria)
1998	Takanobu Okabe, Hiroya Saito, Masahiko Harada, Kazuyoshi Funaki (Japan)	Sven Hannawald, Martin Schmitt, Hansjörg Jäkle, Dieter Thoma (Germany)	Reinhard Schwarzenberger, Martin Höllwarth, Stefan Horngacher, Andreas Widhölzl (Austria)
2002	Sven Hannawald, Stephan Hocke, Michael Uhrmann, Martin Schmitt (Germany)	Matti Hautamäki, Veli-Matti Lindström, Risto Jussilainen, Janne Ahonen (Finland)	Damjan Fras, Primož Peterka, Robert Kranjec, Peter Žonta (Slovenia)

Year	Gold	Silver	Bronze
2006	Andreas Widhölzl, Andreas Kofler, Martin Koch, Thomas Morgenstern (Austria)	Tami Kiuru, Janne Happonen, Janne Ahonen, Matti Hautamäki (Finland)	Lars Bystøl, Bjørn Einar Romøren, Tommy Ingebrigtsen, Roar Ljøkelsøy (Norway)
2010	Wolfgang Loitzl, Andreas Kofler, Thomas Morgenstern, Gregor Schlierenzauer (Austria)	Michael Neumayer, Andreas Wank, Martin Schmitt, Michael Uhrmann (Germany)	Anders Bardal, Tom Hilde, Johan Reme Evensen, Anders Jacobsen (Norway)

Snowboarding

Men's Halfpipe

Year	Gold	Silver	Bronze
1998	Gian Simmen (Switzerland)	Daniel Franck (Norway)	Ross Powers (United States)
2002	Ross Powers (United States)	Danny Kass (United States)	Jarret Thomas (United States)
2006	Shaun White (United States)	Danny Kass (United States)	Markku Koski (Finland)
2010	Shaun White (United States)	Peetu Piiroinen (Finland)	Scotty Lago (United States)

Men's Giant Slalom

Year	Gold	Silver	Bronze
1998	Ross Rebagliati (Canada)	Thomas Prugger (Italy)	Ueli Kestenholz (Switzerland)

Men's Parallel Giant Slalom

Year	Gold	Silver	Bronze
2002	Philipp Schoch (Switzerland)	Richard Richardsson (Sweden)	Chris Klug (United States)
2006	Philipp Schoch (Switzerland)	Simon Schoch (Switzerland)	Siegfried Grabner (Austria)
2010	Jasey-Jay Anderson (Canada)	Benjamin Karl (Austria)	Mathieu Bozzetto (France)

Men's Snowboard Cross

Year	Gold	Silver	Bronze
2006	Seth Wescott (United States)	Radoslav Židek (Slovakia)	Paul-Henri de Le Rue (France)
2010	Seth Wescott (United States)	Mike Robertson (Canada)	Tony Ramoin (France)

Women's Halfpipe

Year	Gold	Silver	Bronze
1998	Nicola Thost (Germany)	Stine Brun Kjeldaas (Norway)	Shannon Dunn-Downing (United States)
2002	Kelly Clark (United States)	Doriane Vidal (France)	Fabienne Reuteler (Switzerland)
2006	Hannah Teter (United States)	Gretchen Bleiler (United States)	Kjersti Buaas (Norway)
2010	Torah Bright (Australia)	Hannah Teter (United States)	Kelly Clark (United States)

Women's Giant Slalom

Year	Gold	Silver	Bronze
1998	Karine Ruby (France)	Heidi Maria Renoth (Germany)	Brigitte Köck (Austria)

Women's Parallel Giant Slalom

Year	Gold	Silver	Bronze
2002	Isabelle Blanc (France)	Karine Ruby (France)	Lidia Trettel (Italy)
2006	Daniela Meuli (Switzerland)	Amelie Kober (Germany)	Rosey Fletcher (United States)
2010	Nicolien Sauerbreij (Netherlands)	Ekaterina Ilyukhina (Russia)	Marion Kreiner (Austria)

Women's Snowboard Cross

Year	Gold	Silver	Bronze
2006	Tanja Frieden (Switzerland)	Lindsey Jacobellis (United States)	Dominique Maltais (Canada)
2010	Maëlle Ricker (Canada)	Déborah Anthonioz (France)	Olivia Nobs (Switzerland)

Short-Track Speed Skating

Men's 500-Meter

Year	Gold	Silver	Bronze
1994	Chae Ji-Hoon (South Korea)	Mirko Vuillermin (Italy)	Nicky Gooch (Great Britain)
1998	Takafumi Nishitani (Japan)	An Yulong (China)	Hitoshi Uematsu (Japan)
2002	Marc Gagnon (Canada)	Jonathan Guilmette (Canada)	Rusty Smith (United States)
2006	Apolo Anton Ohno (United States)	François-Louis Tremblay (Canada)	Ahn Hyun-Soo (South Korea)
2010	Charles Hamelin (Canada)	Sung Si-Bak (South Korea)	François-Louis Tremblay (Canada)

Men's 1,000-Meter

Year	Gold	Silver	Bronze
1992	Kim Ki-Hoon (South Korea)	Frédéric Blackburn (Canada)	Lee Joon-Ho (South Korea)
1994	Kim Ki-Hoon (South Korea)	Chae Ji-Hoon (South Korea)	Marc Gagnon (Canada)
1998	Kim Dong-Sung (South Korea)	Li Jiajun (China)	Éric Bédard (Canada)
2002	Steven Bradbury (Australia)	Apolo Anton Ohno (United States)	Mathieu Turcotte (United States)
2006	Ahn Hyun-Soo (South Korea)	Lee Ho-Suk (South Korea)	Apolo Anton Ohno (United States)
2010	Lee Jung-Su (South Korea)	Lee Ho-Suk (South Korea)	Apolo Anton Ohno (United States)

Men's 1,500-Meter

Year	Gold	Silver	Bronze
2002	Apolo Anton Ohno (United States)	Li Jiajun (China)	Marc Gagnon (Canada)
2006	Ahn Hyun-Soo (South Korea)	Lee Ho-Suk (South Korea)	Li Jiajun (China)
2010	Lee Jung-Su (South Korea)	Apolo Anton Ohno (United States)	J. R. Celski (United States)

Men's 5,000-Meter Relay

Year	Gold	Silver	Bronze
1992	Kim Ki-Hoon, Lee Joon-Ho, Mo Ji-Soo, Song Jae-Kun (South Korea)	Frédéric Blackburn, Laurent Daignault, Michel Daignault, Sylvain Gagnon, Mark Lackie (Canada)	Yuichi Akasaka, Tatsuyoshi Ishihara, Toshinobu Kawai, Tsutomu Kawasaki (Japan)
1994	Maurizio Carnino, Orazio Fagone, Hugo Herrnhof, Mirko Vuillermin (Italy)	Randy Bartz, John Coyle, Eric Flaim, Andrew Gabel (United States)	Steven Bradbury, Kieran Hansen, Andrew Murtha, Richard Nizielski (Australia)
1998	Éric Bédard, Derrick Campbell, François Drolet, Marc Gagnon (Canada)	Chae Ji-Hoon, Lee Jun-Hwan, Lee Ho-Eung, Kim Dong-Sung (South Korea)	Li Jiajun, Feng Kai, Yuan Ye, An Yulong (China)
2002	Éric Bédard, Marc Gagnon, Jonathan Guilmette, François-Louis Tremblay, Mathieu Turcotte (Canada)	Michele Antonioli, Maurizio Carnino, Fabio Carta, Nicola Franceschina, Nicola Rodigari (Italy)	An Yulong, Feng Kai, Guo Wei, Li Jiajun, Li Ye (China)
2006	Ahn Hyun Soo, Lee Ho-Suk, Oh Se-Jong, Seo Ho-Jin, Song Suk-Woo (South Korea)	Éric Bédard, Jonathan Guilmette, Charles Hamelin, François-Louis Tremblay, Mathieu Turcotte (Canada)	Alex Izykowski, J. P. Kepka, Apolo Anton Ohno, Rusty Smith (United States)

Year	Gold	Silver	Bronze
2010	Charles Hamelin, François Hamelin, Olivier Jean, François-Louis Tremblay, Guillaume Bastille (Canada)	Kwak Yoon-Gy, Lee Ho-Suk, Lee Jung-Su, Sung Si-Bak, Kim Seoung-Il (South Korea)	J. R. Celski, Travis Jayner, Jordan Malone, Apolo Anton Ohno, Simon Cho (United States)

Women's 500-Meter

Year	Gold	Silver	Bronze
1992	Cathy Turner (United States)	Li Yan (China)	Hwang Ok-Sil (North Korea)
1994	Cathy Turner (United States)	Zhang Yanmei (China)	Amy Peterson (United States)
1998	Annie Perreault (Canada)	Yang Yang* (China)	Chun Lee-Kyung (South Korea)
2002	Yang Yang** China)	Evgenia Radanova (Bulgaria)	Wang Chunlu (China)
2006	Wang Meng (China)	Evgenia Radanova (Bulgaria)	Anouk Leblanc-Boucher (Canada)
2010	Wang Meng (China)	Marianne St-Gelais (Canada)	Arianna Fontana (Italy)

* Often referred to as Yang Yang (S) to differentiate her from the other prominent Chinese short-track speed skater named Yang Yang.

** Often referred to as Yang Yang (A) or Yang Yang (L) to differentiate her from the other prominent Chinese short-track speed skater named Yang Yang.

Women's 1,000-Meter

Year	Gold	Silver	Bronze
1994	Chun Lee-Kyung (South Korea)	Nathalie Lambert (Canada)	Kim So-Hui (South Korea)
1998	Chun Lee-Kyung (South Korea)	Yang Yang* (China)	Won Hye-Kyung (South Korea)
2002	Yang Yang** (China)	Ko Gi-Hyun (South Korea)	Yang Yang* (China)
2006	Jin Sun-Yu (South Korea)	Wang Meng (China)	Yang Yang** (China)
2010	Wang Meng (China)	Katherine Reutter (United States)	Park Seung-Hi (South Korea)

* Often referred to as Yang Yang (S) to differentiate her from the other prominent Chinese short-track speed skater named Yang Yang.

** Often referred to as Yang Yang (A) or Yang Yang (L) to differentiate her from the other prominent Chinese short-track speed skater named Yang Yang.

Women's 1,500-Meter

Year	Gold	Silver	Bronze
2002	Ko Gi-Hyun (South Korea)	Choi Eun-Kyung (South Korea)	Evgenia Radanova (Bulgaria)
2006	Jin Sun-Yu (South Korea)	Choi Eun-Kyung (South Korea)	Wang Meng (China)
2010	Zhou Yang (China)	Lee Eun-Byul (South Korea)	Park Seung-Hi (South Korea)

Women's 3,000-Meter Relay

Year	Gold	Silver	Bronze
1992	Angela Cutrone, Sylvie Daigle, Nathalie Lambert, Annie Perreault (Canada)	Darcie Dohnal, Amy Peterson, Cathy Turner, Nikki Ziegelmeyer (United States)	Yuliya Allagulova, Natalya Isakova, Viktoriya Taranina, Yuliya Vlasova (Unified Team)
1994	Chun Lee-Kyung, Kim So-Hui, Kim Yoon-Mi, Won Hye-Kyung (South Korea)	Christine Boudrias, Isabelle Charest, Sylvie Daigle, Nathalie Lambert (Canada)	Karen Cashman, Amy Peterson, Cathy Turner, Nikki Ziegelmeyer (United States)
1998	Chun Lee-Kyung, Won Hye-Kyung, An Sang-Mi, Kim Yun-Mi (South Korea)	Yang Yang**, Yang Yang*, Wang Chunlu, Sun Dandan (China)	Christine Boudrias, Isabelle Charest, Annie Perreault, Tania Vicent (Canada)
2002	Choi Eun-Kyung, Choi Min-Kyung, Joo Min-Jin, Park Hye-Won (South Korea)	Sun Dandan, Wang Chunlu, Yang Yang**, Yang Yang* (China)	Isabelle Charest, Marie-Eve Drolet, Amélie Goulet-Nadon, Alanna Kraus, Tania Vicent (Canada)
2006	Byun Chun-Sa, Choi Eun-Kyung, Jeon Da-Hye, Jin Sun-Yu, Kang Yun-Mi (South Korea)	Alanna Kraus, Anouk Leblanc-Boucher, Amanda Overland, Kalyna Roberge, Tania Vicent (Canada)	Marta Capurso, Arianna Fontana, Katia Zini, Mara Zini (Italy)

Year	Gold	Silver	Bronze
2010	Sun Linlin, Wang Meng, Zhang Hui, Zhou Yang (China)	Jessica Gregg, Kalyna Roberge, Marianne St-Gelais, Tania Vicent (Canada)	Allison Baver, Alyson Dudek, Lana Gehring, Katherine Reutter, Kimberly Derrick (United States)

* Often referred to as Yang Yang (S) to differentiate her from the other prominent Chinese short-track speed skater named Yang Yang.

** Often referred to as Yang Yang (A) or Yang Yang (L) to differentiate her from the other prominent Chinese short-track speed skater named Yang Yang.

Biathlon

Men's 10-Kilometer

Year	Gold	Silver	Bronze
1980	Frank Ullrich (East Germany)	Vladimir Alikin (Soviet Union)	Anatoly Alyabyev (Soviet Union)
1984	Eirik Kvalfoss (Norway)	Peter Angerer (West Germany)	Matthias Jacob (East Germany)
1988	Frank-Peter Roetsch (East Germany)	Valery Medvedtsev (Soviet Union)	Sergey Tchepikov (Soviet Union)
1992	Mark Kirchner (Germany)	Ricco Groß (Germany)	Harri Eloranta (Finland)
1994	Sergey Tchepikov (Russia)	Ricco Groß (Germany)	Sergey Tarasov (Russia)
1998	Ole Einar Bjørndalen (Norway)	Frode Andresen (Norway)	Ville Räikkönen (Finland)
2002	Ole Einar Bjørndalen (Norway)	Sven Fischer (Germany)	Wolfgang Perner (Austria)
2006	Sven Fischer (Germany)	Halvard Hanevold (Norway)	Frode Andresen (Norway)
2010	Vincent Jay (France)	Emil Hegle Svendsen (Norway)	Jakov Fak (Croatia)

Men's 20-Kilometer

Year	Gold	Silver	Bronze
1960	Klas Lestander (Sweden)	Antti Tyrväinen (Finland)	Aleksandr Privalov (Soviet Union)
1964	Vladimir Melanin (Soviet Union)	Aleksandr Privalov (Soviet Union)	Olav Jordet (Norway)
1968	Magnar Solberg (Norway)	Alexander Tikhonov (Soviet Union)	Vladimir Gundartsev (Soviet Union)
1972	Magnar Solberg (Norway)	Hansjörg Knauthe (East Germany)	Lars-Göran Arwidson (Sweden)
1976	Nikolay Kruglov (Soviet Union)	Heikki Ikola (Finland)	Aleksandr Yelizarov (Soviet Union)
1980	Anatoly Alyabyev (Soviet Union)	Frank Ullrich (East Germany)	Eberhard Rösch (East Germany)
1984	Peter Angerer (West Germany)	Frank-Peter Roetsch (East Germany)	Eirik Kvalfoss (Norway)
1988	Frank-Peter Roetsch (East Germany)	Valery Medvedtsev (Soviet Union)	Johan Passler (Italy)
1992	Eugeni Redkine (Unified Team)	Mark Kirchner (Germany)	Mikael Löfgren (Sweden)
1994	Sergey Tarasov (Russia)	Frank Luck (Germany)	Sven Fischer (Germany)
1998	Halvard Hanevold (Norway)	Pier Alberto Carrara (Italy)	Alexei Aidarov (Belarus)
2002	Ole Einar Bjørndalen (Norway)	Frank Luck (Germany)	Viktor Maigourov (Russia)
2006	Michael Greis (Germany)	Ole Einar Bjørndalen (Norway)	Halvard Hanevold (Norway)
2010	Emil Hegle Svendsen (Norway)	Ole Einar Bjørndalen (Norway) Sergey Novikov (Belarus)	Not awarded

Men's 12.5-Kilometer Pursuit

Year	Gold	Silver	Bronze
2002	Ole Einar Bjørndalen (Norway)	Raphaël Poirée (France)	Ricco Groß (Germany)
2006	Vincent Defrasne (France)	Ole Einar Bjørndalen (Norway)	Sven Fischer (Germany)
2010	Björn Ferry (Sweden)	Christoph Sumann (Austria)	Vincent Jay (France)

Men's 15-Kilometer Mass Start

Year	Gold	Silver	Bronze
2006	Michael Greis (Germany)	Tomasz Sikora (Poland)	Ole Einar Bjørndalen (Norway)
2010	Evgeny Ustyugov (Russia)	Martin Fourcade (France)	Pavol Hurajt (Slovakia)

Men's 4 × 7.5-Kilometer Relay

Year	Gold	Silver	Bronze
1968	Alexander Tikhonov, Nikolay Puzanov, Viktor Mamatov, Vladimir Gundartsev (Soviet Union)	Ola Wærhaug, Olav Jordet, Magnar Solberg, Jon Istad (Norway)	Lars-Göran Arwidson, Tore Eriksson, Olle Petrusson, Holmfrid Olsson (Sweden)
1972	Alexander Tikhonov, Rinnat Safin, Ivan Byakov, Viktor Mamatov (Soviet Union)	Esko Saira, Juhani Suutarinen, Heikki Ikola, Mauri Röppänen (Finland)	Hansjörg Knauthe, Joachim Meischner, Dieter Speer, Horst Koschka (East Germany)
1976	Alexander Yelizarov, Ivan Byakov, Nikolay Kruglov, Alexander Tikhonov (Soviet Union)	Henrik Flöjt, Esko Saira, Juhani Suutarinen, Heikki Ikola (Finland)	Karl-Heinz Menz, Frank Ullrich, Manfred Beer, Manfred Geyer (East Germany)
1980	Vladimir Alikin, Alexander Tikhonov, Vladimir Barnachov, Anatoly Alyabyev (Soviet Union)	Matthias Jung, Klaus Siebert, Frank Ullrich, Eberhard Rösch (East Germany)	Franz Bernreiter, Hans Estner, Peter Angerer, Gerhard Winkler (West Germany)
1984	Dmitri Vasilyev, Yuri Kashkarov, Algimantas Šalna, Sergey Bulygin (Soviet Union)	Odd Lirhus, Eirik Kvalfoss, Rolf Storsveen, Kjell Søbak (Norway)	Ernst Reiter, Walter Pichler, Peter Angerer, Fritz Fischer (West Germany)
1988	Dmitri Vasilyev, Sergey Tchepikov, Alexander Popov, Valery Medvedtsev (Soviet Union)	Ernst Reiter, Stefan Höck, Peter Angerer, Fritz Fischer (West Germany)	Werner Kiem, Gottlieb Taschler, Johann Passler, Andreas Zingerle (Italy)
1992	Ricco Groß, Jens Steinigen, Mark Kirchner, Fritz Fischer (Germany)	Valery Medvedtsev, Alexander Popov, Valeri Kiriyenko, Sergey Tchepikov (Russia)	Ulf Johansson, Leif Andersson, Tord Wiksten, Mikael Löfgren (Sweden)
1994	Ricco Groß, Frank Luck, Mark Kirchner, Sven Fischer (Germany)	Valeri Kiriyenko, Vladimir Dratchev, Sergey Tarasov, Sergey Tchepikov (Russia)	Thierry Dusserre, Patrice Bailly-Salins, Lionel Laurent, Hervé Flandin (France)
1998	Ricco Groß, Peter Sendel, Sven Fischer, Frank Luck (Germany)	Egil Gjelland, Halvard Hanevold, Dag Bjørndalen, Ole Einar Bjørndalen (Norway)	Pavel Muslimov, Vladimir Dratchev, Sergey Tarasov, Viktor Maigourov (Russia)
2002	Halvard Hanevold, Frode Andresen, Egil Gjelland, Ole Einar Bjørndalen (Norway)	Ricco Groß, Peter Sendel, Sven Fischer, Frank Luck (Germany)	Gilles Marguet, Vincent Defrasne, Julien Robert, Raphaël Poirée (France)
2006	Ricco Groß, Michael Rösch, Sven Fischer, Michael Greis (Germany)	Ivan Tcherezov, Sergey Tchepikov, Pavel Rostovtsev, Nikolay Kruglov Jr. (Russia)	Julien Robert, Vincent Defrasne, Ferréol Cannard, Raphaël Poirée (France)
2010	Halvard Hanevold, Tarjei Boe, Emil Hegle Svendsen, Ole Einar Bjørndalen (Norway)	Simon Eder, Daniel Mesotitsch, Dominik Landertinger, Christoph Sumann (Austria)	Ivan Tcherezov, Anton Shipulin, Maxim Tchoudov, Evgeny Ustyugov (Russia)

Women's 15-Kilometer

Year	Gold	Silver	Bronze
1992	Antje Misersky (Germany)	Svetlana Davidova (Unified Team)	Myriam Bédard (Canada)
1994	Myriam Bédard (Canada)	Anne Briand (France)	Uschi Disl (Germany)
1998	Ekaterina Dafovska (Bulgaria)	Olena Petrova (Ukraine)	Uschi Disl (Germany)
2002	Andrea Henkel (Germany)	Liv Grete Poirée (Norway)	Magdalena Forsberg (Sweden)
2006	Svetlana Ishmouratova (Russia)	Martina Glagow (Germany)	Albina Akhatova (Russia)
2010	Tora Berger (Norway)	Elena Khrustaleva (Kazakhstan)	Darya Domracheva (Belarus)

Women's 7.5-Kilometer

Year	Gold	Silver	Bronze
1992	Anfisa Reztsova (Unified Team)	Antje Misersky (Germany)	Yelena Belova (Unified Team)
1994	Myriam Bédard (Canada)	Svetlana Paramygina (Belarus)	Valentyna Tserbe-Nessina (Ukraine)
1998	Galina Koukleva (Russia)	Uschi Disl (Germany)	Katrin Apel (Germany)
2002	Kati Wilhelm (Germany)	Uschi Disl (Germany)	Magdalena Forsberg (Sweden)
2006	Florence Baverel-Robert (France)	Anna Carin Olofsson (Sweden)	Lilia Vaygina-Efremova (Ukraine)
2010	Anastasiya Kuzmina (Slovakia)	Magdalena Neuner (Germany)	Marie Dorin (France)

Women's 10-Kilometer Pursuit

Year	Gold	Silver	Bronze
2002	Olga Pyleva (Russia)	Kati Wilhelm (Germany)	Irina Nikulchina (Bulgaria)
2006	Kati Wilhelm (Germany)	Martina Glagow (Germany)	Albina Akhatova (Russia)
2010	Magdalena Neuner (Germany)	Anastasiya Kuzmina (Slovakia)	Marie-Laure Brunet (France)

Women's 12.5-Kilometer Mass Start

Year	Gold	Silver	Bronze
2006	Anna Carin Olofsson (Sweden)	Kati Wilhelm (Germany)	Uschi Disl (Germany)
2010	Magdalena Neuner (Germany)	Olga Zaitseva (Russia)	Simone Hauswald (Germany)

Women's 3 × 7.5-Kilometer Relay

Year	Gold	Silver	Bronze
1992	Corinne Niogret, Véronique Claudel, Anne Briand (France)	Uschi Disl, Antje Misersky, Petra Schaaf (Germany)	Yelena Belova, Anfisa Reztsova, Yelena Melnikova (Unified Team)

Women's 4 × 7.5-Kilometer Relay

Year	Gold	Silver	Bronze
1994	Nadezhda Talanova, Nataliya Snytina, Luiza Noskova, Anfisa Reztsova (Russia)	Uschi Disl, Antje Misersky, Simone Greiner-Petter-Memm, Petra Schaaf (Germany)	Corinne Niogret, Véronique Claudel, Delphyne Heymann, Anne Briand (France)
1998	Uschi Disl, Martina Zellner, Katrin Apel, Petra Behle (Germany)	Olga Melnik, Galina Koukleva, Albina Akhatova, Olga Romasko (Russia)	Ann-Elen Skjelbreid, Annette Sikveland, Gunn Margit Andreassen, Liv Grete Skjelbreid Poirée (Norway)
2002	Katrin Apel, Uschi Disl, Andrea Henkel, Kati Wilhelm (Germany)	Ann-Elen Skjelbreid, Linda Tjørhom, Gunn Margit Andreassen, Liv Grete Skjelbreid Poirée (Norway)	Olga Pyleva, Galina Koukleva, Svetlana Ishmouratova, Albina Akhatova (Russia)

Women's 4 × 6-Kilometer Relay

Year	Gold	Silver	Bronze
2006	Anna Bogaliy-Titovets, Svetlana Ishmouratova, Olga Zaitseva, Albina Akhatova (Russia)	Martina Glagow, Andrea Henkel, Katrin Apel, Kati Wilhelm (Germany)	Delphyne Peretto, Florence Baverel-Robert, Sylvie Becaert, Sandrine Bailly (France)
2010	Svetlana Sleptsova, Anna Bogaliy-Titovets, Olga Medvedtseva, Olga Zaitseva (Russia)	Marie-Laure Brunet, Sylvie Becaert, Marie Dorin, Sandrine Bailly (France)	Kati Wilhelm, Simone Hauswald, Martina Beck, Andrea Henkel (Germany)

Military Patrol

Year	Gold	Silver	Bronze
1924	Adolf Aufdenblatten, Alphonse Julen, Antoine Julen, Denis Vaucher (Switzerland)	Väinö Bremer, August Eskelinen, Heikki Hirvonen, Martti Lappalainen (Finland)	Georges Berthet, Camille Mandrillon, Maurice Mandrillon, André Vandelle (France)
1928	Ole Reistad, Leif Skagnæs, Ole Stenen, Reidar Ødegaard (Norway)	Eino Hjalmar Kuvaja, Kalle Tuppurainen, Esko Järvinen, Veikko Hannes Ruotsalainen (Finland)	Otto Furrer, Anton Julen, Fritz Kuhn, Hugo Lehner (Switzerland)
1932: Event not held			
1936	Luigi Perenni, Stefano Sertorelli, Enrico Silvestri, Sisto Scilligo (Italy)	Kalle Arantola, Olli Huttunen, Eino Kuvaja, Olli Remes (Finland)	Seth Olofsson, John Westberg, Johan Wiksten, Gunnar Wåhlberg (Sweden)
1940–1944: Olympics not held			
1948	Robert Zurbriggen, Heinrich Zurbriggen, Xavier Vouardoux, Arnold Andenmatten (Switzerland)	Tauno Honkanen, Mikko Meriläinen, Eero Naapuri, Vilho Ylönen (Finland)	H. Borgh*, Edor Hjukström, O. F. Larssen*, K. G. Ljungquist* (Sweden)

* Full name not known.

Speed Skiing

Men's Individual

Year	Gold	Silver	Bronze
1992	Michael Prufer (France)	Philippe Goitschel (France)	Jeffrey Hamilton (United States)

Women's Individual

Year	Gold	Silver	Bronze
1992	Tarja Mulari (Finland)	Liss Pettersen (Norway)	Renata Kolarova (Switzerland)

Winners and Champions
of Major World Sporting Events

National Football League/American Football League/Super Bowl

Year	Winner(s)
2011 (Super Bowl XLV)	Green Bay Packers
2010 (Super Bowl XLIV)	New Orleans Saints
2009 (Super Bowl XLIII)	Pittsburgh Steelers
2008 (Super Bowl XLII)	New York Giants
2007 (Super Bowl XLI)	Indianapolis Colts
2006 (Super Bowl XL)	Pittsburgh Steelers
2005 (Super Bowl XXXIX)	New England Patriots
2004 (Super Bowl XXXVIII)	New England Patriots
2003 (Super Bowl XXXVII)	Tampa Bay Buccaneers
2002 (Super Bowl XXXVI)	New England Patriots
2001 (Super Bowl XXXV)	Baltimore Ravens
2000 (Super Bowl XXXIV)	St. Louis Rams
1999 (Super Bowl XXIII)	Denver Broncos
1998 (Super Bowl XXXII)	Denver Broncos
1997 (Super Bowl XXXI)	Green Bay Packers
1996 (Super Bowl XXX)	Dallas Cowboys
1995 (Super Bowl XXIX)	San Francisco 49ers
1994 (Super Bowl XXVIII)	Dallas Cowboys
1993 (Super Bowl XXVII)	Dallas Cowboys
1992 (Super Bowl XXVI)	Washington Redskins
1991 (Super Bowl XXV)	New York Giants
1990 (Super Bowl XXIV)	San Francisco 49ers
1989 (Super Bowl XXIII)	San Francisco 49ers
1988 (Super Bowl XXII)	Washington Redskins
1987 (Super Bowl XXI)	New York Giants
1986 (Super Bowl XX)	Chicago Bears
1985 (Super Bowl XIX)	San Francisco 49ers
1984 (Super Bowl XVIII)	Los Angeles Raiders
1983 (Super Bowl XVII)	Washington Redskins
1982 (Super Bowl XVI)	San Francisco 49ers
1981 (Super Bowl XV)	Oakland Raiders
1980 (Super Bowl XIV)	Pittsburgh Steelers
1979 (Super Bowl XIII)	Pittsburgh Steelers
1978 (Super Bowl XII)	Dallas Cowboys
1977 (Super Bowl XI)	Oakland Raiders
1976 (Super Bowl X)	Pittsburgh Steelers
1975 (Super Bowl IX)	Pittsburgh Steelers
1974 (Super Bowl VIII)	Miami Dolphins

Year	Winner(s)
1973 (Super Bowl VII)	Miami Dolphins
1972 (Super Bowl VI)	Dallas Cowboys
1971 (Super Bowl V)	Baltimore Colts
1970 (Super Bowl IV)	Kansas City Chiefs
1969 (Super Bowl III)	New York Jets
1968 (Super Bowl II)	Green Bay Packers
1967 (Super Bowl I)	Green Bay Packers
1966	AFL: Kansas City Chiefs NFL: Green Bay Packers
1965	AFL: Kansas City Chiefs NFL: Green Bay Packers
1964	AFL: Buffalo Bills NFL: Cleveland Browns
1963	AFL: San Diego Chargers NFL: Chicago Bears
1962	AFL: Dallas Texans NFL: Green Bay Packers
1961	AFL: Houston Oilers NFL: Green Bay Packers
1960	AFL: Houston Oilers NFL: Philadelphia Eagles
1959	Baltimore Colts
1958	Baltimore Colts
1957	Detroit Lions
1956	New York Giants
1955	Cleveland Browns
1954	Cleveland Browns
1953	Detroit Lions
1952	Detroit Lions
1951	Los Angeles Rams
1950	Cleveland Browns
1949	Philadelphia Eagles
1948	Philadelphia Eagles
1947	Chicago Cardinals
1946	Chicago Bears
1945	Cleveland Rams
1944	Green Bay Packers
1943	Chicago Bears
1942	Washington Redskins
1941	Chicago Bears
1940	Chicago Bears
1939	Green Bay Packers
1938	New York Giants
1937	Washington Redskins
1936	Green Bay Packers
1935	Detroit Lions
1934	New York Giants
1933	Chicago Bears
1932	Chicago Bears
1931	Green Bay Packers
1930	Green Bay Packers
1929	Green Bay Packers
1928	Providence Steam Roller

Year	Winner(s)
1927	New York Giants
1926	Frankford Yellow Jackets
1925	Chicago Cardinals
1924	Cleveland Bulldogs
1923	Canton Bulldogs
1922	Canton Bulldogs
1921	Chicago Staleys
1920	Akron Pros

Compiled by Charles Parrish

National Basketball Association

Year	Winner	Runner-up
2011	Dallas Mavericks	Miami Heat
2010	Los Angeles Lakers	Boston Celtics
2009	Los Angeles Lakers	Orlando Magic
2008	Boston Celtics	Los Angeles Lakers
2007	San Antonio Spurs	Cleveland Cavaliers
2006	Miami Heat	Dallas Mavericks
2005	San Antonio Spurs	Detroit Pistons
2004	Detroit Pistons	Los Angeles Lakers
2003	San Antonio Spurs	New Jersey Nets
2002	Los Angeles Lakers	New Jersey Nets
2001	Los Angeles Lakers	Philadelphia 76ers
2000	Los Angeles Lakers	Indiana Pacers
1999	San Antonio Spurs	New York Knicks
1998	Chicago Bulls	Utah Jazz
1997	Chicago Bulls	Utah Jazz
1996	Chicago Bulls	Seattle Super Sonics
1995	Houston Rockets	Orlando Magic
1994	Houston Rockets	New York Knicks
1993	Chicago Bulls	Phoenix Suns
1992	Chicago Bulls	Portland Trail Blazers
1991	Chicago Bulls	Los Angeles Lakers
1990	Detroit Pistons	Portland Trail Blazers
1989	Detroit Pistons	Los Angeles Lakers
1988	Los Angeles Lakers	Detroit Pistons
1987	Los Angeles Lakers	Boston Celtics
1986	Boston Celtics	Houston Rockets
1985	Los Angeles Lakers	Boston Celtics
1984	Boston Celtics	Los Angeles Lakers
1983	Philadelphia 76ers	Los Angeles Lakers
1982	Los Angeles Lakers	Philadelphia 76ers
1981	Boston Celtics	Houston Rockets
1980	Los Angeles Lakers	Philadelphia 76ers
1979	Seattle Super Sonics	Washington Bullets
1978	Washington Bullets	Seattle Super Sonics
1977	Portland Trail Blazers	Philadelphia 76ers
1976	Boston Celtics	Phoenix Suns
1975	Golden State Warriors	Washington Bullets
1974	Boston Celtics	Milwaukee Bucks

Year	Winner	Runner-up
1973	New York Knicks	Los Angeles Lakers
1972	Los Angeles Lakers	New York Knicks
1971	Milwaukee Bucks	Baltimore Bullets
1970	New York Knicks	Los Angeles Lakers
1969	Boston Celtics	Los Angeles Lakers
1968	Boston Celtics	Los Angeles Lakers
1967	Philadelphia 76ers	San Francisco Warriors
1966	Boston Celtics	Los Angeles Lakers
1965	Boston Celtics	Los Angeles Lakers
1964	Boston Celtics	San Francisco Warriors
1963	Boston Celtics	Los Angeles Lakers
1962	Boston Celtics	Los Angeles Lakers
1961	Boston Celtics	St. Louis Hawks
1960	Boston Celtics	St. Louis Hawks
1959	Boston Celtics	Minneapolis Lakers
1958	St. Louis Hawks	Boston Celtics
1957	Boston Celtics	St. Louis Hawks
1956	Philadelphia Warriors	Fort Wayne Pistons
1955	Syracuse Nationals	Fort Wayne Pistons
1954	Minneapolis Lakers	Syracuse Nationals
1953	Minneapolis Lakers	New York Knicks
1952	Minneapolis Lakers	New York Knicks
1951	Rochester Royals	New York Knicks
1950	Minneapolis Lakers	Syracuse Nationals
1949	Minneapolis Lakers	Washington Capitals
1948	Baltimore Bullets	Philadelphia Warriors
1947	Philadelphia Warriors	Chicago Stags

Compiled by Andy Mackay

Women's National Basketball Association Champions

Year	Winner	Runner-up
2011	Minnesota Lynx	Atlanta Dream
2010	Seattle Storm	Atlanta Dream
2009	Phoenix Mercury	Indiana Fever
2008	Detroit Shock	San Antonio Silver Stars
2007	Phoenix Mercury	Detroit Shock
2006	Detroit Shock	Sacramento Monarchs
2005	Sacramento Monarchs	Connecticut Sun
2004	Seattle Storm	Connecticut Sun
2003	Detroit Shock	Los Angeles Sparks
2002	Los Angeles Sparks	New York Liberty
2001	Los Angeles Sparks	Charlotte Sting
2000	Houston Comets	New York Liberty
1999	Houston Comets	New York Liberty
1998	Houston Comets	Phoenix Mercury
1997	Houston Comets	New York Liberty

Compiled by Andy Mackay

Major League Baseball World Series

Year	Winner
2011	St. Louis Cardinals
2010	San Francisco Giants
2009	New York Yankees
2008	Philadelphia Phillies
2007	Boston Red Sox
2006	St. Louis Cardinals
2005	Chicago White Sox
2004	Boston Red Sox
2003	Florida Marlins
2002	Anaheim Angels
2001	Arizona Diamondbacks
2000	New York Yankees
1999	New York Yankees
1998	New York Yankees
1997	Florida Marlins
1996	New York Yankees
1995	Atlanta Braves
1994	Series canceled due to player strike
1993	Toronto Blue Jays
1992	Toronto Blue Jays
1991	Minnesota Twins
1990	Cincinnati Reds
1989	Oakland Athletics
1988	Los Angeles Dodgers
1987	Minnesota Twins
1986	New York Mets
1985	Kansas City Royals
1984	Detroit Tigers
1983	Baltimore Orioles
1982	St. Louis Cardinals
1981	Los Angeles Dodgers
1980	Philadelphia Phillies
1979	Pittsburgh Pirates
1978	New York Yankees
1977	New York Yankees
1976	Cincinnati Reds
1975	Cincinnati Reds
1974	Oakland Athletics
1973	Oakland Athletics
1972	Oakland Athletics
1971	Pittsburgh Pirates
1970	Baltimore Orioles
1969	New York Mets
1968	Detroit Tigers
1967	St. Louis Cardinals
1966	Baltimore Orioles
1965	Los Angeles Dodgers
1964	St. Louis Cardinals
1963	Los Angeles Dodgers
1962	New York Yankees
1961	New York Yankees

Year	Winner
1960	Pittsburgh Pirates
1959	Los Angeles Dodgers
1958	New York Yankees
1957	Milwaukee Braves
1956	New York Yankees
1955	Brooklyn Dodgers
1954	New York Giants
1953	New York Yankees
1952	New York Yankees
1951	New York Yankees
1950	New York Yankees
1949	New York Yankees
1948	Cleveland Indians
1947	New York Yankees
1946	St. Louis Cardinals
1945	Detroit Tigers
1944	St. Louis Cardinals
1943	New York Yankees
1942	St. Louis Cardinals
1941	New York Yankees
1940	Cincinnati Reds
1939	New York Yankees
1938	New York Yankees
1937	New York Yankees
1936	New York Yankees
1935	Detroit Tigers
1934	St. Louis Cardinals
1933	New York Giants
1932	New York Yankees
1931	St. Louis Cardinals
1930	Philadelphia Athletics
1929	Philadelphia Athletics
1928	New York Yankees
1927	New York Yankees
1926	St. Louis Cardinals
1925	Pittsburgh Pirates
1924	Washington Nationals
1923	New York Yankees
1922	New York Giants
1921	New York Giants
1920	Cleveland Indians
1919	Cincinnati Reds
1918	Boston Red Sox
1917	Chicago White Sox
1916	Boston Red Sox
1915	Boston Red Sox
1914	Boston Braves
1913	Philadelphia Athletics
1912	Boston Red Sox
1911	Philadelphia Athletics
1910	Philadelphia Athletics
1909	Pittsburgh Pirates

Year	Winner
1908	Chicago Cubs
1907	Chicago Cubs
1906	Chicago White Sox
1905	New York Giants
1904	No championship
1903	Boston Americans

Compiled by Emily J. Houghton

National Hockey League

Year	Winner	Runner-up
2011	Boston Bruins	Vancouver Canucks
2010	Chicago Blackhawks	Philadelphia Flyers
2009	Pittsburgh Penguins	Detroit Red Wings
2008	Detroit Red Wings	Pittsburgh Penguins
2007	Anaheim Ducks	Ottawa Senators
2006	Carolina Hurricanes	Edmonton Oilers
2005	Stanley Cup was not awarded due to NHL lockout	
2004	Tampa Bay Lightning	Calgary Flames
2003	New Jersey Devils	Mighty Ducks of Anaheim
2002	Detroit Red Wings	Carolina Hurricanes
2001	Colorado Avalanche	New Jersey Devils
2000	New Jersey Devils	Dallas Stars
1999	Dallas Stars	Buffalo Sabres
1998	Detroit Red Wings	Washington Capitals
1997	Detroit Red Wings	Philadelphia Flyers
1996	Colorado Avalanche	Florida Panthers
1995	New Jersey Devils	Detroit Red Wings
1994	New York Rangers	Vancouver Canucks
1993	Montreal Canadiens	Los Angeles Kings
1992	Pittsburgh Penguins	Chicago Blackhawks
1991	Pittsburgh Penguins	Minnesota North Stars
1990	Edmonton Oilers	Boston Bruins
1989	Calgary Flames	Montreal Canadiens
1988	Edmonton Oilers	Boston Bruins
1987	Edmonton Oilers	Philadelphia Flyers
1986	Montreal Canadiens	Calgary Flames
1985	Edmonton Oilers	Philadelphia Fyers
1984	Edmonton Oilers	New York Islanders
1983	New York Islanders	Edmonton Oilers
1982	New York Islanders	Vancouver Canucks
1981	New York Islanders	Minnesota North Stars
1980	New York Islanders	Philadelphia Flyers
1979	Montreal Canadiens	New York Rangers
1978	Montreal Canadiens	Boston Bruins
1977	Montreal Canadiens	Boston Bruins
1976	Montreal Canadiens	Philadelphia Flyers
1975	Philadelphia Flyers	Buffalo Sabres
1974	Philadelphia Flyers	Boston Bruins
1973	Montreal Canadiens	Chicago Blackhawks
1972	Boston Bruins	New York Rangers

Year	Winner	Runner-up
1971	Montreal Canadiens	Chicago Blackhawks
1970	Boston Bruins	St. Louis Blues
1969	Montreal Canadiens	St. Louis Blues
1968	Montreal Canadiens	St. Louis Blues
1967	Toronto Maple Leafs	Montreal Canadiens
1966	Montreal Canadiens	Detroit Red Wings
1965	Montreal Canadiens	Chicago Blackhawks
1964	Toronto Maple Leafs	Detroit Red Wings
1963	Toronto Maple Leafs	Detroit Red Wings
1962	Toronto Maple Leafs	Chicago Blackhawks
1961	Chicago Blackhawks	Detroit Red Wings
1960	Montreal Canadiens	Toronto Maple Leafs
1959	Montreal Canadiens	Toronto Maple Leafs
1958	Montreal Canadiens	Boston Bruins
1957	Montreal Canadiens	Boston Bruins
1956	Montreal Canadiens	Detroit Red Wings
1955	Detroit Red Wings	Montreal Canadiens
1954	Detroit Red Wings	Montreal Canadiens
1953	Montreal Canadiens	Boston Bruins
1952	Detroit Red Wings	Montreal Canadiens
1951	Toronto Maple Leafs	Montreal Canadiens
1950	Detroit Red Wings	New York Rangers
1949	Toronto Maple Leafs	Detroit Red Wings
1948	Toronto Maple Leafs	Detroit Red Wings
1947	Toronto Maple Leafs	Montreal Canadiens
1946	Montreal Canadiens	Boston Bruins
1945	Toronto Maple Leafs	Detroit Red Wings
1944	Montreal Canadiens	Chicago Blackhawks
1943	Detroit Red Wings	Boston Bruins
1942	Toronto Maple Leafs	Detroit Red Wings
1941	Boston Bruins	Detroit Red Wings
1940	New York Rangers	Toronto Maple Leafs
1939	Boston Bruins	Toronto Maple Leafs
1938	Chicago Blackhawks	Toronto Maple Leafs
1937	Detroit Red Wings	New York Rangers
1936	Detroit Red Wings	Toronto Maple Leafs
1935	Montreal Maroons	Toronto Maple Leafs
1934	Chicago Blackhawks	Detroit Red Wings
1933	New York Rangers	Toronto Maple Leafs
1932	Toronto Maple Leafs	New York Rangers
1931	Montreal Canadiens	Chicago Black Hawks
1930	Montreal Canadiens	Boston Bruins
1929	Boston Bruins	New York Rangers
1928	New York Rangers	Montreal Maroons
1927	Ottawa Senators	Boston Bruins

Compiled by Jessica Bohince

National Collegiate Athletic Association Football

Champions as recognized by the National Collegiate Athletic Association

Year	Winner
2010	Auburn University
2009	University of Alabama
2008	University of Florida
2007	Louisiana State University
2006	University of Florida
2005	University of Texas
2004	University of Southern California
2003	Louisiana State University & University of Southern California
2002	Ohio State University
2001	University of Miami (Florida)
2000	University of Oklahoma
1999	Florida State University
1998	University of Tennessee
1997	University of Michigan & University of Nebraska
1996	University of Florida
1995	University of Nebraska
1994	University of Nebraska
1993	Florida State University
1992	University of Alabama
1991	University of Miami (Florida) & University of Washington
1990	University of Colorado & Georgia Institute of Technology
1989	University of Miami (Florida)
1988	University of Notre Dame
1987	University of Miami (Florida)
1986	Penn State University
1985	University of Oklahoma
1984	Brigham Young University
1983	University of Miami (Florida)
1982	Penn State University
1981	Clemson University
1980	University of Georgia
1979	University of Alabama
1978	University of Alabama & University of Southern California
1977	University of Notre Dame
1976	University of Pittsburgh
1975	University of Oklahoma
1974	University of Oklahoma & University of Southern California
1973	University of Notre Dame & University of Alabama
1972	University of Southern California
1971	University of Nebraska
1970	University of Nebraska, University of Texas, & Ohio State University
1969	University of Texas
1968	Ohio State University
1967	University of Southern California
1966	University of Notre Dame & Michigan State University
1965	University of Alabama & Michigan State University
1964	University of Alabama, University of Arkansas, & University of Notre Dame
1963	University of Texas

Year	Winner
1962	University of Southern California
1961	University of Alabama & Ohio State University
1960	University of Minnesota & University of Mississippi
1959	Syracuse University
1958	Louisiana State University & University of Iowa
1957	Auburn University & Ohio State University
1956	University of Oklahoma
1955	University of Oklahoma
1954	Ohio State University & University of California Los Angeles
1953	University of Maryland
1952	Michigan State University
1951	University of Tennessee
1950	University of Oklahoma
1949	University of Notre Dame
1948	University of Michigan
1947	University of Notre Dame
1946	University of Notre Dame
1945	Army
1944	Army
1943	University of Notre Dame
1942	Ohio State University
1941	University of Minnesota
1940	University of Minnesota
1939	Texas A&M
1938	Texas Christian University
1937	University of Pittsburgh
1936	University of Minnesota
1935	University of Minnesota
1934	University of Minnesota
1933	University of Michigan
1932	University of Southern California
1931	University of Southern California
1930	University of Notre Dame & University of Alabama
1929	University of Notre Dame
1928	Georgia Institute of Technology
1927	University of Illinois & Yale University
1926	University of Alabama & Stanford University
1925	University of Alabama
1924	University of Notre Dame
1923	University of Illinois & University of Michigan
1922	Cornell University, University of California, & Princeton University
1921	Cornell University & University of California
1920	University of California
1919	Harvard University, University of Illinois, University of Notre Dame, & Texas A&M
1918	University of Pittsburgh & University of Michigan
1917	Georgia Institute of Technology
1916	University of Pittsburgh
1915	Cornell University
1914	Army
1913	Harvard University
1912	Harvard University & Penn State University
1911	Princeton University & Penn State University

Year	Winner
1910	Harvard University & Pittsburgh University
1909	Yale University
1908	University of Pennsylvania & Louisiana State University
1907	Yale University
1906	Princeton University
1905	University of Chicago
1904	University of Pennsylvania & University of Michigan
1903	Princeton University & University of Michigan
1902	University of Michigan
1901	University of Michigan
1900	Yale University
1899	Harvard University
1898	Harvard University
1897	University of Pennsylvania
1896	Princeton University & Lafayette College
1895	University of Pennsylvania
1894	Yale University
1893	Princeton University
1892	Yale University
1891	Yale University
1890	Harvard University
1889	Princeton University
1888	Yale University
1887	Yale University
1886	Yale University
1885	Princeton University
1884	Yale University
1883	Yale University
1882	Yale University
1881	Yale University
1880	Princeton University & Yale University
1879	Princeton University
1878	Princeton University
1877	Yale University
1876	Yale University
1875	Harvard University
1874	Yale University
1873	Princeton University
1872	Princeton University
1871	None
1870	Princeton University
1869	Princeton University

Compiled by Kelsey Moore

National Collegiate Athletic Association Basketball

Men

Year	Winner	Runner-up
2011	University of Connecticut	Butler University
2010	Duke University	Butler University
2009	University of North Carolina	Michigan State University
2008	University of Kansas	University of Memphis
2007	University of Florida	Ohio State University
2006	University of Florida	University of California–Los Angeles
2005	University of North Carolina	University of Illinois
2004	University of Connecticut	Georgia Institute of Technology
2003	Syracuse University	University of Kansas
2002	University of Maryland	Indiana University
2001	Duke University	University of Arizona
2000	Michigan State University	University of Florida
1999	University of Connecticut	Duke University
1998	University of Kentucky	University of Utah
1997	University of Arizona	University of Kentucky
1996	University of Kentucky	Syracuse University
1995	University of California–Los Angeles	University of Arkansas
1994	University of Arkansas	Duke University
1993	University of North Carolina	University of Michigan
1992	Duke University	University of Michigan
1991	Duke University	University of Kansas
1990	University of Nevada Los Vegas	Duke University
1989	University of Michigan	Seton Hall University
1988	University of Kansas	University of Oklahoma
1987	Indiana University	Syracuse University
1986	University of Louisville	Duke University
1985	Villanova University	Georgetown University
1984	Georgetown University	University of Houston
1983	North Carolina State University	University of Houston
1982	University of North Carolina	Georgetown University
1981	Indiana University	University of North Carolina
1980	University of Louisville	University of California–Los Angeles
1979	Michigan State University	Indiana State University
1978	University of Kentucky	Duke University
1977	Marquette University	University of North Carolina
1976	Indiana University	University of Michigan
1975	University of California–Los Angeles	University of Kentucky
1974	North Carolina State University	Marquette University
1973	University of California–Los Angeles	Memphis State University
1972	University of California–Los Angeles	Florida State University
1971	University of California–Los Angeles	Villanova University
1970	University of California–Los Angeles	Jacksonville University
1969	University of California–Los Angeles	Purdue University
1968	University of California–Los Angeles	University of North Carolina
1967	University of California–Los Angeles	University of Dayton
1966	Texas Western University	University of Kentucky
1965	University of California–Los Angeles	University of Michigan
1964	University of California–Los Angeles	Duke University

Year	Winner	Runner-up
1963	Loyola University (Chicago)	University of Cincinnati
1962	University of Cincinnati	Ohio State University
1961	University of Cincinnati	Ohio State University
1960	Ohio State University	University of California
1959	University of California	West Virginia University
1958	University of Kentucky	Seattle University
1957	University of North Carolina	University of Kansas
1956	University of San Francisco	University of Iowa
1955	University of San Francisco	La Salle University
1954	La Salle University	Bradley University
1953	Indiana University	University of Kansas
1952	University of Kansas	St. John's University
1951	University of Kentucky	Kansas State University
1950	City College of New York	Bradley University
1949	University of Kentucky	Oklahoma A&M
1948	University of Kentucky	Baylor University
1947	College of the Holy Cross	University of Oklahoma
1946	Oklahoma A&M	University of North Carolina
1945	Oklahoma A&M	New York University
1944	University of Utah	Dartmouth College
1943	University of Wyoming	Georgetown University
1942	Stanford University	Dartmouth College
1941	University of Wisconsin	Washington State University
1940	Indiana University	University of Kansas
1939	University of Oregon	Ohio State University

Women

Year	Winner	Runner-up
2011	Texas A&M	University of Notre Dame
2010	University of Connecticut	Stanford University
2009	University of Connecticut	University of Louisville
2008	University of Tennessee	Stanford University
2007	University of Tennessee	Rutgers University
2006	University of Maryland	Duke University
2005	Baylor University	Michigan State University
2004	University of Connecticut	University of Tennessee
2003	University of Connecticut	University of Tennessee
2002	University of Connecticut	University of Oklahoma
2001	University of Notre Dame	Purdue University
2000	University of Connecticut	University of Tennessee
1999	Purdue University	Duke University
1998	University of Tennessee	Louisiana Tech University
1997	University of Tennessee	Old Dominion University
1996	University of Tennessee	University of Georgia
1995	University of Connecticut	University of Tennessee
1994	University of North Carolina	Louisiana Tech University
1993	Texas Tech University	Ohio State University
1992	Stanford University	Western Kentucky University
1991	University of Tennessee	University of Virginia
1990	Stanford University	Auburn University
1989	University of Tennessee	Auburn University

Year	Winner	Runner-up
1988	Louisiana Tech University	Auburn University
1987	University of Tennessee	Louisiana Tech University
1986	University of Texas	University of Southern California
1985	Old Dominion University	University of Georgia
1984	University of Southern California	University of Tennessee
1983	University of Southern California	Louisiana Tech University
1982	Louisiana Tech University	Cheyney State University

Compiled by Andy Mackay

FIFA World Cup

Men's

Year	Winner	Runner-up	Score
2010	Spain	Netherlands	1–0 (overtime)
2006	Italy	France	1–1 (5–3 penalties)
2002	Brazil	Germany	2–0
1998	France	Brazil	3–0
1994	Brazil	Italy	0–0 (3–2 penalties)
1990	West Germany	Argentina	1–0
1986	Argentina	West Germany	3–2
1982	Italy	West Germany	3–1
1978	Argentina	Netherlands	3–1 (overtime)
1974	West Germany	Netherlands	2–1
1970	Brazil	Italy	4–1
1966	England	West Germany	4–2 (overtime)
1962	Brazil	Czechoslovakia	3–1
1958	Brazil	Sweden	5–2
1954	West Germany	Hungary	3–2
1950	Uruguay	Brazil	2–1
1938	Italy	Uruguay	4–2
1934	Italy	Czechoslovakia	2–1 (overtime)
1930	Uruguay	Argentina	4–2

Women's

Year	Winner	Runner-up	Score
2011	Japan	United States	2–2 (3–1 penalties)
2007	Germany	Brazil	2–0
2003	Germany	Sweden	2–1 (golden goal)
1999	United States	China PR	0–0 (5–4 penalties)
1995	Norway	Germany	2–0
1991	United States	Norway	2–1

Compiled by Christopher Vigotsky

International Rugby Board Rugby World Cup

Men

Year	Winner	Runner-up
2011	New Zealand	France
2007	South Africa	England
2003	England	Australia
1999	Australia	France
1995	South Africa	New Zealand
1991	Australia	England
1987	New Zealand	France

Women

Year	Winner	Runner-up
2010	New Zealand	England
2006	New Zealand	England
2002	New Zealand	England
1998	New Zealand	United States
1994	England	United States
1991	United States	England

Compiled by Charles Parrish

Rugby League World Cup

Year	Winner	Runner-up
2008	New Zealand	Australia
2000	Australia	New Zealand
1995	Australia	England
1989–1992	Australia	United Kingdom
1985–1988	Australia	New Zealand
1977	Australia	United Kingdom
1975	Australia	England
1972	United Kingdom	Australia
1970	Australia	United Kingdom
1968	Australia	France
1960	United Kingdom	Australia
1957	Australia	United Kingdom
1954	United Kingdom	France

Compiled by Ludek Lhotsky

International Cricket Council Cricket World Cup

Year	Winner	Runner-up
2011	India	Sri Lanka
2007	Australia	Sri Lanka
2003	Australia	India
1999	Australia	Pakistan
1996	Sri Lanka	Australia
1992	Pakistan	England
1987	Australia	England
1983	India	West Indies
1979	West Indies	Australia
1975	West Indies	Australia

Compiled by Jatin P. Ambegankar

Association Football, England (Premier League)

Year	Winner
2009–2010	Chelsea FC
2008–2009	Manchester United
2007–2008	Manchester United
2006–2007	Manchester United
2005–2006	Chelsea FC
2004–2005	Chelsea FC
2003–2004	Arsenal FC
2002–2003	Manchester United
2001–2002	Arsenal FC
2000–2001	Manchester United
1999–2000	Manchester United
1998–1999	Manchester United
1997–1998	Arsenal FC
1996–1997	Manchester United
1995–1996	Manchester United
1994–1995	Blackburn Rovers
1993–1994	Manchester United
1992–1993	Manchester United
1991–1992	Leeds United
1990–1991	Arsenal FC
1989–1990	Liverpool FC
1988–1989	Arsenal FC
1987–1988	Liverpool FC
1986–1987	Everton FC
1985–1986	Liverpool FC
1984–1985	Everton FC
1983–1984	Liverpool FC
1982–1983	Liverpool FC
1981–1982	Liverpool FC
1980–1981	Aston Villa
1979–1980	Liverpool FC
1978–1979	Liverpool FC
1977–1978	Nottingham Forest
1976–1977	Liverpool FC
1975–1976	Liverpool FC

Year	Winner
1974–1975	Derby County
1973–1974	Leeds United
1972–1973	Liverpool FC
1971–1972	Derby County
1970–1971	Arsenal FC
1969–1970	Everton FC
1968–1969	Leeds United
1967–1968	Manchester City
1966–1967	Manchester United
1965–1966	Liverpool FC
1964–1965	Manchester United
1963–1964	Liverpool FC
1962–1963	Everton FC
1961–1962	Ipswich Town
1960–1961	Tottenham Hotspur FC
1959–1960	Burnley FC
1958–1959	Wolverhampton Wanderers
1957–1958	Wolverhampton Wanderers
1956–1957	Manchester United
1955–1956	Manchester United
1954–1955	Chelsea FC
1953–1954	Wolverhampton Wanderers
1952–1953	Arsenal FC
1951–1952	Manchester United
1950–1951	Tottenham Hotspur FC
1949–1950	Portsmouth
1948–1949	Portsmouth
1947–1948	Arsenal FC
1946–1947	Liverpool FC
1938–1939	Everton FC
1937–1938	Arsenal FC
1936–1937	Manchester City
1935–1936	Sunderland
1934–1935	Arsenal FC
1933–1934	Arsenal FC
1932–1933	Arsenal FC
1931–1932	Everton FC
1930–1931	Arsenal FC
1929–1930	Sheffield Wednesday
1928–1929	Sheffield Wednesday
1927–1928	Everton FC
1926–1927	Newcastle United
1925–1926	Huddersfield Town
1924–1925	Huddersfield Town
1923–1924	Huddersfield Town
1922–1923	Liverpool FC
1921–1922	Liverpool FC
1920–1921	Burnley FC
1919–1920	West Bromwich Albion
1914–1915	Everton FC
1913–1914	Blackburn Rovers
1912–1913	Sunderland

Year	Winner
1911–1912	Blackburn Rovers
1910–1911	Manchester United
1909–1910	Aston Villa
1908–1909	Newcastle United
1907–1908	Manchester United
1906–1907	Newcastle United
1905–1906	Liverpool FC
1904–1905	Newcastle United
1903–1904	Sheffield Wednesday
1902–1903	Sheffield Wednesday
1901–1902	Sunderland
1900–1901	Liverpool FC
1899–1900	Aston Villa
1898–1899	Aston Villa
1897–1898	Sheffield United
1896–1897	Aston Villa
1895–1896	Aston Villa
1894–1895	Sunderland
1893–1894	Aston Villa
1892–1893	Sunderland
1891–1892	Sunderland
1890–1891	Everton FC
1889–1890	Preston North End
1888–1889	Preston North End

Compiled by Kelsey Moore

Association Football, Germany (Bundesliga)

Year	Winner
2009–2010	FC Bayern Munich
2008–2009	VfL Wolfsburg
2007–2008	FC Bayern Munich
2006–2007	VfB Stuttgart
2005–2006	FC Bayern Munich
2004–2005	FC Bayern Munich
2003–2004	SV Werder Bremen
2002–2003	FC Bayern Munich
2001–2002	Borussia Dortmund
2000–2001	FC Bayern Munich
1999–2000	FC Bayern Munich
1998–1999	FC Bayern Munich
1997–1998	FC Kaiserslautern
1996–1997	FC Bayern Munich
1995–1996	Borussia Dortmund
1994–1995	Borussia Dortmund
1993–1994	FC Bayern Munich
1992–1993	SV Werder Bremen
1991–1992	VfB Stuttgart
1990–1991	FC Kaiserslautern
1989–1990	FC Bayern Munich
1988–1989	FC Bayern Munich

Year	Winner
1987–1988	SV Werder Bremen
1986–1987	FC Bayern Munich
1985–1986	FC Bayern Munich
1984–1985	FC Bayern Munich
1983–1984	VfB Stuttgart
1982–1983	Hamburger SV
1981–1982	Hamburger SV
1980–1981	FC Bayern Munich
1979–1980	FC Bayern Munich
1978–1979	Hamburger SV
1977–1978	FC Koln
1976–1977	Borussia Mönchengladbach
1975–1976	Borussia Mönchengladbach
1974–1975	Borussia Mönchengladbach
1973–1974	FC Bayern Munich
1972–1973	FC Bayern Munich
1971–1972	FC Bayern Munich
1970–1971	Borussia Mönchengladbach
1969–1970	Borussia Mönchengladbach
1968–1969	FC Bayern Munich
1967–1968	FC Nuremberg
1966–1967	Eintracht Braunschweig
1965–1966	TSV 1860 Munchen
1964–1965	SV Werder Bremen
1963–1964	FC Koln

Compiled by Kelsey Moore

Association Football, Spain (La Liga)

Year	Winner
2009–2010	FC Barcelona
2008–2009	FC Barcelona
2007–2008	Real Madrid
2006–2007	Real Madrid
2005–2006	FC Barcelona
2004–2005	FC Barcelona
2003–2004	Valencia CF
2002–2003	Real Madrid
2001–2002	Valencia CF
2000–2001	Real Madrid
1999–2000	Deportivo La Coruña
1998–1999	FC Barcelona
1997–1998	FC Barcelona
1996–1997	Real Madrid
1995–1996	Atletico Madrid
1994–1995	Real Madrid
1993–1994	FC Barcelona
1992–1993	FC Barcelona
1991–1992	FC Barcelona
1990–1991	FC Barcelona
1989–1990	Real Madrid

280 | Winners and Champions of Major World Sporting Events

Year	Winner
1988–1989	Real Madrid
1987–1988	Real Madrid
1986–1987	Real Madrid
1985–1986	Real Madrid
1984–1985	FC Barcelona
1983–1984	Atletico Bilbao
1982–1983	Atletico Bilbao
1981–1982	Real Sociedad
1980–1981	Real Sociedad
1979–1980	Real Madrid
1978–1979	Real Madrid
1977–1978	Real Madrid
1976–1977	Atletico Madrid
1975–1976	Real Madrid
1974–1975	Real Madrid
1973–1974	FC Barcelona
1972–1973	Atletico Madrid
1971–1972	Real Madrid
1970–1971	FC Barcelona
1969–1970	Atletico Madrid
1968–1969	Real Madrid
1967–1968	Real Madrid
1966–1967	Real Madrid
1965–1966	Atletico Madrid
1964–1965	Real Madrid
1963–1964	Real Madrid
1962–1963	Real Madrid
1961–1962	Real Madrid
1960–1961	Real Madrid
1959–1960	FC Barcelona
1958–1959	FC Barcelona
1957–1958	Real Madrid
1956–1957	Real Madrid
1955–1956	Atletico Bilbao
1954–1955	Real Madrid
1953–1954	Real Madrid
1952–1953	FC Barcelona
1951–1952	FC Barcelona
1950–1951	Atletico Madrid
1949–1950	Atletico Madrid
1948–1949	FC Barcelona
1947–1948	FC Barcelona
1946–1947	Valencia CF
1945–1946	Sevilla FC
1944–1945	FC Barcelona
1943–1944	Valencia CF
1942–1943	Atletico Bilbao
1941–1942	Valencia CF
1940–1941	Atletico Madrid
1939–1940	Atletico Madrid
1935–1936	Atletico Bilbao
1934–1935	Betis Seville

Year	Winner
1933–1934	Atletico Bilbao
1932–1933	Real Madrid
1931–1932	Real Madrid
1930–1931	Atletico Bilbao
1929–1930	Atletico Bilbao
1928–1929	FC Barcelona

Compiled by Kelsey Moore

Association Football, Italy (Serie A)

Year	Winner
2009–2010	Internazionale
2008–2009	Internazionale
2007–2008	Internazionale
2006–2007	Internazionale
2005–2006	Internazionale (Juventus original winner, but legal dispute changes league final results)
2004–2005	Revoked from Juventus
2003–2004	Milan
2002–2003	Juventus
2001–2002	Juventus
2000–2001	Roma
1999–2000	Lazio
1998–1999	Milan
1997–1998	Juventus
1996–1997	Juventus
1995–1996	Milan
1994–1995	Juventus
1993–1994	Milan
1992–1993	Milan
1991–1992	Milan
1990–1991	Sampdoria
1989–1990	Napoli
1988–1989	Internazionale
1987–1988	Milan
1986–1987	Napoli
1985–1986	Juventus
1984–1985	Hellas Verona
1983–1984	Juventus
1982–1983	Roma
1981–1982	Juventus
1980–1981	Juventus
1979–1980	Internazionale
1978–1979	Milan
1977–1978	Juventus
1976–1977	Juventus
1975–1976	Torino
1974–1975	Juventus
1973–1974	Lazio
1972–1973	Juventus
1971–1972	Juventus
1970–1971	Internazionale

Year	Winner
1969–1970	Cagliari
1968–1969	Fiorentina
1967–1968	Milan
1966–1967	Juventus
1965–1966	Internazionale
1964–1965	Internazionale
1963–1964	Bologna
1962–1963	Internazionale
1961–1962	Milan
1960–1961	Juventus
1959–1960	Juventus
1958–1959	Milan
1957–1958	Juventus
1956–1957	Milan
1955–1956	Fiorentina
1954–1955	Milan
1953–1954	Internazionale
1952–1953	Internazionale
1951–1952	Juventus
1950–1951	Milan
1949–1950	Juventus
1948–1949	Torino
1947–1948	Torino
1946–1947	Torino
1945–1946	Torino
1943–1945	Suspended (World War II)
1942–1943	Torino
1941–1942	Roma
1940–1941	Bologna
1939–1940	Internazionale
1938–1939	Bologna
1937–1938	Internazionale
1936–1937	Bologna
1935–1936	Bologna
1934–1935	Juventus
1933–1934	Juventus
1932–1933	Juventus
1931–1932	Juventus
1930–1931	Juventus
1929–1930	Internazionale
1928–1929	Bologna
1927–1928	Torino
1926–1927	Revoked from Torino
1925–1926	Juventus
1924–1925	Bologna
1923–1924	Genoa
1922–1923	Genoa
1921–1922	Novese (Federazione Italiana Gioco Calcio [FIGC])
1921–1922	Pro Vercelli (Confederazione Calcistica Italiana [CCI])
1920–1921	Pro Vercelli
1919–1920	Internazionale
1916–1919	Suspended (World War I)

Year	Winner
1914–1915	Genoa
1913–1914	Casale
1912–1913	Pro Vercelli
1911–1912	Pro Vercelli
1910–1911	Pro Vercelli
1909–1910	Internazionale
1909	Pro Vercelli
1908	Pro Vercelli
1907	Milan
1906	Milan
1905	Juventus
1904	Genoa
1903	Genoa
1902	Genoa
1901	Milan
1900	Genoa
1899	Genoa
1898	Genoa

Compiled by Andrea Giampiccoli

Association Football, France (Ligue 1)

Year	Winner
2009–2010	Olympique de Marseille
2008–2009	Girondins de Bordeaux FC
2007–2008	Olympique de Lyon
2006–2007	Olympique de Lyon
2005–2006	Olympique de Lyon
2004–2005	Olympique de Lyon
2003–2004	Olympique de Lyon
2002–2003	Olympique de Lyon
2001–2002	Olympique de Lyon
2000–2001	Football Club de Nantes
1999–2000	Association Sportive de Monaco
1998–1999	Girondins de Bordeaux FC
1997–1998	Racing Club de Lens
1996–1997	Association Sportive de Monaco
1995–1996	Association de la Jeunesse Auxerroise
1994–1995	Football Club de Nantes
1993–1994	Paris Saint-Germain Football Club
1992–1993	Marseille (Revoked)
1991–1992	Olympique de Marseille
1990–1991	Olympique de Marseille
1989–1990	Olympique de Marseille
1988–1989	Olympique de Marseille
1987–1988	Association Sportive de Monaco
1986–1987	Girondins de Bordeaux FC
1985–1986	Paris Saint-Germain Football Club
1984–1985	Girondins de Bordeaux FC
1983–1984	Girondins de Bordeaux FC
1982–1983	Football Club de Nantes

Year	Winner
1981–1982	Association Sportive de Monaco
1980–1981	Association Sportive de Saint-Étienne
1979–1980	Football Club de Nantes
1978–1979	Racing Club de Strasbourg
1977–1978	Association Sportive de Monaco
1976–1977	Football Club de Nantes
1975–1976	Association Sportive de Saint-Étienne
1974–1975	Association Sportive de Saint-Étienne
1973–1974	Association Sportive de Saint-Étienne
1972–1973	Football Club de Nantes
1971–1972	Olympique de Marseille
1970–1971	Olympique de Marseille
1969–1970	Association Sportive de Saint-Étienne
1968–1969	Association Sportive de Saint-Étienne
1967–1968	Association Sportive de Saint-Étienne
1966–1967	Association Sportive de Saint-Étienne
1965–1966	Football Club de Nantes
1964–1965	Football Club de Nantes
1963–1964	Association Sportive de Saint-Étienne
1962–1963	Association Sportive de Monaco
1961–1962	Stade de Reims
1960–1961	Association Sportive de Monaco
1959–1960	Stade de Reims
1958–1959	Olympique Gymnaste Club de Nice
1957–1958	Stade de Reims
1956–1957	Association Sportive de Saint-Étienne
1955–1956	Olympique Gymnaste Club de Nice
1954–1955	Stade de Reims
1953–1954	Lille Olympique Sporting Club
1952–1953	Stade de Reims
1951–1952	Olympique Gymnaste Club de Nice
1950–1951	Olympique Gymnaste Club de Nice
1949–1950	Football Club des Girondins de Bordeaux
1948–1949	Stade de Reims
1947–1948	Olympique de Marseille
1946–1947	Club Olympique de Roubaix-Tourcoing
1945–1946	Lille Olympique Sporting Club
1944–1945	Football Club de Rouen
1943–1944	Lens-Artois (Federal teams Championship partly unfinished)
1942–1943	Racing Club de Lens (North), Toulouse Football Club (South)
1941–1942	Stade de Reims (North), Football Club de Sète (South)
1940–1941	Red Star Olympique Audonien (North), Olympique de Marseille (South)
1939–1940	Football Club Rouen (North), Girondins ASP (South)
1938–1939	Football Club de Sète
1937–1938	Football Club de Sochaux-Montbéliard
1936–1937	Olympique de Marseille
1935–1936	Racing Club de Paris
1934–1935	Football Club de Sochaux-Montbéliard
1933–1934	Football Club de Sète
1932–1933	Olympique Lillois
1931–1932	Football Club de Mulhouse
1930–1931	Football Club de Sochaux-Montbéliard

Year	Winner
1928–1929	Olympique de Marseille
1927–1928	Stade Français (Paris)
1926–1927	Cercle Athlétique de Paris
1915–1916	Olympique de Pantin
1913–1914	Olympique Lillois
1912–1913	Cercle Athlétique de Paris
1911–1912	Étoile des Deux Lacs
1910–1911	Cercle Athlétique de Paris
1909–1910	Cercle Athlétique de Vitry
1908–1909	Jeanne d'Arc de Saint-Ouen
1907–1908	Patronage Olier
1906–1907	Racing Club de France
1905–1906	Racing Club de Roubaix
1904–1905	Gallia Club
1903–1904	Racing Club de Roubaix
1902–1903	Racing Club de Roubaix
1901–1902	Racing Club de Roubaix
1900–1901	Standard Athletic Club
1899–1900	Havre Athletic Club Football Association
1898–1899	Havre Athletic Club Football Association
1897–1898	Standard Athletic Club
1896–1897	Standard Athletic Club
1896	Club Français
1895	Standard Athletic Club
1894	Standard Athletic Club

Compiled by Daniel Zimmet

Association Football, Netherlands (Eredivisie)

Year	Winner
2009–2010	FC Twente
2008–2009	AZ
2007–2008	PSV
2006–2007	PSV
2005–2006	PSV
2004–2005	PSV
2003–2004	Ajax
2002–2003	PSV
2001–2002	Ajax
2000–2001	PSV
1999–2000	PSV
1998–1999	Feyenoord
1997–1998	Ajax
1996–1997	PSV
1995–1996	Ajax
1994–1995	Ajax
1993–1994	Ajax
1992–1993	Feyenoord
1991–1992	PSV
1990–1991	PSV
1989–1990	Ajax

Year	Winner
1988–1989	PSV
1987–1988	PSV
1986–1987	PSV
1985–1986	PSV
1984–1985	Ajax
1983–1984	Feyenoord
1982–1983	Ajax
1981–1982	Ajax
1980–1981	AZ 67
1979–1980	Ajax
1978–1979	Ajax
1977–1978	PSV
1976–1977	Ajax
1975–1976	PSV
1974–1975	PSV
1973–1974	Feyenoord
1972–1973	Ajax
1971–1972	Ajax
1970–1971	Feyenoord
1969–1970	Ajax
1968–1969	Feyenoord
1967–1968	Ajax
1966–1967	Ajax
1965–1966	Ajax
1964–1965	Feyenoord
1963–1964	DWS
1962–1963	PSV
1961–1962	Feyenoord
1960–1961	Feyenoord
1959–1960	Ajax
1958–1959	Sparta Rotterdam
1957–1958	DOS Atrecht
1956–1957	Ajax
1950–1956	PSV (50–51), Willem II (51–52), RCH Harleem (52–53), FC Eindhoven (53–54), Willem II (54–55), Rapid JC Herenveen (55–56)
1949–1950	Limburgia
1948–1949	SVV Schieden
1947–1948	BVV Hertogenbosch
1944–1945	Not held (44–45), Haarlem (45–46), Ajax (46–47)
1943–1944	De Volewijckers
1942–1943	ADO Den Haag
1939–1942	Feyenoord (39–40), Heracles (40–41), ADO Den Haag (41–42)
1938–1939	Ajax
1937–1938	Feyenoord
1936–1937	Ajax
1935–1936	Feyenoord
1934–1935	PSV
1933–1934	Ajax
1932–1933	Go Ahead Deventer
1931–1932	Ajax
1930–1931	Ajax
1929–1930	Go Ahead Deventer

Year	Winner
1928–1929	PSV
1927–1928	Feyenoord
1926–1927	Heracles
1925–1926	SC Enschende
1924–1925	HBS Den Haag
1921–1924	Go Ahead Deventer
1920–1921	NAC Breda
1919–1920	Be Quick Groningen
1918–1919	Ajax
1917–1918	Ajax
1916–1917	Go Ahead Deventer
1915–1916	Willen II
1914–1915	Sparta Rotterdam
1913–1914	HVV Den Haag
1912–1913	Sparta Rotterdam
1910–1912	Sparta Rotterdam
1910–1911	Sparta Rotterdam
1909–1910	HVV Den Haag
1908–1909	Sparta Rotterdam
1907–1908	Quick Den Haag
1906–1907	HVV Den Haag
1905–1906	HBS Den Haag
1904–1905	HVV Den Haag
1903–1904	HBS Den Haag
1902–1903	HVV Den Haag
1901–1902	HVV Den Haag
1900–1901	HVV Den Haag
1899–1900	HVV Den Haag
1898–1899	RAP Amsterdam

Compiled by Molly McManamon

Association Football, Scotland (Premier League)

Year	Winner
2010	Glasgow Rangers
2009	Glasgow Rangers
2008	Celtic Glasgow
2007	Celtic Glasgow
2006	Celtic Glasgow
2005	Glasgow Rangers
2004	Celtic Glasgow
2003	Glasgow Rangers
2002	Celtic Glasgow
2001	Celtic Glasgow
2000	Glasgow Rangers
1999	Glasgow Rangers
1998	Celtic Glasgow
1997	Glasgow Rangers
1996	Glasgow Rangers
1995	Glasgow Rangers
1994	Glasgow Rangers

Year	Winner
1993	Glasgow Rangers
1992	Glasgow Rangers
1991	Glasgow Rangers
1990	Glasgow Rangers
1989	Glasgow Rangers
1988	Celtic Glasgow
1987	Glasgow Rangers
1986	Celtic Glasgow
1985	Aberdeen
1984	Aberdeen
1983	Dundee United
1982	Celtic Glasgow
1981	Celtic Glasgow
1980	Aberdeen
1979	Celtic Glasgow
1978	Glasgow Rangers
1977	Celtic Glasgow
1976	Glasgow Rangers
1975	Glasgow Rangers
1974	Celtic Glasgow
1973	Celtic Glasgow
1972	Celtic Glasgow
1971	Celtic Glasgow
1970	Celtic Glasgow
1969	Celtic Glasgow
1968	Celtic Glasgow
1967	Celtic Glasgow
1966	Celtic Glasgow
1965	Kilmarnock
1964	Glasgow Rangers
1963	Glasgow Rangers
1962	Dundee FC
1961	Glasgow Rangers
1960	Heart of Midlothian
1959	Glasgow Rangers
1958	Heart of Midlothian
1957	Glasgow Rangers
1956	Glasgow Rangers
1955	Aberdeen
1954	Celtic Glasgow
1953	Glasgow Rangers
1952	Hibernian Edinburgh
1951	Hibernian Edinburgh
1950	Glasgow Rangers
1949	Glasgow Rangers
1948	Hibernian Edinburgh
1947	Glasgow Rangers
1946	No competition
1945	No competition
1944	No competition
1943	No competition
1942	No competition

Year	Winner
1941	No competition
1940	No competition
1939	Glasgow Rangers
1938	Celtic Glasgow
1937	Glasgow Rangers
1936	Celtic Glasgow
1935	Glasgow Rangers
1934	Glasgow Rangers
1933	Glasgow Rangers
1932	Motherwell
1931	Glasgow Rangers
1930	Glasgow Rangers
1929	Glasgow Rangers
1928	Glasgow Rangers
1927	Glasgow Rangers
1926	Celtic Glasgow
1925	Glasgow Rangers
1924	Glasgow Rangers
1923	Glasgow Rangers
1922	Celtic Glasgow
1921	Glasgow Rangers
1920	Glasgow Rangers
1919	Celtic Glasgow
1918	Glasgow Rangers
1917	Celtic Glasgow
1916	Celtic Glasgow
1915	Celtic Glasgow
1914	Celtic Glasgow
1913	Glasgow Rangers
1912	Glasgow Rangers
1911	Glasgow Rangers
1910	Celtic Glasgow
1909	Celtic Glasgow
1908	Celtic Glasgow
1907	Celtic Glasgow
1906	Celtic Glasgow
1905	Celtic Glasgow
1904	Third Lanark AC
1903	Hibernian Edinburgh
1902	Glasgow Rangers
1901	Glasgow Rangers
1900	Glasgow Rangers
1899	Glasgow Rangers
1898	Celtic Glasgow
1897	Heart of Midlothian
1896	Celtic Glasgow
1895	Heart of Midlothian
1894	Celtic Glasgow
1893	Celtic Glasgow
1892	Dumbarton FC
1891	Dumbarton FC & Celtic Glasgow

Compiled by Kelsey Moore

Association Football, Portugal (Primeira Liga)

Year	Winner	Runner-up
2009–2010	SL Benfica	Braga
2008–2009	FC Porto	Sporting Clube de Portugal
2007–2008	FC Porto	Sporting Clube de Portugal
2006–2007	FC Porto	Sporting Clube de Portugal
2005–2006	FC Porto	Sporting Clube de Portugal
2004–2005	SL Benfica	Porto
2003–2004	FC Porto	SL Benfica
2002–2003	FC Porto	SL Benfica
2001–2002	Sporting Clube de Portugal	SL Benfica
2000–2001	Boavista FC	Porto
1999–2000	Sporting Clube de Portugal	Porto
1998–1999	FC Porto	Boavista FC
1997–1998	FC Porto	SL Benfica
1996–1997	FC Porto	Sporting Clube de Portugal
1995–1996	FC Porto	SL Benfica
1994–1995	FC Porto	Sporting Clube de Portugal
1993–1994	SL Benfica	FC Porto
1992–1993	FC Porto	SL Benfica
1991–1992	FC Porto	SL Benfica
1990–1991	SL Benfica	FC Porto
1989–1990	FC Porto	SL Benfica
1988–1989	SL Benfica	FC Porto
1987–1988	FC Porto	SL Benfica
1986–1987	SL Benfica	FC Porto
1985–1986	FC Porto	SL Benfica
1984–1985	FC Porto	Sporting Clube de Portugal
1983–1984	SL Benfica	FC Porto
1982–1983	SL Benfica	FC Porto
1981–1982	Sporting Clube de Portugal	SL Benfica
1980–1981	SL Benfica	FC Porto
1979–1980	Sporting Clube de Portugal	FC Porto
1978–1979	FC Porto	SL Benfica
1977–1978	FC Porto	SL Benfica
1976–1977	SL Benfica	Sporting Clube de Portugal
1975–1976	SL Benfica	Boavista
1974–1975	SL Benfica	FC Porto
1973–1974	Sporting Clube de Portugal	SL Benfica
1972–1973	SL Benfica	Belenenses
1971–1972	SL Benfica	Vitoria de Setubal
1970–1971	SL Benfica	Sporting Clube de Portugal
1969–1970	Sporting Clube de Portugal	SL Benfica
1968–1969	SL Benfica	FC Porto
1967–1968	SL Benfica	Sporting Clube de Portugal
1966–1967	SL Benfica	Academica de Ciombra
1965–1966	Sporting Clube de Portugal	SL Benfica
1964–1965	SL Benfica	FC Porto
1963–1964	SL Benfica	FC Porto
1962–1963	SL Benfica	FC Porto
1961–1962	Sporting Clube de Portugal	FC Porto
1960–1961	SL Benfica	Sporting Clube de Portugal

Year	Winner	Runner-up
1959–1960	SL Benfica	Sporting Clube de Portugal
1958–1959	FC Porto	SL Benfica
1957–1958	Sporting Clube de Portugal	FC Porto
1956–1957	SL Benfica	FC Porto
1955–1956	FC Porto	SL Benfica
1954–1955	SL Benfica	Belenenses
1953–1954	Sporting Clube de Portugal	FC Porto
1952–1953	Sporting Clube de Portugal	SL Benfica
1951–1952	Sporting Clube de Portugal	SL Benfica
1950–1951	Sporting Clube de Portugal	FC Porto
1949–1950	SL Benfica	Sporting Clube de Portugal
1948–1949	Sporting Clube de Portugal	SL Benfica
1947–1948	Sporting Clube de Portugal	SL Benfica
1946–1947	Sporting Clube de Portugal	SL Benfica
1945–1946	Belenenses	SL Benfica
1944–1945	SL Benfica	Sporting Clube de Portugal
1943–1944	Sporting Clube de Portugal	SL Benfica
1942–1943	SL Benfica	Sporting Clube de Portugal
1941–1942	SL Benfica	Sporting Clube de Portugal
1940–1941	Sporting Clube de Portugal	FC Porto
1939–1940	FC Porto	Sporting Clube de Portugal
1938–1939	FC Porto	Sporting Clube de Portugal

Compiled by Daniel Zimmet

Australian Football League Grand Final

Season	Winner	Runner-up
2010	Collingwood	St Kilda
2009	Geelong	St Kilda
2008	Hawthorn	Geelong
2007	Geelong	Port Adelaide
2006	West Coast	Sydney
2005	Sydney	West Coast
2004	Port Adelaide	Brisbane
2003	Brisbane	Collingwood
2002	Brisbane	Collingwood
2001	Brisbane	Essendon
2000	Essendon	Melbourne
1999	North Melbourne	Carlton
1998	Adelaide	North Melbourne
1997	Adelaide	St Kilda
1996	North Melbourne	Sydney
1995	Carlton	Geelong
1994	West Coast	Geelong
1993	Essendon	Carlton
1992	West Coast	Geelong
1991	Hawthorn	West Coast
1990	Collingwood	Essendon
1989	Hawthorn	Geelong
1988	Hawthorn	Melbourne
1987	Carlton	Hawthorn

Year	Winner	Runner-up
1986	Hawthorn	Carlton
1985	Essendon	Hawthorn
1984	Essendon	Hawthorn
1983	Hawthorn	Essendon
1982	Carlton	Richmond
1981	Carlton	Collingwood
1980	Richmond	Collingwood
1979	Carlton	Collingwood
1978	Hawthorn	North Melbourne
1977	North Melbourne	Collingwood
1976	Hawthorn	North Melbourne
1975	North Melbourne	Hawthorn
1974	Richmond	North Melbourne
1973	Richmond	Carlton
1972	Carlton	Richmond
1971	Hawthorn	St Kilda
1970	Carlton	Collingwood
1969	Richmond	Carlton
1968	Carlton	Essendon
1967	Richmond	Geelong
1966	St Kilda	Collingwood
1965	Essendon	St Kilda
1964	Melbourne	Collingwood
1963	Geelong	Hawthorn
1962	Essendon	Carlton
1961	Hawthorn	Footscray
1960	Melbourne	Collingwood
1959	Melbourne	Essendon
1958	Collingwood	Melbourne
1957	Melbourne	Essendon
1956	Melbourne	Collingwood
1955	Melbourne	Collingwood
1954	Footscray	Melbourne
1953	Collingwood	Geelong
1952	Geelong	Collingwood
1951	Geelong	Essendon
1950	Essendon	North Melbourne
1949	Essendon	Carlton
1948	Melbourne	Essendon
1947	Carlton	Essendon
1946	Essendon	Melbourne
1945	Carlton	South Melbourne
1944	Fitzroy	Richmond
1943	Richmond	Essendon
1942	Essendon	Richmond
1941	Melbourne	Essendon
1940	Melbourne	Richmond
1939	Melbourne	Collingwood
1938	Carlton	Collingwood
1937	Geelong	Collingwood
1936	Collingwood	South Melbourne

Year	Winner	Runner-up
1935	Collingwood	South Melbourne
1934	Richmond	South Melbourne
1933	South Melbourne	Richmond
1932	Richmond	Carlton
1931	Geelong	Richmond
1930	Collingwood	Geelong
1929	Collingwood	Richmond
1928	Collingwood	Richmond
1927	Collingwood	Richmond
1926	Melbourne	Collingwood
1925	Geelong	Collingwood
1924	Essendon	Richmond
1923	Essendon	Fitzroy
1922	Fitzroy	Collingwood
1921	Richmond	Carlton
1920	Richmond	Collingwood
1919	Collingwood	Richmond
1918	South Melbourne	Collingwood
1917	Collingwood	Fitzroy
1916	Fitzroy	Carlton
1915	Carlton	Collingwood
1914	Carlton	South Melbourne
1913	Fitzroy	St Kilda
1912	Essendon	South Melbourne
1911	Essendon	Collingwood
1910	Collingwood	Carlton
1909	South Melbourne	Carlton
1908	Carlton	Essendon
1907	Carlton	South Melbourne
1906	Carlton	Fitzroy
1905	Fitzroy	Collingwood
1904	Fitzroy	Carlton
1903	Collingwood	Fitzroy
1902	Collingwood	Essendon
1901	Essendon	Collingwood
1900	Melbourne	Fitzroy
1899	Fitzroy	South Melbourne
1898	Fitzroy	Essendon
1897	Essendon	Geelong

Compiled by Jessica Bohince

Australia Rugby League Grand Final

Year	Winner	Runner-up
2010	St. George	Roosters
2009	Melbourne*	Parramatta
2008	Manly	Melbourne
2007	Melbourne*	Manly
2006	Brisbane	Melbourne
2005	West Tigers	Cowboys
2004	Bulldogs	Roosters
2003	Penrith	Roosters
2002	Roosters	Warriors
2001	Newcastle	Parramatta
2000	Brisbane	Roosters
1999	Melbourne	Dragons
1998	Brisbane	Canterbury
1997	Newcastle	Manly

Super League Grand Final

Year	Winner	Runner-up
1997	Brisbane	Canterbury
1996	Manly	St. George
1995	Bulldogs	Manly
1994	Canberra	Canterbury
1993	Brisbane	St. George
1992	Brisbane	St. George
1991	Penrith	Canberra
1990	Canberra	Penrith
1989	Canberra	Balmain
1988	Canterbury	Balmain
1987	Manly	Canberra
1986	Parramatta	Canterbury
1985	Canterbury	St. George
1984	Canterbury	Parramatta
1983	Parramatta	Manly
1982	Parramatta	Manly
1981	Parramatta	Newtown
1980	Canterbury	Easts
1979	St. George	Canterbury
1978	Manly	Cronulla
1977	St. George	Parramatta
1976	Manly	Parramatta
1975	Easts	St. George
1974	Easts	Canterbury
1973	Manly	Cronulla
1972	Manly	Easts
1971	Souths	St. George
1970	Souths	Manly
1969	Balmain	Souths
1968	Souths	Manly
1967	Souths	Canterbury
1966	St. George	Balmain
1965	St. George	Souths

Year	Winner	Runner-up
1964	St. George	Balmain
1963	St. George	Wests
1962	St. George	Wests
1961	St. George	Wests
1960	St. George	Easts
1959	St. George	Manly
1958	St. George	Wests
1957	St. George	Manly
1956	St. George	Balmain
1955	Souths	Newton
1954	Souths	Newton

* Revoked due to salary cap breach.

Compiled by Charles Parrish

Rugby League Challenge Cup Champions (England)

Year	Winner
2010	Warrington
2009	Warrington
2008	St. Helens
2007	St. Helens
2006	St. Helens
2005	Hull FC
2004	St. Helens
2003	Bradford Bulls
2002	Wigan Warriors
2001	St. Helens
2000	Bradford Bulls
1999	Leeds Rhinos
1998	Sheffield Eagles
1997	St. Helens
1996	St. Helens
1995	Wigan
1994	Wigan
1993	Wigan
1992	Wigan
1991	Wigan
1990	Wigan
1989	Wigan
1988	Wigan
1987	Halifax
1986	Castleford
1985	Wigan
1984	Widnes
1983	Featherstone Rovers
1982	Hull
1981	Widnes
1980	Hull KR
1979	Widnes
1978	Leeds
1977	Leeds

Year	Winner
1976	St. Helens
1975	Widnes
1974	Warrington
1973	Featherstone Rovers
1972	St. Helens
1971	Leigh
1970	Castleford
1969	Castleford
1968	Leeds
1967	Featherstone Rovers
1966	St. Helens
1965	Wigan
1964	Widnes
1963	Wakefield Trinity
1962	Wakefield Trinity
1961	St. Helens
1960	Wakefield Trinity
1959	Wigan
1958	Wigan
1957	Leeds
1956	St. Helens
1955	Barrow
1954	Warrington
1953	Huddersfield
1952	Workington Town
1951	Wigan
1950	Warrington
1949	Bradford Northern
1948	Wigan
1947	Bradford Northern
1946	Wakefield Trinity
1945	Huddersfield
1944	Bradford Northern
1943	Dewsbury
1942	Leeds
1941	Leeds
1940	Not held
1939	Halifax
1938	Salford
1937	Widnes
1936	Leeds
1935	Castleford
1934	Hunslet
1933	Huddersfield
1932	Leeds
1931	Halifax
1930	Widnes
1929	Wigan
1928	Swinton
1927	Oldham
1926	Swinton
1925	Oldham

Year	Winner
1924	Wigan
1923	Leeds
1922	Rochdale Hornets
1921	Leigh
1920	Huddersfield
1916–1919	Rugby League suspended due to World War I
1915	Huddersfield
1914	Hull
1913	Huddersfield
1912	Dewsbury
1911	Broughton
1910	Leeds
1909	Wakefield Trinity
1908	Hunslet
1907	Warrington
1906	Bradford
1905	Warrington
1904	Halifax
1903	Halifax
1902	Broughton
1901	Batley
1900	Swinton
1899	Oldham
1898	Batley
1897	Batley

Compiled by Charles Parrish

Six Nations Rugby Champions (Home Nations, Five Nations, Six Nations)

Six Nations

Year	Winner
2011	England
2010	France
2009	Ireland
2008	Wales
2007	France
2006	France
2005	Wales
2004	France
2003	England
2002	France
2001	England
2000	England

Five Nations

Year	Winner
1999	Scotland
1998	France
1997	France

Year	Winner
1996	England
1995	England
1994	Wales
1993	France
1992	England
1991	England
1990	Scotland
1989	France
1988	France & Wales
1987	France
1986	France & Scotland
1985	Ireland
1984	Scotland
1983	France & Ireland
1982	Ireland
1981	France
1980	England
1979	Wales
1978	Wales
1977	France
1976	Wales
1975	Wales
1974	Ireland
1973	England, France, Ireland, Scotland, & Wales
1972	Not held
1971	Wales
1970	France & Wales
1969	Wales
1968	France
1967	France
1966	Wales
1965	Wales
1964	Scotland & Wales
1963	England
1962	France
1961	France
1960	England & France
1959	France
1958	England
1957	England
1956	Wales
1955	France & Wales
1954	England, France, & Wales
1953	England
1952	Wales
1951	Ireland
1950	Wales
1949	Ireland
1948	Ireland
1947	England & Wales
1946	Not held due to World War II
1945	Not held due to World War II

Year	Winner
1944	Not held due to World War II
1943	Not held due to World War II
1942	Not held due to World War II
1941	Not held due to World War II
1940	Not held due to World War II

Home Nations

Year	Winner
1939	England, Ireland, & Wales
1938	Scotland
1937	England
1936	Wales
1935	Ireland
1934	England
1933	Scotland
1932	England, Ireland, & Wales

Five Nations

Year	Winner
1931	Wales
1930	England
1929	Scotland
1928	England
1927	Ireland & Scotland
1926	Ireland & Scotland
1925	Scotland
1924	England
1923	England
1922	Wales
1921	England
1920	England, Scotland, & Wales
1919	Not held due to World War I
1918	Not held due to World War I
1917	Not held due to World War I
1916	Not held due to World War I
1915	Not held due to World War I
1914	England
1913	England
1912	England & Ireland
1911	Wales
1910	England

Home Nations

Year	Winner
1909	Wales
1908	Wales
1907	Scotland
1906	Ireland & Wales
1905	Wales
1904	Scotland
1903	Scotland

Year	Winner
1902	Wales
1901	Scotland
1900	Wales
1899	Ireland
1898	None
1897	None
1896	Ireland
1895	Scotland
1894	Ireland
1893	Wales
1892	England
1891	Scotland
1890	England & Scotland
1889	None
1888	None
1887	Scotland
1886	England & Scotland
1885	None
1884	England
1883	England
1882	England

Compiled by Charles Parrish

All-Ireland Gaelic Football

Year	Winner	Runner-up
2010	Cork	Down
2009	Kerry	Cork
2008	Tyrone	Kerry
2007	Kerry	Cork
2006	Kerry	Mayo
2005	Tyrone	Kerry
2004	Kerry	Mayo
2003	Tyrone	Armagh
2002	Armagh	Kerry
2001	Galway	Meath
2000	Kerry	Galway
1999	Meath	Cork
1998	Galway	Kildare
1997	Kerry	Mayo
1996	Meath	Mayo
1995	Dublin	Tyrone
1994	Down	Dublin
1993	Derry	Cork
1992	Donegal	Dublin
1991	Down	Meath
1990	Cork	Meath
1989	Cork	Mayo
1988	Meath	Cork
1987	Meath	Cork
1986	Kerry	Tyrone

Year	Winner	Runner-up
1985	Kerry	Dublin
1984	Kerry	Dublin
1983	Dublin	Galway
1982	Offaly	Kerry
1981	Kerry	Offaly
1980	Kerry	Roscommon
1979	Kerry	Dublin
1978	Kerry	Dublin
1977	Dublin	Armagh
1976	Dublin	Kerry
1975	Kerry	Dublin
1974	Dublin	Galway
1973	Cork	Galway
1972	Offaly	Kerry
1971	Offaly	Galway
1970	Kerry	Meath
1969	Kerry	Offaly
1968	Down	Kerry
1967	Meath	Cork
1966	Galway	Meath
1965	Galway	Kerry
1964	Galway	Kerry
1963	Dublin	Galway
1962	Kerry	Roscommon
1961	Down	Offaly
1960	Down	Kerry
1959	Kerry	Galway
1958	Dublin	Derry
1957	Louth	Cork
1956	Galway	Cork
1955	Kerry	Dublin
1954	Meath	Kerry
1953	Kerry	Armagh
1952	Cavan	Meath
1951	Mayo	Meath
1950	Mayo	Louth
1949	Meath	Cavan
1948	Cavan	Mayo
1947	Cavan	Kerry
1946	Kerry	Roscommon
1945	Cork	Cavan
1944	Roscommon	Kerry
1943	Roscommon	Cavan
1942	Dublin	Galway
1941	Kerry	Galway
1940	Kerry	Galway
1939	Kerry	Meath
1938	Galway	Kerry
1937	Kerry	Cavan
1936	Mayo	Laois
1935	Cavan	Kildare
1934	Galway	Dublin

Year	Winner	Runner-up
1933	Cavan	Galway
1932	Kerry	Mayo
1931	Kerry	Kildare
1930	Kerry	Monaghan
1929	Kerry	Kildare
1928	Kildare	Cavan
1927	Kildare	Kerry
1926	Kerry	Kildare
1925	Galway	Cavan
1924	Kerry	Dublin
1923	Dublin	Kerry
1922	Dublin	Galway
1921	Dublin	Mayo
1920	Tipperary	Dublin
1919	Kildare	Galway
1918	Wexford	Tipperary
1917	Wexford	Clare
1916	Wexford	Mayo
1915	Wexford	Kerry
1914	Kerry	Wexford
1913	Kerry	Wexford
1912	Louth	Antrim
1911	Cork	Antrim
1910	Louth	Kerry
1909	Kerry	Louth
1908	Dublin	London
1907	Dublin	Cork
1906	Dublin	Cork
1905	Kildare	Kerry
1904	Kerry	Dublin
1903	Kerry	London
1902	Dublin	London
1901	Dublin	London
1900	Tipperary	London
1899	Dublin	Cork
1898	Dublin	Waterford
1897	Dublin	Cork
1896	Limerick	Dublin
1895	Tipperary	Meath
1894	Dublin	Cork
1893	Wexford	Cork
1892	Dublin	Kerry
1891	Dublin	Cork
1890	Cork	Wexford
1889	Tipperary	Laois
1888	Not completed	
1887	Limerick	Louth

Compiled by Ashley Hartnet

All-Ireland Hurling

Year	Winner	Runner-up
2010	Tipperary	Kilkenny
2009	Kilkenny	Tipperary
2008	Kilkenny	Waterford
2007	Kilkenny	Limerick
2006	Kilkenny	Cork
2005	Cork	Galway
2004	Cork	Kilkenny
2003	Kilkenny	Cork
2002	Kilkenny	Clare
2001	Tipperary	Galway
2000	Kilkenny	Offaly
1999	Cork	Kilkenny
1998	Offaly	Kilkenny
1997	Clare	Tipperary
1996	Wexford	Limerick
1995	Clare	Offaly
1994	Offaly	Limerick
1993	Kilkenny	Galway
1992	Kilkenny	Cork
1991	Tipperary	Kilkenny
1990	Cork	Galway
1989	Tipperary	Antrim
1988	Galway	Tipperary
1987	Galway	Kilkenny
1986	Cork	Galway
1985	Offaly	Galway
1984	Cork	Offaly
1983	Kilkenny	Cork
1982	Kilkenny	Cork
1981	Offaly	Galway
1980	Galway	Limerick
1979	Kilkenny	Galway
1978	Cork	Kilkenny
1977	Cork	Wexford
1976	Cork	Wexford
1975	Kilkenny	Galway
1974	Kilkenny	Limerick
1973	Limerick	Kilkenny
1972	Kilkenny	Cork
1971	Tipperary	Kilkenny
1970	Cork	Wexford
1969	Kilkenny	Cork
1968	Wexford	Tipperary
1967	Kilkenny	Tipperary
1966	Cork	Kilkenny
1965	Tipperary	Wexford
1964	Tipperary	Kilkenny
1963	Kilkenny	Waterford
1962	Tipperary	Wexford

Year	Winner	Runner-up
1961	Tipperary	Dublin
1960	Wexford	Tipperary
1959	Waterford	Kilkenny
1958	Tipperary	Galway
1957	Kilkenny	Waterford
1956	Wexford	Cork
1955	Wexford	Galway
1954	Cork	Wexford
1953	Cork	Galway
1952	Cork	Dublin
1951	Tipperary	Wexford
1950	Tipperary	Kilkenny
1949	Tipperary	Laois
1948	Waterford	Dublin
1947	Kilkenny	Cork
1946	Cork	Kilkenny
1945	Tipperary	Kilkenny
1944	Cork	Dublin
1943	Cork	Antrim
1942	Cork	Dublin
1941	Cork	Dublin
1940	Limerick	Kilkenny
1939	Kilkenny	Cork
1938	Dublin	Waterford
1937	Tipperary	Kilkenny
1936	Limerick	Kilkenny
1935	Kilkenny	Limerick
1934	Limerick	Dublin
1933	Kilkenny	Limerick
1932	Kilkenny	Clare
1931	Cork	Kilkenny
1930	Tipperary	Dublin
1929	Cork	Galway
1928	Cork	Galway
1927	Dublin	Cork
1926	Cork	Kilkenny
1925	Tipperary	Galway
1924	Dublin	Galway
1923	Galway	Limerick
1922	Kilkenny	Tipperary
1921	Limerick	Dublin
1920	Dublin	Cork
1919	Cork	Dublin
1918	Limerick	Wexford
1917	Dublin	Tipperary
1916	Tipperary	Kilkenny
1915	Laois	Cork
1914	Clare	Laois
1913	Kilkenny	Tipperary
1912	Kilkenny	Cork
1911	Kilkenny	Tipperary

Year	Winner	Runner-up
1910	Wexford	Limerick
1909	Kilkenny	Tipperary
1908	Tipperary	Dublin
1907	Kilkenny	Cork
1906	Tipperary	Dublin
1905	Kilkenny	Cork
1904	Kilkenny	Cork
1903	Cork	London
1902	Cork	London
1901	London	Cork
1900	Tipperary	London
1899	Tipperary	Wexford
1898	Tipperary	Kilkenny
1897	Limerick	Kilkenny
1896	Tipperary	Dublin
1895	Tipperary	Kilkenny
1894	Cork	Dublin
1893	Cork	Kilkenny
1892	Cork	Dublin
1891	Kerry	Wexford
1890	Cork	Wexford
1889	Dublin	Clare
1888	(Unfinished)	
1887	Tipperary	Galway

Compiled by Ashley Hartnet

SANZAR Tri-Nations Rugby Champions

Year	Winner	Runner-up
2011	Australia	New Zealand
2010	New Zealand	Australia
2009	South Africa	New Zealand
2008	New Zealand	Australia
2007	New Zealand	Australia
2006	New Zealand	Australia
2005	New Zealand	South Africa
2004	South Africa	Australia
2003	New Zealand	Australia
2002	New Zealand	Australia
2001	Australia	New Zealand
2000	Australia	New Zealand
1999	New Zealand	Australia
1998	South Africa	Australia
1997	New Zealand	South Africa
1996	New Zealand	South Africa

Compiled by Andrea Giampiccoli

Super Rugby (14, 12, 10)

Super 14

Year	Winner	Runner-up
2010	Bulls	Stormers
2009	Bulls	Chiefs
2008	Crusaders	Waratahs
2007	Bulls	Sharks
2006	Crusaders	Hurricanes

Super 12

Year	Winner	Runner-up
2005	Crusaders	Waratahs
2004	Brumbies	Crusaders
2003	Blues	Crusaders
2002	Crusaders	Brumbies
2001	Brumbies	Sharks
2000	Crusaders	Brumbies
1999	Crusaders	Highlanders
1998	Crusaders	Blues
1997	Blues	Brumbies
1996	Blues	Sharks

Super 10

Year	Winner	Runner-up
1995	Queensland	Transvaal
1994	Queensland	Natal
1993	Transvaal	Auckland

Compiled by Charles Parrish

European Rugby Championships

Heineken Cup

Year	Winner	Runner-up
2009–2010	Toulouse	Biarritz
2008–2009	Leinster	Leicester Tiger
2007–2008	Munster	Toulouse
2006–2007	London Wasps	Leicester Tiger
2005–2006	Munster	Biarritz
2004–2005	Toulouse	Stade Français
2003–2004	London Wasps	Toulouse
2002–2003	Toulouse	Perpignan
2001–2002	Leicester Tigers	Munster
2000–2001	Leicester Tigers	Stade Français
1999–2000	Northhampton Saints	Munster
1998–1999	Ulster	Colomiers
1997–1998	Bath	Brive
1996–1997	Brive	Leicester Tigers
1995–1996	Toulouse	Cardiff

European Challenge Cup

Year	Winner	Runner-up
2009–2010	Cardiff Blues	Toulon
2008–2009	Northampton Saints	Bourgoin
2007–2008	Bath	Worcester Warrors
2006–2007	Clermont Auvergne	Bath
2005–2006	Gloucester	London Irish
2004–2005	Sale	Pau
2003–2004	NEC Harlequins	Montferrand
2002–2003	London Wasps	Bath
2001–2002	Sale	Pontypridd
2000–2001	NEC Harlequins	Narbonne
1999–2000	Pau	Castres
1998–1999	Montferrand	Bourgoin
1997–1998	Colomiers	Agen
1996–1997	Bourgoin	Castres

Compiled by Daniel Zimmet

World Ice Hockey Champions

Year	Winner	Runner-up
2010	Czech Republic	Russia
2009	Russia	Canada
2008	Russia	Canada
2007	Canada	Finland
2006	Sweden	Czech Republic
2005	Czech Republic	Canada
2004	Canada	Sweden
2003	Canada	Sweden
2002	Slovakia	Russia
2001	Czech Republic	Finland
2000	Czech Republic	Slovakia
1999	Czech Republic	Finland
1998	Sweden	Finland
1997	Canada	Sweden
1996	Czech Republic	Canada
1995	Finland	Sweden
1994	Canada	Finland
1993	Russia	Sweden
1992	Sweden	Finland
1991	Sweden	Canada
1990	Soviet Union	Sweden
1989	Soviet Union	Canada
1987	Sweden	Soviet Union
1986	Soviet Union	Sweden
1985	Czechoslovakia	Canada
1983	Soviet Union	Czechoslovakia
1982	Soviet Union	Czechoslovakia
1981	Soviet Union	Sweden
1979	Soviet Union	Czechoslovakia
1978	Soviet Union	Czechoslovakia

Year	Winner	Runner-up
1977	Czechoslovakia	Sweden
1976	Czechoslovakia	Soviet Union
1975	Soviet Union	Czechoslovakia
1974	Soviet Union	Czechoslovakia
1973	Soviet Union	Sweden
1972	Czechoslovakia	Soviet Union
1971	Soviet Union	Czechoslovakia
1970	Soviet Union	Sweden
1969	Soviet Union	Sweden
1968	Soviet Union	Czechoslovakia
1967	Soviet Union	Sweden
1966	Soviet Union	Czechoslovakia
1965	Soviet Union	Czechoslovakia
1964	Soviet Union	Sweden
1963	Soviet Union	Sweden
1962	Sweden	Canada
1961	Canada	Czechoslovakia
1960	USA	Canada
1959	Canada	Soviet Union
1958	Canada	Soviet Union
1957	Sweden	Soviet Union
1956	Soviet Union	USA
1955	Canada	Soviet Union
1954	Soviet Union	Canada
1953	Sweden	FR Germany
1952	Canada	USA
1951	Canada	Sweden
1950	Canada	USA
1949	Czechoslovakia	Canada
1948	Canada	Czechoslovakia
1947	Czechoslovakia	Sweden
1940–1946	No championships (World War II)	
1939	Canada	USA
1938	Canada	United Kingdom
1937	Canada	United Kingdom
1936	United Kingdom	Canada
1935	Canada	Switzerland
1934	Canada	USA
1933	USA	Canada
1932	Canada	USA
1931	Canada	USA
1930	Canada	Germany
1928	Canada	Sweden
1924	Canada	USA
1920	Canada	USA

Compiled by Ludek Lhotsky

UEFA Champions League and European Cup

UEFA Champions League

Year	Winner	Runner-up
2010	Inter Milan	Bayern Munich
2009	Barcelona	Manchester United
2008	Manchester United FC	Chelsea FC
2007	AC Milan	Liverpool
2006	FC Barcelona	Arsenal
2005	Liverpool	AC Milan
2004	FC Porto	AS Monaco FC
2003	AC Milan	Juventus FC
2002	Real Madrid	Bayer Leverkusen
2001	FC Bayern Munich	Valencia CF
2000	Real Madrid CF	Valencia CF
1999	Manchester United FC	FC Bayern München
1998	Real Madrid CF	Juventus FC
1997	Borussia Dortmund	Juventus FC
1996	Juventus FC	AFC Ajax
1995	AFC Ajax	AC Milan
1994	AC Milan	FC Barcelona
1993	Olympique de Marseille	AC Milan
1992	FC Barcelona	Sampdoria UC

European Champions Clubs' Cup

Year	Winner	Runner-up
1991	Red Star Belgrade	Marseille
1990	AC Milan	Benfica
1989	AC Milan	Steaua Bucharest
1988	PSV Eindhoven	Benfica
1987	Porto	Bayern Munich
1986	Steaua Bucharest	Barcelona
1985	Juventus	Liverpool
1984	Liverpool	Roma
1983	Hamburg	Juventus
1982	Aston Villa	Bayern Munich
1981	Liverpool	Real Madrid
1980	Nottingham Forest	Hamburg
1979	Nottingham Forest	Malmö
1978	Liverpool	Club Brugge
1977	Liverpool	Borussia Mönchengladbach
1976	Bayern Munich	Saint-Etienne
1975	Bayern Munich	Leeds United
1974	Bayern Munich	Atlético de Madrid
1973	Ajax	Juventus
1972	Ajax	Inter Milan
1971	Ajax	Panathinaikos
1970	Feyenoord	Celtic
1969	AC Milan	Benfica
1968	Manchester United	Benfica
1967	Celtic	Inter Milan

Year	Winner	Runner-up
1966	Real Madrid	Partizan Belgrade
1965	Inter Milan	Benfica
1964	Inter Milan	Real Madrid
1963	AC Milan	Benfica
1962	Benfica	Real Madrid
1961	Benfica	Barcelona
1960	Real Madrid	Eintracht Frankfurt
1959	Real Madrid	Stade de Reims
1958	Real Madrid	AC Milan
1957	Real Madrid	Fiorentina
1956	Real Madrid	Stade de Reims

Compiled by Jørgen B. Kjaer

UEFA Europa League Champions

Year	Winner	Runner-up
2010	Atlético Madrid	Fulham
2009	Shakhtar Donetsk	Werder Bremen
2008	Zenit St. Petersburg	Rangers
2007	Sevilla	Espanyol
2006	Sevilla	Middlesbrough
2005	CSKA Moscow	Sporting CP
2004	Valencia	Marseille
2003	FC Porto	Celtic
2002	Feyenoord	Borussia Dortmund
2001	Liverpool	Alavés
2000	Galatasaray	Arsenal
1999	Parma	Marseille
1998	Internazionale	Lazio
1997	Schalke 04	Internazionale
1996	Bayern Munich	Bordeaux
1995	Parma	Juventus
1994	Internazionale	Austria Salzburg
1993	Juventus	Borussia Dortmund
1992	Ajax	Torino
1991	Internazionale	Roma
1990	Juventus	Fiorentina
1989	Napoli	Stuttgart
1988	Bayer Leverkusen	Espanyol
1987	IFK Goteborg	Dundee United
1986	Real Madrid	FC Koln
1985	Real Madrid	Videoton
1984	Tottenham Hotspur	Anderlecht
1983	Anderlecht	Benfica
1982	IFK Goteborg	Hamburg
1981	Ipswich Town	AZ Alkmaar
1980	Eintracht Frankfurt	Borussia Monchengladbach
1979	Borussia Monchengladbach	Red Star Belgrade
1978	PSV Eindhoven	Bastia
1977	Juventus	Athletic Bilbao
1976	Liverpool	Club Brugge

Year	Winner	Runner-up
1975	Borussia Monchengladbach	Twente Enschede
1974	Feyenoord	Tottenham
1973	Liverpool	Borussia Monchengladbach
1972	Tottenham Hotspur	Wolverhampton Wanderers

Compiled by Charles Parrish

CONMEBOL Copa Libertadores

Year	Winner	Runner-up
2010	Internacional (Brazil)	Guadalajara (México)
2009	Estudiantes de La Plata (Argentina)	Cruzeiro (Brazil)
2008	Liga de Quito (Ecuador)	Fluminense (Brazil)
2007	Boca Juniors (Argentina)	Gremio (Brazil)
2006	Internacional (Brazil)	São Paulo (Brazil)
2005	São Paulo (Brazil)	Atlético Paranaense (Brazil)
2004	Once Caldas (Colombia)	Boca Juniors (Argentina)
2003	Boca Juniors (Argentina)	Santos (Brazil)
2002	Olimpia (Paraguay)	São Caetano (Brazil)
2001	Boca Juniors (Argentina)	Cruz Azul (México)
2000	Boca Juniors (Argentina)	Palmeiras (Brazil)
1999	Palmeiras (Brazil)	Deportivo de Cali (Colombia)
1998	Vasco de Gama (Brazil)	Barcelona (Ecuador)
1997	Cruzeiro (Brazil)	Sporting Cristal (Peru)
1996	River Plate (Argentina)	América de Cali (Colombia)
1995	Gremio (Brazil)	Atlético Nacional (Colombia)
1994	Vélez Sarsfield (Argentina)	São Paulo (Brazil)
1993	Sâo Paulo (Brazil)	Universidad Católica (Chile)
1992	Sãa Paulo (Brazil)	Newell's Old Boys (Argentina)
1991	Colo-Colo (Chile)	Olimpia (Paraguay)
1990	Olimpia (Paraguay)	Barcelona (Ecuador)
1989	Atlético Nacional (Colombia)	Olimpia (Paraguay)
1988	Nacional (Uruguay)	Newell's Old Boys (Argentina)
1987	Peñarol (Uruguay)	América de Cali (Colombia)
1986	River Plate (Argentina)	América de Cali (Colombia)
1985	Argentinos Juniors (Argentina)	América de Cali (Colombia)
1984	Independiente (Argentina)	Gremio (Brazil)
1983	Gremio (Brazil)	Peñarol (Uruguay)
1982	Peñarol (Uruguay)	Cobreloa (Chile)
1981	Flamengo (Brazil)	Cobreloa (Chile)
1980	Nacional (Uruguay)	Internacional (Brazil)
1979	Olimpia (Paraguay)	Boca Juniors (Argentina)
1978	Boca Juniors (Argentina)	Deportivo Cali (Colombia)
1977	Boca Juniors (Argentina)	Cruzeiro (Brazil)
1976	Cruzeiro (Brazil)	River Plate (Argentina)
1975	Independiente (Argentina)	Unión Española (Chile)
1974	Independiente (Argentina)	São Paulo (Brazil)
1973	Independiente (Argentina)	Colo-Colo (Chile)
1972	Independiente (Argentina)	Universitario (Peru)
1971	Nacional (Uruguay)	Estudiantes de La Plata (Argentina)
1970	Estudiantes de La Plata (Argentina)	Peñarol (Uruguay)
1969	Estudiantes de La Plata (Argentina)	Nacional (Uruguay)

Year	Winner	Runner-up
1968	Estudiantes de La Plata (Argentina)	Palmeiras (Brazil)
1967	Racing Club (Argentina)	Nacional (Uruguay)
1966	Peñarol (Uruguay)	River Plate (Argentina)
1965	Independiente (Argentina)	Peñarol (Uruguay)
1964	Independiente (Argentina)	Nacional (Uruguay)
1963	Santos (Brazil)	Boca Juniors (Argentina)
1962	Santos (Brazil)	Peñarol (Uruguay)
1961	Peñarol (Uruguay)	Palmeiras (Brazil)
1960	Peñarol (Uruguay)	Olimpia (Paraguay)

Compiled by Charles Parrish

World Soccer Club Champions

FIFA World Club Cup (2000, 2005–)

Year	Winner	Runner-up
2010	Internazionale (Italy)	TZ Mazembe (DR of Congo)
2009	Barcelona (Spain)	Estudiantes de La Plata (Argentina)
2008	Manchester United (England)	Liga de Quito (Ecuador)
2007	Milan (Italy)	Boca Juniors (Argentina)
2006	Internacional (Brazil)	Barcelona (Spain)
2005	São Paulo (Brazil)	Liverpool (England)
2000	Corinthians (Brazil)	Vasco de Gama (Brazil)

Toyota Cup (1980–2004)

Year	Winner	Runner-up
2004	Porto (Portugal)	Once Caldas (Colombia)
2003	Boca Juniors (Argentina)	Milan (Italy)
2002	Real Madrid (Spain)	Olimpia (Paraguay)
2001	Bayern Munich (Germany)	Boca Juniors (Argentina)
2000	Boca Juniors (Argentina)	Real Madrid (Spain)
1999	Manchester United (England)	Palmeiras (Brazil)
1998	Real Madrid (Spain)	Vasco de Gama (Brazil)
1997	Borrusia Dortmund (Germany)	Cruzeiro (Brazil)
1996	Juventus (Italy)	River Plate (Argentina)
1995	Ajax (Netherlands)	Grémio (Brazil)
1994	Vélez Sarsfield (Argentina)	Milan (Italy)
1993	São Paulo (Brazil)	Milan (Italy)
1992	São Paulo (Brazil)	Barcelona (Spain)
1991	Red Star Belgrade (Yugoslavia)	Colo-Colo (Chile)
1990	Milan (Italy)	Olimpia (Paraguay)
1989	Milan (Italy)	Atlético Nacional (Colombia)
1988	Nacional (Uruguay)	PSV Eindhoven (Netherlands)
1987	Porto (Portugal)	Peñarol (Uruguay)
1986	River Plate (Argentina)	Steaua Bucuresti (Romania)
1985	Juventus (Italy)	Argentinos Juniors (Argentina)
1984	Independiente (Argentina)	Liverpool (England)
1983	Grémio (Brazil)	Hamburger Sport-Verein (West Germany)
1982	Peñarol (Uruguay)	Aston Villa (England)
1981	Flamengo (Brazil)	Liverpool (England)
1980	Nacional (Uruguay)	Nottingham Forest (England)

Intercontinental Cup (1960–1979)

Year	Winner	Runner-up
1979	Olimpia (Paraguay)	Malmo Fotbolforening (Sweden)
1978	Not held	
1977	Boca Juniors (Argentina)	Borussia Monchengladbach (West Germany)
1976	Bayern Munich (West Germany)	Cruzeiro (Brazil)
1975	Not held	
1974	Atlético Madrid (Spain)	Independiente (Argentina)
1973	Independiente (Argentina)	Juventus (Italy)
1972	Ajax (Netherlands)	Independiente (Argentina)
1971	Nacional (Uruguay)	Panathinaikos (Greece)
1970	Feyenoord (Netherlands)	Estudiantes de La Plata (Argentina)
1969	Milan (Italy)	Estudiantes de La Plata (Argentina)
1968	Estudiantes de La Plata (Argentina)	Manchester United (England)
1967	Racing Club (Argentina)	Celtic (Scotland)
1966	Peñarol (Uruguay)	Real Madrid (Spain)
1965	Internazionale (Italy)	Independiente (Argentina)
1964	Internazionale (Italy)	Independiente (Argentina)
1963	Santos (Brazil)	Milan (Italy)
1962	Santos (Brazil)	Benfica (Portugal)
1961	Peñarol (Uruguay)	Benfica (Portugal)
1960	Real Madrid (Spain)	Peñarol (Uruguay)

Compiled by Charles Parrish

Tour de France Winners

Year	Winner
2010	Alberto Contador
2009	Alberto Contador
2008	Carlos Sastre
2007	Alberto Contador
2006	Oscar Pereiro
2005	Lance Armstrong
2004	Lance Armstrong
2003	Lance Armstrong
2002	Lance Armstrong
2001	Lance Armstrong
2000	Lance Armstrong
1999	Lance Armstrong
1998	Marco Pantani
1997	Jan Ullrich
1996	Bjarne Riis
1995	Miguel Indurain
1994	Miguel Indurain
1993	Miguel Indurain
1992	Miguel Indurain
1991	Miguel Indurain
1990	Greg Lemond
1989	Greg Lemond
1988	Pedro Delgado
1987	Stephen Roche

Year	Winner
1986	Greg Lemond
1985	Bernard Hinault
1984	Laurent Fignon
1983	Laurent Fignon
1982	Bernard Hinault
1981	Bernard Hinault
1980	Joop Zoetemelk
1979	Bernard Hinault
1978	Bernard Hinault
1977	Bernard Thévenet
1976	Lucien Van Impe
1975	Bernard Thévenet
1974	Eddy Merckx
1973	Luis Ocana
1972	Eddy Merckx
1971	Eddy Merckx
1970	Eddy Merckx
1969	Eddy Merckx
1968	Jan Janssen
1967	Roger Pingeon
1966	Lucien Aimar
1965	Felice Gimondi
1964	Jacques Anquetil
1963	Jacques Anquetil
1962	Jacques Anquetil
1961	Jacques Anquetil
1960	Gastone Nencini
1959	Federico Bahamontes
1958	Charly Gaul
1957	Jacques Anquetil
1956	Roger Walkowiak
1955	Louison Bobet
1954	Louison Bobet
1953	Louison Bobet
1952	Fausto Coppi
1951	Hugo Koblet
1950	Ferdi Kübler
1949	Fausto Coppi
1948	Gino Bartali
1947	Jean Robic
1946	Not held due to World War II
1945	Not held due to World War II
1944	Not held due to World War II
1943	Not held due to World War II
1942	Not held due to World War II
1941	Not held due to World War II
1940	Not held due to World War II
1939	Sylvère Maes
1938	Gino Bartali
1937	Roger Lapépie
1936	Sylvère Maes
1935	Romain Maes

Year	Winner
1934	Antonin Magne
1933	Georges Speicher
1932	André Leducq
1931	Antonin Magne
1930	André Leducq
1929	Maurice Dewaele
1928	Nicolas Frantz
1927	Nicolas Frantz
1926	Lucien Buysse
1925	Ottavio Bottecchia
1924	Ottavio Bottecchia
1923	Henri Pélissier
1922	Firmin Lambot
1921	Léon Scieur
1920	Philippe Thys
1919	Firmin Lambot
1918	Not held due to World War I
1917	Not held due to World War I
1916	Not held due to World War I
1915	Not held due to World War I
1914	Philippe Thys
1913	Philippe Thys
1912	Odile Defraye
1911	Gustave Garrigou
1910	Octave Lapize
1909	François Faber
1908	Lucien Petit-Breton
1907	Lucien Petit-Breton
1906	René Pottier
1905	Louis Trousselier
1904	Henri Cornet
1903	Maurice Garin

Compiled by Andrea Giampiccoli

Africa Cup of Nations Soccer

Year	Winner	Runner-up
2010	Egypt	Ghana
2008	Egypt	Cameroon
2006	Egypt	Ivory Coast
2004	Tunisia	Morocco
2002	Cameroon	Senegal
2000	Cameroon	Nigeria
1998	Egypt	South Africa
1996	South Africa	Tunisia
1994	Nigeria	Zambia
1992	Ivory Coast	Ghana
1990	Algeria	Nigeria
1988	Cameroon	Nigeria
1986	Egypt	Cameroon
1984	Cameroon	Nigeria

Year	Winner	Runner-up
1982	Ghana	Libya
1980	Nigeria	Algeria
1978	Ghana	Uganda
1976	Morocco	Guinea
1974	Congo DRC (Zaire)	Zambia
1972	Congo (Republic of the)	Mali
1970	Sudan	Ghana
1968	Congo DRC (Zaire)	Ghana
1965	Ghana	Tunisia
1963	Ghana	Sudan
1962	Ethiopia	Egypt
1959	Egypt	Sudan
1957	Egypt	Ethiopia

Compiled by Andrea Giampiccoli

Major Champions of Golf

Amateur Championship (Britain), Men

Year	Winner	Runner-up
2010	Jin Jeong	James Byrne
2009	Matteo Manassero	Sam Hutsby
2008	Reinier Saxton	Tommy Fleetwood
2007	Drew Weaver	Tim Stewart
2006	Julien Guerrier	Adam Gee
2005	Brian McElhinney	John Gallagher
2004	Stuart Wilson	Lee Corfield
2003	Gary Wolstenholme	Raphael De Sousa
2002	Alejandro Larrazabal	Martin Sell
2001	Michael Hoey	Ian Campbell
2000	Mikko Ilonen	Christian Reimbold
1999	Graeme Storm	Aran Wainwright
1998	Sergio García	Craig Williams
1997	Craig Watson	Trevor Immelman
1996	Warren Bladon	Roger Beames
1995	Gordon Sherry	Michael Reynard
1994	Lee James	Gordon Sherry
1993	Iain Pyman	Paul Page
1992	Stephen Dundas	Bradley Dredge
1991	Gary Wolstenholme	Bob May
1990	Rolf Muntz	Michael Macara
1989	Stephen Dodd	Craig Cassells
1988	Christian Hardin	Ben Fouchee
1987	Paul Mayo	Peter McEvoy
1986	David Curry	Geoff Birtwell
1985	Garth McGimpsey	Graham Homewood
1984	José María Olazábal	Colin Montgomerie
1983	Philip Parkin	Jim Holtgrieve
1982	Martin Thompson	Andrew Stubbs
1981	Phillipe Ploujoux	Joel Hirsch

Year	Winner	Runner-up
1980	Duncan Evans	David Suddards
1979	Jay Sigel	Scott Hoch
1978	Peter McEvoy	Paul McKellar
1977	Peter McEvoy	H. M. Campbell
1976	Dick Siderowf	J. C. Davies
1975	Vinny Giles	Mark James
1974	Trevor Homer	Jim Gabrielsen
1973	Dick Siderowf	Peter H. Moody
1972	Trevor Homer	Alan Thirlwell
1971	Steve Melnyk	Jim Simons
1970	Michael Bonallack	Bill Hyndman
1969	Michael Bonallack	Bill Hyndman
1968	Michael Bonallack	Joe Carr
1967	Bob Dickson	Ron Cerrudo
1966	Bobby Cole	Ronnie Shade
1965	Michael Bonallack	Clive Clark
1964	Gordon Clark	Michael Lunt
1963	Michael Lunt	John Blackwell
1962	Richard Davies	John Povall
1961	Michael Bonallack	James Walker
1960	Joe Carr	Robert Cochran
1959	Deane Beman	Bill Hyndman
1958	Joe Carr	Alan Thirlwell
1957	Reid Jack	Harold Ridgley
1956	John Beharrell	Leslie Taylor
1955	Joe Conrad	Alan Slater
1954	Douglas Bachli	William C. Campbell
1953	Joe Carr	Harvie Ward
1952	Harvie Ward	Frank Stranahan
1951	Dick Chapman	Charles Coe
1950	Frank Stranahan	Dick Chapman
1949	Samuel McCready	Willie Turnesa
1948	Frank Stranahan	Charles Stowe
1947	Willie Turnesa	Dick Chapman
1946	James Bruen	Robert Sweeny Jr.
1940–1945	Not played due to World War II	
1939	Alexander Kyle	A. A. Duncan
1938	Charles Yates	Cecil Ewing
1937	Robert Sweeny Jr.	Lionel Munn
1936	Hector Thomson	Jim Ferrier
1935	Lawson Little	William Tweddell
1934	Lawson Little	J. Wallace
1933	Hon. Michael Scott	T. A. Bourn
1932	John De Forest	Eric Fiddian
1931	Eric Martin-Smith	John De Forest
1930	Bobby Jones	Roger Wethered
1929	Cyril Tolley	J. Nelson Smith
1928	Phil Perkins	Roger Wethered
1927	William Tweddell	D. E. Landale
1926	Jess Sweetser	A. F. Simpson
1925	Robert Harris	Kenneth F. Fradgley
1924	Ernest Holderness	E. F. Storey

Year	Winner	Runner-up
1923	Roger Wethered	Robert Harris
1922	Ernest Holderness	John Caven
1921	Willie Hunter	Allan Graham
1920	Cyril Tolley	Robert A. Gardner
1915–1919	Not played due to World War I	
1914	J. L. C. Jenkins	Charles O. Hezlet
1913	Harold Hilton	Robert Harris
1912	John Ball	Abe Mitchell
1911	Harold Hilton	E. A. Lassen
1910	John Ball	C. C. Aylmer
1909	Robert Maxwell	C. K. Hutchison
1908	E. A. Lassen	H. E. Taylor
1907	John Ball	C. A. Palmer
1906	James Robb	C. C. Lingen
1905	Arthur Barry	Osmund Scott
1904	Walter Travis	Edward Blackwell
1903	Robert Maxwell	Horace Hutchinson
1902	Charles Hutchings	Sidney Fry
1901	Harold Hilton	John L. Low
1900	Harold Hilton	James Robb
1899	John Ball	Freddie Tait
1898	Freddie Tait	S. Mure Fergusson
1897	Jack Allan	James Robb
1896	Freddie Tait	Harold Hilton
1895	Leslie Balfour-Melville	John Ball
1894	John Ball	S. Mure Fergusson
1893	P. C. Anderson	Johnny Laidlay
1892	John Ball	Harold Hilton
1891	Johnny Laidlay	Harold Hilton
1890	John Ball	Johnny Laidlay
1889	Johnny Laidlay	Leslie Balfour-Melville
1888	John Ball	Johnny Laidlay
1887	Horace Hutchinson	John Ball
1886	Horace Hutchinson	Henry Lamb
1885	Allen MacFie	Horace Hutchinson

Amateur Championship (Britain), Women

Year	Winner	Runner-up
2010	Kelly Tidy	Kelsey MacDonald
2009	Azahara Muñoz	Carlota Ciganda
2008	Anna Nordqvist	Caroline Hedwall
2007	Carlota Ciganda	Anna Nordqvist
2006	Belen Mozo	Anna Nordqvist
2005	Louise Stahle	Claire Coughlan
2004	Louise Stahle	Anna Highgate
2003	Elisa Serramia	Pia Odefey
2002	Rebecca Hudson	Lindsey Wright
2001	Marta Prieto	Emma Duggleby
2000	Rebecca Hudson	Emma Duggleby
1999	Marine Monnet	Rebecca Hudson
1998	Kim Rostron	Gwladys Nocera

Year	Winner	Runner-up
1997	Alison Rose	Mhairi McKay
1996	Kelli Kuehne	Becky Morgan
1995	Julie Wade Hall	Kristel Mourgue D'Algue
1994	Emma Duggleby	Cecilia Mourgue D'Algue
1993	Catriona Lambert	Kirsty Speak
1992	Pernille Pedersen	Joanne Morley
1991	Valerie Michaud	Wendy Doolan
1990	Julie Wade Hall	Helen Wadsworth
1989	Helen Dobson	Elaine Farquharson
1988	Joanne Furby	Jule Wade Hall
1987	Janet Collingham	Susan Shapcott
1986	Marnie McGuire	Louise Briers
1985	Lillian Behan	Claire Waite
1984	Jody Rosenthal	Julie Brown
1983	Jill Thornhill	Regina Lautens
1982	Kitrina Douglas	Gillian Stewart
1981	Belle Robertson	Wilma Aitken
1980	Anne Quast Sander	Liv Wollin
1979	Maureen Madill	Jane Lock
1978	Edwina Kennedy	Julia Greenhalgh
1977	Angela Uzielli	Vanessa Marvin
1976	Cathy Panton	Alison Sheard
1975	Nancy Roth Syms	Suzanne Cadden
1974	Carol Semple	Angela Bonallack
1973	Ann Irvin	Mickey Walker
1972	Mickey Walker	Claudine Clos-Rubin
1971	Mickey Walker	Beverly Huke
1970	Dinah Oxley	Belle Robertson
1969	Catherine Lacoste	Ann Irvin
1968	Brigitte Varangot	Claudine Clos-Rubin
1967	Elizabeth Chadwick	Mary Everard
1966	Elizabeth Chadwick	Vivien Saunders
1965	Brigitte Varangot	Belle Robertson
1964	Carol Sorenson	Bridget Jackson
1963	Brigitte Varangot	Philomena Garvey
1962	Marley Spearman	Angela Bonallack
1961	Marley Spearman	Diane J. Robb
1960	Barbara McIntire	Philomena Garvey
1959	Elizabeth Price	Belle McCorkindale
1958	Jessie Valentine	Elizabeth Price
1957	Philomena Garvey	Jessie Valentine
1956	Wiffi Smith	Mary Patton Janssen
1955	Jessie Valentine	Barbara Romack
1954	Frances Stephens	Elizabeth Price
1953	Marlene Stewart	Philomena Garvey
1952	Moira Paterson	Frances Stephens
1951	Catherine MacCann	Frances Stephens
1950	Vicomtesse de St Sauveur	Jessie Valentine
1949	Frances Stephens	Valerie Reddan
1948	Louise Suggs	Jean Donald
1947	Babe Zaharias	Jacqueline Gordon
1946	Jean Hetherington	Philomena Garvey

Year	Winner	Runner-up
1940–1945	Not played due to World War II	
1939	Pamela Barton	Mrs. T. Marks
1938	Helen Holm	Elsie Corlett
1937	Jessie Anderson	Dorothy Park
1936	Pamela Barton	Bridgett Newell
1935	Wanda Morgan	Pamela Barton
1934	Helen Holm	Pamela Barton
1933	Enid Wilson	Diana Plumpton
1932	Enid Wilson	Clem Purvis-Russell-Montgomery
1931	Enid Wilson	Wanda Morgan
1930	Diana Fishwick	Glenna Collett-Vare
1929	Joyce Wethered	Glenna Collett-Vare
1928	Nanette le Blan	S. Marshall
1927	Simone de la Chaume	Dorothy Pearson
1926	Cecil Leitch	Marjorie Ross Garon
1925	Joyce Wethered	Cecil Leitch
1924	Joyce Wethered	Mrs. F. Cautley
1923	Doris Chambers	Muriel Dodd Macbeth
1922	Joyce Wethered	Cecil Leitch
1921	Cecil Leitch	Joyce Wethered
1920	Cecil Leitch	Molly Griffiths
1915–1919	Not played due to World War I (1915–1918) and a rail strike (1919)	
1914	Cecil Leitch	Gladys Ravenscroft
1913	Muriel Dodd	Evelyn Chubb
1912	Gladys Ravenscroft	Stella Temple
1911	Dorothy Campbell	Violet Hezlet
1910	Elsie Grant Suttie	Lily Moore
1909	Dorothy Campbell	Florence Hezlet
1908	Maud Titterton	Dorothy Campbell
1907	May Hezlet	Florence Hezlet
1906	Alice Kennion	Bertha Thompson
1905	Bertha Thompson	Maud E. Stuart
1904	Lottie Dod	May Hezlet
1903	Rhona Adair	Florence Walker-Leigh
1902	May Hezlet	Elinor C. Neville
1901	Molly Graham	Rhona Adair
1900	Rhona Adair	Isabel Neville
1899	May Hezlet	Jesse Magill
1898	Lena Thomson	Elinor C. Neville
1897	Edith C. Orr	Theodora Orr
1896	Amy Pascoe	Lena Thomson
1895	Lady Margaret Scott	Emma M. Lythgoe
1894	Lady Margaret Scott	Issette Pearson
1893	Lady Margaret Scott	Issette Pearson

US Amateur, Men

Year	Winner	Runner-up
2010	Peter Uihlein	David Chung
2009	An Byeong-Hun	Ben Martin
2008	Danny Lee	Drew Kittleson
2007	Colt Knost	Michael Thompson
2006	Richie Ramsay	John Kelly

Year	Winner	Runner-up
2005	Edoardo Molinari	Dillon Dougherty
2004	Ryan Moore	Luke List
2003	Nick Flanagan	Casey Wittenberg
2002	Ricky Barnes	Hunter Mahan
2001	Bubba Dickerson	Robert Hamilton
2000	Jeff Quinney	James Driscoll
1999	David Gossett	Sung Yoon Kim
1998	Hank Kuehne	Tom McKnight
1997	Matt Kuchar	Joel Kribel
1996	Tiger Woods	Steve Scott
1995	Tiger Woods	Buddy Marucci
1994	Tiger Woods	Trip Kuehne
1993	John Harris	Danny Ellis
1992	Justin Leonard	Tom Scherrer
1991	Mitch Voges	Manny Zerman
1990	Phil Mickelson	Manny Zerman
1989	Chris Patton	Danny Green
1988	Eric Meeks	Danny Yates
1987	Billy Mayfair	Eric Rebmann
1986	Buddy Alexander	Chris Kite
1985	Sam Randolph	Peter Persons
1984	Scott Verplank	Sam Randolph
1983	Jay Sigel	Chris Perry
1982	Jay Sigel	David Tolley
1981	Nathaniel Crosby	Brian Lindley
1980	Hal Sutton	Bob Lewis
1979	Mark O'Meara	John Cook
1978	John Cook	Scott Hoch
1977	John Fought	Doug Fischesser
1976	Bill Sander	C. Parker Moore Jr.
1975	Fred Ridley	Keith Fergus
1974	Jerry Pate	John R. Grace
1973	Craig Stadler	David Strawn
*1972	Vinny Giles	Mark Hayes & Ben Crenshaw
*1971	Gary Cowan	Eddie Pearce
*1970	Lanny Wadkins	Tom Kite
*1969	Steve Melnyk	Vinny Giles
*1968	Bruce Fleisher	Vinny Giles
*1967	Bob Dickson	Vinny Giles
*1966	Gary Cowan	Deane Beman
*1965	Bob Murphy	Bob Dickson
1964	William C. Campbell	Edgar M. Tutwiler
1963	Deane Beman	R. H. Sikes
1962	Labron Harris Jr.	Downing Gray
1961	Jack Nicklaus	Dudley Wysong
1960	Deane Beman	Robert W. Gardner
1959	Jack Nicklaus	Charles Coe
1958	Charles Coe	Tommy Aaron
1957	Hillman Robbins	Dr. Frank M. Taylor
1956	Harvie Ward	Chuck Kocsis
1955	Harvie Ward	Bill Hyndman
1954	Arnold Palmer	Robert Sweeny Jr.

Year	Winner	Runner-up
1953	Gene Littler	Dale Morey
1952	Jack Westland	Al Mengert
1951	Billy Maxwell	Joseph F. Gagliardi
1950	Sam Urzetta	Frank Stranahan
1949	Charles Coe	Rufus King
1948	Willie Turnesa	Raymond E. Billows
1947	Skee Riegel	Johnny Dawson
1946	Stanley E. Bishop	Smiley Quick
1942–1945	Not held due to World War II	
1941	Bud Ward	Pat Abbott
1940	Dick Chapman	W. B. McCullough Jr.
1939	Bud Ward	Raymond E. Billows
1938	Willie Turnesa	Pat Abbott
1937	Johnny Goodman	Raymond E. Billows
1936	John Fischer	Jack McLean
1935	Lawson Little	Walter Emery
1934	Lawson Little	David Goldman
1933	George Dunlap	Max R. Marston
1932	Ross Somerville	Johnny Goodman
1931	Francis Ouimet	Jack Westland
1930	Bobby Jones	Eugene V. Homans
1929	Harrison R. Johnston	Oscar F. Willing
1928	Bobby Jones	Phil Perkins
1927	Bobby Jones	Chick Evans
1926	George Von Elm	Bobby Jones
1925	Bobby Jones	Watts Gunn
1924	Bobby Jones	George Von Elm
1923	Max R. Marston	Jess Sweetser
1922	Jess Sweetser	Chick Evans
1921	Jesse P. Guilford	Robert A. Gardner
1920	Chick Evans	Francis Ouimet
1919	S. Davidson Herron	Bobby Jones
1917–1918	Not held due to World War I	
1916	Chick Evans	Robert A. Gardner
1915	Robert A. Gardner	John G. Anderson
1914	Francis Ouimet	Jerome Travers
1913	Jerome Travers	John G. Anderson
1912	Jerome Travers	Chick Evans
1911	Harold Hilton	Fred Herreshoff
1910	William C. Fownes Jr.	Warren Wood
1909	Robert A. Gardner	Chandler Egan
1908	Jerome Travers	Max H. Behr
1907	Jerome Travers	Archibald Graham
1906	Eben Byers	George Lyon
1905	Chandler Egan	Daniel Sawyer
1904	Chandler Egan	Fred Herreshoff
1903	Walter Travis	Eben Byers
1902	Louis N. James	Eben Byers
1901	Walter Travis	Walter Egan
1900	Walter Travis	Findlay S. Douglas
1899	H. M. Harriman	Findlay S. Douglas
1898	Findlay S. Douglas	Walter B. Smith

Year	Winner	Runner-up
1897	H. J. Whigham	W. Rossiter Betts
1896	H. J. Whigham	Joseph G. Thorp
1895	Charles B. Macdonald	Charles Sands

* Stroke Play (1965–1972)

US Amateur, Women

Year	Winner	Runner-up
2010	Danielle Kang	Jessica Korda
2009	Jennifer Song	Jennifer Johnson
2008	Amanda Blumenherst	Azahara Muñoz
2007	Maria José Uribe	Amanda Blumenherst
2006	Kimberly Kim	Katharina Schallenberg
2005	Morgan Pressel	Maru Martinez
2004	Jane Park	Amanda McCurdy
2003	Virada Nirapathpongporn	Jane Park
2002	Becky Lucidi	Brandi Jackson
2001	Meredith Duncan	Nicole Perrot
2000	Marcy Newton	Laura Myerscough
1999	Dorothy Delasin	Jimin Kang
1998	Grace Park	Jenny Chuasiriporn
1997	Silvia Cavalleri	Robin Burke
1996	Kelli Kuehne	Marisa Baena
1995	Kelli Kuehne	Anne-Marie Knight
1994	Wendy Ward	Jill McGill
1993	Jill McGill	Sarah LeBrun Ingram
1992	Vicki Goetze	Annika Sörenstam
1991	Amy Fruhwirth	Heidi Voorhees
1990	Pat Hurst	Stephanie Davis
1989	Vicki Goetze	Brandie Burton
1988	Pearl Sinn	Karen Noble
1987	Kay Cockerill	Tracy Kerdyk
1986	Kay Cockerill	Kathleen McCarthy
1985	Michiko Hattori	Cheryl Stacy
1984	Deb Richard	Kimberly Williams
1983	Joanne Pacillo	Sally Quinlan
1982	Juli Inkster	Cathy Hanlon
1981	Juli Inkster	Lindy Goggin
1980	Juli Inkster	Patti Rizzo
1979	Carolyn Hill	Patty Sheehan
1978	Cathy Sherk	Judith Oliver
1977	Beth Daniel	Cathy Sherk
1976	Donna Horton	Marianne Bretton
1975	Beth Daniel	Donna Horton
1974	Cynthia Hill	Carol Semple
1973	Carol Semple	Anne Quast Sander
1972	Mary Budke	Cynthia Hill
1971	Laura Baugh	Beth Barry
1970	Martha Wilkinson	Cynthia Hill
1969	Catherine Lacoste	Shelley Hamlin
1968	JoAnne Gunderson	Anne Quast Welts
1967	Mary Lou Dill	Jean Ashley

Year	Winner	Runner-up
1966	JoAnne Gunderson	Marlene Stewart Streit
1965	Jean Ashley	Anne Quast Welts
1964	Barbara McIntire	JoAnne Gunderson
1963	Anne Quast Welts	Peggy Conley
1962	JoAnne Gunderson	Ann Baker
1961	Anne Quast Decker	Phyllis Preuss
1960	JoAnne Gunderson	Jean Ashley
1959	Barbara McIntire	Joanne Goodwin
1958	Anne Quast	Barbara Romack
1957	JoAnne Gunderson	Ann Casey Johnstone
1956	Marlene Stewart	JoAnne Gunderson
1955	Patricia Lesser	Jane Nelson
1954	Barbara Romack	Mickey Wright
1953	Mary Lena Faulk	Polly Riley
1952	Jackie Pung	Shirley McFedters
1951	Dorothy Kirby	Claire Doran
1950	Beverly Hanson	Mae Murray
1949	Dorothy Germain Porter	Dorothy Kielty
1948	Grace Lenczyk	Helen Sigel
1947	Louise Suggs	Dorothy Kirby
1946	Babe Zaharias	Clara Sherman
1942–1945	Not held due to World War II	
1941	Betty Hicks Newell	Helen Sigel
1940	Betty Jameson	Jane S. Cothran
1939	Betty Jameson	Dorothy Kirby
1938	Patty Berg	Estelle Lawson Page
1937	Estelle Lawson Page	Patty Berg
1936	Pamela Barton	Maureen Orcutt
1935	Glenna Collett Vare	Patty Berg
1934	Virginia Van Wie	Dorothy Traung
1933	Virginia Van Wie	Helen Hicks
1932	Virginia Van Wie	Glenna Collett Vare
1931	Helen Hicks	Glenna Collett-Vare
1930	Glenna Collett	Virginia Van Wie
1929	Glenna Collett	Leona Pressler
1928	Glenna Collett	Virginia Van Wie
1927	Miriam Burns Horn	Maureen Orcutt
1926	Helen Stetson	Elizabeth Goss
1925	Glenna Collett	Alexa Stirling
1924	Dorothy Campbell	Mary Browne
1923	Edith Cummings	Alexa Stirling
1922	Glenna Collett	Margaret Gavin
1921	Marion Hollins	Alexa Stirling
1920	Alexa Stirling	Dorothy Campbell
1919	Alexa Stirling	Margaret Gavin
1917–1918	No championships due to World War I	
1916	Alexa Stirling	Mildred Caverly
1915	Florence Vanderbeck	Margaret Gavin
1914	Katherine Harley	Elaine Rosenthal
1913	Gladys Ravenscroft	Marion Hollins
1912	Margaret Curtis	Nonna Barlow
1911	Margaret Curtis	Lillian B. Hyde

Year	Winner	Runner-up
1910	Dorothy Campbell	Mrs. F. M. Martin
1909	Dorothy Campbell	Nonna Barlow
1908	Katherine Harley	Mrs. T. H. Polhemus
1907	Margaret Curtis	Harriot Curtis
1906	Harriot Curtis	Mary B. Adams
1905	Pauline Mackay	Margaret Curtis
1904	Georgianna M. Bishop	Mrs. E. F. Sanford
1903	Bessie Anthony	J. Anna Carpenter
1902	Genevieve Hecker	Louisa A. Wells
1901	Genevieve Hecker	Lucy Herron
1900	Frances C. Griscom	Margaret Curtis
1899	Ruth Underhill	Margaret Fox
1898	Beatrix Hoyt	Maude Wetmore
1897	Beatrix Hoyt	Nellie Sargent
1896	Beatrix Hoyt	Mrs. Arthur Turnure
1895	Lucy Barnes Brown	Nellie Sargent

US Open, Men

Year	Winner
2010	Graeme McDowell
2009	Lucas Glover
2008	Tiger Woods
2007	Ángel Cabrera
2006	Geoff Ogilvy
2005	Michael Campbell
2004	Retief Goosen
2003	Jim Furyk
2002	Tiger Woods
2001	Retief Goosen
2000	Tiger Woods
1999	Payne Stewart
1998	Lee Janzen
1997	Ernie Els
1996	Steve Jones
1995	Corey Pavin
1994	Ernie Els
1993	Lee Janzen
1992	Tom Kite
1991	Payne Stewart
1990	Hale Irwin
1989	Curtis Strange
1988	Curtis Strange
1987	Scott Simpson
1986	Raymond Floyd
1985	Andy North
1984	Fuzzy Zoeller
1983	Larry Nelson
1982	Tom Watson
1981	David Graham
1980	Jack Nicklaus
1979	Hale Irwin

Year	Winner
1978	Andy North
1977	Hubert Green
1976	Jerry Pate
1975	Lou Graham
1974	Hale Irwin
1973	Johnny Miller
1972	Jack Nicklaus
1971	Lee Trevino
1970	Tony Jacklin
1969	Orville Moody
1968	Lee Trevino
1967	Jack Nicklaus
1966	Billy Casper
1965	Gary Player
1964	Ken Venturi
1963	Julius Boros
1962	Jack Nicklaus
1961	Gene Littler
1960	Arnold Palmer
1959	Billy Casper
1958	Tommy Bolt
1957	Dick Mayer
1956	Cary Middlecoff
1955	Jack Fleck
1954	Ed Furgol
1953	Ben Hogan
1952	Julius Boros
1951	Ben Hogan
1950	Ben Hogan
1949	Cary Middlecoff
1948	Ben Hogan
1947	Lew Worsham
1946	Lloyd Mangrum
1945	Not held due to World War II
1944	Not held due to World War II
1943	Not held due to World War II
1942	Not held due to World War II
1941	Craig Wood
1940	Lawson Little
1939	Byron Nelson
1938	Ralph Guldahl
1937	Ralph Guldahl
1936	Tony Manero
1935	Sam Parks Jr.
1934	Olin Dutra
1933	Johnny Goodman
1932	Gene Sarazen
1931	Billy Burke
1930	Bobby Jones
1929	Bobby Jones
1928	Johnny Farrell
1927	Tommy Armour

Year	Winner
1926	Bobby Jones
1925	Willie MacFarlane
1924	Cyril Walker
1923	Bobby Jones
1922	Gene Sarazen
1921	Jim Barnes
1920	Ted Ray
1919	Walter Hagen
1918	Not held due to World War I
1917	Not held due to World War I
1916	Chick Evans
1915	Jerome Travers
1914	Walter Hagen
1913	Francis Ouimet
1912	John McDermott
1911	John McDermott
1910	Alex Smith
1909	George Sargent
1908	Fred McLeod
1907	Alec Ross
1906	Alex Smith
1905	Willie Anderson
1904	Willie Anderson
1903	Willie Anderson
1902	Laurie Auchterlonie
1901	Willie Anderson
1900	Harry Vardon
1899	Willie Smith
1898	Fred Herd
1897	Joe Lloyd
1896	James Foulis

US Open, Women

Year	Winner
2010	Paula Creamer
2009	Eun-Hee Ji
2008	Inbee Park
2007	Cristie Kerr
2006	Annika Sörenstam
2005	Birdie Kim
2004	Meg Mallon
2003	Hilary Lunke
2002	Juli Inkster
2001	Karrie Webb
2000	Karrie Webb
1999	Juli Inkster
1998	Se Ri Pak
1997	Alison Nicholas
1996	Annika Sörenstam
1995	Annika Sörenstam
1994	Patty Sheehan

Year	Winner
1993	Lauri Merten
1992	Patty Sheehan
1991	Meg Mallon
1990	Betsy King
1989	Betsy King
1988	Liselotte Neumann
1987	Laura Davies
1986	Jane Geddes
1985	Kathy Baker
1984	Hollis Stacy
1983	Jan Stephenson
1982	Janet Anderson
1981	Pat Bradley
1980	Amy Alcott
1979	Jerilyn Britz
1978	Hollis Stacy
1977	Hollis Stacy
1976	JoAnne Carner
1975	Sandra Palmer
1974	Sandra Haynie
1973	Susie Berning
1972	Susie Berning
1971	JoAnne Carner
1970	Donna Caponi
1969	Donna Caponi
1968	Susie Berning
1967	Catherine Lacoste
1966	Sandra Spuzich
1965	Carol Mann
1964	Mickey Wright
1963	Mary Mills
1962	Murle Lindstrom
1961	Mickey Wright
1960	Betsy Rawls
1959	Mickey Wright
1958	Mickey Wright
1957	Betsy Rawls
1956	Kathy Cornelius
1955	Fay Crocker
1954	Babe Zaharias
1953	Betsy Rawls
1952	Louise Suggs
1951	Betsy Rawls
1950	Babe Zaharias
1949	Louise Suggs
1948	Babe Zaharias
1947	Betty Jameson
1946	Patty Berg

British Open, Men

Year	Winner
2010	Louis Oosthuizen
2009	Stewart Cink
2008	Pádraig Harrington
2007	Pádraig Harrington
2006	Tiger Woods
2005	Tiger Woods
2004	Todd Hamilton
2003	Ben Curtis
2002	Ernie Els
2001	David Duval
2000	Tiger Woods
1999	Paul Lawrie
1998	Mark O'Meara
1997	Justin Leonard
1996	Tom Lehman
1995	John Daly
1994	Nick Price
1993	Greg Norman
1992	Nick Faldo
1991	Ian Baker-Finch
1990	Nick Faldo
1989	Mark Calcavecchia
1988	Seve Ballesteros
1987	Nick Faldo
1986	Greg Norman
1985	Sandy Lyle
1984	Seve Ballesteros
1983	Tom Watson
1982	Tom Watson
1981	Bill Rogers
1980	Tom Watson
1979	Seve Ballesteros
1978	Jack Nicklaus
1977	Tom Watson
1976	Johnny Miller
1975	Tom Watson
1974	Gary Player
1973	Tom Weiskopf
1972	Lee Trevino
1971	Lee Trevino
1970	Jack Nicklaus
1969	Tony Jacklin
1968	Gary Player
1967	Roberto DeVicenzo
1966	Jack Nicklaus
1965	Peter Thomson
1964	Tony Lema
1963	Bob Charles
1962	Arnold Palmer
1961	Arnold Palmer
1960	Kel Nagle

Year	Winner
1959	Gary Player
1958	Peter Thomson
1957	Bobby Locke
1956	Peter Thomson
1955	Peter Thomson
1954	Peter Thomson
1953	Ben Hogan
1952	Bobby Locke
1951	Max Faulkner
1950	Bobby Locke
1949	Bobby Locke
1948	Henry Cotton
1947	Fred Daly
1946	Sam Snead
1945	Not held due to World War II
1944	Not held due to World War II
1943	Not held due to World War II
1942	Not held due to World War II
1941	Not held due to World War II
1940	Not held due to World War II
1939	Dick Burton
1938	Reg Whitcombe
1937	Henry Cotton
1936	Alf Padgham
1935	Alf Perry
1934	Henry Cotton
1933	Denny Shute
1932	Gene Sarazen
1931	Tommy Armour
1930	Bobby Jones
1929	Walter Hagen
1928	Walter Hagen
1927	Bobby Jones
1926	Bobby Jones
1925	Jim Barnes
1924	Walter Hagen
1923	Arthur Havers
1922	Walter Hagen
1921	Jock Hutchison
1920	George Duncan
1919	Not held due to World War I
1918	Not held due to World War I
1917	Not held due to World War I
1916	Not held due to World War I
1915	Not held due to World War I
1914	Harry Vardon
1913	John Henry Taylor
1912	Ted Ray
1911	Harry Vardon
1910	James Braid
1909	John Henry Taylor
1908	James Braid

Year	Winner
1907	Arnaud Massy
1906	James Braid
1905	James Braid
1904	Jack White
1903	Harry Vardon
1902	Sandy Herd
1901	James Braid
1900	John Henry Taylor
1899	Harry Vardon
1898	Harry Vardon
1897	Harold Hilton
1896	Harry Vardon
1895	John Henry Taylor
1894	John Henry Taylor
1893	Willie Auchterlonie
1892	Harold Hilton
1891	Hugh Kirkaldy
1890	John Ball Jr.
1889	Willie Park Jr.
1888	Jack Burns
1887	Willie Park Jr.
1886	David Brown
1885	Bob Martin
1884	Jack Simpson
1883	Willie Fernie
1882	Bob Ferguson
1881	Bob Ferguson
1880	Bob Ferguson
1879	Jamie Anderson
1878	Jamie Anderson
1877	Jamie Anderson
1876	Bob Martin
1875	Willie Park Sr.
1874	Mungo Park
1873	Tom Kidd
1872	Young Tom Morris
1871	Not played
1870	Young Tom Morris
1869	Young Tom Morris
1868	Young Tom Morris
1867	Old Tom Morris
1866	Willie Park Sr.
1865	Andrew Strath
1864	Old Tom Morris
1863	Willie Park Sr.
1862	Old Tom Morris
1861	Old Tom Morris
1860	Willie Park Sr.

British Open, Women

Year	Winner
2010	Yani Tseng
2009	Catriona Matthew
2008	Ji-Yai Shin
2007	Lorena Ochoa
2006	Sherri Steinhauer
2005	Jeong Jang
2004	Karen Stupples
2003	Annika Sörenstam
2002	Karrie Webb
2001	Se Ri Pak

PGA Championship

Year	Winner
2010	Martin Kaymer
2009	Yang Yong-eun
2008	Pádraig Harrington
2007	Tiger Woods
2006	Tiger Woods
2005	Phil Mickelson
2004	Vijay Singh
2003	Shaun Micheel
2002	Rich Beem
2001	David Toms
2000	Tiger Woods
1999	Tiger Woods
1998	Vijay Singh
1997	Davis Love III
1996	Mark Brooks
1995	Steve Elkington
1994	Nick Price
1993	Paul Azinger
1992	Nick Price
1991	John Daly
1990	Wayne Grady
1989	Payne Stewart
1988	Jeff Sluman
1987	Larry Nelson
1986	Bob Tway
1985	Hubert Green
1984	Lee Trevino
1983	Hal Sutton
1982	Raymond Floyd
1981	Larry Nelson
1980	Jack Nicklaus
1979	David Graham
1978	John Mahaffey
1977	Lanny Wadkins
1976	Dave Stockton
1975	Jack Nicklaus
1974	Lee Trevino

Year	Winner
1973	Jack Nicklaus
1972	Gary Player
1971	Jack Nicklaus
1970	Dave Stockton
1969	Raymond Floyd
1968	Julius Boros
1967	Don January
1966	Al Geiberger
1965	Dave Marr
1964	Bobby Nichols
1963	Jack Nicklaus
1962	Gary Player
1961	Jerry Barber
1960	Jay Hebert
1959	Bob Rosburg
1958	Dow Finsterwald
1957	Lionel Hebert
1956	Jack Burke Jr.
1955	Doug Ford
1954	Chick Harbert
1953	Walter Burkemo
1952	Jim Turnesa
1951	Sam Snead
1950	Chandler Harper
1949	Sam Snead
1948	Ben Hogan
1947	Jim Ferrier
1946	Ben Hogan
1945	Byron Nelson
1944	Bob Hamilton
1943	Not held due to World War II
1942	Sam Snead
1941	Vic Ghezzi
1940	Byron Nelson
1939	Henry Picard
1938	Paul Runyan
1937	Denny Shute
1936	Denny Shute
1935	Johnny Revolta
1934	Paul Runyan
1933	Gene Sarazen
1932	Olin Dutra
1931	Tom Creavy
1930	Tommy Armour
1929	Leo Diegel
1928	Leo Diegel
1927	Walter Hagen
1926	Walter Hagen
1925	Walter Hagen
1924	Walter Hagen
1923	Gene Sarazen
1922	Gene Sarazen

Year	Winner
1921	Walter Hagen
1920	Jock Hutchison
1919	Jim Barnes
1918	Not held due to World War I
1917	Not held due to World War I
1916	Jim Barnes

LPGA Championship

Year	Winner
2010	Cristie Kerr
2009	Anna Nordqvist
2008	Yani Tseng
2007	Suzann Pettersen
2006	Se Ri Pak
2005	Annika Sörenstam
2004	Annika Sörenstam
2003	Annika Sörenstam
2002	Se Ri Pak
2001	Karrie Webb
2000	Juli Inkster
1999	Juli Inkster
1998	Se Ri Pak
1997	Christa Johnson
1996	Laura Davies
1995	Kelly Robbins
1994	Laura Davies
1993	Patty Sheehan
1992	Betsy King
1991	Meg Mallon
1990	Beth Daniel
1989	Nancy Lopez
1988	Sherri Turner
1987	Jane Geddes
1986	Pat Bradley
1985	Nancy Lopez
1984	Patty Sheehan
1983	Patty Sheehan
1982	Jan Stephenson
1981	Donna Caponi
1980	Sally Little
1979	Donna Caponi
1978	Nancy Lopez
1977	Chako Higuchi
1976	Betty Burfeindt
1975	Kathy Whitworth
1974	Sandra Haynie
1973	Mary Mills
1972	Kathy Ahern
1971	Kathy Whitworth
1970	Shirley Englehorn
1969	Betsy Rawls

Year	Winner
1968	Sandra Post
1967	Kathy Whitworth
1966	Gloria Ehret
1965	Sandra Haynie
1964	Mary Mills
1963	Mickey Wright
1962	Judy Kimball
1961	Mickey Wright
1960	Mickey Wright
1959	Betsy Rawls
1958	Mickey Wright
1957	Louise Suggs
1956	Marlene Hagge
1955	Beverly Hanson

Master's (Men Only)

Year	Winner
2010	Phil Mickelson
2009	Ángel Cabrera
2008	Trevor Immelman
2007	Zach Johnson
2006	Phil Mickelson
2005	Tiger Woods
2004	Phil Mickelson
2003	Mike Weir
2002	Tiger Woods
2001	Tiger Woods
2000	Vijay Singh
1999	José María Olazábal
1998	Mark O'Meara
1997	Tiger Woods
1996	Nick Faldo
1995	Ben Crenshaw
1994	José María Olazábal
1993	Bernhard Langer
1992	Fred Couples
1991	Ian Woosnam
1990	Nick Faldo
1989	Nick Faldo
1988	Sandy Lyle
1987	Larry Mize
1986	Jack Nicklaus
1985	Bernhard Langer
1984	Ben Crenshaw
1983	Seve Ballesteros
1982	Craig Stadler
1981	Tom Watson
1980	Seve Ballesteros
1979	Fuzzy Zoeller
1978	Gary Player
1977	Tom Watson

Year	Winner
1976	Raymond Floyd
1975	Jack Nicklaus
1974	Gary Player
1973	Tommy Aaron
1972	Jack Nicklaus
1971	Charles Coody
1970	Billy Casper
1969	George Archer
1968	Bob Goalby
1967	Gay Brewer
1966	Jack Nicklaus
1965	Jack Nicklaus
1964	Arnold Palmer
1963	Jack Nicklaus
1962	Arnold Palmer
1961	Gary Player
1960	Arnold Palmer
1959	Art Wall Jr.
1958	Arnold Palmer
1957	Doug Ford
1956	Jack Burke Jr.
1955	Cary Middlecoff
1954	Sam Snead
1953	Ben Hogan
1952	Sam Snead
1951	Ben Hogan
1950	Jimmy Demaret
1949	Sam Snead
1948	Claude Harmon
1947	Jimmy Demaret
1946	Herman Keiser
1945	Not held due to World War II
1944	Not held due to World War II
1943	Not held due to World War II
1942	Byron Nelson
1941	Craig Wood
1940	Jimmy Demaret
1939	Ralph Guldahl
1938	Henry Picard
1937	Byron Nelson
1936	Horton Smith
1935	Gene Sarazen
1934	Horton Smith

Kraft Nabisco Championship (Women Only)

Year	Winner
2010	Yani Tseng
2009	Brittany Lincicome
2008	Lorena Ochoa
2007	Morgan Pressel
2006	Karrie Webb

Year	Winner
2005	Annika Sörenstam
2004	Grace Park
2003	Patricia Meunier-Lebouc
2002	Annika Sörenstam
2001	Annika Sörenstam

Nabisco Championshop (Women Only)

Year	Winner
2000	Karrie Webb
1999	Dottie Pepper
1998	Pat Hurst
1997	Betsy King
1996	Patty Sheehan
1995	Nanci Bowen
1994	Donna Andrews
1993	Helen Alfredsson
1992	Dottie Mochrie
1991	Amy Alcott
1990	Betsy King
1989	Juli Inkster
1988	Amy Alcott
1987	Betsy King
1986	Pat Bradley
1985	Alice Miller
1984	Juli Inkster
1983	Amy Alcott

Du Marier Classic (Women Only)

Year	Winner
2000	Meg Mallon
1999	Karrie Webb
1998	Brandie Burton
1997	Colleen Walker
1996	Laura Davies
1995	Jenny Lidback
1994	Martha Nause
1993	Brandie Burton
1992	Sherri Steinhauer
1991	Nancy Scranton
1990	Cathy Johnston
1989	Tammie Green
1988	Sally Little
1987	Jody Rosenthal
1986	Pat Bradley
1985	Pat Bradley
1984	Juli Inkster
1983	Hollis Stacy
1982	Sandra Haynie
1981	Jan Stephenson
1980	Pat Bradley
1979	Amy Alcott

Title Holders Championship

Year	Winner
1972	Sandra Palmer
1971	No tournament
1970	No tournament
1969	No tournament
1968	No tournament
1967	No tournament
1966	Kathy Whitworth
1965	Kathy Whitworth
1964	Marilynn Smith
1963	Marilynn Smith
1962	Mickey Wright
1961	Mickey Wright
1960	Fay Crocker
1959	Louise Suggs
1958	Beverly Hanson
1957	Patty Berg
1956	Louise Suggs
1955	Patty Berg
1954	Louise Suggs
1953	Patty Berg
1952	Babe Zaharias
1951	Pat O'Sullivan
1950	Babe Zaharias
1949	Peggy Kirk
1948	Patty Berg
1947	Babe Zaharias
1946	Louise Suggs
1945	Not held due to World War II
1944	Not held due to World War II
1943	Not held due to World War II
1942	Dorothy Kirby
1941	Dorothy Kirby
1940	Helen Hicks
1939	Patty Berg
1938	Patty Berg
1937	Patty Berg

Women's Western Open

Year	Winner
1967	Kathy Whitworth
1966	Mickey Wright
1965	Susie Maxwell
1964	Carol Mann
1963	Mickey Wright
1962	Mickey Wright
1961	Mary Lena Faulk
1960	Joyce Ziske
1959	Betsy Rawls
1958	Patty Berg
1957	Patty Berg

Year	Winner
1956	Beverly Hanson
1955	Patty Berg
1954	Betty Jameson
1953	Louise Suggs
1952	Betsy Rawls
1951	Patty Berg
1950	Babe Zaharias
1949	Louise Suggs
1948	Patty Berg
1947	Louise Suggs
1946	Louise Suggs
1945	Babe Zaharias
1944	Babe Zaharias
1943	Patty Berg
1942	Betty Jameson
1941	Patty Berg
1940	Babe Zaharias
1939	Helen Dettweiler
1938	Bea Barrett
1937	Helen Hicks
1936	Opal Hill
1935	Opal Hill
1934	Marian McDougall
1933	June Beebe
1932	Jane Weiller
1931	June Beebe
1930	Lee Mida

Compiled by Sasha Sutherland

European Order of Merit (Golf)

Year	Race to Dubai Leader
2010	Martin Kaymer (Germany)
2009	Lee Westwood (England)

Year	Order of Merit Leader
2008	Robert Karlsson (Sweden)
2007	Justin Rose (England)
2006	Pádraig Harrington (Ireland)
2005	Colin Montgomerie (Scotland)
2004	Ernie Els (South Africa)
2003	Ernie Els (South Africa)
2002	Retief Goosen (South Africa)
2001	Retief Goosen (South Africa)
2000	Lee Westwood (England)
1999	Colin Montgomerie (Scotland)
1998	Colin Montgomerie (Scotland)
1997	Colin Montgomerie (Scotland)
1996	Colin Montgomerie (Scotland)
1995	Colin Montgomerie (Scotland)
1994	Colin Montgomerie (Scotland)

Year	Order of Merit Leader
1993	Colin Montgomerie (Scotland)
1992	Nick Faldo (England)
1991	Seve Ballesteros (Spain)
1990	Ian Woosnam (Wales)
1989	Ronan Rafferty (Northern Ireland)
1988	Seve Ballesteros (Spain)
1987	Ian Woosnam (Wales)
1986	Seve Ballesteros (Spain)
1985	Sandy Lyle (Scotland)
1984	Bernhard Langer (West Germany)

Year	Official Money List Leader
1983	Nick Faldo (England)
1982	Greg Norman (Australia)
1981	Bernhard Langer (West Germany)
1980	Sandy Lyle (Scotland)

Year	Order of Merit Leader
1979	Sandy Lyle (Scotland)
1978	Seve Ballesteros (Spain)
1977	Seve Ballesteros (Spain)
1976	Seve Ballesteros (Spain)
1975	Dale Hayes (South Africa)
1974	Peter Oosterhuis (England)
1973	Peter Oosterhuis (England)
1972	Peter Oosterhuis (England)
1971	Peter Oosterhuis (England)

Compiled by Daniel Zimmet

Major Champions of Tennis

Australian Open, Men's Singles

Year	Winner	Runner-up
2011	Novak Djokovic	Andy Murray
2010	Roger Federer	Andy Murray
2009	Rafael Nadal	Roger Federer
2008	Novak Djokovic	Jo-Wilfried Tsonga
2007	Roger Federer	Fernando Gonzalez
2006	Roger Federer	Marcos Baghdatis
2005	Marat Safin	Lleyton Hewitt
2004	Roger Federer	Marat Safin
2003	Andre Agassi	Rainer Schuttler
2002	Thomas Johansson	Marat Safin
2001	Andre Agassi	Arnaud Clement
2000	Andre Agassi	Yevgeny Kafelnikov
1999	Yevgeny Kafelnikov	Thomas Enqvist
1998	Petr Korda	Marcelo Rios
1997	Pete Sampras	Carlos Moya
1996	Boris Becker	Michael Chang
1995	Andre Agassi	Pete Sampras
1994	Pete Sampras	Todd Martin

Year	Winner	Runner-up
1993	Jim Courier	Stefan Edberg
1992	Jim Courier	Stefan Edberg
1991	Boris Becker	Ivan Lendl
1990	Ivan Lendl	Stefan Edberg
1989	Ivan Lendl	Miloslav Mecir
1988	Mats Wilander	Pat Cash
1987	Stefan Edberg	Pat Cash
1986	None	
1985	Stefan Edberg	Mats Wilander
1984	Mats Wilander	Kevin Curren
1983	Mats Wilander	Ivan Lendl
1982	Johan Kriek	Steve Denton
1981	Johan Kriek	Steve Denton
1980	Brian Teacher	Kim Warwick
1979	Guillermo Vilas	John Sadri
1978	Guillermo Vilas	John Marks
1977	Roscoe Tanner (January)	Guillermo Vilas
1977	Vitas Gerulaitis (December)	John Lloyd
1976	Mark Edmondson	John Newcombe
1975	John Newcombe	Jimmy Connors
1974	Jimmy Connors	Phil Dent
1973	John Newcombe	Onny Parun
1972	Ken Rosewall	Malcolm Anderson
1971	Ken Rosewall	Arthur Ashe
1970	Arthur Ashe	Dick Crealy
1969	Rod Laver	Andres Gimeno

Australian Open, Women's Singles

Year	Winner	Runner-up
2011	Kim Clijsters	Li Na
2010	Serena Williams	Justine Henin
2009	Serena Williams	Dinara Safina
2008	Maria Sharapova	Ana Ivanovic
2007	Serena Wililams	Maria Sharapova
2006	Amelie Mauresmo	Justin Henin
2005	Serena Williams	Lindsay Davenport
2004	Justin Henin	Kim Clijsters
2003	Serena Williams	Venus Williams
2002	Jennifer Capriati	Martina Hingis
2001	Jennifer Capriati	Martina Hingis
2000	Lindsay Davenport	Martina Hingis
1999	Martina Hingis	Amelie Mauresmo
1998	Martina Hingis	Conchita Martinez
1997	Martina Hingis	Mary Pierce
1996	Monica Seles	Anke Huber
1995	Mary Pierce	Arantxa Sanchez Vicario
1994	Steffi Graf	Arantxa Sanchez Vicario
1993	Monica Seles	Steffi Graf
1992	Monica Seles	Mary Joe Fernandez
1991	Monica Seles	Jana Novotna
1990	Steffi Graf	Mary Joe Fernandez
1989	Steffi Graf	Helena Sukova

Year	Winner	Runner-up
1988	Steffi Graf	Chris Evert
1987	Hana Mandlikova	Martina Navratilova
1986	None	
1985	Martina Navratilova	Chris Evert
1984	Chris Evert	Helena Sukova
1983	Martina Navratilova	Kathy Jordan
1982	Chris Evert	Martina Navratilova
1981	Martina Navratilova	Chris Evert
1980	Hana Mandlikova	Chris Evert
1979	Barbara Jordan	Sharon Walsh
1978	Chris O'Neil	Betsy Nagelsen
1977	Kerry Melville Reid	Dianne Fromholtz Balestrat
1977	Evonne Goolagong Cawley	Helen Gourlay Cawley
1976	Evonne Goolagong Cawley	Renata Tomanova
1975	Evonne Goolagong Cawley	Martina Navratilova
1974	Evonne Goolagong Cawley	Chris Evert
1973	Margaret Court	Evonne Goolagong Cawley
1972	Virginia Wade	Evonne Goolagong Cawley
1971	Margaret Court	Evonne Goolagong Cawley
1970	Margaret Court	Kerry Melville Reid
1969	Margaret Court	Billie Jean King

Wimbledon, Men's Singles

Year	Winner	Runner-up
2010	Rafael Nadal	Tomas Berdych
2009	Roger Federer	Andy Roddick
2008	Rafael Nadal	Roger Federer
2007	Roger Federer	Rafael Nadal
2006	Roger Federer	Rafael Nadal
2005	Roger Federer	Andy Roddick
2004	Roger Federer	Andy Roddick
2003	Roger Federer	Mark Philippoussis
2002	Lleyton Hewitt	David Nalbandian
2001	Goran Ivanisevic	Patrick Rafter
2000	Pete Sampras	Patrick Rafter
1999	Pete Sampras	Andre Agassi
1998	Pete Sampras	Goran Ivanisevic
1997	Pete Sampras	Cedric Pioline
1996	Richard Krajicek	MaliVai Washington
1995	Pete Sampras	Boris Becker
1994	Pete Sampras	Goran Ivanisevic
1993	Pete Sampras	Jim Courier
1992	Andre Agassi	Goran Ivansevic
1991	Michael Stich	Boris Becker
1990	Stefan Edberg	Boris Becker
1989	Boris Becker	Stefan Edberg
1988	Stefan Edberg	Boris Becker
1987	Pat Cash	Ivan Lendl
1986	Boris Becker	Ivan Lendl
1985	Boris Becker	Kevin Curren
1984	John McEnroe	Jimmy Connors
1983	John McEnroe	Chris Lewis

Year	Winner	Runner-up
1982	Jimmy Connors	John McEnroe
1981	John McEnroe	Bjorn Borg
1980	Bjorn Borg	John McEnroe
1979	Bjorn Borg	Roscoe Tanner
1978	Bjorn Borg	Jimmy Connors
1977	Bjorn Borg	Jimmy Connors
1976	Bjorn Borg	Ilie Nastase
1975	Arthur Ashe	Jimmy Connors
1974	Jimmy Connors	Ken Rosewall
1973	Jan Kodes	Alex Metreveli
1972	Stan Smith	Ilie Nastase
1971	John Newcombe	Stan Smith
1970	John Newcombe	Ken Rosewall
1969	Rod Laver	John Newcombe
1968	Rod Laver	Tony Roche

Wimbledon, Women's Singles

Year	Winner	Runner-up
2010	Serena Williams	Vera Zvonereva
2009	Serena Williams	Venus Williams
2008	Venus Williams	Serena Williams
2007	Venus Williams	Marion Bartoli
2006	Amelie Mauresmo	Justine Henin
2005	Venus Williams	Lindsay Davenport
2004	Maria Sharapova	Serena Williams
2003	Serena Williams	Venus Williams
2002	Serena Williams	Venus Williams
2001	Venus Williams	Justin Henin
2000	Venus Williams	Lindsay Davenport
1999	Lindsay Davenport	Steffi Graf
1998	Jana Novotna	Nathalie Tauziat
1997	Martina Hingis	Jana Novotna
1996	Steffi Graf	Arantxa Sanchez Vicario
1995	Steffi Graf	Arantxa Sanchez Vicario
1994	Conchita Martinez	Martina Navratilova
1993	Steffi Graf	Jana Novotna
1992	Steffi Graf	Monica Seles
1991	Steffi Graf	Gabriela Sabatini
1990	Martina Navratilova	Zina Garrison
1989	Steffi Graf	Martina Navratilova
1988	Steffi Graf	Martina Navratilova
1987	Martina Navratilova	Steffi Graf
1986	Martina Navratilova	Hana Mandlikova
1985	Martina Navratilova	Chris Evert
1984	Martina Navratilova	Chris Evert
1983	Martina Navratilova	Andrea Jaeger
1982	Martina Navratilova	Chris Evert
1981	Chris Evert	Hana Mandlikova
1980	Evonne Goolagong Cawley	Chris Evert
1979	Martina Navratilova	Chris Evert
1978	Martina Navratilova	Chris Evert
1977	Virginia Wade	Betty Stove

Year	Winner	Runner-up
1976	Chris Evert	Evonne Goolagong Cawley
1975	Billie Jean King	Evonne Goolagong Cawley
1974	Chris Evert	Olga Morozova
1973	Billie Jean King	Chris Evert
1972	Billie Jean King	Evonne Goolagong Cawley
1971	Evonne Goolagong Cawley	Margaret Court
1970	Margaret Court	Billie Jean King
1969	Ann Haydon Jones	Billie Jean King
1968	Billie Jean King	Judy Tegart Dalton

French Open, Men's Singles

Year	Winner	Runner-up
2010	Rafael Nadal	Robin Soderling
2009	Roger Federer	Robin Soderling
2008	Rafael Nadal	Roger Federer
2007	Rafael Nadal	Roger Federer
2006	Rafael Nadal	Roger Federer
2005	Rafael Nadal	Mariano Puerta
2004	Gaston Gaudio	Guillermo Coria
2003	Juan Carlos Ferrero	Martin Verkerk
2002	Albert Costa	Juan Carlos Ferrero
2001	Gustavo Kuerten	Alex Corretja
2000	Gustavo Kuerten	Magnus Norman
1999	Andre Agassi	Andrei Medvedev
1998	Carlos Moya	Alex Corretja
1997	Gustavo Kuerten	Sergi Bruguera
1996	Yevgeny Kafelnikov	Michael Stich
1995	Thomas Muster	Michael Chang
1994	Sergi Bruguera	Alberto Berasategui
1993	Sergi Bruguera	Jim Courier
1992	Jim Courier	Petr Korda
1991	Jim Courier	Andre Agassi
1990	Andres Gomez	Andre Agassi
1989	Michael Chang	Stefan Edberg
1988	Mats Wilander	Henri Leconte
1987	Ivan Lendl	Mats Wilander
1986	Ivan Lendl	Mikael Pernfors
1985	Mats Wilander	Ivan Lendl
1984	Ivan Lendl	John McEnroe
1983	Yannick Noah	Mats Wilander
1982	Mats Wilander	Guillermo Vilas
1981	Bjorn Borg	Ivan Lendl
1980	Bjorn Borg	Vitas Gerulaitis
1979	Bjorn Borg	Victor Pecci
1978	Bjorn Borg	Guillermo Vilas
1977	Guillermo Vilas	Brian Gottfried
1976	Adriano Panatta	Harold Soloman
1975	Bjorn Borg	Guillermo Vilas
1974	Bjorn Borg	Manuel Orantes
1973	Ilie Nastase	Nikola Pilic
1972	Andres Gimeno	Patrick Proisy

Year	Winner	Runner-up
1971	Jan Kodes	Ilie Nastase
1970	Jan Kodes	Zeljko Franulovic
1969	Rod Laver	Ken Rosewall
1968	Ken Rosewall	Rod Laver

French Open, Women's Singles

Year	Winner	Runner-up
2010	Francesca Schiavone	Samantha Stosur
2009	Svetlana Kuznetsova	Dinara Safina
2008	Ana Ivanovic	Dinara Safina
2007	Justine Henin	Ana Ivanovic
2006	Justine Henin	Svetlana Kuznetsova
2005	Justine Henin	Mary Pierce
2004	Anastasia Myskina	Elena Dementieva
2003	Justine Henin	Kim Clijsters
2002	Serena Williams	Venus Williams
2001	Jennifer Capriati	Kim Clijsters
2000	Mary Pierce	Conchita Martinez
1999	Steffi Graf	Martina Hingis
1998	Arantxa Sanchez Vicario	Monica Seles
1997	Iva Majoli	Martina Hingis
1996	Steffi Graf	Arantxa Sanchez Vicario
1995	Steffi Graf	Arantxa Sanchez Vicario
1994	Arantxa Sanchez Vicario	Mary Pierce
1993	Steffi Graf	Mary Joe Fernandez
1992	Monica Seles	Steffi Graf
1991	Monica Seles	Arantxa Sanchez Vicario
1990	Monica Seles	Steffi Graf
1989	Arantxa Sanchez Vicario	Steffi Graf
1988	Steffi Graf	Natalia Zvereva
1987	Steffi Graf	Martina Navratilova
1986	Chris Evert	Martina Navratilova
1985	Chris Evert	Martina Navratilova
1984	Martina Navratilova	Chris Evert
1983	Chris Evert	Mima Jausovec
1982	Martina Navratilova	Andrea Jaeger
1981	Hana Mandlikova	Sylvia Hanika
1980	Chris Evert	Virginia Ruzici
1979	Chris Evert	Wendy Turnbull
1978	Virginia Ruzici	Mima Jausovec
1977	Mima Jausovec	Florenta Mihai
1976	Sue Barker	Renata Tomanova
1975	Chris Evert	Martina Navratilova
1974	Chris Evert	Olga Morozova
1973	Margaret Court	Chris Evert
1972	Billie Jean King	Evonne Goolagong Cawley
1971	Evonne Goolagong Cawley	Helen Gourlay Cawley
1970	Margaret Court	Helga Niessen Masthoff
1969	Margaret Court	Ann Haydon Jones
1968	Nancy Richey	Ann Haydon Jones

US Open, Men's Singles

Year	Winner	Runner-up
2010	Rafael Nadal	Novak Djokovic
2009	Juan Martin del Potro	Roger Federer
2008	Roger Federer	Andy Murray
2007	Roger Federer	Novak Djokovic
2006	Roger Federer	Andy Roddick
2005	Roger Federer	Andre Agassi
2004	Roger Federer	Lleyton Hewitt
2003	Andy Roddick	Juan Carlos Ferrero
2002	Pete Sampras	Andre Agassi
2001	Lleyton Hewitt	Pete Sampras
2000	Marat Safin	Pete Sampras
1999	Andre Agassi	Todd Martin
1998	Patrick Rafter	Mark Philippoussis
1997	Patrick Rafter	Greg Rusedski
1996	Pete Sampras	Michael Chang
1995	Pete Sampras	Andre Agassi
1994	Andre Agassi	Michael Stich
1993	Pete Sampras	Cedric Pioline
1992	Stefan Edberg	Pete Sampras
1991	Stefan Edberg	Jim Courier
1990	Pete Sampras	Andre Agassi
1989	Boris Becker	Ivan Lendl
1988	Mats Wilander	Ivan Lendl
1987	Ivan Lendl	Mats Wilander
1986	Ivan Lendl	Miloslav Mecir
1985	Ivan Lendl	John McEnroe
1984	John McEnroe	Ivan Lendl
1983	Jimmy Connors	Ivan Lendl
1982	Jimmy Connors	Ivan Lendl
1981	John McEnroe	Bjorn Borg
1980	John McEnroe	Bjorn Borg
1979	John McEnroe	Vitas Gerulaitis
1978	Jimmy Connors	Bjorn Borg
1977	Guillermo Vilas	Jimmy Connors
1976	Jimmy Connors	Bjorn Borg
1975	Manuel Orantes	Jimmy Connors
1974	Jimmy Connors	Ken Rosewall
1973	John Newcombe	Jan Kodes
1972	Ilie Nastase	Arthur Ashe
1971	Stan Smith	Jan Kodes
1970	Ken Rosewall	Tony Roche
1969	Rod Laver	Tony Roche
1968	Arthur Ashe	Tom Okker

US Open, Women's Singles

Year	Winner	Runner-up
2010	Kim Clijsters	Vera Zvonareva
2009	Kim Clijsters	Caroline Wozniacki
2008	Serena Williams	Jelena Jankovic
2007	Justine Henin	Svetlana Kuznetsova

Year	Winner	Runner-up
2006	Maria Sharapova	Justine Henin
2005	Kim Clijsters	Mary Pierce
2004	Svetlana Kuznetsova	Elena Dementieva
2003	Justine Henin	Kim Clijsters
2002	Serena Williams	Venus Williams
2001	Venus Williams	Serena Williams
2000	Venus Williams	Lindsay Davenport
1999	Serena Williams	Martina Hingis
1998	Lindsay Davenport	Martina Hingis
1997	Martina Hingis	Venus Williams
1996	Steffi Graf	Monica Seles
1995	Steffi Graf	Monica Seles
1994	Arantxa Sanchez Vicario	Steffi Graf
1993	Steffi Graf	Helena Sukova
1992	Monica Seles	Arantxa Sanchez Vicario
1991	Monica Seles	Martina Navratilova
1990	Gabriela Sabatini	Steffi Graf
1989	Steffi Graf	Martina Navratilova
1988	Steffi Graf	Gabriela Sabatini
1987	Martina Navratilova	Steffi Graf
1986	Martina Navratilova	Helena Sukova
1985	Hana Madlikova	Martina Navratilova
1984	Martina Navratilova	Chris Evert
1983	Martina Navratilova	Chris Evert
1982	Chris Evert	Hana Mandlikova
1981	Tracy Austin	Martina Navratilova
1980	Chris Evert	Hana Mandlikova
1979	Tracy Austin	Chris Evert
1978	Chris Evert	Pam Shriver
1977	Chris Evert	Wendy Turnbull
1976	Chris Evert	Evonne Goolagong Cawley
1975	Chris Evert	Evonne Goolagong Cawley
1974	Billie Jean King	Evonne Goolagong Cawley
1973	Margaret Court	Evonne Goolagong Cawley
1972	Billie Jean King	Kerry Melville Reid
1971	Billie Jean King	Rosemary Casals
1970	Margaret Court	Rosemary Casals
1969	Margaret Court	Nancy Richey Gunter
1968	Virginia Wade	Billie Jean King

Compiled by Molly McManamon

Open Era of Tennis Year-End #1 Rankings

Men's Year-End #1 Rankings (Open Era)

2010	Rafael Nadal	Spain
2009	Roger Federer	Switzerland
2008	Rafael Nadal	Spain
2007	Roger Federer	Switzerland
2006	Roger Federer	Switzerland

2005	Roger Federer	Switzerland
2004	Roger Federer	Switzerland
2003	Andy Roddick	USA
2002	Lleyton Hewitt	Australia
2001	Lleyton Hewitt	Australia
2000	Gustavo Kuerten	Brazil
1999	Andre Agassi	USA
1998	Pete Sampras	USA
1997	Pete Sampras	USA
1996	Pete Sampras	USA
1995	Pete Sampras	USA
1994	Pete Sampras	USA
1993	Pete Sampras	USA
1992	Jim Courier	USA
1991	Stefan Edberg	Sweden
1990	Stefan Edberg	Sweden
1989	Ivan Lendl	Czechoslovakia
1988	Mats Wilander	Sweden
1987	Ivan Lendl	Czechoslovakia
1986	Ivan Lendl	Czechoslovakia
1985	Ivan Lendl	Czechoslovakia
1984	John McEnroe	USA
1983	John McEnroe	USA
1982	John McEnroe	USA
1981	John McEnroe	USA
1980	Bjorn Borg	Sweden
1979	Bjorn Borg	Sweden
1978	Jimmy Connors	USA
1977	Jimmy Connors	USA
1976	Jimmy Connors	USA
1975	Jimmy Connors	USA
1974	Jimmy Connors	USA
1973	Ilie Nastase	Romania
1972	Stan Smith	USA
1971	Stan Smith (USA), John Newcombe (Australia)	
1970	Rod Laver (Australia), Ken Rosewell (Australia), John Newcombe (Australia)	
1969	Rod Laver	Australia
1968	Rod Laver	Australia

Women's Year-End #1 Rankings (Open Era)

2010	Caroline Wozniacki	Denmark
2009	Serena Williams	USA
2008	Jelena Jankovic	Serbia
2007	Justine Henin	Belgium
2006	Justine Henin	Belgium
2005	Lindsay Davenport	USA
2004	Lindsay Davenport	USA
2003	Justine Henin	Belgium
2002	Serena Williams	USA
2001	Lindsay Davenport	USA
2000	Martina Hingis	Switzerland
1999	Martina Hingis	Switzerland
1998	Lindsay Davenport	USA

1997	Martina Hingis	Switzerland
1996	Steffi Graf	Germany
1995	Steffi Graf (Germany) and Monica Seles (USA)	
1994	Steffi Graf	Germany
1993	Steffi Graf	Germany
1992	Monica Seles	Yugoslavia
1991	Monica Seles	Yugoslavia
1990	Steffi Graf	Germany
1989	Steffi Graf	Germany
1988	Steffi Graf	Germany
1987	Steffi Graf	Germany
1986	Martina Navratilova	USA
1985	Martina Navratilova	USA
1984	Martina Navratilova	USA
1983	Martina Navratilova	USA
1982	Martina Navratilova	USA
1981	Chris Evert	USA
1980	Chris Evert	USA
1979	Martina Navratilova	Czechoslovakia
1978	Martina Navratilova	Czechoslovakia
1977	Chris Evert	USA
1976	Chris Evert	USA
1975	Chris Evert	USA
1974	Chris Evert and Billie Jean King	USA
1973	Margaret Court	Australia
1972	Billie Jean King	USA
1971	Billie Jean King (USA) and Evonne Goolagong Cawley (Australia)	
1970	Margaret Court	Australia
1969	Margaret Court	Australia
1968	Billie Jean King	USA

Compiled by Elizabeth Ryan

Golf Year-End #1 Rankings

Rolex Women's Year-End #1 World Golf Rankings

2010	Jiyai Shin	Korea
2009	Lorena Ochoa	Mexico
2008	Lorena Ochoa	Mexico
2007	Lorena Ochoa	Mexico
2006	Annika Sorenstam	Sweden

Men's Year-End #1 Official World Golf Ranking

2010	Lee Westwood	England
2009	Tiger Woods	USA
2008	Tiger Woods	USA
2007	Tiger Woods	USA
2006	Tiger Woods	USA
2005	Tiger Woods	USA
2004	Vijay Singh	Fiji
2003	Tiger Woods	USA

2002	Tiger Woods	USA
2001	Tiger Woods	USA
2000	Tiger Woods	USA
1999	Tiger Woods	USA
1998	Tiger Woods	USA
1997	Greg Norman	Australia
1996	Greg Norman	Australia
1995	Greg Norman	Australia
1994	Nick Price	Zimbabwe
1993	Nick Faldo	England
1992	Nick Faldo	England
1991	Ian Woosnam	Wales
1990	Greg Norman	Australia
1989	Greg Norman	Australia
1988	Seve Ballesteros	Spain
1987	Greg Norman	Australia
1986	Bernhard Langer	West Germany

Compiled by Elizabeth Ryan

NASCAR Cup Champions

Year	Driver	Manufacturer
2010	Jimmie Johnson	Chevrolet
2009	Jimmie Johnson	Chevrolet
2008	Jimmie Johnson	Chevrolet
2007	Jimmie Johnson	Chevrolet
2006	Jimmie Johnson	Chevrolet
2005	Tony Stuart	Chevrolet
2004	Kurt Busch	Ford
2003	Matt Kenseth	Ford
2002	Tony Stuart	Pontiac
2001	Jeff Gordon	Chevrolet
2000	Bobby Labonte	Pontiac
1999	Dale Jarrett	Ford
1998	Jeff Gordon	Chevrolet
1997	Jeff Gordon	Chevrolet
1996	Terry Labonte	Chevrolet
1995	Jeff Gordon	Chevrolet
1994	Dale Earnhardt	Chevrolet
1993	Dale Earnhardt	Chevrolet
1992	Alan Kulwicki	Ford
1991	Dale Earnhardt	Chevrolet
1990	Dale Earnhardt	Chevrolet
1989	Rusty Wallace	Pontiac
1988	Bill Elliot	Ford
1987	Dale Earnhardt	Chevrolet
1986	Dale Earnhardt	Chevrolet
1985	Darrell Waltrip	Chevrolet
1984	Terry Labonte	Chevrolet
1983	Bobby Allison	Buick
1982	Darrell Waltrip	Buick
1981	Darrell Waltrip	Buick

Year	Driver	Manufacturer
1980	Dale Earnhardt	Chevrolet
1979	Richard Petty	Chevrolet
1978	Cale Yarborough	Oldsmobile
1977	Cale Yarborough	Chevrolet
1976	Cale Yarborough	Chevrolet
1975	Richard Petty	Dodge
1974	Richard Petty	Dodge
1973	Benny Parsons	Chevrolet
1972	Richard Petty	Plymouth
1971	Richard Petty	Plymouth
1970	Bobby Isaac	Dodge
1969	David Pearson	Ford
1968	David Pearson	Ford
1967	Richard Petty	Plymouth
1966	David Pearson	Dodge
1965	Ned Jarrett	Ford
1964	Richard Petty	Plymouth
1963	Joe Weatherly	Pontiac
1962	Joe Weatherly	Pontiac
1961	Ned Jarrett	Chevrolet
1960	Rex White	Chevrolet
1959	Lee Petty	Plymouth
1958	Lee Petty	Oldsmobile
1957	Buck Baker	Chevrolet
1956	Buck Baker	Chrysler
1955	Tim Flock	Chrysler
1954	Lee Petty	Chrysler
1953	Herb Thomas	Hudson
1952	Tim Flock	Hudson
1951	Herb Thomas	Hudson
1950	Bill Rexford	Oldsmobile
1949	Red Byron	Oldsmobile

Compiled by Charles Parrish

Formula One World Champions

Year	Driver	Constructors' Championship
2010	Sebastian Vettel (Germany)	Red Bull
2009	Jenson Button (United Kingdom)	Brawn
2008	Lewis Hamilton (United Kingdom)	Ferrari
2007	Kimi Raikkonen (Finland)	Ferrari
2006	Fernando Alonso (Spain)	Renault
2005	Fernando Alonso (Spain)	Renault
2004	Michael Schumacher (Germany)	Ferrari
2003	Michael Schumacher (Germany)	Ferrari
2002	Michael Schumacher (Germany)	Ferrari
2001	Michael Schumacher (Germany)	Ferrari
2000	Michael Schumacher (Germany)	Ferrari
1999	Mika Hakkinen (Finland)	Ferrari
1998	Mika Hakkinen (Finland)	McLaren
1997	Jaques Villeneuve (Canada)	Williams

Year	Driver	Constructors' Championship
1996	Damon Hill (United Kingdom)	Williams
1995	Michael Schumacher (Germany)	Benetton
1994	Michael Schumacher (Germany)	Williams
1993	Alan Prost (France)	Williams
1992	Nigel Mansell (United Kingdom)	Williams
1991	Ayrton Senna (Brazil)	McLaren
1990	Ayrton Senna (Brazil)	McLaren
1989	Alan Prost (France)	McLaren
1988	Ayrton Senna (Brazil)	McLaren
1987	Nelson Piquet (Brazil)	Williams
1986	Alan Prost (France)	Williams
1985	Alan Prost (France)	McLaren
1984	Niki Lauda (Austria)	McLaren
1983	Nelson Piquet (Brazil)	Ferrari
1982	Keke Rosberg (Finland)	Ferrari
1981	Nelson Piquet (Brazil)	Williams
1980	Alan Jones (Australia)	Williams
1979	Jody Sheckter (South Africa)	Ferrari
1978	Mario Andretti (United States)	Lotus
1977	Niki Lauda (Austria)	Ferrari
1976	James Hunt (United Kingdom)	Ferrari
1975	Niki Lauda (Austria)	Ferrari
1974	Emerson Fitipaldi (Brazil)	McLaren
1973	Jackie Stewart (United Kingdom)	Lotus
1972	Emerson Fitipaldi (Brazil)	Lotus
1971	Jackie Stewart (United Kingdom)	Tyrrell
1970	Jochen Rendt (Austria)	Lotus
1969	Jackie Stewart (Great Britain)	Matra
1968	Graham Hill (United Kingdom)	Lotus
1967	Danny Hulme (New Zealand)	Brabham
1966	Jack Brabham (Australia)	Brabham
1965	Jim Clark (United Kingdom)	Lotus
1964	John Surtees (United Kingdom)	Ferrari
1963	Jim Clark (United Kingdom)	Lotus
1962	Graham Hill (United Kingdom)	BRM
1961	Phil Hill (United States)	Ferrari
1960	Jack Brabham (Australia)	Cooper
1959	Jack Brabham (Australia)	Cooper
1958	Mike Hawthorne (United Kingdom)	Vanwall
1957	Juan Manuel Fangio (Argentina)	
1956	Juan Manuel Fangio (Argentina)	
1955	Juan Manuel Fangio (Argentina)	
1954	Juan Manuel Fangio (Argentina)	
1953	Alberto Ascari (Italy)	
1952	Alberto Ascari (Italy)	
1951	Juan Manuel Fangio (Argentina)	
1950	Nino Farina (Italy)	

Compiled by Charles Parrish

Indy Car Series Champions

Year	Driver	Team
2010	Dario Franchitti (United Kingdom)	Chip Ganassi Racing
2009	Dario Franchitti (United Kingdom)	Chip Ganassi Racing
2008	Scott Dixson (New Zealand)	Chip Ganassi Racing
2007	Dario Franchitti (United Kingdom)	Andretti Green Racing
2006	Sam Hornish Jr. (United States)	Penske Racing
2005	Dan Wheldon (United Kingdom)	Andretti Green Racing
2004	Tony Kanaan (Brazil)	Andretti Green Racing
2003	Scott Dixson (New Zealand)	Chip Ganassi Racing
2002	Sam Hornish Jr. (United States)	Panther Racing
2001	Sam Hornish Jr. (United States)	Panther Racing
2000	Buddy Lazier (United States)	Hemelgarn Racing
1999	Greg Ray (United States)	Team Menard
1998	Kenny Brack (Sweden)	A. J. Foyt
1997	Tony Stewart (United States)	Team Menard
1996	Scott Sharpe (United States)	A. J. Foyt
1996	Buzz Calkins (United States)	Bradley Motorsports

Compiled by Charles Parrish

North American Soccer League and Major League Soccer

Major League Soccer

Year	Winner	Runner-up
2011	L.A. Galaxy	Houston
2010	Colorado Rapids	FC Dallas
2009	Real Salt Lake	L.A. Galaxy
2008	Columbus Crew	New York Red Bull
2007	Houston Dynamo	New England Revolution
2006	Houston Dynamo	New England Revolution
2005	L.A. Galaxy	New England Revolution
2004	D.C. United	Kansas City Wizards
2003	San Jose Earthquakes	Chicago Fire
2002	L.A. Galaxy	New England Revolution
2001	San Jose Earthquakes	L.A. Galaxy
2000	Kansas City Wizards	Chicago Fire
1999	D.C. United	L.A. Galaxy
1998	Chicago Fire	D.C. United
1997	D.C. United	Colorado Rapids
1996	D.C. United	L.A. Galaxy

North American Soccer League

Year	Winner	Runner-up
1984	Chicago Sting	Toronto Blizzard
1983	Tulsa Roughnecks	Toronto Blizzard
1982	New York Cosmos	Seattle Sounders
1981	Chicago Sting	New York Cosmos
1980	New York Cosmos	Ft. Lauderdale Strikers
1979	Vancouver Whitecaps	Tampa Bay Rowdies
1978	New York Cosmos	Tampa Bay Rowdies

Year	Winner	Runner-up
1977	New York Cosmos	Seattle Sounders
1976	Toronto Metros-Croatia	Minnesota Kicks
1975	Tampa Bay Rowdies	Portland Timbers
1974	Los Angeles Aztecs	Miami Toros
1973	Philadelphia Atoms	Dallas Tornado
1972	New York Cosmos	St. Louis Stars
1971	Dallas Tornado	Atlanta Chiefs
1970	Rochester Lancers	Washington (D.C.) Darts
1969	Kansas City Spurs	Atlanta Chiefs
1968	Atlanta Chiefs	San Diego Toros

Compiled by Charles Parrish

Association Football, Argentina (Primera División)

Year	Winner
2010 (Aperatura)	Estudiantes de La Plata
2010 (Clausura)	Argentinos Juniors
2009 (Apertura)	Banfield
2009 (Clausura)	Vélez Sársfield
2008 (Apertura)	Boca Juniors
2008 (Clausura)	River Plate
2007 (Apertura)	Lanús
2007 (Clausura)	San Lorenzo de Almagro
2006 (Apertura)	Estudiantes de La Plata
2006 (Clausura)	Boca Juniors
2005 (Apertura)	Boca Juniors
2005 (Clausura)	Vélez Sarsfield
2004 (Apertura)	Newell's Old Boys
2004 (Clausura)	River Plate
2003 (Apertura)	Boca Juniors
2003 (Clausura)	River Plate
2002 (Apertura)	Independiente
2002 (Clausura)	River Plate
2001 (Apertura)	Racing Club
2001 (Clausura)	San Lorenzo de Almagro
2000 (Apertura)	Boca Juniors
2000 (Clausura)	River Plate
1999 (Apertura)	River Plate
1999 (Clausura)	Boca Juniors
1998 (Apertura)	Boca Juniors
1998 (Clausura)	Vélez Sarsfield
1997 (Apertura)	River Plate
1997 (Clausura)	River Plate
1996 (Apertura)	River Plate
1996 (Clausura)	Vélez Sarsfield
1995 (Apertura)	Vélez Sarsfield
1995 (Clausura)	San Lorenzo de Almagro
1994 (Apertura)	River Plate
1994 (Clausura)	Independiente
1993 (Apertura)	River Plate
1993 (Clausura)	Vélez Sarsfield

Year	Winner
1992 (Apertura)	River Plate
1992 (Clausura)	Newell's Old Boys
1991 (Clausura)	Boca Juniors
1991 (Apertura)	Newell's Old Boys
1989–1990	River Plate
1988–1989	Independiente
1987–1988	Newell's Old Boys
1986–1987	Rosario Central
1985–1986	River Plate
1985 (Nacional)	Argentinos Juniors
1984 (Nacional)	Ferro Carril Oeste
1984 (Metropolitano)	Argentinos Juniors
1983 (Nacional)	Estudiantes de La Plata
1983 (Metropolitano)	Independiente
1982 (Nacional)	Ferro Carril Oeste
1982 (Metropolitano)	Estudiantes de La Plata
1981 (Nacional)	River Plate
1981 (Metropolitano)	Boca Juniors
1980 (Nacional)	Rosario Central
1980 (Metropolitano)	River Plate
1979 (Nacional)	River Plate
1979 (Metropolitano)	River Plate
1978 (Nacional)	Independiente
1978 (Metropolitano)	Quilmes
1977 (Nacional)	Independiente
1977 (Metropolitano)	River Plate
1976 (Nacional)	Boca Juniors
1976 (Metropolitano)	Boca Juniors
1975 (Nacional)	River Plate
1975 (Metropolitano)	River Plate
1974 (Nacional)	San Lorenzo de Almagro
1974 (Metropolitano)	Newell's Old Boys
1973 (Nacional)	Rosario Central
1973 (Metropolitano)	Huracán
1972 (Nacional)	San Lorenzo de Almagro
1972 (Metropolitano)	San Lorenzo de Almagro
1971 (Nacional)	Rosario Central
1971 (Metropolitano)	Independiente
1970 (Nacional)	Boca Juniors
1970 (Metropolitano)	Independiente
1969 (Nacional)	Boca Juniors
1969 (Metropolitano)	Chacarita Juniors
1968 (Nacional)	Vélez Sarsfield
1968 (Metropolitano)	San Lorenzo de Almagro
1967 (Nacional)	Independiente
1967 (Metropolitano)	Estudiantes de La Plata
1966	Racing Club
1965	Boca Juniors
1964	Boca Juniors
1963	Independiente
1962	Boca Juniors
1961	Racing Club

Year	Winner
1960	Independiente
1959	San Lorenzo de Almagro
1958	Racing Club
1957	River Plate
1956	River Plate
1955	River Plate
1954	Boca Juniors
1953	River Plate
1952	River Plate
1951	Racing Club
1950	Racing Club
1949	Racing Club
1948	Independiente
1947	River Plate
1946	San Lorenzo de Almagro
1945	River Plate
1944	Boca Juniors
1943	Boca Juniors
1942	River Plate
1941	River Plate
1940	Boca Juniors
1939	Independiente
1938	Independiente
1937	River Plate
1936	River Plate
1935	Boca Juniors
1934	Boca Juniors
1933	San Lorenzo de Almagro
1932	River Plate
1931	Boca Juniors

Compiled by Charles Parrish

Association Football, México (Primera División)

Year	Winner
2010 (Apertura)	Monterrey
2010 (Clausura)	Toluca
2009 (Apertura)	Monterrey
2009 (Clausura)	UNAM (Pumas)
2008 (Apertura)	Toluca
2008 (Clausura)	Santos
2007 (Apertura)	Atlante
2007 (Clausura)	Pachuca
2006 (Apertura)	Guadalajara
2006 (Clausura)	Pachuca
2005 (Apertura)	Toluca
2005 (Clausura)	América
2004 (Apertura)	UNAM (Pumas)
2004 (Clausura)	UNAM (Pumas)
2003 (Apertura)	Pachuca
2003 (Clausura)	Monterrey

Year	Winner
2002 (Apertura)	Toluca
2002 (Summer)	América
2001 (Winter)	Pachuca
2001 (Summer)	Santos
2000 (Winter)	Morelia
2000 (Summer)	Toluca
1999 (Winter)	Pachuca
1998 (Summer)	Toluca
1997 (Winter)	Cruz Azul
1997 (Summer)	Guadalajara
1996 (Winter)	Santos
1995–1996	Necaxa
1994–1995	Necaxa
1993–1994	UAG
1992–1993	Atlante
1991–1992	León
1990–1991	UNAM (Pumas)
1989–1990	Puebla
1988–1989	América
1987–1988	América
1986–1987	Guadalajara
México 1986	Monterrey
1985	América
1984–1985	América
1983–1984	América
1982–1983	Puebla
1981–1982	Tigres
1980–1981	UNAM (Pumas)
1979–1980	Cruz Azul
1978–1979	Cruz Azul
1977–1978	Tigres
1976–1977	UNAM (Pumas)
1975–1976	América
1974–1975	Toluca
1973–1974	Cruz Azul
1972–1973	Cruz Azul
1971–1972	Cruz Azul
1970–1971	América
México 1970	Cruz Azul
1969–1970	Guadalajara
1968–1969	Cruz Azul
1967–1968	Toluca
1966–1967	Toluca
1965–1966	América
1964–1965	Guadalajara
1963–1964	Guadalajara
1962–1963	Oro
1961–1962	Guadalajara
1960–1961	Guadalajara
1959–1960	Guadalajara
1958–1959	Guadalajara
1957–1958	Zacatepec

Year	Winner
1956–1957	Guadalajara
1955–1956	León
1954–1955	Zacatepec
1953–1954	Marte
1952–1953	Tampico
1951–1952	León
1950–1951	Atlas
1949–1950	Veracruz
1948–1949	León
1947–1948	León
1946–1947	Atlante
1945–1946	Veracruz
1944–1945	España
1943–1944	Asturias

Compiled by Charles Parrish

Association Football, Brazil

Brazil National Championships

Campeonato Brasileiro Série A

Year	Winner
2010	Fluminense
2009	Flamengo
2008	São Paulo
2007	São Paulo
2006	São Paulo
2005	Corinthians
2004	Santos
2003	Cruzeiro
2002	Santos
2001	Atlético Paranaense
2000	Vasco de Gama
1999	Corinthians
1998	Corinthians
1997	Vasco de Gama
1996	Grémio
1995	Botafogo
1994	Palmeiras
1993	Palmeiras
1992	Flamengo
1991	São Paulo
1990	Corinthians
1989	Vasco de Gama
1988	Bahia
1987	Recife
1986	São Paulo
1985	Coritiba
1984	Fluminense
1983	Flamengo

Year	Winner
1982	Flamengo
1981	Grémio
1980	Flamengo
1979	Internacional
1978	Guarani
1977	São Paulo
1976	Internacional
1975	Internacional
1974	Vasco de Gama
1973	Palmeiras
1972	Palmeiras
1971	Atlético Mineiro

Torneio Roberto Gomes Pedrosa (1967–1970)

Year	Winner
1970	Fluminense
1969	Palmeiras
1968	Santos
1967	Palmeiras

Taca Brazil (1959–1968)

Year	Winner
1968	Botafogo
1967	Palmeiras
1966	Cruzeiro
1965	Santos
1964	Santos
1963	Santos
1962	Santos
1961	Santos
1960	Palmeiras
1959	Bahia

São Paulo State Championship (Paulista)

Year	Winner
2010	Santos
2009	Corinthians
2008	Palmeiras
2007	Santos
2006	Santos
2005	São Paulo
2004	São Caetano
2003	Corinthians
2002	Ituano
2001	Corinthians
2000	São Paulo
1999	Corinthians
1998	São Paulo
1997	Corinthians
1996	Palmeiras
1995	Corinthians

Year	Winner
1994	Palmeiras
1993	Palmeiras
1992	São Paulo
1991	São Paulo
1990	Bragantino
1989	São Paulo
1988	Corinthians
1987	São Paulo
1986	Inter de Limeira
1985	São Paulo
1984	Santos
1983	Corinthians
1982	Corinthians
1981	São Paulo
1980	São Paulo
1979	Corinthians
1978	Santos
1977	Corinthians
1976	Palmeiras
1975	São Paulo
1974	Palmeiras
1973	Santos/Portuguesa
1972	Palmeiras
1971	São Paulo
1970	São Paulo
1969	Santos
1968	Santos
1967	Santos
1966	Palmeiras
1965	Santos
1964	Santos
1963	Palmeiras
1962	Santos
1961	Santos
1960	Santos
1959	Palmeiras
1958	Santos
1957	São Paulo
1956	Santos
1955	Santos
1954	Corinthians
1953	São Paulo
1952	Corinthians
1951	Corinthians
1950	Palmeiras
1949	São Paulo
1948	São Paulo
1947	Palmeiras
1946	São Paulo
1945	São Paulo
1944	Palmeiras
1943	São Paulo

Year	Winner
1942	Palmeiras
1941	Corinthians
1940	Palestra Itália
1939	Corinthians
1938	Corinthians
1937	Corinthians
1936	Palestra Itália
1935	Santos

Rio de Janeiro State Championship (Carioca)

Year	Winner
2010	Botafogo
2009	Flamengo
2008	Flamengo
2007	Flamengo
2006	Botafogo
2005	Fluminense
2004	Flamengo
2003	Vasco de Gama
2002	Fluminense
2001	Flamengo
2000	Flamengo
1999	Flamengo
1998	Vasco de Gama
1997	Botafogo
1996	Flamengo
1995	Fluminense
1994	Vasco de Gama
1993	Vasco de Gama
1992	Vasco de Gama
1991	Flamengo
1990	Botafogo
1989	Botafogo
1988	Vasco de Gama
1987	Vasco de Gama
1986	Flamengo
1985	Fluminense
1984	Fluminense
1983	Fluminense
1982	Vasco de Gama
1981	Flamengo
1980	Fluminense
1979	Flamengo
1978	Flamengo
1977	Vasco de Gama
1976	Fluminense
1975	Fluminense
1974	Flamengo
1973	Fluminense
1972	Flamengo
1971	Fluminense

Year	Winner
1970	Vasco de Gama
1969	Fluminense
1968	Botafogo
1967	Botafogo
1966	Bangu
1965	Flamengo
1964	Fluminense
1963	Flamengo
1962	Botafogo
1961	Botafogo
1960	América
1959	Fluminense
1958	Vasco de Gama
1957	Botafogo
1956	Vasco de Gama
1955	Flamengo
1954	Flamengo
1953	Flamengo
1952	Vasco de Gama
1951	Fluminense
1950	Vasco de Gama
1949	Vasco de Gama
1948	Botafogo
1947	Vasco de Gama
1946	Fluminense
1945	Vasco de Gama
1944	Flamengo
1943	Flamengo
1942	Flamengo
1941	Fluminense
1940	Fluminense
1939	Flamengo
1938	Fluminense
1937	Fluminense
1936	Fluminense
1935	América
1934	Vasco de Gama
1933	Bangu

Compiled by Charles Parrish

FIBA World Basketball Championships

Year	Winner (Gold Medal)
2010	United States
2006	Spain
2002	Yugoslavia
1998	Yugoslavia
1994	United States
1990	Yugoslavia
1986	United States
1982	Soviet Union

Year	Winner (Gold Medal)
1978	Yugoslavia
1974	Soviet Union
1970	Yugoslavia
1967	Soviet Union
1963	Brazil
1959	Brazil
1954	United States
1950	Argentina

Compiled by Charles Parrish

FIBA European Basketball Championships

Year	Winner (Gold Medal)
2009	Spain
2007	Russia
2005	Greece
2003	Lithuania
2001	Yugoslavia
1999	Italy
1997	Yugoslavia
1995	Yugoslavia
1993	Germany
1991	Yugoslavia
1989	Yugoslavia
1987	Greece
1985	Soviet Union
1983	Italy
1981	Soviet Union
1979	Soviet Union
1977	Yugoslavia
1975	Yugoslavia
1973	Yugoslavia
1971	Soviet Union
1969	Soviet Union
1967	Soviet Union
1965	Soviet Union
1963	Soviet Union
1961	Soviet Union
1959	Soviet Union
1957	Soviet Union
1955	Hungary
1953	Soviet Union
1951	Soviet Union
1949	Egypt
1947	Soviet Union
1946	Czechoslovakia
1941–1945	Not held due to World War II
1939	Lithuania
1937	Lithuania
1935	Latvia

Compiled by Charles Parrish

Select Bibliography

General

Allison, L., ed. 2005. *The Global Politics of Sport: The Role of Global Institutions in Sport.* London: Routledge.

Arnaud, P., and G. Garrier, eds. 1992. *Jeux et sports dans l'histoire.* 2 vols. Paris: CTHS.

Arnaud, P., and T. Terret. 1996. *Histoire du sport féminin.* Paris: L'Harmattan.

Bairner, A. 2001. *Sport, Nationalism and Globalization: European and North American Perspectives.* Albany: SUNY Press.

Baker, W. 1988. *Sports in the Western World.* Urbana and Chicago: University of Illinois Press.

Baker, W. 2007. *Playing with God: Religion and Modern Sport.* Cambridge, MA: Harvard University Press.

Bale, J., and M. Cronin, eds. 2003. *Sport and Postcolonialism.* Oxford: Berg.

Bateman, A., and J. Bale, eds. 2008. *Sporting Sounds: Relationships between Sport and Music.* London: Routledge.

Booth, D. 2001. *The Field: Truth and Fiction in Sports History.* London: Routledge.

Burstyn, V. 1999. *The Rites of Men: Manhood, Politics, and the Culture of Sport.* Toronto: University of Toronto Press.

Carter, J. M. 1988. *Sports and Pastimes of the Middle Ages.* Lanham, MD: University Press of America.

Carter, J. M., and A. Krüger, eds. 1990. *Ritual and Record: Sports Records and Quantification in Pre-Modern Societies.* Westport, CT: Greenwood.

Chandler, T. J. L., and J. Nauright, eds. 1999. *Making the Rugby World: Race, Gender, Commerce.* London: Routledge.

Coakley, J., and P. Donnelly, eds. 1999. *Inside Sports.* London: Routledge.

Coakley, J., and E. Dunning, eds. 2000. *Handbook of Sports Studies.* London: Sage.

Cox, R., G. Jarvie, and W. Vamplew, eds. 2000. *Encyclopedia of British Sport.* Oxford: ABC-CLIO.

Decker, W., and J.-P. Thullier, 2004. *Le sport dans l'Antiquité: Égypt, Grèce et Rome.* Paris: Picard.

Diem, C. 1960. *Weltgeschichte des Sports.* Stuttgart: Cotta.

Donnelly, P., and J. Coakley. 2011. *Sport: A Short Introduction.* London: Routledge.

Eichberg, H., J. Bale, and C. Philo. 1998. *Body Cultures: Essays on Sport, Space and Identity.* London: Routledge.

Elias, N., and E. Dunning. 1986. *Quest for Excitement: Sport and Leisure in the Civilizing Process.* Oxford: Blackwell.

Foer, F. 2005. *How Soccer Explains the World: An Unlikely Theory of Globalization.* New York: HarperCollins.

Giulianotti, R. 2004. *Sport and Modern Social Theorists.* Harlow, UK: Palgrave.

Giulianotti, R., and R. Robertson. 2007. *Globalization and Sport.* Oxford: Blackwell.

Gruneau, R. 1999. *Class, Sports and Social Development.* 2nd ed. Champaign, IL: Human Kinetics.

Guttmann, A. 1978. *From Ritual to Record: The Nature of Modern Sports.* New York: Columbia University Press.

Guttmann, A. 1991. *Women's Sports: A History.* New York: Columbia University Press.

Guttmann, A. 1992. *The Olympics: A History of the Modern Games.* Urbana: University of Illinois Press.

Guttmann, A. 1994. *Games and Empires: Modern Sports and Cultural Imperialism.* New York: Columbia University Press.

Guttmann, A. 2004. *Sports: The First Five Millennia.* Amherst: University of Massachusetts Press.

Hall, M. A. 1996. *Feminism and Sporting Bodies: Essays on Theory and Practice.* Champaign, IL: Human Kinetics.

Hargreaves, J. 1994. *Sporting Females: Critical Issues in the History and Sociology of Women's Sports.* London: Routledge.

Hargreaves, J. 2000. *Heroines of Sport: The Politics of Difference and Identity.* London: Routledge.

Hargreaves, J., and P. Vertinsky, eds. 2006. *Physical Culture: Power and the Body.* London: Routledge.

Hill, J. 2007. *Sport and the Literary Imagination: Essays in History, Literature and Sport.* New York: Peter Lang.

Hoberman, J. 1992. *Mortal Engines: The Science of Human Performance and the Dehumanization of Sport.* New York: Free Press.

Hoberman, J. 2005. *Testosterone Dreams: Rejuvenation, Aphrodisia, Doping.* Berkeley: University of California Press.

Huizinga, J. 1950. *Homo Ludens: A Study of the Play Element in Culture.* Boston: Beacon.

James, C. L. R. 1963. *Beyond a Boundary.* London: Stanley Paul.

Kyle, D. 2007. *Sport and Spectacle in the Ancient World.* London: Blackwell.

LaFeber, W. 2002. *Michael Jordan and the New Global Capitalism.* New and expanded ed. New York: Norton.

Magdalinski, T., and T. J. L. Chandler, eds. 2002. *With God on Their Side: Sport in the Service of Religion.* London: Routledge.

Maguire, J. 1999. *Globalization and Sports.* Cambridge: Polity.

Mandell, R. 1984. *Sport: A Cultural History.* New York: Columbia University Press.

Mangan, J. A. 1981. *Athleticism in the Victorian and Edwardian Public School.* Cambridge: Cambridge University Press.

Mangan, J. A. 1987. *The Games Ethic and Imperialism: Aspects of the Diffusion of an Ideal.* Harmondsworth, UK: Viking.

Messner, M. 1992. *Power at Play: Sports and the Problem of Masculinity.* Boston: Beacon.

Messner, M., and D. Sabo, eds. 1990. *Sport, Men, and the Gender Order: Critical Feminist Perspectives.* Champaign, IL: Human Kinetics.

Miller, T., G. Lawrence, J. McKay, and D. Rowe. 2001. *Globalization and Sport: Playing the World.* London: Sage.

Miller, T. 2002. *Sportsex.* Philadelphia: Temple University Press.

Møller, V., and J. Nauright, eds. 2003. *The Essence of Sport.* Odense: University Press of Southern Denmark.

Nauright, J., and T. J. L. Chandler, eds. 1996. *Making Men: Rugby and Masculine Identity.* London: Frank Cass.

Nauright, J., and S. W. Pope, eds. 2009. *The New Sport Management Reader.* Morgantown, WV: Fitness Information Technology.

Nauright, J., and K. Schimmel, eds. 2005. *The Political Economy of Sport.* Basingstoke, UK: Palgrave Macmillan.

Phillips, M., ed. 2006. *Deconstrucing Sports History: A Postmodern Analysis.* Albany: SUNY Press.

Pope, S. W., and J. Nauright, eds. 2010. *The Routledge Companion to Sports History.* London: Routledge.

Riordan, J., and A. Krüger, eds. 1999. *The International Politics of Sport in the Twentieth Century.* London: Routledge.

Sansone, D. 1988. *Greek Athletics and the Genesis of Sport.* Berkeley: University of California Press.

Senn, A. 1999. *Power, Politics, and the Olympic Games: A History of the Power Brokers, Events, and Controversies That Shaped the Games.* Champaign, IL: Human Kinetics.

Simson, V., and A. Jennings. 1992. *The Lords of the Rings: Power, Money and Drugs in the Modern Olympics.* New York: Simon and Schuster.

Van Bottenburg, M. 2001. *Global Games.* Urbana: University of Illinois Press.

Vertinsky, P. 1994. *The Eternally Wounded Woman: Women, Doctors and Exercise in the Late Nineteenth Century.* Urbana: University of Illinois Press.

Wagg, S., and D. Andrews, eds. 2007. *East Plays West: Sport and the Cold War.* London: Routledge.

Young, D. 1984. *The Olympic Myth of Greek Amateur Athletics.* Chicago: Ares.

Africa (Sub-Sahara)

Alegi, P. 2004. *Laduma! Soccer, Politics and Society in South Africa.* Durban, South Africa: University of KwaZulu-Natal Press.

Alegi, P. 2010. *African Soccerscapes: How a Continent Changed the World's Game.* Athens: Ohio University Press.

Archer, R., and A. Bouillon. 1987. *The South African Game: Sport and Racism.* London: Zed.

Baker, W., and J. A. Mangan, eds. 1987. *Sport in Africa.* New York: Africana Books.

Bale, J. 2002. *Imagined Olympians: Body Culture and Colonial Representation in Rwanda.* Minneapolis: University of Minnesota Press.

Bale, J., and J. Sang. 1996. *Kenyan Running.* London: Frank Cass.

Black, D. R., and J. Nauright. 1998. *Rugby and the South African Nation.* Manchester, UK: Manchester University Press.

Booth, D. 1998. *The Race Game: Sport and Politics in South Africa.* London: Frank Cass.

Cobley, A. G. 1997. *The Rules of the Game: Struggles in Black Recreation and Social Welfare Policy in South Africa.* Westport, CT: Greenwood.

Iliffe, J. 1979. *A Modern History of Tanganyika.* Cambridge: Cambridge University Press.

Jarvie, G. 1986. *Class, Race and Sport in South Africa's Social Development.*

Martin, P. 1995. *Leisure and Society in Colonial Brazzaville.* Cambridge: Cambridge University Press.

Murray, B., and C. Merrett. 2004. *Caught Behind: Race and Politics in Springbok Cricket.* Durban and Pietermaritzburg, South Africa: University of Kwa-Zulu Natal Press; Johannesburg: University of Witwatersrand Press.

Nauright, J. 2010. *Long Run to Freedom: Sport, Cultures and Identities in South Africa.* New ed. Morgantown, WV: Fitness Information Technology.

Odendaal, A. 2003. *The Story of an African Game.* Cape Town: David Phillip.

Powe, E. L. 1994. *Combat Games of Northern Nigeria.* Madison, WI: Dan Aiki.

Asia

Geertz, C. 1972. "Deep Play: Notes on the Balinese Cockfight." In *The Interpretation of Cultures,* edited by C. Geertz, 412–454. New York: Basic Books.

Hamid, A., ed. 2008. *The Encyclopedia of Malaysia,* Vol. 15, *Sports and Recreation.* Singapore: Archipelago.

Hong, F. 2009. "China." In *Routledge Companion to Sports History,* edited by S. Pope and J. Nauright, 405–419. Oxford: Routledge.

Kelly, W. "Caught in the Spin Cycle: An Anthropological Observer at the Sites of Japanese Professional Baseball." In *Moving Targets: Ethnographies of Self and Community in Japan,* edited by S. O. Long, 144. Ithaca, NY: Cornell University Press.

Light, R. 2009. "Japan." In *Routledge Companion to Sports History,* edited by S. Pope and J. Nauright, 472–486. Oxford: Routledge.

Little, C. 2009. "South East Asia." In *Routledge Companion to Sports History,* edited by S. Pope and J. Nauright, 587–598. Oxford: Routledge.

Little, C., and J. Nauright. 2008. "Globalization and Development in Sport: Perspectives from South East Asia." In *Development in Asia: Interdisciplinary, Post-neoliberal and Transnational Perspectives,* edited by D. Nault, 195–214. Boca Raton, FL: BrownWalker.

Majumdar, B., and N. Mehta. 2008. *India and the Olympics.* London: Routledge.

Mangan, J., and F. Hong, eds. 2002. *Sport in Asian Society: Past and Present.* London: Frank Cass.

Morris, A. 2004. *Marrow of the Nation: A History of Sport and Physical Culture in Republican China.* Berkeley and Los Angeles: University of California Press.

Orwell, G. 1950. *Shooting an Elephant and Other Essays.* London: Secker and Warburg.

Perera, S. 1979. *History of a Hundred Years of Rugby Football in Sri Lanka, 1879–1979.* Colombo: Sri Lanka Rugby Football Union.

Reeves, J. 2002. *Taking In a Game: A History of Baseball in Asia.* Lincoln: University of Nebraska Press.

Valiotis, C. 2009. "South Asia." In *Routledge Companion to Sports History,* edited by S. Pope and J. Nauright, 571–586. Oxford: Routledge.

Wagner, E., ed. 1989. *Sport in Asia and Africa: A Comparative Handbook.* Westport, CT: Greenwood.

Whiting, R. 1989. *You Gotta Have Wa.* New York: Vintage Departures.

Middle East and North Africa

Amara, M. 2007. "When the Arab World Was Mobilised around the FIFA 2006 World Cup." *Journal of North African Studies* 12(4): 417–438.

Arkoun, M. 2001. "Present-Day Islam between Its Tradition and Globalisation." In *Intellectual Traditions in Islam,* edited by F. Daftary, 179–221. London: I. B. Tauris.

Arkoun, M. 2002. *The Unthought in Contemporary Islamic Thought.* London: Saqi Books in association with the Institute of Ismaili Studies.

Arkoun, M. 2005. *Humanism et Islam, Combats et Propositions.* Paris: Vrin.

Couze, V. 2006. *The Postcolonial Challenge: Towards Alternative Worlds.* London: Sage.

Di-Capua, Y. 2005. "Women, Gender, Sports and the Female Body: Arab States." In *Encyclopedia of Women in Islamic Cultures,* Vol. 3, edited by S. Joseph and A. Najmabadi, 440–441. Leiden: Brill.

Fox, W. J., N. M. Sabbah, and M. al-Mutawa. 2006. *Globalisation and the Gulf.* London: Routledge.

Freeman, S. 2006. *Baghdad F.C., Iraq's Football Story: A Hidden History of Sport and Tyranny.* London: John Murray.

Le Sueur, J. D. 2001. "Jaques Berque: The Other, the Orient, and the Collège de France—The Politics of Othering." In *Uncivil War, Intellectuals and Identity Politics During the Decolonization of Algeria,* 217–224. Philadelphia: University of Pennsylvania Press.

Said, E. W. 2001. *Reflections on Exile and Other Essays.* Cambridge, MA: Harvard University Press.

Schotté, M. 2002. "Les déterminants sociaux de la 'domination' des coureurs marocains dans l'athlétisme français (1980–2000)." *STAPS* 57: 21–37.

Schotté, M., and C. Érard. 2007. "Retour sur une 'contribution' coloniale: Le succès des coureurs nord-africains dans l'athlétisme français des années 1950." *Loisir et Société* [Society and Leisure], 29(2): 423–448.

Touraine, A 2005. *Un Nouveau Paradigme pour Comprendre le Monde d'Aujourd'hui.* Paris: Fayard.

Australia, New Zealand, and Oceania

Adair, D., and W. Vamplew. 1998. *Sport in Australian History.* Melbourne: Oxford University Press.

Blainey, G. 2003. *A Game of Our Own: The Origins of Australian Football.* Melbourne: Black.

Booth, D. 2001. *Australian Beach Cultures: A History of Sun, Sand and Surf.* London: Routledge.

Booth, D., and C. Tatz. 2000. *One-Eyed: A View of Australian Sport.* Sydney: Allen, and Unwin.

Cashman, R. 1984. *'Ave a Go Yer Mug: Australian Cricket Crowds from Larrikin to Ocker.* Sydney: HarperCollins.

Cashman, R. 1995. *Paradise of Sport.* Sydney: University of New South Wales Press.

Cashman, R., and A. Hughes. 1999. *Staging the Olympics: The Event and Its Impact.* Sydney: University of New South Wales Press.

Cashman, R., and A. Weaver. 1991. *Wicket Women.* Sydney: University of New South Wales Press.

Collins, C., ed. 2000. *Sport in New Zealand Society.* Wellington: Dunmore.

de Moore, G. 2008. *Tom Wills: His Spectacular Rise and Tragic Fall.* Sydney: Allen, and Unwin.

Gordon, H. 2003. *The Time of Our Lives: Inside the Sydney Olympics, Australia and the Olympic Games, 1994–2002.* Brisbane: University of Queensland Press.

Hess, R., M. Nicholson, B. Stewart, and G. de Moore. 2008. *A National Game: The History of Australian Rules Football.* Camberwell, Victoria: Penguin Australia.

Hibbins, G. M. 2007. *Sport and Racing in Colonial Melbourne: The Cousins and Me; Colden Harrison, Tom Wills and William Hammersley.* Richmond, Victoria: Lynedoch.

Hogan, T., ed. 2005. *Reading the Game: An Annotated Guide to the Literature and Films of Australian Rules Football.* Melbourne: Australian Society for Sports History.

McKay, J. 1991. *No Pain, No Gain: Sport and Australian Culture.* Sydney: Prentice Hall.

Mangan, J. A., and J. Nauright, eds. 2000. *Sport in the Australasian World.* London: Frank Cass.

Nauright, J., ed. 1995. *Sport, Power and Culture in New Zealand.* Sydney: Australian Society for Sports History.

Nauright, J., and T. J. L. Chandler, eds. 1996. *Making Men: Rugby and Masculine Identity.* London: Frank Cass.

O'Hara, J. 1988. *A Mug's Game: A History of Gaming and Betting in Australia.* Sydney: University of New South Wales Press.

Phillips, J. O. C. 1996. *A Man's Country? The Image of the Pakeha Male; A History.* Revised ed. Melbourne: Penguin Australia.

Phillips, M. G. 2000. *From Sideline to Centrefield: A History of Sports Coaching in Australia.* Sydney: University of New South Wales Press.

Phillips, M. G. 2008. *Swimming Australia: 100 Years.* Sydney: University of New South Wales Press.

Ryan, G. 2004. *The Making of New Zealand Cricket, 1832–1914.* London: Routledge.

Ryan, G., ed. 2005. *Tackling Rugby Myths: Rugby and New Zealand Society, 1854–2004.* Dunedin, NZ: University of Otago Press.

Sandercock, L., and I. Turner 1981. *Up Where, Cazaly? The Great Australian Game.* London: Granada.

Stewart, B., ed. 2007. *The Games Are Not the Same: The Political Economy of Football in Australia.* Carlton: Melbourne University Press.

Stewart, B., M. Nicholson, A. Smith, and H. Westerbeek. 2005. *Australian Sport: Better by Design?* London: Routledge.

Stoddart, B. 1986. *Saturday Afternoon Fever: Sport in the Australian Culture.* Sydney: HarperCollins.

Stoddart. B. 2009. *Sport in the Australian Culture Revisited: Saturday Afternoon Fever II.* London: Routledge.

Tatz, C. 1995. *Obstacle Race: Aborigines and Sport.* Sydney: University of New South Wales Press.

Vamplew, W., and B. Stoddart, eds. 1994. *Sport in Australia: A Social History.* Melbourne: Cambridge University Press.

British Isles

Bateman, A. 2009. *Cricket, Literature and Culture: Symbolising the Nation, Destabilising Empire.* Aldershot, UK: Ashgate.

Burnett, J., 2000. *Riot, Revelry and Rout: Sport in Lowland Scotland before 1860.* East Linton: Tuckwell.

Cronin, M. 1999. *Sport and Nationalism in Ireland: Gaelic Games, Soccer and Irish Identity Since 1884.* Dublin: Four Courts.

Hargreaves, J. 1986. *Sport, Power and Culture.* Cambridge: Polity.

Hargreaves, J. 1994. *Sporting Females: Critical Issues in the History and Sociology of Women's Sports.* London: Routledge.

Hill, J. 1996. *Sport, Leisure and Culture in Twentieth Century Britain.* Basingstoke, UK: Palgrave.

Holt, R. 1989. *Sport and the British.* Oxford: Clarendon.

Huggins, M. 2004. *The Victorians and Sport.* London: Hambledon.

Huggins, M., and Williams, J. 2005. *Sport and the English, 1918–1939.* London: Routledge.

Jarvie, G., and J. Burnett. 2000. *Sport, Scotland and the Scots.* East Linton, UK: Tuckwell.

Johnes, M., 2005. *A History of Sport in Wales.* Cardiff: University of Wales Press.

Jones, S. 1986. *Workers at Play: A Social and Economic History of Leisure, 1918–1939.* London: Routledge and Kegan Paul.

Jones, S. 1988. *Sport, Politics and the Working Class: Organised Labour and Sport in Interwar Britain.* Manchester, UK: Manchester University Press.

Mangan, J. A. 1981. *Athleticism in the Victorian and Edwardian Public School.* Cambridge: Cambridge University Press.

Mason, T. 1980. *Association Football and English Society, 1865–1915.* Brighton, UK: Harvester.

Nauright, J., and T. J. L. Chandler, eds. 1996. *Making Men: Rugby and Masculine Identity.* London: Frank Cass.

Parratt, C. 2001. *More Than Mere Amusement: Working-Class Women's Leisure in England, 1750–1914.* Boston: Northeastern University Press.

Polley, M. 1998. *Moving the Goalposts: A History of Sport and Society since 1945.* London: Routledge.

Sugden, J., and A. Bairner. 1993. *Sport, Sectarianism and Society in a Divided Ireland.* Leicester, UK: Leicester University Press.

Tranter, N. 1998. *Sport, Economy and Society in Britain, 1750–1914.* Cambridge: Cambridge University Press.

Vamplew, W. 1988. *Pay Up and Play the Game: Professional Sport in Britain, 1875–1914.* Cambridge: Cambridge University Press.

Europe

Arnaud, P., and G. Garrier, eds. 1992. *Jeux et sports dans l'histoire.* 2 vols. Paris: CTHS.

Arnaud, P., and T. Terret. 1996. *Histoire du sport féminin.* Paris: L'Harmattan.

Bairner, A. 2001. *Sport, Nationalism and Globalization: European and North American Perspectives.* Albany: SUNY Press.

Baker, W. 1988. *Sports in the Western World.* Urbana: University of Illinois Press.

Carter, J. 1988. *Sports and Pastimes of the Middle Ages.* Lanham, MD: University Press of America.

Coakley, J., and E. Dunning, eds. 2000. *Handbook of Sports Studies.* London: Sage.

Decker, W., and J.-P. Thullier. 2004. *Le sport dans l'Antiquité: Égypt, Grèce et Rome.* Paris: Picard.

Diem, C. 1960. *Weltgeschichte des Sports.* Stuttgart: Cotta.

Edelman, R. 1993. *Serious Fun: A History of Spectator Sport in the USSR.* New York: Oxford University Press.

Edelman, R. 2009. *Spartak Moscow: A History of the People's Team in the Workers' State.* Ithaca, NY: Cornell University Press.

Eichberg, H., J. Bale, and C. Philo. 1998. *Body Cultures: Essays on Sport, Space and Identity.* London: Routledge.

Elias, N., and E. Dunning. 1986. *Quest for Excitement: Sport and Leisure in the Civilising Process.* Oxford: Blackwell.

Giulianotti, R., and R. Robertson. 2007. *Globalization and Sport.* Oxford: Blackwell.

Guttmann, A. 1978. *From Ritual to Record: The Nature of Modern Sports.* New York: Columbia University Press.

Guttmann, A. 1991. *Women's Sports: A History.* New York: Columbia University Press.

Guttmann, A. 1992. *The Olympics: A History of the Modern Games.* Urbana: University of Illinois Press.

Guttmann, A. 2004. *Sports: The First Five Millennia.* Amherst: University of Massachusetts Press.

Hoberman, J. 1992. *Mortal Engines: The Science of Human Performance and the Dehumanization of Sport.* New York: Free Press.

Hoberman, J. 2005. *Testosterone Dreams: Rejuvenation, Aphridesia, Doping.* Berkeley: University of California Press.

Holt, R. 1981. *Sport and Society in Modern France.* London: Macmillan.

Holt, R. 1989. *Sport and the British: A Modern History.* Oxford: Clarendon.

Huizinga, J. 1950. *Homo Ludens: A Study of the Play Element in Culture.* Boston: Beacon.

Krüger, A., and W. Murray, eds. 2003. *The Nazi Olympics: Sport, Politics and Appeasement in the 1930s.* Urbana and Chicago: University of Illinois Press.

Kyle, D. 2007. *Sport and Spectacle in the Ancient World.* London: Blackwell.

Mandell, R. 1984. *Sport: A Cultural History.* New York: Columbia University Press.

Møller, V., and J. Nauright, eds. 2003. *The Essence of Sport.* Odense: University Press of Southern Denmark.

Pope, S. W., and J. Nauright, eds. 2010. *The Routledge Companion to Sports History.* London: Routledge.

Riordan, J. 1977. *Sport and Soviet Society.* London: University of Cambridge Press.

Sansone, D. 1988. *Greek Athletics and the Genesis of Sport.* Berkeley: University of California Press.

Van Bottenburg, M. 2001. *Global Games.* Urbana and Chicago: University of Illinois Press.

Wagg, S., and D. Andrews, eds. 2007. *East Plays West: Sport and the Cold War.* London: Routledge.

Young, D. 1984. *The Olympic Myth of Greek Amateur Athletics.* Chicago: Ares.

Latin America and Caribbean

Alabarces, P., R. Di Giano, and J. Frydenberg, eds. 1998. *Deporte y sociedad.* Buenos Aires: Editorial Universitaria de Buenos Aires.

Alabarces, P., ed. 2003. *Futbologías: fútbol, identidad y violencia en América Latina.* Buenos Aires: CLACSO.

Almeida, B. 1986. *Capoeira, a Brazilian Art Form: History, Philosophy, and Practice.* Berkeley: North Atlantic Books.

Arbena, J. 1988. *Sport and Society in Latin America: Diffusion, Dependency, and the Rise of Mass Culture.* Westport, CT: Greenwood.

Arbena, J. 1989. *An Annotated Bibliography of Latin American Sport: Pre-Conquest to the Present.* Westport, CT: Greenwood.

Arbena, J. 1999. *Latin American Sport: An Annotated Bibliography (1988–1998).* Westport, CT: Greenwood.

Arbena, J., and D. LaFrance, eds. 2002. *Sport in Latin America and the Caribbean.* Wilmington, DE: Jaguar Books.

Archetti, E. P. 1999. *Masculinities: Football, Polo, and the Tango in Argentina.* New York: Berg.

Bale, J., and J. Maguire, eds. 1994. *The Global Sports Arena: Athletic Talent Migration in an Interdependent World.* London: Frank Cass.

Beckles, H. McD. 1998. *The Development of West Indian Cricket.* Barbados: Press of the University of the West Indies.

Bellos, A. 2002. *Futebol, the Brazilian Way of Life.* London: Bloomsbury.

Birbalsingh, F. 1996. *The Rise of West Indian Cricket: From Colony to Nation.* St. John's, Antigua: Hansib.

Bjarkman, P. C. 1994. *Baseball with a Latin Beat.* Jefferson, NC: McFarland.

Breda, E. A. 1962. *Juegos y deportes entre los indios del Rio de la Plata.* Buenos Aires: Ediciones Theoría.

Cárdenas, C., and G. García. 1993. *Venezolanos en el Ring: La Historia de nuestros campeones mundiales y medallistas Olímpicos.* Caracas: Editorial Torino.

Cobley, A. 2009. "The Caribbean." In *Routledge Companion to Sports History,* edited by S. W. Pope and J. Nauright. London: Routledge.

Corson, R. 1979. *Champions at Speed.* New York: Dodd, Mead.

DaMatta, R. 2006. *A Bola Corre Mais Que Os Homens.* Rio de Janeiro: Editora Rocca.

Dundes, A. 1994. *The Cockfight: A Casebook.* Madison: University of Wisconsin Press.

Ferguson, J. 2006. *World Class: An Illustrated History of Caribbean Football.* Oxford: Macmillan Caribbean.

Ferreiro Toledano, A. 1986. *Centroamérica y el Caribe a Través de sus Juegos.* Mexico City: Artes Gráficas Rivera.

Finn, G., and R. Giulianotti. 2000. *Football Culture: Local Contests, Global Visions.* Portland: Frank Cass.

Gaffney, C. 2008. *Temples of the Earthbound Gods: Stadiums in the Cultural Landscapes of Buenos Aires and Rio de Janeiro.* Austin: University of Texas Press.

Galeano, E. 1995. *El fútbol a sol y sombra.* Madrid: Siglo XXI.

Goble, R., and K. A. P. Sandiford, eds. 2004. *75 Years of West Indies Cricket: 1928–2003.* London: Hansib.

Goldblatt, D. 2008. *The Ball Is Round: A Global History of Soccer.* New York: Penguin.

González Echevarria, R. 1999. *The Pride of Havana: A History of Cuban Baseball.* New York: Oxford University Press.

James, C. L. R. 1963. *Beyond a Boundary.* London: Stanley Paul and Co.

Klein, A. 2006. *Growing the Game: The Globalization of Major League Baseball.* New Haven, CT: Yale University Press.

Lever, J. 1983. *Soccer Madness.* Chicago: University of Chicago Press.

Mangan, J. A., and L. P. Da Costa, eds. 2002. *Sport in Latin America: Past and Present.* London: Frank Cass.

Manley, M. 1995. *A History of West Indies Cricket.* London: André Deutsch.

Marín, E., ed. 2007. *Historia del deporte chileno: Entre la ilusión y la pasión.* Santiago, Chile: Cuadernos Bicentenario. Presidencia de la República.

Mason, T. 1995. *Passion of the People? Football in South America.* London: Verso.

McGehee, R. V. 2009. "Central America." In *Routledge Companion to Sports History,* edited by S. W. Pope and J. Nauright, 487–497. *Routledge Companion to Sports History.* London: Routledge.

Miller, R., and L. Crolley, eds. 2007. *Football in the Americas: Futbol, Futebol, Soccer.* London: Institute for the Study of the Americas.

Mitchell, T. J. 1991. *Blood Sport: A Social History of Spanish Bullfighting.* Philadelphia: University of Pennsylvania Press.

Montesinos, E. 1991. *Juegos Deportivos Panamericanos: Ruta de 36 años.* Ciudad de La Habana: Editorial Científico-Técnica.

Murray, B. 1998. *The World's Game: A History of Soccer.* Urbana: University of Illinois Press.

Pereira, L. A-M. 2000. *Footballmania: Uma historia social do futebol no Rio de Janeiro, 1902–1938.* Rio de Janeiro: Nova Fonteira.

Raffo, V. 2004. *El Origen Británico del Deporte Argentino.* Buenos Aires: private printing.

Regalado, S. O. 1998. *Viva Baseball! Latin Major Leaguers and Their Special Hunger.* Urbana: University of Illinois Press.

Riordan, J., and A. Krüger, eds. 1999. *The International Politics of Sport in the 20th Century.* London: Taylor and Francis.

Ruck, R. 1998. *The Tropic of Baseball: Baseball in the Dominican Republic.* Lincoln: University of Nebraska Press.

Ruck, R. 2011. *Raceball: How the Major Leagues Colonized the Black and Latin Game.* Boston: Beacon.

Salatino, G. 2006. *El Séptimo Game.* Buenos Aires: Del Nuevo Extremo.

Sandoval García, C. 2006. *Fuera De Juego: Fútbol, Identidades Nacionales y Masculinidades en Costa Rica.* San José: Editorial UCR, Instituto de Investigaciones Sociales.

Scarborough, V. L., and D. R. Wilcox, eds. 1991. *The Mesoamerican Ballgame.* Tucson: University of Arizona Press.

Stoddart, B., and H. Beckles, eds. 1995. *Liberation Cricket: West Indies Cricket Culture.* Manchester, UK: Manchester University Press.

Sugden, J. P. 1996. *Boxing and Society: An International Analysis.* Manchester, UK, and New York: Manchester University Press.

Taylor, C. 1998. *The Beautiful Game.* London: Phoenix.

Torres, C., and D. G. Campos, eds. 2006. *La Pelota No Dobla? Ensayos Filosoficos en Torno al Futbol.* Buenos Aires: Libros del Zorzal.

Torres, C. 2009. "South America." In *Routledge Companion to Sports History,* edited by S. W. Pope and J. Nauright, 553–570. London: Routledge.

Whittington, E. M., ed. 2001. *The Sport of Life and Death: The Mesoamerican Ballgame.* New York: Thames and Hudson.

Wood, D., and P. L. Johnson, eds. 2009. *Sporting Cultures: Hispanic Perspectives on Sport, Text and the Body.* London: Routledge.

North America

Adelman, M. 1986. *A Sporting Time: New York City and the Rise of Modern Athletics, 1820–1870.* Urbana and Chicago: University of Illinois Press.

Baker, W. 1986. *Jesse Owens: An American Life.* New York: Free Press.

Bouchier, N. 2003. *For the Love of the Game and the Honour of the Town: Amateur Sport and Middle Class Culture in Nineteenth Century Ontario Towns, 1838–1895.* Montreal: McGill-Queen's University Press, 2003.

Boyle, R. H. 1963. *Sport: Mirror of American Life.* Little, Brown.

Cahn, S. 1994. *Coming On Strong: Gender and Sexuality in Twentieth-Century Women's Sport.* Cambridge, MA: Harvard University Press.

Darby, P. 2010. *Gaelic Games, Nationalism, and the Irish Diaspora in the United States.* Dublin: University College of Dublin Press.

Donnelly, P., ed. 2011. *Taking Sports Seriously: Social Issues in Canadian Sport.* 3rd ed. Toronto: Thompson Educational.

Dyreson, M. 1998. *Making the American Team: Sport, Culture and the Olympic Experience.* Urbana and Chicago: University of Illinois Press.

Dyreson, M. 2008. *Crafting Patriotism: America at the Olympic Games.* London: Routledge.

Gorn, E. 1989. *The Manly Art: A History of Bare-Knuckle Prize Fighting in America.* Ithaca, NY: Cornell University Press.

Gorn, E., and W. Goldstein. 2004. *A Brief History of American Sports.* 2nd ed. Urbana and Chicago: University of Illinois Press.

Gruneau, R. 1983. *Class, Sports, and Social Development.* Amherst: University of Massachusetts Press.

Gruneau, R. 1999. *Class, Sports, and Social Development.* 2nd ed. Champaign, IL: Human Kinetics.

Gruneau, R., and D. Whitson. 1993. *Hockey Night in Canada: Sport, Identities and Cultural Politics.* Toronto: Garamond.

Guttmann, A. 1991. *Women's Sports: A History.* New York: Columbia University Press.

Guttmann, A. 2002. *The Olympics: A History of the Modern Games.* 2nd ed. Chicago: University of Illinois Press.

Guttmann, A. 2004. *Sports: The First Five Millennia.* University of Massachusetts Press.

Hall, A. M. 1996. *Feminism and Sporting Bodies: Essays on Theory and Practice.* Champaign, IL: Human Kinetics.

Hall, A. M. 2002. *The Girl and the Game: A History of Women's Sport in Canada.* Peterborough, Ontario: Broadview.

Howell, C. 2001. *Blood, Guts and Glory: Sport in the Making of Modern Canada.* Toronto: University of Toronto Press.

Howell, N., and M. Howell. 1969. *Sports and Games in Canadian Life: 1700 to the Present.* Toronto: Macmillan of Canada.

Kidd, B. 1996. *The Struggle for Canadian Sport.* Toronto: University of Toronto Press.

King, C. R., ed. 2008. *Native Americans and Sport in North America: Other People's Games.* London: Routledge.

Lenskyj, H. 1986. *Out of Bounds: Women, Sport and Sexuality.* Toronto: Women's Press.

Manchester, H. 1931. *Four Centuries of Sport in America, 1490–1890.* New York: Benjamin Blom.

Morrow, D., M. Keyes, W. Simpson, F. Cosentino, and R. Lappage. 1989. *A Concise History of Sport in Canada.* Toronto: Oxford University Press.

Morrow, D., and K. B. Wamsley. 2010. *Sport in Canada: A History.* 2nd ed. Toronto: Oxford University Press.

Mrozek, D. 1982. *Sport and American Mentality, 1880–1910.* Knoxville: University of Tennessee Press.

Oriard, M. 1993. *Reading Football: How the Popular Press Created an American Spectacle.* Chapel Hill: University of North Carolina Press.

Oriard, M. 2003. *King Football: Sport and Spectacle in the Golden Age of Radio and Newsreels, Movies and Magazines, the Weekly and the Daily Press.* Chapel Hill: University of North Carolina Press.

Pope, S. W., ed. 1997. *The New American Sport History: Recent Approaches and Perspectives.* Urbana and Chicago: University of Illinois Press.

Pope, S. W. 2007. *Patriotic Games: Sport and the American Imagination 1876–1926.* New Edition. Knoxville: University of Tennessee Press.

Pope, S. W., and J. Nauright, eds. 2010. *The Routledge Companion to Sports History.* London: Routledge.

Rader, B. 1999. *American Sports: From the Age of Folk Games to the Age of Televised Sports.* 4th ed. New York: Prentice Hall.

Rader, B. 2008. *Baseball: A History of America's Game.* 3rd ed. Urbana and Chicago: University of Illinois Press.

Riess, S. 1988. *City Games: The Evolution of American Urban Society and the Rise of Sports.* Urbana and Chicago: University of Illinois Press.

Roxborough, H. 1957. *Great Days in Canadian Sport.* Toronto: Ryerson.

Roxborough, H. 1966. *One Hundred-Not Out: The Story of Nineteenth-Century Canadian Sport.* Toronto: Ryerson.

Senn, A. 1999. *Power, Politics, and the Olympic Games: A History of the Power Brokers, Events, and Controversies That Shaped the Games.* Champaign, IL: Human Kinetics.

Struna, N. 1996. *People of Prowess: Sport, Leisure, and Labor in Early Anglo-America.* Urbana and Chicago: University of Illinois Press.

Watterson, J. S. 2000. *College Football: History, Spectacle, Controversy.* Baltimore: Johns Hopkins University Press.

Wiggins, D. K. 1997. *Glory Bound: Black Athletes in a White America.* Syracuse, NY: Syracuse University Press.

Wiggins, D. K., ed. 1995. *Sport in America: From Wicked Amusement to National Obsession.* Champaign, IL: Human Kinetics.

Editors and Contributors

Editors

John Nauright, PhD, is director of the Academy of International Sport and a professor of sport management at George Mason University in Virginia and is a visiting professor of cultural studies at the University of the West Indies, Cave Hill, in Barbados. He holds a PhD in history from Queen's University in Canada and is the author or editor of 12 books, including *Long Run to Freedom: Sport, Cultures and Identities in South Africa; The New Sport Management Reader;* and *The Routledge Companion to Sports History.*

Charles Parrish is a lecturer in the School of Recreation, Health, and Tourism at George Mason University in Virginia. He holds a master's degree in sport management from Georgia Southern University and is currently completing PhD work studying supporter groups of Major League Soccer clubs. He has also recently completed research on expressions of masculinity among male Argentinean soccer fans.

Contributors

Driss Abbassi
France

Harvey Abrams
International Institute for Sport and
    Olympic History
United States

Daryl Adair
University of Technology, Sydney
Australia

Sine Agergaard
University of Copenhagen
Denmark

Daniel Allen
Independent Scholar
Sandhurst, Berkshire
England

Dean Allen
University of Stellenbosch
South Africa

Siham Al-Maskari
Loughborough University
England

Bruno Altieri
ESPN Deportes
Argentina

Mahfoud Amara
Loughborough University
England

Jatin P. Ambegaonkar
George Mason University
United States

N. G. Aplin
National Institute of Education
Singapore

Razan Baker
United Kingdom

Robert E. Baker
George Mason University
United States

John Bale
Keele University
England

Dominique Banville
George Mason University
United States

Ellyn L. Bartges
University of Illinois
United States

Susan Barton
United Kingdom

Anthony Bateman
United Kingdom

Heather L. Bell
University of Florida
United States

Andre Beneteau
Laurentian University
Canada

Alexander Bennett
Japan

Peter C. Bjarkman
Independent Scholar
United States

David Black
Dalhousie University
Canada

Chris Bolsmann
Aston University
England

Gherardo Bonini
European University Institute, Florence
Italy

Joe Bradley
Sterling University
Scotland

Gonzalo Bravo
West Virginia University
United States

Pieter Breuker
Catholic University of Leuven
Belgium

Katrin Bromber
Germany

Rachael Brooks
University of Ulster
Northern Ireland

Harko Brown
Maori Advisor, Physical Education, New Zealand
New Zealand

Toni Bruce
University of Waikato
New Zealand

Betsy Burke Parker
Community Times
United States

Mary Bushby
Australia

Austin Stair Calhoun
United States

Jason Carlson
George Mason University
United States

Jayne Caudwell
University of Brighton
England

Ciannon Cazaly
Australia

Timothy J. L. Chandler
Kent State University
United States

Alex Channon
Loughborough University
England

Patrick Chaplin
Anglia Ruskin University, Cambridge
England

Efthalia (Elia) Chatzigianni
University of Peloponnese
Greece

Younghan Cho
Hankuk University of Foreign Studies
South Korea

Anthony Church
Laurentian University
Canada

Martyn Clark
Queen's University
Canada

Jim Clough
University of Gloucestershire
England

James R. Coates Jr.
University of Wisconsin–Green Bay
United States

Alan Gregor Cobley
University of the West Indies, Cave Hill
Barbados

Bruce Coe
Univeristy of Canberra
Australia

Bradley Congelio
University of Western Ontario
Canada

James Connor
University of New South Wales
Australia

Scarlett Cornelissen
University of Stellenbosch
South Africa

Bradley Cutler
Laurentian University
Canada

Braham Dabscheck
University of Melbourne
Australia

Paul Darby
University of Ulster
Northern Ireland

Simon C. Darnell
Dalhousie University
Canada

Paul deLoca
Greensboro, North Carolina
United States

Andrew Denning
University of California, Davis
United States

R. F. Dewey Jr.
Depauw University
United States

Philip Dine
National University of Ireland, Galway
Ireland

Wendi A. Dunlap
Slumberland Annex
United States

Mark Dyreson
Pennsylvania State University
United States

Malika Ed-Dahbi
France

K. D. Edwards
Australia

Henning Eichberg
University of Southern Denmark
Denmark

Chris Elzey
George Mason University
United States

Ahmed Al-Emadi
Qatar University
Qatar

Lynn Embrey
Murdoch University
Australia

Craig Esherick
George Mason University
United States

John D. Fair
Georgia College and State University
United States

Youcef Fates
Université Paris Ouest, UFR STAPS
France

Bouhal Fayçal
Algeria

J. A. Ferguson
Australia

Gabriel E. Fidler
Lee University
United States

Russell Field
University of Manitoba
Canada

Raul Figueroa
George Mason University
United States

Thomas Fletcher
Leeds Metropolitan University
England

Philip Forde
University of the West Indies, Cave Hill
Barbados

Nicholas Foster
University of Canberra
Australia

Babak Fozooni
Open University
United Kingdom

Stephen Frawley
Australia

Christopher Gaffney
Universidade Federal Fluminense
Brazil

Yvan Gastaut
France

Gerald Gems
North Central College
United States

Andrea Giampiccoli
South Africa

Shane Gibson
University of Canberra
Australia

Steven P. Gietschier
Lindenwood University
United States

Bieke Gils
Canada

Terry Gitersos
University of Western Ontario
Canada

John R. Gold
Oxford Brookes University
England

Margaret M. Gold
London Metropolitan University
England

Hilary Gordon
Laurentian University
Canada

Rommel Green
University of the West Indies, Cave Hill
Barbados

Nick Guoth
Australian National University
Australia

Jørn Hansen
University of Southern Denmark
Denmark

Luke J. Harris
Canterbury Christ Church University
England

David Hassan
University of Ulster
Northern Ireland

Sandra Heck
Ruhr University, Bochum
Germany

Judy Hemming
University of New South Wales
Australia

Rob Hess
Victoria University
Australia

Thomas Hickie
Australia

Nicole Hitpas
George Mason University
United States

Mouloud Houaoura
Algeria

Emily J. Houghton
University of Minnesota
United States

P. David Howe
Loughborough University
England

Mike Huggins
University of Cumbria
England

Linda Elaine Hughes
University of Gloucestershire
England

Brett Hutchins
Monash University
Australia

Line Jensen
Aarhus University
Denmark

Naila Jinnah
Queen's University
Canada

Cristian Job
University of Calgary
Canada

Lise Joern
Aarhus University
Denmark

Bo Kampmann Walther
University of Southern Denmark
Denmark

Anna Kavoura
University of Jyväskylä
Finland

P. J. Kitchen
University of Ulster
Northern Ireland

Jørgen B. Kjær
George Mason University
United States

Brendan Knott
Cape Peninsula University of Technology
South Africa

Jordan Kobritz
Eastern New Mexico University
United States

Jordan R. Koch
University of Alberta
Canada

Robert Kossuth
University of Lethbridge
Canada

James C. Kozlowski
George Mason University
United States

Arnd Krüger
Georg-August University
Germany

Ryuta Kudo
Japan

Simona Kustec Lipicer
University of Ljubljana
Slovenia

Monia Lachheb
Tunisia

Robert J. Lake
St. Mary's University College
England

Michael Lariscy
Armstrong Atlantic State University
United States

Daryl Leeworthy
Oxford University
England

Andrew Lemon
Australia

Richard Light
Leeds Metropolitan University
England

Charles Little
London Metropolitan University
England

Matthew P. Llewellyn
Pennsylvania State University
United States

Michael Lomax
University of Georgia
United States

Lynn Hunt Long
Armstrong Atlantic State University
United States

Malcolm MacLean
University of Gloucestershire
England

Louise Mansfield
Canterbury Christ Church University
England

James W. Martens
Red Deer College
Canada

Courtney W. Mason
University of Calgary
Canada

Fred Mason
University of New Brunswick
Canada

James A. McBean
Johns Hopkins University
United States

Keith McClellan
United States

John McClelland
University of Toronto
Canada

Robin McConnell
Massey University
New Zealand

Fletcher McEwen
Australia

Richard V. McGehee
University of Texas–Austin
United States

Douglas W. McLaughlin
California State University, Northridge
United States

Molly McManamon
George Mason University
United States

Robert Messenger
Australia

Lisa M. Miller
Harvard University
United States

Graeme Moir
United Kingdom

Verner Møller
Aarhus University
Denmark

Eric Monnin
University of Franche-Comté France

Kelsey Moore
George Mason University
United States

Ashlee Morgan
University of Technology, Sydney
Australia

Bill Murray
La Trobe University
United States

Dave Nadel
Australia

Mark Nagel
University of South Carolina
United States

Nadim Nassif
Lebanon

Hamish Neal
Australia

Jim Nendel
United States

Philani Nongogo
Tshwane University of Technology
South Africa

Sean O'Connor
Automobile and Touring Club of the United Arab
    Emirates
United Arab Emirates

Jaime Orejan
Winston-Salem State University
United States

Carol A. Osborne
University of Cumbria
England

Gary Osmond
University of Queensland
Australia

Dorothy Ours
United States

Anna Outratova
Charles University
Czech Republic

Victoria Paraschak
University of Windsor
Canada

Maria Leticia Herrera de Parrish
United States

Byron Peacock
Dalhousie University
Canada

Robin Peake
University of Ulster
Northern Ireland

Ann Pegoraro
Laurentian University
Canada

Bob Petersen
University of Sydney
Australia

Gertrud Pfister
University of Copenhagen
Denmark

Jari Piirainen
JAMK University
Finland

Robin Poke
University of Canberra
Australia

Kate Polasek
State University of New York, Cortland
United States

S. W. Pope
West Virginia University
United States

Brian Prueger
United States

Robert Pruter
Lewis University
United States

Cobus Rademeyer
National Institute of Higher Education
South Africa

Abdel Rahman Hamed
Creator, Palestinian National Football Team Blog

Anand Rampersad
University of the West Indies, St. Augustine
Trinidad and Tobago

Risto Rasku
JAMK University
Finland

Michel Raspaud
France

Barbara Ravel
Laurentian University
Canada

Erin Reilly
Auburn University, Montgomery
United States

Abderrahim Rharib
Morocco

Toby C. Rider
University of Western Ontario
Canada

Ian Ritchie
Brock University
Canada

R. Pierre Rodgers
George Mason University
United States

Greggory M. Ross
University of Western Ontario
Canada

Petr Roubal
Academy of Sciences
Czech Republic

Kobus Roux
University of Johannesburg
South Africa

Rob Ruck
University of Pittsburgh
United States

Trevor Ruddell
Melbourne Cricket Club
Australia

Elizabeth Ryan
George Mason University
United States

Greg Ryan
Lincoln University
New Zealand

Melvile Saayman
South Africa

Saad Saloom
MASARAT Magazine
Iraq

Newton César de Oliveira Santos
Freelance Journalist, São Paulo
Brazil

Eric C. Schwarz
St. Leo University
United States

Amanda Schweinbenz
Laurentian University
Canada

Rebecca Sheehan
Australia

Kaitlin Sheridan
Laurentian University
Canada

Fumiaki Shishida
Waseda University
Japan

Rwany Sibaja
George Mason University
United States

Michelle Sikes
Oxford University
England

Michael Silk
University of Bath
England

Valeria Silvestrini
Florida Institute of Technology
United States

Jill Singleton
George Mason University
United States

Neil Skinner
De Montfort University
England

Jacqueline Smith
Syracuse University
United States

Dae Song
George Mason University
United States

Nancy E. Spencer
Bowling Green State University
United States

Tobias Stark
Linnaeus University
Sweden

Julie Stevens
Brock University
Canada

John Stockstill
Georgia Southern University
United States

Megan Stronach
University of Technology, Sydney
Australia

Sasha Sutherland
University of the West Indies, Cave Hill
Barbados

Stephen Swain
University of Western Ontario
Canada

Kamilla Swart
Cape Peninsula University of Technology
South Africa

Colin Tatz
Macquarie University
Australia

Sarah Teetzel
University of Manitoba
Canada

Thierry Terret
University of Lyon
France

Alberto Testa
Brunel University
England

Michael Toohey
New Zealand

Cesar R. Torres
State University of New York, Brockport
United States

Brady Trombly
Laurentian University
Canada

Robert J. Turpin
United States

Martin Urruty
ESPN Deportes
Argentina

Chris Valiotis
University of New South Wales
Australia

Maarten van Bottenburg
University of Utrecht
Netherlands

Floris van der Merwe
University of Stellenbosch
South Africa

Hans Vandergrunderbeek
Catholic University of Leuven
Belgium

Travis Vogan
Indiana University
United States

Christoph Wagner
De Montfort University
England

Marek Waic
Charles University
Czech Republic

Wanda Wakefield
State University of New York, Brockport
United States

Kristin Walseth
Norway

Geoff Watson
Massey University
New Zealand

Charlene Weaving
St. Francis Xavier University
Canada

Ann-Marie White
White Consultants
Australia

David K. Wiggins
George Mason University
United States

David Williams
De Montfort University
England

Jean Williams
De Montfort University
England

John Williams
Australian Institute of Sport
Australia

Terry Williams
Australia

Mihaela Wood
United States

Ying Wushanley
Millersville State University
United States

Daniel Zimmet
George Mason University
United States

Aaron Zipp
State University of New York, Cortland
United States

Sarah Zipp
State University of New York, Cortland
United States

Diego Zorrilla
ESPN Deportes
Argentina

Index

Aaron, Hank (1934–), 3:158–159
  home run production, 3:158–159
  image of, 3:159
  place of birth, 3:158
  racism and, 3:159
  statistics for, 3:158
  teams played for, 3:158
ABC's Wide World of Sports, 3:159–160
Aboriginal mascot issue, North America, 3:160–161
  assimilation and, 3:160
  commodification of, 3:160–161
  protest on, 3:160 (image)
  schools removing aboriginal mascot, 3:161
  stereotyping, 3:161
  vested interests in, 3:161
Aborigines in sport (Australia), 1:327–329
  Aboriginal cricket tour (1868), 1:327
  athletics and, 1:327
  Australian Football League (AFL) and, 1:327–328
  boxing and, 1:327
  Cathy Freeman, 1:328 (image)
  importance of sport to aborigines, 1:329
  inequity, inequality, and imbalance, 1:328
  men, 1:329
  notable Aboriginal athletes, 1:327, 1:328–329
  percentage of Aborigines in AFL, 1:328
  percentage of Aborigines in population, 1:327
  Queensland Amateur Athletic Association and, 1:327
  racism, 1:327, 1:328
  women, 1:328–329
Accra Sports Stadium disaster (Ghana), 1:80–81
  acquittal of police, 1:80
  casualties in, 1:80
  contributing factors to, 1:81
  description of, 1:80
  as symptomatic of African football, 1:80
Adidas, 1:157

Africa Cup of Nations Soccer winners, 4:315–316
African Games, 1:81–83
  athletes with disabilities, 1:82
  history of, 1:82–83
  importance of regional games, 1:81–82
  opening ceremonies, 1:81 (image)
  organizers of, 1:82
African Nations Cup, Association Football, 1:83–84
aikido, 1:184–185
  independent systems of, 1:185
  Kishomaru Ueshiba and, 1:184
  Morihei Ueshiba and, 1:184, 1:185
  purpose of techniques, 1:185
  reputation of, 1:184
  training, 1:184
  uniqueness of, 1:184–185
Ali, Muhammad (1942–), 3:161–163
  adulation of, 3:162
  birth name of, 3:161
  boxing career of, 3:161–163
  draft evasion, 3:162
  final record of, 3:163
  image of, 3:162
  postboxing career, 3:163
Alianza Lima air tragedy (Peru), 3:12–13
All American Girls Professional Baseball League, 3:163–164
  image of, 3:163–164
  importance of, 3:164
  Philip K. Wrigley and, 3:163
  unique femininity principle of, 3:163
All Blacks (Māori–New Zealand), 1:329–330
  ancestry and, 1:329
  current status of, 1:330
  international play of, 1:329–330
  "Natives" team of 1888–1889, 1:329
  notable players, 1:330

All Blacks (Māori–New Zealand) (*continued*)
  racial discrimination and, 1:329
  reputation of, 1:329
  uniform of, 1:329
All Blacks (New Zealand National Rugby Team), 1:330–331
  acquisition of moniker, 1:330
  as "chokers," 1:331
  commercialization and, 1:331
  national pride and, 1:331
  nomenclature and emblem, 1:330
  notable players, 1:331
  success of, 1:330–331
  team uniform, 1:330
  television and, 1:330
All-Ireland Gaelic Football champions, 4:300–302
All-Ireland Hurling champions, 4:303–305
altitude ban, FIFA, 3:13–14
  reaction to, 3:13
  reason for, 3:13
  repeal of, 3:13
America's Cup, Australia and New Zealand, 1:331–332
  Australia and, 1:331
  Deed of Gift challenge, 1:332
  Louis Vuitton Cup challenger elimination series, 1:331, 1:332
  New Zealand and, 1:331–332
  origin of Cup, 1:331
America's Cup, United States, 3:164–165
  eras and races, 3:164–165
  future races, 3:165
  Hundred Pound Cup, 3:164
  New York Yacht Club and, 3:164
  number of chronological eras of, 3:164
ancient Olympic Games and Greek sporting festivals, 2:226–230
  apene race, 2:228
  boxing, 2:227
  calpe horse racing, 2:228
  chariot racing, 2:227, 2:228
  Delian Games, 2:229
  dolichos, 2:227
  hoplitodromos, 2:228
  horse racing, 2:227
  hosts of, 2:227
  International Federation of Associated Wrestling Styles, 2:227–228
  Isthmian Games, 2:229
  last known Olympic celebration, 2:228

Nemean Games, 2:229
  number of events in, 2:228
  number of years celebrated, 2:226
  Olympiad cycle, 2:226
  Panathenaic amphoras, 2:229
  pankration, 2:227–228
  pentathlon, 2:227
  pentathlon for boys, 2:228
  Pythian Games, 2:229
  stade racing, 2:227
  synoris horse racing, 2:228
  Theodosius I and, 2:228–229
  Theodosius II and, 2:229–230
  warfare and truce, 2:227
  warfare training, 2:228
  women and the Olympia, 2:229
  wrestling, 2:227
  Zeus and, 2:226, 2:227
ancient Roman sport, 2:230–233
  certamina, 2:230
  Circus Maximus charioteers, 2:231 (image)
  class and, 2:233
  execution, 2:231
  exercitationes, 2:230
  gladiators, 2:231–232
  importance of, 2:233
  ludi (games), 2:230–231
  munera, 2:230, 2:231–232
  Olympic-style athletics, 2:232–233
  pankratio, 2:230
  professional athletes and, 2:233
  spectator sports, varieties of, 2:230–231
  sphaeristerium, 2:233
  trigon, 2:233
  venatores, 2:231
Andres Escobar murder (Colombia), 3:14
animal blood sports, British Isles, 2:13–15
  attraction to, 2:13–14
  beagling, 2:14
  bearbaiting and bullbaiting, 2:14
  "blood sports" term, 2:13
  cockfighting and dogfighting, 2:14
  The Cockpit, (Hogarth), 2:14 (image)
  Cruelty to Animals Act, 2:14
  "fairness" notion, 2:14
  foxhunting, 2:14, 2:15
  hare coursing, 2:15
  Humanitarian League, 2:13
  Hunting with Dogs Act (2004), 2:15

hunting with hounds, 2:14
otter hunting, 2:14
shooting, 2:15
stag hunting, 2:14
antiapartheid movement (British Isles), 2:15–17
aparthéid defined, 2:15
Basil D'Oliveira Affair, 2:16
Boycott Movement, 2:16
British Anti-Apartheid Movement (AAM), 2:16
"Gleneagles Agreement," 2:16
antiapartheid sports movement (South Africa), 1:84–89
aims of nonracial sports movement, 1:85
ANC and, 1:89
Anti-Apartheid Movement (AAM), 1:85, 1:86, 1:87, 1:89
Basil D'Oliveira, 1:86
Bayo Hamed Lawal, 1:88
black consciousness movement, 1:89
Campaign Against Racial Exploitation (CARE), 1:87
Chris de Broglio, 1:86
Dennis Brutus, 1:86
F. W. De Klerk, 1:88
Fédération Internationale de Football Association (International Federation of Football Associations, FIFA), 1:86
first documented response to racial segregation, 1:85
Halt All Racist Tours (HART), 1:87
international support, 1:87
International Table Tennis Federation, 1:86
IOC initiatives, 1:87–88
John Harris, 1:86
Juan Antonio Samaranch, 1:87
Mluleki George, 1:88
National Party (NP) segregation, 1:85
National Sport Congress (NSC), 1:87, 1:88
nonracial sports movement and the IOC, 1:86, 1:88
nonracial sports movement division, 1:88–89
Sam Ramsamy, 1:88
"SANROC-NSC clique," 1:88
South Africa Council on Sport (SACOS), 1:87, 1:89
South African Cricket Board of Control (SACBOC), 1:87
South African Non-Racial Olympic Congress (SANROC), 1:85, 1:86, 1:88
South African Rugby Union (SARU), 1:87
South African Sports Association (SASA), 1:85, 1:86
sports boycotts, 1:86, 1:87, 1:88, 1:89
Steven Bantu Biko, 1:89

T. Ragasamy and, 1:85
UN General Assembly and, 1:86
apartheid and sports in South Africa, 1:90–93
B. J. Vorster, 1:91
Dennis Brutus, 1:90, 1:91
Errol Tobias, 1:92
F. W. de Klerk, 1:93
Football Association of Southern Africa (FASA), 1:91
Gleneagles Agreement, 1:92
Group Areas Act, 1:90
Hassan Howa, 1:92
IOC intervention, 1:93
multinationalism, 1:91–92
National Party (NP), sports policy of, 1:90
National Sports Congress (NSC), 1:93
ostracized from international events, 1:91
Piet Koornhof, 1:91
Population Registration Act, 1:90
race and the development of sport, 1:90
resistance to, 1:90–91
South African Council of Sport (SACOS), 1:92
South African Football Association (SAFA), 1:90–91
South African Football Association (SAFA) Constitution, 1:90
South African Non-Racial Olympic Committee (SANROC), 1:91, 1:92
South African Table Tennis Board, 1:90
sports boycott, 1:92, 1:93
T. E. Dönges, 1:90
United Nations' Committee Against Apartheid Sport, 1:92
apartheid campaigns (Australia and Aotearoa/New Zealand), 1:332–334
in Aotearoa/ New Zealand, 1:333
in Australia, 1:332–333
Australian Anti-Apartheid Movement (AAAM), 1:333
central factor shaping the campaigns, 1:332
development of campaigns, 1:333
HART: the New Zealand Anti-Apartheid Movement, 1:333
International Cricket Conference (ICC), 1:332
International Rugby Board, 1:333
National Anti-Apartheid Committee, 1:333
New Zealand Rugby Football Union, 1:333
rugby union and, 1:333
similarities in, 1:332
sporting contact and social friction, 1:332–333
themes of public debate about relations with South Africa, 1:332

Arab women and the Olympic Games, 1:272–273
  discrimination issue, 1:273
  marketing and, 1:273
  Nawel Moutawake, 1:272
  notable women athletes, 1:273
  Turkey and, 1:272
archery, 2:17–18
  Ancient Scorton Arrow, 2:17
  equipment and scoring, 2:18
  International Archer Federation (Fédération Inter-
    nationale de Tir à l'Arc), 2:17
  International Archer Federation (FITA), 2:18
  international rules, 2:17–18
  as an Olympic sport, 2:17–18
  origins of, 2:17
  World Championships, 2:18
archery, Olympic medalists (Summer)
  Men's Au Chapelet, 33-Meter, 4:1
  Men's Au Chapelet, 50-Meter, 4:1
  Men's Au Cordon Doré, 33-Meter, 4:1
  Men's Au Cordon Doré, 50-Meter, 4:1
  Men's Continental Style, 50-Meter, 4:1
  Men's Double FITA Elimination Round, 4:5
  Men's Double York Round, 4:1
  Men's Individual, FITA Olympic Round 70-Meter, 4:3
  Men's Individual FITA Round, 4:4
  Men's Individual Fixed Bird Target, Large Birds, 4:2
  Men's Individual Fixed Bird Target, Small Birds, 4:2
  Men's Individual Moving Bird Target, 28-Meter, 4:2
  Men's Individual Moving Bird Target, 33-Meter, 4:2
  Men's Individual Moving Bird Target, 50-Meter, 4:2
  Men's Sur la perche à la herse, 4:4
  Men's Sur la perche à la pyramide, 4:5
  Men's Team Elimination Round, 4:5
  Men's Team, FITA Olympic Round 70-Meter, 4:3
  Men's Team FITA Round, 4:4
  Men's Team Fixed Bird Target, Large Birds, 4:2
  Men's Team Fixed Bird Target, Small Birds, 4:2
  Men's Team Moving Bird Target, 28-Meter, 4:3
  Men's Team Moving Bird Target, 33-Meter, 4:3
  Men's Team Moving Bird Target, 50-Meter, 4:3
  Men's York Round, 4:1
  Women's Double Columbia Round, 4:2
  Women's Double National Round, 4:2
  Women's Individual, FITA Olympic Round 70-Meter,
    4:3
  Women's Individual FITA Round, 4:4
  Women's National Round, 4:2
  Women's Team Elimination Round, 4:5

  Women's Team, FITA Olympic Round 70-Meter, 4:4
  Women's Team FITA Round, 4:4
Arena football, 3:165–166
  Arena Football League (AFL) and, 3:165
  description of, 3:165–166
  James F. Forster and, 3:166
  Kurt Warner and, 3:166
  marketing of, 3:166
  popularity, 3:166
  suspension of operations, 3:166
Armand Césari Stadium Disaster, 2:233–234
  cause of, 2:233
  criminality in, 2:234
  date and place of, 2:233
  number of dead and injured, 2:233
Armstrong, Lance (1971–), 3:166 (image), 3:166–167
Army Physical Training Corps (Great Britain), 2:18–19
  Archibald MacLaren, 2:18
  date of founding, 2:18
  Malcolm Fox, 2:18
  purpose of, 2:18
  W. J. Hammersley, 2:18
artistic gymnastics, Olympic medalists (Summer)
  Men's Club Swinging, 4:13
  Men's Combined Four Events, 4:13
  Men's Combined Three Events, 4:13
  Men's Floor Exercise, 4:13
  Men's Horizontal Bar, 4:16–17
  Men's Indian Clubs, 4:17
  Men's Individual All-Around, 4:10
  Men's Parallel Bars, 4:15–16
  Men's Pommel Horse, 4:13–14
  Men's Rings, 4:14–15
  Men's Rope Climbing, 4:17
  Men's Sidehorse Vault, 4:17
  Men's Team Event (by year), 4:5–4:8
  Men's Team Free System, 4:18
  Men's Team Horizontal Bar, 4:17
  Men's Team Swedish System, 4:18–19
  Men's Triathlon, 4:19
  Men's Vault, 4:15
  Women's Balance Beam, 4:11
  Women's Floor Exercise, 4:12
  Women's Individual All-Around, 4:10–11
  Women's Team Event (by year), 4:8–9
  Women's Team Portable Apparatus, 4:19
  Women's Uneven Bars, 4:12
  Women's Vault, 4:11
Ascot, 2:19

Ashe, Arthur (1943–1993), 3:167–168
  accolades for, 3:168
  commitment to humanitarian causes, 3:167–168
  image of, 3:167
  statistics for, 3:167–168
The Ashes, 1:334–335
  creation of, 1:335
  image of, 1:334
  imperishable names of, 1:335
  Ivo Bligh, 1:334
Asian Beach Games, 1:185
Asian Football Confederation (AFC), 1:185–186
  Asian Club Championship, 1:186
  Asian Cup and, 1:186
  Asian Ladies Football Confederation and, 1:186
  diversity of, 1:186
  formation of, 1:185
  growth of, 1:186
  internal politics of, 1:186
  Israel and, 1:186
  Taiwan and, 1:186
Asian Games, 1:186–188
  2010 edition of, 1:186
  challenge to, 1:187
  China and, 1:187
  growth of, 1:188
  Guru Dutt Sondhi and, 1:187
  incorporation of Asian sports, 1:188
  organizational problems, 1:187
  precursors to, 1:186–187
  women and, 1:188
Asian Games Federation (AGF). *See* Olympic Council of
  Asia (OCA)
Asian Winter Games, 1:188–189
Association football, Argentina, 3:14–24
  1950–1970, 3:18–19
  Alexander Watson Hutton and, 3:15
  Alfredo Di Stéfano, 3:17
  amateurism, and of, 3:17–18
  Apertura (Opening Tournament) and the Clausura
    (Closing Tournament), 3:19–20
  Asociación Argentina de Football (AAF), 3:16
  Asociación del Fútbol Argentino (AFA), 3:17, 3:19,
    3:20, 3:21
  athletic clubs and schools, 3:15–16
  "big five clubs" of, 3:19
  Boca Juniors, 3:17, 3:18
  Cesár Luis Menotti and, 3:22
  challenges in, 3:20–21

Club Atlético River Plate, 3:17, 3:18, 3:20, 3:21
  diffusion and early development of, 3:14–16
  Eduardo Archetti on, 3:16–17
  El Monumental, 3:17
  Estadio Juan Domingo Peron, 3:18
  Estudiantes de La Plata, 3:18
  Ezequiel Lavezzi in action, 3:15 (image)
  football clubs of, 3:16
  foreign investment and immigration, 3:14–15
  la nuestra, 3:14, 3:16–17
  la nuestra, players representing, 3:17
  La Selección and the World Cup, 3:21–23
  Metropolitano and Nacional tournaments, 3:19
  modern era of, 3:19–20
  Old Boys of Rosario, 3:19
  Peron and, 3:18, 3:19
  players strike, 3:17
  professionalism, 3:17–18, 3:22
  Racing Club, 3:18
  Ramón Cereijo and, 3:18
  sale of players, 3:21
  significance of, 3:14
  television and, 3:20
  two-season format of the AFA, 3:19
  Uruguay and, 3:21–22
  violence and, 3:18–19, 3:20–21
  women and, 3:21
  World Cup play, 3:22–23
Association football, Argentina (Primera División)
  winners, 4:354–356
Association football, Australia, 1:335–338
  Australian Rules, 1:335
  Australian SFA, 1:336
  Commonwealth Football Association (CFA),
    1:336
  ethnic clubs, 1:337–338
  first "official" game, 1:335
  Frank Lowy, 1:337
  immigration and, 1:336
  A-League, 1:337, 1:338
  Lowy Revolution, 1:338
  Melbourne Hakoah, 1:336
  National League, 1:337
  Queensland FA, 1:335
  rule of David Hill, 1:337
  in Tasmania, 1:336
  Western Australia British Football Association
    (WABFA), 1:335–336
Association football, Bolivia, 3:24–25

Association football, Brazil, 3:25–32
  1920–1950, consolidation, professionalization, and national identity, 3:26–28
  1950–1970, the golden years, 3:28–29
  1971–2002, the modern era, 3:29–31
  2003–2014, the new capitalism, boom, and return, 3:31–32
  Alex Bellos on, 3:28
  Campeonato Brasiliero (Brazilian National Championship), 3:29
  capoeira style of play, 3:27
  the *cartolas*, 3:30
  CBF, 3:29, 3:30, 3:31
  Charles Miller and, 3:25
  development of, 3:25
  ethics and, 3:28
  futsal, 3:30
  Liga Metropolitana of Rio de Janeiro, 3:27
  linguistics of, 3:27–28
  nationalism, 3:28–29
  Nike/Ronaldo controversy, 3:30, 3:31
  Pelé, 3:28–29
  politics/politicians and, 3:29
  professionalization, 3:27
  proliferation of, 3:26
  racial discrimination, 3:27
  Ronaldo, 3:30
  São Paulo, 3:25–26
  São Paulo Railway, 3:25
  stadium projects for the 2014 FIFA World Cup, 3:31 (table)
  state championships, 3:29
  state involvement in, 3:28
  superstars of, 3:28
  World Cup play, 3:28, 3:29, 3:30
Association football, Brazil National championship winners
  Campeonato Brasileiro Série A, 4:358–359
  Rio de Janeiro State Championship (Carioca), 4:361–362
  São Paulo State Championship (Paulista), 4:359–361
  Taca Brazil (1959–1968), 4:359
  Torneio Roberto Gomes Pedrosa (1967–1970), 4:359
Association football, Cameroon, 1:94–95
  development of, 1:94
  notable players, 1:94
  statistics for, 1:94
  success of, 1:94

Association football, Caribbean, 3:32–34
  Eff Ray and, 3:33
  Francophone territories, 3:33
  notable players, 3:34
  popularity of, 3:32–33, 3:34
  University of the West Indies (UWI) Inter-Campus Games, 3:33
  women and, 3:34
Association football, Central America, 3:34–36
  Catholic Church and, 3:34
  Central American Games, 3:35
  Club Sport La Libertad, 3:34
  Costa Rica, 3:34, 3:35
  Diriangén club of Diriamba, 3:35
  El Salvador, 3:35
  FIFA World Cup and, 3:36
  futsal World Cups, 3:35
  Guatemala, 3:34, 3:35
  Honduras, 3:35
Association football, Central Asia, 1:189
Association football, China, 1:189–190
  Chinese Football Association (CFA), 1:190
  Chinese Super League, 1:190
  distinct periods in the modern era, 1:190
  history of, 1:189–190
  South China Athletic Association (SCAA), 1:190
  success of, 1:190
  women and, 1:190
Association football, Egypt, 1:273–274
  in African play, 1:274
  biggest Egyptian clubs, 1:273–274
  Egypt versus Paraguay, 1:274 (image)
  history of, 1:273
  statistics for, 1:274
Association football, England and Wales, 2:19–26
  Anglo-German rivalry, 2:25
  Arsenal FC, 2:24
  Carling Cup, 2:22
  Conference, 2:23–24
  English Football Association (FA), 2:20
  Everton FC, 2:24
  FA Challenge Cup, 2:22
  fans of, 2:24
  FC United of Manchester, 2:24
  Football League, 2:23–24
  football rules, codification of, 2:20–21
  George Best, 2:23
  Heysel tragedy, 2:25, 2:26
  Hillsborough tragedy, 2:21

history of, 2:19–21

hooliganism, 2:25–26

International Football Association Board, 2:20

introduction to, 2:19

Liverpool FC, 2:24

Manchester City, 2:24

Manchester Union, 2:24

Matthews final, 2:23

national governing bodies of, 2:20

Premier League, 2:23

professionalism in, 2:24

religious rivalry, 2:24–25

rivalries, 2:24–25

stadiums, history of, 2:21

stadiums and churches, 2:21–22

top four divisions of, 2:22

violence and, 2:25–26

Welsh FA, 2:20

Wembley Stadium, 2:22, 2:23

White Horse Final, 2:22–23

Association football, England (Premier League) champions, 4:276–278

Association football, France, 2:234–235

French Football Federation, 2:234

governing body of, 2:234

Ligue de Football Professionnel, 2:234

market size of, 2:234

media and, 2:234

Michel Platini and, 2:234

nationalism and, 2:235

Olympic de Marseille, 2:235

Paris St. Germain, 2:235

pervasiveness of, 2:234

reputation of, 2:234

success of, 2:234

Zinedine Zidane and, 2:235

Association football, France (Ligue 1) champions, 4:283–285

Association football, Germany, 2:235–236

beginning of, 2:235

Bundesliga, 2:235, 2:236

company clubs, 2:236

East Germany and, 2:235

first international match, 2:235

importance of 2006 World Cup, 2:236

international competition and, 2:235–236

notable clubs, 2:236

notable players, 2:236

professionalism and, 2:235

structure of soccer clubs, 2:236

success of, 2:235

Association football, Germany (Bundesliga) champions, 4:278–279

Association football, Ghana, 1:95–96

corporate sponsorship, 1:95

Ghanaian Amateur Football Association, 1:95

growth of, 1:95

Kwame Nkrumah and, 1:95

state support of, 1:95

success of, 1:95

Association football, Italy, 2:236–239

Azzuri jersey, 2:237

decline of, 2:239

fascism and, 2:237

Federazione Italiana Football (FIF), 2:237

Federazione Italiana Gioco Calcio (Italian Football Federation, FIGC), 2:237

FIFA World Cup (1934), 2:237

FIFA World Cup (1982), 2:238

FIFA World Cup (2006), 2:239

founders of, 2:236–237

Juventus Football Club, 2:237, 2:239

match-fixing scandal, 2:239

Mitropa Cup, 2:237

professionalism in, 2:237

racism, 2:238

Serie A championship, 2:237, 2:238

Silvio Berlusconi and, 2:239

success of, 2:236, 2:238

tactic of, 2:238

World Champion status, 2:237

Association football, Italy (Serie A) champions, 4:281–283

Association football, Japan, 1:190–191

All-Japan Soccer Championship, 1:190

company-sponsored teams, 1:191

development of, 1:190

Football Association of Japan formation, 1:190

international success of, 1:191

Japan Soccer League, 1:191

J-League, 1:191

Olympic competition and, 1:191

professionalism and, 1:191

Association football, Korea, 1:191–192

Korea Football Association (KFA), 1:192

nationalism and, 1:192

North Korean football, 1:192

South Korean football, 1:192

Association football, Korea (*continued*)
women's team, 1:192
YMCA and, 1:192
Association football, Mexico, 3:36–38
Central American and Caribbean Games wins, 3:38
Champions Cup, 3:38
clubs occupying first division of, 3:37
CONCACAF championship wins, 3:38
development of, 3:36
Federación Mexicana de Fútbol Asociación (Mexican
Federation of Association Football), 3:36–37
first championship, 3:36
national team captain Rafa Márquez, 3:37 (image)
Pan American Games and, 3:37–38
World Cup play, 3:37
Association football, México (Primera División) winners,
4:356–358
Association football, Netherlands (Eredivisie) champions,
4:285–287
Association football, New Zealand, 1:338–339
British migrants and, 1:338
class composition of, 1:338
domestic infrastructure, 1:338
international football and, 1:338–339
Oceania Football Confederation and, 1:338
popularity of, 1:338
women's football, 1:338
Association football, Nigeria, 1:96–97
Challenge Cup, 1:96
national team success, 1:96
Nigeria Football Association, 1:96
origins of, 1:96
Association football, Nordic countries, 2:240–241
Dansk Boldspil-Union (Danish Football Association,
DBU), 2:240–241
Norges Fotballforbund (Football Association of Norway,
NFF), 2:240
Svenska Fotbollförbundet (Swedish Football Associa-
tion, SvFF), 2:240
Association football, North Africa, 1:274–275
Ahmed Ben Bella and, 1:275
Algeria/Egypt rivalry, 1:275
Algerian war and, 1:275
characterizing feature of, 1:275
Larbi Ben M'barek and, 1:275
Morocco and, 1:275
Rachid Mekhloufi and, 1:275
settler and indigenous club matches, 1:274–275
Tunisia and, 1:275
Zinedine Zidane and, 1:275

Association football, Pacific coast of South America,
3:38–47
in Chile, 3:39–40
in Columbia, 3:44–46
in Ecuador, 3:42–44
in Peru, 3:40–42
Association football, Palestine, 1:275–276
center of Palestinian football, 1:276
connection with Chile, 1:276
earliest account of football in Palestine, 1:275
Gaza, 1:276
international status of, 1:276
Israel Football Association, 1:276
Palestine Football Federation, 1:275, 1:276
West Bank, 1:276
Association football, Paraguay, 3:47–48
Cope América, 3:47
major clubs of, 3:47
notable players, 3:48
Olympic competition, 3:48
politics/politicians and, 3:47–48
violence and, 3:48
World Cup play, 3:47, 3:48
Association football, Portugal, 2:241–242
"big three" domestic powers in, 2:241
Brazilian players restriction, 2:242
British influence on, 2:241
financial problems of, 2:241
inefficiency of, 2:241
Premeira Liga (Premier League), 2:241
recent stars of, 2:242
style of play, 2:241
Association football, Portugal (Primeira Liga) champions,
4:290–291
Association football, Saudi Arabia, 1:276–277
Al-Ittihad founding, 1:276
number of football clubs in, 1:276
number of professional football players in, 1:277
popularity of football in, 1:276
privatization of clubs, 1:277
reputation of Saudi Arabian football, 1:277
Saudi Arabia Football Federation (SAFF) formation,
1:276–277
Association football, Scotland, 2:26–29
Aberdeen, 2:28–29
Celtic and Rangers, 2:27, 2:28, 2:29
Dundee United, 2:28–29
enthusiasm for, 2:26–27
famous managers/coaches, 2:27
Ferguson McCann, 2:29

Glasgow and, 2:27–28
Graeme Souness, 2:29
Hampden Park, 2:27, 2:28
Hampden Riots, 2:28
Ibrox disaster, 2:28
Lawrence Marlborough, 2:29
the New Firm, 2:29
the Old Firm, 2:29
professionalism in, 2:27
Queen's Park, 2:27
record crowds for, 2:28
rivalries with England, 2:27
television money and, 2:29
Association football, Scotland (Premier League) champions, 4:287–289
Association football, South Africa, 1:97–100
amateur level administration of, 1:98
apartheid and, 1:97, 1:98
Bafana men's senior team, 1:99
Banyana Banyana, 1:99
controversy in, 1:99
Football Association of South Africa (FASA), 1:98
image of, 1:97
introduction into South Africa, 1:97
Johannesburg Bantu Football Association (JBFA), 1:97
National Soccer League (NSL), 1:98
number of registered football players in South Africa, 1:99
political mobilization and, 1:97–98
professional level administration of, 1:98
Professional Soccer League (PSL), 1:98, 1:99
professionalization/commercialization, 1:98
South African Soccer Federation (SASF), 1:97–98, 1:99
support of the founding of, 1:97
Association football, South Asia, 1:193
colonialism and, 1:193
current status of, 1:193
development of, 1:193
Durand Football Tournament, 1:193
globalization and, 1:193
South Asian Football Federation (SAFF), 1:193
Association football, Southeast Asia, 1:193–194
Burma and, 1:194
colonialization and, 1:193–194
English Premier League and, 1:194
Indonesia and, 1:194
popular interest in, 1:194
status of men's football, 1:194
status of women's football, 1:194

Association football, Spain, 2:242–244
Atlético Bilbao, 2:243
Atlético Madrid, 2:243
Barcelona, 2:242, 2:243, 2:244
contemporary Spanish football, 2:243–244
Copa del Rey (King's Cup), 2:243
Di Maria of Real Madrid, 2:243 (image)
FIFA World Cup title (2010), 2:244
at international level, 2:244
origins of, 2:242–243
popularity of, 2:242, 2:243
professionalization of, 2:243
public perception of, 2:243
Real Madrid, 2:242–243, 2:244
regional identities and, 2:242, 2:243
rules, codification of, 2:243
Spanish League (La Liga) structure, 2:244
Association football, Spain (La Liga) champions, 4:279–281
Association football, Sub-Saharan Africa in general, 1:100–101
colonialism and, 1:100
current status of, 1:100
diffusion of football in, 1:100
first recorded matches, 1:100
independence and, 1:100
white supremacy of football, 1:100
Association football, the Netherlands, 2:239–240
Ajax Amsterdam, 2:239, 2:240
Amsterdam Arena, 2:239
championships of, 2:239
De Kuip Stadium, 2:240
Dutch team jerseys, 2:240
impact on global soccer, 2:239
Jewish identity and Ajax, 2:240
Koninklijke Nederlandse Voetbalbond, 2:239
Phillips Stadion, 2:240
"total football" style, 2:239, 2:240
Vitesse Stadium, 2:239
Association football, United States and Canada, 3:168–171
amateur level (U.S.), 3:169
British culture and, 3:168
Canada, 3:170
Canadian national team achievements, 3:170
Canadian Soccer Association (CSA), 3:170
Major Indoor Soccer League (MISL), 3:169
Major League Soccer (MLS), 3:168, 3:169, 3:170
North American Soccer League (NASL), 3:169, 3:170
popularity in Canada, 3:170
postrevolutionary America and, 3:168–169

Association football, United States and Canada (*continued*)
    Puritans and, 3:168
    United States, 3:168–169
    United States Soccer Federation, 3:169
    Women's United Soccer Association (WUSA), 3:169
Association football, Uruguay, 3:48–50
    American Football Confederation (CONMEBOL), 3:49
    Carlos Gardel legend, 3:49
    Copa América tournament, 3:49
    Copa Libertadores, 3:48
    development of, 3:48
    Gabriel Terra and, 3:49
    Héctor Rivadavia, 3:49
    international competition, 3:49
    largest teams of, 3:48
    lexicon of, 3:49
    Nacional, 3:48, 3:49
    Peñarol, 3:48–49
    popularity of, 3:48
    Uruguayan football association teams, 3:48
    World Cup and, 3:49, 3:50
Association football, Zambia, 1:101–102
    current status of, 1:101
    decline of, 1:101
    Football Association of Zambia (FAZ), 1:101
    Kenneth Kaunda and, 1:101
    reputation of, 1:101
    Zambia Consolidated Copper Mines Ltd. (ZCCM), 1:101
athletics, Asia, 1:194–195
    Asian Athletic Association (AAA), 1:194
    notable athletes, 1:195
    P. T. Usha and, 1:195
    Seiko Yasuda and, 1:194–195
athletics, Australia and New Zealand, 1:339–341
    Adelaide Amateur Athletic Club (AAC), 1:340
    Amateur Athletic Union of Australasia (AAU of A), 1:340
    Australasian Championships, 1:340
    Australian Institute of Sport, 1:341
    class and sports, 1:339
    competitive exchanges between, 1:340
    Edwin Flack and, 1:340
    indigenous competitors, 1:339–340
    influence of handicapping, 1:340
    Olympic competition and, 1:340, 1:341
    organized professional running, 1:339
    professional challenges and match races, 1:339
    South Canterbury AAC, 1:340
    women's athletics, 1:340–341

athletics, British Isles, 2:29–31
    Amateur Athletic Association (AAA), 2:30
    British running renaissance, 2:30–31
    Eamonn Coughlan, 2:30–31
    Eric Liddell, 2:30
    Harold Abrahams, 2:30
    Jonathan Edwards, 2:31
    Linford Christie, 2:31
    London Athletic Club, 2:30
    London Marathon, 2:31
    Olympic Games and, 2:30, 2:31
    origins of track and field, 2:30
    Roger Bannister, 2:30
    Sonia O'Sullivan, 2:31
    Tessa Sanderson, 2:31
athletics, Caribbean, 3:50–53
    Austin Sealy and, 3:51
    Bahamas, 3:51–52
    Caribbean Free Trade Area (CARIFTA) Games, 3:51, 3:52
    conclusion concerning, 3:52
    Cuba, 3:52
    Eric Williams and, 3:51
    Fidel Castro and, 3:52
    Golden Girls of the Bahamas, 3:51–52
    Jamaica and, 3:51
    popularity of, 3:50
    Trinidad and Tobago, 3:52
    Usain Bolt and, 3:51
athletics, Kenya, 1:102–104
    Catherine Ndereba, 1:103
    distance running and, 1:102
    future outlook for, 1:103
    geography of Kenya, 1:103
    Henry Rono, 1:102
    Kalenjin tribe and, 1:103–104
    Kenya Amateur Athletics Association (KAAA), 1:102
    Kipchoge Keino and, 1:102
    notable female athletes, 1:102
    notable male athletes, 1:102
    running clubs (private), 1:103
    women and sports, 1:102–103
athletics, Middle East and North Africa, 1:277–280
    2008 (Beijing) Games, 1:279
    Ahmed El Ouafi, 1:277, 1:278
    Alain Mimoun, 1:278
    Barcelona Games, 1:278–279
    Driss El Himer, 1:279
    Hassiba Boulmerka, 1:279
    Hicham El Guerrouj, 1:279

introduction of, 1:277–278
Khalid Skah, 1:278
Mehdi Baala, 1:279
Mohammed Gammoudi, 1:278
Noureddine Morceli, 1:279
Pierre de Coubertin and, 1:278
running and, 1:278–279
Saïd Aouita, 1:278
success of North African men, 1:277
Tunisian, 1:278
athletics, Olympic medalists (Summer)
Men's 1,500-Meter, 4:22–23
Men's 1,500-Meter Wheelchair, 4:39
Men's 2,500-Meter Steeplechase, 4:36
Men's 2,590-Meter Steeplechase, 4:36
Men's 3,000-Meter Steeplechase, 4:25
Men's 3,000-Meter Team Race, 4:37
Men's 3,200-Meter Steeplechase, 4:36
Men's 3,500-Meter Walk, 4:37
Men's 3-Mile Team Race, 4:37
Men's 4 × 100-Meter Relay, 4:26–27
Men's 4 × 400-Meter Relay, 4:27–28
Men's 4,000-Meter Steeplechase, 4:36
Men's 4-Mile Team Race, 4:37
Men's 5,000-Meter, 4:23
Men's 5,000-Meter Team Race, 4:37
Men's 5-Mile Race, 4:37
Men's 6.4-Kilogram Stone Throw, 4:49
Men's 10,000-Meter, 4:23–24
Men's 10,000-Meter Walk, 4:38
Men's 10-Mile Walk, 4:38, 4:49
Men's 20-Kilometer Walk, 4:29
Men's 50-Kilometer Walk, 4:29–30
Men's 56-Pound Weight Throw, 4:38
Men's 60-Meter, 4:36
Men's 100-Meter, 4:19–20
Men's 110-Meter Hurdles, 4:24
Men's 200-Meter, 4:20–21
Men's 200-Meter Hurdles, 4:36
Men's 400-Meter, 4:21
Men's 400-Meter Hurdles, 4:24–25
Men's 800-Meter, 4:21–22
Men's Decathlon, 4:35–36
Men's Discus, 4:33–34
Men's Discus, Ancient Style, 4:39
Men's Discus, Two-handed, 4:39
Men's Hammer Throw, 4:34–35
Men's High Jump, 4:31–32
Men's Individual Cross-Country, 4:39
Men's Javelin, 4:35
Men's Javelin, Freestyle, 4:39
Men's Javelin, Two-handed, 4:39
Men's Long Jump, 4:30
Men's Marathon, 4:28–29
Men's Medley Relay, 4:37
Men's Pentathlon, 4:38
Men's Pole Vault, 4:32–33
Men's Shot Put, 4:33
Men's Shot Put, Two-handed, 4:39
Men's Standing High Jump, 4:38
Men's Standing Long Jump, 4:38
Men's Standing Triple Jump, 4:38
Men's Team Cross-Country, 4:39
Men's Triathlon, 4:38
Men's Triple Jump, 4:31
Women's 1,500-Meter, 4:41–42
Women's 3,000-Meter, 4:49
Women's 3,000-Meter Steeplechase, 4:43
Women's 4 × 100-Meter Relay, 4:43–44
Women's 4 × 400-Meter Relay, 4:44–45
Women's 5,000-Meter, 4:42
Women's 10,000-Meter, 4:42
Women's 10,000-Meter Walk, 4:49
Women's 20-Kilometer Walk, 4:45
Women's 80-Meter Hurdles, 4:48
Women's 100-Meter Dash, 4:39–40
Women's 100-Meter Hurdles, 4:42
Women's 200-Meter, 4:40
Women's 400-Meter, 4:40–41
Women's 400-Meter Hurdles, 4:43
Women's 800-Meter, 4:41
Women's 800-Meter Wheelchair, 4:49
Women's Discus, 4:47
Women's Hammer Throw, 4:48
Women's Heptathlon, 4:48
Women's High Jump, 4:45
Women's Javelin, 4:47–48
Women's Long Jump, 4:46
Women's Marathon, 4:42
Women's Pentathlon, 4:49
Women's Pole Vault, 4:46
Women's Shot Put, 4:46–47
Women's Triple Jump, 4:46
athletics, rest of Africa, 1:104–105
Confederation of African Athletics (CAA), 1:104
female athletes, 1:105
Haile Gebrselassie, 1:104–105
Tirunesh Dibaba, 1:105

athletics, South Africa, 1:105–107
  African Amateur Athletics and Cycling Association
    (SAAA&CA), 1:107
  black athletes and, 1:106–107
  British Empire Games, 1:106
  Cape Town Amateur Athletic Club formation,
    1:105–106
  cycling, 1:106–107
  Frank Diamond, 1:106
  Humphrey Khosi and, 1:107
  Laurens Meintjes, 1:106
  notable female athletes, 1:106
  notable men athletes, 1:106, 1:107
  Olympic competition, 1:106
  pedestrian events, 1:106
  South African Amateur Athletic Association (SAAAA)
    founding, 1:106
  South African Amateur Athletic Union (SAAAU), 1:107
  sports days, 1:105–106
athletics, United States (field events), 3:171–175
  broad/long jump, 3:171–172
  discus throw, 3:174
  division of, 3:171
  hammer throw, 3:174
  high jump, 3:172–173
  javelin throw, 3:174
  jumping events, 3:171–174
  jumping events, primary elements in, 3:171
  pole vault, 3:173–174
  shot put, 3:174–175
  standing high jump, 3:173
  triple jump, 3:172
  weight-throwing events, 3:174–175
athletics, United States (track events), 3:175–177
  Amateur Athletic Union (AAU), 3:175–176
  amateurism and, 3:176
  governing body of, 3:175
  Intercollegiate Association of Amateur Athletics of
    America, 3:175
  International Track Association (ITA), 3:176
  Jesse Owens, 3:176
  Olympic competition, 3:176
  performance-enhancing drug and, 3:176–177
  scandals and, 3:176–177
  USA Track and Field, 3:176
  USA Track and Field (USATF), 3:175
  Visa Championship Series, 3:176
Attouga (1945–), 1:280
Augusta National Golf Club, 3:177

Australia Rugby League Grand Final champions, 4:294
  Super League Grand Final, 4:294–295
Australian Cricket Board (ACB), 1:474–475
Australian Football League (AFL), 1:341–343
  awards, 1:342
  date established, 1:342
  length of season, 1:341
  popularity of, 1:341–342
  regulation of, 1:342
  Tasmania and, 1:342
  Victorian Football League (VFL) and, 1:342, 1:343
Australian Football League Grand Final champions,
  4:291–293
Australian Institute of Sport (AIS), 1:343–347
  aim of, 1:345
  Australian Sports Commission and, 1:344
  criticism of, 1:344
  development of facilities, 1:344–345
  directors of, 1:344, 1:345
  disabled athletes and, 1:345
  establishment of, 1:343–344
  inspiration for, 1:343
  National Training Centre program, 1:344
  opening date of, 1:343
  programs operated by, 1:345–346
  research in sport sciences, 1:346
  scholarships of, 1:343, 1:345, 1:346
Australian Olympic Committee, 1:347–348
Australian Open (Tennis), 1:348–349
  image of, 1:348
  popularity of, 1:348
  prize money, 1:349
  reputation of, 1:348
Australian Rules football, 1:349–354
  Australasian Football Council, 1:352
  Australian Football League (AFL), 1:354
  changing nomenclature for, 1:352
  commercialism, 1:354
  Coulter Law (1930), 1:353, 1:354
  dimensions of playing failed, 1:351
  experimentation with rules and forms, 1:349–350
  first formal rules, 1:350–351
  Geelong Football Club, 1:350
  interwar decades and, 1:353
  jubilee events of August 1908, 1:352
  Melbourne Football Club, 1:350
  myths about origin of, 1:350
  origins of Australian code of football, 1:350
  progenitor of, 1:350

Victorian Football Association (VFA), 1:351
Victorian Football League (VFL), 1:351–352, 1:353–354
women's football, 1:353
Australian Society for Sports History, 1:355
Australian Sports Commission (ASC), 1:355–360
Active After-school Communities program, 1:358–359
Active Australia, 1:358
Active Girls campaign, 1:360
amalgamation and, 1:356
Aussie Sports, 1:358
Coaching Athletes with Disabilities, 1:359
establishment of, 1:355–356
Indigenous Sports program, 1:359
mandate of, 1:356
national sporting organizations (NSOs) and, 1:356–357
National Sports Information Centre, 1:360
objectives of, 1:356
Olympic Athlete Program (OAP) of, 1:357
role of, 1:356
Sports CONNECT, 1:359
Willing and Able program, 1:359
Women in Sport, 1:360
auto racing, Asia, 1:195–196
development of, 1:195–196
Formula One racing, 1:195, 1:196
Honda, 1:195–196
Japanese manufacturers and, 1:195, 1:196
Macau Grand Prix, 1:195
auto racing, Formula One, 2:312–315
Bernard Charles Ecclestone and, 2:313–314
as big business, 2:313–314
cars of, 2:314
champions of, 2:312–313
dominance in, 2:314
FIA-FOTA dispute, 2:315
financial troubles in, 2:314
first world championship race, 2:312
Formula One Administration Ltd. (FOA), 2:314
history of (early), 2:312
image of, 2:313
privateers and, 2:314–315
sponsorship, 2:312, 2:314
World champions of, 4:351–352
auto racing, Indy Car Series champions, 4:353
auto racing, Latin America, 3:53–55
in Argentina, 3:53, 3:54
Argentinia Tourismo Carretera (TC) racing circuit, 3:53
in Brazil, 3:53
Formula 1 racing, 3:54

Juan Manuel Fangio and, 3:54
limitations of, 3:54
in Mexico, 3:53, 3:54
NASCAR and, 3:54
rally racing, 3:54
Raúl Recalde and, 3:54
South American Grand Prix, 3:53–54
"special cars," 3:53
world champion drivers, 3:54
auto racing, NASCAR Cup champions, 4:350–351
Azteca Stadium (Mexico), 3:55
capacity of, 3:55
ownership of, 3:55
reputation of, 3:55

badminton, Asia, 1:196–197
Badminton Association of Malaya, 1:196
China and, 1:196, 1:197
International Badminton Federation, 1:196
introduction and spread of, 1:196
Penang Badminton Association, 1:196
Thomas Cup, 1:196
Uber Cup, 1:196
women's badminton, 1:196–197
badminton, British Isles, 2:31–32
America and, 2:32
Asian influences, 2:31–32
Canadian badminton diaspora, 2:32
evolution of, 2:31
Hugh Forgie, 2:32
Ken Davidson, 2:32
"ludic diffusion" of badminton, 2:32
Paul Newman on, 2:31
Shirley Marie, 2:32
badminton, Olympic medalists (Summer)
Men's Doubles, 4:50
Men's Singles, 4:49
Mixed Doubles, 4:50
Women's Doubles, 4:50
Women's Singles, 4:50
Badminton House, 2:32–33
badminton and, 2:33
Badminton horse trials, 2:33
The Badminton Library of Sports and Pastimes, 2:33
Ballesteros, Severiano (1957–2011), 2:244–245
death of, 2:245
reputation of, 2:244–245
Seve Trophy and, 2:245
statistics for, 2:244, 2:245

bandy, 2:33–34
   bandy men World Championships, 2:34
   codification of rules for, 2:34
   explanation of, 2:33
   Federation of International Bandy (FIB), 2:34
   Minnesota and, 2:34
   National Bandy Association (NBA), 2:34
   Olympic Games and, 2:34
   origins of, 2:33
   women's bandy World Championshipswomen's bandy
      World Championships, 2:34
Bantu Sports Club (Johannesburg, South Africa),
      1:107–108
Barmy Army, 2:34–35
   business operations of, 2:34
   criticism of, 2:35
   evolution of, 2:34
   importance of, 2:35
   purpose of, 2:34
   website of, 2:34
baseball, Australia, 1:360–361
   Australian Baseball League (ABL), 1:361
   beginning of, 1:360
   Claxton Shield and, 1:360–361
   date of first overseas tour, 1:360
   international level play, 1:361
baseball, Central and South America, 3:55–57
   in Guatemala, 3:56
   Major League Baseball (MLB) and, 3:55
   Miguel Cabrera, 3:56 (image)
   in Nicaragua, 3:56
   popularity of, 3:55
   in Venezuela, 3:55–56
   Venezuelan players in MLB, 3:55–56
   Venezuelan Professional Baseball League, 3:55
baseball, Cuba, 3:57–60
   baseball creation myths, 3:57
   communist revolution and, 3:59
   Cuban National Baseball Team (2010 squad), 3:58
   Cuban national team successes, 3:57, 3:59–60
   Cuban professional league, 3:57–58
   Cuban winter the baseball, 3:59
   Cuba–Orioles exhibitions, 3:60
   "fathers"of Cuban baseball, 3:57
   independence from Spain and, 3:58
   MLB WBC tournament, 3:60
   myths surrounding, 3:57
   National Series Cuban League, 3:59
   national significance of, 3:57

North American Negro ballplayers, 3:59
   notable Cuban players, 3:57, 3:60
   popularity of, 3:59
   professional baseball in, 3:58–59
baseball, Dominican Republic, 3:60–64
   buscones and young players, 3:63–64
   Caballeros, 3:62
   Campo Las Palma's success, 3:63
   Ciudad Trujillo, 3:62
   the Cocolos and, 3:63
   Cuba and, 3:62
   development of, 3:61
   Dominican winter league, 3:64
   economic significance of, 3:64
   Felipe Alou and, 3:62–63
   foundational teams of, 3:61
   free agency, 3:63
   local identities and, 3:62
   Major League Baseball (MLB) control, 3:64
   Mundiales, participation in, 3:62
   national amateur tournaments, 3:62
   national significance of, 3:60–61
   notable Dominican players in the U.S., 3:62, 3:63
   notable Negro players in, 3:62
   Rafael Trujillo, 3:61, 3:62
   San Pedro de Macorís, 3:63
   signing bonuses, 3:63
   U.S. occupation and, 3:61
baseball, Dutch West Indies, 3:64–65
baseball, Europe, 2:245–246
   connection with U.S. baseball, 2:245
   Italy and, 2:246
   Netherlands and, 2:245–246
   popularity of, 2:246
baseball, Finnish, 2:246–249
   first test game of pesäpallo, 2:247
   Lauri "Tahko" Pihkala and, 2:246
   managers and, 2:248
   name change, 2:247
   national league of pesäpallo, 2:247
   pesäpallo version of, 2:246
   popularity of, 2:247, 2:248
   rules of, 2:247–248
   scoring, 2:248
   Superpesis league, 2:247
   women and, 2:247
   World Cup of, 2:247
baseball, Japan, 1:197–200
   amateur baseball, 1:198

in comparison with U.S. baseball, 1:198–200

introduction of, 1:197

National High School Baseball Championship Series, 1:198

Nippon Professional Baseball League (NPB), 1:197, 1:199

samurai mentality and, 1:199

Yomiuri Giants, 1:198

baseball, Korea, 1:200–202

Baseball Restriction Law, 1:201

Chan-ho Park, 1:201

introduction of, 1:200

Korean Baseball Organization (KBO), 1:201

popularity of, 1:201

baseball, Major League Baseball World Series champions, 4:265–267

baseball, Mexico, 3:65–66

Asociación Nacional de Beisbolistas (National Association of Baseball Players, ANABE), 3:66

Caribbean Series and, 3:66

Cuban contributions to, 3:65

decline in, 3:65–66

Jorge Pascual and, 3:65

Liga Mexicana de Béisbol (Mexican Baseball League), 3:65

Little League World Series wins, 3:65

Mexican Baseball Hall, 3:66

Mexican League, 3:66

notable Cuban players in, 3:65

notable Mexican players in the MLB, 3:65

origins of, 3:65

popularity of, 3:65

World Cup play, 3:66

baseball, Olympic medalists (Summer), 4:51–52

baseball, Puerto Rico, 3:66–68

development of, 3:66

economic significance of, 3:68

Escuela Superior de Ponce, 3:66

first baseball clubs, 3:66

José "Pepe" Santana, 3:66

notable Puerto Rican players in the MLB, 3:67–68

Orlando Cepeda, 3:67 (image)

Puerto Rican Baseball League, 3:66

Roberto Clemente, 3:67–68

William Guzman, 3:66

baseball, South Africa, 1:108–109

baseball, Taiwan, 1:202–203

Chinese Professional Baseball League, 1:203

international success of, 1:202

introduction of, 1:202

Little League baseball, 1:202

baseball, United States, 3:177–184

1903 rules of, 3:181

1920 rules of, 3:181

1931 rules of, 3:181

1973 rules of, 3:181

Allan (Bud) Selig, 3:179

Babe Ruth, 3:183

beginning of Organized Baseball, 3:182–183

Boston Braves, 3:183

broadcasting and, 3:183

Byron Bancroft Johnson, 3:183

codification of rules, 3:180

collective bargaining, 3:184

current problems of, 3:184

description of game, 3:177–178

designated hitter, 3:179, 3:181

divisions of major leagues, 3:179

Doubleday myth, 3:180

equipment and rules, 3:181

expansion of major league baseball, 3:183–184

"farm system," 3:180

formation of National/American leagues, 3:182–183

franchising, 3:182

growth of Minor League Baseball, 3:183

home-field advantage, 3:179

image of World Series 1924, 3:179

Jim Creighton, 3:182

Kenesaw Mountain Landis, 3:178–179

Knickerbocker Base Ball Club, 3:180

leagues of, 3:178

Major League Baseball (MLB), 3:178

Major League Baseball Players Association, 3:184

Minor League Baseball (MiLB), 3:178

minor leagues, 3:180

modern era of, 3:183

National Association of Base Ball Players (NABBP), 3:182

National Association of Professional Base Ball Players (NAPBBP), 3:182

National Baseball Hall Of Fame, 3:183

nationalism and, 3:182

number of competing teams, 3:178

origins of, 3:180

performance-enhancing drug and, 3:184

popularity of, 3:182, 3:183

postseason play, 3:179–180

professionalism, 3:182

baseball, United States (*continued*)
   segregation and, 3:184
   U.S. Supreme Court decision on, 3:178
   William A. Hulbert and, 3:182
   World Series play, 3:180
baseball Hall of Fame (United States), 3:185–186
   election two, 3:185–186
   independence of, 3:185
   location of, 3:185
   main attractions of, 3:185
   number of members (2009), 3:186
   year of founding, 3:185
basketball, Australia and New Zealand, 1:361–362
   in Australia, 1:361
   Australian women's team, 1:361
   men's National Basketball League in New Zealand, 1:362
   National Basketball League (NBL), 1:361–362
   New Zealand men's team, 1:361
   in Oceania, 1:361, 1:362
   St Kilda Saints, 1:361, 1:362
   Women's National Basketball League (WNBL), 1:362
basketball, British Isles, 2:35–36
   Amateur Basket Ball Association of England and Wales (ABBA), 2:35
   Birmingham YMCA and, 2:35
   British Basketball League (BBL), 2:35
   Brixton TopCats, 2:35
   European Basketball Championships, 2:36
   growth of, 2:35
   Hoylake YMCA, 2:35
   London and, 2:35
   NBA and, 2:36
   Newcastle Eagles, 2:35
   Olympic Games and, 2:36
   popularity of, 2:35–36
basketball, China, 1:203–205
   American influence on, 1:204
   Chinese Basketball Association (CBA), 1:204
   communist ideology and, 1:204
   introduction of, 1:203
   National Basketball Association (NBA) and, 1:204
   popularity of, 1:204
   women's basketball, 1:203, 1:204
basketball, Europe, 2:249–251
   Antonio Diaz Miguel, 2:250
   Dirk Nowitski, 2:250
   Ernest Hermann, 2:250
   Euroleague, 2:250

   F. W. Fricke, 2:250
   Fédération Internationale de Basket-ball, 2:249
   in France, 2:250
   in Germany, 2:250
   in Greece, 2:250–251
   growth of, 2:249
   Konrad Koch, 2:250
   Nikos Galis, 2:251
   Panathanaikos, 2:251
   professionalism in, 2:249
   in Spain, 2:250
   U.S. players in, 2:250
   YMCA and, 2:249–250
basketball, FIBA European Basketball championship winners, 4:363
basketball, FIBA World Basketball championship winners, 4:362–363
basketball, Israel, 1:280–281
   first play of, 1:280
   Hapoel club, 1:280
   image of, 1:281
   international competition, 1:280
   Maccabi club, 1:280
   Maccabi Tel Aviv, 1:280
   Maccabiah Games, 1:281
   Mickey Berkowitz and, 1:281
   notable players of, 1:280
   Omri Casspi and, 1:280
   professional league of, 1:280
   Shay Doron and, 1:280
   Tal Brody and, 1:280–281
basketball, Italy, 2:251–253
   Bill Bradley, 2:252
   Cantu club, 2:252
   Dino Meneghin, 2:252
   Fédération Internationale de Basket-ball, 2:251
   Ignis Vareze club, 2:252
   image of, 2:252
   Liliana Ronchetti, 2:253
   Milan club, 2:252
   Olympic program and, 2:251
   Pierluigi Marzorati, 2:252
   Roma club, 2:252
   Sandro Gamba, 2:252
   Serie A club league, 2:253
   U.S. players in, 2:252, 2:253
   women and, 2:253
basketball, Latin America, 3:68–70
   in Argentina, 3:69

in Brazil, 3:69, 3:70
Brazil and women's basketball, 3:69
FIBA World Championships, 3:68–69
international tournaments, 3:69
Latin Americans in the NBA, 3:69–70
local leagues, 3:69
Olympic Games, 3:69
women and, 3:69
basketball, Lebanon, 1:281–282
basketball, National Basketball Association champions,
    4:263–264
basketball, National Collegiate Athletic Association
    champions
    Men, 4:272–273
    Women, 4:273–274
basketball, Olympic medalists (Summer)
    Men's Basketball, 4:52–55
    Women's Basketball, 4:55–56
basketball, Russia, the former Soviet Union, and the Baltic
    countries, 2:253–255
    Bolshevik Revolution, 2:253
    Cold War and, 2:253
    Frank Lubin, 2:254
    Latvia, 2:254
    Lithuania, 2:254
    Men's Russian National Team, 2:255
    Olga Shukhamnova, 2:254–255
    origins of, 2:253
    Soviet Union Olympic competition, 2:254, 2:255
    Soviet Women's National Team, 2:254–255
    Uljona Semjonova, 2:254
basketball, Women's National Basketball Association
    champions, 4:264
basketball, Yugoslav countries, 2:255–257
    Boris Stankovic, 2:256–257
    current state of, 2:257
    Drazen Petrovic, 2:256
    Kresimir Cosic, 2:256
    players of (distinguished), 2:256
    reputation of, 2:255–256
    Toni Kukoc, 2:256
    Vlade Divac, 2:256
    Yugoslavian Basketball Federation, 2:257
basque pelota, Olympic medalists (Summer)
    Men's Cesta Punta, 4:56–57
    Men's Frontenis, 4:57
    Men's Fronton, Bare-handed, 4:58
    Men's Fronton, Doubles Bare-handed, 4:58
    Men's Fronton, Paleta, 4:58

Men's Pala Corta, 4:57
Men's Paleta, Leather Pelote, 4:57
Men's Paleta, Rubber Pelote, 4:57–58
Men's Trinquet, Doubles Bare-handed, 4:58
Women's Frontenis, 4:57
basquette, 3:186–187
    Clara Gregory Baer and, 3:186
    description of play, 3:186
    emphasis of, 3:186
    Iowa Girls High School Athletic Union (IGHSAU) and,
        3:186
    origins of, 3:186
    rules of, 3:186
    Title IX legislation and, 3:186
"Battle of the Sexes" (tennis match), 3:187–188
beach volleyball, Olympic medalists (Summer)
    Men's Beach Volleyball, 4:58
    Women's Beach Volleyball, 4:59
beach volleyball (United States and Canada), 3:188–189
    development of, 3:188
    Olympic competition, 3:189
    popularity of, 3:188
    professionalism, 3:188
    recognition of, 3:188
    uniform regulations controversy, 3:189–190
    William G. Morgan and, 3:188
Beckenbauer, Franz (1945–), 2:257
Becker, Boris (1967–), 2:257–258
    date and place of birth, 2:258
    prize money standings, 2:258
    reputation of, 2:257–258
    statistics for, 2:258
Beckham, David (1975–), 2:36–38
    AC Milan and, 2:37
    achievements of, 2:36–37
    early career of, 2:36
    iconic status of, 2:37
    image of, 2:37
    Los Angeles Galaxy and, 2:37
    Los Blancos and, 2:37
    Manchester United and, 2:36
    personal life of, 2:37
    Real Madrid and, 2:37
Ben M'barek, Larbi (1914–1992), 1:282
Best, George (1946–2005), 2:38
biathlon, Olympic medalists (Winter)
    Men's 4 × 7.5-Kilometer Relay, 4:257
    Men's 10-Kilometer, 4:256
    Men's 12.5-Kilometer Pursuit, 4:256

biathlon, Olympic medalists (Winter) (*continued*)
  Men's 15-Kilometer Mass Start, 4:257
  Men's 20-Kilometer, 4:256
  Military Patrol, 4:259
  Women's 3 × 7.5-Kilometer Relay, 4:258
  Women's 4 × 6-Kilometer Relay, 4:258
  Women's 4 × 7.5-Kilometer Relay, 4:258
  Women's 7.5-Kilometer, 4:258
  Women's 10-Kilometer Pursuit, 4:258
  Women's 12.5-Kilometer Mass Start, 4:258
  Women's 15-Kilometer, 4:257
billiards, 2:38–39
  8/9-ball, 2:39
  "balkline," 2:39
  classes of, 2:38
  history of, 2:38–39
  Michael Phelan, 2:38
  Olympic Games and, 2:39
  origins of, 2:38
  snooker, 2:38, 2:39
  women and, 2:38
  World Confederation of Billiard SportsWorld Confederation of Billiard Sports, 2:39
Black Sox Scandal (1919), 3:189–190
Blatter, Joseph S. (1936–), 2:258–259
bobsled. *See* sliding sports (bobsleigh, luge, and skeleton)
bodybuilding, 3:190–192
  Arnold Schwarzenegger, 3:192
  Charles Atlas, 3:190
  dietary supplements, 3:192
  Eugen Sandow and, 3:190
  Gold's Gym, 3:192
  image of body building competition, 3:191
  Mr. America Contest, 3:190–191
  Mr. Universe Contest, 3:191
  performance-enhancing substances and, 3:192
  promoters of, 3:191–192
  Weider brothers, 3:191
  women and, 3:192
Bodyline (1932–1933), 1:362–363
  Douglas Jardine, 1:362, 1:363
  effect of, 1:363
  Harold Larwood, 1:362, 1:363
  purpose of, 1:362
Bolivarian Games, 3:70–71
Bolt, Usain (1986–), 3:71
Book of the Courtier (Castiglione), 2:259–260
Borg, Björn (1956–), 2:260–261

Bosman Ruling (1995), 2:261–263
  Belgian Court of First Instance finding, 2:261
  European Court of Justice (ECJ) finding, 2:261–262
  explanation of Bosman case, 2:261
  explanation of ruling, 2:262
  importance of, 2:262
  Jean-Marc Bosman, 2:261
  Royal Club Liégeois, 2:261
  Rule 46 (5a), 2:261
  Treaty of Rome Articles, 2:261–262
  Union Royale Belge des Sociétés de Football Association (URBSFA) and, 2:261, 2:262
  US Dunkerque, 2:261
Boston Marathon, 3:192–193
  current course, 3:193
  first running of, 3:192
  John Graham and, 3:192
  John J. McDermott and, 3:192
  media coverage, 3:193
  qualifications, 3:192–193
Botham, Sir Ian (1955–), 2:39–40
Bourguibism and sport (Tunisia), 1:283
boxing, Australia, 1:363–364
  history of, 1:363–364
  image of, 1:363
  recent developments in, 1:364
boxing, British Isles, 2:40–44
  amateur boxing, 2:42
  Amateur Boxing Association (ABA), 2:42
  bare-knuckle prize fighting, 2:40–42
  Benn, Eubank, and Watson fights, 2:43
  British Boxing Board of Control (BBBC), 2:43
  British Pakistanis and, 2:44
  "Broughton's Rules," 2:40, 2:41
  Cribb/Molyneaux fight, 2:41
  Duke of Cumberland, 2:40
  the Fancy, 2:40
  image of, 2:41
  Jack Broughton, 2:40, 2:42
  Johnson/Wells flight, 2:43
  Lonsdale belts, 2:43
  middle classes and, 2:41–42
  National Sporting Club (NSC), 2:43
  "New Rules of the London Ring," 2:41
  Olympic Games and, 2:42
  pay-per-view boxing, 2:43
  popularity decline, 2:43
  popularity of, 2:40, 2:42
  professional boxing, 2:42–43

racism and, 2:43
  Sayers/Heenan fight, 2:42
  Scottish champions, 2:43
  television and, 2:43
  women's boxing, 2:44
boxing, Latin America, 3:71–78
  in Argentina, 3:74
  in Brazil, 3:74–75
  Central American and Caribbean Games, 3:76–77
  in Chile, 3:75
  in Columbia, 3:74
  in Cuba, 3:73
  Federation of Latin American Professional Boxing
    Commissions (FEDELATIN), 3:71
  in Guatemala, 3:72
  Hall of Fame Latin American boxers, 3:75
  international amateur boxing competition, 3:75–77
  Men's World Amateur Boxing Championships, 3:77
  in Mexico, 3:71–72
  in Nicaragua, 3:72–73
  Olympic Games, 3:75–76
  Pan American Games, 3:76
  in Panama, 3:73
  popularity of, 3:71
  in Puerto Rico, 3:73–74
  in Venezuela, 3:74
  women's boxing, 3:77
boxing, Olympic medalists (Summer)
  Bantamweight, 4:60–61
  Featherweight, 4:61–62
  Flyweight, 4:59–60
  Heavyweight, 4:66–67
  Light Flyweight, 4:59
  Light Heavyweight, 4:66
  Light Middleweight, 4:64–65
  Light Welterweight, 4:63
  Lightweight, 4:62–63
  Middleweight, 4:65
  Super Heavyweight, 4:67
  Welterweight, 4:63–64
boxing, Philippines, 1:205–206
  Ceferino Garcia and, 1:205
  Edwin "Eddie" Tai and, 1:205
  Frank Churchill and, 1:205
  introduction of, 1:205
  Manny Pacquiao and, 1:205–206
  notable Filipino boxers, 1:205
  social acceptance of, 1:205
  Stuart Churchill and, 1:205

boxing, South Africa, 1:109–112
  amateur boxing, 1:111–112
  professional boxing, 1:109–111
Bradman, Sir Donald (1908–2001), 1:364–365
  batting average of, 1:365
  birthplace of, 1:364
  coaching manual of, 1:364
  hometown of, 1:365
  professionalism and, 1:364
  questions about, 1:365
  statistics for, 1:364
Brazilian Soccer Match–Fixing Scandal of 2005, 3:78
British Commonwealth Games of 1974 (Christchurch,
  New Zealand), 1:365
British Empire and Commonwealth Games of 1962 (Perth,
  Australia), 1:365–366
British Empire Games of 1938 (Sydney), 1:366
British imperialism and sport, 2:44–50
  Athletic News on, 2:46
  Australia, 2:48–49
  basis for imperialism, 2:44
  British racial superiority, 2:44
  C. B. Fry on, 2:49
  C. Gurdon on sporting education, 2:46
  C. L. R. James on, 2:45
  Charles Box on, 2:45
  Church of England and, 2:47
  cricket, 2:48
  Derek Birley on imperialism, 2:45
  duty and, 2:47
  E. W. Hornung on, 2:46–47
  elite schools and, 2:47
  at the end of the 19th century, 2:49
  evolution of, 2:45
  The Field on, 2:47–48
  India, 2:48
  J. A. Mangan on, 2:46
  Joseph Chamberlain on, 2:44
  legacy of, 2:49
  Lord Harris on, 2:48
  Lord Hawke on, 2:47
  morality and, 2:44, 2:46
  Muscular Christianity, 2:47
  nationalism, 2:48
  public schools and, 2:46–47
  racism, 2:48
  reality of empire, 2:44–45
  relationship between sport and empire, 2:45
  schools and, 2:46–47

British imperialism and sport (*continued*)
South Africa, 2:48
Thomas Hughes on, 2:47
Victorian age, 2:44
West Indies, 2:48
British imperialism and sports in Asia, 1:206–207
athleticism and games ethic, 1:206
British Empire Games, 1:207
Calcutta Cricket Club, 1:206
cricket, 1:206, 1:207
Empire and Commonwealth Games, 1:207
exclusivity, 1:206
football, 1:207
Hong Kong Cricket Club, 1:206
interport games, 1:206–207
racket games, 1:206
Singapore Cricket Club, 1:206
British Olympic Association (BOA), 2:50–51
broomball, 3:193–194
history of, 3:193
popularity of, 3:193
rules and play of, 3:193–194
Brownlow Medal (Australia), 1:366–367
Brundage, Avery (1887–1975), 3:194–195
1972 Munich Games and, 3:194–195
athletic administrator career, 3:194
as IOC president, 3:194–195
Olympic career of, 3:194
place of birth, 3:194
Bryant, Kobe (1978–), 3:195–196
birthplace of, 3:195
early career of, 3:195
image of, 3:195
origin of name, 3:195
scandal, 3:196
statistics for, 3:195–196
Bryant, Paul "Bear" (1913–1983), 3:196
Bueno, Maria (1939–), 3:78–79
bullfighting, 2:263–264
controversy over, 2:264
enthusiasm for, 2:263
explanation of Spanish-style bullfighting, 2:263–264
origins of, 2:263
Bundesliga match-fixing scandal of 2005 (Germany), 2:264–265
jail sentences for, 2:265
matches involved in, 2:264
number of people investigated, 2:265
organized crime syndicate and, 2:264, 2:265

Robert Hoyzer, 2:264–265
Torsten Koop and, 2:265

Cairo Football Derby: Al-Ahly–Zamalek, 1:283–284
camel racing, 1:284–285, 1:285 (image)
camogie (Ireland), 2:51–52
100th anniversary of, 2:51
All-Ireland Final, 2:51
camogie and hurling differences, 2:52
Camogie Association of Ireland, 2:51
Dublin, 2:51–52
first public match, 2:51
Gaelic Athletic Association (GAA), 2:51
hurling and, 2:51, 2:52
main competitions of, 2:51
National League, 2:51
O'Duffy Cup, 2:51
official launch of, 2:51
Camp, Walter (1859–1925), 3:196–197, 3:197–199
All-American football teams and, 3:197
death of, 3:198
image of, 3:198
impact of, 3:198
Intercollegiate Football Rules Committee and, 3:197
post-playing career of, 3:198
as primary architect of American football, 3:197
at Yale University, 3:196–197
Camp Nou (Spain), 2:265–266
inauguration date, 2:265
reputation of, 2:265
seating capacity, 2:265
Camus, Albert (1913–1960), 1:285–286
canoe/kayak, flatwater, Olympic medalists (Summer)
Men's Canoe, Double 1,000-Meter, 4:69
Men's Canoe, Double 10,000-Meter, 4:70
Men's Canoe, Double 500-Meter, 4:68–69
Men's Canoe, Single 1,000-Meter, 4:68
Men's Canoe, Single 10,000-Meter, 4:68
Men's Canoe, Single 500-Meter, 4:68
Men's Folding Kayak, Double 10,000-Meter, 4:70
Men's Folding Kayak, Single 10,000-Meter, 4:70
Men's Kayak, Double 1,000-Meter, 4:71–72
Men's Kayak, Double 10,000-Meter, 4:72
Men's Kayak, Double 500-Meter, 4:71
Men's Kayak, Single 1,000-Meter, 4:70–71
Men's Kayak, Single 4 × 1,000-Meter, 4:72–73
Men's Kayak, Single 4 × 500-Meter, 4:72
Men's Kayak, Single 10,000-Meter, 4:71
Men's Kayak, Single 500-Meter, 4:70

Women's Kayak, Double 500-Meter, 4:74
Women's Kayak, Fours 500-Meter, 4:74
Women's Kayak, Single 500-Meter, 4:73
canoe/kayak, slalom, Olympic medalists (Summer)
Men's Canoe, Double, 4:75
Men's Canoe, Single, 4:75
Men's Kayak, Single, 4:75
Women's Kayak, Single, 4:75
capoeira, Brazil, 3:79–81
Afro-Brazilian identity and, 3:79
formal academies of, 3:79
image of, 3:80
luta livre of, 3:79
origin of, 3:79
schools of, 3:79
universal element of, 3:79
Cardiff Arms Park, 2:52–53
cost of, 2:52
designers of, 2:52
development of, 2:52
importance of, 2:52
pitch of, 2:52
Central American and Caribbean Games, 3:81–82
administrative organization for, 3:81
confusion of terminology, 3:81
first edition of, 3:81
growth of, 3:81
Organization for Central American and Caribbean
University Games, 3:81–82
Central American Games, 3:82–83
2010 games, 3:82
Central American Sports Organization, 3:82
current series of, 3:82
events in, 3:82
political and economic problems and, 3:82
Central Council for Physical Recreation (CCPR), 2:53–54
expansion of, 2:53
key objectives of, 2:53
purpose of, 2:53
role of, 2:53
Champions League, 2:266–267
current play of, 2:267
former name of, 2:266
group phase popularity, 2:266
L'Equipe and, 2:266
most successful teams, 2:267
Chariots of Fire (1981), 2:54–55
Chávez, Julio César (1962–), 3:83–84
Alejandro Páez Varela on, 3:83

birthplace, 3:83
reputation of, 3:83
statistics for, 3:83
Clemente, Roberto (1934–1972), 3:84 (image), 3:84–85
coaching in sport, 1:1–4
in the ancient world, 1:1
coaches as cultural icons, 1:3
evolution of coaching, 1:1–2
independent and community-based grassroots sport
programs, 1:2
modern era of coaching, 1:1–2
preparation and certification of coaches, 1:2
primary role of a coach, 1:2–3
sport clubs, 1:2
state-sponsored sport systems, 1:2
Coast to Coast Race (New Zealand), 1:367–368
Coca-Cola, 1:157
Comăneci, Nadia (1961–), 2:267–268
Commonwealth Games, African nations, 1:112–114
1977 Gleneagles Agreement, 1:113
1986 Commonwealth Games, 1:113
conflict over cricket, 1:112
impact of African nations at Commonwealth Games,
1:113–114
rugby revivals, 1:113
Commonwealth Games, Asia, 1:207–208
boycott, 1:208
Burma (Myanmar), 1:208
Ceylon, 1:207
first appearance of Asian competitors, 1:207
India, 1:208
Malaysia, 1:208
Pakistan, 1:207
Sri Lanka, 1:208
Commonwealth Games, Australia, 1:368–369
1938 Sydney Games, 1:368, 1:369
1962 Perth Games, 1:368
1982 Brisbane Games, 1:368
2006 Melbourne Games, 1:368
competition with England, 1:368–369
contributions to the Games, 1:368
Institute of Sport in Canberra, 1:369
notable athletes, 1:369
public belief in, 1:368
success of Games in, 1:368
Commonwealth Games, Canada, 3:199–200
1954 version of, 3:199
1978 version of, 3:199
British Empire Games, 3:199

Commonwealth Games, Canada (*continued*)
   M. M. (Bobby) Robinson and, 3:199
   Norton Crow and, 3:199
   South Africa and, 3:200
Commonwealth Games, England, 2:55–56
   amateurism, 2:55, 2:56
   Bobby Robinson and, 2:55
   dates of, 2:55
   evolution of, 2:55
   first competition, 2:55
   John Astley-Cooper and, 2:55
   origins of, 2:55
   South Africa and, 2:55–56
   White City, London, 2:56
Commonwealth Games, Northern Ireland, 2:56–57
   boxing, 2:56
   importance of, 2:56
   lawn bowling, 2:56
   Mary Peters, 2:57
   metal success in, 2:56
   most successful year, 2:56
   shooting disciplines, 2:56–57
   Sports Institute for Northern Ireland (SINI), 2:56
Commonwealth Games of 1958 (Cardiff), 2:59–60
Commonwealth Games of 1966 (Jamaica), 3:85–86
   Caribbean medal count, 3:85
   gender verification testing, 3:85
   importance to Jamaica, 3:85
   significance of, 3:85
   success of, 3:85
Commonwealth Games of 1982 (Brisbane), 1:369–370
   Aboriginal protest, 1:370
   Gleneagles Agreement and, 1:370
   martial law and, 1:370
   political and racial conflict, 1:369–370
Commonwealth Games of 1990 (Auckland), 1:370–371
Commonwealth Games of 1998 (Kuala Lumpur),
   1:208–209
Commonwealth Games of 2006 (Melbourne), 1:371–372
   closing ceremony image, 1:371
   medals awarded, 1:372
   number sports contested, 1:371
   total expenditure for, 1:371
Commonwealth Games of 2010 (New Delhi), 1:209–210
   controversies, 1:209
   cost of, 1:209
   number of athletes in, 1:209
   significant sporting outcomes of, 1:210
   withdrawal of athletes, 1:209–210

Commonwealth Games, Scotland, 2:57–58
   1970 games, 2:57
   1986 games, 2:57
   Glasgow and, 2:57
   as host of, 2:57
   new sports added to, 2:57
Commonwealth Games, Wales, 2:58–59
   1958 Games, 2:58–59
   Commonwealth Games Council of Wales, 2:58
   flag of, 2:59
   hosting of, 2:58
   medals won, 2:59
   Queen's Baton Relay, 2:59
   Youth Games, 2:59
Comrades Marathon (South Africa), 1:114
Conejo, Luis Gabelo (1960–), 3:86
CONMEBOL, 3:86–87
   headquarters of, 3:87
   member nations, 3:87
   purpose of, 3:87
   reputation of, 3:87
CONMEBOL Copa Libertadores, 4:311–312
Copa América, 3:87–88
   challenges in early days, 3:87–88
   format of, 3:88
   longevity of, 3:88
   member nations, 3:87
   notable players in, 3:88
   participation in, 3:87
   reputation of, 3:87
Copa Libertadores, 3:88–89
   Atlantic coast domination, 3:89
   club victories, 3:89
   first edition of, 3:88
   popularity of, 3:89
   purpose of, 3:88
   sponsorship, 3:89
   structure of, 3:88–89
Corinthians, 2:60
Cotswold Games (England), 2:60–61
   reestablishment of, 2:61
   revival of, 2:61
   Robert Dover and, 2:60–61
   Robert Dover's Games Society, 2:61
coursing (British Isles), 2:61
Court, Margaret (1942–), 1:372
cricket, Australia, 1:372–378
   Australian cricket today, 1:378
   blind/deaf cricket, 1:378

Bodyline Series, 1:375
cricketers and controversies, 1:375–376
governing body of, 1:374
image of, 1:373
Imparja Cup (Footprint), 1:377
indigenous cricket, 1:377–378
legendary Australian cricket players, 1:375
origins of, 1:372–374
outstanding women Cricketers, 1:377
Shane Warne, 1:376
Test matches, 1:374–375
underarm bowling, 1:375–376
women's Ashes/Tests, 1:377
women's cricket, 1:376–377
World Series Cricket, 1:375
cricket, Bangladesh, 1:210
cricket, England, 2:61–68
amateurism, and of, 2:66
"The Ashes," 2:63–2:64
Ashes (1930), 2:64
Ashes (2005–2009), 2:67
Australian-England tours, 2:63, 2:66–67
Basil D'Oliveira, 2:66
Benson and Hedges, 2:66, 2:67
Bert Oldfield, 2:64
Bill Woodfull, 2:64–65
Birmingham League, 2:63
bodyline tactics, 2:64
Central Lancashire League, 2:63
County Championship, 2:63
Cricket World Cup, 2:66
Dennis Compton, 2:65
division between amateur and professional, 2:62
Don Bradman, 2:64, 2:65
Douglas Jardine, 2:64, 2:65
Duncan Fletcher, 2:67
first "laws of cricket," 2:62
Gillette Cup, 2:65
after the Great War, 2:64
Hambledon Cricket Club, 2:61–62
Harold Larwood, 2:64, 2:65
Ian Botham, 2:66
ICC World Twenty20, 2:67
Indian Premier League, 2:67
Jack Hobbs, 2:63
Jim Laker, 2:65
"John Player County League," 2:65–66
Len Hutton, 2:65
Marylebone Cricket Club (MCC), 2:62

North Staffordshire League, 2:63
North-East Lancashire League, 2:63
One-Day cricket, 2:65
P. F. Warner, 2:64
Pakistan and, 2:67
shamateurism, 2:62, 2:66
Tony Greig, 2:66
touring other countries, 2:63
Twenty20 competitions, 2:67
"Victory Tests," 2:65
W. G. Grace and, 2:62, 2:63
the West Indies and, 2:66
World Series of cricket, 2:66
cricket, India, 1:210–213
history of, 1:211–212
image of, 1:211
Indian Premier League (IPL), 1:212–213
popularity of, 1:212
significance of, 1:210, 1:212
style of play, 1:212
cricket, International Cricket Council Cricket World Cup
champions, 4:276
cricket, Kenya, 1:114–115
Cricket Kenya, 1:115
current status of, 1:115
decline of, 1:115
first recorded match, 1:114–115
International Cricket Council (ICC) and, 1:115
introduction of, 1:114
Kenyan Cricket Association, 1:115
notable players, 1:115
rebuilding of, 1:115
success of, 1:115
cricket, Netherlands, 2:268–269
current condition of, 2:269
date of first recorded match, 2:268
development of, 2:268
Free Foresters, 2:269
German occupation and, 2:269
popularity of, 2:269
World War I and, 2:268
cricket, New Zealand, 1:378–381
during the 19th century, 1:379
colonization, 1:379
New Zealand Cricket Council (NZCC), 1:379, 1:380
obstacles to, 1:379–380
outlook for, 1:380
Test cricket, 1:379, 1:380
touring teams, 1:379

cricket, New Zealand (*continued*)
    transmission of, 1:380
    women's cricket, 1:380
cricket, Olympic medalists (Summer), 4:76
cricket, Pakistan
    Board of Control for Cricket in Pakistan, 1:213, 1:214
    gambling and, 1:215
    history of, 1:213
    international success of, 1:214, 1:215
    organizational and structural problems., 1:213–214
    popularity of, 1:214
    women's cricket, 1:214
cricket, South Africa, 1:115–121
    Abe Bailey and, 1:118, 1:119
    the African game, 1:119
    Bloemfontein Cricket Club, 1:117
    cricket in the Afrikaner Republics, 1:117–118
    Cricket South Africa (CSA), 1:120
    early history of, 1:115–117
    Graeme Smith, Captain of the Proteas, 1:116 (image)
    Imperial Cricket Conference (ICC), 1:118, 1:119
    James Logan and, 1:118–119
    literature and, 1:116
    the modern era, 1:119–120
    Natal Cricket Union, 1:116
    notable Afrikaner players, 1:118
    notable modern players, 1:120
    racial politics and, 1:119–120
    South African Cricket Association (SACA), 1:118, 1:120
    Transvaal Cricket Union, 1:118
    United Cricket Board of South Africa (UCBSA), 1:120
    unsuccessful adoption of cricket, 1:117
cricket, Sri Lanka, 1:215–217
    governing body of, 1:216
    history of, 1:215–216
    international success of, 1:216
    women's cricket, 1:216
cricket, Trobriand Islands, 1:381–382
cricket, West Indies, 3:89–94
    1928–1939 period, 3:91–92
    1947–1960 postwar period, 3:92
    1960–1974 independence period, 3:92
    1974–1900 period, 3:92–93
    1995–2011 period, 3:93–94
    bases of appeal for cricket, 3:89–90
    Clive Lloyd, 3:93
    decline of, 3:93

    dominance of, 3:92–93
    five phases of, 3:91
    importance of, 3:89–90
    introduction of the game, 3:91
    Kensington Oval grounds, 3:90 (image)
    notable players, 3:91, 3:91–92, 3:93
    professionalism, 3:92–93
    quota selection policy, 3:92
    socioeconomic and political changes and, 3:90–91
    West Indies Cricket Board of Control, 3:91
    women's team, 3:93–94
cricket, Zimbabwe, 1:121–122
    current state of, 1:122
    history of, 1:121–122
    introduction of, 1:121
    Robert Mugabe and, 1:122
croquet, 2:68–69
    All- England Lawn Tennis and Croquet Club, 2:68
    development of, 2:68
    national championships of, 2:68
    types of, 2:68
croquet, Olympic medalists (Summer)
    Men's Croquet Doubles, 4:76
    Men's Croquet Singles, One Ball, 4:76
    Men's Croquet Singles, Two Balls, 4:76
Cruyff, Johan (1947–), 2:269–270
    accolades for, 2:270
    the "Cruyff turn," 2:270
    as local folk hero, 2:270
    post-playing career of, 2:270
    reputation is, 2:269
    teams play for, 2:269
curling, North America, 3:200–202
    in Canada, 3:201
    membership in curling clubs, 3:202
    number of Canadian curlers, 3:201
    number of United States curlers, 3:201
    Olympic competition and, 3:201, 3:202
    origin of, 3:200
    playing of, 3:200–201
    popularity of, 3:202
    in the United States, 3:201–202
curling, Olympic medalists (Winter)
    Men's Curling, 4:233
    Women's Curling, 4:233–234
curling, Scotland, 2:69
    birthplace of, 2:69
    medal count for, 2:69
    Olympic competition, 2:69

Royal Caledonian Curling Club (RCCC), 2:69
women and, 2:69
cycling, Australia and New Zealand, 1:382–383
cash racing, 1:382
long-distance racing and touring, 1:382
Melbourne Bicycle Club, 1:382
outstanding athletes of, 1:383
popularity of, 1:383
cycling, BMX, Olympic medalists (Summer)
Men's BMX, 4:76
Women's BMX, 4:76
cycling, North Africa, 1:286–287
cycling, North America, 3:202–203
BMX racing, 3:203
cyclocross, 3:203
innovations, 3:202–203
Marshall "Major" Taylor and, 3:203
the safety bike, 3:202–203
six-day race, 3:203
track racing, 3:203
velodromes, 3:203
cycling, road, Olympic medalists (Summer)
Men's Individual Road Race, 4:77
Men's Team Road Race, 4:77–78
Men's Time Trial, Individual, 4:78
Men's Time Trial, Team, 4:78
Women's Individual Road Race, 4:78–79
Women's Individual Time Trial, 4:79
cycling, track, Olympic medalists (Summer)
Men's ⅓-Mile, 4:79
Men's 1,980-Yard Team Pursuit, 4:85
Men's 1-Kilometer Pursuit, 4:85
Men's 1-Kilometer Time Trial, 4:82
Men's 1-Mile, 4:79
Men's 2-Mile, 4:79
Men's 5-Kilometer, 4:80
Men's 5-Mile, 4:79
Men's 10-Kilometer, 4:80
Men's 12-Hour Race, 4:80
Men's 20-Kilometer, 4:80
Men's 25-Kilometer, 4:80
Men's 25-Mile, 4:79
Men's 50-Kilometer, 4:80
Men's 100-Kilometer, 4:80
Men's 660-Yard, 4:80
Men's ¼-Mile, 4:79
Men's ½-Mile, 4:79
Men's Individual Pursuit, 4:81
Men's Individual Sprint, 4:84

Men's Keirin, 4:82
Men's Madison, 4:80
Men's Olympic Sprint, 4:85
Men's One Lap (660-Yard) Sprint, 4:85
Men's Point Race, 4:80–81
Men's Tandem, 4:81
Men's Team Pursuit, 4:82–83
Men's Team Sprint, 4:84
Women's 3,000-Meter Individual Pursuit, 4:85
Women's 500-Meter Time Trial, 4:85
Women's Individual Sprint, 4:84
Women's Points Race, 4:85

Dakar Rally, 1:123
DanceSport, 2:270–273
disciplines of, 2:272
examples of, 2:270
formal definition of, 2:270
image of, 2:271
International Dance Organization (IDO), 2:272
International DanceSport Federation (IDSF), 2:270,
2:272
Olympic competition and, 2:270, 2:272
origins of popular music styles and associated dance
styles (20th century), 2:272
popularity of, 2:272
World Rock'n'Roll Confederation, 2:272
darts, 2:69–71
British Darts Organisation (BDO), 2:70
dart boards, 2:69–70
National Darts Association (NDA), 2:70
News of the World Individual Darts Championship, 2:70
popularity of, 2:70
Professional Darts Corporation (PDC), 2:70–71
rules of play, 2:70
scarring of, 2:70
in the U.S., 2:70
World Darts Federation (WDF), 2:70
Dassler Family (Adidas and Puma), 2:273–274
Davis Cup (tennis), 3:204–205
Australia and, 3:205
Bill Tilden, 3:205
diffusion of, 3:204
Dwight Davis and, 3:204
elitism, 3:204
first play of, 3:204
governing body for, 3:204
Great Britain and, 3:205
lawn tennis, 3:204

Davis Cup (tennis) (*continued*)
  reputation of, 3:204
  structure of, 3:205
  U.S. wins in, 3:204, 3:205
De Coubertin, Pierre Frédy, Baron (1863–1937), 2:274–275
  image of, 2:274
  International Olympic Committee (IOC) and, 2:274, 2:275
  life's work of, 2:274
  Olympic ceremonies and, 2:275
  parents of, 2:274
Dempsey, William Harrison "Jack" (1895–1983), 3:205–207
  death of, 3:207
  famous fights of, 3:206
  image of, 3:206
  popularity of, 3:205
  segregation and, 3:206–207
Deutsche Demokratische Republik (East Germany) and sport, 2:275–280
  Birgit Boese case, 2:279, 2:280
  Carl Diem, 2:277
  declaration of sovereignty, 2:277
  Deutschen Turn- und Sportbund (German Gymnastics and Sporting Union, GGSU), 2:276
  doping and GDR elite sports system, 2:278–280
  Freie Deutsche Jugend (Free German Youth, FGY), 2:276
  GDR and the IOC, 2:276–278
  Heidi Krieger case, 2:279
  Karl Ritter von Halt, 2:277
  Leipziger Sporthochschule, 2:279
  Manfred Ewald, 2:280
  Manfred Hoeppner, 2:280
  NATO recognition of, 2:275
  sporting system and aim of youth work, 2:275–276
  summer camps, 2:276
Deutscher Olympischer Sportbund, 2:280–283
  Deutscher Olympischer Sportbund (German Olympic Sports Federation, DOSB), 2:280, 2:282
  Deutscher Sportbund (German Sports Federation, DSB), 2:280, 2:281, 2:282
  facilities, 2:282
  Golden Plans, 2:282
  government support, 2:281
  memberships, 2:280, 2:282
  Olympische Komitee (National Olympic Committee, NOK), 2:280
  origin of, 2:280

Di Stéfano, Alfredo (1926–), 3:94
Didrikson, Mildred Ella (1911–1956), 3:207–208
  death of, 3:208
  femininity and, 3:208
  image of, 3:208
  in Olympic competition, 3:207
  reputation of, 3:207
Diem, Carl (1882–1962), 2:283
DiMaggio, Joe (1914–1999), 3:208–209
  death of, 3:209
  early playing career of, 3:209
  Italian American loyalty question, 3:209
  in popular culture, 3:209
  reputation of, 3:209
  statistics for, 3:209
disabled and sport, 1:4–6
  organization of Paralympic Sport, 1:5
  wheelchair race, 1:4 (image)
disc golf, 3:209–210
  governing body of, 3:210
  number of courses in the U.S., 3:210
  Professional Disc Golf Association (PDGA), 3:210
  rules and scoring in, 3:209–210
  "Steady" Ed Headrick and, 3:209
diving, Olympic medalists (Summer)
  Men's 3-Meter Springboard, 4:87
  Men's 10-Meter Platform, 4:86
  Men's Plain High Diving, 4:88
  Men's Plunge for Distance, 4:88
  Men's Synchronized 3-Meter Springboard, 4:87
  Men's Synchronized 10-Meter Platform, 4:87
  Women's 3-Meter Springboard, 4:88–89
  Women's 10-Meter Platform, 4:88
  Women's Synchronized 3-Meter Springboard, 4:89
  Women's Synchronized 10-Meter Platform, 4:89
Doggett's Coat and Badge (England), 2:71
doping, Tour de France, 2:283–26
  blood doping, 2:285
  catalyst for antidoping, 2:284
  definition of doping, 2:283, 2:284
  doping drug of choice, 2:285
  drug raid (1998), 2:285
  first doping scandal, 2:284
  Floyd Landis, 2:285
  Henri Pélissier and, 2:284
  International Cycling Union (UCI) and, 2:283
  Jean Malléjec, 2:284
  Lance Armstrong, 2:285

Lucien Petit-Breton and, 2:284
  method for avoiding antidumping regime, 2:285
  Operacion Puerto, 2:285
  Pierre Dumas, 2:284
  reaction to antidoping legislation, 2:284–285
  scandal of 2006, 2:285
  scandal of 2007, 2:286
  Tom Simpson, death of, 2:285
drag racing, 3:210
Dragon boat racing, 1:217–219
  history of, 1:217
  image of, 1:218
  international competition, 1:218
  paddling, 1:217
  racing, 1:217–218
Dubai Sports City, 1:287
Dubin Inquiry, 3:210–211
  Ben Johnson and, 3:210–211
  cost of, 3:211
  reason for, 3:211
  recommendations of, 3:211

East Germany. *See* Deutsche Demokratische Republik
  (East Germany) and sport
Ederle, Gertrude (1906–2003), 3:211–213
  deafness, 3:212
  early years of, 3:211
  English Channel swim, 3:212
  image of, 3:212
  last public appearance of, 3:213
  professional career of, 3:212
Egypt, sports and Nasserism, 1:287–288
Elliott, Herb (1938–), 1:383–384
  birthplace of, 1:383
  post-running achievements, 1:384
  reputation of, 1:383, 1:384
  start date of competitive career, 1:383
  statistics for, 1:383–384
Ellis Park Stadium Disaster (South Africa), 1:123–124
England and Wales Cricket Board, 2:34–35
Epsom Downs Racecourse (England), 2:71–72
  the Derby, 2:71, 2:73
  first recorded race, 2:71
  image of, 2:72
  as a political stage, 2:73
  reputation of, 2:71
equestrian, Olympic medalists (Summer)
  Men's High Jump, 4:89
  Men's Jumping, 4:89

  Men's Long Jump, 4:90
  Mixed Individual Dressage, 4:90
  Mixed Individual Eventing, 4:91–92
  Mixed Individual Figure Riding, 4:96
  Mixed Individual Jumping, 4:93–94
  Mixed Individual Vaulting, 4:95
  Mixed Team Dressage, 4:90–91
  Mixed Team Eventing, 4:92–93
  Mixed Team Figure Riding, 4:96
  Mixed Team Show Jumping, 4:94–95
  Mixed Team Vaulting, 4:95
Estadio Centenario (Uruguay), 3:94–95
  capacity of, 3:95
  design of, 3:95
  inauguration date, 3:95
  national identity and, 3:95
Estadio Mateo Flores disaster of 1996 (Guatemala),
    3:94–95
  accounts of, 3:95
  casualty count, 3:95
  cause of, 3:95
  consequences of, 3:96
Estadio Monumental (Argentina), 3:96
  capacity of, 3:96
  importance of, 3:96
  inauguration date, 3:96
  location of, 3:96
Estadio Nacional (Chile), 3:97
  capacity of, 3:97
  location of, 3:97
  primary purpose of, 3:97
  renaming of, 3:97
Estadio Nacional disaster of 1964 (Lima, Peru),
    3:97–98
  casualty count, 3:97
  cause of, 3:97–98
  Negro Bomba and, 3:97
ethnicity and sectarianism in divided societies in the
    Middle East (case study of Lebanon), 1:288–290
Eton Wall Game (England), 2:73
  explanation of, 2:73
  rules of, 2:73
  St. Andrew's Day game, 2:73
European Committee for Sports History, 2:286–287
European Cup. *See* Champions League
European Order of Merit (golf) winners, 4:339–340
European Rugby championships
  European Challenge Cup winners, 4:307
  Heineken Cup winners, 4:306

European Union and sport, 2:287–289
  competencies in, 2:287
  EU role in sport, 2:287
  "The European Model of Sport" document, 2:288
  European Year of Education through Sport, 2:288
  Helsinki Report on Sport, 2:288
  importance of sport to EU, 2:287
  institutions of, 2:287
  Nice Declaration on Sport, 2:288
  sports program of, 2:288
  Treaty of Lisbon, Article 165, 2:288
  "The White Paper on Sport" document, 2:288
extreme sports, 3:213–214
  air category sports, 3:213
  definition of, 3:213
  general categories of, 3:213
  general judging standards, 3:213
  Joe Tomlinson on, 3:213
  land category sports, 3:213
  Olympic competition, 3:214
  training, 3:213
  water category sports, 3:213–214
  X Games, 3:214

Fangio, Juan Manuel (1911–1995), 3:98
  nickname of, 3:98
  reputation of, 3:98
  statistics for, 3:98
fanzines (British Isles), 2:73–74
  evolution of, 2:74
  first appearance of, 2:74
  language of, 2:74
  popularity of, 2:74
  tribal quality names of, 2:74
  When Saturday Comes, 2:74
Far Eastern Championship Games, 1:219
fast bowling, West Indies (cricket), 3:98–99
  decline of, 3:99
  importance of, 3:98–99
  notable players, 3:98, 3:99
Fédération Internationale de Football Association, 1:6–8
  Carl Hirschman and, 1:6
  commercialization, 1:7
  current status of, 1:8
  Football Association (FA) relationship, 1:6–7
  growth of membership in, 1:7
  João Havelange and, 1:7
  Jules Rimet and, 1:7
  list of presidents of, 1:7

  Robert Guérin and, 1:6
  Sepp Blatter and, 1:7–8
  Union of Football Associations (UEFA) and, 1:7–8
  World Cup and, 1:7
Fédération Internationale de Natation, 2:289–290
  disciplines of, 2:289
  Natation magazine, 2:289
  open-water races, 2:290
  structure of, 2:290
  swimsuit controversy, 2:290
  synchronized swimming, 2:289
  women and, 2:290
Federation of Basque Pelota, 3:5
Federer, Roger (1981–), 2:290–291
  birthplace of, 2:291
  earnings of, 2:291
  Federer/Nadal rivalry, 2:290–291
  record of, 2:291
  reputation of, 2:290
fencing, 2:291–293
  dominant countries in, 2:293
  the epee, 2:291, 2:292, 2:293
  equipment concerns, 2:292
  Fédération Internationale d'Escrime (FIE), 2:291–292
  the French foil, 2:291
  Gérard Six on, 2:291
  influence of France on, 2:291–292
  Olympic competition, 2:291
  origins of, 2:291
  professionalism and, 2:293
  the saber, 2:291, 2:292
  signalization, 2:292
  women and, 2:292
  women's team competition, 2:292 (image)
fencing, Olympic medalists (Summer)
  Men's Amateurs-Masters Épée, 4:103
  Men's Individual Épée, 4:98–99
  Men's Individual Foil, 4:96
  Men's Individual Saber, 4:101
  Men's Masters Épée, 4:99
  Men's Masters Foil, 4:97
  Men's Masters Saber, 4:101
  Men's Single Stick, 4:103
  Men's Team Épée, 4:99–101
  Men's Team Foil, 4:97–98
  Men's Team Sabre, 4:102–103
  Women's Individual Épée, 4:105
  Women's Individual Foil, 4:103–104
  Women's Individual Saber, 4:105

Women's Team Épée, 4:105
Women's Team Foil, 4:104–105
Women's Team Saber, 4:105
Fenway Park, 3:214–215
  features of, 3:215
  ownership of, 3:215
  reputation of, 3:214
  restoration of, 3:215
  tours of, 3:215
FIBA European Basketball championships, 4:363
FIBA World Basketball championships, 4:362–363
field hockey, Argentina, 3:99
  championship competition, 3:99
  current status of, 3:99
  governing body for, 3:99
  Las Leonas, 3:99
  Luciana Aymar and, 3:99
field hockey, Asia, 1:219–221
  China and, 1:220
  countries dominating at elite level, 1:219–220
  India and, 1:219–220
  Malaysia and, 1:267
  Pakistan and, 1:219–220
  South Korea and, 1:220–221
  women and, 1:220
field hockey, Australia and New Zealand, 1:384–385
  All Australian Women's Hockey Association, 1:384
  Australian women's team, 1:384
  earliest known Australian men's and women's clubs, 1:384
  earliest known New Zealand men's and women's clubs, 1:384
  Hockey Australia, 1:385
  international competition, 1:384–385
  New Zealand Hockey Association, 1:384
  New Zealand Hockey Federation, 1:385
  New Zealand Ladies Hockey Association, 1:384
field hockey, British Isles, 2:74–76
  All England Women's Hockey Association (AEWHA), 2:75, 2:76
  association game, 2:75
  Blackheath Club, 2:75
  England Hockey Association (EHA), 2:76
  Hockey Association (HA), 2:75, 2:76
  interclub competition, 2:75
  International Hockey Federation (FIH), 2:75
  Irish Hockey Association, 2:76
  ladies' teams, 2:75
  National Curriculum and, 2:76
  Olympic competition and, 2:75
  origins of, 2:74–75
  popularity of, 2:75, 2:76
  Teddington Cricket Club, 2:75
field hockey, Olympic medalists (Summer)
  Men's Field Hockey, 4:117–120
  Women's Field Hockey, 4:121–122
field hockey, South Africa, 1:124–125
  apartheid and, 1:125
  club hockey, 1:124–125
  date of establishment of first women's hockey club, 1:124
  development of, 1:125
  international competition successes, 1:125
  Western Province Union, 1:124
Field of Dreams (1989), 3:215–216
field sports, Australia and New Zealand, 1:385–387
  fishing, 1:386–387
  fox hunting, 1:386
  hunting, 1:385–386
  shooting, 1:387
field sports, British Isles, 2:76–80
  angling, 2:78
  British Field Sports Society, 2:79
  British landscape and, 2:78–79
  British royal family and, 2:76–77
  chronology of, 2:77
  controversy and, 2:76, 2:80
  Countryside Alliance, 2:80
  cultural expectations and, 2:76
  dogs and, 2:79, 2:80
  elements of, 2:76
  employment and, 2:79
  Game Act, 2:77
  game shooting, 2:78
  Ground Game Act, 2:77, 2:78
  hare coursing, 2:77–78
  Hunt Saboteurs Association, 2:80
  Hunting with Dogs Act of 2004, 2:80
  land use and landlord goodwill, 2:77
  League Against Cruel Sports, 2:79–80
  legislation and, 2:79–80
  National Coursing Club, 2:78
  poaching, 2:79
  Prevention of Poaching Act, 2:79
  publications for, 2:77
  Scottish Highlands and, 2:79
  trespassing and, 2:79
  Waterloo Cup, 2:78

field sports, British Isles (*continued*)
  women and, 2:77
  Working Men's Anglers' Association, 2:78
field sports, South Africa, 1:125–127
  angling, 1:126
  canine activities, 1:126–127
  equestrian, 1:126
  horse racing, 1:125–126
FIFA World Cup champions
  Men's, 4:274
  Women's, 4:274
FIFA World Cup of 1930 (Uruguay), 3:99–100
  final match of, 3:100
  participating teams, 3:100
  venues for, 3:100
FIFA World Cup of 1950 (Brazil), 3:100–102
  average attendance of, 3:101
  "failure in the Maracanã," 3:102
  final round-robin group, 3:101
  image of, 3:101
  stadiums for, 3:101
FIFA World Cup of 1958 (Sweden), 2:293–294
  Argentina and, 2:293
  Brazil and, 2:293
  British teams, 2:293, 2:294
  countries participating in, 2:293
  Garrincha, 2:294
  Germany and, 2:294
  Helmuth Rahn, 2:293
  Israel and, 2:293
  Just Fontaine, 2:293, 2:294
  Pelé, 2:293, 2:294
  spectatorship, 2:293
  Wales and, 2:293
FIFA World Cup of 1962 (Chile), 3:102–103
  Carlos Dittborn and, 3:102
  notable players in, 3:102
  participating teams, 3:102
  winner of, 3:100, 3:102
FIFA World Cup of 1966 (England), 2:80–83
  African nations forfeit, 2:80
  Alf Ramsey and, 2:80, 2:81, 2:82
  final game of, 2:82
  importance of, 2:80–81
  Jules Rimet trophy disappearance, 2:81
  Norbert "Nobby" Peter Stiles, 2:81
  referees and, 2:81–82
  significant events of, 2:81
  television and, 2:80

"wingless wonders" formation, 2:81
  World Cup Willie mascot, 2:81
FIFA World Cup of 1970 (Mexico), 3:103
  extra period of, 3:103
  Pelé and, 3:103
  performance of Mexico, 3:103
  winner of, 3:103
FIFA World Cup of 1974 (West Germany), 2:294–297
  Ajax Amsterdam, 2:296
  Chile and, 2:295–296
  East Germany and, 2:296
  image of, 2:295
  Netherlands and, 2:296–297
  participating countries, 2:295
  Poland and, 2:296
  Soviet Union, 2:295–296
  spectatorship, 2:295
  West Germany and, 2:296
FIFA World Cup of 1978 (Argentina), 3:103–104
  controversy and political grandstanding, 3:104
  Mario Kempes, 3:103, 3:104
  Peru match, 3:104
  winner of, 3:104
FIFA World Cup of 1982 (Spain)
  Algeria and, 2:297
  brutal foul, 2:298
  France and, 2:297, 2:298
  Germany and, 2:298
  goals scored in final round, 2:297
  Italy and, 2:298
  length of final round, 2:297
  participating countries, 2:297
  Spain and, 2:297
  spectatorship for final round, 2:297
  top scorer, 2:297
  West Germany and, 2:297, 2:298
FIFA World Cup of 1986 (Mexico), 3:104–107
  Diego Maradona and, 3:106
  earthquake damage, 3:106
  format of, 3:106
  "the hand of God" goal, 3:106
  image of, 3:105
  winner of, 3:106
FIFA World Cup of 1990 (Italy), 2:298–300
  Argentina and, 2:299–300
  Cameroon and, 2:299
  Germany and, 2:300
  goals scored in final round, 2:299
  Italian Series A League, 2:299

length of final round, 2:299
participating countries, 2:299
quarterfinal teams, 2:299
semifinal teams, 2:299–300
spectatorship, 2:299
FIFA World Cup of 1998 (France), 2:300–301
Brazil and, 2:301
expansion of the final round, 2:300
France and, 2:301
French victory, 2:301
Jean Marie Le Pen, 2:301
length of final round, 2:300
Netherlands and, 2:301
Nike sponsorship, 2:301
participating countries, 2:300
quarterfinal teams, 2:301
semifinal teams, 2:301
spectatorship, 2:300
Zinédine Zidane in, 2:301
FIFA World Cup of 2002 (Japan and South Korea),
   1:221–222
FIFA World Cup of 2006 (Germany), 2:301–303
final play, 2:303
final round success, 2:303
genesis of, 2:301–302
image of, 2:302
length of final round, 2:303
participating countries, 2:303
quarterfinal teams, 2:303
semifinal play, 2:303
spectatorship, 2:303
FIFA World Cup of 2010 (South Africa), 1:127–129
FIFA World Cup of 2014 (Brazil), 3:107
Brazilian attitude toward, 3:107
dates of, 3:107
stadiums and, 3:107
figure skating, North America, 3:216–218
in 1976 Olympics, 3:217
in 1988 Olympics, 3:217
in 1994 Olympics, 3:217–218
in 2002 Olympics, 3:218
Avery Brundage and, 3:216
Cold War and, 3:217
Dick Button, 3:217
fairness of judging, 3:217
first Olympic competition, 3:216
Montgomery Wilson, 3:217
Sale and Pelletier controversy, 3:218
scoring system, 3:218

Sonja Henie, 3:216
Soviet skaters and, 3:217
Tenley Albright, 3:217
Toller Cranston, 3:217
figure skating, Olympic medalists (Winter)
Men's Singles, 4:240
Men's Special Figures, 4:241
Mixed Ice Dancing, 4:240
Mixed Pairs, 4:241–242
Women's Singles, 4:241
fistball, 2:304
first German championship of, 2:304
International Fistball Association, 2:304
modern development of, 2:304
origin of, 2:304
popularity of, 2:304
fives, England, 2:83
explanation of, 2:83
Fives Federation, 2:83
Old Fives Court of College Hall at Eton College, 2:84
   (image)
popularity of, 2:83
variations of, 2:83
folk sports and traditional games, Europe, 2:304–312
capoeira, 2:310
countercultural innovation and sport for all, 2:309–310
Danish traditional games movement, 2:309
development of modern folk sports, 2:309
diffusions and fusions of, 2:310
dyst, 2:307
European Traditional Sport and Games Association,
   2:310
falling, 2:307
Flemish volkssport, 2:309
flirtation and, 2:306
folk boating, 2:307
folk sports and democratic revolutions, 2:310
folk sports, basis of, 2:304
folks sports, patterns of, 2:310–311
food and carnival, 2:307–308
gender and, 2:306
hindering and tumbling, 2:307
histories, 2:304–305
International Sport and Culture Association, 2:309–310
International Traditional Sports and Games Association,
   2:310
laughter and folk culture, 2:306–307
laughter at failure, 2:308
marking differences, 2:306

folk sports and traditional games, Europe (*continued*)
measurement and, 2:307
modern folk sports, 2:309
modern sport against folk sports, 2:308–309
pencak silat, 2:310
premodern folk games and festivals, 2:305–306
terminology and, 2:304–305
traditional folk sports, erotic and gender relations, 2:305
traditional games, roots of, 2:304
tsan, 2:305
tug-of-war, 2:307
UNESCO and, 2:310
women and folk competitions, 2:305–306
women's sports, 2:306
wushu, 2:310
football (soccer), Olympic medalists (Summer)
Men's Football (Soccer), 4:106–111
Women's Football (Soccer), 4:111–112
football, American, 3:218–225
AFL, formation of, 3:222
American football outside of America, 3:224
American Professional Football Association (APFA), 3:222
Big Ten Conference, 3:220
blackout policy, NCAA, 3:224
blackout policy, NFL, 3:223–224
"Bloody Monday," 3:218
Boston Game rules, 3:219
Bowl Championship Series (BCS), 3:221
bowl games, 3:221
broadcasting, 3:222, 3:223–224
college football, beginnings of, 3:218–221
conclusion concerning, 3:224
development of the NFL, 3:222
dollar amount paid to NFL, 3:223
extension of hosting teams, 3:220
first intercollegiate football game, 3:218
first professional game of, 3:221
"flying wedge" and violence, 3:220
formation of college conferences, 3:221
"Greatest Game Ever Played," 3:222
Harvard University and, 3:218, 3:219
Intercollegiate Football Association, 3:219
Jim Thorpe and, 3:222
McGill University and, 3:219
merger of NFL and AFL, 3:223
National Collegiate Athletic Association (NCAA), 3:220
National Football League Players Association, 3:223

NCAA and broadcasting, 3:224
NFL Europe league, 3:224
notable collegiate coaches, 3:220
overseas expansion of, 3:224
Princeton University and, 3:219
Princeton/Rutgers football games, 3:218–219
professional football, development of, 3:221–223
rugby and, 3:218
rules reform, 3:219–220
Super Bowl, 3:223
television contracts, 3:223–224
Thanksgiving Day Championship, 3:220
Theodore Roosevelt and, 3:218
unionization, 3:223
violence and, 3:218, 3:220
Walter Camp and, 3:220
William Chase Temple, 3:222
William "Pudge" Heffelfinger and, 3:221
Yale/Princeton football match, 3:219 (image)
football, Canadian, 3:225–229
amateurism and, 3:227–228
American influence on, 3:227, 3:228
Argonaut Football Club, 3:226
Burnside's rules, 3:227
Canadian Football Council (CFC), 3:228
Canadian Football League (CFL), 3:228
Canadian Intercollegiate Rugby Football Union (CIRFU), 3:227
Canadian Interuniversity Sport (CIS), 3:228
Canadian Rugby Union (CRU), 3:226–227
early football matches, 3:225
employment of naturalized Canadian players in, 3:228
expansion into America, 3:228
federal government legislation concerning, 3:228
formation of new unions, 3:226
Grey Cup games, 3:227
Harvard University and, 3:226
heel back rule, 3:226
Interprovincial Rugby Football Union (IRFU), 3:227
J. T. M. "Thrift" Burnside and, 3:227
markers in the history of, 3:225
McGill University and, 3:225–226
Ottawa football club, 3:225
professionalism in, 3:228
roots of, 3:225
rugby football and, 3:225
Rugby Football Union (RFU) rules, 3:225–226
rule changes, 3:226, 3:227
Toronto Argonaut Rowing Club and, 3:225

University of Toronto and, 3:226

Western Canada Rugby Football Union (WCRFU), 3:227

football, Gaelic, 2:83–85

All-Ireland Championship, 2:85

All-Ireland final, 2:83

All-Ireland Gaelic Football champions, 4:300–302

amateurism and, 2:85

Australian football and, 2:85

as a code of football, 2:83

Combined Irish Rugby Union, 2:83

explanation of, 2:84–85

Gaelic Athletic Association (GAA), 2:83–84

Gaelic football championship (first), 2:84

Irish diaspora communities and, 2:85

Irish Football Association, 2:83

Irish Republican Brotherhood (IRB), 2:83

popularity of, 2:83

football, National Collegiate Athletic Association champions, 4:269–271

football, National Football League/American Football League/Super Bowl champions, 4:261–263

Football Association of England (FA), 1:157

Football War (El Salvador and Honduras), 3:107–108

Footballers' Wives, 2:85–86

Formula One World champions, 4:351–352

foxhunting, British Isles, 2:87–89

adaptation to rural environment, 2:87

artificiality of, 2:86

attitudes toward, 2:88

barbed wire, 2:87–88

British identity and, 2:87

class and, 2:86

Countryside Alliance march, 2:88

criticism of, 2:88

"drag hunting," 2:89

exclusivity, 2:86, 2:88

hill foxes, 2:87

Hugh Meynell and, 2:86

Hunting with Dogs Act of 2004, 2:88–89

opposition to, 2:86, 2:88–89

rider with pack of beagles, 2:87 (image)

Royal Society for the Protection of Cruelty to Animals, 2:88

social change and, 2:88

women and, 2:87

foxhunting, North America, 3:229–230

Alexander Hamilton and, 3:229

American hound strains, 3:229

first subscription pack, 3:229

Fort Gibson Hunt, 3:229

George Washington and, 3:229

Gloucester Foxhunting Club, 3:229

history of, 3:229–230

horses, 3:230

importation of hounds, 3:229

livery of, 3:230

Masters of Foxhounds Association (MFHA), 3:230

number of registered foxhound packs, 3:230

scent hounds and, 3:230

structure of, 3:230

Thomas Jefferson and, 3:229

Fraser, Dawn (1937–), 1:388

Freeman, Cathy (1973–), 1:388–389

freestyle skating, Olympic medalists (Winter)

Men's Aerials, 4:242–243

Men's Ballet, 4:243

Men's Moguls, 4:242

Men's Ski Cross, 4:243

Women's Aerials, 4:243

Women's Ballet, 4:243

Women's Moguls, 4:243

Women's Ski Cross, 4:243

freestyle wrestling, Olympic medalists (Summer)

Men's Bantamweight, 4:209–210

Men's Featherweight, 4:210

Men's Flyweight, 4:214

Men's Heavyweight, 4:212–213

Men's Light Flyweight, 4:214

Men's Light Heavyweight, 4:214–215

Men's Lightweight, 4:210–211

Men's Middleweight, 4:212

Men's Super Heavyweight, 4:213

Men's Welterweight, 4:211

Women's Flyweight, 4:213

Women's Heavyweight, 4:213

Women's Lightweight, 4:213

Women's Middleweight, 4:213

French Open tennis championships, 2:315–317

Andrea Agassi, 2:316

champions of the Open era, 2:316

champions prior to the Open era, 2:315

Chang/Lendl match, 2:316

dates of, 2:315

the Four Musketeers, 2:316

Michael Chang, 2:316

playing surface of, 2:316, 2:317

Serena and Venus Williams, 2:317

French Open tennis championships (*continued*)
    Stade Roland Garros, 2:315
    Suzanne Lenglen, 2:316
frontier sports, Canada, 3:230–231
    Calgary Stampede, 3:231
    defining of, 3:230
    North West Mounted Police (NWMP) and, 3:230, 3:231
    rodeo and cattle-ranching competitions, 3:231
futsal (Uruguay), 3:108–109
    description of, 3:108
    Federación Internacional de Fútbol de Salón (International Federation of Indoor Football, FIFUSA), 3:109
    FIFA Futsal World Cup, 3:109
    first world championship, 3:109
    history of, 3:108
    key difference between indoor soccer and, 3:108
    spread of, 3:108

Gaelic Athletic Association, 2:89–93
    Anglo-Irish Treaty, 2:91
    Bloody Sunday and, 2:91
    Croke Park, 2:91, 2:92
    definition of games, 2:92
    Easter Rising, 2:90–91
    establishment of rules, 2:90
    ethos of, 2:90
    finances of, 2:92
    formation of, 2:89
    Gaelic Players Association (GPA), 2:92
    home rule and, 2:91
    importance of key principles of, 2:92–93
    inaugural gathering, 2:89–90
    Irish Amateur Athletic Association (IAAA), 2:90
    Irish Republican Brotherhood (IRB), 2:90
    John McKay and, 2:89, 2:90
    Maurice Davin and, 2:89, 2:90
    Michael Collins, 2:91
    Michael Cusack and, 2:89, 2:90
    murder of members of, 2:93
    popularity of, 2:90
    principal aim of, 2:90
    propaganda and, 2:90
    rival body, 2:90
    Rule 21, 2:92
    Sean Brown, 2:93
    Six Nations Championship, 2:92
    suspicion of, 2:90
    themes in the history of (dominant), 2:91–92
    in Ulster, 2:90

Games of the Newly Emerging Forces (GANEFO), 1:222–224
Gehrig, Lou (1903–1941), 3:231–232
    illness and death of, 3:232
    image of, 3:232
    reputation of, 3:231, 3:232
    statistics for, 3:232
gender and sport, Asia, 1:224–225
    China, 1:225
    India, 1:225
    Japan, 1:224
    Malaysia, 1:225
    Moslem women, 1:225
    Thailand, 1:225
gender and sport, British Isles, 2:93–98
    Alicia Thornton, 2:94
    aristocratic leisure class and modern sport, 2:93–94
    auto racing, 2:97
    blood paternity, 2:94
    boxing, 2:94
    Charlotte Cooper, 2:96
    consumerism and, 2:96
    Denis Brailsford on, 2:94
    in the early 19th century, 2:94–95
    education and sports, 2:95–96
    female sporting autobiography, 2:97
    football, 2:97
    gender terminology, 2:93
    gender testing and verification, 2:97
    horseracing, 2:94
    hygiene and health and sports, 2:95
    industrialization, 2:95
    Jennifer Hargreaves on, 2:96
    Lily Parr, 2:96–97
    major characteristics of preindustrial popular sports, 2:95
    Martina Bergman-Österberg, 2:96
    Mary Anne Talbot, 2:94
    Olympic Games and, 2:96, 2:97
    Olympic marathon, 2:97
    privatization, 2:94
    religion and sports, 2:95
    royal patronage, 2:94
    Royal Society of the Prevention of Cruelty to Animals (RSPCA), 2:95
    ski jumping, 2:97
    sports clubs, 2:94
    swimming and diving, 2:96
    transnational network of women's sporting interest, 2:96

Victor Bruce, 2:97

wrestling, 2:94

gender and sport, Canada, 3:232–234

    construction of women's bodies, 3:233

    culturally sanctioned displays of heterosexual femininity in sport, 3:233–234

    dominant discourse in, 3:233

    effeminate and gay athletes, 3:234

    forms of masculinity, 3:233

    ice hockey and, 3:233

    "Matchless Six," 3:233

gender and sport, Europe, 2:317–320

    biological determinism, 2:319

    contemporary issues in relation to, 2:319–320

    ethnic background and participation in sports, 2:318–319

    homosexuality and sport, 2:320

    masculinity concept, 2:318, 2:319–320

    obesity, 2:319

    scope of sport as gender normative, 2:318–319

    sex vs. gender, 2:317–318

    "sport is a feminist issue," 2:319

gender and sport, Latin America and the Caribbean, 3:109–111

    advocacy for equality, 3:110

    Brighton Convention, 3:110

    exclusion, 3:109

    femininity concept, 3:109–110

    masculinity concept, 3:109

    Women and Sport Commission, 3:110

gender and sport, Middle East and North Africa, 1:290–291

    Arwa Mutabagani and, 1:291

    Ghada Shouaa and, 1:290

    Hassiba Boulmerka and, 1:290

    image of, 1:290

    the Internet and, 1:291

    in the media, 1:291

    Nawal El Moutawakel and, 1:290

    recognition of women, 1:291

    religion and, 1:290–291

    Sheikha Naima Al-Ahmad Al-Sabah and, 1:291

gender and sport, United States, 3:234–239

    African American women and, 3:237

    All American Girls' Professional Baseball League, 3:236

    Babe Didrickson Zaharias, 3:236

    in basketball, 3:237

    construction of women's bodies, 3:234–235

    "female apologetic," 3:238

    gay men and, 3:238

    gender verification testing, 3:236

    historical overview of, 3:234–237

    homophobia, 3:238

    individual sports and femininity, 3:236

    institutionalized gender differences, 3:237

    Katie Hnida, 3:235 (image)

    lesbianism, 3:238

    male dominance, 3:236

    mass media and, 3:238

    race and, 3:234–235, 3:237

    regendering, 3:237–238

    selected gender comparison, 3:237–238

    in tennis, 3:237

    Title IX Education Amendment and, 3:237

German Olympic Sports Federation. *See* Deutscher Olympischer Sportbund

Gibson, Althea (1927–2003), 3:239

Gleneagles Agreement, 2:98

    apartheid and, 2:98

    approval of, 2:98

    importance of, 2:98

    Olympic Games and, 2:98

glima. See wrestling, Iceland (*glima*)

globalization and sport, 1:8–15

    collective affinity between global sponsors and sporting events, 1:10–12

    the corporo-economicus, 1:14

    embeddedness of sport and global corporatism, 1:11

    end of the nation question, 1:9–12

    genealogy of the nation, 1:9–10

    Indian Premier League, 1:11

    national cultures, 1:14

    negotiating differences, 1:14–15

    negotiating the nation, 1:12–13

    Olympic sponsorship, 1:11

    Red Bull Air Race World Series, 1:11

    representative subjectivities, 1:14

    single, multivocal, multinationally oriented texts, 1:15

    sport in a global world, 1:13

    Trans National Basketball Association, 1:11

golf, British Isles, 2:98–105

    Amateur Championship, 2:101

    ban on, 2:99–100

    British and Irish golf, 2:105

    British and U.S. golf, 2:104

    caddies, 2:104

    Champion's Belt, 2:101

golf, British Isles (*continued*)
the Claret Jug, 2:101
Edinburgh Silver Club, 2:99
equipment and production changes, 2:103
expansion of golf, 2:101–102
formal organization of, 2:99
golf clubs, 2:100, 2:101
golf course location and design, 2:101
golf industry, 2:101–102
golf-themed novel (first), 2:102
Grand National Tournament, 2:101
"The Great Triumvirate," 2:102, 2:103
gutta-percha golf ball, 2:100–101
Harry Vardon, 2:102, 2:103
Haskell ball, 2:103
Honourable Company of Edinburgh Golfers, 2:100
industrialization of the golf equipment production, 2:103–104
in Ireland, 2:102
Ireland and Scotland, 2:105
James Braid, 2:102
John Henry "J. H." Taylor, 2:102, 2:103
London and West Counties Golf Professionals Association, 2:103
multiple championship winners, 2:100
National Insurance Act (1923) and, 2:104
negative impacts on, 2:104
popularity of, 2:99, 2:100, 2:101
Prestwick Golf Club, 2:101
private golf clubs, 2:102
professional golfers, 2:102–103
Professional Golfers' Association (PGA), 2:103
professional tournament (first), 2:100
professional tournaments, 2:100–101
publications for, 2:102
railroads and, 2:102
Royal and Ancient (R&A) Golf Club, 2:103, 2:104
Royal Portrush Golf Club, 2:102
rubber core ball, 2:103
rules, first known set of, 2:100
Rules of Golf Committee, 2:103
Ryder Cup matches, 2:104
Schenectady putter, 2:103
Scottish clubs, 2:100
Society of St. Andrews Golfers, 2:100
Sphere and Tatler Cups, 2:103
St. Andrews, 2:99, 2:100, 2:104
teeing off at Kirkcaldy (1898), 2:99 (image)
television and, 2:105

Tom Morris, Old and Young, 2:101
tourism and, 2:105
U.S. Golf Association (USGA), 2:103, 2:104
Vardon Flyer, 2:103
Walker Cup matches, 2:104
women and, 2:104–105
written reference to (first), 2:99
golf, Europe, 2:321–322
continental golfing expansion, 2:321–322
European Ryder Cup, 2:322
famous golf courses in, 2:321
PGA European Tour, 2:322
sponsorship and purses, 2:322
golf, European Order of Merit
Official Money List Leader, 4:340
Order of Merit Leader, 4:339–340
Race to Dubai Leader, 4:339
golf, Latin America and the Caribbean, 3:111–112
Argentine Amateur Championship, 3:111
Asociación Argentina de Golf, 3:111
diffusion of, 3:111
elite-level golfing champions, 3:111–112
elite-level training centers, 3:112
first amateur championship, 3:111
introduction of, 3:111
leisure-oriented golf development, 3:112
Tour de Las Américas, 3:112
golf, major championships winners
Amateur Championship (Britain), Men, 4:316–318
Amateur Championship (Britain), Women, 4:318–320
British Open, Men, 4:329–331
British Open, Women, 4:322
Du Marier Classic (Women Only), 4:337
Kraft Nabisco Championship (Women Only), 4:336–337
LPGA Championship, 4:334–335
Master's (Men Only), 4:335–336
Nabisco Championshop (Women Only), 4:337
PGA Championship, 4:322–334
Title Holders Championship, 4:338
US Amateur, Men, 4:320–323
US Amateur, Women, 4:323–325
US Open, Men, 4:325–327
US Open, Women, 4:327–328
Women's Western Open, 4:338–339
golf, Oceana, 1:389–390
Australia, 1:389
New Zealand, 1:389
outlook for, 1:390

outstanding golfers from, 1:389, 1:390
women's golf, 1:390
golf, Olympic medalists (Summer)
  Men's Individual, 4:112
  Men's Team, 4:112
  Women's Individual, 4:112
golf, Sub-Saharan Africa, 1:129–131
  black golfers and, 1:130
  Bobby Locke and, 1:130
  Cape Golf Club, 1:130
  Gary Player and, 1:130, 1:131
  history of, 1:130
  notable black golfers from, 1:131
  notable white golfers from, 1:129
  Papa" Sewgolum and, 1:131
  racial segregation, 1:131
  Royal and Ancient Golf Club and, 1:131
  Royal Cape Club, 1:130
  Royal Nairobi Golf Club, 1:130
  Sun City and, 1:131
  Vincent Tshabalala and, 1:131
  Zanzibar Golf Club, 1:130
golf, United States and Canada, 3:240–246
  All-American Open, 3:242
  criticism of, 3:245
  first Amateur Championship, 3:240
  first golf courses, 3:240
  first PGA tournament, 3:241
  first U.S. Women's Amateur Championship, 3:241
  Junior Amateur Championship, 3:242
  the Masters, 3:242, 3:245
  National Negro Open, 3:244
  popularity of, 3:243
  Professional Golfers' Association of America (PGA),
    3:241, 3:242, 3:244
  public courses, 3:242
  race and, 3:244–245
  resort courses, 3:241–242
  Ryder Cup, 3:242, 3:243
  United Golfers Association (UGA), 3:244
  United States Golf Association (USGA), 3:240–241
  U.S. Open 1913, 3:241
  U.S. Open, early era of, 3:241
  Walker Cup, 3:241
  women's golf, 3:245
golf year-end #1 rankings
  men's year-end #1 official world golf ranking, 4:349–340
  Rolex women's year-end #1 official world golf ranking,
    4:349

Goolagong-Cawley, Evonne (1951–), 1:390–391
gouren. See wrestling, Brittany (gouren)
Grace, W. G. (1848–1915), 2:105–106
  career longevity, 2:105
  cheating and, 2:106
  date of birth, 2:105
  portrait of, 2:106
  reputation of, 2:105
  scoring records, 2:106
  technical innovations, 2:105
Graf, Stefanie Maria "Steffi " (1969–), 2:322–323
  birthplace of, 2:322
  post-playing career, 2:322–323
  statistics for, 2:322
  tax evasion, 2:322
Grand National, 2:106–107
  amount of purse, 2:107
  Becher's Brook fence, 2:107
  famous horse of, 2:107
  female riders, 2:107
  fences of, 2:107
  founding of, 2:107
  George Stevens, 2:107
  official running of (first), 2:107
  reputation of, 2:106–107
  severity of course, 2:107
  sponsor of (current), 2:107
Grange, Harold (1903–1991), 3:246–247
  birthplace of, 3:246
  image of, 3:246
  nickname of, 3:246
  place of death, 3:246
  post playing career of, 3:246–247
  reputation of, 3:246
Greco-Roman wrestling, 2:323–325
  famous Greco-Roman wrestlers, 2:324
  freestyle wrestling, 2:323
  governing body of, 2:323
  ground wrestling, 2:323
  image up, 2:324
  Olympic competition and, 2:323
  popularity of, 2:324
  rules of, 2:323
  upright wrestling, 2:323
  weight class, 2:323
  wrestling styles, 2:323
Greco-Roman wrestling, Olympic medalists (Summer)
  Men's Bantamweight, 4:215
  Men's Featherweight, 4:215–216

Greco-Roman wrestling, Olympic medalists (Summer)
    (*continued*)
  Men's Flyweight, 4:219
  Men's Heavyweight, 4:218
  Men's Light Flyweight, 4:219
  Men's Light Heavyweight, 4:219–220
  Men's Lightweight, 4:216–217
  Men's Middleweight, 4:217–218
  Men's Open, 4:220
  Men's Super Heavyweight, 4:218–219
  Men's Welterweight, 4:217
Green Bay Packers, 3:247
Gretzky, Wayne (1961–), 3:247–248
  controversy, 3:248
  image of, 3:248
  post-playing career of, 3:248
  reputation and, 3:247
  statistics for, 3:247
Gulf Cooperation Council Games (GCCG), 1:292
gymnastics, Czech, 2:325–326
  communist and, 2:326
  Miroslav Tyrš and, 2:325
  Olympic competition and, 2:325–326
  Sokol Organization and, 2:325
  Sokol teams, 2:325
gymnastics, Danish, 2:326–327
  Danish Gymnastics Federation (DGF), 2:326
  federations of, 2:327
  folk high schools and, 2:326, 2:327
  German gymnastics, 2:326
  J. C. F. GutsMuths and, 2:326
  Swedish gymnastics, 2:327
gymnastics, German (*Turnen*), 2:327–331
  adapting *Turnen* for schools, 2:328
  association founding, 2:328–329
  beginnings of, 2:327–328
  internationalization of, 2:330
  Nazism, 2:330
  Turnen faces competition, 2:329–330
  Turnen today, 2:330–331
  Turner federation, 2:330
  Turner movement, 2:329, 2:330
  Turnfeste and *Turnen*, 2:329, 2:330–331
  women and, 2:329
gymnastics, Romania, 2:331–333
  Andrea Raducan, 2:331 (image)
  history of, 2:331
  men and Olympic competition, 2:332

  Montreal Olympics 1976 and, 2:332
  Romanian Gymnastics Federation (RGF), 2:331
  women and Olympic competition, 2:331–332
gymnastics, Soviet/Russian, 2:333–334
  Alexandr Ditiatin, 2:334
  Elena Mukhina's injury, 2:334
  female gymnasts (1950s), 2:333
  female gymnasts (1980), 2:334
  Helsinki games (1952), 2:333
  Larissa Latynina, 2:333
  Larissa Petrik, 2:333
  Ludmilla Tourischeva, 2:333
  male gymnasts (1970s), 2:334
  Montreal Olympics and, 2:333–334
  Nelli Kim, 2:333–334
  Oksana Chusovitina, 2:334
  Olga Korbut, 2:333
  Soviet training programs, 2:334
  Svetlana Boginskaya, 2:334
gymnastics, Swedish, 2:334–335
  Franz Nachetegall, 2:335
  gymnastic system of, 2:335
  Pehr Henrik Ling and, 2:334–335
  physical activity in schools and, 2:335

Hadlee, Sir Richard (1951–), 1:391–392
the haka (New Zealand), 1:392–393
  "Ka Mate Ka Mate" haka, 1:392
  New Zealand All Blacks and, 1:392
  trademark rights, 1:392
  "war haka," 1:392
  women and, 1:392
Hamia, Cherif (1931–), 1:292–293
Hamm, Mia (1972–), 3:248–250
  accomplishments of, 3:248–249
  commercialization and, 3:249
  image of, 3:249
  philanthropy of, 3:249–250
Hammond, Wally (1903–1965), 2:107–108
  date of birth, 2:107
  reputation of, 2:107, 2:108
  scoring of, 2:107–108
Hampden Park, 2:108
Hampden Park Riot (1909), 2:108–109
handball, North Africa, 1:293
handball, Olympic medalists (Summer)
  Men's Handball, 4:113–115
  Women's Handball, 4:115–116

handball, team, 2:335–338
  European Handball Federation (EHF), 2:337
  governing bodies of, 2:337
  indoor version of, 2:335–336
  Olympic competition, 2:337
  outdoor versions of, 2:336
  playing of, 2:336–337
  purpose of, 2:336
  rules of, 2:336
  world championships, 2:337
handball, United States, 3:250–251
  competition types, 3:250
  governing body of, 3:250
  types of courts, 3:250
  U.S. Handball Association (USHA), 3:250
Hanlan, Edward (1855–1908), 3:251
Hansie Cronje match fixing scandal (South Africa), 1:131–132
Harlem Globetrotters, 3:251–252
  history of, 3:251
  image of, 3:252
  influence of, 3:252
  retired numbers of, 3:252
  uniqueness of, 3:251
Havelange, João (1916–), 3:112–113
Henie, Sonja (1912–1969), 2:338
Henley Royal Regatta, England, 2:109
  control of, 2:109
  course of, 2:109
  date of founding, 2:109
  reputation of, 2:109
Henley-on-Todd Regatta, 1:393
Heysel Stadium Disaster (Belgium), 2:338–339
Highland Games, Scotland, 2:109–111
  caber toss, 2:111
  at celebration, 2:110, 2:111
  dancing competition, 2:111
  events of, 2:110–111
  hammer throw, 2:111
  image of, 2:110
  migration of, 2:110
  oral tradition of, 2:109
  piping competition, 2:111
  popularity of, 2:110
  purpose of, 2:109
  "putting of the stone," 2:111
  records of (earliest), 2:110
  sheaf throw, 2:111
  weight throw, 2:111

Hillary, Sir Edmund (1919–2008), 1:393
Hillsborough Disaster, England, 2:111–112
  Bernard Murray and, 2:111
  David Duckenfield and, 2:111, 2:112
  death toll, 2:111
  effect of, 2:112
  reasons for, 2:111–112
Hobbs, Sir John Berry (1882–1963), 2:112–113
  image of, 2:112
  reputation of, 2:112
Hockey Night in Canada, 3:252–253
Hong Kong Sevens, 1:226
hooliganism, British Isles, 2:113–115
  BBC documentary on, 2:114
  cages and, 2:113
  club owners and, 2:113–114
  the "English Disease," 2:113
  Football Disorder Act, 2:114
  Heysel stadium disaster, 2:114
  Hillsborough disaster, 2:114
  "the Kop," 2:113
  Margaret Thatcher on, 2:114
  media and, 2:114
  memoirs of ex-hooligans, 2:114
  middle-class professionals, 2:114
  nickname for, 2:113
  origins of, 2:113
  rules of mayhem, 2:114
  as "self-fulfilling prophecy," 2:113
  Tony Blair on, 2:114
  Union of European Football Associations (UEFA), 2:114
hooliganism, European football (soccer), 2:339–342
  in Belgium, 2:340
  in Britain, 2:339–340
  British disease of, 2:339
  civil liberties and, 2:341
  club-level matches and, 2:341
  control measures, 2:340
  countries with fewer instances of, 2:340
  early history of, 2:339
  European Convention on Spectator Violence and Misbehaviour at Sports Events and in Particular Football Matches, 2:341
  in France, 2:340
  gang rivalries and, 2:339
  in Germany, 2:340
  in Greece, 2:340

hooliganism, European football (soccer) (*continued*)
  Heysel Stadium disaster, 2:340, 2:341
  hooligan cultures, existence of, 2:340
  influences on soccer-related violence, 2:341
  in Italy, 2:340
  in the Netherlands, 2:340
  as organized and disengaged from the game, 2:339
  organized violence, 2:340
  policy and, 2:341
  premediated violence, 2:340
  in Scotland, 2:340
  in Spain, 2:340
  stages of, 2:340
  Ultra groups, 2:341
  in Yugoslavia, 2:340
Hopman Cup (Australia), 1:394
horse racing, Australian and New Zealand, 1:394–396
  Australian Racing Board, 1:394
  Australian Special Metals Brisbane Cup Horse Race, 1:395 (image)
  Flemington racecourse, 1:395
  gambling laws, 1:394, 1:396
  international trends in, 1:396
  jumps racing, 1:394
  Melbourne Cup, 1:396
  New Zealand Thoroughbred Racing Inc., 1:394
  number of courses in, 1:394
  popularity of, 1:394, 1:396
  racing prize money, 1:396
  Sandy Race Course, 1:395
  sprint racing, 1:396
  Sydney Turf Club, 1:395
  Victoria Racing Club, 1:396
horse racing, British Isles, 2:115–121
  Aintree, 2:120
  amateur point-to-point cross-country races, 2:115
  betting interests, 2:117
  bookmaking, 2:120
  breeders, 2:121
  British Class races (traditional), 2:115
  British Horseracing Authority, 2:118
  British Horseracing Board, 2:118
  Cheltenham Gold Cup, 2:120
  Chester, 2:120
  class and, 2:115–1116
  conservatism in, 2:120
  Coolmore, 2:121
  courses in Britain, 2:119–120
  Curragh in Kildare, 2:121

economics, 2:118–119
  Fred Archer, 2:120
  General Stud Book, 2:118
  Gordon Richards, 2:120
  groupings of, 2:115
  Horse Racing Betting Levy Board, 2:119
  Horseracing Regulatory Authority (HRA), 2:118
  image of Epsom Races, 2:116
  Ireland and, 2:121
  Ireland's National Stud, 2:121
  Irish Derby, 2:121
  Irish National Hunt Steeplechase Committee, 2:121
  Jockey Club, 2:117, 2:118, 2:119
  jockeys, 2:120–121
  Joe Magrath, 2:121
  jump jockeys, 2:121
  jump races, 2:115
  length of season, 2:115
  Master of Hounds Point-to-point Association, 2:118
  modern sire bloodlines, 2:116
  National Hunt Committee, 2:118
  National Hunt racing, 2:120
  Newmarket, 2:119–120
  number of courses (2000), 2:119
  number of flats and fixtures in (2010), 2:120
  number of racing days, 2:119
  Paddy Prendergast, 2:121
  Peter Scudamore, 2:121
  photo finish, 2:120
  pony racing, 2:115
  Pony Racing Authority, 2:115
  popularity of, 2:115
  prestigious courses, 2:119
  prize money, 2:119
  public funding, 2:119
  public interest in, 2:117
  Racecourse Betting Control Board, 2:119
  Racing Calendar, 2:117–118, 2:121
  racing hunting horses over fences, 2:115
  racing organizations, 2:117–118
  regulation of, 2:118
  in Scotland, 2:115, 2:120
  starting stalls, 2:120
  Sunday racing, 2:120
  thoroughbred breeding, 2:116
  Tony McCoy, 2:121
  totalisator ("Tote") betting, 2:119, 2:120
  training stables, 2:120

type of, 2:115
Vincent O'Brien, 2:121
in Wales, 2:115
women and, 2:117
horse racing, United States, 3:253–263
American Stud Book, 3:258
American thoroughbred racing, important dates in, 3:262
Arabian racing, 3:261–262
Belmont Stakes, 3:258–259
betting, 3:255–256
Breeders' Cup, 3:259
Bulle Rock, 3:254
early history of, 3:254–255
facts about, 3:262–263
first "post parade," 3:259
harness racing, 3:259–260
Janus, 3:254
Kentucky and, 3:256–257
Kentucky Derby, 3:258
numbers/statistics for, 3:257
Preakness Stakes, 3:258
Quarter Horse, 3:254
Quarter Horse racing, 3:261
repopulating racing, 3:257–258
steeplechasing, 3:260–261
Triple Crown, 3:258
types of races in, 3:254
horseshoes (horseshoe pitching), 3:263–264
first governing body for, 3:263
National Horseshoe Pitchers Association of America (NHPA), 3:264
popularity of, 3:264
rules of, 3:263–264
Hungary vs. Soviet Union Olympic Water Polo match of 1956, 2:342–343
hurling, 2:121–122
bandy and, 2:122
cammag and, 2:122
camogie, 2:122
decline of, 2:121–122
extent of playing of, 2:122
Gaelic Athletic Association (GAA) and, 2:122
Gaelic football similarities, 2:122
history of the game, 2:121
Irish folklore and, 2:122
playing of, 2:122
relationship with other games, 2:122
revival of, 2:122

shinty and, 2:122
women's version of, 2:122
hurling, All-Ireland Hurling champions, 4:303–305

iaidō, 1:226
ice hockey, British Isles, 2:122–123
Berlin Olympic Games and, 2:122
British Ice Hockey Association, 2:123
British Universities Ice Hockey Association, 2:123
Carl Erhardt, 2:122–123
Colin Shields, 2:123
Elite Ice Hockey League (EIHL), 2:123
Ice Hockey World, 2:123
International Ice Hockey Federation, 2:122
Jimmy Foster, 2:122
popularity of, 2:123
Tony Hand, 2:123
unruliness and, 2:123
World Championship play, 2:123
ice hockey, Canada, 3:264–271
Allan Cup, 3:265
Canadian Amateur Hockey Association (CAHA), 3:265, 3:266, 3:267, 3:269, 3:270
commodification of, 3:265–266
cultural role of, 3:269
development of men's ice hockey, 3:265–267
development of women's ice hockey, 3:267–268
Hockey Canada, 3:266, 3:267, 3:269, 3:270
"McGill Rules," 3:264–265
National Hockey League (NHL), 3:265–266
Ontario Women's Hockey Association, 3:270
organization of, 3:269–270
origins of, 3:264–265
"Program of Excellence" (POE) program, 3:269–270
Stanley Cup, 3:265
women's national team (NWT), 3:270
ice hockey, Europe, 2:343–348
Czech Republic, 2:346
Finland, 2:347
Germany, 2:347
historical overview of, 2:343–346
major countries, overview of, 2:346–348
Russia/Soviet Union, 2:347–348
Sweden, 2:348
ice hockey, National Hockey League champions, 4:267–268
ice hockey, Olympic medalists (Winter)
Men's Ice Hockey, 4:234–238
Women's Ice Hockey, 4:239

ice hockey, United States, 3:271–274
  Amateur Hockey League (AHL), 3:271, 3:272
  college hockey, 3:273
  disabled hockey forms, 3:274
  first official hockey game, 3:271
  first professional hockey game, 3:271
  globalization and, 3:273
  International Professional Hockey League (IHL), 3:271
  memorable events in, 3:274
  National Hockey Association (NHA), 3:272
  National Hockey League (NHL), 3:272–273
  Olympic debut, 3:272
  origins of, 3:271
  Pacific Coast Hockey Association (PCHA), 3:272
  popularity of, 3:273, 3:274
  semiprofessional hockey, 3:271
  Sled (or sledge) Hockey program, 3:274
  Stanley Cup, 3:272
  U.S. Amateur Hockey Association (USAHA), 3:272
  Western Pennsylvania Hockey League (WPHL), 3:271
  women and, 3:273
ice hockey, World Ice Hockey champions, 4:307–308
Iditarod dogsled race, 3:274–275
  approximate length of, 3:274
  image of, 3:275
  Joe Redington Sr. and, 3:275
  reputation and, 3:275
Imperial/International Cricket Council (ICC), 2:123–125
  Anti-Corruption and Security Unit (ACSU), 2:124–125
  Anti-Doping Committee, 2:124
  categories of members, 2:124
  colonial mentality and, 2:124
  duties of, 2:124
  executive governing council, 2:124
  founding members of, 2:124
  ICC Code of Conduct, 2:124
  international tournaments, importance of, 2:124, 2:125
  Marylebone Cricket Club (MCC) and, 2:123
  purpose of, 2:124
  responsibilities of, 2:123
  satellite television and, 2:124
  taxation and, 2:124
imperialism and sport, 1:15–23
  sport and American imperialism, 1:19–22
  sport and British imperialism, 1:16–19
imperialism and sport, British Colonial Africa, 1:132–136
  Andre Odendaal on, 1:133, 1:134
  Cain and Hopkins on (2002), 1:132
  cricket and, 1:133, 1:134

"cultural diffusion," 1:132–133
  discrimination, 1:134
  elite schools and, 1:133
  indigenous clubs, 1:134
  J. A. Mangan on (1998), 1:132
  Rhodesian Cricket Union, 1:134
  Williams on (2001), 1:133
indigenous (Aboriginal Australian) Cricket Tour of England (1868), 1:396–398
Indurain, Miguel (1964–), 2:348–349
Indy Car Series champions, 4:353
IndyCar auto racing, 3:275–278
  AAA Championship race series, 3:276, 3:277
  "The Brickyard" legacy, 3:276, 3:277
  Brooklands racecourse, 3:276
  documentation of, 3:276
  early auto races, 3:276
  Formula One World Championship, 3:277
  "Gasoline Alley," 3:277
  Indianapolis 500, 3:277
  Indianapolis 500, inaugural race, 3:276
  Indianapolis Speedway, 3:276, 3:277
International Amateur Athletic Federation, 2:349–351
  administration of, 2:350
  amateurism, 2:349
  congress of, 2:350
  Green Project of, 2:350
  growth of, 2:349
  headquarters of, 2:350
  Kids' Athletics program, 2:350
  program expansion, 2:349–350
  purpose of, 2:349
  responsibility of, 2:350
  World Athletics Day, 2:350
International Cricket Council Cricket World Cup champions, 4:276
International Olympic Committee, 1:23–26
  See also Olympic movement
international relations and sport, 1:26–28
  1936 Olympic Games example, 1:26
  boycotts/sanctions, 1:27
  disapproval/punishment and, 1:27
  domestic/internal lawless and, 1:28
  Olympic movement and, 1:26, 1:28
  political recognition and, 1:27–28
  politically motivated violence, 1:27
  public diplomacy/propaganda, 1:27
  rapprochement and diplomatic dialogue, 1:26–27
  rapprochement within conflict affected countries, 1:27

social change and, 1:28

symbolic power of sport, 1:26

United Nations Educational, Scientific, and Cultural Organization (UNESCO), 1:28

United Nations special advisor, 1:28

International Rugby Board Rugby World Cup champions

Men, 4:275

Women, 4:275

International Rules football, 1:398

International Society for the History of Physical Education and Sport, 2:351

"The Invincibles." *See* New Zealand All Blacks of 1924 ("The Invincibles")

Iowa Girls High School Athletic Union (IGHSAU), 1857 rules of, 3:180–181

Iran and sport since the Islamic "Revolution," 1:293–295

chaos and mutual distrust (ca. 1978 to early 1980s), 1:293–294

uneasy compromise (ca. early 1980s to mid-1990s), 1:294

open conflict (mid-1990s to present), 1:294–295

Iraq, Baath regime and sport in, 1:295–296

Nadi El Rachid, 1:295

Oudaye, 1:295, 1:296

sanction against, 1:295–296

Irish diaspora and sport, 2:125–126

in Australia, 2:125

baseball and, 2:125

basketball and, 2:125

boxing and, 2:125

Celtic Football Club, 2:126

Gaelic Athletic Association (GAA), 2:125

in New Zealand, 2:125–126

in the United States, 2:125

Islamic Solidarity Games of 2005 (Saudi Arabia), 1:296–297

Al-Saud family and, 1:296

image of, 1:297

patronage of, 1:296

purpose of, 1:296

Islamism and sport, 1:297–299

conclusion concerning, 1:298–299

importance of sport in, 1:298

Islamic Brotherhood in Egypt, 1:298

Islamist movements, 1:298

Islamist movements, range of, 1:297–298

Kuwaiti Islamic Constitutional Movement, 1:298

Tunisian Islamic Party, El-Nahdha, 1:298

Isle of Man motorcycle races, 2:126

Italian Football Scandal of 2006 (Calciopoli), 2:351–352

match-fixing allegations, 2:351–352

outcome of, 2:352

punishments for, 2:352

teams involved in, 2:352

Jack Johnson–Tommy Burns Fight, Sydney (1908), 1:398–399

Jackson, Marjorie (1931–), 1:399

jai alai, 3:278

amateurism and, 3:278

betting, 3:278

gender and, 3:278

International Jai Alai Player Association, 3:278

origins of, 3:278

playing of, 3:278

James, C. L. R. (1901–1989), 3:113–114

James, LeBron (1984–), 3:278–279

jeu de paume, Olympic medalists (Summer), 4:122

Jeux de la Francophonie, 2:352–353

Jeux de la Francophonie of 2005 (Niger), 1:136

Johnson, Ben, scandal at the 1988 Olympics, 3:279 (image), 3:279–280

Johnson, Jack (1878–1946), 3:280–281

arrest of, 3:281

death of, 3:281

early career of, 3:280–281

"Fight of the Century," 3:281

image of, 3:280

racism and, 3:281

Jones, Robert (Bobby) Tyre (1902–1971), 3:281–282

accomplishments of, 3:281–282

legacy of, 3:282

post-playing career, 3:282

Jordan, Michael (1963–), 3:282–284

as basketball icon, 3:282

community involvement, 3:284

economic impact of, 3:283–284

image of, 3:283

Jordan brands, 3:283

jousting, 2:353–355

description of, 2:354–355

early form of, 2:354

early goal of, 2:354

fictional model of, 2:353–354

historical form of, 2:353

as historical pageant, 2:354

the horse, 2:354

joules produced in, 2:355

jousting (*continued*)
    the lance, 2:354
    pas d'armes, 2:354
    pretexts for, 2:353–354
    psychological barrier, 2:355
    round-robin jousting, 2:354
    scoring, 2:354
    the shield, 2:354
    as substitute for battle, 2:354
    training exercises, 2:355
    varieties of, 2:355
    water jousting, 2:355
judo, 1:226–227
judo, Olympic medalists (Summer)
    Men's Half Heavyweight, 4:124–125
    Men's Half Lightweight, 4:123
    Men's Half Middleweight, 4:124
    Men's Heavyweight, 4:125
    Men's Individual, 4:122–123
    Men's Lightweight, 4:123
    Men's Middleweight, 4:124
    Men's Open Category, 4:125–126
    Women's Extra Lightweight, 4:126
    Women's Half Heavyweight, 4:127
    Women's Half Lightweight, 4:126
    Women's Half Middleweight, 4:126–127
    Women's Heavyweight, 4:127
    Women's Lightweight, 4:126
    Women's Middleweight, 4:127
jujitsu, 1:227–228
jukskei (South Africa), 1:136–137

kaatsen, 2:355–356
    distribution of, 2:355–356
    history of, 2:356
    number of players of, 2:356
    origin of, 2:356
    tennis and, 2:356
    understanding of, 2:356
kabaddi (aka Hu-Tu-Tu, Ha-Do-Do), 1:228
Kahanamoku, Duke (1890–1968), 3:284–25
    accomplishments of, 3:284–285
    death of, 3:285
    honors to, 3:285
Karaiskakis Stadium disaster, 2:356–357
karate, 1:228–229
    name change, 1:228–229
    popularity of, 1:229

roots of, 1:228
schools of, 1:229
kendo, 1:229–231
    grading system of, 1:230
    image of, 1:230
    main elements of, 1:229
    popularity of, 1:230
    roots of, 1:229
Kentucky Derby, 3:285–286
    date of, 3:285
    distance of, 3:285
    popularity of, 3:285
    reputation of, 3:285
    tragic accident at, 3:285
Khan, Imran (1952–), 1:231–232
    birthplace of, 1:231
    charity work and, 1:232
    controversies and, 1:231
    criticism of, 1:232
    education of, 1:231
    image of, 1:231
    Pakistan and, 1:231
    politics and, 1:231–232
    statistics for, 1:231
Killy, Jean-Claude (1943–), 2:357
King, Billie Jean (1943–), 3:286–287
    "Battle of the Sexes" match, 3:286
    personal life, 3:286
    plaudits for, 3:286–287
    reputation of, 3:286
    women's tennis and, 3:286
Kisumu Youth Football Association (KYFA), 1:157
Klammer, Franz (1953–), 2:358
Knight, Philip Hamson (1938–), and Nike Corporation,
        3:287–288
    brand development, 3:287
    competition with Reebok, 3:287
    controversies, 3:288
    marketing and, 3:287–288
    Nike logo, 3:287
    Nike's net worth, 3:287
    reputation of, 3:287
    slogan development, 3:287–288
knur and spell, England, 2:126–127
    betting and, 2:127
    course for, 2:127
    Joseph Strutt on, 2:127
    playing of, 2:126

spring trap, 2:126–127
    stick for, 2:127
kolven, 2:358–359
    origins of, 2:358
    playing of, 2:358
    popularity of, 2:358
    women and, 2:359
Korbut, Olga (1955–), 2:359
korfball, 2:360
    distinguishing rules of, 2:360
    Nico Broekhuysen, 2:360
    popularity of, 2:360
kurash, 1:232–233

L' équipe FLN (Algeria), 1:299
la crosse, Olympic medalists (Summer), 4:128
La Liga, 2:361–362
    dominant teams of, 2:361
    FC Barcelona, 2:361
    La Liga trophy, 2:362 (image)
    original clubs of Primera División, 2:361
    politics and, 2:361–362
    proper name of, 2:361
    ranking of, 2:361
    Real Madrid, 2:361
la soule, 2:363–364
    date of origin, 2:363
    games related to, 2:363
    playing of, 2:363
    revival of, 2:364
    rules of, 2:363
Lacoste, René (1904–1996), 2:360–361
lacrosse, 3:288–290
    Beers's "Laws of Lacrosse," 3:289
    in Canada, 3:289, 3:290
    Canadian nationalism and, 3:289
    current status of, 3:290
    indoor version of, 3:290
    Mohawk boys playing lacrosse, 3:289 (image)
    Montreal Shamrocks and, 3:289–290
    Native American versions of, 3:288
    origins of, 3:288
    popularity of, 3:289–290
    restructuring of, 3:289
Langer, Bernhard (1957–), 2:362–363
    accolades for, 3:363
    birthplace of, 2:362
    statistics for, 2:362

lapta, 2:363
    revival of, 2:363
    Russia and, 2:363
    similar games to, 2:363
Laver, Rod (1938–), 1:399–400
lawn bowling, Australia and New Zealand, 1:400–402
    Asia Pacific Bowls Championship, 1:401 (image)
    Auckland Bowling Club, 1:400
    first recorded game in Australasia, 1:400
    first set of bowls, 1:400
    Melbourne Bowls Club, 1:400
    New South Wales Bowling Association, 1:400
    women competitors, 1:400
    World Championships, 1:402
lawn bowling, British Isles, 2:127–128
    cash prizes, 2:128
    decline of, 2:128
    English Bowling Association, 2:127
    English Women's Bowling Association, 2:127
    history of, 2:127
    image of, 2:128
    indoor game of, 2:127–128
    international competition, 2:127
    London County Cricket Club, 2:127
    popularity of, 2:127
    Scottish Bowling Association, 2:127
    Southampton Bowling Club, 2:127
    Southsea Open Bowls Tournament, 2:127
    W. G. Grace and, 2:127
legal liability in sport, 1:28–34
    assumption of risk, 1:31
    landowner liability, 1:32–33
    liability waivers and releases, 1:30–31
    negligence liability principles, 1:28–29
    participant liability, 1:31
    postinjury duty, 1:30
    primary assumption of risk, 1:31–32
    spectator liability, 1:30
    sports coach legal duties, 1:29–30
Lenglen, Suzanne (1899–1938), 2:364
Lillee, Dennis Keith (1949–), 1:402
Linares, Omar "El Niño" (1967–), 3:114–115
Lindrum, Walter (1898–1960), 1:402–403
literature and sport, British Isles, 2:128–132
    Alec Waugh, 2:131
    Alexander Pope on, 2:130
    angling and, 2:129
    Arsenal Football Club, 2:132

literature and sport, British Isles (*continued*)
Arthur Conan Doyle, 2:131
The Blinder (Hines), 2:131
The Castle of Health (Elyot), 2:129
cockfighting and, 2:129
The Compleat Angler, or the Contemplative Man's Recreation (Walton), 2:129
cricket and, 2:129, 2:130, 2:131
The Cricket Match (de Selincourt), 2:131
The Cricketers of My Time (Nyren and Cowden-Clarke), 2:130
The Damned United (Clough), 2:131
Daniel Defoe on, 2:130
The Dunciad (Poe), 2:130
Edmund Spenser on, 2:129
England, Their England (Macdonnell), 2:131
Fever Pitch (Hornby), 2:132
Finnegan's Wake (Joyce), 2:131
football and, 2:129, 2:131
The Football Factory (King), 2:131
George Whyte-Melville, 2:130
Goalkeepers Are Crazy (Glanville), 2:131
The Governour (Elyot), 2:129
horse racing and, 2:132
hunting and, 2:129, 2:130
importance of, 2:132
Joseph Addison on, 2:130
jousting and, 2:129
Le Morte D'Arthur (Malory), 2:129
The Loneliness of the Long Distance Runner (Sillitoe), 2:131
northern rugby league, 2:131
P. G. Wodehouse, 2:131
Pierce Egan, 2:130
poets of the interval period, 2:131
poets on, 2:132
Pro: An English Tragedy (Hamilton), 2:131
pugilism and, 2:130
R. S. Surtees, 2:130
Robert Bridges, 2:131
Robinson Crusoe (Defoe), 2:130
Samuel Pepys on, 2:129–130
Sir Gawain and the Green Knight, 2:129
soccer and, 2:131
The Son of Grief (Carew), 2:131
specialist sporting fiction, 2:130
Steve Redhead on, 2:132
This Sporting Life (Storey), 2:131
The Thistle and the Grail (Jenkins), 2:131
Tom Brown's Schooldays (Hughes) and, 2:130
voices of dissent in, 2:130, 2:131
Windsor Forest (Poe), 2:130
yachting and, 2:129
Lombardi, Vince (1918–1970), 3:290–291
birthplace of, 3:290
college coaching career, 3:290
Green Bay Packers and, 3:290–291
New York Giants and, 3:290
popular culture and, 3:291
Lomu, Jonah (1975–), 1:403–404
London Marathon, 2:132–133
charity and, 2:132, 2:133
image of, 2:133
London Marathon Charitable Trusty, 2:133
participation in, 2:132
sponsorship, 2:133
Louis, Joe (1914–1981), 3:291–292
birthplace of, 3:291
burial of, 3:291
popularity of, 3:291
postretirement life of, 3:291
ring record, 3:291
Lovelock, Jack (1910–1949), 1:404
luge. *See* sliding sports (bobsleigh, luge, and skeleton)
luta livre (Brazil), 3:115
equipment, 3:115
globalization of, 3:115
Mexico's *lucha livre* and, 3:115
origins of, 3:115
Ultimate Fighting Championship (UFC) and, 3:115

Macau Grand Prix, 1:233
Maccabiah Games, 2:364–366
1932 games, 2:365
1935 games, 2:365
1950 games, 2:366
1973 games, 2:366
1997 games, 2:366
2001 games, 2:366
2009 games, 2:366
athlete defections, 2:365
date of first games, 2:365
divisions of, 2:364
image of, 2:365
Maccabi World Union (MWU), 2:365
sports of, 2:364–365
Maghrebin Games, 1:299–300
inter-Maghrebin political relations and, 1:300

purpose of, 1:299
violence and, 1:300
Major League Baseball, 3:292–294
    American League, 3:292
    American League teams, 3:292
    Babe Ruth, 3:293
    Babe Ruth at bat, ca. 1920, 3:292 (image)
    Boston Braves, 3:293
    Byron Bancroft "Ban" Johnson, 3:292
    as a cartel, 3:292, 3:293
    Cincinnati Red Stockings, 3:292
    commissioner of baseball, 3:293
    current status of, 3:294
    development of, 3:292–293
    financial growth of, 3:293–294
    financial strategy of, 3:293
    "the great baseball war," 3:292
    Jackie Robinson, 3:293
    legends of, 3:293
    National Association of Professional Baseball Players,
        3:292
    national commission, 3:292–293
    National League of Professional Base Ball Clubs
        (National League), 3:292
    National League teams, 3:292
    New York Yankees, 3:292, 3:293
    special status of, 3:293
    Sport Broadcasting Act (1983), 3:293
    Supreme Court ruling on, 3:293
    television and, 3:293
Major League Baseball World Series champions,
    4:265–267
Major League Soccer, United States, 3:294–295
    current status of, 3:295
    "designated player rule " (Beckham Rule),
        3:295
    development of, 3:294
    FIFA World Cup (1994) and, 3:294
    Landon Donavan and, 3:295
    marginalization of, 3:294
    MLS championship, 3:295
    notable players for, 3:294
    soccer specific stadiums, 3:295
Makybe Diva (1999–), 1:404–405
    Melbourne Cup wins, 1:404
    original name, 1:404
    significance of Melbourne Cup wins, 1:404
    sire of, 1:404
    trainers of, 1:404–405

Man o' War (1917–1947), 3:295–296
    grave site of, 3:296
    image of, 3:296
    jockey of, 3:296
    nickname of, 3:295
    owner of, 3:296
    record of, 3:296
    reputation of, 3:295–296
Manchester United Munich Air Disaster, 2:133–134
Mantle, Mickey (1931–1995), 3:296–297
    birthplace of, 3:296
    death of, 3:297
    nickname of, 3:297
    popularity of, 3:297
    record of, 3:297
Maracanã Stadium (Brazil), 3:115–116
    capacity of, 3:115
    image of, 3:116
    management of, 3:115
    new investments in, 3:115
    reforms of, 3:115
Maradona, Diego (1960–), 3:116–117
    accomplishments of, 3:117
    birthplace of, 3:116
    controversy and, 3:117
    post-playing careers, 3:117
    reputation of, 3:117
    World Cup play (1986), 3:117
Marciano, Rocky (1923–1969), 3:297–297
    amateur record of, 3:297
    birth name, 3:297
    Joe Louis fight, 3:298
    place of birth, 3:297
    posthumous honors, 3:298
    professional record of, 3:298
martial arts, Europe, 2:366–367
    definition of, 2:366
    globalization and, 2:367
    Historical European martial arts, 2:366–367
    Olympic competition and, 2:367
Marylebone Cricket Club (MCC), 2:134–135
    club colors, 2:135
    club sides, 2:135
    England and Wales Cricket Board, 2:135
    founding of, 2:134
    grounds of, 2:135
    importance of, 2:134
    membership of (current), 2:134
    prestige of, 2:135

Marylebone Cricket Club (MCC) (*continued*)
 Spirit of Cricket Test Series, 2:135
 Thomas Lord and, 2:134, 2:135
 Victorian pavilion of, 2:135
 William Nicholson and, 2:135
 William Ward and, 2:135
Massey, Arnaud (1877–1950), 2:367–368
Matthews, Sir Stanley (1915–2000), 2:135–136
Mays, Willie (1931–), 3:298–299
 accolades for, 3:299
 birthplace of, 3:298
 "The Catch," 3:299
 military service, 3:298
 in the Negro American League, 3:298
 New York Giants and, 3:298–299
 posts playing career, 3:299
 statistics for, 3:299
 in Triple-A ball, 3:298
McKay, Heather (1941–), 1:405
Meads, Colin Earl (1936–), 1:406
media and sport, 1:34–37
 cultural politics of transnational sports media, 1:35–36
 transnational media sport structures, 1:34–35
media and sport (Asia), 1:233–235
 newspapers, 1:233
 politics and, 1:234
 television, 1:234
media and sport in the Arab World, 1:300–301
 Abu-Dhabi Sport, 1:301
 Al Jazeera Sport, 1:301
 ART Sport, 1:301
 Canal Plus, 1:301
 liberalization process of TV broadcasting, 1:300
 Showtime Arabia, 1:301
Mediterranean Games of 1975 (Algiers), 1:301–302
Mekhloufi, Rachid (1936–), 1:302
Melbourne Cricket Ground (MCG), 1:406–407
Melbourne Cup, 1:407–408
 image of, 1:407
 popularity of, 1:407, 1:408
 sponsor of, 1:408
 Victoria Racing Club (VRC) and, 1:407
 Victoria Turf Club and, 1:407
Merckx, Eddy (1945–), 2:368
migrations, diasporas, and sports in the Middle East and
 North Africa, 1:302–305
 colonialism, 1:303–304
 conclusion concerning, 1:305
 Hassiba Boulmerka, 1:303 (image)

 immigrant identity crisis, 1:304–305
 labor migration, 1:304
 nationality, 1:304
Milla, Roger (1952–), 1:137–138
Miller, Keith Ross (1919–2004), 1:408–409
miniature golf, 3:299–301
 boom in, 3:300
 collapse of market, 3:300
 expansion of, 3:299–300
 Fairyland course, 3:300
 Fairyland Manufacturing, 3:300
 Miniature Golf Courses of America (MGCA), 3:300
 names for, 3:299
 Putt-Putt, Inc., 3:301
 roots of, 3:299
 survival and globalization of, 3:300–301
 Thistle Dhu course, 3:299
 Tom Thumb Golf, 3:300
"Miracle on Ice" of 1980, 3:301 (image), 3:301–302
missionaries and sport in Africa, 1:138–139
Mitchell Report. *See* steroid scandal in baseball and the
 Mitchell Report
modern pentathlon, 2:369
 disciplines of, 2:369
 governing body of, 2:369
 marginalization of, 2:369
 modification of rules, 2:369
 scoring, 2:369
 women and, 2:369
modern pentathlon, Olympic medalists (Summer)
 Men's Individual, 4:128–129
 Men's Team, 4:129
 Women's Individual, 4:129
Monday Night Football, United States, 3:302–303
motorcycle racing (Europe), 2:369–371
 championships of, 2:370
 dominant manufacturers, 2:371
 European stars of, 2:371
 first international competitions, 2:370
 Gottlieb Daimler and, 2:369
 governing body of, 2:370
 image of, 2:370
 Nikolaus Augustus Otto and, 2:370
mountain bike, Olympic medalists (Summer)
 Men's Cross-Country, 4:86
 Women's Cross-Country, 4:86
mountain climbing, British Isles, 2:136–139
 Alpine Club, 2:136, 2:137
 Alpine Journal, 2:136

Climbers' Club, 2:137
Climbing in Britain (Barford), 2:138
domestic rock climbing, 2:136–137
Fell and Rock Climbing Club, 2:137
Geoffrey Winthrop Young, 2:137
impact on British public psyche, 2:136
innovations in, 2:137
Joe Brown, influence of, 2:138
Ladies Alpine Club, 2:137
Ladies Scottish Climbing Club, 2:137
Leslie Stephen on, 2:137
Mountain Heritage Trust, 2:138
Mountaineering Council (BMC), 2:137
Mountaineering Council of Scotland (MCofS),
    2:138
Mountaineering Ireland (MI), 2:138
Napes Needle ascent, 2:136
Pinnacle Club, 2:137
Scottish Mountaineering Club, 2:137
women in, 2:137
mountaineering (Himalayas), 1:235–236
muay thai, 1:236
Much Wenlock Games, England, 2:139
Murrayfield Stadium, 2:139–140
    reputation of, 2:139
    Scottish Rugby Union (SRU), 2:139
    seating capacity of, 2:139
    significant changes to, 2:139
Muscular Christianity, 2:140–143
    Beyond a Boundary (James), 2:143
    "Broad Church" movement, 2:141
    C. A. R. James on, 2:143
    Charles Kingsley and, 2:140, 2:141–142
    Christian Socialism, 2:141
    cult of athleticism, 2:141, 2:142
    evolving idea of, 2:140
    explanation of, 2:140
    influence of, 2:142–143
    Man and Wife (Collins), 2:142
    morality and, 2:140
    origins of, 2:140
    Pierre de Coubertin, 2:142
    Rugby School, 2:141
    Thomas Arnold, 2:141
    Thomas Hughes and, 2:140, 2:142
    Tom Brown's Schooldays (Hughes) and, 2:141, 2:142,
        2:143
    Wilkie Collins on, 2:142
music and sport, 1:37–39

Nadal, Rafael (1986–), 2:371–372
Nakache, Alfred (1915–1983), 1:305
Namath, Joseph William (1943–), 3:303–304
    birthplace of, 3:303
    celebrity status of, 3:304
    image of, 3:303
    significance of, 3:304
NASCAR Cup champions, 4:350–351
National Association for Stock Car Auto Racing
        (NASCAR), 3:304–308
    Bill France Sr. and, 3:304, 3:305, 3:307
    car/racer development, 3:306
    compared with Formula One racing, 3:304
    Dale Earnhardt's death, 3:308
    date of first race, 3:305
    foundational ethic of, 3:304
    founding of, 3:304
    Grand National, 3:305–306
    Greg Biffle and race car, 3:305 (image)
    important races and racetracks, 3:306
    incorporation of, 3:305
    Nextel Cup, 3:307
    notable drivers in, 3:307–308
    point system, 3:306
    popular culture and, 3:304–305, 3:308
    R.J. Reynolds tobacco company and, 3:307
    sponsorship, 3:306–307
    Sprint Cup, 3:307
    "Strictly Stock" series, 3:305, 3:306
    television and, 3:307
    Winston Cup series, 3:307
National Basketball Association, 3:308–310
    American Basketball Association (ABA) and, 3:309
    Basketball Association of America (BAA), 3:308
    date of establishment, 3:308
    difficulties of (1970s), 3:309
    difficulties of (early), 3:308
    the "Dream Team," 3:310
    expansion of, 3:309
    genesis of, 3:308
    internationalization of, 3:310
    notable players, 3:309–310
    notable rivalries in, 3:309
    number of teams in (current), 3:310
    racial integration and, 3:309
    rejuvenation of, 3:309–310
    success of (current), 3:310
National Basketball Association champions,
        4:263–264

National Collegiate Athletic Association, 3:310–312
  Association for Intercollegiate Athletics for Women (AIAW), 3:311
  as a cartel, 3:311
  compliance and enforcement powers, 3:310, 3:311
  distribution of revenue, 3:311
  divisions in (1973), 3:311
  as an economic agency, 3:312
  eligibility and amateurism, 3:310
  Executive Committee of, 3:311
  executive directors of (current), 3:312
  governance and regulatory power, 3:311
  headquarters of, 3:312
  operating expenses (current), 3:312
  original name of, 3:310
  original purpose of, 3:310
  Sanity Code of Ethical Practices, 3:310
  television and, 3:310, 3:311
  Title IX of the Education Amendments and, 3:311
  Walter Byers and, 3:310–311
National Collegiate Athletic Association Basketball champions
  Men, 4:272–273
  Women, 4:273–274
National Collegiate Athletic Association Football champions, 4:269–271
National Football League championship game of 1958, 3:315
  criticism of, 3:315
  description of game, 3:315
  importance of, 3:315
National Football League (NFL), 3:312–313
  Alvin "Pete" Rozelle and, 3:314
  American culture and, 3:314
  American Football League (AFL) formation, 3:313
  Arizona Cardinals, 3:312
  Chicago Bears, 3:312
  date of first championship game, 3:312
  date of formal organization, 3:312
  European development leagues, 3:314
  Green Bay Packers, 3:312
  Jim Thorpe and, 3:312
  merger of leagues, 3:313
  number of franchises, 3:312
  popularity of (current), 3:314
  popularity of (early), 3:312–313
  postmerger challenges to, 3:313–314
  racial integration and, 3:312
  Super Bowl, 3:314

Super Bowl (first), 3:313 (image)
  television and, 3:314
National Football League/American Football League/Super Bowl winners, 4:261–263
National Hockey League champions, 4:267–268
National Hockey League (NHL), 3:315–317
  Boston Bruins, 3:316
  date of formal organization of, 3:316
  expansion of, 3:316
  labor issues, 3:316
  national culture and, 3:316–317
  number of teams in, 3:315
  "Original Six," 3:316
  "Pond Hockey," 3:316
  racial integration and, 3:316
  Stanley Cup, 3:315–316
  toughness and, 3:316
  Wayne Gretzky, 3:316
  World Hockey Association (WHA), 3:316
Native American sports, 3:317–320
  Aboriginal Sport Circle, 3:318, 3:319
  Beers's "Laws of Lacrosse," 3:318
  Choctaw Indians playing lacrosse, 3:318 (image)
  establishment and promotion of, 3:318–319
  lacrosse, 3:317–318
  Montreal Lacrosse Club (MLC), 3:318
  National Lacrosse Association (NLA), 3:318
  Native American Sports Council (NASC), 3:319
  North American Indigenous Games (NAIG), 3:319
  notable Indian sports, 3:317
Navratilova, Martina (1956–), 2:372
Negro Baseball Leagues, 3:320–322
  Association of Amateur Baseball Players (PAABBP), 3:320
  attempts to organize leagues, 3:321
  Chicago American Giants, 3:321
  Chicago Unions, 3:321
  Cuban Giants, 3:320, 3:321
  Cuban X Giants, 3:321
  Eastern Colored League (ECL), 3:322
  the Great Depression and, 3:322
  National Association of Colored Baseball Clubs of the United States and Cuba (NACBC), 3:321
  National League of Colored Base Ball Players, 3:321
  Negro American League, 3:322
  Negro National League (NNL), 3:321–322
  Negro National League (NNL), second, 3:322
  Negro Southern League (NSL), 3:322
  Negro World Series, 3:322

nucleus teams of Negro Leagues, 3:321
Page Fence Giants, 3:321
Philadelphia Pythians, 3:320
reason for, 3:320
Southern League of Colored Baseballists, 3:320–321
St. Louis Black Stockings, 3:320
Nepia, George (1905–1986), 1:409
netball, Australia, 1:409–411
All Australian Women's Basketball Association, 1:410
ANZ Championship, 1:410
Fast Net competition, 1:410
origins of, 1:409–410
outstanding players of, 1:411
popularity of, 1:409, 1:410
World Championships dominance, 1:410
netball, British Isles, 2:143–146
All England Netball Association, 2:145
All England Netball Association (AENA), 2:145
All England Women's Association for Net Ball and
Other Hand Ball Games, 2:145
date of foundation of, 2:145
Dorothie Malone and, 2:145
emancipation of women and, 2:144
emergence of, 2:144
England Netball, 2:145
growth and development of, 2:145
Netball Ireland, 2:145
Netball Scotland, 2:145
organization of netball in, 2:145
playing area of, 2:143
playing of, 2:143
relationship with basketball, 2:144
rules of, 2:144
traditional form of, 2:143–144
versions of, 2:143
netball, New Zealand, 1:411–412
first national tournament, 1:411
international competition, 1:412
New Zealand Basketball Association (NZBA), 1:411,
1:412
origins of, 1:411
provincial associations, 1:411
salaries of top players, 1:412
netball, Pacific Islands, 1:412–413
netball, South Africa, 1:139–140
apartheid and, 1:139
distinct style of, 1:140
image of, 1:140
prominence of, 1:140

netball, West Indies, 3:117–118
Barbados and, 3:118
Caribbean Netball Association, 3:118
gender stereotypes and, 3:118
George Cabral and, 3:118
international rankings, 3:118
introduction of, 3:117
Jamaica and, 3:117, 3:118
Lystra Lewis and, 3:117–118
prominence of, 3:117
Trinidad and Tobago and, 3:117, 3:118
West Indies Netball Board of Control, 3:117
New Zealand All Blacks of 1905 ("The Originals"),
1:413–415
first use of name, 1:413
image of, 1:414
loss to Wales, 1:414
revolutionary playing style of, 1:413–414
New Zealand All Blacks of 1924 ("The Invincibles"),
1:415
New Zealand Olympic Committee, 1:415–416
Newmarket, England, 2:146
classic races at, 2:146
facilities of, 2:146
Jockey Club and, 2:146
July Course, 2:146
Rowley Mile Course, 2:146
Nga Taonga Takaro (traditional Māori games, New
Zealand), 1:416–422
colonialization, 1:421
games revivals, 1:418
Great Polynesian migrations, 1:416–417
Ki-o-Rahi (open field ball game), 1:418–420
Ki-o-Rahi Akotanga Iho, 1:420
Māori social order, 1:417
Nga Taonga Takaro, 1:417–418
Pakaukau (gliding wings), 1:420–421
Whakahekeheke (surfing), 1:421
Nicklaus, Jack (1940–), 3:322–323
important contributions of, 3:323
nickname of, 3:323
notable matches, 3:323
statistics for, 3:322–323
Nike, 1:157
Nordic combined, Olympic medalists (Winter)
Men's 3 × 10-Kilometer Team, 4:245
Men's 4 × 5-Kilometer Team, 4:246
Men's 7.5-Kilometer Sprint, 4:246
Men's 10-Kilometer Individual Large Hill, 4:246

Nordic combined, Olympic medalists (Winter) (*continued*)
    Men's 10-Kilometer Individual Normal Hill, 4:245
    Men's 18-Kilometer/15-Kilometer Individual Gunder-
      sen, 4:245
Norman, Greg (1955–), 1:422–423
    birthplace of, 1:422
    Great White Shark Enterprises, 1:422
    nickname of, 1:422
    players rights and, 1:422
    statistics for, 1:422
Norman, Peter (1942–2006), 1:423
North Africa and the FIFA World Cup (Association
      Football), 1:305–306
    Algeria, 1:306
    Egypt, 1:305–306
    Morocco, 1:306
    Tunisia, 1:306
North American Soccer League, 3:323–324
    demise of, 3:324
    expansion of, 3:324
    legacy of, 3:324
    stability and, 3:323
North American Soccer League and Major League
      Soccer champions
    Major League Soccer, 4:353
    North American Soccer League, 4:353–354
North American Society for Sport History,
      3:324–325
    abstracts, submission date for, 3:325
    conferences, 3:325
    current membership in, 3:325
    date of first conference, 3:324
    date of founding, 3:324
    goals of, 3:324
    Journal of Sport History and, 3:324–325
    steering committee of, 3:324
    topics of, 3:325
Northern Ireland, sport and sectarianism in, 2:146–148
    Anglo-Irish Agreement, 2:147
    association football, 2:147
    athletics, 2:147
    basketball, 2:147
    Belfast Celtic Football Club, 2:147
    Belfast Good Friday Agreement, 2:148
    Cliftonville Football Club, 2:147
    Derry City Football Club, 2:147
    divide in Northern Ireland, 2:146
    division of Ireland, 2:146
    domestic soccer league, 2:147

    field hockey, 2:147
    FIFA World Cup finals, 2:147
    Gaelic Athletic Association (GAA), 2:148
    Gaelic games and, 2:147
    ice hockey, 2:147
    Irish Republican Army (IRA), 2:146
    Irish sovereignty, 2:146–147
    rugby union, 2:147
    Ulster Defence Association (UDA), 2:146–147
Nurmi, Paavo (1897–1973), 2:372–374
    date and place of birth, 2:372
    death of, 2:374
    guiding principle of, 2:373
    as a historical concept, 2:374
    last competition of, 2:373
    Olympic ban on, 2:373
    physique of, 2:372–373
    in Summer Olympics (1920), 2:373
    in Summer Olympics (1924), 2:373
    in Summer Olympics (1928), 2:373
    systematic training and, 2:373
    tour of the United States, 2:373

Ochoa, Lorena (1981–), 3:118–119
O'Dea, Pat (1872–1962), 3:325
The Old Firm: Glasgow Celtic and Glasgow Rangers
      Football Clubs, Scotland, 2:148–150
    Bosman judgment, 2:149
    Celtic, founding of, 2:148–149
    Celtic as an Irish Catholic club, 2:149
    Celtic popularity, 2:149
    David Murray, 2:149
    Dundee Harp and Edinburgh Hibernians, 2:149
    effect of free competition on, 2:150
    Graham Souness, 2:149
    Mark Walters, 2:149
    Masonic Lodge, 2:149
    Mo Johnston, 2:149
    "The Old Firm," 2:148
    Orange Order, 2:149
    Rangers, founding of, 2:148
    Rangers' anti-Catholic practices, 2:149
    Unionist Party, 2:149
Olympic boycott of 1976 (African nations), 1:141
Olympic Council of Asia (OCA), 1:236–237
Olympic Games of 1896 (Athens), 2:374–375
    date of the opening of, 2:374
    first medal winner, 2:375
    first race of, 2:375

marathon race, 2:375
number of competitions in, 2:375
Pierre de Coubertin on, 2:374, 2:375
Olympic Games of 1900 (Paris), 2:376–377
curiosities of, 2:376–377
failure of, 2:376
Paris exhibition and, 2:376
Pierre de Coubertin on, 2:376
Ray Ewry, 2:376
Olympic Games of 1908 (London), 2:150–151
British-American athletic battle, 2:151
closing date of, 2:151
controversies in, 2:151
first time Olympic sports, 2:150
number of participants in, 2:150
number of sports and events in, 2:151
Shepherd's Bush Stadium, 2:150
sports excluded from, 2:151
Summer Games, 2:150
Winter Games, 2:150–151
world records set in, 2:151
Olympic Games of 1912 (Stockholm), 2:377–379
artwork prizes, 2:378
Avery Brundage, 2:378
Bohemia protest, 2:378
first photo-finish, 2:378
German protest, 2:378
image of, 2:377
Jim Thorpe, 2:378
Pierre de Coubertin and, 2:378
Olympic Games of 1920 (Antwerp), 2:379–380
American participation in, 2:379
Henri de Baillet-Latour, 2:379
impact of First World War, 2:379
Olympic flag and, 2:379
Olympic oath, 2:379
Paavo Nurmi and, 2:380
soccer tournament play, 2:379–380
Olympic Games of 1924 (Paris), 2:380–381
closing ceremony first, 2:381
countries excluded from, 2:380
date of opening ceremony, 2:381
gold medalists, 2:381
Johnny Weissmuller, 2:381
Paavo Nurmi and, 2:381
Pierre de Coubertin on, 2:380
rugby competition, 2:381
soccer tournament play, 2:381
winter sports and, 2:380

Olympic Games of 1928 (Amsterdam), 2:381–383
communists and, 2:382
dates of, 2:382
Henri Baillet-Latour and, 2:381–382
Olympic flame and, 2:382
Pierre de Coubertin on, 2:382
profit and, 2:382–383
soccer tournament play, 2:383
social class and, 2:382
sponsorship, 2:382
women and, 2:382
Olympic Games of 1936 (Berlin), 2:383–386
Amateur Athletic Union and, 2:383
Avery Brundage, 2:383, 2:384
Carl Diem, 2:383, 2:385–386
concern for Jewish athletes, 2:383–384, 2:385
dates of, 2:386
games in Berlin, 2:386
German defeats in, 2:386
German propaganda, 2:384–385
Hitler's games, 2:383–384
image of opening ceremony, 2:384
Jesse Owens and, 2:386
stadium of, 2:385–386
success of, 2:386
Theodor Lewald, 2:383
Olympic Games of 1940 (Tokyo), 1:237–238
Olympic Games of 1948 (London), 2:151–153
bidding process, 2:151–152
disability sport and, 2:152
economic difficulties, 2:152
intangible legacies of, 2:152
as a landmark event, 2:151
medal count, 2:152
number of athletes participating, 2:152
success of, 2:152
Olympic Games of 1952 (Helsinki), 2:387–389
additional countries anticipating in, 2:388
Avery Brundage, 2:388–389
competition between the superpowers, 2:388
dates of, 2:388
Emil Zátopek, 2:388
female Soviet contestants performances, 2:388
Israel and, 2:388
Nina Romashkova, 2:387 (image)
People's Republic of China and, 2:388
Olympic Games of 1956 (Melbourne), 1:423–425
boxing events, 1:425
closing date, 1:425

Olympic Games of 1956 (Melbourne) (*continued*)
    equestrian events, 1:423
    Frank Beaurepaire and, 1:423
    friendship concept, 1:425
    gymnastic events, 1:424
    main stadium site, 1:423
    nations making Olympic debut in, 1:424
    notable athletes in, 1:424
    opening ceremony, 1:424 (image)
    opening date of, 1:423
    sculling, 1:425
    significant international events affecting, 1:423–424
    swimming events, 1:424
    television and, 1:425
    track and field, 1:424
Olympic Games of 1960 (Rome), 2:389–390
    Abeba Bikila, 2:389
    the Cold War and, 2:389
    Danish tragedy at, 2:390
    dates of, 2:389
    Knud Enemark, 2:390
    number of participants, 2:389
    Paul Elvstrøm, 2:389
    Wilma Rudolph, 2:389
Olympic Games of 1964 (Tokyo), 1:238–240
    Avery Brundage, 1:238
    dates of, 1:238
    exclusion of South Africa, 1:238
    external political influences on, 1:239
    importance to Japan, 1:238
    judo, introduction of, 1:239
    participation in, 1:238
    significant advances in Olympic broadcasting, 1:239
    urban regeneration and, 1:238–239
    volleyball, introduction of, 1:239
Olympic Games of 1968 (Mexico City), 3:119–120
    black power salute, 3:119 (image)
    drug testing, 3:120
    financial burden of, 3:120
    José de Jesús Clark and, 3:119
    new records achieved, 3:120
    political aspects of, 3:119–120
    political unrest and, 3:119
    protests against, 3:119
Olympic Games of 1972 (Munich), 2:390–392
    Avery Brundage, 2:390, 2:391–392
    Black September, 2:391
    Cold War politics and, 2:392

East Germany and, 2:391
    gender testing, 2:391, 2:392
    gold medal winners, 2:392
    Mark Spitz, 2:392
    number of athletes involved in, 2:390
    racial discrimination and, 2:390
    Rhodesia, exclusion of, 2:390–391
    South Africa, exclusion of, 2:390
    systematic doping, 2:391
    terrorism, 2:391–392
Olympic Games of 1980 (Moscow), 2:392–394
    boycott of, 2:393
    Cold War politics and, 2:392–393
    gold medal winners, 2:393–394
    Jimmy Carter and, 2:392, 2:393
    Juan Antonio Samaranch, 2:394
    opening ceremony, 2:393 (image)
    reaction to boycott, 2:394
Olympic Games of 1988 (Seoul, Republic of Korea), 1:240–242
    Ben Johnson, 1:240, 1:242
    bid process of, 1:240
    Carl Lewis performing the Long Jump, 1:241 (image)
    North Korea and, 1:240
    Paralympic Games, 1:242
    performance-enhancing drugs, 1:240, 1:242
    political reform and, 1:240
    propaganda and, 1:240
    success of South Korea in, 1:242
    tae kwon do debut, 1:242
Olympic Games of 1992 (Barcelona), 2:394–396
    400-meter hurdles, 2:395
    1500-meter race (men), 2:395
    1500-meter race (women), 2:395
    criticism of the IOC, 2:394–395
    Derartu Tutu, 2:395
    Matchrace competition, 2:395
    number of participants in, 2:395
    optimism and, 2:394
    professionalism, 2:395
Olympic Games of 2000 (Sydney), 1:425–427
Olympic Games of 2004 (Athens), 2:396–397
    Caroline Klüft, 2:397
    cost of, 2:396
    doping, 2:396
    Hicham El Guerrouj, 2:396
    Michael Phelps, 2:397
    number of participants, 2:396

success of, 2:396
  Vanderlei de Lima, 2:397
  World Anti-Doping Agency (WADA), 2:396
Olympic Games of 2008 (Beijing), 1:242–243
  air pollution, 1:243
  Beijing National Stadium, 1:242
  date of closing ceremony, 1:243
  medal count, 1:243
  Michael Phelps, 1:242–243
  official emblem of, 1:243 (image)
  opening ceremony, 1:242
  scandal and, 1:243
  Usain Bolt, 1:243
Olympic Games of 2012 (London), 2:153–155
  dates of, 2:153
  environmental concerns, 2:153
  London Organising Committee of the Olympic and
    Paralympic Games (LOCOG), 2:154
  main Olympic site, 2:153
  Mandeville mascot, 2:154
  Olympic mascots, 2:154 (image)
  regeneration and, 2:153
  transport infrastructure, 2:154
  Wenlock mascot, 2:154
Olympic Games of 2016 (Rio de Janeiro), 3:120–121
  amount of guaranteed funding, 3:121
  candidature dossier of, 3:121
  expense of, 3:121
  opposition to planned investments, 3:121
  Public Olympic Authority, 3:120
  Rio de Janeiro Organizing Committee of the Olympic
    Games (RJOCOG), 3:121
Olympic medalists. *See specific sport*
Olympic movement, 1:39–45
  Baron Pierre de Coubertin, 1:40
  future concerns for, 1:45
  medals and medal presentations, 1:44–45
  Olympic Movement and the International Olympic
    Committee (IOC), 1:43–44
  Olympic symbols, 1:44
  opening and closing ceremonies, 1:44
  postage stamp celebrating, 1:41 (image)
  See also International Olympic Committee
Olympic Summer Games of 1904, 3:325–327
  American domination of, 3:326
  Anthropology Days event, 3:326
  archives of photographs, 3:326
  awards at, 3:326
  image of, 3:326

  Louisiana Purchase Exposition and, 3:325, 3:326
  records of, 3:326
Olympic Summer Games of 1932, 3:327–328
  attendance figures for, 3:327
  legacy of, 3:327–328
  national gold medal count, 3:327
  site of, 3:327
  William May Garland and, 3:327
Olympic Summer Games of 1976, 3:328
  cost of, 3:328
  East Germany and, 3:328
  Nadia Coma¢neci and, 3:328
  New Zealand and, 3:328
  Soviet Union and, 3:328
  United States and, 3:328
Olympic Summer Games of 1984, 3:328–331
  American gold medal count, 3:330
  athletic exploits in, 3:330–331
  Carl Lewis, 3:330
  commercialization, 3:329–330
  date of, 3:328
  Edwin Moses, 3:330–331
  endorsements and television revenue revenue, 3:329
  Evelyn Ashford, 3:331
  Evelyn Ashford, U.S.A., 3:329 (image)
  funding controversy, 3:329
  Joan Benoit, 3:331
  Joaquim Cruz, 3:330
  lack of interest in, 3:329
  legacy of, 3:331
  Li Ning, 3:330
  Los Angeles and, 3:329
  Los Angeles Coliseum, 3:330
  Los Angeles Olympic Organizing Committee (LAOOC),
    3:329–330
  Maricica Puica, 3:331
  Mary Lou Retton, 3:330
  Michael Gross, 3:330
  number of competitors, 3:328
  opening ceremonies of, 3:330
  Peter V. Ueberroth and, 3:329
  Sebastian Coe, 3:331
  Soviet Union boycott of, 3:330
  sports included, 3:328–329
  success of, 3:330
  Valerie Brisco-Hooks, 3:331
Olympic Summer Games of 1996, 3:331–333
  Billy Payne and, 3:331–332
  city of Atlanta and, 3:331–332

Olympic Summer Games of 1996 (*continued*)
  criticism of, 3:332
  Olympic structures, current use of, 3:332
  site of, 3:331
  successes of, 3:332
  terrorism and, 3:331, 3:332
  transportation and commercialization issues, 3:332
Olympic Winter Games of 1924 (Chamonix), 2:397–398
  Charles Jewtraw, 2:397
  Germany and, 2:397
  ice hockey championship, 2:397–398
  Norway and, 2:397
  number of participants in, 2:397
  success of, 2:398
Olympic Winter Games of 1928 (St. Moritz), 2:398–399
  Norway and, 2:398
  number of participants in, 2:398
  Sonja Heine, 2:398
  William Meade Lindsay III, 2:398
Olympic Winter Games of 1932, 3:333–334
  bobsled run controversy, 3:333
  fundraising, 3:333
  goals medals won, 3:334
  Godfrey Dewey and, 3:333
  number of competitors in, 3:333–334
  number of events held, 3:334
  poster advertising, 3:333 (image)
  site of, 3:333
  success of, 3:333
Olympic Winter Games of 1936 (Garmisch-Partenkirchen), 2:399–400
  dates of, 2:399
  Norway and, 2:399
  ski jumping, 2:399
  Sonja Heine, 2:399
  success of, 2:399
Olympic Winter Games of 1948 (St. Moritz), 2:400
  dates of, 2:400
  Gretchen Frazer, 2:400
  Henri Oreiller, 2:400
  media coverage, 2:400
  Norway and, 2:400
  number of participants, 2:400
Olympic Winter Games of 1952 (Oslo), 2:400–401
  dates of, 2:401
  figure skating, 2:401
  Germany and, 2:400–401
  ice hockey, 2:401
  Norway and, 2:401
  Sondre Norheim, 2:401

Olympic Winter Games of 1956 (Cortina), 2:401–402
  dates of, 2:402
  David Allan, 2:402
  Hayes Allan, 2:402
  Norway and, 2:402
  political rivalries, 2:401–402
  Sixten Jernberg, 2:402
  Soviet Union and, 2:401
  Toni Sailer, 2:402
Olympic Winter Games of 1964 (Innsbruck), 2:402–403
  deaths in, 2:403
  France and, 2:403
  Karl Ritter von Halt, 2:403
  Soviet Union and, 2:403
  speed skating, 2:403
  Viekko Hakulinen, 2:403
Olympic Winter Games of 1968 (Grenoble), 2:403–404
  advertisements, 2:403
  dates of, 2:403
  Eugenio Monti, 2:404
  Jean-Claude Killy, 2:404
  media coverage of, 2:403
  Norway and, 2:403–404
  Peggy Fleming, 2:404
Olympic Winter Games of 1972 (Sapporo, Japan), 1:243–244
  Avery Brundage and, 1:244
  environmental issues, 1:243
  expenditure for, 1:244
  International Ski Federation (FIS), 1:244
  population density, 1:243–244
  professionalism debate, 1:244
Olympic Winter Games of 1976 (Innsbruck), 2:404–405
  Axel Laser accident, 2:405
  cross-country events, 2:405
  dates of, 2:405
  East Germany, 2:405
  Franz Klammer, 2:405
  Norway and, 2:405
  number of participants, 2:405
  product development, 2:405
  protest and referendum against, 2:404
  Sheila Young, 2:405
  ski jumping, 2:405
  Soviet Union and, 2:405
  speed skating, 2:405
Olympic Winter Games of 1980, 3:334
  dates of, 3:334
  "Miracle on Ice" hockey team, 3:334

notable performances, 3:334
site of, 3:334
Olympic Winter Games of 1984 (Sarajevo), 2:406–407
    Alpine skiing competition, 2:406–407
    cross-country competitions, 2:406
    dates of, 2:406
    East Germany and, 2:406
    ice dance, 2:406
    Katarina Witt, 2:406
    ski jumping competition, 2:406
    sponsorship money, 2:406
Olympic Winter Games of 1988, 3:334–335
    date of, 3:334
    impressive athletic performances in, 3:335
    negative issues with, 3:335
    significant events in, 3:335
Olympic Winter Games of 1992 (Albertville), 2:407–408
    Alberto Tomba, 2:408
    Bjørn Dæhlie, 2:408
    competitions added, 2:407
    dates of, 2:407
    German and, 2:408
    ice hockey competition, 2:408
    Kjetil André Aamodt, 2:408
    Ljubov Yegorova, 2:408
    minimum performance requirements, 2:407
    nations without winter sports traditions, 2:407
    Norway and, 2:408
    number of participants, 2:407
    Toni Niemenin, 2:408
    Vegard Ulvang, 2:408
Olympic Winter Games of 1994 (Lillehammer), 2:408–410
    alteration of rules, 2:408
    American media concerns, 2:408
    cost-benefit, 2:409
    cross-country competition, 2:409
    Dan Jansen, 2:409
    ice hockey competition, 2:409–410
    Johan Olav Koss, 2:409
    Juan Antonio Samaranch and, 2:410
    Kerrigan/Harding scandal, 2:409
    number of participants in, 2:409
    opening ceremonies, 2:409
    Russia and, 2:409
    spectatorship, 2:409
Olympic Winter Games of 1998 (Nagano, Japan), 1:244–245
    curling and, 1:245
    dates of, 1:244
    exclusion of women, 1:245

number of women competing in, 1:245
    professionalism, 1:244
    regional focus of, 1:244
    Ross Rebagliati, 1:245
    snowboarding debut, 1:244
    women's ice hockey, 1:245
Olympic Winter Games of 2002, 3:335–337
    bidding scandal, 3:335
    bobsled competition, 3:337
    figure skating controversy, 3:336
    long-track speed skating, 3:337
    luge competition, 3:336
    men's hockey competition, 3:337
    skeleton competition, 3:336–337
    snowboarding and, 3:336
Olympic Winter Games of 2006 (Turin/Torino), 2:410–412
    attendance, lack of, 2:411
    Australia and, 2:411
    consensus opinion of, 2:412
    cross-country competition, 2:412
    dates of, 2:411
    doping scandal, 2:411
    Evgeny Plushenko, 2:411
    Germany and, 2:411
    Kjetil André Aamodt, 2:412
    Kristian Ghedina holding Olympic torch, 2:410 (image)
    Marc Hodler and, 2:410
    number of participants, 2:411
    opening ceremony, 2:411
    Turin's bid for, 2:410–411
    Uschi Disl, 2:411
    World Anti-Doping Agency, 2:411
Olympic Winter Games of 2010, 3:337–339
    dates of, 3:337
    death of Nodar Kumaritashvili, 3:338
    medal count by nation (top 10), 3:339 (table)
    Men's Alpine Skiing competition medalists, 3:338 (image)
    notable performances, 3:338–339
    overall success of, 3:339
    site of, 3:337
    television coverage of, 3:338
    venues for, 3:337–338
Oman, sport in, 1:306–308
    description of Oman, 1:306
    government funding, 1:307
    hosting sports events, 1:308
    individual achievements, 1:307, 1:308
    Olympic level competition, 1:307

Oman, sport in (*continued*)
    soccer game in Nakal oasis, 1:307 (image)
    team achievements, 1:307
Open Championship (British Open), 2:155–156
    beginning of, 2:155
    courses of, 2:156
    date of, 2:155
    Jack Nicklaus, 2:156
    most successful champions, 2:156
    Padraig Harrington, 2:156
    players in (dominant), 2:155–156
    prestige of, 2:155, 2:156
    professionalism in, 2:155
    television and, 2:156
    Tom Watson, 2:156
    uniqueness of, 2:156
Open Era of Tennis Year-End #1 Rankings
    Men's Year-End #1 Rankings (Open Era), 4:347–348
    Women's Year-End #1 Rankings (Open Era), 4:348–349
"The Originals." *See* New Zealand All Blacks of 1905 ("The Originals")
Orkney Stadium disaster, 1:141–142
outrigger canoe racing, 3:339–340
    description of canoes, 3:339
    Hawaiian Canoe Racing Association, 3:339
    international competition, 3:340
    paddling the canoe, 3:339
    spread of, 3:339
    types of races, 3:340
    women and, 3:340
Owens, Jesse (1913–1980), 3:340–341
    birthplace of, 3:340
    image of, 3:341
    at Ohio State University, 3:341
    at Olympic Games (1936), 3:341
    reputation of, 3:341

paddleball, 3:341–342
    associations for, 3:342
    original name of, 3:341
    popularity of, 3:342
    versions of, 3:341–342
paintball, 3:342–343
    equipment used, 3:342
    playing of, 3:342
Palmer, Arnold (1929–), 3:343–344
    accolades for, 3:343
    Arnold Palmer Gold-Medal Act, 3:343

    birthplace of, 3:343
    business enterprises, 3:343
    Mark McCormick and, 3:343
    playing record, 3:343
Pan American Games, 3:121–124
    Argentina and, 3:121–122
    challenges to, 3:123
    disabled athletes and, 3:123
    drug testing, 3:123
    first edition of, 3:122
    gender equality, 3:123
    Greater Texas and Pan American Exposition, 3:121
    host cities and countries, 3:122–123
    organizational and financial instability, 3:122
    origins of, 3:121–122
    Pan American Sports Organization (PASO), 3:121
    Pan American Winter Games, 3:123
    Parapan American Games, 3:123
    participation of women, 3:123
    postponements of, 3:122
Pan-Africanism and sport, North Africa, 1:308–309
    African Confederation of Football, 1:309
    African Football Confederation (AFC), 1:308
    Algeria, 1:309
    High Council of African Sport (HCAS), 1:308–309
    Morocco, 1:309
    Pan-African solidarity, 1:309
Pan-Arab Nationalism and the Pan Arab Games, 1:309–310
    Pan-Arab Games, 1:309
    Pan-Arab Games, challenges for, 1:309–310
    Saudi Arabia, 1:309
Pankration, 2:412–413
    banning of, 2:412
    historical record of, 2:412
    rebirth of, 2:412–413
pato (Argentina), 3:124–125
    Argentine Pato Open championship, 3:124
    bans on, 3:124
    in France, 3:125
    governing body of, 3:124
    horse-ball, 3:125
    image of, 3:124
    Juan Peron on, 3:124
    national identity and, 3:124
    origins of, 3:124
    World Cup of Pato-Horse Ball, 3:125
Patrick, Danica (1982–), 3:344–345
    birthplace of, 3:344
    controversy and, 3:344–345

early racing career, 3:344

image of, 3:344

importance of, 3:345

Indy 500 and, 3:344

pedestrianism, 2:156–157

drug use, 2:157

endurance events, 2:157

Foster Powell, 2:157

funding of, 2:156

popularity of, 2:156

Robert Barclay, 2:157

wagering, 2:157

Pelé (1940–), 3:125–126, 3:126 (image)

accomplishments of, 3:125

early career of, 3:125

formal name of, 3:125

importance to U.S. soccer, 3:125

important contributions of, 3:125–126

professional career of, 3:125

pelota, 2:413–414

betting and, 2:413

disciplines of, 2:413

governing bodies of, 2:413

as an Olympic game, 2:413

origins of, 2:413

variations of, 2:413

women and, 2:413

petanque, bocce, boules, 2:414–415

bocce, as a Paralympic sport, 2:414

bocce, governing body of, 2:414

boules, historical roots of, 2:414

common principle of, 2:414

Confédération Mondiales des Sports de Boules (World Confederation of Bowling Sports), 2:414–415

lawn bowling and, 2:414

petanque, governing bodies of, 2:414

petanque, origin of, 2:414

petanque, popularity of, 2:414

popularity of, 2:415

Phar Lap (1926–1932), 1:427–428

attempt on his life, 1:428

death of, 1:428

fame of, 1:427

Harry Telford and, 1:427

sire of, 1:427

wins, 1:427–428

Phelps, Michael (1985–), 3:345–346

accolades for, 3:345

birthplace of, 3:345

controversy, 3:345–346

early childhood of, 3:345

early training of, 3:345

Olympic competition and, 3:345

philosophy of sport, 1:45–47

academic discipline of, 1:45

aesthetics, 1:46

competition, 1:46

ethics, 1:46

future of, 1:47

kinesiology and, 1:47

Olympic Games, 1:46–47

Philosophical Society for the Study of Sport (PSSS), 1:45

physical harm and violence, 1:46

publications for, 1:45

purpose of, 1:45

value of sport, 1:46

pigeon racing, 3:346

electric-timing of, 3:346

object of, 3:346

origins of, 3:346

Sun City Million-Dollar Pigeon Race, 3:346

ping-pong diplomacy, 3:346–347

Platform for International Development, 1:157

Platini, Michel (1955–), 2:415

Player, Gary (1935–), 1:142–143

accolades for, 1:143

birthplace of, 1:142

criticism of, 1:142

fitness and training regime, 1:142

golf course design, 1:143

record of, 1:142

Pollock, Graeme (1944–), 1:143

polo, Argentina, 3:126–128

10-goal handicap players, 3:128

Adolfo Cambiaso, 3:128

Argentine Open Polo Championships, 3:126

development of, 3:126–127

diffusion of, 3:126, 3:127

Ellerstina polo team, 3:128

governing body of, 3:127

Hurlingham Club, 3:127

international championship play, 3:127

La Dolfina polo team, 3:128

nationalism and, 3:127

Olympic competition, 3:127

petiseros, 3:127

polo ponies, 3:127

Venado Tuerto Polo and Athletic Club, 3:126–127

polo, Britain, 2:157–159
    club formation, 2:157
    County Cup, 2:158
    female players, 2:159
    first appearance in England, 2:157
    Fulham's Hurlingham Club, 2:158
    Hurlingham Polo Committee, 2:158
    image of, 2:158
    Lillie Bridge, 2:158
    postwar changes in, 2:159
    rules of, 2:158
    sponsorship, 2:159
    Westchester Cup championship, 2:158
polo, India, 1:245–247
    expansion of, 1:245
    image of, 1:246
    masculine associations of, 1:246
    popularity of, 1:245–246
    roots of, 1:245
    withdrawal of the British military and, 1:247
polo, Olympic medalists (Summer), Men's Polo, 4:129–130
pool (pocket billiards), North America, 3:347–348
    in the 1920s, 3:347
    in the 1930s, 3:347–348
    in the 1980s, 3:348
    classification of, 3:347
    discrimination against African Americans, 3:348
    gambling and, 3:347
    number of participants in, 3:348
    social stigma and, 3:347
    women and, 3:347
Porta, Hugo (1951–), 3:128–129
    accomplishments of, 3:128–129
    Banco Nación and, 3:128
    birthplace of, 3:128
    date of retirement, 3:129
    debut of, 3:128
    in government, 3:129
    Laureus World Sports Academy, 3:129
    reputation of, 3:128
Premier League, 2:159–160
    club in (dominant), 2:160
    commodification of football, 2:159
    foreign players and managers, 2:160
    founding of, 2:159
    initial league competition, 2:160
    number of teams in, 2:160
    ownership of clubs, 2:160
    profits generated by, 2:159

    sponsorship, 2:160
    television and, 2:159, 2:160
    wages for players, 2:159, 2:160
President's Council on Fitness, Sports, and Nutrition, 3:348–349
    awards and recognition programs of, 3:348
    changes in, 3:348
    composition of Council, 3:348
    date of establishment of, 3:348
Prost, Alain (1955–), 2:415–416
Puerta 12 Tragedy (Buenos Aires, Argentina), 3:129–130
    casualty count, 3:129
    explanations for, 3:129
    symbolic change following, 3:129–130
punting, England, 2:160–161
    explanation of, 2:160
    Thames Punting Club, 2:161
Pure Martial Athletic Association (Jingwu Tryuhui), 1:183
Puskas, Ferenc (1927–2006), 2:460

Qatar Asian Games of 2006, 1:310
Qatar sports development and the bid for the 2016 Olympic Games, 1:310–311
quoits, Great Britain, 2:161–162
    image of target, 2:161
    playing of, 2:161
    popularity of, 2:162
    scoring, 2:161–162
    variations of, 2:162

race and sport, British Isles, 2:162–167
    black and South Asian players and, 2:163–164
    British Asians and, 2:165
    Burley and Fleming's (1997) on, 2:164, 2:166
    conclusion concerning, 2:166
    cricket and race, 2:163
    Dimeo and Finn (2001) on, 2:164, 2:166
    emergence of concept of race, 2:163
    empirical reportage on, 2:162–163
    ethnic minority women and, 2:163, 2:165
    "Islamophobia," 2:164
    minority participation in sports, 2:165
    "new" racism, 2:163
    racial difference, conceptualizations of, 2:163
    racism, denial of, 2:164
    racism, overt, 2:164
    racism and national identity in Scottish football, 2:164
    racism and the media, 2:165
    racism as institutional, 2:165

racism in Ireland and Scotland, 2:164
racism in the 1980s/90s, 2:164
racism in Wales, 2:164
racism within individual sports, 2:164–165
terminology, clarification of, 2:162
white supremacy, 2:165
race and sport, North America, 3:349–356
African American education, 3:350
African American women and, 3:355
all-black teams, 3:350–351
Althea Gibson, 3:355
baseball, 3:350–351, 3:353, 3:355
basketball, 3:352, 3:355
Bill Richmond, 3:349
Black Athletic Revolt, 3:354–355
boxing, 3:351
Brown v. Board of Education of Topeka, Kansas
    decision, 3:350
the "color line," 3:350, 3:352
Cornell University, 3:353
Curt Flood, 3:354–355
cycling, 3:352
de facto segregation, 3:354
Flood v. Kuhn decision, 3:355
Florence Griffith Joyner, 3:355
football, 3:352, 3:355
Fritz Pollard, 3:352
George Dixon, 3:351
Harlem Globetrotter, 3:352
higher educational institutions for blacks, 3:350
horse racing, 3:351
integration, 3:353–354
Isaac Murphy, 3:351
"Jack" Johnson and, 3:351–352
Jackie Joyner-Kersee, 3:355
Jackie Robinson and integration, 3:353–354
Jesse Owens, 3:353
Joe Louis, 3:352, 3:353
John Carlos, 3:354
Ku Klux Klan, 3:349
Marion Jones, 3:355
Marshall "Major" Taylor, 3:352
Muhammad Ali, 3:354
NASCAR racing, 3:354
National Association for the Advancement of Colored
    People (NAACP), 3:352
Negro National Baseball League, 3:352–353
New York Renaissance team, 3:352
Paul Robeson, 3:352

Plessey v. Ferguson decision, 3:349
Proposition 48, 3:355
racial segregation, 3:349
slave participation in sport, 3:349, 3:351
southern schools recruitment of blacks, 3:354
Tom Molyneaux, 3:349
Tommie Smith, 3:354
track and field, 3:352
Tuskegee Institute, 3:355
Venus and Serena William, 3:355
voting rights, 3:349
Walker brothers, importance of, 3:350
Wendell Scott, 3:354
white supremacy in boxing, 3:351–352
William Henry Lewis, 3:352
Wilma Rudolph, 3:355
YMCA, 3:350
racewalking, 2:168
importance of, 2:168
Olympic competition, 2:168
rules of, 2:168
rackets, Olympic medalists (Summer)
Men's Doubles, 4:130
Men's Individual, 4:130
racquetball, 3:356–357
Earl Riskey and, 3:356
International Racquetball Federation, 3:357
Michigan and, 3:356
National Paddleball Association (NPA), 3:357
origin of, 3:356
paddleball and, 3:356, 3:357
playing of, 3:356
popularity of, 3:356–357
World Championships, 3:357
Rally Argentina, 3:130
rallying/World Rally Championship, 2:416–417
cars of, 2:417
governing body of, 2:416
scoring, 2:417
special stages (SS), 2:417
WRC, establishment of, 2:416
WRC promoter, 2:417
WRC rallies itinerary, 2:417
Ranfurly Shield (New Zealand), 1:428
Ranjitsinhji, K. S. (1872–1933), 2:168–169
real tennis, 2:169
features of, 2:169
popularity of, 2:169
scoring in, 2:169

rebel sports tours, South Africa, 1:143–144
rhythmic gymnastics, Olympic medalists (Summer)
    Women's Individual All-Around, 4:130
    Women's Team All-Around, 4:131
Richard Riot, the, 3:357–358
    Clarence Campbell and, 3:357
    costs of, 3:358
    date of, 3:357
    Maurice "the Rocket" Richard and, 3:357, 3:358
    reason for, 3:357
    site of, 3:357
ringette, 3:358–359
    founders of, 3:358
    history of, 3:358
    international play, 3:358
    popularity of, 3:358
    rules and play, 3:358–359
Ripken, Cal, Jr. (1960–), 3:359
Robben Island Sports Club (South Africa), 1:144–146
    African National Congress (ANC) and, 1:145
    benefits of, 1:146
    Bucks-Rangers match, 1:145
    Pan-Africanist Congress (PAC) and, 1:145
    sports played on, 1:145
    unification and, 1:145
Robinson, Jackie (1919–1972), 3:360–361
    autobiography of, 3:361
    birthplace of, 3:360
    Branch Rickey and, 3:360
    death of, 3:361
    image of, 3:360
    postathletic career of, 3:360–361
    school career of, 3:360
rock climbing, 2:417–418
    indoor climbing walls, 2:417
    notable climbers, 2:417
    outdoor sport climbing, 2:418
    sport climbing, 2:417, 2:418
    variations in, 2:418
Rockne, Knute (1888–1931), 3:361–316
Rocky, 3:362–363
    critical acclaim of, 3:362
    explanation of, 3:362
    sequels to, 3:362–363
    Sylvester Stallone and, 3:362, 3:363
rodeo, 3:363–364
    cowboys controlling wild horse, 3:364 (image)
    definition of, 3:363
    first cowboy organization, 3:363

National Finals Rodeo (NFR), 3:363
Professional Bull Riders (PBR), 3:363
Professional Rodeo Cowboys Association (PRCA), 3:363
Rodeo Association of America (RAA), 3:363
Spanish influence on, 3:363
roller derby, 3:364–365
    current status of, 3:365
    evolution of, 3:364–365
    Leo Seltzer and, 3:364, 3:365
    origin of, 3:364
    Transcontinental Roller Derby, 3:364
    women and, 3:365
roque, Olympic medalists (Summer), 4:131
Rose, Lionel (1948–), 1:428–429
    birthplace of, 1:428
    legacy of, 1:429
    records of, 1:428–429
    singing career of, 1:429
Rose Bowl, 3:365–366
    Bowl Championship Series (BCS) and, 3:365–366
    date of first radio broadcast of, 3:365
    inauguration date, 3:365
    Pac-10/Big Ten competition, 3:365
    reputation of, 3:366
    segregation and, 3:365
    site of, 3:365
rowing, Olympic medalists (Summer)
    Men's Coxed Fours, 4:137–138
    Men's Coxed Fours, Inriggers, 4:138
    Men's Coxed Pairs, 4:134–135
    Men's Coxless Fours, 4:135–136
    Men's Coxless Pair, 4:133–134
    Men's Double Sculls, 4:132–133
    Men's Eights, 4:138–141
    Men's Lightweight Coxless Fours, 4:142
    Men's Lightweight Double Sculls, 4:141
    Men's Quadruple Sculls, 4:133
    Men's Single Sculls, 4:131–132
    Women's Coxed Fours, 4:144
    Women's Coxless Fours, 4:144
    Women's Coxless Pairs, 4:143
    Women's Double Sculls, 4:142
    Women's Eights, 4:144–145
    Women's Lightweight Double Sculls, 4:145
    Women's Quadruple Sculls, 4:143
    Women's Single Sculls, 4:142
rowing/sculling, Australia and New Zealand, 1:429–431
    at the elite performance level, 1:431

imperial rowing links, 1:430
King's Cup, 1:430
Maadi Cup, 1:430
manual laborers, 1:430
Olympic competition, 1:429–430
rowing/sculling, British Isles, 2:169–171
Amateur Rowing Association (ARA), 2:170, 2:171
British social elite and, 2:170
Doggett's Coat and Badge Race, 2:169
early Oxford v. Cambridge boat race (1863), 2:170
(image)
Hammersmith Sculling Club for Girls, 2:171
Henley Women's Regatta, 2:171
Leander Rowing Club at Henley-on-Thames, 2:170, 2:171
London Rowing Club, 2:170
National Amateur Rowing Association (NARA), 2:170
popularity of, 2:171
Stephen Wagg on, 2:170
Steve Redgrave and, 2:171
style rowing, 2:170–171
Thames Rowing Club, 2:170
women and, 2:170–171
Women's Amateur Rowing Association (WARA), 2:171
World Rowing Championships (2010), 2:169–170
rowing/sculling, Canada, 3:366–367
amateurism, 3:366
Canadian Association of Amateur Oarsmen, 3:366
Edward "Ned" Hanlan and, 3:366
Olympic competition and, 3:366, 3:367
"Paris Crew," 3:366
popularity of, 3:366
Silken Laumann and, 3:367
Tricia Smith and, 3:367
women and, 3:366, 3:367
rowing/sculling, United States, 3:367–369
amateurism, 3:368
Anita DeFrantz, 3:368–369
commercialism and gambling, 3:367
development of, 3:367–368
Harry Parker, 3:368
Harvard-Yale race, 3:368
notable American rowers, 3:368
Title IX and women's intercollegiate rowing, 3:368
women and, 3:368
Yale University women's rowing program, 3:368
Royal and Ancient Golf Club, 2:171–172
Royal Dutch Football Association (KNVB), 1:157

rugby, Australia Rugby League Grand Final champions, 4:294
rugby, Australia Rugby League Super League Grand Final champions, 4:294–295
rugby, European Rugby championship winners
European Challenge Cup, 4:307
Heineken Cup, 4:306
rugby, International Rugby Board Rugby World Cup champions
Men, 4:275
Women, 4:275
rugby, Olympic medalists (Summer), 4:146–147
rugby, Rugby League Challenge Cup champions (England), 4:295–297
rugby, SANZAR Tri-Nations Rugby champions, 4:305
rugby, Six Nations Rugby champions (Home Nations, Five Nations, Six Nations)
Five Nations, 4:297–299, 4:299
Home Nations, 4:299, 4:299–300
Six Nations, 4:297
rugby, Super Rugby (14, 12, 10) champions
Super 10, 4:306
Super 12, 4:306
Super 14, 4:306
rugby league football, Australia, 1:431–433
first season clubs, 1:431
Gold Coast, 1:432
at the international level, 1:432
National Rugby League (NRL), 1:431, 1:432
outlook for, 1:432–433
Rabbitohs, 1:432
rugby union, 1:431
South Queensland, 1:432
State of Origin football, 1:432
Super League War, 1:431–432
rugby league football, New Zealand, 1:433–434
All Golds tour, 1:433
national team (Kiwis), 1:433
new rugby code, 1:433
women and, 1:433–434
rugby league, Great Britain, 2:172–175
amateur rugby league growth, 2:174–175
Americanized nicknames, 2:174
Arthur Cockerham, 2:173
British Amateur Rugby League Association (BARLA), 2:174
Challenge Cup, 2:173–174
development of, 2:172
divisions of professional/semiprofessional clubs, 2:175

rugby league, Great Britain (*continued*)
    expansion of, 2:173
    international competition, 2:173
    Jason Robinson, 2:174
    News Limited involvement in, 2:174
    Northern Union, 2:172, 2:173
    Parliamentary Rugby League Group, 2:174
    professionalism, open, 2:174
    Rugby Football League (RFL), 2:173
    Rugby Football Union (RFU), 2:172, 2:174
    rule changes, 2:172–173
    "shamateurism," 2:173
    spectatorship, 2:174
    Super League, 2:174, 2:175
    "Super League War," 2:174
    Wales and, 2:173
    women's rugby league, 2:175
Rugby League World Cup champions, 4:275
rugby sevens, 1:434
Rugby Union Football, Argentina
    amateurism, 3:134
    Buenos Aires Cricket Club (BACC), 3:130
    Buenos Aires Rugby Union (URBA), 3:132–133
    Campeonato Argentino, 3:132
    championship format change, 3:132
    domestic championships, 3:132–133
    domestic structure, 3:131–132
    Ferrocarril Oeste (Western Railway) Club, 3:131
    first rugby competition in, 3:131
    international rugby–Los Pumas, 3:133–134
    Nacional de Clubes tournament, 3:132
    Old Polo Grounds, 3:131
    origins of, 3:130–131
    Pampas XV, 3:134
    professionalism, 3:134–135
    Unión Argentina de Rugby (UAR), 3:134
    Unión de Rugby de Buenos Aires (URBA), 3:132
Rugby Union Football, Australia, 1:434–439
    Australian Rugby Championship, 1:438
    Australian Rugby Union (ARU), 1:438
    Australian Rules, 1:439
    Concord Oval, 1:437
    District competition, 1:436, 1:437
    first recorded game, 1:434–435
    first recorded Rugby football club, 1:435
    First World War and, 1:436
    innovation, 1:437
    Kentwell Cup Division, 1:437
    outlook for, 1:439

    ownership models, 1:439
    presuburban clubs, 1:435
    professionalism in, 1:436, 1:438
    Rugby Union Players Association (RUPA), 1:438
    rules, 1:435–436
    Rupert Murdoch and, 1:438
    Southern Rugby Football Union, 1:435
    struggles between NSW and Queensland, 1:437
    Sydney Football Club, 1:435
    Sydney Rugby Union (SRU), 1:437
    women and, 1:438
    World Rugby Corporation, 1:438
Rugby Union Football, Canada, 3:369–370
    current status of, 3:370
    first matches in, 3:369
    Halifax City Rugby League, 3:369
    Halifax Football Club, 3:369
    Montreal Football Club, 3:369
    Rugby Union of Canada, 3:369–370
    Winnipeg Football Club, 3:369
Rugby Union Football, England, 2:175–179
    All Blacks victories, 2:177, 2:178
    amateurism, 2:177
    Association Football, 2:176
    A. D. Stoop, 2:177–178
    elitism, 2:175
    English XV, 2:178
    first rugby game in north of England, 2:175
    Harlequin mania, 2:178
    international success and, 2:176
    Law 34 revisions, 2:178
    northern clubs affiliated with, 2:175
    postwar years, 2:178
    professionalism, 2:176, 2:178
    purpose of, 2:175
    "shamateurism," 2:177
    "The Split," 2:176
    "The Split," effect of, 2:177
    structure of northern clubs, 2:176
    tactics, development of, 2:176
    violence, 2:177
Rugby Union Football, France, 2:418–422
    aesthetic sensibility, 2:419
    André and Guy Boniface, 2:421
    British and Irish rugby unions reaction to French game, 2:420–421
    commercial interests revenue, 2:422
    European Rugby Cup, 2:422
    evolution of French game, 2:419–420

Fédération Française de Rugby (French Rugby Federation, FFR), 2:420, 2:421
Five Nations Championship, 2:421
foul play and, 2:421
France-Wales international match (1930), 2:420
French flair and, 2:418–419
golden age of French game, 2:421
Jacques Fouroux, 2:421
Jean Prat, 2:421
Ligue Nationale de Rugby, 2:421–422
Pierre Villepreux, 2:421
popularity of, 2:418
professionalism, 2:421, 2:422
social significance of, 2:418
Stade Français, 2:422
Stade Toulousain, 2:420, 2:422
Top 14, 2:422
transformation of French game, 2:420
Union Française de Rugby Amateur, 2:420
Vichy regime and, 2:421
World Cup semifinal match triumph (1999), 2:418
Rugby Union Football, Ireland, 2:179–182
alternative national anthem, 2:181
caid and, 2:179
as culturally anglicized, 2:181
development of, 2:179–180
Gaelic Athletic Association's (GAA) and, 2:180–181
Heineken European Cup, 2:181
Irish Football Union, 2:180
Lansdowne Road, 2:181
Methodist College and, 2:181
present players of, 2:181
provincial teams, 2:181
Royal Belfast Academical Institution, 2:181
social class and, 2:181
successes of, 2:181
Trinity College rugby football club and, 2:179
Willie Ofahengaue, photo of, 2:180
Rugby Union Football, Italy, 2:422–425
current status of, 2:422–423, 2:424
Fascism and, 2:423, 2:424
Fédération Internationale de Rugby Amateur (International Amateur Rugby Federation, FIRA), 2:423, 2:424
Fiamme Oro, 2:424
revitalized Italian rugby, 2:424
Roy Bish, 2:424
Rugby Italy Cup play, 2:423 (image)
towns influenced by rugby, 2:424

after World War II, 2:424
worldwide credit for, 2:424
Rugby Union Football, New Zealand, 1:439–445
All Blacks perform the Haka, 1:440 (image)
future of, 1:445
influence abroad, 1:444–445
New Zealand rugby into the 20th century, 1:441–442
origins of, 1:439–441
post–World War II, 1:442–443
professional era, 1:443
Rugby World Cup, 1:443–444
women's rugby, 1:444
Rugby Union Football, Pacific Islands, 1:445–447
competitive crisis in, 1:446–447
Federation of Oceania Rugby Unions (FORU), 1:445
Fiji Rugby Union, 1:445
first Pacific Test matches, 1:446
Pacific Islands Rugby Alliance (PIRA), 1:446
Tonga Rugby Football Union, 1:445
Rugby Union Football, rest of Africa, 1:146–147
African Cup, 1:146
African Rugby Charter, 1:146
colonialism and, 1:146–147
Confederation of African Rugby (CAR), 1:146
current status of, 1:147
Rugby Football Union of East Africa (RFUEA), 1:146–147
Tunisian rugby, 1:146
Rugby Union Football, Scotland, 2:182–183
Border League, 2:182
Calcutta Cup, 2:182
Celtic League, 2:183
democratization of rugby football, 2:182
development of international rules, 2:182–183
formation of, 2:182
Home Nations, 2:182
institutions of learning and, 2:182
International Rugby Football Board, 2:182
nationalism and, 2:183
problems in, 2:183
professionalism, transition to, 2:183
rivalry with England, 2:182
Rugby Sevens, 2:182
Scottish Borders and, 2:182
Rugby Union Football, South Africa, 1:147–152
1906—the First Springboks in Britain, 1:149
1995 and the future, 1:150–151
Danie "Doc" Craven, 1:150
early tours, 1:148–149

Rugby Union Football, South Africa (*continued*)
popularity of rugby, 1:148
rugby domination and politics of race, 1:149–150
significance of rugby in, 1:147–148
Rugby Union Football, United States, 3:370–372
beginning of, 3:370
Chicago Lions Club, 3:371
club formation, 3:371
collegiate roots of, 3:370
commercialization and, 3:370–371
counterculture and, 3:371
current status of men's national team, 3:372
Dartmouth College Rugby Football Club, 3:371
Fred Foster and, 3:371
growth in, 3:371
Intercollegiate Football Association and, 3:370
New York Rugby Football Club (NYRFC), 3:371
New Zealand All Black rugby team, 3:370
Olympic competition, 3:371
Southern California Rugby Football Union, 3:371
Stanford University and, 3:370, 3:371
Thanksgiving Weekend Sevens Tournament, 3:371
United States of America Rugby Football Union (USARFU), 3:371–372
University of California, Berkeley, 3:370
Washington Rugby Football Club (WRFC), 3:371
women and, 3:372
Rugby Union Football, Wales, 2:183–188
All Blacks, 2:186
amateurism and, 2:185
Arthur "Monkey" Gould, 2:185
the clergy on, 2:184
cnappan and, 2:185, 2:186
D. Smith and G. Williams on, 2:186, 2:187
decline of, 2:187
Gareth Williams on, 2:186
importance of, 2:184
introduction of rugby to Wales, 2:183–184
patriotism, 2:186–187
resurgence of, 2:187
rugby and Welshness, 2:184, 2:186
stages in the history of Welch rugby, 2:185–186
success and, 2:184, 2:186
Wales and Welsh identity, 2:184
Welshness, 2:184, 2:185–186, 2:187
Rugby World Cup of 1987 (New Zealand and Australia), 1:447
Rugby World Cup of 1991 (United Kingdom and France), 2:188–189

Rugby World Cup of 1995 (South Africa), 1:152–153
Rugby World Cup of 1999 (Wales), 2:189
Rugby World Cup of 2003 (Australia), 1:447–448
Rumble in the Jungle (1974), 1:153–154
image of, 1:154
Mobutu Sésé Seko and, 1:153–154
significance of, 1:153
Running of the Bulls, 2:425–426
casualties and, 2:425
historical roots of, 2:425
image of, 2:425
purpose of, 2:425
Ruth, George Herman (1895–1948), 3:372–374
Baltimore Orioles and, 3:373
birthplace of, 3:372
Boston Red Sox and, 3:373
"The Curse of the Bambino," 3:373
death of, 3:374
image of, 3:373
legacy of, 3:374
New York Yankees and, 3:373–374
physical description of, 3:374
records of, 3:374
salary of, 3:374
St. Mary's Industrial School for Boys and, 3:372–373
Ryder Cup, 3:374–380
in 1957, 3:375
in 1961, 3:375–376
in 1963, 3:376
in 1979, 3:376
in 1985, 3:376
in 1991, 3:376
in 1993, 3:377
in 1995, 3:377
in 1997, 3:377
in 1999, 3:377–378
Alan Campbell on, 3:379
American dominance in, 3:376
Dai Rees and, 3:375
determining eligibility, 3:375
development of, 3:374–375
dramatic win, most, 3:376
European dominance in, 3:378–379
European success in, 3:376, 3:377
first four competitions, 3:375
format changes, 3:375, 3:376
funding of, 3:375
Jim Harnett and, 3:375
Lee Trevino on, 3:379

S. P. Jermain and, 3:375
    Samuel Ryder and, 3:375
    spectatorship, changed nature of, 3:379
    television and, 3:376
    type of competition, 3:374

Sabatini, Gabriela (1970–), 3:135
sailboarding, 3:380
    Darby sailboard, 3:380
    invention the "Windsurfer," 3:380
    typical rig of, 3:380
sailing, Australia and New Zealand, 1:448–449
    Auckland and, 1:449
    in Australia, 1:448
    governing bodies for, 1:448
    Marlborough Sound, 1:449
    mullet boats, 1:448
    and New Zealand, 1:448
    New Zealand (YNZ), 1:448
    notable yacht designers, 1:448
    the Whitsundays, 1:448
    Yachting Australia (YA), 1:448
sailing, North America, 3:380–382
    Canadian Yachting Association (CYA), 3:382
    general concept of sailing, 3:380
    International Federation for Disabled Sailing (IFDS), 3:381
    International Sailing Federation (ISAF), 3:381
    modern developments in, 3:380
    North American Yacht Racing Union (NAYRU), 3:381
    popular sailing destinations (Canada), 3:382
    racing and, 3:381
    sailing in Canada, 3:381–382
    sailing in the United States, 3:381
    uniqueness of, 3:382
    U.S. Sailing organization, 3:381
sailing, Olympic medalists (Summer)
    Men's 470 Two-Person Dinghy, 4:149
    Men's Board (Division II), 4:152
    Men's Board (Lechner), 4:152
    Men's Board (Windglider), 4:152
    Men's Laser One-Person Dinghy, 4:154
    Men's RS:X Windsurfer, 4:154
    Men's Single-handed Dinghy (Finn), 4:155
    Men's Star, 4:155–156
    Mixed 2–3-Ton, 4:148
    Mixed 3–10-Ton, 4:149
    Mixed .5–1-Ton, 4:147
    Mixed 5.5-Meter, 4:150

Mixed .5-Ton, 4:147
Mixed 6.5-Meter, 4:150
Mixed 6-Meter, 4:150–151
Mixed 7-Meter, 4:151
Mixed 8-Meter, 4:151–152
Mixed 10–20-Ton, 4:147
Mixed 10-Meter, 4:147
Mixed 12-Foot Dinghy, 4:148
Mixed 12-Meter, 4:148
Mixed 18-Foot Dinghy, 4:148
Mixed 30-Square Meter, 4:149
Mixed 40-Square Meter, 4:149
Mixed 49er Skiff, 4:150
Mixed Dragon, 4:152–153
Mixed Finn Heavyweight Dinghy, 4:153
Mixed Firefly Class, 4:153
Mixed Fleet (Soling), 4:153
Mixed Fleet (Yngling), 4:153
Mixed Flying Dutchman, 4:153–154
Mixed Individual 12-Foot Dinghy, 4:148
Mixed Olympic Class Monotype, 4:154
Mixed Open Class, 4:154
Mixed Sharpie 12-Meter, 4:154
Mixed Swallow (Golondrina), 4:156
Mixed Tempest, 4:156
Mixed Tornado Multihall, 4:156
Women's 470 Two-Person Dinghy, 4:149
Women's Board (Mistral), 4:152
Women's Laser Radial One-Person Dinghy, 4:154
Women's RS:X Windsurfer, 4:154
Women's Single-handed Dinghy, 4:155
Samaranch, Juan Antonio (1920–2010), 2:426
Samsung, 1:157
San Siro Stadium, 2:426–427
    AC Milan and, 2:426, 2:427
    capacity of, 2:427
    location of, 2:427
    renovation of, 2:427
Sánchez, Hugo (1958–), 3:136
Sandow, Eugen (1867–1925), 3:382–383
Santiago Bernabéu Stadium, 2:427
SANZAR Tri-Nations Rugby champions, 4:305
Schmeling, Max (1905–2005), 2:427–428
Schumacher, Michael (1969–), 2:428
schwingen (Switzerland), 2:428–429
    clothing and, 2:429
    festivals of, 2:429
    governing body of, 2:429
    origin of name, 2:428–429

schwingen (Switzerland) (*continued*)
　　prizes in, 2:429
　　women and, 2:429
sculling. *See* rowing/sculling, Australia and New Zealand;
　　rowing/sculling, British Isles; rowing/sculling,
　　Canada; rowing/sculling, United States
Seabiscuit (1933–1947), 3:383–384
　　"Big Cap" victory, 3:383
　　Charles Hallward and Seabiscuit, 3:384 (image)
　　death of, 3:383
　　relationships to Man O'War, 3:383
　　Seabiscuit/War Admiral match, 3:383
Secretariat (1970–1989), 3:383
　　death of, 3:384
　　sire of, 3:384
　　statistics for, 3:385
　　syndication of, 3:384
Senna, Ayrton (1960–1994), 3:136–137
sepak takraw, 1:247–248
　　forms of, 1:247, 1:248
　　image of, 1:248
　　status of the game, 1:247–248
Serie A (Italy), 2:429–430
　　dominant teams, 2:430
　　format of, 2:429–430
　　sponsorship of, 2:429
　　teams and titles, 2:429
sexuality and sport, North America, 3:385–386
　　Gay Games, 3:385
　　legislation and, 3:385
　　lesbianism, 3:385
　　LGBT participation in sport, 3:385–386
　　male athleticism and homosexuality, 3:385
　　openly gay athletes, 3:385
　　openly lesbian athletes, 3:385
　　World Outgames, 3:385
sexuality and sports, 1:47–50
　　Gay Games, 1:49–50
　　Gay Games in New York (1994), 1:48 (image)
Sheffield Shield, 1:449–450
shooting, Olympic medalists (Summer)
　　Men's 1,000-Yard Free Rifle, Prone, 4:157, 4:164
　　Men's 10-Meter Air Pistol, 4:158
　　Men's 10-Meter Air Rifle, 4:158
　　Men's 10-Meter Running Target, 4:159
　　Men's 25-Meter Military Pistol, 4:159
　　Men's 25-Meter Rapid-Fire Pistol, 4:159
　　Men's 25-Meter Small-Bore Rifle, Disappearing Target,
　　　4:163–164

Men's 25-Yard Rifle, Disappearing Target, 4:163
Men's 25-Yard Rifle, Moving Target, 4:163
Men's 50-Meter Pistol, 4:167–168
Men's 50-Meter Rifle, 3 Positions, 4:160–161
Men's 50-Meter Rifle, Prone, 4:161
Men's 50-Meter Running Target, 4:163
Men's 50-Yard + 100-Yard Rifle, Stationary Target,
　　4:163
Men's 300-Meter Military Rifle, Kneeling, 4:168
Men's 300-Meter Military Rifle, Prone, 4:168
Men's 300-Meter Military Rifle, Standing, 4:168
Men's 300-Meter Rifle, 3 Positions, 4:164
Men's 600-Meter Rifle, Prone, 4:164
Men's Individual 25-Meter Military Pistol, 4:162
Men's Individual 25-Meter Small Bore Rifle, 4:159
Men's Individual 100-Meter Running Deer, Combined,
　　4:158
Men's Individual 100-Meter Running Deer, Double
　　Shot, 4:157
Men's Individual 100-Meter Running Deer, Single Shot,
　　4:157
Men's Individual 200-Meter Rifle, 4:162
Men's Individual 300-Meter Free Rifle, 4:162
Men's Individual 600-Meter Military Rifle, 4:163
Men's Individual Double Trap, 4:166
Men's Individual Trap, 4:166
Men's Rifle, Moving Target, 4:168
Men's Skeet, 4:167
Men's Small-Bore Rifle, 4:160
Men's Team 25-Meter Rifle, 4:165
Men's Team 25-Meter Small-Bore Rifle, 4:160
Men's Team 30-Meter Pistol, 4:164
Men's Team 50-Meter Military Pistol, 4:162
Men's Team 50-Meter Pistol, 4:164
Men's Team 50-Meter Rifle, 4:165
Men's Team 100-Meter Running Deer, Double Shot,
　　4:157
Men's Team 100-Meter Running Deer, Single Shot,
　　4:157
Men's Team 300-Meter Military Rifle, 4:162–163
Men's Team 300-Meter Rifle, 4:165
Men's Team 600-Meter Military Rifle, 4:163
Men's Team Trap, 4:165–166
Mixed 50-Meter Pistol, 4:168
Mixed 50-Meter Rifle, 3 Positions, 4:161
Mixed 50-Meter Rifle, Prone, 4:161
Mixed 50-Meter Running Target, 4:163
Mixed 300-Meter Rifle, 3 Positions, 4:160, 4:164
Mixed Individual Track, 4:166

Mixed Skeet, 4:167
Women's 10-Meter Air Pistol, 4:158
Women's 25-Meter Pistol, 4:162
Women's 50-Meter Rifle, 3 Positions, 4:161–162
Women's Individual Double Trap, 4:167
Women's Skeet, 4:167
Women's Trap, 4:167
short-track speed skating, Australia, 1:450
short-track speed skating, Olympic medalists (Winter)
Men's 1,000-Meter, 4:254
Men's 1,500-Meter, 4:254
Men's 5,000-Meter Relay, 4:254–255
Men's 500-Meter, 4:254
Women's 1,000-Meter, 4:255
Women's 1,500-Meter, 4:255
Women's 3,000-Meter Relay, 4:255–256
Women's 500-Meter, 4:255
Singh, Vijay (1963–), 1:450–451
Six Nations Rugby Champions (Home Nations, Five
    Nations, Six Nations) champions
Five Nations, 4:297–299, 4:299
Home Nations, 4:299, 4:299–300
Six Nations, 4:297
Six Nations Rugby Championship, 2:190
skating, short-track speed (Asia), 1:248–249
skeleton. *See* sliding sports (bobsleigh, luge, and skeleton)
ski jumping, Olympic medalists (Winter)
Men's Individual Large Hill, 4:252
Men's Individual Normal Hill, 4:251–252
Men's Team Large Hill, 4:252–253
skiing, Alpine (Europe), 2:430–435
artificial snow, 2:434
Central European Skiing Association, 2:432, 2:433
class and, 2:433
commodification of, 2:434
development of, 2:430–432
disciplines of, 2:430
environmental problems and, 2:434
Fédération Internationale de Ski (International Ski
    Federation, FIS), 2:433
French Ski Federation, 2:433
Fridtjof Nansen and, 2:431
future of, 2:434
image of, 2:431
as an industry, 2:434
international competition and, 2:433
IOC position on, 2:433
Italian Ski Federation, 2:433
mass media and, 2:433

national ski clubs, early, 2:432
Nordic style skiing and, 2:432
popularity of, 2:433, 2:434
ski clubs, early, 2:432
ski lifts, 2:433–434
as a social sport, 2:432
techniques debate, 2:432
television and, 2:434
World War I and, 2:433
skiing, Alpine, Olympic medalists (Winter)
Men's Alpine Combined, 4:221
Men's Downhill, 4:223
Men's Giant Slalom, 4:223–224
Men's Slalom, 4:224
Men's Super G, 4:224
Women's Alpine Combined, 4:221
Women's Downhill, 4:221–222
Women's Giant Slalom, 4:222–223
Women's Slalom, 4:222
Women's Super G, 4:223
skiing, cross-country, Olympic medalists (Winter)
Men's 1.5-Kilometer Sprint, 4:229
Men's 4 × 10-Kilometer Relay, 4:228–229
Men's 10-Kilometer Classical Interval + 10-Kilometer
    Freestyle Pursuit, 4:229
Men's 10-Kilometer Classical Interval + 15-Kilometer
    Freestyle Pursuit, 4:229
Men's 10-Kilometer Pursuit, 4:233
Men's 15-Kilometer, 4:227
Men's 15-Kilometer Classical Interval + 15-Kilometer
    Freestyle Pursuit, 4:229
Men's 18-Kilometer, 4:227
Men's 30-Kilometer Mass Start, 4:232
Men's 50-Kilometer, 4:227–228
Men's Team Sprint, 4:229
Women's 3 × 5-Kilometer Relay, 4:230
Women's 4 × 5-Kilometer Relay, 4:230–231
Women's 5-Kilometer, 4:232
Women's 5-Kilometer Pursuit, 4:233
Women's 10-Kilometer, 4:230
Women's 15-Kilometer, 4:232
Women's 20-Kilometer, 4:231
Women's 30-Kilometer, 4:231
Women's Combined 5-Kilometer + 5-Kilometer Pursuit,
    4:231
Women's Combined 5-Kilometer + 10-Kilometer
    Pursuit, 4:231
Women's Combined 7.5-Kilometer + 7.5-Kilometer
    Pursuit, 4:231

skiing, cross-country, Olympic medalists (Winter)
(*continued*)
    Women's Individual Sprint, 4:232
    Women's Team Sprint, 4:232
skiing, Nordic, 2:435–438
    biathlon competition, 2:436, 2:437
    competitions, 2:436–437
    cross-country skiing, 2:435, 2:436
    disciplines of, 2:435
    equipment for, 2:435–436
    FIS World Cup competition, 2:437
    future of, 2:437
    hunting, 2:435
    International Ski Federation (FIS), 2:436
    military use, 2:435
    Nordic combined, 2:435, 2:436
    popularity of, 2:437
    ski jumping, 2:435, 2:436
    ski wax, 2:437
    techniques, 2:437
    Telemark skiing, 2:435
    television and, 2:437
sliding sports, bobsled, Olympic medalists (Winter)
    Men's Five-Man, 4:226
    Men's Four-Man, 4:224–225
    Men's Two-Man, 4:226
    Women's Two-Man, 4:227
sliding sports (bobsleigh, luge, and skeleton), 2:438–442
    bobsled, 2:440–441
    Cresta Run, 2:438–439
    Davos Toboggan Club, 2:438
    luge, 2:441
    skeleton, 2:439–440
    St. Moritz Toboggan Club, 2:438
    Symonds Cup, 2:438
    toboggan, 2:438–439
    women and, 2:439–441, 2:441
sliding sports, luge, Olympic medalists (Winter)
    Men's Singles, 4:243–244
    Mixed Doubles, 4:244–245
    Women's Singles, 4:244
sliding sports, skeleton, Olympic medalists (Winter)
    Men's Skeleton, 4:251
    Women's Skeleton, 4:251
Snell, Peter (1938–), 1:451, 1:452 (image)
snooker, 2:190–192
    famous players of, 2:191
    governing bodies of, 2:190, 2:191
    International Snooker and Billiards Federation, 2:190

    Joe Davis and, 2:191
    origin of, 2:191
    playing of, 2:190
    popularity of, 2:190
    scoring of, 2:190
    On Snooker (Richler), 2:192
    television and, 2:191
    in the United States, 2:191
    USA Snooker, 2:191
    World Professional Billiards and Snooker Association
      (WPBSA), 2:190
    World Professional Championships, 2:191
snowboarding, 3:386–387
    controversy and, 3:386
    modern history of, 3:386
    Olympic competition and, 3:386
    Shaun White, 3:386
    women and, 3:386
snowboarding, Olympic medalists (Winter)
    Men's Giant Slalom, 4:253
    Men's Halfpipe, 4:253
    Men's Parallel Giant Slalom, 4:253
    Men's Snowboard Cross, 4:253
    Women's Giant Slalom, 4:253
    Women's Halfpipe, 4:253
    Women's Parallel Giant Slalom, 4:253
    Women's Snowboard Cross, 4:254
Sobers, Sir Garfield (1936–), 3:137
sociology of sport, 1:50–54
    the Cold War, 1:51–52
    development of, 1:50
    as a discipline, 1:50, 1:53
    early sport sociologists, 1:52
    feminism, 1:53
    formal institutionalization of, 1:52
    Olympic Games movement, 1:51
    publications for, 1:52
    socialization, 1:53
    structural functionalist paradigm, 1:52–53
    Workers' Olympic Games, 1:51
softball, 3:387–389
    the All-American Girls Professional Baseball League,
      3:388
    Amateur Softball Association of America (ASA), 3:387,
      3:388
    Canada Amateur Softball Association (Softball Canada),
      3:389
    development of variations of, 3:388
    Great Depression and, 3:387–388

International Softball Federation (ISF), 3:389
International Women's Professional Softball Association, 3:388
National Diamond Ball Association, 3:387
National Pro Fastpitch, 3:389
Olympic competition, 3:389
origins of, 3:387
popularity of, 3:387, 3:389
slow-pitch 12-inch game, 3:388
standardization of rules, 3:387
United States Slow-Pitch Softball Association (USSSA), 3:388
women in, 3:388
Women's Pro Softball League (WPSL), 3:388–389
world competition in, 3:389
softball (women's), Olympic medalists (Summer), 4:169
softball, Australia, 1:451
softball, Latin America, 3:137–138
gender inequity, 3:138
Olympic competition and, 3:138
popularity of, 3:137
regional gains and, 3:137–138
women's fast-pitch achievements, 3:138
Women's Softball World Championship, 3:138
Sokol Movement (Czech Republic, Slovakia, Czechoslovakia), 2:442–443
communist rule and, 2:443
current status of, 2:443
Czech Sokol Organization in the U.S., 2:442–443
Miroslav Tyrš and, 2:442
nationalism and, 2:442, 2:443
Nazi occupation and, 2:443
Sorenstam, Annika (1970–), 2:443–444
South Africa and the Olympic games, 1:154–156
formalized racial segregation, 1:155
lackluster performances, 1:156
National Olympic Committee of South Africa (NOCSA), 1:156
South African National Olympic Committee (SANOC), 1:155
South African Sports Confederation and Olympic Committee (SASROC), 1:156
South American Games, 3:138–139
events in, 3:138
Latin American Congress and, 3:138–139
longevity of, 3:139
name change, 3:138
Organización Deportiva Suramericana (South American Sports Organization, ODESUR), 3:139
resilience of, 3:139
YMCA and, 3:138
South Sydney District Rugby League Club Ltd vs. News Limited, 1:453–454
Southeast Asian Games, 1:249–250
Spalding, Albert Goodwill (1850–1915), 3:389–390
business career of, 3:389
foundational myth of baseball and, 3:389–390
Harry Vardon and, 3:389
image of, 3:390
importance of, 3:389
playing career of, 3:389
rulebooks of, 3:389
ruthlessness of, 3:390
Spalding Library of American Sports, 3:389
Spalding World Baseball Tour, 3:390–391
Spartakiads, 2:444–445
Czechoslovak Spartakiads, 2:444–445
events of, 2:444, 2:445
mass gymnastic tradition, 2:444
origin of, 2:444
participation in, 2:445
postcommunist Sokol movement, 2:445
purpose of, 2:444
Spartakiad of the Peoples of the USSR, 2:445
Strahov Stadium, 2:444–445
types of, 2:445
speed skating, Europe, 2:445–448
400-meter refrigerated ovals, 2:447
Atje Keulen-Deelstra, 2:447
British National Skating Association, 2:447
class and, 2:447
commercialization, 2:448
development of ice skating, 2:445–446
Eric Heiden, 2:448
governing body of, 2:447
image of, 2:446
innovation, 2:448
International Skating Union (ISU), 2:447
ISU speed-skating championships, 2:447
local skating traditions, 2:447
long track speed skating, 2:448
National Skating Association of Great Britain, 2:447
Olympic competition and, 2:447
professionalism, 2:448
short track speed skating, 2:448
specialization, 2:447–448
speedskating competitions, early, 2:446
World Single Event Championships, 2:447–448

speed skating, North America, 3:391–393
  Amateur Skating Association in Canada, 3:392
  Amateur Skating Union of America (ASU), 3:392
  American Skating Congress, 3:391
  Casey FitzRandolph, 3:392 (image)
  development of, 3:391–392
  inauguration date of, 3:391
  International Skating Union of America (ISUA), 3:392
  major centers for, 3:392
  notable North American skaters, 3:392–393
  Olympic competition, 3:392, 3:393
  short track skating, 3:393
  United States International Speed Skating Association, 3:393
speed skating, Olympic medalists (Winter)
  Men's 1,000-Meter, 4:247
  Men's 1,500-Meter, 4:247
  Men's 5,000-Meter, 4:248
  Men's 10,000-Meter, 4:248
  Men's 500-Meter, 4:246–247
  Men's All-Around, 4:251
  Men's Individual, 4:259
  Men's Team Pursuit, 4:249
  Women's 1,000-Meter, 4:249
  Women's 1,500-Meter, 4:250
  Women's 3,000-Meter, 4:250
  Women's 5,000-Meter, 4:250
  Women's 500-Meter, 4:249
  Women's Individual, 4:259
  Women's Team Pursuit, 4:251
speedball, 3:393–394
  creation of, 3:393
  development of rules, 3:393
  Elmer Mitchell and, 3:393
  origin of name, 3:393
  popularity of, 3:394
  promotion of, 3:393–394
  women and, 3:394
speedway, 2:192–193
Spitz, Mark (1950–), 3:394–395
sport and international development in Africa, 1:156–158
  Football Association of England (FA), 1:157
  Kisumu Youth Football Association (KYFA), 1:157
  in northern Uganda, 1:157
  Royal Dutch Football Association (KNVB), 1:157
  in Sierra Leone, 1:157
  soccer and, 1:157
  United Nations Sport for Development and Peace program, 1:157
  in West Africa, 1:157

sport labor migration, 1:54–55
sport psychology, 1:55–59
  history of sport psychology in Europe, 1:55–56
  history of sport psychology in North America, 1:56–58
sports history, culture, and practice in Asia, 1:173–184
  Central Asia, 1:181–182
  colonization and, 1:176
  conclusion concerning, 1:183–184
  diasporas, 1:183
  East Asia, 1:176–178
  Formula 1 motorsport, 1:174–175
  map of agent, 1:174
  opportunities and oversights in Asian sports history, 1:182–183
  political reality and, 1:176
  South Asia, 1:178–180
  Southeast Asia, 1:180–181
  sporting Asia concept, 1:175–176
  sporting transformation, 1:173–174
  traditional sports, 1:175–176
sports history, culture, and practice in British Isles, 2:1–13
  in the 1980s/1990s, 2:12
  Alex Higgins, 2:11
  amateurism, 2:5–6
  amateur-professional conflict, 2:6
  Austerity Olympics, 2:11
  baseball, 2:9
  basketball, 2:9
  Benjamin Disraeli, 2:5
  Blaine N. Sexton, 2:9
  Bloody Sunday, 1920, 2:7
  British Isles defined, 2:1
  British Workers' Sports Federation (BWSF), 2:10
  Christmas Eve football matches, 2:8
  class and, 2:1, 2:5
  cnappan, 2:4
  codification of sports, 2:1
  conclusion concerning sport in the British Isles, 2:12–13
  "Condition of England" question, 2:5
  cricket, 2:3–4
  darts, 2:11
  Dynamo Moscow, 2:11
  film and sports, 2:8
  folk football, 2:4
  football hooliganism, 2:12
  Football World Cup (1966), 2:11
  Frederick Hall Thomas (Freddie Welsh), 2:7–8
  Gaelic Athletic Association, 2:11
  Gaelic Athletic Association (GAA), 2:6–7
  Gaelic handball, 2:4

gender and, 2:1, 2:3
George Orwell, 2:1, 2:11
the Great War, 2:8
greyhound racing, 2:9
handball (fives), 2:4
Harringay Arena, 2:9
Heysel Stadium Disaster, 2:12
hurling, 2:7
ice hockey, 2:9
International Rugby Football Board (IRFB), 2:6
interwar years and, 2:9–10
Junior Imperial League, 2:10
Lord's Cricket Ground, 2:4
map of the British Isles, 2:2
Marylebone Cricket Club (the MCC), 2:4
Melvyn Bragg, 2:1
Miners' Welfare Fund, 2:10
Mitchell and Kenyon film company, 2:8
Muscular Christianity, 2:5
national identity and, 2:1
Northern Football Union, 2:6
politics on sport, 2:10
Premier League, 2:12
price fighting (boxing), 2:3
Public Health Act (1875), 2:5
Queen's Park Football Club, 2:5
Republic of Ireland defined, 2:1
rugby football, 2:4, 2:5, 2:8, 2:11
rugby Grand Slam (Ireland), 2:11
Rugby School, 2:4
shinty, 2:7
Sky Television, 2:12
snooker, 2:11
socialization of the teenager, 2:3
speedway, 2:9
Telefís Éireann, 2:11
television, free-to-view sports, 2:12
television age, 2:11–12
themes in the study of sporting activity, 2:1, 2:3
Thomas Arnold, 2:4
Twenty20 cricket, 2:12
unionism, 2:9–10
Welsh Rugby Union, 2:6
workers' sport, 2:10
Young Men's Christian Association (YMCA), 2:5
sports history, culture, and practice in Europe, 2:219–226
ancient Greece and, 2:219
auto racing, 2:226
badminton, 2:224
ball games, 2:222–224

basketball, 2:224
cold climate sports, 2:221
common fiber and, 2:224
cycling, 2:225
Football Association, 2:223
Friedrich Ludwig Jahn, 2:219
German physical culture, 2:219–220
golf, 2:224–225
handball, 2:223–224
ice hockey, 2:221
introduction to, 2:219–221
Johan C. F. GuthsMuths and, 2:219, 2:220
la soule, 2:222–223
map of Europe, 2:220
mob football, 2:223
modern sports, 2:225–226
origins of physical training in Europe, 2:219–220
Per Henrik Ling, 2:219–220
rules, 2:223
sailing, 2:225
Shrovetide football, 2:223
skiing, 2:221
soccer, 2:223
sports for the wealthy, 2:224–225
swimming, 2:221–222
tennis, 2:224
volleyball, 2:224
welfare and, 2:219
sports history, culture, and practice in Latin America and
    the Caribbean, 3:1–12
amateur sporting ideology, 3:7–8
association football and, 3:9
athletic clubs, 3:7
auto racing and, 3:10
ball games of Mesoamerica, 3:3
baseball and, 3:9–10
basketball and, 3:10–11
batey, 3:3
boxing and, 3:10
British influence, 3:5
bullfighting, 3:4
capoeira, 3:5
cockfighting, 3:4
in colonial era, 3:3–5
commercialization, 3:8
conclusion concerning, 3:11–12
cricket and, 3:5, 3:10
cultural imperialism, 3:1
diffusion of cultural practices, 3:7
educational institutions and, 3:7–8

sports history, culture, and practice in Latin America and the Caribbean (*continued*)
"elite sport"and, 3:11
emulation of foreign leisure activities, 3:1
equestrian activities, 3:4
financial burden of, 3:8
first versions of ball games (*juego de la pelota*), 3:3
foreign investment and immigration, 3:6, 3:7
fronttennis, 3:5
geographical classifications, 3:1
golf and, 3:11
Iberian influence on, 3:3–5
indigenous sport forms marginalized, 3:7
initial settlement of region, 3:2–3
international competition, 3:8–9
jai alai and *pelota a paleta*, 3:5
maps of Latin America and the Caribbean, 3:2
men's rugby side, 3:11
nationalism, 3:8
overview of foundation and major development trends (19th century to present), 3:7–11
pato, 3:4
political instability, 3:6
in postcolonial and modern era, 3:5–12
in pre-Columbian era, 3:2–4
professionalism, 3:8
spot forms (pre-Columbian), 3:3
spread of modern sports in, 3:7–8
suppression of colonial sport practices, 3:7
tennis and, 3:11
time periods of, 3:1–2
vaquejada, 3:4
volleyball and, 3:11
women's field hockey, 3:11
sports history, culture, and practice in Middle East and North Africa, 1:269–272
academic study of, 1:272
important historical phases of, 1:269–271
map of Middle East (1945–1990), 1:270
modernity and, 1:271–272
sports history, culture, and practice in North America, 3:147–158
amateur regulation, 3:149
American football, 3:148, 3:153
appropriate femininities and masculinities in, 3:152–153
baseball, 3:150–151
Ben Johnson scandal, 3:155
Bob Beamon, 3:155
coaching and women, 3:150

Cold War politics and, 3:152
definition of amateur, early, 3:149
earliest records of sport in, 3:147
early European sports, 3:148–149
emancipation of women, 3:150
European settlers and, 3:148–150
George William Beers, 3:147–148
ice hockey, 3:151–152
Jim Thorpe, 3:149
Jose Canseco, 3:156
Kobe Bryant, 3:156
lacrosse, 3:147–148
map of North America, 3:147
Marion Jones, 3:156
Mark McGwire, 3:156
Michael Vick, 3:156
Montréal Olympics, 3:154
national identity and, 3:150–153
Native Americans and, 3:147
Olympic Games and, 3:153–157
Olympic scandals, 3:155–156
Peter Ueberroth, 3:154
professional sports in, 3:153
Puritans and, 3:149
racial exclusion, 3:151
scandals, 3:155–157
segregation and, 3:149, 3:151
substance abuse, 3:155–156
Tiger Woods, 3:156–157
Title IX legislation and women, 3:150
Todd Bertuzzi, 3:156
ullamalizti, 3:147
women's sport, 3:150
sports history, culture, and practice in Oceania, 1:315–327
Aotearoa/New Zealand: beyond boys and balls, 1:324
Aotearoa/New Zealand: comparison, 1:323–324
Aotearoa/New Zealand: history and culture of sport in, 1:322
Aotearoa/New Zealand: national distinctiveness, 1:322–323
Aotearoa/New Zealand: research priorities in support of, 1:325
Australia: geography and self-image through sport, 1:315–317
Australia: indigenous people, nonwhites, and ethnic minorities in sport, 1:319–321
Australia: norms of participation in sport, 1:317–319
Australia: research priorities in sport history, 1:321–322
conclusion concerning, 1:325–326

map of Oceana, 1:316

Pacific islands, 1:325

sports history, culture, and practice in sub-Saharan Africa, 1:73–80

African body cultures, 1:77–78

African sporting histories, 1:79–80

colonialism and imperialism, 1:75–78

history of European interaction with Africa, 1:73–77

map of Africa, 1:74

sports medicine, 1:59–63

1900s to World War II, 1:60–61

histories of some sports medicine organizations, 1:61–62

money and sports medicine, 1:62

Post-World War II: the Cold War era, 1:61

revival of modern sports medicine via the modern Olympics, 1:60

sports medicine for all physically active individuals, 1:62

sports medicine in the old world, 1:59–60

summary of, 1:62

sports museums and heritage collections, 1:63–67

All England Lawn Tennis Club's Wimbledon Lawn Tennis Museum, 1:65

America's Pro Football Hall of Fame, 1:64

Australia's National Sports Museum, 1:65, 1:66

Gaelic Athletic Association Museum, 1:65

International Tennis Hall of Fame and Tennis Museum, 1:64

Johnny Mullagh Cricket Centre, 1:66

Marylebone Cricket Club, 1:63

Melbourne Cricket Club, 1:64

Melbourne Cricket Ground, 1:65

Musèe Olympique, 1:65

Naismith Memorial Basketball Hall of Fame, 1:64

National Art Museum of Sport, 1:65

National Baseball Hall of Fame and Museum, 1:64

National Football Museum, 1:66

Real Madrid Football Club's Archives Centre, 1:66

Richmond Football Club Museum, 1:66

River and Rowing Museum, 1:66

Sports Museum of America, 1:65

Suomen Urheilumuseo, 1:65

World Rugby Museum, 1:64

Springbok emblem (South Africa), 1:158

Springbok Tour of New Zealand (1981) (South African Rugby Tour), 1:454–456

squash, Asia, 1:250

squash, British Isles, 2:193

steroid scandal in baseball and the Mitchell Report, 3:395–396

extent of scandal, 3:395

full title of Mitchell Report, 3:395

main informants, 3:396

number of players named in report, 3:396

prominent players involved in, 3:395

recommendations of the Mitchell Report, 3:396

Sammy Sosa/Mark McGwire, 3:395 (image)

validity of Mitchell Report, 3:396

stick fighting, Africa and Caribbean, 1:158–159

stoolball, 2:193–194

early written references to, 2:193–194

explanation of play, 2:194

Stoolball Association for Great Britain, 2:194

in the United States, 2:194

written rules for, 2:194

Sullivan, John L. (1858–1918), 3:396–397

iconic status of, 3:396

Kilrain/Sullivan fight, 3:396–397

mass media and, 3:396–397

as self-promoter, 3:396

Summit on Ice of 1972 (Canada–Soviet Union Ice Hockey Series), 3:397–398

final contest of, 3:398

importance of, 3:398

Montreal games, 3:397

Moscow games, 3:397–398

notable players in, 3:397

sumo, 1:250–252

contemporary form of, 1:251

history of, 1:251

image of, 1:251

popularity of, 1:252

religious asociation, 1:251

Sun City (South Africa), 1:159–160

Super 15 Rugby, 1:456

Super Bowl, 3:398–399

1969 game, 3:398, 3:399

date of first Super Bowl, 3:398

Green Bay Packers and, 3:398, 3:399

Kansas City Chiefs and, 3:398

New York Jets and, 3:398, 3:399

Pittsburgh Steelers and, 3:399

selection of site of, 3:399

television ratings and advertising revenue, 3:399

Super League "War," 1:456–457

Super Rugby (14, 12, 10) champions, 4:306

Supreme Council for Sport in Africa (SCSA), 1:160–161

surf lifesaving, Australia, 1:460–462
  criticism of, 1:461
  New South Wales Surf Bathing Association, 1:460
  philosophy of, 1:461
  On the Same Wave program, 1:462
  Surf Life Saving Australia (SLSA), 1:461, 1:462
  virtue of, 1:461
  women and, 1:461
surfing, Australia and New Zealand, 1:457–460
  competitive surfing leaders, 1:458, 1:459
  Duke Kahanamoku, 1:458
  International Surf Life Saving Carnival, 1:458
  professional surfing competition, 1:458 (image)
  Surf Life Saving Association (SLSA), 1:458
  Surf NZ, 1:459–460
  Surfing Australia, 1:459
surfing, South Africa, 1:161
swimming, Australia, 1:462–464
  Annette Kellerman, 1:462–463
  Charles Perkins, 1:463
  elite swimmers, 1:463–464
  indigenous people and, 1:463
  Swimming Australia Ltd (SAL), 1:464
  women in competitive swimming, 1:463
swimming, Canada, 3:399–400
  Canadian Amateur Swimming Association (CASA),
    3:399
  Canadian National Swim Team, 3:400
  Swimming Canada, 3:399, 3:400
swimming, England, 2:194–196
  Annette Kellermann, 2:196
  "bungee jumps," 2:194
  dogs and, 2:195
  the English Channel, 2:195, 2:196
  great swimmers of, 2:195, 2:196
  London and, 2:194
  Matthew Webb, 2:195, 2:196
  nudity and, 2:195
  Olympic swim team gold medalists, 2:195 (image)
  pride in, 2:194–195
swimming, Olympic medalists (Summer)
  Men's 1,000-Meter Freestyle, 4:169
  Men's 1,200-Meter Freestyle, 4:173
  Men's 1,500-Meter Freestyle, 4:174
  Men's 4 × 00-Meter Freestyle Relay, 4:184–186
  Men's 4 × 50-Yard Freestyle Relay, 4:186
  Men's 4 × 100-Meter Freestyle Relay, 4:182
  Men's 4 × 100-Meter Medley Relay, 4:182–183
  Men's 4,000-Meter Freestyle, 4:178

Men's 50-Meter Freestyle, 4:186
  Men's 100-Meter Backstroke, 4:170–171
  Men's 100-Meter Breaststroke, 4:171
  Men's 100-Meter Butterfly, 4:172
  Men's 100-Meter Freestyle, 4:172–173
  Men's 100-Meter Freestyle for Sailors, 4:173
  Men's 200-Meter Backstroke, 4:174–175
  Men's 200-Meter Breaststroke, 4:175
  Men's 200-Meter Butterfly, 4:176
  Men's 200-Meter Freestyle, 4:177
  Men's 200-Meter Individual Medley, 4:178
  Men's 200-Meter Obstacle Event, 4:178
  Men's 200-Meter Team Swimming, 4:178
  Men's 400-Meter Breaststroke, 4:178
  Men's 400-Meter Freestyle, 4:178–179
  Men's 400-Meter Individual Medley, 4:180
  Men's 880-Yard Freestyle, 4:187
  Men's Marathon 10-Kilometer, 4:187
  Men's Underwater Swimming, 4:187
  Women's 4 × 100-Meter Freestyle Relay, 4:180–181
  Women's 4 × 100-Meter Medley Relay, 4:183–184
  Women's 4 × 200-Meter Freestyle Relay, 4:184
  Women's 50-Meter Freestyle, 4:186
  Women's 100-Meter Backstroke, 4:169–170
  Women's 100-Meter Breaststroke, 4:171
  Women's 100-Meter Butterfly, 4:171–172
  Women's 100-Meter Freestyle, 4:173
  Women's 200-Meter Backstroke, 4:174
  Women's 200-Meter Breaststroke, 4:175–176
  Women's 200-Meter Butterfly, 4:176–177
  Women's 200-Meter Freestyle, 4:177
  Women's 200-Meter Individual Medley, 4:177–178
  Women's 400-Meter Freestyle, 4:179
  Women's 400-Meter Individual Medley, 4:180
  Women's 800-Meter Freestyle, 4:186–187
  Women's Marathon 10-Kilometer, 4:187
swimming, southern Africa, 1:162–163
  swimming in South Africa, 1:162–163
  swimming in Zimbabwe, 1:163
swimming, United States, 3:400–405
  Amateur Athletic Union (AAU) and, 3:401
  Amateur Swimming Association (ASA), 3:402
  "American crawl," 3:401
  backstroke, 3:402
  butterfly stroke, 3:402
  Charlie Daniels and, 3:401
  community level swimming, 3:400–401, 3:404–405
  competitive swimming, 3:401–403
  David Armbruster, 3:402

disciplines of, 3:400
diving, 3:402
electronic timing, 3:403
first plain high-diving competition, 3:402
flip turn (tumble turn), 3:403
front crawl, 3:402
goggles, 3:403
Greg Louganis, 3:402
International Swimming Hall of Fame, 3:403–404
Jack Sieg, 3:402
Mark Spitz, 3:403, 3:404
Masters Swimming program, 3:405
men's backstroke, 3:402
Michael Phelps, 3:404
Mike Peppe and, 3:402
municipal pools, 3:401
National Collegiate Athletic Association (NCAA), 3:403
notable female swimmers, 3:404
Olympic competition, 3:401, 3:402, 3:405
overarm technique, 3:402
Pan Am Games, 3:403
paralympic swimming, 3:404
public baths, 3:401
racial segregation and, 3:401
Shirley Babashoff, 3:403, 3:404
springboard diving, 3:402
starting blocks, 3:403
swimsuits, 3:403
Sybil Bauer and, 3:402
synchronized diving, 3:402
"Trudgen stroke," 3:401
types of strokes, 3:400
underwater limitation, 3:403
U.S. Aquatic Sports, 3:405
water polo, 3:403
women and, 3:402
Sydney Organising Committee for the Olympic Games, 1:464–465
Sydney Paralympic Organising Committee, 1:465–466
Sydney to Hobart Yacht Race (Australia), 1:466
synchronize swimming, Olympic medalists (Summer)
Women's Duet, 4:187
Women's Solo, 4:187
Women's Team, 4:188
synchronized swimming, 3:405–406
Annette Kellerman and, 3:405
Esther Williams, 3:405
founding of, 3:405

international competition, 3:406
Katherine Curtis and, 3:405
Margaret Sellers and, 3:405
Marion Kane and, 3:406
Olympic competition status, 3:405–406
origin of term, 3:405
World Synchronized Swimming Conference, 3:406

TAB (Totalisator Agency Board), Australia, 1:466–468, 1:467 (image)
table tennis, Asia, 1:252–253
All-Japan Ping-Pong Association, 1:252
India and, 1:252
International Table Tennis Federation (ITTF), 1:252
Japan and, 1:252
Malaysia and, 1:252
Olympic competition, 1:252–253
People's Republic of China and, 1:252–253
Ping-Pong Diplomacy, 1:252
Wang Hao (China), world champion, on attack, 1:253 (image)
table tennis, Europe, 2:448–450
alterations to, 2:450
Asian dominance in, 2:448, 2:449
the celluloid ball, 2:449
English "Ping-Pong fever," 2:449
genesis of, 2:448–449
International Table Tennis Federation (ITTF), 2:449
national associations, 2:449
Olympic competition winners, 2:449–450
Ping- Pong Association (PPA), 2:449
Ping-Pong, 2:448, 2:449
popularity of, 2:450
speed glue, 2:450
Swaythling Cup, 2:449
Table Tennis Association (TTA), 2:449
World Table Tennis Championships, 2:449
table tennis, Olympic medalists (Summer)
Men's Doubles, 4:188
Men's Singles, 4:189
Men's Team, 4:189
Women's Doubles, 4:188–189
Women's Singles, 4:189
Women's Team, 4:189
tae kwon do, 1:253–255
alternative names for, 1:254
history of, 1:253–254
landmarks in, 1:254–255
popularity of, 1:254

taekwondo, Olympic medalists (Summer)
    Men's Flyweight, 4:189
    Men's Heavyweight, 4:190
    Men's Lightweight, 4:190
    Men's Middleweight, 4:190
    Women's Flyweight, 4:190
    Women's Heavyweight, 4:190
    Women's Middleweight, 4:190
tai chi, 1:255
Tartan Army, Scotland, 2:196–197
Taylor Report, 2:197–198
    Football Spectators Act, 2:197
    Hillsborough Stadium disaster and, 2:197
    hooliganism, 2:197
    importance of, 2:198
    reason for, 2:197
    recommendations of, 2:197–198
Tendulkar, Sachin (1973–), 1:255–256
    image of, 1:256
    popularity of, 1:256
    reputation of, 1:255
    statistics for, 1:255
tennis, Africa, 1:163–165
    All Africa Games, 1:164
    in Nigeria, 1:164
    notable South African tennis players, 1:164
    Olympic competition and, 1:164
    "Scramble for Africa," 1:163–164
    South Africa and, 1:164
tennis, Asia, 1:256–257
    Agent Tennis Federation (ATF), 1:256–257
    All India Lawn Tennis Association, 1:256
    development of, 1:256
    Michael Chang, 1:256
    outlook for, 1:257
    popularity of, 1:256
tennis, British Isles, 2:198–202
    All England Club (AEC), 2:198
    amateur play, 2:200
    C. C. Pyle, 2:200
    championships and tournaments, 2:198
    commercialization, 2:201
    Davis Cup competition, 2:200
    decline in popularity of lawn tennis, 2:199–200
    Dwight Davis, 2:199–200
    Fitzwilliam Lawn Tennis Club, 2:198, 2:199
    Fred Perry, 2:200
    grassroot level rebuilding, 2:201
    history of, 2:198

    in Ireland, 2:198–199
    Irish Lawn Tennis Association, 2:199
    Lawn Tennis Association (LTA), 2:199
    marketing of (early), 2:198
    players of (dominant), 2:199, 2:201
    Reginald and Lawrence Doherty, 2:199
    shamateurism, 2:201
    South of Ireland Men's Singles Championship, 2:198
    style of play, 2:199
    Suzanne Lenglen, 2:200
    Wimbledon, 2:199, 2:200, 2:201
    Wimbledon singles successes, 2:201
    women's game, 2:199
tennis, Latin America, 3:139–141
    Davis Cup team triumphs, 3:140
    international triumphs, 3:139
    notable Latin American players, 3:139–140
    popularity and support for, 3:140–141
    reputation of, 3:139
tennis, major champions of
    Australian Open, Men's Singles, 4:340–341
    Australian Open, Women's Singles, 4:341–342
    French Open, Men's Singles, 4:344–345
    French Open, Women's Singles, 4:345
    US Open, Men's Singles, 4:346
    US Open, Women's Singles, 4:346–347
    Wimbledon, Men's Singles, 4:342–343
    Wimbledon, Women's Singles, 4:343–344
tennis, Olympic medalists (Summer)
    Men's Doubles, 4:191
    Men's Doubles Indoor, 4:193
    Men's Singles, 4:192
    Men's Singles Indoor, 4:193
    Mixed Doubles, 4:193
    Mixed Doubles Indoor, 4:194
    Women's Doubles, 4:191–192
    Women's Singles, 4:192–193
    Women's Singles Indoor, 4:193
tennis, Open Era of Tennis Year-End #1 Rankings
    Men's Year-End #1 Rankings (Open Era), 4:347–348
    Women's Year-End #1 Rankings (Open Era), 4:348–349
ten-pin bowling, 3:406–408
    American Bowling Congress (ABC), 3:407
    "Dutch pins" bowling, 3:407
    English form of bowling, 3:407
    extreme form of bowling, 3:407
    first formal bowling alley, 3:407
    origin of bowling, 3:406
    popularity of, 3:407

religious ceremony and, 3:406

technology and, 3:407

television and, 3:407

Women's International Bowling Congress (WIBC), 3:407

This Sporting Life (Storey), 2:202

Thorpe, Ian (1982–), 1:468

Thorpe, Jim (1888–1953), 3:408–410

in 1912 Olympics, 3:408

accolades for, 3:408

beginning of athletic career, 3:408

birthplace of, 3:408

image of, 3:409

versatility of, 3:408

Title IX, 3:410–411

Birch E. Bayh and, 3:410

Edith S. Green and, 3:410

genius of, 3:410

language of, 3:410

new areas of interpretation, 3:410

Patsy T. Mink and, 3:410

purpose of, 3:410

renaming of, 3:410

special interests and, 3:410

three prongs of, 3:410–411

Tonya Harding–Nancy Kerrigan scandal, 3:411–412

total football (Netherlands), 2:450

Tour de France, 2:450–456

Best Young Riders competition, 2:454–455

bonus seconds, 2:453

defunct jerseys, 2:455

Eddy Merckx, 2:452

first Tour de France, 2:450

French nationalism and, 2:452

the green jersey, 2:453

harassment and violence in, 2:452

Henri Desgrange and, 2:451, 2:452, 2:454, 2:456

image of, 2:451

Lance Armstrong and, 2:450

longest total distance of, 2:451

measured time and, 2:452–453

mythological events of, 2:452

origins of, 2:451–452

other competitions in, 2:455

polka dot jersey, 2:454

popularity of, 2:452

recent conflicts, 2:456

shortest total distance of, 2:451

symbolic jerseys of, 2:453–455

tradition versus innovation, 2:456

winners of, 2:450–451, 4:313–315

the yellow jersey, 2:453

tourism and sport, 1:67–69

sports tourist: hard definition, 1:68–69

sports tourist: soft definition, 1:69

tourism sport: hard definition, 1:69

tourism sport: soft definition, 1:69

track and field. *See* athletics, United States (field events);
athletics, United States (track events)

tractor pulling. *See* truck and tractor pulling

traditional sports and games, Latin America, 3:141–144

canicas (marbles), 3:141

charreada, 3:142–143

jai alai, 3:142

la víbora del mar (the sea snake), 3:142

las estatuas de marfi l (the marble statues), 3:142

Mesoamerican ball game, 3:142

oral tradition and, 3:141

tejo, 3:143

traditional games, 3:141–142

traditional sports, 3:142–143

trompo (tops), 3:141–142

traditional sports, Asia, 1:257–259

geographic scope of, 1:257–258

international popularity of, 1:258

multiple meanings in, 1:258

traditional sports, Australian Aboriginal and Torres Strait
Islander Peoples, 1:468–472

Aboriginal people term, 1:468

activities observed among, 1:470–471

Alfred Haddon (1912) on, 1:469

Australian Rules football, 1:471

Australian Sports Commission (ASC), 1:471

childhood and, 1:469–470

colonization and, 1:469

games identified, 1:469

marn-grook ball game, 1:471

Michael Salter (1967) on, 1:469

oral accounts of traditional games, 1:469

Torres Strait Islander people term, 1:468

Walter Roth (1902) on, 1:469

traditional sports, southern Africa, 1:165–168

Xhosa, 1:165–166

Zulu, 1:166–168

Trampoline, 2:202–203

trampoline, 3:412

trampoline, Olympic medalists (Summer)

Men's Individual, 4:194

Women's Individual, 4:194

Tretiak, Vladislav (1952–), 2:456–457

triathlon, 3:412–413

    equipment and costs, 3:413

    first reference to, 3:412

    International Triathlon Union (ITU), 3:412

    Ironman triathlon, 3:413

    Olympic competition, 3:412

    popularity of, 3:413

    Sprint triathlon, 3:412–413

    transitions in, 3:412

    World Triathlon Corporation (WTC), 3:413

triathlon, Olympic medalists (Summer)

    Men's Individual, 4:194

    Women's Individual, 4:194

truck and tractor pulling, 3:413–414

    basis for judging, 3:413

    classes of tractors, 3:413

    competition categories, 3:413–414

    National Tractor Pullers Association, 3:413

    origins of, 3:413

    terminology in, 3:413

Trumper, Victor Thomas (1877–1915), 1:472

tug-of-war

    first world championship, 2:202

    future of sport, 2:203

    image of, 2:203

    Olympic medalists (Summer), 4:194–195

    rules of, 2:202–203

    Tug of War International Federation (TWIF), 2:202

    weight categories, 2:202

Tunis 2001 Mediterranean Games, 1:311–312

Turnen. *See* gymnastics, German (*Turnen*)

Tutsi high jumping (Rwanda), 1:168–169

Twenty20 cricket (India), 1:259

Twickenham Stadium, 2:203–204

two Chinas issue, 1:260–261

UEFA Champions League and European Cup

    European Champions Clubs' Cup, 4:309–310

    UEFA Champions League, 4:309

UEFA Europa League champions, 4:310–311

ultimate, 3:414–115

    beginning of, 3:314

    governing body of, 3:415

    image of, 3:414

    Joel Silver and, 3:314

    playing of, 3:314

    Spirit of the Game (SOTG) philosophy, 3:414–415

    World Flying Disc Federation, 3:415

underarm bowling incident, cricket (Australia), 1:472–473

underwater hockey, 2:204–205

    governing body of, 2:204

    mix of competitors, 2:204–205

    playing of, 2:204

    popularity of, 2:204

Union of European Football Associations, 2:457–458

    disputes of, 2:457

    founding of, 2:457

    guiding principle of, 2:457

    purpose of, 2:457

Unitas, Johnny (1933–2002), 3:415

United Nations and sport, 1:69–72

    dimensions of, 1:70

    Millennium Development Goals, 1:70

    recognition of sports as a fundamental right, 1:70

    UN-IOC cooperation, 1:71

U.S. imperialism and sport in Asia, 1:261–263

    baseball, 1:262

    in China, 1:261–262

    in Japan, 1:262

    missionaries and, 1:261–262

    in the Philippines, 1:262–263

    YMCA and, 1:262, 1:263

US Open Golf Championship, 3:415–416

    date of, 3:415

    design of, 3:416

    early winners of, 3:415

    first play of, 3:415

    notable winners of, 3:416

    television coverage of, 3:416

    U.S. Golf Association (USGA), 3:415

US Open of 1913 (golf), 3:417

US Open Tennis Championship, 3:417–421

    in 1968, 3:418

    in 1969, 3:418

    in 1970, 3:418

    in 1979, 3:419

    in 1991, 3:419

    advent of "Open" tennis, 3:417–418

    Althea Gibson and, 3:420

    Arthur Ashe and, 3:418

    Arthur Ashe Stadium, 3:420, 3:420 (image)

    Billie Jean King and, 3:418, 3:419

    Billie Jean King National Tennis Center,, 3:420

    Chris Evert and, 3:419

    Court of Champions inaugural inductees, 3:420

    date and site of inaugural, 3:417

    Flushing Meadows site of, 3:418

grass court era winners, 3:418
Har-tru surface winners, 3:418
Jack Kramer and, 3:418
Jimmy Connors and, 3:418, 3:419
John McEnroe, 3:419
memorable matches and/or days of competition, 3:419
Pete Sampras, 3:419
Poncho González, 3:420
predecessor of, 3:417
Renee Richards and, 3:419
Serena Williams, 3:419
"shamateurism," 3:418
"Super Saturday," 3:419
tennis innovations and, 3:418–419
types of court surfaces played on, 3:418
U. S. National Championships, 3:417
Venus Williams, 3:419
Virginia Wade, 3:419

Vardon, Harry (1870–1937), 2:205–206
burial place, 2:206
The Complete Golfer, 2:205
A. G. Spalding Company and, 2:205
reputation of, 2:205
statistics for, 2:206
in the United States, 2:205–206
Vasco da Gama Stadium disaster of 2000 (Brazil), 3:144
Eurico Miranda and, 3:144
reason for, 3:144
significance of, 3:144
Vilas, Guillermo (1952–), 3:144–145
"Vitaï Lampada," 2:206
volata, 2:452
volleyball, Asia, 1:263–265
in China, 1:263–264
image of, 1:264
introduction of, 1:263
in Japan, 1:263
significance of, 1:263
volleyball, Brazil, 3:145–146
beach volleyball, 3:146
Brazilian Sports Confederation (CBD), 3:145
Brazilian Volleyball Confederation (CBV), 3:145
Denis Rupert Hathaway and, 3:145
dissemination of, 3:145
Fédération Internationale de Volleyball (International Volleyball Federation, FIVB), 3:145
first Brazilian States Championship, 3:145
Hollywood Volley competition, 3:146

Liga de Volley Ball do Rio de Janeiro (Volleyball League of Rio de Janeiro), 3:145
national tournament, 3:146
Olympic competition, 3:146
professionalism, 3:146
world championship play, 3:146
volleyball, Olympic medalists (Summer)
Men's Volleyball, 4:195–197
Women's Volleyball, 4:197–199
volleyball, United States, 3:421–422
current status of, 3:422
early playing of, 3:421
in the Far East, 3:421–422
Federation Internationale de Volleyball (FIVB), 3:422
George Fisher and, 3:421
innovations, 3:421–422
international governing body for, 3:422
international play of, 3:422
name change, 3:421
new volleyball techniques, 3:422
Olympic competition and, 3:422
Pan Am Games and, 3:422
popularity of, 3:421, 3:422
professionalism, 3:422
rules, 3:421
Soviet contribution to, 3:422
substantive changes to, 3:422
two-person beach volleyball, 3:422
U.S. military and, 3:421
U.S. Volley Ball Association (USVBA), 3:421
William G. Morgan and, 3:421
YMCA and, 3:421
vuvuzela (South Africa), 1:169–170

Walker Cup, 2:206–207
formal competition (first), 2:206
format of, 2:207
George Herbert Walker and, 2:206
great players of, 2:207
uniqueness of, 2:207
Warne, Shane (1969–), 1:473
Warner, Sir Pelham (1873–1963), 2:207
water motorsports, Olympic medalists (Summer)
Men's Class B, 4:199
Men's Class C, 4:199
Men's Open Class A, 4:199
water polo, 2:207–208
Olympic Games and, 2:208
rules for, 2:208

water polo (*continued*)
   spread of, 2:208
   William Wilson and, 2:208
water polo, Olympic medalists (Summer)
   Men's Water Polo, 4:199–202
   Women's Water Polo, 4:203
water skiing, Olympic medalists (Summer)
   Men's Figure Skiing, 4:203
   Men's Jump, 4:203
   Men's Slalom, 4:203
   Women's Figure Skating, 4:203
   Women's Jump, 4:203
waterskating, 3:422–423
   competitive categories of, 3:422–423
   Fred Waller and, 3:422
   governing body for, 3:422
   hydrofoiling, 3:422
   Olympic competition and, 3:422
   Ralph Samuelson and, 3:422
Weah, George (1966–), 1:170
weightlifting (Europe), 2:458–459
   European Weightlifting Federation (EWF), 2:459
   famous European stars, 2:459
   first official European championships, 2:459
   France and, 2:458
   Germany and, 2:459
   International Weightlifting Federation (IWF), 2:458
   renumbering of championships, 2:459
   styles of, 2:458
   women and, 2:459
weightlifting, Olympic medalists (Summer)
   Men's All-Around Dumbbell, 4:204
   Men's Bantamweight, 4:204
   Men's Featherweight, 4:204–205
   Men's First Heavyweight, 4:208
   Men's Flyweight, 4:204
   Men's Heavyweight, 4:207
   Men's Light Heavyweight, 4:206
   Men's Lightweight, 4:205
   Men's Middle Heavyweight, 4:207
   Men's Middleweight, 4:206
   Men's One-hand Lift, 4:204
   Men's Super Heavyweight, 4:208
   Men's Two-hand Lift, 4:204
   Women's Featherweight, 4:208
   Women's Flyweight, 4:208
   Women's Heavyweight, 4:209
   Women's Light Heavyweight, 4:209
   Women's Lightweight, 4:208
   Women's Middleweight, 4:208
   Women's Super Heavyweight, 4:209
Weissmuller, Johnny (1904–1984), 3:423–424
   birthplace of, 3:423
   death of, 3:423
   movie career of, 3:423
   pinnacle of his career, 3:423
   statistics for, 3:423
Wembley Stadium, 2:208–209
Wenlock Olympian Games. *See* Much Wenlock Games, England
Wightman Cup, 2:209–210
   Hazel Hotchkiss Wightman and, 2:209, 2:210
   history of, 2:209–210
   suspension of, 2:210
Wilding, Anthony (1883–1915), 1:473–474
Williams, Esther (1921–), 3:424
Wimbledon, 2:210–215
   1973 boycott of, 2:213
   centenary anniversary, 2:213
   championships (early), 2:211–212
   championships, opening the, 2:212–213
   changes to, 2:213–214
   fashion and, 2:214
   format of, 2:212
   golden era of, 2:212
   Ladies' Doubles and Mixed Doubles, 2:212
   layout of the grounds of, 2:211
   modern era records, 2:214
   Open Championship, first official, 2:213
   reputation of, 2:210
   Roger Federer vs Richard Gasquet at, 2:211 (image)
   site of, 2:210–211
   television rights, 2:214
   World Wars and, 2:212
winter sports, Asia, 1:265
Wisden Cricketers' Almanack, 2:215
Witt, Katerina (1965–), 2:459–460
Wolfenden Committee Report (1960), 2:215–216
   John Wolfenden and, 2:215
   outcome of, 2:216
   reason for, 2:215
   recommendations, 2:216
Women Islamic Games (Iran), 1:312–314
   controversies over, 1:313
   date established, 1:312
   founder of, 1:312
   image of, 1:313

popularity of, 1:312
resistance to, 1:312–313
Women's National Basketball Association, 3:424–425
collective bargaining agreement of, 3:424
expansion of, 3:424
marketing strategy of, 3:424–425
modification of men's basketball, 3:424
popularity and profitability of, 3:424
Women's National Basketball Association champions,
4:264
Women's Olympics, 2:460–461
Alice Milliat, 2:460, 2:461
"alternative internationalism," 2:460
Dick, Kerr ladies' football, 2:460
first edition of, 2:461
gender boycotted Olympics, 2:461
IOC and, 2:460, 2:461
as Jeux Féminines (Women's World Games), 2:461
La Femme Sportive Fédération des Sociétés Féminines
Sportives de France (FSFSF), 2:461
popularity of, 2:461
separatist initiative, 2:461
Women's Sports Foundation, 3:425
Billie Jean King and, 3:425
Donna de Varona and, 3:425
mission of, 3:425
primary programming focus of, 3:425
works of, 3:425
woodchopping, 1:474
Wooden, John (1910–2010), 3:425–426
accolades for, 3:426
birthplace of, 3:425
coaching career of, 3:425–426
hallmark of, 3:425
playing career of, 3:425
"Pyramid of Success," 3:426
Woods, Tiger (1975–), 3:426–427
controversy and, 3:427
early life of, 3:426–427
image of, 3:426
mixed heritage of, 3:427
statistics for, 3:426, 3:427
worker sport, Europe, 2:461–464
Confédération Sportive Internationale du Travail
(International Worker Sports Federation, CSIT),
2:462
international Social Democratic worker sport movement, 2:463
Olympiada Popular in Barcelona (1936), 2:462–463

Red Sport International (RSI), 2:462, 2:463
Socialist Worker Sport International (SASI), 2:462
Solidarity federation, 2:463
Soviet Union and, 2:462, 2:463
statistics of worker sports worldwide, 2:462
Switzerland and, 2:462
Winter Olympiad of the Workers competitive level,
2:463
Winter Olympiad of the Workers, first, 2:462
Winter Olympiad of the Workers, second, 2:462
Winter Olympiad of the Workers, third, 2:463
Worker Summer Olympiad, first, 2:462
World War I and, 2:462
workers' sport, British Isles, 2:216–217
British Workers' Sports Federation (BWSF), 2:216–217
Clarion Cycle Club, 2:216
Junior Imperial League, 2:217
National Workers' Sports Association, 2:216
politics and, 2:217
popularity of, 2:217
Red Sports International, 2:216
sponsors of, 2:216
World Anti-Doping Agency, 2:464–465
advisory committees of, 2:464
Copenhagen Declaration on Anti-Doping in Sport, 2:464
criteria of doping list, 2:464
definition of doping, 2:464
Executive Committee of, 2:464
extraordinary powers and, 2:464
Foundation Board of, 2:464
headquarters of, 2:464
pragmatic definition of doping, 2:464
purpose of, 2:464
reason for, 2:464
World Hockey Association, 3:427–428
date of disbandment, 3:427
fame of, 3:427
legal battle with the NHL, 3:428
rivalry with the NHL, 3:427
significance of, 3:428
World Ice Hockey champions, 4:307–308
World Rally Championship. See rallying/World Rally
Championship
World Series Cricket (WSC), 1:474–475
World Series (United States), 3:428–429
development of structure of, 3:428
memorable games and plays, 3:429
original name of, 3:428
winner of the first World Series, 3:428

World Soccer Club champions
    FIFA World Club Cup (2000, 2005–), 4:312
    Intercontinental Cup (1960–1979), 4:313
    Toyota Cup (1980–2004), 4:312
wrestling, Brittany (*gouren*), 2:465–466
    Breton culture and, 2:465
    Charles Cotonnec and, 2:465
    governing body of, 2:465
    on the international level, 2:465
    as a modern sport, 2:465
    mythology of, 2:465
    playing of, 2:465
    women and, 2:465
wrestling, Iceland (*glima*), 2:466
    governing body of, 2:466
    historical roots of, 2:466
    Icelandic wrestling forms, 2:466
    Icelandic Youth Federation and, 2:466
    International Glima Association (IGA), 2:466
    playing of, 2:466

    Viking Glima Federation, 2:466
    women and, 2:466
wrestling, Mongolian, 1:265 (image), 1:265–266
wushu, 1:266

X Games, 3:429–430
    first winter games, 3:429
    original name of, 3:429
    success of, 3:429
    superstars of, 3:429

Yao, Ming (1980–), 1:267
Yashin, Lev Ivanovic (1929–1990), 2:466–467
Yemen, sport in the Republic of, 1:314

Zambian National Football Team disaster (1993), 1:171
Zatopek, Emil (1922–2000), 2:467
Zidane, Zinedine (1972–), 2:467–468, 2:468 (image)
Zoff, Dino (1942–), 2:468–469